THE 1994 IEEE INTERNATIONAL CONFERENCE ON NEURAL NETWORKS

IEEE WORLD CONGRESS ON COMPUTATIONAL INTELLIGENCE

June 27 - June 29, 1994

IEEE
NEURAL
NETWORKS
COUNCIL

Walt Disney World Dolphin Hotel
Orlando, Florida

IEEE

Volume VII
Pages 4180-4777

The 1994 IEEE International Conference on Neural Networks

IEEE Catalog Number: 94CH3429-8
ISBN Softbound: 0-7803-1901-x
Casebound: 0-7803-1902-8
Microfiche: 0-7803-1903-6
Library of Congress Number: 94-75611

Additional copies of this publication are available from

IEEE Service Center
445 Hoes Lane
P.O. Box 1331
Piscataway, NJ 08855-1331
1-800-678-IEEE

ICNN TABLE OF CONTENTS
VOLUME I

FAST LEARNING FOR NEURAL NETWORKS-INVITED SESSION

SUPERVISED LEARNING

VOLUME II

UNSUPERVISED LEARNING

LEARNING AND MEMORY

LEARNING AND MEMORY (Continued)

NEURODYNAMICS

ASSOCIATIVE MEMORY

VOLUME III

ARCHITECTURE

WHO MAKES THE RULES?-INVITED SESSION

ARTIFICIALLY INTELLIGENT NEURAL NETWORKS

FUZZY NEURAL SYSTEMS

HYBRID SYSTEMS

ANALOG NEURAL CHIPS AND MACHINES-INVITED SESSION

NEURAL SYSTEMS HARDWARE-INVITED SESSION

ADVANCED ANALOG NEURAL NETWORKS AND APPLICATIONS-INVITED SESSION

NEURAL NETWORKS IMPLEMENTATIONS

HARDWARE IMPLEMENTATIONS-INVITED SESSIONS

VOLUME IV

ANALOG IMPLEMENTATIONS-INVITED SESSION

PARALLEL ARCHITECTURES-INVITED SESSION

MODULAR/DIGITAL IMPLEMENTATIONS

IMPLEMENTATION FOR SPECIAL PURPOSES

ANALOG IMPLEMENTATIONS

SOCIAL AND PHILOSOPHICAL IMPLICATIONS OF COMPUTATIONAL INTELLIGENCE-INVITED SESSION

COMPUTATIONAL INTELLIGENCE

ARTIFICIAL LIFE

INTELLIGENT NEURAL CONTROLLERS: ALGORITHMS AND APPLICATIONS-INVITED SESSION

NEUROCONTROL RESEARCH: REAL-WORLD PERSPECTIVES-INVITED SESSION

NEURAL NETWORKS FOR CONTROL-INVITED SESSION

LEARNING AND RECOGNITION FOR INTELLIGENT CONTROL-INVITED SESSION

INTELLIGENT CONTROL-INVITED SESSION

INTELLIGENT ROBOTICS-INVITED SESSION

VOLUME V

ROBOTICS

PATTERN RECOGNITION

TIME SERIES PREDICTION

SYSTEM IDENTIFICATION

APPLICATIONS

VOLUME VI

MEDICAL APPLICATIONS

COMMUNICATIONS APPLICATION

ECONOMIC/FINANCE/BUSINESS APPLICATIONS

NEURAL SYSTEMS HARDWARE

MOTION ANALYSIS

CHARACTER RECOGNITION

OPTIMIZATION/GRAPH PROBLEMS

COMPUTER APPLICATIONS

FILTERING

PARALLEL ARCHITECTURES

HARDWARE/MISCELLANEOUS

IMAGE PROCESSING

IMAGE PROCESSING/MACHINE VISION

VOLUME VII

IMAGE RECOGNITION-INVITED SESSION

APPLICATIONS IN IMAGE RECOGNITION

MACHINE VISION

SPEECH

OPTIMIZATION

OPTIMIZATION USING HOPFIELD NETWORKS

NEURAL NETWORK APPLICATIONS TO ESTIMATION AND IDENTIFICATION: ALGORITHMS AND CASE STUDIES

IEEE WORLD CONGRESS ON COMPUTATIONAL INTELLIGENCE

NEURAL-KNOWLEDGE BASE OBJECT DETECTION IN HYBRID LUNG NODULE DETECTION (HLND) SYSTEM

Y. S. Peter Chiou*+, Fleming Y. M. Lure*# and Panos A. Ligomenides+

* Caelum Research Corporation, 11229 Lockwood Dr., Silver Spring, MD 20901
(TEL) 301-593-1748, (FAX) 301-593-3951

+ Cybernetic Research Lab., Electrical Eng. Dept., University of Maryland, College Park, MD 20742

e-mail: CWYFL @ charney.gsfc.nasa.gov

Abstract. A "Hybrid Lung Nodule Detection (HLND) system" based on artificial neural network architecture and interactive knowledge-base system is developed for object detection in noisy image environments. This paper describes the system architecture and its application to detection and classification of nodules in lung cancerous pulmonary radiology. The configuration of the HLND system includes the following processing phases: (1) pre-processing to enhance the figure-background contrast; (2) Morphology based quick selection of nodule object suspects based upon the most prominent feature of nodules; and (3) feature space determination and neural network based suspect fields reduction; (4) interactive knowledge base and knowledge fusion processing and final classification of nodule suspect fields. Preliminary results from the approach are also reported.

INTRODUCTION

This paper describes a Computer Aided Diagnosis (CAD) system to improve the accuracy and speed of object recognition in cluttered and noisy image background. The detection and diagnosis is based on a hybrid scheme of artificial neural network and knowledge base synergy. This CAD tool was applied to early detection of cancerous pulmonary nodule from X-ray films. The resulting hybrid system is a robust, effective and fast Hybrid Lung Nodule Detection (HLND) System. Lung cancer, next to the heart disease, is the second highest cause of death in the United States. Early detection and diagnosis of cancerous tumors from chest X-ray films is essential for successful treatment of the illness. Dr. Doi and Dr. Giger of University of Chicago have shown that it is feasible to automate the lung nodule detection process by searching in the chest X-ray radiography for a set of preselected nodule features [1,3-7]. Moderate successes have since been achieved in lung nodule detection, with the help of modern digital computer and digital image processing techniques, from digitized chest X-ray images [2,8,9,11,12,14]. Although the digital processing method correctly identified cancerous nodules, it also misidentified numerous other anatomic structures in the image as nodules.

Despite the vast improvements in digital computer technology in the past few years, differentiation between the object of interest and the image background which contains similar attributes as the object of interest (e.g., true-positive and false-positive of nodules from radiography) still remains a challenging problem. Artificial neural network (ANN) techniques are chosen for this class of problems because of its capability to learn and generalize from training data set. By applying ANN techniques, the common features of the true-positive objects and the false-positive objects can be extracted and used internally by the ANN in the learning process to differentiate between true and false objet of interest. The generalization property of the ANN suggest that the features learned from the training data set would be applicable to other data set as well. By applying knowledge base techniques, the logic reasoning of experts' knowledge for making diagnosis can be extracted and simulated during the detection process. In the case of lung nodule detection, the patient's age, history of smoking, living environment and work condition may become a factor in deciding true-positives nodules. A Hybrid Lung Nodule Detection (HLND) system is developed to integrate the robustness of ANNs and the logic reasoning of knowledge bases with the accuracy of digital signal/image processing techniques in a single system for shape feature analysis in diagnostic radiology which provides accurate and robust recognition performance in the presence of noise and object-to-background sensory uncertainty [2]. The configuration of the HLND system includes the following processing phases: (1) pre-processing to enhance the figure-background contrast; (2) Morphology based quick selection of nodule object suspects based upon the most prominent feature of nodules; and (3) feature space determination and neural network based suspect fields reduction; (4) interactive knowledge base and knowledge fusion processing for final classification of nodule suspect fields.

0-7803-1901-X/94 $4.00 ©1994 IEEE

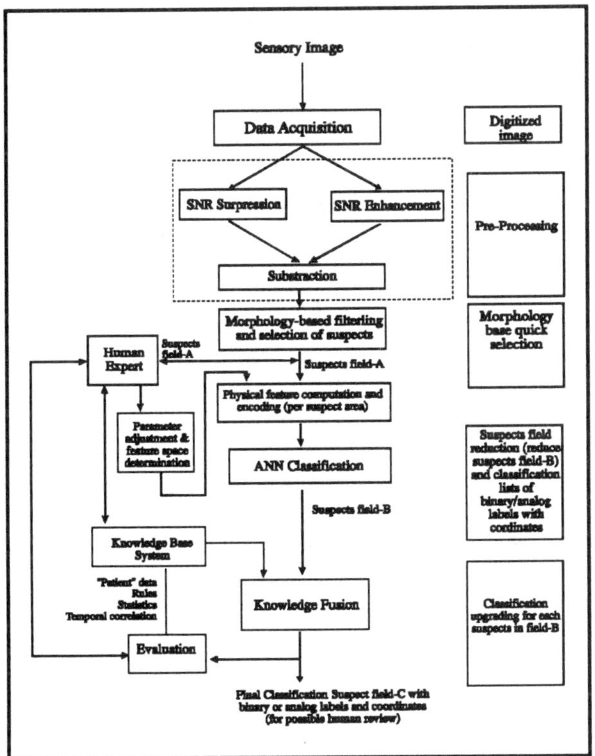

Figure 1. Schematic Diagram of Hybrid Lung Nodule Detection System

PRE-PROCESSING

The digital chest images were obtained from Georgetown University Hospital and University of Maryland Medical Center. Each pulmonary radiograph was digitized to 2000x2048x12 bits where each pixel represents about 200 μm for a 14" by 17" X-ray film. The images are later reduced to 500x512x12 bits image for computational speed. Each image contains at least one nodule. The actual location of the nodules are verified by computed tomography (CT) or followed by radiologists. A reversible contrast scaling function is used to obtain a constant contrast between lung space and the mediastinum area. Potential nodule information in a pulmonary radiograph is enhanced by a differential technique which subtracts a nodule suppressed image (through a median filter) from a nodule enhanced image (through a matched filter with a spherical profile) [2-7]. This approach would reduce the camouflaging anatomic background in the difference image, containing nodule-enhanced signal, is used for morphology base selection processing phase.

Median filtering technique tends to smoothen the image by reducing the intensity of abnormal phenomenon (e.g., nodules). Match filtering technique, which correlates the energy of the synthetical nodule image with original image, generates resultant images with highest values corresponding to the locations of potential nodule suspects. The matched filtering technique, shown in Fig. 2, involves fast Fourier transform, complex conjugate, and complex matrix multiplication with assumption of white noise (i.e., Fourier spectrum equals constant). A spherical profile with diameter of 3mm is used to synthesize the ideal nodule images. Subtraction between the resultant images derived from median and matched filtering methods further enhanced the nodule-to-background information [5].

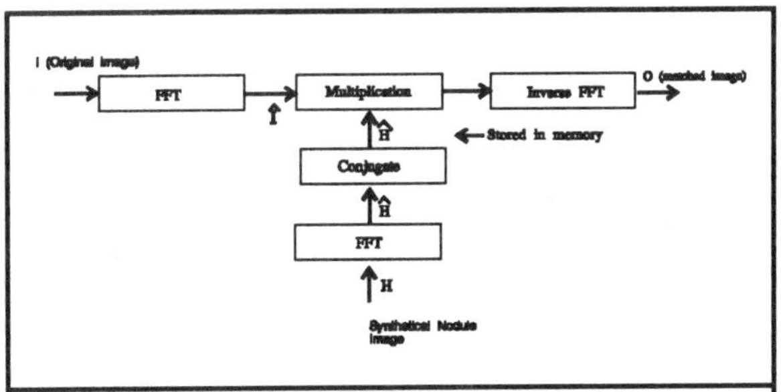

Figure 2. Schematic Diagram of Matched Filtering

MORPHOLOGY BASED QUICK SELECTION

A search algorithm is applied for quick (pre-) selection of all possible nodule suspects based mainly upon the most prominent feature of nodule - the spherical profile [4,5,6]. The difference image is processed by locally-adaptively area extraction process using edge and gray value tracking with different gray values for thresholding and morphological operations. It provides an initial determination of features, arising from nodules and arising from anatomic background. Circularity and effective radius of the segmented image block are evaluated at different thresholding levels to determine the location and the size of the nodule suspects. All the suspect areas (blocks) with dense area (high gray values) equivalent to 3 mm of diameter or less are captured in 32x32x12 bits images for further evaluation.

A morphological filtering sequence of erosion followed by dilation is performed by using 3 mm diameter circular kernel during each stage of testing circular parameters *r*, *C*, and I_r on the difference images. Here both erosion (*e*) and dilation (*d*) are defined as:

$$e = \min\{I_{i,j}\} \qquad (1)$$

$$d = \max\{I_{i,j}\} \qquad (2)$$

$$\forall\sqrt{(i^2+j^2)} < \frac{l}{2}$$

where *l* is the diameter of circular kernel. The matrix *I* corresponds to pixel values of the digital input image. Such filtering is used to eliminate the presence of small vascular structures while retaining the relatively large structures of ribs and nodules.

A quick selection is performed on the difference image based upon circular parameters describing **disk shape,** namely, equi-area radius (*r*), degree of circularity (*C*), and degree of irregularity (I_r) at certain contour lines. Assuming the area of grown region is identical to an round area, the *r*, *C*, and I_r of such equivalent round area are defined as followed:

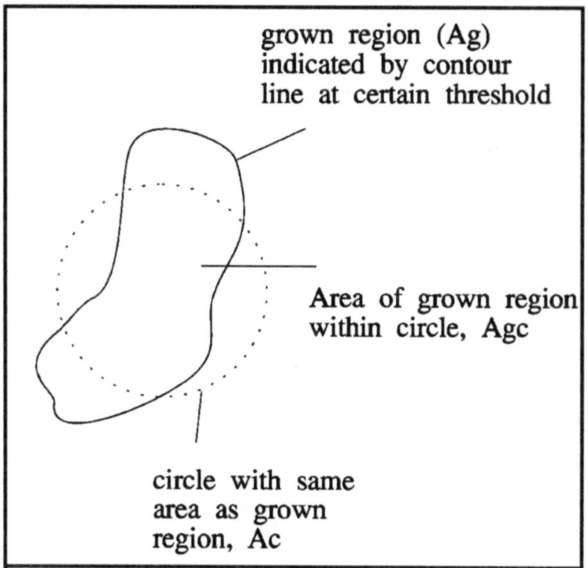

Figure 3. Grown Region of Lung Nodule Suspect

$$r = \sqrt{\left(\frac{A_g}{\pi}\right)} \tag{3}$$

$$D = \frac{A_{gc}}{A_g} \tag{4}$$

$$I_r = \frac{P_c}{P_g} \tag{5}$$

where A_g denotes area of grown region, A_{gc} area of grown region within circle, P_c perimeter of circle, and P_g perimeter of grown region (Figure 3). At both erosion and dilation filtering, grown region at which the variation of r, C, and I_r are small are subject to the further test at 10 different contrast values which are selected based on cumulative distribution curve of the gray value level in difference image. Nodule candidates are selected if test for r, C, and I_r of grown region are met within pre-defined threshold for at least 7 times. The selected nodule candidates are then segmented into 32x32 image blocks for further feature determination and neural classification.

FEATURE DETERMINATION AND SUSPECTS REDUCTION

Image Feature Extraction

Since the quick selection process are based on the general features of lung nodules -- the spherical profile, a classification algorithm based on localize anatomic features is needed. We developed an algorithm for localized feature extraction and classification based on gradient edge analysis of local anatomic structure in the 32x32 image blocks [2,10,17]. After the processing of morphology based quick selection filtering, specific geometric features (the spherical profile in X-ray images) of the nodule suspects, denoted as Field-A, is further utilized in both feature extraction and human expert processing phases, as shown in Fig. 1. In order to define a feature space in which the ANN architecture can be trained to derive a decision surfaces for separating different classes of anatomic structures, a feature extraction function that can complement the major search algorithm (morphology based filter) is needed. Such feature extraction algorithm should minimize the homogeneous effect among the suspect Field-A selected from quick selection process, yet maximize the geometric differences among the suspect Field-A. Therefore we designed a feature extraction algorithm based on Sobel operators to respond to the gradient in the image.

After first two processing phases (pre-processing and morphology based quick selection), nodule suspect Field-A are determined from each image. Typically, there are 15-30 suspects on a radiograph. The nodule suspect is extracted into a 32x32 pixel image (larger than 9 mm in diameter) sufficient for the ANN-based development. After processing 31 radiographs, more than 380 nodule suspects in **original** and **difference** image blocks (32x32 pixel) are obtained for further development of the ANN classification. Among the nodule suspects, 22.2% of them are true positive nodules. Since sufficient data base for various anatomic structures are required for analysis, many false positive nodules are included for further investigation. With properly adjustment of parameters, the success rate in detection of nodule can achieve 70% after first two phases.

Anatomic Class								
	RX	RV	VC	EV	RE	BO	VS	TN
No. of samples	96	40	41	43	28	42	15	87
Total suspect image blocks: 392								

Table 1. Eight Types of Anatomic Classes

The suspect image blocks are first classified into 8 classes: true nodule (TN), rib crossing (RX), rib-vessel crossing (RV), vessel cluster (VC), end-vessel (EV), rib edge (RE), bone (BO), and vessel (VS), based on the content of the image and previous related works [2,11]. Generally, the suspect image blocks contains more than one class of information. It is found that among 392 images 24.5% are rib crossing and 22.2% are true, as shown in Table 1. Since eight (8) categories of anatomic classes are obtained from real radiographs, overlapping of several phenomenon in single image block is quite common. The classification is primarily based on the most dominant anatomic structure in the image. Based on these image blocks, several features are analyzed and extracted.

A 1-D histogram of gradient component (either amplitude or orientation) has been applied by Matsumoto et al., [11] for analysis of subtracted image block. In this analysis, we investigated both elements of gradient vector (amplitude and orientation) from original image block. A 3x3 Sobel operator for image edge enhancement is applied to the original image block to obtained two 32 x 32 images: one is amplitude image and another one is orientation image. The orientation angles are within the range between 0 and 360 degree, whereas the amplitude varies from 0 to 1024. Feature

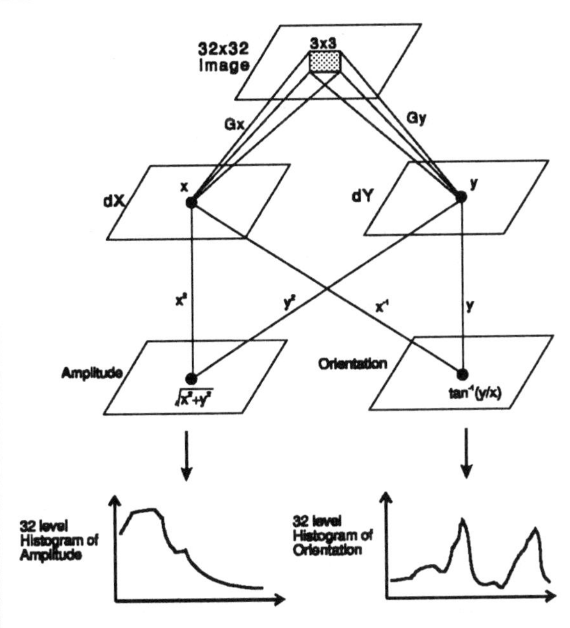

Figure 4. Schematic Diagram of Feature Extraction

vector pairs are generated from histogram of orientation and amplitude. It was found that most non-nodule 32x32 images contain identifiable histogram features in amplitude and orientation gradient image.

By performing the histogram operation on gradient image, two sets of marginal distribution curves are obtained: one for orientation distribution and another one for amplitude distribution. The feature vectors from the nodule curves (both in orientation and amplitude) is quite distinct from rest of other structures. Each distribution is normalized to enhance its variation through performing division by ten, which is the deviation of these curves, and followed by taking its square. These feature vectors are then used for development of supervised neural classifier in this study.

It is found that for true nodules the distribution of orientation angles is relative uniform compared with other false positive cases and the magnitude of gradient amplitude of true nodules is mostly concentrated in smaller magnitude. Most types of false positive nodules demonstrate two peaks separated at around 180 degree in orientation angle axis except for vessel cluster. Because bone is wider than vessel in the 32 x 32 images and the contrast between bone and anatomic background is stronger than that for vessel, one peak at distribution of orientation is typically smaller than another one for bone whereas they are within similar range for vessel class. Each peak in bone gradient images is sharper (i.e., smaller standard deviation) than that in vessel images. Rib-edge gradient image shows one stronger amplitude distribution at certain angle because of the orientation of the rib in the 32 x 32 image. Gradient distribution for rib-vessel crossing also demonstrates one stronger peak with relatively larger standard deviation at orientation axis. Although it is expected to obtain one sharper peak at angle axis, it shows very insignificant effect due to the low contrast of end vessel. Vessel-cluster gradient image shows more rough contour (i.e., larger standard deviation along the amplitude axis) than this from nodule. This type of analysis and classification algorithm perform well in noisy conditions, because the distribution enhancement tends to smooth out the noise contribution to the feature vector. Images containing mixed features will be easily analyzed. Parameters derived from standard deviation, curtosis, skewness, multi-scale/multi-resolution wavelet method and other texture information from the feature vectors are currently extracted for further supervised neural network applications.

Neural Network Based Suspect Reduction

A supervised back-propagation (BP) neural network classifier is developed for classification of each anatomic structure. The BP ANN classifier contains four layers. Input layer consists of 64 neurons corresponding to combination of both amplitude and orientation bins of marginal distribution. Two hidden layers contains 128 and 64 neurons, which are chosen as multiple of eight (pre-determined anatomic structure classes) since the properties of each class are desired to be coded evenly within the network. Finally a two-neuron output layer is used to classify either true positive or false positive nodules.

Since BP ANN **learned** from the training data set presented to it during learning phase (weight adaptation phase), the resulting class samples which presented to the BP ANN should have equal probability among classes. Thus the BP ANN will not biased toward any result classes (in our case, TRUE nodule class and FALSE nodule class). In our case, 87 of the 392 samples (22.5%) are TRUE nodule, while 305 samples (77.8%) are FALSE nodule. The BP ANN will biased toward FALSE nodule class if the data set is applied for training. Therefore the TRUE nodule sample was replicated 7 times and FALSE nodule samples was duplicated twice based upon the statistical properties of the training set. As a result, 609 out of 1219 samples (49.95%) are TRUE nodules and 610 out of 1219 samples (50.05%) are FALSE nodules in the resulting data set. 40% of the data set are used as training set depending on the results of image shape feature analysis [2].

INTERACTIVE KNOWLEDGE BASE AND KNOWLEDGE FUSION

Interactive Knowledge Base

An expert's expertise knowledge toward the specific problem domain should not be treated lightly. In the case of medical diagnosis, the physicians' expertise and experiences can never be replaced. Therefore we designed an interactive mechanism to **learn** from the experts. The interactive knowledge extraction, as demonstrated in Fig. 1, occurred in four possible ways during HLND training process: (1) by having the expert examine the suspects field-A and give suggestion to remove suspects and/or introduce suspects from/to suspects field-A; (2) By adjusting the parameter for feature space determination; (3) By providing production rules, group statistics, patient's data and the correlation between data and X-ray images; (4) By evaluating the final classification (suspect field-C) and provide new rule or new data into knowledge base [16].

Successful development of knowledge base requires sufficient knowledge provided by the experts. However, most of the expertise and experiences will only **activate** by similar cases, the expert will only remember the rules or exceptions when a similar case presented to him/her. The interactive nature of HLND CAD system let the expert teaches the system on a case by case basis during the system's training process [16].

Knowledge Fusion

Knowledge fusion processor is designed to integrate different decision from different decision maker to obtain the optimal classification accuracy. As the data fusion processor, which has been used widely in communication theory and satellite remote sensing applications. The knowledge fusion processor fuse classification from ANN classification (suspect field-B) and expert diagnosis (through knowledge base inference), the fusion parameter can be controlled by the expert through evaluation process to modify knowledge base (on a case by case basis) or by statistical evaluation of the detection performance.

EXPERIMENTAL RESULTS

The knowledge base is still under construction. Therefore, the knowledge fusion process has little effect on the experimental results. The ANN classification result are report herein. It takes around 130 epoches to train the BP ANN classifier to learn up to 100% accuracy of the training data set. With a fully-trained BP ANN, True-positive classification accuracy can reach 93.3% over the overall image base as shown in Table 2. It is found that the trained BP ANN increases the detection accuracy of true nodule up to 93% with around 7% false detection. By examining the weight matrix, the effect due to different feature (either amplitude or orientation) can be determined. Such implementation can also be easily implemented in a highly parallel, reconfigurable, and scalable, neural network co-processor called MNR [15] for fast and real time processing.

		Actual Structure	
		True Nodule	False Nodule
Classified	True Nodule	93.3%	6.7%
	False Nodule	1.3%	98.7%

Table 2. Classification Accuracy for Nodule Detection

SUMMARY

A neural-knowledge base analysis and detection algorithms are developed for improvement of the performance of Hybrid Lung Nodule Detection (HLND) system. The configuration of the proposed system includes the following processing phases: (1) pre-processing to enhance the figure-background contrast; (2) Morphology based quick selection of nodule object suspects based upon the most prominent feature of nodules; and (3) feature space determination and neural network based suspect fields reduction; (4) neural network based knowledge fusion processing and final classification of nodule suspect fields. After first processing phases, several suspect image blocks are captured. Extraction of shape features is performed through edge enhancement, evaluation of marginal distribution curves and feature extraction. A pair of feature vectors is determined based on the analysis of image blocks. A supervised back-propagation-trained neural network is developed for recognition of the derived feature curve, a marginal distribution curves. A interactive knowledge extraction method and knowledge fusion processor is under development to include prior information not inherent in the X-ray image into HLND system. Preliminary results show that this feature set is able to identify most true nodule at accuracy of 93% with around 7% false detection. More data set are still needed for further improvement of the HLND system.

ACKNOWLEDGEMENT

This work is supported by grant number 1 R43 CA58116-01 from the National Cancer Institute, National Institute of Health. Its contents are solely the responsibility of the authors and do not necessarily represent the official view of the NCI/NIH.

REFERENCES

[1]Chan, H.P., Doi, K., Vybomy, C.J., et al.: "Improvement in Radiologists' Detection of Clustered Microcalcification Mammograms: The Potential of Computer- Aided Diagnosis," Inves. Radio., Vol. 25, 1990, pp. 1102-1110.

[2]Chiou, Y.-S. P., J.-S. J. Lin, Lure, Y.-M. F., P. A. Ligomenides, M. T. Freedman, and S. Fritz, ''Shape Feature Analysis Using Artificial Neural Networks for Improvements of Hybrid Lung Nodule Detection (HLND) System '', SPIE Medical Imaging 1993 Symposium, Newport Beach, CA.

[3]Doi, K.: "Feasibility of Computer-Aided Diagnosis in Digital Radiography," Jap. J. Radio. Technol. Vol. 45, 1989, pp. 653-663.

[4]Doi, K., Giger, M.L., MacMahon, H., et al.: "Clinical Radiology and Computer- Aided Diagnosis: Potential Partner in Medical Diagnosis?," RSNA 1990, Scientific Exhibit, Space 129.

[5]Giger, M.L., Doi, K., and MacMahon H.: "Image Feature Analysis and Computer-Aided Diagnosis in Digital Radiography. 3. Automated Detection of Nodules in Peripheral Lung Field," Med. Phy. Vol. 15, 1988, pp. 158-166.

[6]Giger, M.L., Doi, K., and MacMahon, H., et al.: "Pulmonary Nodules: Computer- Aided Detection in Digital Chest Images," RadioGraphics, Vol. 10, 1990, pp. 41- 51.

[7]Giger, M.L., Ahn, N., Doi, K., MacMahon, H., Metz, C.E.: "Computerized Detection of Pulmonary Nodules in Digital Chest Images: Use of Morphological Filters in Reducing False-Positive Detections" Med. Phys., Vol. 17, 1990, pp. 861-865.

[8]Heelan, R.T., Flechinger, B.J., Melamed, M.R., et al.: "Non Small Cell Lung Cancer: Results of the New York Screening Program." Radiology, 1984; 151: 289- 293.

[9]Lin, J.S., Ligomenides, P.A., Lure, Y.M.F., Lo, B.S. and Freedman, M.T.: "Application of Artificial Neural Networks for Improvements of Lung Nodule Detection," Proc. Symposium for Computer Assisted Radiology, S/CAR '92, SCAR, Baltimore, June 14-17, 1992.

[10]Chiou, Y.S.P., Lure, Y.M.F., et al, "Neural Network Based Hybrid Lung Nodule (HLND) System", IEEE International Conference on Neural Network, San Francisco, CA, March 28-April 1, 1993.

[11]Matsumto, T., H. Yoshimura, K. Doi, M. L. Giger, A. Kano, H. MacMahon, K. Abe, and S. Montner, "Image Feature Analysis of False-Positive Diagnosis Produced by Automated Detection of Lung Nodules", Investigative Radiology, 1992, pp. 587-597.

[12]Montain, C.F.: "Value of the New TNM Staging System for Lung Cancer," 5th World Conference on Lung Cancer, CHEST:96/1, 1989, pp. 47s-49s.

[13]Rumelhart, D.E., McClelland, J.L., Parallel Distributed Processing: Explorations in the Microstructure of Cognition, MIT Press, 1986.

[14]Stitik, F.P., Tockman, M.S. and Khouri, N.F.: "Chest Radiology," in Miller, A.B. (Ed.): Screening for Cancer, New York, Academic Press, 1985, 163-191.

[15]Ligomenides, P.A., Jump, L. B. and Chiou, Y-S: "A Reconfigurable Ring Architecture for Large Scale Neural Networks," Conf. Fuzzy and Neual System and Vehi. Appli., 1991, Tokyo, Japan.

[16]Chiou, Yun-Shu: "A Neural-Knwoeldge Base System for Diagnosis in Noisy Image Background", PhD Dissertation, Dept. of Electrical Engineering, University of Maryland, College, MD. (in progress)

[17]Chiou, Y.-S. and Lure, Y.-M. F. ''Hybrid Lung Nodule Detection (HLND) System '', To be published in Cancer Letters, Elsevier Scientific Pub. Ire. Ltd., 1994.

Edge-preserving and Scale-space Filtering by Saddle-node Dynamics

Yiu-fai Wong[1], *Member, IEEE*

***Abstract*— Using maximum entropy principle and statistical mechanics, we derive and demonstrate the use of saddle-node dynamics for edge-preserving filtering. The nonlinear dynamics allows the clustering filter to achieve three tasks: a) removing noise; b) preserving edges and c) improved smoothing of nonimpulsive noise. For each datum in a signal, a neighborhood of weighted data is used for clustering. The cluster center becomes the filter output. This filter presents a new mechanism for preserving discontinuities differing from techniques based on local gradients and line processes. We demonstrate the filter using real images. This work provides a framework within which further image processing, image coding and computer vision problems can be investigated.**

I. Introduction

One problem in image and speech processing is to filter out noise in the data while preserving the edges. This problem is also important in multiresolution systems because as resolution decreases, some information is necessarily classified as "noise" and discarded or relegated to the higher resolution description. If one desires the low-resolution description to resemble the original data, it is important to preserve as many edges as possible because edges carry so much information. From the coding point of view, do we need to represent edges by a set of linear components and then re-assemble them at the receiver end?

Without any *a priori* knowledge, however, it is not clear what constitutes noise or an edge. Intuitively, at a very fine scale, every pixel is a signal itself. At a very coarse scale, a nonlinear averaging effect comes into play. Thus, a sensible solution requires one to specify a level of description or scale. That is, one can only distinguish noise versus signal in the scale space.

The author is affiliated with the Institute for Scientific Computing Research, Lawrence Livermore National Laboratory, Livermore, CA 94550, USA, e-mail: wong@redhook.llnl.gov

In this work, we present a new approach [1] to edge-preserving and scale-space filtering. We derive a clustering filter based on information theory and statistical mechanics. This filter is governed by a single scale parameter and has two additional features: 1) noise reduction and improved smoothing of nonimpulsive noise; and 2) edge preservation. These are achieved through saddle-node dynamics, which presents a new mechanism for edge preservation distinct from local gradients and line processes.

This paper is organized as follows: We first discuss related previous approaches, followed by a rigorous derivation of the clustering filter. We then discuss the scale parameters and fine details about the filter. Demonstrations using real data are then presented.

II. Related Previous Work

Gaussian scale-space filtering was introduced in [2] and has generated substantial interest in the computer vision community [3, 4]. But it suffers the major difficulty of blurring across the edges. This drawback is not surprising because the scale parameter is, in fact, a blurring parameter. Clearly, one can treat the Gaussian as the point spread function of the sensors used to detect the input signals. However, from the viewpoint of the human visual system, an image at a coarse scale, though blurred and missing the fine details, still have well-defined boundaries and edges.

To prevent blurring across the edges, anisotropic diffusion [5] and its variants were introduced such that diffusion is very slow across adjacent pixels with large gradients. There are at least three difficulties with these methods: 1) Impulsive noise will have large gradients in all directions and hence will not be removed; 2) the schemes tend to produce piecewise constant surfaces and thus the images appear blocky; 3) It is not clear how scale is defined.

Median filtering was first proposed by Tukey [6] for smoothing data. It has been used for speech processing and image restoration. Its generalized versions, order-statistic (OS) filters [7] and variations have also been widely studied and applied. However, it is known that median or OS filters do not

0-7803-1901-X/94 $4.00 ©1994 IEEE

provide sufficient smoothing for nonimpulsive noise. Another recent approach was the line processes introduced in [8]. A line process is a binary variable which signals the presence of a discontinuity and inhibits the interaction between the neighboring pixels. This idea has been applied to both segmentation and data smoothing in the form of weak membrane models [9].

III. A Clustering Filter

Seeing things in scale space inevitably involves the removal of signal which could include both noise and signal. Once a scale is selected, the task then is to estimate what one sees, i.e. the output. Presumably, the output should be a good representative of the original data. This process can be cast as robust estimation. A cluster center is naturally a robust estimate of the data associated with it. To give a robust estimate, one can either exclude the outliers from the cluster membership or assigning them negligible weights in the final estimate. However, it is known that clustering depends on scale too. Hence, scale-space clustering and scale-space filtering are naturally related.

Let $\mathbf{x}$ be the coordinate of a pixel in an image[2] and y its real-valued attribute. Since the pixels are highly redundant due to spatial correlation, we can in principle estimate the true pixel value y at position x by its neighboring pixels. Common sense tells us that the data points near $(\mathbf{x}, y)$[3] should give more information at lower cost while those far away should give less at higher cost. To make this estimate robust, the information should be spread among the neighboring data. If we treat the contributions to the determination of y from the neighboring data as a probability distribution, this means that the entropy of this distribution should be maximized subject to linear cost constraints.

The above reasoning implies that we can estimate each pixel independently. Say we are given a neighborhood of data points $S = \{(\mathbf{x}_i, y_i) : i = 1, \dots, N\}$. Let P_i denote the contribution of $(\mathbf{x}_i, y_i)$ to $(\mathbf{x}, y)$. To specify the cost function, we note that the input and output domains should be treated differently because the former is fixed and known but the latter is really environment-dependent. Thus, let the cost function have two components $e_x(\mathbf{x}_i)$ and $e_y(y_i)$. Our criterion seeks to maximize the entropy $S = -\sum_i P_i \log P_i$, subject to the linear constraints

$$\sum_i P_i e_x(\mathbf{x}_i) = C_x, \sum_i P_i e_y(y_i) = C_y \qquad (1)$$

[2] $\mathbf{x} = (i, j)$ for an image with rectangular grids. We choose this notation for simplicity.

[3] We use $(\mathbf{x}, y)$ to denote the joint image plane and intensity space.

which are obtained by averaging the costs in the neighborhood. Using Lagrangian multipliers, one obtains

$$P_i = e^{-\alpha e_x(\mathbf{X}_i) - \beta e_y(y_i)}/Z \qquad (2)$$

where $Z = \sum_i e^{-\alpha e_x(\mathbf{X}_i) - \beta e_y(y_i)}$. To make the connection with statistical mechanics, we call $\beta = 1/T$ the "inverse temperature" and Z the "partition function". Naturally, the "free energy" is defined as

$$F = -\frac{1}{\beta} \log Z. \qquad (3)$$

Let us choose the cost functions $e_x(x_i) = \|\mathbf{x} - \mathbf{x}_i\|_2^2$ and $e_y(y_i) = (y - y_i)^2$. At equilibrium, a thermodynamical system always settles into a state which minimizes its free energy. That is, we want $\partial F / \partial y = 0$, or equivalently

$$y = \sum_i \frac{y_i w_i e^{-\beta(y_i - y)^2}}{\sum_j w_j e^{-\beta(y_j - y)^2}}, \qquad (4)$$

where $w_i = e^{-\alpha\|\mathbf{X}_i - \mathbf{X}\|_2^2}$.

A. Two Scales and Saddle-node dynamics

From [10, 11], we can interpret y as a cluster center given the data y_is and w_i as either the *weight* given to y_i or the *relative multiplicity* of y_i. Note that the data used for clustering differ from pixel to pixel because the w_is differ.

Let us now explain what α means. When $\alpha = \infty$, $w_i = 1$ if $\mathbf{x}_i = \mathbf{x}$ and 0 otherwise. Every pixel is preserved perfectly. Conversely, a small α implies that more neighbors of $\mathbf{x}$ can contribute. Hence, α is a measure of scale in the input space.

Given a scale α in the input space, β is identical to the scale parameter in the scale-space clustering algorithm [10, 11]. When $\beta = \infty$, every datum y_i with nonzero w_i is a solution of (4). As β decreases, the number of solution decreases. Eventually when $\beta = 0$, there is only one solution. Hence, β is a measure of scale in the output space.

Given a fixed α and allow β to vary from a large to a small value, there are critical temperatures β_c's at which the fixed points of (4) become unstable and bifurcate. This results in the merging of the clusters. The merging of clusters as β varies can be rigorously analyzed using local bifurcation techniques [12]. It may thus be helpful to summarize the relevant results in [10] regarding the dynamics of (4) here.

1. Given any initial y, the iterative map (4) always converges.
2. There are two types of local bifurcations for (4) as β varies: saddle-node and pitchfork bifurcations.

3. A saddle-node indicates an inhomogeneous spatial distribution in the data. Their bifurcation diagrams are shown in Figure 1.

The particular estimate y one obtains depends on the initial y and β. Intuitively, β should be related to the variations of the pixel intensities in the spatial window defined by the scale α in the input domain. In fact, the variation in the allowed output space (pixel intensity) should be inversely proportional to β. Therefore, a natural method to initialize y and choose β is as follows:

Let $\bar{y} = \sum_i y_i w_i / \sum_i w_i$ and

$$\sigma_y^2 = \sum_i (y_i - \bar{y})^2 w_i / \sum_i w_i.$$

Intuitively, $\bar{y}$ is the average of the pixel values in the neighborhood of x, while σ_y^2 is a measure of its local variance. A small σ_y^2 implies that the local region is quite smooth, while a large σ_y^2 implies that the local region may contain outliers or an edge. Hence for every pixel location, one can choose $\beta = (2\sigma_y^2)^{-1}$. The initial y can be set to $\bar{y}$. One then iterate (4) and the converged value is the filter output.

Before we demonstrate this filter on both artificial and real data in the next section, we make the following remarks:

- One can easily extend the above analysis to data with multiple attributes;
- Although all discussions are made with images for simplicity and clarity, the clustering filter is applicable to any kind of data or computed data with a spatial or temporal domain, such as curves and speech signals. The data points do not need to lie on a regular grid, as required by most algorithms in digital image processing.
- Although our formulation starts with two parameters, the clustering filter has, in effect, only one scale parameter. The other scale parameter is determined by the local variations in the data. This data-driven selection of β gives a family of adaptive filters. We remark that β can be further modified to suit one's needs.

IV. Demonstrations

Example 1. The circles in Figure 2 show a "hat" of height 0.5, corrupted by a Gaussian noise of variance 0.001 and two very noisy pieces of data. The solid line shows the clustering filtered output with $\alpha = 1/32$. One can see that edges are well preserved and the non-edge portions are very smooth. The dashed line shows the output when a median filter with window of size 9 is used. The dot-dashed line is the Gaussian filtered output. The superiority of our method over both median filtering and Gaussian filtering is clearly demonstrated.

Example 2. To see the effect of β on the filter output, let us set $\alpha = 0$. That is, the estimate is the same for every pixel. To see the estimates as β varies, we set β to a large number (fine scale) and initialize every datum y_i as a cluster. Equation (4) is iterated until it converges for all the clusters. Then β is decreased and the iterations are repeated using the previous clusters as the initial clusters. Figure 3a shows the tree of clusters in the scale space as β decreases. Data are plotted as $\star$'s on the vertical axis. The procedure of calculating all the clusters at all scales is called *melting* in [10]. From the tree, we see two robust clusters: one at the zero level and the other at 0.5. They remain stable for a long range of scales. The zero-level cluster is more robust because it contains more points. When the less robust cluster bifurcates through saddle-node bifurcation and merges with the other cluster, the center of the more robust cluster is hardly affected. This is the *key mechanism* for preserving discontinuities.

Example 3. Scale-space clustering with nonzero α: We set $\alpha = 1/32$ which corresponds to a window of 8 pixels wide. Suppose we want to estimate the pixel at $i = 9$. The w_is are computed and melting is carried out in a manner similar to that in Example 2 except that w_is are nonuniform. Figure 3b shows the tree of clusters in the scale space. Since the w_is are concentrated on the relatively flat zero level, it is seen that the merging of the two clusters is very sharp. Figure 3c shows the tree when the window is centered at $i = 19$. Note that the merging is less sharp due to the sharing of weights w_i around the edge.

Example 4: Figure 4a shows a series of filtered outputs for $\alpha = 1/2, 1/8, 1/32$, and $1/128$ respectively. The data is shown on the lowest plot. Figure 4b shows the outputs when Gaussians with identical α's are used. We note two differences: 1) Gaussian filtering simply smoothes across the data while the clustering filter can preserve the "bumps" much better; 2) Gaussian filtering also reduces the contrast much faster than the cluster filtering.

Real Data: Figure 5a shows the Lena image. Figures 5b and 5c show the images obtained by the clustering filter with $\alpha = (2 \times 2^2)^{-1}, (2 \times 4^2)^{-1}$ respectively. Figures 5d shows the Gaussian filtered image with $\alpha = (2 \times 4^2)^{-1}$. Indeed, while the Gaussian filter blurs across the whole image, the cluster filter generates smoother blobs, yet the edges are sharp. It is also clear that Figure 5c carries much more information about the original image than Figure 5d. Our results differ vastly from those produced by diffusion schemes, which produce blocky and piece-wise constant images.

The above examples demonstrates that the clustering filter not only preserves edges, it also removes impulsive noise and provides improved smoothing of nonimpulsive noise.

The crucial difference between Gaussian filtering and our scheme is the nonlinear feedback term in (4). There are intuitive arguments why scale space filtering is neither associative nor commutative. For example, suppose we quantize an interval into 5 levels and then further quantize the 5 levels into 2 levels. A signal passing through this two-stage quantizer differs from its passing through a one-stage quantizer with 2 levels. In scale-space, a "hard" decision has to be made. Moreover, the anisotropy is handled by nonlinear dynamics though the cost function is isotropic. The above comparison shows that the clustering filter constitutes a new scale-space filter.

V. Summary

We have derived and demonstrated a nonlinear clustering filter based on information theory and statistical mechanics. The filter has only one parameter, which governs the size of the spatial or temporal neighborhood of data that can influence the filter output. This, together with local characteristics of the signal, determine the scale parameter in the output space. The result is adaptive filtering of the data in an unsupervised manner. The relation of this filter to scale-space clustering has been emphasized. The filter is shown to be able to remove noise, preserve edges and smooth data. It also presents a new mechanism to preserve discontinuities in the data.

Comparisons with Gaussian filtering and median filtering demonstrated that this clustering filter gives better performance than the other techniques. This filter may be a more appropriate approach to scale-space filtering. This work shows that scale-space filtering, nonlinear filtering and scale-space clustering are closely related and provides a framework within which further image processing, image coding and computer vision problems can be investigated.

VI. Acknowledgement

I am deeply indebted to the late Edward C. Posner for his encouragements for this research. I thank Carver Mead for teaching me the magic of exponentials. This work was performed while Wong was at Caltech and was supported in part by a grant from Pacific Bell to Caltech and the Caltech Communications Consortium.

References

[1] Yiu-fai Wong, "A Nonlinear Scale-space Filter by Physical Computation," *Proc. IEEE Workshop on Neural Networks for Signal Processing*, September, 1993.

[2] A. Witkin, "Scale-space filtering," in *Int. Joint Conf. Artificial Intelligence*, Karlsruhe, West Germany, 1983, 1019–1021.

[3] Jan J. Koenderink, "The Structure of Images," *Biol. Cybern.*, 50, 363-370, 1984.

[4] A. Yuille and T. Poggio, "Scaling theorems for zero crossings," *IEEE Trans. Patt. Anal. and Mach. Intell.*, 8, 15-25, 1986.

[5] P. Perona and J. Malik, "Scale-space and edge detection using anisotropic diffusion," *IEEE Trans. Patt. Anal. and Mach. Intell.*, 12, 629-639, 1990.

[6] J.W. Tukey, *Exploratory Data Analysis*, Reading, Addison-Wesley, MA, 1977.

[7] A.C. Bovik, T.S. Huang and D.C. Munson, Jr., "A generalization of median filtering using linear combinations of order statistics," *IEEE Trans. Acoust., Speech, Signal Processing*, 31, 1342-1350, 1983.

[8] S. Geman and D. Geman, "Stochastic relaxation, Gibbs distribution, and the Bayesian restoration of images," *IEEE Trans. Patt. Anal. and Mach. Intell.*, 6, 721–741, 1984.

[9] A. Blake and A. Zisserman, *Visual Reconstruction*. MIT Press, Cambridge, MA, 1987.

[10] Yiu-fai Wong, *Towards a Simple and Fast Learning and Classification System*, Ph.D Thesis, Caltech, Electrical Engineering, January, 1992.

[11] Yiu-fai Wong, "Clustering Data by Melting," *Neural Computation*, vol. 5, 89-104, 1993.

[12] S. Wiggins, *Introductions to Applied Nonlinear Dynamical Systems and Chaos,* Springer-Verlag, New York, 1990.

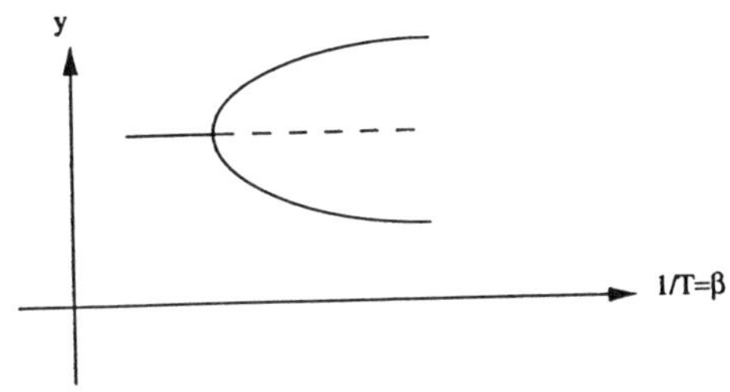

Figure 1a Pitchfork Bifurcation in scale-space clustering

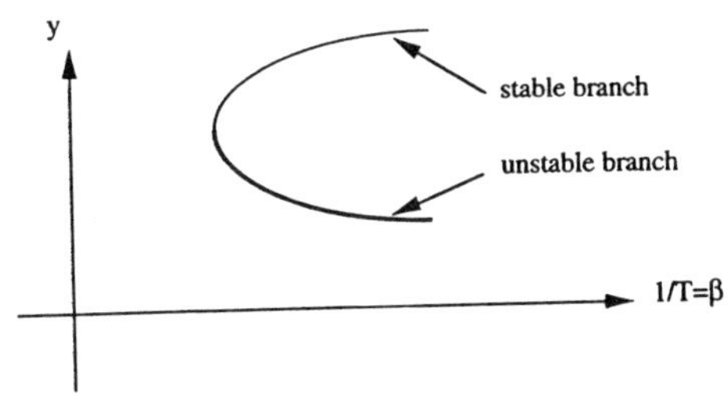

Figure 1b Saddle-node bifurcation in scale-space clustering

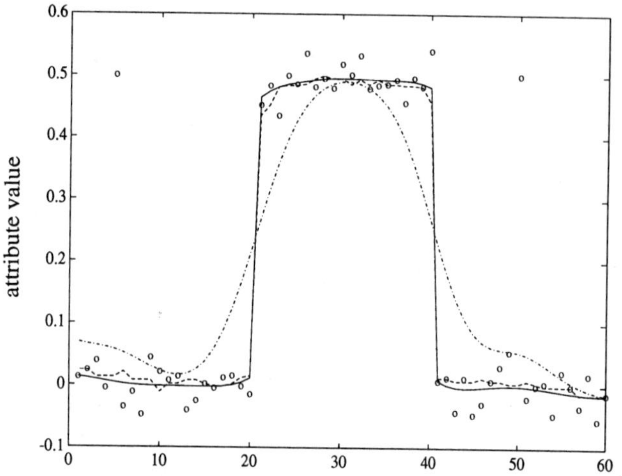

Figure 2. A corrupted hat and various filtered outputs.

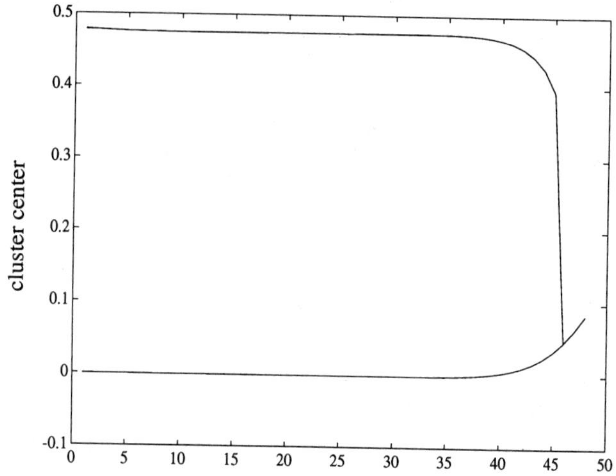

Figure 3c. Cluster centers versus scale for window centered at i=19.

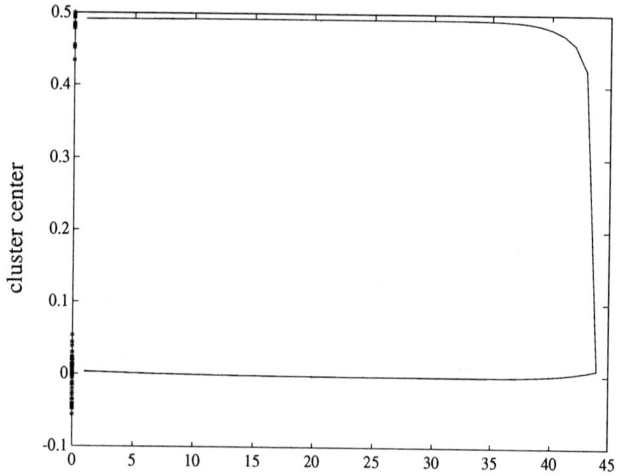

Figure 3a. Cluster centers versus scale.

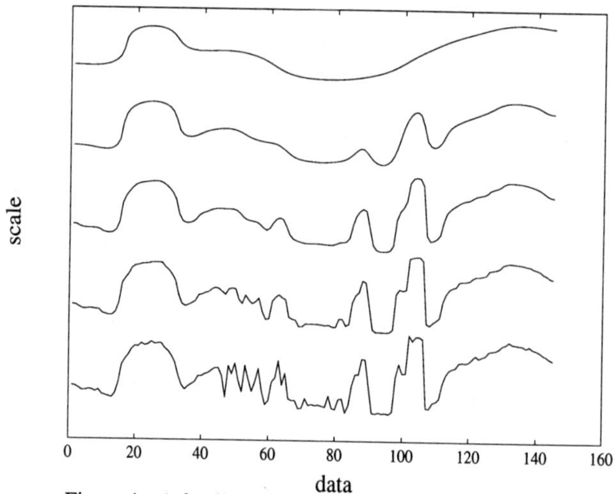

Figure 4a. A family of cluster filtered outputs as scale varies.

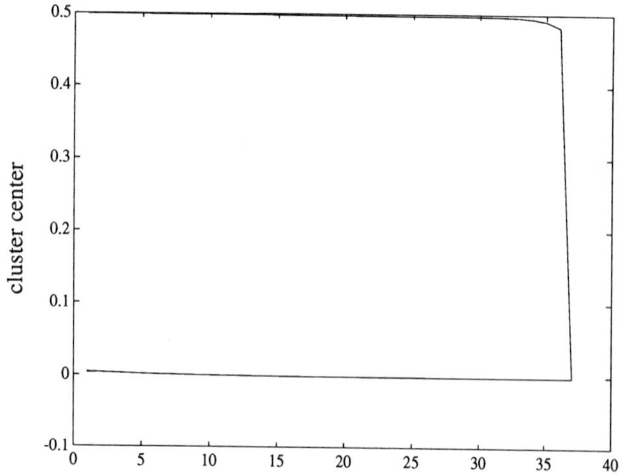

Figure 3b. Cluster centers versus scale for window centered at i=9.

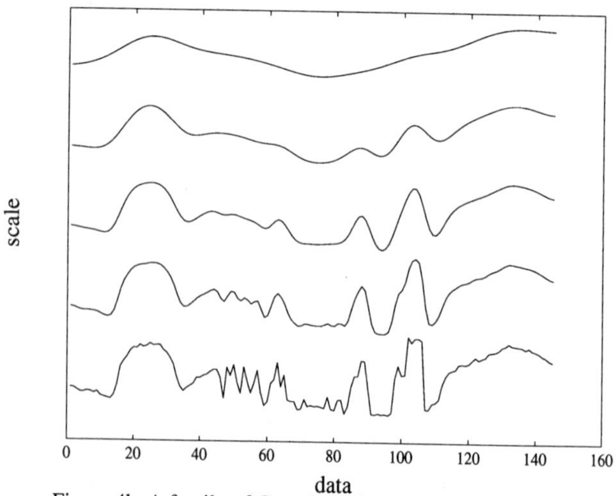

Figure 4b. A family of Gaussian filtered outputs as scale varies.

INTENTIONALLY LEFT BLANK

Digital Movies Using Optimized Feature Maps

YASUO MATSUYAMA† AND MASAYOSHI TAN*

† Department of Computer and Information Sciences, Ibaraki University, Hitachi, Japan 316
(† also, RWC Sympat Committee)
* Hitachi Cable, Ltd., Hitachi, Japan 316

Abstract

Steps from DC (data compression) to AC (animation coding) are discussed. This means that a digital movie is generated from a single still image using data compression. Such processing is made possible by the multuiply optimized competitive learning (multiply descent cost competitive learning). A key point is the usage of the optimized feature map. This optimized feature map groups nearby pixels together. Therefore, it is also called grouping feature map. Since this grouping feature map is optimized with respect to the source image and standard weight vectors, it possesses the ability of source data recovery. This property can not be realized by plain feature maps. The grouping feature map and standard weight vectors are metamprphic. Given information to move vertices in the grouping feature map, modified images can be produced. Thus, by generating temporal key frames, digital movies are realized. An initial trial toward 3D image processing is also given.

I. INTRODUCTION

MULTIPLY optimized competitive learning (multiply descent cost competitive learning [MAT90]) generates two feature maps of different levels at the same time. The upper-level feature map apparently looks like a plain one generated by a ubiquitous algorithm. However, the total map pattern is optimized with respect to the source input and weight vectors. An important property here is that each subregion of this optimized feature map is accompanied by a selected standard weight vector. This merit can not be found in usual feature maps. Therefore, the optimized feature map together with the standard weight vector set possesses an ability to reproduce the source input with good quality. This property matches to applications to sensory information processing. We treat the case of image processing. Usage of the optimized feature map is quite meritorious to image processing. For instance, the optimized feature map allows non-rectilinear segmentations. Since the optimized feature map collects nearby pixels, it is also called grouping feature map.

There are further merits of the grouping feature map. It is flexible in shape. This property is applicable to image transformation. Our main interest here is to generate a different image by modifying the grouping feature map. Thus, the new image is the result of the following mixture:

$$\text{New\_Image} = \text{Data\_Compressed\_Image} + \text{External\_Information}. \tag{1}$$

Since the new image can be created without using any images other than the original, the whole process is extrapolative in this sense. The interpolation between the data-compressed and the new image generates a series of frames. The grouping feature map plays the main role of this interpolation. The significance of our approach is summarized as follows:

- The presented method is based on a single still image:
  - Our method is totally different from animation systems where full background knowledge on personae etc. are specified.
  - Our movies do not use any prepared wire-frames [AIZ87] which is a weaker version of the above background knowledge.

0-7803-1901-X/94 $4.00 ©1994 IEEE

Figure 5a. Lena Image

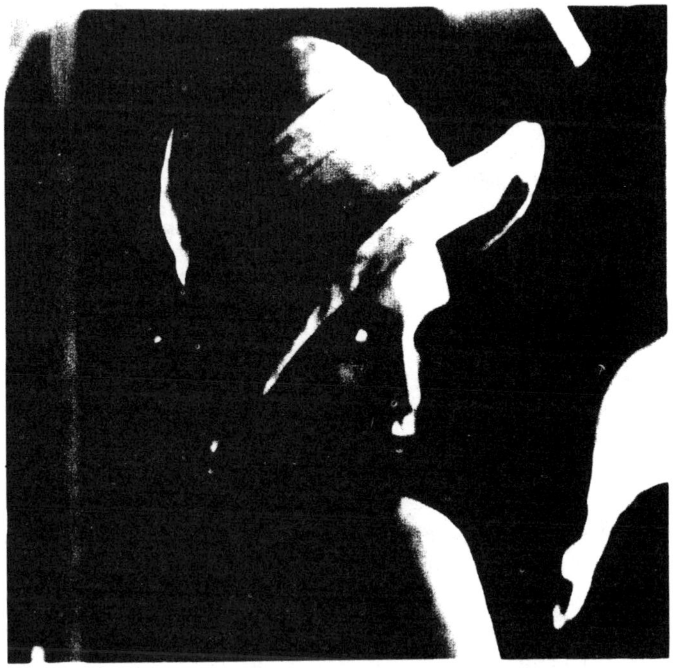

Figure 5b. Cluster filtered image of Fig. 5a.

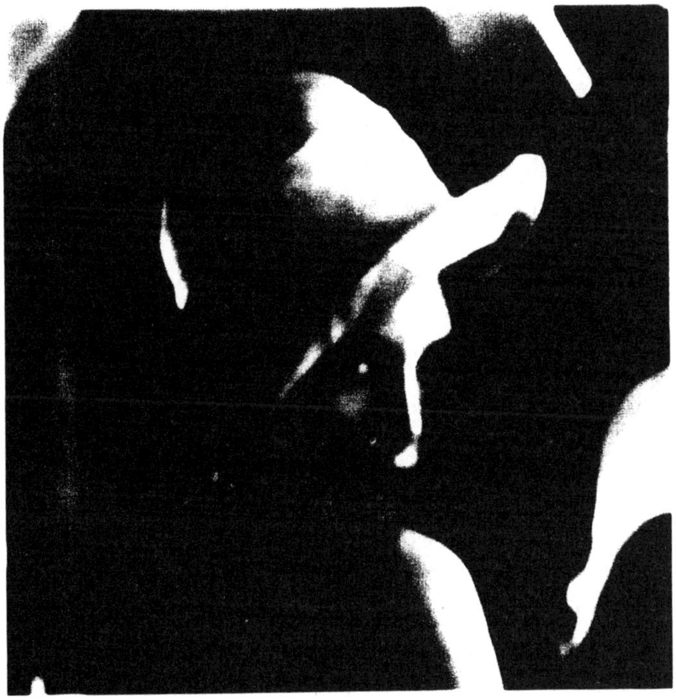

Figure 5c. Cluster filtered image at a coarser scale.

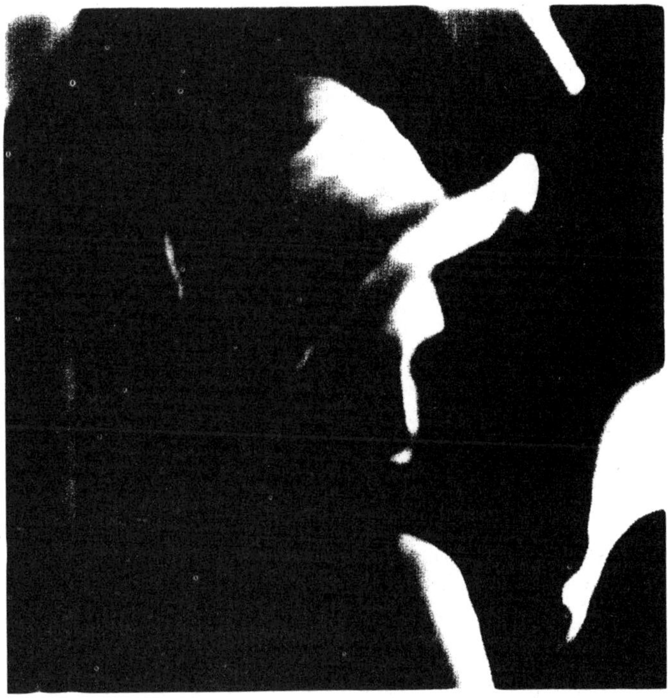

Figure 5d. Gaussian filtered image.

- Unlike our method, simple feature maps are unable to reproduce the source data.
- The grouping feature map together with the set of standard weight vectors reproduces the source data with good approximation with a high compression ratio. Adding extra information generates a series of frames for digital movies. Thus, the description required for the movie is very few in comparison with generated scenery.
- Facial emotion [ECK78] is discussed. However, this case is just one of many possible applications.
- The persented method has steps towards 3D images.

II. PRELIMINARIES

2.1 Multiply Optimized Competitive Learning

The multiply optimized competitive learning (multiply descent cost competitive learning) [MAT90] is as follows:

Step 1 (t=0; initialization)

A set of atomic data for training $\boldsymbol{x}_i$, $(i = 0, \ldots, I-1)$ is given. This is utilized to form a family of weight supervectors $\boldsymbol{v}_j(u_0)$, $(j = 0, \ldots, J-1)$ according to the initial grouping pattern $u_0 \in \mathcal{U}$. The class $\mathcal{U}$ is a set of admissible groupings. This is the total class of grouping feature maps. There is one more set given at the beginning: $\mathcal{C}^0 = \{\mathbf{c}_0^0, \ldots, \mathbf{c}_{N-1}^0\}$. This is the set of neural weight supervectors as standard patterns. The set of standard patterns forms a prespecified topology $\mathcal{N}$, whose evolved structure is the weight vector feature map.

Step 2 (t-th iteration; update the lower level feature map)

A portion of supervectors $\boldsymbol{v}_j(u_{t-1})$ is given. An evolved grouping feature map u_t is computed by the *competitive* optimization on the cost between $\boldsymbol{v}_j(u_{t-1})$ and $\mathcal{C}_{t-1}$. Here, the winning standard pattern in $\mathcal{C}_{t-1}$ is simultaneously decided.

Step 3 (update weight-supervectors and higher-level feature map)

Using the newly obtained supervector $\boldsymbol{v}_j(u_t)$, the winning neuron is updated:

$$\boldsymbol{c}_n^t = \boldsymbol{c}_n^{t-1} + \alpha^{t-1}\Delta\boldsymbol{c}_n.$$

Other neighborhood neurons in the sense of the topology $\mathcal{N}$ are also updated:

$$\boldsymbol{c}_m^t = \boldsymbol{c}_m^{t-1} + \beta^{t-1}\Delta\boldsymbol{c}_m.$$

Step 4 (update learning parameters)

If the predefined termination condition is met, stop the learning. Otherwise, update the learning parameters α^{t-1}, β^{t-1} and others. Then, replace $t \leftarrow t-1$. Go to Step 2.

2.2 Grouping Feature Map and Weight Vector Feature Map

There are two different classes of feature maps. The first one is the converged grouping pattern u_t. As is given in 2.1, this grouping feature map is optimized with respect to the source data and the standard weight vector set $\mathcal{C}^t$. The optimization in this case is executed by the minimization of the total error

$$D = \sum_{\text{all pixels}} \|\text{Original\_ Pixel - Recovered\_ Pixel}\|^2. \tag{2}$$

Another feature map of a different level is the evolved topology $\mathcal{N}$. This weight vector feature map is reduced to the usual feature map if $\boldsymbol{v}_j = \boldsymbol{x}_j$. We will use only the grouping feature map of the above. That is, there is no topology required to elements in $\mathcal{C}^t$.

III. Still Image Processing

3.1 Metamorphic Patches

The converged $\mathcal{C}^t$ is simply denoted by $\mathcal{C}$ hereafter. So is u_t by u. It is important to note that each element in $\mathcal{C}$ is possible to be metamorphic. This property keeps (2) meaningful. It is further important for data compression and generation of images. The regional shape of each weight vector is selected to be the right-angled isosceles triangle with a unit length edge (standard triangle). Inside of this triangle, learned pixels are packed. The standard triangles are metamprphic so that similar image portion is generated. The patches are transformed according to the bilinear transformation. Let (x, y) be an interior point specified by $(u, v) \in (0,1)^2$. Let its pixel value be p. If there are four vertices $(a_x, a_y) = (0,0)$, (b_x, b_y), (c_x, c_y) and (d_x, d_y) around (x, y), the following equations are used.

$$\begin{cases} x = vb_x(1-u) + \{d_x - (c_x - d_x)v\}u, \\ y = vb_y(1-u) + \{d_y - (c_y - d_y)v\}u, \end{cases} \tag{3}$$

$$p = (1-x)(1-y)p_0 + (1-x)yp_1 + xyp_2 + (1-x)yp_3. \tag{4}$$

If there are only three points $(a_x, a_y) = (0,0)$, (b_x, b_y) and (c_x, c_y) around (x, y), we use

$$\begin{cases} x = c_x u + b_x v, \\ y = c_y u + b_y v, \end{cases} \tag{5}$$

$$p = (1-x-y)p_0 + yp_1 + xp_2. \tag{6}$$

3.2 Data Compression via Inside-Training and Outside-Training

The original image is approximated by a grouping feature map and a set of standard weight vectors to be filled in the mesh of the map. Thus, the recovered image is described using

- bits to describe $\mathcal{C}$,
- bits to describe u,
- bits to describe filling elements drawn from $\mathcal{C}$.

In this case, the standard weight set $\mathcal{C}$ is computed for each original image. Thus, $\|\mathcal{C}\| = N$ can be made small (e.g., $N = 32$). But, training needs to be performed for each image. This is called *inside-training*. On the other hand, we can obtain the set of weight vectors $\mathcal{C}$ which works well for a wide class of images. In this case, the training data needs to be fairly large and contain rich image patches. The number of elements N is also larger in this case. The most important property is that the training data to obtain $\mathcal{C}$ is required only one time. This $\mathcal{C}$ is applicable to any images. Thus, the bits to describe $\mathcal{C}$ is not necessarily required for each image. Therefore, the outside training is meritorious in the sense of data compression. However, large training data, large main memory and computational power are required. Thus, for full-color images, inside training is used so far. If we prepare a product set $\mathcal{C}_{\text{red}} \times \mathcal{C}_{\text{green}} \times \mathcal{C}_{\text{blue}}$, the outside training has been possible using only a small computer.

3.3 Movement, Insertion and Deletion of Feature Map Vertices

The metamorphic patches (3)~(6) generate a new image by moving vertices of the grouping feature map. This is equivalent to elastically modify the original pattern. The main part of External_Information of (1) corresonds to specify such vertex transformation.

A class of images generated in terms of the vertex movement is pretty wide. But, it has natural limitations. Consider the case of facial action expression. Most expressions result from such vertex movement. However, there are cases that insertion and deletion of vertices are required. Erasure of one patch is achieved by moving one vertex onto another or onto an edge. Insertion of one patch is possible by adding extra vertices. Addition of vertices generates blank regions where something should be imbedded.

IV. Examples and Possibilities

4.1 Modification of Facial Expressions

The multiply optimized competitive learning is not a dedicated algorithm to facial expression coding. Such an instance is just one example drawn from applicable cases. However, it is an appealing exemplification. Human facial expressions are results of muscle movements [ECK78]. This process matches well to the modification of the optimized feature map which leads to a different expression. Our process starts from a single still image by the following steps.

Step 1

A still image containing a face is prepared.

Step 2

The multiply optimized competitive learning is applied to this source image. The grouping feature map, corresponding weight vectors (image patches) and a data-compressed image are obtained.

Step 3

External information to specify new vertex positions is given.

Step 3′

External information to specify vertex insertion/deletion is given. The vertex insertion is accompanied by extra pathces.

Step 4

Execute the midification of the feature map.

Step 5

Corresponding patches are filled into the grouping feature map. This process generates a new image.

Two data compressed images generated at Step 1 and Step 5 are used for digital movie generation.

4.2 Digital Movies

Let the image obtained at Step 1 of 4.1 be a frame for $t = 0$. On the other hand, let the image at $t = 1$ be the one generated at Step 5 of the above. Frames at $t = \tau \in (0, 1)$ are generated by temporal interpolation of two grouping feature maps corresponding to these two images. Therefore, the frame at $t = \tau$ is generated by imbedding image patches. Since the movement is based on the grouping feature map, the frame at $t = \tau$ is *not* a cross-fading image. We can prepare a necessary number of key frames in the time interval $[0, 1]$. Additional frames are automatically generated by a usual digital movie system. Thus, the obtained digital movie is smoothly generated using only the following information bits:

$$[\text{bits to specify data-compressed still image for } t = 0] + [\text{bits to specify vertex modification for } t = 1]$$

If the vertex insertion is specified, bits to specify accompanied patches are needed.

Fig. 0 is the full image of the grouping feature map. Fig. 1 is a data-compressed image for $t = 0$, and two generated images for $t = 0.5$ and $t = 1$. Fig. 2 is a series of differential images at key frames. Fig. 3 is a series of differential patterns of the grouping feature maps. One can observe the evidence that our movie generation which does not use cross fading.

V. Concluding Remarks - - Towards 3D Processing

We realized a total system of generating a digital movie from a single still image. The method is based on the mogification of an optimized grouping feature map. Given examples in this paper were on human facial images. However, the presented algorithm is not limited to such emotional feature transformations. Processing of a wide variety of images is possible. Giving such examples is an interesting next step.

There is another intriguing class of problems - - steps towards 3D images and movies. A first step to this issue has been initiated by our group. The problem is described as follows. Consider the diagram below:

$$\boxed{\text{2D} \xrightarrow{t} \text{2D}\times\text{frames} \Longrightarrow \text{extrapolative digital movie}}$$

This was the case that we presented by examples of 2D digital movies. The problems on 3D processing and 3D movies are expressed by the following diagram:

$$2D \xrightarrow{z} 3D \xrightarrow{t} 3D\times\text{frames} \Longrightarrow 3D \text{ digital movie}$$

That is, inferences which help to obtain depth of a 2D image are tried. However, perfect estimation from only a 2D image is not our target. We try to make an inference system which accepts external information as a guidance. This is because we have a famous exemple: Consider a case of a stereogram. By adjusting our focus, an object can be identified either convex or concave. Another difficulty is the estimation of nose length from a make-up face. Considering these facts, we try to make a system to help a person to give depth to an 2D image. Thus, the system estimates depth to an 2D image first. If the estimeted value is inappropriate, then the user corrects it to be an admissible one interactively. This system is yet helpful since any user can not specify depth data to every pixel (the number of pixels is at least 256 × 256). The above inference subsystem is generated by supervised learning on depth images.

ACKNOWLEDGEMENTS

The authors are grateful to Mr. Y. Kurosawa of Kawasaki Steel, Co., for his early contributions and discussions. Mr. S. Saito receives thanks for his programming support. The Ministry of Education's Grant-in-Aid for Scientific Research and NEC partially supported this study.

REFERENCES

[AIZ87] Aizawa, K., Yamada, Y., Harashima, H. and Saito, T., Model-based synthesis image coding system: Modeling a person's face and synthesis of facial expressions, Convention Record of GLOBECOM'87, Vol. 1, pp. 45-49 (1987).

[ECK78] Eckman, P. and Friesen, W. V., Facial Action Coding System, Psychlogists Press, Palo Alto, CA (1978).

[MAT90] Matsuyama, Y., Multiple descent cost competitive learning: Batch and successive self-organization with excitatory and inhibitory connectins, Proc. IJCNN, San Diego, Vol. II, pp. 299-306 (1990).

[MAT92] Matsuyama, Y. and Kurosawa, Y., Coordination of optimal feature map and supervisory concept, Proc. IJCNN, Beijin, Vol. II, pp. 734-741 (1992).

[MAT93] Matsuyama, Y. and Tan, M., Multiply descent cost competitive learning as an aid for multimedia processing, Proc. IJCNN, Nagoya, Vol.3, pp.2061-2064 (1993).

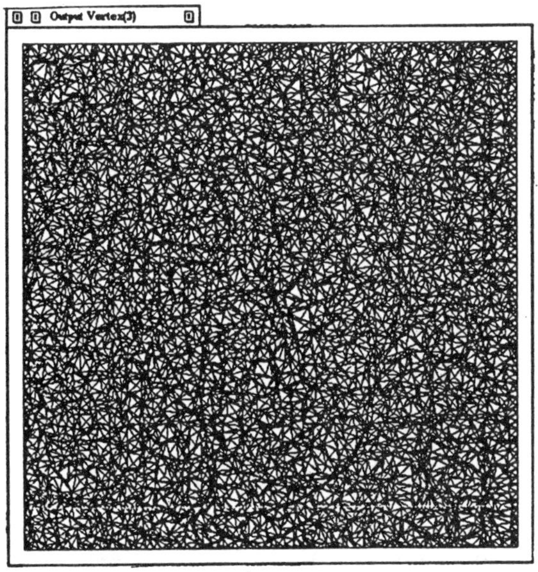

Fig.0 Full image of the grouping feature map.
(The outline can be observed.)

(a) $t = 0$. (b) $t = 0.5$. (c) $t = 1$.

Fig.1 Data-compressed and modified images.

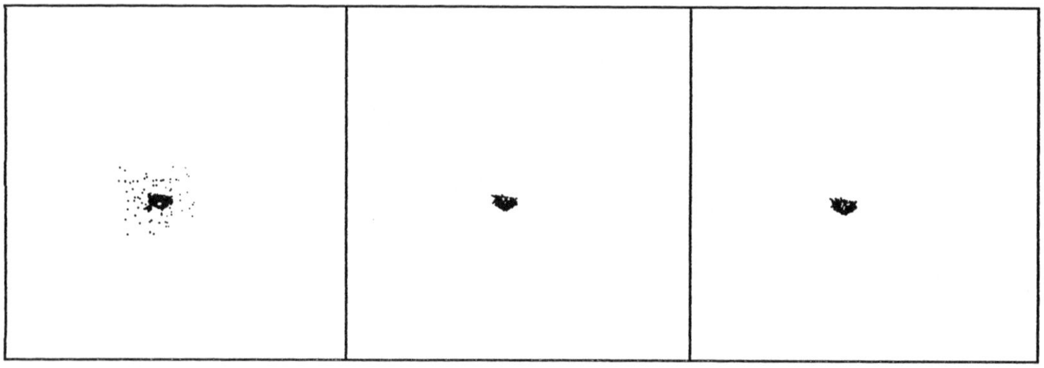

(a) $t = 0$. (b) $t = 0.5$. (c) $t = 1$.

Fig.2 Difference of image frames.

(a) $t = 0$. (b) $t = 0.5$. (c) $t = 1$.

Fig.3 Difference of grouping feature maps.

INTENTIONALLY LEFT BLANK

Pattern Theory for Character Recognition

Jack S.N. Jean* Kefu Xue† Shailendra Goel*
Wright State University
Dayton, OH 45435

Abstract

Pattern Theory is an engineering theory of algorithm design which provides a robust characterization of all types of patterns. Similar to logical neural networks, the Theory can be used to generalize from a set of training data. However, it *optimizes network architectures* as well as the "weights" of the resulting machine. In this paper, the application of the Theory to character recognition is considered. The application requires a simple extension to the Theory and a faster algorithm to perform a basic decomposition operation. Such an algorithm is developed and described in the paper. Some simulation results of the algorithm are also included.

1 Introduction

Pattern Theory is an engineering theory of algorithm design which provides a robust characterization of all types of patterns [3]. Given a problem description in terms of a truth table and a special measure of pattern-ness, called Decomposed Function Cardinality (DFC), the Theory conjectures that the desired solution among a set of candidates is the one that possesses the lowest DFC. The application of the Theory is similar to that of neural networks. A finite set of observed data, represented as a truth table, is analyzed to extract some *patterns*, or a model of the data. The resulting model is then applied to unseen input data so to predict their outputs. The conjecture is that, due to the minimization of criteria such as DFC, the Theory would automatically lead to a machine that generalizes from the observed data set.

Compared to neural network approaches, Pattern Theory has two technical merits. It *optimizes* the architecture as well as the "weights" of the resulting machine. Note that this is different from simply ruling out architectures that contradict with a chosen network topology and a training data set as used by some logical neural network developments [2]. Another advantage is about the speed of the resulting machine. Since the resulting machine operation involves only table lookups, it is expected to be very fast. The machine speed after training is important for many applications.

Pattern Theory was invented by Ross et. al. [3]. They developed a software called FLASH to implement the Theory [4]. The current implementation of FLASH is for single bit output and is not suitable for applications which require multi-value or multi-bit outputs. This paper describes an extension to the Theory and discusses an algorithm to speed up the training process.

In Section 2, the Theory is briefly reviewed. In Section 3, the extension to the The-

*The authors are with the Department of Computer Science and Engineering.

†The author is with the Department of Electrical Engineering.

0-7803-1901-X/94 $4.00 ©1994 IEEE

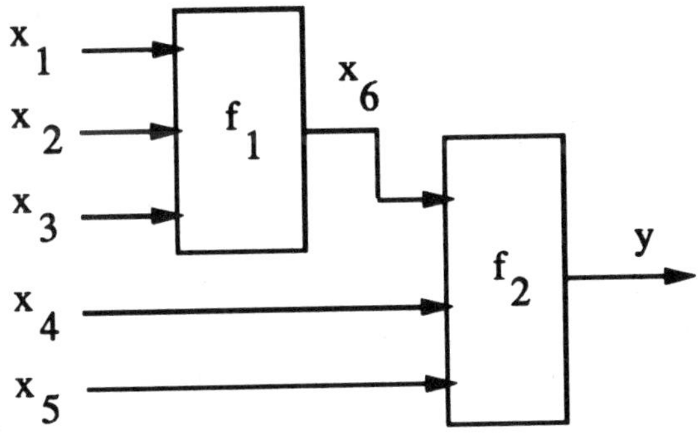

Figure 1: Partition

		x_1	0	0	0	0	1	1	1	1
		x_2	0	0	1	1	0	0	1	1
x_4	x_5	x_3	0	1	0	1	0	1	0	1
0	0		1	1	1	x	1	1	x	1
0	1		0	x	0	0	1	x	1	1
1	0		1	1	x	x	x	0	0	x
1	1		x	1	x	1	0	x	x	0

Table 1: A partition table where an 'x' means a don't care, or an undefined entry.

x_1	x_2	x_3	x_6
0	0	0	0
0	0	1	0
0	1	0	0
0	1	1	0
1	0	0	1
1	0	1	1
1	1	0	1
1	1	1	1

x_6	x_4	x_5	y
0	0	0	1
0	0	1	0
0	1	0	1
0	1	1	1
1	0	0	1
1	0	1	1
1	1	0	0
1	1	1	0

Table 2: The truth tables for $f_1()$ and $f_2()$.

ory and the algorithm are described. Some preliminary implementation results are also included. Section 4 concludes the paper.

2 Review of Pattern Theory

Given a problem description in terms of a truth table, or equivalently a (partial) function $f()$, there are many different ways to partition the input variables into two sets and decompose function into two (partial) functions f_1 and f_2 as shown in Figure 1. (This paper concentrates on this form of partition even though there exist other forms of partition.) For a large system, the truth table specification can be recursively partitioned. The first partition produces two tables which can be further partitioned individually. The Pattern Theory suggests that the partition with the lowest complexity in its decomposed form can best extract the inherent "patterns" from the training data set, i.e., it can best generalize from the training data set. The Theory also suggests that the complexity of a decomposed form can be measured as the total table size for all the decomposed functions [3]. Since each level can be partitioned in many ways, the search for an optimized combination of partitions is computationally expensive and is usually done heuristically.

Here an example is used to illustrate the operations involved in the partitioning process. Suppose a stateless system has five binary input variables $(x_1, x_2, \ldots, x_5)$ and one binary output variable y. A truth table of 32 entries would be enough to specify the system. Suppose there are only 20 entries of data in the training data set and, with a partition of the input variables into two sets $\{x_1, x_2, x_3\}$ and $\{x_4, x_5\}$, the truth table can be represented as a *partition table* as shown in Table 1. Note that if suitable values are assigned to the entries with don't cares, the first four columns of the partition table can be made the same as (1 0 1 1)' while the last four columns can be made the same as (1 1 0 0)'. This is called the *merging* of columns. Therefore, as indicated in Figure 1, an intermediate variable x_6 may be introduced to distinguish the two types of columns and the two functions, $f_1()$ and $f_2()$, may be described by the two tables as shown in Table 2.

Since both $f_1()$ and $f_2()$ are fully defined, the 12 previously undefined entries have been assigned some values. Whether the output values are assigned correctly or not determines the generalization capability of the decomposed system. Note that to store the truth table for complete functions such as $f_1()$ and $f_2()$, there is no need to store the table of input combinations.

3 Extension to Pattern Theory

For the character recognition problem, there are 96 input variables when a 12×8 binary image is used and the output has more than two different values to represent all the different types of characters. Therefore two issues need to be addressed. One is to extend the Theory for multi-value outputs. The other is about the memory storage and execution speed.

3.1 Multi-Value Outputs

One simple way to handle a multi-value output is to encode its levels with multiple binary variables and treat the variables independently. This converts a single system with a muitl-value output into multiple systems, each with a binary output. Each of the binary-output system can then be decomposed individually. However, the resulting system complexity would be higher than necessary because those multiple binary systems could have shared some common decomposed functions. Furthermore, once binary encoded with n bits, all the levels of outputs are placed in an n-dimensional space and some degree of asymmetry among the levels is arbitrarily introduced. This extra asymmetry may influence the system generalization capability.

Another way to handle multi-value outputs is to allow non-binary entries in the partition table. Partition of the table or merging of columns can be processed in a similar way. This is the approach adopted in our current study.

A related question is whether the intermediate variables should be binary or not. In the previous example, x_6 is introduced because there are two types of columns after merging. If there were three types of columns instead, should two binary intermediate variables or a three-value one be used? By applying the same argument in using non-binary entries in the partition table, we chose to use a three-value variable in this case.

3.2 Memory Storage and Execution Speed

For an implementation of Pattern Theory to be able to handle 8,000 96-bit training patterns, some considerations to the memory requirement and execution speed are necessary.

- Memory Requirement: Although there are only around 8000 training data, the size of a partition table is usually much large and depends on the partition of input variables. For example, if the 96 bits are partitioned into two sets, one with the first 24 bits and the other with the rest of the bits, simulation shows that the table can be of 2276 rows and 7114 columns, or equivalently, 16,191,464 entries. That means the table is very sparse and a data structure of two-dimensional array is a waste. Instead a set of linked lists is more appropriate. Another implementation issue about memory requirement is the way to store a 96-bit binary pattern in C (or C++) language. (The current implementation of Pattern Theory, FLASH [4], is in C++ language.) Using one character, or one byte, to store each bit would simplify programming while increase the storage by a factor of eight. It also increases memory access time and slows down the computation. Therefore, a program has been developed which uses three 32-bit integers in C to store 96 bits at the expense of increased program complexity.

- Execution Speed: Experience from neural network research shows that, although it takes exponential amount of time to find the optimal solution, it normally takes much less amount of time to find a "satisfactory" solution. This should be also true when applying Pattern theory to the character recognition problem. Furthermore, in the 96-dimensional space, the 8000 or so training data should be very sparse and well clustered. This property can be used to speed up the merging of column variables, a very basic operation required for Pattern Theory.

3.3 Column Merging Algorithm

To find a good partition, the operation to merging columns of a partition table may need to be performed millions of times. To make things worse, the execution time of the operation is normally of order $O(C^2)$ where C is the number of non-empty columns in a partition table and it may be greater than a thousand. Thus a new algorithm based on a divide-and-conquer concept has been developed for the operation.

In this section, the data structure for the algorithm is first described. It is then shown that the column merging problem can be translated into a graph coloring problem and solved in $O(C^2)$ time complexity. The effects of applying a divide-and-conquer concept are also demonstrated.

Data Structure As stated previously, some linked lists instead of 2-D arrays are necessary for the storage of partition tables. In our current implementation, a partition table is stored as a set of *row-ordered hashed lists* where a linked list is used for each row and hashing is performed on the row variables to store the large number of linked lists. For any 96-bit image entry, the hashing greatly speeds up the locating of its corresponding linked list. Note that a set of row-ordered hashed lists can be constructed in roughly linear time from a set of training data.

Graph Coloring Formulation If two entries on a row of a partition table correspond to two valid but different characters, then the two columns where the two entries belong to cannot be merged. Two columns in a partition table can be merged *if and only if* there exists no row where the two columns have valid but different characters. Therefore for a partition table of R rows and C columns, it is possible to construct a undirected graph G(V, E) where V is the set of vertices, each corresponding to a column, and E is the set of edges. There exists an edge between two vertices if the two corresponding columns cannot be merged.

1. To construct the graph, it is assumed that the partition table is stored as a set of row-ordered hashed lists and the number of training data is much smaller than RC. In this case, the number of entries in each row is usually very small and it takes only a small amount of time to add edges to the graph for each row.

2. Once the graph is constructed, the problem of merging columns can be translated into the problem of using minimal number of colors to color all the vertices so that no two connected vertices share the same color. The graph coloring problem is NP-complete [1]. In our implementation, a heuristic algorithm with $O(C^2)$ time complexity and $O(C^2)$ space storage

is used. The algorithm calculates the degree for each vertex and colors the vertices in the sequence of descending degrees.

Divide-and-Conquer For the character recognition problem, R and C can be in the order of thousands. That makes column merging a very expensive operation. To reduce the complexity, it is noted that

1. There exist a lot of *single-entry rows.* A single-entry row contains only one entry and does not influence the column merging decision at all.

2. For rows with multiple entries, they do not influence the column merging decision if characters on the same row are of the same type. They are called *single-character rows.*

3. For the remaining rows, after some shuffling of rows and columns, there exists a block structure where different blocks share no common rows and columns. In this case, the coloring algorithm can be independently applied to each small block which has a much smaller R and C values. Note that the speedup will be significant only if the operation to breaking into small blocks is relatively fast and each small block is much smaller than the original partition table.

For the last case, to obtain the small blocks starting from a set of *row-ordered hashed lists* is equivalent to putting all the rows sharing some columns into a block and, at the same time, putting rows sharing no column into different blocks. The operation goes row by row and, for each row, entry by entry. It checks if the column of an entry is the same as that of entries from all previously processed rows. The checking can be done in (close to) constant time by using hashing on column variables. Therefore getting all the small blocks can be done in liner time in the number of training data.

As to the processing of each small block, it is noted that many *single-entry columns* exist in each small block. Since these single-entry columns may be colored very easily after the other multi-entry columns are colored, there is no need to include them in the graph coloring process. Therefore the coloring process may focus on the multi-entry columns in each block.

Simulation Results To verify the feasibility of the approach, a program was written and applied to a set of training data. A total of 22,644 alphanumeric data samples were collected from 35 commonly-used fonts using a 300 dpi scanner. Among them, 8508 characters were used for training and the remaining data were used for testing. All characters were normalized into 12×8 low-resolution bitmaps by a linear shrinking process. Because of the normalization and low resolution, some characters became indistinguishable. Therefore duplicate patterns were removed and some different types of characters were considered as equivalent. For example, 'H' is considered equivalent to 'X'. The final training set contains 7695 data belonging to 49 classes of characters.

The program can partition the table for training data into two tables according to a given partition of the input variables. Table 3 summarizes the preliminary results of the program on the training data set with several different partitions. Here the first entry of the table is used as an example to explain the results. When the 96 input variables are partitioned into two sets, 24 as inputs to $f_1()$ (refer to Figure 1) and 72 to $f_2()$, the partition table has 2276 rows and 7114 columns. Among the rows, 1149 are single-entry rows and 532 are single-character rows. Therefore

No. of Variables (Row/Column)	R (Row)	C (Col.)	Single-Entry Rows	Single-Character Rows	C'	C"	B	M
24/72	2276	7114	1149	532	4525	210	47	15
28/68	3117	7022	1804	744	3413	173	40	13
32/64	3908	6846	2587	881	2350	134	40	12
40/56	5225	6427	3975	998	976	75	12	9
48/48	5913	5947	4872	885	528	49	9	6
52/44	6180	5611	5224	827	396	40	8	4

Table 3: Simulation results: After the removal of single-entry and single-character rows, C' is the number of remaining columns and C" is the number of columns with multiple entries. B is the maximal number of columns used in the graph coloring process and M is the number of columns (colors) after merging.

only 595 (= 2276 − 1149 − 532) rows which occupy 4525 columns need to go through the process of breaking into small blocks. Among the 4525 columns, only 210 of them contain multiple entries. The largest block after the divide-and-conquer technique has 47 multi-entry columns. After merging, there are 15 columns. That means, the output of $f_1()$ has 15 output values. From the results, it is clear that the divide-and-conquer technique did reduce the block size drastically.

4 Conclusion

In this paper, Pattern Theory is reviewed and extended to handle character recognition problem. The discussion focuses on the basic partition operations required for Pattern Theory. Preliminary results of a program to perform the basic operation are summarized to show that the presented algorithm to merging columns of a partition table is very effective for the first level of decomposition. Not implemented yet is a program to perform the decomposition recursively and to search for an satisfactory solution. The generalization capability is not discussed in the paper.

Acknowledgement

The authors would like to thank Timothy D. Ross, Mark L. Axtell, David A. Gadd, and Michael J. Noviskey for their introduction to Pattern Theory and many helpful discussions.

References

[1] S. Even, GRAPH ALGORITHMS, Computer Science Press, 1979.

[2] T.J. Stonham and R. Al-Alawi, "A Design Strategy for Logical Neural Networks," in Proc. of IEEE International Conference on System Engineering, pp. 355–358, 1991.

[3] Timothy D. Ross, Michael J. Noviskey, Timothy N. Taylor, and David A. Gadd, "Pattern Theory: An Engineering Paradigm for Algorithm Design," Final Technical Report WL-TR-91-1060, Wright Laboratory, USAF, WL/AART, WPAFB, OH 45433-6543, August 1991.

[4] Timothy D. Ross, Michael J. Noviskey, Mark L. Axtell, and David A. Gadd, "FLASH User's Guide," Wright Laboratory, USAF, WL/AART-2, WPAFB, OH 45433-6543, November 1993.

SHOSLIF: A Framework for Object Recognition from Images

John (Juyang) Weng
Department of Computer Science
Michigan State University
East Lansing, MI, 48824 USA

Abstract

A new framework called Self-organizing Hierarchical Optimal Subspace Learning and Inference Framework (SHOSLIF) is introduced for recognizing and segmenting real-world objects from images. It addresses critical problems in real-world recognition including visual attention, feature representation efficiency, shape variation in unsegmented data (including size, position and orientation), decision optimality, and geometric inference.

1 Introduction

The performance of a neural network trained with the back-propagation method is typically not predictable, due to the problem with local minima. The work of Neocognitron by Fukushima [1] was designed for recognizing a small number of segmented patterns such as numerals and alphabets. It is based on local-to-global analysis while the backpropagation training is based on nonlinear global optimization. The Cresceptron by Weng *et al* [3] uses a multi-level local-to-global analysis retinotopic network. It is different from the Neocognitron in that the network configuration of the Cresceptron is *automatically* determined during learning, and it is for recognizing *real-world objects* from intensity images, among other structural differences.

Although the local-to-global analysis networks are relatively free from the local minima problem, its efficiency is an unsolved problem. A real-world recognition system must recognize hundreds and thousands of objects. It is computationally intractable to keep all intermediate-level feature structures, because the number increases exponentially with the size of the receptive field it covers. The SHOSLIF introduced here addresses this key issue of feature representation, along with other critical issues of efficiency, visual attention, shape variation in unsegmented data (including size, position and orientation), decision optimality, and visual inference.

2 An Outline of the SHOSLIF

The SHOSLIF is fully adaptive in the sense that there is little constraint on the shape of the objects the system can deal with. The structure of the network itself is a function of learning. Fig. 1 shows a functional view of the SHOSLIF. Each invocation of the

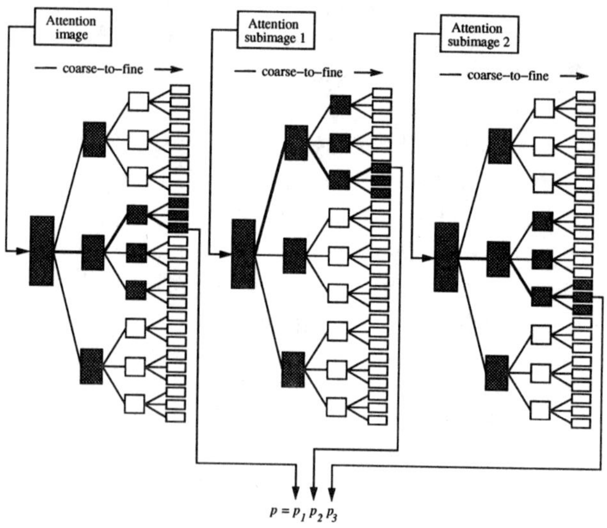

Figure 1: A functional view of the SHOSLIF. The hierarchical network is invoked several times (3 in the figure) according to the visual saccades sequence specified by the human operator during the learning phase. Within each network, the coarse-to-fine hierarchy recursively subdivides the learned visual objects into finer and finer subclasses. The darkened paths are traversed paths. In actuality, each tree is not necessarily a complete tree.

network corresponds to the examination of an area. The first network is typically for the entire region of the object and the following ones are to examine some subregions of the object with a higher resolution. The final confidence for recognizing an object is measured by a product of the probabilities computed from every invocation.

0-7803-1901-X/94 $4.00 ©1994 IEEE

Fig 2 is a more detailed structural illustration of the SHOSLIF network. At lower levels, the input is

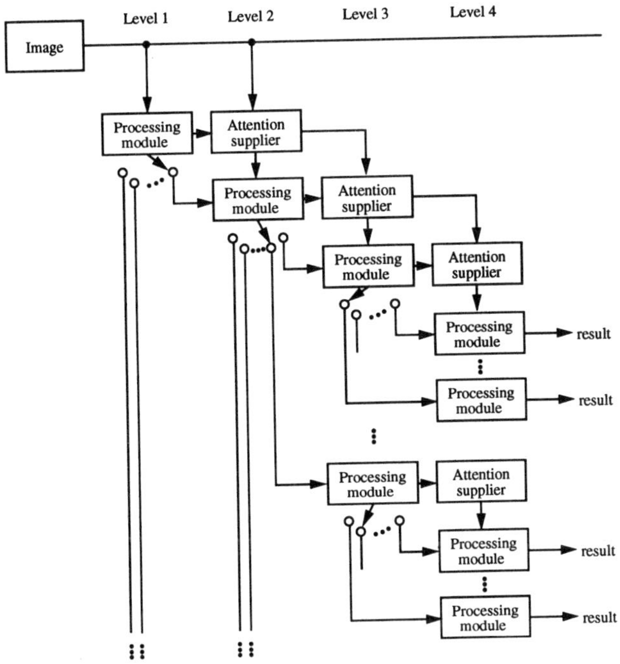

Figure 2: The network structure of the SHOSLIF. Each level may have several processing modules. Each module at level l_0 has a subtree at levels $l > l_0$. In the figure, only one processing module is shown for levels 1 and 2. Each processing module may activate one processing module at the next higher level, as indicated by a multiplex in the figure. Each processing module controls an attention module which is responsible for supplying proper re-normalized subimages (called attention images) to the activated processing module.

classified into rough categories, at higher levels finer classification is performed. For example, the first level is to detect a possible human face; and the following levels detect faces with specific viewing angle, size, and position, etc.

The processing module is illustrated in Fig. 3. The module uses optimal subspace in the sense that the subspace is spanned by a set of automatically generated optimal features with minimal loss of useful information but with a drastic reduction of the number of features.

The attention supplier shown in Fig. 4 has two basic steps. The first is to use the parameters supplied by the associated processing module to re-normalize the subimage so that the region of interest is centered at the attention window and the scale is standard (the same as that learned). The second is to generate a list

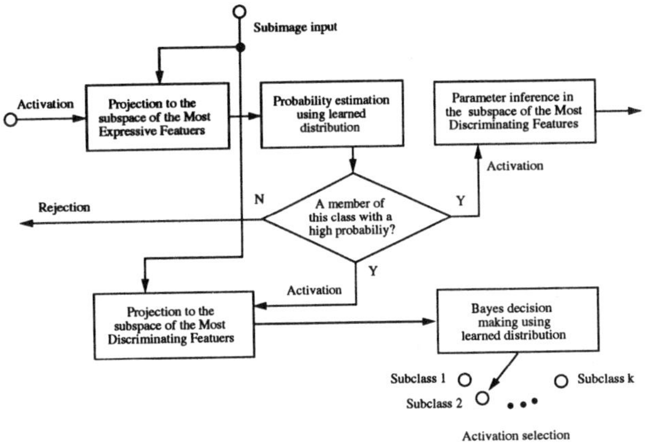

Figure 3: The action flow chart of the processing module.

of attention image according to the learned attention list, by linearly mapping the desired attention area in the normalized image to the attention window. The first on the list typically correspond to the current visual attention and thus, the current network is further traversed. The remainder in the list each requires a new invocation of the network as shown in Fig 1.

2.1 Automatic visual attention

2.2 The tasks of visual attention.

In the proposed SHOSLIF, fovea image is defined with a fixed resolution (according to the experiment with the Cresceptron, 64 × 64-pixel resolution is a good candidate). Visual attention supplier provides a subimage, defined by the attention window and called attention image, in which the object of interest is, as much as possible, centered and fills almost the entire window. The attention image is linearly mapped to the fovea image and then fed into the processing module for recognition. A close examination of subregions of an object is made possible by mapping each part to the entire fovea. For example, the image of an eye in a face image can be mapped to the entire fovea for close examination. Such subregions of interest can be recursively defined in the learning phase.

Specifically, visual attention involves two levels:

1. Visual attention for estimating position and size of the object of interest, which is accomplished by: (a) A set of coarse grid points are defined in position-size space. Each grid point defines an attention window. The recognition is applied to a grid point if it passes a simple test on the intensity variance (to save computation, grid points in uniform regions are skipped). (b) The fovea

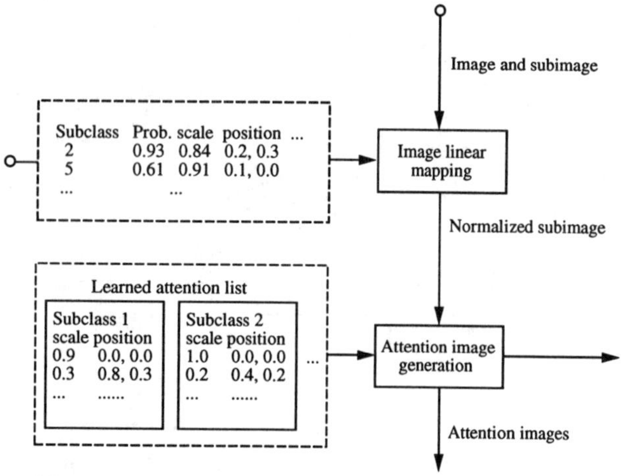

Figure 4: A simplified illustration of the attention supplier.

recognition can tolerate the position-size variation that corresponds to the spacing between the grid points.

2. Saccadic examination of subregions of the object of interest, which is accomplished by: (a) For each type of object, human teacher specifies a sequence of subregion of interest, which is learned by the system. (b) For each subregion of interest, the fovea recognition can tolerate the position-size variation among different individuals in the same class.

2.3 Recognition of admissible attention image and estimation of object's position and size

Fovea recognition must be able to tolerate certain variation in position and size within a certain *tolerance range*. (For example, the size can vary 20%, and the position can vary 10% in each direction from the center of the fovea.) An attention image in which the relative size and position of the object of interest fall into this tolerance range is called *admissible image*. The tolerance range is accomplished by the first few levels of the SHOSLIF. Each attention image is first properly blurred to allow distortion for recognition and produce a smooth trajectory in geometric inference (see Section 6). The amount of blurring should be larger at a coarse level (low level number) and smaller at a fine level (higher level number). The blurred attention images with several different position-size combinations are used to train Level 1. Each level thus estimates the position-size parameters with a better accuracy from the previous level and then the subimage is renormalized for the next level.

2.4 Shallow invocation of the SHOSLIF on coarse grid

Let us consider the task of finding learned objects from the real world scenes. The first stage is to define a set of equally spaced grid points in (position, scale) space. The spacing between the grid points is small enough so that the variation represented by the spacing just falls into position-size tolerance range of the fovea recognition. The coarsest level (Level 1) in the SHOSLIF is applied to only those grid points that pass the simple intensity variation test. Only those grid points that lead to a large probability (say, above 0.8) at level 1 are further computed by the next levels. The computation is terminated as soon as it is confident that the corresponding grid point does not hit an object of interest.

2.5 Automatic generation of network through self-organization in learning

At each level, the extent of sample variation accepted by a processing module is automatically controlled by specifying an upper bound on the trace of the covariance matrix in the feature space (the most expressive feature as explained in the next section). This bound is reduced by a factor of $q < 1$ from the current level to the next.

The graphic description in Fig. 5 gives a simplified and intuitive explanation of the idea. The feature space of the visual world with all the possible objects that can occur is divided recursively into "cells". At a low level, the cells are large, as shown by thick lines in Fig. 5. The children of a parent subdivide the parent's cell into smaller cells, as shown by thin lines in Fig. 5. The grandchildren subdivide their parent's cell further. The finer the cell is, the more specific recognition (classification) can be obtained.

2.6 Segmentation

Segmentation is to locate the region in the image that is covered by the recognized object. During the learning phase, the human operator identifies the area to be learned from the image by drawing a polygon using, say, a computer mouse. Magnitude of the image gradient is used for training. During the recognition phase, the segmentation works in the same way as in Cresceptron. Background regions in each attention image is masked off by the feature vector projections when the size and position estimates of the input is improved through the levels. The mask is automatically created because the corresponding components

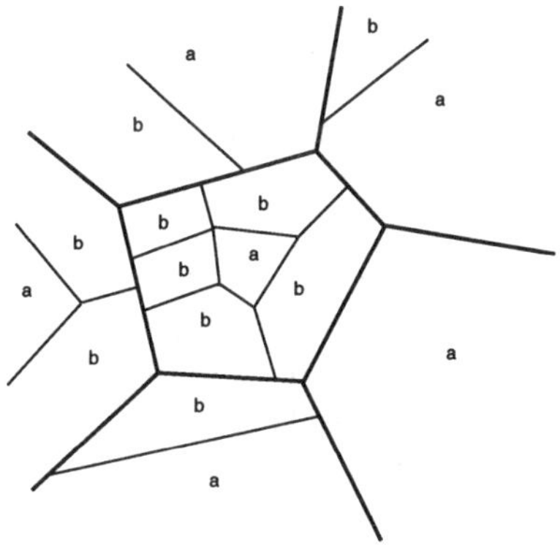

Figure 5: A simplified illustration of the hierarchical visual concept decomposition in the optimal feature space. a's and b's represent the mean vector of each cell at levels 1 and 2, respectively. The decomposition of space is like a Voronoi diagram. But, the actual space decomposition in SHOSLIF is different from Voronoi diagram: (1) It is hierarchical. (2) It is based on Bayes principle instead of Euclidean distance. (3) The centers and extent of the cells are recursively updated during learning. (4) Each cell in each level uses a different set of features (MEF and MDF as defined later).

in each of MEF and MDF are zeros. A back tracking of the network from top level to level 1 records the non-zero components in the feature vector space. Finally the recorded non-zero pixels in the fovea image are marked back to the input image.

3 The Most Expressive Features

The Karhunen-Loeve projection [2] can be used to select the most expressive features. Images of objects in a category (e.g., human faces) can be considered as samples represented by an n-dimensional random vector $\mathbf{X}$. $\mathbf{X}$ can be expanded exactly by n orthonormal vectors, $\mathbf{v}_1, \mathbf{v}_2, ..., \mathbf{v}_n$, so that

$$\mathbf{X} = \sum_{i=1}^{n} y_i \mathbf{v}_i = V\mathbf{Y} \qquad (1)$$

where V is an orthogonal $n \times n$ square matrix consisting of orthonormal column vectors $\mathbf{v}_i$. Without loss of generality, we can assume that the mean of the random vector $\mathbf{Y}$ is a zero vector, since we can always redefine $\mathbf{Y} - E\mathbf{Y}$ as the new feature vector.

We can expect that a relatively small number of features is sufficient to characterize a class. Suppose we use m features, each is a component of $\mathbf{Y}$. The approximate representation is $\hat{\mathbf{X}}(m) = \sum_{i=1}^{m} y_i \mathbf{v}_i$. It has been proved [2] that the best $\mathbf{v}_1\ \mathbf{v}_2\ ...\ \mathbf{v}_m$ that minimize

$$\epsilon^2(m) = E\|\delta\mathbf{X}(m)\|^2 = E\|\mathbf{X} - \hat{\mathbf{X}}(m)\|^2 \qquad (2)$$

are the m unit eigenvectors of the covariance matrix of $\mathbf{X}$, $\Sigma_X = E[(\mathbf{X} - E\mathbf{X})(\mathbf{X} - E\mathbf{X})^t]$, associated with the m largest eigenvalues. After $\mathbf{v}_i$'s are computed, these m features values y_i can be computed from

$$y_i = \mathbf{v}_i^t \mathbf{X} \qquad i = 1, 2, ..., m \qquad (3)$$

Since the m features y_i's in (3) give the minimum mean-square error, we can call them the *most expressive features* (MEF) in that they best describe the sample population in the sense of linear transform.

We can choose m so that the ratio of the mean-square error over the total variance,

$$\sum_{i=m+1}^{n} \lambda_i / \sum_{i=1}^{n} \lambda_i$$

is smaller than a given percentage (e.g., 95%).

If we are given k discrete training images, typically $k < n$ and n is very large. Instead, we can find the eigenvector and eigenvalues of a smaller $k \times k$ matrix U^tU, which has the same non-zero eigenvalues as $S = UU^t$. If $\mathbf{w}_i$ is an eigenvector of U^tU associated with the eigenvalue λ_i, then $\mathbf{v}_i = U\mathbf{w}_i$ is the eigenvector of $S = UU^t$ with the same eigenvalue.

4 The Most Discriminating Features

4.1 Weakness of the MEF's for classification

The MEF's are, in general, not the best ones for classification, because that features that describe some major variations in the class may be irrelevant to how the subclasses are divided, as shown in Fig. 6. The MEF along y_1 cannot separate the two subclasses. The direction along the difference of the two means cannot either. Although the variation along z_1 is not large, it catches the major feature that is crucial for classifying subclasses. The theory for this issue is called discriminant analysis in mathematical statistics.

4.2 Hyperplanes are sufficient for space decomposition

A natural question arises here is whether the classes are linearly separable. Note that we want to use hyperplanes to obtain hierarchical space decomposition as shown in Fig. 5, instead of separating two predefined classes. The region of a class can be approximated to within any given accuracy by the union of a

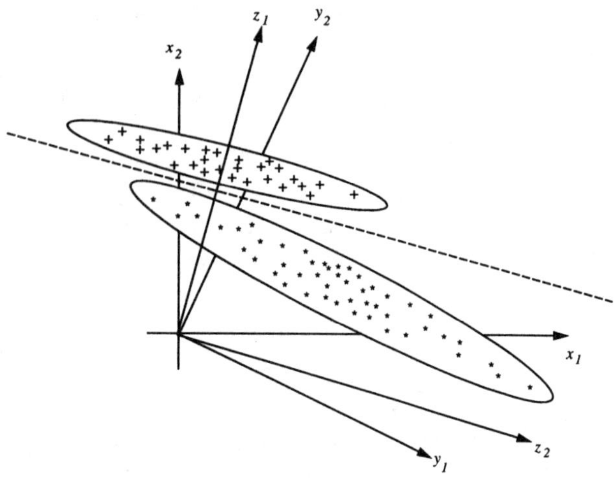

Figure 6: A 2-D illustration of the most discriminating features (MDF). The MDF is the projection along z_1. The MEF along y_1 cannot separate the two subclasses.

number of hyper-plane defined cells (i.e., polyhedron) at proper levels, although the number of cells could be large.

Of course, we would like to decompose the space in an efficient way. If visually similar objects mostly fall into the same cell, the network tends to be small because relatively few nodes at a coarse levels can cover the type of objects in the training set. Therefore, the MDF is crucial for reducing the network size.

4.3 Fisher's discriminant analysis and the MDF's

Suppose samples $\mathbf{Y}$'s are m-dimensional random vectors from c classes. The ith class has a probability p_i, a mean vector $\mathbf{m}_i$ and a scatter matrix Σ_i. The *within-class scatter matrix* is defined by

$$S_w = \sum_{i=1}^{c} p_i E\{(\mathbf{Y} - \mathbf{m}_i)(\mathbf{Y} - \mathbf{m}_i)^t \mid \omega_i\} = \sum_{i=1}^{c} p_i \Sigma_i \quad (4)$$

The *between-class scatter matrix* is $S_b = \sum_{i=1}^{c} p_i(\mathbf{m}_i - \mathbf{m})(\mathbf{m}_i - \mathbf{m})^t$ where $\mathbf{m}$ is defined as $\mathbf{m} = E\mathbf{Y} = \sum_{i=1}^{c} p_i M_i$. The *mixture scatter matrix* is defined by $S_m = E\{(\mathbf{Y} - \mathbf{m})(\mathbf{Y} - \mathbf{m})^t\} = S_w + S_b$. We want to maximize the between-class scatter with respect to the within-class scatter. In the discriminant analysis [4], an objective function we wish to maximize is

$$\mathrm{trace}\{S_w^{-1} S_b\} \quad (5)$$

In other words, we want to find features in which the scatter between classes is large but the scatter within every class is small. Suppose we use k-dimensional linear features $\mathbf{Z} = W^t\mathbf{Y}$ where W is an $m \times k$ rectangular matrix whose column vectors are linearly independent. The above mapping represents a linear projection from m-dimensional space to k dimensional space. The objective is to determine an $m \times k$ matrix W so that in the new space, the objective function in (5) $f_Z(m) = \mathrm{trace}\{S_{Zw}^{-1} S_{Zb}\}$ is minimized. Alternatively, we can also consider another objective function. Note that $\det\{S_{Zw}\}$ and $\det\{S_{Zb}\}$ measures the hyperellipsoidal scattering volume of S_{Zw} and S_{Zb}, respectively. We may maximize their ratio

$$\frac{\det\{S_{Zb}\}}{\det\{S_{Zw}\}} = \frac{\det\{W^t S_{Yb} W\}}{\det\{W^t S_{Yw} W\}} \quad (6)$$

It has been proved that both objective functions (5) and (6) lead to the same projection matrix W whose column vectors are the eigenvectors of $S_{Yw}^{-1} S_{Yb}$ associated with the first k largest eigenvalues. Since the rank of S_{Yb} is at most $c-1$, we know that only at most $c-1$ features are needed and others do not contribute to the maximum of the objective functions.

4.4 The curse of dimensionality and the new DKL projection

The discriminant analysis procedure breaks down when the within-class scatter matrix S_w becomes degenerate, which is our case due to a high dimension of the input image and a much smaller number of training samples.

The Karhunen-Loeve projection that includes all the eigenvectors associated with non-zero eigenvalues is a sufficient statistic for normal distributions (in the sense of Bayes decision). The projection of discriminant analysis is now based on the space of Karhunen-Loeve projection (i.e., MEF space), where the degeneracy typically does not occur. We first project the n-dimensional $\mathbf{X}$-space onto m-dimensional $\mathbf{Y}$-space using the Karhunen-Loeve projection. m is such that $m + c$ is not larger than the number of training samples s. We define the new *DKL projection* (short for Discriminant Karhunen-Loeve projection) as $\mathbf{Z} = W^t V^t \mathbf{X}$ with an appropriate m ($k \leq c - 1 \leq m \leq s - c$). The details are omitted due to the space limit.

5 Determining Subclass Using the Bayes Decision Theory

The remaining issue is how to determine which class an input belongs to using the corresponding MDF values. In the SHOSLIF, we use Bayes decision theory, using a multidimensional Gaussian distribution model and the estimated mean and covariance matrix as the learned knowledge. Given a feature vector, the Bayes theory determines which class number i should be chosen to minimize the conditional average loss. The detail is omitted here due to the space limit.

6 Geometric Inference

We need to estimate the parameters of the input subimage. The parameters include, e.g., the relative size of the face in the attention window, the x- and y-coordinates of the center of the face in the subimage, etc. It is reasonable to assume that the MDF values vary continuously and slowly with these parameters. Fig. 7 gives a schematic illustration. We can define

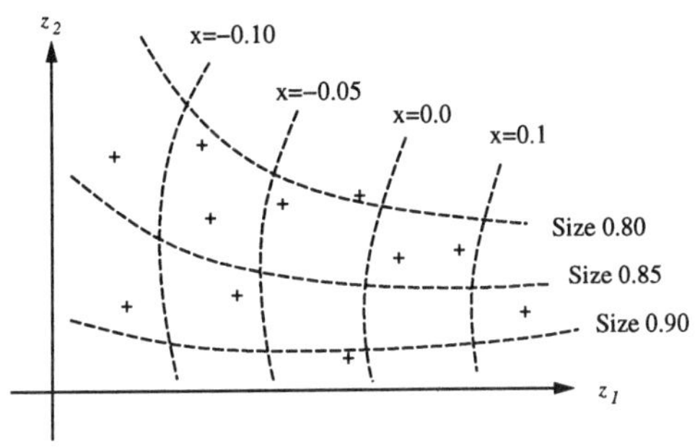

Figure 7: A schematic illustration of geometric inference via function fitting and interpolation through training points in the MDF space. The plus signs indicate the MDF values of the training samples from a person.

a vector-valued function $\mathbf{S}(\mathbf{Z})$ which maps from MDF space to the parameter space.

A set of basis function $\mathbf{s}_i(\mathbf{Z})$, $i = 1, 2, ...n$ (i.e., interpolants) is used to linearly span the function $\mathbf{S}(\mathbf{Z})$ to be approximated:

$$\mathbf{S}(\mathbf{Z}) = \sum_{i=1}^{n} \mathbf{c}_i s_i(\mathbf{Z}) \qquad (7)$$

A generalized multiquadratics that has desirable properties has the form of $s(\mathbf{Z}) = (||\mathbf{Z}||^2 + d)^\alpha$ where α is a nonzero real number, d is a positive damping factor, and $||\cdot||$ is the Euclidean distance. We use $\alpha = -1/2$. A very small d tends to force the function to pass the data points.

Given feature vector $\mathbf{Z}_i$ with parameter $\mathbf{S}_i$, the corresponding interpolant is $s_i(\mathbf{Z}) = (||\mathbf{Z} - \mathbf{Z}_i||^2 + d)^\alpha$. Thus, with $m \geq n$ training samples, we have m vector equations $\mathbf{S}_i = \sum_{i=1}^{n} \mathbf{c}_i s_i(\mathbf{Z})$, $j = 1, 2, ..., m$, that are linear with respect to the vector efficients $\mathbf{c}_i$'s, from which $\mathbf{c}_i$'s can be solved using a noniterative procedure for linear least squares problems. Once the training is done, the parameters for an input with feature vector $\mathbf{Z}$ can be estimated by (7) using the coefficients determined in the learning phase.

7 Complexity of the SHOSLIF

Due to the tree structure of the SHOSLIF as shown in Figs. 1 and 2, a tremendous reduction in space and time complexities is achieved. In other words, the network is built to adaptively devote space for concepts that are important for each application. Consider a complete tree of level l with a branching factor of b. The number of classes classified by the tree corresponds to the number of leaf nodes, which is b^l. The number of total nodes is equal to $(b^{l+1} - 1)/(b - 1)$. In the case of linear indexing to find the model, at least a half of class needs to be examined on average. Thus, the complexity is in the order of b^l. With the SHOSLIF, only a path of width b is traversed and the number of nodes visited is equal to bl. The rate of reduction is $b^l/(bl)$. The DKL projection reduces drastically the number of computation at each node (module).

The Cresceptron [3] has indicated the promising performance of the self-organizing approach. The result of experiment with the SHOSLIF is to appear.

8 Summary

In this article, we introduced the new self-organizing SHOSLIF approach designed for general object recognition. The new representation scheme is general and can virtually represent any object in the image. The method of using function fitting and interpolation in the MDF space can infer geometric information (such as size, position, orientation).

References

[1] K. Fukushima, S. Miyake, and T. Ito, "Neocognitron: A neural network model for a mechanism of visual pattern recognition," *IEEE Trans. Sys., Man, Cyber.*, vol. 13, no. 5, pp. 826-834, 1983.

[2] M. M. Loeve, *Probability Theory.* Princeton, NJ: Van Nostrand, 1955.

[3] J. Weng, N. Ahuja and T. S. Huang, "Learning recognition and segmentation of 3-D objects from 2-D images," in *Proc. 4th Int'l Conf. Computer Vision*, pp. 121-128, May, 1993.

[4] S. S. Wilks, *Mathematical Statistics.* Wiley, New York, 1963.

A weather radar image prediction method in local parallel computation

Kazuhiko Shinozawa†, Masaharu Fujii‡ and Noboru Sonehara†

†NTT Human Interface Laboratories
1-2356 Take, Yokosuka-Shi, Kanagawa 238-03 Japan
‡Sapporo Information Network
10F Sapporo MN bldg.
Kita 1, Nishi 3, Chuoh-Ku, Sapporo-Shi, Hokkaido 060 Japan

Abstract

This paper proposes a new method for the short term weather radar image prediction which depends on local information of images. A conventional method, called a kinetic method, estimates a moving vector of two radar echo images and predicts future radar echo images. This method cannot predict local changes of radar echoes in the image because they calculate the average radar echo velocity of the whole image.

The proposed method treats local changes of radar echoes as local mapping between the images and predicts future radar echo images using a neural network as a non-linear mapping. The performance of the proposed method is 12% better than a conventional method in the best case of Critical Success Index (CSI) evaluation. We propose a linear approximation including terms of diffusion, translation and a sink and source to decrease the calculating costs. This approximation method provides almost the same prediction performance as the non-linear method, and the calculating time is about 25% less than a non-linear one.

1 Introduction

Clearing snow costs a lot. A short term prediction for snowfall is effective in planing to clear snow and necessary to decrease the costs. The radar echo image reflects the snowfall regions, and their images can be predicted and used for snowfall prediction.

A conventional prediction method, called a kinetic method, estimates a moving vector that has the maximum correlation between two radar echo images as the vector of the whole radar echo image ([1],[2],[3]). To predict future images, its method moves a current radar image along the estimated vector. The method is effective for the radar echo image when its shape won't change and rotate until several hours later. However, its shape changes according to the time of day, and the source and sink happen realistically. Methods that solve these problems are needed.

This paper proposes a new method for weather radar image prediction. Section 2 describes the proposed method and its prediction performance. Section 3 describes an inspection of the assumption that local changes of radar echo images can be treated as local mapping.

2 Prediction method

This method treats the radar image as the mapping between local data of time and space, and predicts future images using this mapping.

The current image $I(x,y,t)$ is assumed to be $\overline{I}(x,y,t)$. $\overline{I}(x,y,t)$ is represented by the previous neighborhood $I(x+\Delta x, y+\Delta y, t-\Delta t)$ as shown in Equation (1).

$W_{x,y,\Delta x,\Delta y,\Delta t}$ and $\sigma(x,y)$ are parameters.

$$I(x,y,t) \cong \overline{I}(x,y,t) = f(\sum_{\Delta t}^{n_t}\sum_{\Delta x}^{n_x}\sum_{\Delta y}^{n_y} W_{x,y,\Delta x,\Delta y,\Delta t} I(x+\Delta x, y+\Delta y, t-\Delta t) + \sigma(x,y)) \quad (1)$$

Prediction image $\overline{I}(x,y,t+\Delta t), \overline{I}(x,y,t+2\Delta t), \cdots$ is obtained by repeating mapping f.

$$\overline{I}(x,y,t+(n+1)\Delta t) = f(\sum_{\Delta t}^{n_t}\sum_{\Delta x}^{n_x}\sum_{\Delta y}^{n_y} W_{x,y,\Delta x,\Delta y,\Delta t} I(x+\Delta x, y+\Delta y, t+n\Delta t) + \sigma(x,y)) \quad (2)$$

0-7803-1901-X/94 $4.00 ©1994 IEEE

n_t means a time neighborhood. In Figure 1, n_x and n_y are indexes of space neighborhood shown in three space neighborhoods.

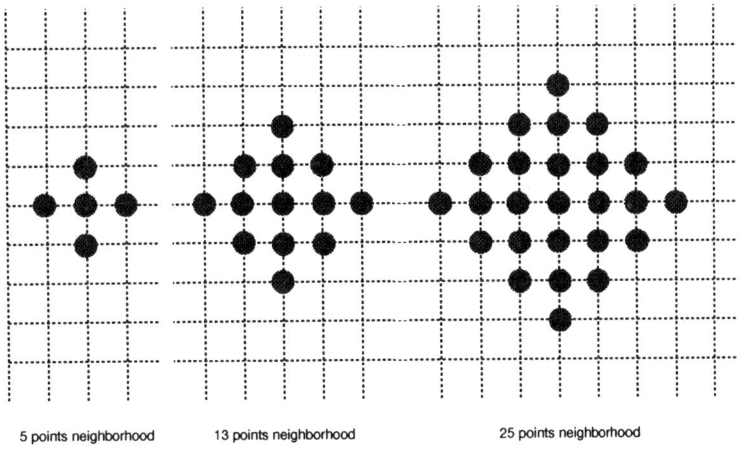

Figure 1: Space neighborhoods

2.1 Mapping with non-linear function

The radar image reflects the snowfall region whose change is represented as a non-linear system, so it is expected that by using a non-linear mapping a better prediction will be obtained.

This method uses a three-layered perceptron and the back propagation method [4] as a non-linear mapping.

$$z_i(x,y,t-\Delta t) = f(\sum_{\Delta x}^{n_x}\sum_{\Delta y}^{n_y} W_{x,y,\Delta x,\Delta y,i} I(x+\Delta x, y+\Delta y, t-\Delta t) + c_{(x,y)}) \quad (3)$$

$$\overline{I}(x,y,t) = f(\sum_i \omega_i z_i(x,y,t-\Delta t) + \theta) \quad (4)$$

Where, $\overline{I}(x,y,t)$ shows the approximated value of each point (x,y) at time t. Parameters ($W_{x,y,\Delta x,\Delta y,i}$, $\omega, \theta, c_{(x,y)}$) are determined using the back propagation method, which minimized the squared error E in Equation (5).

$$E = \sum_x\sum_y \left(I(x,y,t) - \overline{I}(x,y,t)\right)^2 \quad (5)$$

Future images are predicted using the estimated parameters. Five points neighborhood data for space neighborhood, and three hidden units for the perceptron are used. The radar image data are given every five minutes. It consists of 340 × 340 meshes. Its mesh size is 1 km.

To quantitatively evaluate the results, we use the CSI [2] defined as Equation (6). The CSI is used for evaluating weather prediction.

$$CSI(\%) = \frac{N_{11}}{N_{10}+N_{01}+N_{11}} \cdot 100 \quad (6)$$

N_{11}, N_{10} and N_{01} mean the number of image points which are shown in Table 1.

Figure 2 shows the relationship between the prediction time and the value of CSI. The evaluated area is the center of the total image area, which is 240 × 240 in the 340 × 340. This method which uses neural networks is 12% better than a conventional method in the best case.

symbol	prediction	reality
N_{11}	It snows.	It snows.
N_{10}	It snows.	It does not snow.
N_{01}	It does not snow.	It snows.

Table 1: Symbol table

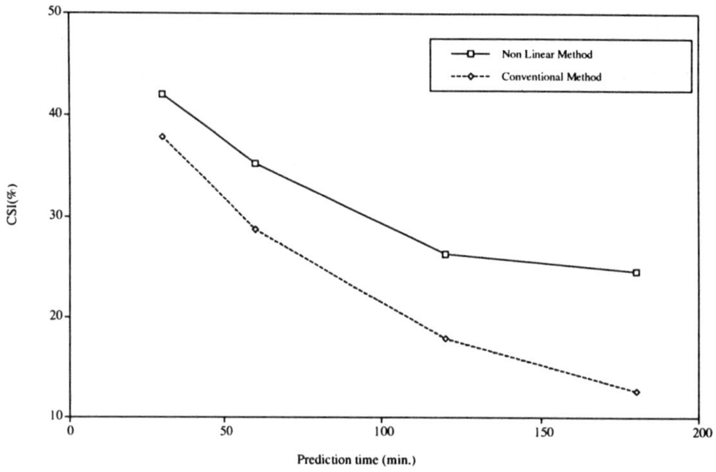

Figure 2: Average CSI data on 12/10

2.2 The mapping with linear function

The method with neural networks increases the calculating costs which consist of estimating $5\times3+3+3+1 = 22$ parameters at each point of the image and calculates the non-linear function. Therefore, we introduce the linear approximation that changes at each image point according to time, which consists of the linear summation of diffusion, translation and a sink and source of the image. This approximation can be defined as Equation (7).

$$\frac{dI}{dt} = \alpha(x,y)\nabla^2 I(x,y,t) + \vec{\beta}(x,y)\nabla I(x,y,t) + \gamma(x,y)I(x,y) + \varepsilon(x,y) \quad (7)$$

Parameters $(\alpha(x,y), \vec{\beta}(x,y), \gamma(x,y), \varepsilon(x,y))$ show the degree of diffusion, translation and a sink and source at a point of the image, respectively.

We get the following equation by translating this differential equation into a difference one with the central difference method and the mesh's sizes set to 1.

$$\begin{aligned} I_{x,y}^{t+1} = & \left(\alpha(x,y) + \frac{1}{2}\beta(x,y)_x\right) I_{x+\Delta x,y}^t - \left(\alpha(x,y) - \frac{1}{2}\beta(x,y)_x\right) I_{x-\Delta x,y}^t + \\ & \left(\alpha(x,y) + \frac{1}{2}\beta(x,y)_y\right) I_{x,y+\Delta y}^t - \left(\alpha(x,y) - \frac{1}{2}\beta(x,y)_y\right) I_{x,y-\Delta y}^t + \\ & \left(\gamma(x,y) - 4\alpha(x,y)\right) I_{x,y}^t + \varepsilon(x,y) \end{aligned} \quad (8)$$

Here, $\vec{\beta}(x,y) = (\beta(x,y)_x, \beta(x,y)_y)$.

There are two constraints to represent Equation (8) with Equation (1). One is Equation (9), the other is the function approximation $f(x) = x$ in Equation (1).

$$W_{x,y,\Delta x,0,-\Delta t} + W_{x,y,-\Delta x,0,-\Delta t} - (W_{x,y,0,\Delta y,-\Delta t} + W_{x,y,0,-\Delta y,-\Delta t}) = 0 \quad (9)$$

Therefore, the parameters in Equation (1) are estimated such that E in Equation (10) is minimized.

$$E = \sum_y \sum_x \left(\left(I_{x,y}^t - \sum_{\Delta x} \sum_{\Delta y} W_{\Delta x,\Delta y,5} I_{x+\Delta x,y+\Delta y,t-5}^{t-5} \right)^2 \right) + \lambda \sum_x \sum_y (W_{x,y,\Delta x,0,-5} + W_{x,y,-\Delta x,0,-5} - (W_{x,y,0,\Delta y,-5} + W_{x,y,0,-\Delta y,-5}))^2 \quad (10)$$

Here, λ is a constant. Figure 3 shows the results using this linear prediction method. Figure 3 shows that the

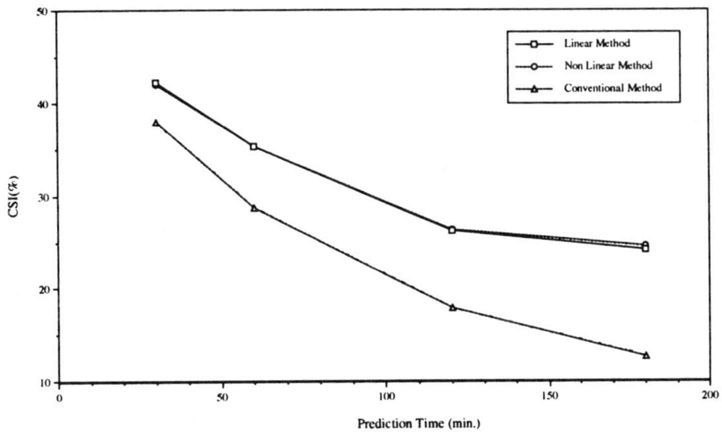

Figure 3: Average CSI on 12/10

performance of this linear approximation method is almost equal to the non-linear method. Table 2 shows the comparison between the linear approximation method and non-linear prediction method for a number of operations and calculating time. The calculating time is measured on a CM-200 which is a SIMD type massively parallel computer. It is shown that the performance of the linear method is nearly equal to the

	operations	calculating time(sec)
non-linear method	846720×10^5	556.4
linear method	190740×10^5	146

Table 2: calculating cost

non-linear one, and the calculating time is about 25% less than the non-linear one.

The difference between the non-linear and linear method, which almost never appeared in the CSI evaluation, is discussed below. The squared error evaluation is used to evaluate these performances from another point of view. The squared error evaluation is defined in Equation (11).

$$Error = \frac{\sum_y^M \sum_x^N \left(I(x,y,t) - \overline{I}(x,y,t) \right)^2}{N\ M} \quad (11)$$

Here, N and M mean the number of meshes, and both of them are set to 240. Figure 4 shows the results of the squared error evaluation. Figure 4 shows the large difference in performance between the linear and non-linear methods. Each image point data has a value from 0 to 255. However, the CSI evaluation divided the value in whether it snows or not as follows. It does not snow when the point has a value from 0 to 20,

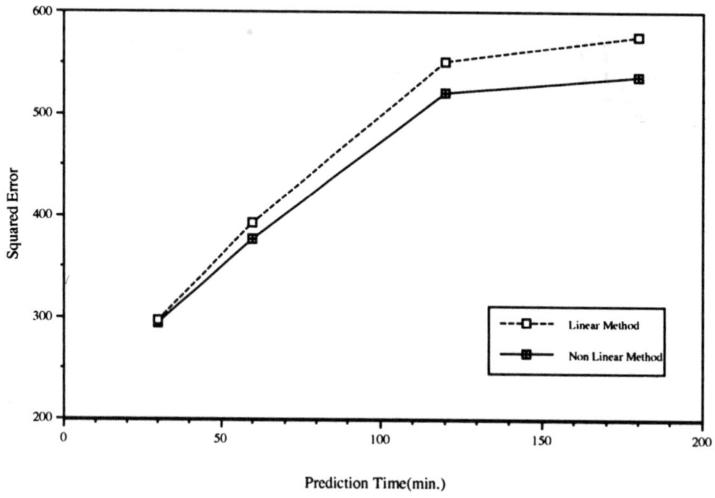

Figure 4: Squared error on 12/10

and it snows when it has a value over 20. In addition, only the three cases shown in Table 1 are considered. The case where it does not snow in both prediction and reality is ignored, so the difference between the linear and non-linear method did not appear clearly in the CSI evaluation.

3 Prediction with the repetition of estimated mapping

We assumed that the change in radar images depends only on local space and time neighborhood of the image. In the used data, there are some invalid areas where the mapping can not be estimated when a 5 space neighborhood and a 1 time neighborhood are used. We investigated real data to illuminate which is more effective in predicting more correctly; that is, the number of time neighborhood must be increased, or the number of space must be increased. To quantitatively evaluate the invalid area, we introduced the rate of invalid areas in all areas as shown in the following equation.

$$R(\%) = \frac{N_i}{N_a} \times 100 \qquad (12)$$

Here, R, N_i, and N_a mean the rate of invalid areas, the number of invalid points, and the number of all points (340×340), respectively. In the used data, the 39.7% of the whole image is an invalid area. The proposed method estimates the next time value on a point of the image using neighborhood values of the point. As the prediction time extends longer, using the repetition of mapping, the invalid area spreads larger. Figure 5 shows the relationship between the prediction time and the rate of the invalid area. The 5-1 in Figure 5 means using a 5 points neighborhood of a space neighborhood and a 1 point neighborhood as a time neighborhood when the mapping is estimated. The time neighborhood means the number of frames used for estimation. Similarly, 25-1, and 5-10 mean a 25 points space neighborhood and a 1 point time neighborhood, and a 5 points space neighborhood and a 10 points neighborhood, respectively.

The 5-1 in Figure 5 also shows that the invalid area is over 85% at two hours of prediction time, and is over 92% at three hours of prediction time. In this case, even if the mapping is estimated exactly at where it can be estimated, the performance decreases at three hours prediction time.

Here, we discuss increasing the points of a space neighborhood. 25-1 in Figure 5 shows that the space where the mapping cannot be estimated decreases to 24.6%. However, the invalid area spreads more widely because more neighborhoods are used for the prediction. This prediction performance for 10 minutes later is worse than the one for a 5 points neighborhood.

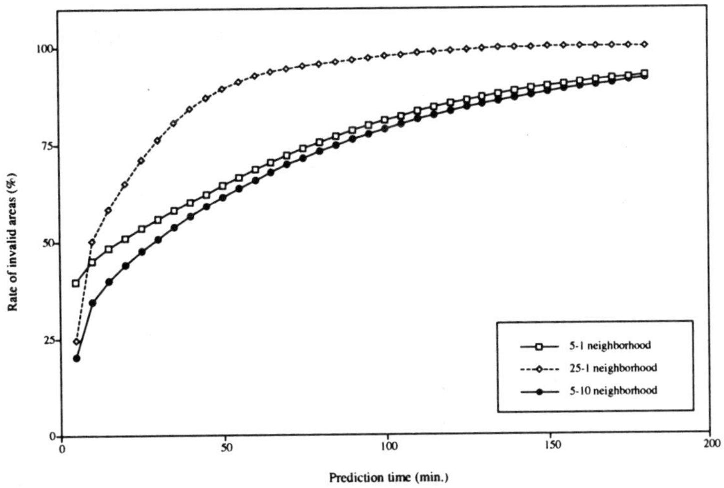

Figure 5: Rate of invalid space

Next, we discuss increasing the points of a time neighborhood. 5-10 in Figure 5 shows such a case. The invalid space where the mapping cannnot be estimated decreases to 20.3%, and also decreases to 83.5% at three hours prediction. Increasing the points of a time neighborhood is more effective than one for a space neighborhood for prediction with the repetition of estimated mapping.

4 Conclusion

We proposed a new method with the assumption that a change of radar images can be treated as a local mapping between the image frames, and estimated the mapping using non-linear parallel computation. The performance of the proposed method is 12% better than a conventional method in the best case of CSI evaluation. In addition, we introduced a linear approximation, and showed that this method can predict a future radar image faster than the non-linear method, while maintaining the same performance as non-linear's one.

Radar images are investigated to inspect prediction with the repetition of estimated mapping, and the investigation showed that increasing the points of a time neighborhood is more effective for the prediction than that of a space neighborhood.

References

[1] Yoshio Asuma, Katsuhiro Kikuchi and Hisashi Kon *"Experiments for a Very-short-range Prediction of Snowfall Using a Simple Weather Radar System Part 1. -Outline and Possibility-", Geophysical Bulletin of Hokkaido University, Sapporo, Japan, Vol.44. October. 1984. p35-51*

[2] Yoshio Asuma, Katsuhiro Kikuchi and Hisashi Kon *"Experiments for a Very-short-range Prediction of Snowfall Using a Simple Weather Radar System Part 2. -Examples of Actual Prediction-", Geophysical Bulletin of Hokkaido University, Sapporo, Japan, Vol.44. October.1984. p53-65*

[3] Yoshio Asuma, Katsuhiro Kikuchi and Hisashi Kon *"A Method for Estimating the Advection Velocity of Radar Echoes Using a Simple Weather Radar System", Geophysical Bulletin of Hokkaido University, Sapporo, Japan, Vol.44. October. 1984. p23-34*

[4] Rumelhart D.E., Hinton G.E. and Williams R.J. *"Learning internal representations by error propagation", Parallel Distributed Processing, 1, pp.318-362 The MIT Press (1986)*

A Neural-Network-Based Classifier Applied to Real-world Aerial Images

Greenberg S. and Guterman H.
Department of Electrical and Computer Engineering
Ben-Gurion University of The Negev
P.O.B. 653, Beer-Sheva, 84105, ISRAEL.

Abstract

The classification and recognition of real-world aerial images, independently of their position and orientation, by using neural network are discussed. Invariance feature spaces which have been used in conjunction with neural nets are not invariant to all possible transformations and required an extensive computational preprocessing. In the proposed method the invariance is achieved by training a Neural Network (NN) with a large number of appropriate distorted scene samples. The performance of the neural network classifier is compared with the classical correlation based techniques. Invariant classification of shifted and rotated real scene image is shown to be feasible.

1. Introduction

Correlation is often used as an approach to determine similarity between a pair of images in order to classify a given image. The principal weakness of the classical correlator is that its performance rapidly degrades as geometric distortions are present in the input image. Although correlation methods are invariant to a relatively small shift between images [1], this is not the case when rotation or a combination of rotation and scale is discussed. In such case the correlation plane contains un-sharp random peaks. This makes the detection of the correlation peak and its discrimination from the wide random peaks extremely difficult. To achieve distortion invariant characteristics, alternative correlation approaches have been proposed [2,3,4]. However, they have failed to achieve the desired performance in terms of both distortions invariant and noise rejection.

Neural Networks (NN) have been proven to be extremely powerful as classifier. Three major methods exist for invariant neural network recognition: Invariance by structure, invariance by training and using invariant feature spaces [5]. Both invariance feature spaces and invariance by net structure methods, are not invariant to all possible transformations, required extensive computational preprocessing and are restricted to a certain type of images such as binary images [6,7]. In the proposed method the invariance of real-world aerial image is achieved by training a Neural Network with a large number of appropriate distorted scene samples.

2. Preprocessing

A classical approach to pattern recognition, using neural networks, is to extract some set of features from the raw image [8]. These features are then presented to the classifier network. In the present case several features were considered as possible inputs to the network. Primarily, two dimensional Fourier transform (FT) was applied to the input images. The FT space allows significant data compression [9]. In order to remove the DC component, the mean value of the image was subtracted from each pixel before applying the FFT algorithm. The high frequency components were filtered out by selecting a low-pass window in the frequency domain. In the quest for the optimal low pass filter, windows of several sizes were selected.

Previous work in image processing has shown that the phase in the Fourier plane contains significantly more information than its amplitude [3,10]. Also, it is a well-known fact that the human visual system is attuned to the phase spectrum [11]. For these reasons the phase spectrum of the image given by :

$$P = \frac{F(\omega_x, \omega_y)}{|F(\omega_x, \omega_y)|} = \cos(\phi) + j\sin(\phi) \qquad (1)$$

was employed here. As the basic information is contained in the phase, and according to the work of Horner and Leger [12], only the real part of the phase spectrum ($\cos(\phi)$) was employed.

This preprocessing method that has been previously employed for shift invariance classification [1] enables also invariance to a combination of rotation and shift. This is due to the fact that translation and rotation

This work was supported in part by the Paul Ivanier Center for Robotics and Production Management, Ben-Gurion University, Beer-Sheva, Israel

0-7803-1901-X/94 $4.00 ©1994 IEEE

relationship are linearly preserved in the FT domain. Therefore, by training the network with a large number of samples shift and rotation invariant might be achieved. Rotation invariant only is achieved by a discrete log-polar transformation and by Zernike moments.

3. Classical correlator vs NN based correlator

A classical technique used to determine similarity between a pair of images is to estimate a correlation measure between the images and determine the location of the maximum correlation [2]. A pattern that is close to the reference image produces a higher Signal-to-Noise Ratio (SNR) in the correlation plane than other pattern. The SNR is used as a decision criterion for classification using an appropriate decision threshold.

The correlator based classifier has been designed to obtain optimal classification using a new method of signal to noise ratio calculation. This was done by using an edge detection based on Laplacian subtraction. In order to make a sketch of the peak region in the correlation plane, the result was segmented using a signum function. Then the signal to noise ratio was calculated as the ratio of the peak power and the side lobe power.

The proposed NN correlator, as shown in Fig. 1, consists of two 2-layer feed forward networks. Learning was carried out by a previously described algorithm [13], which automatically selected the initial conditions of the training. Primarily, the algorithm analyzes the *a-priori* information contained in the covariance matrix. Based on this information the algorithm selects the number of neurons in the hidden layer, and provides an educated guess of the initial weight matrices. This algorithm has shown better performance than the conventional back propagation in terms of both speed and convergence.

The performance of a correlator is graded in terms of discrimination and peak localization. Correlation filters are generally unable to optimize both criteria, so we used two different neural networks. One was trained to perform a discrimination function for classification, using the cos(ϕ) components of the Fourier plane as input. The second network was trained for peak localization determination using the cos(ϕ) of the correlation plane as input instead of the generally employed correlation plane [14]. This approach allowed us to perform fewer calculations and have good noise rejection properties. Translation and rotation invariant classification was obtained from these networks. Only the results of the NN classifier are shown in this paper.

The correlation peak value was used to determine if the image under test belongs to the reference In_Class set. By using the correlation peak criteria for training the supervised network we might constrain the network to be not better than a classical correlator. We avoided this problem by training the network with high correlation doubtless In_Class images. A special output neuron was assigned the task of identify the No_Class images (which did not belong to one of the pre defined classes). Training for the No_Class was accomplished by a special set of images obtained from the background of the In_Class images. This "well selected" No_Class training set improved the classifier discrimination.

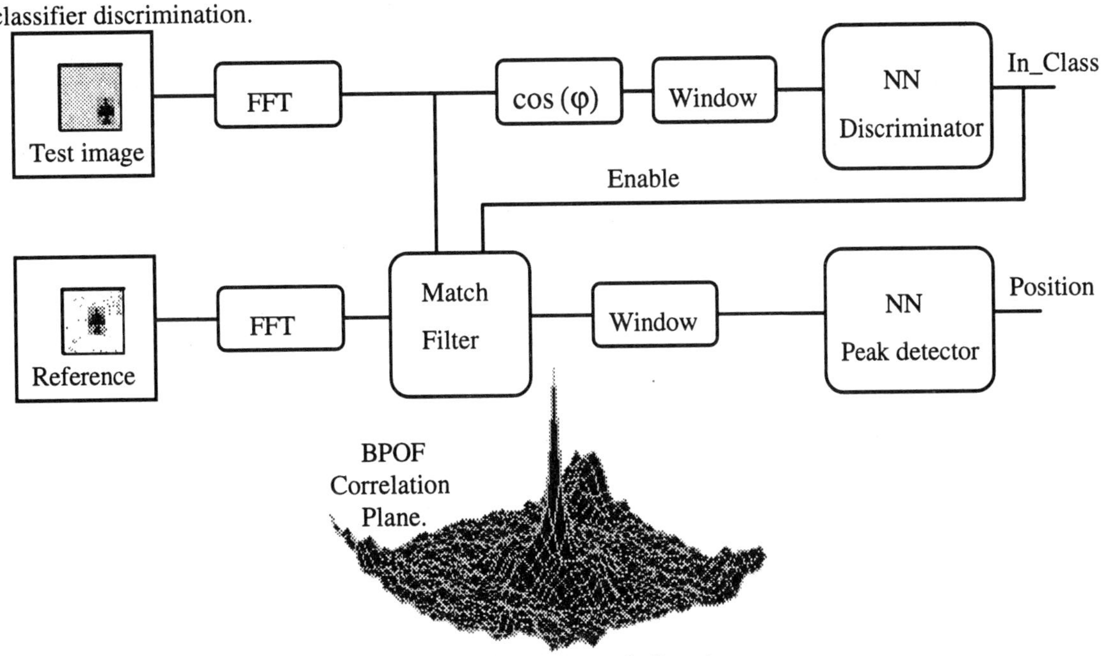

Fig. 1. Neural Network Correlator

4. Results

4.1. Rotation Invariant

Rotation invariant only is successfully achieved by a discrete log-polar transformation and by Zernike moments. A unique discrete polar transform is used for efficient mapping a low dimension sub-image (64x64 pixels) from Cartesian to log-polar coordinates. A window of 30x30 pixels is chosen to be input to a neural net consist of 50 hidden neurons (900:50:3). The key advantage of this method is the low number of pictures (30 pictures) needed for the training. The success rate of the trained network as a function of different degrees of random noise and random exchange of pixels is shown in Fig.2. The success rate for the training set was almost perfect. The classification success rate for the test was about 95%.

As an alternative method for rotation-invariant-only the orthonormal moments of Zernike are used. Thirty two moments are calculated and used as an input to a NN. This approach applied to aerial images seem to be very sensitive to noise (specially the odd and the high-order moments).

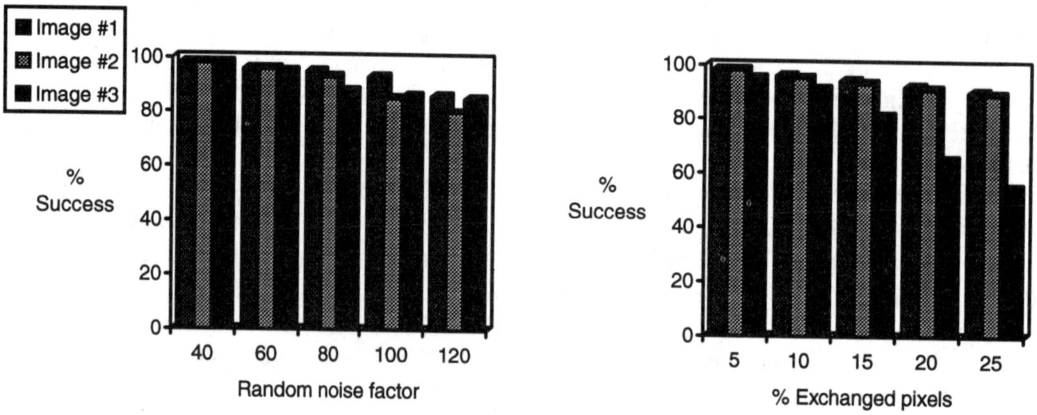

Fig. 2. Discrete Polar Transform

4.2. Shift Rotation Invariant

The data set consisted of 1541 shifted and rotated images (64x64 pixels each) extracted from two images (512x512 pixels) and pictures that overlap part of the two original images. To generate the data set a reference sub window of size 64x64 was chosen and the shifted and rotated images were created. The selected window was taken from the original image by performing pyramid averaging (4x4 pixels). This operation eliminates the "black edges" effect caused by translation and rotation.

The image discriminator consists of a fully connected two layer perceptron configuration. The input feature vector consisted of 220 $\cos(\phi)$ elements. The number of neurons in the hidden layer was chosen to be 53 by using the PCA covariance matrix of the pattern and target matrixes, using a quality factor of 80%, which means that 80% of the input information has been taken into consideration [15]. The number of neurons in the output layer was 3. Training was carried out by an improved Back-Propagation (BP) algorithm [16].

The results obtained by the correlation based classifier are shown in Fig. 3. Results for 4 different signal to noise ratio thresholds are shown. An optimal success rate of about 72% was achieved for a signal to noise ratio threshold of -4 dB. The goodness of classification was graded as follows:

- **Miss#1:** In_Class image classified as No_Class.
- **Miss#2:** No_Class image classified as In_Class.
- **Success rate:** The percentage of correctly classified images.

As above described, preprocessing involved removing the mean, performing FFT, computing the phase, taking the real part of it and implementing a low-pass filter. The NN based classifier results for the test set are shown in Fig.4 for 2000 and 8000 training epochs.

Due to the high correlation between the overlap images and the two known categories the success rate for the unknown images (Out_Of_Class) is relatively low. The perfect score for the first image may be explain by the fact that it contains very well define edges. The NN based classifier has an overall success rate of about 95%, which is about 23% higher than the correlator based classifier.

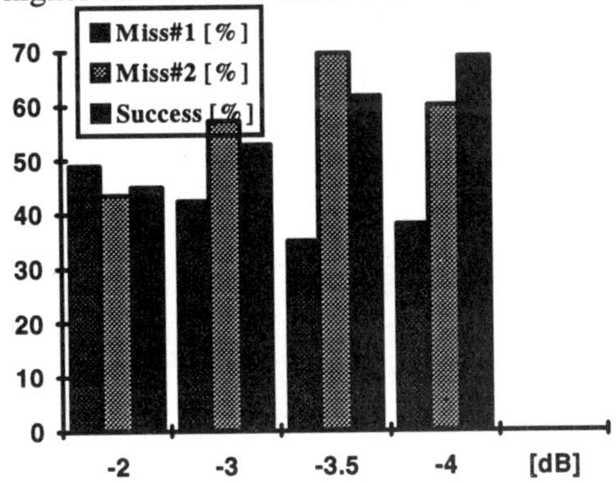

Fig. 3. Classical correlator performance

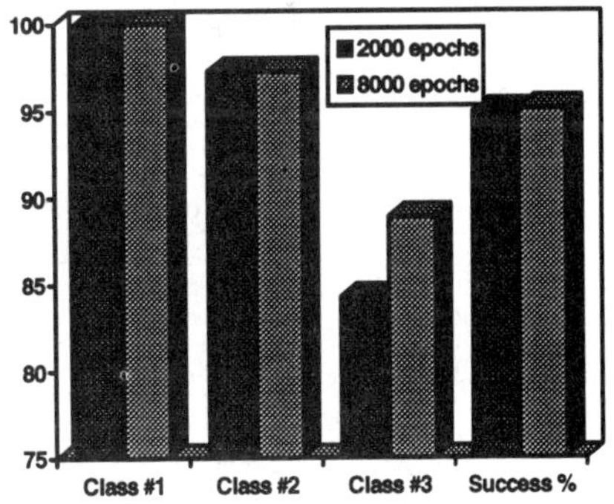

Fig. 4. NN based classifier results

5. Conclusions

The neural network performance was obviously better that the correlator. The use of the phase rather than the magnitude for achieving shift-rotation-invariant classification has shown to be a feasible approach. The invariance is obtained by training from examples and is independent of the kind of image. Using this approach special *tailored* classifiers might be implemented in real time.

Acknowledgment

We would like to acknowledge Eliezer Oron from I.A.I., for support and interesting discussions. The support of Israel Aircraft's Industry is gratefully acknowledged.

References

[1] S. Greenberg and H. Guterman ,"*Position Invariant Correlation Using a Neural Network* ," World Congress on Neural Networks, Vol. 3, pp. 745-748, July 1993.

[2] W. K. Pratt, "*Correlation Techniques of Image Registration*," Trans. IEEE, Aerosp. Electron. Syst., vol. AES-10, pp. 353-358, May 1974.

[3] D. L. Flannery and J. L. Horner, "*Fourier Optical Signal Processors*," Proc. IEEE, vol. 77, No. 10, Oct.1989.

[4] D. Casasent and D. Psaltis, "*Position, Rotation and Scale invariant optical correlation*," Applied optics, vol. 15, No. 7, July 1976.

[5] E. Barnard and D. Casasent, "*Invariance and Neural Nets,*" IEEE Trans. on Neural Networks, vol. 2, No. 5, September 1991.

[6] A. Khotanzad and J. Lu ,"*Classification of Invariant Image Representation Using a Neural Network,*" IEEE Trans.Acoust.Speech.Signal Processing, vol.38, No.6, pp.1028-1038, June 1990.

[7] C. Zetzsche and T. Caelli ,"*Invariant Pattern Recognition Using Multiple Filter Image Representation* ," Computer Vision, Graphics and Image Processing 45, pp. 251-262, 1989.

[8] M. W. Roth, "*Survey of Neural Network Technology for Automatic Target Recognition,*" IEEE Trans. on Neural Networks, vol. 1, No. 1, March 1990.

[9] E. Oran Brigham, "*The fast Fourier Transform,*" Prentice-Hall, Inc.

[10] A. Oppenheim and J. Lim, "*The importance of phase in signals,*" Proc. IEEE, vol. 69, pp. 529-541, 1981.

[11] B. Jahne, "*Digital Image Processing. Concepts, Algorithms and Scientific Applications,*" Springer-verlag.

[12] J. L. Horner and J. R. Leger, "*Pattern recognition with Binary Phase Only filters,*" App. Opt., Vol. 24, pp. 609-611, Mar. 1985.

[13] H. Guterman, "*Application of Principal Component Analysis to the design of Neural Networks,*" (submitted)

[14] S. C. Gustafson, D. L. Flannery, and D. M. Simon, "*Neural Networks with Optical Correlation Inputs for Recognizing Rotated Targets,*" Proc. SPIE, vol. 1294, pp. 171-179, 1990.

[15] P. J. B. Hanckok, R. J. Beddely and L. S. Smith ,"*The Principal Components of Natural Images* ," Network 3, pp.61-70, 1992.

[16] T. P. Volg, J. K. Mangis, A. K. Rigler, W. T. Zink and D. L. Alkon, "*Accelerating the convergence of the backpropagation method,*" Biological Cybernetics, vol. 59, pp. 257-263, 1988.

DIFFUSION NEURAL NETWORK MODEL FOR IMAGE-PREPROCESSING

Yool Kwon, Ki Gon Nam, Tae-Hoon Yoon, Jae Chang Kim
Department of Electronics Engineering
Pusan National University
Pusan 609-735, Korea

H.-K. Liu
Jet Propulsion Laboratories
California Institute of Technology
Pasadena, CA 91109-8099

ABSTRACT

In this letter we propose a neural network model that performs the Gaussian operation efficiently by the diffusion process. Diffusion of an external spot excitation to the neighbouring pixels results in a Gaussian distribution. We apply this diffusion model to the DOG (Difference of Gaussian) operation to detect the intensity changes in an image. In this model each cell has four fixed-weighted interconnections to the neighboring cells for a two-dimensional image. A different spatial frequency component can be obtained in each step of a sequential diffusion process. Therefore, the diffusion model is simpler and more efficient than the well-known LOG masking method. As far as we know, this is the only model for edge detection that can be implemented in hardware.

I. INTRODUCTION

The function of the receptive field of an eye is known as the DOG operation that enhances the contrast of an image and detects the intensity changes. The Laplacian of Gaussian (LOG) operator [1],[2], which is similar to the DOG operator, has been widely used for the detection of intensity changes. However, this method requires long processing time because of the large mask size[3]. Moreover, the hardware implementation is complicated because the mask size is usually very large and each value of the mask is not fixed-valued.

In this letter we propose a neural network model that performs the Gaussian operation efficiently by the diffusion process. A Gaussian distribution is obtained by diffusing an external spot excitation to the surrounding neighbouring pixels. Then, we apply this in producing the DOG function by the superposition of two different Gaussians, which can detect spatial frequency components in an image. It can be used as a preprocessor for the detection of edges or lines of an image.

In this model each neuron cell has four connections to the neighboring cells for a two-dimensional image, while in the well-known LOG masking method each cell has more than one hundred connections. Furthermore, in the former the connection weights are fixed-valued, while in the latter they depend on the size of the mask. Although several diffusion steps are required to detect the intensity changes by the proposed model, the number of total computations is smaller than that of the LOG masking method. Furthermore, different spatial frequency components can be obtained in each step of a sequential diffusion process, while in the LOG masking method each frequency component requires separate calculations with the corresponding mask. Therefore, the proposed model is simpler and more efficient than the LOG masking method, especially in hardware implementation.

II. DIFFUSION NEURAL NETWORK MODEL

0-7803-1901-X/94 $4.00 ©1994 IEEE

In this chapter we propose a neural network model that forms a Gaussian distribution when a spot excitation is transferred to the surround. A typical one-dimensional example describing this process, which we call 'diffusion,' is shown in Fig. 1. In each step of diffusion, 2/3 of a given excitation in a neuron is kept to itself and a sixth is transferred to each of the two neighboring cells. As shown in Fig. 1, a unit impulse excitation applied to a neuron results in the state $(\frac{1}{6}, \frac{2}{3}, \frac{1}{6})$ after the first step of diffusion, and the state $(\frac{1}{36}, \frac{2}{9}, \frac{1}{2}, \frac{2}{9}, \frac{1}{36})$ after the second step, and so forth. After several steps of diffusion the intensity distribution of the response approaches a Gaussian.

This diffusion process can be realized by a simple network shown in Fig. 2. In this network each neuron cell has connections of weight α to the two neighboring cells, a self-decay loop with the decay rate of $1-2\alpha$, an external input path, and an output path. The diffusion process shown in Fig. 1 corresponds to the response of the network shown in Fig. 2 with $\alpha = 1/6$ when a unit impulse excitation is applied to a neuron. We note here that the connection weights are fixed-valued throughout a diffusion process.

Now we derive the analytic expression for the variance of a Gaussian in our model from the diffusion equation which describes the energy transfer from the high- to the low-potential region [4],[5];

$$\frac{\partial^2 v(x,t)}{\partial x^2} = \frac{1}{\alpha}\frac{\partial v(x,t)}{\partial t}, \tag{1}$$

where $v(x,t)$ is the potential function and α the diffusivity. The solution of this one-dimensional partial differential equation with an impulse input $\delta(x,t)$ in the free space is given by a Gaussian function with the variance $\sigma^2 = 2\alpha t$ [6].

The discrete diffusion equation can be derived from Eq.(1) as,

$$v(m,n+1) = \alpha v(m+1,n) + \alpha v(m-1,n) + (1-2\alpha)v(m,n) + I(m,n) \tag{2}$$

where $v(m,n)$ and $I(m,n)$ stand for the state value and the input excitation of the mth neuron at the nth diffusion step, respectively. It is clear that Eq.(2) is the mathematical representation of the model shown in Fig. 2. The diffusivity α in Eq.(2) corresponds to the connection weight in the model shown in Fig. 2. We can show that the solution of Eq.(2) for an impulse input $\delta(m,n)$ is given by a Gaussian function $G(m,n)$;

$$G(m,n) = \frac{1}{\sqrt{4\pi\alpha n}} \exp(-\frac{m^2}{4\alpha n}), \tag{3}$$

with the variance

$$\sigma^2 = 2\alpha n. \tag{4}$$

Equation (4) shows that the variance of the Gaussian is changeable by the number of diffusion steps n with a fixed connection weight α, and vice versa. The fixed-valued connection weights make the hardware implementation very efficient.

III. DIFFUSION MODEL BASED DOG PROCESSING

Now we apply the diffusion model given above to the DOG operation to detect the intensity changes in an image. The DOG operation can be performed by subtracting the state value $v(m,n)$ after n diffusion steps from the state value $v(m,n')$ after $n'(<n)$ diffusion steps.

According to Eq.(4), the standard deviation of a Gaussian after n [n'] steps of diffusion is $\sigma=\sqrt{2\alpha n}$ [$\sigma'=\sqrt{2\alpha n'}$]. If we let $\Delta\sigma=\sigma-\sigma'$, the two Gaussians may be represented as $G(x,\sigma)$ and $G(x,\sigma-\Delta\sigma)$, respectively. In case $n \cong n'$(i.e., $\Delta\sigma \ll \sigma$), the DOG function $DOG(x,\sigma) \equiv G(x,\sigma-\Delta\sigma)-G(x,\sigma)$ can be written as the differential of a Gaussian $G(x,\sigma)$ with respect to σ;

$$DOG(x,\sigma) \cong -\Delta\sigma \frac{\partial}{\partial\sigma}G(x,\sigma), \tag{5}$$

that is,

$$DOG(x,\sigma) \cong \frac{1}{\sqrt{2\pi}} \frac{\Delta\sigma}{\sigma^2} (1 - \frac{x^2}{\sigma^2}) \, exp(-\frac{x^2}{2\sigma^2}). \tag{6}$$

The DOG function given by Eq.(6) is the same as the LOG function, which means that results of the DOG operation by the proposed method will be the same as that of the LOG operation.

For simplicity, we choose here $n'=n-1$. Then, the DOG operation can be performed by subtracting the current state value $v(m,n)$ from state value $v(m,n-1)$ of the a-step-earlier state.

Because both diffusion and subtraction are linear processes, instead of subtraction after the diffusion, the operation can be performed by diffusing the difference between the state value $v(m,1)$ after a diffusion and the initial state value $v(m,0)$. For a unit impulse (0, 1, 0), a step of diffusion with the diffusivity α results in the state (α, $1-2\alpha$, α). The input convolved with the difference ($-\alpha$, 2α, $-\alpha$) between these two state values is taken as the initial values of diffusion.

A neural network model capable of diffusing the initial values for the DOG operation may be constructed by two layers shown in Fig. 3; a 'distribution layer' and a 'diffusion layer'. To set the initial values of the diffusion layer, each neuron in the distribution layer is connected to the directly facing neuron in the diffusion layer with the weight of 2α, and to the neighboring neurons with the weight of $-\alpha$. The results of diffusion after each step are shown in Fig. 4.

IV. COMPARISON BETWEEN THE DIFFUSION NEURAL NETWORK MODEL AND THE LOG MASKING METHOD

As shown in Table 1, the diffusion neural network not only is simple and easy in hardware implementation, but also reduces the number of multiplications as compared with the LOG method. The LOG masking method requires the mask size of $6\sqrt{2}\sigma$ to detect the intensity changes with the spatial center frequency ω_o of $\sqrt{2}/\sigma$ in an input image [2],[3]. We can show that this calculation involves $72\sigma^2$ multiplications per pixel. The diffusion method needs five multiplications per each step of diffusion. To detect the intensity changes with the spatial center frequency $\sqrt{2}/\sigma$ in an input image, $\sigma^2/2\alpha$ steps of diffusion are needed. Then, the number of multiplications N per pixel is $5\sigma^2/2\alpha$. In case $\alpha=1/6$, the processing time of the diffusion method ($N = 15\sigma^2$) is about 20% of the LOG masking method.

Small number of fixed-weighted connections makes both hardware and software implementation of our model very efficient.

In order to obtain the intensity changes of many different spatial frequency components by the LOG masking method, each frequency component requires separate calculation with the corresponding mask. In our diffusion method, the variance of the Gaussian increases linearly with the repetition of the diffusion process for a fixed value of α. Each step of a sequential diffusion process brings about a Gaussian with the variance increase of 2α per each step. Therefore, a different spatial frequency component can be obtained in each step of a sequential diffusion process.

By applying the proposed diffusion neural network model to the 128 X 128 Lena picture shown in Fig. 5(a), we detected the intensity changes in an image as shown in Fig. 5(b). It is very similar to the result of the LOG masking method.

V. CONCLUSIONS

We have proposed a diffusion neural network model by which the Gaussian function can be formed efficiently. We have applied this model to the DOG processing to detect the intensity changes in an image. We have shown that the simulation results of the DOG processing by the proposed model are the same as that of the LOG masking method. Small number of fixed-weighted connections makes the realization of the proposed model very simple and efficient, especially in hardware implementation.

REFERENCES

[1] D. Marr and E. C. Hildreth, "Theory of edge detection," *Proc. R. Soc. London B207*, pp. 187-217, 1980.

[2] D. Marr, *Vision*, Freeman, 1982.

[3] A. Huertas and G. Medioni, "Detection of intensity changes with subpixel accuracy using Laplacian-Gaussian mask," *IEEE Trans. Pat. Anal. Machine Intel., vol. PAMI-8, no. 5,* pp. 651-664, Sept. 1986.

[4] R. N. Bracewell, *The Fourier Transform and Its Application, 2nd ed.*, McGraw-Hill, 1978.

[5] J. P. Holman, *Heat Transfer*, McGraw-Hill, 1989.

[6] E. Kreyszig, *Advanced Engineering Mathematics, 5th ed.*, John Wiley & Sons, 1983.

Table 1. Comparison of the number of multiplication and the complexity in hardware implementation between the two-dimensional diffusion neural network model with α=1/6 and the LOG masking method.

variance σ^2	center spatial frequency ω_o	software implementation		hardware implementation			
		number of multiplications		number of connections		connection weights	
		LOG	diffusion	LOG	diffusion	LOG	diffusion
1	1.4	72	15	72	5	σ-dependent	fixed
2	1.0	144	30	144	5		
4	0.71	288	60	288	5		
8	0.50	576	120	576	5		

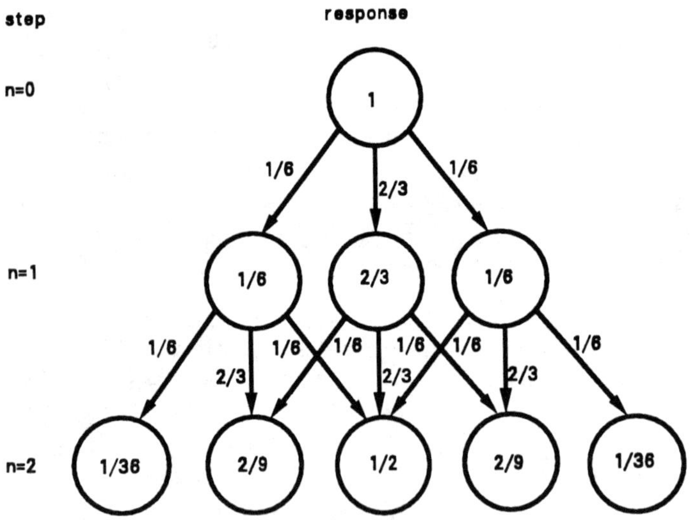

Fig. 1. Diffusion process.

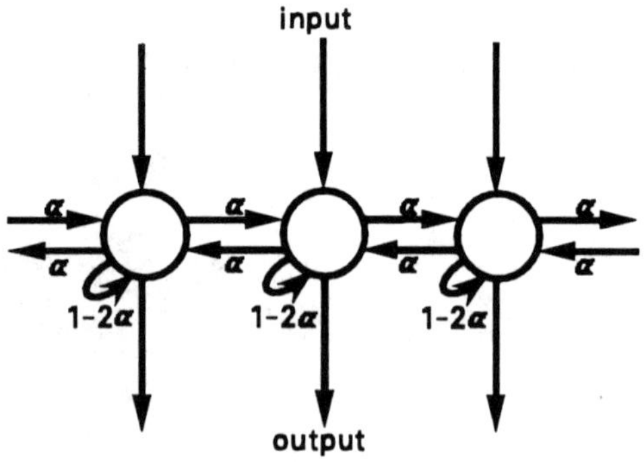

Fig. 2. The diffusion neural network model.

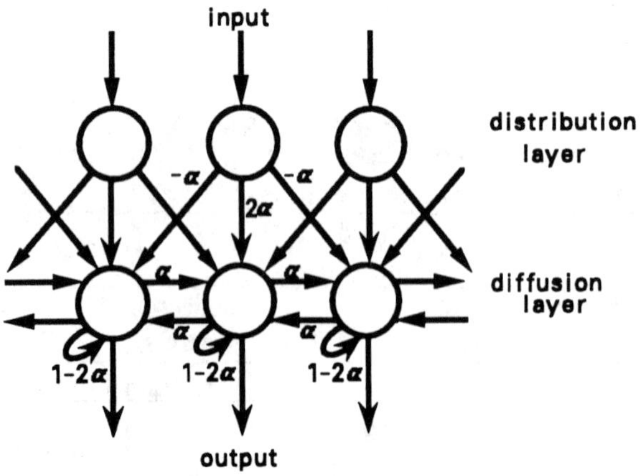

Fig. 3. The diffusion neural network model for the DOG operation.

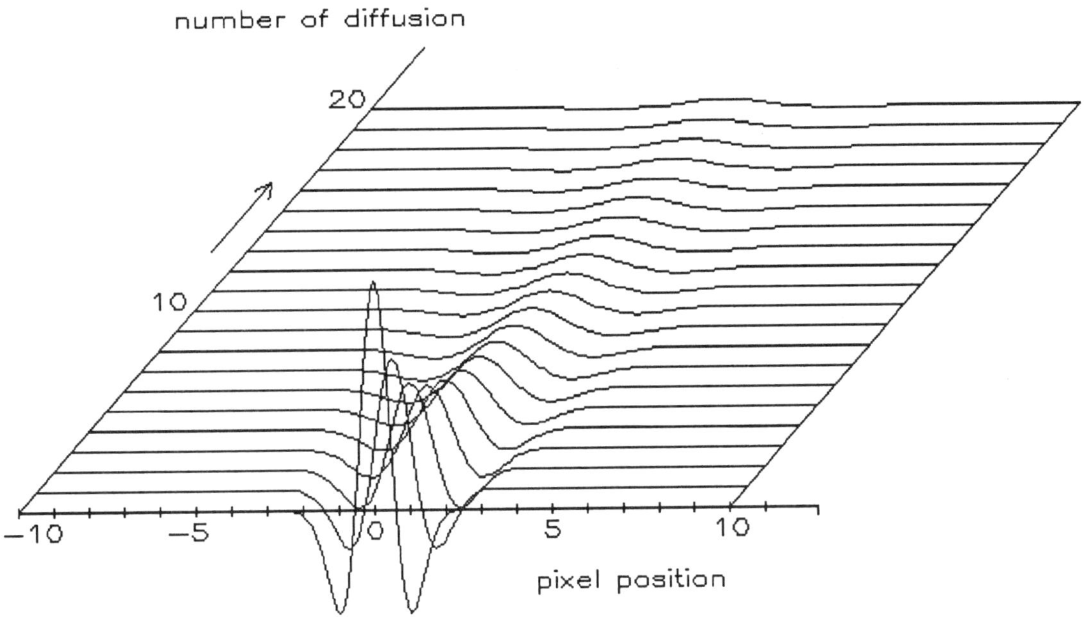

Fig. 4. The responses of the network shown in Fig. 3 to a spot excitation with $\alpha=1/6$.

(a)

(b)

Fig. 5. (a) The Lena picture as an input image, (b) the response of the proposed model with $\alpha=1/6$ and $n=12$.

Detection of Highway Warning Signs in Natural Video Images
Using Color Image Processing and Neural Networks

1LT David L. Kellmeyer, United States Army Environmental Hygiene Agency,
Building 4411, Fort Meade, MD 20755-5225
Helmut T. Zwahlen, Ph.D., Russ Professor, Department of Industrial and Systems Engineering,
Stocker Center, Ohio University, Athens, OH 45701-2979

I. INTRODUCTION. This study reports on the development of a system that incorporates color image processing and neural networks to detect and locate highway, warning signs in natural roadway images. Such a system could reduce the need for redundant or oversized signs by assisting drivers in acquiring roadway information. Transportation agencies could use such a system as the first step in an automated, highway sign, inventory system. Presently, a human operator must watch hours of highway videos to complete this inventory. While only warning signs were considered in this study, the procedure was designed to be easily adapted to all highway signs.

According to Lewis [1], it is unfortunate that no current, computer-based, segmentation technique can provide the discrimination required to distinguish many objects from their natural backgrounds. Furthermore, Lewis [1] states that "Automatic scene segmentation represents the single most difficult step in modern image processing." This system uses neural networks to accomplish complicated, image processing tasks including color scene segmentation and pattern recognition. Standard, image processing techniques are incorporated to increase the quality of information provided to the neural networks and to incorporate apriori knowledge of highway warning signs into the system.

Color is a common means of quickly transmitting information to humans, especially on roadways. When developing intelligent machines to perform tasks in environments designed for humans, the perception of color, as humans perceive it, is vitally important. Psychophysics tries to relate one's perception of a color with the physical color spectrum. This attempt to relate spectral color with one's perception of a color is where the study of color generally breaks down [2]. The perceived color of an object is a product of the human mind, not, an equation that can be devised from the physical properties of a color [3]. This lack of a mathematical equation is the major reason for choosing a neural network to learn from examples the relationship between spectral color and human color perception. A primary advantage of color is that it is not as susceptible to changes in the illumination and geometry of an object, as are luminance values [4,5,6,7]. Furthermore, color analysis usually produces a set of regions that are more "meaningful" to the goals of most imaging systems [4,5,7].

Figure 1. Saturation Enhancement Using a Natural Log Function

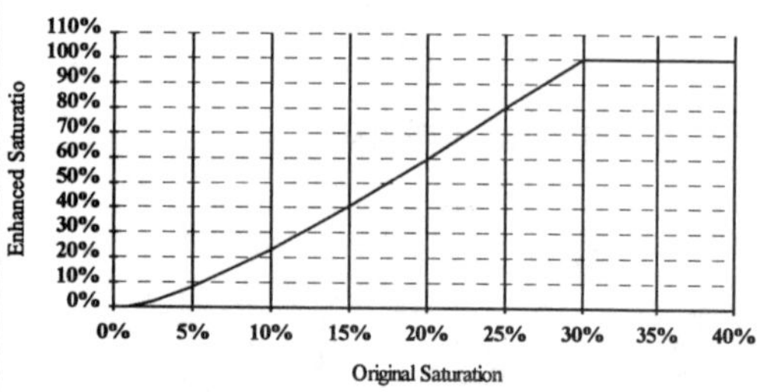

II. SYSTEM OVERVIEW. The basic approach is to digitize a roadway image and segment this image, using a back-propagation neural network, into eight colors that are important to highway sign detection. Next, the system scans the image for color regions that may possibly represent highway warning signs. Upon finding possible warning sign regions, these regions are further analyzed by a second back-propagation neural network to determine if their shape corresponds to that of a highway warning sign.

III. COLOR SEGMENTATION NEURAL NETWORK PRE-PROCESSING. The system begins by digitizing a roadway video scene as a 16 bit color image with a resolution of 640x480 pixels. This degree of resolution is required to recognize symbols or messages on a sign, a future goal of the system, but is not required for the detection of highway signs. By reducing the image resolution to 160x120, the amount of unneeded information is reduced by 94%.

The next pre-processing step prepares the image to be color segmented by converting each pixel's red, green and blue (RGB) color values to hue, saturation and intensity (HSI) values. Then the saturation of colorful pixels is increased and the saturation of non-colorful pixels is decreased using a natural log function (Figure 1):

IF original_saturation% <= 1% THEN enhanced_saturation% = 0;
ELSE enhanced_saturation% = original_saturation%* ln(original_saturation%*100).

This transformation results in pixels saturated above approximately 30% being assigned an enhanced saturation of 100% and those under 1% being assigned a saturation of 0%. This allows the 1-30% range to be stretched between 0-100%, providing the color segmentation network with greater differentiation of these more difficult to classify pixels.

IV. COLOR SEGMENTATION NEURAL NETWORK. Next, the color segmentation neural network reduces the color resolution of the image from 65,500 colors to a universal palette of eight colors: red, orange, yellow, green, blue, violet, brown and achromatic (non-color). These eight colors were chosen as those most useful in detecting highway signs and for providing an approximately even span of the color space. The color segmentation network attempts to simulate the way a person would segment an image given the same standard palette of eight colors. By using a universal palette that evenly spans the color space instead of a custom palette, the chance of ignoring small, meaningful regions of color is reduced. The reason for this is that a custom palette tends to place the reduction error on infrequently occurring pixels, whereas, a universal palette distributes a small portion of the error to all pixels, thus, representing each pixel with reasonable fidelity. A universal color palette was also chosen to produce segmented images consisting of a standard set of colors. The use of a universal palette was the key reason for using a supervised neural network for color segmentation, since a known group of outputs was required. An unsupervised neural network would probably be better suited for developing a custom color palette for each image.

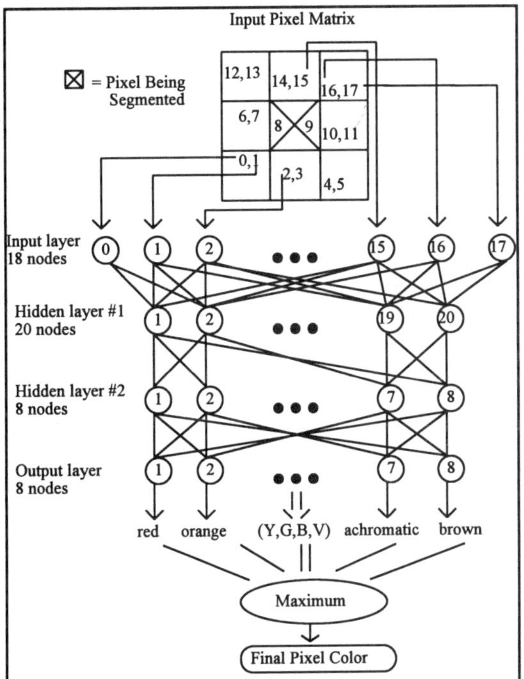

Figure 2. Color Segmentation back-propagation neural network with 18 inputs, 2 hidden layers, and 8 output colors

A. Color Segmentation Neural Network Inputs. Eighteen inputs provide the network with color information for the pixel to be classified and its 3x3 neighborhood of surrounding pixels (Figure 2). Neighboring pixels were incorporated because surrounding colors influence our perception of a color and because in cases of high resolution, the human eye cannot distinguish the color of a single pixel. Also, incorporating neighborhood pixels makes this procedure similar to a local smoothing operation by blending irrelevant pixels into larger color groups.

Two color difference values, similar to those presumably used by the human eye to encode color information [8], are used to denote each pixel's color. Each pixel's color values were converted back to the RGB format. The first color input for each pixel is the difference between the percentage of red and the percentage of green in a pixel:

$$\text{input\_1} = \%R - \%G.$$

Positive values represent the pixel's degree of reddishness and negative values represent its degree of greenishness. The second input is the color difference between the percentage of blue and the percentage of yellow (R+G) in a pixel:

$$\text{input\_2} = 2*\%B - (\%R + \%G) = 2*\%B - \%Y.$$

Positive values denote the degree of blueishness and negative values denote the degree of yellowishness, greenishness, or reddishness depending on the value of input_1. Blue values were multiplied by a factor of two to force input_1 = 0 and input_2 = 0 for achromatic pixels (red = green = blue = 1/3). While this color representation excludes the intensity of each pixel, this reduction in information was seen as more beneficial than the intensity values. It was observed that a network trained using hue and saturation values did not learn as effectively as the same network using color difference inputs. We hypothesize that the color difference values provided more meaningful information since positive/negative and larger/smaller input values directly corresponded to greater or lesser amounts of colors. Conversely, the abstract notation of a hue as an angle was more difficult for the network to decipher because smaller or greater hues did not represent more or less of anything, only a different state.

B. Color Segmentation Neural Network Outputs. The color neural network uses a separate output node for each of the eight colors in the universal palette. Since the value of each output node ranges from zero to one, it can be used to determine the network's "confidence" of each output being the correct color choice. The final pixel color is determined by the greatest output value. The network thus reduces the color resolution form 16 bits ($H = \log_2 65{,}500$) to 3 bits ($H = \log_2 8$), which is an 81% reduction in color information. In many cases, the sign becomes even more apparent in the segmented image because irrelevant information is removed.

C. Color Segmentation Neural Network Learning. The color network was taught using a training set of 2,400 color examples. Approximately 3% red, 10% orange, 21% yellow, 18% green, 10% blue, 3% purple, 5% brown and 30% achromatic. The different percentages of each color reflect the approximate abundance of that color in natural highway scenes and/or its importance in detecting highway warning signs. The human perception of each pixel's color was used as the correct answer for each example. The development of this type of training set is an extremely tedious task which emanated in the development of a mouse-driven program to quicken the process and to reduce the number of errors. In this program, the user selects one of the eight colors from a swatch of colors and then clicks on any pixel in the image that appears to be this color. Upon each selection, a training example is automatically generated. The network learned for approximately 200,000 trials (83 repetitions/training set) but proved unable to converge. However, the segmentation network did learn the overall color segmentation rules to the point of producing images that were easily identifiable to viewers.

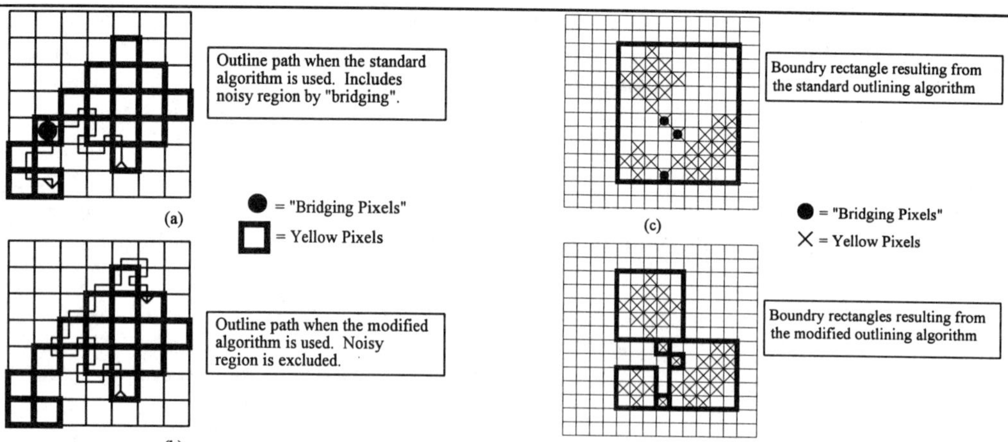

Figure 3. Outlining procedure for (a) standard procedure, (b) modified procedure, (c) standard procedure, (d) modified procedure

V. DETECTION OF POSSIBLE WARNING SIGN REGIONS. Next, a scanning procedure keys on the colors produced by the color segmentation network to detect possible regions of interest (yellow regions). Detected yellow regions were bounded using a modified version of an outlining procedure described by Nevatia [3]. The original procedure bounds yellow regions by making a left turn if one is located on a yellow pixel, or a right turn if one is located on a pixel of some other color (Figure 3a). This procedure ends upon returning to the beginning pixel.

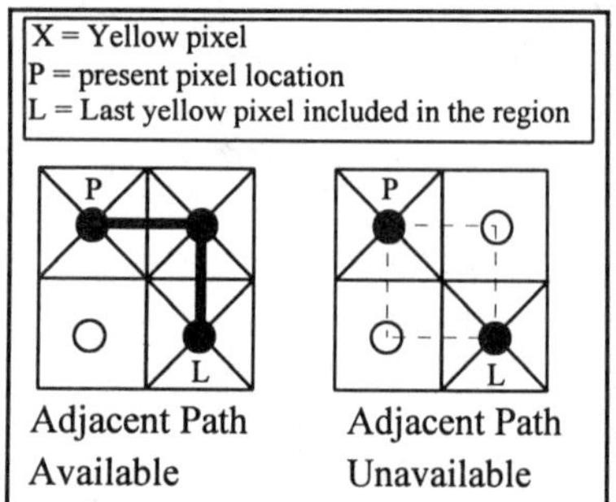

Figure 4. Adjacent paths

This results in two pixels located cady-corner to each other being defined as adjacent and thus components of the same region ("bridging pixels", Figures 3a & 3c). The modified algorithm enforces a more stringent definition of adjacent pixels by checking each pixel of desired color for a truly adjacent path to the most recently included pixel in the region (Figure 4). If an adjacent path is available, this pixel is included in the region and the standard left turn is made to the next pixel. Otherwise, a right turn is made (Figure 3b). Finally, a bounding rectangle is drawn around the bounded regions (Figures 3c & 3d).

Parametric features are then used to exclude regions that are obviously not signs. Only the horizontal and vertical dimensions of the selected regions were used, as other parametric features proved too restrictive in real-world images. If the horizontal and vertical sizes of the bounding rectangle were within the expected size range of a highway warning sign, this region was selected as a possible sign location. A standard warning sign was within our camera's field of view at a minimum distance of 50 feet (Figures 5a & 5b). At this distance, a 3' by 3' sign would be 28x28 pixels in a 160x120 image. Thus, a maximum height and width of 30 pixels was chosen as the largest area that could possibly represent a warning sign. A minimum height and width of seven pixels was chosen as the smallest group of pixels that could accurately represent a warning sign's shape to the sign recognition network. Given these size restrictions, signs are detectable between the distances of approximately 50 and 200 feet (Figure 5b). Traveling at 55 mph, this translates into approximately two seconds of viewing time or 60 frames in which to detect a warning sign.

VI. PREPROCESSING OF POSSIBLE WARNING SIGN REGIONS. The requirement for a proficient pre-processing routine for proper neural learning was again realized when trying to detect the presence of a sign in the segmented image. The original method of sign detection consisted of a 20x20 pixel "eye" that moved throughout the entire image in 10 pixel increments using a neural network to look for warning signs. Once a sign was detected, the above outlining routine was used to bound this region. The neural network was able to "memorize" the examples given, but performed poorly on images it had not seen before. Three major hypotheses were drawn to explain the network's poor performance. First, the sign was not always located entirely within the "eye". So, the network did not always get a "look" at the entire sign but rather only a piece of the sign. Second, signs were located at multiple locations within the "eye". Finally, each input to the network could be any of the basic eight colors. This use of analog inputs required the network to consider not only shape, but color as well. This detection system created a wide variety of input patterns that represented warning sign regions.

To obtain regions of interest that were centered within a window, the method of the previous approach needed only to be reversed. The scanning and outlining routines were used first to locate regions of proper color and size. A neural network was then called upon to recognize if the shape of these regions was that of a warning sign (a diamond). Yellow pixels were represented with a one and other colors with a zero to provide shape information to the network. This is an example of how our apriori knowledge, of highway warning signs being yellow and of a certain size, can be incorporated into the system and not have to be learned by the neural network.

A new problem emerged since these regions where now of varying sizes. This problem of varying-sized boundary rectangles was solved by converting each rectangle to a standard-sized square of 10x10, 20x20, or 30x30 pixels (Figure 6). For 10x10 regions, each pixel is inputted to the network in a one-to-one fashion. For 20x20 regions, a single input neuron must represent 4 pixels. For 30x30 regions, each input neuron must represent 9 pixels (Figure 6). The algorithm adopted to achieve this states that for each 2x2 or 3x3 square, if at least 2 or 3 pixels respectively are yellow, the entire square is represented by a one. Otherwise, a zero input is used to represent the square.

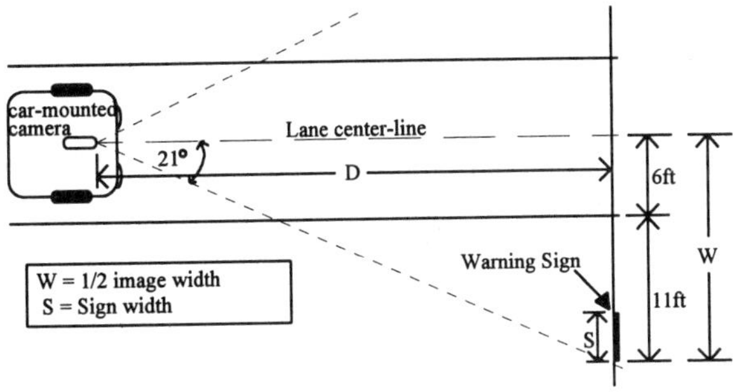

(a)

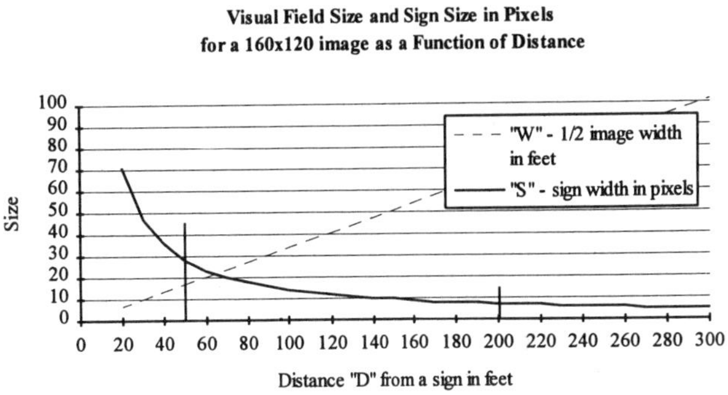

(b)

Figure 5. (a) Top view of a typical roadway image. (b) Size of the visual field and a 3 ft. warning sign in pixels for a 160 x 120 image as a function of distance.

VII. SIGN RECOGNITION NEURAL NETWORK. While parametric features can be used effectively to exclude regions that are not signs, it is difficult to use parametric features to recognize signs in real-world images. A back-propagation neural network was used to recognize the shape of warning signs because of its ability to generalize and handle noisy conditions. The detection network must be able to recognize degraded signs since shape degradation occurs when the background of the sign contains noisy yellow pixels, a tree obstructs the sign, or a sign is distorted by heavy shadows. Degradation also occurs when larger boundary squares are reduced to the standard 10x10 square.

A. Sign Recognition Neural Network Inputs. The sign recognition network is composed of 100 binary inputs that represent the shape of the yellow region inside the 10x10 boundary square (Figure 6). Since binary inputs are used, a sigmoid transfer function that ranges between 0 and 1 is used throughout the network.

B. Sign Recognition Neural Network Outputs. The network uses two outputs to represent the two possible outcomes that consist of the region being a sign or a non-sign (Figure 6). Two outputs were used as it was conjectured that by utilizing a separate output for the two possible outcomes, the trade-off between type I and type II errors could be better adjusted. However, the network proved its ability to provide probabilistic outcomes better than expected as the two outputs always summed to approximately 100 percent. This leads to the conclusion that for networks with only two mutually exclusive outcomes, using a single output node is just as effective as having one output node for each outcome.

C. Sign Recognition Network Post-Processing. The effectiveness of the sign detection neural network can be tailored to individual situations by determining the consequences of type I and type II errors. Since our final goal is to recognize the symbol on a warning sign, the consequences of sending non-sign regions to be further processed (type II error) is not extreme. However, the consequences of ignoring sign regions (type I error) results in the failure of the system. However, for testing purposes a threshold of 50% was used to determine the system's effectiveness, independent of type I and II error consequences.

Table 1: Processing times established using a 486/25MHz processor equipped with a Targa+/64 video capture board.

Operation	Resolution	Time
Digitize Image	640x480, 65,500 colors	< 1/30 second
Resolution Reduction	160x120, 65,500 colors	48 seconds
Saturation Enhancement	160x120, 65,500 colors	10 seconds
Color Segmentation	160x120, 8 colors	1 minute 27 seconds
Search for Possible Signs	160x120, 8 colors	2-5 seconds
Sign Recognition	160x120, 8 colors	< 1/30 second
Total Time		**2 minutes 30 seconds**

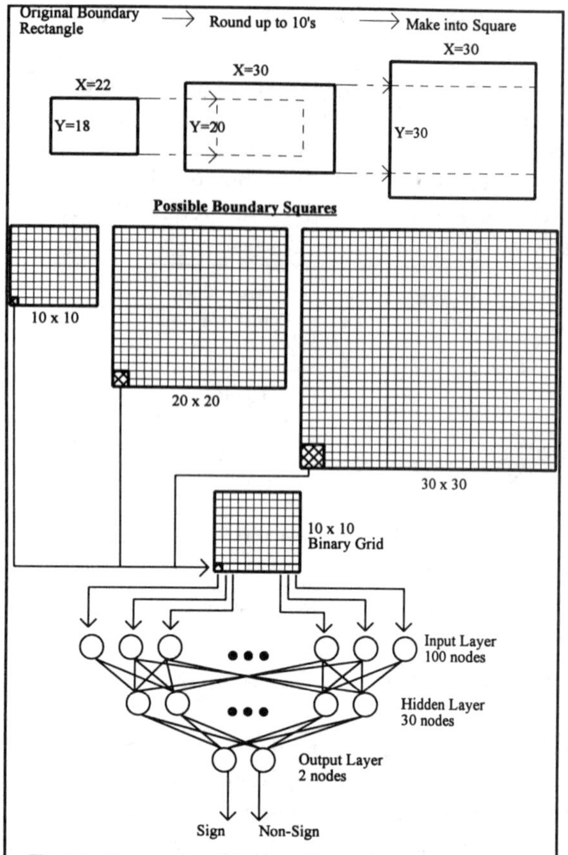

Figure 6. Pre-processing and sign recognition neural network

VIII. RESULTS. A video tape of continuous roadway scenes taken from within a vehicle traveling at posted speeds was used to test the system. The video tape contained a total of 40 separate highway warning signs. The system operator selected images to be analyzed until either the sign(s) was detected or it was determined the system had failed to detect the sign(s). This resulted in a total of 55 images being analyzed during the testing procedure. The system was able to detect 55% of the warning signs within the 55 images. However, the system detected and located 30 of the 40 possible signs which corresponds to a 75% detection rate. This demonstrates how being able to view each sign at different distances and angles as the car approaches greatly increases the reliability of the system. Furthermore, only 35 of the possible 40 signs where large enough in the image to be detected by the system. Thus, the program should not be blamed for these errors, but rather, the video camera's field of view should be altered to alleviate this problem. If only large enough signs are considered, then the reliability of the system increases to 86%. Within the 55 total images, the system only produced three false alarms (selecting regions that actually were not signs), which translates into a 5% false alarm rate. The authors recognize that this test only represents a single day's viewing conditions and that these results should not be extrapolated for all conditions. However, the test was conducted on natural video images not previously seen by the system, which, provides encouragement that this methodology could be used as an effective target detection tool for any object of a known color and shape.

As seen above, sequential images increase the reliability of the system. If real-time imaging can be achieved, the system would have between 40 and 80 sequential "looks" at each sign. The sequential probabilities that a sign is within an image could be further utilized with Baysien theory and/or incorporated back into the sign recognition network to provide temporal information. These sequential images could also provide information about the size and placement of the sign. As an added feature, the system effectively located highway lane striping which could prove useful in the further development of an automated vehicle navigation system.

IX. CONCLUSIONS. Preliminary results suggest that a fairly robust warning sign detection and location system has been developed through the use of color image processing and neural networks. The robustness of the developed method is attributed to the use of color as an identification feature and the implementation of neural networks to accomplish standard image processing tasks that usually tend to fail because of required thresholds. With processing times of around 2 minutes 30 seconds on a 486/25MHz PC, the potential for real-time operation is within today's technology if implemented in dedicated hardware. Such a system, with additional modules, could be implemented for automatic inventorying of highway signs and/or for use as an in-car information system to assist drivers in obtaining roadway information. As a more general conclusion, this methodology could prove beneficial to any image processing task requiring color reduction or the detection of objects of a known color and shape.

X. REFERENCES

[1] Lewis, R.. Practical Digital Image Processing. New York: Ellis Horwood, 1990.

[2] Sheppard, J.. Human Color Perception: a critical study of the experimental foundation. New York: American Elsevier, 1968.

[3] Nevatia, R. Machine Perception. Englewood Cliffs, NJ: Prentice - Hall, 1982.

[4] Malowany, M.E. and Malowany, A.S.. "Color-edge Detectors for a VLSI Convolver." *Visual Communications and Image Processing IV* SPIE v.1199 (Nov. 8, 1989).

[5] Healey and Binford. "A Color Metric for Computer Vision." *Proceedings of the DARPA Image Understanding Workshop* v.2 (Apr. 1988).

[6] Tominaga, S.. "Color Classification of Color Images Based on Uniform Color Spaces." *Human Vision and Electronic Imaging: Models, Methods, and Applications* SPIE v.1249 (Feb. 12, 1990).

[7] Nevatia, R.. "A Color Edge Detector and Its Use in Scene Segmentation." *IEEE Transaction on Systems, Man, and Cybernetics* v.SMC-7 n.11 (Nov. 1977).

[8] Hunt, R.W.G.. Measuring Color. New York: Wiley, 1987.

Template 1. An original digitized test image (the blue box around the sign would not be present). Template 1 also shows the final image with a blue box around the only region with a sign output over 50%, and thus designated as a warning sign.

Template 2. The test image after having the resolution reduced to 160x120 and the saturation enhanced using a natural log function.

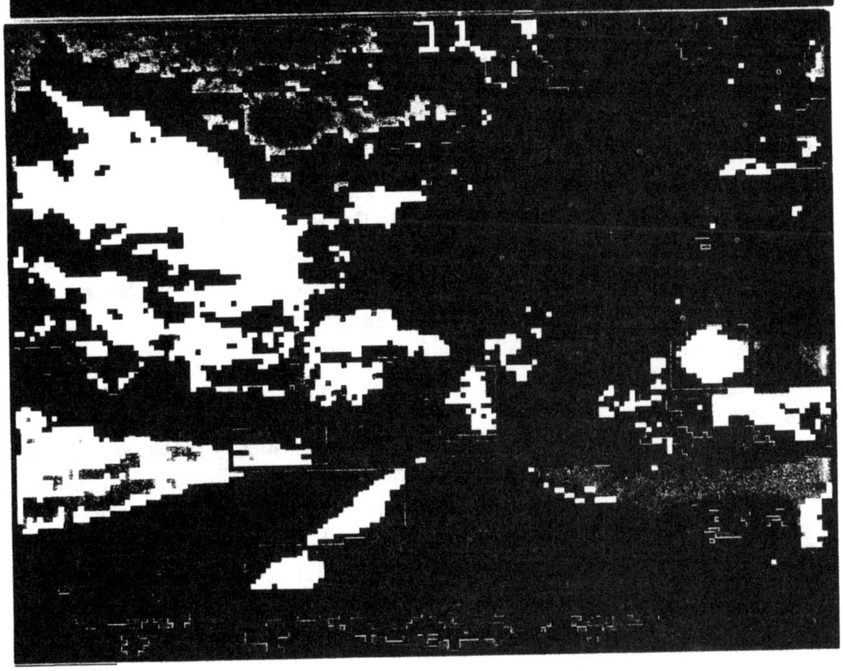

Template 3. The test image after the color neural network has segmented the image into basic color regions. The blue bounding rectangles represent possible warning sign regions found by the scanning routine (see Template 1 for those regions designated to be warning signs by the sign recognition neural network).

Multi-Layer Perceptron ensembles for pattern recognition: some experiments

M.Costa, E. Filippi and E.Pasero

Dipartimento di Elettronica, Politecnico di Torino, C. Duca degli Abruzzi 24, 10129-Torino, ITALY

***Abstract*— All global optimization methods trying to select the best model for a given task have to face the problem of the bias introduced during learning by several factors (e.g., overfitting problems or local minima) which may lead to poor generalization. Multiple models can reduce this problem by combining the results of a population of differently trained networks. Unfortunately, nonlinear adaptive systems like Multi-Layer Perceptrons cannot be integrated in the parameter (weight) space. Therefore, a key issue in the development of efficient network ensembles is the trade-off between performance improvement and the required resource overhead with respect to standard optimal model selection techniques. In this work several approaches to the design of multiple Multi-Layer Perceptrons classifiers are compared, and their robustness to some implementation constraints is evaluated.**

I. Introduction

Multi-Layer Perceptrons (MLPs) when trained by means of a backpropagation algorithm perform a regression estimate of a target function $T(x)$ from a finite set of examples $\{x_p, T(x_p)\}$. In classification tasks, $T(x)$ is typically a multidimensional stochastic function taking M different values T_i (where M is the number of classes), so that $T(x) = T_i$ if $x \in C_i$, and the MLP can be viewed as an approximation of the Bayes optimal classifier [1, 2]. The off-training probability of error is theoretically bound by the Bayes limit, but different sources of errors reduce their performance. Among them: the inadequate or insufficient sampling of the training data, the sensitivity to the initial conditions, the inaccuracies in the learning procedure, the noise and constraints imposed by the hardware platforms.

A careful design can reduce the extent of these problems: for instance, pruning and smoothing strategies have been suggested to optimize either the network architecture or the learning procedure [3, 4]; cross-validation schemes are often used for optimal model selection [3]. Almost all these techniques are based on a probabilistic interpretation of the MLP [5, 6] and correspond to variations of well-established statistical methods (e.g., hypothesis testing, regularization, resampling methods).

In the last years many authors [6]-[13] have suggested that significant improvements could be obtained by using some of these statistical techniques for model integration instead of single model selection. Unfortunately, due to their non-linearity, MLPs cannot be combined in the parameter (i.e. weight) space, and their integration involves the generation of a new large "stacked" feed-forward network [14]. Therefore, from a practical point of view, the trade-off between performance improvement and resource overhead must be carefully evaluated.

In general, during the training phase, the computational requirements of the ensemble methods are comparable to those of the standard techniques (which usually take the form of selecting the best net among some trials). From this point of view, the generation of a multiple model is a worthwhile job compared with the "winner-takes-all" approach, because it provides a more efficient use of all the available information [13].

During normal operation, however, a resource overhead may appear due to the fact that all the component nets must be stored in memory. In the following we will show that this problem can be largely compensated either by the performance improvement or by the relaxation of some hardware constraints (such as the required precision).

This work summarize our experience with simple MLP committees on a non-toy problem: optical recognition of handwritten numerals.

II. Overview

Different frameworks can be provided for MLP combination if we consider them either as regression estimators or as classifiers. The first approach is not limited to pattern classification problems, while the second one can be applied to a large variety of neural or traditional classifiers, thus providing

This work was partly supported by "Progetto finalizzato sistemi informatici e Calcolo Parallelo" and "Progetto strategico Reti Neurali" of CNR

0-7803-1901-X/94 $4.00 ©1994 IEEE

methods for the generation of very heterogeneous hybrid models. In any case, an ensemble is characterized by the features which distinguish its component (in other words, by the component training and selection strategies), and by the result integration rule. Let us point out the fact that model integration techniques are sometimes addressed as the dual problem of task partitioning and architecture modularization (as in [10]). In the following the basic solutions are briefly described.

A. Component net selection

Many of the existing works [7, 8, 10, 12] implement some resampling algorithms on the input data, building an ensemble of networks which differ in the training data subset. The input samples are distributed to the component nets of an ensemble according to a random process [7, 12] as well as to a self-organized process embedded into the learning procedure [8, 10].

A second broad class of works is based on the randomness stemming from initial conditions in optimization problems with multiple minima, and generate an ensemble of networks which differ in the initial weight vectors [9, 13].

A third approach is based on the fact that for a specific recognition problem, usually numerous types of features could be used to represent and recognize patterns, each one attaining a different degree of success under different conditions. Therefore, the component nets in an ensemble can be differentiate in the input or output data representation [15].

B. Integration rules

B.1. Multiple MLP regressors

In the "regression estimator" approach, if K nets share the same target function $T(x)$, we can directly average their output vectors $Y_k(x)$:

$$Y_{ens}(x) = \frac{1}{K}\sum_{k=1}^{K} Y_k(x) \qquad (1)$$

and select the final winner class on these new outputs. As shown in [13], the mean square error (MSE) of the averaged estimator is less or equal to the average MSE of the individuals, and the reduction is maximal if these are mutually independent. A natural extension of the simple average is a linear combination of the output vectors. Some methods to find the weighting coefficients are suggested in [11, 13].

B.2. Multiple MLP classifiers

In the "classifier" approach, we can further distinguish between two main types of classifiers [15]:

1. classifiers providing a "degree of confidence" (e.g. a measurement value) for each class, like Bayes classifiers.
2. classifiers providing just a label for the selected class, like syntactic classifiers.

To define a Multiple MLP classifier of type 1, an additional stage is required to obtain a set of estimated post-probabilities $P(x \in C_i/x)$, $i = 1,..M$ from the network outputs. For example, in the case of the standard "one-shot" target coding, the post-probabilities are expressed as Softmax functions of the output activations [1].

A simple way to combine a set of K classifiers is to build an average classifier with the new post-probabilities

$$P_{ens}(x \in C_i/x) = \frac{1}{K}\sum_{k=1}^{K} P_k(x \in C_i/x) \qquad (2)$$

A second approach is to search for the maximum upon i of the joint post-probabilities that $x \in C_i$ given x and given the answers of the K classifiers. If we suppose the networks to be statistically independent, then these are proportional to the product of the individual post-probabilities:

$$P_{ens}(x \in C_i/x) = \eta \prod_{k=1}^{K} P_k(x \in C_i/x) \qquad (3)$$

were η is a normalization factor.

Otherwise, if we consider the MLP as a classifier of type 2, then its response will be just a label indicating the most probable class. When conflicts exist among the individual decisions, a voting rule (a plurality or majority consensus scheme) can be adopted. Also in this case, the network error independence plays a very important role [9]. In the following we will not consider other more sophisticated approaches in the integration of classifiers of type 2 [15] because they essentially try to estimate a "measurement level" information for each class, which is directly available in the case of MLPs by considering them as classifiers of type 1.

III. Application to handwritten digit recognition

In this section, an application of the described methods to the recognition of isolated handwritten numerals is reported.

Our experiments have been carried out on the database provided by NIST for the worldwide contest organized in 1992. It consists of a main set of 223,125 samples (the suggested training set) and of a test set of 58,646 samples purposely drawn from a quite different population (we will address it as the "hard" test set).

In the first part of the work we randomly selected 20,000 samples from the main NIST Database. Of these, 10,000 made up a small training set, 5,000 a cross-validation set, 5,000 an "easy" test set. In addition, we tested our nets on the "hard" test set: due to the very small size of the training set, the results have only the purpose of analyzing the performance improvement of the MLP ensembles in a situation of heavy data undersampling. Then we checked the effectiveness of the most promising solution by training a MLP ensemble on the whole main set. We performed only scaling operations on the original data to produce 8x8 images with 64 gray levels, through two different algorithms. The first one (called "distorting") forces the output character to "touch" all four borders of the image, while the other one (called "non-distorting") preserves the original aspect ratio.

We used both classical "One-Shot" output target encoding and random binary encoding. In order to combine MLPs that are heterogeneous in the target encoding, we defined a a similarity measure $s_i, i = 1, ..M$ between the raw output vector Y and the target vector T_i corresponding to the i-th class as their normalized dot product. If we regard s_i as a membership function for a fuzzy set, then we can estimate the post-probabilities according to the following formula:

$$P(x \in Ci/x) = \eta s_i \prod_{j \neq i}(1 - s_j) = \eta' \frac{s_i}{1 - s_i} \quad (4)$$

where η, η' are normalizing constants.

A. Performance evaluation

Using the small training set, we generated several population of 5 up to 10 MLPs. Individuals in each population could differ in the training data subset, or in the weight initialization, or in the input data features, or in the output target encoding. On the whole, the individual nets achieved widely varying results (at 0% rejection rate): from 2.53% to 5.2% error rate on the easy test set, and from 9.74% to 15.38% error rate on the hard test set. Then we built different ensembles with the methods described in section II.B.

We observed very small differences between averaging in the output (Eq. 1) or in the probability (Eq. 2) space. Moreover, in our experiments we never obtained an appreciable improvement by using weighted sum instead of simple average. Thus we selected simple average in the probability space as our reference rule for the family of averaging methods.

Table 1 compares averaging, product-of-probability and voting rules. We show the relative improvement (defined as the percentage error reduction with respect to the best individual in the ensemble), that we obtained with some of the tested ensembles. Ensemble 1 consists of 5 nets with different weight initialization, ensemble 2 consists of 5 nets with different random target encoding, and ensemble 3 consists of 5 nets with different training data subsets. All the nets were trained with "distorted" data by means of on-line backpropagation. The best individual in the ensemble 1, 2 and 3 achieved respectively 2.53%, 3.80% and 4.5% error rate on the easy test set, and 9.74%, 11.38% and 14.28% error rate on the hard test set.

	ens. 1		ens. 2		ens. 3	
rule	easy	hard	easy	hard	easy	hard
aver.	17	11	64	28	38	27
prod.	8	6	67	28	38	23
voting	9	3	32	9	19	13

Table 1: relative improvement % achieved with different combination rules (easy and hard test).

The relative improvement is very variable with respect to either the combining rule or the nature of the ensemble. It tends to be higher when the individual performance of the components is not very good. As an example, combining nets with different random subsets of the training data (table 1, ensemble 3) is quite effective, but in our experiments the improvement cannot compensate the individual worsening due to the training set reduction. This problem is sometimes solved in the literature by an ad-hoc generation of additional synthetic training prototypes [8].

In general, we obtained the best results with the average technique. The product rule seems to be more sensitive than average to network mutual dependence, while voting is the least effective technique, probably due to the smaller quantity of information carried by each net.

We also extensively analyzed the trade-off between individual performance and mutual independence. Some results are reported in figure 1, showing the error rate versus the number of nets, for different ensembles built with the averaging rule.

Ensembles A and B consist of nets trained with different initial weights, with distorted and non-distorted data respectively. Ensemble C consists of nets with different random target encodings (trained with distorted data). Ensemble D consists for one half of individuals from population A and for the other half of individuals from population B. Nets are added to the ensemble according to their performance on the cross-validation set: thus the ensemble of one net is the best individual of the population. Our experiences clearly show that combining nets

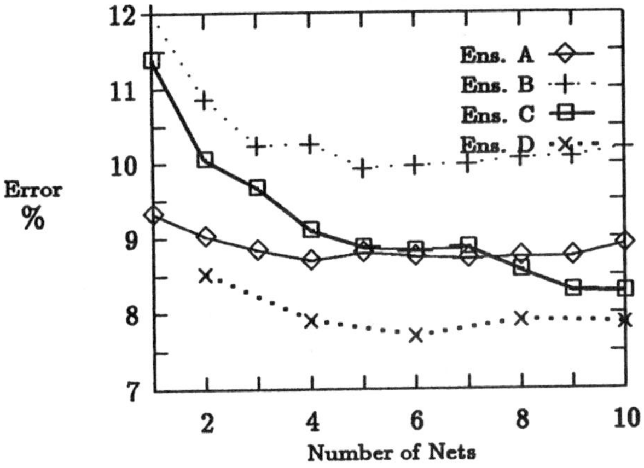

Figure 1: error rate versus number of component nets (hard test).

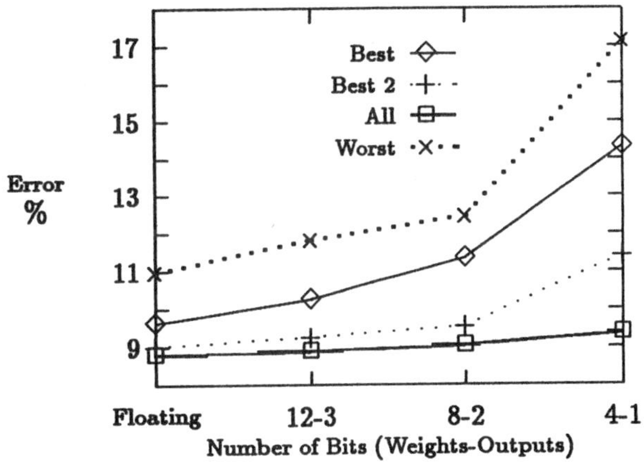

Figure 2: error rate versus precision (hard test).

with different initial weights is not as effective as combining nets with different output or input features, whatever the individual net performance is. Let us point out that, while the generation of more input features may be very expensive (or infeasible), the cost of differentiating the output targets is equivalent to the cost of differentiating the initial weights.

Moreover, as already noted in [13], a critical number of components exists which limits the "useful" size of the ensemble. This parameter is related with the network independence.

On the basis of the above results, we trained two 2-layer Perceptrons (with $\approx 10,000$ synapses each) on the whole training database, with standard back-propagation. We then combined them by averaging their outputs. The two nets were fed with data preprocessed by means of two different scaling algorithms (i.e. with different input features), and the best one achieved 4.0% error rate on the hard test set. The whole system, which is in effect a 3-layer locally connected feed-forward network with about 20,000 synapses, reached 3.4%. This result ranks well among the best ones obtained in the NIST 1992 world contest.

B. Effects of limited resolution and faulty connections

In some applications, the weight and output resolution may be a very critical parameter: for example, in bit-serial digital implementations, or in analog implementations using analog EEPROM as the weight memory [16, 17]. In this case, ensemble methods allow to reach a dramatic reduction of the requested resolution.

We trained five networks with floating point precision and different weight initializations, then we simply reduced the parameter resolution (without any additional training). Fig. 2 shows the error rate on the hard test set versus precision when both weights and logistic functions are quantized (in this case we used linear output units). The performance of the best and worst individuals, of a 2-net ensemble and of a 5-net ensemble are reported, which highlight the excellent behavior of the multiple models. This result is remarkable in that it suggests that the quantization error enhances the network independence: this is probably due to the fact that the weight matrices are usually much more uncorrelated than the network outputs (we verified this effect in all our ensembles). In other words, "spurious" local minima (e.g. due to permutation in the hidden units) uncorrelate the weights even in presence of highly coincident output errors.

We obtained comparable results when analyzing the behavior in presence of random faulty connections: Table 2 shows the error rate versus the percentage of faulty (open) synaptic links.

fault %	best net		worst net		5-net ens.	
	easy	hard	easy	hard	easy	hard
0	2.5	9.7	2.9	11.0	2.2	8.8
5	3.6	12.0	6.4	17.7	2.4	9.6
10	8.7	18.8	13.2	25.3	2.8	10.3

Table 2: error rate versus percentage of connection faults (easy and hard test).

The performance of the best and worst individuals, and of a 5-net ensemble are reported on both the easy and the hard test sets. Again, the multiple models give a considerable improvement with respect to the best single model in presence of the same percentage of faults. This result is not surprising due to the natural redundancy of the ensembles.

IV. Conclusions

As already stated by previous works, network ensembles provide good performance improvement at a reasonable cost, allowing the designer to better utilize available data and to better fit implementation constraints. The robustness and inherent redundancy (fault tolerance) of the multiple models can become winning features in the hardware implementation of high-speed and low-cost neural systems.

In spite of these encouraging results, the component selection criteria appear to be very application-dependent: for example, as one can expect, in our OCR tests we obtained the best performance by varying the input features, but this result cannot be extended to other fields. Moreover, the different combination rules have shown different degrees of sensitivity to coincident errors. Whatever the chosen solution is, the ensemble performance relies on the component network mutual independence at least as much as on their individual performance. Therefore, novel model selection criteria are needed to really exploit the potentiality of these methods.

References

[1] J.S. Bridle, "Probabilistic Interpretation of Feedforward Classification Network Outputs, with Relationships to Statistical Pattern Recognition", in *"Neurocomputing - Algorithms, Architecture and Applications"*, F.F. Soulie et al. eds, NATO ASI Series vol. F68, pp. 227-236, Springer-Verlag, Berlin (1988).

[2] E.A. Wan, "Neural Network Classification, A Bayesian Interpretation", *IEEE Trans. on Neural Networks*, vol. 1, pp. 303-304, 1990.

[3] W. Finnoff, F.Hergert, H.G.Zimmermann, "Improving Model Selection by Nonconvergent Methods", *Neural Networks*, vol.6, pp. 771-783, 1993.

[4] J. Moody, "Generalization, weight decay and architecture selection for nonlinear learning systems", in *Advances in Neural Information Processing Systems 4*, pp.471-479, J. Moody et al. eds., San Mateo, CA, Morgan Kaufmann Publishers, 1992.

[5] D.J.C. MacKay, "A practical Bayesian framework for backpropagation networks", *Neural Computation*, vol. 4, pp. 448-472, 1992.

[6] R.M. Neal, "Bayesian Learning via Stochastic Dynamics", in *Advances in Neural Information Processing Systems 5*, pp.475-482, S.J. Hanson et al. eds., San Mateo, CA, Morgan Kaufmann Publishers, 1993.

[7] M. Banan, K.D. Hjelmstad, "Self-Organization of architecture by simulated hierarchical adaptive random partitioning", *Proc. of Int. Joint Conf. on Neural Networks, III*, pp. 823-828, 1992.

[8] H. Drucker, R. Shapire, P. Simard, "Improving Performance in Neural Networks Using a Boosting Algorithm", in *Advances in Neural Information Processing Systems 5*, pp.43-49, S.J. Hanson et al. eds., San Mateo, CA, Morgan Kaufmann Publishers, 1993.

[9] L.K Hansen, P.Salamon, "Neural Network Ensembles", *IEEE Trans.on Pattern Analysis and Machine Intelligence*, vol. 12, pp. 993-1001, 1990.

[10] R.A. Jacobs, M.I. Jordan, S.J. Nowlan, G.E. Hinton, "Adaptive mixtures of local experts", *Neural Computation*, vol. 3, pp. 79-87, 1991.

[11] W.P. Lincoln, J. Skrzypek, "Synergy of clustering multiple back propagation networks", in *Advances in Neural Information Processing Systems 2*, pp. 650-657 , D.S. Touretzky ed., San Mateo, CA, Morgan Kaufmann Publishers, 1990.

[12] G. Paass, "Assessing and Improving Neural Networks Predictions by the Bootstrap Algorithm", in *Advances in Neural Information Processing Systems 5*, pp.197-203 , S.J Hanson et al. eds., San Mateo, CA, Morgan Kaufmann Publishers, 1993.

[13] M.P. Perrone, L.N. Cooper, "When Network Disagree, Ensemble Method for Neural Networks", in *"Neural Networks for Speech and Image processing"*, R.J. Mammone ed., Chapman-Hall, 1993.

[14] D.H. Wolpert, "Stacked Generalization", *Neural Networks*, vol. 5, pp. 241-259, 1992.

[15] L. Xu, A. Krzyzak, C.Y. Suen, "Methods of Combining Multiple Classifiers and Their Applications to Handwriting Recognition", *IEEE Trans. on Systems, Man, and Cybernetics*, vol. 22, pp. 418-435, 1992.

[16] L.M. Reyneri, E. Filippi, "An analysis on the performance of silicon implementations of backpropagation algorithms for artificial neural networks", *IEEE Trans. on Computers*, vol. 40, pp. 1380-1389, 1991.

[17] E. Pasero, "Floating Gates as Adaptive Weights for Artificial Neural Networks", in *Silicon Architectures for Neural Networks*, pp.125-135, M. Sami and J. Calzadilla eds., Elsevier Science Publishers, 1991.

A WEIGHTED COMPETITIVE LEARNING METHOD EXTRACTING SKELETON PATTERN FROM JAPANESE KANJI CHARACTERS

Kenji NAKAYAMA **Takuo KATO**

Dept. of Electrical and Computer Eng.,
Faculty of Tech., Kanazawa Univ.
2-40-20, Kodatsuno, Kanazawa 920 JAPAN
E-mail: nakayama@haspnn1.ec.t.kanazawa-u.ac.jp

ABSTRACT: A weighted competitive learning (WCL) method was proposed by authors for extracting skeleton patterns from digit and alphabet characters. The extracted pattern is essential in character recognition. It can satisfy the following important requirements. (a) Insensitive to irregular edge lines. (b) Non-structure patterns are not extracted. (c) Insensitive to non-uniform line width. (d) Line information should be held even though the line width widely changes in a character.

In this paper, the previous WCL method is improved for application to more complicated characters, such as Japanese Kanji characters. Furthermore, a PDP model, implements the WCL method, is provided.

I INTRODUCTION

Neural networks (NN) have been successfully applied to signal processing, pattern recognition and others based on waveform analysis [1]. Handprinted and handwritten character recognition are also important application fields of NNs. Many methods have been proposed [2]-[5]. However, performance of recognition are easily affected by distortion, non-uniform line width and blurred lines. Therefore, it is very important to extract essential structure of the character pattern to be recognized.

Conventional skeletonizing methods are based on shaving bold lines. Therefore, when line width is non-uniform, and blurred lines are included, it is difficult to obtain accurate skeleton patterns. Extracting unnecessary structures and missing important parts easily occur [5],[6].

A weighted competitive learning (WCL) method was proposed by authors for extracting essential structure of character patterns. It is insensitive to the above distortions. The idea behind this method is quite different from existing methods.

In this paper, the WCL method is improved in order to be applied to more complicated patterns, such as Japanese Kanji characters. Furthermore, implementation of this method based on a PDP model is discussed. Computer simulation using many distorted characters is demonstrated.

II BASIC STRATEGY

In handprinted or handwritten character recognition, requirements for skeletonization can be summarized as follows:

(a) Insensitive to irregular edge lines.
(b) Non-structure patterns are not extracted.
(c) Insensitive to non-uniform line width.
(d) Line information should be held.

The WCL method has been developed so as to satisfy the above require-

0-7803-1901-X/94 $4.00

ments [7],[8]. Regarding **(a)** and **(b)**, unnecessary pattern information is removed by representing some region of the pattern by a representative point, denoted 'RP'. This is a sort of 'vector quantization'. In order to optimize the RPs, the competitive learning was employed [9].

For the requirement **(c)**, the range, covered by a RP, is adaptively changed according to the line width. Therefore, this method is called 'weighted competitive learning (WCL)'. The winner is evaluated using this region, that is a weighting factor.

The condition **(d)** is satisfied by connecting the RPs along the pattern and also through the border of the regions covered by them.

III WEIGHTED COMPETITIVE LEARNING

3.1 Generation and Movement of Representative Points

The WCL method [7],[8] is described for reader's reference here.

A pixel of a pattern is abbreviated as 'point' in this paper. A pattern and a pixel are denoted P and p_I, respectively. At the initial state, there is no RP. In the learning process, RPs are generated and moved toward the optimum position. The process is described step by step in the following.

(1) One point p_I of the pattern is randomly selected.

(2) Look for the RP, whose region includes this point. When a RP is found, this RP is shifted toward the above point by

$$\delta_{IK} = \mu (p_I - r_K) \qquad (1)$$

μ is a learning coefficient. Where p_I and r_K are assumed to be 2-dimensional vectors, expressing the coordinates of the ith pixel of P and RP_K, respectively.

If there is no such a RP, then a new RP is generated on the same position as the point p_I.

(3) Repeat the above steps for all points in the pattern.

(4) When the RPs locate close to each other, as shown in Eq.(2), after shifting, they are combined, resulting in a new RP.

$$|r_K - r_{K'}| < C(r_K + r_{K'}) \qquad (2)$$

$$r_K = (r_K + r_{K'})/2 \qquad (3)$$

$|x|$ is the Euclidian distance of a vector x.

The process including **(1)** through **(4)** is counted as one iteration. The above steps are repeated until RPs converge to the stable state. How to evaluate convergence will be described later. After the RPs reach the optimum positions, their movement become very small.

In this method, some parameters, used in adjusting the regions, are determined before the learning. However, the number of RPs and their location are automatically optimized through the WCL.

3.2 Adjusting Region Covered by Representative Point

In order to extract the precise structural pattern from the distorted pattern with non-uniform line width, it is very important how to control the region covered by a single RP. If the region is narrow, then a zigzag line will be extracted. On the other hand, when the region is wide, fine structure cannot be extracted. This relation is shown in Fig.1.

In the WCL method, the region is adjusted according to the line width of each part of the pattern. Length of the lines crossing the RP are measured as shown in Fig.2.

They include the horizontal and vertical lines, and slopes with ± 45

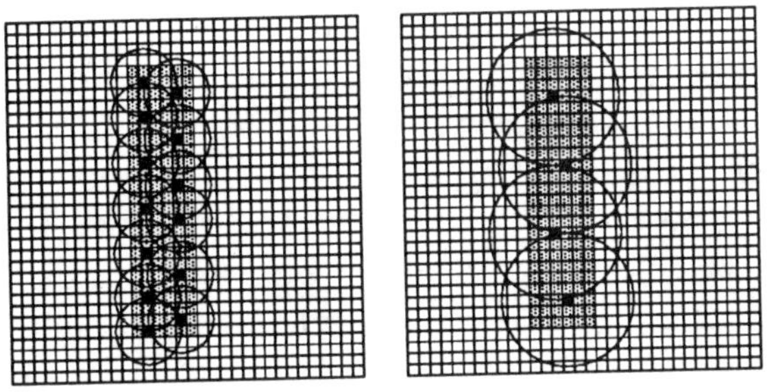

Fig.1 Relation between region covered by RP and extracted structure.

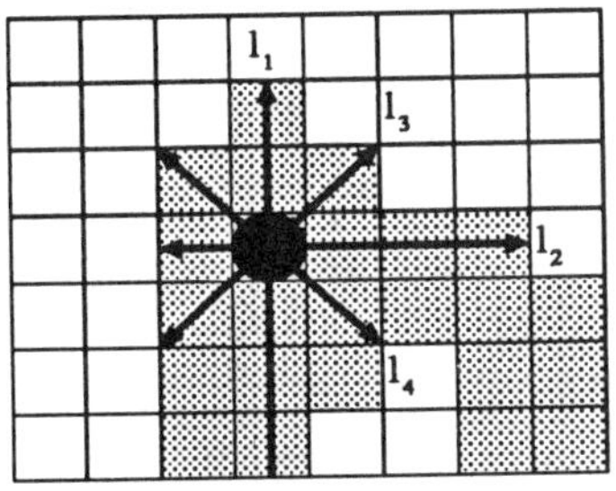

Fig.2 Detection of line width in four directions.

degrees. Length of these lines are expressed l_1, l_2, l_3 and l_4, respectively. The minimum distance is taken as the line width around this RP. By introducing some parameter, a radius of the region is determined by

$$R_K = \alpha \cdot \min_i\{l_i\} \tag{4}$$

R_K corresponds to the kth RP. α is determined taking pattern complexity and noise into account. Usually, $\alpha = 1 \sim 2$ can be widely used.

Figure 3 shows an example of the RPs and their region.

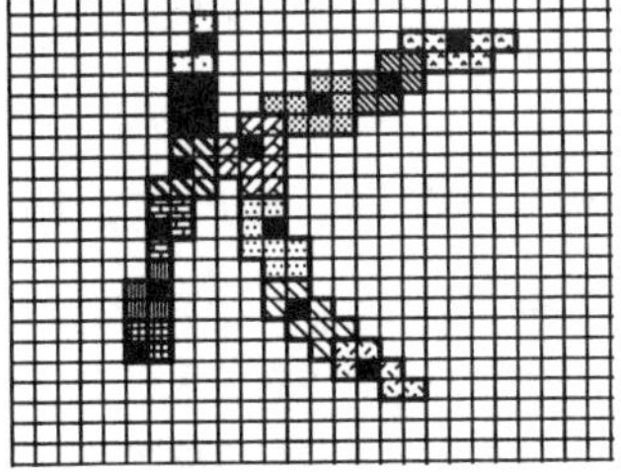

Fig.3 Example of RPs and their region.

3.3 Convergence of Learning

Efficiency of the RPs is evaluated the following error function.}

$$E_K = \sum_i |r_K - p_{Ki}| / R_K \tag{5}$$

$$E = \sum_K E_K \tag{6}$$

p_{Ki} is a point included in the RP_K region. This error function can be reduced as the RPs approach to the optimum positions. Finally, the optimum allocation of all RPs will produce the minimum error.

Since the minimum value of E is slightly different for the distorted patterns. Therefore, instead of E, the relative change of E is used.

$$\Delta E = \left| \frac{E(n) - E(n-1)}{E(n)} \right| < \varepsilon \tag{7}$$

E(n) is the error at n iteration. After ΔE satisfies the above condition, the learning process is regarded as converges. ε takes a small value. Its actual value is also determined by experience. Figure 4 shows an example of a learning curve.

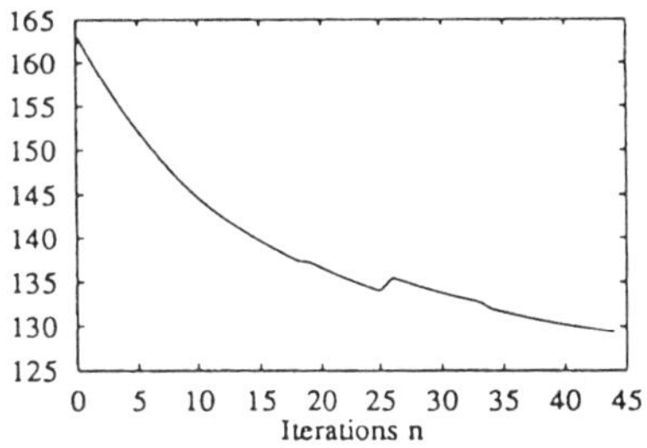

Fig.4 Example of learning curve.

3.4 Linkage of Representative Points

The optimized RPs are linked along the pattern and through the border of the regions. Figure 5 shows an example of linkage of the RPs.

As shown in Fig.4, a triangle is some time issued at the junction point. This is incorrect structure, and is replaced by a junction point as shown in Fig.6.

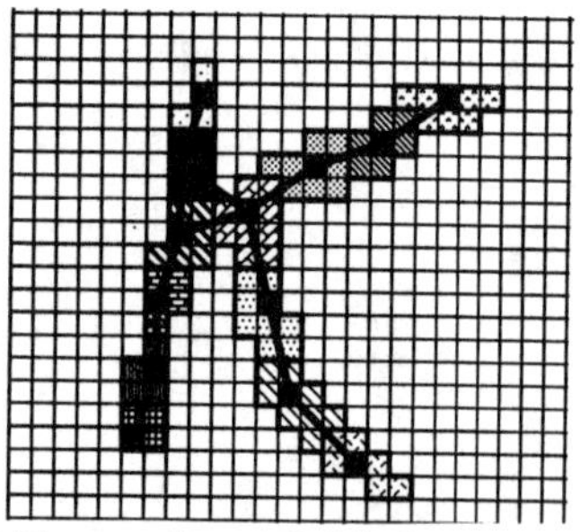

Fig.5 Example of linkages of RPs.

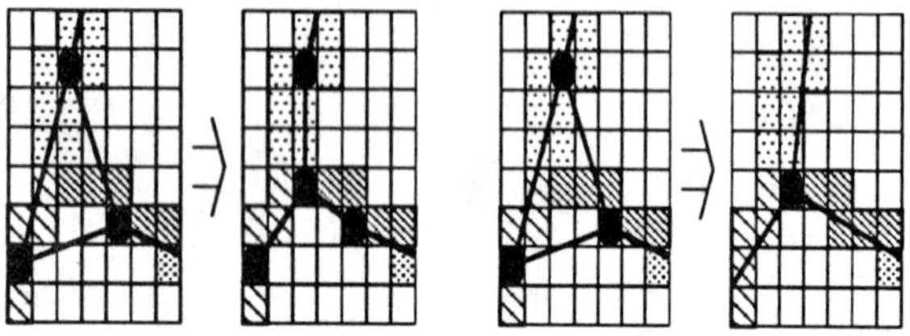

Fig.6 Unnecessary triangle is replaced by the central point.

IV APPLICATION TO COMPLICATED CHARACTERS

In this paper, the WCL method is further applied to more complicated characters, such as Japanese Kanji characters.

4.1 Property of Japanese Kanji Characters

Japanese Kanji characters, for instance 「謙」「藤」「雄」, have square structures, They are composed of small sub-patterns. Size of sub-patterns are not the same. Thus, small and complicate sub-patterns should be precisely extracted. At the same time, it should be insensitive to non-uniform line width and noise.

For this reason, how to control the region of RPs becomes very important.

4.2 Extracting Small Square Structure

The region has a circle form, actually not exactly a circle form, as described in **Sec.3.2.** In the case of Japanese Kanji characters, it is necessary to extract small corners and cross points. For this purpose, the region is modified as follows:.

Suppose a selected point p_I is included in the region of RP_K. If a straight line connecting both points p_I and r_K crosses non-pattern region, then this point p_I is not included in the RP_K region. An example is shown in Fig.6. ○ is a point locates on the pattern, ◎ is a selected point p_I, and ● is RP_K. In this example, ◎ is not represented by ●.

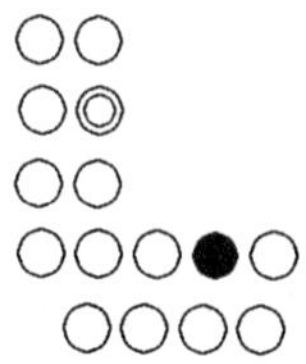

Fig.7 Example of point ◎, which is not included in region of RP ●.

4.3 Lower Bound of Region

In a fine pattern, the radius R_K of the region some time takes 1. This narrow region is not always useful. Therefore, the lower bound for the region is set.

$$R_K \geqq R_{min} \qquad (8)$$

R_{min} is used for all RPs, regardless of the line width. R_{min}=2～3[dots] can be widely used.

4.4 Overlap Regions

When the selected point p_I is included in several RP regions, the winner is determined by a ratio of the distance between p_I and r_K. and R_K.

$$d_{IK} = |p_I - r_K| \qquad (9)$$

$$\eta_{IK} = d_{IK}/R_K \qquad (10)$$

The RP, which has the minimum η_{IK}, is selected as the winner.

V IMPLEMENTATION OF WCL METHOD

5.1 Network Structure and Operation

The WCL method can be implemented using a PDP model. It consists of the input layer and the competitive layer as shown in Fig.8.

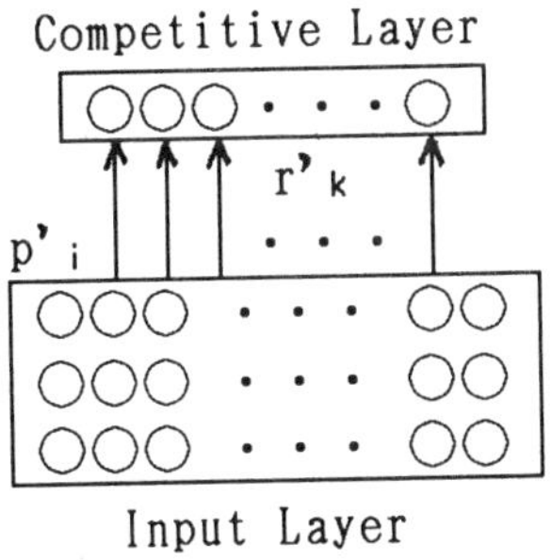

Fig.8 A PDP model for WCL method.

The input layer expresses the character patterns to be processed. Each unit outputs a 2-dimensional vector $p_i=(p_{i1},p_{i2})$. This vector is normalized to unity by adding the following auxiliary element a_i [10].

$$D > \max_i \{|p_i|\} \quad (11)$$

$$a_i = (D^2 - |p_i|^2)^{1/2} \quad (12)$$

$$p'_i = (a_i, p_{i1}, p_{i2})/D \quad (13)$$

D is constant for all p_i. The connection weight r'_k also includes $r_k=(r_{k1},r_{k2})$ and an auxiliary element. The input of the competitive layer is an inner product of p'_i and r'_k.

$$net_k = p'_i \cdot r'_k \quad (14)$$

The maximum net_k indicates the shortest distance between p_i and r_k. Therefore, if the k'th unit in the competitive layer the maximum input,

$$net_{k'} = \max_k\{net_k\} \quad (15)$$

then it can be the winner.

5.2 Adjusting Connection Weights

If RP_k becomes the winner, its connection weights are updated.

$$r_k(n) = r_k(n-1) + \mu(p_i - r_k(n-1)) \quad (16)$$

$r_k(n)$ is the component of RP_k at the nth update cycle.

VI SIMULATION RESULTS

6.1 Alphabet and Digit Patterns

Figure 9 shows examples of alphabet and digit patterns (a1) ~ (c1), and their skeleton patterns extracted by conventional methods (a2) ~ (c2) [11], and (a3) ~ (c3) [6], and (a4) ~ (c4) the WCL method. The WCL method can successfully extract the essential structural patterns.

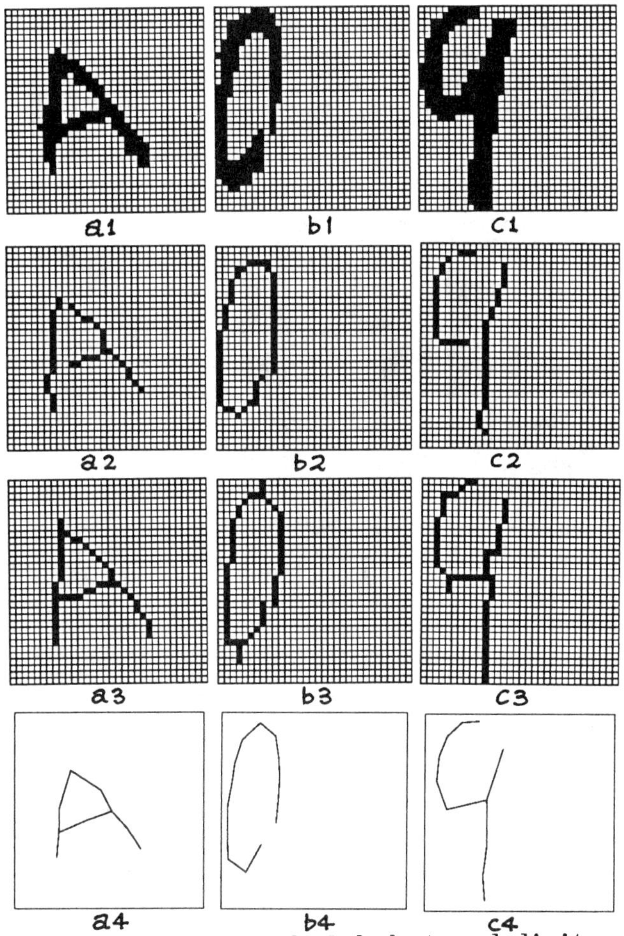

Fig.9 Examples of alphabet and digit patterns and their skeleton patterns.

6.2 Alphabet Patterns with Edge Noise

Figure 10 shows alphabet patterns with edge noise (a). The skeleton patterns obtained by (b) the conventional [6] and (c) the WCL method are shown. The WCL method can provide essential patterns.

6.3 Japanese Kanji Characters

Figure 11 shows examples of Japanese Kanji Characters and their skeleton pattern extracted by the improved WCL method. $\alpha=2$ and $R_{min}=2$ are used. Efficiency of the proposed

WCL method can be confirmed.

Fig.10 Examples of alphabet patterns with edge noise and their skeleton pattern.

Ⅶ CONCLUSIONS

The WCL method has been improved for applications to complicated characters, such as Japanese Kanji characters. Furthermore, its implemention based on a PDP model has been proposed. Through computer simulation efficiency of the proposed WCL method has been confirmed.

REFERENCES

[1]A.Maren et al.,Handbook of Neural Computing Applications, Academic Press, Inc., 1990.

[2]K.Fukushima, et al., IEEE Trans. vol.SMC-13, pp.826-834, 1983.

[3]T.P.Vogl et al., Proc., IJCNN'91 Seattle, pp.I-97-102, 1991.

[4]Y.Idan et al., Proc. IJCNN'91 Singapore, pp.2576-2581, 1991.

[5]K.Nakayama, Y.Chigawa and O.Hasegawa, Proc. IJCNN'92, Baltimore, pp.Ⅳ235-Ⅳ239, June 1992.

[6]H.Harrer et al., Proc. ISCAS'92 San Diego, pp.2897-2901, May 1992.

[7]T.Kato et al, Proc., IEICE Japan, Tech. Meeting of Neuro-Computing, vol.NC93-1, pp.1-8, May 1993.

[8]K.Nakayama et al, Proc., IJCNN'93 Nagoya, pp.2480-2483, Oct. 1993.

[9]T.Kohonen, Self-Organization and Associative Memory, 3rd Ed., Springer-Verlag 1989.

[10]J.Dayhoff,Neural Network Architectures,Van Nostrand Reinhold, 1990.

[11]N.Funakubo, Processing and Recognition of Visual Patterns (in Japanese), Keigaku Press, Japan 1990.

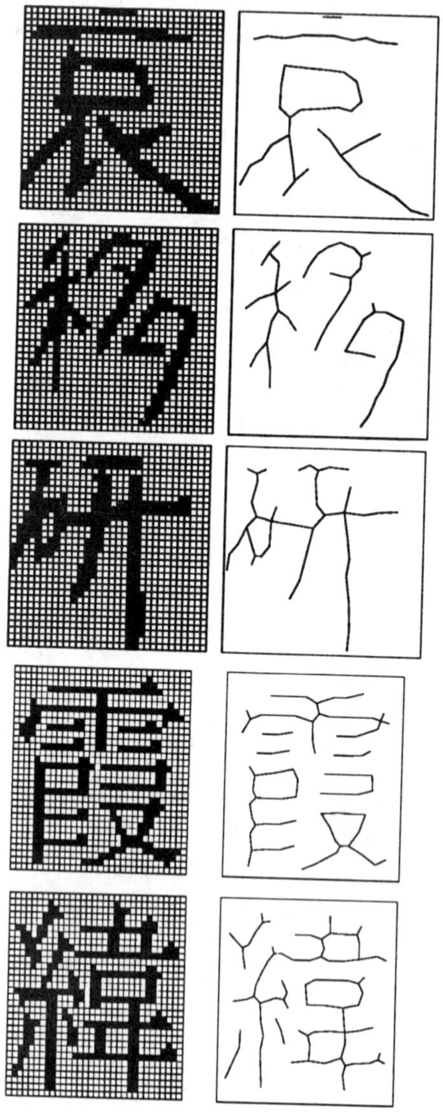

Fig.11 Examples of Japanese Kanji characters and their skeleton patterns extracted by WCL method.

A Paper Currency Recognition Method by a Small Size Neural Network with Optimized Masks by GA

*Fumiaki Takeda, **Sigeru Omatu, *Saizo Onami
*Takashi Kadono, *Kengo Terada

*GLORY LTD. Development Center 3-1 Shimoteno 1-Chome, Himeji, 670, Japan
Phone:+81-792-92-8455 Fax:+81-792-94-9603
**University of Tokushima Faculty of Engineering, 2-1 Minami-josanjima, Tokushima, 770, Japan
Phone:+81-886-26-4739 Fax:+81-886-26-4739

ABSTRACT

Many researchers have applied neural networks (NNs) to pattern recognition and the results have prove that NNs are effective recognition methods. However, compactness, transaction speed, and cost are important design factors when we apply neural networks to commercial products. We have proposed a structure reduction method for NNs. We adopt slab values which are sums of input pixels as characteristics of the inputs. But there is the possibility of generating the same slab values even when the inputs are different. To avoid this problem, we adopt a mask which covers some parts of input. This enables us to reflect the difference of input pattern to slab values with masks. Still more, we adopt the genetic algorithm (GA) to optimize the masks. We can generate various effective masks automatically. Finally, we show that the proposed method by neuro-recognition with masks can be applied effectively to paper currency recognition machine using the GA.

1. INTRODUCTION

In this paper, we discuss paper currency recognition by the small size NN to aim at commercializing of NNs. Generally, when we implement the NN to current paper currency recognition machines, the size of NN becomes a serious problem. In order to solve this problem, various methods with FFT have been proposed [1]. But for current recognition machines, such methods need complex pre-processing which is not preferable for implementation.

Here, we introduce a slab-like architecture [2] and propose a method which condenses input pixels in a simple way. In order to get information on a two-dimensional input image from various directions, we introduce masks [3]-[6] which cover some parts of input pixels. Then we input not pixel values but sum of them which have been passed through the various masks to the NN. First, we explain the basic idea of the proposed method. Second, we adopt genetic algorithm (GA) [7] to optimize these masks. Namely, we regard the position of mask as a gene. And we operate "crossover", "selection", and "mutation" to some genes on the computer. By repeating a series of these operations, we can get effective masks for paper currency recognition. Finally, we show this matter with computer simulation using the real data of US dollar.

2. BASIC IDEA OF NEURO-RECOGNITION METHOD WITH MASKS

In the present method, We suppose paper currency image as the figure on

0-7803-1901-X/94 $4.00 ©1994 IEEE

16 × 8 matrix in Fig.1. We can get 31 as the slab value in Fig.1(a) and 25 as the slab value in Fig.1(b). Using the slab values, we can separate "$1" and "¥1000". However, it may generate the same slab value even when the inputs are different. For example, slab value corresponding to "¥5000" in Fig.2(a) is 23 but the one corresponding to "W1000" in Fig.2(b) is also 23. In this case, we can not separate "¥5000" and "W1000". This problem can be solved by adopting a mask which cover some parts of the input in Fig.3(c). We can get

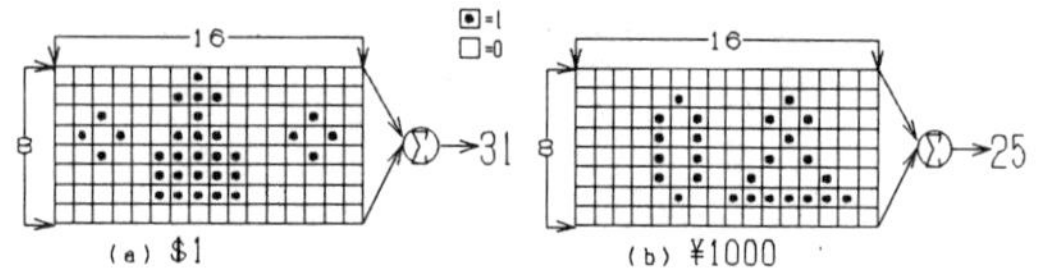

Fig. 1. Different inputs and different slab values.

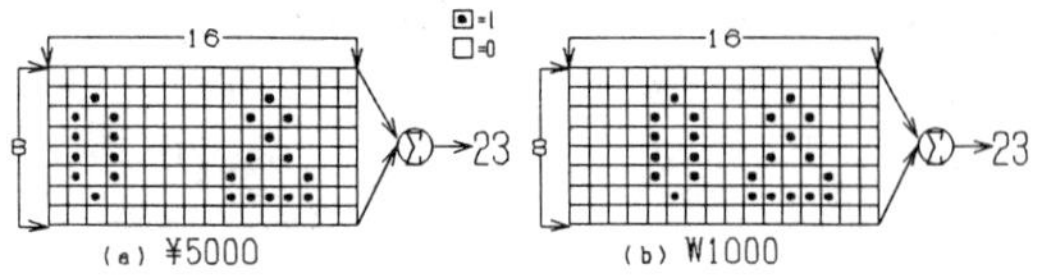

Fig. 2. Different inputs and same slab values.

13 as the slab value when the input in Fig.2(a) is covered with the mask in Fig.3(c). Otherwise, by the same method we can get 23 as the slab value from the input in Fig.3(b). In this way, we can separate "¥5000" and "W1000". We can get different values using various different masks even if the inputs are the same. It is possible to increase separability of the inputs in a stochastic sense. We show the configuration of the proposed NN with masks in Fig.4. Some parts of input are covered with various masks in pre-processing. The sum of pixels which are not masked becomes one slab value which is taken as an input of NN.

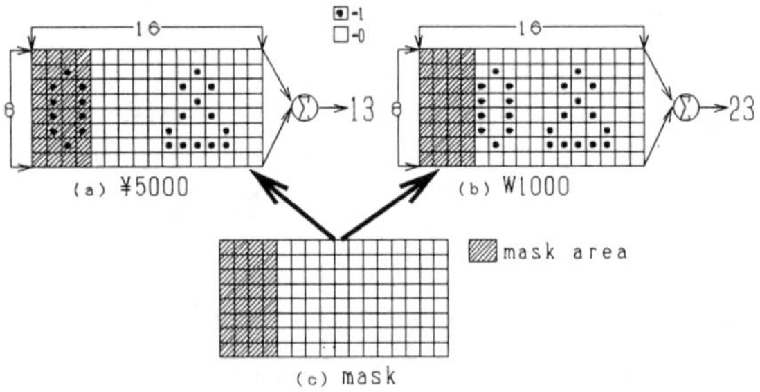

Fig. 3. Mask and slab values.

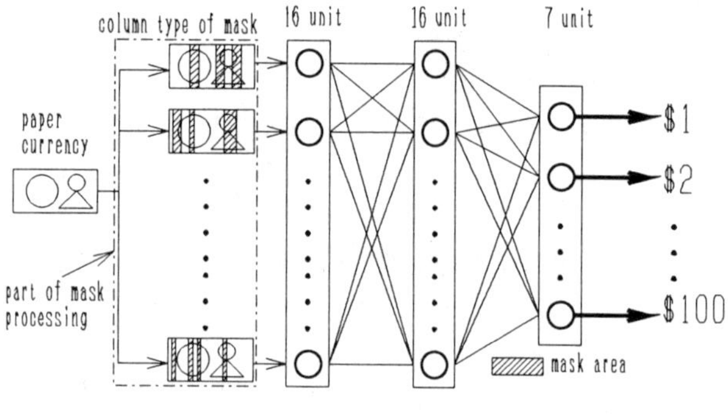

Fig. 4. Configuration of NN with masks.

3. MASK OPTIMIZATION BY GA

Here, we explain how to adopt the GA [7] to mask generation based on Fig.5. First, we prepare the some random masks (for example: A,B,C). We represent the masked part as "1" and non-masked part as "0" for each mask, respectively. We recombine their parts (for example: 1/2) of genes in these

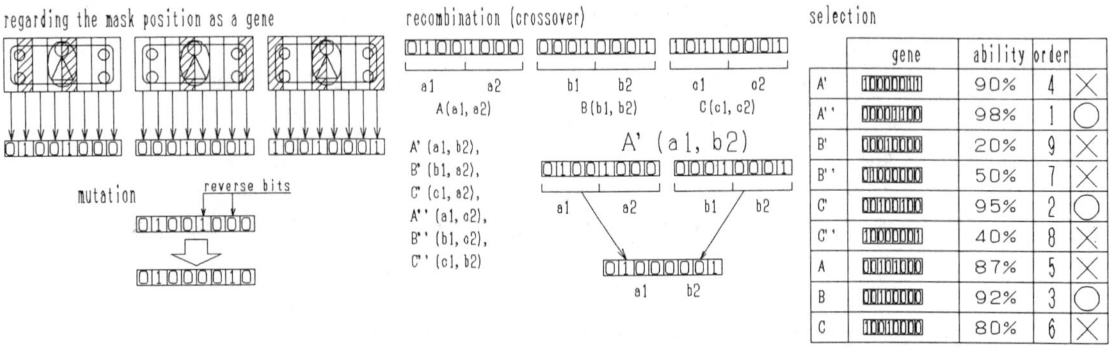

Fig. 5. Various GA operations.

three parental masks for each other. Then, we make inputs for NN using these initial masks. Learning is executed using the above inputs.

After learning, we investigate the generalization of each NN with masks using unknown data. We select upper three candidates including the parental masks considering their ability. Finally, we regard these masks as the masks of the next generation. By repeating a series of these operations, the masks are optimized gradually. Furthermore, to provide the variety to recombined masks, mutation which reverses the some bits of the genes of masks is operated randomly during the generation of new masks. In this way, we can effectively reflect the difference of input image to inputs of NN by adopting the GA. These effective masks enable to shorten the learning time and to improve the generalization

4. EXPERIMENT USING THE US DOLLAR

4.1. EXPERIMENTAL SYSTEM

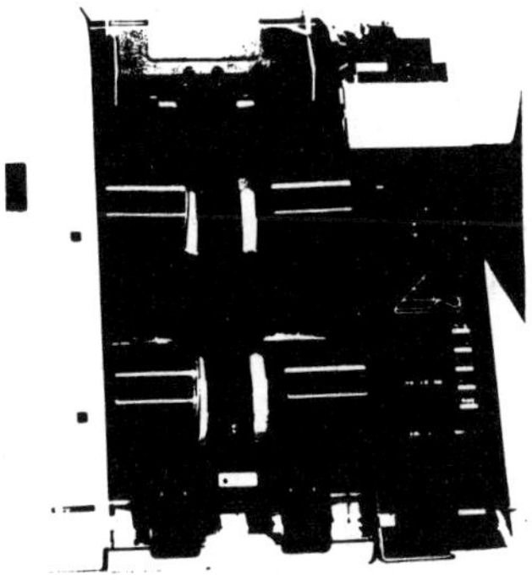

Fig. 6. Data sampling system.

Here we construct the experimental system by the proposed method using the current paper currency recognition machine as shown in Fig.6 but this machine can not recognize US dollar. This machine has been already commercialized. It can sample image data such as 216×30 pixels which are represented by 1 byte grey level. Paper currency is conveyed in the parallel direction of its short part and its conveyed speed is 10 pieces per second. The recognized paper currency kinds are US $1, $2, $5, $10, $20, $50, and $100 [5][6].

4.2. CONSTRUCTION OF NN WITH MASKS

We show the construction of NN with masks in Fig.4. We adopt the column type of mask because slab values are almost robust for the rotation (maximum $\pm 8^\circ$) compared with other types of masks [3]. We select 16 as the number of masks [3][6]. We mask columns on the input image. We define that one column denotes a series of 30 pixels in the parallel direction of short part of paper currency. Both numbers of input units and the hidden units are 16. We decide 7 as the number of output units which corresponds to paper currency kinds.

4.3. EXPERIMENT OF MASK OPTIMIZATION

Here we adopt the error back-propagation method. We execute the learning to classify different kind of US dollars for tail upright figure. For US dollars, they are much similar each other and each paper currency is the same size and have the similar tone of colour [5][6]. We use 10 pieces of paper currency as learning data to reflect their conveyed deviation for learning. We execute the US dollar recognition using the proposed method with the above excellent weights. We evaluate other 30 pieces of paper currency for each currency kind. We continue to optimize masks till 10 generation. Here, 1 generation denotes a series of "crossover", "mutation", "NN learning", "NN evaluation", and "selection".

Table 1 shows the ability of each mask and frame denotes the ability of upper three candidates of the masks. We can confirm the appearance of the masks which have the highest ability (target: 7 kind × 30 pieces=210 pieces)in the group 2 and group 4. Fig.7 shows one of the group of the masks which have highest ability and its group of the initial masks.

Table 1. Results of optimizing masks by GA.

	masks 1	masks 2	masks 3	masks 4	masks 5	masks 6
generation 1	164	[184]	[187]	176	175	[185]
generation 2	169	[186]	168	[186]	155	[184]
generation 3	167	[184]	164	[187]	152	[181]
generation 4	142	[186]	170	[185]	152	[178]
generation 5	149	[187]	170	[193]*	153	[181]
generation 6	171	[190]	148	[186]	152	[184]
generation 7	167	[193]*	164	[187]	152	[181]
generation 8	171	[190]	148	[186]	152	[184]
generation 9	167	[193]*	164	[187]	152	[181]
generation 10	171	[190]	148	[186]	152	[184]

target:7currencyX30pieces=210pieces □: upper 3 candidates * : the supreme

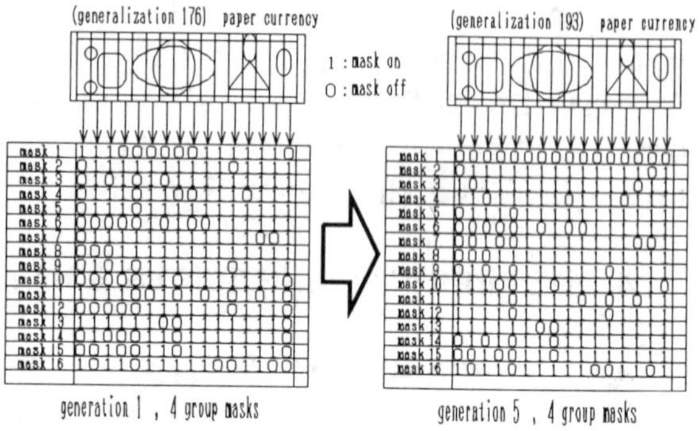

Fig. 7. Initial masks and final masks.

5. CONCLUSIONS

In this paper, we have proposed the structure reduction method of NN and applied recognition of US dollars. First, we have described its basic idea. Especially, by reflecting input patterns to slab values that are sum of pixels, we adopted masks to measure inputs from various directions and we could get the characteristic slab values. Furthermore, we optimized these masks by the GA. By use of this new technique, we confirmed that effective masks could be generated. Finally, we suppose that the GA makes easy to apply neuro-recognition method with masks to commercial products.

REFERENCE

[1] F.Takeda,S.Omatu,T.Inoue, and S.Onami, "Bill Money Recognition Using Neural Network with FFT as Pre-processor, "Trans. on ISCIE of Japan, Vol.5, No.7, pp.265-273, 1992 (in Japanese).

[2] B.Widrow,R.G.Winter, and R.A.Baxter, "Layered Neural Nets for Pattern Recognition, "IEEE Trans. on Acoust., Speech & Signal Process., Vol.36, No.7, pp.1109-1118, 1988.

[3] F.Takeda, S.Omatu, T.Inoue, and S.Onami, "A Structure Reduction of Neural Network with Random Masks and Bill Money Recognition," Proceedings of the 2nd International Conference on Fuzzy Logic and Neural Networks, IIZUKA, Japan, Vol.2,pp.809-813, 1992.

[4] F.Takeda, S.Omatu, T.Inoue, and S.Onami, "High Speed Conveyed Bill Money Recognition with Neural Network, "Proceedings of the IMACS/SCINE International Symposium on Robotics, Mechatronics and Manufacturing Systems '92 Kobe, Japan, Vol.1, pp.16-20, 1992.

[5] F.Takeda and S.Omatu, "Bank Note Recognition System Using Neural Network with Random Masks, "Proceedings of the World Congress on Neural Networks, Portland, USA, Vol.1, pp.241-244, 1993.

[6] F.Takeda and S.Omatu, "Recognition System of US Dollars Using a Neural Network with Random Masks, "Proceedings of the International Joint Conference on Neural Networks, Nagoya, Japan, Vol.2, 1993.

[7] D.E. Goldberg, Genetic Algorithms in Search, Optimization and Machine Learning, Addison-Wesley, 1989.

Object Recognition by Saccadic Parts Verification

Oleg G. Jakubowicz
Jireh Systems
23 Mayfield Dr., Leola, PA 17540[1]

Abstract - A model for the sequential processing of image 'parts' alias subobjects for the purpose of identifying visual objects is presented. The implementation uses three different coherently working neural networks to accomplish the task. One is for coarse resolution hypothesizing, one for verification via fine resolution subobject identification and the third is a sequentially processing saccade generation net. The mathematical/architectural model is implemented on a UNIX computer with MOTIF interface. In addition a comprehensive set of positional, scale and rotational invariance (PSRI) conditions are tested using CCD camera inputs of real world objects. Data collected from experiments describe the system to have 100% PSRI for real photographs. Samples over a wide range of other real world conditions such as varied illumination and cluttered scenes are recognized correctly also.

1. INTRODUCTION

Psychological experiments have shown that object components or subobjects are important in the human visual identification of objects (Biederman, 1985). While computerized Gestalt recognition of objects is rapidly approaching maturity for binary drawings (Perantonis & Lisboa 1992; Spirkovsk & Reid, 1993) and real photographic images (Jakubowicz, 1991) there practically aren't any implemented systems (Baron, 1987) operating on the principle of recognition by components. In this paper we describe the development and experimental results of SIGHT, a system capable of identifying positional, scale, rotationally and illumination invariant (hence termed PSR-II) real world objects in real world photographed scenes using recognition by Markov-like sequentially identified components. A comparison with several other recent PSRI models is presented at the end.

2. SYSTEM DESCRIPTION

2.1. Modules

The system model consists of three main modules; an object and location hypothesizer, a subobject identifier, also called a verifier here, and a sequential control system used to pick appropriate subobject locations for applying the subobject verifier. The object hypothesizer and subobject verifier in earlier instantiations were used in image identification systems while versions of the sequential control module were used in robotics and natural language processing systems. A diagram of the processing relationships among the three modules in the current vision model is presented in Figure 1. The processing relationship is described in the following paragraphs.

2.2. Inputs, Outputs And Flow Of Control

The inputs are currently presented to the system as 250x250 pixel images with 8-bit gray scale encoding. Visual objects in the images should be about 140 pixels across : +- 50% permissible by scale invariance. A 196x196 pixel window from a X11/MOTIF interface screen is chosen by using a mouse. The input is first passed to the 'object class, location and rotation hypothesizer'. This object hypothesizer presents a first guess for the 'subobject verifier' which works iteratively with the 'sequencer'. The sequencer iteratively provides locations and subobject classes for further search by the subobject verifier.

If an adequate number of subobjects are found for object identification the system outputs the identification of which of three trained objects is present in the input image. Also the location and orientation of the input object is detected and presented.

2.3. Preprocessing Layers

Processing proceeds upwardly through layers of 2 dimensional planes of nodes. Each of the bottom two layers has two center-surround opponent processing planes; one for on-center off-surround and the other for off-center on-surround. The first one mimics retinal horizontal-bipolar contrasting via a small 3x3 input window matrix consisting of one cell/node for the center and eight cell/nodes for the surround. The second layer is intended to perform the larger center-surround integrations and contrasting physiologically observed in laminar layer IV of the V1 visual neocortex area. The lateral geniculate nucleus intermediate processing stage is not used in the model since experiments in primates show comparatively little change for foveal processing regions other than a small degree of contrast enhancement. The nonlinear logistic activation function is used since it offers well controllable

---

[1] This work was supported in part by the Navy under N60921-92-C-A343.

0-7803-1901-X/94 $4.00 ©1994 IEEE

contrasting properties without requiring iterative processing that would be required in lateral inhibition implemented via differential equations.

The function used for these two layers are of the form :

$$Output(i,j) = \frac{1}{1 + \exp(\lambda*(\xi - pw \bullet v_{in}))}$$

were the weight matrix pw produces opponent center-surround processing over 3x3 areas for the first (retina) layer and 9x9 areas for the second (laminar IV) layer and λ and ξ are constants.

2.4. The Object Hypothesizer

Including the preprocessing the object hypothesizer is a 7 layer neural network with spatially distributed redundantly processing nodes having overlapping input areas. It is a network of the Fukushima Neocognitron class (Fukushima, Miyaki & Takayuki, 1983) , with similar simple and complex sublayers within each layer, aperture input windows for each node and similar processing equations and learning rules. A diagram of the module is presented in figure 2.

The preprocessing feeds into the first layer simple nodes in the V1 processing planes where each node has a 9x9 input across both opponent processing planes in the V1 laminar layer IV system layer. This represents the 12x20 retinal cones receptive areas observed in Macaque monkeys (Dow, Bauer, Snyder and Vautin, 1984). The output of each node in all simple-like layers is calculated by the standard Neocognitron simple node equation ,

$$Output(i+1) = r\frac{1 + \overrightarrow{w_{in}} \bullet \overrightarrow{v_{in}}}{1 + \frac{r}{r+1} b\ sumsr} - 1$$

where the sumsr is

$$sumsr = \sqrt{c_{in} \bullet \left(\overrightarrow{v_{in}} \bullet \overrightarrow{v_{in}}\right)}$$

c is a normalized gaussian matrix, r is a positive constant determining the efficiency of the inhibition v cells, b is a variable inhibitory connection to v cells and w is the input weight matrix. sumsr represents the output of the v inhibitory cells. In the third layer v_{in} is the 9x9x2 input window to each node taken over all the second layer preprocessing nodes.

These nodes are trained with a teacher to be sensitive to bars, edges and end stops (Hubel & Wiesel, 1968) that are found in primate natural cortex. The training equations are also the standard Neocognitron learning equations for w and b weights. The winner locations are supervised but the features are not.

The second sublayer in the V1 processing area contains Neocognitron-like complex nodes that are sensitive to small positionally invariant simple sublayer features. A layer of oriented contrast-insensitive nodes is placed at the top of the V1 layers in a manner similar to that reported by Grossberg et. al. (Grossberg & Mingolla, 1985).

There are two layers in the V2 level. Each contains nodes sensitive to more complicated features. In contrast to the previous (V1) layer the V2 'simple-like' layer was trained without a teacher. The training and propagation equations are the same as in the previous layer but contain different parameter values. Up to 100 self organizing features may be formed during training. The upper V2 layer contains 'complex-like' planes of nodes which do not need to be trained but perform localized integration based on Gaussian matrices.

Finally the highest layer contains 12 output planes, four for each trained object. There are four for each object because there are four rotations trained for each object; 0, 30, 60 and 90 degrees. Since a single rotation system is found to be invariant to + or - 20 degrees, these four rotations are sufficient to cover the entire range of rotations from 0 to +90 degrees. This model can be expanded to recognize objects rotated from 0 to 360 degrees by placing (4x4 =) 16 planes for each object at this top level. This layer was trained with a teacher using the aforementioned learning equations. Propagation proceeds with the same equations.

Implementations of this module in previous projects have demonstrated near 100% detection accuracy for input objects spanning approximately 60% to 150% of the trained images in scale, rotated between 0 to 90 degrees, and having their center translated anywhere within the input plane (Jakubowicz, 1991). Identical results for this hypothesizer will be presented in the second half of this paper.

2.5. The Subobject Verifier

The subobject verifier is identical to the object hypothesizer already outlined except that it is missing the V2 complex-cell layer and it has an increased number of planes in the output layer. The increase in number of planes accommodates the larger set of subobjects in relation to the number of objects.One major reason the V2 complex-cell layer is missing is because a neural net having more layers will have a larger input field of view for each output node at the top layer. Since the input image does not propagate through as many levels as it does through the object hypothesizer module the effective spatial extent of each output node is over a much smaller portion of the input image.

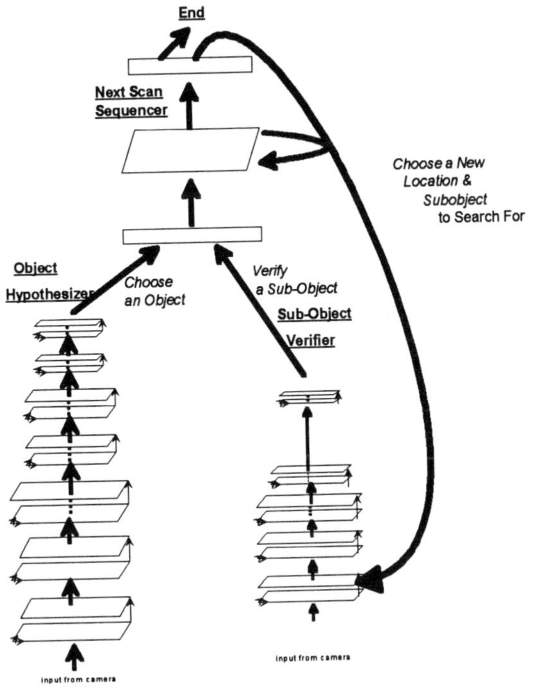

Figure 1 The entire system showing the relationship among the three modules/neural networks. Initially the camera input processes through the hypothesizer module. Then the recurrent sequential module iteratively directs the location where the verifier module searches/ saccades to. One of three additional output nodes of the sequential network wins when a final object is decided.

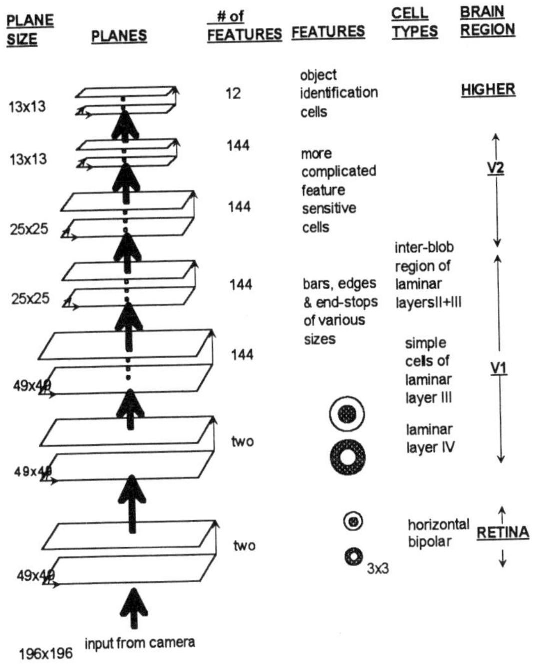

Figure 2 Diagram of 'Object Class, Location and Orientation Hypothesizer'. There are two layers involved with fixed weights preprocessing. One in the retina region and one at the start (laminar layer IV) of the V1 area both consisting of center surround opponent processing. Subsequently a simple layer and complex layer of bars, edges and endstops completes V1 processing. Afterwards complicated training set dependent features are processed in two V2 layers. Finally the Higher layer produces information leading to a hypothesized object.

In the current implementation of the module each of the three objects are appropriated with 5 subobjects and each subobject is detectable over 0 to 90 degrees of rotations. The subobject sensitive nodes have been trained at 0, 30, 60 and 90 degrees. These conditions necessitate the 3x5x4 = 60 planes or different types of features to be detected.

The subobject recognition system is also designed to be invariant over the range of 0 to +90 degrees rotationally and approximately 60% to 150% in scale. Subobjects which were translated anywhere within a 9x9 pixel window centered on the hypothesized location for the subobject where recognized most of the time. A quantitative table of statistical recognition rates for subobjects hasn't been assimilated yet.

2.6. The Sequencing Controller

The sequential control of focus of attention for the subobject verifier is provided by a neural network model developed by (Samarabandu & Jakubowicz, 1990). A 10x10 internal feature map representation has been shown to have a high capacity for distinguishing among input patterns and sequences of input patterns. The sequencing controller module is the upper sub modules in the system diagram in figure 1.

The combination of two different sets of nodes into one equation is accomplished by

$$Output(i+1) = r\frac{1+\overrightarrow{\mathbf{w}_{in}}\bullet\overrightarrow{v_{in}}+\overrightarrow{\mathbf{w}_{fb}}\bullet\overrightarrow{v_{fb}}}{1+\frac{r}{r+1}b\ sumsr} - 1 + \Theta\ Output(i)$$

b, sumsr and the learning equations are described in a journal article, (Jakubowicz, 1994). Neocognitron-like equations are used mainly because of their nonlinear sharpness of recognition.

The sequencer is first invoked after the object hypothesizer has chosen an object class as its best guess for the object in the input image. One of three nodes on the input to the sequencer becomes activated. Next a pattern is generated on the 10x10 internal feature map and one of the 15 (3 objects x 5 subobjects each) output nodes is activated for the purpose of reporting relationally where to start searching and what subobject to search for to the subobject verifier. When the subobject verifier returns, the results are placed onto the 15 other input nodes to the sequencer and the sequencer mixes this information with feedback of what its done already to pick a new subobject and location to search. When all the subobjects for the hypothesized object are found then the sequencer indicates the system is finished processing.

2.7. Subobject Relational Representation

During sequential search a different object may be hypothesized due to subobjects other than the ones originally proposed being detected/verified . One reason a switch in focus of attention in midstream can occur is because in the system's current relational modeling all objects have their subobjects in roughly the same places. In this way an alternate object may be hypothesized during any scan if several subobjects of a different object are found in or near appropriate locations; i.e. if a face is hypothesized initially but the center location verifies the center of an aircraft and the top of the face verifies the nose of an aircraft then the hypothesis will very likely take a midcourse correction to search according to another object paradigm for aircraft alternate subobjects.

3. TRAINING

The system described in the previous sections was trained to recognize the three objects shown in Figure 3. First images of these three objects at 30° increments would be trained into the object hypothesis system. Then the subobject recognition system was trained to recognize five subobjects from each of these same three objects.

The trained objects were a F108 jet fighter aircraft, a F14, and a human face. The two aircraft are similar, so the hypothesis mechanism would occasionally in some extreme situations not be able to distinguish correctly between the two. But the verifier improves identification. Both the hypothesizer and verifier never confuses the face with the aircraft, in the tests we conducted, since they is so dissimilar.

Object #0 F108 Object #1 F14 Object #2 Face

Figure 3 TRAINING OBJECTS - This figure shows the three objects that were trained to the coarse/hypothesizer network for the tests performed in this paper. Subobjects of these objects were trained into the subobject verifier network. Saccade sequences were trained to the sequential network. Object # 1 (the F14 aircraft) was used for most of the PSRI tests reported in the paper. Other tests on the remaining objects produced similar results.

4. TESTING

4.1. Method Of Processing

A CCD camera collected 8 bit images of real world objects in the various testing situations. A 196x196 pixel section of the image transformed into a 49x49 coarse pixel representation would be presented to the recognition system. The testing objects that are to be recognized in the images were typically from 15 to 45 coarse pixels in length since the trained objects were approximately 35 coarse pixels in length.

Either the object type or object class would be correctly identified by the hypothesizer. Then its location and orientation (angle of rotation) would be hypothesized. Finally the subobject/parts verifier and sequential subsystem would pick locations and test for subobject types to complete the search process.

4.2. PSR Invariance

An aircraft #1 (F-14) was tested at 11 different positions (from 27 pixels to the right of center to 26 pixels to the left) by moving the CCD camera to as many locations. The correct object was both hypothesized and then verified for all the translations between -24 to +27 pixels.

Previously, nowhere is the Neocognitron reported to demonstrate 100% translational invariance for real world images; only sporadic translations are demonstrated. The reason this offspring model is able to perform 100% translational invariance is because of a 2x2 redundancy of processing at the interface between simple to complex levels.

For scale tests an aircraft #1 was photographed at lens magnifications that produced object images between 19 to 49 coarse pixels long. The proper group type of objects, aircraft, is hypothesized correctly in each of these cases. The correct aircraft was not always hypothesized. However all objects between 72% to 132% of the original trained size were identified correctly through the verification process.

This demonstrates that an appropriate representation of similarities of subparts between similar objects is necessary in order to arrive at correct verification when the hypothesizer picks a close but not optimal object to start the sequential search. It also displays the advantage of having a parts verification system in addition to the Gestalt object hypothesis system.

For the rotational invariance test eleven pictures of aircraft#1 were taken at rotational angles from -13° to +101°. The aircraft was close to center, scale was close to 1.00 of the training set for this aircraft and the illumination level and source were varying in these tests. The hypothesizer was able to recognize that an aircraft was present 100% of the time from -13° to +101°. However the finer discrimination between the two similar fighter aircraft did not occur until full utilization of the system sequential capabilities.

4.3. Various Other Tests

There were 9 images tested for additional capabilities as illustrated in figure 4. The same aircraft#1 was used in the input in each of these tests. All 9 tests represent 'must' capabilities for a real world operating system besides having PSR invariance. These tests demonstrate the system's ability to operate in the presence of 1) different angles of the sun, 2) different times of the day resulting in varying illumination levels, 3) objects out of focus, diffused by clouds or smoke, 4) objects interspersed among other objects or background as for example on an airfield, and also 5) object/background illumination inversions.

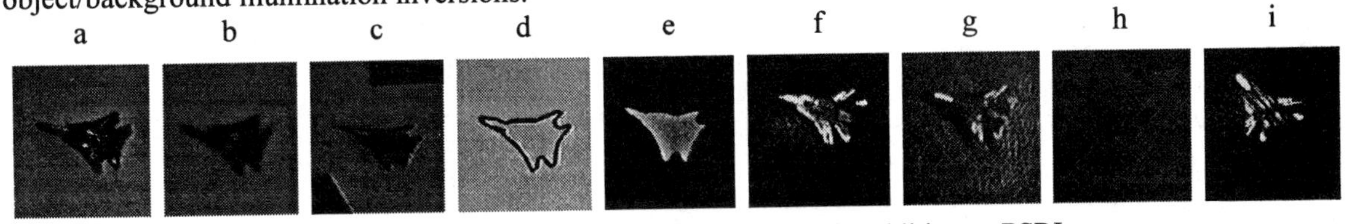

Figure 4 Various other tests were performed in addition to PSRI.

Of the images in figure 4 tests a to d identified the correct aircraft. Tests e to g where identified as aircraft but the exact type of aircraft was mis-identified. Tests h and i resulted in all final winner object identification outputs producing '0.0', null result. Both the h and i images would probably be likewise difficult for a casual human observer to identify also.

5. CONCLUSIONS

SIGHT has extended the capabilities of the Neocognitron to exhibit 100% PSRI as in several other currently researched neural net vision systems including Perantonis and Lisboa's TON (P+L TON) (Perantonis & Lisboa, 1992) and Spirkovska and Reid's HONN (S+R HONN) (Spirkovska & Reid, 1993). However in this paper SIGHT has demonstrated its effectiveness with real world objects in real world scenes. This includes gray level encoding and cluttered scenes. In contrast the P+L TON uses binary-1 bit typed and written characters for input while the S+R HONN uses binary-1 bit hand-drawn outlines of two aircraft or cars at a time. SIGHT is able to discriminate between minutely differing objects by utilizing a fine resolution parts verification processing level. Note the two fighter aircraft used in SIGHT are much more similar than HONN's most similar objects which is probably the blunt space shuttle-sharp F18 test. And finally efficiency in processing is enhanced by sequential saccadic movements based on which parts/subobjects have been verified/recognized at each step.

A table summarizing the capabilities of the TON, HONN and SIGHT, is presented in table 1.

Additional real world examples show that SIGHT is able to identify objects illuminated from various 3-d source angular locations and intensities, on various backgrounds which even result in intensity reversal (light on dark verses dark on light, outlined objects), having missing parts (e.g. translated half off of the screen), noise or unfocused. Also objects may be placed nearby and not obstruct identification.

Since SIGHT performs spatially and rotationally localized processing as opposed to TON's and HONN's global processing, it is able to perform segmentation in cluttered scenes and maintain knowledge of the orientation of the objects and subobjects it views. Based on these properties SIGHT exhibits the characteristics required for real world object segmentation, identification and scene understanding systems.

TABLE 1 PSR INVARIANCE COMPARISON

Property	SIGHT Hypothesizer	SIGHT Verifier	SIGHT Intergrated	P+L TON	R+S HONN
Positional	100%	100%	100%	100%	100%
Scale	2.5x	2.5x	2x	1.5-2.5x	3.0x
Rotational	360°	360°	360°	360°	360°
Real Images	YES	YES	YES	NO	NO

SIGHT is similar to TON & HONN in PSRI, but works with real images, discriminates well among highly similar aircraft and maintains knowledge of the orientation of parts and objects for later scene analysis purposes.

References

Baron,R.J. (1987). *The Cerebral Computer: An Introduction to the Computational Structure of the Human Brain*, Hillsdale NJ: Lawrence Erlbaum Associates.

Biederman,I. (1985). Human image understanding: Recent research and a theory, *Computer Vision, Graphics, and Image Processing*, **32**, 29-73.

Dow,B.M., Bauer,R., Snyder,A.Z., and Vautin,R.G. (1984). Receptive fields and orientation shifts in the foveal Striate Cortex of the awake Macaque monkey,. In *Dynamical Aspects of Neocortical Function*, Edelman,G.M., Gall,EW.E., and Cowan,W.M., eds.., pp.41-65, John Wiley and Sons, New York, New York

Fukushima, K., Miyake, S., and Takayuki, I. (1983), Neocognitron: A neural network model for a mechanism of visual pattern recognition, *IEEE Transactions on Systems, Man and Cybernetics*, **13**, 826-834.

Grossberg, S. and Mingolla, E. (1985). Neural Dynamics of perceptual grouping: Textures, boundaries, and emergent segmentations, *Perception and Psychophysics*, **38**, 141-171.

Hubel, D.H., and T.N. Wiesel (1968). Receptive fields and functional architecture of monkey striate cortex., *Journal Physiology,* **195**, 215-243.

Jakubowicz,O. (1989). Efficiency in the generation of hierarchical feature detectors in neural nets, *Proceedings of SPIE-Sensor Fusion II: Human and Machine Strategies*, **1198**, 430-434, Bellingham, WA: SPIE.

Jakubowicz, O. (1991). Foveal mapping and sequential steps of parallel attribute testing, presented at the *Neural Networks and Automatic Target Recognition Conference of Boston University*, Wang Institute of the Boston University.

Perantonis,S.J. and Lisboa,P.J.G. (1992). Translation, Rotation, and Scale Invariant Pattern Recognition by High-Order Neural Networks and Moment Classifiers, *IEEE Transactions on Neural Networks*, **3**, 241-251.

Samarabandu, J. and Jakubowicz, O. (1990). Principles of sequential feature maps in multi-level problems, *Proceedings of the International Joint Conference on Neural Networks*, **2**, 683-686 Hillsdale, NJ: Erlbaum.

Spirkovska,L. and Reid,M.B. (1993). Coarse-Coded Higher-Order Neural Networks for PSRI Object Recognition, *IEEE Transactions on Neural Networks*, **4**, 276-283.

Axially Symmetric Neural Network Architecture for Rotation-Invariant Pattern Recognition

Hidefumi SAWAI

Information and Communication
Research and Development Center, Ricoh Co., Ltd.
3-2-3, Shin-Yokohama, Kohoku-ku, Yokohama, 222 Japan
Email: sawai@ipe.rdc.ricoh.co.jp

Abstract

We propose axially symmetric Neural Network archtecture capable of detecting orientations for *rotation-invariant* pattern recognition. This is a class of multi-layer perceptrons, where the synaptic weights "in parallel" between the lower layer and the succesive upper layer all have the same values (i.e., symmetric with respect to the principal axis of the network architecture). This network can be trained by the back-propagation procedure under the above weight constraints using any patterns (e.x., 10-digit or 26 alphabet characters) in a standard position, which automatically makes it possible to recognize test patterns with different orientations (i.e., rotated patterns), simultaneously detecting orientation.

1 Introduction

Several studies on rotation-, scaling-, translation- and distortion-invariant neural network architecture in the field of pattern recognition have been reported. Among them, the MADALINE is a network which is designed to recognize patterns invariant to translation and to rotation by 90 degrees[1]. The Neocognitron is a hierarchical network capable of recognizing deformed handwritten alphaneumeric characters[2]. Translation, rotation, scaling and distortion-invariant recognition of handwritten numerals is also reported[3]. The TDNN (Time-Delay Neural Nework)[4] incorporates shift-invariance originally designed for high-performance phoneme recognition, and has been applied to several speech recognition tasks[5][7]. The FTDNN (Frequency-Time-Shift-Invariant TDNN) architecture[6] was designed for robust continuous speech recognition. The BWNN (Block Windowed Neural Network) architecture[6] is an alternative architecture to the FTDNN.

The newly proposed architecture has axial symmetry with respect to the pricipal axis of the network, which enables it to extract rotation-invariant features from input patterns and recognize those regardless of orientation (rotation angles of input patterns). Furthermore, that architecture can automatically detect the orientation (i.e., the angle from a standard position) of an input pattern.

2 Axially Symmetric Architecture

The Axially Symmetric Neural Network (ASNN) architecture is shown in Fig.1. The network comprises five layers: an input layer, two hidden layers and two split output layers. In the input layer, neurons are arranged in a circular and radial lattice shape (i.e., along polar coordinates) with proper separations. A similar situation is also realized in the upper layers including

0-7803-1901-X/94 $4.00 ©1994 IEEE

the first and second hidden layers and the second output layer. Both first and second hidden layers consist of some sublayers in which neurons are arranged in a circular lattice shape. The number of sublayers in the first hidden layer is set to three for both digit and letter recognition. Each sublayer in the second hidden layer corresponds to a category neuron in the first output layer. So, there are ten sublayers for digit recognition and 26 sublayers for letter recognition. The first output layer has a number of neurons corresponding to the number of categories (i.e., 10 for digits or 26 for letters). The second output layer is arranged for detecting the angle of departure from a standard position of input patterns (in the case of Fig.1, detection of orientation is possible every 45 degrees. Note that higher angular resolution can be possible if more neurons are arranged in a circular lattice shape). The synapses are fully connected between the input layer and the first hidden layer, between the first and second hidden layers, and between the second hidden layer and the second output layer. However, symmetric weight constraints ("tied" connections) with respect to the principal axis (i.e., the vertical axis) are introduced among the *"parallel"* connections (in Fig.1, respective solid, broken and dotted lines are *"parallel"*) between the each two layers. The synaptic weight values between the second hidden layer and a category neuron in the first output layer are all the same, thus summing up the outputs from the second hidden layer.

In summary, the network for digit recognition has 155 units (including 33 inputs, 104 hidden units and 18 outputs) and 3,530 weight connections (450 different values of connections), and the network for letter recognition has 299 units (including 33 inputs, 232 hidden units and 34 outputs) and 7,898 weight connections (1,010 different values of connections). This *"axial symmetry"* in arranged neurons and synaptic connections makes it possible for the network not only to recognize any input patterns rotated from a standard position (i.e., the position of training patterns), but also to detect the orientation of input patterns.

Fig.1 shows an example of an input pattern "M" correctly recognized. Of course, any 45 degree-rotated patterns can be recognized as well. Fig.2 shows an example of input pattern representation. The left side of the figure is an input pattern "M" fed to the input layer, where twelve neurons out of 32 neurons arranged in polar coordinates (r, θ) with proper separations become active (i.e., represented as black neurons). The right side of the figure shows the conversion from polar coordinates to rectangular coordinates.

3 Experiments

3.1 Training of the ASNNs

3.1.1 Training of the ASNN for Ten-digit Recognition

Fig.3 shows training patterns in a standard position for 10 digit recognition. The training of the ASNN is performed using an accelerated algorithm[9] based on the back-propagation procedure[8]. This modified accelerated algorithm is based on a dynamical change of momentum (α) and step size (η) in the back-propagation procedure, which is one of the most effective algorithms proposed so far.

Fig.4 shows two curves of error and recognition rates for classification of digits as a function of Epochs (an "Epoch" is a short period presenting 10 training patterns); the solid line shows the Euclidian error between output values of two output layers and target values, and the broken line shows recognition rates for classification of training patterns. Training was successfully performed for classification of categories as well as detecting standard orientations, although temporary degradation around the 55th Epoch was observed due to a slightly too large step size(η).

3.1.2 Training of the ASNN for Letter Recognition

Fig.5 shows training patterns in a standard position for 26 letter recognition. Among the shape of alphabets, there are some point-symmetric patterns, such as "H", "I", "N", "O", "S", "X" and "Z". Some consideration is needed when we set the target values for detecting orientation in the second output layer. For example, the target values of $\vec{\theta} \equiv (0°, 45°, 90°, 135°, 180°, 225°, 270°, 315°)$ should be set to $(1,0,0,0,1,0,0,0)$ for the patterns "H", "I", N", "S" and "Z". Similary, let the target value of $\vec{\theta}$ be $(1,1,1,1,1,1,1,1)$ for the pattern "O", $\vec{\theta}$ be $(1,0,1,0,1,0,1,0)$ for the pattern "X" (Note that the target value $(1,0,0,0,1,0,0,0)$ was also set for the pattern "0(zero)" in digit recognition). The training scheme is otherwise the same as the training of 10-digit patterns.

Fig.6 shows two curves of error and recognition rates for classification of letters as a function of Epochs. Similarly to the case of training 10-digit patterns, training for classification of letters was successfully performed, although temporary degradation in around the 120th epoch was observed. In the training of orientation detection, only two patterns("B" and "I") were not successfully trained, because some confusion of such patterns with others occurred. Nevertheless, if various other procedures are considered such as a slight modification of structure in the hidden layers or the learning parameters in back-propagation, training of the exceptional cases might be successfully performed.

3.2 Testing of the ASNNs

Fig.7 and Fig.8 are examples of test patterns for 10 digit and 26 alphabet recognition, respectively. The test patterns are arranged in order rotating every 45 degree, except the standard position (i.e., $\theta = 0°$). All patterns in Figures 7 and 8 are correctly classified, and orientations of all patterns except "B" and "I", whose orientations were not correctly detected in the training phase, were successfully detected.

4 Conclusion

We proposed a novel neural network architecture for rotation-invariant pattern recognition. That architecture has axial symmetry which enables the network to automatically recognize input patterns regardless of the orientation of the training patterns. Furthermore, the network is capable of detecting the angle of departure from a standard position of training patterns. We verified the performance of the architecture through two kinds of pattern recognition tasks: ten-digits recognition and alphabet recognition. The next stage will focus on integration of modular neural network architecture, which will enable to recognize patterns with rotation-, scaling-, translation- and distortion-invariance as the extension of this study.

Acknowledgement

The author would like to express his gratitude to Mr.Erik McDermott of ATR Human Information Processing Research Laboratories for his poofreading of this manuscript.

References

[1] B.Widrow and R.Winter, "Neural Nets for Adaptive Filtering and Adaptive Pattern Recognition," IEEE Trans. on Computer, pp25-39, Mar. 1988.

[2] K.Fukushima and S.Miyake, "Neocognitron: A New Algorithm for Pattern Recognition Tolerant of Deformations and Shifts in Position," Pattern Recognition, vol.15, no.6, 1984.

[3] S.Lee and Y.Choi, "Translation, Rotation, Scaling, and Distortion Invariant Recognition of Handwritten Numerals," Proceedings of IJCNN'92, vol.2, pp185-196, Beijing, Nov.1992.

[4] A.Waibel, T.Hanazawa, G.Hinton, K.Shikano and K.Lang, "Phoneme Recog-

nition Using Time-Delay Neural Networks," IEEE Trans. on ASSP, vol.37, no.3, pp328-339, Mar. 1989.

[5] A.Waibel, H.Sawai and K.Shikano, "Modularity and Scaling in Large Phonemic Neural Networks," IEEE Trans. on ASSP, vol.37, no.12, pp1888-1898, Dec. 1989.

[6] H.Sawai, "Frequency-Time-Shift Invariant Time-Delay Neural Networks for Robust Continuous Speech Recognition, " Proceedings of ICASSP-91, in Toronto, May. 1991.

[7] H.Sawai, Y.Minami, M.Miyatake, A.Waibel and K.Shikano, "Connectionist Approaches to Large Vocabulary Continuous Speech Recognition," IEICE Trans. vol.E 74, no.7, pp1834-1844, July 1991.

[8] D.E.Rumelhart, J.E.McClelland and the PDP Research Group, "Parallel Distributed Processing," Chap.8, MIT Press, 1986.

[9] M.Nakamura and K.Shikano, "A New Method to Speed up the Back-Propagation Algorithm," ATR Technical Report, TR-I-0119, Oct.1989.

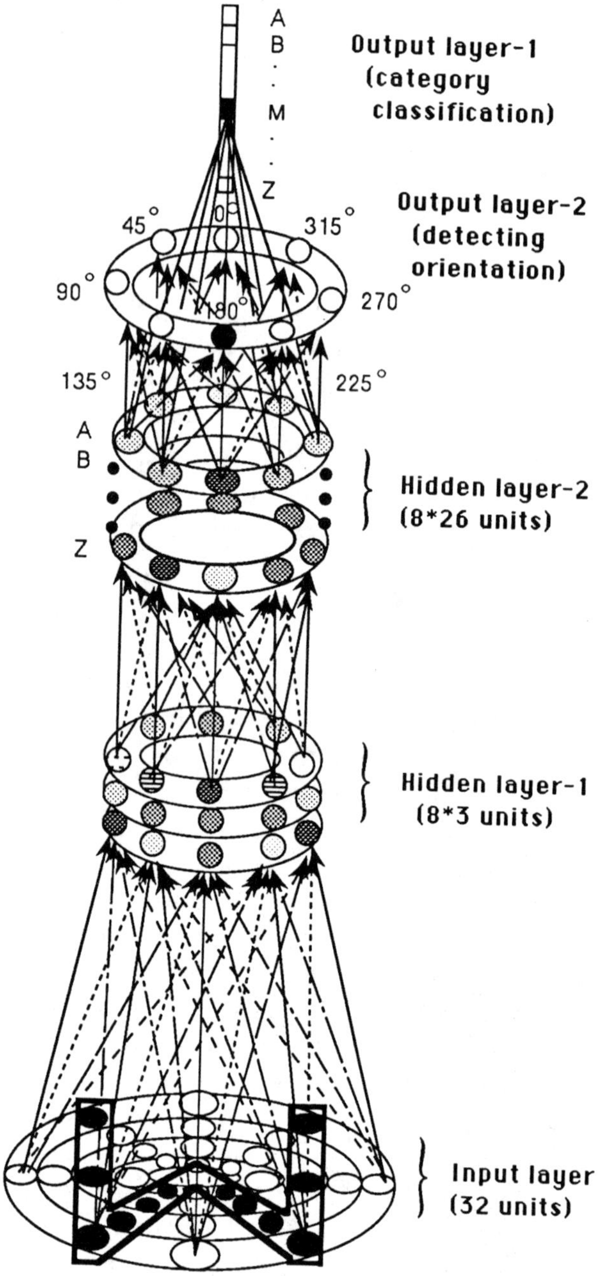

Fig.1 Axially Symmetric Neural Network Architecture

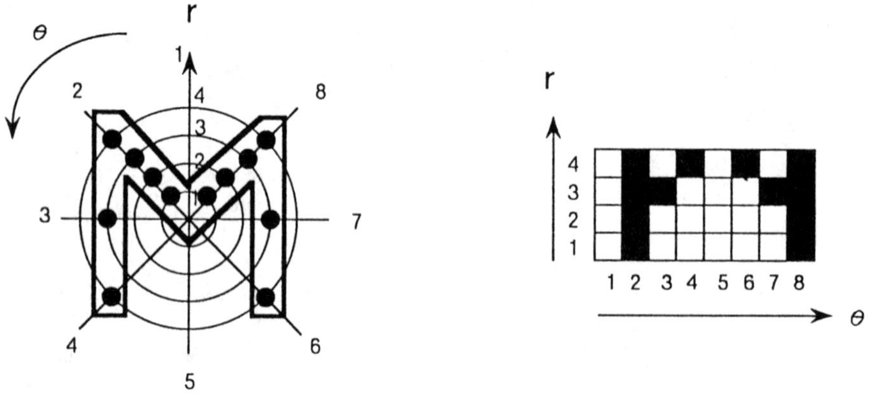

Fig.2 An Input Pattern represented by Polar Coordinates

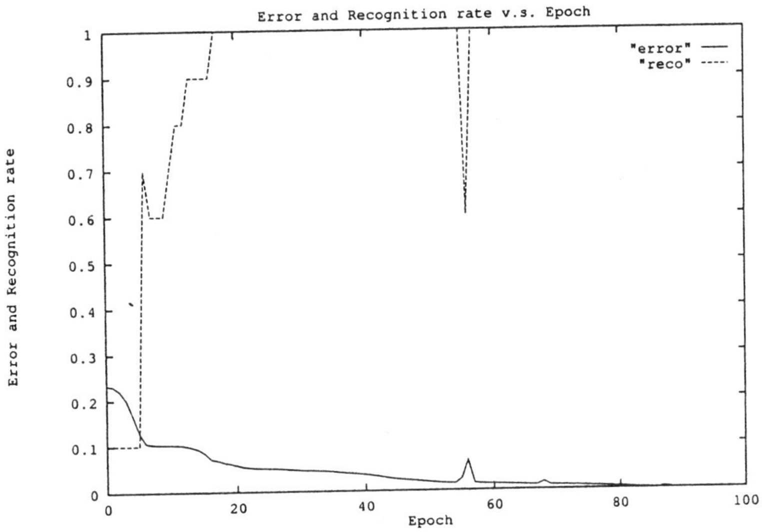

Fig.4 Error and Recognition Rates v.s. Epochs in Training Ten-digit Patterns

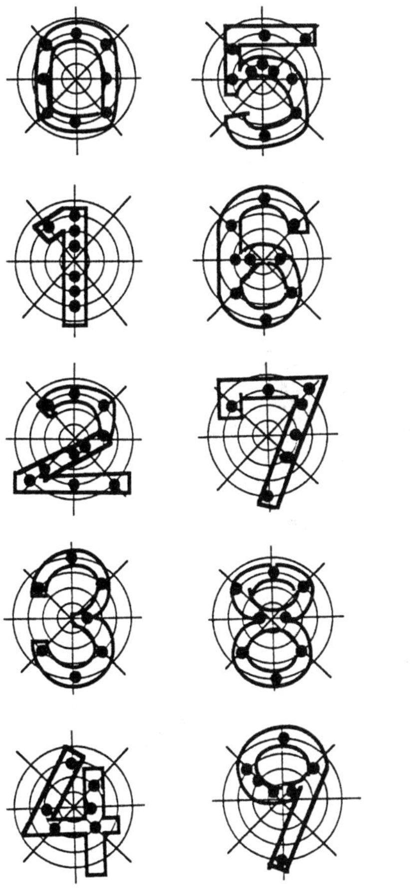

Fig.3 Training Patterns for Ten-digit Recognition

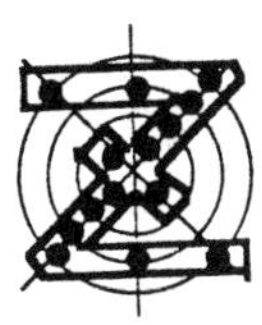

Fig.5. Training Patterns for Alphabet Recognition

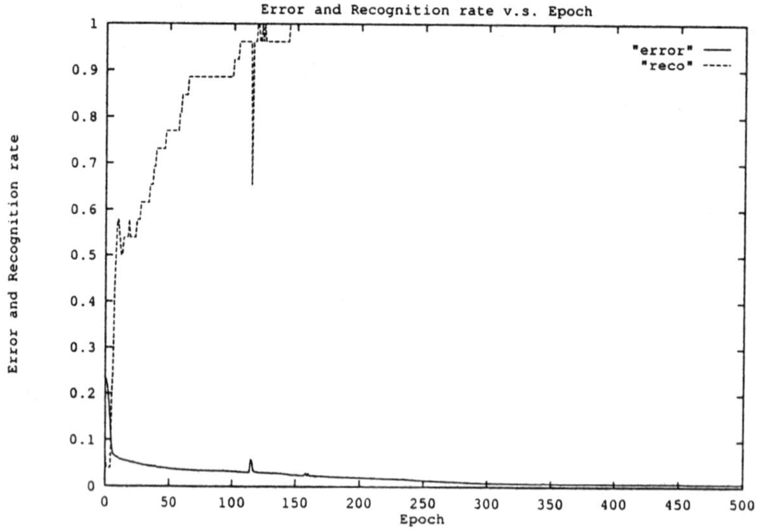

Fig.6 Error and Recognition Rates v.s. Epochs in Training Alphabet Patterns

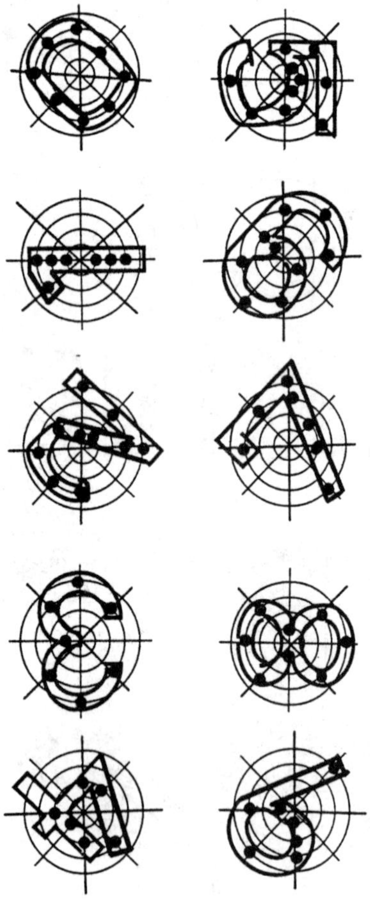

Fig.7 Test Patterns for Ten-digit Recognition

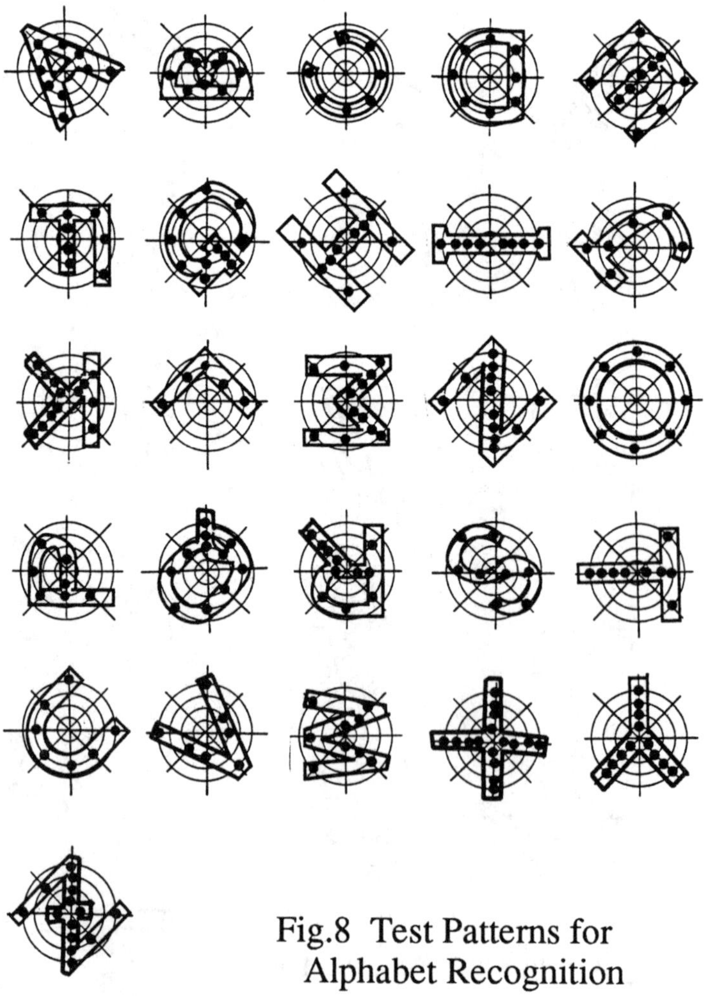

Fig.8 Test Patterns for Alphabet Recognition

Segmentation and Classification of Domestic Moving Objects using a Syntactic Approach

Gek Lim Michael D. Alder Christopher J.S. deSilva
Centre for Intelligent Information Processing Systems
The University of Western Australia
Nedlands W.A. 6009, AUSTRALIA
email : gek@ee.uwa.edu.au mike@maths.uwa.edu.au chris@ee.uwa.edu.au

Abstract

In this paper, we propose a method for segmenting and classifying domestic moving objects using a syntactic approach. The problem is to recognise moving objects in front of the camera in a domestic environment such as human beings, curtains blown by the wind and external events such as tree branches, and the aim is to distinguish moving human heads from moving curtains or tree branches. In real-world images, the situation where a human being is moving in the foreground and at the same time the curtains and/or tree branches are moving in the background, often arises.

We use quadratic neurons (represented by quadratic forms) as our simple pattern primitives and extract the structural information based on the relationships between the forms. We call this the *UpWrite* process, and it can be applied any number of times. To achieve our aim of recognising moving heads, we require two levels of the *UpWrite* process. We hypothesise that the syntactic *UpWrite* is implemented in wetware by distinct layers of neurons.

1 Introduction

We are trying to identify human heads moving in front of a video camera, under normal lighting condition, in a domestic environment. In the real environment, finding other moving objects such as curtains blown by the wind and external events such as moving tree branches as seen through the windows is inevitable. In real-world images, the situation where a human being is moving in the foreground and at the same time, the curtains and/or tree branches are moving in the background often arises. This requires segmentation of the moving objects, then recognising the segmented parts, and finally distinguishing moving heads from the other moving objects.

We propose a method for segmenting and classifying moving objects, from consecutive frames, using a syntactic approach. The idea of the syntactic approach is to extract structural information about subobjects and the relationship between them in order to specify the higher level objects, which can then be classified using some decision-theoretic approach. More generally, we observe that an object can be described in terms of simpler subobjects or parts, and each part can be described in terms of even simpler subparts, etc., where the simplest parts are known as the primitives, in a hierarchical fashion. The structural information is extracted from the relationships between the primitives at the lower level and passed on to the next level for further processing. We call this the *UpWrite* process, and it can be applied any number of times depending on the type and specification of the problem. This is analogous to the syntax of language, where a sentence is built up by concatenating words and a word is built up by concatenating characters. Only certain combinations of the characters make up words that are found in the dictionary, and there are rules governing the composition of the words to build a sentence, rules which constitute the grammar of the language.

In this application, we choose quadratic neurons as our simple pattern primitives and they are represented by positive semi-definite quadratic forms. We have described this in earlier work [1]. The representation of the state of a quadratic neuron as a point in $\mathbf{R}^n$ for some n means that we can represent a set of neurons at one level, each measuring some part of a complex object, as input

0-7803-1901-X/94 $4.00 ©1994 IEEE

to a second layer of neurons. This corresponds to the *UpWrite* process. This provides an easy way to extract structural information of the objects by looking at the relationship between the forms. This will become more apparent when we describe the *UpWrite* proccess in Section 3.

2 Preprocessing

The functions of the preprocessing are, (i) to detect moving objects; (ii) to 'simplify' and compress the image data for further processing.

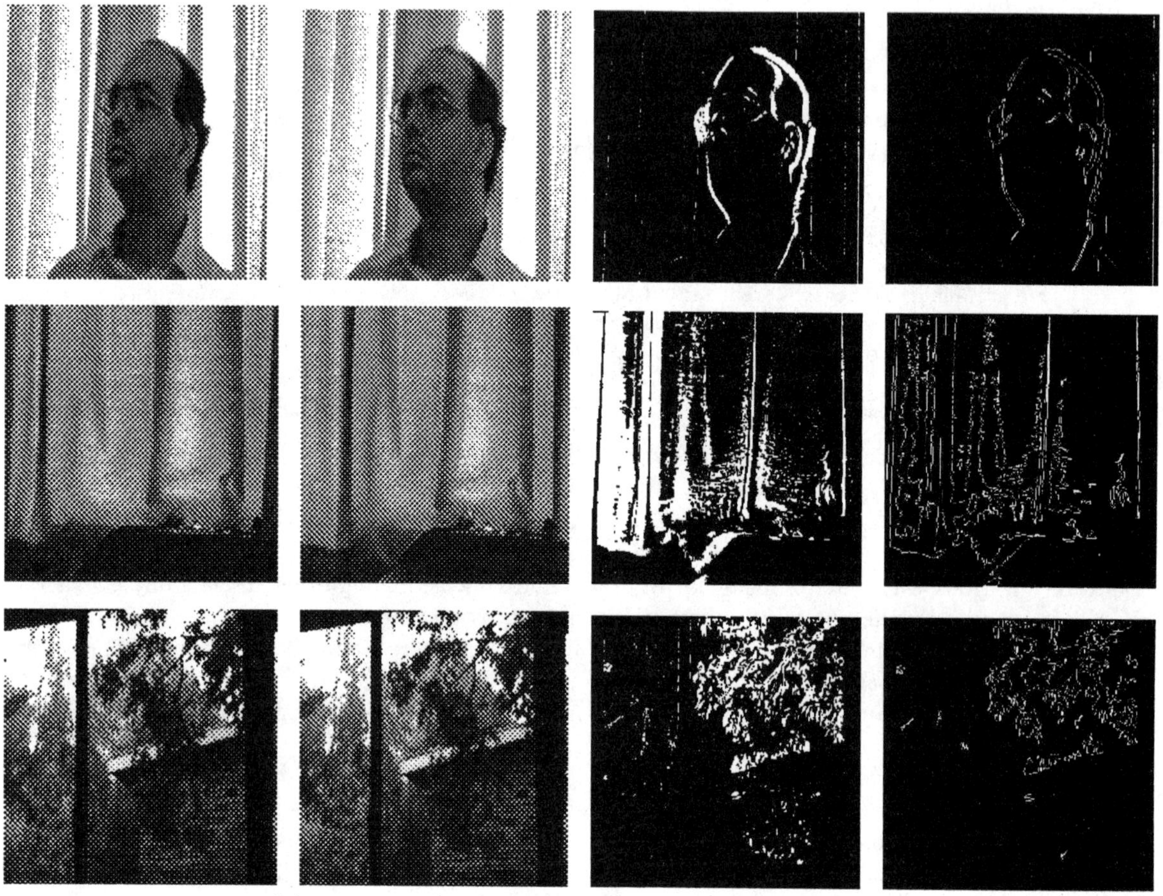

(a) (b) (c)

Figure 1: Examples of images: (a) Original images, (b) Difference image, (c) Border Image

The first function makes sure that we only process objects that are of interest, i.e. objects that moved in front of the video camera. This is easily achieved by applying differencing on consecutive frames, **Figure 1(a)**. It is done by comparing the pixel value of the two images, if there is a significance difference in the value, we set it to white, otherwise it is black. This process results in a difference image, **Figure 1(b)**, showing the moving parts of the objects in white.

The next function is to 'simplify' and compress the pixel representation of the moving object, so that it is more efficient for processing in the later stage. We describe the moving parts of the objects using a border tracing algorithm [2]. This results in isolated regions being segmented and represented by their starting point and the chaincode along the border, **Figure 1(c)**. Noisy images can then be cleaned up by eliminating 'short' chaincode.

3 The *UpWrite* Process

The *UpWrite* process first represents the preprocessed image by a set of primitives and then extracts the structural information and codes that into a point in $\mathbf{R}^n$ for further processing.

Our application requires two levels of *UpWrite*. First we extract the strokes of the object. These strokes are then treated as input to the second level of *UpWrite* to the object. We postulate that the action of a single neuron is to perform a local *UpWrite* on some part of the data, and hence to represent some subset of the image as a point in $\mathbf{R}^n$ for some n. Then the second *UpWrite* is performed, with input from the first layer of neural outputs, on the set of points in $\mathbf{R}^n$. Thus the layers of neural processing correspond explicitly to increasing levels of abstraction, as in the *Neocognitron*, but the process in our case is wholly automated.

3.1 Stroke Extraction

First, we represent the preprocessed image, **Figure 1(c)**, by a set of primitives. In our case, we have chosen to use the positive semi-definite, symmetric, quadratic forms as our primitives. These are easy to compute and it is easy to construe a single neuron as implementing such a process.

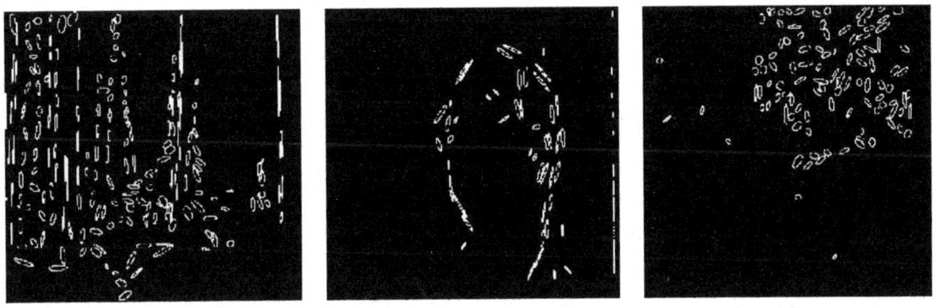

(a) (b) (c)

Figure 2: Examples of ellipses along the border of the difference image from **Figure 1(c)** : (a) curtain, (b) head, (c) tree

We segment the chaincode representation of the objects into sequences of quadratic forms. This is done by taking K consecutive elements of the chaincode for some suitable K, and computing the mean, $\mathbf{m}$, and the covariance matrix, $\mathbf{C}$, for the set in $\mathbf{R}^2$. K must be chosen so that the forms are not degenerate, but not so large that the structure is distorted. Each form may be visualised by drawing the ellipse given by the equation

$$\{\mathbf{x} \in \mathbf{R}^2 : (\mathbf{x} - \mathbf{m})^T \mathbf{C}^{-1} (\mathbf{x} - \mathbf{m}) = 1\}$$

where $\mathbf{m}$ is the mean and $\mathbf{C}$ is the matrix giving the quadratic form, **Figure 2**. The effect of this is to smooth the noisy border contour and also compress the representation of the objects.

The first *UpWrite* after this preprocessing is the extraction of strokes, that is to say sequences of ellipses which form some approximation to a smooth curve. It is plain that tree images provide virtually no stroke structure, curtains provide a vertical linear stroke structure, and heads provide structure with notable curvature. In addition there is considerable non-stroke 'noise' in all images.

This is accomplished as follows: from the sequences of ellipses, we find sets of three consecutive ellipses, triples, that are close to each other and *UpWrite* them into a point in $\mathbf{R}^n$. The idea is to generate different clusters of triples in the *UpWrite* space. We expect to obtain two different classes of triples, one of them contains *smooth* triples, where there is a constant change of angle from one ellipse to another as shown in **Figure 3(a)**. The other class contains *chaotic* triples where there is much variation in the change of angle from one ellipse to another, as shown in **Figure 3(b)**.

A triple of consecutive ellipses $\mathbf{e}_1, \mathbf{e}_2, \mathbf{e}_3$, can be specified as a vector $(\theta 1, \theta 2, \alpha 1, \alpha 2)$ in $\mathbf{R}^4$, where

$\theta 1$ is the angle between the principal eigenvectors of ellipse **e1** and ellipse **e2**
$\theta 2$ is the angle between the principal eigenvectors of ellipse **e2** and ellipse **e3**
$\alpha 1$ is the angle between the principal eigenvector of ellipse **e1** and the vector from **c1** to **c2** and
$\alpha 2$ is the angle between the principal eigenvector of ellipse **e2** and the vector from **c2** to **c3**.

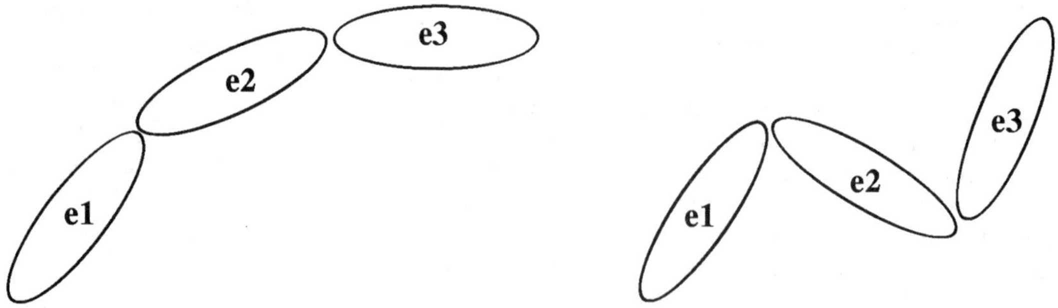

(a) Smooth Triple (b) Chaotic Triple

Figure 3: Examples of triples

The smooth triples formed a cluster in the *UpWrite* space, distinct from the chaotic triples. We fitted a gaussian to the cluster of smooth triple *UpWrite* vectors and used it to decide for any given triple whether it was smooth or chaotic. We then went through all the sequences of ellipses to find the strokes. A stroke is simply a set of ellipses or forms such that each consecutive triple in it is smooth.

It should be noted that we can justify the procedure of *chunking* adjacent ellipses (or forms) into strokes by an entropic criterion: each form may be regarded as a predictor of points, and when a triple is not smooth, the information supplied by the divergent ellipses is high. This is precisely analogous to the way in which characters in natural language text chunk into words, as was pointed out by Shannon.

In **Figure 4** we show the smooth triples that will eventually be represented by strokes and used in the next level of *UpWrite*, using the above method based on the images in **Figure 2**. The reason for not showing any smooth triples from the tree branches class is because there aren't any. The structure of the tree branches is more complex and chaotic and thus almost all of the triples are chaotic. We are thus able to filter out the tree branches object from the other two classes, curtains and faces.

Finally, each stroke must be described as a point in $\mathbf{R}^n$ for some n so as to be available for an iteration of the same process. We may do this in a variety of ways; the simplest is to use low order moments to characterise the pixel set comprising the stroke, another is to characterise the quadratic forms comprising the stroke, regarded as points in $\mathbf{R}^5$, by computing low order moments for the smaller set. We chose, in order to minimise the computation, to compute low order moments for the centres of the quadratic forms. Again, in order to establish the feasibility of the method, we chose moments of order 1 and 2, the centre and covariance matrix for the set. The strokes are now represented by ellipses graphically as shown in **Figure 5**.

It is to be expected that this will give only a very coarse description of the stroke set, but this has the merit of robustness under noise, and turns out to be adequate for the relatively simple classification task described. Thus each stroke becomes converted to a point in $\mathbf{R}^5$. We stored this in the form of a centre for each stroke, the two eigenvalues, the larger one first, and the angle between the X-axis and the principal eigenvector. Curved strokes associated with edges of heads have noticeably larger second eigenvalues than the straight strokes normally associated with curtains. The set of points in $\mathbf{R}^5$ will be passed on to the next level for further processing.

3.2 Object Extraction

We next wish to describe the sets of strokes, represented by a set of points in $\mathbf{R}^5$, produced by the previous level of *UpWrite* which characterise the object consisting of the boundary of a moving head, and the object consisting of the boundary of a moving curtain. We apply essentially the same process as before. The object which is a head now comprises some number of points in $\mathbf{R}^5$, where

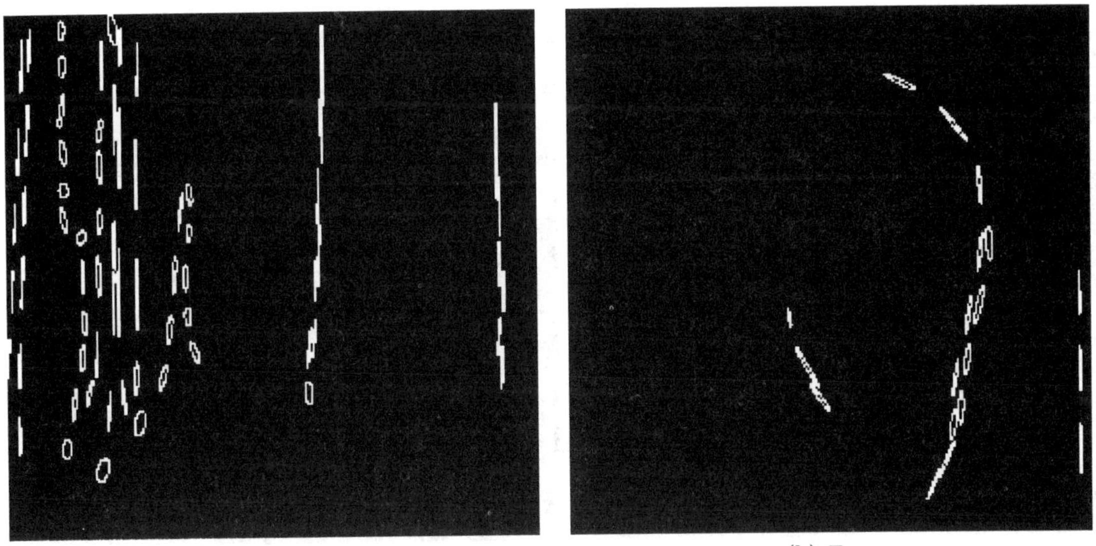

(a) Curtain (b) Face

Figure 4: Smooth triples of a curtain and a face extracted from **Figure 2**

the number of points is at least two. Normally the head decomposes into two sides, occasionally with extra components representing shoulders, spectacles, *et cetera.*

We compute first and second order central moments for the sets of strokes. Again, the choice of order two as a limit on the precision of the description was for simplicity and to restrict the computation. In the training process, we extracted by eye those strokes which comprised a head or a significant part of a head to specify the head images, and likewise with the curtains.

The resulting data contains five values for the centres and fifteen values for the symmetric 5 by 5 matrix: in fact we ignored the off-diagonal terms because we expected little information from them, and we also ignored the data saying where the geometric position of the centre on the screen was, so we would have translation invariance built into the recognition system. This leaves six terms; we add the zeroth order moment, the count of the number of strokes. Thus the object, head or curtain, is UpWritten to a point in $\mathbf{R}^7$. We then fit gaussian distribution on the set of points in $\mathbf{R}^7$ for both head and curtain.

4 Classification and Results

In doing the recognition, we had the problem of extracting a subset of a stroke set which corresponded to an object, since our test images contain both heads and curtains. This is clear from **Figure 5(b)** where the right most ellipse is part of a curtain. During the training, the strokes that make up the object had been selected manually but this process has to be automated for the testing phase. We used a neighbourhood of each stroke as a prospective region in which to look for the rest of an object, and selected all possible combinations of strokes inside such a ball. These were coded as a point, $\mathbf{x}$, in $\mathbf{R}^7$ and we computed the Mahalanobis distance, $MD = \sqrt{(\mathbf{x} - \mathbf{m}_i)^T \mathbf{C}_i^{-1} (\mathbf{x} - \mathbf{m}_i)}$ where $\mathbf{m}_i$ is the mean of the gaussian distribution of object i; $\mathbf{C}_i$ is the covariance matrix of the gaussian distribution of object i, where object i is one of the two object classes, head or curtain. MD is the distance of the point $\mathbf{x}$ from the centre of the two gaussian distributions of the head and curtain. The point $\mathbf{x}$ is classified according to the smaller of the two distances.

The results were encouraging that in only 3 out of 32 cases was an image of a curtain interpreted as a head. In none out of 34 cases was a head interpreted as a curtain. We believe that the accidental 'seeing' of heads in curtain folds would be easily eliminated by using more temporal information.

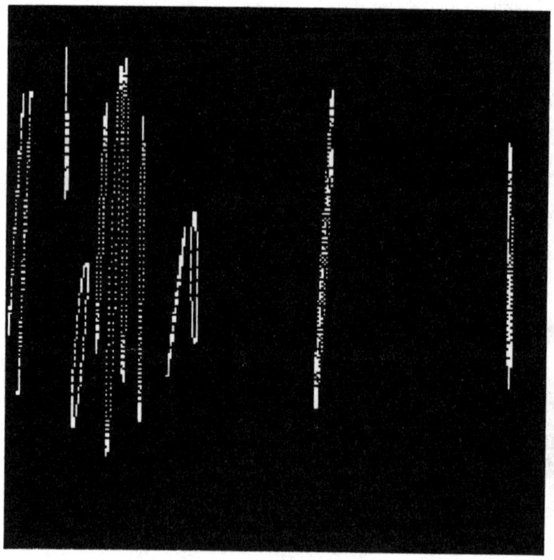

(a) Curtain

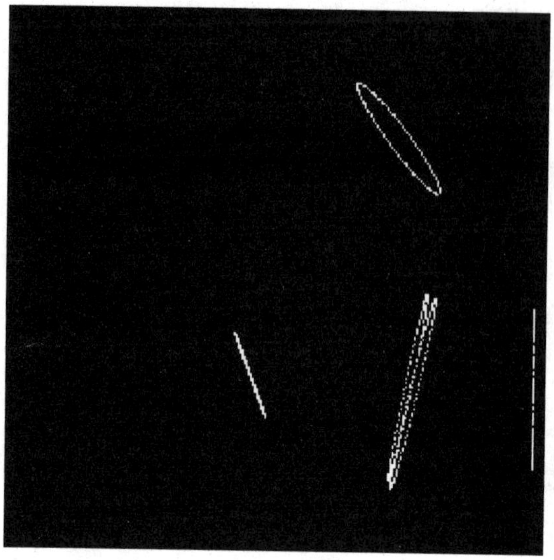

(b) Face

Figure 5: Stroke representation for a curtain and a face from **Figure 4**

5 Conclusion

We applied a two-level quadratic neural net to the task of classifying moving objects in a domestic environment and had no difficulty in extracting very complex objects such as tree branches. We were reasonably successful in distinguishing heads from folds in curtains on the basis of motion alone on a small data set.

6 References

[1] Lim, S.G., Alder, M. and Hadingham, P. *Adaptive Quadratic Neural Net* Pattern Recognition Letters 13, pp. 325-329, May, 1992.

[2] Haig, T.D., Attikiouzel, Y. and Alder, M.D. *Border Following: New Definition Gives Improved Border* IEE Proc-I, Vol. 139, No.2, pp. 206-211, April 1992.

Texture Analysis for Foreign Object Detection using a single layer Neural Network

D. Patel, I. Hannah and E.R. Davies
Royal Holloway, University of London
Machine Vision Group, Department of Physics
Egham, Surrey, TW20 0EX, United Kingdom.
e-mail: d.patel@uk.ac.rhbnc

1. Introduction

Inspection of food products for quality control to ensure that products are free from impurities such as stone, glass or metal is a demanding part of a production process. The foreign objects (FOs) occur extremely rarely, but their presence causes alarm to both the consumer and the food manufacturer. This paper presents a method to detect FOs in bags of frozen vegetables and in particular using bags of frozen corn kernels. The inspection process is at the final stage of the production process, where the bags have been packed and sealed. X-ray imaging is then used to view the contents of the bag. Typically inspection tasks are performed by humans or by simple thresholding techniques. Decisions based on these techniques cannot be relied upon in a stringent quality control process.

FOs which can potentially occur in food products vary in form and size; they range from hard contaminants such as slivers of glass to soft contaminants such as small pieces of wood. In the approach described here, we have aimed to make the image analysis as generic as possible, by not assuming any knowledge of the FOs. An example of an X-ray image is shown in figure 1. The FO in the bag is a small piece of metal (size $4 \times 1 \times 0.3$ mm), at the top left of the image, on the edge of the food substrate and the conveyor background. The food substrate has a strong textural appearance and lends itself naturally to analysis via texture discrimination. The emphasis is on characterising texture and detecting any differences highlighted from the texture analysis. Convolution masks sensitive to the particular local structural attributes are used to extract texture features and, based on these features, the FOs in the image are detected and segmented. For texture characterisation we do not use standard masks with pre-set coefficients, but use masks whose coefficients have been "learnt" from an example of the food substrate with no contaminants. These filters respond to the peculiarities of the structure of the texture and subsequently detect any anomalies, such as FOs within the food substrate. We use principal component analysis (PCA) techniques to find orthogonal vectors in data space that account for as much as possible of the variance of the data. The vectors are then used as the coefficients of the convolution masks.

Figure 1: An example X-ray image

In section two of this paper, we briefly mention the various texture analysis methods using PCA and describe the artificial neural network (ANN) texture description method used in this study. Section three presents the overall FO detection scheme and also illustrates the overall method for detecting FOs such as metal, stone and glass. The detection of soft contaminants such as wood and plastics has been presented elsewhere [Patel, Hannah and Davies, 1993]. Finally, in section four we offer some conclusions and suggest avenues for further research.

2. Texture characterisation

Several researchers have used convolution filter methods for texture characterisation. These masks are designed to act as matched filters for certain types of variations found in textures. Laws (1980) defined an empirical set of masks and used then to generate feature images. These masks are derived from one dimensional vectors which are sensitive to characteristics such as edges and spots. Ade (1983), presented a method where the mask coefficients are adaptively generated via the calculation of eigenvectors. Unser (1986) proposed a filter bank analysis approach, where the problem of texture analysis was approached by taking some local linear transform such as the discrete cosine transform over each sub-image. More recently several researchers (Turner, 1986; Fogel and Sagi, 1989; Jain and Farrokhnia, 1992) have used Gabor filters as masks. The motivation here has been to show that the receptive field profiles of certain simple cells in the visual cortex approximate the Gabor functions. However, these methods have not proved to be any better with respect to recognition or computational needs to existing texture analysis methods (Ohanian and Dubes, 1992).

After calculating the variance-covariance matrix of a homogeneous texture region, Ade(1983) obtained the mutually orthogonal eigenvectors of the matrix. These vectors best characterise the structure of the underlying texture and are used as coefficients of the masks. His approach may be criticised for its computational demand. This is particularly true for large input as this requires eigenvector calculation of a higher dimension.

A 2-layer (1 hidden layer) Multi-Layer Perceptron (MLP) using the Back-Propagation (BP) rule can be trained to perform an identity mapping with fewer nodes in the hidden layer than input nodes; this network can be used to approximate the principal components (Cotterell, Munro and Zipser, 1987). The hidden units project onto the subspace of the M principal components. The major difference as indicated by Sanger (1989) is that the Generalised Hebbian Algorithm (GHA) produces the first M eigenvectors themselves in eigenvalue order, whereas the MLP produces a linear combination of the M eigenvectors. Other factors regarding the BP algorithm such as; training times, local minima, selection of the number of hidden nodes, further reduces the usefulness of the MLP.

The GHA algorithm mentioned above was developed, to train neural networks in order to find the eigenvectors of the autocorrelation matrix of the input data, given only samples from that input distribution. Each output of the trained network represents the response to one eigenvector and the outputs are ordered in decreasing value. The method does not require the calculation of the correlation matrix, since the eigenvectors are derived directly from the data. This has a considerable computational speed and memory advantage over conventional methods particularly if the input dimensions are large. The GHA is given by:

$$W_{nq}(t+1) = W_{nq}(t) + \eta V_q \left(X_n - \sum_{j=1}^{q} V_j W_{nj} \right)$$

$$V_q = \sum_{n=1}^{N} W_{nq} X_n$$

where V_q is the output at each node and W_{nq} are the inter-connection weights. The learning rate η can decrease with time or can be held constant. The outputs project the input vector X, of dimension N, onto the space of the first M principal components.

3. Foreign object detection scheme

The ANN topology used in this work has 9 input nodes and 8 output nodes. The training data consists of 6600 samples, extracted from 3×3 mapping window which scans across a small section of an image with no FO. The learning rate η is held constant at 0.1, although is could be made to decrease to zero as t increases. The weights which the network learns are represented as eight, 3×3 masks. The masks are the rows W_n of the 8×9 weight matrix.

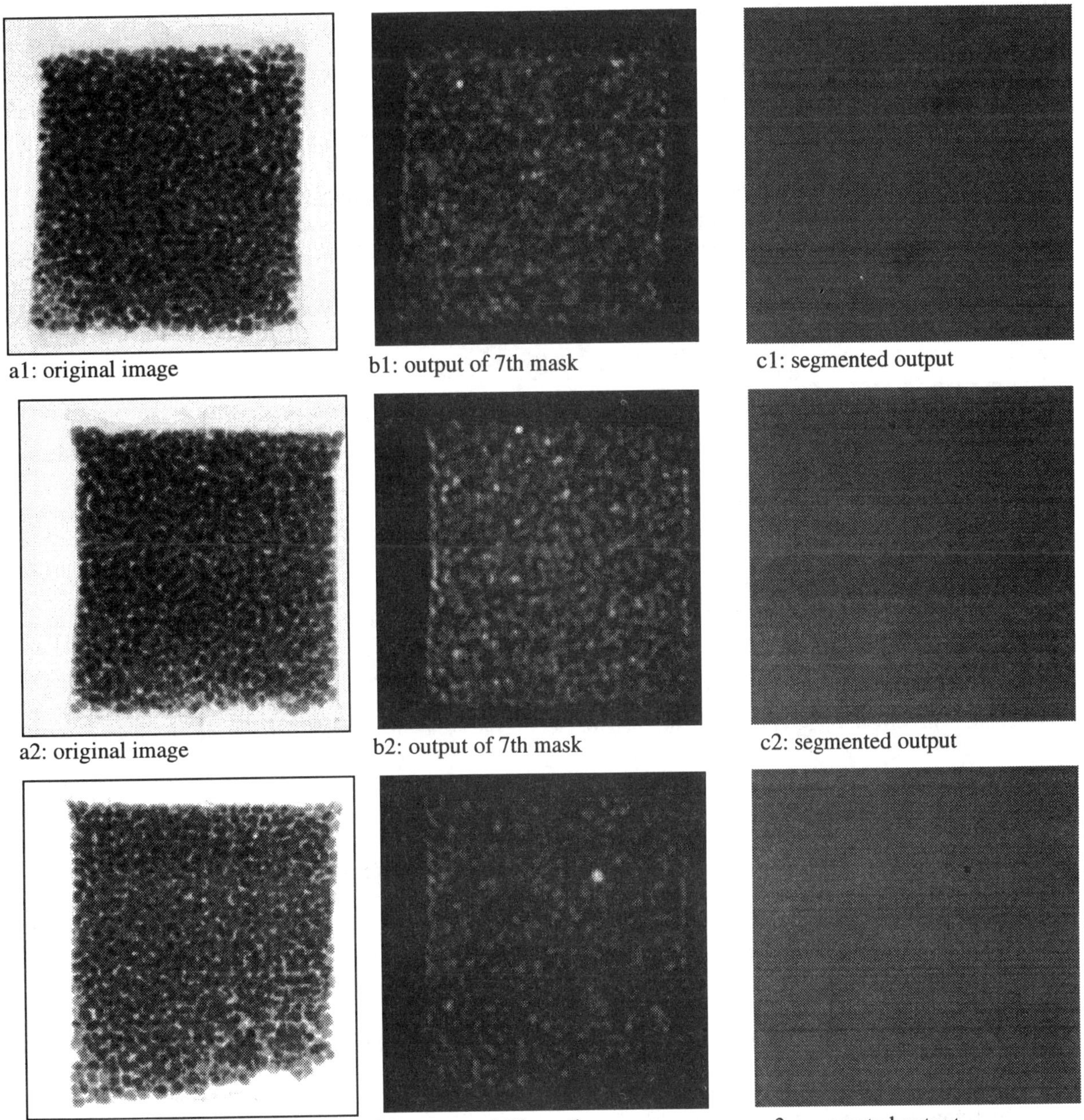

a1: original image b1: output of 7th mask c1: segmented output

a2: original image b2: output of 7th mask c2: segmented output

a3: original image b3: output of 7th mask c3: segmented output

Figure 2: Detection of (1) glass, (2) metal and (3) stone.

In the overall FO detection scheme, the images are passed through a log filter pre-processing stage. This increases the grey-level contrast between the FO and the food substrate. This is particularly useful for hard contaminants where the FOs appear darker than the food substrate. The images are then convolved with masks whose coefficients are the principal components generated using the ANN described in section 2. The convolution transforms the texture segmentation problem from the spatial domain to the feature space domain. The eight, 3×3 masks are not all sensitive to the textural variations on the images. For the images used in this study, masks 5, 7 and 8 generate the most discriminable features and are used in the convolution process. Masks 5 and 7 can be seen as diagonal edge detectors in opposite orientation, and mask 8 can be seen as a ripple detector. These feature images are then smoothed to remove any noise. The resulting feature images can then detect any variations on the textured food substrate as a different output from the general learnt texture area. Thresholding can then be used to segment the FO from the food. However, in the post-processing stage before the thresholding, a maximising filter is used to enhance the contrast between any detected FO and the filtered food substrate. Finally, after segmentation, the three resulting images are then passed through a majority operator where the final pixel assignment corresponds to the majority label of the three pixels in the segmented images.

The FOs detected were small pieces of stone, metal and glass. Figure 2/a shows three X-ray images, resolution 256×256×8, taken of 1 lb. bags of frozen corn kernels with one FO inserted in each. Image a1 contains a splinter of coffee jar glass (size 7.5×4.0×1.12 mm), in the top left quadrant of the image. The bag in figure a2 has a small piece of metal inserted in it (size 4.0×1.0×0.3 mm) in the top left part of the bag. The last sample bag in figure a3 is contaminated with a piece of stone (9.0×6.0×6.0 mm) in the top right quadrant of the bag. The log filtered images are convolved with the principal component masks, then smoothed and maximised. These filtered feature images then highlight any discrepancy within the food substrate. Typical filtered outputs using the 7th principal component mask, for all three images are given in figures b1, b2 and b3. These images show the detected FOs which are indicated by a lighter intensity than the food substrate. Finally the thresholded images illustrating FO segmentation are given in figures c1, c2 and c3.

4. Summary

The results obtained using the FO detection method described earlier have been promising and the method has been successfully applied to several other images. The texture characterisation is based on a convolution operator which "adapts" and "learns" from representation of food samples containing no contaminants using the generalised Hebbian rule. The detected FOs are discrepancies within the food substrate which are highlighted by the convolution process. Such a method offers a fast and computationally efficient method for calculating principal components of the input distribution. A comparison between the traditional method for texture analysis using Ade's eigenfilter method and the GHA for the detection of FOs is proposed (Hannah and Patel, 1993).

The training data for the GHA contained 6600 samples and was iterated once through the network with the learning rate held constant. The ANN generalisation achieved using these parameters was adequate. However, we need to investigate the effect of training until the network converges and the effect of reducing the learning rate as t increases.

References

F. Ade (1983), "*Characterization of textures by Eigenfilters,*" Signal Processing, vol. 5, pp. 451-457.
G.W. Cotterell, P. Munro and D. Zipser (1987), "*Learning internal representations from gray-scale images: An example of extensional programming,*" Proc. 9th Annual Conf. on Cognitive Science, Seattle, USA, pp. 461-473.
I. Fogel and D. Sagi (1989), "*Gabor filters as texture discriminator,*" Biological Cybernetics, vol. 61, pp. 103-113.
I. Hannah and D. Patel (1993), "*Texture analysis using PCA derived from Eigen analysis or neural networks,*" [in preparation].
A. K. Jain and F. Farrokhnia (1991), "*Unsupervised texture segmentation using Gabor filters,*" Pattern Recognition, vol. 24, no. 12, pp. 1167-1186.
K.I. Laws (1980), "*Texture image segmentation,*" Ph.D. Thesis, University of Southern California, USA.
P.P Ohanian and R.C. Dubes (1992), "*Performance evaluation for four classes of textural features,*" Pattern Recognition, vol. 25, no. 8, pp. 819-833.
D. Patel, I. Hannah and E.R. Davies (1993), "*Foreign object detection via texture recognition and a neural classifier,*" in Visual Communication and Image Processing '93, Proc. SPIE 2094. 1291-1299.
T.D. Sanger (1989), "*Optimal unsupervised learning in a single-layer linear feedforward neural network,*" Neural Networks, Vol. 2, pp. 459-473.
M. Turner (1986), "*Texture discrimination by Gabor filters,*" Biological Cybernetics, vol. 55, pp. 71-82.
M. Unser (1986), "*Local linear transforms for texture measurements,*" Signal Processing, vol. 11, pp. 61-69.

Acknowledgements

The authors are grateful to the ACME Directorate of the UK Science and Engineering Council for financial support during the course of this project.

A Hybrid Method for Recognizing Handwritten Numbers*

Ye Meng, Fan Junbo and Jin Fan

Institute of Neural Networks and Information Techniques
Southwest Jiaotong University, Chengdu, Sichuan, 610031, P.R.China

Abstract

In this paper, a hybrid method for recognizing handwritten numbers is proposed. This method exploits the power of neural networks, tree classifiers, fuzzy feature extraction and topologic feature extraction. Simulation results demonstrate that this method is efficient.

I. Introduction

Recognizing handwritten numbers is an interesting problem, with which many papers have been dealing. In recent years, neural network, a powerful tool for pattern recognition, is used to solve this problem frequently and some good results are got [2]-[3]. In most of these methods, the feature vectors, which are extracted by a certain method from all teaching samples, are sent to a certain type of neural network that is used as a nonlinear classifier. Because there are too many teaching samples, it is difficult to design a suitable structure for the neural network and the training time is too long. Our method discussed below overcomes these diffculties. In our method, first of all, classification tree technique is adopted to split the teaching sample set into some subsets according to some topologic features, such as the number of endpoints and the number of circles. Each subset includes only part of the teaching samples and for the elements of a certain subset, there is remarkable shape difference. Second, a fuzzy feature extraction method [4] is adopted to get the feature vectors of each subset. At last, a group of small multilayer neural networks are used to learn these feature vectors and the trained neural networks can be used to identify the unlearned samples.

II. Methology

A. Overview of Our Method

Our method can be represented as a classification tree that has different decision methods in its decision nodes, as shown in Fig.1. In Fig.1, the leaf nodes that have only one element are the results and those nodes that include the handwritten numbers will be identified by neural networks based on fuzzy features extraction.

B. Topologic Feature Extraction

Topologic features are extracted from thinned binary images. There are three kinds of topologic feature :

1) The number of endpoints
   A endpoint is a point , which is connected with only one other point.
2) The number of circles
   A circle is a group of points that enclose an area in the image.

---

* This work is partly supported by National Nature Science Foundation of China, National 863 High Technology Plan of China.

3) The number of the points that do not belong to the circles
Fig.2 shows examples of endpoint, circle and the points that out of a circle.

C. Fuzzy Feature Extraction

There are 56 fuzzy features, which are extracted from 32*32 binary image, belong to three kinds. Number '1' in the image denotes a pixel in primiary image of a handwritten number. Let $F_i=\{f_{i0},\ldots,f_{i55}\}$ denote the feature vector of the ith teaching sample.

1) Horizontal Features

There are 32 horizontal features. Let l be the lth row of the image, L_l (R_l) be the horizontal coordinate of the leftest(rightest) point of l, W_l be the width of l, and C_l be the number of the intersection times of '1' and '0' of l. The left (right) membership function, $UL_l(UR_l)$, is defined by

$$UL_l=\begin{cases}1 & L_l\leqslant 10\\ (27-L_l)/17 & 10<L_l\leqslant 27\\ 0 & L_l>27\end{cases} \quad (1) \qquad UR_l=\begin{cases}0 & R_l\leqslant 10\\ (R_l-10)/17 & 10<R_l<27\\ 1 & R_l\geqslant 27\end{cases} \quad (2)$$

Fig.3 shows the two functions.

Similarly, the width membership function, UW_l, and the cross membership function, UHC_l, are defined by

$$UW_l=\begin{cases}0 & W_l\leqslant 10\\ (W_l-10)/17 & 10<L_l<27\\ 1 & L_l\geqslant 27\end{cases} \quad (3) \qquad UHC_l=\begin{cases}0 & C_l=0\\ 0.5 & C_l=1\\ 1 & C_l\geqslant 2\end{cases} \quad (4)$$

Fig.4 shows the two functions.

For each of the membership functions defined by (1),(2),(3) and (4), we take a average value of each four adjacent rows to construct a subset of F_i with 8 elements.

$$f_{ij}=\sum_{l=4k+1}^{4(k+1)} UL_l\ /4 \quad k=0,1,\ldots,7 \quad j=0,1,\ldots,7 \quad (5) \qquad f_{ij}=\sum_{l=4k+1}^{4(k+1)} UR_l\ /4 \quad k=0,1,\ldots,7 \quad j=8,9,\ldots,15 \quad (6)$$

$$f_{ij}=\sum_{l=4k+1}^{4(k+1)} UW_l\ /4 \quad k=0,1,\ldots,7 \quad j=16,17,\ldots,23 \quad (7) \qquad f_{ij}=\sum_{l=4k+1}^{4(k+1)} UHC_l\ /4 \quad k=0,1,\ldots,7 \quad j=24,25,\ldots,31 \quad (8)$$

2) Vertical Feature

There are 8 vertical features. Let m be the mth column of the image, Cm be the number of the intersection times of '1' and '0' of m. The vertical cross membership function, UVC_m, is defined by

$$UVC_m=\begin{cases}VC_m/3 & VC_m\leqslant 3\\ 1 & VC_m\geqslant 3\end{cases} \quad (9)$$

For the membership function defined by (9), we take a average value of each four adjacent column to construct a subset of F_i with 8 elements.

$$F_{ij}=\sum_{m=4k+1}^{4(k+1)} UVC_m\ /4 \quad k=0,1,\ldots,3 \quad j=33,34,\ldots,39 \quad (10)$$

3) Dots Distribution Feature

There are 16 dots distribution features. A certain sample image is divided into sixteen 8*8 areas. Let D_n be the number of '1' in the nth area, D_{max} (D_{min}) be the maxnium (minnium) number of Dn(n=1,2,...,16). The dots distribution feature is defined by

$$F_{ij}=(D_n-D_{min})/(D_{max}-D_{min}) \quad n=1,2,\ldots,16 \quad j=40,41,\ldots,55 \tag{11}$$

Fig.5 showes the division of a certain image.

D. Training Neural Networks

We use the normal BP net [1]. There are 56 neurons in its input layer. The number of the neurons in the hidden layer and in the output layer are determined by the number of the elements of a specific subset of the teaching sample set with the maxnium number 15 and 8. Fig. 6 shows the structure of the neural network.

III. Simulation

A LOGITECH hand-held scanner (Model 32 for IBM) is used to obtain the grayscale image of the handwritten number and a preprocession program is used to change the image to 32*32 binary image. From the binary image, the topologic features and fuzzy features are extracted using the methods proposed above. The topologic features are used to determine which subset that the image belongs to. The fuzzy features are used to train the neural networks and the trained neural networks are used to idtenfy which number that the image represents.

For each type of handwritten numbers, we use only 5 training samples and get very high recognition accuracy. The results are shown in Tab. 1.

IV. Conclusion

Based on fuzzy feature extraction, tree classifier and neural networks, a hybrid method for handwritten numbers recognition is investigated. Simulation results show that the method is very efficient. Furthermore, experiments show that the method can also be used to recognize handwritten alphebets. The detail results will be reported in our next paper.

References

[1] Jin Fan , Fan Junbo, Tan Yongdong, "Neural Networks and Neurocomputers" , published by Southwest Jiaotong University Press, 1992.

[2] Dr. Gilles BUREL & Isabelle POTTIER & Dr. Jean- Yves CATROS & Thomson CSF- LER, "Recognition of Handwritten Digits by Image Processing and Neural Network ", Proceedings of IJCNN 92, Baltimore, Maryland.

[3] Heng Guo and Saul B.Gelfand "Classification Trees with Neural Network Feature Extraction", IEEE Transactions on Neural Networks, vol 3, No.6, November 1992

[4] Du Yu, Chang Liming, "A Neural Network Method for Handwritten Numbers Recognition Based on Fuzzy Feature Extraction", The 3rd China Conference on Neural Network, 1993, Xian.

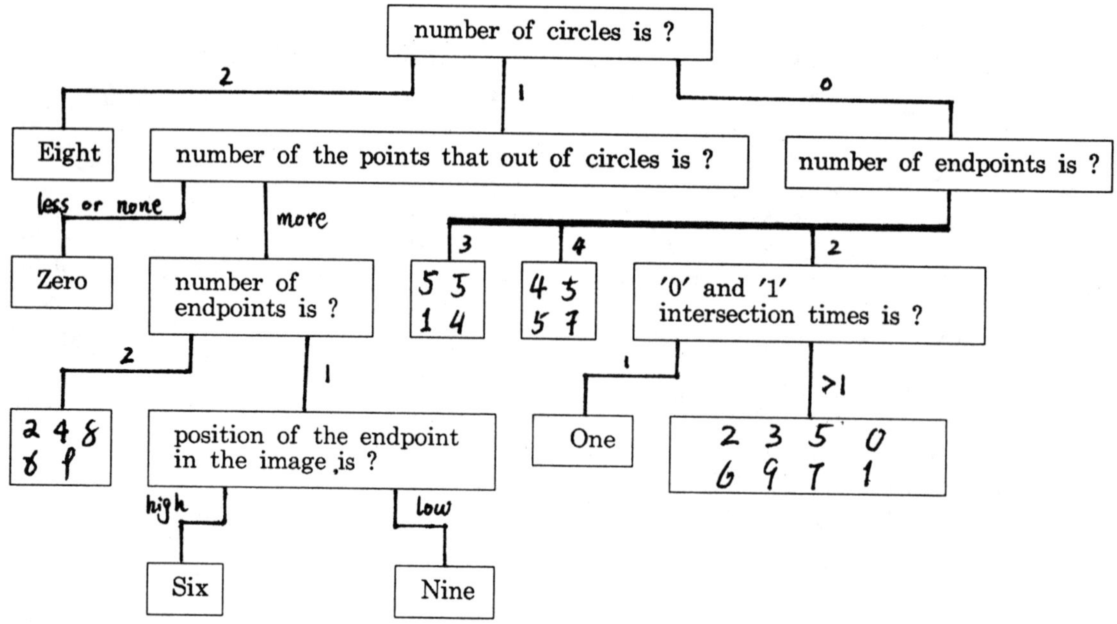

Fig.1 Outline of our method

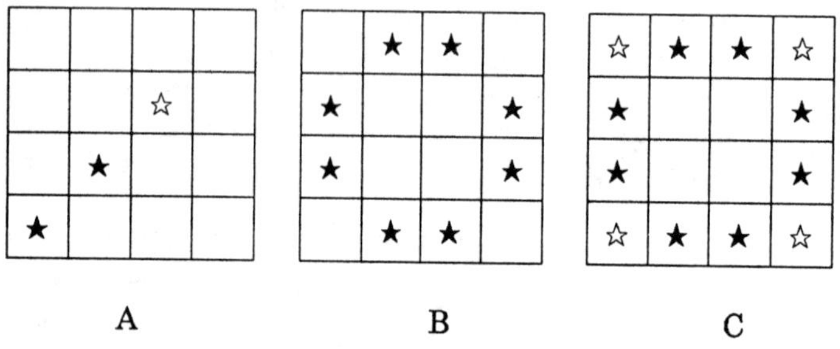

A :☆ endpoint B :★ circle
C :☆ the points that out of a circle
Fig.2 Examples of ednpoint, circle and the points that out of a circle

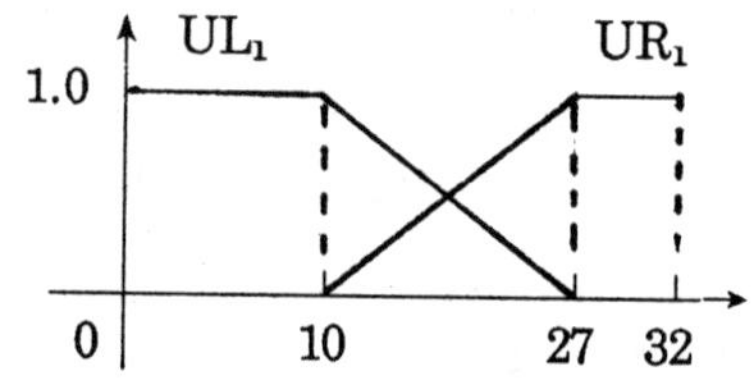

Fig.3 UL_1 and UR_1

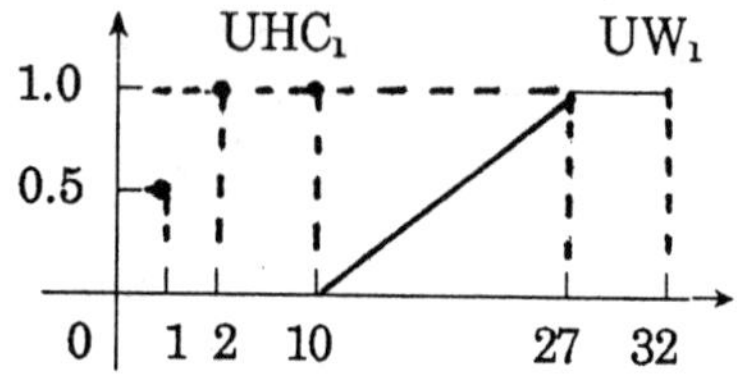

Fig.4 UW_1 and UHC_1

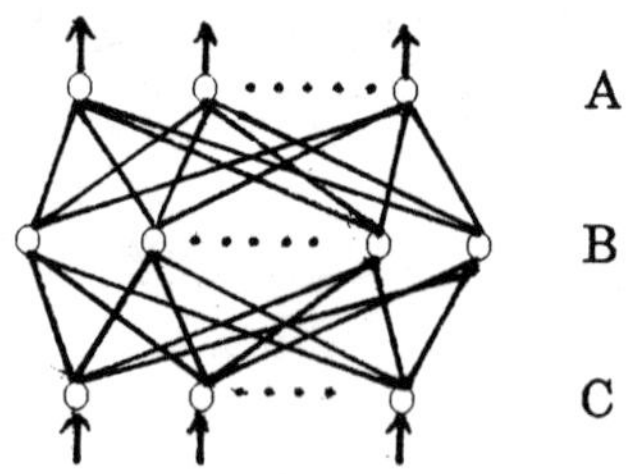

A :output layer
B :hidden layer C:input layer
Fig.6 Structure of the neural net

Number	Error Rate	Recognition Rate
105 Training Data	0%	100%
78 Test Data	7.69%	92.31%

Tab.1 Simulation Result

1	2	3	4
5	6	7	8
9	10	11	12
13	14	15	16

Fig.5 Split of a certain image

A LEARNING RULE FOR FUZZY ASSOCIATIVE MEMORIES *

Fan Junbo, Jin Fan and Shi Yan
Inst. of Neural Networks & Information Techniques
Southwest Jiaotong University
Chengdu, Sichuan 610031, P. R. China

Abstract

In this paper a learning rule for multiple pattern pairs in fuzzy associative memories (FAMs) with Max-Min composition units is presented. Under a certain condition, the proposed rule can efficiently encode multiple fuzzy pattern pairs in a single FAM and perfect association of these pairs can be achieved. The correctness of the proposed rule is proved and illustrative examples are given.

1 Introduction

It is well known that neural networks can efficiently model subjective phenomena such as perception, image and memory while fuzzy logic is another powerful tool to model phenomena associated with perception and thinking. In recent years, several models that combine neural networks and fuzzy logic, called fuzzy neural networks, have been developed and widely applied to prospective fields such as control, pattern recognition, decision making and expert systems[1-5]. The FAM introduced by Kosko, which involves Max-Min composition units, is one of the most useful and important paradigms[1, 2]. Such a FAM is characterized by the subset recall when trained using the fuzzy Hebian rule. The inability to reliably store more than one pair is its enssential drawback.

Some endeavors have given brith to overcoming this drawback. Hirota and Pedrycz used a gradient descent algorithm with two-value derivatives under some constraints [6]. Authors of this paper ever suggested an iterative learning algorithm that employed a so- called hill -climbing search strategy to conduct connection weight adjustments[7]. However, both algorithms may easily get struck at local minima of a defined index function although satisfactory performence of the trained FAM can usually be achieved. We propose here another learning rule that employs a suitable fuzzy logical-implication operation different from the fuzzy Hebbian rule used by Kosko. The proposed rule is capable of encoding multiple pattern pairs in the weight matrix of a FAM if there exists some weight matrix that properly forms the fuzzy relation between the input and output of the given pairs.

2 FAMs with Max-Min Composition Units

A FAM is designed to store p fuzzy (unit-interval valued) pattern pairs (A_1, B_1), ..., (A_p, B_p) in the weight matrix W, where the kth pair is represented by the vectors $A_k = (a_1^k, \ldots, a_n^k)$ and $B_k = (b_1^k, \ldots, b_m^k)$ respectively. The topology of a FAM is shown in Fig. 1.

In the FAM with Max-Min composition units, perfect association implies that eq. (1) should hold

*This work is partly supported by both the National Natural Science Foundation of China and the 863-High Technology Programme of China

$$A_k \circ W = B_k \qquad (k=1, 2, \ldots, p) \tag{1}$$

where the symbol '$\circ$' denotes the Max-Min composition operation. Generally, there are two kinds of methods to find the weight matrix W. One is to define a performence index, for instance, the sum of squared errors

$$E = 1/2\sum_{k=1}^{p}\sum_{j=1}^{m}(b_j^k - b_j)^2 \tag{2}$$

where b_j^k and b_j are the desired output and actual output of the jth output unit. Weight adjustment is aimed at minimizing the index function[6]. The other is to encode the single pair (A_k, B_k) into the matrix W_k and then to superimpose the matrices W_k s in a single matrix W, i.e., W may be found using the following equation

$$W = \bigcap_{k=1}^{p} W_k = \bigcap_{k=1}^{p} (A_k \rightarrow B_k) \tag{3}$$

where the symbol '$\rightarrow$' denotes some implication operation, and '$\cap$' denotes a generalized superimposition (e.g., maxima, minima etc). Kosko adopted a fuzzy Hebbian (the minimum implication R_c) rule pointwise to encode the kth pair (A_k, B_k) in the W_k, then superimposed the matrices W_ks in a single matrix W by the maximum operation. That is

$$w_{ij} = \bigvee_{k=1}^{p} w_{ij}^k = \bigvee_{k=1}^{p} (a_i^k \overset{R_c}{\rightarrow} b_j^k) = \bigvee_{k=1}^{p} (a_i^k \wedge b_j^k) \tag{4}$$

where the symbols '$\vee$' and '$\wedge$' stand for the maximum and minimum operations respectively, and w_{ij}s are components of the W. Obviously, multiple pairs can not be reliably stored in the FAM. An approach to overcoming the problem is that a bank of FAMs is used, each of which seperately store only one pair. But this results in consuming space of storage.

3 The Proposed Learning Rule

As usual, we wish to distributively and reliably store multiple fuzzy pattern pairs (A_k, B_k) in a single FAM such that each B_k can be perfectly recalled when each corresponding A_k is presented. Instead of using the minimum implication R_c, we associate here B_k with A_k usng the implication R_g, and we replace the maximum superimposition by the minimum one as well. In this way, we obtain the following learning rule

$$W = \bigwedge_{k=1}^{p} W_k$$

$$= \bigwedge_{k=1}^{p} (A_k \xrightarrow{R_g} B_k) \tag{5}$$

In pointwise notation, that is

$$w_{ij}^k = a_i^k \xrightarrow{R_g} b_j^k$$

$$= \begin{cases} b_j^k & \text{if } a_i^k > b_j^k \\ 1 & \text{otherwise} \end{cases} \tag{6}$$

$$w_{ij} = \bigwedge_{k=1}^{p} (a_i^k \rightarrow b_j^k) \tag{7}$$

Obviously, the complexity of the proposed learning rule is equivalent to the rule used by Kosko.

As we know, there doesn't always exist the weight matrix of a FAM, which makes eq. (1) hold for arbitrary set of input-output pairs. In other words, these pairs have to satisfy a certain condition for the purpose of perfect association. On the other hand, even if there exists some desired weight matrix, the Kosko's rule is not guaranteed to yield the desired matrix, as shown in [1,2]. Based on analyzing the condition for existence of desired weight matrix, we show below that the proposed learning rule can yield the desired matrix if it indeed exists.

Since the m units in the output layer of the FAM are independent one another, we can consider only one output unit. For the jth output unit, we have

$$\begin{bmatrix} a_1^1 & a_2^1 & \cdots & a_n^1 \\ a_1^2 & a_2^2 & \cdots & a_n^2 \\ \cdot & \cdot & \cdot & \cdot \\ \cdot & \cdot & \cdot & \cdot \\ \cdot & \cdot & \cdot & \cdot \\ a_1^p & a_2^p & \cdots & a_n^p \end{bmatrix} \circ \begin{bmatrix} w_{1j} \\ w_{2j} \\ \cdot \\ \cdot \\ \cdot \\ w_{nj} \end{bmatrix} = \begin{bmatrix} b_j^1 \\ b_j^2 \\ \cdot \\ \cdot \\ \cdot \\ b_j^p \end{bmatrix} \tag{8}$$

We define the following sets and value

$$K = \{ 1, 2, \ldots, p\} \tag{9}$$

$$I = \{ 1, 2, \ldots, n\} \tag{10}$$

$$G_{ij} = \{ k \in K \mid a_i^k > b_j^k \} \tag{11}$$

$$E_{ij} = \{ k \in K \mid a_i^k = b_j^k \} \tag{12}$$

$$m_{ij} = \begin{cases} \bigwedge_{k \in G_{ij}} b_j^k & \text{if } G_{ij} \neq \varphi \\ 1 & \text{if } G_{ij} = \varphi \end{cases} \tag{13}$$

$$S_{ij} = \{ k \in G_{ij} \cup E_{ij} \mid b_j^k \leqslant m_{ij} \} \tag{14}$$

Then the necessary and sufficient condition for existence of the desired weight vector that enables eq. (8) to hold can be expressed as follows[8]

$$\bigcup_{i \in I} S_{ij} = K \tag{15}$$

If there exists some weight vector enabling eq. (8) to hold such that some $k' \in K$ but $k' \notin S_{ij}$ for all $i \in I$. By definition, $a_i^{k'} < b_j^{k'}$ or $w_{ij} \leq m_{ij} < b_j^{k'}$. Hence we have $b_j^{k'} = \bigvee_{i \in I} (a_i^{k'} \wedge w_{ij}) = \bigvee_{i|k \notin S_{ij}} (a_i^{k'} \wedge w_{ij}) < b_j^{k'}$. This is obviously a contradiction. Vice versa, assume that $\bigcup_{i \in I} S_{ij} = K$. For any $k \in K$, $a_i^k < b_j^k$, or $w_{ij} \leq m_{ij} < b_j^k$ for all i as $k \notin S_{ij}$, but $a_i^k = b_j^k$ and $m_{ij} \geq b_j^k$ or $a_i^k > b_j^k$ and $m_{ij} = b_j^k$ for all i as $k \in S_{ij}$. Hence, if let $w_{ij} = m_{ij}$, we have $\bigvee_{i \in I} (a_i^k \wedge w_{ij}) = \{\bigvee_{i|k \in S_{ij}} (a_i^k \wedge w_{ij})\} \vee \{\bigvee_{i|k \notin S_{ij}} (a_i^k \wedge w_{ij})\} \bigvee_{i|k \in S_{ij}} (a_i^k \wedge w_{ij}) = \bigvee_{i|k \in S_{ij}} (a_i^k \wedge m_{ij}) = b_j^k$. This means that there exists a weight vector enabling eq. (8) to hold.

So, there exists a weight matrix W enabling eq. (1) to ho, if and only if eq. (15) holds for any j. The proposed learning rule expressed by eq. (6) and (7) is in accordance with eq. (13). From above analysis, we can conclude that the proposed rule can yield the desired weight matrix enabling eq. (1) to hold if it exists.

4 Examples

Two sets of fuzzy pattern pairs (Data1 and Data2) to be stored are shown in Tab. 1 and 2.

For Data1, we can obtain the weight matrix of the FAM using the proposed rule

$$W = \begin{bmatrix} 0.6 & 0.5 & 1.0 & 0.9 & 1.0 & 0.5 \\ 0.4 & 0.5 & 0.4 & 0.4 & 0.6 & 0.4 \end{bmatrix}^T \tag{16}$$

The FAM with the above matrix can perfectly each output pattern B_k when presented with each input pattern A_k. But the Kosko's rule produces the following weight matrix

$$W = \begin{bmatrix} 0.9 & 0.7 & 0.6 & 0.9 & 0.7 & 0.7 \\ 0.6 & 0.6 & 0.6 & 0.6 & 0.6 & 0.6 \end{bmatrix}^T \tag{17}$$

With the matrix, the trained FAM can not perfectly all pairs in Data1.

For Data2, two rules yield matrices

$$W = \begin{bmatrix} 0.2 & 0.8 & 1.0 & 1.0 & 1.0 & 0.4 \\ 0.6 & 0.5 & 1.0 & 0.4 & 0.4 & 0.5 \end{bmatrix}^T \tag{18}$$

and

$$W = \begin{bmatrix} 0.4 & 0.8 & 0.5 & 0.7 & 0.6 & 0.6 \\ 0.6 & 0.5 & 0.5 & 0.4 & 0.5 & 0.5 \end{bmatrix}^T \tag{19}$$

It is easy to confirm that eq. (1) holds with eq. (18), but it dosen't with the weight matrix eq. (19).

5 Conclusion

A learning rule for multiple fuzzy pattern pairs in FAMs with Max-Min composition units is presented. Under a certain condition, multiple pairs can be reliably stored in a single FAM and perfect associations can be achieved. The correctness of the proposed rule is demonstrated. Due to the simple complexity, the proposed rule may be much of use in the design of fuzzy systems where multiple inference rules need to be reliably stored.

References

[1] Kosko, B. (1987). Fuzzy Associative Memories, In Kandel, A. (Ed.), Fuzzy Expert Systems Reading, MA: Addison-Wesley.

[2] Kosko, B. (1991). Neural Networks and Fuzzy Systems: a dynamical systems approach to machine intelligence.

[3] Jin, F., FAN, J. B. and TAN, Y. D. (1991). Neural Networks and Neurocomputers: Principles and Applications, Southwest Jiaotong University Press.

[4] Fan, J. B., Jin, F. and Yuan, X. (1992) . A New Neuro- Fuzzy Network for Pattern Classification, Proc. of the ICIIPS'92 (Beijing).

[5] Fan, J. B., Jin, F. and Shi, Y. (1992). A New Model of Fuzzy Associative Memories, Proc. of the IJCNN'92 (Beijing), Vol. 3.

[6] Hirota, K. and Pedrycz, W. (1991). Fuuzy Logic Neural Networks: Design and Computations, Proc. of the IJCNN'91 (Singapore).

[7] Fan, J. B., Jin, F. and Yuan, X. (1992). A Learning Algorithm for Multiple Fuzzy Pattern pair Associations, Proc. of IJCNN'92 (Beijing), Vol. 3.

[8] Saito, T. and Mukaidono, M. (1991). A Learning Algorithm for Max- Min Network and Its Application to Solve Fuzzy Relation Equation, Proc. of the IFSA'92 (Bussels).

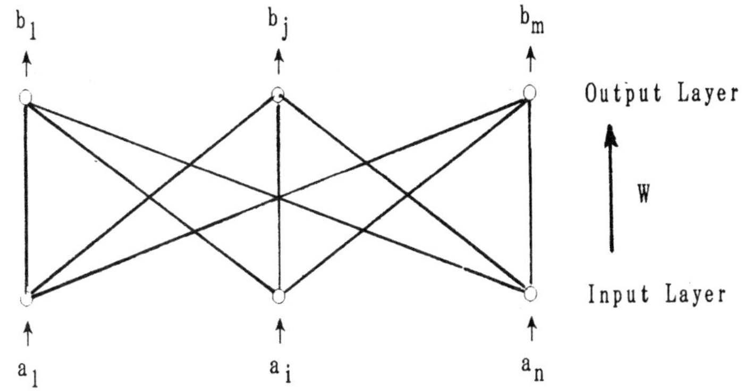

Fig. 1 The topology of a FAM

Tab. 1 Data1

k	A_k	B_k
1	(0.7 0.2 0.4 0.6 0.3 0.8)	(0.6 0.4)
2	(0.9 0.4 0.5 1.0 0.7 0.0)	(0.9 0.6)
3	(0.3 0.6 0.4 0.5 0.2 0.9)	(0.5 0.5)
4	(0.1 0.7 0.4 0.7 0.7 0.7)	(0.7 0.6)
5	(0.3 0.6 0.4 0.8 0.2 0.4)	(0.8 0.5)
6	(0.7 0.9 0.6 0.1 0.7 0.4)	(0.7 0.6)
7	(0.8 0.1 0.6 0.5 0.4 0.3)	(0.6 0.4)

Tab. 2 Data2

k	A_k	B_k
1	(0.1 0.9 0.5 0.4 0.5 0.6)	(0.8 0.5)
2	(0.3 0.2 0.4 0.3 0.6 0.4)	(0.6 0.4)
3	(0.9 0.2 0.2 0.1 0.3 0.0)	(0.3 0.6)
4	(0.4 0.0 0.4 0.7 0.4 0.1)	(0.7 0.4)
5	(0.8 0.2 0.2 0.1 0.0 0.2)	(0.2 0.6)
6	(0.4 0.1 0.5 0.3 0.2 0.9)	(0.5 0.5)
7	(0.5 0.2 0.0 0.3 0.2 0.6)	(0.4 0.5)

A New Connetionist Approach for Facial Identification

P.G Luebbers*, A.S. Pandya** and R. Sudhakar*
*Department of Electrical Engineering
**Department of Computer Science and Engineering
Florida Atlantic University
Boca Raton, Florida 33431

Abstract

A new artificial neural network architecture called Power Net (PWRNET) and Orthogonal Power Net (OPWRNET) has been developed. Based on the Taylor series expansion of the hyperbolic tangent function, this novel architecture can approximate multi-input multi-layer feed-forward perceptrons, while requiring only a single layer of hidden nodes. This allows a compact representation with only one layer of hidden layer weights. The resulting trained network can be expressed as a polynomial function of the input nodes. The degree of non-linearity of the network can be controlled directly by adjusting the number of hidden layer nodes, thus avoiding problems of over-fitting which restrict generalization.

The OPWRNET architecture was applied to the task of facial image recognition. An architecture of one and two hidden layer nodes were trained and compared to a linear discriminator. Features were extracted from the images using normalized centralized regular moments. The extracted moments were combined into individual features for each order of the moment by generating receptive fields for each feature. It is shown that the performance of the OPWRNET architectures is superior to that of the linear discriminator.

I. Introduction

Commercially available Biometric Identification Devices (BID) currently use fingerprints, hand geometry, retinal vascular patterns and voice as the means for discrimination and classification (Holmes, *et al.* (1991)). BIDs which use facial images are just beginning to become available and are typically in the prototype stage. Facial recognition verification systems present certain advantages when compared to other BIDs, among these is the ability to operate in a less obtrusive nature than other types of BID systems. For example, in the case of fingerprints, hand geometry, retinal vascular patterns or voice recognition systems, the individual to be identified must actively cooperate with the identification device. In contrast, a facial recognition verification system could be designed so that the person being identified takes a passive role.

Machine recognition of facial images has been investigated for many years by many researchers, (Samal and Iyengar (1992)), with limited success. A system which can locate and recognize faces would have uses in the areas of identification of criminals (as from mug shot photos, or in prison settings), authentification for secure systems (such as secure computer terminals or bank teller machines) or any application where the identification of an individual is required.

II. Facial Recognition Procedure

In this paper a simple, yet non-trivial application of an artificial neural network architecture called the Orthogonal Power Net (OPWRNET) to facial recognition is presented. The images consist of three sets of images (baseline, corners and talkers) for three individuals (Tim, Bill and Neil), with 256 images for each set (3x3x256, or 2304 total images). For the first set the individuals look directly at the camera. For the second set the individuals look at the four corners of a computer monitor and for the third set the individuals are talking. Of the 2304 images, 900 were chosen arbitrarily to be used for a training set, and the rest were reserved for testing the final trained neural network.

The original images (128x128 at 256 bits per pixel (bpp)) were compressed to 64x64x4bpp and adjusted for any bias in the brightness of the image. These images were processed and features were extracted based on centralized regular moments, up to 10-th order. It was determined that image moments could adequately represent a facial image, and that an image could be reconstructed from them with reasonable accuracy, and can be made to be invariant to translations and scaling (Gonzalez and Wintz (1977). The individual moments for each order were combined in a manner in which they produced a "receptive field" for each order of the moments extracted (see figure 1). Receptive fields are

0-7803-1901-X/94 $4.00 ©1994 IEEE

areas of the feature space which are particularly receptive to the presence of features from a particular class. Figures 1 shows a three dimensional plot of the

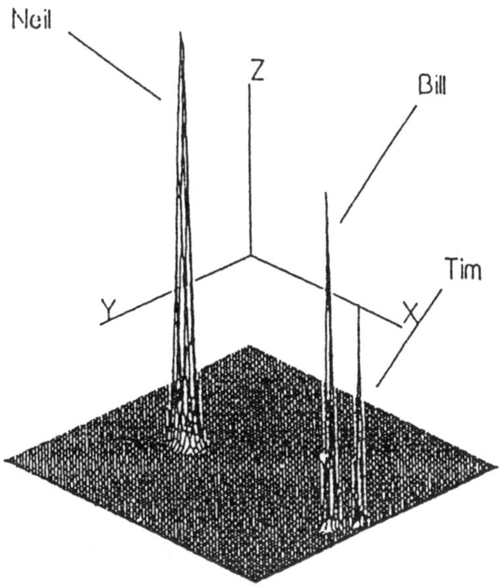

Figure 1. 3-D plot of second order feature space for three classes with spread equal to one

receptive fields for each of the individuals using the second order moments (these moments are defined with respect to the x and y spatial coordinate axes of the image). These two images are for a narrow receptive field which allows very little variation in the features used to construct the receptive fields. This narrow receptive field helps to avoid false positive identifications, however at the same time increase the number of false negative identifications. Figure 2 shows a receptive field plot for the same individuals but with a wider receptive field. This wider receptive field encourages more generalization and allows more variation in the features (fewer false negatives identifications), while at the same time allowing for more false positive identifications. The details of the feature extraction are contained in a NeuroMetric Vision Systems, Inc. Technical Report (Luebbers (1993)). During the processing of the image moments, the information contained in the 0-th and 1-st order moments is lost. The remaining 9 features (2-nd order through 10-th order) are used as inputs to the OPWRNET.

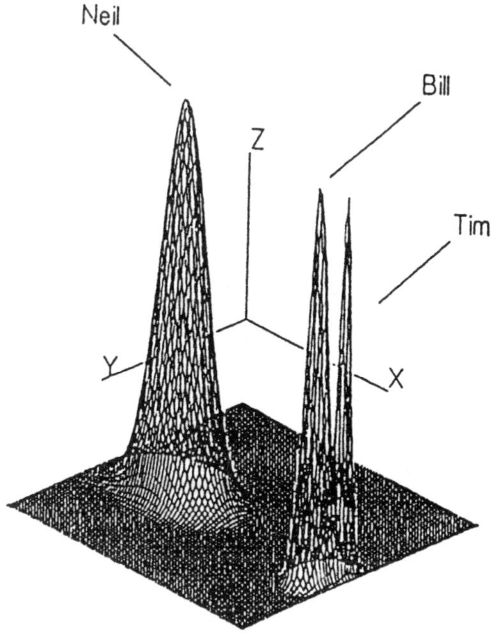

Figure 2. 3-D plot of second order feature space for three classes with spread equal to sixteen

III. OPWRNET Architecture

The architecture used is shown in Figure 3. The architecture shown consists of an input layer, an expansion layer of nodes containing orthogonal polynomials (we use Legendre Polynomials in this implementation), a hidden layer of nodes containing simple power functions and an output node containing a linear combining or summation function. The weights from the input layer to the expansion layer are fixed. The weights from the expansion layer to the hidden layer are adjusted using the familiar error back propagation training algorithm. The weights from the hidden layer to the output node are adjusted using the delta rule training algorithm (Rumelhart and McClelland (1988)).

This novel architecture has the following characteristics:

a. It approximates multi-layered feed-forward perceptron with multiple hidden layers and multiple hidden layer nodes.
b. It has only one hidden layer, and therefore is potentially easier to train compared to ANNs with multiple hidden layers.
c. The degree of non-linearity represented by

OPWRNET can be controlled directly, and can thereby avoid a common over-training situation experienced by traditional multi-layer neural networks, known as 'brittleness'.

d. Once the network has been trained, the networks functionality can be expressed in the form of a polynomial of the network inputs.

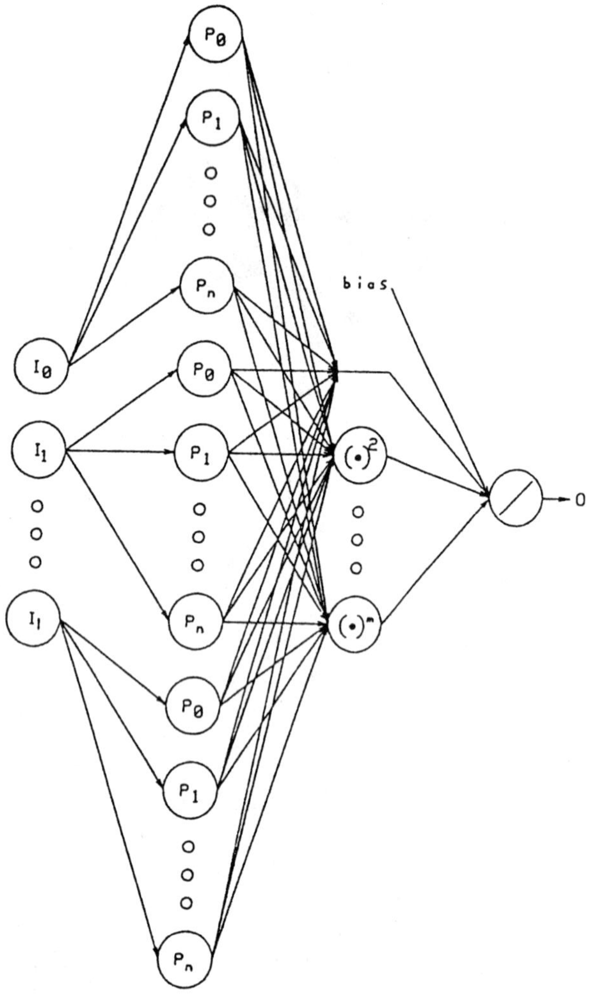

Figure 3. OPWRNET Architecture

The architecture used for this implementation consists of one hidden layer node (second order node), however an architecture with two hidden layer nodes (second and third order) was also used.

It has been shown that this architecture can approximate a general feed-forward multi-input multi-layer single output perceptron. Details of the development of the OPWRNET architecture can be found in the technical report FAU TR-CSE-93-51 (Luebbers *et al.* (1993)).

IV. Results of Facial Recognition

Besides the two OPWRNET architectures used, a linear discriminant was used to compare the neural network results. The feature extraction procedure is designed to be invariant to minor changes in face pose, translation, change in scale, and variation in contrast. These variations represent a fairly difficult task for a facial recognition system, and accounts for most of the variations typically encountered in a face recognition implementation.

The output of the discriminators were scaled to be either 1.0 (positive identification) or -1.0 (negative identification). The results are for discriminators trained to recognize Subject A (Tim), however the performance is similar for discriminators trained to recognize the other individuals. Two criterion were used to compare the relative performance of the different classifiers: 1) Use the 0.0 line as a threshold for classification (positive number means positive identification, negative number means negative identification), and 2) Use of a 90% criterion, i.e. the output of the classifier above 0.8 (90% of the [-1,1] range), means positive identification, and output of the classifier below -0.8 means negative identification. For the first criterion, an incorrect classification is obvious, in the second, any value in the [-0.8,0.8] range is counted as a misclassification. This second criterion helps to determine if a particular discriminator has been able to separate the classes (maximize a between class variance to with-in class variance ratio). For practical applications this is preferred.

Figures 4 through 6, present the results of classifying the "training" data for the linear discriminator, the one node OPWRNET, and the two node OPWRNET respectively. Note that for the first performance criterion, only the linear discriminant had any misclassifications, and then only one (although there is a second one which is almost a misclassification as well). Since there are a total of 900 images, the performance is 99.89% for the linear discriminant and 100% for both of the OPWRNET architectures. The results are summarized in Table 1 for the second performance criterion. The OPWRNET classifiers performed much better than the linear discriminator for the second performance criterion. The two OPWRNET classifiers performed about equally well.

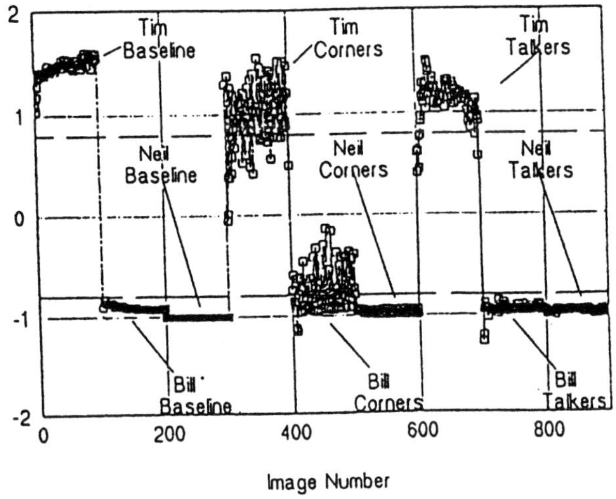

Figure 4. Training results for Linear Discriminant

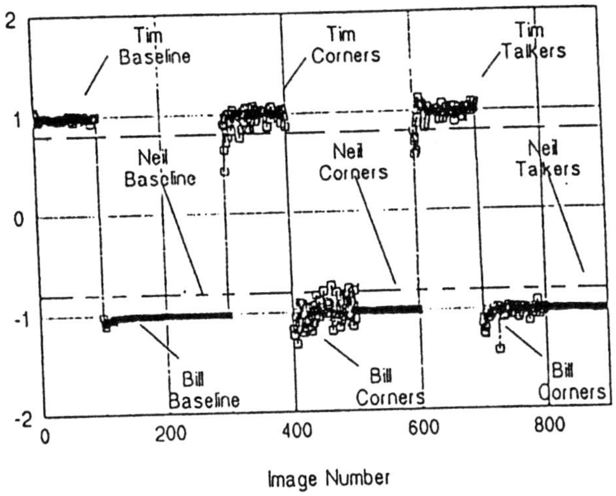

Figure 5. Training results for one node OPWRNET

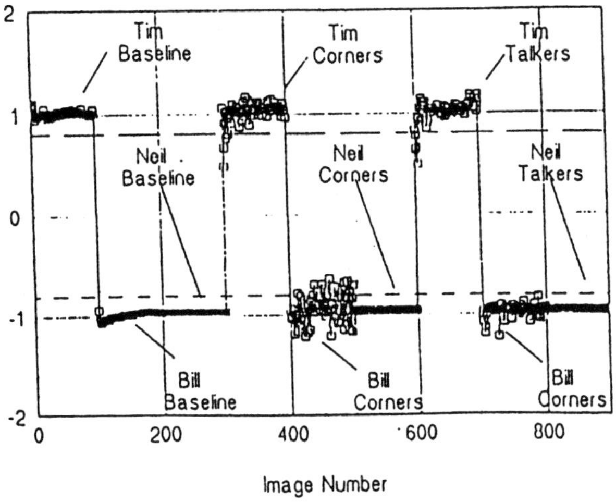

Figure 6. Training results for two node OPWRNET

Table 1 Classification Results for the Training Data Set

	Linear	One Node	Two Nodes
False Positive	54	4	16
False Negative	36	10	8
Total	90	14	24
Percent	90.00%	98.44%	97.33%

Table 2 Classification Results for the Test Data Set

	Linear	One Node	Two Nodes
False Positive	56	9	18
False Negative	122	17	11
Total	178	26	29
Percent	87.32%	98.15%	97.93%

The task of classifying images which were not contained in the training set is a more rigorous test of the performance of the discriminators. The results of these tests are presented in Figures 7 through 9. Similar to the results for the training set, only the linear discriminant had any misclassifications for the first performance criterion for the test set. The linear discriminator had three misclassifications in the "test" set of data. Since there are a total of 1,404 images in the test set of data; the performance is 99.79% for the linear discriminant and 100% for both of the OPWRNET architectures. The results for the test set for the second performance criterion are summarized in Table 5.2.

As before the OPWRNET classifiers performed much better than the linear discriminator for the second performance criterion. The two OPWRNET classifiers performed about equally well.

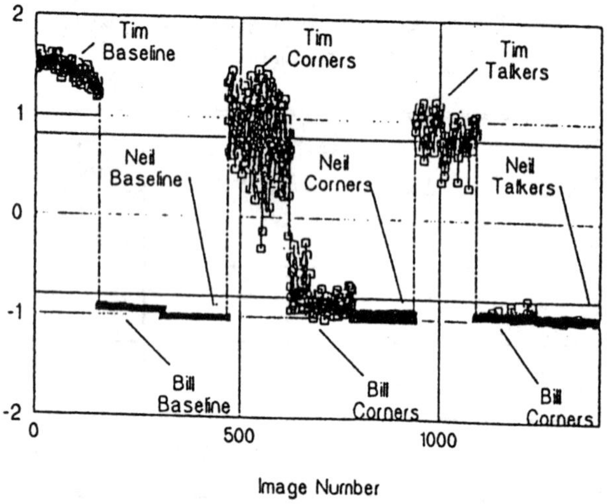

Figure 7. Test results for Linear Discriminant

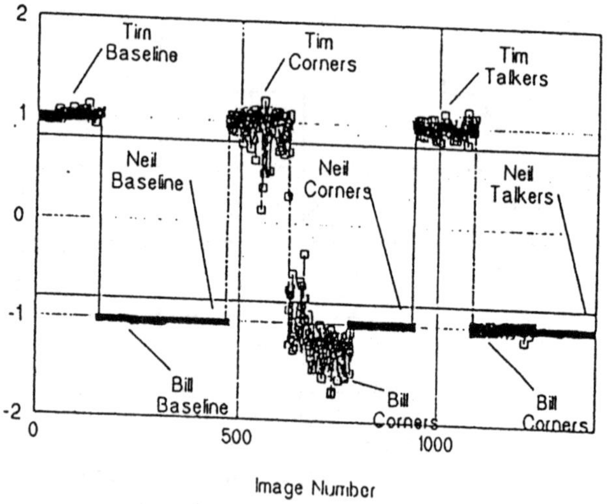

Figure 8. Test results for one OPWRNET

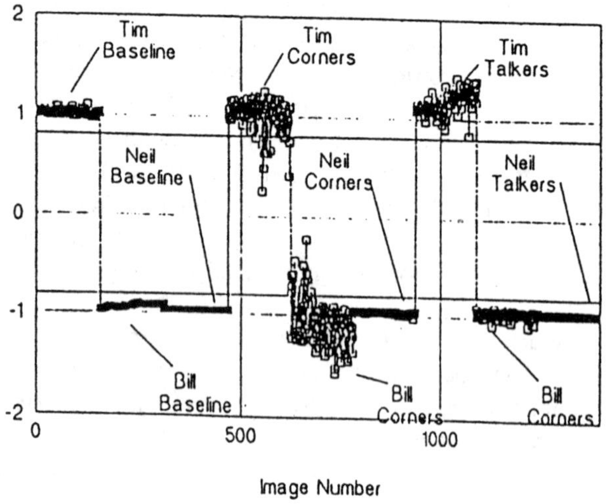

Figure 9. Test results for two node OPWRNET

V. Conclusion

Note that for most security access systems, such as for secure computing terminals or door access systems, a false positive identification is a more serious problem than a false negative identification. In cases of a false negative identification, a user may merely need to try to access the secure system again (this assumes that the user tries to look more like his baseline or training data set). On the other hand, a false positive identification would allow a presumably unauthorized person to access a secure system. In light of this, the linear discriminator performed even worse than indicated by the overall percent performance. This limited case shows that the OPWRNET with one hidden node ($OPWRNET_1$) performs better than the OPWRNET with two hidden nodes ($OPWRNET_2$).

This phenomenon may be due to what is called "brittleness" or overtraining of the network. The concept of brittleness is sometimes observed in artificial neural networks and results in a reduction in the network's ability to generalize the nonlinear mapping. This inability to generalize is attributed to the order of the non-linearity of the network. The degree of the non-linearity can be controlled directly for OPWRNET, and thereby control the brittleness of the network directly.

VI. References

Gonzalez, R.C. and Wintz, P. (1977), *Digital image processing,* Addison-Wesley Publishing Co. Reading, MA.

Holmes, J.P., Wright, L.J. and Maxwell, R.L. (1991), A performance evaluation of bio-metric identification devices, Sandia Report, SAND91-0276, Sandia National Laboratories, Albuquerque, NM.

Luebbers, P (1993), A feature extraction procedure for facial identification using regular, centralized moments, NeuroMetric Vision Systems, Technical Report, NMVS-TR-9301.

Luebbers, P., Pandya A. and Sudhakar, R. (1993), A Connectionist Approach for Interpolation and Function Approximation, *FAU Technical Report,* FAU TR-CSE-93-51.

Rumelhart, D. E. and McClelland, J.L. (1988). *Parallel Distributed Processing.* The MIT Press, Cambridge MA.

Samal, A. and Iyengar, P.A. (1992), Automatic recognition and analysis of human faces and facial expressions: A survey, *Pattern Recognition,* vol. 25, **1**, 65-77.

Reduced Shift Invariant Second Order Neural Networks using Principal Component Analysis and Pixel Combinations

Bong-Kyu Lee , Dong-Kyu Kim,Yoo-Kun Cho
Dept. of Computer Engineering
Seoul National University,Shinlim-Dong,Gwanak-Ku
Seoul 151-742,KOREA
e-mail : bklee@dosa1.snu.ac.kr

Heong-Ho Lee
Dept.of Electrical Engineering
Chung Nam University,Daejeon,Korea

Hee-Yeung Hwang
Dept of Electrical Engineering
Hoseo University,Chunan,Korea

Abstract

When two dimensional images are used as input to a neural network, the noise from the input device and small deformations in the end parts that occur in the processes of separating each pattern and size normalization lead to images shifted from the original learned image being input to the neural network which is a maijor cause of misrecognition. In existing multi-layer perceptrons using standard EBP, it is difficult to solve shift invariant problems because pattern pixel values are presented directly to the neural network input nodes. Second order neural network inputs consist of geometrically related nonlinear combinations of two pixels, and can be used for shift invariant pattern recognition. But the number of Second order neural network input nodes increases in proportion to N^2, where N is the dimension of the input patterns, even if we only consider shift invariance. Such large number of input nodes lead to slower learning and recognition.

In this paper, we propose a method for reducing the number of shift invariant second order neural network input nodes using combinations of input pattern pixels and PCA(Principle Component Analysis). Using the proposed method, we are able to implement a shift invariant second order neural network with 2/5*N nodes. Due to the reduced number of input nodes, a 50% reduction in the learning and recognition time was obtained.

I. Introduction

Multi-layer perceptrons using EBP(Error Back Propagation) learning rule have attracted a great deal of interest recently in the field of pattern recognition where solutions using existing algorithmic methods, because of it's simplicity and superior problem solving capabilities. But the perceptron has a low rate of recognition for patterns which has been geometrically transformed (rotation, scaling, shifting). This shows that the multi-layer perceptron model has a weak point in recognizing geometrically transformed patterns, one of the basic problems of pattern recognition[2]. Geometric invariance is important in pattern recognition because the target location and orientation is usually unknown. Among all the variations, shift variation generally occurs in two dimensional pattern recognition. Shift variation refer to the shifting of the entire extracted pattern as a result of a small amount of noise at the end points of the pattern that occur during the process of extracting indivisual patterns from the entire scene[1].

To overcome such geometric variations, researches on using higher order neural networks, which can learn variations by itself, have been actively conducted. Recent research has shown that because invariances can be built into the architecture of higher order neural networks, they can be effectively used for invariant pattern recognition[2,3]. But straightforeward use of higher order neural networks is limited in actual implementations because of the combinatorial explosion of the number of input layer nodes in proportion to the input pattern dimension. If the input pattern to be learned is of dimension N, the number of input layer nodes increases in

0-7803-1901-X/94 $4.00 ©1994 IEEE

$O(N^2)$, even if we only consider the second order neural networks. This is the major obstacle to actual implementation. Also, such large number of input nodes lead to slower learning and recognition[5,7].

There have been many approaches which maintain the geometric invariance properties of higher order networks while reducing the number of input nodes. For example, sigma-pi networks use a hidden layer of higher order nodes[10]. This strategy retains the higher order network properties, but its learning speed is slower. Another approach is to use a priori information to remove the terms which are irrelevant to the problem in a single layer of higher order nodes[5,7]. However since it is often difficult to find the properties of input pattern space a priori, this stretegy has limited applications.

Recently, the problems of the above methods have been overcome be representing pixel combinations in the same relation in the context of the invariance wanted by a single representative node[1,4,6]. Using such methods allow an O(N) implementation of high order neural networks with N dimensional input patterns. For example, shift invarient second order neural networks have 2*N input nodes for N dimensional input patterns. But even such methods still need a large number of input nodes necessitating longer learning and recognition time.

In this paper, as a part of an on going research to reduce the number of high order neural network input nodes, we propose a method for reducing the number of shift invariant second order neural network input nodes to close to the input pattern dimension N using PCA(Principal Component Analysis) and pattern pixel combinations. Using the proposed method, we are able to implement a shift invariant second order neural network only with 2/5*N nodes. Experiments using the implemented neural network on shifted Korean Munjo character set resulted in about 95% recognition rate. Due to reduced number of input nodes, reduction in the learning and recognition time was also obtained.

The rest of the paper is structured as followes. In section II, we show an O(N) shift invariant second order neural network implementation using pixel combinations. Section III details the process of implementating a further reduced shift invariant second order neural network using principal component analysis on the pixel combinations obtained in section II. Section IV presents the experimental results that show the proposed reduced second order neural network is superior to the existing non-reduced second order neural network. The paper ends with a conclusion in section V.

II. Shift Invariant Second Order Neural Network using Pixel Combinations.

Second order neural networks have the lowest order among higher order neural networks and have shift and size invariant properties. These properties are due to the fact that second order neural networks perceives the relationship between two pixels combinations.

The operation equation for second order neural network is shown in equation (1). To obtain shift invariance, we need only to take the two dimentional corelation terms of equation (1) into account. Equation (2) shows the terms of equation (1) that affect the relative positions of the inputs, only these terms need be taken into account for shift invariance[2,3].

$$h_i = \sum_{j=1}^{n} W_{i(jj)}\xi_j^2 + \sum_{j=1}^{n-1}\sum_{k=j+1}^{n} W_{i(jk)}\xi_j\xi_k + \sum_{j=1}^{n} W_{ij}\xi_j + W_i \quad (1)$$

$$h_i = \sum_{j=1}^{n-1}\sum_{k=j+1}^{n} W_{ijk}\xi_j\xi_k \quad (2)$$

For shift invariant learning, weights in shifted positions are updated simultaneously according to equation (3). So equation (2) can be rewritten as equation (4).

$$W_{ijk} = W_{i|j-k|} \quad (3)$$

$$h_i = \sum_{j=1}^{n-1}\sum_{k=j+1}^{n} W_{i(k-j)}\xi_j\xi_k \quad (4)$$

In shift invariant second order neural networks, since all weights in shifted positions have the same values, all the two pixel combinations are added beforehand and the cumulative value can be represented by a single input node of the second order neural network. This feature, summation of all the two pixel combinations for given relative position, is called SOP(Summation Of Products) or second order feature[1,7].

$$SOP = \sum[\prod(\xi_{jk}\xi_{kl}.....)] \qquad (5)$$

In obtaining second order features, the direction must be taken into account. There are four directions which two pixel combinations can have. So, second order feature can be represented by a 2*N - (L+M) dimensional vector with each element representing the numbers of the relative position pixel combinations. Fig 1. shows the possible directions of two pixel combinations and an example of the second order feature.

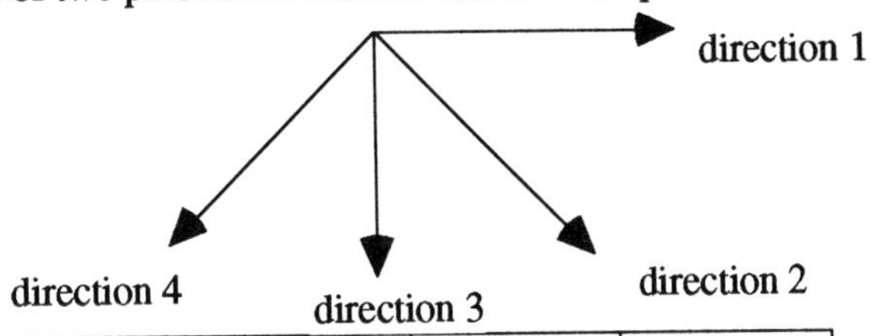

		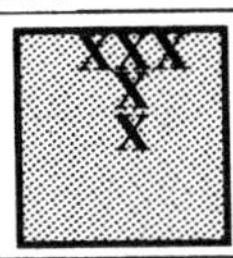	vector size
direction 1	21000	21000	(L-1)
direction 3	21000	21000	(M-1)
direction 2	10000 10000 00000 00000 00000	10000 10000 00000 00000 00000	(L-1)(M-1)
directin 4	10000 10000 00000 00000 00000 00000	10000 10000 00000 00000 00000 00000	(L-1)(M-1)

Fig 1. Directions of two pixel combinations and example of second order feature

As can be seen above, shift invariant second order neural network can be implemented by first order multi-layer perceptron which has about 2*N input nodes when using the second order features.

III. Reduction of Second order Neural Network using PCA(Principal Component Analysis)

Shift invariant second order neural network using second order features considering position and directional correlations has O(N) input nodes. But the size of the neural network increases twice as fast as the dimension of the real pattern. To be realistically applied to pattern recognition systems, the learning and recognition process must be achieved as quickly as possible. Thus it is preferable to reduce the number of input nodes of second order neural networks as much as possible.

PCA(Principal Component Analysis) is a statistical tool which yields substantial data reduction by representing each pattern in terms of a relatively small subset of orthonormal features(Principal Component) extracted from the input set[8,9]. The Principal Components are eigenvectors of the covariance matrix formed from the pattern set. Each eigenvalue is equal to the variance of the projections of the patterns onto the corresponding principal component. The principal components can be obtained by using the diagonal terms from the diagonalized covariance matrix. Then the values obtained from the PCA are equivalent to the variance of each dimension of each pattern. So, the variances of each dimension can be used as Principal Components[8,9].

Fig. 2 shows the top 80% of the variance of each dimension from 990 chracter patterns from the Korean Munjo chracter set. As can be seen from Fig 2. dimensions of smaller variances differ very little for most of the patterns. Therefore such dimentions only increase the learning and recognition time while contributing very little to the overall recognition rate. By eliminating these dimension from the second order features, improvement for learning and recognition time can be obtained without adversely affecting the recognition rates.

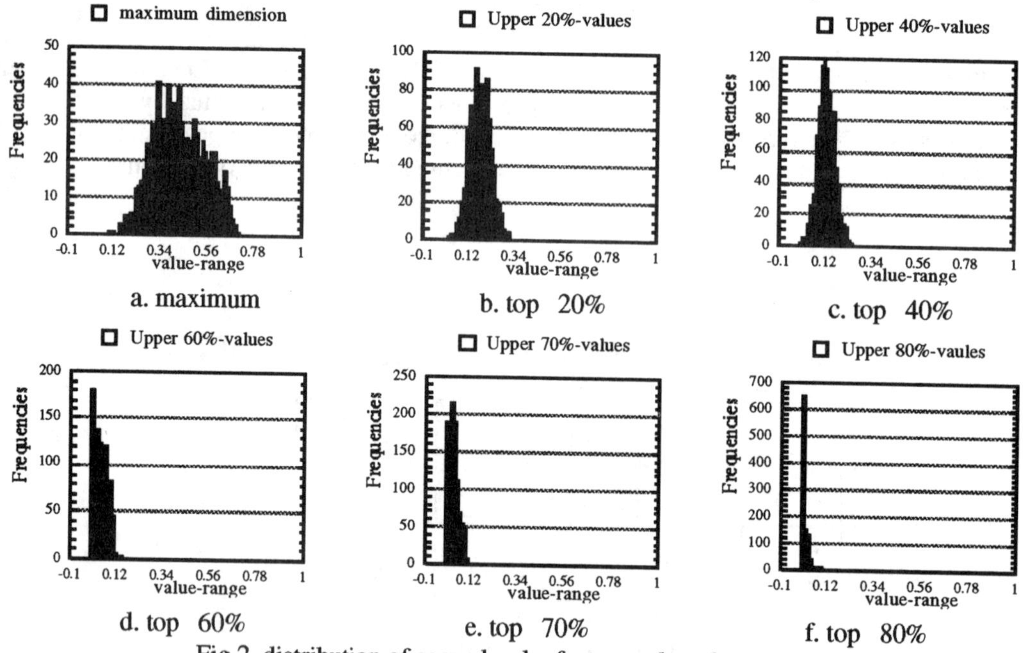

Fig 2. distribution of second order feature values for each dimension

IV. Experimental results

Second order neural networks reduced to 2*N input nodes using pixel combinations are shown to be further reducible by using PCA without adversely affecting the recognition rate through experiments of 990 patterns from the Korean Mungjo charcter set. The experiments compared the results of using a fixed percentage of the second order features with the highest variance values. We have conducted experiments using the top 10%, 20%, 30%, 40%, 50%, 70%, and 100% of the second order features. Fig. 3 shows the resulting recognotion rate, learning time and recognition time.

First of all, using second order neural networks rather than first order neural networks show a far higher recognition rate proving that theshift invariance problem has been overcome. Also, comparing the results of using the top 20% with the results of using all second order features, we can see that using only the top 20% of the features results in a 80% reduction in the number of the input nodes and a 50% reduction in learning and recognition time.

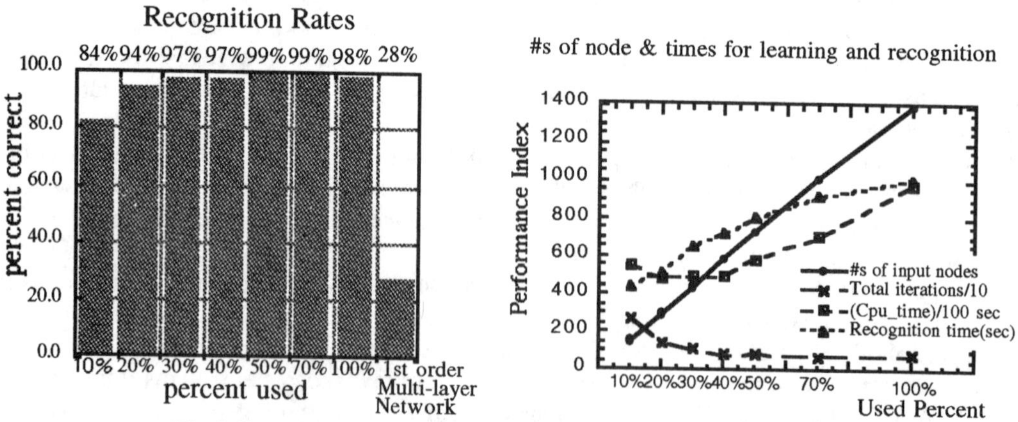

Fig 3. Results of Experiments using reduced second order neural networks.

From the experimental results, we can see that the second order features obtained through pixel combination still has redundant information that does not contribute to improving the recognition rate. Eliminating such redundant information through PCA can lead to a further reduction in the number of input nodes without adversely affection the recognition rate while also improving the learning and recognition speed.

V.Conclusion

In this paper, we propose a method for reducing the number of second order neural network input nodes for solving the problems caused by the $O(N^2)$ increase in the number of input nodes -- difficulties in implementations, increases in learning and recognition time -- through pixel combination and PCA. Using the proposed method, we are able to implement second order network with only 2/5*N input nodes. Reduction in the learning and recognition time is also obtained.

Because geometric invariances are important for the pattern recognition, there are many researches being conducted on using higher order neural network. But combinatorial explosion of input nodes is the main obsticle to research. So, researches for solving this problem is progressively increasing. In the proposed method, we adopt a statistical tool(PCA) to reduce the number of higher order neural network input nodes. So the proposed method can be used regardless of the given pattern class.

References

[1] B.C. Kim,H.Y. Kwon,D.K. Kim, H.Y.Hwang,D.S. Cho, " Shift invariant character feature extraction using second order neural network characteristics," WCNN'93 , vol. IV , pp. 28 - 32.

[2] S.J. Perantonis ,P.J.G. Lisboa , "Translation,Rotation,and Scale Invariant Pattern Recognition by Higher order Neural Networks and Moment Classifier," IEEE Transactions on Neural Network,March,vol. 3 , No. 2, pp. 241-251,1992.

[3] C.L. Giles ,T. MAxwell, "Learning,invariance,and generalization in high-order neural networks," Applied Optics,vol. 25,pp. 4972 - 4978,1987.

[4] Y. Shin , J. Fhosh , "The pi-sigma network : an Efficient Higher-Order Neural Network for pattern classification and function approximation," , Proc. IJCNN 91 , vol. , pp. 13 - 18.

[5] L. Spirkovska , M.B. Reid, "Connectivity Strategies for Higher-Order Neural Networks applied pattern recognition,"Proc. IJCNN 90,vol.1 , pp. 21 - 26.

[6] W. A.C. Schmidt , J.P. Davis, "Pattern Recognition Properties of various feature spaces for higher order Neural Networks," IEEE Transaction on PAMI , vol. 15,No. 8, pp. 795 - 801,1993.

[7] H. Yang , C.C. Guest, "High order Neural Networks with reduced numbers of interconnection weights," Proc. IJCNN 91 , vol. 3 , pp. 281 - 286.

[8] J. Hertz, A. Krogh , R.G. Palme , Introduction to the Theory of Neural Computation, Addision-Wesely , 1991.

[9] S.D. Hyman , T.P. Vogl , K.T. Blackwell , G.S. Barbour , J.M. Irvine , D.L. Alkon, "Classification of Japanese Kanji using Principal Component Analysis as a preprocessor to an artificial neural network,",IJCNN 91,vol.1 , pp.233- 238.

[10] D.E. Rumelhart and J.L. McClelland, Parallel Distributed Processing,MIT,1986.

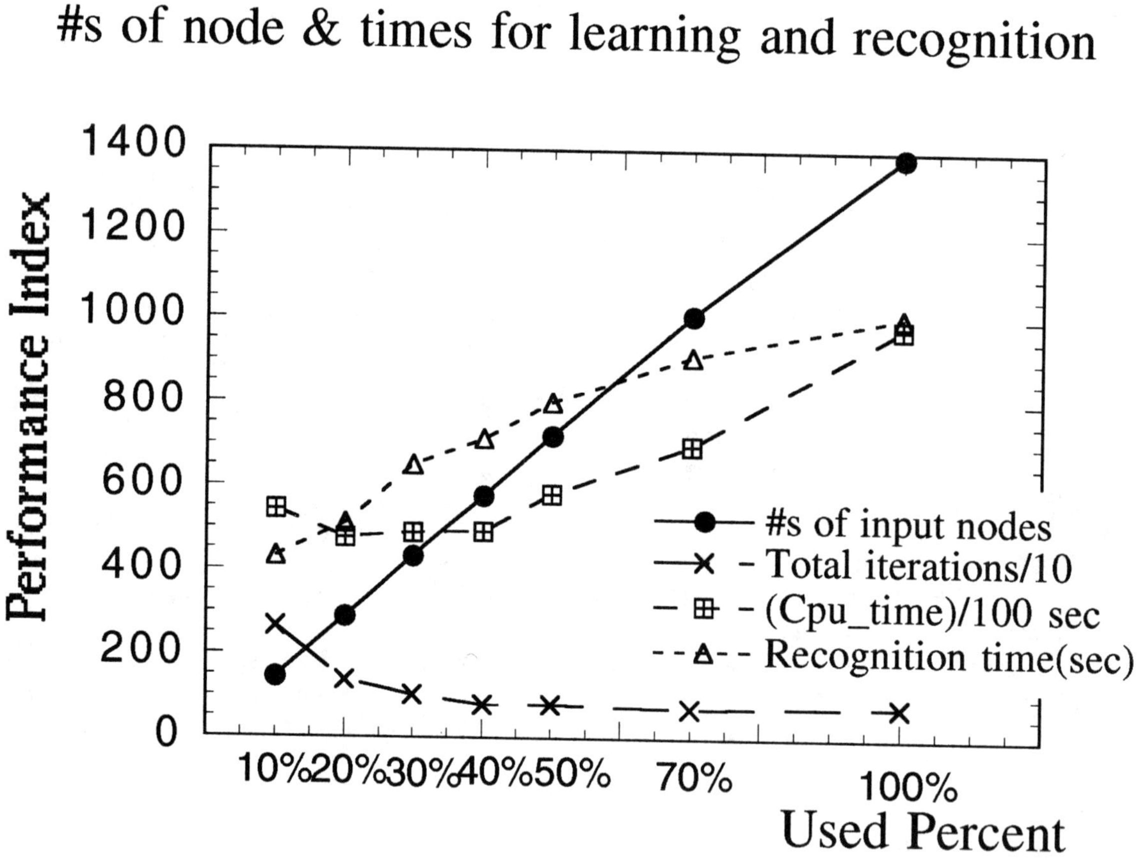
#s of node & times for learning and recognition
Performance Index
1400
1200
1000
800
600
400
200
0
10%20%30%40%50%
70%
100%
Used Percent
#s of input nodes
Total iterations/10
(Cpu_time)/100 sec
Recognition time(sec)

INTENTIONALLY LEFT BLANK

Recognising Aircraft: Automatic Extraction of Structure by layers of Quadratic Neural Nets

Robert A. McLaughlin and Michael D.Alder
ram@ciips.ee.uwa.edu.au mike@maths.uwa.edu.au
Centre for Intelligent Information Processing Systems
Department of Electrical and Electronic Engineering
The University of Western Australia
Nedlands W.A. 6009, AUSTRALIA

Abstract

This paper explores a method of recognition applicable to a wide range of problems. It adopts a syntactic or structural approach, which involves viewing an object in terms of its simpler components. In the specific example of aircraft recognition, this entails decomposing an aircraft into entities such as a nose, fuselage, tail and wings. Each component may then be further decomposed as a set of pixels. The process of recognition requires finding sets of pixels forming such components and then sets of these components forming an aircraft. This is implemented by a Quadratic Neural Network.

keywords: Syntactic Pattern Recognition, Quadratic Neural Networks.

1 Introduction

Consider the problem of recognising the aircraft of *fig. 1.* Each aircraft may be thought of as comprising a collection of components, such as wings, a nose, fuselage and tail. Each of the components may in turn be viewed as a collection of yet simpler sub-components, in this case pixels. This allows us to rephrase the recognition problem thus:

- Find a collection of pixels forming a wing, nose, fuselage or tail.
- Find a collection of such components forming one of the aircraft shown below.

Such an approach to a recognition problem is termed *Syntactic* or *Structural* and was pioneered by K.S. Fu [1].

We propose implementing this structural recognition with a construct termed a *Quadratic Neural Network.* In such a network, a neuron models its inputs with low order moments. The term *Quadratic* stems from a correspondence between the first and second order central moments of a set and a quadratic form. This is expanded upon in the next section, where it is utilised to give a graphical representation of the state of the network. In the network proposed, the pixel level description of an

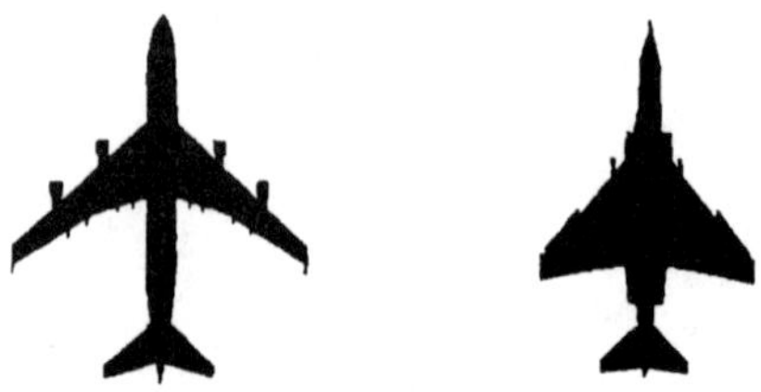

Figure 1: Aircraft for recognition

0-7803-1901-X/94 $4.00 ©1994 IEEE

image is fed to a layer of these neurons, each of which models a subset or component of the image such as a nose, fuselage, tail or wing. The output of this layer is then treated as the input to the next, and it is here that relationships between these components are characterised and embedded as a point in a high dimensional space. This point represents the high level structure of the image and facilitates the recognition of entities such as aeroplanes.

The two subtasks listed in the first paragraph are obviously conceptually very similar. In both, a collection of components are being formed into a single, higher level entity. A single method capable of achieving both of these subtasks is outlined in this paper. This method possesses a high degree of generality. This generality allows it to be used with many different types of components forming many different types of objects. To appreciate the power of this generality, consider if the aircraft of *fig. 1* were replaced with silhouettes of a left and a right hand. As with the aircraft, each hand can be decomposed into components, fingers and a palm. Each component can then be seen as a collection of pixels. Differentiating left hands from right is essentially the same problem as differentiating passenger and fighter aircraft, only the components have been changed. Replacing these images with hand drawn cubes or letters of the alphabet again reduce to essentially the same tasks, although the number of stages in the decomposition of the objects may be increased. Equivalently, the number of layers in the corresponding neural network may increase. The method presented in this paper is, in principle, capable of both reading the postcode on a letter and differentiating between aircraft. This method has been explored in the context of the aircraft problem.

2 Representations and UpWrites

Begin with a black and white image and abstract the black pixels as a point set in $\mathcal{R}^2$. Our task is to find those subsets of points which form an object such as a wing, nose, fuselage or tail. We then must represent this set of points as a single entity. Let us begin with the latter of these problems.

Let us assume that we have a set of points in $\mathcal{R}^2$ forming an object such as a wing. Such a set may be described by taking central moments of the points. The first order moment is the mean, the second order central moment being the covariance matrix of the points. Let us restrict ourselves to first and second order central moments. Taking higher order moments would give a more accurate description of the set, but for our purposes we have found first and second order moments to be adequate. These moments may be parameterised by several numbers. The mean requires two numbers i.e. (x, y). The covariance matrix is a 2x2 symmetric matrix and an obvious way to parameterise it would be to record its three distinct entries. However an equally valid method, and the one chosen here, is to record the two eigenvalues (λ_1, λ_2) of the matrix and the angle of the dominant eigenvector $(\theta_{\lambda 1})$. This angle is somewhat ambiguous as the same eigenvector could map to any of a number of angles differing by $n\pi$ radians (n $\epsilon \mathbb{Z}$). Thus we define the transformation

$$\theta_{\lambda 1} \quad \longmapsto \quad [cos(2\theta_{\lambda 1}), sin(2\theta_{\lambda 1})]$$

which maps each angle to a point on the unit circle.

The first and second order central moments are now parameterised by six numbers, which may be interpreted as a point in $\mathcal{R}^6$

$$[x, y, \lambda_1, \lambda_2, cos(2\theta_{\lambda 1}), sin(2\theta_{\lambda 1})]^T$$

This single point corresponds to a description of a set of points in $\mathcal{R}^2$ and that set of points represents an object such as a wing. Thus we have abstracted an object such as a wing as a point in $\mathcal{R}^6$.

These operations may be viewed in terms of the actions of a single neuron. Fundamentally, this neuron takes an input, operates upon it and produces an output. The input here is the point set in $\mathcal{R}^2$ that forms an object such as a wing. The neuron performs the operation of taking low order moments of the input, these moments being embedded as a single point in $\mathcal{R}^6$. This point constitutes the output of the neuron and will be fed as input to later layers of the network.

This still leaves the problem of deciding which of the subsets of points in $\mathcal{R}^2$ form a component of an aircraft. To address this problem, first note that such a subset will be described by a mean and a covariance matrix. Note also that a mean and a covariance matrix uniquely define a gaussian probability density function. Thus we could view our description process of a set of points in $\mathcal{R}^2$ as fitting a two dimensional gaussian probability density function to the points. Given an object such as

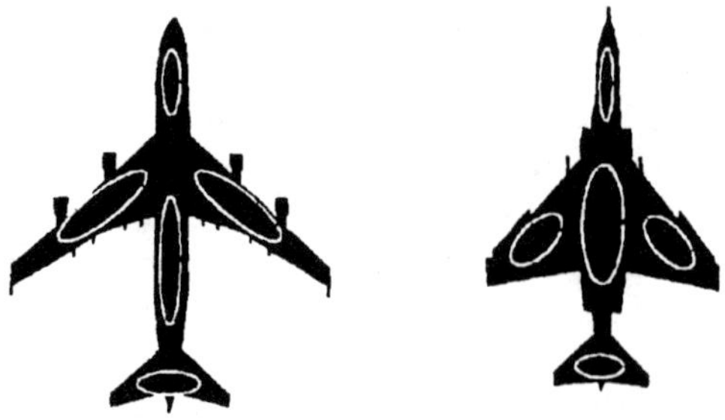

Figure 2: Gaussian mixture model of aircraft

an aeroplane, make the assumption that each black pixel (or the corresponding point in $\mathcal{R}^2$) belongs to a component such as a nose, fuselage, tail or wing. Finding the subset of points corresponding to each component then reduces to the task of finding the maximum likelihood gaussian mixture model for the image. This is a standard problem in statistics and may be solved with the aid of algorithms such as the E.M. algorithm [2]. The mixture model will model the subset of pixels forming each of the nose, fuselage, tail and each wing with a separate gaussian.

To represent such a gaussian mixture model graphically, we note that each gaussian of mean $\mathbf{m}$ and covariance matrix $\mathbf{C}$ defines an associated quadratic form

$$\begin{aligned} F : \mathcal{R}^2 &\longrightarrow \mathcal{R} \\ \mathbf{x} &\longmapsto (\mathbf{x}-\mathbf{m})^T \mathbf{C}^{-1} (\mathbf{x}-\mathbf{m}) \end{aligned}$$

and plot the points $\{\mathbf{x} : F(\mathbf{x}) = 1\}$. This set of points forms an ellipse centred on the mean of the gaussian and with a radius in any direction indicative of the gaussian's variance. The gaussian mixture model of the aircraft of *fig. 1* results in the graphical representation shown in *fig. 2*.

We have now identified the various components of an object such as an aeroplane. It has already been outlined in this paper how these may be embedded as points in $\mathcal{R}^6$, thus the object is now described as a set of points in $\mathcal{R}^6$. This set constitutes the output of the first layer of the network.

Having begun with an image described as a large set of points in $\mathcal{R}^2$, we have identified subsets forming individual components of the image and abstracted each component as a single point in $\mathcal{R}^6$. This process of mapping a set of points in some space to a single point in a different, generally higher dimensional space, has been termed an *UpWrite*. It results in what could be interpreted as a higher level representation of the data. We conjecture that this is implemented in wetware by sequential layers of neurons. In the present example, an image originally described in terms of black and white pixels (abstracted as points in $\mathcal{R}^2$) has been UpWritten to a description in terms of a nose, fuselage, tail and wings (abstracted as points in $\mathcal{R}^6$). The next step will be to UpWrite this to a description of the image as a single entity, an aeroplane, abstracted as a single point in some different space. This will involve implementing a second layer of the network, a layer whose input is the point set in $\mathcal{R}^6$ and whose output will be a point in a higher dimensional space.

As before, we choose to take the first and second order central moments of the point set that constitutes the input. The first order moment results in a six dimensional mean which may be parameterised by six numbers. The second order central moment results in a 6x6 covariance matrix. Such a matrix may be parameterised by its six eigenvalues and a sufficient number of angles to define its eigenvectors. Note that as the eigenvectors are by definition perpendicular to each other, five angles are required to define the first eigenvector but only four to define the second, three for the third etc. Mapping each angle, as before, to a point on the unit circle

$$\theta \longmapsto [cos(2\theta), sin(2\theta)]$$

we obtain a parameterisation of the first and second order central moments requiring forty two numbers. This defines an embedding of a set of points in $\mathcal{R}^6$ as a single point in $\mathcal{R}^{42}$.

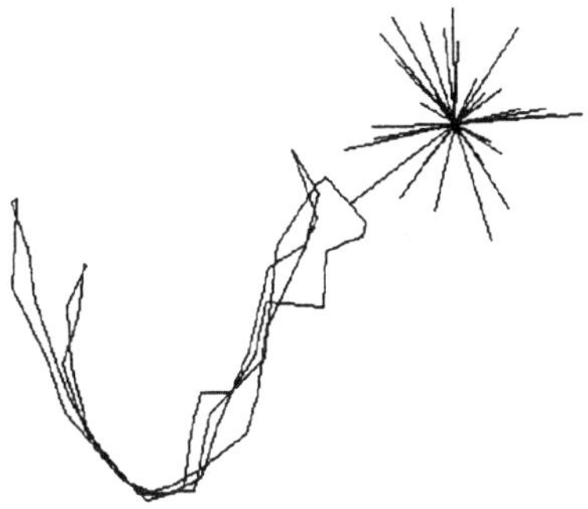

Figure 3: Curve in $\mathcal{R}^{42}$ produced by rotating an aircraft

3 Recognition

In the previous section we outlined a method which took an object such as an aeroplane described as a set of points in $\mathcal{R}^2$ and mapped it to a single point in $\mathcal{R}^{42}$. Imagine that we were to take a second image of the same aeroplane but were to rotate it slightly. This image would then map to a slightly different point in $\mathcal{R}^{42}$. Repeating this process and rotating the aeroplane through 2π radians, we would trace out a curve in $\mathcal{R}^{42}$. In other words, the process of presenting the same image rotated produces a discrete approximation to an embedding of the Lie group $SO(\mathcal{R}, 2)$ in the top level space. An example of such a curve, projected on to the two dimensional plane of this page, is shown in *fig. 3*. The axes of the space are shown in the top right of the figure. This particular curve was generated by rotating the passenger aircraft of *fig. 1*. If we were to repeat the entire process of rotating the aircraft and tracing out a curve in $\mathcal{R}^{42}$, but were to do so with a slightly smaller image of the aircraft, we would trace out a very similar curve which was displaced slightly in space. If we were then to translate the aircraft (i.e. move it about in the two dimensional plane of the page) and map each resulting image to a point in $\mathcal{R}^{42}$, we would trace out a surface in $\mathcal{R}^{42}$.

A little thought will lead the reader to conclude that a particular type of aircraft could not be made to map to all points in $\mathcal{R}^{42}$ regardless of how it is translated, rotated or scaled. All points in $\mathcal{R}^{42}$ corresponding to a particular aircraft will in fact lie on a manifold. This manifold will be topologically equivalent to

$$\mathcal{R}^2 \quad X \quad SO(2, \mathcal{R}) \quad X \quad \mathcal{R}^+$$

which corresponds to the operations of translation, rotation and scaling respectively. The curve of *fig. 3* can be thought of as a projection of a part of this manifold. In order to recognise if a given image is of a particular aircraft we map it to a point in $\mathcal{R}^{42}$. If this point lies on (or very near) the appropriate manifold, then the image is deemed to resemble the appropriate aircraft.

This raises the question of how do we find this manifold. In order to distinguish between the two aircraft of *fig. 1*, we found it sufficient to approximate the manifold corresponding to each aircraft with a twenty dimensional affine subspace. To obtain the subspace for the passenger aircraft, a large number of images of the aircraft translated, rotated and scaled were mapped to points in $\mathcal{R}^{42}$. The mean of the resulting set of points was specified as the origin of the affine subspace. The covariance matrix of these points was then calculated and the eigenvectors of the matrix were found. The eigenvalue corresponding to each eigenvector gives an indication of the amount of variation of the points in that direction, a small eigenvalue indicating very little variation. The eigenvectors corresponding to eigenvalues above a threshold value were selected, these representing the directions in which the points exhibited greatest variation. These eigenvectors were defined as the basis vectors for the affine subspace. This process was then repeated with examples of the fighter aircraft, generating a second twenty dimensional affine subspace.

The process of recognition may now be described as follows. An image is mapped to a point in $\mathcal{R}^{42}$ as outlined in *Section 2: Representation and UpWrites.* This point is then considered in relation to the twenty dimensional affine subspaces corresponding to each type of aircraft. If the

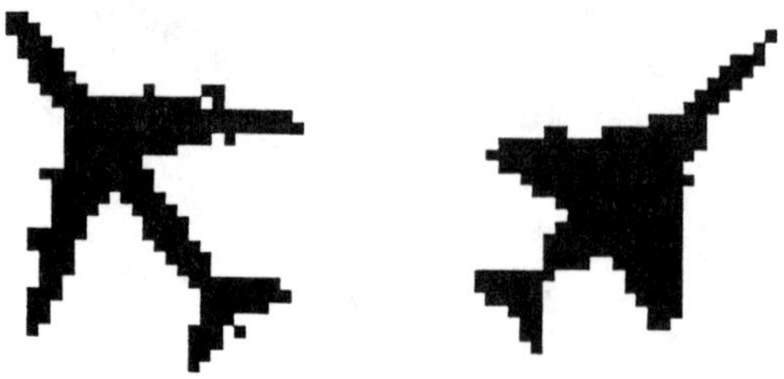

Figure 4: Noisy aircraft

point lies in or very near to one of the subspaces, then the original image is judged to resemble that type of aircraft. A point which lies near neither subspace is deemed not to represent an aircraft.

4 Invariance, Extrapolation and Noise

An attraction of the method outlined in this paper is that invariance is not built into the system, it is learnt. To appreciate why this is important, consider the operation of rotation and the problem of recognising alpha-numeric digits. The letter **A** obviously remains a letter **A** even when rotated. However, the digit **6** becomes a **9**. Therefore which invariances are allowable depends upon the objects being recognised. If such invariances are built into the recognition system, its applicability to a wide range of objects is immediately limited. No such invariances are built into the system outlined here.

A second attraction of this system is that all invariances are handled in a uniform way. In the example that we have explored, translation, rotation and scale invariance of aircraft were learnt. Each type of invariance influenced the manifold in $\mathcal{R}^{42}$ to which the objects mapped. More complicated forms of invariance will merely give rise to a higher dimensional manifold.

A third notable point of this method is its ability to extrapolate upon what it has learnt. The computer program written to explore this method was shown examples of two types of aircraft. These were translated, rotated and scaled. The scaling was at 60%, 80%, 100%, 120% and 140% of some base size. Not only was the program able to recognise images at scales in between those seen during training, but it was tested on and found to recognise images scaled from 20% to 200%. Thus it was able to extrapolate upon what it was shown during training.

A point must also be made regarding noise. Images which were heavily distorted at the pixel level were shown to the computer. An example of such images is shown in *fig. 4*. The computer was able to classify all such images correctly. This is because, whilst the image may be distorted, the underlying structure of the object is intact and it is this structure which the computer extracts and upon which recognition is based.

Much of the robustness of this system is due to its ability to handle different types of noise at an appropriate level. Consider again the problem of recognising alpha-numeric digits and the situation of a system which has been trained on several different fonts and is now required to read a new, previously unseen font. The characters, at the pixel level, will bear little resemblance to their counterparts in different fonts. However, at the stroke level, similarities will be pronounced. As the method presented in this paper would assemble sets of pixels into strokes and then sets of strokes into individual characters, a certain robustness against such variations as change of font is inherent in the system. It is for this reason that we have chosen to use low order moments and treated the problem in several levels in preference to attempting to solve the problem in a single level by taking high order moments of the original pixel set.

5 Results and Conclusions

In this paper, we have presented a method applicable to a wide range of recognition problems and explored it in the context of the recognition of two types of aircraft. A system using the method outlined here was implemented on a Sun Sparc workstation. The training set consisted of 900 examples of each aircraft type, varying in position, orientation and scale. The scale varied from 60% to 140% of some base size. The system was then tested upon a different set of 900 images of each class, exhibiting the same variations in position, orientation and scale. All images were identified correctly. 170 images of each class varying in scale from 20% to 200% were then shown to the system. Again all images were identified correctly. Finally, 30 images distorted to the level illustrated in *fig. 4* were shown to the system. Again all images were identified correctly.

This method has several interesting features. It has exhibited a high level of accuracy and robustness. It has not required the programmer to build in invariances but learns these from examples. All forms of invariance are treated in a uniform manner. This suggests that more complex forms of invariance are possible, such as the OCR example of tolerance to different fonts. Finally and most importantly, the method was not designed to be specific to the task of aircraft recognition. Applying it to different recognition problems requires no alteration in the method, as is demonstrated in its successful application to the tasks of recognising hand drawn cubes [3] and differentiating between silhouettes of left and right hands [4].

The method outlined here models a neuron as a primitive element whose output corresponds to low order moments of its input. This is in some contrast to the more generally accepted model of a neuron as a primitive element whose output corresponds to a weighter sum of its input which has been operated upon by some non-linear function. The model used here has been previously suggested elsewhere. Both the quadratic neural network of [5] and the probabilistic neural network of [6] assume fundamentally similar models of a neuron. By utilising this model, we have outlined a network which takes the pixels of an image (abstracted as points in $\mathcal{R}^2$) as its initial input. The first layer of the network groups these into entities such as a nose, fuselage, tail and wings (abstracted as points in $\mathcal{R}^6$). These form the input to the next layer, which groups these components into an entity such as an aeroplane. More structurally complex objects may require further layers of processing.

6 References

1 Fu, K. S., *Syntactic Pattern Recognition and Applications*, Prentice-Hall, New Jersey, 1982.

2 Dempster, A.P., N.M. Laird and D.B. Rubin, *Maximum Likelihood from Incomplete Data via the EM Algorithm*,Proc.Roy.Stat.Soc., **B**,39(1), (1977), pp 1-38.

3 McLaughlin, R.A., M.D. Alder, *Recognising Cubes in Images*, Pattern Recognition in Practice IV, Vlieland, Holland, June 1-3 1994.

4 McLaughlin, R.A., M.D. Alder, *Inference of Structure: Hands*, submitted for publication to Pattern Recognition Letters, Elsevier Science Publishers B.V.

5 Lim, G.S., M. Alder, P. Hadingham, *Adaptive quadratic neural networks*, Pattern Recognition Letters, 13 (1992), pp 325-329, Elsevier Science Publishers B.V.

6 Specht, D., *Probabilistic neural networks*, Neural Networks, 3 (1990), 109.

Evaluation of a Training Method and of Various Rejection Criteria for a Neural Network Classifier Used for Off-line Signature Verification

Jean-Pierre Drouhard, Robert Sabourin and Mario Godbout

Laboratoire d'imagerie et de modélisation tridimensionnelle
École de technologie supérieure
Département de génie de la production automatisée
4750, avenue Henri-Julien, Montréal (Québec), H2T 2C8, CANADA

Abstract

This paper addresses the problems related to the design of a neural network classifier used in the first stage of an Automatic Handwritten Signature Verification System (AHSVS). We used the directional Probability Density Function (PDF) as a global shape vector, and its discriminating power was enhanced by a pretreatment. The training phase of the BackPropagation Network (BPN) was conducted by using the global classification error in memorization and in generalization. To improve the global performance of the BPN classifier, various rejection criteria were evaluated and the number of hidden neurons optimized by means of experimental protocols. The BPN classifier is better than the threshold classifier, and compares favourably with the k Nearest Neighbour classifier.

1. Introduction

The design of a complete Automatic Handwritten Signature Verification System (AHSVS) that will be able to take into account all classes of forgeries is a very difficult task [1]. Since random and simple forgeries represent almost 95 % of the cases usually encountered in practice [2], a better solution might be to subdivide the verification process in such a way as to rapidly eliminate gross forgeries. The first stage of the AHSVS would be responsible for this rapid elimination and the second stage used only in complicated cases. To eliminate only random and simple forgeries, a characteristic dealing with the overall shape of handwritten signatures seems appropriate. Accordingly, we have chosen to use the directional Probability Density Function (PDF) as a global shape vector [3]. Its discriminating power is not optimum because, even if it is invariant in translation and in scale, it is not invariant in rotation. To make a rapid decision, we have chosen to use a Neural Network (NN) as a signature classifier. Indeed, once trained, unlike conventional classifiers such as the k Nearest Neighbour (kNN) classifier, it has a very fast response time since it does not have to memorize all signature specimens. However, the training phase of these classifiers is a relatively difficult task in this application. As a matter of fact, we must know a priori all the false signatures and have many examples prior to training. In addition, due to the very high variability of handwritten signatures, the separation between true and false signatures is not a sharp one. This results in very long convergence times and the overall performance will never be perfect. Nevertheless, as shown in a feasibility study [4], these difficulties can be diminished if some precautions are taken.

2. Neural network classifier

Neural Networks (NN) present a computational paradigm for constructing classifiers that can perform as accurately as conventional techniques [5]. For the first stage of the AHSVS, we used a completely connected feed-forward neural network with the classical backpropagation learning algorithm, more simply known as the BackPropagation Network (BPN). However, with the BPN the training phase is critical, especially when the data to be classified are not clearly distinguishable and when there are not enough examples to conduct training. In this case, the training phase can be very long and it may even be impossible to obtain an acceptable performance. Since this is the case for our application (few signatures with high variability), we will define a criterion for stopping the training phase. After that, we will evaluate several rejection methods to improve the decision taken by this kind of classifier. Finally, we will adjust the number of neurons in the hidden layer of the BPN in order to increase the global performance of the first stage of the AHSVS.

2.1. Backpropagation network definition

The BPN is a multilayered neural network with an input layer that receives the data to be classified, an output layer that gives the result of the classification, and one or more hidden layers that are used to represent the domain's knowledge. Each layer contains

0-7803-1901-X/94 $4.00 ©1994 IEEE

several neurons which are fully interconnected to the neurons of the next layer via a weight. Since network weights are initially undetermined, a training process is needed to set their values. To do this, a learning law is used to modify weight values based on an output error signal propagated back through the network. From random initial values, the weights are changed according to this learning law that uses a learning rate and a smoothing rate which sometimes allows a faster convergence of the training phase. This learning law is applied for each of the training pairs (input pattern and desired output pattern) and stopped when the error (individual or global) is reduced below a preestablished limit.

To build a BPN, there are many parameters to choose from dealing with the network size or the learning law. Unfortunately, there is no way to determine them rigorously since they are strongly dependent on the application. The number of neurons on the input layer (N_i) is eighteen, which corresponds to the dimension of the PDF vector after applying a pretreatment. The goal of pretreatment on the full directional PDF is to enhance its discriminating power. A classifier will be more efficient if the dimension of the input vector is not too big (unnecessary data) and if the variations in the input vector are not too abrupt (noisy data). Unfortunately, the full directional PDF does not have these characteristics. So, pretreatment including filtering and compression, must be made. To find the pretreatment that improves the discriminating power of the directional PDF the most, we must use a classifier. We cannot use a NN classifier since its training and its performance depend strongly on the input vector (dimension and noise). So, we have to choose from among the conventional classifiers. Even though this requires a great deal of computer time when the reference set is enough large, the kNN classifier was selected because it permits the evaluation of a lower limit of the total error rate when the maximum available information is kept in memory [6]. To find the best pretreatment, an experimental protocol was developed and a rigorous analysis with statistical methods (ANOVA and LSD tests) was carried out [7]. From this analysis, we retained the integration filter with a compression step of ten. By applying this pretreatment on the full directional PDF, we increase its discriminating power roughly twofold and, overall, we reduce the input vector dimension from 180 to 18. The number of neurons on the output layer (N_o) is two since we have two classes (ω_1 and ω_2) and we want to study various rejection methods. The number of hidden layers was set to one since generally a single hidden layer is sufficient for most applications. Up to now, only rules of thumb have been proposed to determine the number of neurons on the hidden layer (N_h). We have arbitrarily set N_h = 12, a number included between the maximum and the minimum proposed by the various methods. Concerning the learning law, there are two parameters to choose: the learning rate and the smoothing rate. Again, there is no way to find a rigorous value for these parameters. Consequently, after a few preliminary trials, we arbitrarily decided to settle the learning rate = 0.6 and the smoothing rate = 0.0. In order to facilitate the start of the training phase, the weights was initialized to random values in the -0.1 and 0.1 range, and a bias term was used for the hidden and output layers to avoid a saturation of the output of the neurons [5]. We have normalized between 0 and 1 all training, test and validation sets used by the BPN classifier to improve the convergence time of the BPN during the training phase [8].

2.2. Data set definition

A standard signature database of 40 signatures written by 20 individuals (800 images) is used in this study. For the design of the NN classifier, the first 20 signatures were used to build the training set, and the last 20 signatures were divided into two groups to build the test set (first 10) and the validation set (last 10). The training set was composed of 280 examples: 140 related to the genuine signatures of an individual (class ω_1) and other 140 related to random forgeries defined as a subset of signatures from all the other individuals (class ω_2). For each writer, the 140 examples in class ω_1 were obtained by rotating all the full directional PDF issued from its 20 reference signatures in a circular fashion from -6° to +6° in 2° increments. This was done to increase the number of examples in class ω_1 that facilitate the training phase of the NN classifier, and to introduce a pseudo-invariance in rotation for the directional PDF which is, by definition, already invariant in translation and in scale. In the case of class ω_2, the 140 examples were obtained by choosing 7 or 8 reference signatures at random from 19 other individuals. The cardinality of classes ω_1 and ω_2 is equal in order not to favour one class over the other. The test and validation sets were built up in the same way. They were composed of 105 examples: 10 genuine signatures (class ω_1) and 95 signatures taken at random from all the other writers (class ω_2). The 10 examples of class ω_1 are the 10 signatures of one individual, and the 95 examples of class ω_2 are 5 random examples of 19 other individuals. The cardinality of class ω_2 were reduced to offset the diminution in the cardinality of class ω_1, but not too much in order not to affect the accuracy of the performance measure. Unlike the training and test sets, the validation set is not used to design the NN classifier, but only to compare the performances of each NN configuration.

2.3. Performance measures

The performance of each classifier is evaluated globally for the 20 writers and for 25 experiments for which the training and test sets are changed each time. Thus, in each experiment, class ω_1 will be always the same, but class ω_2 will be always different. In this way, it is possible to reduce the bias that may have been introduced by particular random forgeries. Classifier performance is measured by means of the total error rate ϵ_t expressed in terms of ϵ_1 (type I error rate, the false classification of genuine signatures) and ϵ_2 (type II error rate, the false classification of random forgeries) and $P[\omega_i]$ the a priori probability of classes ω_i, which is set at 0.5 in our case: $\epsilon_t = ((\epsilon_1 \times P[\omega_1]) + (\epsilon_2 \times P[\omega_2]))$. When appropriate, we use the total rejection rate R_t which is obtained with an equation similar to the latter one where error rates ϵ_i are substituted with rejection rates R_i (R_1 rejection of genuine signatures and R_2 rejection of random forgeries). Finally, in order to take into account in a single parameter the total error and rejection rates, a reliability factor [9] ($RF = [100 - \epsilon_t - R_t] / [100 - R_t]$) is used to find the best configuration of the NN classifier.

3. Training method

3.1. Definition

It is well known that the training phase is crucial in the design of a NN classifier, especially when we use a BPN. The major difficulty is to decide on what basis to stop training. For the BPN, training is conducted in the supervised mode, that is, during the training phase we give the input pattern and its desired output pattern, and it is the difference between this and the actual output pattern that is used to adjust the weights. When this difference is small enough, we can consider that the network has correctly learned this example. We can thus use this error value ϵ to stop training when it is lower than a preestablished limit (ideally 0) for all examples included in the training set. However, it is not always possible to reach this stopping criterion, especially when the input data are not clearly separated. A variant of this method, which takes this problem into account, is to stop training when the Root Mean Square (RMS) error on the training set is lower than a fixed threshold (ideally 0). This very popular method was not selected because it is not well suited to our application. Indeed, it is not absolutely necessary for us to have a small RMS error to obtain an acceptable performance of the classifier. In other words, we do not want the BPN to learn to give the exact output level but to make a good decision. This may be done well before the RMS error becomes weak. Consequently, we have based our stopping criterion on the performance measure ϵ_t defined in section 2.3. Thus, the network weights were adjusted for each example of the training set, and once all examples have been presented to the network (later referred to as a presentation), we freeze the weights and we evaluate ϵ_t on this training set (later referred to as ϵ_{tm}). In this way, we measure the memorization performance of the NN classifier. But the first objective of the NN classifier is to have a good generalization performance, that is, on examples not seen during the training phase. It is thus logical to stop training on the generalization performance measure of the NN classifier. To do this, we evaluate ϵ_t on the test set (later referred to as ϵ_{tg}). The drawback of the BPN which is called the "overtraining phenomenon"([10]) implies that we must stop training when ϵ_{tg} goes through a global minimum. We have not retained this criterion since preliminary results showed that for our data ϵ_{tg} was quite noisy and the curve was relatively flat after a few hundred presentations, and that the overtraining phenomenon was often imperceptible even after many thousands of presentations. Under these conditions, it would be best to stop training as soon as ϵ_{tm} and ϵ_{tg} are both almost stable. However, this method needs a great deal of computing time and is very unstable when the data are noisy. For these reasons, we decided to stop training when ϵ_{tg} is stable for all twenty writers. This consists of finding the number of presentations ($NBP = T_p$) after which the generalization performance for each writer is not significantly improved with longer training. Nevertheless, in some cases the training phase could be greatly reduced if we stopped it when the memorization and generalization performances are acceptable, that is, when $\epsilon_{tm} < T_m$ **and** $\epsilon_{tg} < T_g$. In summary, the stopping criterion adopted in this study is the following: "The training phase will be stopped when ($\epsilon_{tm} < T_m$ **and** $\epsilon_{tg} < T_g$) **or** when $NBP > T_p$."

3.2. Determination of T_m, T_g and T_p

Since we do not want to impose a limit to the NN classifier's performance either in memorization or in generalization, T_m and T_g must be set to 0. In this way, the NN classifier so obtained will always be the best one. Moreover, if this condition is met first, the NN classifier will be perfect both in memorization and in generalization. T_p, the maximum number of presentations used in the training phase, is determined by means of an experimental protocol [7]. Fig.1 illustrates the results found with this experimental protocol. We can see that the mean global error curves for ϵ_{tg} and ϵ_{tm} are very noisy, that the standard deviation (SD) of these curves is weak enough to justify a posteriori the 25 experiments and that ϵ_{tg} is more stable than ϵ_{tm} and, overall, sharply higher ($\epsilon_{tg} \approx 4\%$ and $\epsilon_{tm} \approx 0.3\%$), thus confirming the choice of ϵ_{tg} for finding T_p. To find T_p for which the slope of this curve is very weak, we

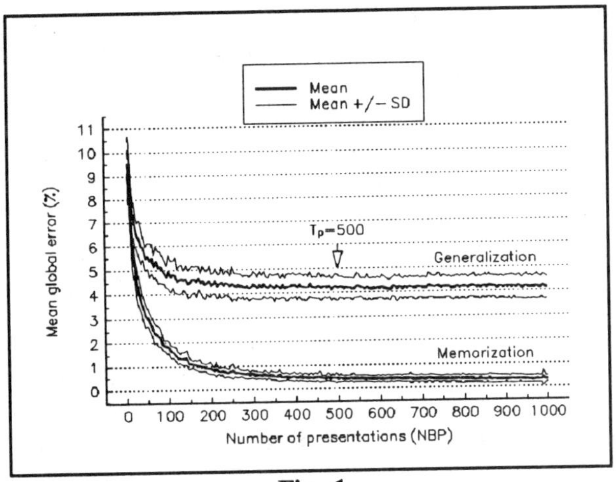

Fig. 1

have smoothed this curve by curve fitting. We have tried the two following slope values 10^{-3} and 10^{-4} and the resulting T_p values were 250 and 650, respectively. As we can see in Fig.1, the first value is quite low and the second one is a little too high. So, we have set T_p at 500 to obtain a sufficiently stable curve without excessive computation time.

4. Rejection criteria

4.1. Definition

For systems not requiring an immediate decision, the addition of a rejection criterion to the decision rule allows significant improvement in the classifier's performance by refusing to classify doubtful cases [11]-[12]. However, even if the cost of a rejection is lower than that of an error [11], the rejection rate must be as weak as possible, for two reasons. The first is that we can also reject good decisions and if the rejection rate of good decisions becomes higher than that of bad decisions, the classifier performance will be decreased instead of increased. The second concerns classifier utility. Indeed, in an extreme case, the classifier can have an error rate of 0% but a rejection rate of 100%. In this case, the classifier is useless. A way to take this phenomenon into account is to use the reliability factor (RF) as defined in section 2.3. With this measure, we consider the error rate as well as the rejection rate in evaluating the classifier's performance.

The definition of all rejection criteria used in this study is as follows: RC1 = (MAX $\{o_1, o_2\} < T_M$); RC2 = (ABS $\{o_1 - o_2\} < T_A$); RC3 = ([MAX $\{o_1, o_2\}$ - MIN $\{o_1, o_2\}$] / [MAX $\{o_1, o_2\}$] $< T_{R1}$); RC4 = ([MAX $\{o_1, o_2\}$ - MIN $\{o_1, o_2\}$] / [MIN $\{o_1, o_2\}$] $< T_{R2}$); RC5 = (RC1 **and** RC2), and RC6 = (RC1 **and** RC3) where o_1 and o_2 are the output levels for classes ω_1 and ω_2 respectively and where T_M, T_A, T_{R1} and T_{R2} are adjustable thresholds. The first two are very popular [11]-[12] and deal with the highest output level (RC1) and with the absolute difference between the output levels (RC2) respectively. The next two concern the relative difference between the output levels, either with respect to the maximum value (RC3) or with respect to the minimum value (RC4). Finally, the last two are a combination of the first one and one of the following two. For all rejection criteria, the decision rule used is of the following form: **IF** RC? = YES **THEN** the observation is not classified **ELSE** it is.

4.2. Evaluation

First, we have examined how the rejection area varies when we change the threshold of rejection criteria RC1 to RC4. Except for RC4, the rejection area is a linear function of the threshold value which varies between 0 and 1. This also shows that RC3 and RC4 are equivalent, since in each case we can find a threshold value that gives exactly the same rejection area. Given that we are more familiar with a relative variation included between 0 and 100%, we have used only RC3 in this study. Based on this examination, it is not possible to choose among the rejection criteria RC1 to RC3. Consequently, we have to evaluate them by means of an experimental protocol. We have also examined whether or not a combination of RC1 and RC2 (RC5) or RC3 (RC6) can improve classifier quality. The various rejection criteria were evaluated by using the mean value and standard deviation over the 500 files of 105 examples for ϵ_t, R_t and RF of the NN classifier obtained by varying the thresholds T_M, T_A and T_{R1} for the rejection criteria RC1, RC2, RC3, RC5 and RC6 respectively. All these results show a better performance of the NN classifier when the threshold values increase. This better performance, corresponding to a higher reliability (RF) and a lower total error rate (ϵ_t), is obtained at the expense of a total rejection rate (R_t) that is clearly higher. Unlike RC2 and RC3, RC1 becomes effective only when the threshold T_M is higher than 0.5 (Fig.2). We can also conclude that RC1, RC2

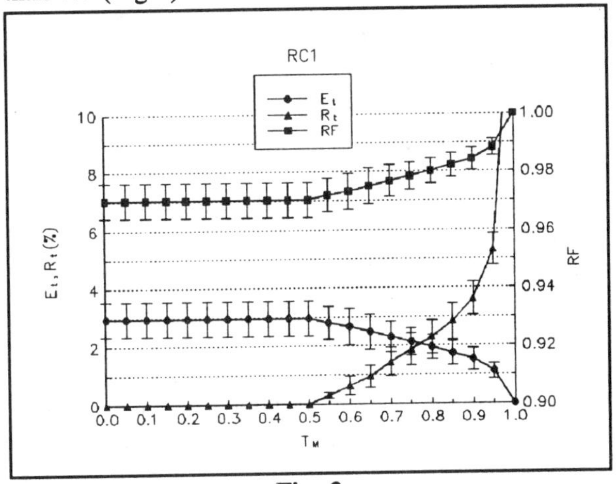

Fig. 2

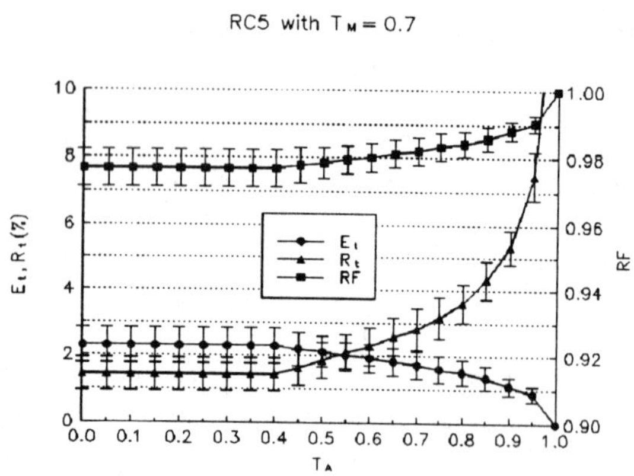

Fig. 3

and RC3 are equivalent when applied to our data. As for RC5 and RC6, they simply show that the addition of RC2 or RC3 to RC1 is only effective when the threshold T_A or T_{R1} is higher than a value for which it allows a better performance than that already obtained with the threshold T_M (Fig.3). This means that below this particular threshold T_A or T_{R1}, the rejection criteria RC1 and RC2 or RC3 reject exactly the same examples. All these results can easily be explained by the fact that our output levels are complementary. Indeed, under these conditions, the output level of one of the output neurons can never be lower than 0.5. This is why the threshold T_M must be higher than 0.5 to be effective. It is also for this reason that the rejection criteria RC1, RC2 and RC3 are equivalent. Finally, we can also explain the results of RC5 and RC6 with the complimentary phenomenon. In conclusion, we can say that, due to the output complementarity, the rejection criteria RC1, RC2 and RC3 are strictly equivalent and the rejection criteria RC5 and RC6 are only useful when we want to impose a lower limit on the NN classifier performance via RC1. Consequently, the rejection criterion RC1 has been chosen only because of its practical aspect. We now have to determine the threshold T_M, but this determination must be made with caution. Indeed, a careful examination of our results showed that if the threshold T_M was too small we could accept bad classifications. On the other hand, if we want to refuse these bad classifications with a higher threshold T_M this often leads to the elimination of good decisions. This proves that the application of a rejection criterion may degrade the NN classifier's performance, and also indicates that the threshold value must be high enough but not too high. Consequently, we chose the threshold T_M according to the following heuristic: "Obtain the best performance with an acceptable rejection rate". For our AHSVS application, a rejection rate of 5% could be considered acceptable. In this case, we find a value of 0.94 for the threshold T_M. In addition, the NN classifier's performance with the RC1 rejection criterion using a threshold T_M of 0.94 (ϵ_t = 1.22%, R_t = 4.83%, RF = 0.987) was also compared to that obtained without a rejection criterion (ϵ_t = 2.96%, RF = 0.97). The introduction of a rejection criterion improves the reliability (RF) of the AHSVS slightly but sharply decreases its total error rate (ϵ_t) via the type I error rate (ϵ_1). In other words, the rejection criterion makes it possible to reduce the false classification of genuine signatures greatly. Nevertheless, there are always genuine signatures that are more difficult to classify with our NN classifier since ϵ_1 is higher than ϵ_2 without a rejection criterion or R_1 is higher than R_2 with a rejection criterion.

5. Neural network optimization

Essentially, there are two ways to optimize a BPN: 1) we can adjust the learning algorithm [13] and 2) we can modify its structure before [14] or during [15] the training phase. In this study we only performed the BPN optimization on the structural aspect of the network. Unfortunately, there are no theoretical means for finding the optimum number of hidden neurons (N_{ho}). However, we know its upper limit, which is $N_{hm} = 2N_i+1$ [10] thus in our case N_{hm} = 37. Consequently, N_{ho} must be found by experimentation in which N_h varies gradually between 0 and N_{hm}. Moreover, to see if the rejection criterion had an effect on N_{ho}, we also conducted this experimentation without rejection. But in order to reduce the simulation time we have varied N_h between 0 and 36 with an increment of 4.

The results of this experimentation showed that the BPN performance clearly improves as soon as we have a hidden layer, and that, for our database, the effect of the number of hidden neurons is not very pronounced with or without a rejection criterion (Fig.4). In order to find the best configuration, a statistical analysis is necessary since the variations are weak. We therefore did an ANOVA test to show whether or not there was a significant difference between the configurations, and a LSD test to find the best configuration. The results of the ANOVA test emphasize two main points: first, with or without a rejection criterion, there is a significant difference between the configurations; second, the use of this rejection criterion reduced twofold the variability of the error rate and the reliability factor at the expense of a very large variability in the rejection rate. The results of the LSD test show that the regrouping obtained with the error rate (ϵ_t) and the reliability factor (RF) are identical with or without the rejection criterion. In addition, the use of a rejection criterion suppresses only the last configuration of the regrouping obtained without a rejection criterion. But, for the

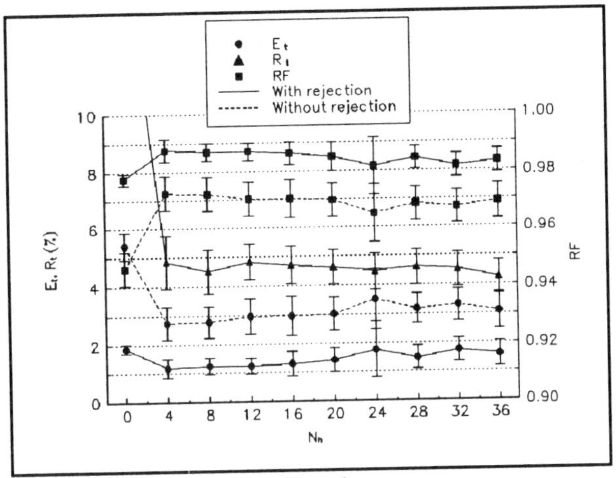

Fig. 4

rejection rate, the regrouping is very different. This result can be explained by the fact that the rejection rate has a higher variability, as indicated by the ANOVA test. Finally, the configuration with 8 hidden neurons has the best combination of the error (ϵ_t = 1.24%) and rejection (R_t = 4.5%) rates and reliability factor (RF = 0.987).

6. Conclusion

The main objective of this work was to determine whether or not a NN classifier could be used in the design of the first stage of a complete AHSVS. To do this, we have chosen the directional PDF as a global shape vector and the BackPropagation Network (BPN). In order to better assess the potential of the BPN classifier, we performed a comparative study [7] with the kNN classifier, which should give an upper limit for the performance, and the threshold classifier which is very popular in spite of its failings. Since these latter do not use a rejection criterion in making their decision, we used a BPN classifier without the rejection criterion previously defined. The conclusion of this comparative study is that the BPN classifier (ϵ_t = 3.22%) behaves better than the threshold classifier with its best reference set of 5 examples (ϵ_t = 5.61%) and worse than the kNN classifier (ϵ_t = 1.68%). In conclusion, we can say that, once trained, the BPN classifier compares favourably with the kNN classifier since it has almost the same performance but with a shorter response time at generalization, especially if we use a hardware implementation of the BPN classifier. The fact of having obtained a mean error rate of around 3% with the directional PDF, which is not the best global shape vector for a signature, clearly shows that the BPN classifier is a very good candidate for the design of the first stage of a complete AHSVS.

Acknowledgments

This work was supported in part by a PSIR grant from the École de technologie supérieure to Jean-Pierre Drouhard and Robert Sabourin, and by grant OGP010456 to Robert Sabourin from the NSERC of Canada. Master's student Mario Godbout also received a scholarship from the École de technologie supérieure.

References

[1] R. Sabourin, Une Approche de Type Compréhension de Scène Appliquée au Problème de la Vérification Automatique de l'Identité par l'Image de la Signature Manuscrite, *Ph.D. Thesis*, École Polytechnique de Montréal (1990).

[2] W.R. Harrison, *Suspect Documents, Their Scientific Examination*, Nelson-Hall Publishers, Chicago (1981).

[3] R. Sabourin and J.-P. Drouhard, Off-line Signature Verification Using Directional PDF and Neural Networks, *Proceedings of the 11th ICPR*, The Hague, 321-325 (1992).

[4] R. Sabourin, J.-P. Drouhard, L. Gagné and N. Paquet, Automatic Handwritten Signature Verification Using Directional PDF and Neural Networks: A Feasibility Study, *Proceedings of the Conference and Exhibition on Industrial Automation*, Montréal, 20.17-20.20 (1992).

[5] D.J. Burr, Experiments on Neural Net Recognition of Spoken and Written Text, *IEEE Transactions on Acoustics, Speech, and Signal Processing* **36**, 1162-1168 (1988).

[6] K. Fukunaga, *Introduction to Statistical Pattern Recognition (Second Edition)*, Academic Press Inc., New York (1990).

[7] M. Godbout, Évaluation de l'applicabilité des réseaux de neurones à la classification des images de signatures manuscrites, *Mémoire de Maîtrise*, École de technologie supérieure (1993).

[8] J. Maren, D. Jones and F. Franklin, Configuring and Optimizing the Back-Propagation Network, in *Handbook of Neural Computing Applications*, Academic Press, Santiago (1990).

[9] L. Xu, A. Krzyzak and C.Y. Suen, Methods of Combining Multiple Classifiers and Their Applications to Handwriting Recognition, *IEEE Trans. on Systems, Man, and Cybernetics* **22**, 418-435 (1992).

[10] R. Hecht-Nielsen, *Neurocomputing*, Addison-Wesley, New York (1990).

[11] M. Nadler and E.P. Smith, *Pattern recognition engineering*, John Wiley & Son, New York (1993).

[12] B. Dubuisson, *Diagnostic et reconnaissance des formes*, Hermès, Paris (1990).

[13] A.V. Ooyen and B. Neinhuis, Improving the convergence of the backpropagation algorithm, *Neural Networks* **5**, 465-471 (1992).

[14] E.B. Baum and D. Haussier, What size net gives valid generalization?, *Neural Computation* **1**, 151-160 (1989).

[15] T. Ash, Dynamic node creation in backpropagation networks, *Proceedings of the International Joint Conference on Neural Networks* **2**, 623-628 (1989).

A Performance Evaluation of Texture Measures for Image Classification and Segmentation Using the Cascade-Correlation Architecture

Marijke F. Augusteijn (mfa@antero.uccs.edu) and Laura E. Clemens
University of Colorado at Colorado Springs

Abstract: The performance of several texture-based measures is compared with respect to their ability to classify and segment images. Texture measures considered are: co-occurrence matrices, features derived from the Fourier spectrum and Gabor filters. The performance of raw pixel gray level values and gray level averages as classification features is also investigated. The Cascade-Correlation Neural Network architecture is used as a classifier. It was found that certain measures derived from the Fourier spectrum outperformed other types. The size of the fragments used for classification played a dominant role with respect to performance.

Introduction

Image segmentation is the technique in computer vision which partitions an image into units which are homogeneous with respect to one or more characteristics. There are two basic strategies: region growing and boundary detection. Each strategy may or may not assign labels to the various regions. When labels are assigned, segmentation becomes equivalent to classification. Neighboring image fragments are classified and will be merged if found to belong to the same class. If, on the other hand, neighboring fragments are classified differently, the existence of a boundary between them is inferred. The methods investigated in this study are all texture-based classification techniques. A classifier is trained to distinguish a pre-defined set of textures. The trained classifier can then scan an image consisting of these same textures and assign a label to each image fragment. Fragments are assumed to contain a single texture. Their size will often be determined by the expected average size of the segments in the image. If the image is known to vary significantly over small distances then the size of the fragments must be small. However, a small size will constrain accurate texture characterization.

A neural network can be used as the classifier. Neural networks have been shown to perform as well or better than other classification techniques. A comparison of neural networks to other methods, like K-nearest neighbor and discriminant analysis, has shown that neural networks can achieve equal performance using a much smaller set of training data (Hepner, 1990). This study will use this approach for the segmentation of a set of Brodatz textures (Brodatz, 1966). The objective is to determine which kind of input data for the neural network leads to the best performance. A set of statistical texture measures will be compared with measures derived from the Fourier spectrum and Gabor filters. Alternatively, it is possible to use the raw pixel gray level values as input patterns or simple features which can be immediately derived from these pixels. Since neural networks are themselves feature extractors and use their hidden node activations as features for classification, it might be advantageous to allow them to extract features directly from the pixels rather than from a different, user-defined feature set. The performance of this simple approach will be compared with that of the more sophisticated texture measures. The influence of the size of the fragments on classification performance will also be investigated.

A feedforward architecture, like back-propagation (Rumelhart *et al.*, 1986), is appropriate for this application. However, standard back-propagation is relatively slow and requires the assignment of a suitable number of hidden units. Determining this number is a matter of trial and error. Many researchers have attempted to improve on this architecture. One of these newer networks, Cascade-Correlation (Fahlman and Lebiere, 1990), is used in this study. Its main distinguishing feature is its dynamic character: it builds an internal structure suitable for its task during training. This architecture is also appreciably faster than standard backpropagation.

The Classification Experiments

All experiments were performed with nine textures from the Brodatz atlas showing different kinds of weaves. The performance of measures extracted from image fragments of sizes 8x8 and 32x32 was studied. The smaller size pushes the limits of texture representation but this size is often required for the segmentation of natural scenes. For example, in the satellite image ground cover study by Augusteijn *et al.* (1993) a fragment size of 8x8 was the largest possible size for which a sufficient number of homogeneous fragments could be found. Twenty fragments of this size were randomly selected from each texture. The larger size is commonly used for the extraction of texture measures. For example, Ohanian and Dubes (1992) use this size in their comparative study. For this size,

0-7803-1901-X/94 $4.00 ©1994 IEEE

ten fragments were selected from each texture. Each set of fragments was partitioned into a training and a test set of equal size. Four different classes of inputs were compared. They are raw pixel patterns and average gray level values derived from these pixels, co-occurrence measures as introduced by Haralick *et al.* (1973), features derived from the Fourier spectrum, and Gabor filters. The Cascade-Correlation network was always trained five times on the same set of data. The weights of each network were randomly initialized which resulted in slightly different performance of each trained network. Both the range of performances and the average value are reported in percentages for each experiment.

Pixel Patterns and Gray Level Averages

The simplest way to characterize the variability in an image segment is by noting the gray level values of the raw pixels. This set of gray values then becomes the feature set on which classification will be based. An important advantage of this approach is the speed which with images can be processed since features need not be calculated. A disadvantage is the size of the feature set. This approach is only feasible for small image fragments since it is important to keep the size of the networks as small as possible. Oversized networks are inclined to store specific details of the training set and often show poor performance on a test set (Baum and Haussler, 1989). Therefore, only very small fragments of size 5x5 were used to establish the performance of raw pixel patterns. The results are shown in the leftmost column of Table 1.

It is also possible to condense the pixel information into a small set of averages. This method will be referred to as Gray Level Averaging (GLA). In this approach, the gray level value of a pixel centrally located in an image fragment is considered a feature and additional features are provided by the average gray level values of increasingly larger neighborhoods. Five features were used in the case of fragment size 8x8. They are the gray level of a pixel centrally located in the fragment, the average gray levels of its 3x3 and 5x5 neighborhoods, and the average gray level and standard deviation of the entire fragment. The performance of this set is shown in the middle column of Table 1. The same technique was used on fragments of size 32x32. Sixteen averages were calculated in this case and combined with the standard deviation of the gray levels. Its performance is shown in the rightmost column of Table 1.

Table 1. Performance of Pixel Patterns and Averaging Features

Performance Range for 5x5 Pixel Patterns	Average Performance for 5x5 Pixel Patterns	Performance Range for GLA Applied to 8x8 Fragments	Average Performance for GLA Applied to 8x8 Fragments	Performance Range for GLA Applied to 32x32 Fragments	Average Performance for GLA Applied to 32x32 Fragments
33.3 - 37.8	35.4	54.4 - 60.6	57.1	46.7 - 51.1	49.6

Co-occurrence Features

Co-occurrence features were introduced by Haralick *et al.* (1973). This method assumes that the texture information is contained in the spatial relationships between gray levels and can be specified by a set of gray-tone spatial-dependence matrices called co-occurrence matrices. These matrices can be computed for various angular relationships and distances between pixel pairs in the image. A co-occurrence matrix measures the frequency of the simultaneous occurrence of two specified gray levels at two designated relative positions in an image segment. Generally, four different matrices are used, each computing the frequency of gray-level co-occurrence at neighboring positions in four different directions (horizontal, vertical, and along the two diagonal directions of the image). Matrices can be calculated that employ other distances between pixels but this study only considers matrices using pixel neighbors.

The first experiment employed thirteen of the fourteen measures introduced by Haralick *et al.* Only the maximal correlation coefficient, which requires calculation of the second largest eigenvalue of the co-occurrence matrix, was not implemented. These thirteen features were combined with the average value and standard deviation of the gray levels of the image fragment. The performance of these measures is shown in the leftmost column of Table 2 for both fragment sizes. The performance of some subsets of these features was also investigated. The middle column of Table 2 shows the results of the four most popular measures: contrast, homogeneity, correlation, and entropy, combined with the average gray level of the fragment. The rightmost column shows the performance of a subset of nine features which were found most useful in a different study of these texture measures (Augusteijn *et al.*, 1993). The features added to the subset of five are: the standard deviation of the gray levels in the fragment and the sum average, the sum variance, and an information measure of correlation as defined by Haralick *et al.* (1973).

Table 2. Performance of Co-occurrence Measures

Fragment Size	Performance Range for 15 Measures	Average Performance for 15 Measures	Performance Range for Subset of 5 Measures	Average Performance for Subset of 5 Measures	Performance Range for Subset of 9 Measures	Average Performance for Subset of 9 Measures
8x8	56.7 - 63.3	58.9	57.2 - 59.4	58.1	57.2 - 59.4	58.4
32x32	82.2 - 91.1	86.2	82.2 - 86.7	84.0	83.3 - 88.9	85.8

Features Derived from the Fourier Transform

The Fourier transform of an image segment $f(x,y)$ is defined by:

$$F(u,v) = \int_{-\infty}^{\infty}\int_{-\infty}^{\infty} e^{-2\pi i(ux+vy)} f(x,y)dxdy,$$

where u and v are the spatial frequencies in the x and y direction, respectively. The FFT algorithm, when applied to an image fragment, will calculate a complex-valued spectrum of the same size as the image fragment. This algorithm performs a transformation from the spatial coordinates (x,y) to the spatial frequencies (u,v).

The amplitudes of the Fourier power spectrum are calculated as $A = |F| = (FF^*)^{1/2}$, where * denotes the complex conjugate. This real-valued power spectrum is used to provide the feature sets. A set of statistical measures can be defined as follows:

Maximum Magnitude: $Max[A(j,k):(j,k) \neq (0,0)]$,

Average Magnitude (A_M) $\sum_{j,k} A(j,k)/N$,

Energy of Magnitude $\left[\sum_{j,k} A(j,k)^2\right]^{1/2}$,

and Variance of Magnitude $\sum_{j,k}\left[A(j,k) - A_M\right]^2 / N$,

in which N is the number of frequency components of the spectrum. These measures were proposed by Phillips[1] and showed good performance in a previous study (Augusteijn *et al.*, 1993). The results of these four measures, applied to the Brodatz weaves, are shown in the leftmost column of Table 3. It is sometimes advantageous to combine these measures with the average value of the gray levels but the addition of this value did not improve the performance in the current application.

It is also possible to use the amplitudes of a set of selected frequencies as a feature set. A variety of selections was investigated. The set giving the best performance may be problem dependent. Two selections gave good results for the current application. They are the amplitudes of the set of unique frequencies in which one frequency is always 0. This set consists of 7 features for the fragment of size 8x8 and of 15 features for size 32x32. The performance of these sets are shown in the middle column of Table 3. Another possibility for this selection is to find a set of *dominant* frequencies; i. e., a set of frequencies which consistently appear with higher amplitudes than other frequencies in the spectra. The current application did not show a clear-cut set of dominant frequencies. For

[1]Dr. Keith Phillips, Department of Mathematics, Univ. of Colorado at Colorado Springs, private communication

each fragment size, a set of frequencies was selected that seemed to appear with higher amplitudes on the average. For the smaller fragment size, this set consisted of 5 amplitudes and for the larger size a set of 14 amplitudes was selected. The performance of these sets is shown in the rightmost column of Table 3.

Table 3. Performance of Features Derived from the Fourier Spectrum

Fragment Size	Performance Range of the 4 Statistical Measures	Average Performance of the 4 Statistical Measures	Performance Range of Amplitudes with Zero Component	Average Performance of Amplitudes with Zero Component	Performance Range of Amplitudes of Dominant Frequencies	Average Performance of Amplitudes of Dominant Frequencies
8x8	52.8 - 56.7	54.9	50.0 - 55.0	53.8	56.7 - 61.2	58.7
32x32	73.3 - 78.9	76.4	88.9 - 94.4	92.4	93.3 - 94.4	93.8

Gabor Filters

The Gabor kernel has properties which make it attractive as a receptive field for image feature extraction (Lu *et al.*, 1991). A symmetrical, two-dimensional Gabor kernel is the product of a Gaussian-shaped window and a complex exponential term:

$$\Psi(x,y;\sigma,u,v) = \left\{ \exp\frac{-(u^2+v^2)}{2\sigma^2}(x^2+y^2) \right\} \exp i(ux+vy),$$

where (x,y) are the variables representing position in the spatial domain, (u,v) are the spatial frequencies, and σ is the width of the Gaussian. A different width may be used in the x- and y-direction which would give the filter a directional preference. Each Gabor filter is specified by three (or four in the case of different widths) parameters: σ, u, and v and is a function of (x,y). The Gabor transform, $G(x,y)$, of an image fragment, $I(x,y)$, is defined as the convolution of a Gabor kernel Ψ with I:

$$G(u,v) = \iint \Psi(x,y;\sigma,u,v) I(x,y) dx dy.$$

The resultant transform is complex. However, only the magnitude is used because the phase information does not seem to improve classification (Lu *et al.*, 1991).

Each experiment in this category required the selection of a set of spatial frequencies and a Gaussian width. The first two experiments used frequency sets selected from the discrete Fourier spectrum defined in the previous section. A variety of selections was tested; the results of the best-performing sets are shown in Table 4. The left-most column of this table shows the performance of features calculated as the dot product of an image segment and a filter of the same size. Six frequency pairs were used in this experiment. The filters for the small fragments were calculated employing a Gaussian width of 2 pixels and a width of 10 pixels was used for the larger filters. The second experiment used the same filters but calculated an actual convolution in a slightly unusual way. The convolution was performed by extending the filter in all directions and translating the image fragment over the filter. The results of this test are shown in the middle column of Table 4. A standard convolution which is calculated by means of translating a filter over the image fragment was also investigated in the case of the larger fragments. Filters of size 8x8 gave an average performance of only 44%. The additional texture information present in the larger fragments is apparently not used when convolving with a small filter.

A different way to select frequencies is by imposing a dyadic relationship. The resulting filters are believed to be reminiscent to the ones that play a role in biological vision (Lu *et al.*, 1991). The third experiment used these kind of filters. If the orientation of a filter is defined as $\theta = \tan^{-1}(v/u)$ and the "modulation frequency" is given by $\omega_0 = (u^2+v^2)^{1/2}$ then each filter can be expressed in terms of the parameters (θ, ω_0). Each experiment in this category used 24 filters of the same size as the image fragments and employed the magnitudes of the dot product as feature sets. For the small fragments, the parameter values $\omega_0 = \pi, \pi/2, \pi/4, \pi/8$ and θ = 0, 30, 60,

90, 120, and 150 degrees were used. For the larger fragments it was found that the values $\omega_0 = \pi/4, \pi/8, \pi/16, \pi/32$ combined with the same orientations gave better performance. The results are shown in the rightmost column of Table 4.

Table 4. Performance of Gabor Filters

Fragment Size	Performance Range Using a Dot Product	Average Performance Using a Dot Product	Performance Range Using a Convolution	Average Performance Using a Convolution	Performance Range Using Dyadic Filters	Average Performance Using Dyadic Filters
8x8	41.1 - 49.4	46.3	40.6 - 46.1	43.8	60.6 - 63.3	62.2
32x32	67.8 - 76.7	73.6	66.7 - 71.1	68.9	77.8 - 85.6	82.0

Comparison of Texture Measures

When comparing the various texture measures, the most striking fact is the difference in performance between the small and large image fragments. Apparently, the size of the small fragments is insufficient to capture the texture information of the Brodatz weaves. Most measures score in the range of 50 to 60 percent when used with the smaller fragments. The raw pixel patterns score considerably lower but this may be due to the use of even smaller fragments of size 5x5. The GLA method is interesting in the sense that this is the only technique showing higher performance on the smaller segments. The results obtained with Gabor filters are also noteworthy. It is seen that these filters give poor results on the smaller fragment size when a set of frequencies from the Fourier spectrum is used. However, Gabor filters employing a set of dyadic frequencies gave the highest performance on the smaller fragments of all measures investigated in this study. Comparable performance was obtained from co-occurrence measures and from the amplitudes of a carefully selected set of frequencies of the Fourier spectrum. In the case of co-occurrence measures, the number of features did not have much effect on performance. Therefore, the subset of four combined with the average gray level seems to be a good feature set. However, the Gabor filters or Fourier measures are preferred because they require considerably less execution time. It should be noted that the selection of the set of frequencies required for these measures does influence performance and a significant number of experiments may be required to determine this set for a particular type of images. Co-occurrence measures do not have this drawback.

When the fragment size is enlarged, most methods show considerable improvement in performance. A notable exception is the GLA method which actually scored lower. This technique is not a true texture method and although it was shown to work well in some applications (e. g., see Augusteijn *et al.*, 1993), it should always be used with great care. The performance of the amplitudes of a set of selected frequencies of the Fourier spectrum clearly outperformed all other methods for these larger fragments. Again, the selection of the frequency set strongly influenced the performance. The results obtained with the co-occurrence measures are also reasonably good. The Gabor filters scored lower. It is noteworthy that feature calculation by means of a convolution gave lower performance than features calculated as a simple dot product. The performance comparison performed by Ohanian and Dubes (1992) also showed disappointing results for Gabor filters. Many researchers have obtained superior performance from co-occurrence measures (see Augusteijn *et al.* for a comparison with the literature). This study shows that certain Fourier measures can outperform co-occurrence features on certain textures.

In order to show the performance of these texture measures as a segmentation tool, a composite image consisting of the nine weaves was created. This image is shown in Figure 1a. Each weave segment had a size of 352x352 pixels and was scanned with a window size of 32x32. Each image fragment was classified using the best set of Fourier measures and the best set of co-occurrence measures. The performance of several networks trained with these features was observed. The networks trained with the Fourier measures showed consistent performance and scored between 92.2 and 93.4 % correct classification. The performance of the co-occurrence measures showed a much larger spread and scored between 82.9 and 87.9 %. To a large extent, this lower performance was caused by the texture shown in the middle position of the bottom row of Figure 1a. This texture could be classified reasonably well using Fourier measures but classification was very poor when using co-occurrence measures. When this texture was eliminated, the average performance of the co-occurrence measures increased by 3% while the performance of the Fourier measures decreased by about 0.5 %. Although the two sets of measures showed considerable differences in performance on only one of the nine textures used in these experiments, this result draws attention to the fact that the conclusions of performance comparisons of this kind will often depend on the data used. Figures 1b and 1c shows the segmentation for the Fourier and co-occurrence measures, respectively.

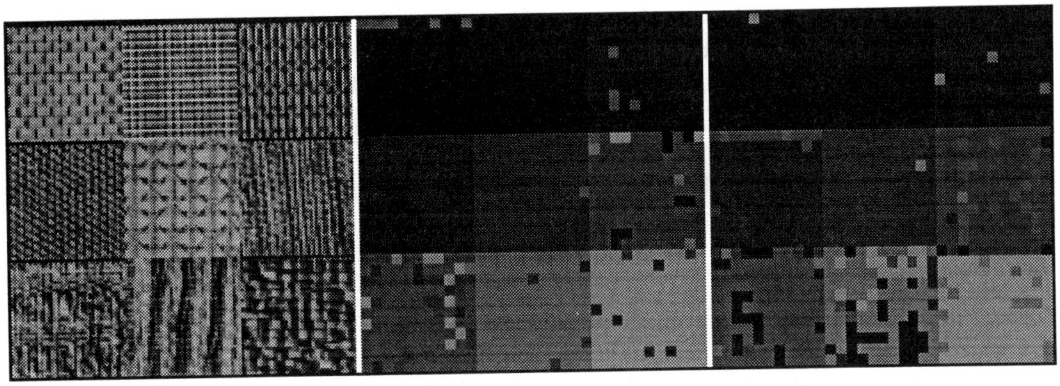

a b c

Figure 1. Segmentation performance of two sets of texture measures: (a) the textures used in the experiments, (b) Fourier features showing a performance of 93.4 %, (c) co-occurrence measures showing a performance of 87.1 %

References

Augusteijn, M. F., Shaw, K. A. and Watson, R. J. (1993). A Study of Neural Network Input Data for Ground Cover Identification in Satellite Images. Proceedings of the International Conference on Artificial Neural Networks (ICANN'93), pp. 1010-1013.

Baum, E. B. and Haussler, D. (1989). What Size Net Gives Valid Generalization? Neural Computation, Vol. 1, pp. 151-160.

Brodatz, P. (1966). Textures: A Photographic Album for Artists and Designers, Dover Publications, Inc. New York, New York.

Fahlman, S. E. and Lebiere, C. (1990). The Cascade-Correlation Learning Architecture. In: Advances in Neural Information Processing Systems 2, D. Touretzky (Ed.), Morgan Kaufmann, San Mateo, pp. 524-532.

Haralick, R. M., Shanmugam, K. and Dinstein, I. (1973). Textural Features for Image Classification. IEEE Transactions on Systems, Man and Cybernetics, Vol. 3, pp. 610-621.

Hepner, G. F. (1990). Artificial Neural Network Classification Using a Minimal Training Set: Comparison to Conventional Supervised Classification. Photogrammetric Engineering and Remote Sensing, Vol. 56, pp. 469-473.

Lu, S., Hernandez, J. E., and Clark, G.A. (1991). Texture Segmentation by Clustering of Gabor Feature Vectors. International Joint Conference on Neural Networks, Vol. I, pp. 683-687.

Ohanian, P. P. and Dubes, R. C. (1992). Performance Evaluation for Four Classes of Textural Features. Pattern Recognition, Vol. 25, pp. 819-833.

Rumelhart, D. E., Hinton, G. E. and Williams, R. J. (1986). Learning Internal Representations by Error Propagation. In: D. E. Rumelhart and J. L. McClelland (Eds) Parallel Distributed Processing: Explorations in the Microstructure of Cognition, Vol. 1: Foundations. Cambridge, Massachusetts: MIT Press, pp. 318-362.

Scale and Rotation Invariant Pattern Recognition using Complex-Log Mapping and Translation Invariant Neural Network

Heung-Ho Lee, Hee-Yong Kwon*, and Hee-Yeung Hwang**

Department of Electrical Engineering, Chung-Nam National University,
Yusung-gu, Taejon, KOREA (302-764)
Tel : +82-42-821-5656, Fax : +82-42-823-7970
E-mail : hykwon@basia.kotel.co.kr
* Research Center, Korea Telecom,
** Department of Electronic Engineering, Ho-Seo University

Abstract

In this paper, we propose a scale and rotation invariant pattern recognition system using Complex-Log Mapping(CLM) and Translation Invariant Neural Network(TINN). CLM is very useful for extracting scale and rotation invariant features. However, the results are given in a wrap-around translated form, which requires subsequent wrap-translation invariant recognition steps. This problem can be solved by using an augmented second order neural network(SONN). It requires, however, a connection complexity $O(n^2)$ for input feature extraction which is too high to be implemented. The proposed method reduces the connection complexity to $O(n*\log(n))$ by using TINN. Experimental results show that the recognition performance of the proposed method is almost the same as that of SONN while its network size is significantly reduced.

I. Introduction

Scale and rotation invariant pattern recognition is a difficult problem because it is essentially third order [1]. CLM is useful for such problems because it can easily extract scale and rotation invariant features [2]. But its drawback is that the results are given in a wrap-around translated form. The following recognition step should be wrap-translation invariant. To solve this problem, conventional approaches use three stage system composed of CLM, Fourier Transform and multilayer perceptron(MLP) [3] or two stage system composed of CLM and second order neural network(SONN) [4]. The former is too complex and not a pure neural network solution. The latter is the first pure neural network solution, however, it has too high connection complexity $O(n^2)$ to be implemented. It is necessary to reduce the connection complexity for realistic applications. In this paper, we propose a new scale and rotation invariant pattern recognition method using CLM, TINN, and MLP. The recognition performance of the proposed method is almost the same as that of SONN while it has a lower complexity $O(n*\log(n))$ compared with that of SONN. Also it can be implemented with pure neural network. The paper is organized as follows : In the next section, we introduce M-transform which is one of the well-known translation invariant transforms. In Section III, we present a wrap-around translation invariant network on 2-dimension. Also we propose a scale and rotation invariant pattern recognition method. Finally, experimental results are shown.

0-7803-1901-X/94 $4.00 ©1994 IEEE

II. M-transform : Translation Invariant Transform

The CLM maps scale and rotational transformations into positional translations with possible wrap-translations. Therefore, the subsequent recognition step should be invariant to such wrap-translations. M-transform is one of the well-known translation invariant transforms [5] and provides a wrap-translation invariance. Also, it can be easily implemented by neural networks. Therefore, we can construct a scale and rotation invariant pattern recognition system using CLM, TINN and MLP. In the following, we introduce the M-transform and describe its neural network implementation method.

Let X be an one-dimensional input pattern vector such as X := {xi}, i = 0,1, .. ,N-1. Then the M-transform of X when N = 8 is shown in Figure 1.

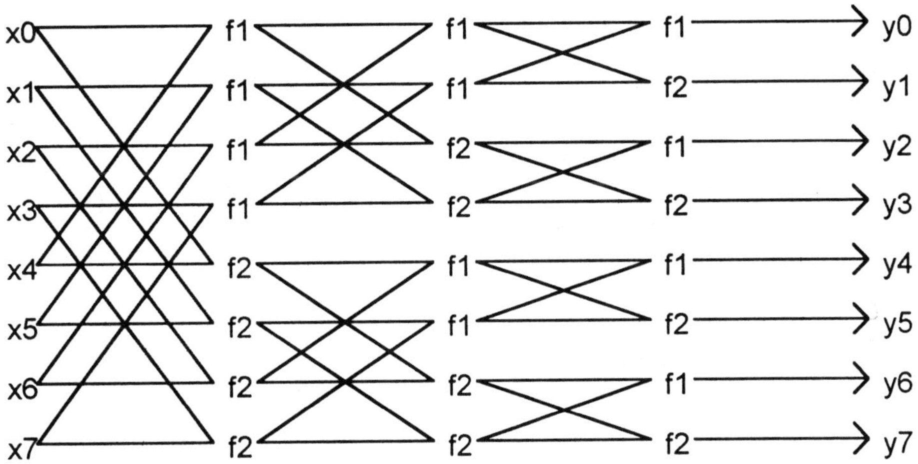

Figure 1. The M-transform of the input X when N = 8.
(f1 : AND network, f2 : OR network, y : output)

In Figure 1, we can easily replace the f1 and f2 with AND and OR neural networks, respectively [6]. Then the above network can be regarded as a neural network which has wrap translation invariant property on one dimensional(1D) space. From now on, we represent this M-transform network as 1D TINN.

III. Scale and Rotation Invariant Pattern Recognition Networks

For image pattern recognition, both the input and the output of a CLM are two-dimensional. Therefore, we need a wrap-translation invariant property for 2D space. If the input pattern passes through the horizontally (vertically) arranged 1D TINNs, H_TIN (V_TIN), the output becomes horizontal (vertical) wrap-translation invariant on 2D space. Therefore, if H_TIN and V_TIN are applied to input pattern sequentially, the output becomes wrap-translation invariant on 2D space. If the order of the applications of H_TIN and V_TIN are changed, the ouptuts are not the same. To solve this problem, we propose the following network shown in Figure 2.

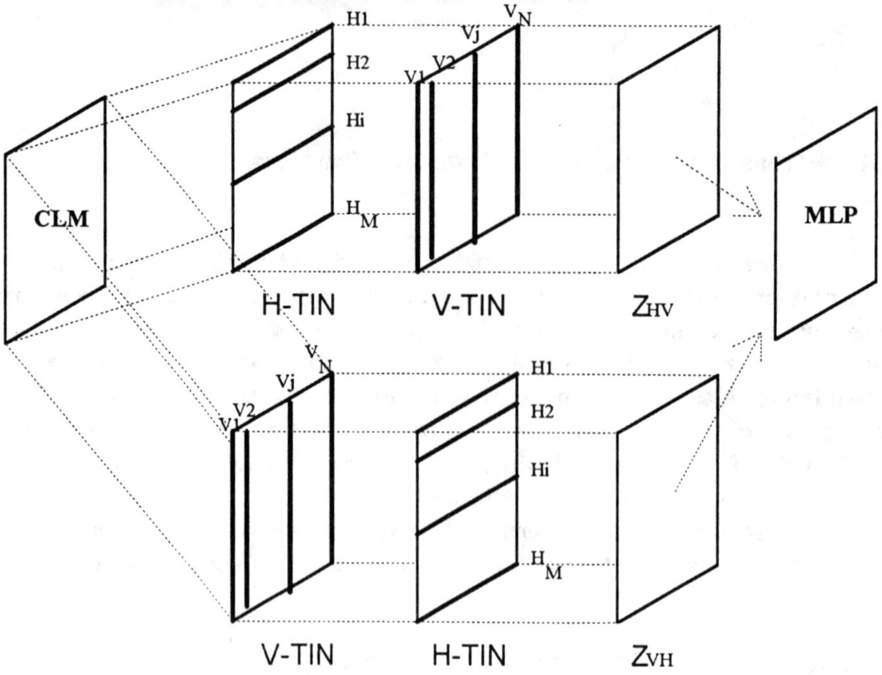

Figure 2. Wrap-translation invariant network

(Hi : horizontally arranged 1D TINN, H_TIN : set of Hi,
Vi : verticall arranged 1D TINN, V_TIN : set of Vi,
Z_{HV} : output obtained by applying V_TIN after H_TIN,
Z_{VH} : output obtained by applying H_TIN after V_TIN)

Then, the output of the above network (Z_{HV}+Z_{VH})has properties of wrap-translation invariance on 2D space. Now we can construct a scale and rotation invariant pattern recognition neural network system as shown in Figure 3.

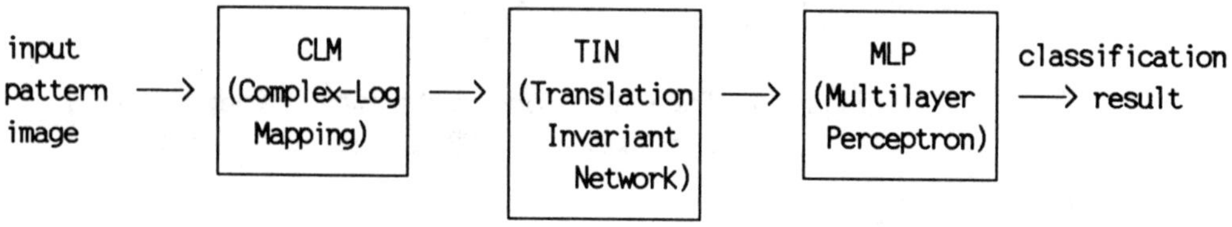

Figure 3. Scale and rotation invariant pattern recogniton system.

IV. Experiments

To evaluate the performance of the proposed system, we have conducted comparison with a two stage system composed of CLM and SONN. Experiments were performed on four types of plane images(Boeing 747, DC-10, F-16c, Mig-25). Each image was scaled from 50% to 150% and arbitrarily rotated to make 30 input image patterns per plane for a total of 120 sample input patterns. Experimental results are given in Table 1 and Table 2. Table 1 shows the difference error at both systems' output units. The average PSS (Pattern Square Sum error) value and the standard deviation of the proposed system are almost the same with those of the two stage system (the performance of the proposed system is slightly lower than that of the compared system). Table 2 shows the recognition rate of the two systems. It shows the same result with table 1.

Table 1. Stability (PSS)

		R	S	C	CC
Proposed System	Avg.	0.05	0.04	0.03	0.00
	Sd.	0.06	0.06	0.05	0.00
Two Stage System	Avg.	0.00	0.00	0.02	0.00
	Sd.	0.00	0.00	0.03	0.00

Table 2. Recognition rate(%)

	R	S	C	CC
Proposed System (Avg.)	100	98	98	100
Two Stage System (Avg.)	100	100	98	100

(R : results for rotated image, S : results for scaled image
C : results for rotated and scaled image, CC : results for increased learning data)

The network size used in experiments are as follows. Both systems have the same 256*256 input image, 64(M)*32(N) CLM output, and MLP network. So we consider only wrap-translation invariant feature extraction networks. While the two stage system case (SONN) has ${}_{M*N}C_2$ * 2 connections for second relation, the proposed system case (TINN) has M*N*(log(M)+log(N)) connections. The recognition performance of the proposed method is almost the same as that of SONN while its network size is significantly reduced.

V. Conclusion

A new scale and rotation invariant pattern recognition system using CLM, TINN and MLP has been proposed. To solve the wrap-translation problem which results from CLM, we have used M-transform. From this, we have been able to propose a wrap-translation invariant TINN. Comparative results with two stage system have been achieved.

Experiments on four types of plane images reveal that our system is very efficient with small network size for the recognition of scaled and rotated patterns. The recognition rate of the proposed system are slightly lower than those of the two stage system. But the network connetion complexity is much lower than that of the compared system. It is expected that the proposed system can be applied to real-time automatic target recognition and automatic visual inspection systems since CLM can be implemented with polar-exponential sampling and the neural network architecture can be parallelized.

References

1. MINSKY, M., PAPERT, S., 'Perceptrons', (MIT Press, Cambridge, MA., 1969)
2. MESSNER, R.A., and SZU, H.H., " An Image Processing Architecture for Real Time Generation of Scale and Rotation Invariant Patterns," CVGIP,1985,Vol.31,pp.50-66
3. KAGEYU, S., OHNISHI, N., and SUGIE,N., " Augmented Multi-layer Perceptron for Rotation-and-Scale Invariant Hand-Written Numeral Recognition," nt. Joint Conf. on Neural Networks, Singapore, Nov., 1991, Vol. I, pp.54 - 59
4. H.Y.Kwon, B.C.Kim, D.S.Cho and H.Y.Hwang, " Rotation and scale invariant pattern recognition using complex-log mapping and augmented second order neural network," Proc. of IJCNN, 1992, Nov., Vol.II, PP. 213-219.
5. Hans Burkhardt and Xaver Muller, " On invariant sets of a certain class of fast translation-invariant transforms," IEEE Trans. on ASSP, 1980, Vol. 28, No. 5, pp. 517-523.
6. J.L.McClelland and D.E.Rumelhart, Parallel Distributed Processing, Vol. 1., Cambridge, MA, MIT Press, 1986.

INTENTIONALLY LEFT BLANK

Occluded Object Recognition By Hopfield Networks

Mengkang Peng and Narendra K Gupta

Dept. of Electrical, Electronic & Computer Engineering
Napier University, Edinburgh, EH14 1DJ
United Kingdom

Abstract A new method to use Hopfield neural network for object recognition is proposed. Object recognition is treated as a subgraph matching. A system consisting of one global network and several sub-networks is constructed. The sub-networks are dynamically changed and the outputs of the global network and the sub-networks are feedbacked to each other to complete the subgraph matching. This method avoids the local minimum problem arising from the use of one single Hopfield network and also uses much less time than simulated annealing algorithm. Computer simulation shows it can efficiently recognize objects in occlusion.

1. Introduction

Hopfield neural network has been used to solve TSP[1] problem and for object recognition[3]. All these applications are based on the fact that starting from an initial state, the network will converge to a stable state, where the so-called energy function is minimized. Most of the time, however, the energy function is just locally minimized and a different initial state may lead to a different local minimum. For object recognition, it means some objects, which are present, may fail to be recognized and some objects, which are not present, may be wrongly recognized. A carefully chosen initial state may improve the situation, but generally, it is very hard to find an appropriate state which will lead to a global minimum. Simulated annealing algorithm[5] can be used to achieve a global minimum, but theoretically, it needs unlimited time.

As in [2] and [3], we'll treat object recognition as a subgraph matching. We'll construct a new system structure consisting of one global network and several sub-networks. The sub-networks are dynamically changed and the outputs of global network and sub-networks are feedbacked to each other to complete subgraph matching. Our method avoids the local minimum problem arising from the use of a single Hopfield network and uses much less time than simulated annealing algorithm. Computer simulation shows that it can efficiently recognize the objects with or without occlusion.

2. System Structure for Labelled Graph matching

Let's assume M model objects are represented by M labelled graphs. The nodes of each graph are labelled by the local features and the links between the nodes by the spatial relationship of features. Assume that Graph K (K=1,2, ... M) has m_K nodes with $F_k^{(K)}$ representing the features and $R_{kl}^{(K)}$ (k,l=1,2, ... m_K) the links. The total number of nodes of M model graphs is T:

0-7803-1901-X/94 $4.00 ©1994 IEEE

$$T=\sum_{i=1}^{M} m_i$$

Assume that a scene graph has S nodes with f_i representing its features and r_{ij} (i,j=1,2, ..., S) its links. Then the problem of object recognition is to find a subgraph matching between the scene graph and M model graphs.

A S×T 2-D binary Hopfield network is constructed, as shown in Fig.1.

Its energy function is defined as:

$$E=\sum_{j=1}^{S}\sum_{k=1}^{T}(f_i-F_k)^2V_{ik}+\frac{\alpha}{2}\sum_{k=1}^{T}\sum_{i=1}^{S}\sum_{j=1,j\neq i}^{S}V_{ik}V_{jk}+\frac{\beta}{2}\sum_{i=1}^{S}(1-\sum_{k=1}^{T}V_{ik})^2 \qquad (1)$$

where α and β are positive constants. F_k represents the model feature.

$$F_k=\begin{cases} F_k^{(1)} & (1\le k\le m_1)\\ F_{k-m1}^{(2)} & (m_1<k\le m_1+m_2)\\ \vdots & \vdots \\ F_{k-(m_1+\ldots+m_{M-1})}^{(M)} & (\sum_{i=1}^{M-1} m_i<k\le\sum_{i=1}^{M} m_i)\end{cases}$$

The first term in expression (1) represents the matching error of the features. The second term represents the constraint that each node of the model graph should have no more than one match with the node of the scene graph. The third one represents the constraint that each node in the scene graph sould have and can only have one match with a model node. Since this network employs all the feature information of the scene and the model graphs, we'll call it a global network.

E can be rewritten in the form of Hopfield energy function (omitting one constant):

$$E=-\frac{1}{2}\sum_{i=1}^{S}\sum_{k=1}^{T}\sum_{j=1}^{S}\sum_{l=1}^{T}T_{ikjl}V_{ik}V_{jl}-\sum_{i=1}^{S}\sum_{k=1}^{T}I_{ik}V_{ik} \qquad (2)$$

with $T_{ikjl}=-\alpha\delta_{kl}(1-\delta_{ij})-\beta\delta_{ij}$ (3)

and $I_{ik}=-(f_i-F_k)^2+\beta$ (4)

where $\delta_{ij}=1$ if i=j and 0 otherwise. Similarly $\delta_{kl}=1$ if k=l and 0 otherwise.

The dynamics of the global network is characterized as follows:

Randomly choose a neuron V_{ik} and update its state according to following rule:

$$V_{ik}=\begin{cases} 1 & \text{if } U_{ik} > -T_{ikik}/2\\ 0 & \text{if } U_{ik} < T_{ikik}/2\\ \text{no change} & \text{otherwise}\end{cases} \qquad (5)$$

where U_{ik} denotes the total input of the neuron V_{ik}:

$$U_{ik}=\sum_{j=1}^{S}\sum_{l=1}^{T} T_{ikjl}V_{jl}+I_{ik} \tag{6}$$

It's easy to show that the energy function E is always decreasing. Therefore, given an initial state, the network will converge to a stable state.

A neuron $V_{ik}=1$ means that the scene node f_i and the model node F_k are matched.

Based on the stable output state of the global network, we'll construct M sub-networks. The column elements of each sub-network just correspond to the nodes of a certain model graph. The row elements, however, depending on the output of the global network, correspond to all the scene nodes, which have matches with the nodes of the above model graph when the global network is stabilized. If S_K scene nodes have matched with model K's nodes, the sub-network K will be constructed as in Fig.2. For the simplicity of expression, we'll use $f_i^{(K)}$ and $r_{ij}^{(K)}$ $(i,j=1,2,\ldots S_K)$ to represent the scene feature and the link in the sub-network K. It is easy to obtain $f_i^{(K)}$ and $r_{ij}^{(K)}$ $(i,j=1,2,\ldots S_K)$ from f_i and $r_{ij}(i,j=1,2,\ldots S)$.

The energy funtion of sub-network K is defined as :

$$E_K=\frac{1}{2}(1-\lambda)\sum_{i=1}^{S_K}\sum_{k=1}^{m_K}\sum_{j=1}^{S_K}\sum_{l=1}^{m_K}(r_{ij}^{(K)}-R_{kl}^{(K)})^2V_{ik}^{(K)}V_{jl}^{(K)}+\lambda\sum_{i=1}^{S_K}\sum_{k=1}^{m_K}(f_i^{(K)}-F_k^{(K)})^2V_{ik}^{(K)}+$$

$$+\frac{1}{2}\alpha_K\sum_{k=1}^{m_K}\sum_{i=1}^{S_K}\sum_{j=1,j\neq i}^{S_K}V_{ik}^{(K)}V_{jk}^{(K)}+\frac{1}{2}\beta_K\sum_{i=1}^{S_K}(1-\sum_{k=1}^{m_K}V_{ik}^{(k)})^2 \tag{7}$$

where α_K, β_K are positive constants. $0\leq \lambda \leq 1$, λ is a control parameter.

E_K can be rewritten in the form of Hopfied energy function:

$$E_K=-\frac{1}{2}\sum_{i=1}^{S_K}\sum_{k=1}^{m_K}\sum_{j=1}^{S_K}\sum_{l=1}^{m_K}T_{ijkl}^{(K)}V_{ik}^{(K)}V_{jl}^{(K)}-\sum_{i=1}^{S_K}\sum_{k=1}^{m_K}I_{ik}^{(K)}V_{ik}^{(K)} \tag{8}$$

with $$T_{ikjl}^{(K)}=-(1-\lambda)(r_{ij}^{(K)}-R_{kl}^{(K)})^2-\alpha_K\delta_{kl}(1-\delta_{ij})-\beta_K\delta_{ij} \tag{9}$$

$$I_{ik}^{(K)}=-(f_i^{(K)}-F_k^{(K)})^2+\beta_K \tag{10}$$

The dynamics of the sub-network K is characterized as:

Randomly choose a neuron $V_{ik}^{(K)}$ and update its state according to following rule:

$$V_{ik}^{(K)}=\begin{cases}1 & \text{if } U_{ik}^{(K)} > -T_{ikik}^{(K)}/2\\ 0 & \text{if } U_{ik}^{(K)} < T_{ikik}^{(K)}/2\\ \text{no change} & \text{otherwise}\end{cases} \tag{11}$$

where $U_{ik}^{(K)}$ denotes the total input of the neuron $V_{ik}^{(K)}$.

$$U_{ik}^{(K)} = \sum_{j=1}^{S_K} \sum_{l=1}^{m_K} T_{ikjl}^{(K)} V_{jl}^{(K)} + I_{ik}^{(K)} \qquad (12)$$

Like the global network, it will converge to a stable state for a given initial state.

The whole system structure is shown in Fig.3 and the subgraph matching algorithm is described as follows:

1) Set control parameter λ=1. Construct the global network according to (3),(4) and randomly set its initial state;

2) Update the state of the global network according to (5) till a stable output state is achieved. Then compare this state with the last circle's output state of the global network. If they are different, go to 3); otherwise reduce the control parameters λ with a small value and check if λ >0. If yes, go to 3); otherwise go to 5);

3) Create M sub-networks according to (9) and (10). The initial states of sub-networks will be set according to following rule: The matched nodes in the global network will remain matched. Therefore, set the states of the equivalent neurons to 1 and all others to 0. Then update the state of each sub-network according to (11) till a stable state is achieved;

4) Feedback the results of all sub-networks to the global network to reset the initial state. The matched nodes in sub-networks will remain matched. Therefore, set the states of the equivalent neurons to 1 and all others to 0. Then go to 2).

5) Output the results. A scene and a model node are said matched only when they are matched in both the global network and the sub-networks.

The choice of parameters α, β, α_K and β_K (K=1,2,... M) is quite flexible. Generally, they should be large enough to guarantee the constraints that each model node cannot have more than one match with the scene nodes and each scene node should have one match with a model node. But a very large value is not favourable. In fact, in the sub-networks, it is better to have those scene nodes, which have no correspondence in that model graph, find no match.

Carefully comparing (3) (4) with (9) (10), it can be seen that when λ=1, the global network is equivalent to the M sub-networks, provided that parameters α, β, α_K and β_K (K=1,2, ..., M) are chosen appropriately. When λ is gradually reduced, the differece between the global network and the sub-networks become greater and greater. When λ is reduced to 0, they become completely independent since the global network uses only the information of feature and the sub-networks only the information of relationship.

In the above system, each single Hopfield network still faces the local minimum problem. However, with the feedback of each other, they can escape from their local minimum state and finally find the correct matching globally.

3. Computer Simulation Experiment

A polygonal approximation[4] is used to represent the object. Fig.5 shows three model objects. The internal angles of the polygon are used as the features. Although Euclidean distance is a simple way to characterize the spatial relationship, it is not invariant to a scale change. In [6], we propose a method to characterize the spatial relationship, which is invariant to position, orientation and scale change. This, then will be used in the experiment. A scene image is shown in Fig.5. The objects included may have arbitrary changes in position, orientation and scale against their models.

The experimental result is shown in Fig.6, where "+" marks the scene nodes which have the correct matches with the model nodes and "o" marks the scene noded which have wrong matches and "*" the scene nodes which have no matches. It can be seen that all scene nodes, which have correspondence in the model graphs, have found the correct matches. The wrong matches or no matches happened only on the scene nodes which are newly created because of the occluding of the objects.

4. Conclusion

The paper investigates the object recognition problem by using Hopfield network. Objects are represented as labelled graphs. Object recognition becomes a problem of subgraph matching. To avoid the local minimum problem arising from the use of one single Hopfield network, a new system structure consisting of one global network and several sub-networks is proposed to do the subgraph matching. Computer simulation has verified that objects can be efficiently recognized even in occlusion. The method, however, is time-consuming because of the feedback between the networks. The future work will try to improve the feedback in order to reduce the calculating time.

5. Acknowledgement

The authors wish to thank Prof. A.E.A. Almaini, the acting Head of the Department of Electrical, Electronic & Computer Engineering at Napier University for the use of the facilities.

Reference

[1] J. J. Hopfield and D. M. Tank, "Neural computation of decisions in optimization", Biol. Cybern., V53, pp.141-152, 1985

[2] C. Von der Malsburg, "Pattern recognition by labbelled graph matching", Neural Networks, vol.1, pp.141-148, 1988

[3] N. M. Nasrabadi and W. Li, "Object recognition by a Hopfield network", IEEE. Trans. Sys. Man. Cybern., vol.21, No.6, pp.1523-1535, Nov/Dec. 1991

[4] M. W. Koch and R.L. Kashyap, "Using polygon to recognze and locate partially occluded objects", IEEE. Trans. Pattern Anal. Machine Intell., vol.PAMI-9, pp.483-494, July 1987

[5] E. Aarts and J. Korst, "Simulated annealing and Boltzmann machine", John Wiley & Son, 1988
[6] M. K. Peng and N. K. Gupta, "Object recognition based on labelled graph and neural network", Proceeding of the First International Symposium of Young Investigators on Information\Computer\Control, Beijing, Feb. 1994 (to be published)

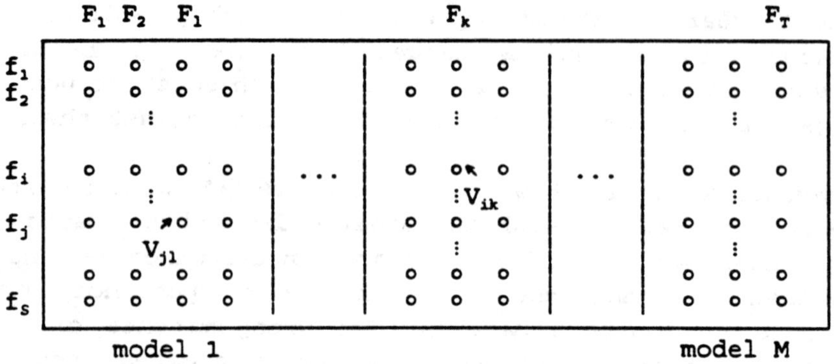

Fig.1. Global Hopfield network.

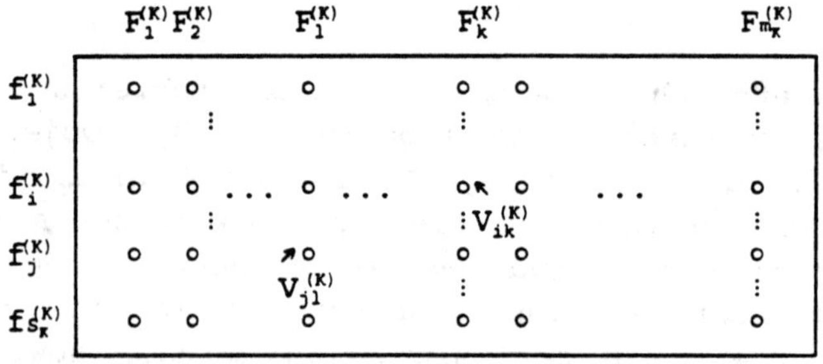

Fig.2. sub-network K.

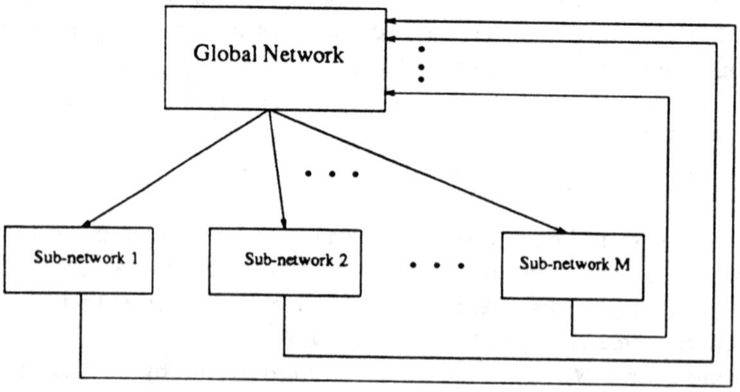

Fig.3. System structure for subgraph matching.

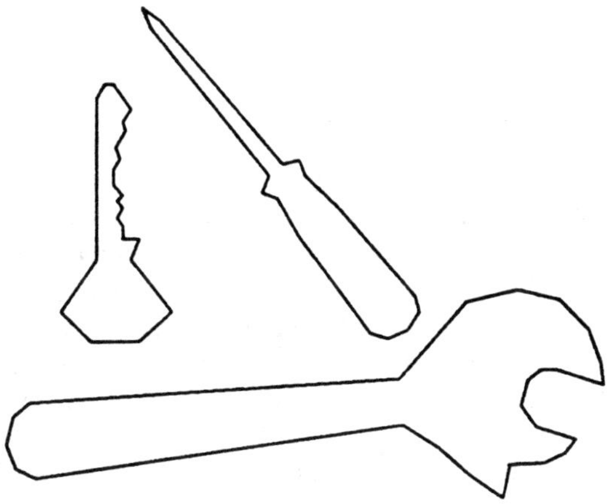

Fig.4. Three model objects.

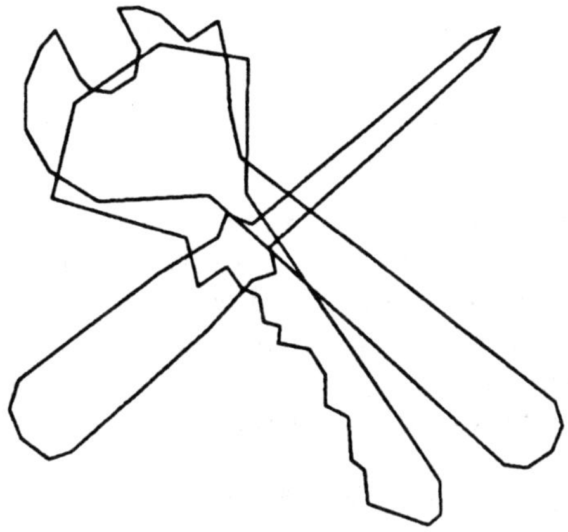

Fig.5.A scene image of three occluded objects.

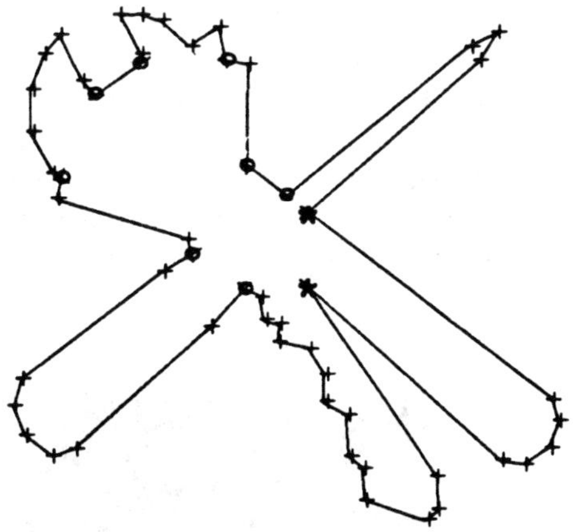

Fig.6. The experimental result. "+" marks the nodes which had correct matches with their correspondence in model graphs. "o" marks the nodes which had wrong matches and "*" marks the nodes which had no matches.

Soft contaminant detection using neural networks: Techniques and limitations

D. Patel, I. Hannah and E.R. Davies
Royal Holloway, University of London
Machine Vision Group, Department of Physics
Egham, Surrey, TW20 0EX, United Kingdom.
e-mail: d.patel@uk.ac.rhbnc

1. Introduction

Impurities such as small pieces of stone, splinters of wood, slivers of glass, bits of plastic, etc. rarely occur in food products. However, when such impurities are detected both the consumer and the manufacturers are greatly concerned and their occurrence is detrimental to the process of quality control. In this research we deal with the detection of contaminants in bags of frozen corn kernels. Foreign objects (FOs) buried in the bags are not visible to a conventional camera and consequently in order to view the contents of the bags we use X-ray imaging. The aim of this research is to develop an image analysis system which detects and segments any FOs that might be in the bags.

FO contaminants which get mixed with vegetables fall into two categories: hard contaminants such as stone, metal and glass, and soft contaminants such as plastic or wood. The detection of hard contaminants is relatively easy and is presented elsewhere [Hannah and Patel, 1993 and Patel, Hannah and Davies, 1993b]. However many soft contaminants have similar X-ray attenuation to the organic foods and consequently the grey level contrast in the image is low. This makes the detection of soft contaminants more difficult. In this paper, we deal with the automatic detection of soft contaminants and furthermore we present the limitations of using X-ray techniques for the detection of soft contaminants. We use frozen corn kernels as the food substrate but the same processing can be adapted to other food substrates such as peas. An example of a X-ray image showing a piece of wood in the centre of the food substrate is illustrated in figure 1. The food substrate and the FO have a strong textural appearance and FO detection based on texture features has given us some promising results [Patel, Hannah and Davies, 1993a]. However, due to a wide variety of FOs, texture analysis techniques have not always ensured acceptable discrimination. The proposed methodology is not dependant on a mathematical texture measure upon which the FO detection is based and has therefore eliminated long processing times that might otherwise be required to characterise texture.

Figure 1: A sample X-ray image

Instead we use artificial neural network (ANN) technology to detect the FOs. ANNs have several advantages over conventional pattern classification techniques [Sethi and Jain, 1991], but the two major benefits are as follows: ANNs are adaptive; they learn from the data presented to them and thus infer solutions by capturing features based on subtle differences between categories in the training data. They have the ability to generalise, i.e. they respond to data which was not included in the training set. Generalisation is particularly useful because the real-world is fuzzy, distorted and noisy. Our aim is to show that ANNs comprised of a few nodes can successfully detect FOs.

0-7803-1901-X/94 $4.00 ©1994 IEEE

2. The Parallel ANN architecture

Representing a wide variety of FOs to an ANN to build an adequate generalisation set is a complex task. As the number of FOs that have to be learnt increases, training complexities and times increase and furthermore there is a possibility that the ANN might not converge to a minimum. In our approach, we do not train a single network to recognise a range of different FOs, but we create sub-networks, each one being trained to recognise one particular FO. After all the sub-nets are trained independently, they are linked together as shown in figure 2. Using this parallel ANN (PANN) architecture improves learning and generates a better representation of each FO. The output from the networks is then fed into a decision unit which determines whether the sample bag is to be accepted or rejected. The decision unit currently is a threshold device; an expert network incorporating other features is being developed.

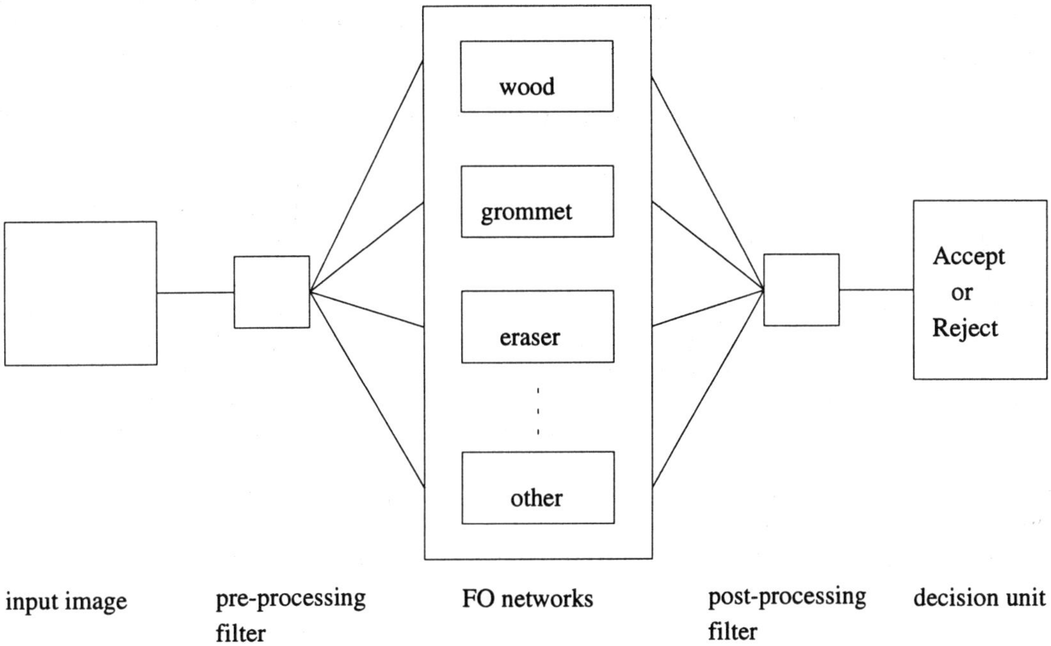

Figure 2: Parallel artificial neural network (PANN) architecture

Each sub-network uses a fully connected multi-layer perceptron (MLP) topology with the Back-Propagation (BP) learning rule [Rumelhart and McClelland, 1986], which comprises a three layer topology with one layer of hidden nodes. It has been shown [Huang and Lippman, 1987; Cybenko, 1989] that it is possible to train MLP networks with one hidden layer using the BP training and sigmoidal non-linearities as output functions to form complex regions. The network is given the input and the corresponding desired output pairs and it learns to minimise the error between the network output and the desired output by automatically adjusting the inter-nodal connection weights.

The input layer nodes have a linear transfer function whereas the input-output characteristics of all other nodes are defined by a sigmoidal non-linearity threshold function:

$$f(x) = \frac{1}{1+e^{-x}}$$

Each layer in the MLP topology is a column of nodes with feed-forward communication between layers. Each layer calculates:

$$y_j = f\left[\sum_{i=1}^{n} w_i x_i\right]$$

and passes that as input to the next layer. The final layer output values are o_j and the desired output values are d_j. The BP algorithm minimises the difference between the desired output and the actual output values:

$$E = \sum_{p} \sum_{j} (o_{pj} - d_{pj})^2,$$

for all nodes in the output layer; $j \in (1,2,\ldots J)$ and the input patterns; $p \in (1,2,\ldots P)$.
The function is minimised by adjusting the inter-nodal connection weights and the nodal thresholds. The detailed algebra for the BP rule is not presented here, but can be found in Rumelhart and McClelland [1986].

3. Foreign object detection and the limitations

Each sub-network from the overall PANN architecture is trained to recognise a specific FO. The networks consist of an input layer of nine nodes and an output layer of three nodes. The network is trained to recognise three regions on the images; foreign object, food substrate and conveyor belt background. The input layers of nodes each yield values from a 3×3 mapping window which scans across the image. The choice of hidden layer nodes for each sub-net is problematic; if there are too many the network will memorise the training samples and consequently not generalise. On the other hand, if there are too few, then the network will not converge during training. In this paper we use the dynamic node creation method suggested previously for networks with one hidden layer [Patel, Hannah and Davies, 1993c].

Classification accuracy for segmentation purposes implies a comparison of the segmented region with that of a visually perceived segmented image. However, it is not possible to draw out a visual boundary segmenting the FOs from each corrupted image. Consequently, data is extracted via a 3×3 mapping window which scans across small subsections of the three categories of a training image. A cross-validation procedure is used where the data is split into training data and test data, and the latter is used to measure the generalisation of the network. The nodes in the middle layer were varied between a lower and an upper bound using the dynamic node generation method in order to achieve good segmentation. During training, the node outputs are set to 0, except for the class from which the current input pattern is taken, which is set to 1. The patterns are iterated through the network until sufficient convergence is achieved. After training, the internodal connection weights and nodal offsets are frozen and the network used to detect FOs. The node with the highest response is the label assigned to the pixels being classified.

The FOs inserted in the food bags include a splinter of pallet wood, a rubber grommet and a desk eraser, examples of these are illustrated in figure 3a. These are typical soft contaminants that occur in the factory environment and there is a minute chance that they will appear on product lines. All images are pre-processed using a 9×9 averaging filter to reduce spot noise and cluster the grey levels; this tends to connect the neighbouring pixels. The training set contained 1500 pattern samples made up of 500 samples each from the food substrate, conveyor background and FO categories. The training data is iterated through the network until the error on each output node is $E_j \leq 0.1$. The test data for the images with the rubber grommet and wooden splinter has 7816 and 7866 samples representing all the three categories respectively. It should be noted that the images used subsequently to test the network's ability to detect the FOs were not the same as those from which the training data was extracted. Three networks each representing a category of FO were set up in the PANN architecture of figure 2. Based on the node generation method, the best generalisation achieved for each of the FO sub-nets was 9-6-3, where the number of hidden layer nodes was 6. The classification rates for the test images of wood and rubber were 97.3% and 92.9% respectively. The individual sub-net segmented images are filtered through a spurious noise removing filter and the results are illustrated in figures 3b. Several other images have also been segmented with similar results.

From the results shown in figure 3, it can be seen that the FO detection for the three categories of soft contaminants was successful. The contrast shown in the original images arises from differences in the atomic numbers between the food and FOs. Small differences are difficult to discriminate due to the presence of system noise such as X-ray detector variations, or density fluctuations in homogeneous food such as uneven layers of food within the bag. In general, the X-ray attenuation of soft contaminants such as wood, plastics and polymers with low density is very similar to the surrounding food substrate. Hence differences can only be detected from large volume FOs which are present. The wood piece used in the experiments is approximately of dimension 48×18×17 mm; smaller pieces could not be substantially discriminated from the food substrate. Furthermore, the edge of the bag where the layers of corn kernels decreases gets mistakenly classified as the FO. This is because the X-rays absorbed by the corn is similar to that absorbed by the FO. However, the threshold decision unit can cope with such an overall discrepancy.

For plastics, we have successfully detected the rubber grommets and erasers. However, the detection of the eraser is straightforward and can be done using simple thresholding techniques. Again, plastics or polymers of low density such as a piece of vehicle indicator lamp reflector, cannot be seen on the X-ray image even with a trained human eye and has thus far eluded machine vision detection. Several techniques to enhance the contrast between the contaminants and the food are being suggested. The possibility of doping likely contaminants with a high atomic number marker is likely to increase detectability to a useful degree. However, the detection of contaminants doped with a marker is not within the scope of this project.

a: Original images b: Segmented output

Figure 3: Foreign object detection

4. Summary

This paper has shown that small MLP networks operating in parallel can be used to detect FOs in food bags. The PANN architecture offers improved training times as each network is only taught to detect one category of FO. We have concentrated on the detection of soft contaminants such as wood and plastic and have shown the limitations of using X-ray imaging for the detection of soft contaminants. Although the results have so far been encouraging, there are areas which require further research. For example, features which are generated by learning the structure of the particular texture can be used to enhance the contrast between the contaminant and the food substrate to a certain degree and the combined features can then be used to drive the expert network.

References

G. Cybenko (1989), "*Approximations by superpositions of sigmoidal functions*", Mathematics of Control, Signals and Systems, vol. 2, pp. 303-314.

I. Hannah and D. Patel (1993), "*The use of variance and entropic thresholding methods for image segmentation*", Pattern Recognition Journal, [paper submitted].

W.Y. Huang and R.P. Lippman (1987), "*Neural networks and traditional classifiers*", Proc. of Conf. on Neural Information Processing Systems, NIPS-87, Denver, U.S.A., vol. 4, pp. 485-493.

D. Patel, I. Hannah and E.R. Davies (1993a), "*Foreign object detection via texture recognition and a neural classifier*", in Visual Communication and Image Processing '93, Proc. SPIE 2094. 1291-1299.

D. Patel, I. Hannah and E.R. Davies (1993b) "*Texture analysis for foreign object detection using a single layer neural network*", IEEE Int. Conf. on Neural Networks, [paper submitted].

D. Patel, I. Hannah and E.R. Davies (1993c), "*A dynamic node creation method*", [paper in preparation].

D.E. Rumelhart and J.L. McClelland (1986), *Parallel Distributed Processing Foundations*, vol. 1, MIT Press, Cambridge.

I. Sethi and A. Jain (1991), *Artificial Neural Networks and Statistical Pattern Recognition*, Eds. I.K. Sethi and A.K. Jain, Elsevier North-Holland.

Acknowledgements

The authors are grateful to the ACME Directorate of the UK Science and Engineering Research Council for financial support during the course of this research.

A FAST LEARNING ALGORITHM FOR GABOR TRANSFORM WITH APPLICATIONS TO IMAGE DATA REDUCTION AND PATTERN CLASSIFICATION

Ayman E. Ibrahim, Mahmood R. Azimi Sadjadi, and Sassan Sheedvash
Electrical Engineering Department
Colorado State University
Fort Collins, CO 80523
Tel:(303)-491-7956
Email:azimi@longs.lance.colostate.edu

Abstract:

A simple neural network-based approach is introduced in this paper which allows the computation of the coefficients of the generalized non-orthogonal 2-D Gabor transform representation. The network is trained using a recursive least squares (RLS) type algorithm. This RLS learning algorithm offers better accuracy and faster convergence when compared to the least mean squares (LMS) based algorithms. The aim is to achieve minimum mean squared error for the reconstructed image from the set of the Gabor coefficients. Applications of this scheme in image data reduction and pattern classification are demonstrated in the simulation results.

I. Introduction:

Image transformation plays an important role in image analysis, segmentation, pattern recognition, and data compression [1], as it extracts the relevant information from the images. Among these transformations is the Gabor transform [2]-[4], which can be viewed as a special case of the short time Fourier transform (STFT) [2] with optimal "time-localization" property. This transform is generated by using a Gaussian window in the STFT. Nonetheless, there is a trade-off between time and frequency resolutions, as the product of time-frequency resolution is lower bounded through the Heisenberg inequality. This implies that improving frequency resolution results in sacrificing the time resolution and vice versa. For the 1-D case, Gabor [2] proved that the lower bound of the inequality is achieved by multiplying the harmonic oscillation of any frequency with a window with the Gaussian shape.

Besides optimal localization in the joint time-frequency domains and the achievement of the lower bound of uncertainty principle, other advantages of the Gabor transform include: compatibility with mammalian visual system [5], and energy packing capability which leads to lower entropy for data compression [6]. The deficiency of the Gabor transform, however, is that the elementary basis functions are not orthogonal. As a result, they can not be easily computed. This precludes the wide spread application of this scheme for signal/image processing problems. Thus, a method for fast computation of the Gabor coefficients is needed.

In [3] Daugman proposed a three layer neural network for extracting the Gabor transform coefficients. Using this method a given pixel is represented optimally by projecting it onto a chosen set of Gabor elementary functions based on minimizing the mean squared of the error (MSE). He then used an LMS-based updating equation to obtain the weights of the network which converge to the optimum Gabor coefficient set. Tenuer and Hosticka [4] presented a complex LMS algorithm for the computation of the Gabor coefficients and studied the convergence behavior of the algorithm. However, the main problem with all the LMS-based scheme is that there is a trade-off between the accuracy and speed of convergence. Specifically, one can increase the convergence speed by sacrificing the accuracy in estimating the weights.

The proposed neural network in this paper has a very simple structure with only a single neuron. The network is trained using the recursive least squares (RLS) learning algorithm which converges to the optimum solution in few iterations and doesn't have the accuracy-speed trade-off problem. Simulation results in this paper show the applications of this approach for image data reduction. In addition, simulation results for cloud detection and classification from satellite imaging data are also presented.

0-7803-1901-X/94 $4.00

II. Image Representation using Discrete 2-D Gabor Transform

The goal of image representation is to find a set of coefficients in the transform domain which closely approximate a discrete image $I[x,y]$ of size P x P . If $\{a_{mnrs}\}$ represents the set of coefficients on the non-orthogonal Gabor elementary functions $\{G_{mnrs}[x,y]\}$, then $I[x,y]$ will be represented with a minimum MSE by projecting it onto the basis of the Gabor space i.e.

$$H[x,y] = \sum_{m=0}^{K-1}\sum_{n=0}^{L-1}\sum_{r=0}^{M-1}\sum_{s=0}^{N-1} a_{mnrs}\, G_{mnrs}[x,y]\,. \quad (1)$$

where $H[x,y]$ is the reconstructed image and should be as close as possible to the original image $I[x,y]$, so that the image can be accurately reconstructed from the Gabor coefficients. The 2-D Gabor elementary functions are generally parameterized [3] for an invariant Gaussian window which is positioned on fully overlapping Cartesian lattice locations $\{x_m, y_m\} = \{mM, nN\}$ where M, N are the lattice cell dimensions, (m,n) represent the index of each lattice, $m \in [0,K-1]$, $n \in [0,L-1]$ and K x L is the number of the lattices inside the image. Thus, if the size of the image is P x P, then K=P/M and L=P/N. The 2-D spatial frequencies $\{u_r, v_s\}$ are equal to $\{r/M, s/N\}$ for integer increments of (r,s) spanning the range inside each lattice $\{0,M-1\}$ and $\{0,N-1\}$, respectively. The Gabor elementary functions in (1) can then be expressed as [3]

$$G_{mnrs}[x,y] = \exp(-\pi\alpha^2[(x-mM)^2+(y-nN)^2]).\exp(2\pi j[(r-\frac{M-1}{2})\frac{x}{M}+(s-\frac{N-1}{2})\frac{y}{N}]) \quad (2)$$

where α defines the scale of the Gaussian window. The larger the size of M and N which leads to fewer the number of spatial sampling positions (m,n), the larger the number of the spatial frequency components required in each cell. The product of the ranges of the indices m,n,r and s should be equal to the number of the pixels inside the image. Note that the value of M,N is affecting the localization in the spatial domain. These 2-D functions achieve the lower bound of the joint uncertainty in the two conjoint domains i.e. (x,y) visual space and (u,v) spatial frequency variables [3]. This is given by

$$\Delta x \Delta y \Delta u \Delta v \geq 1/16\pi^2. \quad (3)$$

From equation (1), it can easily be seen that the reconstructed image $H[x,y]$ is either identical to $I[x,y]$ or approximates this image with an error. The error in the reconstruction is given by

$$\epsilon[x,y] = I[x,y] - H[x,y]\,. \quad (4)$$

If $\{G_{mnrs}[x,y)\}$ forms a complete orthogonal set, then the difference image is zero and a_{mnrs}'s can be calculated by the inner product formula [3]. However, in general the elementary functions may not be orthogonal and the criterion for finding the optimum coefficients is to minimize the MSE

$$E = \sum_x \sum_y |\epsilon(x,y)|^2, \quad (5)$$

by setting its partial derivatives with respect to all the coefficients a_{mnrs}'s equal to zero. This gives the following system of normal equations, which can be solved using either the LMS or the RLS algorithms

$$\sum_{x,y} (I[x,y]\, G^*_{mnrs}[x,y]) = \sum_{x,y} (H[x,y]\; G^*_{mnrs}[x,y])\,. \quad (6)$$

III. Neural Network Implementation and Training

The image is divided into non-overlapping blocks of size M x N and the Gabor transform is taken on each block. In each block there are M x N number of totally overlapping Gabor functions, each of which is extended in the whole lattice. Assuming that the Gaussian windows are truncated outside each lattice, then for the entire image we have

$$H[x,y] = \sum_{m}\sum_{n} H_{mn}(x,y) \quad (7)$$

The equation governing the transform inside each lattice (m,n are now fixed) is given by

$$H_{mn}[x,y] = \sum_{r=0}^{M-1}\sum_{s=0}^{N-1} a_{mnrs}G_{mnrs}[x,y] \qquad for \; x\epsilon\,[mM-\frac{M-1}{2}, mM+\frac{M-1}{2}], y\epsilon\,[nN-\frac{N-1}{2}, nN+\frac{N-1}{2}] \quad (8)$$

$$= 0 \qquad \text{otherwise}$$

The normal equation (6) can be solved to generate the optimal Gabor coefficients, a_{mnrs} 's for each block of the image using the RLS learning [7]. The RLS algorithm is based on the recursive implementation of the method of least squares in conjunction with the matrix inversion lemma. Unlike the LMS which is derived from the ensemble averages, the RLS algorithm involves the use of time averages. It is based on the minimization of the global sum of the squared error and the weights are updated by solving a system of normal equations recursively [7]. This method improves the learning rate significantly when compared to the LMS method as the step size in this algorithm is data dependent.

To implement the operation on a neural network, a single neuron structure can be constructed to extract the Gabor coefficients in each block at its weights. The input data set to the network consists of the Gabor elementary functions at each pixel within the block i.e

$$U_{mn}(x,y) = [\; G_{mn00}(x,y) \quad G_{mn01}(x,y) \; \ldots\ldots\ldots \quad \ldots\ldots\ldots \quad G_{mn,M-1,N-1}(x,y)\;]^t$$

The spatial variables x and y give the time dependency factor, because for each x and y we will have a new input data vector. The desired output is the corresponding pixel value of the original image i.e I[x,y]. If the associated weight vector of the neuron is defined by

$$W_{mn} = [w_{mn00} \quad w_{mn01} \quad \ldots\ldots\ldots \quad \ldots\ldots\ldots \quad w_{mn,M-1,N-1}]$$

Then, the output of the neuron for each pixel inside a lattice takes the form of

$$\hat{H}_{mn}[x,y] = \sum_{r=0}^{M-1}\sum_{s=0}^{N-1} w_{mnrs}G_{mnrs}[x,y] \quad (9)$$

where $\hat{H}_{mn}[x,y]$ is the estimate of $H_{mn}[x,y]$. Upon the completion of the training, the weights associated with these inputs converge to the Gabor coefficients a_{mnrs}'s and $\hat{H}_{mn}[x,y]$ will approach $H_{mn}[x,y]$. The training of all the other blocks can be done concurrently using an RLS-type learning method.

The training equations using the RLS algorithm [7] are given below. Note for simplicity the block index (m,n) is removed. In the following equations $k \;\epsilon\; [1,MN]$, which is a 1-D index obtained by mapping the 2-D spatial indices (x,y) inside each lattice in row-wise fashion, corresponds to the iteration number. The algorithm starts by initializing $P(0)= \delta^{-1}I$, where δ is a very small positive constant ($\delta = 10^{-4}$) and $W(0)=0$. Then iterate

$$K(k) = \frac{\lambda^{-1}P(k-1)\,U(k)}{1+\lambda^{-1}U^{H}(k)\,P(k-1)\,U(k)} \quad (10)$$

$$\alpha(k) = d(k) - \hat{W}(k-1)\,U(k) \quad (11)$$

$$\hat{W}(k) = \hat{W}(k-1) + K(k)\,\alpha^{*}(k) \quad (12)$$

$$P(k) = \lambda^{-1}P(k-1) - \lambda^{-1}K(k)\,U^{H}(k)\,P(k-1) \quad (13)$$

where U(k) is the input data vector at iteration k, d(k) is the desired output, i.e. I[x,y], W(k) is the weight vector at iteration k which contains the estimate of the Gabor transform coefficients, λ is the forgetting factor $0 < \lambda \leq 1$, (in our case $\lambda = 1$, i.e. infinite memory), K(k) is Kalman gain vector and P(k) approaches the inverse of data covariance matrix. This training is performed by consecutive presentation of the training data set to the network and updating the weights according to the above equations. An epoch is completed when all the training data $k \in [1,MN]$ are presented to the network. This process is repeated for a number of epochs until the network converges to an acceptable solution.

IV. Simulation Results:

a. Image Data Reduction

"Lena" image of size 128 x 128 in Fig. 1 was used as a test image. Fig. 2 shows the histogram of this image. The entropy of this image was found to be 7.6. The resulting Gabor coefficients have a symmetry property, i.e the real part has an even symmetry and the imaginary part has an odd symmetry. Thus, half of the coefficients gives a complete information about the transform. The simulations were carried out using both LMS and RLS schemes for various lattice dimensions. For M = N = 16 lattice size with α = .065 and step size or learning factor μ = 0.35, the LMS algorithm converged in 165 epochs as apposed to only two epochs using the RLS method. It is interesting to note that RLS method converged to almost zero MSE in only two epochs. The histogram of the coefficients was well compact, and the entropy decreased to 2.6. About 78% of the coefficients lie in the range [0,3], hence making this transform suitable for data compression by designing a code word length varying inversely with the frequency distribution of the coefficients. Figs. 3 and 4 show the reconstructed image and the histogram of the resultant Gabor coefficients for the new RLS method. Owing to the fact that the energy was contained in few components, the image reconstruction can be made based on only the high energy coefficients. Fig. 5 shows the reconstructed image based on 40 % or actually 20 % of the coefficients because of the symmetry property. The reconstructed image has still a very good visual appearance. The effect of varying the learning factor on the behavior of LMS method was also studied. Increasing the learning factor (μ = 0.40), gives faster convergence in 150 epochs using the LMS learning, but with a higher mean squared error because of the fact that the LMS learning is sensitive to the learning factor. Also the effect of changing α, which is the scale of the Gaussian window, was studied for both the LMS and RLS methods. Decreasing α to .05, with the same learning factor (μ = 0.35), provided faster convergence in 120 epochs for the LMS method, because as α decreases the elementary functions become nearly orthogonal. Using the RLS algorithm, the network converged to almost zero mean squared error in only two epochs irrespective of the choices of α or the lattice size.

b. Cloud Detection and Classification

In this study, a satellite image shown in Fig. 6 of size 451 x 418 is used for the detection and classification of cloud areas. The Gabor coefficients were first computed to extract the textural features attributed to the cloud and no-cloud areas. A small number of coefficients which contain a large fraction of the energy would be sufficient to represent the data in these areas. This reduces the dimensionality of the data which in turn leads to slimmer neural network classifier. Blocks of sizes 11 x 11 were used to extract 121 Gabor coefficients, 37 of which were used as the input to the neural network classifier. A 3-layer back-propagation neural network was used as classifier. The network contained 48 and 72 neurons in the first and the second hidden layers, respectively. The network was trained using 109 blocks taken randomly from the original image which contained a total number of 1558 blocks. The training blocks were chosen such that it covers different areas from the original image. Before presenting the input data i.e the Gabor coefficients to the classifier, they should be normalized. However, this leads to the loss of the intensity information. To overcome this problem an additional input node was added which carries the intensity information. Note that this intensity information can be obtained using the normalization factor. Since this normalization factor is too big to be used as an input to the network, scaling had to be done in order to fit this value to a range comparable to the other input nodes, so that all the inputs have equal importance to the network. The network took 55000 epochs to converge to a mean squared error value of .01 using the adaptive learning with initial learning factor of 0.1 and with a momentum factor 0.9. Then, after the training was completed the network was tested on the whole image. The output of the network is either 1 for cloud blocks or 0 for no-cloud blocks. The output of the classifier was used to generate the processed image by assigning a fixed gray level (black) for the blocks classified as background and leaving the pixel values unchanged for the cloud blocks. The results show a very good performance of the classifier when used in conjunction with the Gabor coefficients extraction network. The misdetection was found to be about 4 % and the false alarm rate was 3%. The processed image is shown in Fig. 7.

V. Conclusion

An RLS - based learning scheme is introduced in this paper for the extraction of Gabor transform coefficients from images. This method offers a faster and more accurate convergence behavior comparing to the LMS method. The energy compaction of the Gabor transform makes this method suitable for data compression applications. The localization in space can be utilized to capture the spatial variations of the image which will be useful in pattern recognition, segmentation, and image analysis based on textural information. The application of the proposed scheme in the areas of image data reduction and cloud detection/classification were demonstrated in the simulation results. This neural network-based method can be applicable to other non-orthogonal transforms such as non-orthogonal Wavelet transform.

References

[1] A. k. Jain, "Fundamentals Of Digital Image Processing", Prentice-Hall, Englewood Cliffs, N.J., 1989.

[2] D. Gabor, "Theory of Communication", J. Inst. Elec. Engr, pp. 429-457, 1946.

[3] J. Daugman, "Complete Discrete 2-D Gabor Transform by Neural Networks for Image Analysis and Compression", IEEE Trans on Acoust. Speech, and Signal Proc., Vol. ASSP36, No. 7, pp. 1169-1179, July 1988.

[4] A. Teuner and B.J. Hosticks, "Adaptive Gabor Transformation for Image Processing", IEEE Trans. on Image Processing, Vol. IP2, No. 1, pp. 112-117, Jan 1993.

[5] J.Daugman, "Uncertainty Relation for Resolution in Space, Spatial Frequency, and Orientation Optimized by Two-dimensional Visual Cortical Filters", J. Opt. Soc. Amec, Vol. 2, No. 7, pp. 1160-1169, 1985.

[6] J. Daugman ,"Entropy Reduction and Decorrelation in Visual Coding by Oriented Neural Receptive Fields", IEEE Trans. Biomed. Eng., Vol. 36, pp. 107-114, Jan 1989.

[7] S. Haykin, "Adaptive Filter Theory", Prentice-Hall, Englewood Cliffs, N.J., Second Edition, 1991.

[8] J. Wexler and S. Raz, "Discrete Gabor Expansion", Signal Processing, Vol. 81, pp. 207-220, 1990.

[9] B. Widrow, J.Mcool and M. Ball, "The Complex LMS Algorithm", Proc. IEEE, Vol. 63, pp. 719-720, April 1975.

[10] I. G. smotroff, T. P. Howells, and S. Lehar, "Meteorlogical classification of satellite imagery using neural network data fusion", in Proceedings of IJCNN, San Diego, CA, pp. II-23-II-28, 1990.

Fig. 1. Original "Lena" Image 128 X 128.

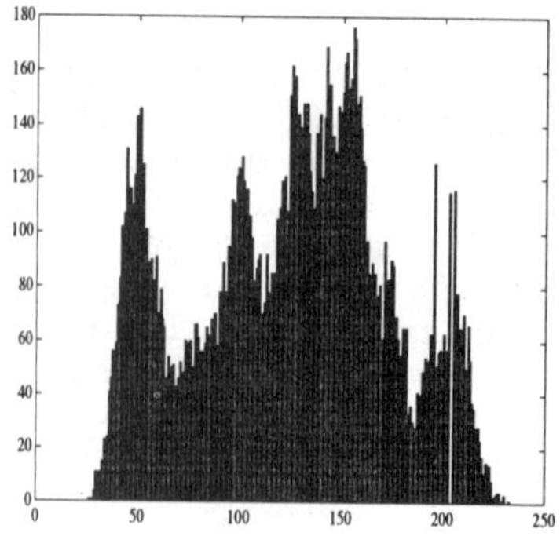

Fig. 2. Histogram of the Original Image.

Fig. 3. Reconstructed Image Using RLS Algorithm.

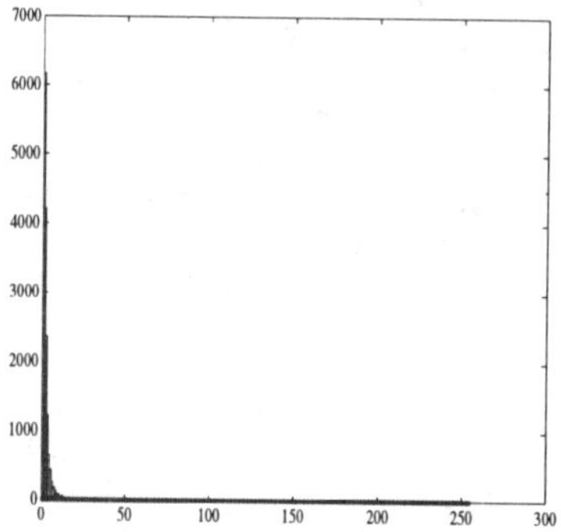

Fig. 4. Histogram of the Gabor Coefficients Using RLS Algorithm.

Fig. 5. Reconstructed Image Based on 40% of the Coefficients.

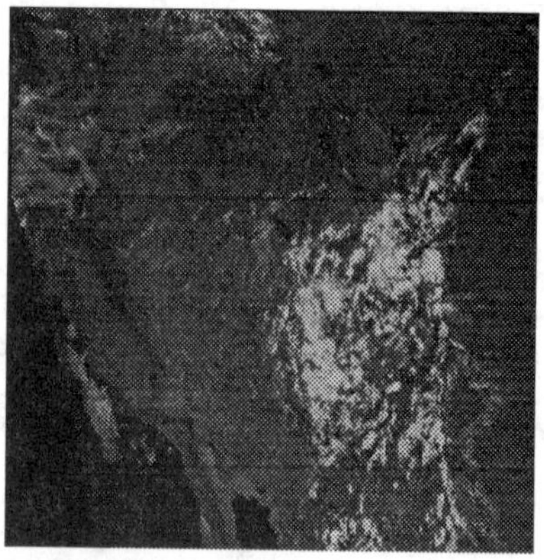

Fig. 6. Original Satellite Image.

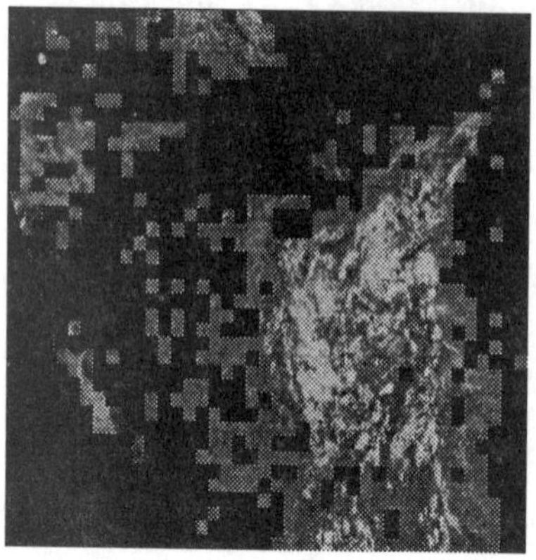

Fig. 7. Processed Satellite Image

Detection and Classification of Cloud Data From Geostationary Satellite Using Artificial Neural Networks

Ren-Jean Liou, Mahmood R. Azimi-Sadjadi*, Donald L. Reinke
Thomas H. Vonder-Haar and Kenneth E. Eis

Cooperative Institute for Research in the Atmosphere
Colorado State University
Fort Collins, CO 80523

*Department of Electrical Engineering
Colorado State University
Fort Collins, CO 80523

Abstract

This paper presents a new approach using neural network-based methods. This approach advances the detection/classification of cloud field from satellite data in both the visible and infrared (IR) range. Unlike many existing cloud detection schemes which use thresholding and statistical methods, this approach uses Singular Value Decomposition (SVD) to extract image textural features in addition to mean value methodologies. The extracted features are then presented to a self-organizing feature map or Kohonen network for automatic detection and classification of cloud areas. The effectiveness of this method is demonstrated under many situations which are considered difficult for the conventional methods. The proposed method also possesses some interesting classification capabilities which can facilitate future studies on global climatology.

I. Introduction

Cloud observations from satellite imagery have been used for several decades. Recently, the large volume of data has mandated the use of automated methods to process the imagery. However, owing to the complicated nature of cloud characteristics and the substantial variations in the background, many problems in this area still remain unsolved. Thresholding techniques and nearest neighbor structure functions are the most common cloud detection method currently being used. This research is aimed at extending this methodology to the full use of texture that has only been used by human analysts in a subjective manner till now.

The emergence of neural network technology has provided very promising means of performing image processing and pattern recognition tasks. Neural networks have the capability to learn from examples and generalize on novel data. Owing to their inherent high parallelism, they are ideally suited for performing real-time decision making and processing tasks. There are several different neural network paradigms which can be used depending on the nature of the problem at hand. When finding an appropriate neural network structure for use, the choices of the learning algorithm, the network architecture, the input representation and the training set play dominant roles for accurate and reliable performance. These choices also determine the network generalization capability.

In this paper, a neural network approach is applied to cloud detection/classification of satellite images at both visible and IR ranges. The intensities of visible images change according to the brightness while the intensities of IR images change according to the sensed temperature. The changes in IR images are more significant and thus more difficult to handle. The block diagram of the proposed processing scheme is illustrated in Fig. 1. SVD is first applied to extract the textural features attributed to the cloud and no-cloud areas. This also reduces the input dimensionality to the neural network which in turn reduces the training time and improves the generalization capability. The extracted eigenvalues are applied to an unsupervised self-organizing feature map which is used for detection and classification purposes. The robustness and generalization capability of neural networks in dealing with some difficult situations are demonstrated in this paper.

The organization of this paper is as follows. The feature extraction scheme using the SVD approach is given in Section II. Section III describes the neural network architecture and the detection/classification processes. The simulation results are presented in Section IV. Finally, conclusions are given in Section V.

0-7803-1901-X/94 $4.00 ©1994 IEEE

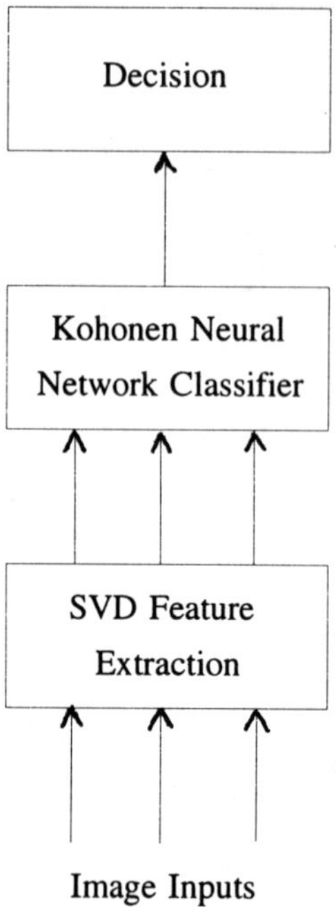

Fig. 1 The processing diagram for cloud detection/classification.

II. Feature Extraction Using SVD Transform

SVD transform is a useful tool in image restoration, power spectrum estimation and data compression areas [3]. As a numerical approach, it is a powerful tool for dealing with sets of equations or matrices that are either singular or very close to being singular. It provides quantitative information about the structure of a system or linear equations. In image processing, it possesses the best information-packing efficiency for any given image. The transformation results can vary drastically from image to image and thus can better represent the features of different images.

Let us consider an $N \times M$ image $\mathbf{X}$ where $N \geq M$. It is possible to represent any such image in an r-dimensional subspace where r is the rank of the matrix $\mathbf{X}$. Let

$$\mathbf{U} = \mathbf{X}\mathbf{X}^T \qquad \text{and} \qquad \mathbf{V} = \mathbf{X}^T\mathbf{X} \tag{1}$$

Matrices $\mathbf{U}$ and $\mathbf{V}$ are thus non-negative, symmetric and have identical eigenvalues $\lambda_1, \lambda_2, \ldots, \lambda_r$, where $\lambda_1 \geq \lambda_2 \geq \cdots \geq \lambda_r$. Matrices $\mathbf{\Psi}$ and $\mathbf{\Phi}$ which are formed from the corresponding eigenvectors will then diagonalize $\mathbf{X}$ as

$$\mathbf{X} = \mathbf{\Psi}\mathbf{\Lambda}\mathbf{\Phi}^T \tag{2}$$

where $\mathbf{\Lambda}$ is the diagonal matrix defined as

$$\mathbf{\Lambda} = \begin{pmatrix} \sqrt{\lambda_1} & 0 & \ldots & 0 \\ 0 & \sqrt{\lambda_2} & \ldots & 0 \\ \vdots & \vdots & \ddots & \vdots \\ 0 & 0 & \ldots & \sqrt{\lambda_r} \end{pmatrix} \tag{3}$$

The SVD transform of the image $\mathbf{X}$ is then given by

$$\mathbf{\Lambda} = \mathbf{\Psi}^T\mathbf{X}\mathbf{\Phi} \tag{4}$$

which is a separable transform that diagonalizes a given image. The eigenvalues provide useful information about the matrix $\mathbf{X}$. If $r < M$ then the matrix is singular and the eigenvalues $\lambda_{r+1} =$

$\cdots = \lambda_M = 0$. The conditional number of a matrix is defined as λ_1/λ_M. A matrix is said to be ill-conditioned if the condition number is large. Therefore, these eigenvalues are not only in proportion to the intensities of $\mathbf{X}$ but also change as the contents of $\mathbf{X}$ change. Thus, it is clear that $\mathbf{\Lambda}$ carries necessary information about $\mathbf{X}$.

In our data, the images are of size 500×430 pixels. To compute the singular values, the entire image was divided into subimages of size 11×11. The subimages which lie on the border of the images were omitted. Ignoring those blocks with zero value pixels there were a total of 1401 blocks for an image to be processed stepwise. The elements of matrix $\mathbf{\Lambda}$ have to be obtained for each block. Since the block size is small, the process does not have the numerical limitations of SVD when dealing with computation of eigenvalues and eigenvectors of large matrices. For a 11×11 matrix, at most 11 eigenvalues can be extracted. These eigenvalues can be used directly for the detection/classification process by presenting them to the neural networks. Since the last few eigenvalues are very small, it would be sufficient to use only the first 8 eigenvalues for training, which possess more than 99% of the image energy.

III. Neural Network Classifiers

The neural network training schemes can be generally divided into supervised and unsupervised [1]. When the number of classes and the desired outputs for each input set are known, supervised networks are preferred; otherwise, unsupervised training is more suitable.

In an unsupervised learning scheme, each output unit is trained to respond to a particular class of input pattern which allows clustering of the patterns. The system extracts the salient statistical features of the input population. Since there is no *a priori* set of categories into which the patterns are to be classified, the system has to develop its own representation of the input stimuli. It is imperative for the cloud classification problem that no desired output has to be specified for each input set by using an unsupervised training. This requirement is stipulated since the cloud classification of every scene can be different. Thus, not only the detection task can be performed but also some classification capabilities may be achieved.

The Kohonen self-organizing feature map [5] is among the most popular unsupervised neural networks. In this network, the weights are adjusted so that the winning output neuron has a weight vector with minimum Euclidean distance from the input vector. The neurons which are close enough to the winning neuron in a neighborhood will also have high output values. Therefore, the weights associated with these neurons undergo changes. As the learning progresses the neighborhood shrinks to declare only one winning neuron. This type of network can produce better results than supervised learning especially for high dimensional data with overlapping class boundaries.

Let the input vector to the network be $\mathbf{X}$ and the weight matrix be $\mathbf{W}$, the winning neuron c is determined such that

$$\|\mathbf{X} - \mathbf{W}_c\| = \min_j \|\mathbf{X} - \mathbf{W}_j\|, \qquad \forall j \tag{5}$$

The weights to the winning neuron j as well as those of its neighbors are updated according to the rule

$$\mathbf{W}_j(t+1) = \begin{cases} \mathbf{W}_j(t) + \alpha[\mathbf{X}(t) - \mathbf{W}_j(t)], & \text{when } j \in N_c; \\ \mathbf{W}_j(t), & \text{otherwise.} \end{cases} \tag{6}$$

where α is the learning rate which decreases linearly to zero during training. The size of neighborhood, N_c, decreases to one winning neuron as the learning proceeds. A Gaussian function is commonly used as the neighborhood function. Due to this collective learning scheme, similar inputs will be mapped on the same or neighboring neurons. Thus, the topology which is inherently present in the inputs will be preserved under this mapping.

In a Kohonen network the number of outputs should be specified before the training process starts. Nine output neurons were used for this detection/classification problem in order to accommodate different possible classes. The SVD outputs of each block from each day constitute a training set. The training sets from different days of the same block are sequentially presented to the network for training. After the training is done, these sequences of images are classified so that input sets with different characteristics are assigned to different categories. Since the characteristics of each block from the entire image are independent, training has to be performed for every block. This can be demonstrated in Fig. 2. The data in block 1 from day 1 to day 15 construct a set of training examples. After the training is done for this block, the training proceeds for data in block 2 from day 1 to day 15.

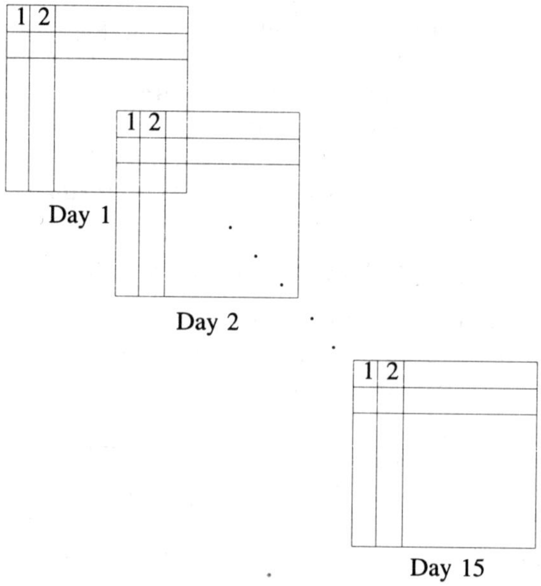

Fig. 2 The training scheme for the entire image.

As stated in Section I, the input data representation by SVD has important effect on the results of training. If the original eigenvalues were used as the input, the network would be able to perform classification based upon both the intensity and the textural information. However, if the training sets contain significant variations, in order to separate these inputs the classification tends to ignore small variations between different input sets and thus produces misclassification. This happens especially often when only a small portion of a block contains cloud.

In many data representation methods, the input data are first normalized. If the input eigenvalues are normalized, the intensity information no longer exists. Only the textural information is available for the networks. Thus, the classification can be achieved even when there are slight variations in texture. Nevertheless, even though two input sets with same normalized eigenvalues may have different intensity levels, they will still be classified into the same class. To remedy this deficiency, the inputs can be arranged to include the normalized eigenvalues together with an additional input node which carries the intensity information. The intensity information can be obtained directly using the normalization factor. However, the normalization factor is too big to use as an input and it has to be scaled in order to have its value comparable to the other inputs so that they are equally important to the network.

IV. Results and Discussions

The GOES satellite images in the visible and IR sensor range for the month of July 1988 were analyzed. The visual and IR data sets contained 21 and 22 days worth of data. For each type, the data of 15 days were selected for training and the rest was used for testing. The training process for IR and visible data took same amount of computation and were done independently. The entire training time for each type of data took approximately 325 minutes CPU time on an IBM RISC/6000 machine. The computation time required for performing SVD operation and neural network testing of an entire image is less than 15 seconds. It should be mentioned that the computation time can be considerably reduced when using a parallel processor or a supercomputer, as most of the computations involved vector processing.

Although after the training the images were classified into different categories, there is no knowledge about which output unit belongs to which cloud class since the training was unsupervised. This map visualization and monitoring task has to be done separately and manually which can become lengthy and tedious. In order to reduce this time consuming process, the output units which correspond to lower input scaled normalization factors, i.e., intensities are set to background, i.e., "no cloud" classes. For the input set that has intensity near the borderline the corresponding eigenvalues are examined. For background these eigenvalues should be close to those with lower intensities which were clearly part of the background. In such a case, it means that the intensities of the background change uniformly. Note that it is possible that more than two output nodes can belong to the background because of the image intensity variations.

Figs. 3 (a) and (c) show the original processed images for IR and visible sensors, respectively. Figs. 3 (b) and (d) show the corresponding processed IR and visible images, respectively. Both types of images exhibited some false alarms and misdetections. The false alarms were caused by background variations which did not satisfy the simple decision rule during the map visualization and monitoring task. The major reason for misdetection is that training data were not properly selected. For example, if the training data for an area only included sunny days, the network will not be able to pick up cloudy days. In order to have good generalization capability, it is desired that all the possible cases can be provided for training which means all seasons, not just a summer month will need to be analyzed.

A traditional but simple rule for cloud detection is that the visible intensities of the background are usually darker than those in the cloud areas. For IR images, colder areas give rise to higher intensity levels while visible images, brighter areas have higher intensities. Difficulties arise when the visible background has higher pixel values or when cloud has lower pixel values. This can be seen from the image histogram where overlapping regions occur between the cloud and the background. The performance of a typical thresholding technique is strongly dependent on the amount of overlap. The approach proposed in this paper considered both intensity and textural information and is very sensitive to input variations, thus it provides better classification in many difficult situations such as cirrus clouds, low clouds and high intensity background. For example, in Fig. 3(c) the images have a big portion of cirrus clouds on the upper-left hand which is difficult to identify by a simple threshold but was detected by the neural networks.

V. Conclusions

This paper presents the results of research on cloud detection and classification from IR and visible images using artificial neural networks. The learning and generalization capability of the neural networks were demonstrated. Excellent results were obtained, especially for the IR images, by effectively utilizing the image textural and intensity information as opposed to many of the conventional methods [2, 4, 6] which are only able to use one of those features.

References

[1] J. A. Freeman and D. M. Skapura, *Neural Networks, Algorithms, Applications and Programming Techniques*, NY: Addison-Wesley, 1991.

[2] A. H. Goodman and A. Henderson-Sellers, "Cloud detection and analysis: A review of recent progress," *Atmospheric Research*, vol. 21, pp. 203–228, 1988.

[3] A. K. Jain, *Fundamentals of Digital Image Processing*, NJ: Prentice-Hall, 1989.

[4] J. Kittler and D. Pairman, "Contextual pattern recognition applied to cloud detection and identification," *IEEE Transaction on Geoscience and Remote Sensing*, vol. 23, no. 6, pp. 855–863, November 1985.

[5] T. Kohonen, *Self-Organization and Associated Memory*, NY: Springer-Verlag, second ed., 1987.

[6] W. B. Rossow, "Measuring cloud properties from space: A review," *Journal of Climate*, vol. 2, pp. 201–213, 1989.

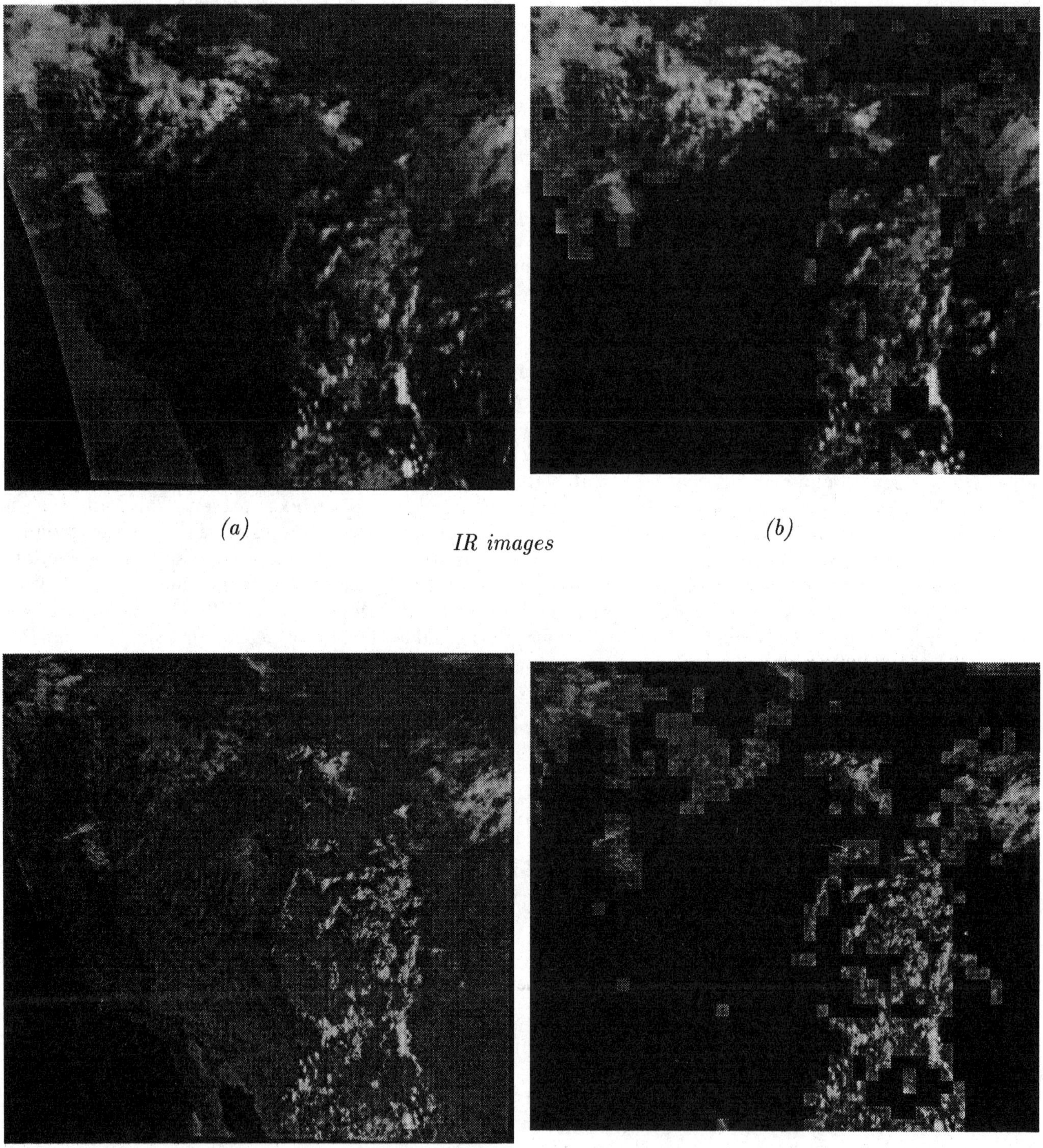

(a) IR images (b)

(c) Visible images (d)

Fig. 3 Four original and processed cloud images.

An Active Vision System for a Location Task Using an Inhomogeneously Blurred Image

T. Yagi †, N. Asano ††, K. Gouhara †††, Y. Uchikawa ††††
† Dept. of Electronic-Mechanical Engineering, Nagoya University, Nagoya, Japan
†† Dept. of Electrical Engineering, Nagoya University, Nagoya, Japan
††† Dept. of Electrical Engineering, Chubu University, Kasugai, Japan
†††† Dept. of Electronic-Information Engineering, Nagoya University, Nagoya, Japan
E-mail : yagi@bioele.nuee.nagoya-u.ac.jp

Abstract–This paper describes a simple method to detect a location of each object using an inhomogeneously blurred image, and the implementation of its method to an active vision system in order to execute a location task. In the proposed method, which based on our previous theoretical study on the early vision, a camera-taken image is processed with high resolution near the optical axis of the camera, and with low resolution in the periphery. Using such inhomogeneously blurred image, we can classify the objects in respect with their location in view. This method is implemented to our proposed mobile camera as the active vision system. The experimental results show that every object in view is easily foveated one after another.

I. INTRODUCTION

Active vision [1][3][4] is expected to solve the ill-posed problem in computation of 3-D information from the 2-D images. An important factor in active vision is literally "active", in other words, "mobile". In order to move a view of a camera (or some other image input device), a target object must be searched among others, and its location should be determined prior to its movement. Therefore the determination of each object's location in the camera-taken image is essential in active vision systems. This task is called a location task [3].

A location task is considered as a part of the image segmentation in the image processing. Among a large number of conventional methods, the segmentation by means of clustering several features in the feature space is probably the most popular one [5][8]. This method, however, needs to obtain various features of each object like brightness, color, edge, and so on. After clustering each features in the feature space, a location of each object is computed. Therefore the more features are necessary, the longer processing time will be required. Moreover, it is more difficult to apply this method in mono-color images than in color ones. On the contrary, a directed split-and-merge procedure is the clustering the location of each object in the image space [6]. This method also needs several steps for processing; however, a location of each object is directly determined without clustering features, and possible to be applied in mono-color images.

Our previous theoretical study in the early vision has shown that an *inhomogeneous* morphological feature in the vertebrates' retina causes the non-uniform spatial resolution in vision, and plays a great role to classify the location of each visual stimulus in a scene [9]. Because of the long processing time, our findings in this previous study are difficult to be implemented for the industrial uses. Therefore we have been seeking a more simple method for a location task [2].

In this paper, focusing on the inhomogenity in vertebrates' vision, and a directed split-and-merge procedure, we develop the previously proposed method. We use partially blurred image, and apply the artificial neural networks to determine the location of each object. Besides, we add the adjustment method. The advantage of our method is its simple processing., and less processing time in order to execute a location task in moon-color images. In this paper, we also apply this method to our active vision system, and make an experiment to foveate each object in view.

II. LOCATION TASK

In order to execute a location task, we introduce the following method. It consists two steps, the approximate determination of the location and the adjustment phase.

A. Eye Field Processing & PNN

For the approximate determination of the location, we use the inhomogeneously blurred image. Because this processing is the imitation of the human vision, we have named it as Eye Field Processing (EFP). In EFP depicted in Fig. 1, every input image is split into relatively smaller size near the optical axis than in the periphery. Therefore EFP makes the resolution in the processing image inhomogeneous. It means that the resolution in the processed images is higher near the optical axis and lower in the periphery. Because the various split sizes are previously determined, the processing time is always constant while it is varied in a directed split-and-merge procedure.

In our previous study [2], it is ambiguous how to split the camera-taken images with various sizes. According to our theoretical study on the early vision [9], the *linearly* increased dendritic field size in the retinal ganglion cells plays a great role in determination of the spatial resolution. Although we have still investigated other neurological and optical

0-7803-1901-X/94 $4.00 ©1994 IEEE

factors to affect the inhomogeneous vision, we have been confirming that the morphological feature mentioned above is the main factor in computing the proximity of the visual stimulus to the optical axis. In this paper, based on our theoretical findings, we make the split size in EFP increase *linearly* with the eccentricity from the center in view. It enables the camera to detect the object near the optical axis at the first.

In each split area, the brightness of each pixel is summed, then summed value is divided with the size of the split area in order to obtain the mean brightness. Because of the inhomogeneous split size, the area which contains the object near the optical axis is expected to have the greater mean value of the brightness. After these processing, the partially blurred image is sent to Position Neural Network (PNN) [7]. PNN is the three layered artificial neural network which outputs the x-y coordinate from the image, using the back-propagation learning method. In this paper, each split area corresponds to input units in PNN (Fig. 2). The network size is 100 units in input layer, 15 units in hidden layer, and 2 units in output layer. Using PNN, the position where the split area has the maximum value among others is computed for the movement of the camera.

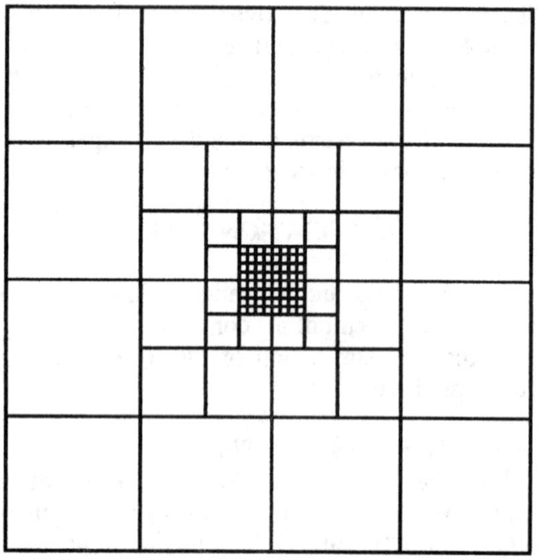

Fig. 1. Schematic diagram of Eye Field.

B. Adjustment of the determined location

Our previous study has shown that EFP is effective to determine the approximate location of the target [2]. The determined location, however, contains some errors even though the training in the network is completed. In order to obtain the precise location for the further processing, for example, identifying the target object, or grasping it with a robot hand, we introduce an adjustment method of the determined location.

After the determination of the approximate location, it is checked if one of the smallest split area, which is the center in view, has the maximum value. If it does not, EFP is taken again. Because the target must be already close to the optical axis after the first movement, the second EFP will be possible to foveate the target at the center in view. If one of the smallest split area already has the maximum value, the optical axis is moved towards that area. After the brightness of each pixel is summed in the smallest areas *only*. The small movement is repeated until the total value in the smallest areas reaches to the maximum. After these adjustment proceedings, the target object is expected to be detected at the center in view.

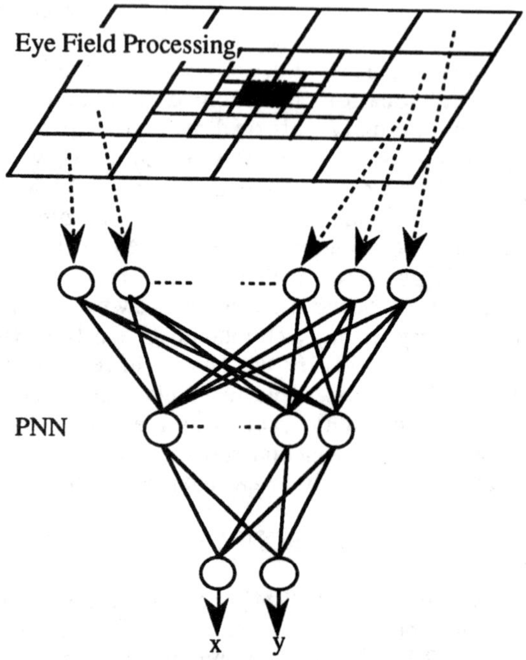

Fig. 2. The determination of the approximate location of the object in view.

III. ACTIVE VISION SYSTEM

Using EFP with the adjustment processing, we constitute an active vision system, called Eye Mover (Fig. 3a). This system does not require the complicated calculation of the position for the movements. Using an X-Y plotter as an actuator, we incorporate a small CCD camera into a ball joint that is linked to the actuator with a sliding rod. The distance between the rotational center and the camera itself is limited to be short (at the maximum, 0.22m), in order to make the inertia small. This simple mechanism enables the camera to foveate the target object with fast speed, and to keep a wide mobile range.

When a focusing point of the camera coincides a rotational center of a ball joint, the moving distance in the X-Y plotter denoted by D_{act} is proportional to the distance on an image plane between the center and the target object, which is denoted by D_{image} (Fig. 3b). Therefore D_{act} is given with the following simple equation;

$$D_{act} = L \tan\theta = \frac{L \cdot D_{image}}{F} \qquad (1)$$

L is defined as the distance between the rotational center and the X-Y plotter, θ as the angle between the optical axis and the target object, and F as the distance between the focusing point and the image plane of the camera. Because L and F are already given, only D_{image} is measured on the image for camera movements.

To avoid the repetitive fixation towards the same object, each movement is checked with the stored past movement data prior to the next movement.

Fig. 3a. Active Vision System, "Eye Mover".

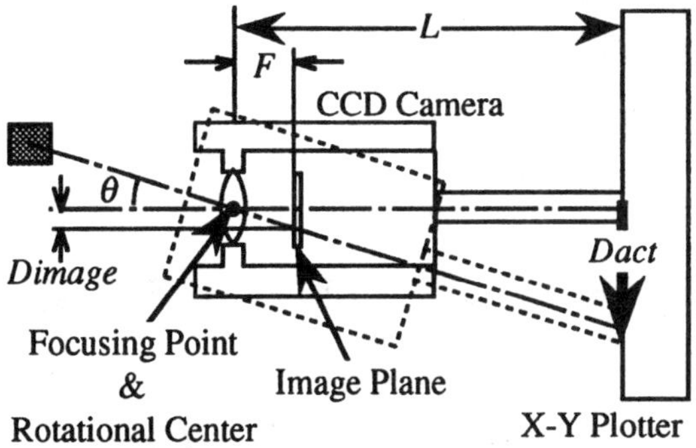

Fig. 3b. Schematic diagram of the mechanism in Eye Mover.

V. EXPERIMENTAL RESULTS

For the experiment at this moment, we use very simple scenes which have simple target objects with plane backgrounds. Fig. 4 shows an example of the displayed scenes. In the scene, several objects (white cubic objects in the figure) were distributed at random. The square symbols in the figure show the determined position of each object, and straight lines denoted the locus of the optical axis of the camera. Starting from the center of the image, Eye Mover moved towards each object, and foveated it at the optical axis within a few movements.

Fig. 5a to 5d displays the camera-taken images (left) and the processed images (right) at position "a" to "d" in Fig. 4. At first, the camera was staring at the center of this scene denoted "a" in Fig. 4, The camera-taken image at this position is depicted in Fig. 5a-left. Fig. 5a-right shows the processed camera-taken image using EFP. The brightness indicates the signal level at each split area. This figure displays the split area located at the upper left of the center has the maximum signal level among others. Applying PNN, the position is computed, then the camera is moved towards it for foveation. Fig. 5b-left is the camera-taken image after the camera movement. This shows the object is almost correctly foveated. The processed image at this position is shown in Fig. 5b-right.

Fig. 5c and 5d show the adjustment phase. Fig. 5c-left shows the camera-taken image after several movements. Because the smallest split areas do not have the maximum level (Fig. 5c-right), the camera moved slightly using the adjustment method. After the second small movement, the object was foveated correctly at the optical axis (Fig. 5d).

V. DISCUSSION AND CONCLUSION

The experimental results above have revealed that the proposed system is able to emulate a location task using EFP when simple scenes are applied. The present brief analysis is showing that the optical axis moves closely enough to each object after the first camera movement, then each object is precisely detected within a few adjustment steps. In EFP, the camera-taken images are split into various sizes, and brightness in each split area is summed only. Therefore three factors; a location, a size and a brightness of each object, might affect the determination of the fixation point. When each object has the almost same size shown in Fig. 4, the object closely located to the optical axis is tend to be detected. When an object is larger or brighter than others, such an object is often foveated earlier. The relation among these three factors is now being evaluated quantitatively as well as the acuity of the detection, and the sequence of the camera movements.

A location task has been focused in our present study. In future, an identification task will be our next step. After each object is foveated at the optical axis with high resolution, it is identified what it is. There are various identification methods. Among them, our laboratory has already developed the identification method using artificial neural networks. We are thinking to apply it to our system.

REFERENCES

[1] Aloimonos, J., and Weiss, I., and Bandyopadhyay, A., "Active vision," Proc. 1st Int. Conf. Computer Vision, 35-54 (1989)

[2] Asano, N., Yagi, T., Gouhara, K., and Uchikawa, Y., "Pattern extraction system using a nonuniformly resolved image," Proc. IJCNN '93 Nagoya, Vol. 2, 1195-1198 (1993)

[3] Bajsy, R., "Active perception vs. passive perception," Proc. IEEE Workshop on Computer Vision, (1985)

[4] Ballard, D.H., "Reference Frame for Animate Vision," Proc. 11th Int. Joint Conf. Artificial Intelligence, 1635-1641 (1989)

[5] Coleman, G.B. and Andrews H.C., "Image segmentation by clustering," Proc. IEEE, 67, 5, 773-785 (1979)
[6] Horowitz, S.L. and Pavlidis, T., "Picture segmentation by a directed split-and-merge procedure," Proc. 2nd IJCPR, 424-433 (1974)
[7] Imai K., Gouhara K., and Uchikawa Y., "Detection of position and size using neural network learning," Trans. of IEICE (D-II), J-74-DII, 6, 784-756 (1991)
[8] Ohlander R., et. al., "Picture segmentation using a recursive region splitting method," CGIP, 8, 3, 313-333 (1978)
[9] Yagi, T., Gouhara, K., and Uchikawa, Y., "An algorithm of eye movements in selective fixation," Proc. IEEE Int. Conf. Neural Networks, 761-765 (1993)

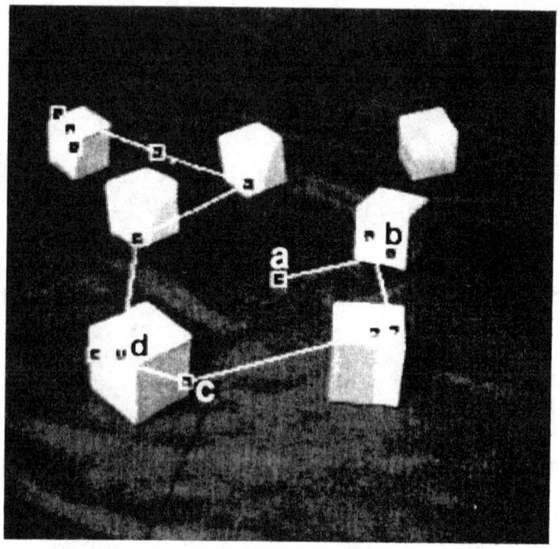

Fig. 4. Displayed image.

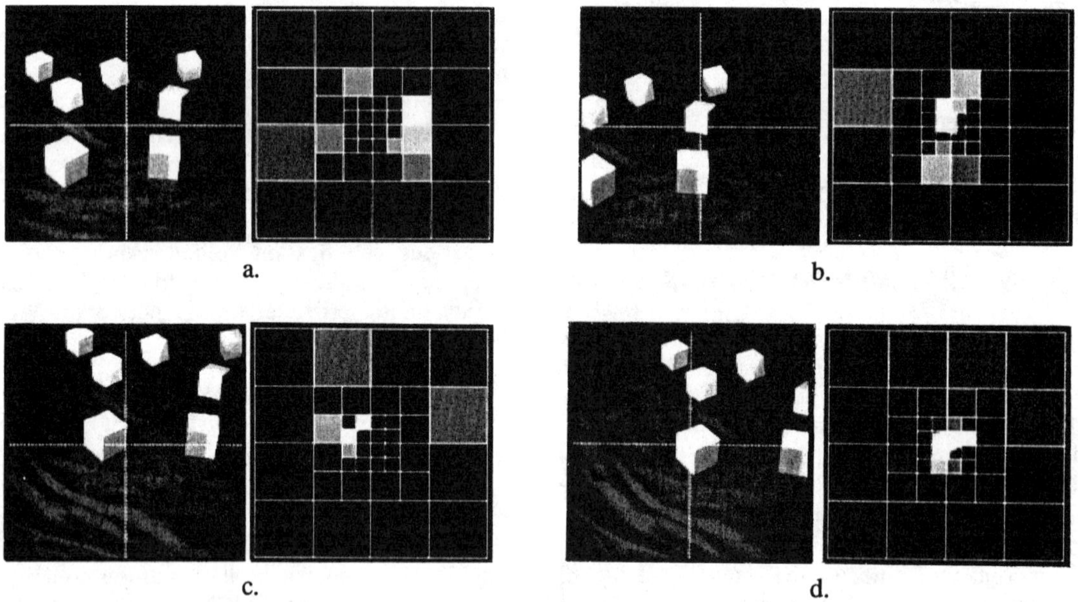

Fig. 5. The camera-taken (left) and the processed (right) images.

A Counterpropagation Neural Network for Determining Target Spacecraft Orientation

Bradley L. Vinz and Dr. Sara J. Graves

Computer Science Department
University of Alabama in Huntsville
Huntsville, AL 35899

Abstract— **This paper describes a concept that integrates a counterpropagation neural network into a video-based vision system employed for automatic spacecraft docking. A brief overview of docking phases, the target orientation problem, and potential benefits resulting from an automated docking system is provided. Issues and challenges of automatic target recognition, as applied to automatic docking, are addressed. Following a review of the architecture, training, and desirable characteristics of the counterpropagation network, an approach for determining the relative orientation of a target spacecraft based on a counterpropagation net is presented.**

I. Introduction

THE ability to determine the rotational displacement of an independent body, relative to a reference orientation, has significant application, especially to the autonomous docking of spacecraft. The process of automating the orientation determination necessitates a vision system to provide an input. In a video-based vision system, an image target scene is captured and compressed into a pattern of pixels. The key to determining the relative orientation of the target lies within the pixel-analyzing process — that is, how the pixel arrangement is interpreted. Due to their strong pattern-matching and pattern-mapping capabilities, artificial neural networks offer a potential role in the determination process. This paper will demonstrate the practical application of a counterpropagation neural net for integration into a chaser spacecraft vision system employed for automatic spacecraft docking. In particular, it will be shown how a counterpropagation net can be constructed and trained for determining the orientation of a target spacecraft relative to a closing chaser spacecraft.

In Sections II and III, background information on automatic docking principles and automatic target recognition issues are discussed. The benefits of a realized automated system are revealed. Section IV describes spacecraft coordinate systems and explains how an image system can be constructed. Section V provides an in-depth review of the counterpropagation network architecture and training procedure. The advantage of applying counterpropagation technology to automatic docking is highlighted. And finally, Section VI describes the functionality of the chaser spacecraft vision system components and presents a counterpropagation net approach for determining target spacecraft orientation.

The research of Bradley L. Vinz is supported by a grant provided by the NASA Graduate Student Researchers Program, Contract Number NGT-50679.

II. Automatic Docking

The automation of the docking procedure between two orbital spacecraft is a sophisticated task involving a high degree of vehicular coordination. After the target spacecraft has been autonomously identified by the chaser spacecraft during rendezvous, the chaser performs a series of maneuvers to accomplish mechanical latching with the cooperative target.

Successful docking relies on the chaser's ability to continuously recognize a target within a scene and produce accurate closing maneuvers (Fig. 1). The vision system, equipped with a video camera and imaging components, captures a target image, processes it, and provides target data to the control system. The control system analyzes this data and issues appropriate six degree-of-freedom maneuvering commands to the propulsion system.

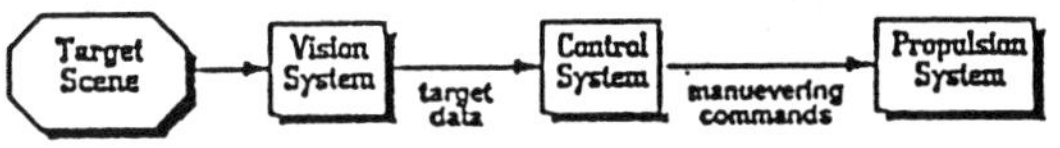

Fig. 1. Recognition/action process of chaser spacecraft

A. Automatic Docking Phases

To make the automated rendezvous and docking task more manageable, the chaser vehicle closure maneuvers may be divided into two distinct phases: approach maneuvers and docking maneuvers [1]. Approach maneuvers begin at about 200 meters from the target vehicle and proceed to approximately 10 meters — the distance at which final docking maneuvers commence (Fig. 2). At the start of the docking maneuvers, it is assumed that an alignment target emblem, located near the docking latch mechanism on the target vehicle, will be within the field of view of the chaser vision system (Fig. 3).

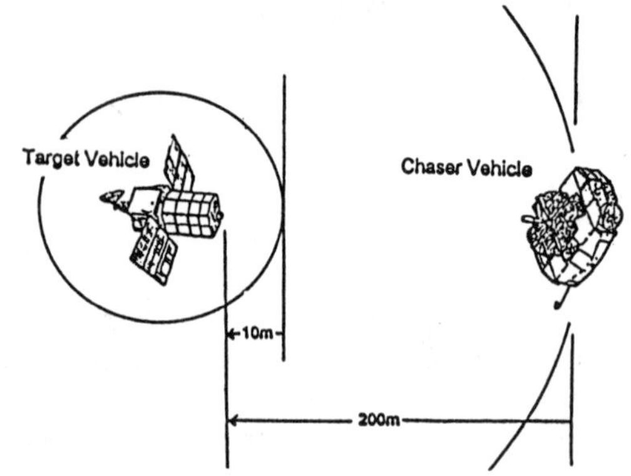

Fig. 2. Target and Chaser Spacecraft at start of Approach Maneuvers Phase

This alignment target can provide visual cues of alignment errors during final docking [2]. As the procedure executes, the video data captured by the camera is processed to determine the translational and rotational misalignment data. Computation systems onboard the chaser spacecraft then designate appropriate thruster firing commands required to control the final closure. The docking maneuvers terminate upon completion of rigidly latching the spacecraft together.

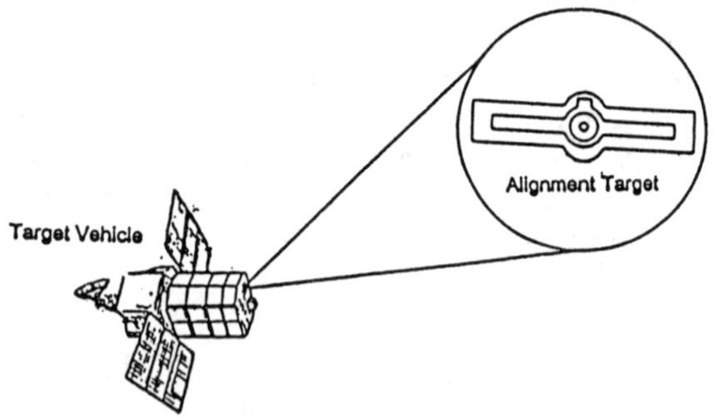

Fig. 3. Location of Alignment Target

B. *The Target Orientation Problem*

As stated in [1], before the docking phase can commence, the problem of determining the orientation of the target spacecraft with respect to the chaser spacecraft must be continually solved during the approach phase. The alignment target on the target vehicle must be located so that the chaser can perform appropriate maneuvers for correct alignment of the chaser and target coordinate systems. Thus, the goal of the approach phase is to maneuver the chaser vehicle about the target vehicle so that the alignment target is in the field of view as required for the docking phase. This paper will offer a neural network solution for determining spacecraft orientation during the approach phase.

C. *Potential Payoffs*

At the present, the U.S. space program has no actual experience in automatic docking, although much research has been accomplished [3] and current efforts are being pursued by NASA to develop an automated system [4].

When successful deployment of automatic docking systems can be realized, many attractive potential payoffs become evident [5], such as reduced costs, extended operational capabilities, and lowered risk factors. For example, high costs are incurred for manned missions — mainly due to added capability (life support systems, software, vehicle durability, etc.) to support the crew at minimize risk to life. With an automated spacecraft, these safety procedures can be relaxed, thus reducing costs.

Operational capabilities of automated spacecraft can be extended to include satellite servicing, space debris collection, and reboosting of low-orbiting (falling) satellites to higher orbits [5]. Other capabilities may include on-orbit refurbishment of the space station [6], orbital assembly [7], and prevention of radioactive materials (e.g. distressed space reactor cores) from reentering the atmosphere [8]. Many of these extended capabilities, such as the servicing of satellites in high orbit, prove too impracticable for manned spacecraft.

III. Automatic Target Recognition

This section identifies useful criteria that necessitates a robust design strategy for the automated visual system of a chaser spacecraft.

A. *Issues*

The objective of video-based target recognition is to identify a target within a scene from a sequence of digitized images. Automating this process can be a very difficult task [9], especially when the images contain scenes with structured background clutter, foreground visual obstruction, and varying intensity levels within the digitized images themselves.

For automatic docking, the recognition task becomes more complicated, since the target may exhibit dynamic behavior [10] — for example, the target vehicle may lose its attitude stabilization and start to spin, cone or tumble. The recognition system is required to produce fast and reliable responses due to the dynamic environment in which it must operate. It must also make efficient use of computational resources due to spacecraft resource restrictions.

B. Fundamental Needs

It has been suggested [9] that a robust automatic target recognition system should satisfy four fundamental needs: 1) target signatures and backgrounds are well represented, 2) the system is able to adapt to target or environmental changes, 3) target representation consists of easily identifiable features, and 4) the system makes use of a priori knowledge about target signatures and backgrounds.

As noted above, fast response times are essential in adapting to dynamic changes in the environment (e.g. sun shadows, tumbling target, embedded objects in background). Also, the more a priori knowledge about the target that is built into the system, the better the chances of successful recognition.

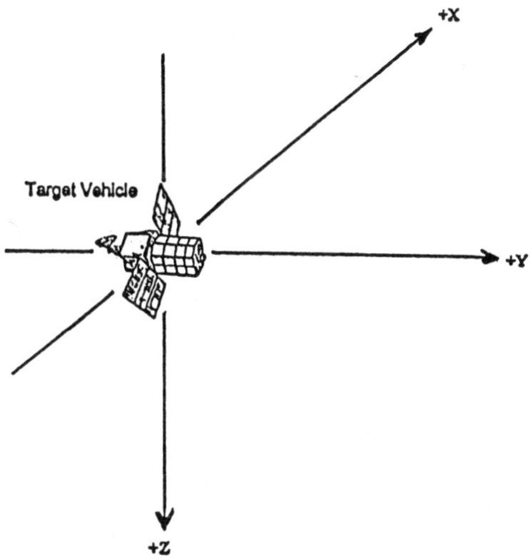

Fig. 4. Target Vehicle Coordinate System

IV. A PRIORI KNOWLEDGE ACQUISITION

After introducing the coordinate reference systems used for orbital docking, this section focuses on the construction of a priori knowledge built into the chaser spacecraft vision system.

A. Coordinate Systems

A spacecraft is capable of exhibiting 6 degrees-of-freedom: 3 degrees of freedom in linear translation (X_T, Y_T, Z_T) and 3 degrees of freedom in body rotation (X_R, Y_R, Z_R). A spacecraft's translation and rotation errors are represented in time using a coordinate reference system (Fig. 4). Since the chaser and target spacecraft can each exhibit 6 degrees-of-freedom, they both possess separate vehicle coordinate systems. For successful docking to occur, the chaser vehicle coordinate system must be aligned (in a predetermined attitude) with the target vehicle coordinate system.

B. Image Construction

In order to build a priori knowledge about the target (vehicle) into an automated target orientation determination method, a collection of image views of the target can be established before a space-based docking mission is attempted. It is assumed that a ground-based facility will provide the means by which the images can be captured and processed. The collection will consist of views of the target vehicle obtained by translating and rotating a video camera about the target in various displacements from the target origin. In actual flight, it is assumed the camera will be mounted in a fixed boresight on the chaser. This method of image construction simulates approximate image captures that a chaser spacecraft could perform during actual docking.

V. THE COUNTERPROPAGATION NETWORK

The simplified feed-forward version of the counterpropagation network [11] combines the Kohonen self-organizing feature map with the Grossberg outstar, resulting in a fully connected three layer paradigm having capabilities beyond the individual scopes of the Kohonen and Grossberg models. This section provides a brief review of the basic counterpropagation network and introduces concepts and terminology discussed in the next section.

A. Architecture

In the feed-forward counterpropagation net, information proceeds through a series of three layers [11]: the input layer, the Kohonen (hidden or middle) layer, and the Grossberg (output) layer. The network accepts an input pattern presented to its input layer, processes this information forward through its Kohonen and Grossberg layers, and produces an output pattern in response to the input pattern. The architecture gives the network this capability of mapping one pattern into another for a whole collection of patterns.

Each layer is composed of a set of artificial neurons (units) which receive, process, and send signals to and from neurons in other layers. A neuron communicates information with another neuron by means of a connection. Since the counterpropagation net is fully-connected, each input layer neuron is connected to every Kohonen layer neuron; likewise, each Kohonen layer neuron is connected to every Grossberg layer neuron. At the receiving end of a connection between two neurons, a modifiable entity called a weight (connection strength) is associated with the neuron receiving the signal over the connection. Typically, the receiving neuron multiplies this signal by its connection strength, producing a weighted signal. The neuron then sums all inbound weighted signals and applies a transfer function, resulting in an output signal.

The network operates in two modes [11]: train (learn) mode and run (recall) mode. During training, the net learns to associate specific input patterns with correct output patterns using a collection of input-target pattern pairs. The input patterns are divided into distinct classes by the Kohonen layer. Each class is associated with a specific output (target) pattern stored in the Grossberg layer. During recall, a trained net will classify an input pattern — even one that has not been presented during training — into the closest matching established class. The stored pattern in the Grossberg layer associated with this class is then output from the network.

B. Training

During training [11], the network is repeatedly presented with the collection of input-target pattern pairs. As each pattern pair is presented, learning occurs through selective modification of the Kohonen and Grossberg weights. Once the correct input-to-target pattern mapping is memorized, training is complete.

For the following discussion, assume the network consists of n input neurons, p Kohonen neurons, and m Grossberg neurons. Each input-target pattern pair consists of an input vector $X=(x_1,x_2,...,x_n)$ and a target vector $Y=(y_1,y_2,...,y_m)$. The set of weights associated with Kohonen neuron i, $1 \le i \le p$, comprise the weight vector $W_i=(w_{i1},w_{i2},...,w_{in})$, where w_{ij} represents the connection strength between input neuron j and Kohonen neuron i. Likewise, the set of weights associated with Grossberg neuron j, $1 \le j \le m$, comprise the weight vector $U_j=(u_{j1},u_{j2},...,u_{jp})$, where u_{ji} represents the connection strength between Kohonen neuron i and Grossberg neuron j. Initially, all weight vector values are randomly assigned [11].

In train mode [11], the network delivers each pattern pair to the input and Grossberg layers, respectively. The input layer then distributes the entries of the input vector to the neurons in the Kohonen layer. The target pattern vector is processed during computation of network output. The procedure proceeds to the next level of processing in which a winner-take-all competition is held among the Kohonen layer neurons.

During competition [11], each Kohonen neuron computes a Euclidean distance metric, $\| W_i - X \|$, which determines how close each neuron's weight vector W_i lies to the input vector X. The neuron with the minimum distance wins the competition and sets its output signal z_i to 1. The remaining neurons set their output to zero.

Following the competition, only the winning neuron's weight vector is modified (using the Kohonen learning rule):

$$W_i^{new} = W_i^{old} + \alpha(X - W_i^{old}) z_i$$

where $z_i = 1$ is the output of the winner and α is the learning rate $(0.0 \le \alpha \le 1.0)$. The learning rate usually starts out high (e.g. $\alpha = 0.8$) and decreases as learning progresses [11].

After processing of the Kohonen layer is completed, the network output vector is calculated [11]. Each Grossberg layer neuron j, $1 \le j \le m$, computes the summation of inbound weighted signals:

$$y_j' = \sum_{i=1}^{p} u_{ji}^{old} z_i$$

producing the network output $Y' = (y_1, y_2, ..., y_m)$. In the comparison of output vector Y' to the target vector Y, the Grossberg layer weights are modified according to:

$$u_{ji}^{new} = u_{ji}^{old} + \mu(y_j - y_j')$$

where μ is a learning rate, $0.0 \le \mu \le 1.0$.

At this point, the next pattern pair is presented and training continues until the input-to-target pattern mapping is learned.

C. A Desirable Characteristic

The counterpropagation net possesses an interesting characteristic that makes it a good candidate for determining the orientation of a spacecraft: its architecture is relatively simple, functioning mainly as a look-up table capable of generalization [12]. Even when presented with a partially incomplete or partially incorrect input vector, the generalization capability of this network permits it to produce a desirable response. To put it another way, an automated vision system (designed for automatic docking) containing a trained counterpropagation network will be able to generalize and adapt to target or environmental changes — such as if the target vehicle is partially casted with sun shadows, resulting in an incomplete digitized image.

VI. THE CHASER SPACECRAFT VISION SYSTEM

This section describes the functionality of the chaser vehicle vision system components and then offers an approach for determining the relative orientation of a target spacecraft based on a counterpropagation net.

A. System Components

The automated chaser vehicle vision system (Fig. 5) for the approach phase consists of five components:

(1) video camera
(2) digitizer
(3) image compression component
(4) image normalization component
(5) target orientation determination component

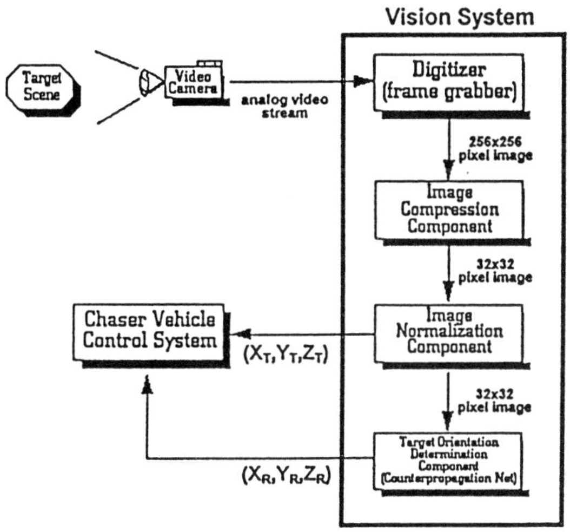

Fig. 5. Chaser spacecraft vision system.

The following example highlights the interaction of these components. The digitizer captures a frame of analog video target data and converts it into a 256 x 256 pixel image. This image is reduced to a 32 x 32 binary pixel image using image compression. The image normalization component then determines the (X_T, Y_T, Z_T) translation misalignment of the target. In the process, the region within the image representing the target is centered and scaled to coincide with images used during a priori knowledge acquisition (i.e. the image presented during training of the counterpropagation network). The (X_T, Y_T, Z_T) translation misalignment is output to the control system. The target orientation determination component accepts the 32 x 32 normalized binary image as input and produces the (X_R, Y_R, Z_R) rotation misalignment data for input to the control system.

B. Target Orientation Determination Component

The orientation displacement of the target spacecraft with respect to the chaser spacecraft can be approximated using a counterpropagation neural network. By orientation displacement, it is meant, the rotational displacement of the target vehicle in 3 degrees-of-freedom (rotation about the X, Y and Z axes, respectively) from a reference position of the target within the target coordinate system. The counterpropagation net accepts a captured 32 x 32 normalized binary image as input and produces the orientation displacement (X_R, Y_R, Z_R) of the target spacecraft.

During training, the network is presented with a collection of input-target pattern vectors representing image views of the target from various orientation displacements. The network requires 1027 neurons in the input layer, of which 1024 (32×32) distribute data (binary image values) to the Kohonen layer and 3 distribute the correct orientation displacement (correction vector) (X_R, Y_R, Z_R) to the 3 neurons in the Grossberg (output) layer. As learning progresses, the Kohonen layer neurons categorize each input pattern vector (image) presented to it into a distinct class. The Grossberg layer neurons associate the correct output (orientation displacement) with this established class. It follows that a collection of p unique training images results in p distinct classes — requiring the net to maintain p neurons in the Kohonen layer. The next step is to determine the number of distinct classes required.

In a simple 2-dimensional spacecraft orientation system, [13] established a set of 12 image classes from a stationary (fixed) location using a rotatable, but non-translatable, target. During training, the system captured video images of a spacecraft model rotated about a principal axis using 30-degree angular increments (0°, 30°, ... 330°). The 2-dimensional configuration used a counterpropagation network that categorized images into 12 distinct classes — requiring 12 neurons in the Kohonen layer. This method can be extended to a more realistic situation where distinct classes are established for images obtained for a target rotated in 3 dimensions.

It should be noted that the translation displacement (X_T, Y_T, Z_T) of the target — that is, the linear movement of the chaser along the X, Y, and Z axes — will be determined by the centering and scaling processes of the Image Normalization Component. This will greatly reduce the number of neurons needed in the Kohonen layer.

In 3 dimensions, an object is not restricted to rotation about a single principal axis, but may freely rotate about three axes (X, Y, and Z) — in any combination of angular displacements. The combined rotation can be expressed as a vector of angular displacements

(X_R, Y_R, Z_R) from a standard reference position $(0°, 0°, 0°)$, where

X_R = angular rotation displacement about X-axis
Y_R = angular rotation displacement about Y-axis
Z_R = angular rotation displacement about Z-axis

Suppose that the 2-dimensional scheme (mentioned above) for capturing images of a target rotated by 30-degree angular increments (during training) is extended to 3 dimensions. Holding X_R and Y_R constant and letting Z_R vary by 30°increments $(0° \leq Z_R \leq 330°)$ results in 12 unique training images. Similarly, holding X_R constant and letting Y_R and Z_R vary by 30°increments $(0° \leq Y_R, Z_R \leq 330°)$ results in 12×12 = 144 unique training images. And finally, varying all three angular displacements results in $12 \times 12 \times 12$ = 1,728 unique training images — which the network will categorize into 1,728 distinct classes (Table 1).

X_R	Y_R	Z_R
0°	0°	0°
0°	0°	30°
⋮	⋮	⋮
0°	0°	330°
0°	30°	0°
⋮	⋮	⋮
0°	30°	330°
⋮	⋮	⋮
330°	330°	330°

Table 1. Possible combinations of angular displacements.

Thus, a trained counterpropagation net using this system of a priori image views will require 1024 neurons in the input layer, 1,728 neurons in the Kohonen layer, and 3 neurons in the Grossberg layer.

VII. Conclusion

Determining the orientation of a target spacecraft relative to a chaser spacecraft during the approach maneuvers phase of automatic docking is a challenging problem. The counterpropagation neural network offers a viable role in the solution. Integrating a counterpropagation net into the chaser spacecraft vision system provides robustness, allowing the system to operate reliably within the dynamic environment in which it is placed.

This paper has demonstrated the practical application of the counterpropagation network to automatic docking — in particular, to determine target spacecraft orientation. Future research will concentrate on developing automated methods for use in the final docking maneuvers. Here, too, the counterpropagation network may provide an invaluable role.

References

[1] Vinz, B.L. (1993). *"An Automated DBMS Approach To The Target Orientation Problem"*. [Graduate Student Paper, Dr. Sara J. Graves, Advisor]. ACM Mid-Southeast Chapter Fall Conference, Gatlinburg, TN, November 11-12, 1993, 12 pages.

[2] Dabney, R.W. (1992). *"Application of Neural Networks to Autonomous Rendezvous and Docking of Space Vehicles"*. American Institute of Aeronautics and Astronautics (AIAA) Paper 92-1516. Space Programs and Technologies Conference, Huntsville, AL, March 24-27, 1992.

[3] Berenji, H.R. and T. Castellano (1991). *"Hybrid Neural Network and Fuzzy Logic Approaches for Rendezvous and Capture in Space"*. In *NASA Automated Rendezvous and Capture Review: A Compilation of Abstracts.* National Aeronautics and Space Administration (NASA). Williamsburg, VA, November 19-21, 1991.

[4] Shannon, E.J. [editor] (1993). "Team to Develop Automated Rendezvous and Capture Technology", National Aeronautics and Space Administration (NASA). Marshall Star, Marshall Space Flight Center (MSFC), Huntsville, AL, Vol. 33, No. 16, January 1993.

[5] Vinz, F.L. (1989). *"Computer Vision for Space Applications"*. In *Intelligent Robots and Computer Vision VIII: Systems and Applications.* Proceedings of the Meeting, Philadelphia, PA, November 9-10, 1989. Society of Photo-Optical Instrumentation Engineers (SPIE), Vol. 1193, p. 100-110.

[6] Bergmann, E. (1991). *"An Automated System for Spacecraft Proximity Operations"*. In *NASA Automated Rendezvous and Capture Review: A Compilation of Abstracts.* National Aeronautics and Space Administration (NASA). Williamsburg, VA, November 19-21, 1991.

[7] Bittel, M.A. (1991). *"Six-Degree of Freedom Test Facility"*. In *NASA Automated Rendezvous and Capture Review: A Compilation of Abstracts.* National Aeronautics and Space Administration (NASA). Williamsburg, VA, November 19-21, 1991.

[8] Buden, D. and J.A. Angelo, Jr. (1991). *"Automated Technologies Needed To Prevent Radioactive Materials From Reentering The Atmosphere"*. In *NASA Automated Rendezvous and Capture Review: A Compilation of Abstracts.* National Aeronautics and Space Administration (NASA). Williamsburg, VA, November 19-21, 1991.

[9] Roth, M.W. (1990). *"Survey of Neural Network Technology for Automatic Target Recognition"*. Institute of Electrical and Electronics Engineers (IEEE). IEEE Transactions on Neural Networks, Vol. 1, Issue 1, March 1990, p. 28-43.

[10] Vinz, F.L., L.L. Brewster, L. D. Thomas (1984). *"Computer Vision for Real-Time Orbital Operations - Center Directors Discretionary Fund Final Report (Project No. 82-27)"*. National Aeronautics and Space Administration (NASA). NASA Technical Memorandum 86457, Marshall Space Flight Center (MSFC), Huntsville, AL, August 1984.

[11] Hecht-Nielsen, R. (1990). Neurocomputing. Addison-Wesley, 1990.

[12] Wasserman, P.D. (1989). Neural Computing: Theory and Practice. Van Nostrand Reinhold, 1989.

[13] Freeman, J.A. (1988). *"Neural Networks for Machine Vision: The Spacecraft Orientation Demonstration"*. e^{x}ponent: Ford Aerospace Technical Journal, Fall 1988, p. 16-20.

Illusory Contour Detection Using MRF Models

Suthep Madarasmi[1], Ting-Chuen Pong[1] and Daniel Kersten[2]
[1]Department of Computer Science, [2]Department of Psychology
University of Minnesota, Minneapolis, MN 55455

***Abstract*— This paper presents a computational model for obtaining relative depth information from image contours. Local occlusion properties such as T-junctions and concavity are used to arrive at a global percept of distinct surfaces at various relative depths. A multi-layer representation is used to classify each image pixel into the appropriate depth plane based on the local information from the occluding contours. A Bayesian framework is used to incorporate the constraints defined by the contours and the prior constraints. A solution corresponding to the maximum posteriori probability is then determined, resulting in a depth assignment and surface assignment for each image site or pixel. The algorithm was tested on various contour images, including two classes of illusory surfaces: the Kanizsa and the the line termination illusory contours.**

I. Introduction

Occluding contours refer to the image contours that correspond to object boundaries. Such contours are an integral part of the construction of the 2.5-D sketch [8] and, therefore, are important in computer vision research. We present an algorithm that uses contour information to segment an image into meaningful regions and to provide a relative depth ordering of the partitioned regions. A model for obtaining shape from occluding contours should be able to explain illusory (subjective) contour perception since these illusions arise from artificially arranged cues to occlusion. The primary objective of our model is to account for such illusions through a cooperative process of computing depth and its segmentation.

Illusory contours have been used as the intuitive proof of several models of perceptual organization. On the other hand, there are several theories which have been proposed to account for illusory contours.

This research was supported in part by a contract between the Army Research Office and the University of Minnesota for the Army High Performance Computing Research Center. Additional support was furnished by Air Force Office of Scientific Research grant 90-0274.

An important question to address is whether illusory contours provide any insight into the computational mechanism of the brain. Equivalently, an interesting issue is if such mechanisms are needed for building a robust vision system. We take the position that illusory contours serve to strengthen edges (or even create edges) where other segmentation properties such as depth suggest their appearance.

Kanizsa [5] provides a thorough analysis of T-junctions and how surfaces are perceived for various arrangements of T-junctions. He demonstrated the perception of terminating lines as a weak form of T-junction and many terminators as a cue for an occluding surface such as in figure 1a. Similarly, corners with aligned edges are viewed as degenerate forms of T-junctions as in the Kanizsa Pac-man illusion in figure 1b. Such figures offer valuable insight into the computational processes involved in the human visual system to complete contours given partial evidence. Kanizsa suggests that a non-local process with knowledge of surfaces and occlusion is involved in the image completion process; thus, accounting for such illusions.

Grossberg and Mingola [4] (see also [3]) use a neural model to explain how segmentation may arise across image regions without any luminance differences. Network interactions between three components namely, the Boundary Contour (BC) system, the Feature Contour (FC) system, and the Object Recognition (OR) system are used to explain the illusory contours and related phenomena. The BC system acts as a hypothesis generator to generate perceptual boundaries for the FC system. They suggest that the visible percepts are the result of the hypothesis confirmation by the FC system using input from the BC system. The OR system is connected to the BC system and provides top-down learned template signals for the conversion of various BC features into FC features. Thus, accounting for the perception of illusory contours. Our algorithm can be related to that of Grossberg and Mingola at this abstraction level.

0-7803-1901-X/94 $4.00 ©1994 IEEE

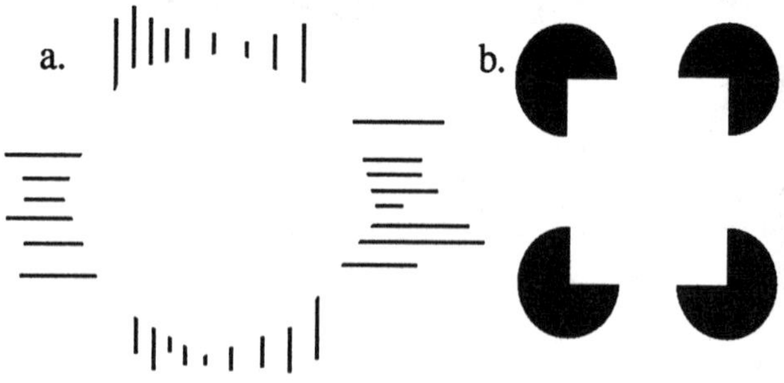

Figure 1: *Subjective contours formed by (a) terminating lines and (b) corners*

II. Multi-Layer Representation

An important feature in our approach lies in the underlying representation for segmentation and surface ordering. Our model uses a different output representation from the commonly used edge or contour based methods. To illustrate our representation for image grouping, consider the input range image of two overlaid surfaces such as a textured, transparent cylinder shown in figure 2a using intensity to code the depth. Figure 2b shows the depth profile of such an image. If the segmentation relied on edges, the result would be multiple spurious edges for such an image due to the local discontinuities as shown in figure 2d. Clearly, this is not desirable since we clearly perceive two overlaid surfaces for such a display. Our multi-surface representation produces an explicit piece-wise smooth segmentation of the image into surfaces while also computing the relative depth of the surfaces. This representation is, in spirit, similar to the one proposed by Darrell and Pentland [1]. Our multi-layer representation for shape has been successfully used in various other low-level vision modules [6, 7].

III. Algorithm

In this section we discuss our segmentation algorithm using the depth information present in occluding contours. Since we are interested in applying this approach to obtain illusory contour perception, we make an assumption that all surfaces in the scene are piece-wise constant or fronto-parallel. To illustrate the modified multi-layer segmentation output representation used here, consider the input image shown in figure 3a. The output shown in part b of the figure consists of three intensity coded labels with layer 1 (background) shown in black, layer 2 (closer surface) shown in gray, and layer 3 (fore-

Figure 2: *The multi-layer representation: An example*

ground surface) shown in white. The layer label also represents the depth value so that layer N has a depth of N where N=1 represents the background. Since each depth layer contains a constant value due to our assumption of piece-wise constant surfaces, their values need not be shown. Stated more formally, given a set of depth values $D_{\{\wp\}}$, the image segmentation representation is modified so that the produced output is $C_{\{\wp\}}, U_{1\{\wp\}}, U_{2\{\wp\}}, \ldots, U_{L\{\wp\}}$ where C is a layer classification image, $\wp$ is the image domain, and each U_l now has a constant depth value of l. Since each U_l has a constant value, we could drop its representation in the output and only look at the layer labels at each pixel given by $C_{\{\wp\}}$. Thus, the desired depth image and the labeling image are the same:

$$D_{\{\wp\}} = C_{\{\wp\}}$$

Our algorithm for segmenting contour images for illusory contour perception involves the confirmation of various local hypothesis. For example, any surface such as the Pac-man in figure 4a may be interpreted as either a circle partly occluded by the corner of a rectangle or as a simple Pac-man shaped object. Line terminations can either be due to an

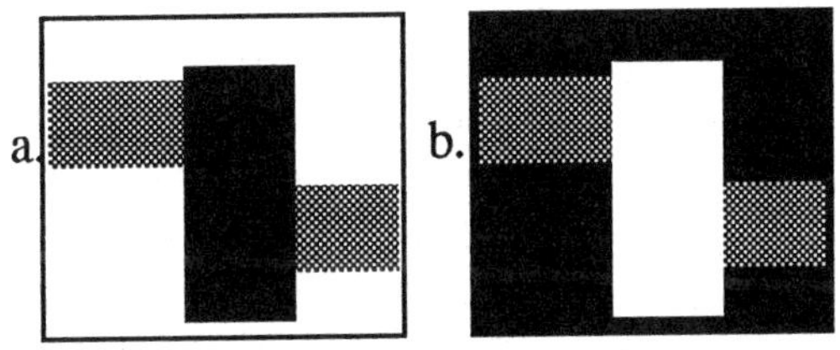

Figure 3: *The multi-layer representation for depth from occluding contours*

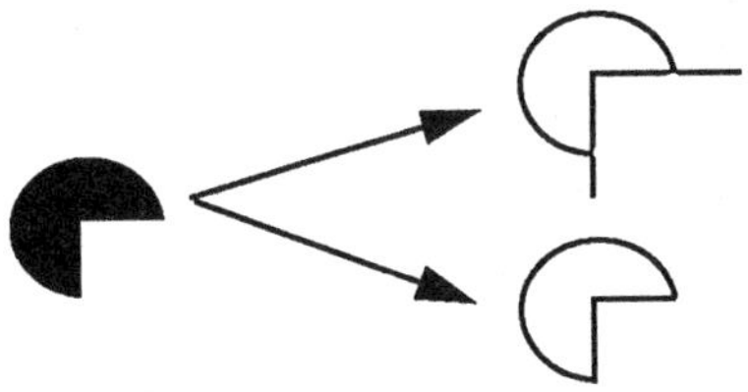

Figure 4: *Examples of the occlusion hypothesis.*

occluding surface or due to a naturally terminating line as shown in figure 4b. In general, the shape of any visible surface may be partly due to an occluding surface or may be due to the surface having exactly that underlying shape to begin with. We define a local cost based on convexity and corner properties so that certain surfaces are preferred to others. For example, surfaces with convex boundaries have lower cost than those with concave boundaries. Surfaces with a corner boundary formed by the meeting of contours at less than 180 degrees angle are preferred. Thus, illusory surfaces are formed by the grouping of hypothesized local evidences of occlusion constraints to form a set of salient surfaces each with a cost.

For a single Pac-man the square region may be hypothesized as an occluding surface. This occluding surface would trigger a grouping in the frontal depth plane by extending the corner of the rectangle. Thus, the four corners may successfully be grouped into a rectangle. Note that the Pac-man image is interpreted as comprised of an illusory, salient rectangle occluding 4 surfaces (discs), instead of 4 high-cost, non-salient Pac-man shapes. Our treatment of the perception of illusory contours involves the minimization of a cost function that involves this type of saliency measure.

Our model for illusory contour perception can be outlined by the following steps:

1. *Image feature extraction.* In this step the edges are obtained and grouped to find features such as T-junctions, corners, convex contours, and line terminations.
2. *Layer and depth assignment to each pixel.* In this step each pixel is assigned an appropriate layer label and, thus, a depth value to minimize a cost defined by the local constraints.
3. *Layer and depth assignment to grouped regions.* Here, the pixels are assumed grouped by the previous step and are moved as regions to minimize the same cost function as in the previous step.
4. *Object completion in the visible depth plane.* Here, extrinsic edges in the visible depth plane are extended to group objects. This is primarily responsible for the grouping of illusory contours.

In our model steps 2,3, and 4 are performed simultaneously, with steps 3 and 4 occurring after longer time intervals than step 2.

A. Bayesian Approach

We use a Bayesian approach to compute the scene attribute, namely the layer assignment l which also has an associated relative depth of l:

$$p(l|I) = \frac{p(I|l)p(l)}{p(I)}$$

where I is the intensity input image data. Each constraint is expressed as a local cost function using the Markov Random Field assumption [2], that pixels values are conditional only on their nearest neighbors. Using the Gibbs-MRF equivalence, the energy function can be written as a probability function:

$$p(x) = \frac{1}{Z}e^{-\frac{E(x)}{T}}$$

where Z is the normalizing constant, T is the temperature, E is the energy cost function, and x is a random variable.

B. The Cost Function

We start with a L layer system each layer representing a different fronto-parallel depth plane. Initially, each pixel is assigned a random layer value and, therefore, a corresponding depth value. After the computations are completed, each pixel is assigned to the layer consistent with the 3-D occlusion cues in the input image.

Using a small $3x3$ window we obtain a feature measure. Using the window we obtain two constraints on the depth of nearest 8 neighboring pixels with respect to the center pixel: Above (A), Below (B) and Same (S). For the T-junction, if the center pixel is at the the occluding part of the junction, all the neighboring pixels with different intensity are constrained to be below. Thus, a cost is assigned to it if the constraint is not met. Neighboring pixels with different contrasts are constrained to be in

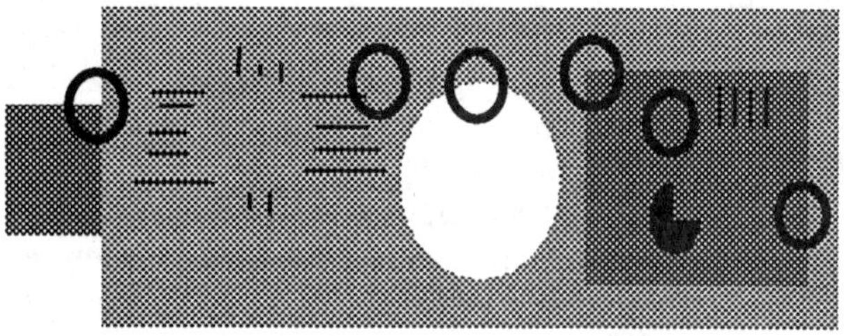

Figure 5: *Examples of regions with occlusion constraints. The circled constraints from left to right include T-junction, line termination, convex contour, corner, illusory L junction and illusory T junction.*

different layers. In addition, we have a constant intensity constraint C that forces neighbors with the same intensity value to have the same depth. Note that this constraint discourages the formation of illusory contours. Another very important cost is what we call the illusory junction cost J. This cost is high if the T-junction or corner is partly (or completely) formed by illusory contours and does not a consistent depth assignment. For example, if a single Pac-man creates an illusory boundary that meets its borders, the T-junction formed would require that the border be above the illusory surface. Since the background is below the illusory surface in this case, the illusory junction is assigned a rather high cost. This cost ensures that a single Pac-man does not form illusory boundaries with the border of the image.

The local occlusion constraints used in our simulations are T-junctions, surround occlusion, and line terminations with examples shown in figure 5. The surround occlusion example includes convex contours and corners that are constrained to be above the background. This is because closed contours are frequently perceived as the inner region of a surface that, therefore, occludes the background. These constraints can be thought of as mere hypothesis which could be rejected to minimize the total system energy. For example, for the single Pac-man shown in figures 4, the hypothesis that an edge of a square occludes the disk both of which are low cost surfaces (i.e. two convex surfaces) may be rejected since it produces illusory junctions and the system may settle at perceiving a high cost surface (i.e. a non-convex surface shaped like a Pacman).

The data constraints A, B, S, C, J costs at each pixel can be converted into an energy function representation as:

$$V_D = \lambda_A V_A + \lambda_B V_B + \lambda_S V_S + \lambda_C V_C + \lambda_J V_J$$

where the λ's are the weighting factors, and V_A, V_B, V_S, V_C, and V_J are the energy associated with the above, below, same, no-edge, and illusory junction constraints, respectively. This energy function is defined locally for each pixel as in the example above.

The V_A constraint is given by:

$$\sum_i^M \sum_{j \in N_i} \delta(d_i, d_j) A_i j(\sigma(l_i, l_j) + \beta\sigma(l_j, l_i))$$

where i is the index for each image pixel, j is the nearest neighbor of i, d_i is the input luminance value at pixel i, $A_i j$ is the local Above constraint A determined initially by the various $3x3$ window configurations. The various functions defined above are given by:

$$\delta(a,b) = \begin{cases} 1 & \text{if } a-b \neq 0 \\ 0 & \text{otherwise} \end{cases} \quad \sigma(a,b) = \begin{cases} 1 & \text{if } a-b > 0 \\ 0 & \text{otherwise} \end{cases}$$

In plain English, the above constraints ensures that if the local intensity defines an Above relationship, the layer assignment should enforce the same.

The V_B constraint is analogous to the V_A constraint with some of the signs reversed:

$$\sum_i^M \sum_{j \in N_i} \delta(d_i, d_j) B_i j(\sigma(l_j, l_i) + \beta\sigma(l_i, l_j))$$

where $B_i j$ is the local *Below* constraint B.

The V_S constraint ensures that if there is an intensity edge, the layer and depth assignments must also be discontinuous,

$$\sum_i^M \sum_{j \in N_i} \delta(d_i, d_j) S_i j(1 - \delta(l_i, l_j))$$

where $S_i j$ is the local *Same* constraint set to a value of 1 in our experiments.

The V_C constraint penalizes the formation of illusory contours by ensuring that if neighboring intensity is the same, then the layer and depth assignments should also be the same:

$$\sum_i^M \sum_{j \in N_i} (1 - \delta(d_i, d_j))\delta(l_i, l_j)\phi_i * \sigma(\phi_j, \phi_i)$$

where ϕ is a feature measure at each pixel. This constraint is active only when the neighboring feature measure ϕ_j is greater than the current ϕ_i. Since ϕ is proportional to the distance to an occluding feature, the regions with constant intensity rely more on their neighbor's values than on their own. The V_J constraint penalizes illusory junctions that have incorrect depth relations.

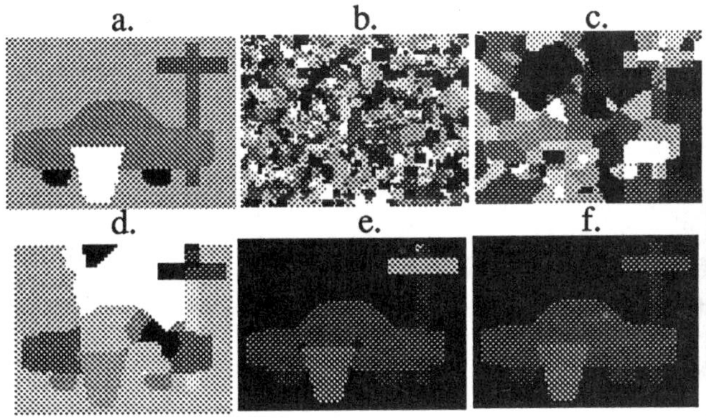

Figure 6: *(a) Input: Cartoon image with depth information. (b-f) Results from selected iterations.*

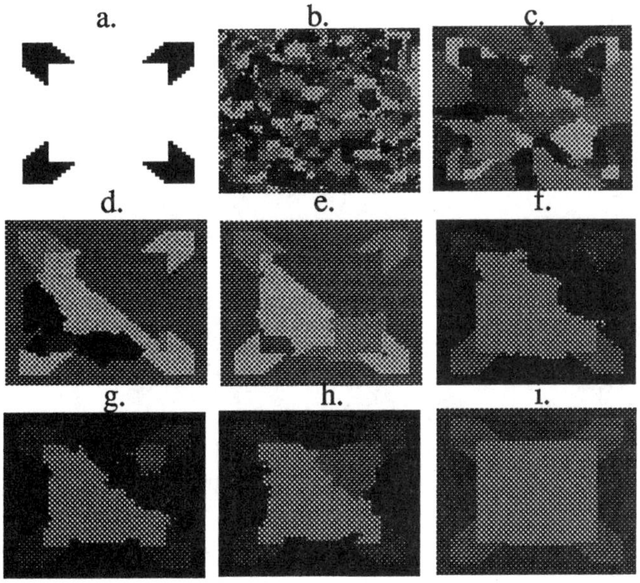

Figure 7: *(a) Input: Kanizsa type of Illusory contours. (b-i) Results from selected iterations.*

IV. Experimental Results

Various test images were used in our simulations including those with and without illusory contours. In figure 6 is the cartoon-like image of various objects with depth relations. Note that to use the minimum number of layers, the tires and the pole are placed in the same depth plane. Since other cues to depth such as familiarity are not available to the system, the objects are placed in the depth plane based purely on their information from occluding contours.

Images with illusory contours were also used in our simulations. Figure 7 shows the segmentation result for a Kanizsa type illusory contour. Note that the 4 dark objects eventually get assigned to a single layer. The V_L cost is primarily responsible for bringing the regions down to the same depth plane. The pixel-based depth assignment allows for new surfaces to be generated while the region-based assignment is responsible for merging these regions or moving the regions to the appropriate depth plane to minimize the global cost. Thus, the corners of the occluding rectangle places the pixel above its background. This depth value is propagated to the various neighbors due to the confidence weighting ϕ and eventually meets in the middle region. The parts are then grouped by the region-based depth assignment process. Note that the boundary saliency term V_E eventually plays a role in assigning the labels to bias the formation of straight line boundaries.

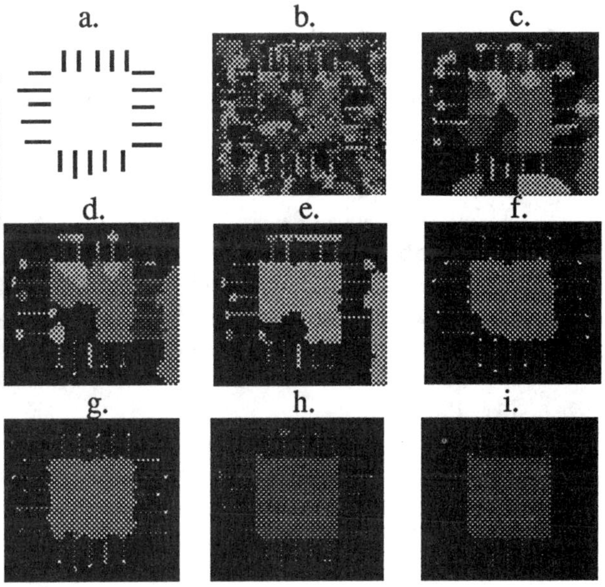

Figure 8: *(a) Input: Illusory contour from line terminations. (b-i) Results from selected iterations.*

A second class of illusory contours is formed by the termination of lines. Figure 8 shows the input to our segmentation algorithm. The result is the formation of a square illusory surface shown in the figure. The background eventually gets assigned to layer 0, the lines get assigned to layer 1, and the center illusory surface to layer 2.

V. Conclusion

We have shown that the depth planes, multi-layer representation which is based on surface completion instead of contour extension is appropriate for the segmentation of illusory contours. The study of illusory contours provides insight into the cooperative mechanisms involved in shape perception and object grouping. Our model can account for the various known classes of illusory contours and the representation is appropriate for the modeling of each.

REFERENCES

[1] T. Darrell and A. Pentland. Discontinuity models and multi-layer description networks. M.I.T. Media Lab Technical Report no. 162, 1991.

[2] S. Geman and D. Geman. Stochastic relaxation, gibbs distribution, and the bayesian restoration of images. *IEEE Transactions on Pattern Analysis and Machine Intelligence*, 6(6):721–741, 1984.

[3] S. Grossberg and E. Mingolla. Neural dynamics of form perceptions: boundary completion, illusory figures, and neon color spreading. *Psychology Review*, 92, 1985.

[4] S. Grossberg and E. Mingolla. Neural dynamics of perceptual grouping: Textures, boundaries, and emergent segmentations. *Perception and Psychophysics*, 38(2), 1985.

[5] G. Kanizsa. *Organization in vision.* Praegar, New York, 1979.

[6] S. Madarasmi, T. C. Pong, and D. Kersten. Stereopsis for opaque and for transparent surfaces. In C.L Giles, S.J. Hanson, and J.D. Cowan, editors, *Advances in Neural Information Processing Systems 5.* San Mateo, CA: Morgan Kaufmann Publishers, 1993.

[7] S. Madarasmi, T.C. Pong, and D. Kersten. Multi-layer surface segmentation through energy minimization. Transactions of the IEEE Conference on Computer Vision and Pattern Recognition 93, 1993.

[8] D. Marr and T. Poggio. Cooperative computation of stereo disparity. *Science*, 194:283–287, 1976.

A Modular Boolean Architecture for Pattern Recognition

A de Carvalho M C Fairhurst D L Bisset

Electronic Engineering Laboratories,
University of Kent,
Canterbury, Kent CT2 7NT, UK
44-227-475413 (tel), 44-227-456084 (fax)
e-mail mcf@ukc.ac.uk

Abstract

This paper describes a modular neural structure where a self-organising Boolean neural network architecture (SOFT) is used as a front-end processor to a feedforward neural architecture based on goal-seeking principles (GSN^f). The characteristics of this architecture are illustrated by considering its application to a character recognition problem.

1 Introduction

Boolean neural networks have been shown to be effective tools for a number of pattern recognition applications [1, 2, 3]. However, in spite of offering a number of advantages over other approaches (in terms, for example, of speed, hardware implementation and simplicity), the recognition performance attainable does not always match that which can be achieved using alternative techniques, and it is therefore desirable to consider ways of improving performance. Boolean neural networks generally function by detecting quantitative similarities between patterns, which leads to a fast deline in performance when pattern diversity increases. Boolean networks operate directly at the pixel level of an image and it is therefore argued that appropriate front-end processing could improve the performance of Boolean networks by mapping N input patterns into $M(<< N)$ binary representations, where similar input patterns would be mapped to the same representation.

An appropriate mapping should make patterns from the same class more similar and patterns from distinct classes more different. This con-

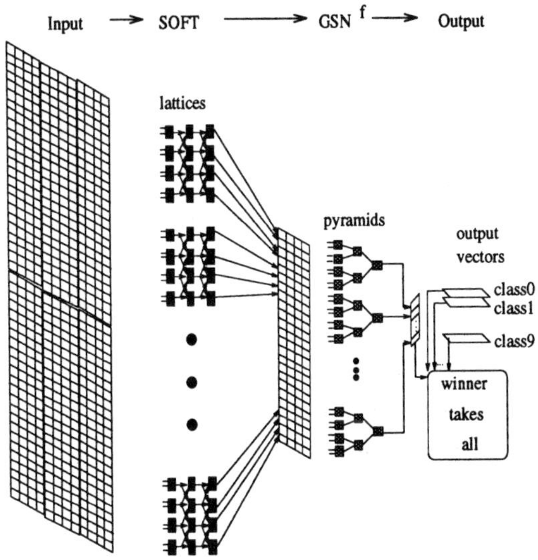

Figure 1: Integrated architecture

cept is similar to the pre-processing performed by the visual cortex, where feature-sensitive cells in the early stages of the visual system detect primitive features such as ends of lines and lines in different orientations, which are used by the later layers in the recognition of a complete visual scene [4]. Feature extraction is an important issue in a number of neural network architectures, either as a main goal [5] or as an intermediate step in achieving some more global function [6]. This paper describes a modular architecture which uses the SOFT feature extractor [7] as a front-end processor and a goal-seeking structure, GSN^f [1], as a classifier. Figure 1 illustrates this architecture.

2 SOFT

SOFT (Self-Organising Feature Extractor) uses a lattice structure and relies on self-organising

0-7803-1901-X/94 $4.00 ©1994 IEEE

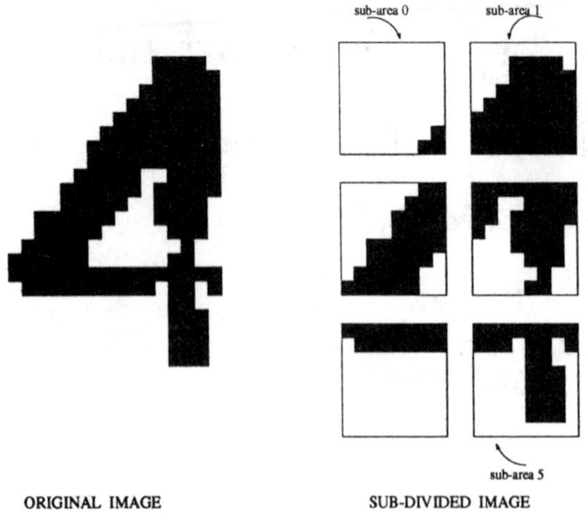

Figure 2: Division of the input in sub-images

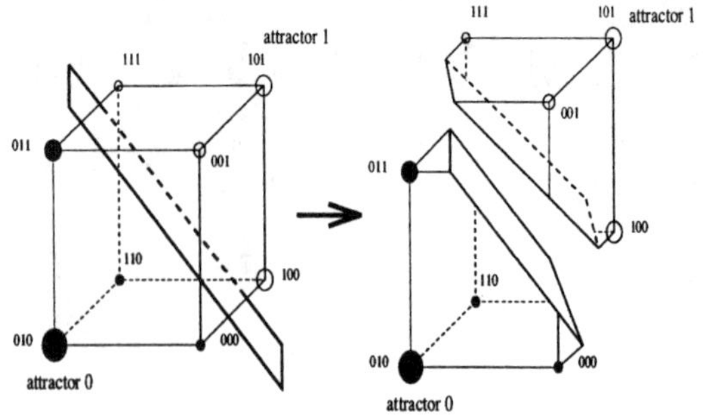

Figure 3: Attractors dividing the input space

properties of local rules at a node level to change the memory content of the nodes and thus the overall function of the network. The design principles adopted are such that they guarantee a fast processing rate with minimum use of memory while ensuring low connectivity, high independence and simple learning and recall rules within the network. As can be seen in Figure 1, each block covers a sub-area of the input image. Its connection mapping will provide more than one path from a given pixel in the input to a given output neuron. This ensures the migration of data across the network and in turn allows the extraction of features filling the input space without high node connectivity. Figure 2 illustrates the division of the input image into six sub-images.

SOFT uses an unsupervised learning algorithm to teach its blocks in parallel. The layers of each neuron block can be trained in a parallel pipeline, starting with the neurons in the first layer and, using the output produced by the already trained previous layer as input, the subsequent layers can be trained. SOFT uses RAM-based neurons [8]. Such a neuron is similar to a Random Access Memory device and uses the input values presented to its input terminals to access one or more of its 2^N memory contents, where N is the number of input terminals. Each neuron can accept, store and generate the values u (an undefined value), 0 and 1 and is trained to work as a very simple feature extractor. A learning rule defines the value to be stored in each addressed content $m_i \in M$ of each neuron by selecting, for each neuron, two memory attractors, which are memory contents with complementary addresses. These attractors are selected by dividing the neuron input space into two halves in such a way that the neuron input patterns with a lower frequency in the training set are situated near to the boundary. The boundary is defined by the addresses whose Hamming distances to both attractors are similar. The SOFT structure can be dynamically redefined during its training by eliminating and replicating neurons, according to the function they perform.

Figure 3 shows an example of how the attractors might divide a particular input space into two halves if connectivity 3 were used. A white circle is drawn for the input patterns that are nearer, in Hamming distance, to the attractor 0, and a black circle is drawn to represent the input patterns nearer, in Hamming distance, to the attractor 1. The larger the circle, the higher the frequency with which that particular input pattern occurs in the training set. Immediately after the attractors for a particular neuron have been chosen, the value to be stored in each of its memory contents will be defined through competition between the attractors. This competition will determine which would be the neuron's most "natural" output. Once the architecture has been trained it can then be used to extract primitive features. The next section describes the second part of the modular architecture, GSN^f.

3 GSN^f

The goal-seeking neuron (GSN) is a deterministic neuron designed to overcome many of the problems found in other Boolean models, maximising the efficiency of storage of values in its memory, storing new information without disrupting previously absorbed information, and employing one-shot (single-pass) learning. The GSN can accept, store and generate values of 0, 1 and u, where u represents an "undefined" value. If there is at least one undefined value on the input terminals of a GSN unit then a set of memory contents, rather than a single storage location, will be addressed, and this is a principal factor in the efficient distribution of stored information across a trained network [1].

GSN networks can be configured in various architectures, and in each a different goal is associated with the neuron. For example, GSN^f [1] is a multi-layer feedforward architecture where the neurons are typically organised into several independent pyramids and the processing is performed by such a system in three different phases. These are a validating phase, which defines which pyramids can be trained, a learning phase, where by using a supervised learning algorithm, defined values can be stored in memory locations holding undefined values, and a recall phase, where the neuron generates as output the predominant value stored in the memory contents addressed from the input.

4 Modular architecture

The main prerequisite for a modular architecture is the compatibility of its internal inputs and outputs. In the SOFT-GSN^f modular architecture, this condition is satisfied, since the SOFT output is directly compatible with the GSN^f input. In the modular architecture the input is first pre-processed by an already trained SOFT to be then directly used without further pre-processing as input to GSN^f. The input image is divided into six areas, where each area covers an 8x8 group of pixels. A three-layer neuron lattice is associated with each area, where each layer has 16 neurons, each with 5 input terminals and either 1 output terminal (when it is the output layer), or 5 output terminals otherwise.

4.1 Recognition performance

In order to evaluate the contribution of SOFT to the recognition performance achieved by GSN^f, both the basic GSN^f architecture and the modular architecture were trained to recognize numeral characters extracted from mail envelopes. In both cases, each network was trained and tested with the original data and with the pre-processed data. In order to evaluate, on a comparative basis, the effectiveness of SOFT pre-processing, experiments were carried out with three different learning algorithms previously used with the GSN feedforward classifier which is to be used as the heart of the proposed modular architecture. These algorithms are the "conventional" GSN^f algorithm (algorithm A [9]) , the "deterministic" algorithm (algorithm B [10]) and the "progressive" algorithm (algorithm C [11]). Table 1 and Table 2 show the recognition performance achieved in each case.

Classification performance			
Number of pyramids	*Correct recognition (%)*		
	Learning strategy		
	A	*B*	*C*
50	70.0	89.5	91.1
100	84.1	93.0	93.5

Table 1: Without pre-processing

Classification performance			
Number of pyramids	*Correct recognition (%)*		
	Learning strategy		
	A	*B*	*C*
50	89.3	93.6	93.4
100	92.5	94.4	94.5

Table 2: With pre-processing

These results clearly show that the SOFT preprocessor provides useful information to the GSN^f classifier. Structurally, it reduces the number of pixels covered by GSN^f from 384 to 96, but the contribution provided by SOFT becomes even more valuable when the number of pyramids used by GSN^f becomes smaller. It is interesting to see that GSN^f with 50 pyramids using pre-processed inputs achieves a recognition performance similar to that achieved by GSN^f with 100 pyramids using the original input patterns.

5 Conclusion

In this paper, a modular Boolean architecture has been described on the basis of an integrated neural classifier. The proposed architecture uses an unsupervised learning algorithm where neuron blocks are trained in parallel and independently of each other as a front-end processor to generate pre-processed input to a GSN^f Boolean classifier.

A number of experiments are reported in order to evaluate SOFT and the results obtained demonstrate that the performance achieved by the modular architecture is better than that achieved by the basic GSN^f, even when a smaller number of pyramids is used in its implementation.

Acknowledgement: A. de Carvalho would like to acknowledge the support of the Brazilian Postgraduate Federal Agency (CAPES).

References

[1] A de Carvalho, M C Fairhurst, and D L Bisset. Classifying images using goal seeking neural network architectures. *IEE Proceedings-I Communications, Speech and Vision*, 40(1):12–18, February 1993.

[2] J D McCauley, B R Thabe, and A D Whittaker. Fat estimation in beef ultrasound images using texture and adaptive logic networks. *To appear in Transactions of ASAE.*

[3] J D Mason, E L Hines, and J W Gardner. Analysis of electronic nose data using weightless neural networks and genetic algorithms. In *Weightless Neural Network Workshop'93, Computing with Logical Neurons*, pages 93–97, University of York, York, UK, April 1993.

[4] D H Hubel and T N Wiesel. Receptive field and functional architecture in two nonstriate visual areas (18 and 19) of the cat. *Journal of Neurophysiology*, 28:229–289, 1965.

[5] T Kohonen. *Self-Organization and Associative Memory*. Springer Verlag, third edition, 1989.

[6] D E Rumelhart and J L McClelland. *Parallel Distributed Processing*, volume 1: Foundations. The MIT Press, 1986.

[7] A de Carvalho, M C Fairhurst, and D L Bisset. SOFT - a Boolean self organising feature extractor. In *Proceedings of the ICANN 92 Conference*, pages 669–672, Brighton, UK, September 1992. Elsevier.

[8] I Aleksander, W V Thomas, and P A Bowden. Wisard: a radical step forward in image recognition. *Sensor Review*, 4(3):120–124, 1984.

[9] E Filho, M C Fairhurst, and D L Bisset. Adaptive pattern recognition using goal-seeking neurons. *Pattern Recognition Letters*, 12:131–138, March 1991.

[10] R G Bowmaker and G G Coghill. Improved recognition capabilities for goal seeking neuron. *Electronics Letters*, 28:220–221, 1992.

[11] A de Carvalho, M C Fairhurst, and D L Bisset. A progressive learning algorithm for GSN feedforward neural architectures. Technical report, Electronic Laboratory, University of Kent, 1993.

Title : A Neural Network Recognition System for Handwritten Chinese Character Using Structured Approach

Authors : Daniel S. Yeung and
Hak-shun Fong,
Department of Computing,
Hong Kong Polytechnic, Hong Kong.
Fax : 7642528 Email : csdaniel@hkpcc.hkp.hk

Abstract

Off-line recognition of handwritten Chinese characters is a formidable challenge. Both structural and non-structural approaches have only achieved limited success. While the non-structural approaches deal with the noise and minor structure-distortions by gathering a large number of character samples, structural ones perform better in handling large structural variations. Recently, neural network is also employed to offer alternative solutions in various manners. However, in these attempts neural network is seldom used to address the handling of the strong structural characteristics of a character set. This paper aims to incorporate structural knowledge of the character set into a neural network, to take advantage of both approaches. Two sets of tests have been carried out. One of them deals with the recognition of seventeen categories of simple Chinese characters. With ten samples in each category written by five individuals, the system achieves a recognition rate of 52.4%. Another test involves the expansion of the system to handle fifty categories. One sample set is used to demonstrate the expandability of this approach. In this test, the system still achieves a recognition rate of 62%. By this approach, potential in learning new writing styles and tolerance to input inexactness are readily achievable by the means of neural network settings. Moreover, techniques in handling large structure variations (as established in structural approaches) can also be realized in the system.

1. INTRODUCTION

Handwritten Chinese character recognition is a formidable challenge because of these characteristics : a large number of frequently used character categories, high pattern complexity, high similarity among categories of characters and great deviation in writing styles. Off-line recognition, i.e., optical recognition, is reckoned to be much more difficult than on-line recognition. On-line recognition systems often rely on the stroke information of the input, such as starting/ending locations of each stroke, the path traced by a stroke and the ordering of the strokes. Lacking these information, off-line recognition approaches depend heavily on other image recognition techniques [1,2]. These approaches can be divided into two major groups, namely structural and non-structural.

The non-structural approaches do not consider the inherent structural properties of a character set. Instead, they often capture either global features through some sorts of transformations on the whole character or local characteristics of different regions of the character [3,4,5]. With these feature-values, representations of the character categories are formed for comparison with input characters. To accommodate various writing styles of a category, the information above must be collected from a pool of sample characters of each category. These approaches are found to be rather insusceptible to noise and minor structure-variations. However, a large number of samples are required to provide representative statistics of a category. The approaches rely solely these features are also found to be sensitive to the large structure deviations which are not uncommon in handwritings. In contrast, attention is paid to the structural properties of Chinese characters in structural approaches. Knowledge of character features, such as feature-points [6], line/curve-segment approximation to a character [7], basic strokes or radicals [8,9] are employed. These features are sometimes organized in structure-tree [10], grammar [11] and graph [12] representations. When integrated with certain matching techniques, e.g., relaxation matching [13] and fuzzy graph matching [12], these approaches offer solutions which are less susceptible to the structure-distortions found in handwritten Chinese characters. Unfortunately, some of these symbolic manipulations involve highly complicated computations. Furthermore, the feature extraction phases involved are often noise-sensitive. Therefore, some approaches proposed recently tend to integrate both structural and statistical techniques [14].

On the other hand, Neural network has demonstrated its abilities in various pattern recognition tasks, including alphanumeric characters recognitions. There are also attempts to employ it in off-line recognition of handwritten Chinese/Kanji characters. According to the roles of neural network in these approaches, three strategies are identified. One strategy is to use a neural network to classify the input feature vectors extracted through conventional methods. For instance, Wang J.F. [15] uses a multi-layer perceptron to classify 48 different radicals, with a recognition rate of 65.6%. Mori Y. [16] adopts a modular approach to organize many small neural networks and also their decisions. Three thousand categories are handled with an accuracy of 74%. Hyman [17] achieves 89.1% recognition with 956 categories. However, increment of the feature vector dimension by about 2.5 times does not lead to

0-7803-1901-X/94 $4.00 ©1994 IEEE

significant improvement. The small improvement arouses a query if this approach is bounded to an unacceptable recognition rate. Indeed, this situation may be due to the fact that no structural property of the character set is considered. In another strategy, neural network is used to extract the relevant features which are to be processed by other mechanisms. Fukushima [18] employs the Neocognitron to the recognition of eight radicals from input characters. It is claimed that, based on the radical information, some Chinese characters are recognized correctly. However, no thorough experimental result is reported. The third strategy employs neural network to recognize the pixel-image of an input character directly. Hildebrandt [19] uses an improved Neocognitron to handle twenty character categories and a recognition rate of 86.9% is achieved. Perfect recognition of 50 categories, using Neocognitron, is also reported by Wang S.D. [20].

Thus, it is found that so far the performance achieved with neural network is quite limited. Either the number of categories attempted is too small to be convincing, or the recognition rate is too low to be acceptable. Moreover, in Hyman's case, the "bounded" performance seems to support the conjecture that structural knowledge consideration is critical for high recognition rate. Nevertheless, the learning capability and tolerance to both noise and input inexactness still make neural network a promising tool to this problem. Therefore, this paper presents an attempt to integrate neural network and structural knowledge of the character set (section 2). The system developed is a cascade of two modules, whose architectures are described in section 3. The first module performs stroke extraction on an input binary thinned character. The results of extraction are then forwarded to the second module. The second module is a modified-Neocognitron which is responsible for recognizing the character structure. Although only seventeen categories of simple characters are handled in the first test, the approach shows certain expandability in the second test (section 4). Discussion on the strengths and weaknesses of this approach is then given. Finally, a concluding section projects some possible future extensions of the work.

2. INTEGRATION OF NEURAL NETWORK & STRUCTURAL KNOWLEDGE

Similar to most conventional practices, the recognition task is decomposed into two subtasks, namely stroke extraction and pattern structure recognition. Basic strokes are chosen as primitive features for two reasons : they are sufficient for the construction of most Chinese characters, and the character representations built upon them are stable. While various approaches adopt different sets of basic strokes [8,21], twenty-two stroke classes are employed here (Fig.1). From the template stroke in every class, at most twenty-seven stroke variants are generated for that class. These stroke variants, generated through horizontal scaling, vertical scaling and rotation, stand for various styles of a basic stroke in handwritings (Fig.2). The extraction of these stroke variants is implemented in a layered network. This network performs hierarchical template matching to detect existence of the stroke variants and their positions in the input character. Every stroke variant is decomposed into a 4-level hierarchy of subpatterns. Each stage in the network is responsible for the matching of subpatterns within one level of this hierarchy. In order to allow for fuzziness in handwritten strokes, a shift tolerating mechanism is adopted in every stage but the output one.

On the other hand, for each character category concerned, one structure template is devised. This template is obtained by considering a machine printed Chinese character in the font "Kai Tai", projected onto a 65x65 grid. A structure template is a hierarchy of basic strokes, multi-stroke patterns and subcharacters. Both multi-stroke pattern and subcharacter are frequently found subpatterns consisting of more than one basic stroke; while a subcharacter is a Chinese character by itself, a multi-stroke pattern is not. As one can see, more than one way of decomposition may exist (Fig.3). At present, the choice is made to maintain maximally the complexity of subpatterns in each level of the hierarchy. An attributed production rule syntax is devised to represent the structural knowledge thus achieved. According to these rules, a modified-Neocognitron [22] is devised to implement structure recognition. This structure recognizer receives input information from the stroke extractor to detect any existing pattern structure. The input character is then identified as the most complicated character that the structure recognizer can detect. In the following section, the stroke extractor and the structure recognizer are elaborated separately.

3. SYSTEM ARCHITECTURE

3.1 Stroke Extractor

As shown in Fig.4, the stroke extractor possesses a layered architecture. There are totally four stages, excluding the input grid. The input grid is a 65x65 binary-pixel matrix for the input image of a Chinese character. The output stage, i.e., the fourth stage, consists of a number of s-planes. Each s-plane in this stage is a 17x17 cell matrix for one stroke variant; each of the cell on the matrix is to detect the stroke variant within a corresponding region on the input grid. A cell is to fire with score of real number in the range from 0 to 1, indicating the degree of match of the associated stroke variant at the particular region.

The stroke detection process is essentially a hierarchical template matching mechanism. The intermediate stages between the input grid and the output stage are responsible for the detection of sets of subpatterns. The closer a stage is to the output stage, the higher the complexity of the set of subpatterns it handles. In each of these three stages, a pattern-detecting s-layer and a response-blurring c-layer coexist. Within every stage, the cells on the c-layer receives input connections from those cells in the s-layer, while the cells in the s-layer receives input connections from the c-layer in the preceding stage (or the input grid, if the stage concerned is the first one). The connections within one stage are simply to offer position-shift tolerance on the subpatterns. On the other hand, to establish connections between two stages, the patterns for each stage are identified first. Then, the geometric relationships between a pattern and its building blocks in the lower stage is approximated in the form of mask/rule. Finally, these relationships are loaded onto the network by assigning weights on the corresponding connections.

3.2 Structure Recognizer

The modified-Neocognitron for structure recognition possesses a layered architecture too. The number of layers is dependent on the subset of characters handled. Its first layer is for the detection of the patterns consisting of two strokes, the second for patterns of three strokes, and so on (Fig.5). For simplicity sake, the layers are labelled as L_2, L_3, ... L_N, where N is the maximum number of strokes of the character being handled. Each layer contains some neuron-planes; one neuron-plane stands for one category of pattern, i.e., multi-stroke pattern or subcharacter. Every neuron-plane is a 17x17 matrix of neuron-modules. All neuron-modules in one plane are assigned the same structural knowledge of one single pattern category. This duplication of modules is to achieve shift-invariant recognition of the input character.

The internal structure of a neuron-module is determined when the corresponding plane is assigned the pattern to be handled. Suppose the assigned pattern is composed of N building blocks, the neuron-module will consist of N p-cells and one s-cells. Each p-cell is responsible for the detection of one building block. Their output scores are then collected by the s-cell to determine the degree of match of the pattern structure. Every neuron-module in the structure recognizer may receive its input connections from either neuron-modules in the preceding layers, or the output stage of the stroke extractor, or both. The connection scheme is governed by a rule-mapping mechanism. The attributed production rule adopted to manipulate the structural knowledge of the patterns take the form as follows :

if A and B and ....then Z;

the antecedents A, B, ... stand for the building blocks of the target pattern Z. Their associated patterns may be stroke variants, multi-stroke patterns or subcharacters. Besides the associated pattern, an antecedent also possesses the attributes specifying the expected location and a tolerable region for that building block to be found.

The structure recognition process is carried out layer by layer. A layer is labelled as a candidate-layer if it has a neuron-plane, associated to a character pattern, fires with non-zero response in one of its neuron-module. After all layers have finished processing, the last candidate-layer is checked. The input character is identified as the character category associated to the neuron-plane in that layer which fires with the highest score. If no candidate-layer is found at all, the input character is rejected.

4. EXPERIMENT & RESULTS

In the first test, structure knowledge of seventeen categories of Chinese characters are implemented in the present system (Fig.6a). Ten testing samples of each category are written by five individuals. Thus, the system is tested with a total of one hundred and seventy samples. The corresponding result is shown in Table I. Although the recognition rate is rather low, one can see in Fig.6b that some of categories possess quite different writing styles.

In the second test, the system is expanded to handle fifty categories. Preliminary results is obtained by testing this system with one set of writing samples (Table II). Although only one writing style variation is involved, this test shows that this approach has the potential to be applied on a larger set of Chinese characters.

5. DISCUSSION

There are a few limitations in the present approach. They are listed as follows :

(1) Structure rules for strokes and character/multi-stroke patterns have to be prepared manually for initial rule-mapping.

(2) The number of neuron-planes, or even the number of layers, in the structure recognizer changes if new character categories are added. Fortunately, for the Chinese character set, roughly speaking, the number of categories and maximum number of strokes in a character is stable.

(3) The present system poses certain constraints on the input characters : for the "narrow" stroke classes (Fig.7a), the lower bound of their height or width is one-fourth; the lower bounds for both the height and width of the other stroke classes are one-fourth. These constraints are set for the correct extraction of short strokes. For dot-stroke (Fig.7b), either the height or width of the stroke must not be less than one-eighth of the dimension of the

input grid. However, this requirement is often violated after thinning. A better extraction scheme for dot-strokes has to be sought.

(4) Since the stroke extractor outputs all the stroke variants which can be matched (Fig.8), there may be lots of irrelevant stroke detections. This can be viewed as certain kind of "system noise" of the stroke extractor, which indeed has lowered the recognition rate of the whole system.

(5) There are certain groups of ambiguous characters which cause trouble to the system. For instance, lets consider the case of an input character "土". Stroke variants in the class of horizontal strokes, from the short to medium ones, can be detected in the middle portion of the character. It is a problem due to the nature of template matching. In this case, both the characters "土" and "上" may be matched. Probably, the character "土" may even be detected with score higher than the character "上".

On the other hand, there are several advantages attained through the current approach.

(1) The approach employs a neural network in the structure recognition phase. Therefore, learning mechanisms can be adopted to allow continuous adaptation to new writing styles of the categories handled.

(2) It is easy to include new character categories for the recognition. Appropriate rules for the templates of the new category are constructed. A neuron-plane is then inserted into the relevant layer and corresponding input connections are established through the rule-mapping mechanism.

(3) The approach does not use a large number of character samples in each category to develop an initial system. Instead, one pattern structure template is constructed. Various degrees of positional shift tolerance of its building blocks are adopted to deal with the fuzziness in handwritings. However, a pattern may indeed be written in very different scales (Fig.9). Hence, it may be desirable and necessary to extend the architecture to incorporate more than one template for each category.

(4) The system offers shift-tolerant recognition of Chinese characters and its subpatterns. Moreover, slight degree of scaling and rotation tolerance is exhibited too (Fig.6b).

(5) Fuzzy matching, a technique widely adopted in structural approaches, is also realized in our system. Similarly, this integration approach may offer a platform to incorporate some newly developed structural techniques in the future.

6. CONCLUSION

In this paper, a neural network based, off-line recognition system for handwritten Chinese characters is presented. Seventeen character categories are handled with a recognition rate of 52.4%. Tolerance to shift, slight rotation and slight scaling of the input character is achieved by the system.

The approach demonstrates an integration of neural computation and structural representation of Chinese characters. Neural network is employed for its tolerance to inexactness and noise contamination of input patterns; structural representation is adopted for its relevance to the construction of Chinese characters. Being a neural network based system, it is expected to be adaptable to accommodate newly encountered writing styles of a category. Moreover, addition of new character categories do not require removal of the established knowledge in the current system. Simple rule construction, neuron-plane insertion and rule-mapping suffice the inclusion of that new category. However, in order to achieve optimal performance with the whole system, interactions between the newly added category and the rest of the system needs to be investigated.

At present, the initial template rules are prepared by considering machine printed characters. It is reasonable to conjecture that more fine tuning towards real handwritings is necessary. Thus, a learning mechanism for the system is surely helpful. Meanwhile, the stroke extractor should be improved to reduce the amount of detection of irrelevant strokes. The recognition rate of the whole system can thus be raised. Furthermore, the system will be tested with a larger set of Chinese character, with characters of more complicated structure.

References

[1] Mori, S., Yamamoto, K. (1984), "Research on Machine Recognition of Handprinted Characters", *IEEE Trans. on Pattern Analysis and Machine Intelligence*, **Vol.6**, No.4, p.386-405.

[2] Hildebrandt, T.H., Liu, W.T. (1993), "Optical Recognition of Handwritten Chinese Characters : Advances since 1980", *Pattern Recognition*, **Vol.26**, No.2, p.205-225.

[3] Leung, C.H. (1985), "A Practical Basis Set for Chinese Character Representation", *IEEE Computer Society Conf. on Computer Vision and Pattern Recognition '85, San Francisco*, p.532-537.

[4] Maeda, K.I., et al. (1982), "Handprinted Kanji Recognition by Pattern Matching Method", *Int. Conf. on Pattern Recognition '82*, **Vol.2**, p.789-792.

[5] Yamashita, Y., et al. (1983), "Classification of

Handprinted Kanji Characters by the Structured Segment Matching Method", *Pattern Recognition Letters*, **Vol.1**, p.475-479.

[6] Kurakake S. (1989), "Predictive Category Learning of Handwritten Kanji Characters", *Computer Processing of Chinese & Oriental Languages*, **Vol.4**, No.2&3, p.99-111.

[7] Lee, H.J., Chen, B. (1992), "Recognition of Handwritten Chinese Characters via Short Line Segments", *Pattern Recognition*, **Vol.25**, No.5, p.543-552.

[8] Tsui, H.T. (1982), "Guided Stroke Structure Extraction for the Recognition of Handprinted Chinese Characters", *The 6th Int. Conf. on Pattern Recognition '82, Munich*, p.786-788.

[9] Lee, S., et al. (1989), "Radical Extraction Methods for Processing and Recognition of Chinese Characters", *Int. Symp. on Computer Architecture and Digital Signal Processing '89, Hong Kong*, p.480-483.

[10] Stallings, W. (1975), "The Morphology of Chinese Characters : A Survey of Models and Applications", *Computers and the Humanities*, **Vol.9**, p.13-24.

[11] Tai, J.W. (1984), "A Syntactic-Semantic Approach for Describing Chinese Characters", *Computer Processing of Chinese & Oriental languages*, **Vol.1**, No.3, p.186-194.

[12] Chan, K.P., Cheung, Y.S. (1992), "Fuzzy-Attribute Graph with Application to Chinese Character Recognition", *IEEE Trans. on Systems, Man, and Cybernetics*, **Vol.22**, No.2, p.402-410.

[13] Ogawa, H. (1983), "Point Pattern Representation and Pattern Matching of Handwritten Characters by Relaxation Technique", *Int. Conf. on Systems, Man and Cybernetics '83*, p.388-392.

[14] Chen, L.H., Lieh, J.R. (1990), "Handwritten Character Recognition using a 2-Layer Random Graph Model by Relaxation Matching", *Pattern Recognition*, **Vol.23**, No.11, p.1189-1205.

[15] Wang, J.F., et al. (1991), "Handwritten Chinese Radical Recognition via Neural Networks", *Int. Conf. on Computer Processing of Chinese and Oriental Languages '91*, p.92-97.

[16] Mori, Y., Yokosawa, K. "A Large-Scale Neural Network which Recognizes Handwritten Kanji Characters", in **Advances in Neural Information Processing Systems 2**, by Touretzky, D.S. (eds.), *MORGAN KAUFMANN PUBLISHERS*, p.415-422.

[17] Hyman, S.D., et al. (1991), "Classification of Japanese Kanji using Principal Component Analysis as a Preprocessor to an Artificial Neural Network", *Int. Joint Conf. on Neural Networks '91, Seattle*, **Vol.1**, p.233-238.

[18] Fukushima, K. (1992), "Character Recognition with Neural Networks", *Neurocomputing*, **Vol.4**, p.221-233.

[19] Hildebrandt, T.H. (1991), Optical Recognition of Handwritten Chinese Characters using an Improved Neural Network Model, **Ph.D. thesis**, *North Carolina State University*, March (1991).

[20] Wang, S.D., Pan, C.C. (1990), "A Neural Network Approach for Chinese Character Recognition", *Int. Joint Conf. on Neural Networks '90, San Diego*, **Vol.2**, p.917-923.

[21] Takahashi, T., et al. (1983), "Handprinted Chinese Character Discrimination using Stroke Extraction Method with referral to Peripheral Structural Information", *Int. Conf. on Text Processing '83*, p.163-168.

[22] Yeung, D., et al. (1992), "A Neocognitron-based Chinese Character Recognition System", *Int. Joint Conf. on Neural Networks '92, Beijing*, **Vol.3**, p.617-622.

Total number of samples	Correct Recognition	Wrong Recognition	Rejected Samples
170	89 (52.4%)	79 (46.5%)	2 (1.1%)

Table I

Total number of samples	50
Correction Recognition	31 (62%)
Wrong Recognition	19 (38%)
Rejection	0

Table II

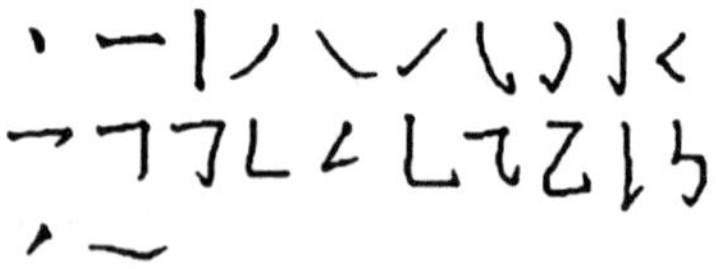

Fig.1 : 22 Basic Stroke Classes

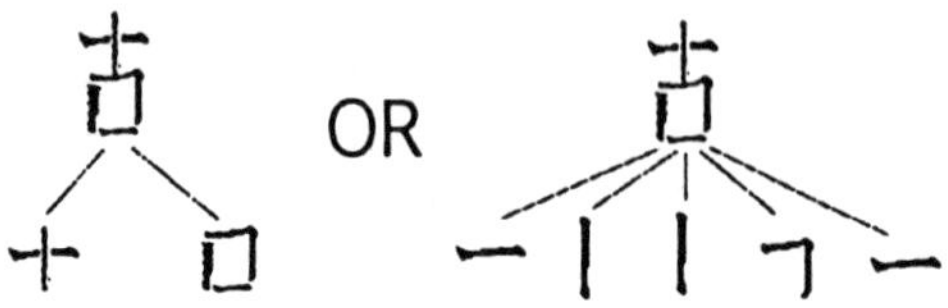

Fig.3 : Different ways of structure Decomposition

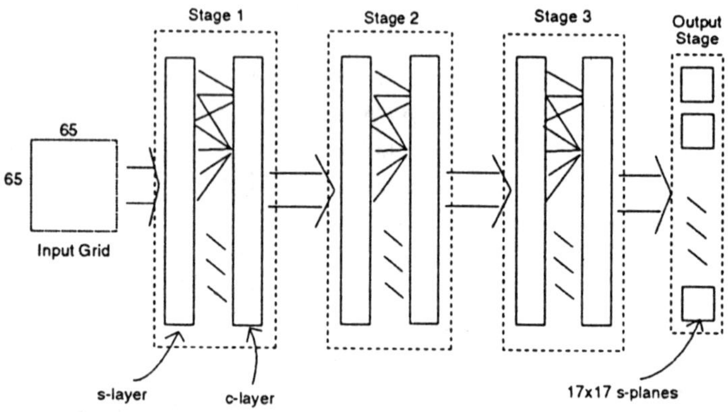

Fig. 4 : Stroke Extractor

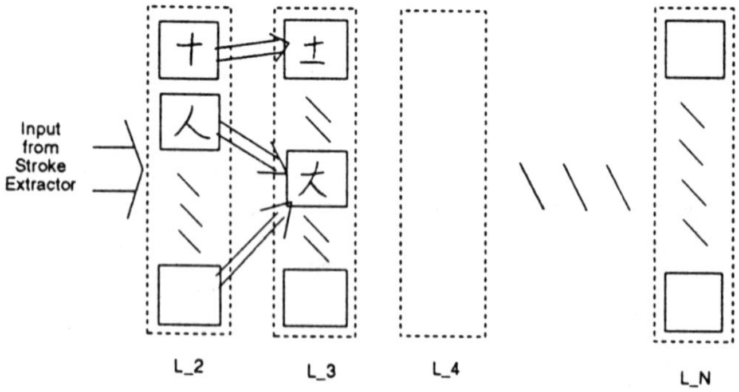

Fig. 5 : Modified-Neocognitron

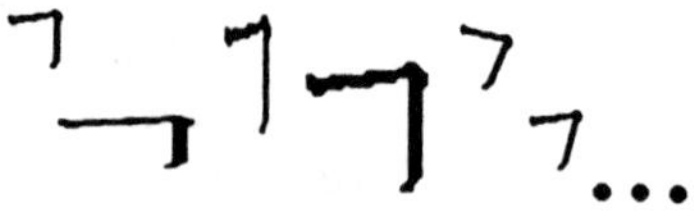

Fig.2 : Sample variants of one stroke class

(a) 17 character categories in test 1

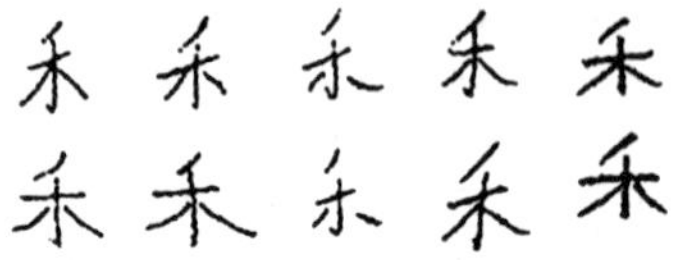

(b) 10 handwritten samples of one category

Fig.6

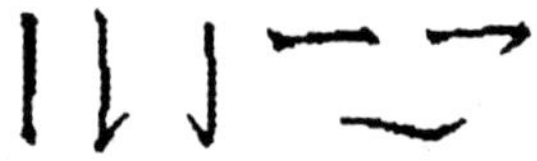

(a) Narrow stroke set

(b) Dot-stroke(in dashed frame)

Fig. 7

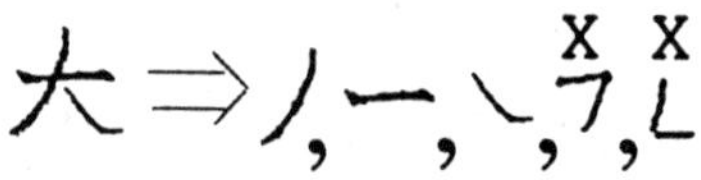

Fig.8 : Extracted irrelevant strokes (with a "X" on top of each of them)

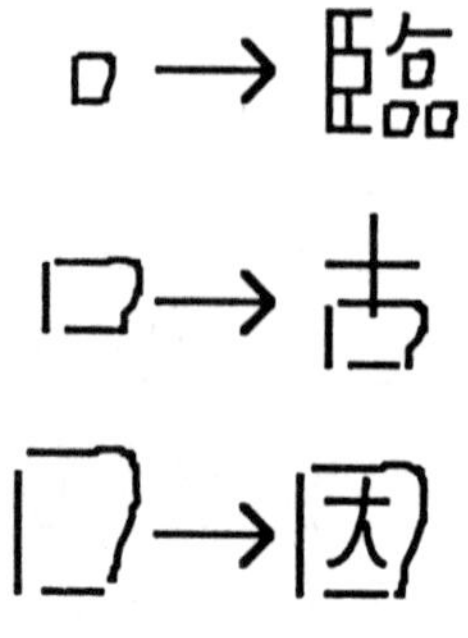

Fig.9 : Different scales of a pattern existing in different characters

A Neural Network Computing Observer's Heading From Optical Flow

M. Brattoli†, G. Convertino†, A. Distante†, A. Branca†
E-mail: Brattoli@astrba.ba.cnr.it
† Istituto Elaborazione Segnali ed Immagini - C.N.R. Bari - Italy

Abstract

In this paper a neural network model is proposed for the computation of the instantaneous direction of translation of an observer moving relative to a static environment. This direction is given by the Focus of Expansion (*FOE*) associated with the radial optical flow pattern arising as a consequence of the translational component of motion. The network is characterized by a feed-forward architecture and is trained through the standard supervised Back-propagation algorithm. Its input signals are the directions of the optical flow vectors, while its output nodes represent the image coordinates of the FOE associated with the input optical flow field. A number of experiments have been performed both for theoretical optical flow fields and for flow signals actually computed from a TV image sequence by an Hopfield network implementing a gradient-based algorithm. The network is able to recover the FOE position of testing flow fields with a mean error of 0.1 pixels and seems resistant to noise.

1 Introduction

The estimation of the motion parameters of a moving vehicle relative to its environment is an interesting application of computer vision in robot passive navigation. Psychophysical evidence exists [1], that two main 3D egomotion parameters, namely the *instantaneous direction of observer's heading* and the *time-to-collision (TTC)* allow living organisms to avoid collision with the objects in their environment or to perform steering, i.e. to make on-line adjustments to their current trajectory and path. This observation makes appealing the use of the information also for the control of artificial vehicles locomotion.

Several approaches in computational vision attempt to compute the 3D motion parameters from the 2D vector field constituted by the projections on the image plane of the 3D scene velocities. They generally assume a perspective projection model in which, for simplicity, the focal length is one unit of measurement, so that a world point $P = (X, Y, Z)$ projects on the image point $(x, y) = (\frac{X}{Z}, \frac{Y}{Z})$. So, if we consider a stationary world in which an observer undergoes rigid movements described by the translational velocity (T_x, T_y, T_z) and by the rotational velocity $(\Omega_x, \Omega_y, \Omega_z)$, the projected velocity (u, v) of a point P on the image plane is given by the following equations:

$$\begin{aligned} u &= -xy\Omega_x + (1+x^2)\Omega_y - y\Omega_z + \frac{T_x - xT_z}{Z} \\ v &= -(1+y^2)\Omega_x + xy\Omega_y + x\Omega_z + \frac{T_y - yT_z}{Z} \end{aligned} \quad (1)$$

Actually, due to the ambiguity of the input data [1] and to the local nature of operators used, any proposed computational technique [2, 3, 4] can only derive an approximation of the theoretical 2D motion field, the **Optical Flow**, which turns to be inadequate to the computation of quantitative motion parameters [5]. Therefore we consider a method for the observer's heading computation that

[1] Typically, the variation of the 2D brightness pattern in a time-varying (TV) image sequence of the 3D scene is the only source of information for an artificial vision system

0-7803-1901-X/94 $4.00 ©1994 IEEE

relies on a purely qualitative property of the optical flow, in the application context of planar passive navigation in which the visual control of locomotion requires only the direction of translation and not the full set of moving parameters. When an observer translates toward (backward) a surface with constant velocity ($T_z \neq 0$), the resulting optical flow vectors radiate outward from (inward to) a singularity called **Focus Of Expansion** (**Focus Of Contraction**) which lie in the direction of translation:

$$(FOE_x, FOE_y) = \left(\frac{T_x}{T_z}, \frac{T_y}{T_z}\right)$$

If ($T_z = 0$) the FOE can be defined as a direction toward infinity defined by (T_x, T_y) and all the flow vectors point in that direction. Since the FOE position is completely determined by the directions of the flow vectors, it is independent of the distances of world surfaces and doesn't require assumptions about surface shape and smoothness, its computation turns to be an important qualitative cue to the observer's heading determination.

Actually the accurate computation of FOE seems to be an hard problem, mainly due to digitization errors, unreliable flow vectors and image noise. Moreover, even a small amount of occasional observer rotation can change the radial shape of the flow field and the true position of the FOE. To manage this situation methods that require a preliminary decomposition of the optical flow field into its translational and rotational components [7] or which compute a 2D region of possible FOE locations (Fuzzy FOE) [8] instead of a single point FOE, have been proposed. In this work we investigate the performance of an artificial neural network for the computation of the FOE of an optical flow field induced by an observer translation relative to a static environment. The present work is inspired to a previous attempt [9] to model the medial superior temporal (MST) area of the macaque visual cortex, in which the presence of cells sensitive to radially expanding, translating and rotating optical patterns, has been shown by psychophysical studies. Our work, however, far from having neurophysiological claims, simply aims to investigate the possibility that the distributed neural paradigm helps in filtering out the noise intrinsic in any artificial vision system. In the following two sections the neural network architecture and some experimental results are shown.

2 The neural network model

The neural network used in this work has a three layers feed-forward architecture. It is trained to map a set of optical flow fields to their corresponding FOE coordinates. Since the heading direction is fully specified by the flow vectors directions, each component of the input pattern is the angular coordinate (in radians) of an optical flow vector in the 2D polar plane. So each input neuron is activated by an analogic signal in the $[-\pi, \pi]$ range. In theory a minimum of two flow vectors is sufficient to determine the FOE position, but we use redundant information to improve the robustness of the model. Furthermore, this choice is sustained by the observation that it is not the locus of outflow per se that specifies heading but rather the global flow pattern [1] . The nodes in the output layer represent the FOE position in such a way that both the case of FOE in the image plane and the case of FOE at infinity are managed. If the input pattern is a radial flow field ($T_z \neq 0$) each image coordinate (FOE_x,FOE_y) of the FOE is distributively coded through the activation value of a preset number N of neurons, associated with N discrete points sampling the linear range $\{0, 1, .., DIM\}$ of image pixels. Each output has an activation value in $[-1, 1]$ range, that is proportional to its distance from the proper FOE coordinate. The following coding rule is used during the supervised training phase to determine it:

$$act_k^h = \frac{out_k^h - FOE_k}{DIM - 1} \; \forall k = x, y \; \forall h = 1, \ldots, N \qquad (2)$$

where act_k^h and out_k^h are, respectively, the activation and the coordinate values associated to the h-th unit.

In the testing phase the following inverse rule is used to reconstruct the FOE coordinates from the output activation:

$$FOE_k = \frac{1}{N}\sum_{h=1}^{N}[out_k^h \; - \; (DIM \; - \; 1)act_k^h] \; \forall k = x, y \; \forall h = 1, \cdots, N \tag{3}$$

The special cases in which the observer moves perpendicular to its line of sight in the four directions up, down, left and right, have also been coded. The four special pairs $\{(0, +\infty), (0, -\infty), (-\infty, 0), (+\infty, 0)\}$ have been associated to each of the above directions. The output coding of these values has been obtained through the addition of two more nodes (one for each coordinate) whose activation is 0 if the FOE is in the image plane, +1 or −1 when the corresponding FOE component is $+\infty$ or $-\infty$. In the latter cases the previous 2N output nodes are all set to 0.

The net input to each neuron is computed as the weighted sum of the activity of the cells which it is connected to; the *sigmoid* and *tanh* transfer functions are used respectively by hidden and output nodes.

The supervised learning rule by which the network is trained is the standard back-propagation algorithm [10]:

$$\Delta w_{ij}(t+1) = \eta \, e_i \, x_{ij} \; + \; \mu \, \Delta w_{ij}(t) \tag{4}$$

The weight change $\Delta w_{ij}(t+1)$ at instant t+1 is proportional to the error e_i computed for the i-th unit, to the input x_{ij} to the connection w_{ij}, and to the weight change at the previous step t. The addition of the momentum term μ is used to help "smooth out" the weight changes. The error e_i in the output layer is computed as the difference between the desired and actual output. This error, transformed by the derivative of the transfer function is "back-propagated" to prior layers where it is accumulated. This back-propagated and transformed error becomes the error term for that prior layer. The back-propagation process continues until the first layer is reached.

3 Experiments

Two kind of simulations have been performed. In the first one theoretical flow fields were used both as training and as testing patterns, to empirically determine the most important architectural and dynamical parameters of the network; in the second one a more interesting test was performed by using optical flow maps computed with a gradient-based technique, for realistic TV image sequences. For each simulation, a learning phase in which a set of training examples were cyclically presented to the network along with the output coding of the correct FOE, was followed by a testing phase in which the FOE associated with new optical flow patterns had to be determined. Since we were interested in the pixel accuracy with which the FOE components can be recovered, the testing results were measured through the average on the testing examples of the *Manhattan distance* between the correct and the computed FOE:

$$AVGERR_{FOE} = \frac{1}{tot}\sum_{j=1}^{tot}\left[\frac{1}{2}(|tFOE_x^j - oFOE_x^j| + |tFOE_y^j - oFOE_y^j|)\right] \tag{5}$$

where:
tot is the total number of testing examples;
tFOE and *oFOE* are the correct and output FOE, respectively.

3.1 Results for theoretical flow fields

In fig.1 some of the results obtained for the theoretical motion fields are shown. Each input pattern consisted of a sample of 2D velocity vectors randomly extracted from a radial motion field 16 × 16 pixels wide. Its associated FOE is in a randomly chosen image point and is coded by 10 output units, 2 of which are used for the coding of translations parallel to the image plane. The input layer size was varied between 30 and 200 units, while the number of hidden nodes was empirically set to the 10% of (*input* + *output*) nodes. This value was chosen as a result of various trials in which its relation with convergence time and testing performances were measured.

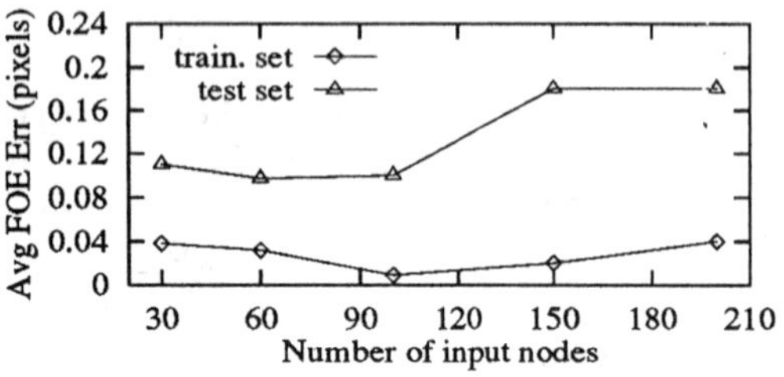

Figure 1: Average testing errors for various input layer sizes

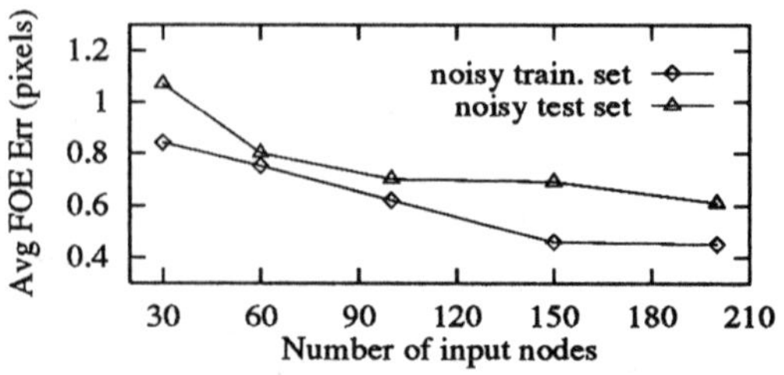

Figure 2: Average testing errors for noisy input patterns

For each simulation, 200 different radial patterns were generated. The 60% of them plus the four parallel patterns were used to train the network, the remaining ones to test it. Moreover the network tolerance of noise was measured by perturbing each component of the input pattern with an additive gaussian noise with mean 0 and a specified variance σ. This is an important test to assess the applicability of the model in a real context in which the input data are corrupted by intrinsic noise. The training phase was stopped when the RMS error between the actual and the desired output met a value of 0.01. This latter was empirically determined through a standard cross-validation procedure in which the learning phase is periodically stopped and the current testing performance is measured. The initial value of the learning coefficient η was set to 0.3 for the hidden layer and to 0.1 for the output layer. They follow an exponential decaying rate with a decay coefficient of 0.5. The momentum term was fixed to 0.4.

The testing results in figg. 1 and 2 show that the network can recover the FOE with a mean error of 0.1 pixels for clean signals and of 0.7 pixel about for signals corrupted by a gaussian noise with σ=0.5. The fundamental role of redundant inputs in improving the network resistance to noise, is evident.

3.2 Results for realistic flow fields

To establish the usefulness of the proposed approach when operating with real data, we measured the model performances for the optical flow fields actually computed with one of the existing computational techniques from a sequence of time-varying images.

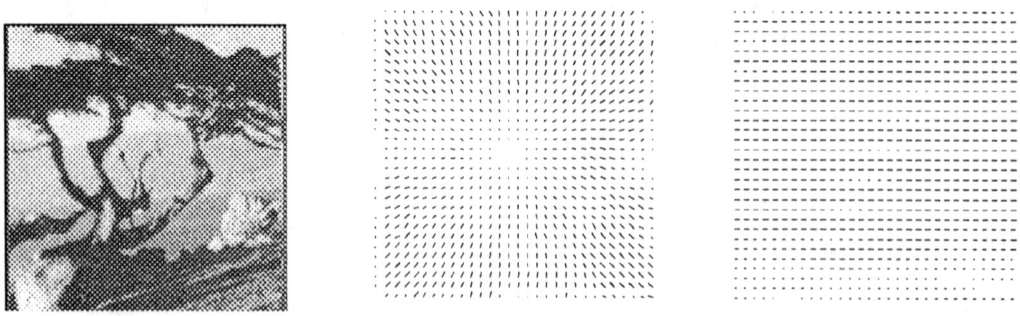

Figure 3: One frame of the Diverging and Translating Tree Sequence along with the computed optical flow fields

In fig.3 an example of the input patterns used in these experiments is shown. The presented image is a textured planar surface used in two sequences simulating translational camera motion, created by [11]. In the *Translating Tree Sequence* the camera moves normal to its line of sight, with velocities all parallel to the image x-axis, while in the *Diverging Tree Sequence* the camera translates along its line of sight and the FOE is at the centre of the image plane whose size is 150×150. The optical flow field shown in the figure were computed with the gradient-based approach proposed by Horn-Schunck [2]. This consists in minimizing the following variational functional on the whole image:

$$\begin{aligned} E(u,v) &= \int\int \left(\frac{\partial I}{\partial x}u + \frac{\partial I}{\partial y}v + \frac{\partial I}{\partial t} \right)^2 dxdy + \\ &+ \lambda \int\int \left[\left(\frac{\partial u}{\partial x}\right)^2 + \left(\frac{\partial v}{\partial x}\right)^2 + \left(\frac{\partial u}{\partial y}\right)^2 + \left(\frac{\partial v}{\partial y}\right)^2 \right] dxdy \end{aligned} \quad (6)$$

where the first term, called *constant-brightness term*, describes the continuity of the gray values in the time-varying sequence, while the second is a *smoothness constraint* used to solve the aperture problem which makes ill-posed the computation of optical flow. The minimization cited above was performed by an Hopfield neural network [12] whose energy function was obtained by mapping the variables in the previous functional on the network components. The values of the current injected in the network depends on the values of the pixels intensity gradients. This current injection induces a relaxation process that minimizes the network's energy. The output potential values of the network nodes are the computed optical flow components [13]. The Hopfield network had been previously used by authors in investigation of neural models for low level TV image processing.
Each of the flow field shown in the image was properly sampled and fed in input to a feed-forward network consisting of 225 input, 30 hidden and 34 output nodes, which had been trained on a set of 450 theoretical motion fields. Each of the radial training patterns had the FOE in an image point randomly chosen on a square of 50×50 pixels centered on the original image.
The translating field was perfectly recognized and the FOE coordinates recovered for the radial flow field were (74,75). This results seems to encourage the applicability of the considered neural architecture in a real context. Our present interest is devoted to the extension of the model to manage the case of more general curvilinear motions producing non-radial optical arrays.

References

[1] J.J. Gibson, *The perception of the visual world*, Boston: Houghton Mifflin, 1950

[2] B.K.P. Horn, B.G. Schunck, *Determining optical flow* Artificial Intelligence, Vol.17, 185-203(1981)

[3] P. Anandan, *A computational framework and an algorithm for the computation of visual motion*, IJCV, vol. 1, 1988

[4] D.J. Heeger, *Optical flow using spatiotemporal filters*, IJCV, vol. 1, 1988

[5] A. Verri, T. Poggio, *Motion Field and Optical Flow: Qualitative Properties* IEEE Transactions on PAMI, 11(5), May 1990

[6] W.H. Warren, Jr. Morris, M. Kalish, *Perception of translational heading from optical flow*, J. of Experimental Psychology: Human Perception and Performance, Vol. 14, No. 4, 1988

[7] K. Prazdny, *Determining the instantaneous direction of motion from optical flow generated by a curvilinearly moving observer*, CGIP, 17, 238-248 (1981)

[8] W. Burger, B. Bhanu, *Estimating 3D egomotion from perspective image sequences*, IEEE Transactions on PAMI, 12(18), Nov. 1990

[9] N.G. Hatsopoulos, W.H. Warren, *Visual navigation with a neural network*, Neural Networks, Vol. 4, 1991

[10] D.E. Rumelhart, J.L. McClelland, PDP Research Group, *Parallel Distributed Processing: Explorations in the Microstructure of Cognition, Volume1: Foundations*, Cambridge: MIT Press

[11] D. Fleet, A. Jepson, *Computation of component image velocity from local phase information,* IJCV, 5, 1990

[12] Hopfield, J.J.: *Neural computation of decision in optimization problems* Biol. Cyber.52,141-152(1985)

[13] J. Hutchinson, C. Koch, J. Luo, C. Mead: *Computing Motion Using Analog and Binary Resistive Networks* IEEE Computer (1988) 52-63

Fast Adaptive Scalar Quantization for Minimal Mean Squared Error Distortion in the High Resolution Case: Extension of the Boundary Adaptation Rule

Marc M. VAN HULLE

Laboratorium voor Neuro- en Psychofysiologie,
Faculteit Geneeskunde, K.U.Leuven,
Campus Gasthuisberg, Herestraat,
3000 Leuven, Belgium

Abstract

Recently we have introduced a new unsupervised competitive learning rule for adaptive scalar quantization [1,2]. The rule, called Boundary Adaptation Rule (BAR), directly adapts the boundary points demarcating the quantization intervals and minimizes mean absolute error (MAE) distortion. In this article we will extend the BAR concept towards mean squared error (MSE) distortion minimization in the high resolution case. The performance of this extended rule is shown for stationary as well as non-stationary input probability density functions, such as speech- and image signals. The rule yields near-optimal performance.

1 Introduction

In analog VLSI and many other signal processing applications there is need for efficient analog to digital (A/D) convertors digitally coding signals for secure storage and transmission. Efficient A/D converters adapt to changing input conditions or to changing input sensor characteristics. For example, speech signals can vary over 40 dB depending on the speaker, and unvoiced sounds can have variances often 20 dB less than voiced sounds [3,4]. This effectively reduces by several bits the range over which non-adaptive converters encode speech signals. Another major field of applications are the so-called smart sensors. In these sensors, A/D conversion is combined with an integrated microcomputer for performing dynamic correction of changes in sensor characteristics and in environmental conditions [5].

Scalar quantization is at the heart of A/D conversion: it converts analog input signals, such as input probability density functions (*p.d.f.*s), into a discrete number of quantization levels. The efficiency of a given quantizer is proportional to how well the *p.d.f.* $p(x)$ is modelled by the N quantization levels. In Artificial Neural Networks (ANNs) adaptive quantization is realized with competitive learning rules changing weights that represent the centroids of N quantization regions partitioning input space so as to minimize mean squared error (MSE) distortion. The quantization regions themselves are defined by nearest-neighbor classification. In the absence of *a priori* knowledge about the desired partition, the rules are of the unsupervised type (unsupervised competitive learning, UCL). We will restrict ourselves to this case. On several occasions the original UCL paradigm, in which only the neuron's weight vector closest to the present input is updated, has proven inadequate: it often generates units that are underutilized or even 'dead units', so-called since they are not used in partitioning the input signal space [6-8]. (Also the most widely used (non-neural) classical quantizer design algorithm called LBG (generalized Lloyd) suffers from this problem and can yield non-optimal partitionings (for references, see [9]). In practical applications of data representation and compression, it is essential to add mechanisms which will avoid dead units and ensure an equitable weight distribution. This has been done in Kohonen learning [10] by adding a 'neighborhood' to each neuron. In another scheme, a 'conscience' is added to frequently updated neurons to feel 'guilty' and reduce their update rate [6,7]. Inspired by the latter mechanism, several other schemes have been introduced (see [11]), usually with the aim of achieving an *equiprobable* weight distribution, and thus implicitly maximizing information-theoretic entropy [1].

In previous articles, we have introduced a novel unsupervised competitive learning rule for adaptive scalar quantization [1,2]. The rule is completely different from other unsupervised competitive learning rules: rather than finding the centroids of the quantization intervals, it directly computes the boundary points separating the (non-overlapping) quantization intervals. Since the rule updates boundary points directly, it

0-7803-1901-X/94 $4.00 ©1994 IEEE

is called Boundary Adaptation Rule (BAR). Since BAR explicitly maximizes information-theoretic entropy regardless of the input $p.d.f.$, it always yields an equiprobable weight distribution. Hence, due to this, it can be analytically shown that it minimizes mean absolute error (MAE) distortion [12]. In the present article, we will extend the BAR concept towards MSE minimization following the principle of High Resolution Quantization (HRQ). We will call this rule BAR_2, the subscript referring to MSE minimization. Also for this rule, we will derive a fast version which we will call fast BAR_2 ($FBAR_2$). We will apply $FBAR_2$ on speech- and image data and show that it yields a near-optimal HRQ performance.

2 High Resolution Quantization

An N-point scalar quantizer is a function which maps a scalar-valued input signal x into one of N quantization levels $y_1, y_2, ..., y_N$. The quantizer is then specified by the values of these quantization levels and the location of the N non-overlapping quantization intervals $R_1, R_2, ..., R_N$. In the case of high-resolution quantization, N is very large so that the input $p.d.f.$ $p(x)$ is roughly constant over the individual intervals. Hence, $p(x) \approx p_i$ in interval R_i, with $p_i = p(R_i)/\Delta_i$, $p(R_i) = \int_{R_i} p(x)\, dx$, and $\Delta_i = x_i - x_{i-1}$ the size of interval $R_i \equiv [x_{i-1}, x_i)$; if x_0 is infinite, then $R_1 \equiv (x_0, x_1)$. In case x takes on values in a finite interval $[a, b)$ with probability (nearly) one, so that we can neglect the overload probability, the mean squared error distortion can approximatively be written as:

$$D_2 \approx \sum_{i=1}^{N} \frac{p(R_i)}{\Delta_i} \int_{x_{i-1}}^{x_i} (x - y_i)^2 \, dx \tag{1}$$

with $x_0 \equiv a$ and $x_N \equiv b$, and $x_{j-1} < x_j$, $j = 1, ..., N$. Following the high-resolution assumption, we can approximate the centroid y_i by the midpoint of the corresponding quantization interval. Integration of eq. (1) and substitution for the midpoints yields:

$$D_2 \approx \frac{1}{12} \sum_{i=1}^{N} p(R_i) {\Delta_i}^2. \tag{2}$$

Finally, the necessary condition which minimizes the previous equation is obtained by taking the first derivatives with respect to the x_i's and setting them equal to zero:

$$\Delta_j \;\, p(R_j) = \Delta_{j+1} \;\, p(R_{j+1}), \quad j = 1, ..., N-1. \tag{3}$$

3 Boundary Adaptation Rule Minimizing MSE

We will now derive an unsupervised learning rule which will minimize eq. (2) and thus satisfy eq. (3). For this, we need some additional definitions. Let $\{x_0^t, x_1^t, ..., x_N^t\}$ be a set of $N+1$ boundary points arranged in increasing order at iteration- or time step t. Let $Act_{R_j}(x)$, $j = 1, ..., N$, be the code membership function of interval R_j so that at time step t:

$$Act^t_{R_j}(x) = \begin{cases} 1 & \text{if } x \in R^t_j \\ 0 & \text{if } x \notin R^t_j, \end{cases}$$

with $R^t_j \equiv [x^{t-1}_{j-1}, x^{t-1}_j)$. At time step t the probability $p(R_j)$ of $x \in R_j$ satisfies:

$$p(R^t_j) = \int_{x_0^{t-1}}^{x_N^{t-1}} Act^t_{R_j} \, p(x)\, dx = \int_{x^{t-1}_{j-1}}^{x^{t-1}_j} p(x)\, dx \equiv E[Act^t_{R_j}], \quad j = 1, ..., N, \tag{4}$$

where $E[.]$ denotes the expectation operator. Assume that for input x at time step t, $Act^t_{R_j} = 1$, we then modify R_j by increasing x^{t-1}_{j-1} and decreasing x^{t-1}_j proportional to the length of the interval spanned by them:

$$\Delta x^t_j = \eta(\Delta^{t-1}_{j+1} Act^t_{R_{j+1}} - \Delta^{t-1}_j Act^t_{R_j}), \quad j = 1, ..., N-1, \tag{5}$$

with η the learning rate, a positive constant. This update rule is then called BAR_2, the Boundary Adaptation Rule minimizing MSE in the high resolution case. Indeed, in case η is small, so that the boundary points preserve their initial ordering during subsequent updates, eq. (2) is minimized by BAR_2. This can be easily shown as follows.

N	Optimal Quantization	BAR_2	Optimal HRQ
2	0.363	1.000 ± 5.0 E-3	0.363
4	0.117	0.131 ± 1.0E-4	0.117
8	0.0345	0.0370 ± 2.8E-4	0.0347
16	0.00950	0.0102 ± 1.0E-4	0.00977
32	0.00250	0.00291 ± 0.5 E-4	0.00269

Table 1: MSE distortion as a function of number of intervals N for a Gaussian with $\overline{x} = 0$ and $\sigma_x = 1$. Comparison between Optimal Quantization, Optimal High Resolution Quantization (HRQ) and BAR_2. The Optimal Quantization results were determined with the Lloyd I algorithm using *a priori* knowledge of the Gaussian [13,14]. The Optimal HRQ results were determined by solving for the boundary points that both satisfy eq. (3) and minimize eq. (1), and also using *a priori* knowledge of the Gaussian; the quantization levels correspond to the intervals' centroids. In case of BAR_2, $\eta = 0.001$, the overload points $a = -5$ and $b = 5$; 500,000 iterations were considered for each run. The MSE values were estimated after convergence, using 100,000 samples. The quantization levels correspond to the intervals' midpoints. The values given are averages over 20 runs with their standard deviations.

Since the ordering is preserved we have, at convergence, on average that $E[\Delta x_j] = 0$, so that:

$$E[\Delta_{j+1}^{t-1} Act_{R_{j+1}}^t] = E[\Delta_j^{t-1} Act_{R_j}^t], \quad \text{and, thus, that} \tag{6}$$

$$\Delta_{j+1}^{t-1} E[Act_{R_{j+1}}^t] = \Delta_j^{t-1} E[Act_{R_j}^t]. \tag{7}$$

Now since $p(R_j) = E[Act_{R_j}]$, eq. (3) is satisfied and eq. (2) minimized. Convergence of the rule is proven in [12].

The fastest rule, called fast BAR_2 ($FBAR_2$), is obtained by updating all boundary points each time an input sample is presented:

$$\Delta x_j^t = \eta\left(\sum_{k=j+1}^{N} \Delta_k^{t-1} \frac{Act_{R_k}^t}{N-j} - \sum_{k=1}^{j} \Delta_k^{t-1} \frac{Act_{R_k}^t}{j}\right) \quad j = 1, ..., N-1. \tag{8}$$

At convergence, $FBAR_2$ also satisfies eq. (3) (see Appendix). In the next section, we will use this rule for quantizing sampled speech and image data 'on the fly', *i.e.* after the presentation of each input sample.

4 Simulation Results

Before we show the performance of $FBAR_2$ in quantizing speech- and image data, we will consider a stationary *p.d.f.* and compare the MSE results for optimal (*i.e.* minimal MSE) quantization with those for high resolution quantization (HRQ) and its approximation, BAR_2. The results are summarized in Table 1 for a Gaussian with $\overline{x} = 0$ and $\sigma_x = 1$. For BAR_2, the quantization levels $y_1, y_2, ..., y_N$ correspond to the intervals' midpoints. We observe that, as N increases, BAR_2 yields a better approximation of the optimal HRQ result, and also of the optimal quantization result. Hence, BAR_2 is a valid technique for quantizing *p.d.f.*s for minimal MSE.

We now show the performance of $FBAR_2$ in quantizing speech signals (adaptive waveform quantization). The signals come from TIMIT, a popular speech data base. Consider the example signal in Fig. 1A. We will quantize this signal with a 5 bit quantizer ($N = 32$) with $\eta = 0.6$; the overload points are $a = -1$ and $b = 1$. We estimate the quantization levels of the overload regions as follows: $y_1 = x_1 - (y_2 - x_1)$ and $y_N = x_{N-1} + (x_{N-1} - y_{N-1})$, in order to avoid the possible occurrence of large peaks in the quantized signal for these regions. The resulting quantized signal is shown in Fig. 1B. The MSE obtained equals 4.36E-05, which corresponds to a 26.38 dB signal-to-quantization-noise ratio (SNR). The corresponding $E[\Delta_i Act_{R_i}]$ distribution is given in Fig. 1C: it shows that, notwithstanding the signal is highly non-stationary, the necessary condition eq. (3) is satified on average (except around the overload regions since for these regions the choice of a and b is arbitrary) and that there are no dead-units. Finally, using the same speech signal, we have compared the SNR performance of $FBAR_2$ with those of uniform- and μ-law ($\mu = 255$) 5 bit quantizers. Note that also for the latter two quantizers the overload points are -1 and 1, respectively. The μ-law quantizer is widely used in digital telephony [15]. The results are given in Table 2. We observe that $FBAR_2$ yields the best SNR result: almost 7 dB better than the μ-law quantizer and more than 10 dB better than the uniform quantizer.

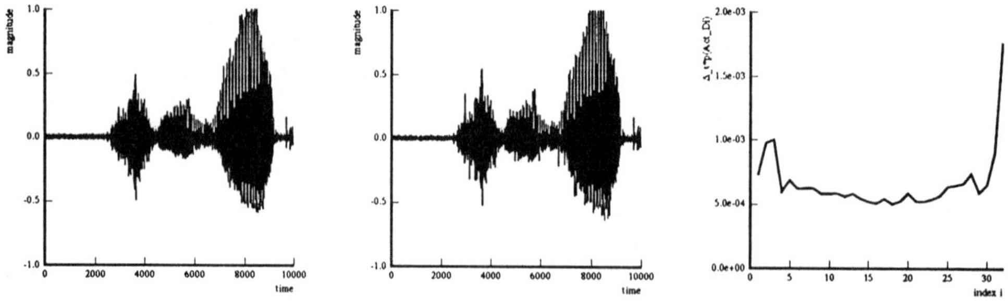

Figure 1: A. Example speech signal *i.e.* the word *she*. Time is expressed in milliseconds. B. Resulting quantized signal. C. $E[\Delta_j \; Act_{R_j}]$ distribution (see text).

Quantizer	SNR @ 5 bits
uniform	16.05 dB
μ law	19.57 dB
$FBAR_2$	26.38 dB

Table 2: SNR performance of $FBAR_2$, uniform and μ-law quantizers on Fig. 1A

We will now apply $FBAR_2$ on greyscale images. Consider the 'Lena' image in Fig. 2A. We quantize this 8 bit signal with a 3 bit quantizer ($N = 8$), also with $\eta = 0.6$. We use the same definition of overload quantization levels as in the speech example. The result is shown in Fig. 2B. The MSE now equals 5.03E-04 and the SNR 17.1 dB; the perceptual quality of the image remains good. If we use the present quantizer in an A/D converter setting and compress its output with non-adaptive Huffman coding, we need only 2.57 bits to store or communicate the image, a compression ratio of 8:2.57 = 3.1.

5 Conclusion

In this article we have extended the Boundary Adaptation Rule (BAR) for scalar quantization towards mean squared error distortion minimization. The new rule is called BAR_2. Furthermore, we have derived a fast version of this extension, called $FBAR_2$, and shown its quantization performance in case of stationary and non-stationary *p.d.f.*s such as speech- and image signals. In particular, we have shown that we can compress by a factor of 3 greyscale images using $FBAR_2$. Notwithstanding it has long been known from Shannon's source coding with a distortion measure [15,16] that better performance can be achieved by coding vectors rather than scalars, we have applied scalar quantization in the present article for two compelling reasons: 1) $FBAR_2$ is very fast and able to quantize in real-time non-stationary signals close to the optimal HRQ result; and 2) the circuit is very simple to implement and can be made part of adaptive A/D converters, a device for which there exists a gamut of signal processing applications such as smart sensors and consumer electronics.

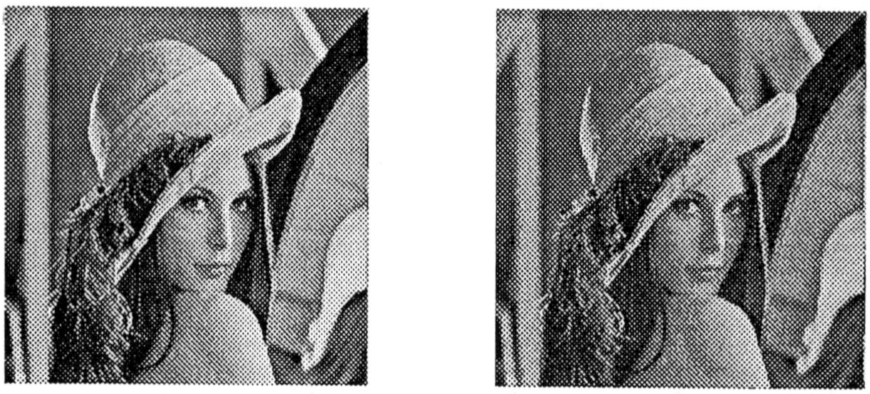

Figure 2: A. 'Lena' image. B. 'Lena' image quantized with $FBAR_2$ using 3 bits ($N = 8$).

Acknowledgement

The author is a postdoctoral researcher of the National Fund for Scientific Research (Belgium).

References

[1] M. M. Van Hulle and D. Martinez, "On an unsupervised learning rule for scalar quantization following the maximum entropy principle," Neural Computation, vol. 5, pp. 939-953, 1993.
[2] M.M. Van Hulle and D. Martinez, "On a novel unsupervised competitive learning algorithm for scalar quantization," IEEE Trans. on Neural Networks, in press.
[3] D. O'Shaughnessy, Speech Communication: Human and Machine, Reading, Mass: Addison-Wesley, 1987.
[4] T. W. Parsons, Voice and Speech Processing, New York: McGraw-Hill, 1987.
[5] D. Estève, F. Baillieu and G. Delapierre, "Integrated Silicon-based sensors: basic research activities in France," Sensors and Actuators A, vol. 33, pp. 1-4, 1992.
[6] S. Grossberg, "Adaptive pattern classification and universal recoding: I Parallel development and coding of neural feature detectors," Biol. Cybern., vol. 23, pp. 121-134, 1976.
[7] S. Grossberg, "Adaptive pattern classification and universal recoding: II Feedback, expectation, olfaction, illusions," Biol. Cybern., vol. 23, pp. 187-202, 1976.
[8] D. E. Rumelhart and D. Zipser, "Feature discovery by competitive learning," Cogn. Sci., vol. 9, pp. 75-112, 1985.
[9] E. Yair, K. Zeger and A. Gersho, "Competitive Learning and Soft Competition for Vector Quantizer design," IEEE Trans. on Signal Processing, vol. 40, pp. 294-308.
[10] T. Kohonen, Self-organization and associative memory, Berlin: Springer, 1989.
[11] J. Hertz, A. Krogh and R. G. Palmer, Introduction to the theory of neural computation, Reading MA: Addison-Wesley, 1991.
[12] D. Martinez and M.M. Van Hulle, "Generalized Boundary Adaptation Rule for minimizing r-th power law distortion in the case of high resolution quantization," submitted.
[13] S. P. Lloyd, Least squares quantization in PCM's. Bell Telephone Laboratories Paper, Murray Hill, NJ, 1957.
[14] J. Max, "Quantizing for minimum distortion," IRE Trans. on Inform. Theory, vol. IT-6, pp. 7-12, 1960.
[15] A. Gersho and R. M. Gray, Vector quantization and signal compression, Boston: Kluwer, 1991.
[16] C. E. Shannon, Coding theorems for a discrete source with a fidelity criterion. In IRE National Convention Record, Part 4, pp. 142-163, 1959.

Appendix

At convergence, $E[\Delta x_j] = 0, j = 1, ..., N-1$, hence eq. (8) becomes:

$$\sum_{k=j+1}^{N} \Delta_k^{t-1} \frac{E[Act_{R_k}^t]}{N-j} - \sum_{k=1}^{j} \Delta_k^{t-1} \frac{E[Act_{R_k}^t]}{j} = 0 \quad j = 1, ..., N-1. \tag{9}$$

Since eq. (9) is a non-homogenous system of linear equations with fewer equations than unknowns, $\Delta_k^{t-1} E[Act_{R_k}^t]$, $k = 1, ... N$, we have the trivial solution and a set of non-trivial solutions. We show that the trivial solution cannot occur and the non-trivial solutions satisfy the necessary condition eq. (3).

Proof:

1) The trivial solution, $\Delta_k^{t-1} E[Act_{R_k}^t] = 0$, $\forall k$, does not occur since at convergence we have that: a) the quantization range, $b-a$, equals $\sum_{j=1}^{N} \Delta_j^{t-1}$, a non-zero quantity, and b) $\sum_{j=1}^{N} E[Act_{R_j}^t] = 1$ with $E[Act_{R_j}^t]$ non-negative, $\forall j$. Furthermore since $p(R_j) = E[Act_{R_j}]$, $\forall j$, and since $p(R_j) = \int_{R_j} p(x)\, dx$, activations are coupled to interval lenghts, we conclude that the trivial solution is not feasible.

2) The necessary condition eq. (3). Assume that we multiply the j-the equation of eq. (9) with $N-j$, $\forall j$, so that we obtain a new set of equations. We can now find eq. (3) recursively, one equality at a time. For this we start with the first two equations of the new set and subtract the second from the first. We then obtain that $\Delta_1^{t-1}\ E[Act_{R_1}^t] = \Delta_2^{t-1}\ E[Act_{R_2}^t]$. By subtracting the third from the second and substituting the equality just found, we obtain that $\Delta_2^{t-1}\ E[Act_{R_2}^t] = \Delta_3^{t-1}\ E[Act_{R_3}^t]$. And so on until we have used the last two equations. Now since $p(R_j) = E[Act_{R_j}]$, $\forall j$, we then have that eq. (3) is satisfied. QED.

OSCILLATOR MEDIA FOR IMAGE PROCESSING ON THE BASE OF NEURAL NETWORKS

Yuri I. Balkarey, Alex S. Cohen, Walter H. Johnson*, Mordukh I. Elinson, Michael G. Evtikhov, Polievkt I. Perov.

Institute of Radio Engineering and Electronics,
Russia Academy of Sciences,
11 Mokhovaya St., Moscow, 103907, Russia.
Tel: (095) 404 6175; Fax: (095) 203 8414
Email: l191@ire.uucp.free.msk.su
*Physics and Engineering Department, Suffolk University,
41 Temple St., Boston, Massachusetts 02114, USA

Transformation of neural networks containing threshold adders into media of oscillator elements and using of such media for image processing are studied. This paper develops our works devoted to connections between active media and neural networks [1].

1. The main equation of modern models of neural networks is the equation of neuron activity, which can be written in the following form:

$$\eta_i(t+\tau) = \tanh\left[\alpha \sum_j \mu_{ij}\eta_j(t)\right] \tag{1}$$

Here η_i is the output of the i- th neuron, τ is the characteristic delay time, μ_{ij} are the synaptic weights, α is the constant. We are further to discuss the case of the fixed μ_{ij}.

Consider a medium of isolated paired neighboring neurons η_i and η_j with $\mu_{ij} \neq 0$, and take $\mu_{ij} = 0$ outside of every pair (Fig. 1). For the pair (i = 1, j = 2) we obtain two equations:

$$\eta_1(t+\tau) = \tanh\left[\alpha\left(\mu_{11}\eta_1(t) + \mu_{12}\eta_2(t)\right)\right] \tag{2}$$

$$\eta_2(t+\tau) = \tanh\left[\alpha\left(\mu_{21}\eta_1(t) + \mu_{22}\eta_2(t)\right)\right] \tag{3}$$

We choose the cases of one stationary point on the phase plane (η_2, η_1). At appropriate μ_{ij} Eqs. (2)-(3) can be transformed into an oscillator equation.

If the time interval τ is the smallest one in the system and suppose $\eta_{1,2}(t+\tau) \simeq \eta_{1,2}(t) + \tau\, d\eta_{1,2}(t)/dt$ after linearization of Eqs. (2)-(3) near the stationary point and eliminating η_2 we obtain:

$$\frac{d^2\eta_1}{dt^2} = \frac{1}{\tau^2}\left[\left(\alpha\,\mu_{11} - 1\right)\left(\alpha\,\mu_{22} - 1\right) - \alpha^2\mu_{12}\mu_{21}\right]\eta_1 = \frac{1}{\tau}\left(\alpha\,\mu_{11} + \alpha\,\mu_{22} - 2\right)\frac{d\eta_1}{dt} \tag{4}$$

0-7803-1901-X/94 $4.00 ©1994 IEEE

If the expression in square brackets is positive we have an equation of an oscillator with frequency

$$\Omega = \tau^{-1} \left[(\alpha \mu_{11} - 1)(\alpha \mu_{22} - 1) - \alpha^2 \mu_{12}\mu_{21} \right]^{1/2} \qquad (5)$$

and damping
$$\nu = \tau^{-1} (2 - \alpha \mu_{11} - \alpha \mu_{22}) \qquad (6)$$

At appropriate parameters damping ν may be small in comparison with Ω. For example, if $\mu_{11} = \mu_{22} = (1 - \varepsilon)\alpha^{-1}$, $\mu_{12} = -\delta\alpha^{-1}$, $\mu_{21} = \delta\alpha^{-1}$ ($\varepsilon \ll 1$, $\delta \ll 1$) we have:

$$\Omega = \tau^{-1} (\varepsilon^2 + \delta^2)^{1/2}, \qquad \nu = 2\varepsilon\tau^{-1}$$

For $\varepsilon \ll \delta$ oscillations damp weakly ($\nu \ll \Omega$).

It is also possible to make ν negative. For example, $\mu_{11} = \mu_{22} = (1 + \varepsilon)\alpha^{-1}$, $\mu_{12} = \delta\alpha^{-1}$, $\mu_{21} = -\delta\alpha^{-1}$ ($\varepsilon \ll 1$, $\delta \ll 1$). Then:

$$\Omega = \tau^{-1} (\varepsilon^2 + \delta^2)^{1/2}, \qquad \nu = -2\varepsilon\tau^{-1}$$

As a result of negative ν the oscillations increase and in the absence of other stationary points a limit cycle of self-sustained oscillations may exist.

The transformation of Eqs. (2)-(3) holds if $\Omega\tau \ll 1$ and $\nu\tau \ll 1$. If $\varepsilon \ll 1$ and $\delta \ll 1$ these conditions are satisfied.

We note that the oscillating regimes may also exist in the initial system (2)-(3). In Fig. 2 results of a numerical modeling of Eqs.(2)-(3) are shown.

For INTEL 80170NX neural network the main time parameter τ is of the order of 10^{-6} s. Therefore the period of oscillations is of the same order.

It is possible to use the input signals for oscillator control. For example, the dynamics of η_1 is described by the following equation

$$\eta_1(t + \tau) = \tanh \left[\alpha \left(\mu_{11}\eta_1(t) + \mu_{12}\eta_2(t) \right) + \xi_1 \right] \qquad (7)$$

The additional signal ξ_1 changes the shape and the frequency of oscillations. Inhomogeneous input signal $\xi(X,Y)$ makes the frequencies of oscillators depending on the coordinates X, Y. Such transformation is the main step in realization of the ideas of the following section. Special periodic input signal $\xi(t)$ may be used for resonant excitation of oscillators.

Besides the neural networks the special arrays of microelectronics analog elements (cellular neural networks [2]), optical bistable elements [3], and microcavity lasers [4] can be used for creation of oscillatory media.

2. We discuss two oscillator regimes for image processing: self- sustained oscillations and weakly damping quasi- harmonic oscillations under resonance pumping. The oscillators may be isolated or interacted.

Suppose all oscillators have optical inputs and outputs

and the illumination changes the oscillator frequency ω_0. If such a medium is illuminated by light, I(X,Y), which contains the information of interest, the frequency ω_0 becomes a function of I(X,Y): $\omega_0 \Rightarrow \omega_{loc} \equiv \omega_0 + \alpha I(X,Y)$. We can use inhomogeneous resonant pumping $H(X,Y) \cos \Omega t$ $(\Omega \sim \omega_0)$. For inhomogeneous parametric resonance pumping the change of frequency is $\omega_0^2 \Rightarrow \omega_{loc}^2 (1 + h(X,Y) \cos 2\Omega t)$ $(\Omega \sim \omega_0)$.

For example, resonant excitation of the medium can be realized by passage of light through a wide aperture modulator with harmonic regime of modulation.

Oscillators inputs and outputs can be also electrical. Then an interface for transformation of optical signals into electrical one is necessary.

For the medium of isolated self- sustained oscillators for many periods of oscillations the image I(X,Y) (which changes the frequency ω_0) gives a large accumulation of inhomogeneous local phase shifts. The noise gives local frequency shifts of different signs and can be fully averaged during many periods. After the information signal I(X,Y) is switched off, the medium becomes a memory since the self- oscillations do not damp. So, it is possible to extract images from intensive noise.

A periodic shift of the image along the medium transforms the small scale static distortions into dynamic noise and they can be also removed by the medium of self- oscillators.

Regime of damping quasi- harmonic oscillations allows us to use resonant excitation of the medium's oscillatory elements. Then it is possible to call all medium's elements by a parallel way. The using of resonances allows us to solve the following problems: halftoning, parallel extraction of regions of equal intensity or color, determination of common and distinct parts of images, moving elements, points of extrema, correlation comparison of patterns, etc. In Fig. 3,b we demonstrate the halftoning of one dimensional image by a medium of isolated parametrically excited oscillators; frequency of pumping is chosen in such a way that the medium extracts only the most intensive part (peak 1 in Fig. 3,a); for frequency corresponding to the resonance with peak 2 the result of binarization is shown in Fig. 3,c.

REFERENCES.

[1].Balkarey Yu.I., Evtikhov M.G., Elinson M.I. (1991). Auto Wave Media and Neural Networks. Proc. SPIE, v. 1621, pp. 238- 249.

[2].Chua L.O., Yang L. (1988). Cellular Neural Networks: Theory. IEEE Transactions on Circuits and Systems, v. CAS 35, pp. 1257- 1272.

[3].Balkarey Yu.I., Cohen A.S., Evtikhov M.G. (1992). Instabilities of Lateral Modes in Semiconductor Fabry-Perot Interferometers. J. of Modern Optics, v. 39, pp.1583-1591.

[4].Jewell J.L., Harbison J.P., Scherer A., Lee Y.H., Florez L.T. (1991). Vertical- Cavity Surface- Emitting Lasers: Design, Growth, Fabrication, Characterization. IEEE J. Quant.Electron., v. QE- 27, pp. 1332- 1346.

FIGURES.

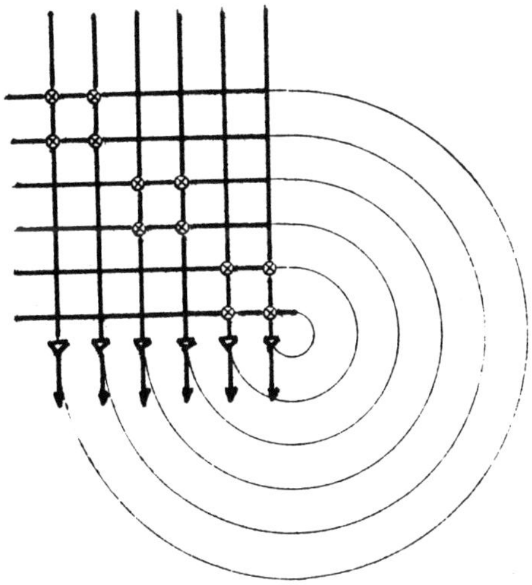

Fig. 1. Neuron pairs which form oscillator medium. In points ⊗ the weights $\mu_{ij} \neq 0$. Other $\mu_{ij} = 0$.

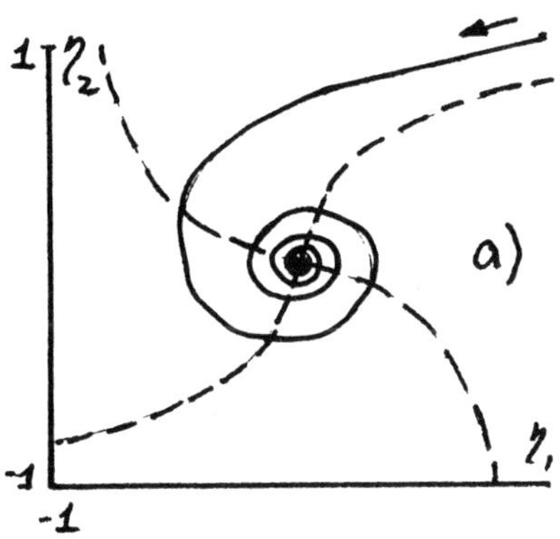

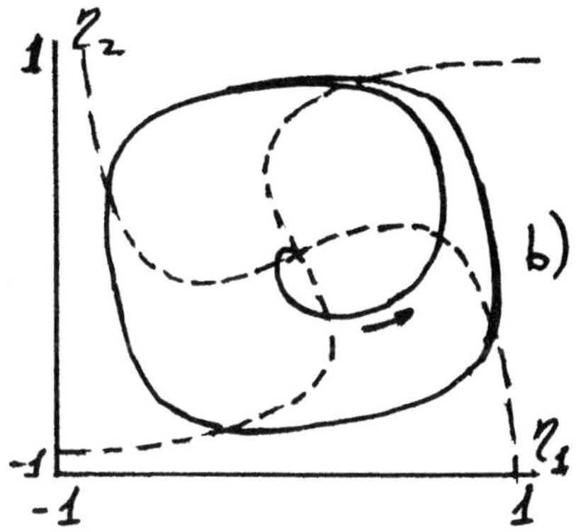

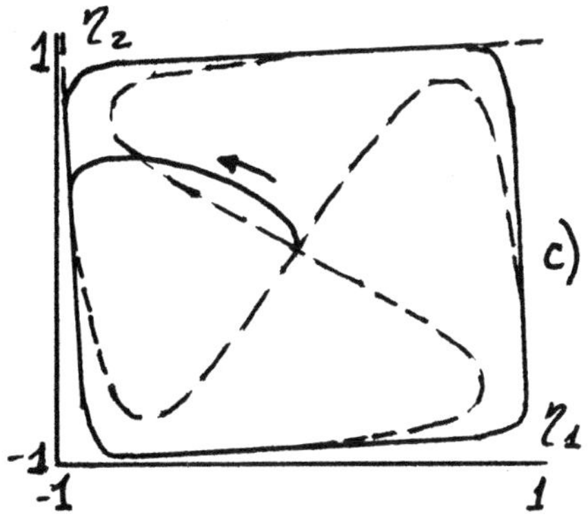

Fig. 2. Stationary solutions of Eqs.(2)-(3) (dashed lines) and phase portraits (solid lines) of oscillations of a neuron pair. Parameters: $\alpha = 4$, $\mu_{12} = -0.1$, $\mu_{21} = 0.1$.

a) Quasi harmonical damped oscillations. $\mu_{11} = \mu_{22} = 0.22$.

b) Quasi harmonical self-sustained oscillations. $\mu_{11} = \mu_{22} = 0.3$.

c) Unharmonious self- sustained oscillations. $\mu_{11} = \mu_{22} = 0.315$.

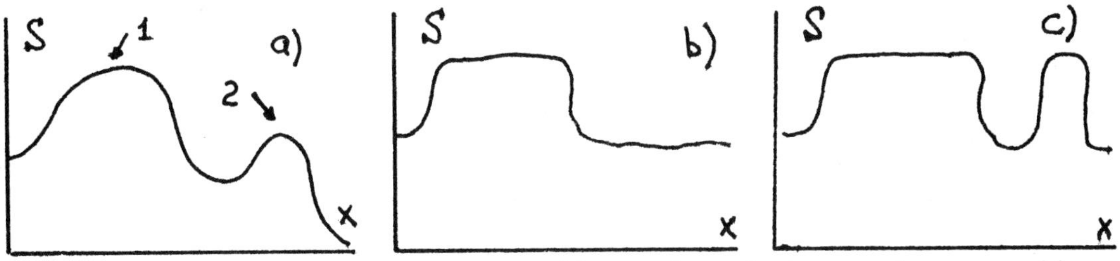

Fig. 3. Halftoning of the one- dimensional image by a medium of isolated parametrically excited oscillators.

a) Initial curve S(X).

b) Frequency of pumping corresponds to the peak 1.

c) Frequency of pumping corresponds to the peak 2.

Learning Texture Discrimination Masks

Anil K. Jain and Kalle Karu
Department of Computer Science
Michigan State University
East Lansing, MI 48824, USA

Abstract

Texture segmentation using multichannel filtering involves applying a set of masks to an input image, and then grouping the pixels based on the responses to these masks. We solve the problem of finding an optimal set of masks by designing a neural network which is trained to maximize a relevant function. Two algorithms – the centroid algorithm [1] and the gradient descent algorithm – are used to train the network. Experimental results on segmenting two natural textures and extracting barcodes in an image are reported and the error rates compared for both the algorithms with different network configurations. The centroid algorithm gives better results in small parameter spaces, whereas the gradient descent algorithm works better with more parameters. Our method of automatically generating texture discrimination masks not only results in a good segmentation performance, but also reduces the dimensionality of the feature space compared to previously published multichannel filtering methods.

1 Introduction

Texture is one of the most important properties of visual surfaces which helps us to discriminate one object from another, an object from the background, and to draw inferences about 3D world. Any machine vision system that tries to compete with or mimic a human visual system, must therefore be able to deal with texture.

Among the main tasks of texture analysis are texture segmentation and classification. Segmentation involves assigning different labels to image points that belong to regions with different textures. Segmentation can be supervised, when the texture types in the image are known beforehand, or unsupervised, when the image consists of unknown textures. An example of texture segmentation is illustrated in Figure 1. Figure 1(a) shows an image composed of two natural textures from Brodatz album [2], and Figure 1(c) shows the output of our segmentation algorithm. The task of texture classification is to assign predefined labels to different textures. In Figure 1(c) we would like a classification algorithm to assign the label 'handmade paper' to the white pixels, and the label 'cotton canvas' to the black pixels.

(a) (b) (c)

Figure 1: Texture segmentation example: (a) input image (256×256) with two different textures; (b) filtered image; (c) smoothed and thresholded image.

0-7803-1901-X/94 $4.00 ©1994 IEEE

There is no widely accepted definition of texture [10]. Unlike other image features, such as intensity or color, texture is not a property of a single pixel, but rather of a spatial neighborhood around the pixel. Different methods of texture analysis are based on different definitions and interpretations of image texture.

Multichannel filtering approach to texture analysis is motivated by psychophysical evidence and ease in parallel implementation. The general setup is as follows. The input image is convolved with each filter from a predefined filter bank. For each pixel, the outputs of filtered images constitute a feature vector which is then used to label the pixel. Three questions arise: (1) how to choose the initial filter bank?, (2) how to select only a few best filters for given textures to reduce the dimensionality of the feature vector?, and (3) how to use the feature vector to segment or classify the textures?

The Gabor transform, essentially a Fourier transform windowed by a Gaussian envelope, has been used to decompose an input image into components of different spatial frequencies and orientations [3, 4, 6, 8, 9, 10]. While the Fourier transform gives the frequency components over the whole image, Gabor transform captures 'local' frequencies. Moreover, it can be shown [5] that Gabor transform possesses optimal bandwidths in both spatial and frequency domains. Similar multichannel filtering and even cells with receptive fields similar to Gabor functions have been found in some biological visual systems.

Dunn *et al.* [3] proposed an effective method of finding the single best Gabor filter for discriminating a given texture pair. Jain and Farrokhnia [4, 8] started with a bank of 28 Gabor filters. The filters were then ranked based on the amount to which the original image could be reconstructed from the filtered image. Only the outputs of a few best filters were selected for image segmentation. Both an unsupervised statistical clustering algorithm and a supervised neural network were used to segment the image. There is, however, no guarantee that the first n highest ranked filters are the best n-tuple of filters possible from the 28 given filters. Greenspan *et al.* [6] also used a bank of Gabor filters to obtain 15-dimensional feature vectors, which were then classified by a rule-based system embedded in a neural network. The network was trained with a combined unsupervised-supervised algorithm. Randen and Husøy [9] have studied other types of filters and concluded that simpler filters, such as IIR and FIR, have performance comparable to that of Gabor filters. To find the best filter, not necessarily of Gabor type, IIR, or FIR, Skinner and Benke [1] have proposed a random search algorithm, called the centroid algorithm, and demonstrated its usefulness in supervised and unsupervised texture segmentation tasks.

In this paper, we study the filtering method for segmenting an image with two textures. The system to accomplish this task is embedded in a neural network architecture, described in Section 2. We address all the three questions mentioned above – the network is first trained to find a set of best filters and then the filter outputs are combined so that the texture discrimination error is minimized. To train the network, we use two methods: the centroid algorithm, and the gradient descent algorithm, implemented as back propagation. The algorithms are described in section 3, experimental results are presented in section 4, and conclusions are drawn in Section 5.

2 Neural Network Architecture

The neural network used to segment a textured image is a multi-layer feed-forward network shown in Figure 2. It receives input from a $(2M+1) \times (2M+1)$ square region around pixel (r,c) of the image to be classified, and feeds this through hidden layers to the output node. We expect the output to be 'high' for one texture type and 'low' for the other. Based on the output value, the center pixel (r,c) of the input region is then assigned to one of the two categories. The weights from the input image to the first layer are conventionally called masks, and the output of the first layer is called a feature vector.

Different nonlinearities can be applied to the summed input in the first layer. Skinner and Benke [1] used the square function to calculate the 'energy' of the masked image, whereas Jain and Farrokhnia [4, 8] applied the absolute value of sigmoid. In the experiments reported here, we have used three types of nonlinearities:

$$o_i = tanh(\beta h_i) \quad (1)$$

$$o_i = h_i^2 \quad (2)$$

$$o_i = tanh(\beta h_i^2) \quad (3)$$

where o_i is the output of the ith node in the first layer, and h_i is its input, the weighted sum from the input image. The activation from the first layer to the second, and so on, is propagated as in a standard

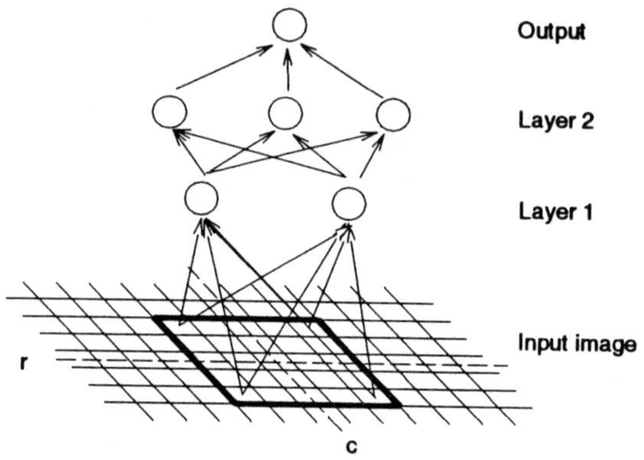

Figure 2: The neural network architecture.

fully connected feed-forward neural network, with each node applying a sigmoidal squashing function to the weighted sum of the outputs of all the nodes in the previous layer.

Training the network means modifying the weights in such a way that an objective function is maximized. In the experiments, we fed all the pixels in the two textured images to the network. From the output values, the means μ_1, μ_2 and standard deviations σ_1, σ_2 for the two textures were calculated. We have utilized two functions to be maximized by the learning procedures: the Fisher ratio, successfully used by Skinner and Benke [1]

$$\frac{(\mu_1 - \mu_2)^2}{\sigma_1^2 + \sigma_2^2} \tag{4}$$

and a simpler squared difference of means

$$(\mu_1 - \mu_2)^2. \tag{5}$$

At every training step, the weights from the input image to the first layer were normalized to zero mean and unit variance. All other weights were clipped to a maximum value. The learning algorithms are described in the next section.

3 Learning Algorithms

In this section, we describe the two learning algorithms. The centroid algorithm, as proposed by Skinner and Benke [1], is a random search algorithm for maximizing an arbitrary merit function $F(\mathbf{x})$, where $\mathbf{x}$ is the parameter vector to be found. We assume that the function F is positive, symmetric: $F(\mathbf{x}) = F(-\mathbf{x})$, and the parameter space is known. The algorithm consists of the following steps:

1. Randomly generate a parameter vector $\mathbf{p}_{best}$ (the current best estimate) and evaluate $F(\mathbf{p}_{best})$.
2. Randomly generate a new vector $\mathbf{p}_{rand}$, and evaluate $F(\mathbf{p}_{rand})$.
3. Form two linear combinations $\mathbf{p}_+$, $\mathbf{p}_-$, and evaluate $F(\mathbf{p}_+)$, $F(\mathbf{p}_-)$, where

$$\mathbf{p}_+ = w_{best}\mathbf{p}_{best} + w_{rand}\mathbf{p}_{rand}, \qquad \mathbf{p}_- = w_{best}\mathbf{p}_{best} - w_{rand}\mathbf{p}_{rand},$$

$$w_{best} = \frac{F(\mathbf{p}_{best})}{F(\mathbf{p}_{best}) + F(\mathbf{p}_{rand})}, \qquad w_{rand} = \frac{F(\mathbf{p}_{rand})}{F(\mathbf{p}_{best}) + F(\mathbf{p}_{rand})}.$$

4. From the four parameter vectors $\mathbf{p}_{best}$, $\mathbf{p}_{rand}$, $\mathbf{p}_+$, and $\mathbf{p}_-$, select the one with the greatest value of F as the next $\mathbf{p}_{best}$.
5. Repeat steps 2-4 a predetermined number of times.

The idea behind calculating the linear combinations of parameter vectors is as follows. If both $\mathbf{p}_{best}$ and $\mathbf{p}_{rand}$ are considered as perturbed from an optimal value $\mathbf{p}^*$ by a small random noise ϵ, then the linear combination should cancel out the noise and be closer to $\mathbf{p}^*$. The average is closest to the optimum $\mathbf{p}^*$ when the weights w_{best} and w_{rand} are inversely proportional to $|\epsilon|^2$. Generally, ϵ is unknown, but assuming a strong negative correlation between the magnitude of ϵ and the value of F at a given point, the function

F can be used to replace ϵ in the calculation of weights. The weighted difference should give an improved approximation when $\mathbf{p}_{best}$ and $\mathbf{p}_{rand}$ are near opposite maximum points $\mathbf{p}^*$ and $-\mathbf{p}^*$. One of the advantages of the centroid algorithm is its simplicity. There are no learning parameters to be adjusted and no tight constraints on the form, modality, or differentiability of the merit function F. We used the centroid algorithm to train the neural network. The parameter vector in this case consisted of all the weights in the network.

The second algorithm for training the network is the gradient descent algorithm, implemented using back propagation. To compare the performance of the two algorithms, we maximized the same function given in Eq.(5). Differentiating the Fisher ratio in Eq.(4) is computationally too expensive, so we could not use it in the gradient descent method. However, maximizing Eq.(5) instead of Eq.(4) did not considerably affect the performance. In the gradient descent algorithm, a constant learning rate and a speed-up momentum term were used.

4 Experimental Results

In this section, we describe the experimental results of applying the learning algorithms to two segmentation tasks: discrimination of a pair of natural textures, and locating barcodes in an image. As was mentioned above, we could not maximize the Fisher ratio using the gradient descent algorithm. Nevertheless, experiments with a number of different texture pairs revealed that the simpler objective function in Eq.(5) had almost the same performance. Also, it became evident that using the plain sigmoid as the nonlinearity in the first layer did very poorly compared with the other two nonlinearities (Eqs. (2) and (3)). Therefore, we do not report the results with Fisher ratio or sigmoidal nonlinearity. Whenever possible, the same parameter values, such as the slope β of the sigmoid function, number of nodes, etc., were used for both the learning methods.

4.1 Segmentation of Two Natural Textures

We applied the two algorithms described above to a variety of natural texture pairs from Brodatz album [2]. In this section, we only report the results on the texture pair shown in Figure 1(a). For this texture pair, three 5×5 masks were sufficient to get a good quality segmentation result. Applying the segmentation algorithms to other textures gave similar results. However, since we use only 5×5 masks (M=2), the textures should possess a 'fine' structure. Earlier studies on texture segmentation (e.g. [4, 8]) used many more filters (masks) to segment similar texture pairs.

To train the network, the input images were divided into training and test sets. We randomly selected a square 64×64 region in the two input images of size 128×128. Pixels from this training set were used to train the network with both the algorithms. The network's performance was then tested on the two 128×128 images as follows. Every pixel in the two input images was fed into the network, and then classified depending on the output value of the network: if it exceeded a threshold θ, the pixel was assigned to class 1, and was assigned to class 2, otherwise. The threshold was taken to be the average of the two means μ_1 and μ_2. We did not use any smoothing before calculating the error rates. Figure 1(b) shows the output of the network, which was then thresholded and used for the error calculations. Figure 1(c) shows the same image smoothed and thresholded.

Figure 3 plots the convergence of the two learning algorithms when applied to two- and three-layer networks with different nonlinear functions. The two-layer networks had three nodes in the first layer (the number of masks was 3), and the three-layer network had three nodes in both the hidden layers. The functions plotted in Figure 3 are not strictly increasing because the objective function that was maximized during training does not have an explicit relationship with the error rate. It is evident from the figures that the centroid algorithm works better when the number of parameters is small. In most cases it provides good parameter estimates after a few hundred steps. Gradient descent method, on the other hand, shows better results with a large number of parameters, especially in the case of a three-layer network. It may be speculated that increasing the dimensionality of the parameter set, the probability of randomly choosing a point near an optimum decreases very rapidly. Gradient descent algorithms seem to give better results with bigger networks, if they are not overtrained.

It is interesting to look at the frequency responses of the learned masks. We selected a trained two-layer network with correct classification rate above 0.9, and applied all the three learned masks (the weight vectors from the input image to the first layer) to the image shown in Figure 4(a), which consists of concentric

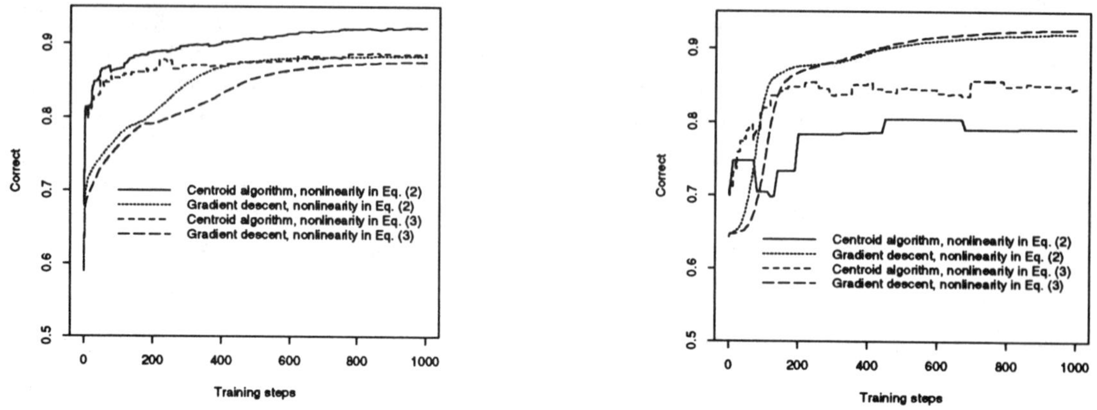

(a) (b)

Figure 3: Correct classification rate: (a) two-layer network; (b) three-layer network.

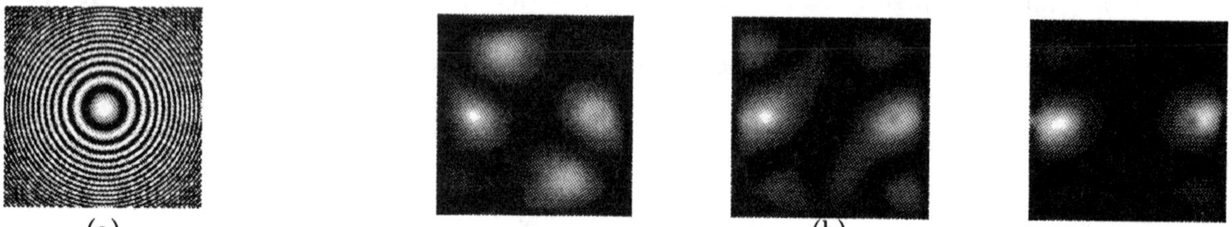

(a) (b)

Figure 4: Frequency responses of the learned masks: (a) the image of concentric sinusoids; (b) the responses of the three learned masks to the image (a).

sinusoids with frequencies increasing linearly from the center towards the borders. In Figure 4(b) the outputs of applying the three masks to the image in Figure 4(a) are shown. A white region in the filtered image means that the mask responds strongly to a certain frequency and orientation. Unlike Gabor filters, all the three masks have high responses to more than one frequency and orientation. The combination of different frequencies and orientations in one mask may be crucial in reducing the number of masks from 28 in [4, 8] to only 3 in our experiments.

4.2 Barcode segmentation

We applied the same two learning methods to the problem of barcode segmentation. Jain and Chen [7] have used a bank of Gabor filters to segment barcodes. They utilized a simple heuristics that in a barcode, only the Gabor filter in one direction should give a high response, whereas the filter corresponding to the orthogonal direction gives no response. Since this is similar to the XOR problem, which cannot be solved by a one-layer network, we expected the network with two layers above the first feature extraction layer (3-layer network in our terminology) to perform better than one with a smaller number of layers.

Figure 5(a) shows an input image with a barcode in it. The segmentation result is shown in Figure 5(b). We wanted the barcode extraction network to be rotation invariant. To achieve this, the network was trained to discriminate the texture in Figure 5(c) from random noise. We trained two- and three-layer networks with 4 nodes in each hidden layer using both the learning algorithms. Again, the centroid algorithm gave better results with the smaller network, and the gradient descent algorithm performed better in case of a large network. The reduction in the number of masks, compared with [7], was achieved because each mask captured more than one frequency and orientation. Also, the size (5×5) of the masks, generated by the two learning algorithms, was much smaller than that of Gabor masks used by Jain and Chen [7].

(a) (b) (c)

Figure 5: Barcode segmentation results: (a) a barcode image (256×256); (b) the same image segmented; (c) input image to the training algorithms.

5 Conclusions

We have implemented a texture segmentation algorithm in a neural network architecture. The performance of two learning algorithms – the centroid and the gradient descent algorithms – was evaluated. We applied the method to the tasks of segmenting two natural textures and locating barcodes in an image.

In the current image processing literature, mostly static masks are used to filter an image. Replacing these general masks with a few specific masks, which are optimal with respect to the problem at hand, will greatly reduce the processing time and error rates. The masks learned by the two algorithms studied in this paper can be used in image processing programs for filtering, which are usually faster than the corresponding neural network simulators. Our approach for learning a set of masks can readily be generalized to the task of segmenting an image containing more than two texture types. For this purpose, we need to add new nodes at the output layer of the network, and define a new objective function to be maximized. By assigning one output node to each texture, and defining an objective function that will minimize the discrimination error over all textures, it is possible to avoid the combinatorial explosion of having one mask to discriminate each pair of textures.

References

[1] K.K. Benke and D.R. Skinner, Segmentation of Visually Similar Textures by Convolution Filtering. *The Australian Computer Journal,* Vol. 19, No. 3, pp. 134-139, 1987.

[2] P. Brodatz, *Textures: A Photographic Album for Artists and Designers.* New York, NY:Dover 1966.

[3] D.F. Dunn, W.E. Higgins and J. Wakeley, Determining Gabor Filter Parameters for Texture Segmentation. In *Proceedings of SPIE Intelligent Robots and Computer Vision* XI, Vol. 1826, pp. 51-63, 1992.

[4] F. Farrokhnia, *Multichannel Filtering Techniques for Texture Segmentation and Surface Quality Inspection,* Ph.D. thesis, Michigan State University, 1990.

[5] D. Gabor, Theory of communication. J. IEE (London), Vol. 93, pp. 429-457, 1946.

[6] H. Greenspan, R. Goodman, R. Chellapa, and C.H. Anderson, Learning Texture Discrimination Rules in a Multiresolution System. To appear in *The IEEE Trans. PAMI,* 1994.

[7] A.K. Jain and Y. Chen, Barcode Localization Using Texture Analysis. *Proc. Second Int'l Conf. on Document Analysis and Recognition, Tsukuba city, Japan,* pp. 41-44, October 1993.

[8] A.K. Jain and F. Farrokhnia, Unsupervised Texture Segmentation Using Gabor Filters. *Pattern Recognition,* Vol 24, No. 12, pp. 1167-1186, 1991.

[9] T. Randen and J.H. Husøy, *Multichannel filtering for image texture segmentation,* Technical report, Rogaland University Center, Norway, 1993.

[10] M. Tuceryan and A.K. Jain, Texture Analysis, Chapter 11 in *The Handbook of Pattern Recognition and Computer Vision,* C.H. Chen, L.F. Pau, P.S.P. Wang (eds.) World Scientific Publishing Co., pp. 235-276, 1993.

Self-Organizing Scaling Filters for Image Segmentation

T. Rozgonyi[†,‡], T. Fomin[†], A. Lőrincz[†]

[†] Departement of Photophysics, Institute of Isotopes
The Hungarian Academy of Sciences, Budapest, Hungary

[‡] Department of Physics, Attila József University, Szeged, Hungary

I. Introduction

Competing neurons are able to create spatial filters of circular shape and of equal sizes, as it was shown in [1]. Our goal was to develop a neural network, that creates filters of different sizes in order to distinguish among patterns of different sizes, even if they are positioned to the same place in the input space. Such network could solve fast segmentation tasks in parallel. There are evidences that neurons of the primary visual cortex (V_1) can perform in similar fashion [2, 3].

II. Description of the model

We have performed our computations on a network consisiting of N_i competing neural units. In the network each neuron received inputs from an input vector $\mathbf{x}$ via Hebbian weights. Let us denote the weight connecting the ith neuron with the jth component of the input vector by q_{ij} ($i = 1, \ldots, N_i$; $j = 1, \ldots, {N_j}^2$). The input vector x_j ($j = 1, \ldots, {N_j}^2$) represents an N_j by N_j pixel sized input space. When an input vector x_j is presented to the network, activities a_i are computed for all the neurons, where

$$a_i = \sum_j q_{ij} x_j, \qquad (1)$$

and the neuron with the maximum a_i is selected as the winner. It is only the winner that can train its Hebbian connections, known as winner-take-all (WTA) mechanism. The adjustment we applied for connections q_{ij} ($j = 1, \ldots, {N_j}^2$) is as follows:

$$\frac{dq_{ij}}{dt} = -a_i q_{ij} + x_j \qquad (2)$$

WTA and equation (2) was chosen by considering that (i) inputs can be more or less frequent and the success of segmentation cannot depend on the frequency of the samples, i.e. postsynaptic learning is needed, (ii) postsynaptic learning is appropriate for making redundant representation, (iii) both small and large receptive field neurons that overlap should be able to win for their appropriate inputs.

To satisfy the last point consider filters of equal weights but different in size. Then any input that has one pixel outside of the receptive field of the 'small neuron' (SN) and inside the receptive field of the 'big neuron' (BN) shall make BN to win. To consider the other crucial extreme assume that all weights are equal within a single receptive field. Assume further, that weights are inversely proportional to the number of connected pixels. Then to any input that covers the receptive field of the SN, the SN shall win over the BN. That is we ought to try to develop connection strengths that scale between n^0 and n^{-1}, where n is the approximate number of pixels within the receptive field. Eqs. (1) and (2) were chosen to have the power of n at $-1/2$.

It may be interesting to note that the model has no adjustable parameter.

To avoid the edge effects the input space was either a 1 dimensional (1D) or a 2 dimensional (2D) torus. Input pattern vectors corresponding to Gaussian spatial excitation with random amplitude between 0 and 2 were presented at random positions to the network. Noisy background was added and inputs were assumed to saturate at the value 1. The patterns were presented according to a probability distribution inversely proportional to the area of the input. In some cases the inputs were presented with identical probabilities. Convergence slowed down for the last case, leaving other properties unchanged.

III. Results on 2D torus

Spatial filters' radii ordered according to their sizes are shown in Fig. (1) for the case of a two dimensional torus with surface area of 18x18 pixels. To every filter the quantity of

$$Q_i = \frac{\sum_j q_{ij}}{r_i} \qquad (3)$$

is plotted also. It can be seen that quantity Q_i is approximately constant as it should be if the $n^{-1/2}$ rule is to be satisfied. 18 input patterns were presented with equidistant area ratios. The radii of the largest and smallest presented input patterns were equal to 4.76 and 0.9, respectively. Both extremes are fairly well matched by the filter distribution.

0-7803-1901-X/94 $4.00 ©1994 IEEE

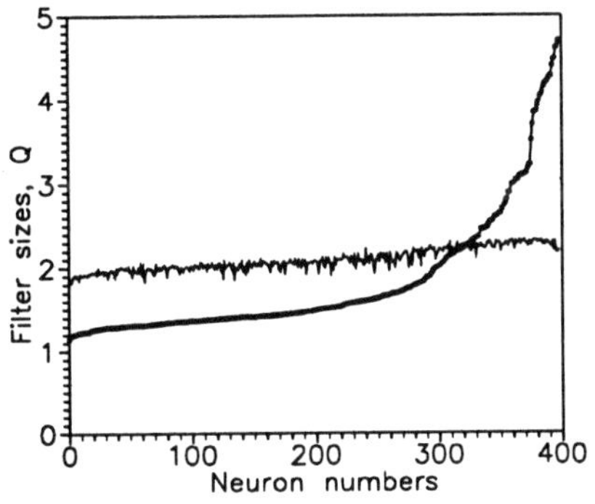

Figure 1: Filter radii, $r_i, i = 1, \ldots, 400$ and $Q_i = \sum_j q_{ij}/r_i$ in increasing order for the 2D torus

Four typical spatial filters are shown in Fig. (2).

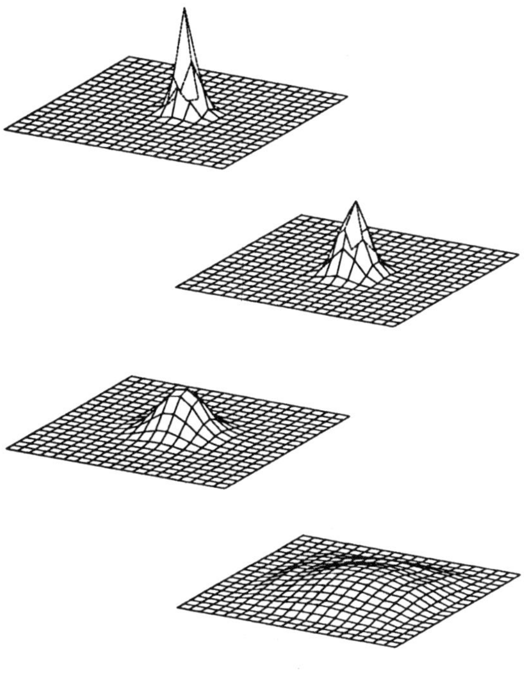

Figure 2: Typical spatial filters. Corresponding radii are 1.2, 1.6, 2.2 and 3.8, respectively

The role of additive noise and saturation seemed to be marginal for the network, apart from the fact that small receptive field neurons learnt the presence of noise, while large receptive field neurons had very clean background due to the $n^{-1/2}$ rule. There is small gap that opens up in the figure around the 380th neural unit. Other points of the figure also show gap forming tendencies. Similar effects were found in computer experiments on 18x18 pixel closed world (not torus). Gap was formed by 'volume' neurons and the gap was conquered by neurons around the edges of the image. Only 'surface' neurons had radii between 2.9 and 3.7 pixels.

The slow convergence of winner-take-all (WTA) networks did not allow us to study the gap effect in 2D.

IV. Results on 1D torus

Gap formation - formation of neuron groups with close receptive fields - was studied in 1D. Inputs of Gaussian shape were generated subject to additive noise and saturation. Fig. (3) shows gap formation vs. training number up to 800,000. Fig. (4) shows stabilized neuron radii curves for different neuron numbers for the same 50 pixel 1D torus.

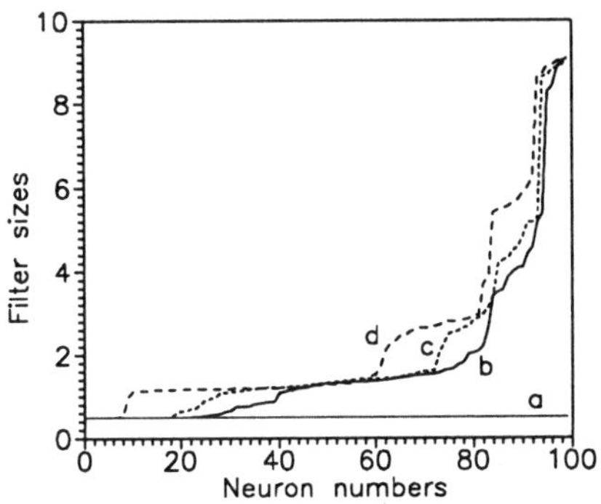

Figure 3: Figure shows the time evolution of filter sizes on a 50 pixel 1D torus. Curves a, b, c and d correspond to 0, 100, 200 and 800 thousands learning steps.

Gaps formed for all cases. Gap structure becomes finer - more groups are formed - as the number of neurons grows. The groups that are formed during the evolution of the network is usually made of neurons that can, together, cover the input field.In all cases the same input patterns were presented. Q_i values were constant for all the filters and for different neural number experiments. The size of the largest filter still suits the size of the largest input pattern.

V. Extension of model to Hebbian-anti-Hebbian (HAH) network

It is challenging to extend the method to HAH networks [4, 5], since HAH provides sotf competition, allows cooperative training and thus learning can be faster [6].

Equations of HAH networks were modified in or-

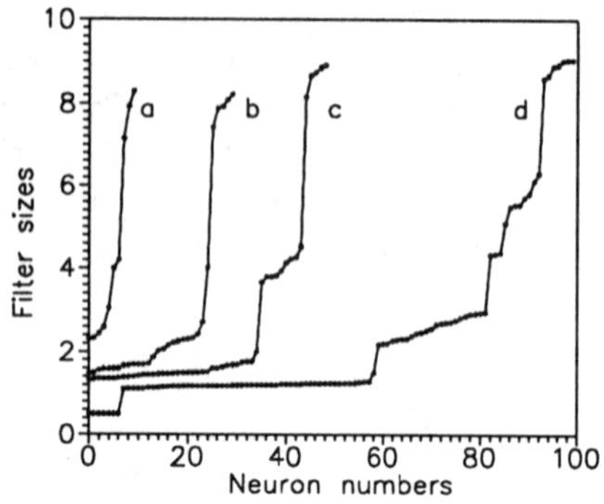

Figure 4: Figure shows magnitude ordered filter radii for different neuron numbers. Curves a, b, c and d correspond to 10, 30, 50 and 100 neurons, respectively.

der to keep the scaling properties. In a HAH network the neurons are connected with each other through the anti-Hebbian connections w_{ik} ($i, k = 1, \ldots, N_i$). When an input is connected to the system the output of the neural units develops through a relaxation process governed by the following non-linear differential equations:

$$\frac{dy_i}{dt} = -y_i + f\left(\sum_j q_{ij}x_j - \sum_{\substack{k\\ i\neq k}} w_{ik}y_k\right), \qquad (4)$$

where y_i and f denote the output of the ith neural unit and the sigmoid function respectively. During the training process both $\mathbf{q}$ and $\mathbf{w}$ are modified (trained) according to the following equations:

$$\epsilon\frac{dq_{ij}}{dt} = y_i(-a_i q_{ij} + x_j), \qquad (5)$$

$$\epsilon\frac{dw_{ik}}{dt} = y_i y_k(-w_{ik} + \alpha\sqrt{a_i a_k}), \qquad (6)$$

Here ϵ stands to remind us that the setting of weights is carried out on a longer timescale than that of the relaxation process.

Equation (5) is a postsynaptic equation. In this sense it is identical to Eq. (2). Equation (6) was made postsynaptical also for the same reason: the frequency of presenting special size samples cannot effect learning. The term $\sqrt{a_i a_k}$ was chosen to make the argument of function f approximately independent of filter size. Without this or a similar choice the inhibition cannot scale with the filter size. Now, there is one parameter, α in the model. If this parameter is zero then there is no competition between neurons and every neuron becomes identical. The higher the value of α the stronger the competition. This was found in the experiments: the smaller the α the more similar the receptive fields are - the smaller range they can span. (Experiments were run on the 50 pixel 1D torus.)

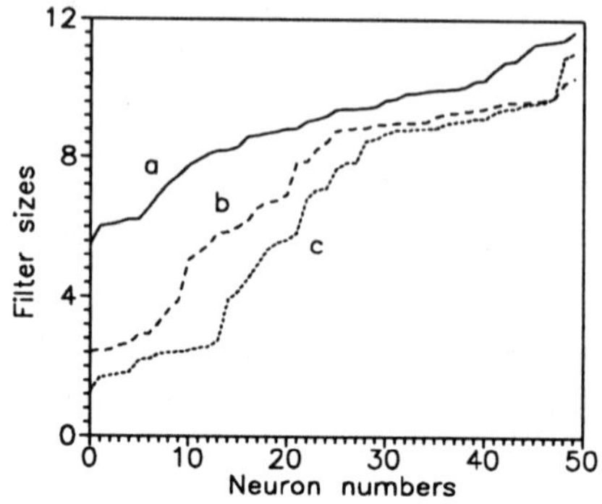

Figure 5: Filter radii. Curve a corresponds to 100 learning steps ($\alpha = 1.0$). Curve b corresponds to 1.5 million learning steps ($\alpha = 1.0$). Curve c corresponds to 420 thousands learning steps with $\alpha = 1.0$ after pretaining through 810 thousands learning steps with $\alpha = 0.2$.

Curve a of Fig. 5 shows that the initial stage of learning is very quick: spatial filters are formed in 100 steps. These filters however do not span the range of input patterns. Efforts of the network to learn smaller filters were not as successful as for the WTA mechanism (Fig. 5, curve b). On the other hand, if one is to increase α then, in principle, the WTA limit is to be reached for Eqs. (4)-(6). Higher α's gave, however, no improvement. The reason relies in the training mechanism: inhibitory connections are postsynaptic and once formed, it becomes hard to change them (the inhibitory connections are "frozen"). That can bring the system into local minima, that are very hard to escape from. There are two ways to avoid this problem: (i) either the non-linearity of function f should be made softer (that would allow more efficient drifting of the inhibitory connections), or (ii) α should be changed as learning goes on. We have made one trial along this latter route, performed pretraining with $\alpha = 0.2$ and then continued training with $\alpha = 1.0$. During pretraining small filters could not developed, since soft competition allows a small filter to learn for larger samples. When α was increased to 1.0 the resulting filter distribution surpassed the one without pretraining (Fig. 5, curve c). To reach WTA results it is then promising to increase competition in a smooth fashion, just like for Kohonen feature maps. It may be interesting to note, that the HAH version of segmentation networks provides a self-organizing feature map, where not only the receptive fields, but the neural connections themselves are self-organizing too. It is expected that HAH is superior to WTA in terms of convergence speed.

VI. Conclusions

WTA learning mechanism and the self-organizing learning rule of Eqs. (1) and (2) seem suitable for developing overlapping circular filters of local Gaussian character. Range of filter sizes can scale with the size of the input samples and show filter size clusters with gaps between. Limitations of our computer experiments include the large variety of input shapes: the question is wether different input shapes would allow the formation of local filters. Experiments on identical filters, however, suggest that a larger variety of input patterns shall not modify performance [6]. Experiments on Hebbian and anti-Hebbian networks show similar, but somewhat inferior results. To reach identical performance results suggest that competition in HAH should be increased in a smooth fashion, just like for Kohonen feature maps. In all cases (WTA and HAH) filters were deistributed evenly over the input space.

The self-organizing network described in this work can perform parallel image segmentation task.

References

[1] Cs. Szepesvári, L. Balázs, and A. Lörincz. Topology learning solved by extended objects: a neural network model. *Neural Computation*, 1993. in press.

[2] D.H. Hubel and T.N. Wiesel. *Proc. Roy. Soc. Lond.*, 198:1–59, 1977.

[3] D. Sagi and B. Julesz. *Science*, 228:1217–1219, 1985.

[4] J.Rubner and P. Tavan. A self-organizing network for principal component analysis. *Europhysics Letters*, 10:693–698, 1989.

[5] P. Földiák. *Biological Cybernetics*, 64:165–170, 1990.

[6] T. Fomin and A. Lörincz. Positioning and feature extraction with Hebbian and anti-Hebbian networks. *Neural Networks*, 1993. submitted.

An Integrated Multiple Neural Network Architecture For Reading Alphanumeric Characters in Complex Scenes

Kong-Wah WAN, Qi TIAN, Kah-Chan LOW,
Soo-Leng LAU, Ho-Chung LUI
Institute of Systems Science, National University of Singapore
Kent Ridge, SIngapore 0511
Tel:(65)772-6705, Fax:(65)774-4998
Email: kongwah@iss.nus.sg

Abstract

An integrated multiple neural network (NN) architecture is proposed to handle the automatic extraction and recognition of machine-printed alphanumeric characters in a complex scene. The computational framework is illustrated by our implementation of a multi-expert, multi-level reading system comprising of five NNs for both segmentation and recognition. A window-based alphanumeric NN (WNN_AD) is trained as a first-pass character-level primary recognizer. A window-based alphabet NN (WNN_A) and a window-based digit NN (WNN_D) are then used as group-level secondary recognizers. To further boost recognition accuracy, a Fourier-Descriptor-based Probabilistic neural network (FDPNN) is trained on characters which were misrecognized by the above three networks. In the event of mis-segmentation of merged or damaged characters, a special Character Horizontal Position Neural Network (CHPNN) is used to detect the horizontal positional occurrence of characters. Our system has been applied to the recognition and verification of the 11 machine-printed alphanumeric ID on containers. In spite of the variations due to character fonts, distortions, background color, image contrast, illuminations and ID layout formats, etc, the system has achieved a container ID-based recognition rate of more than 90% over 3000 images.

1. Introduction

The robust extraction and recognition of characters in complex 3D scenes is an extremely challenging task for computers. A practical reading system must make provisions in effectively handling the tremendous amount of image variation due to character stroke/font variety, environmental changes and acquisition imprecisions. Therefore it is impossible to achieve robust reading based on the traditional segmentation - feature extraction - recognition approach. In this paper, we propose an iterative-refinement strategy to the reading problem and describe our implementation of the approach into a system which reads and verifies the printed alphanumeric IDs on containers [4]. The basic framework propagandizes the necessity of providing "redundancy" to reduce information ambiguity. By using multiple tools and knowledge sources, however, we need to consider integration issues [2,7]. This paper will present our systematized approach to the total solution by the extensive use of multiple neural network segmenter and recognizers, designed with specific functionalities and levels of control to achieve a natural system fit.

2. The Integrated Architecture

Figure 1 shows the multiple NN architecture used in our system. The primary processing pipeline is still the ***Extraction-Recognition*** (ER) process. But the integrated architecture supplements the traditional single-pass ER by an additional ***Character Recovery Engine*** (CRE) [11], which acts upon the current ***global system states*** and performs selection of the appropriate tools to invoke. The system states are a set of system status variables denoting the stage of processing the system is currently in. Hence they also indicate how far is the system from finishing the reading job. These status variables are perpetually updated by the ER process in a continuous iterative refinement fashion until the reading job is done. The CRE also makes extensive use of higher-level model knowledge, such as the character height/width, alphabet/digit groups, inter-group placement, etc.

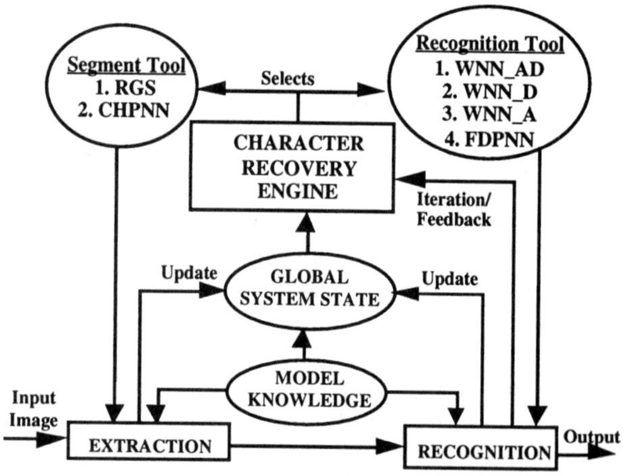

Figure 1. Integrated Multiple NN Architecture
RGS:: Region Growing Segmenter
CHPNN:: Character Horizontal Position Neural Network
WNN_AD/WNN_A/WNN_D:: Window-Based Neural Networks
FDPNN:: Fourier Descriptor-based Probabilistic Neural Network

The tools used in our framework consists of 5 neural networks implemented with specific functionality and performance criteria. Neural network models have been chosen as the character recognizers for their ease of implementation, parallel opportunity and automatic detection of key features and discriminant functions. Integration of the various networks into the entire system requires a knowledge of their functionalities, strengths and weaknesses.. The 5 networks are:

1. A window-based NN, **WNN_AD**, trained and used as an alphanumeric character recognizer;

2. A window-based NN, **WNN_D,** trained and used as a dedicated digit recognizer;
3. A window-based NN, **WNN_A,** trained and used as a dedicated alphabet recognizer;
4. A **FDPNN**, short for a Probabilistic NN, trained on the Fourier-Descriptor features of the character;
5. A **CHPNN**, short for a window-based NN, trained and used as a Character Horizontal Position NN detector.

Several network architecture for character recognition have been tried. Particularly, good results have been obtained using the shared-weights architecture proposed in [13], though at the expense of greater computation cost because of its massive connection. Considering the simplicity and speed factor, we have adopted the window-based approach for a more attractive performance-cost ratio [14].. Figure 2 shows the principle topology of the window-based network. For a full description, please see [5]. The learning algorithm used in training these networks is the popular BackPropagation [8].

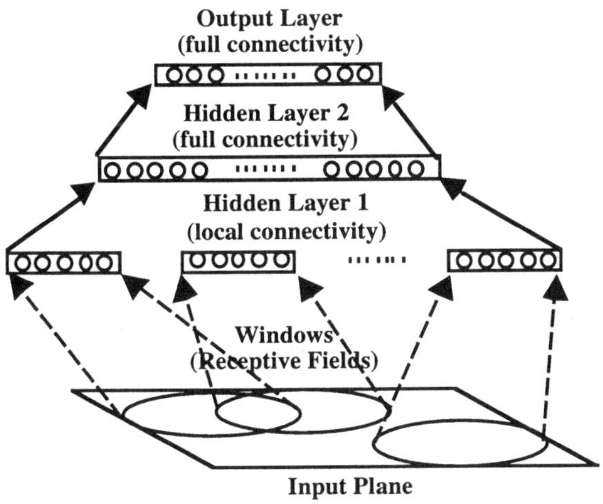

Figure 2. The Window-based Network Architecture

2.1 Network Generality and Specificity

The functional characteristic of these network recognizers are nominally reflective of their operational domain. The WNN_AD is used as a first-pass alphanumeric character recognizer after a low-level Region-Growing Segmenter (RGS) has performed preliminary character extraction. The WNN_A, WNN_D are used as a secondary recognizers, invoked at a later stage of processing, when incremental results and application of model and domain knowledge has narrowed the environment ambiguities. Hence, at the initial stage, the tools must exhibit generality in expectation of the wider range of uncertainty. Tools at a later stage can then move to a higher level of specialization.

In our system, the operative environment is that of iterative refinement. The solution to the reading problem is a function of time. In the initial pass, incomplete information about the domain and object conditions forces the use of a general recognition tool. This come in the form of the WNN_AD, where the network has to contend with close alphabet/digit pairs like "8"/"B","2"/"Z","0"/"D",etc. Recognition precision is expected to rise, however, when the character domain (whether alphabet or digit) is known by the accumulation of object/domain knowledge through time. We put the WNN_A and WNN_D to good use at this stage. Figure 3 shows the networks' performance with training sample size. The graph is indicative of the finer classification acuity of networks with higher specificity.

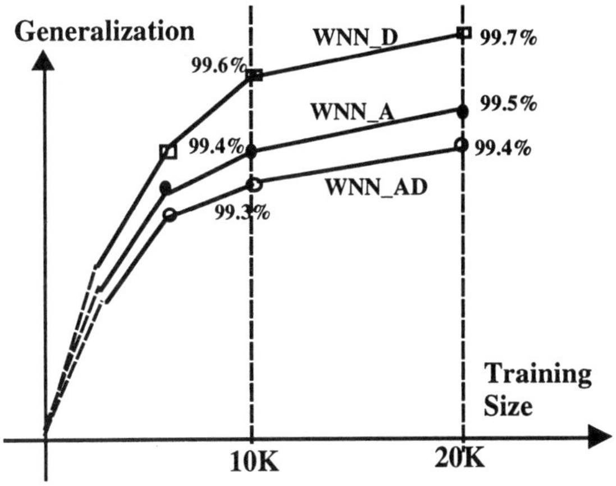

Figure 3. Network Generality and Specificity
The dedicated networks WNN_A and WNN_D have outperformed the larger WNN_AD network across each training sample size used.

2.2 Compounded Performance

The strength of a neural model as a standalone classifier has been much investigated. Our experience has also ratified its propriety in machine-printed character recognition. State-of-the-art high recognition rates are easily achievable for each of our independent networks. However, when implemented as an isolated recognition module in a practical system detecting a *string* or *composition* of characters, then the overall system performance depends on the successful recognition during each and every call. Hence, the system error is compounded. This is justification for continual effort to improve the rate of correct response on each individual call [1].

We can theoretically improve the recognition rate by presenting a large enough training set to the NN during network learning. But it is not always clear how much is enough. We have instead chosen to have a larger testing set in order to generate enough failed recognition samples, and then to examine the pattern of those failed cases. We have generally noticed that the failed cases correspond to genuinely "difficult" samples which exhibit marked variation from the mean training sample. These samples are few in numbers, and hence do not solicit significant weight-updating during network learning. Even upon increase in training epoch, these samples were observed to be still unrecognizable. Also, low-resolution effects are observed, causing closely resembling characters like "0"/"D", which only have separable differences over a small pixmap area, to be unseparable. Under- and over-segmentation effects have also been observed to pull down the NNs' performance.

An additional recognizer was implemented to specially handle these samples. The Fourier Descriptor-based probabilistic neural network is used [6,9,12]. A higher pixmap dimension was preserved and appropriate FD features chosen so as to enable positional, size and rotation-invariance. These features also capture the strokes and curvatures of the characters more efficiently than the former pixmap-based recognizers. The features are then fed into a PNN, which performs final classification. The PNN is memory-based and hence has the capacity to "remember" the rare samples misrecognized by the former pixmap-based recognizers. We have consolidated these samples and use them as training samples for the FDPNN. With an appropriate integration strategy, the overall recognition rate of the system is improved. We have adopted an activation cut-off approach where the FDPNN is invoked whenever the activation of the primary recognizer falls below a prescribed threshold. Section 3 will report on the integration improvements.

2.3 Character Recovery Engine

A recognition problem can be seen as an interpretation problem where hypotheses are made and ratified in a continuous fashion. The CRE looks at the current system state and makes interpretation therein. In our system, during the first-pass ER process, an initial recognition result will be generated and the system state updated. The CRE performs examination and verification on this, making use of target ID and other domain-specific information like knowledge about ID formats, character placement, groupings, etc If it detects a discrepancy, or a violation of some rules, it then undergo a hypothesis scheme which guesses the whereabouts of characters which may have been mis-segmented (e.g. as a result of closeness, low-resolution, merging, etc). Whatever hypothesis it generates, it tries to make good of it by using an exhaustive scanning approach across the hypothesized space. Each time the scanning window resides on a particular hypothesized spot, a recognition call is made to the appropriate NN. Obviously, this approach has limitations. The recovery effort is only as good as the guesses made by the CRE, which is in turn directly dependent on the current system state. Given the extreme condition of total absence of knowledge, the decisions the CRE makes is at best random choices. But given a good preliminary partial information, as the system evolves, it is able to produce intelligent search schemes which may lead to fruitful character recovery.

2.4 The CHPNN

A full fledged exhaustive search and recover scheme is computation-intensive. The CRE may spend unproductive time over many potential regions before getting anywhere near the characters in the right candidate region. Also, it is prone to *false recovery* of characters. This phenomena is a consequence of a false positive response from the NN recognizer, even though presented with an invalid input. To circumvent this problem, we develop an additional NN which serves to detect the positional occurrence of characters along a horizontal image strip, called CHPNN, [10].

The CHPNN is an evolved architecture from MCC's work in reading handwritten characters [3]. The CHPNN is invoked in conjunction with the CRE scanning window which hovers over a horizontal region with probable character occurrence. The window is slid across the entire field, with incremental pixel jump size as dictated by the CRE. At proximity positions near a valid character, returned by an above-average response of the CHPNN, a finer jump size will be taken to exact attentive focus.

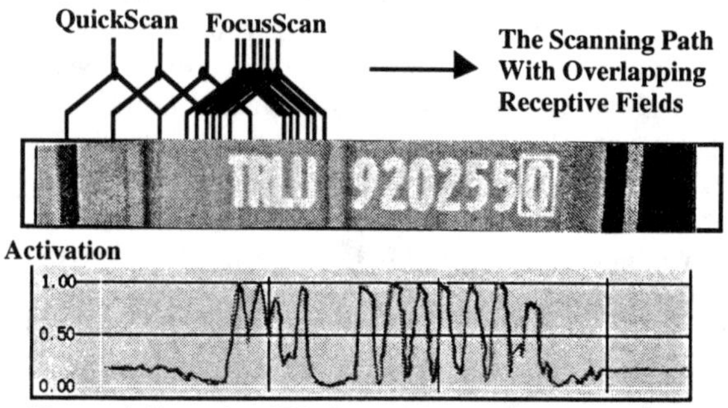

Figure 4. Scanning Window of the CHPNN and its Activation profile along the Image Strip.

A key design principle of the CHPNN is that whenever a valid character is centrally present in the scanning window, it should respond maximally. For all other courses, it should respond minimally. We realize this by presenting the CHPNN strips of character images in their natural context during its network learning phase. These image strips were directly obtainable by our system, but manual labeling need to be performed to encode the horizontal positions of the characters along the image strips. The target activation along the central region around a character is set to maximum, while it tapers off to a minimum moving off the central and down the left-right proximity portion. Hence, activations are maintained at a plateau high at character center, allowing a certain amount of shift tolerance into the CHPNN. The inclusion of the natural context improves the robustness of character detection. As the entire image strip is presented during learning, the CHPNN also learns to respond lowly to blank space, interfering background structures, container signs and logos, etc. It also picks up the ability to detect close, slanting, broken, merging, and low-contrast characters. These were not handled effectively by the general RGS, described in Section 2. Therefore, the CHPNN plays complementary role to the primary segmenter.

We have used the window-based topology for the CHPNN, similar to the one shown in figure 2, apart from just having a single output node in the output layer. Network training is by backpropagation. A total of 1516 image strips were extracted from container images. Character positional occurrences were manually entered into these strips. Out of these, 1091 were used for network training, and 425 for testing. Convergence of network is reached after 50 iterations, where performance on training set reaches 100%, and on the test-set, it is 68.2%. Note that this performance figure is inclusive of the correct network response along non-character positions as well. In other words, if the network detects a character occurrence at a non-character position, it is considered as a misrecognition. Disregarding the false positive response, the network's performance on valid character detection on the entire image strip is 92.0%. On average, we have about 6 characters per image strip. Translating this to the character-level, this means that the network's character detection is about 98.6%.

3. System Test Results

We have implemented the entire computational framework to an application where the alphanumeric characters on a container are to be recognized and verified. A CCD camera takes snapshots of the stationary container, and the digitized image is sent to the reading system. The IDs on the container may come in various fonts and layout. Figure 5 shows some samples of these images.

Though the ID character were machine-printed, they come in various sizes and fonts. Container surfaces may be corrugated, dirty, and characters may suffer from ink-fading. A high-performance system cannot retract from handling these aberrant cases because it is tackling these "difficult" cases that deliver an acceptable level of performance for practical application. Figure 6 shows several typical samples of difficult characters that we have managed to solve.

A large number of images were collected from the actual container sites. The character pixmaps were extracted and compiled to become the training samples for our neural network recognizers. A total of more than 30K character samples and 3000 images had been collected over a period of 2 years since commencement of the work. Testing our system over this large amount of images assured us of the robustness of our algorithms over a variety of image conditions.

We report on the comparative performance of our system at two stages of its operation: the preliminary first-pass and after character recovery. The improvement upon using the WNN_AD+WNN_A+WNN_D combination over the single WNN_AD is mentioned. Also, the advantage of further using the FDPNN is highlighted:-

Single NN system using only **WNN_AD**

System Stage	Performance (%)
First-Pass	60.9, 82.6
Character Recovery	88.0, 93.4

WNN_AD+WNN_A+WNN_D system.

System Stage	Performance (%)
First-Pass	60.9, 82.6
Character Recovery	89.0, 94.0

And upon addition of the **FDPNN**, further improvement are:-

System Stage	Performance (%)
First-Pass	62.8, 83.6
Character Recovery	91.4, 95.0

(All results reported are run over a total of 2965 test images, collected from container sites. The performance figures in each table come in pairs. The first number denotes the percentage of images achieving full ID-based recognition, while the second denotes failure of recognition of ONLY 1 character)

The table clearly shows the incremental performance improvement as the additional networks are integrated. In particular, the CRE search scheme has tremendous pay-off. Our probing investigation into the 10% failed cases reveal that only about 2% of these cases are due to NN failures (others being segmentation problems like under- and over-segmentation). This level of performance at system level translates to an equivalence of 99.8% of recognition rate at the character level. Future work in further improvement of the system performance shall be directed to the enhancement of segmentation tools and recovery schemes.

4. Conclusions

An integrated architecture for reading alphanumeric characters in complex scenes has been presented. The multi-expert multi-level computational framework utilizes multiple neural networks as recognizers and computes the final solution in an iterative refinement fashion. It is proposed that such an overkill strategy be instrumental in solving the complex recognition problem. We have applied the above technology to the recognition and verification of IDs on containers. State-of-the-art performance has been achieved.

Acknowledgement

The authors thank the Port of Singapore Authority for providing the container images.

References

[1] Q.Tian, K.W.Wan, L.N.Teow and H.C.Lui. "Applications of Back-Propagation Neural Networks for High-Accuracy Verification of Industrial Object IDs". In *Proc. of Neural Networks Application for Signal Processing*, pp.382-387, 1993.

[2] C.H.Wang and S.N.Srihari. "A Framework for Object Recognition in a Visually Complex Environment and its Application to Locating Address Blocks on Mail Pieces". In *International Journal of Computer Vision*, Vol.2, pp.125-151, 1988

[3] G.L.Martin and M.Rashid. "Recognizing Overlapping Hand-Printed Characters by Centered-Object Integrated Segmentation and Recognition". In *MCC Technical Report ACT-NN-395-91 (Rev1.0)*, 1991

[4] J.L.Goh, K.C.Low, K.W.Wan, Q.Tian and H.C.Lui. "Recognizing Container Number Using Machine Vision, Parallel and Neural Computing Technologies". In *Proc. IT Works '93*, pp.117-122, Singapore, October 18, 1993

[5] H.C.Lui and S.L.Lau. "Character Recognition On Gray Level Images Using Neural Networks". In *Proc. of International Joint Conference on Neural Networks*, pp.325-330, 1991

[6] M.T.Y.Lai and C.Y.Suen. "Automatic Recognition of Characters by Fourier Descriptors and Boundary Line Encoding". In *Pattern Recognition*, pp.383-393, 1981
[7] L.P.Wesley and A.R.Hanson. "The Use of an Evidential-based Model for Representing Knowledge and Reasoning about Images in the Visions Systems". In *Proc. of the Workshop on Computer Vision: Representation and Control.* Rindge, New Hampshire, pp.14-25, 1982.
[8] D.E.Rumelhart, G.E.Hinton and R.J.Williams. "Learning Internal Representations By Error Propagation". In *Parallel Distributed Processing: Explorations in the Microstructure of Cognition,* chapter 8, MIT Press, Cambridge MA, London, England, 1986.
[9] D.F.Specht. "Probabilistic Neural Networks". In *Neural Networks*, Vol. 3, pp.109-118, 1990.
[10] K.W.Wan and Q.Tian. "A Character Horizontal Position Neural Network for Robust Character ID detection in a Complex Scene". *Technical Report*, Institute of System Science, National University of Singapore.
[11] K.C.Low, K.W.Wan and Q.Tian. "A Model-based Character Recovery Scheme for Robust Character ID reading in a Complex Scene". *Technical Report*, Institute of System Science, National University of Singapore.
[12] S.L.Lau and Q.Tian. "A Fourier-Descriptor-based Probabilistic Neural Network and Applications in Multi-expert Recognition System". *Technical Report,* Institute of System Science, National University of Singapore.
[13] Y.LeCun, B.Boser, J.Denker, D.Henderson and R.E.Howard, W.Hubbard and L.D.Jackel. "Handwritten Digit Recognition with a Backpropagation Networks". In D.S.Touretzky (Ed). *Advances in Neural Information Processing Systems 2.*. Morgan Kaufmann, 1990.
[14] K.W.Wan, S.L.Lau and Q.Tian. "Neural Network Architecture for Character Recognition -- A Comparative Study". *Technical Report*, Institute of System Science, National University of Singapore.

(a). ID **GSTU4657112** amongst other valid characters. A typical 1-Line ID layout with white characters. The ID characters may be black. See (f).

(b). ID **NYKU2573696**. A typical 2-Line ID layout with black characters.

(c). ID **SCXU8073414**. Another 2-Line ID layout with black characters.

(d). ID **APLS278305**. A typical 3-Line ID layout with white characters.

(e). ID **NEPU5024095**, with mixed color characters.

(f). ID **TPHU6130814**. The occluded '6' is successfully recovered by our system.

Figure 5. Typical Samples of Container Images.

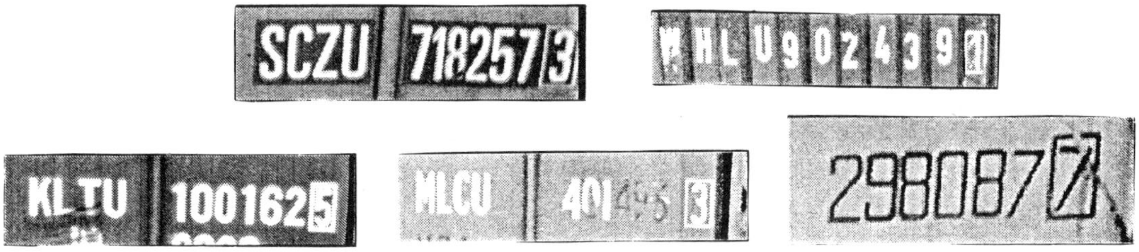

(a). Damaged Characters

(b). Merged Characters

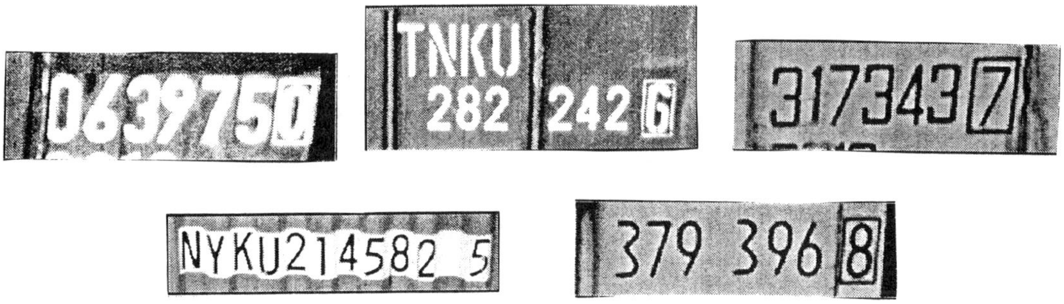

(c). Fonts and Other Domain Variation

Figure 6. Samples of Difficult Character Domain successfully handled by our system.

Rotation Invariant Neural Pattern Recognition System which Can Estimate A Rotation Angle

Minoru Fukumi*, Sigeru Omatu*, and Yoshikazu Nishikawa**
*University of Tokushima, Faculty of Engineering
2-1, Minami-josanjima, Tokushima 770 Japan,
**University of Kyoto, Faculty of Engineering
Yoshida-honmachi, Sakyo-ku, Kyoto 606 Japan

Abstract

This paper presents a rotation invariant neural pattern recognition system, which can recognize a rotated pattern and estimate a rotation angle.

So far, we have considered rotation-invariant neural pattern recognition systems. They are very effective methods for a rotated coin recognition problem, but are poor compared with human performance. It is well known that human sometimes recognizes a rotated pattern by means of the *mental rotation*. Such a fact, however, has never been considered and used in neural pattern recognition systems, especially in rotation invariant systems. Therefore, we examine a principle of the mental rotation to apply it to a rotation invariant pattern recognition system.

The system with such a principle could recognize a rotated pattern and estimate a rotation angle. It is shown that the system is effective to recognize a rotated pattern from results of computer simulation for a coin recognition problem.

1 Introduction

Human has sophisticatedly developed its brain in the process of evolution. We can easily do associative memory, recognition of speech and face, understanding of situation, and so forth, although it is difficult for recent digital computers to do such things. This is due to the difference of basic principle, a serial processing in digital computers and a parallel distributed processing in our brains [1]–[4]. Artificial neural networks and genetic algorithms (GAs) have been a focus of active research owing to such a background [4]–[5]. There has been much work which showed the effectiveness of neural networks and GAs in pattern recognition, optimization, control, and so forth [4]–[20]. Furthermore, a hybrid system of both is also presented [13].

Authors have presented rotation invariant neural pattern recognition systems [7],[9]–[12]. They are very effective for a rotated pattern recognition problem. However, they are poor compared with a performance of human vision system. On the other hand, systems which can estimate a rotation angle have been presented [17][18]. However, as those system use a kind of pattern matching method, it is not clear whether they are effective for a gray scale image, and they are time-consuming to check out every angle to select one.

We therefore consider the mental rotation[3][21][23] and construct a pattern recognition system with its principle. If we can get in the principle of the mental rotation, it would be effective to recognize a rotated pattern, to estimate a rotation angle, and to elucidate a human perceptual process for rotated patterns. The objective of this paper, however, is not to directly model the mental rotation by means of neural networks, but to construct a more sophisticated system by getting the function in and to examine its advantage.

In this paper, in order to show the effectiveness of the system, we apply it to a recognition problem for rotated coin images. The coins classified in this paper are a 500 yen coin in Japan and a 500 won coin in Korea (see Fig.1). Those coins have the same size and shape, the same thickness, and a similar pattern. In relation to such a fact, there was an article on misclassification of those coins [24].

2 Coin Recognition Systems

Coin images taken into a real coin classifying machine are randomly rotated in many cases. In order to recognize such coin images, it is essential to develop a coin recognition system insensitive to rotation by any number of degree.

Authors have presented the coin recognition systems insensitive to rotation by any number of degree

(a)Obverse side of coins

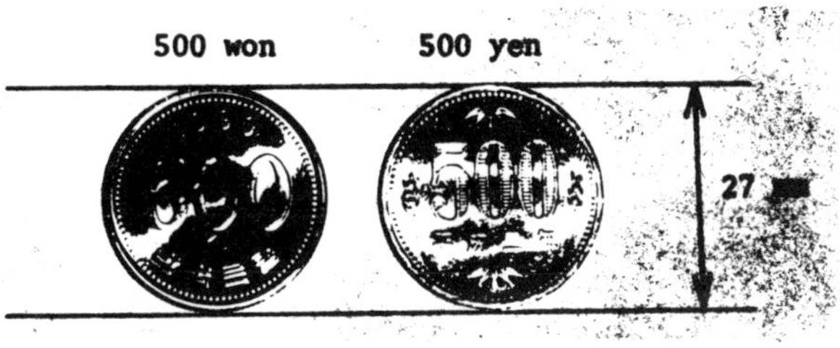

(b)Reverse side of coins

Fig. 1: A 500 yen coin and a 500 won coin.

	element	combination
direction free	**identification** (a)	**arrangement** (c)
direction dependent	**absolute direction**(b)	**relative direction**(d)

Table 1: Four information types.

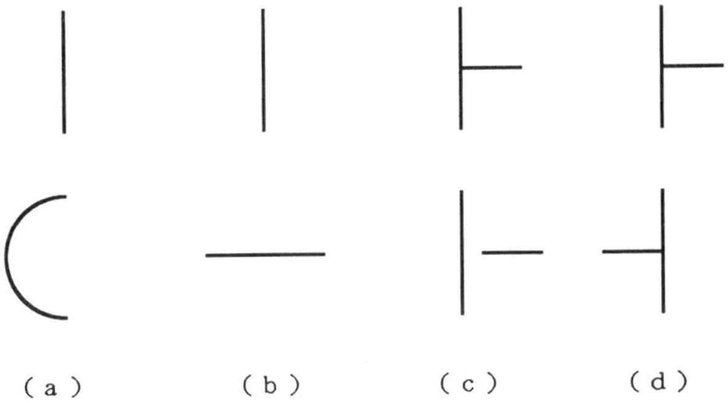

Fig. 2: Examples of four information types.

[7],[9]–[12]. The rotation invariant neural network systems we considered are as follows [12]:

A. preprocessor(Fourier transform) + BP [7],[8].

B. preprocessor(neural network) + BP [9].

C. preprocessor(edge detection) + BP with weight link [10].

D. BP with weight link.

E. recurrent neural network [11].

The BP is the back-propagation algorithm [4]. The preprocessor in the system **B** uses the improved version of the slab structure which Widrow [14] proposed. If the sigmoid functions in the preprocessor are replaced by linear functions, then it is essentially the same as the system [25] using a ring mask. The preprocessor in the **C** detects edge features of coin images with gray level. The BP with weight link is a training algorithm which adds a restriction on network weights so that outputs of network can be insensitive to rotation. In the **D**, however, the network weights could not converge to a solution for the rotation invariant coin recognition. The **E** uses a simple recurrent network to classify coins. Those systems are very effective for engineering problems such as a coin image recognition, but are poor compared with a performance of human vision system. The system **B** and **C** aim at designing a system insensitive to any transform of a pattern as human. In this paper, we try to construct a more sophisticated system by expanding the **C**. The mental rotation is thus considered in the following, which is a important feature in a perceptual process of human.

3 Mental Rotation

It is known that human have a tendency to increase a recognition time with increase of a rotation angle in recognizing a rotated pattern. This phenomenon caused an idea of, what is called, the mental rotation [3][21][23]. The recognition time becomes maximum in rotation by 180°, and is independent of clockwise or not. Some work related to the mental rotation have been presented in psychology and cognitive science [3][21][23]. However, there was no theory that can perfectly explain the mental rotation. The *information type theory* [21] is distinguished as a method which may explain it.

Properties of the mental rotation can be described according to the information type theory. Table 1 shows a classification of information based on it. This is illustrated in Fig.2. (a)~ (d) in Table 1 refer to (a)~ (d) in Fig.2. Note that each word in the Table may be different from the original one, because we could not get the English version [22].

Classifying information types as shown in Table1, we can say the following:

- if figures which we have to classify have mirror writing relation and only a difference of the relative direction information, then the mental rotation is required.
- if figures which we have to classify have a differ-

ence of the identification or arrangement information, then the mental rotation is not required.

Therefore, if there is a difference on the direction free information, then the mental rotation is not used. Practically speaking, however, if we could not find a difference on the direction free information between patterns, then the mental rotation would be necessary.

Furthermore, we human must make an image in rotating it. It is known that a resolution and a capacity in rotating are limited [21]. Thus, there must be a case that we can not believe a recognition result owing to a obscure memory. It seems that we then rotate the image to make sure. The same situation would happen in recognizing similar coins, too. That is to say, there may be a case that we could not be convinced of the truth of a recognition result. Consequently, it seems that we use the mental rotation in such a case. On the other hand, we agree with an opinion which human required both of the direction free and the direction dependent information owing to necessity for existence.

Thus, we suppose the following as a principle to recognize a rotated pattern, considering the mental rotation.

- First, try to recognize a pattern as a standard or slightly rotated one (by a multilayered network).
- Second, try to recognize the pattern by a rotation invariant system and to estimate a rotation angle, if the recognition result in the first step is not clear.
- Third, try to rotate the pattern on the basis of the angle estimation, if the recognition result in the second step is not clear.
- Finally, try to recognize the pattern rotated in the third step (by the multilayered network).

The first and the second steps refer to a pattern recognition based on the direction dependent and the direction free information, respectively. On the one hand, the third step refers to rotation of the image by means of the mental rotation.

4 Rotation Invariant System

The system presented in this paper is shown in Fig.3. It consists of a feature extraction network as a preprocessor and two subnetworks, a first network and a second one. The preprocessor detects an edge feature of an input pattern to activate a set of orientation specificity cells according to edge directions. This activity pattern with a 3-dimensional structure

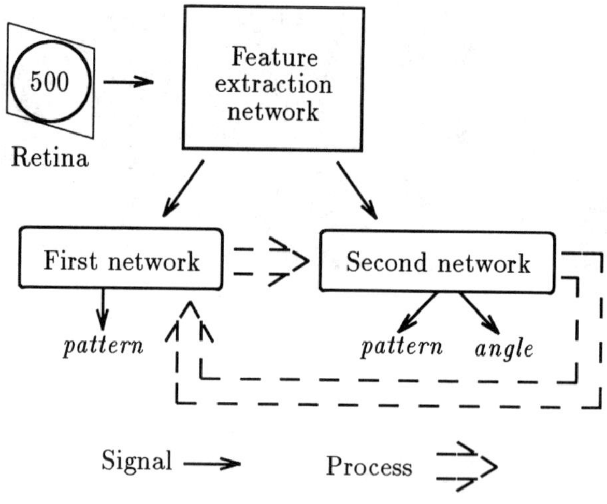

Fig. 3: Rotation invariant pattern recognition system, which includes two subnetworks.

is an input pattern into two subnetworks (multilayered networks). This pattern, however, is not rotationally invariant. The invariance is accomplished in the multilayered network.

The first network, which is a 3-layered network, is to learn and recognize a standard pattern. Practically speaking, a little bit rotated patterns are also learned in the network. As shown in Fig.5, the second one is also a 3-layered network, in which an input pattern is the edge feature from the preprocessor. This network is an extended version of the **C** mentioned in the section 2. The network includes in an output layer two parts, a pattern discrimination part and a rotation angle estimation part. A hidden layer is used in common. In learning, different teacher signals are given to the parts, while their training proceed at the same time. In other word, it can train both the properties sensitive and insensitive to rotation.

4.1 Preprocessing Network

The preprocessor is shown in Fig.4. It consists of an edge detection layer and a 3-dimensional structure of the orientation specificity cells (OSCs), which is described as an OSC-layer on the same level in Fig.4.

A square labeled "EN" indicates the edge detection network. Each EN takes an area of a pattern on the retina to compute edge intensity and direction. Then, it produces the directions with high intensity to activate the cells in the OSC-layer. In Fig,4, a radial and a circumference directions refer to a horizontal and a vertical directions in the edge detection layer and each plane of the OSC-layer, respectively.

In the OSC-layer, the OSCs are arranged in order. The OSC-layer consists of many planes, which include the cells with the same specificity as many as the EN in the edge detection layer. Each cell gets a signal only from the corresponding EN. The number

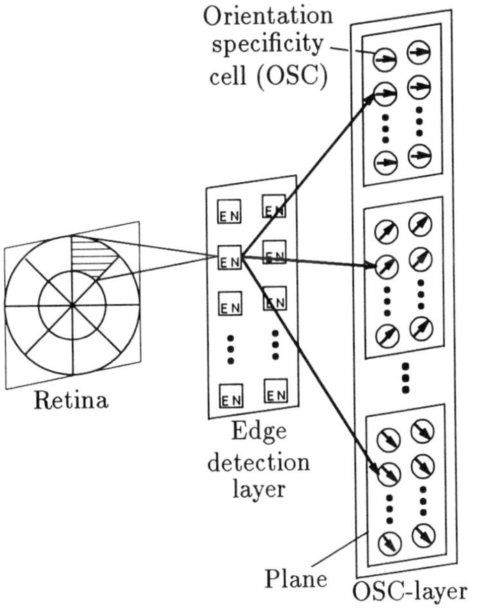

Fig. 4: Feature extraction network. It produces an edge feature to activate the OSCs in the OSC-layer.

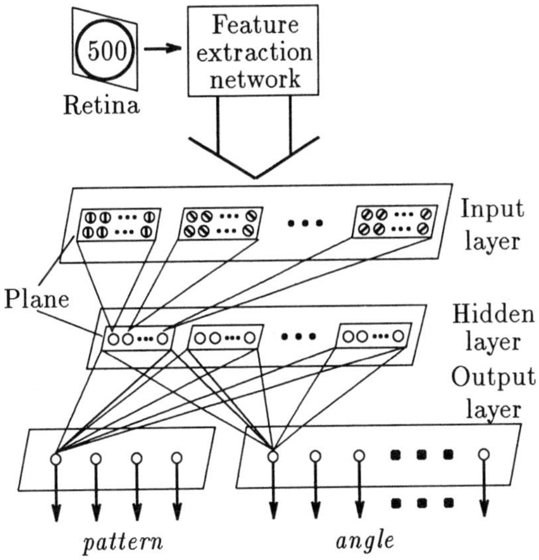

Fig. 5: Neural network (the second network) to recognize a rotated pattern and to estimate a rotation angle. A hidden layer is used by two different parts in common, although it can be divided into two networks.

of planes is the same as the division number of the circumference of the pattern on the retina.

Each EN produces the edge directions of the predefined number to activate the cells with specificity near those. In this paper, the Sobel operator with size of 3×3 is used to detect edges. As a result, the preprocessor can produce a rough edge feature of the pattern.

4.2 The Second Network

The multilayered network with sigmoid type neuron units is trained by the improved BP to produce desired outputs [15][16]. It is trained under restraint in order to achieve a rotational invariance. Also, it has in an output layer two different parts : one can recognize patterns and the other can estimate a rotation angle of patterns.

When an input pattern is rotated, an edge feature to be activated is translated and rotated in the OSC-layer according to a rotation angle. Suppose that the circumference of the retina is divided into 8 segments and a standard pattern is given to the retina to produce the edge feature. Next, if the same pattern except rotated by 45° is given, then this edge feature is translated one on plane and position in the plane, respectively. Therefore, in order to reach rotational invariance, the training algorithm requires a restriction to be invariant to them which vary according to a rotation angle.

The network has three layers, an input, a hidden, and an output layers. The hidden layer also consists of the planes, which include sigmoid neuron units as many as the division number of the circumference of the retina. The neuron units in each plane have the same weights, but their receptive fields are different. Neuron units in another plane have different weights. Let weights of the ith plane be $W_{i,k,m}, m = 1 \sim NTH, k = 1 \sim NR$, where NTH and NR are the number of segments in the circumference and the radius of the retina, respectively. The input layer (OSC-layer) consists of NTH planes, each of which includes an activity pattern made up of NR (subscript k) × NTH (subscript m) OSCs. Let an activity pattern in the input layer be $S_{jj,k,mm}, mm = 1 \sim NTH, k = 1 \sim NR, jj = 1 \sim NTH$, where jj indicates the jjth plane in the input layer.

Then, the net input values Net(L),$L = 1 \sim NTH$ to neuron units of the ith plane in the hidden layer are computed as

$$\text{Net}(L) = \sum_{k=1}^{NR} \sum_{m=1}^{NTH} W_{i,k,m} \times S_{L,k,m+(L-1)}$$

Accordingly, the weights $W_{i,k,m}$ connect between the first plane in the input layer and the first neuron unit of the ith plane in the hidden layer. The second neuron unit with same weights $W_{i,k,m}$ gets inputs from the second plane in the input layer, and the receptive field are translated one to the subscript m. The same procedure is done for the others. The translation to plane and the subscript m correspond to rotation and translation of the edge feature by rotation of the input pattern. In the point of view, this is different from the traditional methods [4][6][19][20].

The quantity of weight change $\Delta W_{i,k,m}$ is given as an average over NTH neuron units in the ith plane as follows:

$$\Delta W_{i,k,m} = \sum_{L=1}^{NTH} (\Delta W_{i,k,m})_L / NTH$$

4.2.1 Pattern Recognition Part

In Fig.5, the part which produces *pattern* is to recognize an input pattern. Weights $W_{n,i}$ from a unit in the ith plane to the nth neuron in the part are also restrained to be the same as the others in the ith. The number of weights which each unit in the output layer has, therefore, is the same as the number of planes in the hidden layer. The net input to the nth output unit is computed as

$$\text{Net}(n) = \sum_{i=1}^{NS} \sum_{j=1}^{NTH} W_{n,i} \times O_{i,j}$$

where $O_{i,j}$ is the output value of the jth unit in the ith plane, and NS is the number of the planes in the hidden layer. The quantity of weight change is given as an average over NTH neuron units in the ith plane:

$$\Delta W_{n,i} = \sum_{L=1}^{NTH} (\Delta W_{n,i})_L / NTH,$$

which is similar to that in the hidden layer.

By using the above training algorithm, a rotational invariance can be achieved in the multilayered network. Presenting a pattern to the retina causes responses from the pattern recognition part. It is clear that those will be unchanged by rotation of the pattern on the retina. Rotation of the pattern by $360° / NTH$ causes an interchange of the role of the units in each planes in making their responses, but since they are all weighted equally and summed by the output units, the output response is unchanged by such a rotation.

4.2.2 Angle Estimation Part

In Fig.5, the part which produces *angle* is to estimate a rotation angle of an input pattern. In this part, rotation of the input pattern causes an interchange of the role of output units unlike the pattern recognition part. This can be achieved by having all the output units had the same weights $W_{i,j}$, where the subscripts i and j refer to an plane in the hidden layer and an unit in the ith plane, respectively. The net input to the nth output unit is computed as

$$\text{Net}(n) = \sum_{i=1}^{NS} \sum_{j=1}^{NTH} W_{i,j} \times O_{i,j+(n-1)}$$

where $O_{i,j+(n-1)}$ is the output value of the $(j+n-1)$th unit in the ith plane. Therefore, a receptive field of the next output unit is translated one in the ith plane. In training, the weights of all the output units are restrained to be the same. The quantity of the weight change is given by

$$\Delta W_{i,j} = \sum_{n=1}^{NTH} (\Delta W_{i,j})_n / NTH,$$

averaged over the output units. The desired signal is 1 for the unit related to a pattern with a standard direction and 0's for the others.

By using such a structure, rotation of the pattern causes an interchange of the role of the units in each planes in making their responses and, as a result, causes an interchanges of the output units, producing 1 and 0's. The number of training samples is only 1 in this case, because coin images used for a simulation are randomly rotated.

5 Simulation Results

Computer simulations for a rotated binary pattern and a coin image recognition are done to show the effectiveness of the system. It can give correct results, including angle estimation, for the binary pattern recognition. Next, in coin recognition, a preprocessing procedure takes out only the coin image from each original image with 256 gray levels by an image scanner in a real coin classifying machine to make an image with 40×40 pixels. A part of the 50 randomly rotated coin images is used to train the system and the rest is used as test samples to compute a recognition accuracy. The number of *NTH, NR,* and *NS* are 20, 7, and 16, respectively. 7 samples rotated by $-3 \times 360° / NTH$ to $3 \times 360° / NTH$ per kind are used to train the first network.

The results are shown in Table2. In the Table, those indicated by "Net1" and "Net2" show the results only by the first and the second networks, respectively. The "max" means the results only by considering the maximum output value in the output layer. On the one hand, the "clear" means the results by considering:

It is a clear result, if $|O_{\text{maximum}} - O_{\text{second}}| > \theta$,

where O is a value of an output unit for pattern classification and θ is a threshold value. Those indicated by "mental" show the results using the method presented in this paper. The "number of samples" indicates the number of training samples for the pattern recognition part. The number of those for the angle estimation part is 1. The difference in the results by the first network is due to the difference in the number of test samples. The choice of initial weights often produces a 100 % recognition accuracy by the method "max" in the second network. The clear correct results in the second network is further improved

No. of samples	Net1		Net2		mental
	max	clear	max	clear	clear
1	58.1	7.7	75.5	28.6	74.5
5	57.8	7.8	95.0	63.9	90.0
10	56.3	8.8	98.1	79.4	93.1

Table 2: Recognition accuracy for coin images. $\theta = 0.5$.(%)

by means of our approach. Note that the rotation of coin images based on an angle estimation in the second network is often repeated several times to get a clear result.

6 Conclusion

This paper considers the rotation invariant neural pattern recognition system, which can estimate a rotation angle, by means of a principle of the mental rotation. From the results of computer simulation, a perfect angle estimation and a perfect pattern recognition can be done for binary patterns. In coin image recognition, the better recognition accuracy is given.

A rotation angle estimation in the second network is about 70 % accuracy only by using a single training sample for the angle estimation part. The improvement of accuracy in angle estimation is important.

The hidden layer in the second network could be divided into two networks, each of which uses as an output layer a different part, namely, a pattern recognition part or a angle estimation part.

References

[1] M.Iriki et al. : *Physiology*, Bunkodo (1986) (in Japanese)

[2] N.Tsukahara et al. : *Information Processing of Brain*, Asakura-shoten (in Japanese)

[3] K.Yazawa : *Brain and AI : Thinking Machines*, Gakken (1992) (in Japanese)

[4] D.E.Rumelhart et al. : *Parallel Distributed Processing*, **1,2**, The MIT Press, Cambridge, MA (1986)

[5] D.Goldberg : *Genetic Algorithms in Search, Optimization, and Machine Learning*, Addison-Wesley (1989)

[6] K.Fukushima, et al. : "Neocognitron: A Neural Network Model for A Mechanism of Visual Pattern Recognition, *IEEE Trans. Syst., Man, Cybern.*, **SMC-13**, pp.826-834 (1983)

[7] M.Fukumi, et al. : "Neural Pattern Recognition System Invariant to Rotation of Input Pattern and Its Application to Coin Recognition", *Trans. ISCIE* Japan, **5**, pp.9-17 (1992) (in Japanese)

[8] S.Kageyu, et al. : "Augmented Multi-layer Perceptron for Rotation-and-Scale Invariant Hand Written Numeral recognition", *Proc. of Int. Joint Conf. Neural Networks*, Singapore, **3**, pp.54-59 (Nov. 1991)

[9] M.Fukumi, et al. : "Rotation-Invariant Neural Pattern Recognition System with Application to Coin Recognition, *IEEE Trans. Neural Networks*, **2**, pp.272-279 (1992)

[10] M.Fukumi, et al. : "Rotation Invariant Neural Network with An Edge Detection Network, *Trans. IEE* Japan, **112-C**, pp.457-464 (1992) (in Japanese)

[11] M.Fukumi and S.Omatu : "Recognition of Coin Images by Neural Networks", *Proc. of 35th Japan Joint Automatic Control Conf.*, 3034, pp.451-452 (1992) (in Japanese)

[12] M.Fukumi et al. : "Rotation Invariant Neural Pattern Recognition Systems with Application to Coin Recognition", *J. SICE Japan*, **33**, (1994) (in Japanese)

[13] M.Fukumi and S.Omatu :" Designing a Neural Network for Coin Recognition by A Genetic Algorithm", *Proc. Int. Joint Conf. Neural Networks*, Nagoya, pp.2109-2112 (1993)

[14] B.Widrow, et al. : "Layered Neural Nets for Pattern Recognition, *IEEE Trans. Acoust, Speech & Signal Process.*, **ASSP-36**, pp.1109-1118 (July 1988)

[15] M.Fukumi, et al. : "A New Neuron Model "CONE" with Fast Convergence Rate and Its Application to Pattern Recognition", *Trans. IEICE* Japan, **D-II-J73**,pp.648-653 (1990) (in Japanese)

[16] M.Fukumi and S.Omatu : "A New Back-Propagation Algorithm with Coupled Neuron, *IEEE Trans. Neural Networks*, **2**, pp.535-538 (1991)

[17] S.D.You and G.E.Ford : " Network Model for Invariant Object Recognition and Rotation Angle Estimation ", *Proc. Int. Joint Conf. Neural Networks*, Nagoya, **3**, pp.2145-2148 (1993)

[18] T.H.Christopher : "Rotation Invariant Neocognitron ", *Proc. Int. Joint Conf. Neural Networks*, Singapore, **3**, pp.2216-2221 (1991)

[19] A.Waibel et al.: "Phoneme Recognition Using Time-Delay Neural Network", *IEEE Trans. Acoust, Speech & Signal Process.*, **ASSP-37**, 3, pp.328-339 (1989)

[20] S.Araya et al. : " A Neural Network for Learning and Recognizing Rotated Patterns ", *Trans. IEE Japan*, **111-C**, 5, pp.202-208 (1991) (in Japanese)

[21] Y.Takano : *Mystery of Rotated Forms*, Tokyo-Univ. Press (1987) (in Japanese)

[22] Y.Takano: "Perception of Rotated Forms : A Theory of Information Types", *Cognitive Psychology*, **21**, pp.1-59 (1989)

[23] R.N.Shepard and J.Metzler : " Mental Rotation of Three-Dimensional Objects ", *Science*, **171**, pp.701-703 (1971)

[24] "Foreign Coins in Toll Change Cause Mix-ups, Anger Drivers" : *The Daily Yomiuri*, (June 30, 1992)

[25] F.Takeda et al. :"Bank Note Recognition System Using Neural Network with Random masks", *Proc. World Cong. Neural networks*, **1**, pp. 241-244 (1993)

A Two-Level TDNN (TLTDNN) Technique for Large Vocabulary Mandarin FINAL Recognition

Gee-Swee Poo

Department of Information Systems and Computer Science,
National University of Singapore, Kent Ridge, Singapore 0511

ABSTRACT

A Two-Level Time-Delay Neural Network (TLTDNN) technique has been developed to recognize all Mandarin Finals of the entire Chinese syllables. The first level discriminates the vowel-group based on (a,e,i,o,u,v) and the nasal-group based on nasal ending, (-n,-ng,-others). Orthogonal combination of the two groupings in the first level enables the second level discrimination of all 35 Mandarin Finals. The technique was thoroughly tested with 8 sets of 1265 isolated Hanyu Pinyin syllables, with 6 sets used for training and 2 sets used for testing. The overall result shows that a high recognition rate of 95.3% for inside testing and 93.9% for outside testing is achievable.

1 Introduction

The Time-Delay Neural Network (TDNN) introduced by Waibel et al [1,2] has achieved high performance in speech recognition. The time-delay architecture is capable of capturing the dynamic nature of speech and able to achieve superior phoneme recognition performance. It is a powerful technique to be applied to Mandarin speech recognition.

The Mandarin speech consists of about 1300 spoken syllables. Each syllable can be divided into two parts: Initial (Consonant) and Final (Vowel). The Initial could be absent, in that case, a Final is just a syllable. There are a total of 35 Finals in Mandarin phonetic system. The Final contains pure vowel, diphthong, triphthong and vowel-nasal compounds as follows:

Vowel: a,e,i,o,u,v,er (v=ü)
Diphthong/Triphthong: ai,ei,ao,ou,ia,ie,ua,uo,ve,ui,iu,iao,uai
Nasal: an,en,in,un,vn,ang,eng,ong,ing,ian,uan,van,iang,iong,uang.

Several attempts have been made for the recognition of Finals [3,4,5,6]. The techniques explored include Karhunen-Loeve Transformation [3], LPC-based Vector Quantisation (VQ)[4], Segmental model [5], Multi-section VQ [5] and VQ-HMM [6]. The above experiments were based on only small partial datasets for the training and testing. The claimed recognition rate is less than 89%.

In this paper, we develop a Two-Level TDNN technique to recognize all 35 Mandarin Finals using a comprehensive database covering the entire spoken syllables of Chinese language.

2 TLTDNN Architecture for Mandarin Finals

The basic TDNN architecture is effective for small recognition tasks. For larger scale recognition tasks. It is then necessary to explore the strategy of modularity and incremental learning [2]. The idea is to break up a large learning neural network into smaller subcomponent networks, each of which can be trained and learned independently.

The modeling of Mandarin Final faces similar difficulties. A straightforward modeling with 35 Finals output would require a large neural network structure. This is computationally prohibitive. Moreover, the complexity of searching a huge configuration space for good solutions is practically unmanageable. The strategy of modularity and incremental learning is therefore adopted.

To assist in modular decomposition, a thorough analysis is made on the time-domain graphical representation of the waveforms for the Finals. It is observed that some patterns are predominately similar. For instance, the time-domain waveforms of /a/, /an/, /ang/ etc are similar, all dominated by the occurrence of /a/. Similarly, the waveforms of /en/, /eng/ etc are dominated by the occurrence of /e/, and so on. By scaning through all the

0-7803-1901-X/94 $4.00 ©1994 IEEE

waveforms, it is found that all the Finals can be classified into the six distinctive vowel-based groups, based on /a/,/e/,/i/,/o/,/u/,/v/ as follows:

/a/:	a,ai,ua,ao,ia,uai,iao,er,an,uan,ang,iang,uang	/o/:	o,uo,ong,iong
/e/:	e,en,eng	/u/:	u,ou,iu,un
/i/:	i,ei,ie,ui,in,ian,ing	/v/:	v,ve,vn,van.

Further observation of time-domain graph reveals that it is possible to distinguish syllables with different nasal ending, i.e. -n or -ng and also those without nasal ending. Thus, a nasal discriminator can be set up to discriminate n, ng and 0t. "ot=others" indicate those without nasal ending.

The above consideration leads to the proposal of a Two-Level Time-Delay Neural Network (TLTDNN) architecture for Mandarin Finals. This is shown in Figure 1. In level 1, two networks are set up, one for the vowel-group discriminator and another for the nasal-group discriminator. These two networks are independent of each other. Thus, orthogonal combination of the two will produce smaller subcomponent networks at the second level. Without nasal-group discriminator, the /a/ subnet at the second level remains very large, making it difficult to model. The presence of nasal-group discriminator further splits the large /a/ subnet into three smaller subnets, making it easy to compute. Thus, at the second level, a total of 15 groupings are produced. Some of them are at the atomic level, giving the Finals as required. These include /e/, /en/, /eng/, /ing/, /un/. For these cases, no more modeling is required. As for the other groups, further subnet modeling is needed. A total of 9 subcomponent networks are to be formed.

The TLTDNN architecture produces 11 component networks, 2 in level 1 and 9 in level 2. Each component network assumes a TDNN structure. Nonetheless, unlike the original TDNN, we use an input matrix of size 16x16 instead of 16x15. Hence, the cell configuration varies. Take the vowel group network for example, the modified cell arrangement will be 16x16 for input layer, 12x14 for first hidden layer, 6x10 for second hidden layer and 6x1 for output layer. The cells in the first hidden layer is chosen to be twice of that in the second hidden layer. This is regarded as a good choice [7]. Likewise, other component networks will have similar cell configurations depending on the number of output to be produced.

3 Data and Training

In order to provide a thorough training and testing, a large database was set up. The database consists of 8 sets of 1265 Mandarin monosyllables spoken by a Beijing female speaker in a quiet environment. Thus, a total of 8x1265=10,120 speech samples were used. Each set of data covers the entire vocabulary of Mandarin speech. Among the 8 sets, 6 sets were used for training and the remaining 2 sets were used for testing. The entire database was phonetically hand labeled. The label marks the beginning point of speech sample, the ending point of speech sample and the separation point between Initial and Final. Special effort was required for the separation of the Initial and the Final for both unvoiced and voiced Initials. The Final portion extracted from each speech sample is then used in the experiment.

To prepare for the input matrix, the speech samples were low-pass-filtered to 5 kHz and sampled at 10 kHz. Each segment of speech was weighted by a Hamming window and a 256-point FFT was computed every 5 ms. From the power spectrum of FFT, 16 melscale spectral coefficients were calculated [8]. Coefficients adjacent in time were averaged to produce an overall frame rate of 10 ms. The coefficients were then normalised between -1 and +1 with the mean set at 0.0.

Each component TDNN network is trained independently using back propagation learning procedure according to a generalisation of the least mean-square (LMS) error principle. The standard Back Propagation is slow in learning. The training of TDNN could be speed up significantly by two means: samples skipping and momentum scaling [7]. These means were adopted and was found to be effective in training. A standard sigmoid was used in the process. The experiments were carried out on an IBM RS/6000 Model 560 Compute Server. The timing is expressed in terms of epochs as well as in hours of machine times.

4 Experimental Results

For the Two-Level TDNN architecture, the training and testing were carried out in three phases. Firstly, the component networks at level 1 were built up. These include the vowel-group network and nasal-group network. This is the crucial stage. A thorough training is needed. As much as 2500 epochs were required for the training using more than 9000 speech samples. Convergence is slow for the two networks. Secondly, the

9 component networks at level 2 were trained and tested independently. Training at this level is less strenuous. It requires half as much epochs and a quarter amount of data. Convergence can be achieved rapidly at this level. A constant learning rate of 0.01 was fixed for training the component networks in both levels. Thirdly, after the completion of level 1 and 2 training, the best weights were extracted and used for the overall testing of the entire architecture. No further training is made. The testing includes inside test and outside test. The inside test refers to testing on the training datasets whereas the outside test refers to testing on the remaining datasets which are never used in training.

Table 1 shows the training and testing results for vowel-group network and the nasal-group networks. For vowel-group network, the TDNN was trained up to 2500 epochs using 5842 speech tokens. The inside test gives 99.8% and the outside test gives 98.2%. For the nasal-group network, it was trained up to 2000 epochs using 9554 tokens. The recognition rate obtained is 99.8% for inside test and 97.5% for outside test respectively. The high accuracy of level 1 component networks confirms the validity of the modeling.

The level 2 involves 9 component networks. These networks were trained and tested independently. About 1000 epochs were used for training. Very high recognition rates are recorded for all the groups. This is because the groups are smaller and involve less training tokens.

From the 11 component networks that were trained, the weight-connections for each network were extracted and used for the overall testing. The results are shown in Table 3 and 4. Table 3 shows individual scores for the 34 Finals for both inside test and outside test. The number of tokens used are also indicated. By and large, the inside test gives better performance than the outside test. The only exception is /er/ which gives better outside test than the inside test. The scores for most Finals are quite high, mostly above 90%. The results are quite consistent for those with high occurrence of speech tokens. A few Finals have lower scores. These are the ones with fewer speech tokens in the datasets, resulting in higher fluctuation in their scores, particularly in the outside test. This trend is confirmed in Table 4 which shows the performance of the Final groups in the Two-Level architecture. All major groups show good performance. Only some minor show weaker results. On the whole, the average recognition rate achieved is 95.3% for inside test and 93.9% for outside test.

5 Conclusions

This paper presents a Two-Level TDNN technique for the recognition of all Mandarin Finals of Chinese syllables. A high recognition rate was obtained, yielding 95.3% for inside test and 93.9% for outside test. The overall performance is much better than that obtained previously using other techniques [3,4,5,6].

The uneven distribution of some Final tokens poses a problem in training. For instance, there are only 10 /vn/, 15 /van/ and 10 /iong/ among a 1265 dataset. These rare tokens have to be presented repeatedly during the training in order to maintain an even input of training tokens. A consequence of this is the poorer generalisation capability as exhibited in Table 3 and 4. The weakness needs to be addressed if further improvement is to be sought.

References

1 Waibel, A., Hanazawa, T., Hinton, G.E., Shikano, K. and Lang, K.J., "Phoneme recognition using Time-Delay Neural Networks", IEEE Trans. Acoust. Speech, Signal Processing, 1989, Vol.37(3), pp.328-339

2 Waibel, A., Sawai, H. and Shikano, K., "Modularity and scaling in large Phoneme Neural Networks", IEEE Trans. Acoust. Speech, Signal Processing, 1989, Vol.37(12), pp.1888-1898

3 Chan, L.C.M., and Cheung, Y.S., "Analysis and Recognition of isolated Putonghua Vowels by Karhunen-Loeve Transformation Techniques", Speech Communications, 1986, Vol.5 (3,4), pp.299-330

4 Lin, L.J. Wang, H.C. & Chang, Y.C. "Recognition of isolated syllable Finals in Mandarin speech", Proc. of Int. Conf. on Chinese and Oriental Language Comput., June 15-17, 1987, Chicago, USA, pp.234-238

5 Hwang, C.H. Hsu,Y.M. Wang, B.C. Tseng,C.Y. & Lee, L.S. "Efficient speech recognition techniques for the Finals of Mandarin syllables", Compu. Proc. of Chinese and Oriental Lang., 3 (3&4) 1988, 257-273.

6 Wu, J.X. Chan, C.K. & Cai, G.L. "Mandarin Final recognition based on VQ and Markov Model method", Proc. of Int. Conf. on Chinese & Oriental Language Comput, June 15-17, 1987, Chicago, USA, 234-238

7 Haffner, P. Waibel, A. Sawai, H. & Shikano, K. "Fast back-propagation learning methods for large Phonemic Neural Networks", Proc. of Euro. Conf. on Speech Comm. & Tech., Paris, Sept. 1989, pp.553-556

8 Davis, S.B. and Mermelstein, P., "Comparison of parametric representation for monosyllabic word recognition in continuously spoken sentences", IEEE Trans. ASSP Vol.28(4), 1980, pp.357-366

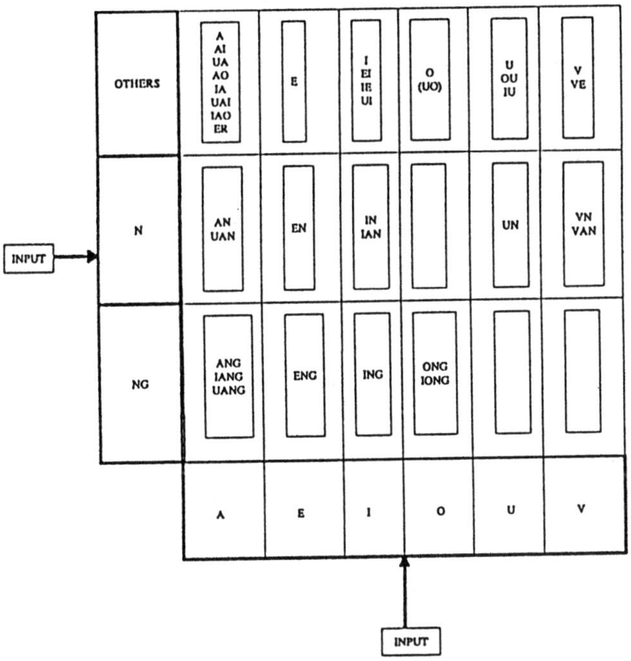

Figure 1 The TLTDNN architecture

Table 2 Final Group Recognition performance

Final Group	Inside Test % correct	Outside Test % correct
(a,e,i,o,u,v)	99.6	98.9
(n,ng,ot)	99.8	98.3
(a,ai,ua,ao, ia,uai,iao,er)	95.2	97.2
(an,uan)	96.7	92.1
(ang,iang,uang)	96.2	91.5
(e)	96.6	98.7
(en)	98.5	91.1
(eng)	93.0	95.0
(i,ei,ie,ui)	94.9	95.0
(in,ian)	88.9	88.6
(ing)	92.1	86.1
(o (uo))	96.7	96.7
(ong,iong)	97.9	84.6
(u,ou,iu)	96.1	96.5
(un)	94.8	98.8
(v,ve)	96.9	94.7
(vn,van)	95.5	86.5

Table 1 Overall test performance on Mandarin Finals

Final	Inside Test # errors/ # Tokens	Inside Test % correct	Outside Test # errors/ # Tokens	Outside Test % correct
a	18/372	95.2	3/124	97.6
e	8/234	96.6	1/78	98.7
i	25/396	93.7	9/132	93.2
o(uo)	12/366	96.7	4/122	96.7
u	20/408	95.1	4/136	94.1
v	4/126	96.8	1/42	97.6
er	7/18	61.1	0/6	100
ai	15/324	95.4	1/108	99.1
ua	4/120	96.7	2/40	95.0
ao	12/402	97.0	1/134	99.3
ia	6/102	94.1	3/34	91.2
ei	9/174	94.8	4/58	93.1
ie	8/210	96.2	3/70	95.7
ui	10/240	95.8	1/80	98.8
ou	7/300	97.7	3/100	97.0
iu	6/138	95.7	3/46	93.5
ve	3/102	97.1	3/34	91.2
an	9/384	97.7	9/128	93.0
en	4/270	98.5	8/90	91.1
in	11/162	93.2	4/54	92.6
un	13/252	94.8	1/84	98.8
vn	4/66	93.9	3/22	86.4
uan	12/258	95.4	8/86	90.7
ian	33/234	85.9	11/78	85.9
van	3/90	96.7	4/30	86.7
ang	16/378	95.8	9/126	92.9
eng	21/300	93.0	5/100	95.0
ing	17/216	92.1	10/72	86.1
ong	5/270	98.2	13/90	85.6
uai	7/120	94.2	3/40	92.5
iao	12/240	95.0	3/80	96.3
iang	2/120	98.3	0/40	100
uang	6/138	95.7	9/46	80.4
iong	2/60	96.7	4/20	80.0
Total	357/7590	95.3	154/2530	93.9

Correlative Training and Recurrent Network Automata for Speech Recognition

Roberto GEMELLO, Dario ALBESANO, Franco MANA
CSELT - Centro Studi e Laboratori Telecomunicazioni
via G. Reiss Romoli, 274 - 10148 Torino - Italia
Tel.: +39-11-2286224 Fax: +39-11-2286207 email: gemello@cselt.stet.it

Abstract

Discriminative training is one of the more distinctive features of Multilayer Perceptron networks when used as classifiers. Although, when dealing with overlapping classes, it may be useful to smooth this feature not compelling the MLP to discriminate where it is impossible. This can be done adaptively, without any prior information about the classes by introducing a straightforward modification of backprop we have named Correlative Training. This new MLP feature has proved to be very useful when training the hybrid Recurrent Network Automata model for speech recognition.

1. Introduction

Neural Networks (NN) have, in the last years, found their place among speech recognition technologies as powerful adaptive non-linear classifiers [Morgan,1991].

As, at present, NN are not yet able to manage well time modelling, they are mainly employed in integration with Hidden Markov Models (HMM). This approach has been investigated by several research teams: [Franzini90,91] have introduced the Connectionist Viterbi Training to enhance HMM based connected digit recognition; [Austin92] has described Segmental Neural Networks for phonetic modelling; [Bourlard93] has proposed connectionist probability estimation to significantly improve a HMM based continuous speech recognition system.

Our contribution to this line was the introduction of Recurrent Network Automata (*) (RNA) [Albesano92,93] which integrates recurrent NN with HMM word modelling, showing the advantages which can be obtained by exploiting the joint contextual information of feedback hidden units and time delayed input.

Discriminative training is the main feature of Multi-layer Percepron (MLP) neural networks, when trained as classifiers. In the field of speech recognition this feature of MLP classifiers is particularly interesting as it represents an alternative to the Maximum Likelihood (ML) training usually employed for HMMs. In fact, while ML training characterises each word model separately, discriminative training tries to find the best separation between them.

However, in some cases, a pure discriminative training can be not advisable: when there are some quite overlapping classes the best policy seems to be smoothing the discriminative training for the correlated classes while maintaining it for the uncorrelated ones. Of course, overlapping is a continue property, and hard decisions are not well suited. To overcome this problem, that we have encountered while training the MLP component of RNAs for word recognition, we conceived and experimented a modification to standard discriminative training that we called *Correlative Training*.

Although it was studied to solve a specific problem, Correlative Training can be applied in all those cases where you are looking for a trade-off between discriminative and characterizing training. Furthermore, it results into a very simple modification to backprop equations.

2. The Recurrent Network Automata model

The RNA recognition model [Albesano92] is a hybrid HMM-NN model devoted to recognise sequential patterns. Each class is described in terms of a left-to-right automaton (with self loops) as in HMM, and the emission probability of the automata states are estimated by a Simple Recurrent Network [Elman88]. The transition probabilities among states are not considered. The RNA has an input window that comprises some contiguous frames of the sequence, one hidden layer with a self-feedback, and an output level where the activation of each unit estimates the probability of the input window to belong to an automaton state.

The hidden neuron dynamics is given by the equation:

$$y_i(t) = F(\Sigma_j w_{ij} x_j(t) + \Sigma_k w_{ik} y_k(t-1))$$

(*) patent pending

where y_i is the activation of a hidden neuron, x_j is an input unit and F is the standard logistic function. The hidden neurons are also called *state neurons* because thanks to the self-feedback they can encode a contextual information about the sequence which is being recognised. The output neurons follow the standard MLP dynamics.

3. Speech Modelling with Recurrent Network Automata

The RNA model was principally conceived for speech recognition, and in particular for modelling words for isolated or connected word recognition with a small vocabulary. In RNA time modelling takes place in two ways: first, by an external modelling, through the HMM like time warping ability of the dynamic programming applied to left-to-right automata corresponding to words; second, by the internal modelling of the recurrent network. In fact, the memory capability of the recurrent network allows to give the states a contextual information, inside the word automaton, and to give a more stable evolution of emission likelihoods, inside the state [Albesano *et al.*, 1992].

The architecture of RNA has many degrees of freedom: the architecture of the NN, the input window width, the number of automaton states for the different words of the vocabulary. A lot of experimental activity has been performed to optimise the architecture for the recognition of small vocabularies (10-20 words) resulting in the structure depicted in fig. 1. The input window is 3-7 frames wide, and each frame contains 26 parameters (log Energy, 12 Cepstral Coefficients, and their first derivatives). The first hidden layer is divided into three feature detectors blocks, one for the central frame, and two for the left and right context. Each block is in its turn divided into four sub-blocks devoted to keep into account the four types of different input parameters. It was empirically found that this a priori structure is generally better than a fully connected layer. The second hidden layer has a fully connected recurrence, like in Elman's nets (the double arrow means a copy of activation values). The neurons of this layer have a twofold function: first, they represent, together with the first hidden layer neurons, a *space transform* between the input parameters and some self-organised internal features, corresponding to acoustic/phonetic characteristics (e.g. silence, stationary sounds, transitions, specific phonemes). Besides, they encode a *state information* related to the temporal context the current input is inserted in, as described in [Albesano *et al.*, 1993]. The output layer estimates the emission probabilities of the states of the word automata, and is virtually divided in several parts, each one corresponding to an automaton.

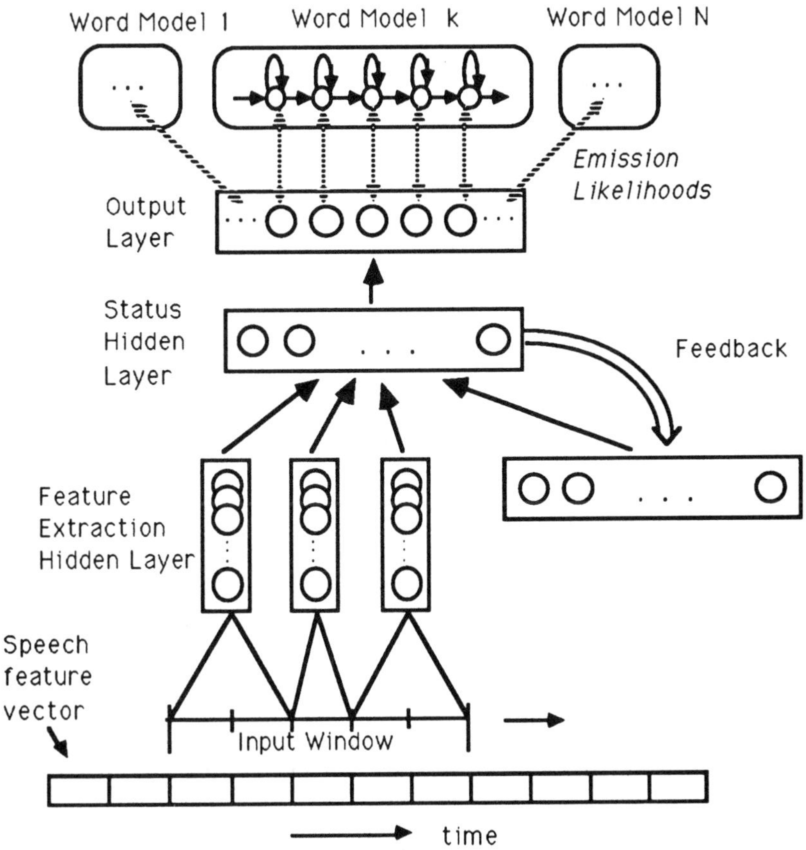

Figure 1: Architecture of a Recurrent Network Automata devoted to word recognition

Typical dimensions for a RNA devoted to recognise the ten Italian digits are:

- 7 frame input window;
- first hidden layer: central block with 24 units (divided in 2+10+2+10 for the four types of parameters), context blocks with 36 units (3+15+3+15).
- second hidden layer: 70 units, with fully connected recurrence.
- output layer: 63 units, corresponding to 63 automata states, pertaining to the 10 word automata, and divided proportionally to the average word length.

4. Correlative Training

4.1 Basic training algorithm

Recurrent Network Automata are trained using an iterative procedure as follows:

Initialisation:

- initialise the RNA with small random weights;
- create the first segmentation by segmenting the training utterances uniformly.

Iterations:

- load the present segmentation;
- train the RNA some epochs to implement the automata which approximates that segmentation;
- obtain a new segmentation by applying the dynamic programming to each utterance in the training set to re-evaluate the transition points proposed by the RNA;
- update the present segmentation by using a function of itself and of the new segmentation: present_segm = F(present_segm, new_segm);

  e.g. $F(s1, s2) = \alpha s1 + (1-\alpha)s2$, with α starting from 1.0 and decreasing during the training.

The input to the RNA is a window sliding on the speech frames, including a central frame and some left and right context frames. The targets are generated according to the present segmentation, putting 1.0 for the active state of the right automaton and 0.0 otherwise. All the automata are trained into a unique net, so performing a discriminative training. The NN basic learning algorithm is the back-propagation.

4.2 Correlative Backpropagation

The training outlined in the previous section is a discriminative training, as usual for MLP networks for classifications. With this kind of training, if two classes C1 and C2 happen to be superimposed, that is the patterns of C1 and the patterns of C2 are not separable, the estimated probability for a generic pattern of C1 or C2 will be only determined by the a priori probability of the class. In fact, as MLP nets used as classifiers were proved to estimate the posterior probability of classes [Bourlard90,93], we have:

$$p(C|X) = \frac{p(X|C)p(C)}{p(X)} \quad \text{with } C = C1, C2$$

but in this case $p(X|C1) = p(X|C2)$, as the two classes C1 and C2 are superimposed, $p(X)$ is a constant, and the only different factors are the a priori probabilities $p(C1)$ and $p(C2)$. Obviously that fact is unacceptable in a recognition system and has to be corrected.

In speech recognition with entire word models, this situation may happen in some cases and with different degrees. For example, as the Italian digits SEI and SETTE (six and seven) begins in the same way, it is foreseeable that the first 2-3 states of the two automata will be associated to overlapping sets of patterns.

To face that cases it is advisable to modify the standard discriminative training in such a way that discriminable classes are trained with a discriminative training, while for non-discriminable classes the discriminative training is adaptively smoothed. That is what we call *Correlative Training.*

The problem of similar states in word automata was already encountered by Smyth [Smyth, 1992] in the recognition of the English alphabet. He started with 26 words and three output units per word, resulting in 78 distinct states, a significant number of these states corresponding to very similar sounds (i.e. the final units of the E-set and A-set). He managed the problem of units correlation by identifying during training (from the confusion matrix) the most confusable states, and clustering them. That method works, and has the advantage of reducing the number of output units. However, it is intrinsically discrete, as two states are clustered or are not. We think that in many cases this hard decision is not advisable, and propose, with Correlative Training a continuous way of letting the natural correlations among output states to emerge.

Correlative training has been developed for speech recognition, but its scope is beyond this application, including the cases in which it is convenient to adaptively tune the discriminative training.

Briefly, Correlative Training consists in changing the definition of the target in function of the correlation of the outputs of the considered unit and of the expected corrected unit.

Let us name:

o_k the output of output unit k;

t_k the target of output unit k;

h the index of the output unit with $t_h = 1.0$

We redefine the target of a generic output unit k as:

$$t_k(o_k, o_h) = \begin{cases} t_h & \text{if } h = k \\ o_k o_h & \text{if } h \neq k \end{cases}$$

where $o_k o_h$ has been chosen as a measure of the correlation of the output of the considered unit k and the output of the unit h the target of which is 1.0 .

This change in the definition of the target leads to a variation in the $\frac{\partial E}{\partial o_j}$ term of backpropagation for output units, that becomes

$$\frac{\partial E}{\partial o_j} = \frac{\partial}{\partial o_j} \frac{1}{2} \sum_k (t_k(o_k, o_h) - o_k)^2$$

and deriving we obtain:

$$\frac{\partial E}{\partial o_j} = (t_j(o_j, o_h) - o_j)\left(\frac{\partial(t_j(o_j, o_h))}{\partial o_j} - 1\right) = \begin{cases} -(t_j - o_j) & \text{if } j = h \\ o_j(o_h - 1)^2 & \text{if } j \neq h \end{cases}$$

This change in backpropagation results in an adaptive smoothing of discriminative training. In fact if two output units o_m and o_n correspond to intrinsically similar acoustic phenomena they will try to respond with a high value on the same input patterns. The correlation substitutes the zero target for the "wrong" unit with the correlation of the two outputs $o_m o_n$, so allowing gradually the two units to respond both with higher and higher values on that input patterns. On the contrary, if two output units o_m and o_n respond with different values (one high and the other low) the product $o_m o_n$,will be low (~0.0) and the correlative training will behave as a regular discriminative training.

5. Recognition Experiments

We used RNA trained with correlative training to face a difficult real problem, i.e. the speaker independent recognition of the digits over the public telephone network. This problem has been already faced in our labs by using Continuous Density Hidden Markov Models (CDHMM) [Canavesio91], so we already have a large training database and some state of the art results to compare with. Preliminary results obtained using RNA and a comparison with HMMs were reported in [Albesano, 1993].

The speech database we used was collected on the Italian public telephone network, each time using a different switching circuit. It is suited for speaker independent training as about 1,000 people evenly distributed between male and female voices contributed to it. The pre-processing technique consists of a Mel-based spectral analysis followed by a Discrete Cosine Transform [Gemello90] to obtain Cepstral coefficients. Together with the cepstral coefficients, the value of the logarithm of the total energy of each frame is retained as it provides some information about distinguishing the voiced parts of the speech input from the unvoiced ones.

A RNA network was trained on a training set containing about 500 repetition for each digit. Several architectures were experimented, with and without feedback. The feedback always improved the performances, both in recognition percentage and in the average distance between the correct model and the second one. Presently, the best RNA architecture has an input window of 7 frames, each containing 26 features (12 Cepstral, Energy, 12 Cepstral derivatives, Energy derivative), a first hidden layer with 96 units, windowed both on time and on features, as described in Fig. 1, a second hidden layer of 70 units, a feedback layer of 70 units and one output layer of 63 units (one for each state of the automata modelling the ten digits). The obtained results are exposed in Table 1.

Architecture	Training	Test
w=3, 2 hidden layers + feedback (Dec. '92)	98.7	98.4
w=7, 2 hidden layer + feedback , as in Fig. 1 (Dec. '93)	99.7	98.7
w=7, 2 hidden layer + feedback, 1 state for word	99.1	97.0

Table 1. - Recognition results of RNA trained with Correlative Training

Correlative training substantially improved the convergence of RNAs and the recognition results, and was used in all the experiment reported here.

The first result with a input window of 3 frames, (98.4) was already reported in [Albesano, 1993] . Using a window of 7 frames the result was enhanced to 98.7.

In the first two experiments the word automata are modelled with a number of states ranging from 5 for short words to 9 for long words. The last experiment, on the contrary, makes use of just one state to model each word: in this way no external modelling is provided, and all the time modelling is made internally by the recurrent net. The obtained results (97.0) are inferior, but not so bad, and outline the possibility, for small vocabularies, of using directly a recurrent network with one output for each word, so avoiding the dynamic programming decoding of automata.

6. Conclusion

Correlative Training has been described as a simple way to soften in an adaptive way the strength of discriminative training for classes that cannot be completely put apart, without compromising its power on separable classes. The correlations which naturally emerge between classes during training are considered, allowing them to gradually arise without disturbing the training process.

Correlative training was applied to the training of RNA for word recognition, allowing an effective training and performances which get over those of continuous HMMs on small vocabulary word recognition.

References

[Albesano92] D. Albesano, R. Gemello and F. Mana, "Word Recognition with Recurrent Network Automata", in *Proc. IJCNN 92*, Baltimore, June 1992, pp. 308-313.

[Albesano93] D. Albesano, R. Gemello and F. Mana, "Recurrent Network Automata for Speech Recognition", in *Proc. WCNN 93*, Portland, July 1993, vol. III, pp. 16-19.

[Austin92] S. Austin, G. Zavaliagkost, J. Makhoul, and R. Schwartz, "Speech Recognition using Segmental Neural Nets", in *Proc. ICASSP*, 1992, pp. 625-628.

[Bourlard90] H. Bourlard, C.J. Wellekens, "Links Between Markov Models and Multilayer Perceptrons", in IEEE Transaction on Pattern Analysis and Machine Intelligence, vol. 12, pp. 1167-1178.

[Bourlard93] H. Bourlard, N. Morgan, *Connectionist Speech Recognition: A Hybrid Approach,* Kluwer Academic Publishers, 1993.

[Elman88] J.L. Elman, "Finding Structure in Time", CRL Technical Report #8801, University of California, San Diego, 1988.

[Canavesio91] F. Canavesio, L. Fissore, M. Oreglia, R. Ruscitti "HMM modeling in the public telephone network environment: experiments and results", in *Proc. EUROSPEECH 91*, Genova, September 1991, pp. 731-734.

[Franzini90] M.A. Franzini, K.F. Lee and A. Waibel, "Connectionist Viterbi Training: A new hybrid method for continuous speech recognition", in *Proc. ICASSP*, Albuquerque,NM, April 1990, pp.425-428.

[Franzini91] M.A. Franzini, A. Waibel and K.F. Lee , "Continuous Speech Recognition with the Connectionist Viterbi Training Procedure: a summary of recent work", in *Proc. IJCNN* , Singapore, 1991, pp.1855-1860.

[Haffner91] P. Haffner, M. Franzini, A. Waibel, "Integrating Time Alignment and Neural Networks for High performance Continuous Speech Recognition", in *Proc. ICASSP*, 1991, pp. 105-108.

[Li92] K.P. Li, J.A. Naylor, and M.L. Rossen, " A Whole Recurrent Neural Network for Keyword Spotting", in *Proc. ICASSP*, 1992, pp. 81-84.

[Morgan91] D.P. Morgan and C.L. Scofield, *Neural Networks and Speech Processing,* Kluwer Academic Publishers, 1991.

[Smyth92] S.G. Smyth, "Segmental sub-word unit classification using a multilayer perceptron", in R. Linggard, D.J. Myers, C. Nightingale editors *Neural Networks for Vision, Speech and Natural Language,* Chapman & Hall, 1992.

Structured Representations Developed by Learning in Recurrent Networks

Mihail Crucianu, LIMSI - CNRS, B.P.133, 91403 Orsay, France

Abstract — **We study the internal representations developed by recurrent networks learning to associate semantic role descriptions with simple sentences. Our analysis of the state-space of the hidden units makes explicit the structure of the representations and shows how it reflects the similarities between the sentences. We find that the representation scheme developed by learning is related to a formally defined one.**

I. Introduction

It was argued (see [5]) that structured representations of complex entities and structure-sensitive processes are required in order to provide effective solutions to high-level tasks. In [7], van Gelder considers that connectionist models can satisfy these strong requirements, while providing composition mechanisms which are more general that the concatenation employed by symbolic AI. The solution would be to reliably translate the structural similarities between external entities into vectorial similarities between their connectionist representations, so that structure-sensitive processes could be implemented as vectorial similarity sensitive processes. Recurrent networks were shown (see e.g. [4], [8], [9], [12], [13]) to be effective in solving some interesting — though simple — sequential high-level tasks. Here, we wanted to better understand the internal non-concatenative representations such models employ. The analysis we present makes explicit the structure of these representations and shows that structural similarities between entities are indeed translated into vectorial similarities between their representations. We find that these internal representations developed by learning are related to a representation scheme which was formally defined in [11], using the tensor product. These results extend the ones in [3].

II. Task, Network Model and Analysis Methods

We want the networks to build *intra-state* representations of entire sentences, as in [9] and [13], so we employ a relatively similar task. Specifically, a sentence without relative clauses is input to a network as a sequence of words; after each word is input, the network must instantiate the semantic roles corresponding to the part of the sentence which was already presented. This task makes use of the schema-like structure model — a schema being regarded as a set of <filler | *role*> bindings — employed by Smolensky when introducing tensor product representations in [11]. We only consider non-recursive structures here.

To tackle the temporal component of the task in a flexible way, we chose recurrent networks (RNs). To ease analysis, the RNs we use have three layers, with only one — recurrent — hidden layer (see figure 1).

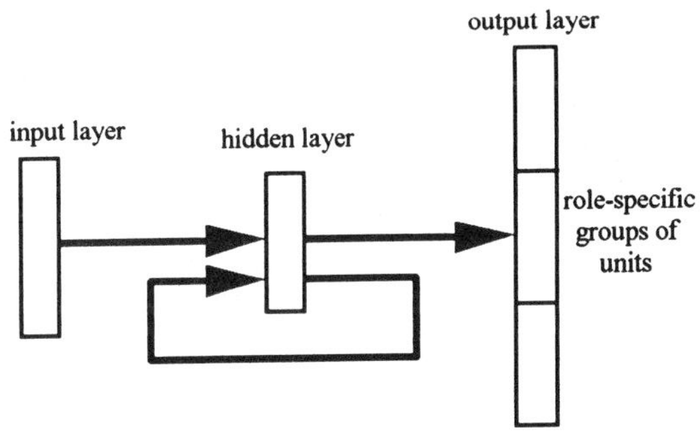

Figure 1: Network architecture

We employ local coding for the words, so the output representation is conjunctive: each active output unit represents the binding of a word to a semantic role. The training sequences (a sequence corresponds to a sentence) are randomly arranged in the corpus, but their presentation always respects the same order, so we can speak of training epochs. The learning algorithm we use is back-propagation through time ([10]). We want the networks to develop representations of whole sentences and avoid any interference between sentences, so we back-propagate the error to the beginning of a sequence and do not cross the frontier between sequences. Weights are updated after the presentation of each sequence. The error measure employed is cross-entropy. Learning policy is as follows: learning proceeds until error reaches a plateau; at that moment, learning rate is decreased and training continues. Learning rate when training starts is 0.02 and momentum 0.0.

Sentences are represented inside the networks by activation vectors of the units in the hidden layer (we call them network states). We want to find whether and how the similarities between sentences are translated into vectorial similarities between their representations. Since many *different* types of similarity can exist between sentences, the global relationships between states — as obtained by hierarchical clustering analysis (see [2], [4]) — can only reflect here a mixture of the similarities. For the task we use, one type of similarity is given by each semantic role: two sentences are similar if they bind the same word to this role. This type of similarity defines a classification of the sentences and, correspondingly, of the set of network states representing them. For each role we must then look for a *subspace* of network state-space that reflects as accurately as possible this classification. This is exactly what a *discriminant analysis* (DA) of the set of network states would do. Given a classification of a set of vectors in some high-dimensional space, DA projects these vectors on a subspace so as to optimise a joint criterion: maximise between-class dispersion while minimising total dispersion. To our knowledge, DA was first proposed as a method for the analysis of network state-space in [1] and [6], but unfortunately has not been much employed since. In our experiments, given the classification induced by one role on the sentences in the corpus, we performed a DA of the set of network states representing them. The pictures show projections of the set of states on 3-dimensional subspaces obtained by DAs. We only used for the analysis network states which are supposed to represent entire sentences; such a state is obtained after the last word of a sentence is input.

III. Analysis of an Experiment

This experiment was devised to study the structure of representations developed for active and passive voice sentences having three semantic roles, *agent*, *action* and *patient*, but allowing the *agent* role to receive two fillers at the same time, as in:

Mary and John followed Dick.

→ *active voice sentence*

Dick was followed by Mary and John.

→ *passive voice sentence*

((Mary&John | *agent*)(follow | *action*)(Dick | *patient*))

→ *associated schema*

Using 8 proper names and 8 transitive verbs we obtained a corpus of 9216 sentences. Each sentence contains bindings for all the roles. The words *and*, *was* and *by* are presented as distinct inputs to the networks. Networks had 25 hidden units and were trained on 67% of the whole corpus. Training was stopped after 200 epochs, when the network mastered the entire corpus perfectly. Networks with only 20 hidden units did not master the corpus even after extensive training. For each semantic role, a discriminant analysis (DA) was performed on the set of network states corresponding to the whole corpus of 9216 sentences — see figures 2 to 4 (DCs stands for *discriminant components*). Each of these figures presents the very same set of network states, but projected on different subspaces, associated by DAs with the different semantic roles in the sentences. For the *agent* role, which can be bound to two fillers at the same time, the first 9 DCs are actually found to be significant.

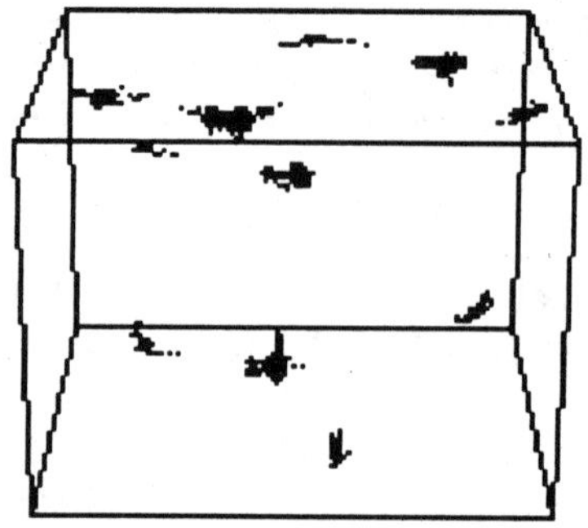

Figure 2: Discrimination between combinations of fillers of the *agent* role (DCs 1 to 3, with 9216 points)

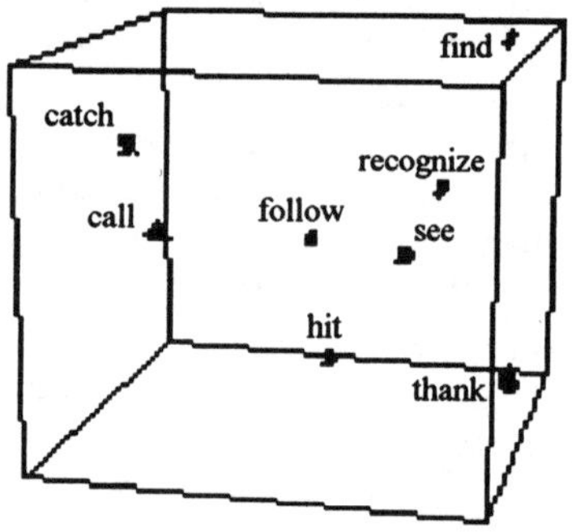

Figure 3: Discrimination between fillers of the *action* role (DCs 1 to 3, with 9216 points)

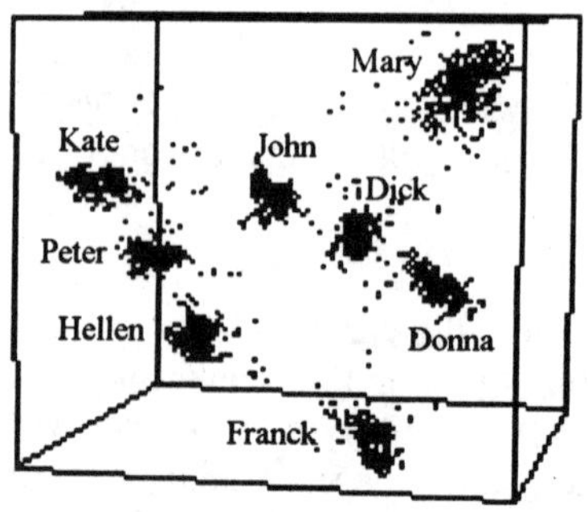

Figure 4: Discrimination between fillers of the *patient* role (DCs 1 to 3, with 9216 points)

For each role, the points corresponding to different fillers make relatively dense and well separated clusters. The networks appear to dedicate independent subspaces of the hidden unit state-space to the semantic roles. When projected on the subspace associated with a given role, the network states which represent sentences having a same word bound to this role form clusters. Since DA makes orthogonal projections of the space on corresponding subspaces, the very good clustering shows that the subspaces associated with the roles tend to be orthogonal.

Our results are in agreement with those obtained in [14] for multi-layer perceptrons trained to perform auto-association on small fragments of highly combinatorial corpora. The task here is significantly more difficult because it is sequential and the sequences corresponding to the active and passive voice versions of a sentence are very different.

For each proper name, a DA was performed on the network states, classified according to the semantic role to which the name is bound. Figure 5 shows the results for *Mary*.

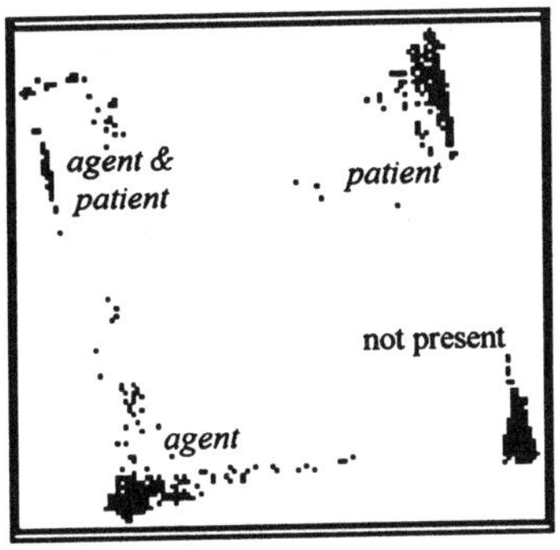

Figure 5: Corpus with *and* — discrimination between the semantic roles for *Mary* (DCs 1 and 2, with 9216 points)

The same good clustering is found for the other names. It appears that the networks also tend to dedicate orthogonal subspaces of the hidden unit state-space to the fillers of the *agent* and *patient* roles.

To better evaluate this result, we performed a similar analysis on networks trained and tested on a corpus whose sentences did not contain multiple bindings of any semantic role. Ten proper names and ten transitive verbs were employed to obtain 2000 active and passive voice sentences. The corresponding picture, presented in figure 6, shows that in this case the clustering associated to the different semantic roles of Mary is significantly worse. The high degree of variation inside each cluster shows that in this case the networks do not dedicate independent subspaces of the hidden unit state-space to the fillers of the *agent* and *patient* roles.

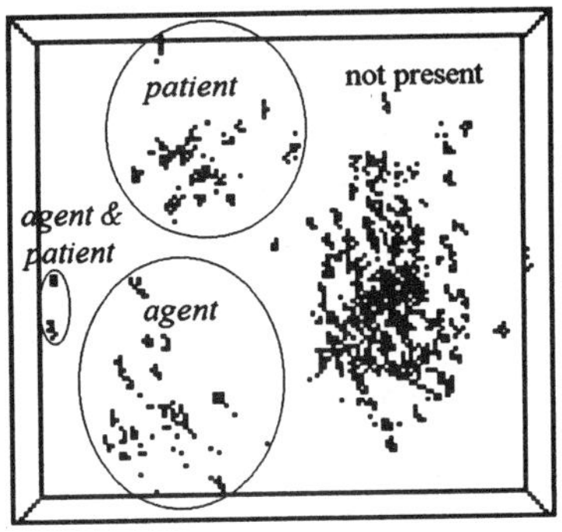

Figure 6: Corpus without *and* — discrimination between the semantic roles for *Mary* (DCs 1 and 2, with 2000 points)

We mention that for this second corpus the results given by DAs associated with the roles (some are presented in [3]) are highly similar to the ones presented here in figures 2 to 4. It follows that the difference between the clustering in figure 5 and the one in figure 6 can only be explained by the use or not of multiple bindings for the *agent* role.

IV. Discussion

In [11], tensor product (TP) representations of schemata regarded as sets of <filler | *role*> bindings were formally defined. If the roles are represented as vectors $\Psi_R(r)$ in a vectorial space V_R and the fillers as vectors $\Psi_F(f)$ in V_F, then the representation of a binding is defined, in a vectorial space V, as

$$\Psi_b\left(f_i \middle| r_j\right) = \Psi_F\left(f_i\right) \otimes \Psi_R\left(r_j\right),$$

$\otimes$ being the tensor product. The representation of a schema containing several bindings is the vectorial sum of the representations of its individual bindings. When the roles are represented by orthogonal vectors, we can say that orthogonal subspaces of V — each having the dimension of V_F — are associated with the roles; the representations of all the schemata containing a given <filler | *role*> binding have identical projections on the subspace associated with the role. When a role can have multiple bindings in a same schema, a sufficient condition for the representation to be non-ambiguous is to employ linearly independent vectors for the fillers.

Quite similarly, the networks we trained tend to dedicate orthogonal subspaces of the hidden unit state-space to the semantic roles; when projected on the subspace associated with a given role, the network states representing sentences with a same word bound to this role form tight clusters. Also, if several fillers can be bound to a same role at the same time, the subspaces associated with these fillers tend to be orthogonal. But can we speak of *individual* representations of the roles and of the fillers, as we did for TP representations? Ideally, we can define the representation of a role, $\Psi_R(r)$, based upon the subspace found by DA to be associated with it. Then, we define the representation of a filler, $\Psi_F(f)$, knowing the centre of the cluster corresponding to this filler in the subspace associated with one of the roles it can be bound to. Now we can define, for each role, a non-linear function Γ allowing us to approximate the representations of a binding by

$$\Psi_b(f_i|r_j) = \Gamma_j[\Psi_F(f_i)] \otimes \Psi_R(r_j).$$

The representation of a sentence is then approximated by the vectorial sum of the representations of its individual bindings.

We can now see the relationship between TP representations, as defined in [11], and an idealisation of the internal representations learning develops in the networks.

The task and network architecture we employed here share important features with the ones in [9], [12] and [13]. We believe that an analysis of the hidden layer of the simple recurrent networks used in [9], and of the *sentence/story gestalt* layer of the networks in [13] and [12] should give essentially similar results.

V. Conclusion

We studied the internal representations developed by RNs learning to translate sequences of words composing sentences into corresponding sets of <word | semantic role> bindings. We showed that these representations do possess an internal structure expressing the corresponding structure of the sentences. Indeed, when the learning corpora allow RNs to correctly infer the presence of independent roles (variables) in the sentences to be represented, orthogonal subspaces are dedicated to these roles. When projected on the subspace dedicated to a given role, the vectors representing sentences having a same word bound to this role form clusters. Also, if the sentences in the training corpus contain multiple bindings for certain roles, networks tend to dedicate orthogonal subspaces to the fillers of these roles.

The analysis allowed us to find a relationship between the internal representations developed by learning and tensor product representations, formally defined in [11].

The reliable translation of structural similarities between entities into vectorial similarities between their representations accounts for at least some of the systematicity required by high-level tasks.

Acknowledgements

The author is grateful to Jean-François Jodouin and Daniel Memmi for very useful discussions and advice. The author is supported by PhD grant 900621 from the French Government.

References

[1] A. Bloesch and J. Wiles, "Data reduction and display techniques for representations in hidden unit space", poster presented at the *First Indiana Conference on Dynamics in Cognition*, November 1991, Indiana University, Bloomington, Indiana.

[2] A. Cleeremans, D. Servan-Schreiber and J. L. McClelland, "Finite state automata and simple recurrent networks", *Neural Computation*, vol. 1, pp. 372-381, 1989.

[3] M. Crucianu, "Looking for structured representations in recurrent networks". In M. C. Mozer, P. Smolensky, D. S. Touretzky, J. L. Elman and A. S. Weigend (Eds.), Proceedings of the 1993 Connectionist Models Summer School (pp. 170-177). Hillsdale, NJ: Erlbaum Associates.

[4] J. L. Elman, "Distributed representations, simple recurrent networks and grammatical structure", *Machine Learning*, vol. 7, pp. 195-224, 1991.

[5] J. A. Fodor and Z. W. Pylyshyn, "Connectionism and cognitive architecture: a critical analysis", *Cognition*, vol. 28, pp. 3-71, 1988.

[6] P. Gallinari, S. Thiria, F. Badran and F. Fogelman-Soulié, "On the relations between discriminant analysis and multilayer perceptrons", *Neural Networks*, vol. 4, pp. 349-360, 1991.

[7] T. van Gelder, "Compositionality : a connectionist variation on a classical theme", *Cognitive Science*, vol. 14, pp. 355-384, 1990.

[8] J.-F. Jodouin, "Réseaux de neurones et traitement du langage naturel: étude des réseaux de neurones récurrents et de leurs représentations", *Thèse de Docteur en Sciences*, Université de Paris-Sud, Orsay, France, 1993.

[9] R. Miikkulainen and M. G. Dyer, "Natural language processing with modular PDP networks and a distributed lexicon", *Cognitive Science*, vol. 15, pp. 343-400, 1991.

[10] D. E. Rumelhart, G. E. Hinton and R. J. Williams, "Learning internal representations by error propagation", in Rumelhart, D. E., McClelland, J. L. (1986, eds.): *Parallel distributed processing: explorations in the microstructure of cognition*, Vol.2: Psychological and biological models, MIT Press, pp. 7-57, 1986.

[11] P. Smolensky, "Tensor product variable binding and the representation of symbolic structures in connectionist systems", *Artificial Intelligence*, vol. 46, pp. 159-216, 1990.

[12] M. F. St. John, "The story gestalt: a model of knowledge-intensive processes in text comprehension", *Cognitive Science*, vol. 16, pp. 271-306, 1992.

[13] M. F. St. John and J. L. McClelland, "Learning and applying contextual constraints in sentence comprehension", *Artificial Intelligence*, vol. 46, pp. 217-256, 1990.

[14] J. Wiles, "Representation of variables and their values in neural networks", presented at the 15th Annual Meeting of the Cognitive Science Society, Boulder, Colorado, June 1993.

[15] J. Wiles and M. Ollila, "Intersecting regions: the key to combinatorial structure in hidden unit space", in Hansen, S. J., Cowan, J. D., Giles, C. L. (eds.): *Advances in Neural Information Processing Systems* 5, pp. 27-33, Morgan-Kaufmann, San Mateo, California, 1993.

Normalizing Internal Representations for Speech Classification

Ramesh R. Sarukkai, and Dana H. Ballard

Abstract—

Speech segments are encoded using an auto-associative network, and the possibility of matching the hidden unit activation sequences for classification is studied. Surprisingly good discrimination can be achieved by matching the lower dimensional projections of the unknown with template speech patterns. The possibility of normalizing the variations of the hidden unit activation sequences is then explored. In particular, experiments demostrate the advantage of the presented technique for single speaker, and multi-speaker syllable distinction tasks. Normalization of the encoded representations of sounds within classes, and across speakers improves results significantly.

I. Introduction

Connectionist models[1] have been applied to speech recognition with reasonable success. Common neural network architectures applied include time delay neural networks (TDNN), recurrent networks, multilayer feed-forward classifiers, and combination techniques with conventional speech recognition techniques such as Hidden Markov Models (HMM).

Although it has been proven that auto-associative feedforward networks with linear units performs Principal Component analysis[3], it seems like networks with sigmoidal units tend to learn equal variance encodings[4]. It would be interesting to know whether this encoded information can itself be used for classification directly by matching, and surprisingly, experiments don't seem to have been performed in that direction. For instance, Elman and Zipser[2] applied auto-associative networks to single speaker speech recognition, and classified the signals using the hidden representation as input to another level, rather than measuring the invariant properties of such encodings by themselves. This paper would throw light on the issue of whether the encoding contains useful information about the training patterns, or whether it is just a complex compressed version of the training speech patterns.

The authors are with the Dept. of Computer Science, University of Rochester, Rochester, NY-14627

In addition, it may be a good idea to refine these representations using additional constraints. One particular constraint that we study in this paper is to match the hidden unit representations for different templates for the same sound. In addition, in the case where templates are from multiple speakers, this process may be viewed as a form of *speaker normalization*.

II. Is Matching Hidden Unit Activation Sequences a Good Idea?

A. Motivation

Elman and Zipser[2] have studied feed-forward architectures that perform simple speech recognition. Their network consisted of 320 input nodes, 2 to 6 hidden nodes, and as many output nodes as there were distinct consonant-vowel sequences to be distinguished. Their set of experiments included labelling of speech samples: i.e. some part of the network was actually trained to activate the correct output (corresponding to a label) for a given input. In one of their experiments, they used an auto-associative scheme to encode the input speech, and used these encodings to adapt another network to perform the labelling task. Surprisingly, they have not tried matching the actual hidden unit activations (auto-associative encoding of the spectrogram) on test data. Although, it is interesting to note that the encodings have captured enough information to be substituted for the original speech, it would be useful to examine the invariance of the low dimensional projections for different samples of speech segments.

An important issue in speech modelling is the choice of the basic unit of representation: In particular, the time window used to divide the speech into different parts with relevant cues is critical. Usually, the whole speech segment (e.g. syllable) is input to the neural network, to get appropriate activations. We propose to increase the temporal resolution of coding, and use the sequence of encodings as a valuable source of representation. The advantages of

0-7803-1901-X/94 $4.00 ©1994 IEEE

finer temporal refinement is one of better parameter sharing, and improved pronunciation optimization.

Given that temporal refinement is a good idea, the appropriate window size should be determined. One would expect that as the window size decreases, the encoding will be able to capture the information quite accurately. As the window size increases, and the dimension (or number of bits) of code remains constant, the reproductions will tend to be less exact than before. Thus, from the point of view of exact replication, small time windows are good. However, encodings using small time windows exhibit very high variability, and are not viable options for matching. Thus, very small time windows is a bad idea. Experiments led us to choose a time window of 20ms.

This study will throw some light on whether auto-associative encodings tend to cluster sounds, which one perceives as similar, nearby in the temporal encoding space, and different ones apart. Input speech is divided into time windows, and an auto-associative network is trained to encode such input patterns. Template sequences of hidden unit encodings are stored for matching later with unknown speech. Unknown speech is fedforward through the auto-associative network, and hidden unit sequences compared with the template sequences. Thus, this scheme is unsupervised in the sense that the auto-association proceeds without any labelling(teaching) signal. However, the template making process can be viewed as *a post-learning labelling* process. The presented approach can be viewed as an intermediate between purely regression based approaches (such as neural networks which construct global decision boundaries), and local, purely memory based (nearest neighbor) approaches to classification.

B. Experimental Results

Speech was sampled at a frequency of 8KHz. The speech signal was filtered through a first order difference filter. Segmentation was done manually, by removing all but 50msec of speech before stop release and after stop release. Fast Fourier transform was performed on the speech signal every sixteen time steps (after being applied to a Hamming window)[1], giving frequency intensity values for 9 frequencies linearly spaced between 0 and 4000. No overlapping time windows were used.

The input to the network consisted of 90 units, corresponding to ten blocks of 9 FFT frequency intensity values. Ten hidden units were used. The auto-associative network consisted of 90 output units. The inputs were normalized between 0 and 1 linearly. *QuickProp*[5], a modified version of back-propagation was used to perform the following experiments. Unless otherwise stated, the learning rate was 0.1, the momentum factor was set to 0.3 after ten epochs, and a weight decay factor of -0.0001 was in effect. All weights were initialized to lie between -0.7 and +0.7. Split epsilon scheme was used. Sigmoid Prime offset was 0.1. Rather than running the learning methods till an error criteria was met, training was carried out for a fixed number of epochs, and the correct classification capability evaluated. This was also done to compare the performances of different trails of the techniques presented. The segmented tokens constituted five sets of inputs to the auto-associative network giving a temporal sequence of five time steps[2].

C. Recorded Tokens

Over fifty samples each of Ba,Pa and Da syllables were recorded from a single speaker. These were edited, and exactly fifty tokens of each were arbitrarily chosen, and single speaker experiments were performed only on these tokens. In the case of multi-speaker data, ten tokens of each syllable were recorded from six speakers, thus a total of 180 speech tokens. The male speaker used for recording the single speaker data was re-recorded as a part of the multi-speaker set. Among the six, three were non-native English speakers, and three were North American native English speakers. One was a woman. Thus, the tokens exhibited a high amount of variability in accent, pitch etc. [3]

D. Ba-Pa Discrimination- Single Speaker Training and Test tokens

Experiment 1 (see figure 1) tests the Ba-Pa distinction task for a single speaker. Ba is a voiced stop whereas Pa is a voiceless stop. Our training set for the auto-associative net was 5 tokens of Ba and 5 tokens of Pa. Our total test set consisted of the remaining 90 speech tokens recorded from the same speaker. Training was performed for a 1000 epochs. Then the training speech tokens were fed-forward, and corresponding hidden activation sequences were stored as templates used for matching with unknown speech encodings. Nearest neighbor classification scheme was used. Figure 1 shows the statistics of ten trials for the single speaker training and test ex-

[1] 800 values were thus obtained in the segmented duration of 100 msec for each syllable.

[2] Since the time window chosen was 20ms, the 100ms segmented syllable token is represented as a sequence of 5 temporal encodings

[3] The segmented Ba, Pa, and Da tokens were randomly presented, and human subjects were asked to classify the tokens in one of 3 classes. Average performance was around 73%. As opposed to the usual practice of discarding tokens misclassified by humans, we chose to retain the "confusing" tokens, since real world speech would include such "production" errors.

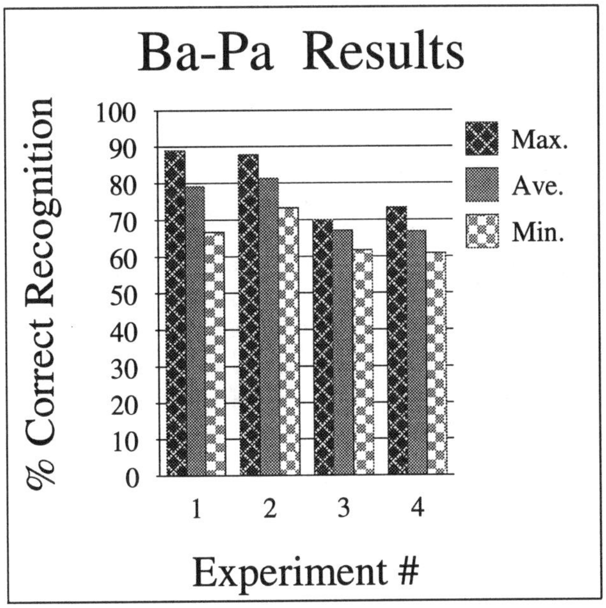

Figure 1: *Recognition results for Ba/Pa syllable Distinction. Single speaker training set. 10 trails were conducted for each experiment*

periment. As can be seen in figure 1, a maximum correct classification of 88.9% was achieved, with an average of 79.11% correct classification.

E. Ba-Pa Discrimination- Single Speaker Training, Multi-speaker test tokens

Experiment 3 (see figure 1) tested whether the auto-associative mapping developed by the network on the single speaker training set could capture some speaker independent properties. The experiment was the same as Experiment 1, except that the multi-speaker tokens were used as the test set. The results were well above chance (see figure 1). A maximum of 70% correct classification was achieved, with the average being 67.08%.

F. Ba-Pa Discrimination- Multi-speaker training and testing

Experiment 5 (figure 2) trained the network with 2 Ba and Pa samples from 3 of the six speakers. Thus, 12 tokens were used to train the network (one speaker was the woman, and the other two training speakers were males). The test set consisted of 112 tokens, with 60 tokens from the 3 untrained speakers. A maximum recognition of 73.2% was achieved with an average of 64.6%.

G. Ba-Da Discrimination- Single Speaker Training and Test tokens

Now consider the problem of Ba-Da distinction. This is a very difficult task, especially since both Ba, and Da are voiced stops. The procedure was as for the Ba-Pa single speaker train and test experiments described previously. A maximum of 83.33% recognition was achieved (see experiment 9, figure 3) and the average classification rate over ten trials was 76.22%.

H. Ba-Da Discrimination- Single Speaker Training, Multi-speaker test tokens

As before, 10 single speaker training tokens were used to train the auto-associative network, and build the templates. Testing was done by classifying the multi-speaker data by matching with the single speaker templates. A maximum of 68.33% correct classification was achieved (experiment 11, figure 3), with the average being 61.67%. The idea behind this experiment was to see if the performance was purely random or not(50%).

I. Ba-Da Discrimination- Multi-speaker training and testing

Lastly, multi-speaker training and testing experiments were done as in the Ba-Pa case. A maximum of 71.3% recognition was achieved, and the average over ten trials was 63.70%. The results are summarized in figure 4 (experiment 13).

J. Discussion

It is clear from the results with single speaker training and test sets that matching sequences of low-dimensional projections (encodings) for classification is promising. In some sense, it is surprising that one layer encoders can produce such uniformly, distinguishable representations of inputs belonging to different classes. Keeping in mind the variability in accent, pitch etc of the multi-speaker data, correct classification rates of over 70% indicate that speaker invariant properties have been captured in the encoding sequences. However, the hidden activation sequence templates of similar sounds for multiple speakers do differ drastically, which prompted us to explore the idea of normalizing the internal representations with the hope of improving performance.

III. Normalizing Hidden Unit Representations

A. Motivation

Additional constraints on the hidden encodings would enable the system to develop a more general representation. For instance, in the Ba-Pa distinction task, the hidden activation sequences for the five training templates differ due to the variability in the speech signals for the same sounds. We propose to add in constraints on the hidden unit representation such as forcing all the five templates for the same sound to have closer representations. This can be done by a *normalization process*, as follows:

1 • Train network to perform auto-association as usual.

2 • Get single template Hidden Activation Sequence for each sound.

3 • Freeze hidden to output weights. Adapt input to hidden weights so that all training speech signals which correspond to the same label produce the maximum-discriminant *fixed* hidden activation sequences.

The idea is to reduce variability in representation across different training samples, and hope to reduce the error on the test set in this process. In the case of multi-speaker training set, the proposed scheme can be expected to perform some form of *speaker normalization*. Thus, the network is trained for distinguishing sounds by presenting sets of sounds belonging to different classes[4]. Thus, after some internal representation of the sounds has been developed, the system chooses the set of samples which have internal representations which are farthest from each other, and use them to normalize the other representations towards the "most discriminant" encoding sequence. Thus speech segments belonging to the same class are associated to each other by sharing a common hidden representation. As the results below indicate, the normalization process improves the correct classification rates significantly in some cases.

B. *Ba-Pa Discrimination- Single Speaker Training and Test tokens*

As in experiment 1, the auto-associative network was trained upto 1000 epochs. After training, the 5 templates of Ba-Pa pairs were made. The pair with the maximum difference in the hidden activation sequence was taken as the *fixed template* to normalize. The input to hidden weights were then adapted so as to force all the remaining syllables to produce the *fixed template* hidden activation sequence. This training was done for 150 epochs with a learning rate of 0.1. Then templates of the 5 Ba and Pa tokens were got after a feed-forward process, and used for matching. This normalization scheme was used in all the following experiments too. The maximum recognition rate achieved (see experiment 2, figure 1) in 10 trials was 87.8%, and the average recognition rate was 81.3%, an improvement of over 2% than the un-normalized version.

C. *Ba-Pa Discrimination- Single Speaker Training, Multi-speaker test tokens*

This experiment (experiment 4, figure 1) is same as the previous one, except that the test set used was

[4]In our actual implementation, speech segments of different classes were randomly paired.

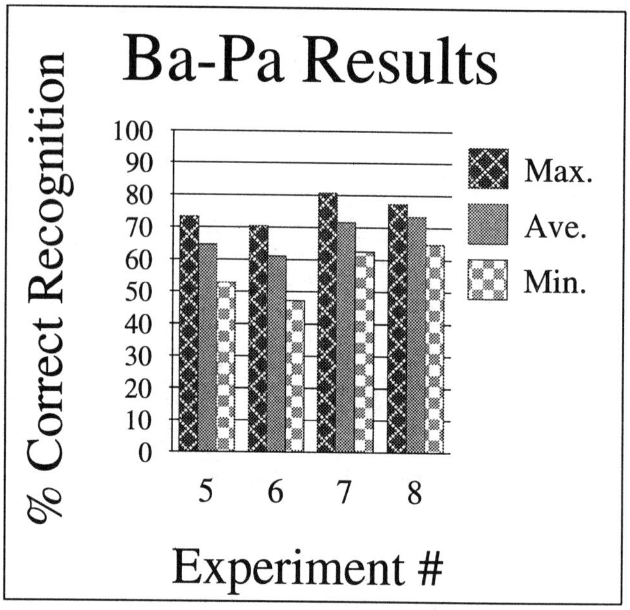

Figure 2: *Recognition results for Ba/Pa syllable Distinction- Multi-speaker Train and Test. 10 trails were conducted for each experiment*

the multi-speaker set. The maximum recognition rate was 73.3%, while the average over ten trials was 66.8%, 0.33% lesser than the un-normalized case.

D. *Ba-Pa Discrimination- Multi-speaker training and testing*

In the case of multi-speaker training data, the normalization process can be viewed as a form of *speaker normalization*. It should be noted that our training set consisted of two male speakers and one woman speaker. The average recognition rate (see experiment 6, figure 2) dropped by 3% from the un-normalized case to 61%. A maximum rate of 70.4% was achieved. This decrease in recognition can be attributed to the fact that highly varied internal representations (normalizing a womans voice to a mans) are being normalized. This led us to conduct experiments on a single gender, and is discussed later.

E. *Ba-Da Discrimination- Single Speaker Training and Test tokens*

The Ba-Da experiments were conducted in a similar fashion to the Ba-Pa experiments explained in the preceding subsections. For the single speaker training set case, normalizing various single speaker speech segments belonging to the same class improved performance by over 3%. The average recognition rate rose to 79.9%, while the maximum went up to 85.6%. Results are summarized for this experiment (expt. 10) in figure 3.

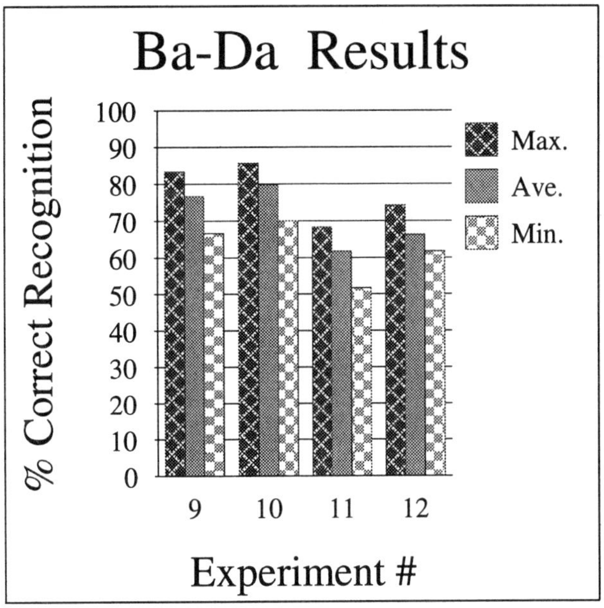

Figure 3: *Recognition results for Ba/Da syllable Distinction. Single speaker training set. 10 trails were conducted for each experiment*

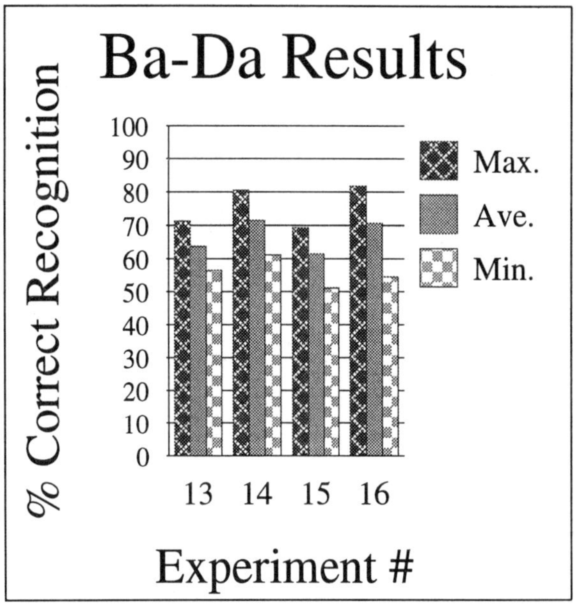

Figure 4: *Recognition results for Ba/Da syllable Distinction. Multi-speaker Train and Test. 10 trails were conducted for each experiment*

F. Ba-Da Discrimination- Single Speaker Training, Multi-speaker test tokens

Normalizing internal representations of various single speaker tokens improved the classification results on multi-speaker test data. The average over 10 trials rose to 66.25%, an improvement of over 4% than the un-normalized case. The maximum rate was 74.17%.(Experiment 12 in figure 3)

G. Ba-Da Discrimination- Multi-speaker training and testing

Multi-speaker recognition results improved significantly in the Ba-Da case when normalization was applied. A maximum of 80.6% was achieved, and the average correct classification rose by over 7% to 71.5%. The results for this experiment (expt. 14) are shown in figure 4.

H. Ba-Pa Discrimination- Normalization within speakers of the same gender

A normalization test over training and test sets of a single gender tokens was done to ascertain that the *speaker normalization* process is useful in correcting for speaker variance. It must be noted that in the multi-speaker train and test results presented previously, one of the training speakers was a woman. Thus, shifting the male templates to accommodate for the woman template could be a possible bottleneck to much higher improvement in performance.

Three male speakers (whose tokens were not used as training samples in the multi-speaker training set experiment discussed previously) were chosen and a 12 token Ba-Pa training set constructed. The test set consisted of 88 Ba and Pa tokens produced by only males. Without normalization, the performance (see figure 2: expt. 7 is un-normalized case, and expt. 8 is normalized case) on the test set was reasonable: average 71.6%, maximum 80.7%. However, with normalization performed, average correct classification over ten trials rose by 1.8% to 73.4%, while the maximum correct classification achieved was 77.3%.

I. Ba-Da Discrimination- Normalization within speakers of the same gender

Without normalization, average correct recognition over 10 trials was 61.4%, and the maximum was 69.3%. However, with the addition of the normalization process, average correct classification rose by over 9% to 70.6%, and the maximum was 81.8%. These results clearly indicate that normalization variations in representations of similar speakers improves overall performance on the test set. Results are summarized in figure 4 (expt. 15 is un-normalized case, and 16 is normalized case).

J. Discussion

Let us discuss the implications of the experimental results obtained in this section. Although performance did improve when normalization was done with hidden unit representations of speech segments of a single speaker, it did not improve significantly.

Normalizing variance of internal representations due to difference in speakers seems to improve performance in some cases. In particular, experiments where representations of speech produced by a woman and two men were normalized improved performance for the Ba-Da distinction task by over 7% on an average, while in the Ba-Pa case performance diminished marginally (0.3%). Normalizing with single gender speakers improved performance in both cases (over 9% in the Ba-Da case).

IV. Conclusions and Future Work

The possibility of encoding speech segments, and using temporal sequences for matching was explored in this paper. In particular, it led us to examine the possibility of refining the internal representations developed by auto-associative networks so as to capture more general properties in the speech segments. The presented approach can be viewed as a combination of purely learning (such as neural networks which construct global decision boundaries), and purely memory based (nearest neighbor) approaches to classification. The invariant properties of internal representations was examined and methods to improve these representations explored. It is interesting to find that matching temporal sequences of internal representations with a few templates of speech tokens projected to a lower dimensions by single layer encoders can give good recognition rates. Scalability issues remain to be explored in the future. In addition, it would be interesting to study matching of internal representations obtained by networks with multi-layered encoders and decoders(eg. 5-layered net with intermediate bottleneck).

References

[1] Richard P. Lippmann, "Review of Neural Networks for Speech Recognition", *Neural Computation*, pp.374-392, 1989.

[2] Jeffrey Elman, and David Zipser, "Learning the hidden structure of speech", *J. Acoust. Soc. Am.*, vol. 83, April 1988.

[3] Pierre Baldi, and Kurt Hornik, "Neural networks and Principal Component Analysis: Learning from examples without local minima", *Neural Networks*, vol. 2, pp. 53-58, 1989.

[4] Suzanna Becker, "Unsupervised Learning Procedures for Neural Networks", *Intl. Jour. of Neural Systems*, vol. 2, Nos. 1 & 2 pp.17-33, 1991.

[5] Scott E. Fahlman, "Faster-Learning Variations on Back-Propagation: An Empirical Study", in **Proceedings of the 1988 Connectionist Models Summer School**, Pittsburg (1988), 38-51, Morgan Kaufmann.

Analysis and Pruning of Temporally Dynamic Neural Networks

Kamran Etemad
Center for Automation Research and
Department of Electrical Engineering
University of Maryland
College Park, MD 20742

***Abstract*— An algorithm for pruning temporally dynamic neural networks is suggested. A set of "Importance and Similarity Measures" are defined for both links and nodes of the network, which are computed recursively from output to input. Pruning and analysis of the network can be performed based on these importance and similarity measures. The suggested algorithm is tested on several networks including a "Multi-rate Temporal Flow Model" which is trained for a speaker independent phoneme recognition task.**

I. INTRODUCTION

Temporally Dynamic Neural Networks with time delay and recurrent structures have been found to be useful in temporal pattern analysis (e.g. speech recognition [1][2][3] and prediction [4], acoustic signal processing and even optical character recognition).

In the design of such networks it is desirable to have a final network that achieves the required performance with a minimum number of parameters. Networks of small size (i.e. number of nodes and links) are less susceptible to over training and have better generalization capability[5].

Suitable network architectures can be obtained if in the process of design knowledge about the structure and nature of desired signal or class of signals is taken into account[6]. Also, since there is no solid theory for optimal selection of network topology (i.e. number of layers and number of nodes in each layer), network growing and network pruning techniques are suggested and used.

The main idea of network pruning is to identify and remove redundancies in the network. Removing redundancies and using a small size network with fewer parameters enable us to achieve better generalization and simplify network analysis. Typically pruning may cause some degradation in the overall performance, so the pruned networks are often post-trained for further fine-tuning.

There have been some studies on pruning neural networks mostly for temporally static networks used in static pattern classification. Methods based on trial and error, sensitivity analysis [7] and second order derivatives of the network energy function [8] have been suggested. Some of the methods suggested for static networks can be extended to or modified for dynamic network pruning.

However, the analysis and pruning of temporally dynamic networks with large number of time varying inputs are more involved and require special considerations. In the following an alternative pruning algorithm for such networks and inputs is proposed and tested.

II. VISUAL INSPECTION OF WEIGHTED ACTIVATIONS

The basic idea relies on the inspection of weighted activations at the input of each neural unit. Basically the objective is to discard all units that are not responsive to desired parts of the input sequences, i.e. those units (or weighted activations) that are almost constant or have very small deviations from their mean value during selected time intervals.

Consider the weighted activations $\{V_{ij} = w_{ij}U_i\}$ as stochastic signals in time whose sum determines the net effect of the previous layer on the output of the destination unit U_j, as shown schematically in Figure 1.

All connections whose corresponding signals are "almost constant" over the selected intervals have negligible effects on the classification performance, so removing those and compensating their effects by threshold adjustments in the destination units should not change the overall performance significantly. Also all but one of the connections whose corresponding signals are "similar" (up to a scalar) are redundant, because they convey the same information. So by retaining just one of those and adjusting its weight nothing should change dramatically. If all connections originating from a unit have negligible dynamic effects on their destination then that unit along with all links connected to it can be removed.

Figure.1 shows the basic idea, where the connections to unit U_6 are inspected. It is clear that w_{46} can be removed because the change in its corre-

0-7803-1901-X/94 $4.00 ©1994 IEEE

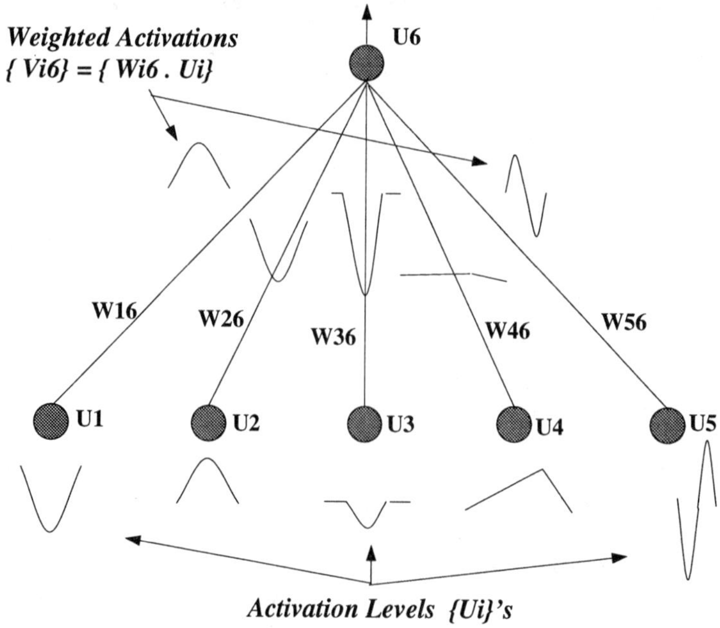

Figure 1: Inspecting the weighted activations at the input of a neural unit.

sponding weighted activation $V_{46} = w_{46}.U_4$ is small. Also w_{26} can be removed because its corresponding weighted activation as a function of time is similar to that of w_{16}, i.e. $V_{26} \propto V_{16}$ approximately. For each unit, the same set of inspections has to be made for all input patterns.

III. Entropy Based Importance and Redundancy Measures

In order to handle a large number of input sequences and to put these ideas into a computational framework, for each connection and unit in the network we define a so-called "Importance Measure"(Imp). Consider again the signals obtained by concatenating weighted activations in time, chopped at selected intervals in the input sequence.

For each of these random signals V_{ij} the importance measure must show the amount of information or activity within selected time intervals. If V_{ij}'s can be considered to be approximately stationary over the selected intervals, one sensible choice would be the entropy of the random signal V_{ij}. Therefore, for connection weight w_{ij}, the link from unit i to unit j,

$$Imp(V_{ij}) \equiv h(V_{ij}) \qquad (1)$$

where $h(.)$ is Shannon's entropy function.

Based on the Imp's for the connection weights one can define the importance of neural units. For the ith neural unit,

$$Imp(U_i) \equiv \sum_j (Imp(w_{ij})\ Imp(U_j)) \qquad (2)$$

which is based on the intuitive idea that the importance of each unit in the network depends on the contributions of the weighted activations emerging from that unit and on the importance of their destinations. Importance measures should be compared within each layer, so they should be normalized for each network layer separately. Using equation (2), the importance values for the units are calculated recursively from the output layer toward the input. Therefore, normalized importance factors have to be assigned to each output unit depending on the purpose of the analysis.

In order to measure the similarity or redundancy $Red(.)$ between any pair of random signals V_{ij} and V_{kj} in terms of their information content, the "Mutual Information" between them is considered. Therefore,

$$Red(V_{ij}, V_{kj}) \equiv I(V_{ij}, V_{kj}) \qquad (3)$$

If we assume the the random signals $\{V_{ij}\}$ are Gaussian we can write,

$$Imp(V_{ij}) \propto\ log(K.w_{ij}^2\ Var(U_i)) \qquad (4)$$

where K is a constant, so that Imp of a link is a monotonically increasing function of the variance of the signal it carries i.e. V_{ij}.

Also, in computing $Red(.)$ since only similarity in information content is considered, without loss of

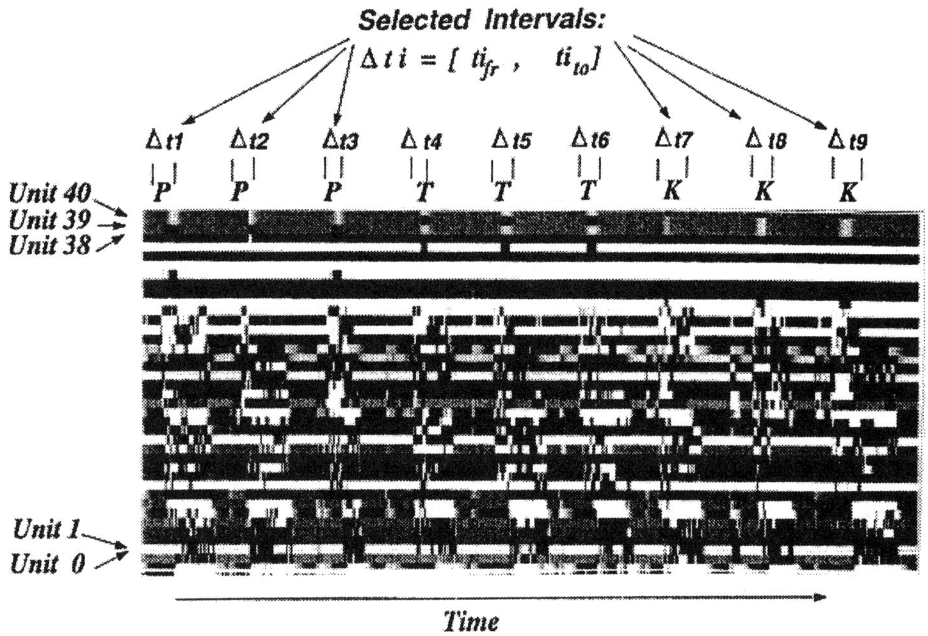

Figure 2: Outputs of hidden and output units for nine input examples. Spotting "desired time intervals" for computing Importance Measures.

generality we may assume (or make) the two random signals to be of zero mean and unit variance. Thus if V_{ij} and V_{kj} are jointly Gaussian with correlation coefficient ρ we have,

$$Red(V_{ij}, V_{kj}) \propto log(K.\frac{1}{1-\rho^2}) \qquad (5)$$

which is monotonically increasing with ρ and $|\rho| < 1$. So in this case, comparatively, one may just look at the variance and correlation coefficient of the signals to measure their activities and "similarities" respectively.

In fact Gaussian assumption is not needed, because this comparison is valid for all random signals for which the entropy and mutual information are monotonically increasing functions of variance and correlation coefficient respectively. Also the arguments, as well as relations (4),(5) and (2), are still valid if $\{V_{ij}\}$'s are not stationary.

IV. Pruning and Analysis

First of all the following consideration has to be taken into acount:

In some cases each input example contains not only the desired frames but also their context frames. For example, in our experiment each input example includes the stop phoneme, its previous closure and the following vowel (Figure 2). Variations of $\{V_{ij}\}$ far from the desired process (i.e. context frames far away from the desired frames) are of no significance. Therefore the first step is to concatenate all input sequences clipped a few frames before and after the desired time intervals and to concentrate on important variations only in those time intervals. Note that some of the preceding and following frames should be included because of the memory span of the network and delays associated with the propagation of activations in the network (Figure 2).

Then based on assumptions in the previous section,

- To compare the information content and importance of each link or node it suffices to look at the variances of the weighted activations as given by (4) and (2) and to normalize them for each layer. One may define a threshold for Imp based on which "less important" units or links are removed.
- To identify and remove "similar inputs" to each unit U_j, one can compute and compare the correlation coefficient of the $\{V_{ij}\}$'s for all i's. A large correlation coefficient ρ shows highly correlated inputs, which means that one of the inputs is redundant and can be removed.
- Removal of each inactive link requires adjustment in the threshold of its destination unit. This adjustment is done by adding the mean value of the weighted activation corresponding to the removed link to the threshold of desti-

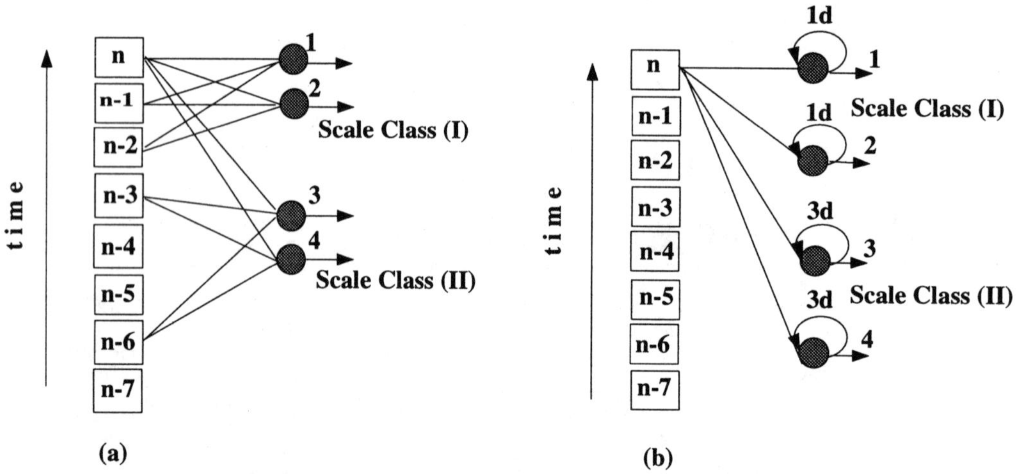

Figure 3: Modifications in (a) TDNN and (b) TFM architectures that provide multi-rate/scale views of input signal. Units in each "scale class" "look" at their incoming activations from previous layers at different rates [6].

nation unit. Also for every set of similar V_{ij}'s the connection weight of the retained one has to be adjusted to compensate for the removal of the others. So, if V_{ij} and V_{kj} are two such similar signals, we may assume approximately that $V_{ij} \approx \alpha.V_{kj}$ for some scalar α. Thus one can remove w_{kj} and change w_{ij} to $(1+\alpha).w_{ij}$.

- As mentioned above because of the recursive form of equation(2) one has to assign a set of values for *Imp*'s for output units. By different such assignments one can perform different kinds of analysis. In our phoneme recognition experiment, outputs correspond to p, t, k. By assigning $\{1,0,0\}$ to their importances respectively, we will be able to look at units and features that are important for detecting *p*'s only. For pruning however, we normally assign (1, 1, 1) to include all important elements involved in classification. Tracing $\{Imp\}$'s recursively back to the input layer, one can estimate the importance of each of input feature vector components.

Note that these kinds of redundancies might not be detected using sensitivity analysis or other static network pruning methods. For example a link of large weight from an almost constant unit can not be considered redundant statically, because it has a large effect on the total input activation to its destination unit. Also several input signals may carry similar but very important information to their destination, so none of them can be considered as redundant and removed without the suggested observations and adjustments.

Thus, based on these relative importance measures one can tell for each unit in the network how important it is compared to the other units in that layer, and which of the links at its input are redundant.

Thus by setting an appropriate threshold one can discard all the inactive units and links and hence prune the initially fully connected network. The result of these computations is an ordered list of important inputs for each unit, along with the importances of units. Based on a preset threshold for the pruning process, a network description for a simplified network can be generated.

As mentioned above one expects to have slightly inferior performance for the resulting network. Performance can be improved by considering the pruned network as an initial network description and post-training it. The final net will have a smaller number of links and by looking at the outputs of the algorithm one can tell which components of the input feature vector have been considered and picked by the network as clues for its discrimination task. The number of removed links and nodes is a function of the pruning threshold and the size of the originally trained network.

V. Experiment, Results and Discussions

Having explained the suggested approach and its plausibility, the results of an experiment on speech data are presented.

The task is speaker independent discrimination of stop phonemes (i.e. $\{p,t,k\}$ and $\{b,d,g\}$, within their contexts (the preceding closure and the following vowel), extracted from the TIMIT database.

Training	/p,t,k/	/b,d,g/
AER.ORG	98%	96%
MSE.ORG	0.001	0.002
AER.PRN	95%	93%
MSE.PRN	0.0015	0.0027

Test	/p,t,k/	/b,d,g/
AER.ORG	88%	85%
MSE.ORG	0.003	0.0035
AER.PRN	87%	84%
MSE.PRN	0.0032	0.0041

Table 1: Average Error Rate and Mean Square Error of the original and pruned networks obtained for $/b,d,g/$ and $/p,t,k/$ discrimination tasks using MTFM. In the pruned network almost 20% of links and two hidden units are removed.

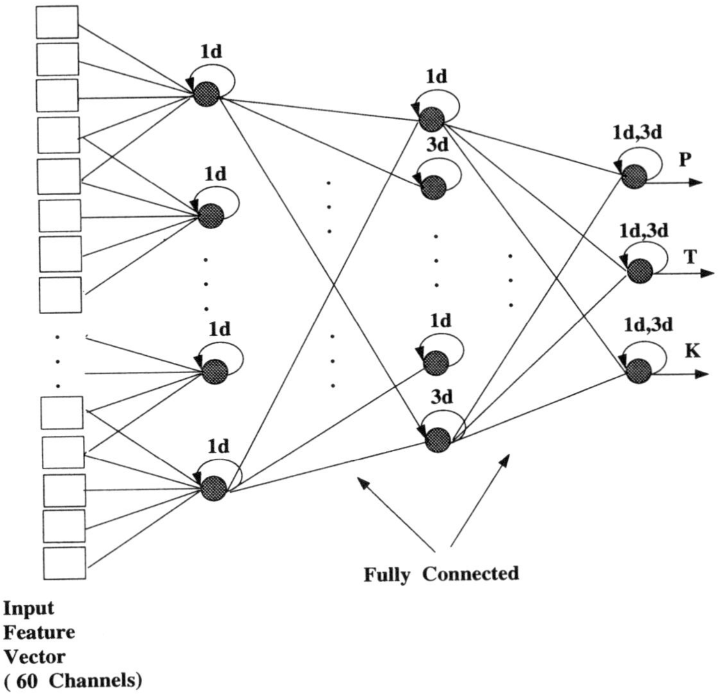

Figure 4: The Multi-rate TFM used in the experiment. The simple TFM network has the same architecture with self-recurrencies of only unit delay.

Input feature vectors are outputs of an auditory model[9] and consist of 60 channels centered at different frequencies.

Several network architectures were used in the experiment, including the Time Delay Neural network (TDNN[1][2]), the Temporal Flow Model (TFM [3]), and their Multi-rate modified forms (Figure. 3)[6]. These multi-rate modifications as well as some other technical issues involved in training such networks are explained in [6].

Fully connected networks with large number of links and delayed links have more redundancies and their pruning results in relatively more simplifications. But generally and in terms of pruning performance similar results were obtained for all cases. Therefore, without any claim of optimality of the network models and performances obtained, the results of pruning of TFM and MTFM are provided.

Both networks have 60 input, 37 hidden, and 3 output units. For the Temporal Flow Model the mean square error converges to 0.0035 on the training set and to 0.006 on the test set. For the Modified TFM [6] the final normalized error per frame was about 0.001, and the average recognition score was about 98% on the training set and about 88% on the test set. By applying the suggested pruning method to MTFM about 20% of the connection weights and two hidden units were removed, and the resulted network was post-trained to give about 0.002 MSE per frame (Table 1). Using similar importance thresholds, the pruning of the simple TFM resulted in almost the same amount of "removals".

The small drop in recognition rate after pruning, on training set and even smaller decrease of performance on the test set shows that the pruned network, despite its small number of parameters, has almost the same performance on the training set with even better generalization to examples in the test set. This result along with similar results obtained on other network architectures show that the suggested method is appropriate for pruning temporally dynamic networks.

Further study has to be carried out about the application of these ideas to network analysis and selection of the "most important" input features. Also more general importance and similarity measures may be suggested and used.

One alternative approach to the analysis of temporally dynamic networks is to use some synthetic input test signals and observe the corresponding patterns of activities in hidden and output layers. A simple example of such an approach for a neural network based phoneme recognizer is given in [10]. A set of synthetically generated input FM signals are used to check if some of the neural units are sensitive to frequency transitions at the input. This kind of analysis can be extended to study the "temporal patterns" learned by the network.

Acknowledgement: I would like to thank Dr. Shihab Shamma and Dr. Raymond Watrous for their excellent ideas and suggestions and for helping me with both theoretical and practical problems.

VI. References

[1] N. Hataoka and A. Waibel,"Speaker independent phoneme recognition on TIMIT database using integrated time delay neural networks" Proc. ICNN 1990, Vol.1 , pp. 57-62.

[2] R.L. Watrous,"Phoneme discrimination using connectionist networks." Journ. of Acoust. Soc. of Am. 87(40) pp. 1753-1772, April 1990.

[3] R.L. Watrous, B. Ladendorf, G. Kuhn,"Complete gradient optimization of a recurrent network applied to /b/,/d/,/g/ discrimination" Journ. of Acoust. Soc. of Am. 87(3) pp. 1301-1309, March 1990.

[4] L. Wu, M.Niranjan and F. Fallside,"Non-linear Predictive Vector Quantization with Recurrent Neural Networks", IEEE Neural Networks for Signal Processing,NNSP'93, pp. 372-381.

[5] E.B. Baum and D. Haussler,"What size net gives valid generalization?", Neural Computation 1,1989, pp. 151-160.

[6] K. Etemad,"Phoneme recognition based on multiresolution and non-causal context", IEEE Neural Networks for Signal Processing,NNSP'93, pp. 343-352.

[7] S. Hashem," Sensitivity Analysis for Feed-forward Artificial Neural Networks with Differentiable Activation Functions", IJCNN 1992, Baltimore, Vol. 1, pp. 419-425.

[8] B. Hassibi, D. G. Stork and G.J. Wolff,"Optimal Brain Surgeon and general network pruning", Proc. ICNN 93, Vol. 1, pp. 293-299.

[9] S. Shamma,"Spatial and temporal processing in central auditory networks",Methods in Neural Modeling, Kock and Segev (editors), MIT Press, 1990. pp. 247-289.

[10] K. Etemad,"Temporally dynamic neural networks for speaker independent phoneme recognition", Masters Thesis, University of Maryland, MD, 1993, Institute for Systems Research Technical Report No. M.S. 93-17.

Diminishing the number of nodes in multi-layered neural networks

Pascal NOCERA, Régis QUELAVOINE

Université d'Avignon et des Pays de Vaucluse,
Laboratoire d'Informatique 33, rue L. Pasteur 84000 Avignon

Abstract.
We propose in this paper two ways for diminishing the size of a multi-layered neural network trained to recognise French vowels. The first deals with the hidden layers : the study of the variation of the outputs of each node gives us information on its very discrimination power, and then allows us to reduce the size of the network. The second involves the input nodes : by the examination of the connecting weights between the input nodes and the following hidden layer, we can determinate which features are actually relevant for our classification problem, and then eliminate the useless ones. Through the problem of recognising the French vowel /a/, we show that we can obtain a reduced structure that still can learn.

1. Introduction.

The aim of our work is to build reduced neural networks for the recognition of the French vowels : the optimal size leads to a fast computable device along with a good generalisation ability. In this paper, we only take a look on the /a/. We cannot cut some output nodes, since we only have one here; we will focus upon hidden layers themselves, keeping the only important nodes in regard of the variation of their outputs, and then upon input nodes, eliminating the useless features through the examination of the connection weights with the following layer.

2. Multi-layered neural networks.

For the classification of the different French vowels, the expert cannot give us simple rules, and signal processing outputs are not easy to understand. Hopefully, neural networks can compensate this ignorance, and multi-layered ones, with backpropagation, appear as very efficient in supervised learning [3], and proved it in many cases [5].

We use the classical sigmoïd function : $f(x) = \frac{1}{1+e^{-x}}$, but in order to decrease the effect of "flat spot", we add a bias (0.1) to its derivative f ' [4].

Also common, the correction of a weight between node i and j at the time t is of the form :

$$0 < \alpha, \beta \le 1 \text{ and } \Delta W_{ij}(t) = \alpha \cdot \Delta W_{ij}(t-1) - \beta \cdot \frac{\partial E}{\partial W_{ij}(t)} ,$$

this allowing to find a solution in a limited number of utterance while learning.
Following [1], it is better to build a network for each vowel, so we can adapt each structure independently for its aim and then obtain better results than with a single generalist network. Moreover, the reduced networks contain the relevant piece of information for each class, by this way they can give the hints the expert cannot. So what we do here with the /a/ is also applicable for other vowels.

In [5], an "ideal" /a/ is used as a reference for finding the other occurrences of this phoneme with an adequate distance. A phoneme is found each time a wide enough area is close to the referent. Nevertheless, the great variability of context leads to use a low threshold, and then many bad detections come. The aim of the network is to decide whether or not a detection is a real /a/.
The inputs we use are 3 vectors (at the beginning, the middle and the end of the phoneme) of 24 features each, corresponding to a Linear Prediction Coding of the signal, grouped on a Mel scale. To be independent from the order of the 409 examples while learning, they are randomly taken into account for each utterance.

0-7803-1901-X/94 $4.00 ©1994 IEEE

3. Normalisation of the inputs.

In order to increase the speed of learning, and decrease the error rate, we study the influence of inputs' variation upon outputs : we notice that a very significant input with low amplitude will have no effect in a network if there are other useless inputs with greater extent [6]. Moreover, we need this normalisation if we want to compare the weights in relation with these inputs.

Example : let us use a 2 - 1 - 1 network (2 inputs, 1 hidden node, 1 output), inputs are of the form (0, 1) or (α, 1). We want to separate those beginning with 0 from the others. Here, the second input is useless. After several randomly generation of weights, we obtain the following averaged values :

α	utterance	|weight 1|	|weight 2|
0.01	4959	52.4	0.1
0.1	270	13.9	0.2
1	34	4.8	1.1

As we can see, the number of utterances needed to reach a solution decrease with the growth of α. Weight 1 takes bigger values while weight 2 keeps constant, this is very interesting because the first feature is actually more important than the second !

So we can notice the direct relation between input extents and the quality and speed of the learning : all data must vary in a same range to avoid one overshadowing an other one.

Consequently, we normalise inputs independently :

let Xi(j) be the jth pattern of example i, min(j) = $\min_i$ Xi(j) and max(j) = $\max_i$ Xi(j), then for all i and j :

$$Xi(j) = \frac{Xi(j) - \min(j)}{\max(j) - \min(j)}$$

All data take range between 0 and 1, but in statistics, variances of different inputs being not equal, we change the relative importance of them. This is mathematically not seen by our neural networks. For a node j :
if

$$\alpha_i = \frac{1}{\max(i) - \min(i)} \quad \text{and} \quad \beta_i = -\alpha_i \min(i)$$

then

$$output_j = f(\sum_i weight_{ij}(\alpha_i input_i + \beta_i) + biasis_j)$$

so

$$output_j = f(\sum_i \alpha_i weight_{ij} input_i + \sum_i weight_{ij}\beta_i + biasis_j)$$

Weights compensate the α_i and biases β_i ! The network is now more efficient to use the width of each input for classification, diminishing the number of remnant errors, and speeding up the learning.
Using this idea with our classification problem gives good results :

> with a 72 - 36 - 1 network, there are still 24 errors while learning after 1000 utterances while 250 are enough to reach 0 error with normalisation.

4. Reducing the number of nodes in a hidden layer.

A node giving always the same output is a constant input for the following layer, varying only with the connection weights. Thus, we can cut it by changing the biases of the connected nodes, by example, the modification for the node j if we cut the node k (the output of node k is a quasi-constant) is of the form :

$$input_j = \sum_{i \neq k} (weight_{ij} \times output_i) + biasis_j + output_k \times weight_{ki}$$

Thus, we only add a constant to the biases of j.

Starting with a 72 - 36 - 1 network, 250 learning utterances to reach 0 error, we find a 72 - 15 - 1 one that needs 300 utterances.
Moreover, a reduced number of nodes in the hidden layer forces the network to use the inputs properly, and then the study of their connection's weights should give us information about their real importance.

5. Reducing the number of input nodes.

Constant or equally distributed features for all classes are of no interest in classification, and in the former example, we saw that weights tended to be proportional to the discrimination power of the corresponding input.
We can see it again in another example : with binary numbers coded with 4 digits, if we look for those greater than 3, the information is in the first and second inputs. With one of them, we can only explain 75% of the examples, so the second must be involved for at least 25%. After 50 different trials of learning, we find the following relative importance of the input's weights of the network.

- for inputs 3 and 4, variation between 1 and 5% of the sum of all input's weights,
- for input 1, between 27 and 70%,
- for input 2, between 27 and 69%,
- the sum of 1 and 2 vary between 90 and 97%.

Thus, we find that the weights are representative of the power of explanation for each feature !

The sum of weights corresponding to the good input are the biggest. This principle gives us a way to find where information is when we use unknown types of examples. We can also reduce the size of the networks with the elimination of inputs having the smallest weights (recognition will be faster). Though, we only can do this while learning remains efficient (not too long, not too many errors). At last, when adding a new input, we can easily compare its separation ability to others.

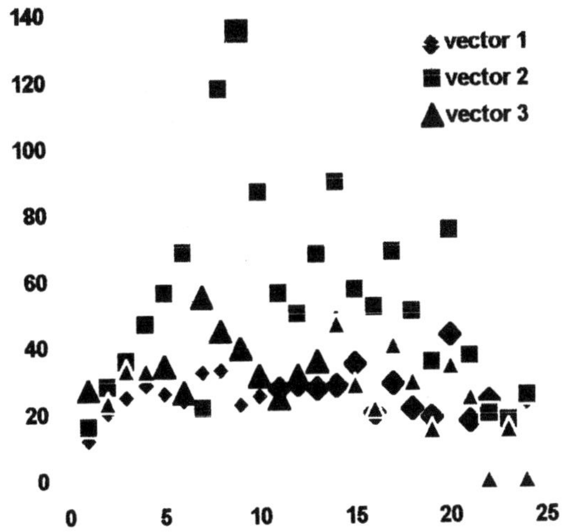

Fig.1

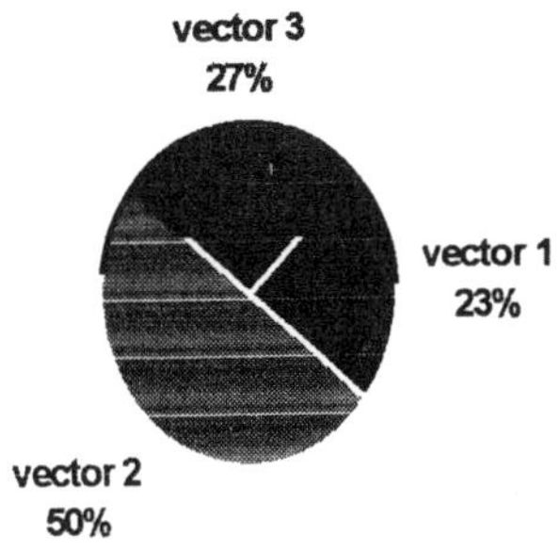

Fig.2

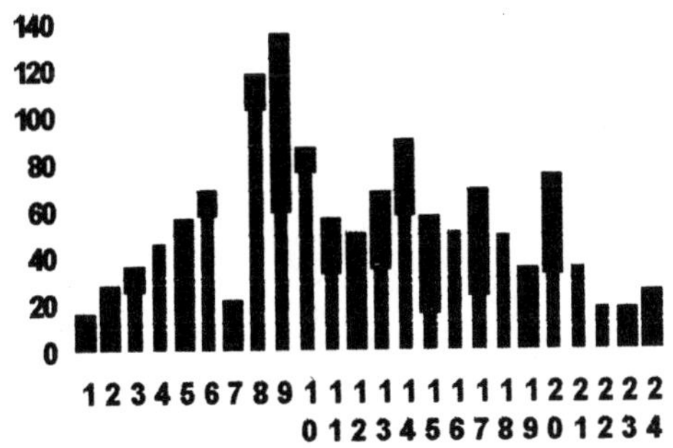

Fig.3

Fig.4

Fig.1 represent the Σ |weights| connected to the different features of each 3 input vectors. As we can see, the second vector (central one) is the most important, then comes the right context and at last the left context (vectors 3 and 1). Fig.2 show it again with the sum of all weights for each vector.

Now, it is interesting to look at the location of the biggest weights for the vector 2. In fact, the shape has got something common with the shape of the /a/ : the peaks are in same channels. Fig.3 is the graph of the weights of vector 2, and Fig.4 of the input values of an /a/ (without normalisation). We can see that the channels 8, 9,10, 13, 14, 17 and 20 denote high values at the same places. The first and last channels are also of poor importance for the classification of vowels, because having quite the same energy for every of these.
So, the direct relationship between inputs' power of classification and their weights is seen here : eliminating the nodes corresponding to the lower weights, thus the less important inputs, allows us to find the relevant features for our classification.

6. Conclusion.

Neural networks are not as easy to use as they seem to be. To achieve fast computing times with good results, we must adapt them to the very problem. Nevertheless, the normalisation of inputs increases greatly a network's power of classification, speeding up its learning time also. Moreover, reducing the number of nodes in the structure allows us to find were the information is through its weights. By this way, we can see what the network actually learns, so we are able to build an efficient structure of specialised networks, giving an accurate classification of the French vowels, with a low error rate.

7. Reference.

[1] Bochereau L., Bourgine P. : A generalist-specialist paradigm for multilayer neural networks. CEMAGREF, Antony.
[2] Bonastre J.F. : Stratégie analytique orientée connaissances pour la caractérisation et la reconnaissance du locuteur. Thèse, Université d'Avignon, jan94.
[3] Caudill M. : Avoiding the great backpropagation trap. AI expert, vol.6, n°7, jul91, pp.29,30,32,34,35.
[4] Fahlman S.E. : Faster learning variations of backpropagation : an empirical study. Connectionist Models Summer School, 1988, pp 38-51.
[5] Nocera P. : Utilisation conjointe de réseaux neuronaux et de connaissances explicites pour le décodage acoustico-phonétique. Thèse, Université d'Avignon, 29jan92, 135p.
[6] Quélavoine R. : Reconnaissance de bruits transitoires sous-marins à l'aide de réseaux de neurones multi-couches. DCN Ingénierie Sud/LSM, Six Fours les Plages.

Neuromorphic Speech Processing for noisy environments

Chalapathy Neti
IBM, internal zip 1211
1000, NW 51 street
Boca Raton, FL 33429-1328

Abstract

Current speech recognition systems perform very poorly in the presence of background noise, particularly for signal-to-noise ratios (SNR) below 10 dB and for certain noise conditions such as cafeteria noise [3]. In this study we investigate the use of acoustic processing based on cochlear models and neural-like processing as a means of arriving at noise robust acoustic representation of speech. However, unlike previous work based on cochlear models that used cochlear filter parameters based on neurophysiological data, we optimize cochlear filter shape and thresholds to reduce the noise contribution in the resulting acoustic representations. Results suggest that average SNR improvements of the order of 5-10 dB can be obtained for noise corrupted signals with SNRs near 0-6 dB for realistic noise such as cafeteria noise. Furthermore, using a neural network to include context and arrive at a lower dimensional representation can lead to further improvements in SNR.

1 Introduction

Current speech recognition systems perform very poorly in the presence of backgroud noise, particularly for signal-to-noise ratios (SNR) below 10 dB and for certain noise conditions such as cafeteria noise [3]. Das et al. [3] also show that the variations in SNR that come about due to microphone variations (a 15 dB degradation going from an expensive noise-cancelling microphone to omnidirectional tie-clip microphone) can cause the recognition error rate to increase from less than 5% to more than 50%. Also, for the same microphone, training in a quiet setting and testing in cafeteria noise setting can again degrade the recognition error rate from less than 1% to more than 50%. ChiWei et al. [2] report that the recognition error of the Sphinx recognition system [6] degrades from 4% to 29% when the close-talking Senheiser microphone at 5 inches, is replaced by a wide-band microphone array at 4 feet.

The use of auditory models to address the problem of speech recognition in the presence of noise has been studied by various groups [5, 9, 11] with some promise. Wang et al. [12] showed that neural representation of complex signals such as speech is derived from a highly reduced version of the wavelet transform and that such an encoding endows the representation of speech with enhanced spectral peaks and superior robustness in the presence of noise [11]. Based on studies of auditory nerve (rate-place) representation for discrimination of complex stimuli, Sachs et al. [8] have suggested that efferent connections from higher processing centers in the auditory pathway can dramatically improve the auditory nerve representation. Studies have shown that the disruption of the efferent feedback to the cochlea (i.e., Olivocochlear bundle) can affect the discrimination of stimuli in noise. Thus, efferent feedback may serve a central role in vowel discrimination in high-noise environments. Stimulation of the Olivocochlear bundle leads to changes in the tuning properties of the auditory nerve fibers characterised by broadening of the bandwidth and increase in threshold [1]. The

0-7803-1901-X/94 $4.00 ©1994 IEEE

similarity of cochlear filtering to multiresolution filtering using the wavelet transform has been pointed out by Yang et al. and Liu [12, 7]. Donoho [4] shows that wavelet shrinkage involving thresholding the wavelet coeffecients is an effective method of de-noising noisy data with superior performance compared to adaptive fourier methods. These studies suggests that suitable modifications of the shape of cochlear filters followed by thresholding may be an effective method for reducing the influence of noise on the resulting representation. In this study we examine the influence of the adaptation of the shape and threshold of the cochlear filters on the robustness of the neural representation in the presence of noise.

2 Problem formulation

2.1 Acoustic processing

The cochlear processing model used in this paper is similar to that used by Liu [7]. Briefly, the processing used has a model of the cochlea, which can be represented by the following steps. A linear filtering operation described as: Let $x(t)$ denote the speech input, and $h(t,s)$ denote the impulse response of the cochlear filters with s denoting the spatial location of the filter on the cochlea. Let $*_t$ denote convolution in time.

$$y_1(t,s) = h(t,s) *_t x(t) \tag{1}$$

In the current implementation $h(t,s)$ is modeled as a lowpass filter followed by a bandpass filter and the filtering is carried out in the time domain by using the bilinear transform on the continous time filter transforms [7]. The next step is a model of the hair cell, which can be represented by a time derivative, a compressive nonlinearity $g(.)$, a lowpass filter $w(t)$ as:

$$y_2(t,s) = g(\partial_t y_1(t,s) *_t w(t) \tag{2}$$

followed by a neurotransmitter reservoir model for characterizing hair cell adaptation [10]. The next step (3) is a spatial derivative operation across the s axis as proposed by Wang et al. [11] followed by channel specific thresholding. The spatial derivative operation models the lateral inhibitory neural processing and is suggested as an important step for noise reduction in the final representation [11].

$$y(t,s) = \partial_s y_2(t,s) *_s v(s) - \theta(s) \tag{3}$$

2.2 Optimization formulation

The problem of estimating optimal parameters to reduce the noise in the acoustic representation is formulated as follows: Let $y_n(t,s)$ denote the noisy output (3) of the acoustic processing corresponding to the noise corrupted signal $x(t)$ and let $y(t,s)$ represent the clean output. If $H(jw,s)$ are the fourier tranforms of $h(t,s)$ in (1), then $H(jw,s)$ are parameterized by a set of parameters as a function of s. Let p denote the set of parameters of $H(jw,s)$ including $\theta(s)$. Define

$$R_t(p) = \frac{1}{S}\sum_{s=1}^{S}[y_n(t,p(s)) - y(t,p(s))]^2. \tag{4}$$

and

$$E(p) = \frac{1}{T}\sum_{t=1}^{T} R_t(p). \tag{5}$$

where S denotes the number of spatial locations, and T denotes the number of time frames. Then the optimization problem solved to estimate optimal parameters p is defined as:

$$\min_{p} E(p) \tag{6}$$

(6) was solved using a simplex method for unconstrained optimization.

2.3 Performance measures

The general measure of quality of a noise reduction system is its improvement in signal-to-noise ratio. This is a useful, though coarse measure. The best method for noise reduction systems for speech recognition is their improvement in speech recognition performance. As our aim is, at this stage, to test the neuromorphic representation as a means to improve the performance of any recognizer trained on nominally quiet data, we will use SNR improvement as a measure of noise reduction. In this paper, SNR is computed by estimating the mean power of the clean signal and mean power of noise averaged over the entire analysis period (and averaged across frequency for the time-frequency representations). Since the experimental method involves adding noise to clean speech signals, the noise component of the representation is estimated by subtracting the clean representation from the noisy representation and computing the resulting average power. From a recognition standpoint, this measure provides an estimate of the amount of distortion from the clean representation. Thus, SNR in dB is:

$$SNR = 10 * log[\frac{< averagesignalpower >}{< averagenoisepower >}] \tag{7}$$

3 Results

Two sets of data were used for experiments. The first dataset consisted of a synthetic chirp signal with frequency varying from 3100 Hz to 300 Hz. White noise was added to generate a noisy chirp signal over the same interval (80 ms) at an SNR of -5.574 dB. The dataset "speech1" consisted of 100 ms of speech signal sampled at 20 kHz (a combination of silence and the begining of the word "imagine"). A more realistic noise collected in a cafeteria during lunch hours (cafeteria noise) was added to generate noisy speech signals at signal to noise ratios of 0.91 dB and -2.45 dB. The dataset "speech2" (the word "imagine") is generated by contaminating 500 ms of speech with cafeteria noise at SNRs of 3.14 and 6.37 dB; and "speech3" (the word "a" with some silence) is generated by contaminating 500 ms of speech with cafeteria noise at SNRs of 3.46 and 6.82 dB, respectively.

Table 1 shows the results of the experiments. Column 2 shows SNR based on short-time fourier transform analysis (STFT); column 3 shows the SNR for the initial values of the cochlear filter parameters based on some neurophysiological data [7]; and column 4 shows the SNR based on optimal filter parameters found by solving the optimization problem. Note that an improvement of about 10 dB is obtained for the chirp signal compared to an STFT representation; about 5 dB for the speech signal at initial SNRs of -2.45 and 0.911 dB; about 4.4 dB for noisy speech signals 'speech2' and 'speech3' at 3.14 and 3.46 dB; and about 7.5 dB for speech signals 'speech2' and 'speech3' at 6.37 and 6.82 dB. Also, note that the repesentations using the starting parameters based on neurophysiology show better SNR compared to the STFT representation except for the speech signal at -2.45 dB SNR.

For a more closer comparison to standard short-time fourier transform (STFT) processing, Figure 1 shows the SNR as a function of time for both STFT processing (denoted by solid line) and the Cochlear model based processing (denoted by broken line). Note that Cochlear model-based processing is clearly superior.

Dataset	SNR (STFT)	SNR(start)	SNR(optimal)
Chirp	-5.57	2.80	5.48
Speech1	0.91	3.93	5.90
Speech1	-2.45	-2.83	3.21
Speech2	3.14	5.98	7.50
Speech2	6.37	9.29	13.85
Speech3	3.46	5.17	7.85
Speech3	6.82	8.00	14.38

Table 1: Signal to noise ratio (SNR) results

3.1 Dimensionality reduction using neural networks

Multilayer neural networks with a single hidden layer which learn by the backpropagation algorithm in supervised autoassociative mode have been shown to be closely connected to Principal component analysis (PCA) by Baldi and Hornik [13] and Boulard and Kamp [14]. In this section we illustrate the use of a single hidden layer neural network in supervised autoassociative mode to extract a lower dimensional representation of the neuromorphic representation described above.

Five succesive frames of the previous stage ($10ms$) are concatenated to represent the input to the network containing 145 input units and the desired output is defined to be the same as the input for each input vector. The number of hidden units is fixed at 50 units.

The training set is generated by contaminating the 'clean' representation by white noise with variances set at 0.1,0.2,0.4 and 0.8 of the maximum input value and normalizing the inputs to 0-1 range. The training was carried out using the backpropagation algorithm using a learning rate of 0.1, a momentum value of 0.9 and a decay of 0.1 to keep the weight values from growing too large. The 50 values represented by the hidden units are treated as the feature vector repesenting the input in a lower dimensional space, since they are approximations to the PCA even in the nonlinear case [15, 13] The solution obtained is tested using the noise reduced representation.

Again, as before, the proximity of the noisy feature vector (as determined by the hidden unit responses to the noise-reduced noisy input) to the clean feature vector is computed as a signal-to-noise ratio:

$$SNR(NN) = 10 * log \frac{\sum_{i=1}^{H} h_i^{c\,2}}{\sum_{1}^{H} (h_i^n - h_i^c)^2} \tag{8}$$

where h_i^c and h_i^n are the clean and noisy hidden unit responses for the ith unit and, H is the number of hidden units.

Table 2 shows the results for three datasets speech1, speech2 and speech3. Column 2 shows the SNR for the neuromorphic representation after cochlear processing (previous stage) and Column 3 shows the SNR for lower dimensional (neural network based) representation. Note that in all three cases a signicant improvement in SNR is achieved.

4 Discussion

Although, the improvement in SNR is encouraging, the true test of the goodness of the noise reduction can be verified only in the context of recognition based on the new representation. We intend to use the model as

Dataset	SNR (optimal)	SNR(NN)
Speech1	5.90	17.79
Speech2	7.50	25.24
Speech3	7.85	20.98

Table 2: SNR results for neural network representation

Dataset	fapex	fbase	qapex	qbase	threshold
Initial	100.0	8000.0	0.50	4.00	0.40
Speech1	194.9	6109.6	6.87	2.54	0.61
Speech2	112.9	7304.0	3.88	1.57	0.49
Speech3	104.8	7598.4	4.22	1.98	0.55

Table 3: Cochlea filter parameters after optimization

a front end to a HMM based speech recognition engine [3] to validate the goodness of the new representation in the presence of noise.

It is instructive to compare the changes in cochlear filters due to the optimization procedure in this paper with that of experimental neurophysiology. It has been shown that the stimulation of COCB or the presence of noise masking broadens the tip of the filter and decreases the center frequency [1]. Changes seen in these experiments indicate that the variations are consistent at high frequencies but are contrary at low frequencies. Table 3 shows the optimal parameters for the cochlear filters and thresholds. Note that in each case the higher (fbase) center frequency decreases with a simultaneous broadening of the tip of the filter (decrease in qbase), while the lower frequency (fapex) increases with a simultaneous sharpening of the filter (increase in qapex). Also in all cases, the threshold increases to a higher value consistent with neurophysiology.

References

[1] M.C. Brown, A.L.Nuttall and R.I. Masta. Intracellular recordings from cochlear inner hair cells: effects of stimulation of the crossed olivocochlear efferents. *Science*, 222, pages 69-72, 1983.

[2] C. Che, M. Rahim and J. Flanagan. A Neural Network system for robust speech recognition in variable acoustic environments. *Preprint*, Nov, 1992.

[3] S. Das, R. Bakis, A. Nadas, D. Nahamoo and M. Picheny. Influence of Background noise and microphone on the performance of the IBM tangora speech recognition system. *Proc. IEEE Intl. Conf. on Acoustics Speech and Signal Processing* , 1993.

[4] David L. Donoho. Wavelet Shrinkage and W.V.D. *To appear in Proc. Toulouse Conf. on Wavelets and Appl.*, S. Roques, Editor, Springer-Verlag, 1993.

[5] O. Ghitza. Auditory nerve representation as a Basis for Speech Processing. In *Advances in Speech Signal Processing* S. Furui and M.M. Sondhi, editors, pages 453-485 ,Marcel Dekker Inc, 1992.

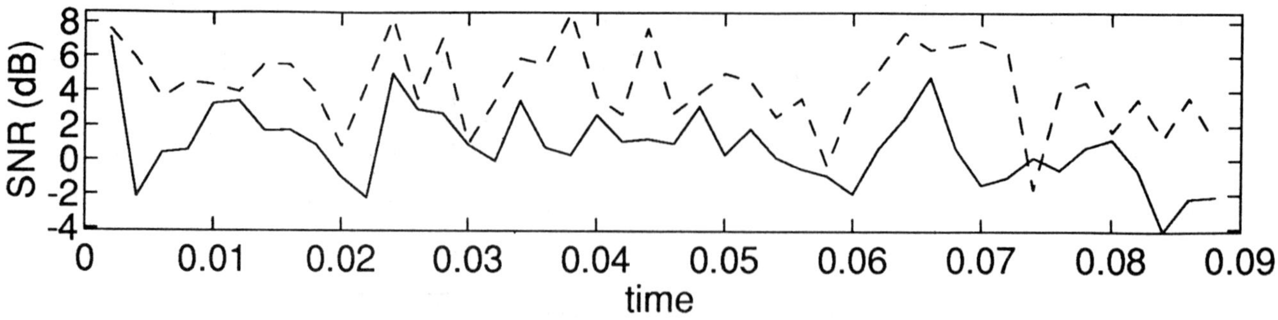

Figure 1: A comparison of signal-to-noise ratios across time between the spect rogram representation (solid line) and time-frequency representation obtained by the cochlear model (dashed line)

[6] K.F. Lee, H.W. Hon and R. Reddy. An overview of the SPHINX speech recognition system. *IEEE trans. on Acoustics speech and signal processing* 38(1), January 1990.

[7] Weimin Liu. An Analog Cochlear Model: Signal representation and VLSI realization. *Ph.D. dissertation*, The Johns Hopkins University, Baltimore, MD, 1992.

[8] M. Sachs, R.L. Winslow and C.C. Blackburn. Representation of Speech in the auditory periphery. In *Auditory function, Neurobiological Bases of Hearing*, G.E. Edelman, W.E.Gall and W.M.Cowan, editors, John Wiley and Sons, New York, pages 747-774, 1988.

[9] S. Seneff. A Joint Synchrony/Mean Rate Model of Auditory Speech processing. *Journal of Phonetics*, 16(1), pages 55-76, 1988.

[10] R.L. Smith and M.L. Brachman Adaptation in auditory-nerve fibers: a revised model. *Biological Cybernetics*, 44, pages 107-120, 1982.

[11] K. Wang, S.A. Shamma and William J. Byrne. Noise robustness in the auditory representations of the speech signals *Proc. IEEE Intl. Conf. on Acoustics Speech and Signal Processing*, 1993.

[12] X. Yang, K. Wang and S. Shamma. Auditory representations of acoustic signals. *IEEE transactions on Information Theory, Special issue on wavelet Tranforms and Multiresolution analysis*, 38(2), 1992.

[13] P. Baldi and K. Hornik. Neural Networks and principal component analysis: Learning from examples without local minima. *Neural Networks* 2, 52-58, 1989.

[14] H. Boulard and Y. Kamp. Auto-association by multilayer perceptrons and singular value decomposition. *Biological Cybernetics* 59, 291-294, 1988.

[15] J.A. Sarat. A fast neural algorithm for principal component analysis and singular value decomposition. *International Journal of Neural Systems*, 2, 147-155, 1991.

A SCALY ARTIFICIAL NEURAL NETWORK FOR SPEAKER INDEPENDENT ISOLATED WORD RECOGNITION USING NON–LINEAR TIME ALIGNMENT

M. J. Creaney and R. N. Gorgui–Naguib

Department of Electrical and Electronic Engineering
University of Newcastle Upon Tyne
Newcastle–Upon–Tyne NE1 7RU
U.K.

ABSTRACT

The use of neural networks for the recognition of isolated letters from the English Alphabet is investigated. A scaly architecture neural network model is used and is trained using the error back propagation algorithm. The architecture is varied by changing the number of inputs to the network, the number of hidden units in the network and the performance of each of these networks is compared. The non–linear time alignment algorithm called Trace Segmentation is used. The use of different transfer functions within the processing units of the neural network is looked at and several versions of the sigmoid function compared.

I. INTRODUCTION

One of the major problems in speech recognition systems has been due to spectral pattern variation [1]. Neural networks have proved to be useful tools for pattern recognition and are therefore suitable for the task of discriminating between different categories of spectral patterns such as those obtained for speech signals. A network with a scaly architecture [2] is investigated in this paper and its ability as a speech recognition tool assessed. A second major problem in speech recognition systems is in dealing with speech pattern time axis variation [1]. A non–linear time alignment algorithm called Trace Segmentation is used here in conjunction with the neural network here to produce a model which has features that deal with both the aforementioned problems.

II. THE SCALY NEURAL ARCHITECTURE

The neural network under consideration is a feed–forward multi–layer neural network [3] with a scaly type architecture [1].

A fully connected, three layer, feed–forward neural network has every node in the input layer connected to every node in the hidden layer and every node in the hidden layer connected to every node in the output layer. Signals flow in the forward direction from the input layer to the hidden layer to the output layer. During training the training phase error signals will be propagated back through the network in the reverse direction.

Krause and Hackbarth [1] showed that a fully connected network is not required to support high recognition rates for isolated word recognition. It was shown that the performance of a neural network does not necessarily improve as the number of connections is increased by applying a scaly type architecture to a neural network. Here the scaly architecture is applied between the input layer and the hidden layer [4] as shown in Figure 1.

The input data is preprocessed and presented to the network such that successive feature vectors or frames are presented to the network inputs, each coefficient of a feature vector being presented to one input neuron. Input frames are grouped into input zones with each zone being associated with a frame of hidden neurons of the same size as an input layer frame. Each hidden neuron in a hidden frame is connected to its equivalent in all the frames of the associated input zone. The input zones are overlapped such that there will be input frames common to adjacent zones.

An example of a scaly architecture neural network used here is shown in Figure 1. All input patterns are warped to fifteen feature vectors each of eight coefficients. To accommodate this an architecture with 120 input neurons is required consisting of 15 frames each of 8 neurons. The number of frames in a zone is 5 frames with an overlap of three frames so the number of frames required in the hidden layer is 6. The hidden layer therefore contains 48 neurons made up of 6 frames each of 8 neurons. The number of output classes is 26 so the output layer therefore requires 26 neurons.

The software used, as described in section IV, offers the choice of three different non–linear activation functions, $f(x)$, these are as follows

standard : $f(x) = 1.71 * tanh(0.666x)$
sigmoid01 : $f(x) = 1 / (1 + exp(-x))$
sigmoid11 : $f(x) = (1 - exp(-x)) / (1 + exp(-x))$

Several possible network architectures are trained using all three functions and the results compared. The function which results in the best performance for these architectures is then used to train several more network architectures.

The neural network is initialised such that all the weights are set to a value between –0.5 and 0.5 assigned using a random number generator.

The weights are changed according to the following rule

$$\Delta p W_{ji} = \varepsilon * \delta_{pj} * O_{pi}$$

where,
$\Delta p W_{ji}$ is the change for the weight joining the jth node to its incoming connection

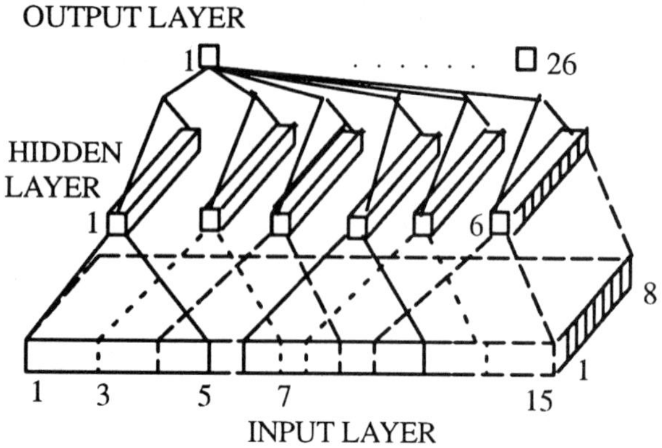

Fig. 1. Scaly Neural Network Architecture

δ_{pj} is the error for this *jth* unit.
O_{pi} is the value of the *ith* incoming connection.
ε is a constant which determines the rate of learning.

A value of $\varepsilon = 0.01$ is used here [4].

III. Time Alignment

Speaking rate variation results in non–linear fluctuations in the speech time axis. The length of the input pattern vector is constrained by the number of input neurons to the network since the structure of the type of network in question cannot be varied after training. Therefore some form of time alignment is required which will modify the input patterns to fit the neural network while retaining these discriminating features. Performance of the network is dependent upon the performance of the time alignment algorithm [5].

Linear algorithms are the simplest time alignment algorithms but they do not take into account the importance of feature vectors within the pattern vector when removing or duplicating them. Important features may therefore be lost.

Non–linear time alignment algorithms are more complicated and result in higher computational cost. Their advantage lies in their ability to recognise the important discriminatory features and to retain them during the time warping process.

Dynamic time warping for time alignment was introduced by Sakoe and Chiba in 1978 [6] and was used in conjunction with dynamic programming techniques. It was used in conjunction with neural networks by Sakoe et al [5] in 1989 for recognition of isolated digit words.

This algorithm removes timing differences between speech patterns by warping the time axis of one speech pattern until it maximally coincides with the other. All pattern vectors are warped against a reference pattern vector of the same category which has the same number of feature vectors as there are frames in the input layer of the neural network.

A major drawback of dynamic time warping is the high computational expenditure it incurs[2]. It also requires the use of a reference pattern to warp the pattern to be recognised. A reference pattern will be required for every pattern the network is required to recognise and the input pattern would have to be warped against all the reference patterns then presented to the network each time before it can be recognised. A method of time alignment called Trace Segmentation removes the need for a reference pattern to carry out time alignment and it is much simpler computationally.

Trace Segmentation was introduced by Kuhn et al in 1981 [2]. It is based on the assumption that despite any timing differences for speech signals of the same category, fluctuations in frequency with time will occur in the same sequence but over different lengths of time. It was used in conjunction with a neural network by Demichelis et al [7] for the recognition of isolated digits and by Smith [8] for the recognition of letters of the English alphabet.

The speech pattern can be expressed as a sequence of feature vectors

$$A = a_1, a_2, ..., a_i, ..., a_K$$

It is also assumed that each feature vector has N features

$$a_i = (a_{i1}, a_{i2}, ..., a_{il}, ..., a_{iN})$$

which can be represented as a point in N–dimensional space.

Where there is no change in frequency there will be a high density of points and where the frequency changes are rapid the frequency points will be widely spaced. The number of feature vectors can be reduced by removing those that occur during the stationary portions of the speech. Kuhn et al [2] achieved this by summing the Euclidean distances between successive feature vectors of a pattern vector to give the total length D of the pattern vector. If F feature vectors are required in the time aligned pattern vector then D is divided into F segments of length L where, $L = D/F$

The most suitable vectors from the pattern vector are selected as follows. The first feature vector of the input pattern vector is taken as the first feature vector of the time aligned pattern vector. Successive feature vectors of the time aligned pattern vector are then chosen such that the euclidean distance between each of them is as close to L as possible. The final time aligned pattern vector should therefore consist of F feature vectors with euclidean distances between them of approximately L.

This algorithm can only be used for the compression of pattern vectors which implies that using it on its own entails warping all pattern vectors to the size of the smallest pattern vector. This can result in a very large pattern vector being warped to a very small length.This, obviously, is a restrictive consequence if all the discriminating features are to be retained in the time aligned pattern vectors. The size to which all the pattern vectors are warped is chosen, approximately, as the mean of all the speech data pattern sizes. This requires compression in some cases and expansion in others. Therefore, a linear time alignment algorithm is used for the expansion of pattern vectors. This algorithm duplicates vectors at regular intervals throughout the pattern vector until it is of the correct length. This version of the time segmentation algorithm is the one used here.

IV. Experimental Procedure and Simulation Results

The source of the data for training and testing the neural network is a database from the British Telecommunications Research Laboratories. It consists of each of the letters of the English alphabet being repeated three times by 104 individual speakers. The spoken English Alphabet is known to be a difficult vocabulary and problematic for a recogniser [4][9][10]. There are several subsets of letters which are which are easily confused with each other. The E set {B, C, D, E, G, P, T, V}, the set {Q, U}, the set {M, N} and the set {A, K, J}. Here we look at the recognition of the E set alone.

There are 53 male and 51 female speakers of various ages.The speech signals are recorded in a low noise environment with high quality recording equipment. They are sampled at 20KHz using a 16–bit A/D converter and the exact start and finish of each utterance have been labelled. Endpoint Mel Frequency Cepstral Coefficients are calculated resulting in each feature vector being characterised by 8 coefficients.

The neural network simulator used in obtaining these following results is called Galatea and is produced as part of a joint EEC project called PYGMALION. The software consists of a set of C libraries which build, train and run different types of neural networks. The Gain Back Propagation algorithm is used to train and test the neural network on a SUN ipc SparC station.

A. Experimental Outline

Neural networks with three different sizes of input layer are trained to recognise the E set ; 15 input frames (120 input neurons), 31 input frames (248 input neurons) and 45 input frames (360 input neurons).

The target values for output nodes to indicate which node represents the current input pattern category are varied. Woodland [9] suggests setting the target value for the output node representing the current input class to 0.9 and the target value for the other output nodes to 0.1. This should lead to an improved generalisation performance which is important for speaker independent recognition. The networks here are trained using the following three sets of target values {0, 1}, {0.1, 0.9}, and {0.01, 0.99} with the high value indicating the current input pattern category and the lower values indicating the categories to which the input pattern does not belong.

Each network is trained over 2500 training sweeps with $\varepsilon = 0.01$ and using the activation function sigmoid01.

The same procedure is then followed using activation function sigmoid11 and the standard sigmoid function.

The activation function sigmoid01 is found to clearly outperform the other two activation functions (see section IV *B*) for the networks over all three input layer sizes. Several more networks of different sized input layers are then trained ; 11 input frames (88 input neurons), 21 input frames (168 input neurons), 25 input frames (200 input neurons), 35 input frames (280 input neurons) and 41 input frames (328 input neurons). These are all trained to recognise the E set over 2500 training sweeps with $\varepsilon = 0.01$ using the three different sets of output node target values and the performances with differing input layer size and output node target values compared.

B. Simulation Results

(i) Activation Function

Tables I, II and III show the performance and error after 2500 sweeps for three networks of different input layer sizes using the three possible activation functions. Performance indicates the percentage of all the utterances presented to the network which the network identifies correctly.

TABLE I

Error And Performance Of Network Of Input Layer Size 15 Frames In Recognising The E-set After 2500 Training Sweeps

Sigmoid Function	Node Target Values		Training Data	Testing Data
Sigmoid01	0 , 1	Error	0.01404	0.02316
		Perf.	84.10%	65.22%
	0.1 , 0.9	Error	0.02299	0.02599
		Perf.	59.73%	48.24%
	0.01 , 0.99	Error	0.01449	0.02339
		Perf.	83.37%	64.07%
Sigmoid11	0 , 1	Error	0.04178	0.04261
		Perf.	13.24%	12.63%
	0.1 , 0.9	Error	0.03336	0.03403
		Perf.	13.96%	13.70%
	0.01 , 0.99	Error	0.04064	0.04151
		Perf.	13.64%	12.72%
Standard	0 , 1	Error	0.04758	0.04784
		Perf.	12.43%	11.81%
	0.1 , 0.9	Error	0.03815	0.03846
		Perf.	12.43%	11.81%
	0.01 , 0.99	Error	0.04686	0.04720
		Perf.	12.43%	11.81%

TABLE II

Error And Performance Of Network Of Input Layer Size 31 Frames In Recognising The E-set After 2500 Training Sweeps

Sigmoid Function	Node Target Values		Training Data	Testing Data
Sigmoid01	0 , 1	Error Perf.	0.00803 93.46%	0.02439 61.03%
	0.1 , 0.9	Error Perf.	0.01633 84.02%	0.02609 53.73%
	0.01 , 0.99	Error Perf.	0.00748 94.83%	0.02383 62.84%
Sigmoid11	0 , 1	Error Perf.	0.04201 15.17%	0.04345 14.19%
	0.1 , 0.9	Error Perf.	0.03414 13.32%	0.03530 12.72%
	0.01 , 0.99	Error Perf.	0.04129 13.64%	0.04253 13.04%
Standard	0 , 1	Error Perf.	0.04741 12.35%	0.04755 11.81%
	0.1 , 0.9	Error Perf.	0.03802 12.35%	0.03821 11.81%
	0.01 , 0.99	Error Perf.	0.04648 12.35%	0.04648 11.81%

Error indicates the difference between the desired outputs and the actual outputs. The sigmoid01 function achieves least error values with error values of less than 0.02299 for the training data and 0.02634 for the testing data.

The sigmoid01 function is clearly the best performer in all cases achieving the highest performances. The other two activation performances fail to achieve performance rates anywhere near acceptable. With the sigmoid01 function a performance of 94.83% is achieved on the training data with the same network achieving 62.84% on the testing data. The networks when trained with the sigmoid11 and standard sigmoid functions fail to perform at a level of greater than about 16%.

(ii) Node Target Values and Input Layer Size

Figure 2 shows the performance with size of input layer for the three possible sets of node target values on the training data and Figure 3 shows the performance on the testing data. Figures 4 and 5 show the error values obtained with size of input layer for the three possible sets of node target values.

TABLE III

Error And Performance Of Network Of Input Layer Size 45 Frames In Recognising The E-set After 2500 Training Sweeps

Sigmoid Function	Node Target Values		Training Data	Testing Data
Sigmoid01	0 , 1	Error Perf.	0.00726 92.82%	0.02364 63.49%
	0.1 , 0.9	Error Perf.	0.01680 81.03%	0.02634 52.34%
	0.01 , 0.99	Error Perf.	0.00905 89.59%	0.02440 60.62%
Sigmoid11	0 , 1	Error Perf.	0.04178 13.24%	0.04261 12.63%
	0.1 , 0.9	Error Perf.	0.03336 13.96%	0.03403 13.70%
	0.01 , 0.99	Error Perf.	0.04064 13.64%	0.04151 12.72%
Standard	0 , 1	Error Perf.	0.04758 12.43%	0.04784 11.81%
	0.1 , 0.9	Error Perf.	0.03815 12.43%	0.03846 11.81%
	0.01 , 0.99	Error Perf.	0.04686 12.43%	0.04720 11.81%

As can be seen, there is not much difference in performance and error when the node target value sets {0 , 1} and {0.01 , 0.099} are used but there is a big difference between these and the performance and error achieved with node target values {0.1 , 0.9}. The target value set {0.1 , 0.9} therefore achieves much lower performance and much higher error and is the most unsuitable of the three.

Furthermore, it can be noticed that performance versus size of network input layer initially increases but then levels off at around 30 input frames. There is slight fluctuation after this. The same is true of the error values. These initially decrease as the size of input layer is increased but level off at around 30 input frames.

V. Discussion and Conclusions

A. *Effect of Activation Function*

One activation function clearly outperforms the others for this recognition task and network. This is the sigmoid function over the range 0 to +1 which performs much better than either the standard sigmoid function or the sigmoid function over the range −1 to +1.

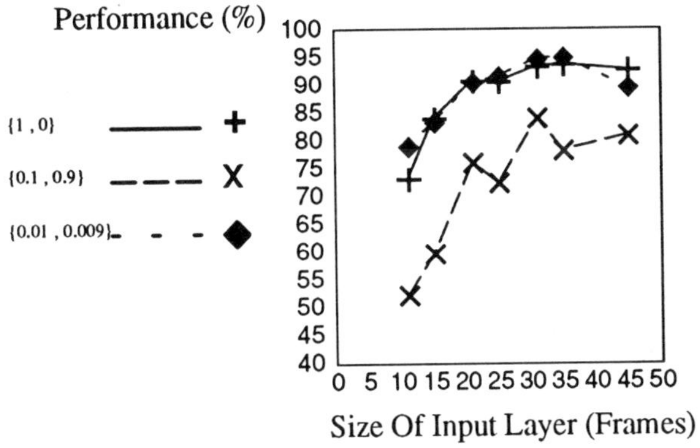

Fig. 2. Performance of Network On Training Data

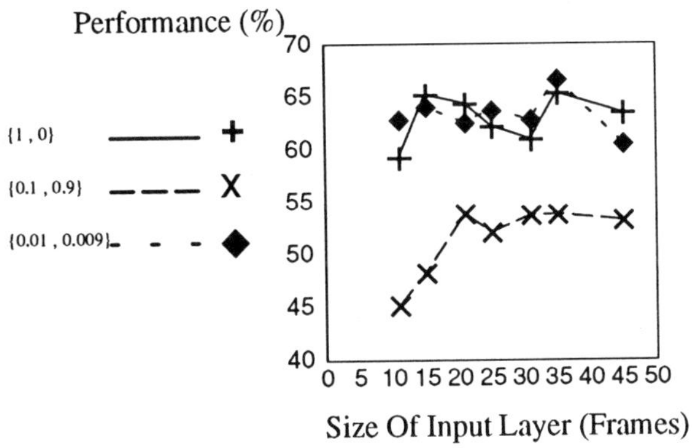

Fig. 3. Performance of Network On Testing Data

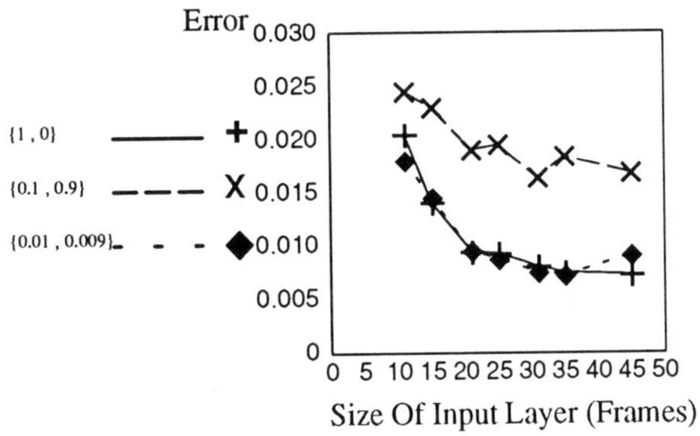

Fig. 4. Network Error with Training Data

B. Effect of the Architecture

High performance rates and low error values are achieved by the scaly architecture over all input layer sizes for the training data and promising results are achieved on the test data.

The results indicate that there exists a point where increasing the network input layer size does not improve the performance significantly. Increasing the input layer size increases the amount of time a network takes to train and also the computational cost in recognition. For the task in question a network input layer of size around 30 input frames proves sufficient.

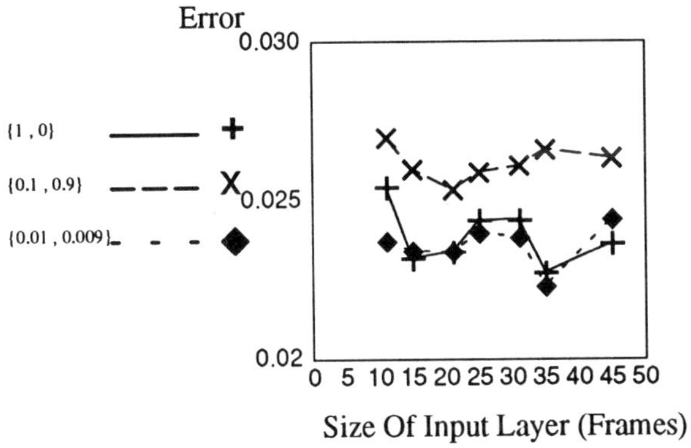

Fig. 5. Network Error with Testing Data

Further investigation of the network architecture would prove useful. The effect of varying the number of frames in an input zone could be investigated as well as varying the overlap between zones both of which lead to varying the number of hidden neurons.

C. Effect of Node Target Values

It can be clearly seen that using node target values of {0 , 1} and {0.01 , 0.99} yield the best results. It is interesting to note that though there is very little difference between the results using either of these there is slightly better performance achieved using {0.01 , 0.99} on the test data when the input layer size is around 30 frames. This is the size suggested to be sufficient for this particular task of isolated word recognition of letters of the English Alphabet.

D. The Time Alignment Method

The results achieved suggest that the non–linear time alignment algorithm used called Trace Segmentation is supportive of high recognition rates for the recognition task being investigated here.

After 2500 training sweeps the learning rate has fallen such that an increase in performance or decrease in error only occurs after a fairly large number of training sweeps, approximately 40 training sweeps for an increase in performance of only 0.2%. It would therefore appear that performance in these networks could not be increased much beyond that at 2500 training sweeps without a large amount of training for a small increase in performance.

High performance rates are achieved on recognition of the training data which the network has already seen but performance on the test data is much lower. The test data is utterances from speakers whose speech the network has not heard examples of before. Therefore, lower performance is to be expected; however, ways to improve the performance on this data are required to be looked at.

In conclusion, the scaly type architecture neural network when used in conjunction with the Trace Segmentation non–

linear time alignment algorithm has been shown to be promising for speaker independent recognition of isolated words in the form of letters of the English Alphabet. The sigmoid activation function over the interval 0 to +1 proves most suitable when used with node target values of {0 , 1} or {0.01 , 0.99}. Using {0.01 , 0.99} with a network input size of 31 frames appears to give the best results for the test data.

References

[1] A. Krause and H. Hackbarth. "Scaly Artificial Neural Networks for Speaker–Independent Recognition of Isolated Words" *Proc. Of The IEEE Int. Conf. On Acoustics, Speech and Signal Processing, ICASSP '89*, pp.21–24, Glasgow, 1989.

[2] M. H. Kuhn, H. Tomaschewski and H. Ney. "Fast Nonlinear Time Alignment For Isolated Word Recognition" *Proc. Of The IEEE Int. Conf. On Acoustics, Speech and Signal Processing, ICASSP '81*, pp.736–740, 1981.

[3] D. E. Rumelhart, G. E. Hinton and R. J. Williams. "Learning Internal Representations by Error Propagation" D. E. Rumelhart and J. L. McLelland, editors, *Parallel Distributed Processing: Explorations in the Microstructure of Cognition. Vol 1. Foundations*, pp. 318–362, MIT Press, 1986.

[4] M. J. Creaney and R. N. Gorgui–Naguib. "A Scaly Neural Network Architecture for Isolated Word Recognition Using The British Telecommunications English Alphabet Database" *Proc. Of The IEEE Int. Conf. on Neural Networks*, ICNN '93, vol. III, pp.1644–1649, San Francisco, 1993.

[5] H. Sakoe, R. Isotani, K. Yoshida, k. Iso and T. Watanabe. "Speaker–Independent Word Recognition Using Dynamic Programming Neural Networks" *Proc. Of The IEEE Int. Conf. On Acoustics, Speech and Signal Processing, ICASSP '89*, pp.29–32, Glasgow, 1989.

[6] H. Sakoe and S. Chiba. "Dynamic Programming Algorithm Optimization for Spoken Word Recognition" *IEEE trans. on Acoustics, Speech and Signal Processing*, vol.26, no.1, pp.43–49, 1978.

[7] P. Demichelis, L. Fissore, P. Laface, G. Micca and E. Piccolo. "On the Use of Neural Networks for Speaker Independent Isolated Word Recognition" *Proc. Of The IEEE Int. Conf. On Acoustics, Speech and Signal Processing, ICASSP '89*, Glasgow, pp.314–317, 1989.

[8] A. D. Smith. "Isolated Word Recognition using gradient backed–propagation neural networks", MEng. Thesis, University Of Newcastle–Upon–Tyne, 1990.

[9] P. C. Woodland. "Isolated Word Speech Recognition based on Connectionist Techniques" *Br. Telecom. Technol. J.*, vol. 8, no. 2, pp.61–66, 1990.

[10] David J.Burr. "Experiments on Neural Net Recognition on Spoken and Written Text" *IEEE trans. on Acoustics, Speech and Signal Processing*, vol.36, no.7, pp.1162–1168, 1988.

Phoneme Recognition Using a Time-Sliced Recurrent Recognizer

Ingrid Kirschning Hideto Tomabechi
Dept. of Information Science & Intelligent Systems
Tokushima University
2-1 Minami Josanjima-Cho, Tokushima Shi 770, JAPAN.
E-Mail : ingrid@j-aoe.is.tokushima-u.ac.jp

Abstract

This paper presents a new method for phoneme recognition using neural networks, the Time-Sliced Recurrent Recognizer (TSRR). In this method we employ Elman's recurrent network with error-backpropagation [1], adding an extra group of units that are trained to give a specific representation of each phoneme while it is recognizing it. The purpose of this architecture is to obtain an immediate hypothesis of the speech input without having to pre-label each phoneme or separate them before the input. The input signal is divided into time-slices which are recognized in a linear sequential fashion. The generated hypothesis is shown in the extra group of units at the same moment the time-slices are passed through the network and being recognized as a certain phoneme. Thus the TSRR is capable of recognizing the phonemes in real-time without discriminatory learning.

I. Introduction

In the last years, a significant effort has been put into the study of automatic speech recognition. There is a worldwide interest in large-vocabulary speech recognition, because of its numerous applications, such as speech-to-speech translation and voice database accesses [2]. Most current recognition systems have the goal of speaker independent, continuous speech recognition and there are three main approaches that have been taken [2][3] : Hidden Markov Models (stochastic approach), Neural Networks and Feature-based approach.

Currently, Hidden Markov Models (HMM) - based methods and TDNN's (Time-Delay Neural Networks) appear to be the most popular ones. Each one has a different application, some are applied to large-vocabulary, speaker-dependent and speaker-independent [4] speech recognition, others to continuous speech [5], high-performance phoneme recognition or word recognition [6]. Neural networks are successful in high-performance phoneme recognition (TDNN - Time-Delay Neural Networks [2][4][7][8]) and for small vocabulary recognition (TDNN's with Dynamic Time Warping [9], Dynamic Programming Neural Networks). For large vocabularies, where a sequential control of sub-word units is required a neural network can be employed as a phonetic classifier whose results are fed into an alignment procedure (Dynamic Programming or Viterbi Alignment [3]). Or, another method is known as Linked Predictive Neural Network (LPNN) [10][11].

Concerning the acoustic preprocessing, the spectral decomposition of a speech signal is the most used method to obtain the data for the input to neural networks [7][8][10][11][12]. It has been shown, that Mel-scaled Fast Fourier Transforms of the input signal seem to produce the best performance [13], because it is fast and accurate, and it performs a metric clustering of the phonemic samples. The speech signal is obtained using a window (Hamming), a FFT is performed on that window and a state vector is constructed that contains the spectral components of the signal.

II. Existing Schemes

Today's most successful schemes for speech recognition using neural networks seem to be TDNN and LPNN, which are sometimes combined with other methods to form hybrid systems or feature based approaches.

a) Linked Predictive Neural Networks (LPNN)

Generally neural networks are being used as pattern classifiers. A LPNN performs phoneme recognition by modeling a phoneme by signal prediction, instead of classification [10][11. The LPNN

0-7803-1901-X/94 $4.00 ©1994 IEEE

system is based on canonical phoneme models, which can be concatenated in any order to create templates for different words. Each phoneme is modeled by a series of states, as in HMM, and each state is implemented by a predictive neural net. So the input is divided into speech frames and each neural network is trained to predict the next speech frame. The LPNN training algorithm consists of three steps : a forward pass, an alignment step and a backward pass. But the phonemes are not classified at that level, instead the prediction scores are stored for several word candidates, and the decision is made at the word level.

b) Time-Delay Neural Networks (TDNN's)

The aim of the TDNN's is a better recognition by incorporating a method to represent relationships between events in time, which does not require precise temporal alignment or segmentation of the labels that are to be learned (Waibel et al.). A TDNN is a feedforward multilayer neural network with time-delayed connections at each hidden layer to relate and compare current input to the past history of events [7].

The learning technique used in TDNN's is the back-propagation learning rule in a "semi-batch" manner, i.e., they first apply the regular backpropagation forward and backward pass to all time-shifted units as if they were separate events and they update each weight on corresponding connections by the average of all corresponding time-delayed weight changes. This applies to all connections and all time shifts. In this way the network is forced to discover useful acoustic-phonetic features in the input, regardless of when in time they actually occurred. This way the network doesn't require the time alignment and/or segmentation of the speech signal.

In both, LPNN and TDNN, the speech input is partitioned into frames that consist of normalized melscale filterbank coefficients (such as frames of 10 ms each, consisting of 16 coefficients). The input speech is normally sampled at 12 or 16 KHz, a Hamming window and a FFT is computed to produce the coefficients. TDNN's seem the best method so far for speech recognition that deals with the dynamic nature of speech. But, as most of the neural networks for pattern recognition, TDNN is a discriminatory network. In other words, in the past and until now the networks needed to be presented with the whole phoneme at one time so that it can train on it. Also at the moment of recognition the entire phoneme, pre-segmented, has to enter the network in order to be recognized. Even when some are dealing with time delay, they require that the input signal length is specifically pre-labeled [6] or separated phoneme by phoneme and fitted into a special format, so that the network can be trained and recognize each phoneme separately. For example, in the case of Waibel et al. [7]'s TDNN the spectral coefficients of the signal are fitted into 15 frames centered around the hand-labeled vowel onset. This makes the continuous recognition of spontaneous speech by TDNN rather difficult.

Also, since the entire phonemic segmentation for each input has to be represented in (each of the time-delayed) neural networks, the size of the network has normally been very large.

Addressing this we developed a new method which is able to recognize a phoneme in a continuous stream of speech without having to fit the signal into a fixed time-format and without having to presented the entire phoneme at one time while training and running the network.

III. Time-Sliced Recurrent Recognizer (TSRR)

As a new alternative for speech recognition using neural networks we present the TSRR method:

The TSRR Architecture

The network is a fully-connected, recurrent net [14] which is trained as a sort of predictive network for the frequency components of a phoneme through time. The network's overall architecture is shown in Figure 1. As can be seen in the figure, it consists of three layers. The first layer contains the input-units and a context-layer. The context layer

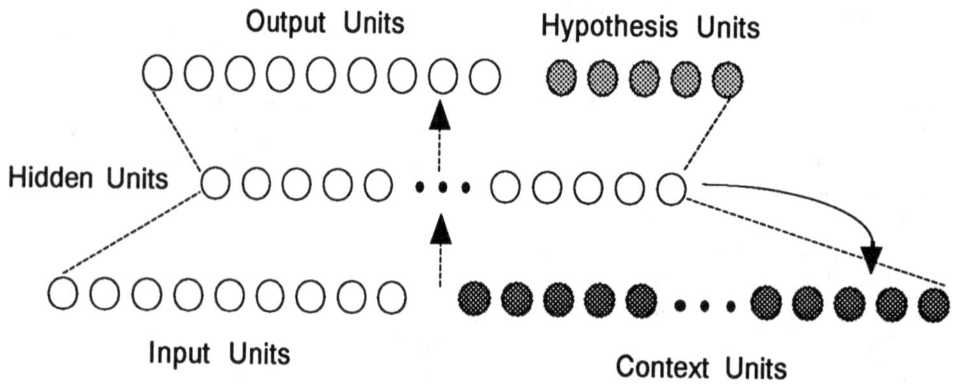

Figure 1 : The architecture of the TSRR

will hold a copy of the activation state of the hidden layer and therefore has to be of the same size as the hidden layer. The second layer is the hidden layer and the third is the output layer, which consists of the output units and a set of, as we call them, hypothesis units. These hypothesis units are actually the ones that show the corresponding representation of the recognized phoneme with a binary string.

The connections are the customary feedforward full connections from input- and context units to hidden units and from hidden units to output- and hypothesis units. All the connections are trainable, with the exception of the connection going from the hidden layer to the context layer, which is a simple copy connection.

The input to the network consists of the spectrum of the recorded phoneme. In our implementation, each phoneme is recorded at a sampling rate of 22 KHz with 8 bit representation, Hamming windowed, and computed with a Fast Fourier Transform (FFT). The resulting spectrum is cut into 'slices' (see figure 2) of approximately 22.22 milliseconds (512 points) each, which are fed sequentially into the network. The actual length of the input signal is not fixed, it depends on the length of the recorded input.

We are using a recurrent neural network, because we want the network to learn the specific sequences of the different slices for each phoneme. This is done by passing each slice through the net and copying, after each epoch, the contents of the hidden layer into the context layer. In the next epoch this information is fed back into the hidden layer together with the next slice. The function of the context units is to provide a short-term memory, in order to have the network learning a sequence of frequencies.

But we don't want the network to only learn the different sequences, we also want it to predict each following slice. To achieve this we train the network with the slice of time 't' as input, and the slice 't+1' as the output.

While training the network to predict the next time-slice for each phoneme, at the same time we are training the network to produce a specific hypothesis for each phoneme in the hypothesis units. So that, after training, the network will be able to show a specific representation for each phoneme that is passed through the net, thus obtaining an immediate hypothesis of the recognized phoneme.

Every time-slice is passed forward through the network and the output is compared to the desired output, which is the next time-slice and the code for the phoneme being trained. Then the error is propagated backwards. But the updating of the weights is done only after each phoneme has passed completely. The backpropagation algorithm we adopted is Fahlman's *Quickprop* [15] which seems to work well with our architecture and learning has been very fast.

IV. Experiment

To train the network we first recorded the phonemes 'a', 'i', 'u', 'e' and 'o' (in Japanese), with a sample rate of 22 KHz and 8 bit representation. Then we transformed the sounds into their spectrum. To do the transformation, the sample is Hamming windowed, passed through a high-pass filter (to boost the high frequency components of the Fourier transform) and the input is squared before transformation (to spread out closely spaced frequency power components). Other parameter settings are : The frequency range is adjusted to 0 - 5000 Hz (for speech), the transform size is set to 32 points and the offset (spacing between transforms) is set to 512 points. The resulting spectral coefficients are then normalized (linear) to

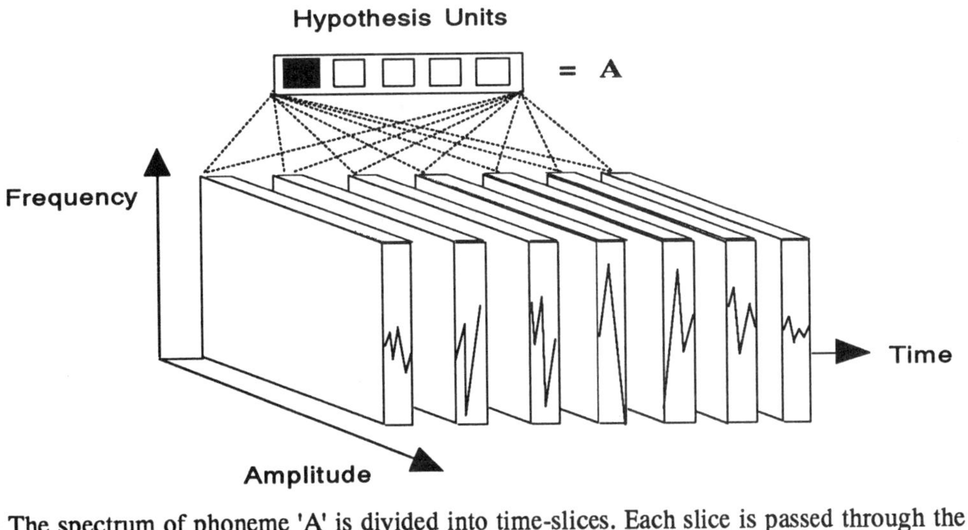

Figure 2 : The spectrum of phoneme 'A' is divided into time-slices. Each slice is passed through the network obtaining an immediate representation of the phoneme in the hypothesis units.

values that lie between 0 and 1. The normalization is done by setting all the values that are greater than 1000 to 1, all those that lie below 10 are set to 0 and the rest is divided by 1000. The obtained spectral data (one file for each phoneme) contains the values of the frequencies (columns) vs. time (rows), where the number of columns is always fixed, but the number of rows depends on the length of the recording. [1]

In our implementation, we represented each one of the 5 vowels as follows : 'a': (1 0 0 0 0), 'e': (0 1 0 0 0), 'i': (0 0 1 0 0), 'o': (0 0 0 1 0) and 'u': (0 0 0 0 1). This code is copied into the hypothesis units for the training of each phoneme.

In the first step of the training process, the context layer is initialized with random values (between -1 and +1) and the hypothesis units are set to the specific code for the phoneme to be trained. This code is kept in the hypothesis units throughout the training of one phoneme to have the network learn the code and reproduce it every time it encounters that specific frequency sequence.

Next, the frequencies are scanned one row at a time and fed into the input layer. Following Elman's methodology [14], when the row#1 is fed into the input layer, row #2 is copied into the output layer. After the forward- and backward pass row #2 becomes input and row#3 is put into the output layer. In other words, when the frequencies of time 't' are the input, the frequencies of 't+1' are in the output layer. This is done in order to train the network to predict the next row of frequencies of a phoneme.

Also, after the activation is passed to the hidden- and then to the output layer, the contents of the hidden layer are copied into the context layer. Where, at the next cycle, this information is fed back into the hidden layer, combining the context with the next row of frequencies [14]. This method was invented by Elman and the aim of which is to maintain a certain memory of the previous frequencies, in order to distinguish between the different sequences of frequencies of each phoneme.

The training is performed having the phonemes passed in varying the order, for example : (a,e,i) - (e,i,a) - (i,a,e), etc.. The preliminary experiment was done for Japanese vowels. We successfully trained the network for 3 different vowels using 200 hidden units and 30 input- and output units.

Our preliminary evaluations of the results are encouraging with the recognition of vowels and we are starting our experiment for consonants. The production of the specific statistical results for speaker independent recognition is to be completed soon when our entire experiment is finished in a few months.

[1] For the experiments we used two different formats, one of 9 columns (transform size 32 points) and another of 30 columns (transform size 128 points) to see if there is a difference in the learning speed and accuracy.

V. Discussion

Once trained, the network is able to perform a real-time recognition of the phonemes without discriminating. That is, that the input to the network doesn't have to be labeled or segmented phoneme by phoneme, instead, the network is trained to recognize the sequence of frequencies (slices) that compose a certain sound, which can be inside a longer stream of spoken language. And simply, when the network recognizes a sound, this is shown in the strong hypothesis it produces. The training itself is done phoneme by phoneme to teach the network the different frequency-sequences and their corresponding representation, but when running the trained network, the input can be a continuous stream of speech.

The recurrent architecture provides the necessary short term memory to analyze and recognize the sequence of frequencies of a specific phoneme. And it is a simple and rather small network which is easy to train. The number of epochs necessary to train the network to recognize 3 different vowels was of about 7000, and the result is a good approximation to the defined hypothesis. This means that the values obtained are above 0.8 when it should be '1', and below 0.1 when it should show a '0'.

The strength of the TSRR method is that the computational cost is lower[2] than other neural net-based methods, since the network only represents a time-slice of a phoneme as opposed to the entire phoneme in the existing methods.

VI. Conclusion

We have proposed a new method for phoneme recognition using neural networks. The Time-Sliced Recurrent Recognizer (TSRR) is able to learn sequences of frequencies and recognize them as one specific phoneme, generating an immediate hypothesis of the recognized phoneme.

The fact, that its computational cost is rather low, makes it possible to run the network on small computers, even PC's.

But the main difference to previous speech recognition systems is that the input to the network doesn't have to be labeled or segmented phoneme by phoneme, instead, the network is trained to recognize the sequence of frequencies (slices) that compose a certain sound, which can be inside a longer stream of spoken language.

To be used by TDNN and other existing neural net-based speech recognizers, the recorded phonemes have to be fitted into a specific format in time (for example, 16 melscale coefficients x 15 frames of 10 ms) and the entire phoneme has to be presented to the network at one time, while in our case, we

[2] Low enough to train and run the network on small computers like a Sparc Station or even a PC.

also perform a FFT but letting the length of the recording to be variable. This input signal is then divided into time-slices, and the network analyzes each slice in a linear sequential fashion. And when the hypothesis is strong enough, it shows the recognized phoneme, which can be long or short but it has not to be presented to the network completely at one time. This makes our network independent of the length of the input at the moment of recognizing separate sounds in a stream of spoken phonemes.

With the inexpensive nature of training due to representing only the time-slice of phonemes, and the linear sequential nature of recognition based on recurrent network, TSRR seems a viable method for continuous spontaneous speech recognition. We are currently working on all five vowels of Japanese and all the consonants. We hope to report the latest experimental results at the 1994 ICNN meeting.

References

[1] D.E. Rummelhart and J.L. McClelland, Parallel Distributed Processing; Explorations in the Microstructure of Cognition, Vol. I, Cambridge, MA: M.I.T. Press, 1986, U.S.A.

[2] C.H. Lee, L. Rabiner, "Automatic Speech Recognition - Current State and Future Directions", Proceedings of the ATR International Workshop on Speech Translation, 1993, Kyoto, Japan.

[3] A.Kuremasu, "Research on Speech Recognition at ATR", Proceedings of Tohoku University Symposium on Automatic Speech Recognition Present and Future, pp. 1-7, 1990.

[4] N. Hataoka, A. Waibel, "Speaker-Independent Phoneme Recognition on TIMIT Database Using Integrated Time-Delay Neural Networks (TDNNs)", Proceedings of the International Joint Conference on Neural Networks (IJCNN), Vol. I, pp. 57-62, 1990.

[5] P. Haffner, M. Franzini, A. Waibel, "Integrating Time Alignment and Neural Networks for High Performance Continuous Speech Recognition", IEEE Proceedings of the International Conference on Acoustics, Speech, and Signal Processing (ICASSP), Vol. I, 1991.

[6] A. Hirai, A. Waibel, "Phoneme-based Word Recognition by Neural Network - A Step Toward Large Vocabulary Recognition", Proceedings of the International Joint Conference on Neural Networks (IJCNN), Vol. III, pp. 671-676, 1990.

[7] A. Waibel, T. Hanazawa, G. Hinton, K. Shikano and K. Lang, "Phoneme Recognition Using Time-Delay Neural Networks", *IEEE Transactions on Acoustics, Speech, and Signal Processing*, Vol. 37, No. 3, March 1989.

[8] K. Lang, A. Waibel, G. Hinton, "A Time-Delay Neural Network Architecture for Isolated Word Recognition", *Neural Networks*, Vol. 3, pp. 33-34, 1990.

[9] N. Botros, S. Premnah, "Speech Recognition Using Dynamic Neural Networks", IEEE Proceedings of the International Conference on Neural Networks (ICNN), 1992.

[10] J. Tebelskis, A. Waibel, "Large Vocabulary Recognition Using Linked Predictive Neural Networks", IEEE Proceedings of the International Conference on Acoustics, Speech, and Signal Processing (ICASSP), April 1990.

[11] J. Tebelskis, A. Waibel, B. Petek, O. Schmidbauer, "Continuous Speech Recognition Using Linked Predictive Neural Networks", IEEE Proceedings of the International Conference on Acoustics, Speech, and Signal Processing (ICASSP), May 1991.

[12] T. Kohonen, "The 'Neural' Phonetic Typewriter", *IEEE Computer* , March 1988, pp. 11-22.

[13] F. Gurgen, K. Aikawa, K. Shikano, "On the Training of Neural Networks for Speech Recognition", IEEE Proceedings of the International Conference on Neural Networks (ICNN), 1992.

[14] J. Elman, "Representation and Structure in Connectionist Models", Center of Research in Language Technical Report # 8903, University of California, August 1989.

[15] S. Fahlman, "An Empirical Study of Learning Speed in Back-Propagation Networks", Technical Report # CMU-CS-88-162, Carnegie Mellon University, September 1988.

A Neural Network Architecture for Speech Segmentation Using Mean Field Annealing

C. G. Jeong and H. Jeong
Department of Electrical Engineering, POSTECH
P.O.Box 125, Pohang 790-600, South Korea

Abstract

As a dual algorithm to the Geiger–Girosi restoration scheme, a new segmentation method is introduced and used to demonstrate an approach to phoneme–boundary detection. Also we introduce a neural network suitable for this algorithm, which consists of sigmoid neurons and Sigma-Pi neurons. Experimental results show that the new algorithm is superior to the *forward-backward* algorithm and the Geiger–Girosi algorithm in terms of position accuracy and recognition accuracy as well as computational speed for phoneme–boundary detection.

I. Introduction

Many segmentation algorithms are based upon the *divergence test* [2], [8], log-likelihood [3] or any other test-statistics [6], [9]. Among them, the *divergence test* shows prominent results. This algorithm is, however, very sensitive to threshold values, and critical misses may occur at vowel to consonant(VC) transitions. In order to detect better the VC transition, Regine [2] proposed the *forward-backward* algorithm by introducing a backward search scheme to the *divergence test.*

On the other hand, Geman and Geman [10] introduced a generic stochastic framework for signal reconstruction, especially for optical images. Since then, some investigators [11] applied this paradigm into the speech signal processing. This approach, however, requires much computation time due to simulated annealing.

Recently Geiger and Girosi [5] proposed a fast method for the Geman algorithm using mean field approximation and *saddle point approximation.* This mean field solution was especially designed for signal restoration, and therefore shows poor estimates of *line processes*; in general, it tends to generate many false-alarms at object boundaries. To overcome this problem, we propose an approach opposite to this scheme, that is tailored to obtain accurate boundaries with the help of less accurate restoration, and that is suitable for neural network implementation.

II. Segmentation Framework

A Markov process together with its boundary process is defined in the *parameter space* (X, L) of size N: $X \triangleq \{X(k); k \in \{1, \cdots, N\}\}$ and $L \triangleq \{L(k); k \in \{1, \cdots, N\}\}$, where $X(k)$ is a signal process in the form of time sequence, cepstrum, or short time Fourier transform defined at time k. Also $L(k) \in \{0, 1\}$ is the so-called *line process* which determines the existence of discontinuity between $X(k-1)$ and $X(k)$. We assume that from the hidden process (X, L), the *observation*, $Y \triangleq \{Y(k);\ k \in \{1, \cdots, N\}\}$, is generated with additive Gaussian noise.

Based upon this stochastic model, we can find the MAP estimate of (X, L) from Y:

$$(\mathbf{x}^*, \mathbf{l}^*) = \arg\max_{(\hat{\mathbf{x}}, \hat{\mathbf{l}})} P(\hat{\mathbf{x}}(\mathbf{y}), \hat{\mathbf{l}}(\mathbf{y})|\mathbf{y}), \tag{1}$$

where $\hat{\mathbf{x}}(\mathbf{y})$ and $\hat{\mathbf{l}}(\mathbf{y})$ are the estimates of the realizations $\mathbf{x}$ and $\mathbf{l}$, respectively. Since X and L

0-7803-1901-X/94 $4.00 ©1994 IEEE

are Markov random fields, $P(\cdot)$ can be represented by the Gibbs distribution [7]:

$$P(\mathbf{x},\mathbf{l}|\mathbf{y}) = \frac{1}{Z_0}\exp[-\beta U_0(\mathbf{x},\mathbf{l}|\mathbf{y})], \tag{2}$$

where $U_0(\cdot)$ is an *energy function*, $1/\beta$ is a *temperature* constant, and Z_0 is a *partition function*:

$$Z_0 \triangleq \sum_{\mathbf{x}}\sum_{\mathbf{l}}\exp[-\beta U_0(\mathbf{x},\mathbf{l}|\mathbf{y})]. \tag{3}$$

Following Geman's strategy [10], we can define $U_0(\mathbf{x},\mathbf{l}|\mathbf{y})$ as

$$U_0(\mathbf{x},\mathbf{l}|\mathbf{y}) \triangleq \sum_{k=1}^{N}\left\{\|x(k)-y(k)\|^2+\lambda(1-l(k))\|x(k)-x(k-1)\|^2+\gamma l(k)+\nu\sum_{i\in N_k}\frac{1}{(k-i)^2}l(k)l(i)\right\}, \tag{4}$$

where λ, γ and ν are weighting parameters, $N_k \triangleq \{k-1, k-2, \cdots, k-d\}$ is a dth neighborhood of $L(k)$, and $\|\cdot\|$ is the L_p norm. Here p is the dimension of the signal process. Notice that this energy function consists of the three terms: *matching*, *smoothness*, and *a priori* knowledge about discontinuity. Considering (1)–(4) together, we note that the MAP estimate $(\mathbf{x}^*, \mathbf{l}^*)$ is a minimizer of the functional $U_0(\mathbf{x},\mathbf{l}|\mathbf{y})$, as was first noticed by Geman [10].

As a special case of (4), a *weak membrane model* is

$$U_0(x,l|y) = \sum_{k=1}^{N}[(x(k)-y(k))^2+\lambda(1-l(k))(x(k)-x(k-1))^2+\gamma l(k)]. \tag{5}$$

To solve this equation, Geman [10] proposed the *Gibbs Sampler*, and Blake and Zisserman [1] the *graduated nonconvexity* (GNC) algorithm, respectively. Recently, Geiger [5] derived a deterministic relaxation solution.

$$\begin{cases} \bar{x}^{\tau+1}(k) &= \bar{x}^{\tau}(k) - \mu\Big[(\bar{x}^{\tau}(k)-y(k)) + \lambda\{(\bar{x}^{\tau}(k)-\bar{x}^{\tau}(k-1))(1-\bar{l}^{\tau}(k)) \\ & \quad -(\bar{x}^{\tau}(k+1)-\bar{x}^{\tau}(k))(1-\bar{l}^{\tau}(k+1))\}\Big], \\ \bar{l}^{\tau}(k) &= \frac{1}{1+\exp[-\beta(\lambda\|\bar{x}^{\tau}(k)-\bar{x}^{\tau}(k-1)\|^2-\gamma(k))]}, \end{cases} \tag{6}$$

where τ is an iteration index, and μ a convergence rate. In particular, note that $\bar{x}^{\tau}(k)$ is recursively improved but $\bar{l}^{\tau}(k)$ is indirectly estimated from $\bar{x}^{\tau}(k)$. As a result, the resolution of $\bar{l}^{\tau}(k)$ is poor and an alternative approach is required.

III. Mean Field Approximation

To begin with, let us introduce an auxiliary process $s(k)$ having continuous value on real line:

$$l(k) \triangleq \frac{1}{1+\exp(-\beta s(k))}, \quad s(k) \in (-\infty, \infty). \tag{7}$$

Next, substituting (4) into (3) yields

$$\begin{aligned} Z_0 &= \int\!\!\int \exp\Big[-\beta\sum_{k=1}^{N}\Big\{\|x(k)-y(k)\|^2+\lambda(1-l(s(k)))\|x(k)-x(k-1)\|^2 \\ &+ \gamma l(s(k))+\nu\sum_{i\in N_k}\frac{1}{(k-i)^2}l(s(k))l(s(i))\Big\}\Big]ds(1)\cdots ds(N)dx(1)\cdots dx(N). \end{aligned} \tag{8}$$

Approximating Z_0 by replacing $x(k-1)$ by the mean field value $\bar{x}(k-1)$ and applying *saddle point approximation* to $s(k)$ will give

$$Z_0 \approx C\prod_{k=1}^{N}\int_{-\infty}^{\infty}\exp\Big\{-\beta(1+\lambda(1-l(\bar{s}(k))))\|x(k)-m(k)\|^2\Big\}dx(k)$$

$$\times \exp\Big\{-\beta\{\frac{\lambda(1-l(\bar{s}(k)))}{1+\lambda(1-l(\bar{s}(k)))}\|y(k)-\bar{x}(k-1)\|^2+\gamma l(\bar{s}(k))+\nu\sum_{i\in N_k}\frac{1}{(k-i)^2}l(\bar{s}(k))l(\bar{s}(i))\}\Big\},$$

(9)

where C is a constant, and $m(k)$ is defined as

$$m(k) \triangleq \frac{y(k)+\lambda(1-l(\bar{s}(k)))\bar{x}(k-1)}{1+\lambda(1-l(\bar{s}(k)))}. \tag{10}$$

Shortly it will be shown that $m(k)$ is indeed the mean of $X(k)$. Note that (10) is a linear combination of the observation and the estimate $\bar{x}(k-1)$, i.e., $m(k)=\alpha y(k)+(1-\alpha)\bar{x}(k-1)$, $0\le\alpha\le 1$, where $\alpha \triangleq 1/\{1+\lambda(1-l(\bar{s}(k)))\}$. Finally noting in (9) that $X(k)$ is a Gaussian process with the mean $m(k)$ and the variance, $1/\{2\beta(1+\lambda(1-l(\bar{s}(k))))\}$, we obtain

$$\begin{aligned} Z_0 \approx\ & C\exp\Big[-\beta\sum_{k=1}^{N}\{\frac{\lambda(1-l(\bar{s}(k)))}{1+\lambda(1-l(\bar{s}(k)))}\|y(k)-\bar{x}(k-1)\|^2+\gamma l(\bar{s}(k)) \\ & + \nu\sum_{i\in N_k}\frac{1}{(k-i)^2}l(\bar{s}(k))l(\bar{s}(i))-\frac{1}{\beta}\log\sqrt{\frac{\pi}{\beta(1+\lambda(1-l(\bar{s}(k))))}}\}\Big]. \end{aligned} \tag{11}$$

We can now derive $\bar{s}(k)$ and $\bar{x}(k)$ from Z_0. First, the mean field $\bar{x}(k)$ can be represented by the partition function:

$$\begin{aligned} \bar{x}(k) &= \int_{-\infty}^{\infty} x(k)\frac{1}{Z_0}\exp\{-\beta U_0(x,l|y)\}\,dx(k), \\ &= y(k)-\frac{1}{2}\nabla_{y(k)}F(\bar{x},\bar{s},y), \end{aligned} \tag{12}$$

where F is the *free energy*: $F \triangleq -\log Z_0/\beta$. As a result, substituting (11) into (12), we have

$$\bar{x}(k) = y(k)+\frac{\lambda(1-l(\bar{s}(k)))}{1+\lambda(1-l(\bar{s}(k)))}(\bar{x}(k-1)-y(k)). \tag{13}$$

Note that (??) is same as (10), and that (13) represents an estimate $\bar{x}(k)$ from $y(k)$ with an innovation $(\bar{x}(k-1)-y(k))$ and a variance $(1+\lambda(1-l(\bar{s}(k))))$ as normalization factor.

Finally, to obtain an equilibrium solution of $\bar{s}(k)$, we set

$$\frac{\partial\bar{s}(k)}{\partial\tau} = -\frac{\partial F(\bar{x},\bar{s},y)}{\partial\bar{s}(k)}. \tag{14}$$

Next putting (11) into (14) results in (15).

Therefore, we have the final result:

$$\left\{\begin{aligned} \bar{s}^{\tau+1}(k) &= \bar{s}^{\tau}(k)+\mu\beta l(\bar{s}^{\tau}(k))(1-l(\bar{s}^{\tau}(k)))\{\tfrac{\lambda}{(1+\lambda(1-l(\bar{s}^{\tau}(k))))^2}\|y(k)-\bar{x}^{\tau}(k-1)\|^2 \\ &\quad -\gamma-\nu\textstyle\sum_{i\in N_k}\tfrac{1}{(k-i)^2}\{l(\bar{s}^{\tau}(i))+\bar{s}^{\tau}(2k-i)\}+\tfrac{\lambda}{2\beta(1+\lambda(1-l(\bar{s}^{\tau}(k))))}\}, \\ \bar{x}^{\tau}(k) &= y(k)+\tfrac{\lambda(1-l(\bar{s}^{\tau}(k)))}{1+\lambda(1-l(\bar{s}^{\tau}(k)))}(\bar{x}^{\tau}(k-1)-y(k)). \end{aligned}\right. \tag{15}$$

Notice that fixed points of these equations are the mean field approximation of the MAP estimates of (1). The importance of this equation is the fact that it is actually dual to the Geiger–Girosi equation (6). The major difference is that which of $X(k)$ and $L(k)$ is pursued at the cost of the other.

As a neural network architecture to implement (15), we show a basic part for a time section k in Fig. 1. In this figure, the disks and boxes denote neurons and the solid disk represents a switch controlled by the line process $L(k)$.

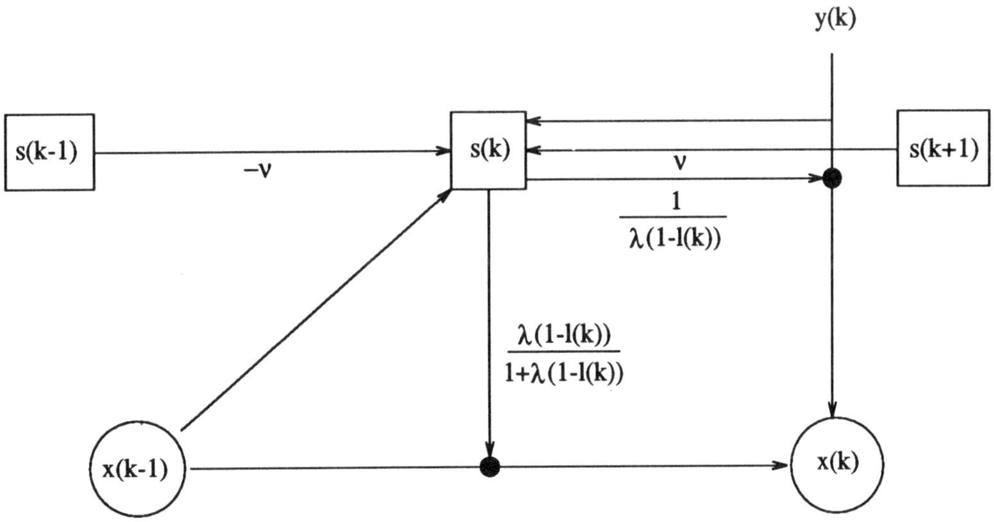

Fig. 1. A neural network at the section k; the neighborhood size $d = 1$ is considered.

IV. Experimental Results

As an application to speech segmentation, we will find phoneme–boundaries. To compare its performance, we chose the *forward-backward* algorithm [2] and the Geiger–Girosi algorithm as typical references among many other segmentation algorithms [6], [8], [9].

The training database consists of 602 phoneme segments and is used to determine the parameters for the three segmentation algorithms. After then, the second database, consisting of 2588 phoneme segments, is used to test the segmentation algorithms.

To begin with, we divide a large speech sample into possibly overlapping blocks of N frames and process each block in a batch. The last detected position of the previous segmentation result will become the starting position of the current N frames. For the purpose of simplicity, we consider only the case where $x(k)$ and $y(k)$ are represented in pth order LPC cepstrum. In this experiment all spectrum analysis are done using 256 point rectangular window spaced with half window size. Cepstrum analysis with $p = 16$ is carried out by the LPC Burg algorithm along with the cepstrum *liftering* [4].

One of the most hardest problems in the MRF framework is to track the Markov parameters. In our case, we estimated the parameters by trial and error. Typical parameters are $\gamma = 0.1$, $\lambda = 0.1$, and $\nu = 1.8$. Also the temperature $1/\beta$ is reduced by the schedule, $1/\beta(i) = T_0/(1 + \log(i))$, $(i = 1, \cdots, 20)$. Here i is an annealing index and T_0 is an initial temperature. In addition, at each fixed temperature, (15) is updated up to 40 times($\tau = 1, 2, \cdots, 40$).

To compare our algorithm with the previous works, we implemented the *forward-backward* algorithm and the Geiger algorithm. Each algorithm is optimized so that it may give about the same number of segments as that of manual segmentation. In the *forward-backward* algorithm, we used $(\delta_v, \lambda_v) = (0.2, 400)$ and $(\delta_u, \lambda_u) = (0.8, 800)$ [2], so as to get phonemic units.

Some snapshot views of our algorithm are illustrated in Fig. 2. Note that the vertical bars in Fig. 2(a) shows the desired segmentation locations. As can be seen from Fig. 2(b) to 2(d), phoneme boundaries of abruptly changing points are detected first, and then less abrupt points appear. In this figures, the length of the vertical bars indicates the likelihood of boundaries.

The comparison with the *forward-backward* algorithm and the Geiger-Girosi algorithm is shown in Fig. 3. As can be seen from this figure, the new algorithm performs very well.

To estimate the performance quantitatively, we computed the miss and false-alarm rates and the position tolerance as shown in Fig. 4. We notice that the new algorithm performs well for any transitions such as CV, VV, VC, and CC on the average.

Table I shows the recognition rate at a typical position tolerance of ± 42 msec. Here the

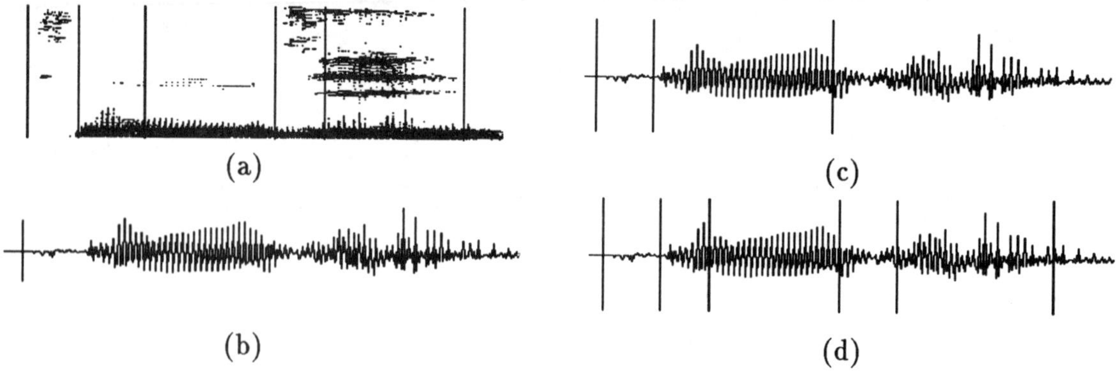

Fig. 2. Segmentation results (b)–(d) with the mannually segmented boundary (a). Here (b) results after 40 iteration($i = 1$), (c) after 80($i = 2$), (d) after 400($i = 10$), respectively.

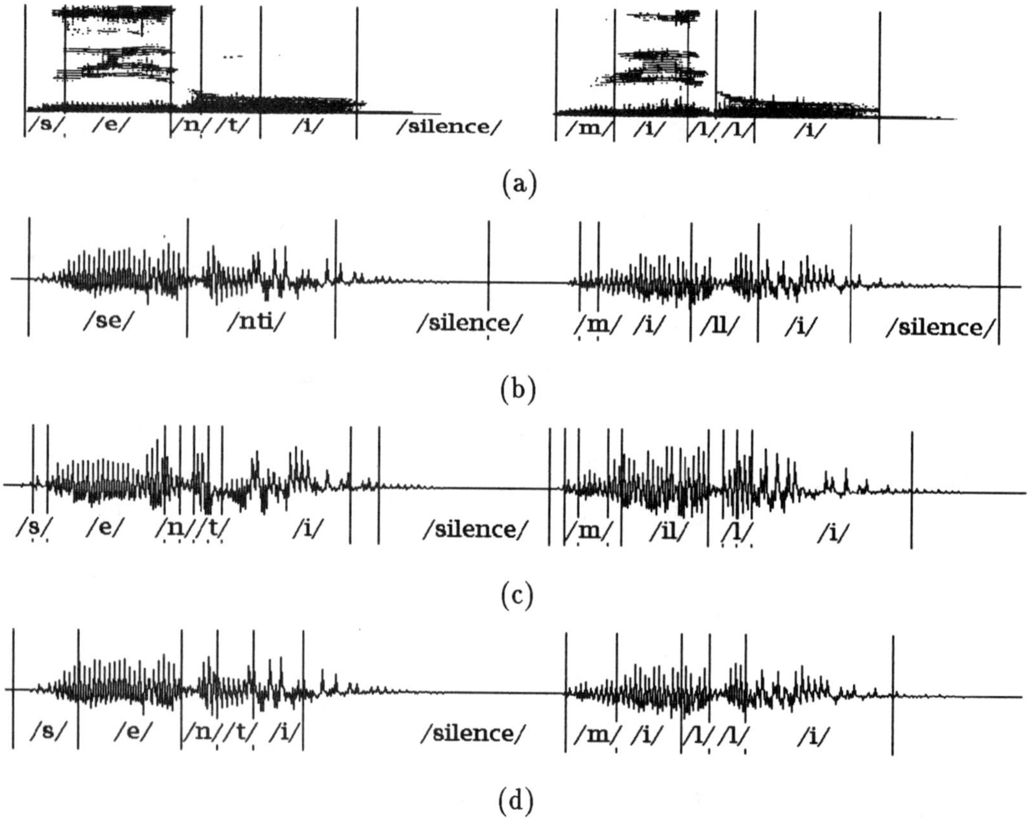

Fig. 3. Segmentation results: (a) a test speech spectrum, (b) the forward-backward algorithm, (c) Geiger-Girosi algorithm, and (d) the new algorithm.

performance index is the average of the *miss* and *false-alarm* rates, and the position tolerance of ± 42 msec corresponds to $d + 1$ window rates(i.e., 512 samples). As can be seen from this table, the new algorithm shows about 5.3% and 33.8% better recognition rate than the *forward-backward* algorithm and the Geiger–Girosi mean field solution, respectively.

Finally the new algorithm is $\mathcal{O}(N^2)$ times faster for N speech frames than the forward-backward method achieving 0.75 phonemes boundaries per second by a 2.3 MFLOPS computer.

V. Conclusion

In conclusion, we derived a robust segmentation algorithm and its neural network architecture starting from the Geman algorithm and showed that it is actually dual to the Geiger–Girosi algorithm which is especially designed to signal restoration.

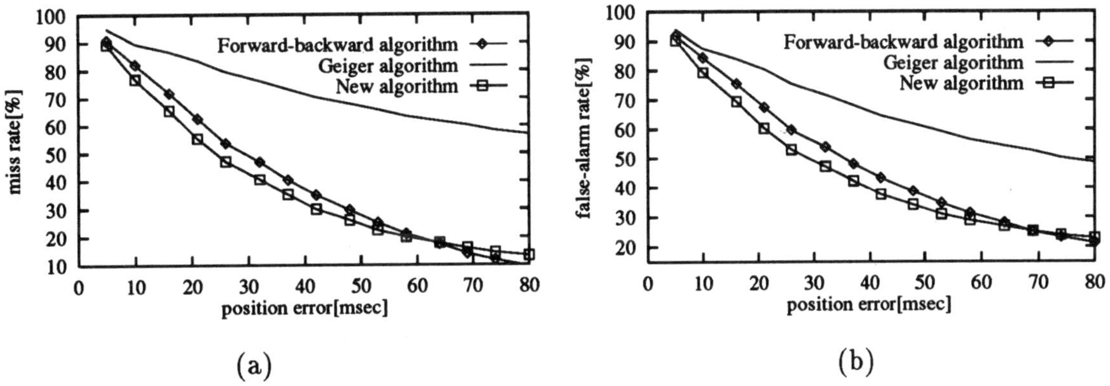

Fig. 4. The miss (a) and false-alarm rates (b) with respect to the position tolerance.

TABLE I

THE RATES OF MISSES AND FALSE-ALARMS WITHIN A ±42 MSEC POSITION TOLERANCE. THE PERFORMANCE INDEX IS THE AVERAGE OF THE MISS AND FALSE-ALARM RATES.

Algorithm \ Recognition rate	Miss	False-alarm	Performance index
Forward-backward algorithm	34.9%(903/2588)	43.3%(940/2171)	39.1%
Geiger algorithm	70.3%(1819/2588)	64.5%(1918/2973)	67.4%
New algorithm	29.9%(774/2588)	37.7%(1128/2991)	33.8%

Also the experimental results show that the new algorithm is better, about 5.3% – 33.8% in recognition rate, than the *forward-backward* algorithm and the Geiger–Girosi mean field solution.

REFERENCES

[1] A. Blake and A. Zisserman, *Visual Reconstruction*, Cambridge. MA: MIT Press, 1987.

[2] A. O. Regine, "A New Statistical Approach for the Automatic Segmentation of Continuous Speech Signals," *IEEE Trans. on ASSP*, Vol. 36, No. 1, Jan. 1988, pp. 29–40.

[3] A. Van Brandt, "Detecting and Estimating Parameter's Jumps Using Ladder Algorithms and Likelihood Ratio Test," *Proc. of ICASSP*, 1983, pp. 1017–1020.

[4] B. H. Juang, L. R. Labiner, and J. G. Wilpon, "On the Use of Bandpass Liftering in Speech Recognition", *IEEE Trans. on ASSP*, Vol. ASSP–35, No. 7, July 1987, pp. 947–1987.

[5] D. Geiger and F. Girosi, "Parallel and Deterministic Algorithms from MRF's: Surface Reconstruction," *IEEE Trans. on PAMI*, Vol. 13, No. 5, May 1991, pp. 401–412.

[6] Jan P. van Hemert, "Automatic Segmentation of Speech," *IEEE Trans. on SP*, Vol. 39, No. 4, April 1991, pp. 1008–1012.

[7] J. E. Besag, "Spatial Interaction and the Statistical Analysis of Lattice Systems," *J. Royal Statis. Soc., Ser. B 36*, 1974, pp. 192–236.

[8] M. Basseville and A. Basseville, "Sequential Detection of Abrupt Changes in Spectral Characteristics of Digital Signals," *IEEE Trans. on Information Theory*, Vol. IT-29, No. 5, Sept. 1983, pp. 709–724.

[9] R. J. Di Francesco, "Real-Time Speech Segmentation Using Pitch and Convexity Jump Models: Application to Variable Rate Speech Coding," *IEEE Trans. on ASSP*, Vol. 38, No. 5, May 1990, pp. 741–748.

[10] S. Geman and D. Geman, "Stochastic Relaxation, Gibbs Distributions, and the Bayesian Restoration of Images," *IEEE Trans. on PAMI*, Vol. 6, No. 6, Nov. 1984, pp. 721–741.

[11] Y. Zhao, et al., "Applying of the Gibbs Distribution to Hidden Markov Modeling in Speaker-Independent Isolated Word Recognition," *IEEE Trans. on SP*, Vol. 39, No. 6, June 1991, pp. 1291–1299.

Speaker-Independent Spoken Digits Recognition Using LVQ

K.Kondo, H.Kamata and Y.Ishida

Department of Electronics and Communication, Meiji University
1-1-1,Higashi-mita, Tama-ku, Kawasaki, 214 Japan

Abstract

In this paper we present a new spoken Japanese digits recognition system using LVQ (Learning Vector Quantization) [1][2]. LVQ is very effective to phoneme recognition and its algorithm is very simple. We try to utilize LVQ algorithm using word, not phoneme, as one unit. Input vectors in our system are the mel-cepstrum coefficients generated from beginning points to end points of spoken digits. In recognition process we only find the closest reference vector to the input vector. Experiments are excuted for two cases. One is for some isolated spoken digits. The other is for some continuous spoken digits (the speech speed, V, is $1 < V < 3$ [word/sec]). The recognition rate of isolated spoken digits was 99.2%. That of continuous spoken digits was 95.4%. Experimental results shows this method is effective for spoken digits recognition.

1. Introduction

There are many studies on speech recognition , for example, continuous speech recognition, speaker-independent recognition and so on. In this paper we plan to especially improve the score rate of speaker-independent and continuous speech recognition.

LVQ is often used for phoneme recognition and it has high performance and can generate some good reference vectors for speaker-independent speech. However, it often lead uncorrect categories of the phonemes in words recognition, because of coarticulation. We use LVQ for words recognition. The speech signals used to recognition experiments are continuous and isolated spoken digits. In both case the beginning and end points of each spoken digit are determined by manual opetation. Input speech is analyzed by Cepstrum method. In learning process category reference vectors are generated by 5 male speakers. Each category has only one reference vector. We find the category which has the closest reference vector to the input vector in recognition process.

This paper is organized as following. Section 2 gives a speech analysis (pre-process for LVQ

0-7803-1901-X/94 $4.00 ©1994 IEEE

). Section 3 describes LVQ and learning process. Section 4 presents recognition results for both isolated and continuous Japanese spoken digits.

2. Speech analysis

Speech signals are converted into 12-bit samples at rate of 10 kHz and pre-emphasized by $(1-z^{-1})$. The beginning and end points of each spoken digit are determined, by hand, based on spectrum energy $P(t)$ as shown in Eq.(1). Each spoken digit is separated into 16 sections between the beginning and end points and is multiplied by a 256 points Hamming window. The input vector is 16×16-dimensional vector with mel-cepstrum coefficients which are normalized for each section.

$$P(t)=\sum_{k=1}^{N} S(t)_k \qquad S(t)_k\text{: Spectrum} \tag{1}$$

where N is 16.

3. LVQ

The learning rule of LVQ is as following: First, we calculate Euclidean distance for all reference vectors $m_i(t)$ and then find the closest reference vector $m_c(t)$ to the input vector $x(t)$.

$$\|x(t)-m_c(t)\| = min\{\|x(t)-m_i(t)\|\} \tag{2}$$

Let the input vector $x(t)$ belong to category S_r and the closest reference vector $m_c(t)$ to $x(t)$ belong to S_S. If S_r belongs to the same category as S_S, $m_c(t)$ is moved closer to $x(t)$ as shown in Eq.(3). Fig.1(a) illustrates this process. If S_r belongs to a category other than S_S, $m_c(t)$ is moved away as shown in Eq.(4) and illustrated in Fig.1(b). All reference vectors except $m_c(t)$ are not updated. The moving direction is $x(t)-m_c(t)$.

$$m_c(t+1)=m_c(t)+\alpha(t)\{x(t)-m_c(t)\} \tag{3}$$

$$m_c(t+1)=m_c(t)-\alpha(t)\{x(t)-m_c(t)\} \tag{4}$$

where the function $\alpha(t)$ ought to be a monotonically decreasing function of time $(0<\alpha(t)<1)$.

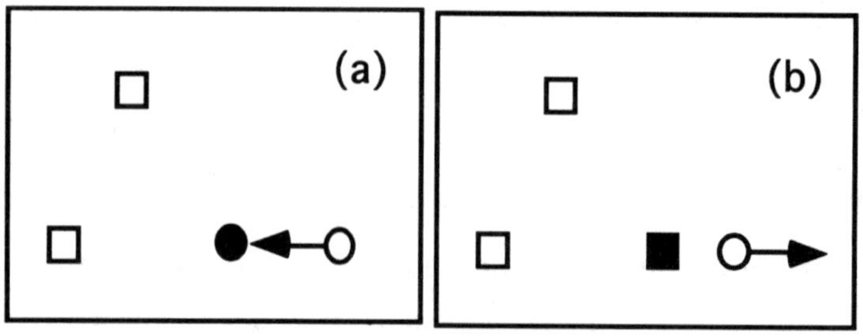

Black : Input vector, White : Reference vector, Shape : Category

Fig. 1 (a): S_r belongs to the same category as S_S.

(b) : S_r belongs to the category other than S_S

The reference vectors are initialized by those sampled randomly from all the input vectors. Then the reference vectors are modified by moving closer to the input vector or away based on Eqs.(3) and (4). In our system, we use LVQ using words different from the conventional one using phonemes.

4. Result

10 Japanese spoken digits are shown in Table 1.

Table 1 10 Japanese digits

0	1	2	3	4	5	6	7	8	9
ZERO	ICHI	NI	SAN	YON	GO	ROKU	NANA	HACHI	KYU

The structure of our system used in the experiments is as following: We use utterances by 5 male speakers in leaning process. One of input vectors is randomly chosen as the reference vector in initial condition. In our system, the reference vector for each category is only one. Learning epochs are 1000. We use spoken digits uttered by 10 speakers(including 5 speakers described above).

Table 2 Recognition rate of isolated Japanese digits

	0	1	2	3	4	5	6	7	8	9	Total
Rate %	100	100	100	100	100	100	92.9	100	100	100	99.2

Table 3 Recognition rate of continuous Japanese digits

	0	1	2	3	4	5	6	7	8	9	Total
Rate %	100	100	100	100	100	100	72.7	100	100	91.7	95.4

The result of isolated spoken Japanese digits recognition in 126 samples is shown in Table 2. The average value of the recognition rates is 99.2%.

The recognition rates of continuous spoken Japanese digits is shown in Table 3. The average value of them is 95.4%. This is less than the isolated case. The recognition rate of /6/ is less than the other. This is why a part, "U", of "ROKU" may be often unvoiced and the beginning and end points are obscurer due to the effect of coarticulation effect.

5. Conclusions

In this paper we have presented a new method for the speaker-independents spoken Japanese digits recognition using LVQ. The proposed method utilizes LVQ algorithm using word, not phoneme, as one unit . The experimental results have shown that this method is effective for both isolated and continuous Japanese digits. We confirm that our method is robust for the obscure estimation of beginning and end points.

Acknowledgment

We wolud like to thank Dr. Mitsuru Endo of Matsusita laboratory for his helpful advice.

6. References

[1] T. Kohonen, "The neural phonetic typewriter", IEEE Computer, 21, 3, pp.11-22, (1988).

[2] E. McDermott, S. Katagiri, "Shift-Invariant, Multi-Category Phoneme Recognition Using Kohonen's LVQ2", IEEE, ICASSP88, 9.S3, pp.81-84, (1986.5).

Neural Computations as Multidimensional Feature Mapping for Acoustic Information Representation

Kuansan Wang, *Student Member IEEE*

***Abstract*— Neurons in the biological systems usually exhibit distinctive response selectivity to certain features in the stimulus. As the neurons are functionally and spatially segregated, one may interpret the computational principles of the neural systems as a mechanism of feature mapping, which represents information in a topographic fashion. In this article, we summarize the physiological findings of the neural selectivities in the primary auditory cortex and, based on which, propose a mathematical framework for mapping the acoustic features conveyed in the power spectrum. We further demonstrate how this model may be employed to explain a series of psychoacoustic experiments that are designed to measure the sensitivity of human auditory system to spectral shape perception, and hypothesize how the measured thresholds may be related to the model parameters.**

I. INTRODUCTION

From the viewpoint of computational architecture, neural networks are a very peculiar structure for signal and information processing. Neural networks often employ extremely high degree of parallelism and massive interconnections. In contrast, the individual computing units (neurons) can usually be modeled with limited varieties of operations that are of moderate complexity. Such a computing architecture is different from conventional computers in many ways, yet the processing required for all the sensory and intellectual capabilities, as remarkable as they are, is achieved within the neural networks in the nervous system. It is widely believed [2] that biological neural networks are not designed and suitable for carrying out exact numerical computations as digital computers. Neural network based systems must employ a totally different set of computational principles for information representation and processing.

Neurons in the biological systems often exhibit distinctive response selectivities to stimulus with certain features. More interestingly, neurons that are functionally similar are usually spatially segregated. In other words, neural responses tend to have a high degree of locality, and the response area can usually be associated with a particular feature. From a functional point of view, the purpose of neural computations seems to transform salient information in terms of the shapes and locations of feature maps, i.e., while information is usually encoded numerically in the conventional computing architecture, it appears to be represented *topographically* in the biological neural systems.

In this article, we demonstrate the feature mapping mechanism in the auditory system with the results from our recent psychophysical studies. Specifically, we focus our discussion here on the analysis of the acoustic spectral shape in the primary auditory cortex (A1). Spectral shape is the most important physical correlate of the percept of timbre [4]. Experimental and theoretical investigations have demonstrated that the early auditory stages of processing basically manifest an enhanced and noise-robust version of acoustic spectrum [7]. There is virtually no loss of the information encoded in the shape of acoustic spectrum. However, as it arrives at A1, the spectral representation undergoes a substantial transformation, which will be the center of discussion of this article.

II. BRIEF REVIEW OF THE AUDITORY FUNCTIONS

As early as in the cochlea of the inner ear, the auditory system evolves a spatial dimension, often known as the *tonotopic axis*, to represent the frequency components of the acoustic signal in a spatial-temporal fashion. The tonotopic axis is preserved all the way up along the auditory pathway, and roughly corresponds to a logarithmic frequency scale. Therefore, the spatial-temporal representation $f(x,t)$ rendered by the auditory periphery may also be regarded as a time-frequency representation of the

The author is with the Institute for Systems Research and Department of Electrical Engineering, University of Maryland, College Park, MD 20742. Phone: (301)405-6596, E-mail: kuansan@src.umd.edu, Fax: (301)405-6707.

0-7803-1901-X/94 $4.00 ©1994 IEEE

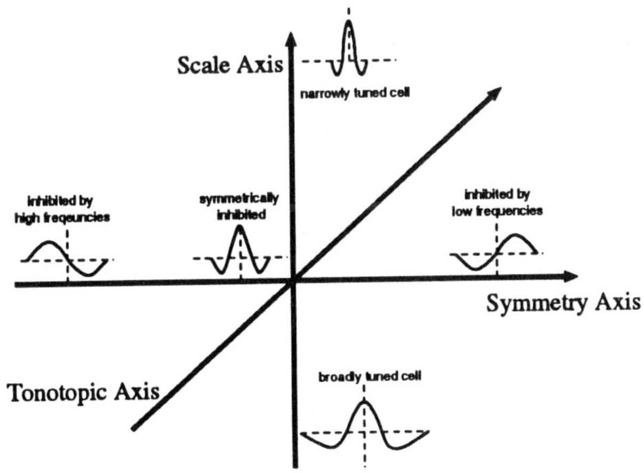

Figure 1: A schematic description of the cortex model. According to the response patterns, the neurons are assumed to be systematically organized on three spatial dimensions that characterize each neuron's tuning frequency and selectivity to spectral symmetry and bandwidth of the stimulus.

sound. Indeed, it is mathematically shown [7] that $f(x,t)$ is very similar to a short-time, logarithmically normalized magnitude spectrum of the sound signal.

Neurons in A1 exhibit organizational characteristics that reflect systematic selectivity to various features in the spectral profile $f(x,\cdot)$. One may usually associate each neuron with a *response function*(RF) $w(\cdot)$ and characterize the neural response with the inner product $< f, w >$ along the x-axis. The response function here is similar to the so-called receptive field in the vision literature. Conceptually, inner product is an operation to quantitatively measure how close two signals match each other. By modeling the response as an inner product, RF dictates the neural response patterns. The sign of the inner product reflects whether the neuron exhibits an excitatory or inhibitory response. The systematic neural selectivity can therefore be studied by examining how RF's are organized.

Through extensive physiological studies, there are at least three spatial dimensions in A1 along which RF's are systematically organized [6]. First, neurons in A1 preserve the tonotopic tuning characteristic as observed earlier in the auditory system. Unlike the one dimensional nature in the auditory periphery, however, neurons tuned to the same frequency (called best frequency BF) are lined up along a two dimensional plane known as *iso-frequency plane* that runs perpendicular to the tonotopic axis. For neurons on the iso-frequency contour, two other organizations in RF's are recently identified. First, it is found that their tuning bandwidths vary systematically and considerably with the location on the iso-frequency contour. Neurons in the center are more sharply tuned than those on the sides of A1. Second, the neural tuning curves are also observed to exhibit systematic change in symmetry. Neurons in the center respond best to stimulus with a symmetric spectral shape, while neurons on the edges of A1 are more selective to stimuli with spectral energy distribution slanted to a higher or lower frequency than BF. A schematic description of these observations is shown in fig. 1. From a functional point of view, the variation in bandwidth indicates that the auditory system may employ a multiscale framework to analyze the acoustic spectrum, and the variation in symmetry suggests that the skewness of spectral energy distribution is a feature explicitly represented by the auditory system.

As elaborated in [6], the variations of RF's along these three spatial dimensions may be closely described by

$$w(x,\phi,s) = w_s(x)\cos\phi - \hat{w}_s(x)\sin\phi \quad (1)$$

$$w_s(x) = a^{s/2} w_m(a^s x) \quad (2)$$

for some symmetric function $w_m(x)$ and some constant a. It is noted that the above equation employs a simple norm-preserving dilation to model the variation in tuning bandwidths. The symmetry variation, on the other hand, is achieved by sinusoidally interpolating the symmetric seed function w_m and its Hilbert transform $\hat{w}_m$, which is antisymmetric but has the same norm as w_m. From physiological data, one suitable candidate for $w_m(x)$ is the (negative) second derivative of a Gaussian function, which is also known as the *Mexican hat* function. The neural response to the stimulus can therefore be modeled by

$$\begin{aligned} r(x,\phi,s) &= < f, w(\cdot - x,\phi,s) > \quad (3) \\ &= \int f(y) w(y-x,\phi,s)\,dy \end{aligned}$$

The response selectivity is clearly dictated by the RF $w(x,\phi,s)$. The time index t is dropped here for notational simplicity.

III. REPRESENTATION REDUCTION AND FEATURE EXTRACTION

It is clear that the multidimensional transformation of the acoustic spectrum in eq. 3 gives rise to a highly redundant representation $r(x,\phi,s)$. It is interesting to note that similar redundant representation also occurs in the early auditory system in which an additional spatial (tonotopic) axis is used to represent sound that is one dimension in nature. From an information processing point of view, redundant representation, when combined with proper reduction algorithms, usually gives rise to two major benefits: (1) noise robustness and (2) making salient features more explicit and easy to access. In the auditory periphery, these are achieved by employing a biologically feasible mechanism called *lateral inhibition* for representation reduction [7]. In the primary auditory cortex, evidence of lateral inhibition is still to be found. However, many psychoacoustic results and biological findings in its visual counterpart all suggest the existence of lateral inhibition (on the isofrequency plane) is highly probable [6]. One salient function of lateral inhibition is to enhance *feature edges* of the signal representation which are believed to contain most important information of the signal. For instance, the feature edges detected by the lateral inhibition in the peripheral auditory system correspond to frequency contents in the acoustic signal [7]. Examples of employing similar feature reduction algorithms are also abundant in many areas of biologically motivated and multidimensional signal processing applications.

For the cortex model, the reduction on the isofrequency (ϕ-s) plane can be analytically approximated in the following steps. First, it can be shown that the cortical response along the ϕ-axis is always a sinusoid. To be more specific,

$$r(x,\phi,s)=p(x,s)\cos(\phi-\phi_o(x,s)), \qquad (4)$$

where

$$\phi_o(x,s)=\tan^{-1}\frac{< f,\hat{w}_s(\cdot-x) >}{< f,w_s(\cdot-x) >}$$

and

$$p(x,s)=\sqrt{< f,w_s(\cdot-x) >^2+< f,\hat{w}_s(\cdot-x) >^2}.$$

Rewritten in the Fourier domain of the spatial dimension, the above two equations can be interpreted as estimating the phase and modulus, respectively, of the signal $F(\omega)$ within the support of $W_s(\omega)$. In the terminology of linear system, $\phi_o(x,s)$ and $p(x,s)$ may be referred to as the *local phase response* and *local magnitude response* of the signal. It is argued that each local maximum at $\phi=\phi_o(x,s)$ for given (x,s) will inhibit other outputs along the ϕ-axis, hence the two dimensional lateral inhibition on the isofrequency (ϕ-s) plane may be effectively approximated by a one-dimensional inhibition on the local magnitude response $p(x,s)$ along the s-axis. If we denote the one dimensional edges of $p(x,s)$ as $\{s_i\}$, then the above process is, in effect, to manifest a set of feature edges

$$\mathcal{F}=\{(x,\phi_i,s_i):\phi_i=\phi_o(x,s_i)\} \qquad (5)$$

that describe the spectral characteristics of the acoustic signal.

The above framework has been demonstrated to provide a useful and complimentary description of spectral shapes for speech classification [6]. In the following, we demonstrate that it may also be employed to render a simple and elegant explanation to a series of psychoacoustic experiments designed to measure the sensitivity of human auditory system to spectral profile.

IV. CORRELATES TO SPECTRAL SHAPE PERCEPTION

Many psychoacoustic experiments have been conducted to investigate how the auditory system is sensitive to various features of the power spectrum of the sound signal. Experiments of this kind are usually lumped under the name of *profile analysis*. A series of experimental results that are directly related to the cortex model are recently reported in [5]. These experiments employ the stimulus that presumably generates a spectrum that can be described by

$$f(x)=e^{-Rx}u(x)+e^{Lx}u(-x) \qquad (6)$$

or equivalently,

$$\begin{aligned} F(\omega) &= \frac{1}{R+j\omega}+\frac{1}{L-j\omega} \\ &= \frac{L+R}{(RL+\omega^2)+j\omega(L-R)} \end{aligned} \qquad (7)$$

Note that we have arbitrarily set $x=0$ for the peak location. The so-called bandwidth factor (BWF) and spectral symmetry factor (SF) are defined as

$$\begin{aligned} \text{BWF} &= 1/L+1/R \\ \text{SF} &= \frac{L-R}{L+R} \end{aligned} \qquad (8)$$

The bandwidth and the symmetry of the stimuli are independently modified by adjusting L and R, and the thresholds to discriminate both factors are measured.

To associate BWF and SF with the cortex model, let us first examine the feature set of the stimulus. Note that the magnitude response of such stimulus is a two-pole pattern, which profile has the largest curvature change located roughly at the logarithmic center of the two poles, i.e.,

$$\Omega_c=\log\omega_c=\frac{\log R+\log L}{2} \qquad (9)$$

or

$$\omega_c=\sqrt{RL}$$

Such a curvature change will be detected as an edge by the lateral inhibition network.

From eq. 8, we have

$$\begin{aligned} \frac{1}{R} &= \frac{\mathrm{BWF}(1+\mathrm{SF})}{2} \\ \frac{1}{L} &= \frac{\mathrm{BWF}(1-\mathrm{SF})}{2} \end{aligned} \quad (10)$$

If we denote the characteristic spatial frequency of $W_m(\omega)$ as ω_m, then from eq. 2, we may associate each scale with a logarithmic spatial frequency in

$$\log\omega = s\log a + \log\omega_m.$$

Therefore,

$$\begin{aligned} \Omega_c &= s_c \log a + \log\omega_m \quad (11) \\ &= \log\sqrt{RL} \\ &= \log 2 - \log(\mathrm{BWF}) - 0.5\log(1-\mathrm{SF}^2). \end{aligned}$$

The experimental results indicate that, when SF is fixed, the threshold to detect the change in bandwidth factor is proportional to BWF, i.e., the threshold of detecting $\Delta\mathrm{BWF}/\mathrm{BWF}$ is constant. Moreover, this trend remains the same regardless the values of SF or BWF. From the above equation, we have

$$\Delta s_c = -\frac{\Delta\log\mathrm{BWF}}{\log a} \propto -\frac{\Delta\mathrm{BWF}}{\mathrm{BWF}}$$

The constant threshold in detecting $\Delta\mathrm{BWF}/\mathrm{BWF}$, therefore, can be explained by assuming a constant threshold in detecting the scale variation in the auditory system. Such assumption seems to suggest that the "scale channels" are uniformly organized in human's auditory system so that the threshold in detecting variation in scale is the same everywhere. In fact, this is the major motivation for assuming a simple dilation for the seed functions (eq. 2). The measured threshold may therefore be closely related to the spatial frequency resolution of the auditory system. The experimental data suggest that the spatial frequency resolution might be around 20%, or equivalently, the dilation factor $a = 0.82$.

This series of experiments also examined the perceptual sensitivity on SF, a parameter designed to reflect the symmetry of the spectral shape of the stimulus. Following our previous argument, the stimulus has one dominant edge. It is therefore reasonable to assume that the "perceived" spectral symmetry is the phase of $F(\omega)$ evaluated at ω_c. According to eqs. 9 and 10, we have

$$\begin{aligned} \tan\phi_c &= \frac{\omega_c(R-L)}{\omega_c^2 + RL} \\ &= -\mathrm{SF}/\sqrt{1-\mathrm{SF}^2} \end{aligned}$$

or

$$\sin\phi_c = -\mathrm{SF}. \quad (12)$$

Therefore, the spectral symmetry factor is represented by $\sin\phi_c$. For small ϕ_c, $\Delta\mathrm{SF} \approx -\Delta\phi_c$. The experimental results regarding the SF can be summarized as follows:

1. When BWF is fixed, the threshold of detecting ΔSF remains constant against SF over a wide range.
2. For large BWF with fixed SF, the threshold also seems to be independent of BWF and remains constant.
3. However, when BWF is small, the threshold increases linearly as BWF decreases.

Similar to our arguments for BWF, eq. 12 suggests that the first and second conclusions can be explained by assuming that the threshold for detecting change in ϕ is constant. Effectively, this may be achieved if the "phase channels" are uniformly organized in the auditory system. However, as the third observation indicates, the resolution of phase seems to decrease for small BWF. Since BWF can be closely associated with Ω_c, this seems to imply a large threshold for detecting phase variation at high spatial frequency. To be more specific, recall that it is the ϕ_c at the scale given by eq. 11 that is assumed to be most significant. Since SF is small in the experiments, the critical scale is determined mostly by BWF. Hence a large BWF implies ϕ_c from a low spatial frequency scale, and a small BWF suggests otherwise. It can thus be hypothesized that the effects of BWF on the detection of ΔSF are similar to the effects of spatial frequency on phase. The experimental results appear to suggest that the auditory system has a constant phase sensitivity at low spatial frequency, and the sensitivity degrades linearly for higher spatial frequencies. Such hypothesis bears remarkable similarity to the analogous findings in vision [1], and has been recently investigated through psychoacoustic experiments reported in [5]. The preliminary data appear consistent with the above hypothesis.

This hypothesis can be explained by the cortex model in a simple and straightforward manner. First note that the spatial position on the tonotopic axis is closely related to its spatial phase. Specifically, the pattern variation in terms of location and phase at spatial frequency ω is given by

$$|\Delta\phi| = \omega|\Delta x|. \quad (13)$$

In the three dimensional space of the cortex model, these two factors $\Delta\phi$ and Δx both account for the measurement of the displacement Δd of the feature edge, i.e., Δd is a combination of Δx and $\Delta\phi$.

Therefore, a feature variation in the cortex model can be detected if either $\Delta\phi$ or Δx of the feature edge exceeds the resolution of the corresponding axis. From eq. 13, it can be concluded that, at a low spatial frequency, Δd will be dominated mostly by $\Delta\phi$, and the trend reverses at high spatial frequencies. Therefore, the constant threshold at low spatial frequency actually may reflect a constant resolution of the ϕ axis, and the linearly increasing threshold measured in the experiments for high spatial frequency may be indeed caused by a also constant resolution on the tonotopic axis, which manifests itself as the slope of the phase sensitivity curve at high spatial frequency region (eq. 13). From the experimental results, it can be estimated that the resolution on the ϕ axis is approximately 6 degrees, and the tonotopic resolution is about 0.016 octave, or 0.5%. The latter is surprisingly close to the results from the frequency resolution experiments reported in [3] which are based on totally different paradigms.

In summary, the stimulus used for this series of experiments is approximated by a feature set that contains only a single point $\{(0, \phi_c, s_c)\}$. Although such interpretation on lateral inhibition is largely simplified, the model is still able to explain the experiments designed to measure the perceptual sensitivity on spectral shape for the human's auditory system. Significantly, the experimental results suggest that the three dimensions in the cortex model seem to be quite *uniformly* organized. This uniform structure may prove helpful for defining a distance measure that is very close to perceptual reality yet with reasonable complexity.

V. CONCLUSIONS

In this article, a mathematical framework modeling the feature mapping in the primary auditory cortex is proposed. The feature mapping is based on the systematically organized response functions that dictate neural response selectivity. It is demonstrated that the acoustic signal is represented by the spatial locations of the feature edges that correspond to the frequency components, spectral symmetry and spectral bandwidth. Such a biologically derived processing principle bears close relationship to human perception of spectral shape, and therefore may be useful in many speech and audio signal processing applications.

References

[1] R. L. De Valois and K. K. De Valois. *Spatial Vision*. Oxford Science Publications, New York, NY, 1990.

[2] S.-Y. Kung. *Digital Neural Networks*. Prentice-Hall, Englewood Cliffs, N.J., 1993.

[3] B. C. J. Moore and B. R. Glasberg. Psychoacoustic abilities of subjects with unilateral and bilateral cochlear hearing impairments and their relationship to the ability to understand speech. Scandinavian audiology supplementum 32, Stockholm, Sweden, 1989. Distributed by the Almqvist and Wiksell periodical company.

[4] R. Plomp. *Aspects of tone sensation: a psychophysical study*, chapter 6, pages 85–110. Academic Press, New York, NY, 1976.

[5] S. Vranić-Sowers, H. Versnel, and S. A. Shamma. Phase sensitivity in psychoacoustical and physiological experiments. In *The 125th Meeting of the Acoustic Society of America*, Ottawa, Canada, May 1993.

[6] K. Wang. *Neural computations in the auditory system for audio information processing*. PhD thesis, Dept. of EE, University of Maryland, 1993.

[7] K. Wang and S. A. Shamma. Self-normalization and noise-robustness in early auditory representations. *IEEE Transactions on Speech and Audio Processing*, July 1994. (Scheduled).

Pitch Determination Considering Laryngealization Effects In Spoken Dialogs

H. Niemann, J. Denzler, B. Kahles, R. Kompe, A. Kiessling, E. Nöth, V. Strom

Abstract— **A frequent phenomenon in spoken dialogs of the information seeking type are short elliptic utterances whose mood (declarative or interrogative) can only be distinguished by intonation. The main acoustic evidence is conveyed by the fundamental frequency or F_0–contour.**

Many algorithms for F_0 determination have been reported in the literature. A common problem are irregularities of speech known as 'laryngealizations'. This article describes an approach based on neural network techniques for the improved determination of fundamental frequency. First, an improved version of our neural network algorithm for reconstruction of the voice source signal (glottis signal) is presented. Second, the reconstructed voice source signal is used as input to another neural network distinguishing the three classes 'voiceless', 'voiced non–laryngealized', and 'voiced laryngealized'. Third, the results are used to improve an existing F_0 algorithm.

Results of this approach are presented and discussed in the context of the application in a spoken dialog system.

I. Introduction

Spoken dialog systems for information seeking enquiries, e.g. train or plane connections, are a current research topic. The importance and the use of intonation (or prosody, or suprasegmental information) in speech recognition and understanding has been discussed, for example, in [11] [12] [13] [14] [15]. It has been shown in [10] that in such dialogs short elliptic utterances occur frequently whose mood can only be determined by prosody. For example, an utterance of an officer or an automatic system 'the train leaves at 16.30' might be answered by the client by 'at 16.30 (!)' signalling to the officer 'ok, I got it' or by 'at 16.30 (?)' signalling to the officer 'please, confirm the time'. In both cases the wording is identical, only the intonation is different. The most important cue to intonation is the course of the fundamental frequency over time, that is, the F_0–contour. Many algorithms for determining the fundamental frequency have been reported [6]. A fairly reliable algorithm using dynamic programming was presented in [9] and employed in a prosodically controlled dialog system [10]. Nevertheless, irregularities of speech known as *laryngealizations* or as *creaky voice* often cause errors in F_0 detection which in turn may cause erroneous reactions of a dialog system. Hence, further improvement is desirable.

A laryngealization is usually characterized by an irregularity of the voiced excitation, manifested in the speech signal by irregular periodicity, strong variations of the amplitude, special form of the damped wave, or very long pitch periods. An example is given in Figure 1. Different types of laryngealizations are distinguished in [7] [2]. Such irregularities in the speech signal are a frequent source of errors in F_0 determination. However, they also occur frequently at phrase boundaries, and therefore, may be a useful cue for parsing of the utterances.

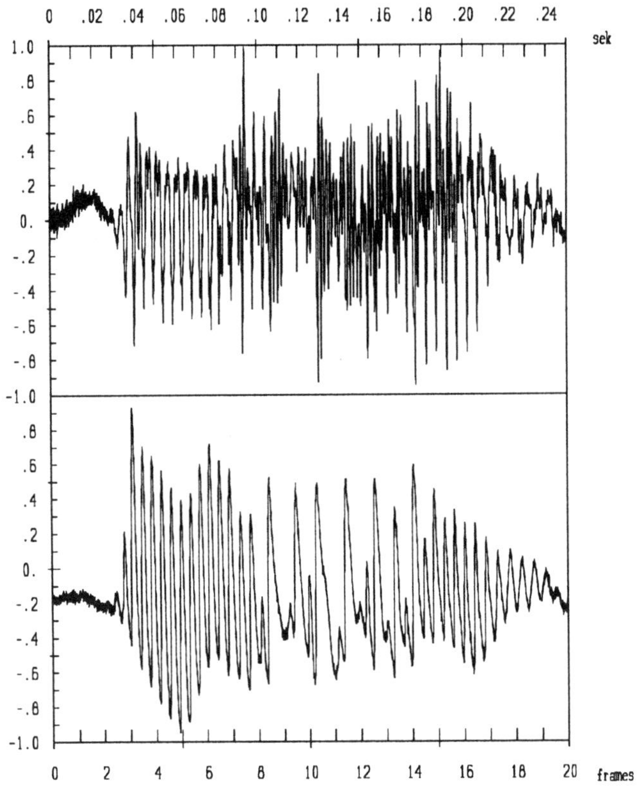

Figure 1. Top: a speech signal with laryngealization Bottom: Voice source signal, recorded with a laryngograph.

In this contribution we describe a neural network based approach to the determination of laryngealizations which in turn are used to improve F_0 extraction. Since many errors in the present version of the F_0 extraction algorithm are caused by laryngealizations, the idea is simply to detect them and to interpolate the F_0–contour over laryngealized portions of speech. Figure 1 indicates that laryngealizations may be detected more easily and reliably in the voice

This research was supported by the German Ministry of Research and Technology (BMFT) in the project VERBMOBIL. Only the authors are responsible for this article.

The authors are with Lehrstuhl für Mustererkennung (Informatik 5), Universität Erlangen–Nürnberg, 91058 Erlangen, Germany, except for V. Strom who is now with Institut für Kommunikationsforschung und Phonetik, Universität Bonn, 53115 Bonn, Germany source signal than in the speech signal. Therefore, the first step is the reconstruction of the voice source signal (VSS) by means of inverse filtering. This is done by a neural network as described in Sect. II; a first version of this approach was presented in [3], and here we present an improved version of this algorithm. Once the VSS has been determined it is classified by a neural network frame by frame into one of the three classes 'voiceless', 'voiced non-laryngealized', and 'voiced laryngealized'; this is described in Sect. III. We show in Sect. IV that these results can be used to improve an existing algorithm for F_0 extraction. A conclusion and outlook is given in Sect. V.

II. Inverse Filtering of the Speech Signal

A. Signal-To-Signal Mapping

Since pitch period calculation and the detection of laryngealizations can be done much easier using the voice source signal (VSS) instead of the speech signal the first step is to reconstruct the VSS. Additionally, the voiced/unvoiced decision is trivial on the VSS. The approach is to map the speech signal *directly* to the VSS, i.e. to apply a signal-to-signal transformation. The input and desired output values are normalized to the range of [0, 1]. One window (containing 78 sample values corresponding to 39 ms) of the speech signal is presented to the input layer of an artificial neural network (ANN) which gives as output one single value of the VSS. If we denote, in a multilayer-perceptron,

- the *input layer* by index $l = 0$ having $i = 0, 1, \ldots, M_0 - 1$ input nodes $n_i^{(0)}$ for signal values x_i,
- the *hidden layers* by indices $l = 1, 2, \ldots, M_{L-1}$ having $i = 0, 1, \ldots, M_l - 1$ hidden nodes $n_i^{(l)}$,
- the *output layer* by index $l = L$ having — in our case — *one* output node n_0^L,

then the relevant equations for computing an output value are:

1. for each layer and each node per layer compute the weighted sum of input values

$$y_j^{(l+1)} = \sum_{i=0}^{M_l - 1} w_{ij}^{(l+1)} f_i^{(l)} - w_j^{(l+1)} \qquad 0 \leq j \leq M_{l+1} - 1\,, \quad l = 0, 1, 2\,, \tag{1}$$

2. compute the output of a node from a *nonlinearity* Θ, in our case the sigmoid function

$$f_j^{(l+1)} = \Theta\left[y_j^{(l+1)}\right] = \frac{1}{1 + \exp(-y_j^{(l+1)})} \tag{2}$$

By shifting the speech signal point-by-point through the input layer, one gets the complete VSS reconstructed by the ANN; the reconstructed VSS is termed here ANN-VSS. Three types of ANN's are investigated, the (non-recursive) multilayer perceptron and the (recursive) Elman and Jordan networks [4] [8]; for each type different configurations were evaluated. As an example we give the structure of an Elman network in Figure 2 which has only one hidden layer of neurons. The output of every hidden neuron is fed back to a recursive node which in turn feeds forward to every hidden node. Hence, the number of hidden nodes and recursive nodes is the same in this network type. There may be additional layers of hidden nodes which in fact were used in our experiments.

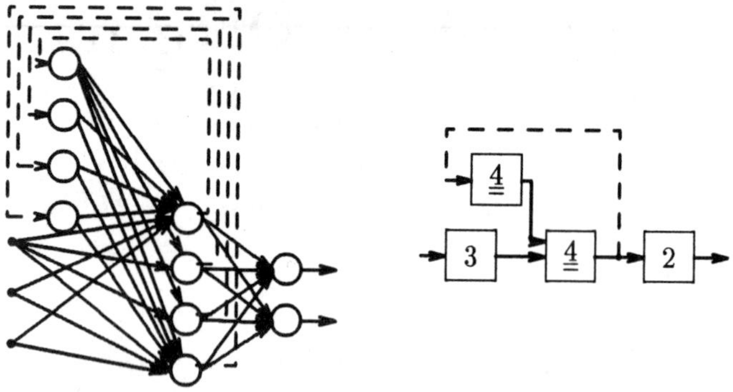

Figure 2. An example of an Elman recursive network having one hidden layer of nodes.

We chose the sigmoid function as the activation function of all the neurons. The network is trained with the quickpropagation algorithm [5]. For training the mean-square-error criterion is used, for testing of the quality of the ANN-VSS we use coarse errors in estimation of F_0. If we denote the iteration step during training by n, the backpropagation training adjusts weights according to

$$w_{ij,n+1} = w_{ij,n} + \alpha \Delta w_{ij,n+1} + \beta \Delta w_{ij,n} \tag{3}$$

where α is the learning rate and β is the momentum term . The quickpropagation algorithm replaces this by

$$w_{ij,n+1} = w_{ij,n} + \Delta w_{ij,n}$$
$$\Delta w_{ij,n} = \frac{\frac{\partial \epsilon}{\partial w_{ij,n}}}{\frac{\partial \epsilon}{\partial w_{ij,n-1}} - \frac{\partial \epsilon}{\partial w_{ij,n}}} \Delta w_{ij,n-1}\,; \tag{4}$$

hence, no choice of α and β is necessary. The term ϵ in the above equation denotes the mean-square-error between input and output values. In the cases $n = 0$ and $\Delta w_{ij,n-1} = 0\,,\ \frac{\partial \epsilon}{\partial w_{ij,n}} > 0$ we use equ. (3).

The speech signal is low-pass filtered with 1000 Hz; to reduce high and low frequencies the VSS is band-pass filtered from 20 Hz to 1000 Hz; and finally the signals are downsampled to 2 kHz, to reduce the amount of data. The processing simply consists of shifting the speech signal point-by-point through the input layer of the ANN, and concatenating the sequence of single output values of the ANN to the ANN-VSS. The output value of the net is interpreted as the value of the ANN-VSS, measured at the middle of the input frame. We use this input/output relationship because the other possible form of relationship, i.e. mapping one frame of the speech signal to one frame of the ANN-VSS, enlarges the net and so the training time. Furthermore, the mapping would be more complex and cause discontinuities at output frame boundaries. The

ANN–VSS is smoothed to reduce noise. We use iteratively 5 average filters the width of which depends on the average pitch period of the ANN-VSS, so that only noisy parts and no period in the ANN-VSS will be smoothed. The average period is estimated by analyzing every frame of the ANN-VSS in the frequency domain, searching for the maximum in the spectrum. Unvoiced frames are ignored for this estimation.

To train the network we use a database S in which speech and voice source signals were recorded in parallel [1]. We got a data set of 114 pairs of speech and voice source signals (recorded by a laryngograph) with sampling frequency of 16 kHz. Within the data set 3 male and 5 female speakers spoke German time of day expressions (for example, "sechzehn Uhr vier", 16.04 o'clock). The database S has a length of 140 seconds of speech. It is divided into three subsets, S1, S2, S3.

The subset S1 consists of 35 sentences from 8 speakers, 40 seconds of speech, 2757 frames, 68620 training patterns; it is used for training the various networks. The subset S2 has a non–laryngealized utterance from each of the 8 speakers. It consists of 1014 frames and is used to test (during training) the ability of a network to discriminate non–laryngealized utterances which were not in the training set. The subset S3 contains from each of the 8 speakers one utterance having at least one laryngealization. It consists of 641 frames and is used to test the ability of the network to discriminate laryngealized utterances which were not in the training set.

The mean–square–errror (MSE) is used to optimize the weights and to judge the quality of the mapping performance by an ANN. However, in this case the MSE is not an useful measure of the quality of the ANN-VSS. Some visually good signals have a greater mean square error than visually poor signals. Hence, the quality of the ANN–VSS is measured in the following way. We first calculate the pitch period of the VSS recorded by a laryngograph on a frame–by–frame basis using a modification of the algorithm given in [1] that searches for relevant maxima in the VSS. The pitch period of an ANN–VSS frame (length of a frame: 12.8 msec) is the average of the distances between all consecutive maxima in the frame. We define an *error* in one frame of the ANN–VSS if its pitch period differs from the reference (created automatically and hand-corrected) by more than 30 Hz. Thus the error is given frame–by–frame not point–by–point. This is done only for frames of voiced speech. This measurement is also close to the intuitive judgment of a person who visually analyzes the ANN–VSS.

The weights are initialized by small random numbers. The ANN is trained a fixed and relatively small number of epochs (15 epochs) with the training set S1. Then we test the ANN with the sets S1, S2, and S3 and record the number of errors. If the error becomes zero or if it increases over several (e.g. 3) iterations, the training stops and otherwise a new cycle is entered. After training the network we compute the error rate, that is the percentage of deviations in F_0 which are larger than 30 Hz, on the full database S.

[1] This database was kindly provided by the Institute of Phonetics of the L.M. Universität, München.

T	I	L	H	O	Rec	W	Error
ML	78	3	80	1	NIL	19361	184 (3.5 %)
ML	78	3	100	1	NIL	28201	159 (3.0 %)
JO	78	2	100	1	10	19131	189 (3.6 %)
EL	78	2	100	1	200	38101	186 (3.6 %)

Table 1. Summary of main results.
T denotes the type of ANN (ML: multilayer perceptron, JO: Jordan recursive network, EL: Elman recursive network); I, H, and O are the number of input nodes, hidden nodes per layer, and output nodes, respectiveley; L is the number of hidden layers; Rec is the number of recursive nodes; W is the number of weights in the ANN; Error gives the absolute number of errors and the percentage.

B. Results

As mentioned above, three types of networks were investigated. Several configurations with different number of hidden layers, different number of nodes per hidden layer, and different number of recursive nodes (for Jordan and Elman networks) were considered. Training times for larger networks were about 3 days on a workstation with about 100 MIPS. The best configurations are summarized in Table 1. This table shows that very reliable F_0 estimation is possible from the ANN–VSS.

An example of a reconstructed ANN–VSS is given in Figure 3. It supports the result given in Table 1 that reconstruction is very good. The irregularites in the voice source signal due to laryngealizations are clearly reconstructed, see frames 32 – 38 in the lower part of Figure 3. The results support the assumption that there are general regularities for mapping a voice source signal to a speech signal, that the inverse mapping exists, and that at least a very good approximation of this inverse mapping can be learned by an appropriate neural network.

Probably most of the remaining errors are caused by voiced/unvoiced transitions and by laryngealizations. The inverse filtering is robust to untrained speakers, different recording conditions, facilities, and vocabularies. Although a large number of network configurations was tested, it may be expected to obtain still better results with larger networks and more training data.

III. Determination of Laryngealizations

Having reconstructed the VSS, the next step is to use it to detect laryngealizations in the speech signal. This is done by a second artificial neural network (ANN) which again is a multilayer perceptron.

The input is the ANN–VSS obtained as described in Section II above. It has a sampling frequency of 2 kHz and is normalized to the interval $[-1, +1]$. Experiments were carried out using 3, 5, and 7 frames (corresponding to 77, 128, and 179 sample values, respectively) as input to an ANN. Training of the ANN's was done with 1329 sentences

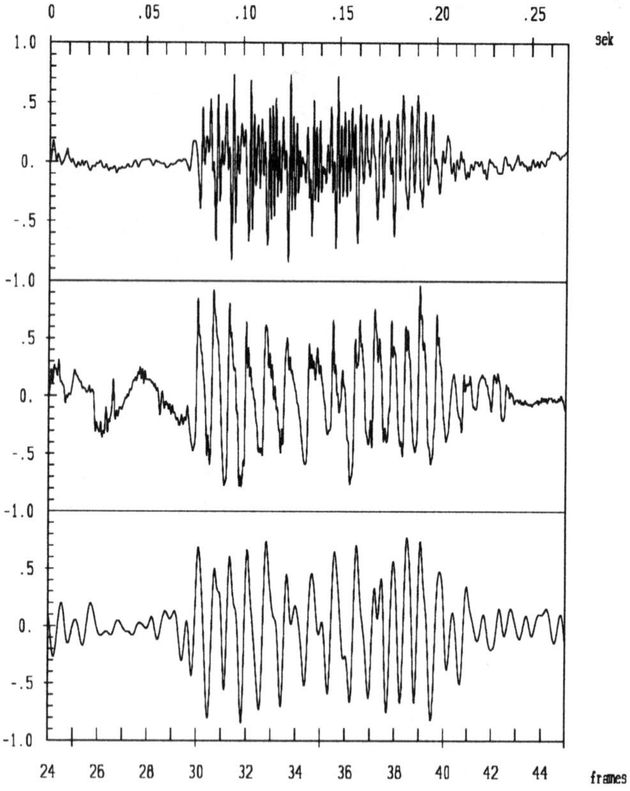

Figure 3. From top to bottom: speech signal, laryngograph VSS, ANN–VSS

(about 30 minutes) of speech spoken by 1 male and 3 female speakers, one third spontaneous and two thirds read speech. Frames of 12.8 ms duration containing laryngealizations were hand–labeled by phoneticians at L.M. University Munich. This hand–labeling is here assumed to be correct. In a first series of experiments the output of the ANN was one out of the three classes 'unvoiced', 'voiced non–laryngealized', and 'voiced laryngealized'. In a second series unvoiced frames were excluded a priori and only the two classes 'voiced non–laryngealized' and 'voiced laryngealized' were distinguished. The experiments are summarized in Figure 4.

Again, various ANN's were tried. It was found to be useful to smooth results with a median filter of width three. The best network consisted of 128 input nodes, two hidden layers each one with 80 nodes, and 3 output nodes (128–80–80–3 ANN); the results are summarized in the confusion matrix given in the upper part of Table 2. In particular, 85.6 % of laryngealized frames are classified correctly, and the false alarm rate consists of 16.1 %. This is considered to be a reasonable compromise between not missing laryngealizations (maximizing correct recognition) and minimizing false alarm rate. Using the hand labeling the unvoiced frames were excluded and a second series of experiments was made. Now the best network consisted of 128 input nodes, two hidden layers each with 100 nodes, and 2 output nodes. The results are given in the lower part of Table 2.

initialize weights by small random numbers, iteration step number $N = 0$, learning rate $\alpha = 0.01$, and correct classifications $p_c = 0$
$N \leftarrow N + 1$
train ANN on training set having an equal number of patterns from the three classes ($\approx$ 6000) for a fixed number of epochs (here: 25)
test on test set of 144 sentences and store $p_{c,N}$, that is correct classifications at iteration step number N
IF $p_{c,N} \leq p_c$
THEN $\alpha \leftarrow \alpha/10$
ELSE $p_c = p_{c,N}$
UNTIL learning rate $\alpha \leq 0.000\,01$
determine iteration step number with maximal recognition rate $p_{c,N}$ and corresponding ANN
determine with this ANN the recognition rate on the full sample of speech

Figure 4 Training and testing for the detection of laryngealizations.

	classified as					
	UV		VN		VL	
	#	%	#	%	#	%
UV	47820	80.2	6327	10.6	5456	9.2
VN	5320	6.9	54906	71.5	16559	21.6
VL	431	7.0	456	7.4	5273	85.6

		classified as			
		VN		VL	
VN		56929	74.1	19856	25.9
VL		424	6.9	5736	93.1

Table 2. Summary of main results for detection of laryngealizations. The abbreviations are UV for 'unvoiced', VN for 'voiced non–laryngealized', and VL for 'voiced laryngealized'. The upper part of the table shows results on three classes, the lower part on two classes.

The recognition rate could be increased to 93.1 %, but the false alarm rate increased to 25.9 %.

In Sect. II we showed an approach to inverse filtering using a neural network. The "classical" approach to inverse filtering is a linear filter and, of course, the question arises, whether anything can be gained from using an ANN instead of a linear filter. Hence, in another experiment we computed the voice source signal from a linear inverse filter and used this VSS to train a 128–80–80–3 ANN, which was the best network type for the ANN–VSS. The result is that 75.9 % of laryngealized frames are correctly classified (instead of 85.6 % for the neural network inverse filter), that the mean recognition rate on all frames drops to 63.1 % (from 76.5 %), and that the false alarm rate is almost the same for both approaches (about 16 %). This result clearly demonstrates the superiority of ANN inverse filtering to linear inverse filtering for the detection of laryngealizations.

	NO	REF	ANN
UV/VO error in %	3.9	3.9	3.8
VO/UN error in %	6.9	7.3	8.3
coarse F_0 error %	10.4	6.5	7.2
av. error in Hz	17	11	12

Table 3 Improved computation of the fundamental frequency by exclusion of laryngealized sections of speech. The abbreviations are: NO for no consideration of laryngealized sections, REF for using the hand labeled laryngealizations, and ANN for using the automatically (ANN) detected laryngealizations.

IV. Improved Pitch Determination

As mentioned in the introduction (Sect. I), the final goal is a reliable estimate of the fundamental frequency F_0. An algorithm for F_0 computation based on dynamic programming has been described elsewhere [9]. It first computes several candidate values for the fundamental frequency using two independent algorithms and then computes an optimal F_0 contour by dynamic programming. A problem are wrong candidate values which often are caused by irregularities of speech, that is laryngealized frames. Therefore, the idea is to detect laryngealizations, as shown above, and then to exclude those frames from the DP-based computation of the fundamental frequency by labeling them as "unvoiced". After computation of the F_0 contour this contour is interpolated linearly in laryngealized frames; if the laryngealized section is at the beginning or end of a voiced section, the F_0 value of the last voiced frame is extrapolated by a constant.

The results for the database of 1329 sentences are summarized in Table 3. The table shows that the coarse error rate, that is fundamental frequency errors of more than 30 Hz, is reduced significantly (from 10.4 % to 7.2 %). Furthermore, there is only a small degradation of performance when using laryngealizations automatically detected by the ANN instead of the hand labeled laryngealizations (from 6.5 % coarse errors to 7.2 %). This result indicates the overall success of reconstructing the voice source signal and detecting laryngealizations by means of neural networks.

V. Conclusions and Outlook

In this paper we showed that the voice source signal can be reconstructed reliably from the speech signal using an artificial neural network. With a network of type (78–100–100–100–1) we achieved a reconstruction giving 3.0 % of coarse errors in fundamental frequency computation. The reconstructed VSS was used to detect laryngealized sections of speech using another neural network. With a network of type (128–80–80–3) 85.6 % of laryngealizations are classified correctly at a false alarm rate of 16.1 %. In addition it was shown that a voice source signal computed from a *linear* inverse filter performs worse. Finally, it was demonstrated that the performance of a dynamic programming based algorithm for the computation of F_0 contours was improved from 10.4 % coarse errors to 7.2 % coarse errors.

We expect that these results will make prosodic control of a spoken dialog system more reliable and in turn improve its user acceptance. However, verification of this expecation will be the subject of future work.

References

[1] P. Alku. An automatic method to estimate the time based parameters of the glottal pulseform. In *Proc. Int. Conf. on Acoustics, Speech, and Signal Processing*, pages II, 29–32, San Francisco CA, 1992.

[2] A. Batliner, S. Burger, B. Johne, A. Kiessling. M"USLI: A Classification Scheme For Laryngealizations. In *Proc. ESCA Workshop on Prosody*, pages 176–179, Lund, Sweden, 1993

[3] J. Denzler, R. Kompe, A. Kiessling, H. Niemann, E. Nöth. Going back to the source: Inverse filtering of the speech signal with ANN's. In *Proc. European Conf. on Speech Communication and Technology*, pages 111–114, Berlin, Germany, 1993.

[4] J.L. Elman. Finding structure in time. *Cognitive Science*, 14:179–211, 1990.

[5] S. Fahlman. An empirical study of learning speeds in backpropagation networks. Technical Report CMU-Cs-88-162, Carnegie Mellon University, Pittsburgh PA, 1988.

[6] W. Hess. *Algorithms and Devices for Pitch Determination of Speech Signals.* Springer, Berlin, 1983.

[7] D. Huber. *Aspects of the Communicative Function of Voice in Text Intonation.* PhD Thesis, Chalmers University, Göteborg/Lund, Sweden, 1988

[8] M. Jordan. Attractor dynamics and parallelism in a connectionist sequential machine. In L. Erlbaum, editor, *Proc. 1986 Cognitive Science Conference*, pages 531–546, 1986.

[9] A. Kiessling, R. Kompe, H. Niemann, E. Nöth, A. Batliner. DP-based determination of f0 contour from speech signals. In *Proc. Int. Conf. on Acoustics, Speech, and Signal Processing*, pages II–17 – II–20, San Francisco, CA, 1992.

[10] R. Kompe, A. Kiessling, T. Kuhn, M. Mast, H. Niemann, E. Nöth, K. Ott, A. Batliner. Prosody takes over: A prosodically guided dialog system. pages 2003–2006, Berlin, Germany, 1993.

[11] W.A. Lea. *Intonational Cues to the Constituent Structure and Phonemics of Spoken English.* PhD thesis, Indiana University, 1972.

[12] E. Nöth. *Prosodische Information in der Sprachverarbeitung, Berechnung und Anwendung.* PhD thesis, Technische Fakultät, Universität Erlangen-Nürnberg, Erlangen, 1990.

[13] J. Vaissiere. The use of prosodic parameters in automatic speech recognition. In H. Niemann, M. Lang, G. Sagerer, editors, *Recent Advances in Speech Understanding and Dialog Systems*, volume 46 of *NATO ASI Series F*, pages 71–100. Springer, Berlin, 1988.

[14] A. Waibel. *Prosody and speech recognition.* PhD thesis, Carnegie-Mellon Univ. Pittsburgh, USA, 1986.

[15] M.Q. Wang, J. Hirschberg. Automatic classification of intonational phrase boundaries. *Computer Speech & Language*, 6:175–196, 1992.

Big Dumb Neural Nets: A Working Brute Force Approach to Speech Recognition

Nelson Morgan

Abstract— **Neural networks with over a million connections have been trained using online backpropagation and a speech corpus with over 6 million training examples (speech frames). These networks provide phonetic probabilistic estimates that are used in a continuous speech recognizer. Issues of the network training and application are discussed in this paper.**

I. Introduction

Over the last 6 years, work at ICSI and collaborating institutions has shown that extremely large networks (ranging from 300,000 to 1,600,000 free parameters) can be successfully trained on large data sets[3] (ranging from 1 to 6 million tokens). For the larger case, training appears to be complete after roughly 2 passes through the data. Cross-validation is used to control the learning rate to avoid overtraining. The resulting networks are used to estimate emission probabilities for an HMM-based 5000-word continuous speech recognizer, and performance appears to be close to that of mainstream recognizers that use far more detailed speech models.

The networks used so far have for the most part been simple, monolithic multi-layer perceptrons with a single large hidden layer (e.g., 4000 hidden units). Certainly, many of us have felt in the past that exponential growth in training time and increased likelihood of falling into extremely suboptimal local minima would make such large networks completely impractical. While we make no claim that either training or recall of these nets is particularly efficient in comparison with more clever schemes, we nonetheless must acknowledge the experimental evidence that in fact these networks can work well.

The gross character of these nets does have some advantages from the system implementation point of view. The nature of the computation is extremely simple and regular, and can be parallelized in a straightforward way. However, training of such nets is still a considerable burden with respect to competitive approaches, necessitating a significant effort in hardware and software development. Furthermore, while we have kept network architecture extremely simple, we have changed our initialization and training strategies over the years, so that we required fully programmable hardware.

These considerations led us through a combined effort of hardware, software, and algorithmic development that has resulted in both our current speech results and a series of systems that we are in the process of designing.

The author is with the International Computer Science Institute and the University of California at Berkeley.

II. Connectionist Probability Estimation for Speech

So far, the best systems for recognizing continuous speech are statistical in nature. For this problem, it is necessary that hard decisions not be made too quickly, and probability theory provides a rich structure for the handling of uncertainty. On the other hand, the mainstream approaches to speech recognition are handicapped by a series of constraining assumptions, for instance of the independence of the speech data from one analysis window to the next, which is a blatantly false perspective. Of course, we all must make incorrect assumptions from time to time in practical analysis of real world data (such as assumptions of linearity or Gaussian distribution), but when the data is a poor match to these assumptions, it is useful to have alternate techniques that do not require them. Since even fairly simple neural networks can integrate information without strong statistical assumptions, we were interested in applying them to estimating probabilities of speech sounds as part of a continuous speech recognizer.

In the mid-eighties, Hervé Bourlard showed [4] that under certain broad conditions a system trained for classification would produce probabilities of each class conditioned on the data. That is, if q_k is the kth class from the set of K classes $\mathcal{Q} = \{q_1, q_2, \ldots, q_K\}$, and x_n is the input data vector for the time n, such systems can provide estimates of $p(q_k|x_n)$. The conditions for this to be true are:

- The system is trained to minimize sum-of-squared error (or relative entropy, a criterion useful for

0-7803-1901-X/94 $4.00 ©1994 IEEE

many problems), as is often the case with neural networks such as multilayer perceptrons.

- The system is trained in classification mode; that is, the targets are all zero except for one that is 1. (Note; with some minor modification, this can work with other targets, such as .1 and .9, except that a transformation must be done after training).
- The system has enough parameters. If the system is too simple to represent the underlying phenomenon (for instance trying to model a circle with a single straight line) it will never converge to a good solution.
- The system is trained to a global minimum.

The last condition is problematic, since we essentially never reach the global minimum in a problem of scale. In fact it is not even clear that we would want to reach the global minimum for the training data, since we wish to generalize to the best possible minimum for previously unseen data, which is what we will be using the net for.

Fortunately, our experience has shown us that we can get fairly good probabilistic estimates from networks so long as we train them properly, i.e.:

- Use enough hidden units - this can be a problem if you have insufficient computational resources, but depending on the precise problem, we have found that we needed hundreds to thousands of hidden units to represent speech sounds.
- Use on-line training (per-pattern back propagation).
- Randomly sample the training data for presentation to the net so that you don't present too many samples of the same class sequentially.
- Cross-validation - use performance of an independent section of the data as a criterion for reducing the learning rate. When there is no further improvement (on the cross-validation set, not training) even when the learning rate has been reduced, training is stopped. Overtraining, particularly with large networks, can result in very poor performance on new data.
- Output nonlinear function - either use a sigmoid or a softmax function; the latter appears to be slightly better for this purpose, and has the added advantage of guaranteeing the outputs will sum to one. The softmax function is defined as

$$f(x_k) = \frac{e^{x_k}}{\sum_{i=1}^{K} e^{x_i}}$$

- Training criterion - again, either use squared error or relative entropy. In practice we have found that the latter speeds training.
- Initialization - we have trained a network to estimate phonetic probabilities given a corpus of hand-marked continuous speech that is widely available to the speech community (TIMIT)[5]. The weights of this network are now used to initialize any training that we do on a new task. This greatly speeds up training. When we go to a new-sized network (or new input features), we must also train up a new TIMIT net. This one training, though, can be used for different tasks or for different segmentations of a given training set, as determined by a statistical algorithm rather than being hand-marked; see next item.
- Learning targets - as noted above, in general we do not know the targets a priori (i.e., the phonetic identity of the speech corresponding to each analysis window). We learn this in an iterative fashion by using the TIMIT net to determine the segmentation of the training data into the known sequence of speech sounds (using dynamic programming); this set of targets is used to train a new network, and so on. Each iteration of this overall procedure improves the score, though we typically only must re-segment once or twice.

III. Applying the Nets to Continuous Speech Recognition

In the recognition phase, we combine the network outputs according to hypothesized sequences of sounds in order to get an overall probability for a string of words. This is done to find the optimal path through the models of pronunciation that have been previously developed. Since we wish to multiply probabilities across this path, we add the logs of network outputs to get the overall scores, using dynamic programming. In practice, when the language and pronunciation models have been derived from sources other than the data used for training, we have found it necessary to divide the network outputs by the prior probability for each class; that is, by the relative frequency of each class as it was presented to the network during training. Note that the learning rate should be the same for each class or else it is equivalent to modifying these relative frequencies.

Using this procedure, then, we have tackled difficult problems in continuous speech recognition. In one experiment, we trained for a 1000-word speaker independent task called Resource Management, training on about 1.3 million feature vectors of speech that were computed once every 10 milliseconds. The typical network used in this task had 1000 hidden units, as much smaller nets did significantly worse. The output layer was 61 units corresponding to phonetic classes, and the input consisted of 9 windows (four from the past and 4 from the future as well as the current frame), 26 features each. Performance on a standard evaluation set of 300 sentences (called the Feb '89 set) is currently in the 4-5% error range (using a wordpair grammar that is standard for this task), which is competitive with systems that learn statistics for thousands of sound classes.

Recently, we have extended this system to a larger task with a 5000 word vocabulary and about 6 million feature vectors. Given the increase in data, we scaled up the network size in fairly obvious ways; we increased the size of the input vectors (from 26 to 39), and we increased the size of the hidden layer (from 1000 to 4000). It is difficult to compare between tasks, but we appear to currently get about 12% to 18% error on various test sets for this task, which is probably about twice the error of the best mainstream systems. However, we have just begun working with this task, and we expect to again reach competitive performance for a much simpler system.

Of course, it would be desirable not only to be simpler than conventional systems, but actually better. In practice this is difficult to show, since test scores can be reduced by many means, as researchers are always working to improve their systems. However, so far we have always observed (since we developed this technique) that any given system we used was greatly improved by substituting in network-generated probabilities rather than ones generated by conventional means (typically by estimating the probabilities for a mixture of Gaussians). See [7] for examples.

IV. Computational Considerations

An obvious limitation to this approach is the amount of computation required to train up the network. While the training approaches described above have reduced the work to about 2 or 3 iterations through the training set, even a single pass is extremely time consuming due to the quantity of data involved (and of course the size of the network). We are in fact currently looking at ways to reduce the network size and/or to constrain what we use from the training set. However, in the short term our approach has been to develop the hardware and software resources necessary to support this approach. Since we are fortunate to have good faculty and student support in this area, this was a feasible approach. This permitted us to develop other aspects of our algorithms without having to tweak the neural architecture significantly.

To give an idea of the scale, a single iteration through the pilot Wall Street Journal data took us about 10 trillion connection updates. A Sparc 10 typically gets about 1 million connection updates per second on this task, which would take about 3 months to complete. Careful coding can provide higher performance, although this improvement is limited for large weight matrices that tend to cause many cache misses.

Recall that this is a single iteration, and we require two or three per phonemic realignment loop. A full training would take 1-2 years. Our current connectionist hardware (the Ring Array Processor, or RAP [6]) takes a few days for an iteration, which is still long enough to constrain the possibilities for experimentation. For this reason we have been working as a group to develop more powerful neurocomputers; these are described elsewhere but a description can be found in [2] and [1].

On the other hand, for recognition the added computation for this approach is comparable to the work required for the search (word recognition) portion of most algorithms (when applied to very large vocabularies), and should not be prohibitive. In particular, the structure of the computation makes it particularly well-suited for blocking of the data in ways that permit high sustained computational rates on SIMD, systolic, or vector architectures.

Further discussion of these system issues can be found in chapters 10 and 11 of [3].

V. Summary

In terms of common neural networks, the systems described here are quite large. However, in comparison to the elaborate systems in use in major laboratories, the complete system size is moderate. On the other hand, it took a number of years to learn how to train and how to use these nets for recognition.

In other words, they ain't so big, and they ain't so dumb.

VI. Acknowledgements

The core developments described here arose from a long-term international collaboration between the author and Hervé Bourlard, originally from Philips Research of Belgium and more recently at Lernout and Hauspie Speech Products, also of Belgium. Additionally, there have been significant contributions from collaborations with colleagues at ICSI (Chuck Wooters, Yochai Konig, and Gary Tajchman), SRI International (primarily Mike Cohen, Horacio Franco, and Victor Abrash), and at Cambridge University in the U.K. (Steve Renals, who was also at ICSI; Tony Robinson, and Mike Hochberg). Funding for this work was provided by ICSI itself, as well as by ARPA contract MDA904-90-C-5253, and the European Community's Esprit Basic Research Project 6487.

References

[1] K. Asanović, J. Beck, T. Callahan, J. Feldman, B. Irissou, B. Kingsbury, P. Kohn, J. Lazzaro, N. Morgan, D. Stoutamire, and J. Wawrzynek, CNS-1 Architecture Specification - A Connectionist Network Supercomputer *ICSI Technical Report* TR-93-021

[2] K. Asanović, J. Beck, J. Feldman, N. Morgan, and J. Wawrzynek A Supercomputer for Neural Computation *Proceedings of the ICNN*, 1994, in prep

[3] H. Bourlard and N. Morgan *Connectionist Speech Recognition - A Hybrid Approach*, Kluwer Academic Press, 1994

[4] H. Bourlard and C. Wellekens Links Between Markov Models and Multilayer Perceptrons, in *Advances in Neural Information Processing Systems 1*, D. Touretzky (ed)., San Mateo, Morgan Kaufmann, pp.502-510

[5] L. Lamel, R. Kassel, and S. Seneff, Speech Database Development: Design and Analysis of the Acoustic-Phonetic Corpus, in *Proceedings of the DARPA Speech Recognition Workshop*, pages 100-109, Ed. L. Baumann, Feb., 1986.

[6] N. Morgan, J. Beck, P. Kohn, J. Bilmes, E. Allman, and J. Beer, The Ring Array Processor (RAP): A Multiprocessing Peripheral for Connectionist Applications, *Journal of Parallel and Distributed Processing*, Special Issue on Neural Networks, 1992, v14, pp.248-259, 1992

[7] S. Renals, N. Morgan, H. Bourlard, M. Cohen, and H. Franco, Connectionist Probability Estimators in HMM Speech Recognition to appear in *IEEE Transactions on Speech and Audio Processing*, Jan 1994.

Auditory Models with Kohonen SOFM and LVQ for Speaker Independent Phoneme Recognition

Timothy R. Anderson, *Member, IEEE*

***Abstract*— Neural networks that employed unsupervised learning were used on the output of two different models of the auditory periphery to perform phoneme recognition. Experiments which compared the performance of these two auditory model representations to Mel-Cepstral Coefficients showed that the auditory models performed significantly better in terms of phoneme recognition accuracy under the conditions tested (high signal-to-noise and a large database of speakers). However, the three representations made different types of broad class recognition errors. The Patterson auditory model representation performed best with the highest overall phoneme and broad class performance.**

I. Introduction

Over the past several years researchers have investigated using biologically based models for feature representation (i.e., auditory models) and biologically based models for classification (i.e., neural networks). This paper represents part of a continuing effort to examine the benefits of using the combination of auditory models and neural networks for speech recognition. A neural network that employed unsupervised learning was used on the output of two different models of the auditory periphery to perform phoneme recognition. Continuous speech from 151 speakers (49 female and 102 male) taken from dialect regions 1 and 2 of the TIMIT database [4] was processed by the auditory models for this experiment. The average firing rate from the auditory models was used to train Kohonen self-organizing feature maps. The resulting context-independent phoneme recognition performance was equal to or better than that of traditional representations.

The author is with the Armstrong Laboratory, Bioacoustics and Biocommunications Branch, 2610 Seventh St., Wright-Patterson AFB, OH 45433-7901, USA.

II. Auditory Model Descriptions

A. Payton

Payton [7] developed a model of peripheral auditory processing that incorporates processing steps describing the conversion from the acoustic pressure-wave signal at the eardrum to the time-course activity in auditory neurons. The model can process arbitrary time-domain waveforms and yield the probability of neural firing. The model contains separate modules for each anatomical section of the periphery. These modules are: a middle ear section, a model of the basilar membrane, and a hair-cell section that includes synaptic connections to auditory-nerve fibers. The predicted membrane displacements, for 20 locations along the basilar membrane, are used as input to subsequent stages of the model. The hair cell/synapse section of Payton's composite model predicts the probability of firing for 20 auditory neurons covering the frequency range 440 Hz to 6600 Hz. The model converts the acoustic pressure wave into action-potential firing probability as a function of time through the stimulus.

B. Patterson

In Patterson's model, know as Auditory Image Model (AIM), the spectral analysis is performed by a gammatone auditory filterbank which converts the incoming wave into a surface that provides a reasonable representation of the motion of the basilar membrane as a function of time. The operation of the inner hair cells is simulated by a module that includes a bank of logarithmic compressors and a bank of adaptive threshold generators. Together they convert the basilar membrane motion into a surface that represents the pattern of activity at the output of the cochlea. The adaptive thresholding mechanism removes the temporal and spectral smearing introduced by the filterbank and it enhances features in the filterbank output.

III. Signal Representations

Historically, the short-time spectrum has played a major role in speech analysis. Specifically, Linear Predictive Coding (LPC) has been used extensively

0-7803-1901-X/94 $4.00 ©1994 IEEE

for speech coding and speech recognition because of it's computational efficiency. Previous work by this author has compared the performance of LPC and auditory models for phoneme recognition using a small database of speakers [1].

For this work the 20 channel output of the hair cell/synapse section of Payton's auditory model (PAM) was averaged over a 16 millisecond window with a 5 millisecond frame rate.

Patterson's model was used to calculate hair cell outputs of 20 filters covering the same frequency range as that of Payton's model. The output of Patterson's model was also averaged over a 16 millisecond window with a 5 millisecond frame rate.

A third representation, Linear Predictive Coding (LPC) derived mel-cepstral coefficients, was used as the baseline. A 16 millisecond Hamming window was used with a 5 millisecond frame rate. Twenty LPC coefficients for each frame were converted to mel-scale using the bilinear transformation method [6].

IV. Database Description

The speech data used for this work comprised a subset of the TIMIT acoustic-phonetic database [4]. The work reported here used all 10 sentences from 114 talkers from dialect regions 1 and 2 (37 female and 77 male) for training and a different 37 talkers from regions 1 and 2 (12 female and 25 male) for testing.

During the development of the SPHINX [5] speech recognition system at Carnegie Mellon University (CMU), the TIMIT phoneme labels were slightly modified. This modified convention was adopted for the present research in order to provide a better means of comparing results with other established systems. This convention yields 39 phones in separate categories.

V. Self-Organizing Feature Maps

The neural network selected for this investigation was the self-organizing feature map [3]. This neural network was selected because of its ability to learn a topological mapping of an input data space into a pattern space which defines discrimination or decision surfaces. This process has been used by Kohonen in a system for phonetic recognition of Finnish and Japanese [2].

The operation of this network resembles the classical vector-quantization method called k-means clustering. Self-organizing feature maps are more general because topologically close nodes are sensitive to inputs that are physically similar. Output nodes will be ordered in a natural manner.

Kohonen's algorithm adjusts weights from common input nodes to output nodes arranged in a two-dimensional grid. Each input node is connected to every output node. Real-valued input vectors are presented sequentially in time to the network without specifying the desired output. After enough input vectors have been presented, each node's weights will specify a cluster center. These cluster centers approximate the probability density function of the input vectors. The weight adjustment is based on a distortion measure. In this work, a mean squared error distortion measure was used, based on the input and stored weights.

Most speech recognition systems employing vector quantization use a codebook size of 256. This codebook size was used in this experiment as well in the form of a 16x16 (two-dimensional) grid. The initial neighborhood of 4x4 and was linearly reduced to 1.5x1.5 during the first 30 speakers' data and held constant at 1.5x1.5 thereafter. The initial learning rate of 0.9, was linearly reduced to 0.1 during the first 30 speakers' data and reduced linearly from 0.1 to 0.0 during the remaining speakers.

The calibration process used in this work was similar to that used by Kohonen. The process consisted of the following steps. Once the self-organizing feature map was trained, learning was turned off (the weights are fixed) and the training data was presented to the feature map a second time. The node that responded to each training token was associated with that token label. The token label that had the largest number of responses for each node was assigned as the label for that node.

Learning Vector Quantization (LVQ) was used on the calibrated codebook to adjust the codewords for improved performance [3]. In this work LVQ3 was used with a window width of 0.2, an epsilon of 0.02, and eta of 0.1.

VI. Performance Measure

Several measures of performance were used to quantify and compare each signal representation. The most common measures of speech recognition performance are the percent correct, percent insertions, percent deletions, and percent substitutions.

Zue and colleagues [8] have shown how phonotactic constraints can provide significant benefit to the speech recognition process. In light of these results, measures of recognition performance at the broad class level were also made. Six broad class categories were used in this work: Vowels, Stops, Nasals, Liquids and Glides, Fricatives, and Silence.

VII. Results

Experiments which compared the performance of the auditory models with mel-cepstral coefficients

(MCC) showed that both auditory-model representations performed significantly better than MCC in terms of phoneme-recognition accuracy under the conditions tested (high signal-to-noise and a large database of speakers). The three representations made different types of broad class recognition errors. Results in the form of average recognition, substitution, deletion, and insertion rates are shown in Table 1. Broad class recognition rates are shown in Table 2.

The AIM representation performed significantly better, [1] in terms of phoneme-recognition performance, than either of the other representations. AIM performed significantly better than MCC in the broad class categories of Fricatives, Silence, Stops and Total broad class performance. AIM performed significantly better than PAM in the broad class categories of Stops, Vowels and Total broad class performance.

The PAM representation performed significantly better than AIM in the broad class categories of Glides and Silence. PAM performed significantly better than MCC in phoneme recognition performance and the broad class categories of Fricatives, Silence, Stops, Vowels, and Total broad class performance.

MCC was significantly better in recognizing the broad class categories of Glides and Nasals than the two auditory model representations. It should be noted that MCC did not recognize any Stops.

VIII. SUMMARY AND CONCLUSIONS

This paper examined different auditory model representations to perform speaker-independent phoneme classification. The study examined the phoneme classification performance using the self-organizing feature map and LVQ. The results indicated that it was possible to assign an acoustic segment to one of 39 phoneme categories with at least 50% recognition accuracy using either auditory model representation. The resulting context-independent phoneme-recognition performance was better than that of the SPHINX System [6] with the same feature set (i.e. cepstral coefficients only, no delta or power features).

This work demonstrated the potential benefits of using an auditory model/neural network combination for phoneme recognition in continuous speech. Although the two auditory models show similar performance advantages compared to MCC, there was a substantial difference in computational cost. AIM required approximately 10 times real time while PAM required approximately 1000 times real time.

[1] Significance in this paper refers to statistically significant at the 95% confidence level with 36 degrees of freedom.

	MCC	AIM	PAM
Correct	49.18	50.87	50.38
Deletions	11.67	7.50	7.38
Insertions	2.20	1.61	1.34
Substitutions	36.95	40.02	40.90

Table 1: Summary Results

	MCC	AIM	PAM
Fricatives	62.42	72.57	72.73
Glides	42.13	34.13	36.49
Nasals	52.08	43.65	45.20
Silence	91.19	93.65	94.73
Stops	0.0	38.05	27.60
Vowels	82.52	87.01	86.07
Total	71.31	76.11	75.71

Table 2: Broad Class Results

The results presented were the first comparing the performance of PAM to MCC and AIM with a large speaker database. These results demonstrated that the auditory models provided a significant improvement over MCC. This could translate into better speech recognition performance as MCC's have been the representation of choice for state-of-the-art speaker-independent speech recognition systems [5]. Present work employs AIM as the front-end for a Hidden Markov Model based recognition system.

Results presented here also indicate potential advantage for use of multiple representations for phoneme recognition. Since each representation has different broad class performance, an additional neural network to fuse the output of these nets or a single network trained on all three representations could provide greater recognition performance. Future work will investigate this approach with neural networks as well as Hidden Markov Models.

IX. ACKNOWLEDGEMENTS

The author would like to express his thanks to Janet Slifka who developed the Kohonen code and many other utilities that greatly aided in the research and for reading and commenting on an earlier version of this paper. The author would also like to thank Dr. Roy Patterson for his help and assistance in the setup and use of the AIM model. This work was supported in part by the Air Force Office of Scientific Research (AFOSR Task 2313V3).

REFERENCES

[1] T. R. Anderson. A comparison of auditory models for speaker-independent phoneme recogni-

tion. In *Int. Conf. on Acoustics, Speech, and Signal Processing*, volume IV, pages 231–234, 1993.

[2] T. Kohonen. The neural phonetic typewriter. *IEEE Computer Magazine*, 21:11–22, 1988.

[3] T. Kohonen. *Self-Organization and Associative Memory*. Springer-Verlag, Berlin, third edition, 1989.

[4] L. Lamel, R. Kassel, and S. Seneff. Speech database developement: Design and analysis of the acoustic-phonetic corpus. In *DARPA Speech Understanding Workshop*, pages 100–109, 1986.

[5] K. F. Lee. *Automatic Speech Recognition: The Developement of the SPHINX System*. Kluwer Academic, Boston, 1989.

[6] K.F. Lee and H.W. Hon. Speaker-independent phone recognition using hidden markov models. *IEEE Trans. ASSP*, 37:1621–1648, November 1989.

[7] K. L. Payton. Vowel processing by a models of the auditory periphery: A comparison to eighth-nerve responses. *J. Acoust. Soc. Amer.*, 83:145–162, 1988.

[8] V. W. Zue. The use of speech knowledge in automatic speech recognition. *Proc. of the IEEE*, 73:1602–1615, November 1985.

A Time Delay Radial Basis Function Network for Phoneme Recognition

Michael R. Berthold *Intel Corporation, Santa Clara, CA95052, USA*

***Abstract*— This paper presents the Time Delay Radial Basis Function Network (TDRBF) for recognition of phonemes. The TDRBF combines features from Time Delay Neural Networks (TDNN) and Radial Basis Functions (RBF). The ability to detect acoustic features and their temporal relationship independent of position in time is inherited from TDNN. The use of RBFs leads to shorter training times and less parameters to adjust, which makes it easier to apply TDRBF to new tasks.**
The recognition of three phonemes with about 750 training and testing tokens each was choosen as an evaluation task. The results suggest an equivalent performance of TDRBF and TDNN presented in [7], but TDRBF require much less training time to reach a good performance and in addition have a clear indication when the minimum error is reached, therefore no danger of overtraining exists.

I. Introduction

To detect features not only present in the input pattern at one point in time, but also features of the input pattern changing over time, is essential for successful recognition of speech. Conventional methods based on Multi Layer Perceptrons often use the Time Delay Neural Network (TDNN) which was first used for the recognition of speech by Waibel et al (see [7] for details). But long training times and multiple parameters which need careful adjustment make it hard to apply this network to new tasks. In contrast Radial Basis Function (RBF) based networks do not require special adjustments and the training time is much shorter than the time required to train a TDNN. But RBF networks are neither shift invariant in time, nor can they detect features in time.
The desire to combine the advantages of Radial Basis Functions with the time shift invariance of the TDNN lead to the Time Delay Radial Basis Function Network presented in this paper.

II. The Architecture

To allow a RBF to detect features over time it is necessary to present inputs not only of one point in time but of several. This leads to the structure shown in figure 1. The RBF gets in-

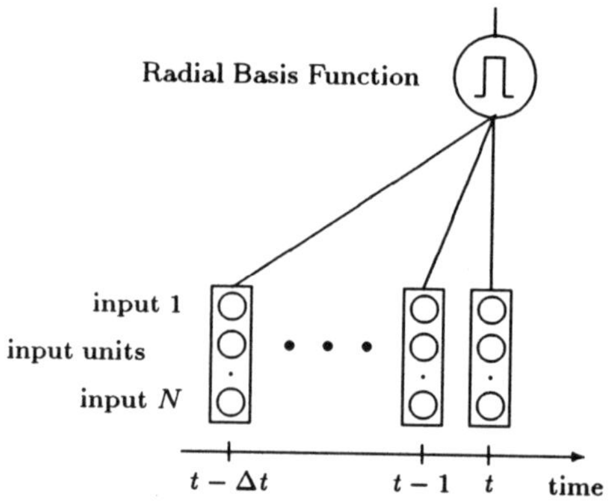

Figure 1: A RBF "looking" onto a window in time

put from several frames at different points in time. In this structure the RBF itself does not care about different frames or inputs, it handles the whole input data as one big vector, computes the distance to its prototype and applies an activation function which, in this case, is a signum function with variable radius[1] (see also

The author is now with: Forschungszentrum Informatik, Gruppe ACID (Prof. D. Schmid) Haid-und-Neu-Strasse 10–14, 76131 Karlsruhe, Germany (eMail: berthold@fzi.de)

[1] An attempt to use Gaussian and triangular activation functions did not result in performance improvements. The Signum function is also much easier (and faster!) to use.

0-7803-1901-X/94 $4.00 ©1994 IEEE

[3]):

$$d(t) = \sum_{\tau=0}^{\Delta t} \sum_{i=0}^{n-1} (o_i^\tau - \mu_{i,\tau})^2$$

$$a(t) = \begin{cases} 1 & d(t) \le r \\ 0 & else \end{cases}$$

$d(t)$ denotes the euclidian distance of the input data (o_i^τ: i-th component of the input vector at time τ) to the reference vector ($\mu_{i,\tau}$) of this RBF. $a(t)$ is the final activation, which depends on the radius r of the signum function.

One obvious problem with this structure is the inability to be invariant against shifts in time. If the pattern presented to the network is equal to the stored prototype but only shifted by one frame, the RBF will not respond as desired. Therefore a second layer which is simply integrating over time is used. Figure 2 shows the structure of the resulting network.

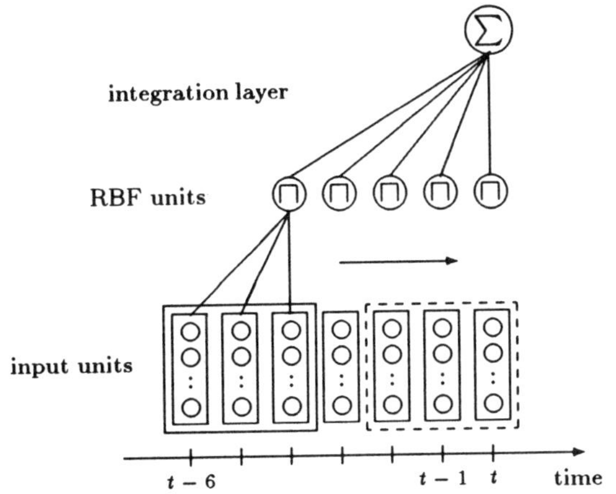

Figure 2: The structure of a 3(5)–TDRBF Network, for simplicity only one RBF for one class is shown. In practice several classes might be used and the training algorithm would have committed probably more than one RBF per class.

The network still contains RBFs looking onto small windows in time, but the second layer sums up activations of several instances of these RBFs over time. The "$x(y)$" notation used in this paper specifies the sizes of these windows in time. x indicates the number of frames each RBF takes as an input, y represents the size of the window in time the second layer is integrating.

This structure leads to the desired response to a pattern even if the pattern is shifted in time against the stored prototype. The input pattern will match the prototype of one of the instances of the corresponding RBF. The activation function of the integration layer is important for the success of this approach. Here a simple "weighted sum + sigmoid"–method was used, but one could also imagine a "winner take all" function which only picks the best response for each class. In our experiments the first approach produced the best results.

The only adjustable parameter of this network is the relation between the time–span of the Radial Basis Functions and the window size of the integration layer. As is shown later this "magic number" can be found by a few simple tries. Because for most speech problems the size of the time window is in the order of 10–20 the number of experiments required to determine the structure of the network is usually below 5–10. And due to the usage of RBFs, the training is done much faster than it is in the case of a Back–Propagation type network.

III. Training

Training this new architecture requires some thoughts about how the integration layer is being used during training. In the following experiments this layer was only used to pass the information to which class a certain window in time belongs down to the RBF layer. In one series of experiments the weights were initially set to 1.0 and were then trained using normal BackProp which did not improve the overall performance of the network significantly. All instances of RBFs in this window in time are then trained to classify the pattern correctly. Several training methods to achieve this are known, one could use an unsupervised clustering algorithm first and do some sort of supervised training during a second phase. It would also be possible to use the "growing cell structure" approach proposed by Fritzke (see [1]) to generate the first layer of the network. The algorithm used in this approach was RCE–training (see [4] and [5]) which introduces new prototypes when necessary and adjusts the radii of existing prototypes to avoid conflicts. RCE is one of the algorithms supported by Intels Ni1000 (see [2]), a Radial Basis Function Coprocessor. This form of training makes the TDRBF much easier to use than a TDNN. It is obvious when training is finished, because the algorithm does not commit any new prototypes. The danger of overtraining, known from BackProp, no longer exists.

IV. Testing with the BDG-task

To allow a comparison, the same phoneme recognition task was used for testing the TDRBF which was used for the introduction of the TDNN (see also [7]). The BDG–task uses a large vocabulary database of 5240 common japanese words. These words were uttered in isolation by one Japanese native male speaker. All utterances were digitized at a 12 kHz sampling rate. The database was then split into a training and a testing set, from which the actual phonetic tokens were extracted. The training tokens were then randomized within each class and the two sets were built by alternating each class to be learned. The phonemes to recognize were the three stop consonants "b", "d" and "g". Each "piece" of speech contained 15 frames, each of them containing 16 Melscale coefficients. The network to recognize these chunks of speech needs from 1 to 15 frames of input for the RBFs (depending on the size of the time window for this layer) and accordingly 15 to 1 frames for the integration layer (to cover the whole input sequence of 15 frames) which finally provides three outputs corresponding to the three phonemes. The only adjustable parameter is the relation of the number of time delays in the RBF layer compared to the number of time delays in the integration layer, which is uncritical to optimize. Figure 3 illustrates the main structure of the BDG-TDRBF.

The bottom layer has 16 inputs per time frame, which are Melscale Coefficients (a logarithmically compressed frequency spectrum). Each of the RBFs in the middle layer (for simplicity only one RBF per class is drawn, the number of RBFs in this layer changes during training, when new prototypes are committed) takes the current and the past 6 frames as an input, resulting in prototypes of dimension $7 * 16 = 112$. The responses of these RBFs are integrated by the last layer, which takes values from the previous and the past eight frames and produces the final output, for each of the three phonemes one value per frame.

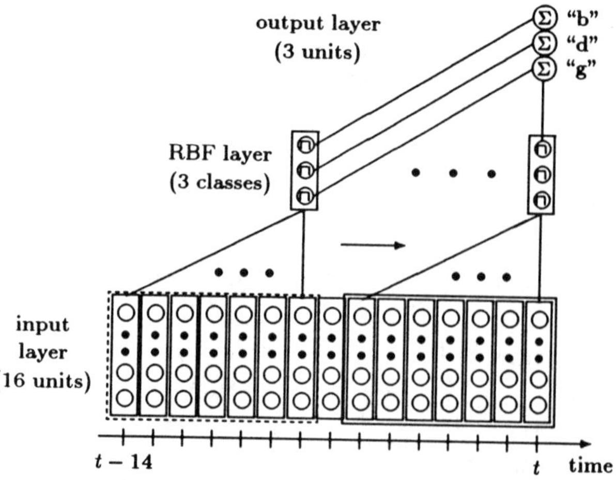

Figure 3: The Structure of the 7(9)–TDRBF used for the BDG–task. The number of RBFs in the second layer grows during training. Here only one RBF per class is drawn.

V. Performance

A. RBF Layer Window Size

Figure 4 shows how the size of the window which is moved over the input signal influences the performance of the whole network. If the number of time delays in the RBF layer is chosen too small, the performance is poor because the network has no opportunity to find features over time. On the other hand, if the number of time delays is chosen too large, the shift invariance over time is lost and the performance degrades also. The optimum performance lies somewhere in between and is easy to spot.

For this specific task, the interesting features are spread out over somewhere between 6 to 9 frames in time. Note that the error–rate for the training data set is a perfect 0% for the interesting networks and the best results for the test data are similar to those achieved with the TDNN mentioned in [7]. All experiments took less than 10 runs over the training data to complete.

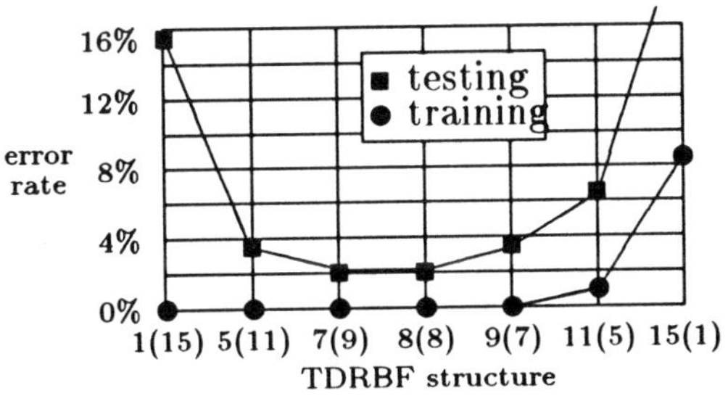

Figure 4: Performance vs. window size

B. Training the Integration Layer

For the previous examples the integration layer was used only to sum activations produced by RBFs for different points in time. One obvious experiment was to train these 1.0–weights. To do so, we used common Error Back Propagation training. Because this includes only a very small number of weights (for this example 3 — 45, depending on the structure of the net) it did not take too long to train this part of the networks. For this experiment we used the 7(9)–network from above. The error rate on the training data stayed at 0% and the error on the test data decreased by 0.3% which corresponds to two more patterns classified correctly. This trend held for other experiments as well, the training of the integration layer always improved performance but never substantially. Nevertheless it seems to be an interesting approach to improve performance, worthwhile to investigate further.

VI. Conclusion and Summary

In this paper a Time Delay Radial Basis Function Network (TDRBF) for the recognition of phonemes was presented. The main advantage over comparable approaches recognizing phonemes with Neural Network based systems is the decrease in time needed to train the network and the absence of hard to optimize parameters.

The TDRBF combines advantages of TDNNs, which are the shift invariance and the ability to recognize features in time, and the training speed and ease to use of RBF–based networks.

It was shown that TDRBF perform as well as TDNN on a phoneme recognition task used in [7] (TDRBF: 98.3% vs. TDNN: 98.5% recognition rate). The TDRBF needed less than 10 epochs to finish training, whereas the TDNN needs around at least 50 epochs to converge. In addition training epochs for TDRBF are faster than one epoch for TDNN, especially in the beginning when the commitment of new prototypes has just started.

VII. Acknowledgment

I would like to thank Mark Holler and Simon Tam for the opportunity to work on this project during my time at Intel. I would also like to thank Jay Diamond for many fruitful discussions. And last, but not least I would like to thank Alex Waibel for introducing me to this interesting field and for providing the BDG–database.

References

[1] B. Fritzke: "Growing Cell Structures – a self–organizing network in k dimensions", ANNs II, I. Aleksander & J. Taylor, eds., Amsterdam, pp. 1051–1056

[2] M. Holler, et al: "A 40,000 Patterns/s Classification Coprocessor with Learning Capability", Proc. Hot Chips V, Stanford, August 1993.

[3] J. Moody, C. Darken: "Fast Learning in Networks of locally–tuned processing units", Touretzky, Hinton and Sejnowsky, editors, Connectionist Models Summer School, 1988, pp. 133–143

[4] D. Morgan, P. Scofield: "Neural Networks for Speech Processing", Kluwer Academic Publishers, Boston, 1991, pp. 63–69

[5] D. Reilly, L. Cooper, C. Elbaum: "A Neural Model for Category Learning", Biol. Cybern., vol. 45, 1982, pp. 35–41

[6] E. Singer, R. Lippmann: "A Speech Recognizer using Radial Basis Function Neural Networks in an HMM Framework", Proc. ICASSP, San Francisco, March 1992.

[7] A. Waibel, T. Hanazawa, G. Hinton, K. Shikano, K. Lang: "Phoneme Recognition Using Time–Delay Neural Networks", Proc. ICASSP, Vol 37, No. 3, March 1989

INTENTIONALLY LEFT BLANK

Artificial Neural Networks for Phoneme Recognition

Peter T. Brunet* A. S. Pandya** Carlos V. Pinera*

*IBM, Internal Zip 5432
Special Needs Systems Development
1000 NW 51 St.
Boca Raton, FL 33431

**Florida Atlantic University
Department of Computer Science and Engineering
500 NW 20 St.
Boca Raton, FL 33431

Abstract

This paper describes the use of a back propagation artificial neural network (ANN) to recognize sustained phonemes. The inputs to the neural network were taken from 74 points of an LPC spectrum. This LPC data was augmented by adding slope information to each point in an attempt to add knowledge of the shape of the spectrum. The approach was verified by merging the ANN into an existing speech therapy product, IBM SpeechViewer™ II[1], and then testing the ANN with a number of male and female speakers. Results are shown which demonstrate the viability of the approach. It was also discovered that the ANN was able to function in a speaker independent manner. However, results are also shown which point out limitations of ANNs in classifying phonemes which are quite similar such as the **m** *and* **n** *phonemes.*

Introduction

An important aspect of a speech therapy system is the ability to work on the generation of sustained phonemes. Therefore, phoneme recognition is an integral part of such a system. Artificial neural networks have been used to some extent in speech recognition efforts [1]. Our goal was to determine if ANNs would be useful as a phoneme classification tool when imbedded into a speech therapy system. The speech therapy system we used for this work is IBM SpeechViewer II.

We were especially interested to see if an ANN could distinguish between phonemes that are very close in spectral makeup. For example, the m and n phonemes are very close. Another related issue is the ability to be able to distinguish between a nasalized and non-nasalized version of the same phoneme.

This paper describes the speech processing system which provides the input to the ANN, the back propagation algorithm used during training, the methods used to train and classify the phonemes, the steps taken to reach the optimum design of the network, the results, and some conclusions.

System Design and Implementation

There were three software elements used in this study:

- SpeechViewer II product software
- A back-propagation algorithm used in training to determine the network weights.
- A forward-propagation neural network that performs the classification task.

The speech processing system used was the one imbedded in SpeechViewer II. This system was used with no modifications. The system is implemented using DSP software running on a TI TMS30C25 DSP chip on an IBM M-Audio Capture Playback Adapter. The DSP software processes speech data producing an LPC spectrum every 17.4 ms. This spectrum has a bandwidth of 7.3 khz consisting of 74 bands of 100 hz each. The amplitude of each of the 74 spectral points is based

[1] SpeechViewer is a trademark of IBM Corporation.

0-7803-1901-X/94 $4.00 ©1994 IEEE

on a logarithmic scale. The 74 LPC spectral points serve as input to the ANN.

The SpeechViewer II module was modified to call the feed-forward network module which calculates the network output based on the spectral inputs. Before being passed to the forward propagation network, the spectra are stored in an array of type double-precision floating point. This array is passed to a neural network consisting of 74 inputs and one output for each phoneme to be classified. When the results are returned, the modified SpeechViewer II module determines which output is largest and displays on the screen which phoneme has been recognized.

The feed-forward network that calculates the phoneme recognition uses the layered network architecture as shown in Figure 1.

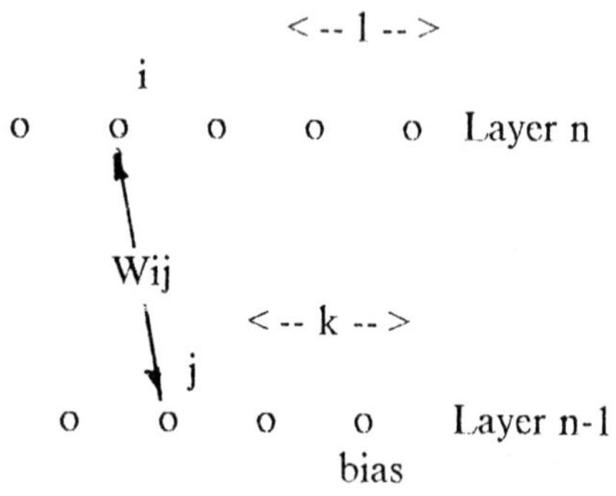

Figure 1. Feed-forward network

We calculate the output at each layer using the following equations:

$$net_i = \sum_{k=1}^{n} w_{ik} out_k - \theta_i$$

$$out_i = \frac{1}{1 + e^{-net_i/\theta_0}}$$

We start at the input layer and work upwards toward the output layer where the final outputs are calculated. A bias node is added with a fixed value of 1 to incorporate the θ_i (threshold) term.

For training the network weights, we used the popular back-propagation algorithm with the layered network architecture as shown in Figure 2.

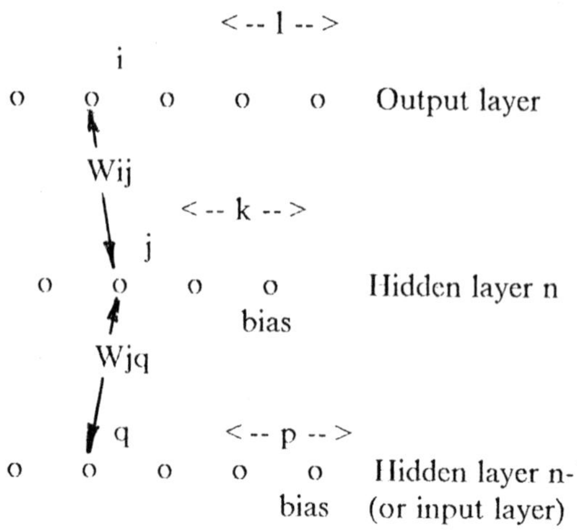

Figure 2. Back-propagation network

The equations for training the weights shown in Figure 2 are given by:

$$w_{(n+1)} = w_{(n)} + \eta \delta_i out_j + \alpha(w_{(n)} - w_{(n-1)})$$
if i is in the output layer
$$w_{(n+1)} = w_{(n)} + \eta \delta_j out_q + \alpha(w_{(n)} - w_{(n-1)})$$
if j is in a hidden layer

where:

η = the learning rate

α = the momentum

θ_0 = temperature

$\delta_i = (d_i - out_i) f'(net_i)$ if i is in the output layer

$\delta_j = (\sum_{l=1}^{n} \delta_l w_{lk}) f'(net_j)$ if j is in a hidden layer

$$net_i = \sum_{j=1}^{n} w_{ij}\, out_j$$

$$f'(net_i) = out_i (1 - out_i)$$

$$out_i = \frac{1}{1 + e^{-net_i/\theta_0}}$$

Convergence is reached if $|d_i - out_i| < 0.1$ for all patterns. The output of the training produces a weights file which is used by the feed-forward network module. The training and classification modules use the same configuration file as input. The values for θ_0 that provided the minimum training time and still had convergence were $\eta = 0.5$ and $\alpha = 0.5 \ldots 0.7$ and $\theta_0 = 1.0$.

Approach

IBM's Neural Network Utility (NNU) was available to us, but we used our own back propagation code and imbedded it into SpeechViewer II, since this approach proved to be the most fruitful for us. Even though NNU offers a lot of flexibility and extensive data logging, it computes so much data that it ran much slower than our C routines which are small and efficient. Since training times are so long, speed is very important. Our C routines ran significantly faster than NNU and we could easily modify our software to add data dumps as needed.

Our approach to the development of the application consisted of several stages:

- Modify SpeechViewer II so that we could capture data in a form useable by our C routines and also by NNU. We also modified SpeechViewer II so that it could be used during the classification process.
- Capture data to be used as a training set.
- Train the neural network.
- Determine the most efficient network architecture by systematically conducting a study.
- Use the neural network to classify data and compare its capability to the existing SpeechViewer II methods.

We took a two-phased approach to training and classification for this project. Training was done using a separate training ANN module we wrote which provided an efficient method of running several concurrent runs under OS/2. While this neural network module has classification code, we found it was better to do the classification in real-time using the modified SpeechViewer II.

The training data was obtained by producing a sustained phoneme into the microphone which was attached to an IBM PC running the SpeechViewer II application software in the data capture mode. The software captured the spectra and the spectral values were compiled into a file to be used as a training set. Figure 3 and Figure 4 show example spectra for different phonemes. In these figures the amplitude scale is logarithmic and the 0 dB point was arbitrarily chosen such that all the data points are positive.

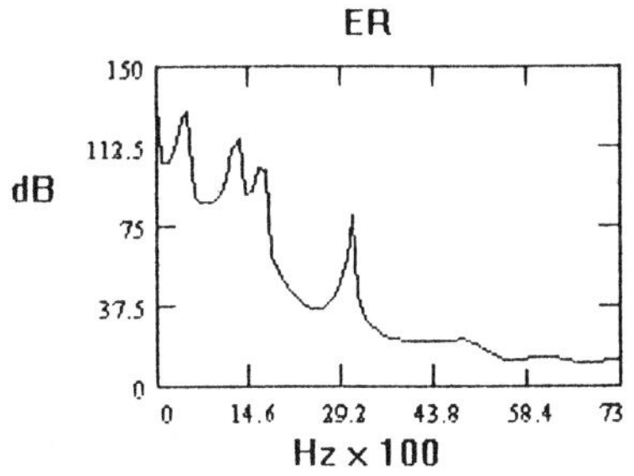

Figure 3. The er phoneme

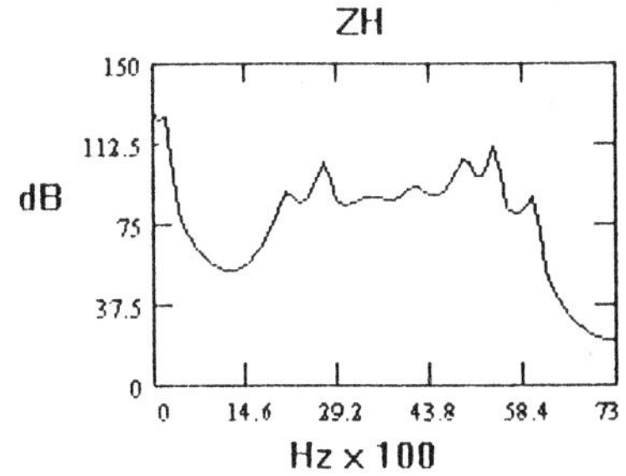

Figure 4. The zh phoneme (as in measure)

Using this utility 74 spectral input values representing 100 hz segments of the frequency range 0 to 7.3 khz were captured for each phoneme and the desired network output was added manually to create the training data set. Then training was preformed using the feed-forward network module and the back-propagation learning module. Upon convergence the weights were stored in a file for use in the testing phase.

During the testing phase the classification ability of the trained network was analyzed. The test data was obtained online by producing sustained phonemes into the microphone. The trained network used the spectra of these phonemes as input. The feed-forward neural network module was run and the recognized phoneme and the ANN output values were displayed on the screen. The phoneme name recognized by the network was checked to determine if it matched the produced phoneme. The output node values were also checked to see how strongly the output indicated the particular phoneme. This phase was repeated for each phoneme and with different test subjects.

This method provided good feedback; we could try different subjects or vary the way we pronounced phonemes and see immediately the effects of the variations.

Results

The first experiment was to train the neural network for two phonemes that were far apart, i.e. **ah**, as in say "ahhh" and **ee** as in bee. We started with a network of 74x127x127x2. The 74 inputs consist of one sensor for each 100 hz of the spectrum from 0 hz to 7.3 khz. These spectral values were available to us from the existing DSP and PC software of SpeechViewer II. The 127 node hidden layers were the maximum size hidden layers available in NNU. (53 nodes is the limit when working with our C routines.) This network converged nicely and successfully differentiated between the ah and ee phonemes. In order to find a more time and space efficient network we tried 74x7x7x2 network and this one also worked successfully. The value of seven for the size of the hidden layer was suggested by a rule of thumb [2] which recommends sizes of two to seven percent for image pattern recognition tasks. Our phoneme recognition task is similar to an image pattern recognition problem.

The next experiment was to try two phonemes that were very close to each other in the spectral input space, i.e. m and n. See Figure 5 and Figure 6 for examples of the m and n spectra.

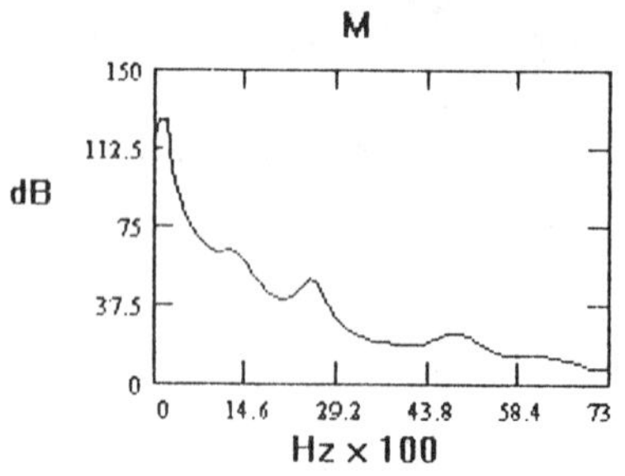

Figure 5. The m phoneme

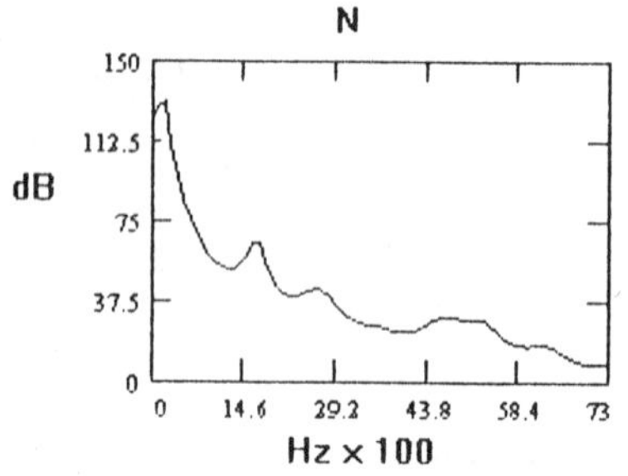

Figure 6. The n phoneme

This experiment was not at all successful even when we increased the number of nodes in the hidden layers to the largest possible values.

We then tried to increase the number of phonemes in the phoneme pool, using ah, er, ee, m, zh (as in measure), and Λ (as in table). This network had 6 outputs, one for each phoneme. While working on this experiment we were also thinking about how to solve the closeness problem. We modified our training set slightly in an attempt to incorporate a more distinctive input pattern for each phoneme. This modification consisted of adding a slope component to each of the existing amplitude components. This was done by computing the first difference between the amplitude of each spectral point and the one just lower in frequency and then adding that difference to the amplitude of each spectral point. This experiment using the larger phoneme pool also converged and classified successfully. However, the number of nodes in the hidden layers had to be increased to forty. This was because of the closeness between the m phoneme and the er phoneme. These two phonemes don't sound too close together when using our ears to distinguish them but their spectral makeup was apparently close enough to cause problems for a neural network with less than 40 nodes in each hidden layer. See Figure 3 on page 3 for an example of the er phoneme and Figure 5 for an example of the m phoneme. For this set of experiments our training set consisted of phonemes uttered by 4 males. This neural network was able to not only successfully distinguish phonemes uttered by the 4 males but also was successful in classifying phonemes uttered by four females, thus showing an indication of speaker independent capabilities.

We continued our experimentation to see if the addition of the slope information would improve the system's ability to distinguish between m and n. Unfortunately, even when raising the number of nodes in the hidden layers to the maximum allowed by our memory constraints, i.e. 53 nodes, the system was unable to distinguish these phonemes. That is not too surprising since the human hearing system has a much larger number of spectral sensors and neural connections to work with and we have noticed that even humans occasionally make mistakes when asked to differentiate between the m and n sounds with no visual cues.

Since the difference between a nasalized and normally produced version of the same phoneme is even closer than the distance between m and n we did not include this experiment.

Conclusions

Artificial neural networks do a good job of distinguishing between orthogonal patterns and we found that when an ANN is applied to a set of phonemes that are sufficiently orthogonal the network was able to do a very good job of differentiating between the phonemes. The system was even able to do its task in a speaker independent manner. However, when dealing with phonemes that are close in their spectral makeup, such as the m and n phonemes, the orthogonality is lost and the ANN is unable to distinguish between them.

One of the concerns with ANNs for this task is the training time involved. With the current (traditional) methods used in SpeechViewer II, the training time is limited to the time taken to capture a set of phonemes that will make up the target phoneme models. When using ANNs, several hours of additional time are needed to train the network.

If ANN hardware were available, the number of nodes could be increased perhaps to the point of allowing sufficient differentiation between "close" phonemes. Also, such hardware would reduce the training times.

We have some ideas for future research. One is to include a much larger number of nodes in the hidden layers. This was beyond the capability of the systems available to us for these tests. Another is to try additional augments to the spectral data along the lines of adding the slope information to each spectral component. One such change might be the use of pure amplitude data rather than logarithms we used. This might help emphasize the peaks in the data since this seems to be of more importance than the other points on the spectrum. An idea that would help improve efficiency is to cut down on the number of inputs. Since the peaks in the spectral envelope are the most important points, we could detect these peaks by finding all positive to negative slope reversals and then use the frequencies of the first five peaks as inputs to the neural network. This would make a dramatic improvement in the efficiency of the network.

References

1. Waibel, Hanazawa, Hinton, Shikano, Lang, Phoneme Recognition Using Time-Delay Neural Networks, IEEE Trans. On Acoustics, Speech and Signal Processing, March 1989, pp. 328-339.

2. Hammerstrom, Working with Neural Networks, IEEE Spectrum, July 1993, pp. 46-53

Table 1. Training results, ah-er-ee-m-zh-Λ

Name	η	α	θ_0	Architecture	Epochs	Type	Notes
test8	0.1	0.2	0.7	74x7x7x6	1,772	alldata	m -> er
test9	0.1	0.2	0.7	74x7x7x6	1,481	alldelta	m -> er
test10	0.3	0.3	1.0	74x7x7x6	626	alldelta	m -> er
test11	0.5	0.2	1.0	74x7x7x6	527	alldelta	m -> er and ah
test12	0.2	0.2	0.7	74x7x7x6	1,121	alldelta	m -> ah
test13	0.7	0.9	1.0	74x10x10x6	-	alldelta	no convergence
test14	0.5	0.2	1.0	74x10x10x6	548	alldelta	m -> er
test15	0.5	0.2	1.0	74x12x12x6	532	alldelta	m -> er
test16	0.5	0.5	1.0	74x12x12x6	387	alldelta	m -> er
test17	0.5	0.7	1.0	74x12x12x6	308	alldelta	m -> er occasionally
test18	0.5	0.5	1.0	74x50x50x6	295	alldelta	works well
test19	0.5	0.9	1.0	74x12x12x6	-	alldelta	no convergence
test20	0.5	0.5	1.0	74x50x50x6	455	alldata	m -> er rarely
test21	0.5	0.5	1.0	74x20x20x6	356	alldelta	m -> er, ah -> er and Λ
test22	0.5	0.5	1.0	74x30x30x6	326	alldelta	m -> er, ah -> er and Λ
test23	**0.5**	**0.5**	**1.0**	**74x40x40x6**	**313**	**alldelta**	**works well**
test24	0.5	0.5	1.0	74x32x32x6	337	alldelta	m -> er occasionally
test25	0.5	0.5	1.0	74x34x34x6	352	alldelta	m -> er occasionally
test26	0.5	0.5	1.0	74x36x36x6	353	alldelta	m -> er occasionally
test27	0.5	0.5	1.0	74x38x38x6	295	alldelta	ah -> m rarely

Notes related to Table 1

The symbol "->" in the **Notes** column should be read as "was classified as".

Tests 8 through 27 were run in a process of determining the right number of nodes in the hidden layer. Test 23 resulted in the optimal number of nodes, i.e. 40 nodes per hidden layer. If less than 40 nodes per hidden layer were used, the ANN would typically detect that an **er** was uttered when an **m** was spoken.

In the **Type** column, alldata refers to spectral data that was not augmented by slope information as described in the paper while alldelta refers to spectral data that was augmented.

Window Structure and Computation of Neural Networks for Speech Recognition

D. Zhang and M.I. Elmasry

VLSI Research Group, Department of Electrical and Computer Engineering
University of Waterloo, Waterloo, Ontario, Canada N2L 3G1

Abstract

Neural networks(NNs), as processors of time-sequence patterns, have been successfully applied to several speaker-dependent speech recognition systems. They can be efficiently implemented by a pipelined architecture. In this paper, we explore its window structure as a computation component in the architecture. Two types of windows, parallel and serial data flow window, and their computation units with both feedforward and feedback paths are developed. The implementations of the windows are easily matched to the VLSI medium. Examples of applications to the NNs and performance analysis are given to illustrate effectiveness of the proposed window computation.

1. Introduction

A variety of NNs for speech recognition have been developed during the past few years [1]. Numerous studies have demonstrated effectiveness of the multilayer networks with time sequences as inputs to the networks [2]. Several typical examples are: Time-delay neural network(TDNN) proposed by Waibel and Lang, et al. [3-4]; Block-windowed neural network (BWNN) by Sawai [5] and Dynamic programming neural network(DNN) by Sakoe, et al. [6].

A common design approach used in these NNs is incorporation of short delays, of temporal integration, or of recurrent connections. Spectral inputs are applied to input nodes sequentially, one frame at a time, and their corresponding input matrix can be formed. The NNs can thus be integrated into real time speech recognizer because only short delays are used.

These NNs can be implemented by a pipelined architecture in [7], where P+1 processing stages are cascaded. In each processing stage, a window is built as a connection to next stage. Loading an input submatrix to the window in a pipeline mode, and mapping the corresponding weight matrix, the output results can be obtained.

Note that two different types of operations, control flow and data flow, are used in the pipelined neural network (PNN) architecture, as shown in Fig.1(a). Master control unit not only gives each sequence of instructions (control flow) to the corresponding processing stage, but also arranges the parameter of each frame of speech input as data flow input to the given window. Once the window is filled, the submatrix obtained will be processed.

Obviously, window in the PNN architecture is an important component and is also a typical feature which differs from other NN architectures. In this paper, we explore its evolutionary computation with implementation efficiency as our goal. The window model and its structure definition are first described. Then, two types of window structures and their building units are discussed. Finally, case studies for the NNs and performance analysis for window structure are given, respectively.

2. Definition and Structure

A multilayer NN with time sequence input of feature parameters for speech recognition is composed of p+2 layers, which includes an input layer, p hidden layers, and an output layer. Both the input and the hidden layer are characterized by time sequence input matrix of speech parameters, built by m_s x n_s (s = 1, 2, ..., p+1) memory units, where $m_{p+1} = q$ is the number of pattern classes. The output layer consists in q units. The relation between nodes x_{ij} in Layer s and nodes y_{kl} in Layer s+1 can be defined as:

$$y_{kl} = f\left(\sum_{i=k}^{k+e_s-1} \sum_{j=l}^{l+r_s-1} x_{ij}\, w^{(kl)}{}_{i-k+1,j-l+1} + \theta^{(kl)} \right) \tag{1}$$

where f is a sigmoid function; $w^{(kl)}$ and $\theta^{(kl)}$, $1 \le k \le m_{s+1}$ and $1 \le l \le n_{s+1}$, are referred to as weight value and bias value from a small input submatrix, called "window", where the size is e_s x r_s($e_s \le m_s$ and $r_s \le n_s$) in Layer s to the nodes y_{kl} in Layer s+1, respectively. There will be m_{s+1} x n_{s+1} windows formed from the input matrix(m_s x n_s) in Layer s.

Based on the window operation model in Eq.(1), only an input window built by e_s x r_s units is given in Layer s. Instead of moving such a window to the whole input matrix, speech parameters in time sequence are arranged to pass through the window in pipeline. Thus, the relation in Eq.(1) can be rewritten as

$$y_{kl} = f\,(\Sigma W_{kl} X^T) = f\,(\Sigma X W_{kl}{}^T) \tag{2}$$

where **X** is an input submatrix given by such a fixed window, and can be represented as

$$\mathbf{X} = \begin{pmatrix} X_1 \\ X_2 \\ \cdots\cdots \\ X_{es} \end{pmatrix} = \begin{pmatrix} x_{11} & x_{12} & \ldots & x_{1rs} \\ x_{21} & x_{22} & \ldots & x_{2rs} \\ & \cdots\cdots & & \\ x_{es1} & x_{es2} & \ldots & x_{esrs} \end{pmatrix} \tag{3}$$

and $\mathbf{W}_{kl}$ is the corresponding weight matrix from the window in Layer s to nodes y_{kl} in Layer s+1, i.e.

$$\mathbf{W}_{kl} = \begin{pmatrix} w^{(kl)}_{11} & w^{(kl)}_{12} & \ldots & w^{(kl)}_{1rs} \\ w^{(kl)}_{21} & w^{(kl)}_{22} & \ldots & w^{(kl)}_{2rs} \\ & \cdots\cdots & & \\ w^{(kl)}_{es1} & w^{(kl)}_{es2} & \ldots & w^{(kl)}_{esrs} \end{pmatrix} \tag{4}$$

It is evident that there are m_{s+1} x n_{s+1} different weight matrices from Layer s to Layer s+1. Their sizes are equal to the size of the window in Layer s.

The NNs discussed above can be implemented by a pipelined architecture with p+1 processing stages, each with its own sequence of instructions (See Fig.1(a)). In each processing stage, a fixed window is built as a connection to next stage. Loading an input submatrix, **X**, to the window in a pipeline mode, and mapping the corresponding weight matrix, $\mathbf{W}_{kl}$ ($k = 1, 2, \ldots, m_{s+1}$; $l = 1, 2, \ldots, n_{s+1}$), the output results, y_{kl}, can be obtained. Such a window model is shown in Fig.2. In the pipelined neuron structure (Fig.1(b)), the inputs, X_i ($i = 1, 2, \ldots, e_s$), are underlayed or delayed D_t ($=\sum_{j=1}^{t-1} D_j + \Delta$; D is a delay unit and Δ is its increment, $t = 1, 2, \ldots, r_s-1$). The inputs will be multiplied by several weights, one for each delay and one for the underlayed input.

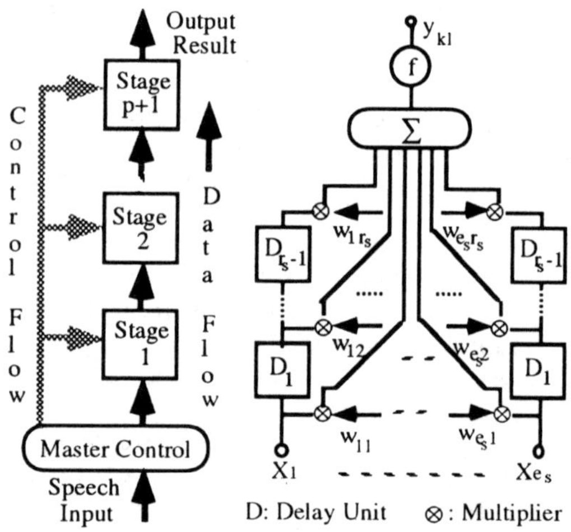

Fig.1 Pipelined NN architecture and its neuron

3. Window Computation

Depending on the nature of the speech input, two types of window computations using parallel or serial data flow can be defined.

Parallel Data Flow Window (Fig.3): The window built by m_s x r_s computation units is used to receive the input data flow from its previous stage, and m_{s+1} neurons are used to send the output results to the next stage in parallel. In other words, the input data flow is passed through the window and transformed by this stage to generate the corresponding output data flow. Their widths are m_s and m_{s+1}, respectively. A new feature parameter obtained by each neuron is represented as

$$y_i\,(s+1) = f\,(\,\Sigma W_i(s)\; X^T(s)\,) \tag{5}$$

where $s = 1, 2, \ldots, p+1$; $i = 1, 2, \ldots, m_{s+1}$; $W_i(s)$ is the i-th weight matrix and X(s) is the input submatrix formed by the window in Stage s.

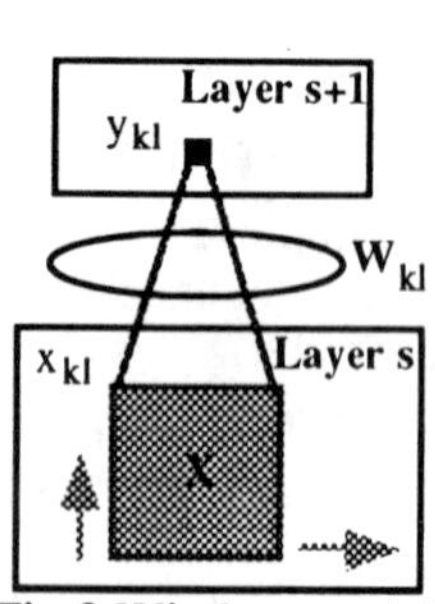

Fig.2 Window model

Serial Data Flow Window(Fig.4): A pipe with single parameter width is made by a chain of serial shifting units. The window consists of e_s x r_s computation units. The neuron associated with the window is represented as

$$y(s+1) = \mathrm{OR}(y_i(s+1)) \tag{6}$$

where $i = 1, 2, \ldots, m_{s+1}$; $s = 0, 1, \ldots, p+1$. This means that the output can be in turn obtained and that there is either a single output, $y_i(s+1)$, or no output within a single clock interval. The output order in a cycle is: $y_1(s+1), \ldots, y_{m_{s+1}}(s+1), *_1, \ldots, *_{e_s-1}$, where $m_{s+1} + e_s - 1 = m_s$ and " * " indicates no output. There are a total of n_{s+1} ($= n_s - r_s + 1$) processing cycles for each given speech input matrix (m_s x n_s). Some select cells are used in this window to obtain a common output, y(s+1).

Note that in both window computations, the line delays are used to receive a data stream of parameters and to construct the window required. There are a total of $\{m_s\,(m_s-1)\}\,/\,2$ and $\{(2m_s-2e_s-r_s)\,(r_s-1)\}\,/\,2$ shifting units in parallel and serial data flow window, respectively. The adder arrays are to use as the accumulators to compress the output results of the window as the inputs to the neurons. Obviously, They can be implemented by regular shifting registers and adders.

Since the computation unit is a key component in window structure, we will discuss its building block with on-line learning. In fact, the computation units used in both Fig.3 and Fig.4 have the identical structure definition. It can be built in Fig.5, where special feedforward and feedback paths are given in the block.

It is mainly composed of weight memory (W_i) (i = 1, 2, ..., m_{s+1}), adder (⊕) and multiplier (⊗). A control clock indicates which phase the unit is, i.e. CLK = 0, searching phase; CLK = 1, learning phase. Three data inputs, x, $\{z_i\}$ and $\{\delta_i\}$, and their outputs, x', $\{Z_i\}$ and $\{\Omega_i\}$, are given, where $\{z_i\}$ and $\{Z_i\}$ are used for CLK = 0; $\{\delta_i\}$ and $\{\Omega_i\}$ for CLK = 1. It is notice that each input (output) is transmitted by m_{s+1} data except x (x'). When CLK = 0, the output of the unit is

$$Z_i = x\ w_i + z_i \quad (7)$$

Otherwise,

$$\Omega_i = w_i\ \delta_i \quad (8)$$

and at the same time, W_i is changed in terms of the rule

$$w_i = w_i + \eta\ \delta_i\ x \quad (9)$$

Attaching simple selectors to the unit, some multipliers can be saved.

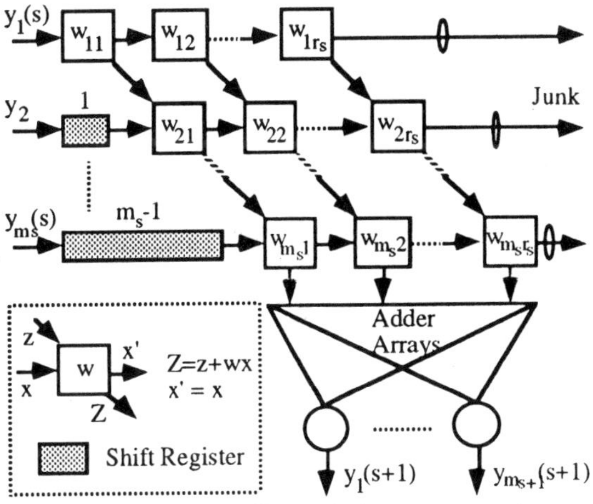

Fig.3 Parallel data flow window computation

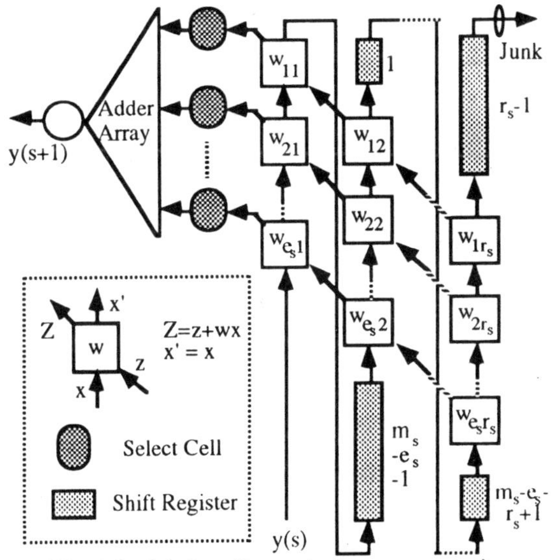

Fig.4 Serial data flow window computation

4. Application and Analysis

We provide the results of our study on three types of NNs using the window computation. The NNs selected are motivated by speech recognition applications and they have been widely used by speech recognition researchers.

The basic TDNN [3] and the BWNN [5] can be implemented by the parallel and serial data flow window structure, respectively. Here, we will focus on the DNN [6] with three processing stages, which the parallel and serial data flow window are used in the first two stages and the last stage (See Fig.6). An input pattern, x_1, ..., x_i, ..., x_I, is defined as a warping function i = i(j) between input pattern time i and window unit j, where j = 1, 2, ..., J. The window is built by 2 x J units and J neurons are used in the first stage. When the input patterns x_i and x_{i-1} pass through the window, the corresponding output for each neuron can be represented as: $y_{ij} = f(w_{j0}\ x_i + w_{j1}\ x_{i-1})$, where w_{j0} and w_{j1} are weighs from two shifting units in window unit j to neuron j. In the second stage, a window with J x 1 window is used to receive y_{ij} (j = 1, 2, ..., J), in parallel. Each neuron in the stage is used as a multiplier, i.e. $q_{ij} = w_j\ y_{ij}$. The third stage is built by a serial data flow window. Its input data, q_{ij}, is arranged in a pipeline of a single parameter like $q_{iJ} \rightarrow \cdots \rightarrow q_{ij} \rightarrow \cdots \rightarrow q_{i1}$. It is composed of a four-unit window, two J-1 line delays and a processing element(PE). The initial condition is $g_{11} = q_{11}$. Then, data is processed according to DP-equation: $g_{ij} = q_{ij} + \max(g_{i,j-1}, g_{i-1,j-1}, g_{i-2,j-1})$. Given q_{ij}, its corresponding g_{ij} obtained by the PE is fed into the given window to generate the new values. This process is continued until the total cumulation value, Z = g(I, J), is reached.

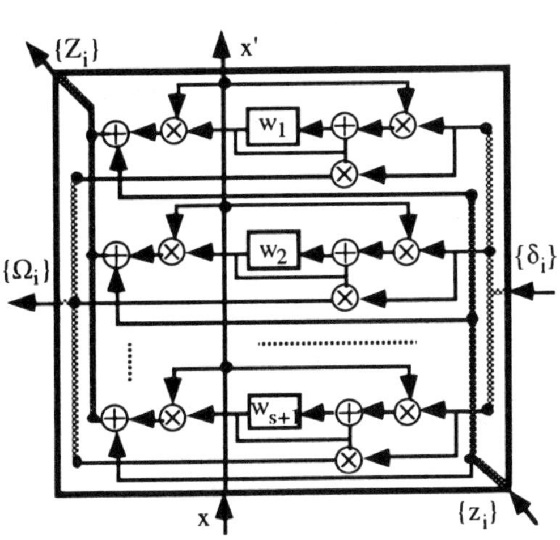

Fig.5 Computational unit building block (⊗: multipliers; ⊕: adder)

The window structure can greatly reduce the memory units in each layer of the NN to a small number of computation units with feedforward and feedback path, because only a limited window is connected to its next stage and the parameters shifted out from the window are discarded. Since the speech feature parameters applied to each layer sequentially one frame at a time, this reduction of memory units is easily implementable. Especially, this window structure which combines weight computation makes the real speech recognition become possible.

The window size has a direct relation to the properties of the PNN, such as the number of computation units, Φ, and the time delay, Ψ. The smaller the window, the fewer number of computation units, but the greater length of time delay are required.

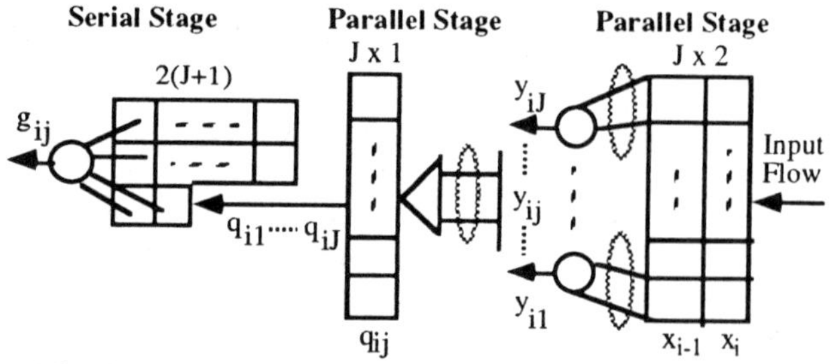

Fig.6 Window structure of the DNN implementation

In parallel data flow window (Type 1), these two trade-off properties for Stage s are

$$\begin{cases} \Phi_{Type\ 1} = r_s \times m_s \\ \Psi_{Type\ 1} = n_s - r_s + 1 \end{cases} \tag{10}$$

We define their product as $E(r_s) = \Phi_{Type\ 1} \times \Psi_{Type\ 1} = (r_s \times m_s)(n_s - r_s + 1)$. To maximize the $E(r_s)$ function, take derivative with the window size r_s, i.e., $E'(r_s) = m_s n_s - 2 m_s r_s + m_s$. Let $E'(r_s) = 0$, the optimal size of window for Type 1 can be selected as $r_s = (n_s+1)/2$. Note that this optimal window size is not a function of the length of the window, m_s (See Fig.7(a)).

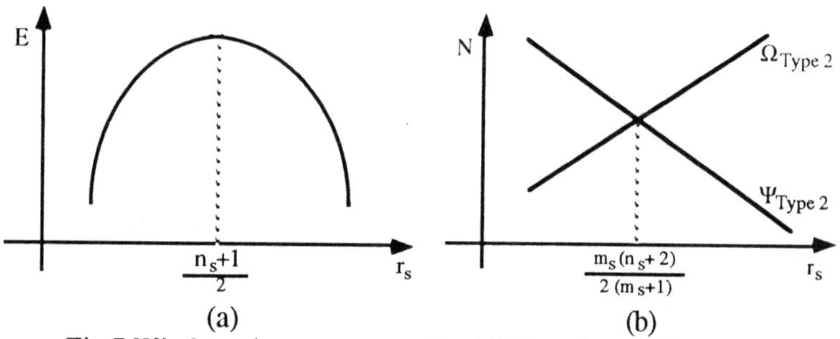

Fig.7 Window size parameters for (a) Type 1 and (b) Type 1

In the same way, the two trade-off properties in serial data flow window (Type 2) can be written as:

$$\begin{cases} \Phi_{Type\ 2} = (r_s - 1)\, m_s + r_s \\ \Psi_{Type\ 2} = m_s n_s - (r_s - 1)\, m_s - r_s \end{cases} \tag{11}$$

where $r_s = e_s$, i.e., a square window is used. The size of the window can be selected directly from the relation $\Phi_{Type\ 2} = \Psi_{Type\ 2}$ (See Fig.7(b)), which leads to $(r_s - 1)\, m_s + r_s = m_s n_s - (r_s - 1)\, m_s - r_s$. Hence, the choice of the window size for Type 2 is $r_s = \{m_s(n_s + 2)\} / 2(m_s + 1)$.

5. Conclusion

In this paper, a novel window model which can be used for solving speech recognition problem is proposed. Two efficient window structures, parallel and serial data flow windows, are developed and their computation units with both feedforward and feedback paths are built. The implementations of these windows are easily matched to the VLSI medium. Examples of applications and performance analysis are given to illustrate effectiveness of the proposed window computation.

6. References

[1] S. Furui and M.M. Sondhi (eds.), 1992. Advances in speech signal processing, *Marcel Dekker Inc.*, N. Y.

[2] R.P. Lippmann, 1989. Review of neural networks for speech recognition, *Neural Computing* 1, 1-38.

[3] A. Waibel, et al., 1989. Phoneme recognition using time-delay neural networks, *IEEE Trans. on ASSP* 37, 3, 328-339.

[4] K.J. Lang, and A.H. Waibel, 1990. A time-delay neural networks architecture for isolanted word recognition, *Neural Networks*. 3, 23-43.

[5] H. Sawai, 1991. Frequency-time-shift-invariant time-delay neural networks for robust continuous speech recognition, *IEEE, Proceeding of ICASSP-91*, S-2.1, 45-48.

[6] H. Sakoe, R. Isotani, K. Yoshida, K. Iso, and T. Watanabe, 1989. Speaker-independenct word recognition using dynamic programming neural networks, *Speech Recognition*, 439-442.

[7] D. Zhang, L. Deng and M.I. Elmasry, 1994. Pipelined architecture for neural-network-based speech recognition", *Neural, Parallel & Scientific Computation*, (in print).

Classification of Speech Accents with Neural Networks

Mike V. Chan, Xin Feng, James A. Heinen and Russell J. Niederjohn
Department of Electrical and Computer Engineering
Marquette University
Milwaukee, WI 53233

Abstract - Several neural network models including competitive learning, counter propagation, and counter propagation are developed to identify individuals as either native or non-native speakers based on their accents. Some important speech features, such as pitch period and the first three formant frequencies, are used as inputs to the neural networks. Comparison results based on experiments are also presented. The primary contribution is that it provides a feasible approach for assisting automatic speech recognition system in an environment in which different English accents may be used. Such approaches have not been seen in the literature.

I. INTRODUCTION

In spite of various accents of English speakers, listeners are still able to recognize the speech of a non-native English speaker most of the time [1]. However, a computer-based automatic speech recognition system may not have such flexibility built in when it was specifically designed for native English speaking people. Furthermore, English accents vary widely, even within the same English-speaking country. Therefore, there is a need for a subsystem that can identify accents so that an automatic speech recognition system may better be able to process the input speech signal.

It is believed that the artificial neural network (ANN) does have the potential to identify different accents. In this paper, several ANN models are proposed to identify the accents. These models include competitive learning [2], back-propagation [3], and counter propagation [4]. The primary contribution is that it provides a feasible approach for assisting automatic speech recognition systems in an environment in which different English accents may be used. There are many practical applications of the proposed approach, such as automatic speech recognition systems.

II. NEURAL NETWORK ARCHITECTURES

Both supervised and unsupervised learning neural networks have the capabilities of pattern recognition and have been applied in speech signal recognition [5]. These two architectures are fundamentally different in architecture as well as in training strategies. The significance of unsupervised competitive learning is that it can automatically identify the hidden features in the input patterns without supervision and thus it can automatically classify the patterns into categories [6]. Figure 1 illustrates a two-layer unsupervised competitive learning ANN architecture.

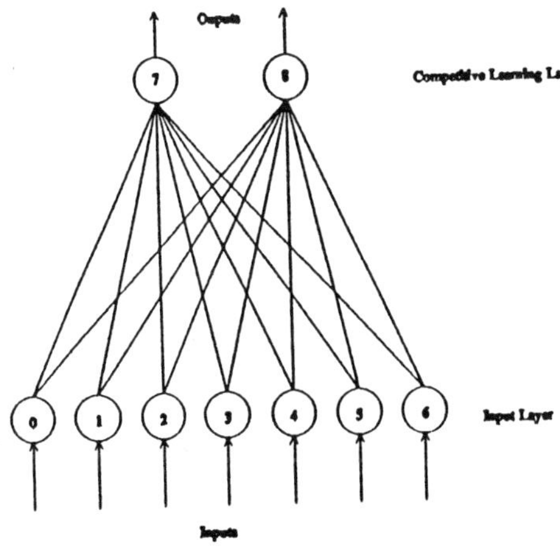

Figure 1 competitive neural network

On the other hand, the performance of the supervised learning ANN scheme is well known, and the applications of the back-propagation ANN, the typical supervised learning ANN, for speech

0-7803-1901-X/94 $4.00 ©1994 IEEE

recognition have also been reported [7]. While competitive learning ANN is relatively simple in architecture and training is less time consuming, the training for a typical BP neural network requires more time. However, due to its supervised training nature, the results are generally more stable than these obtained by unsupervised ANNs.

Another type of ANN architecture is the counter propagation ANN, which was proposed by Nielson [4], this type of ANN integrates competitive learning and back-propagation together and is designed to take advantage of both learning schemes. Readers are referred to [4] for details.

It is unclear, however, which ANN has better performance in the application of speech processing, especially in accent identification. At the present time, no comparison reports have been seen for the performance of three ANN architectures.

III. TRAINING AND TESTING

The three mentioned ANNs are implemented in the laboratory environment for the experimental purposes using NeuralWare Professional II/Plus neural network package [8]. The first implemented ANN uses the competitive learning training approach with categorization. The second ANN is the counter-propagation. Finally, the third one is back-propagation.

A. Selection of Features and Training Patterns

To the input layer, the demographic data from 22 speakers (10 native English speakers and 12 non-native English speakers) and features of their speech are fed. The data includes age at which English was first used, the percentage of time on a typical day during which English is used as the only communication medium, and the number of years in which English has been used. The speech features include the pitch frequencies averaged over time, and the first three formant frequencies of the speech averaged over time. Therefore, there are totally seven input neurons in the input layer. The speech features are extracted from the spoken phrase "correct mandatory collection" using existing software. Figure 2 shows the pitch frequency distributions of the two groups of speakers.

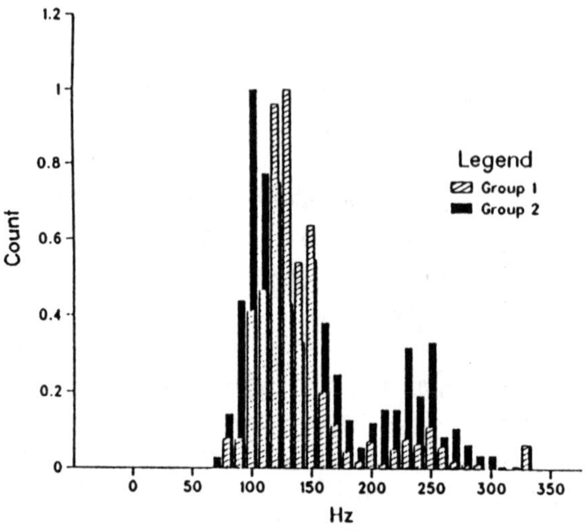

Fig. 2 Pitch frequency distribution of speakers

Also group one consists of native speakers and group two non-native English speakers. Figures 3 and 4 show the normalized formant frequency distributions of the two groups of the speakers. It is interesting to note considerable amount of overlap in the pitch frequency histograms shown in Figure 2. On the other hand, there are distinct differences in the formant frequency distributions shown in Figures 3 and 4., particularly for the second and third formants.

For comparison purpose, same architectures are used for all three ANNs: 7 input neurons in the first layer, 3 neurons in the hidden layer, and 2 neurons in the output layer. The hidden layer uses a hyperbolic tangent function. The stop criterion is set to 0.0001 for weight changes in all ANNs.

To each of the three neural networks, two training sets and two testing sets were presented. The first training set included the inputs from all 22 speakers; the inputs of the native English speakers were interlaced with those of the non-native English speakers. When this was the training set, all the inputs were used again for the testing set. The second training set included only the inputs from 11 speakers: 5 native English speakers interlaced with 6 non-native English speakers. The testing set then consisted of the inputs from the rest of the speakers.

From the table, the back propagation ANN demonstrates superior performance, followed by counter propagation ANN. The competitive learning has an acceptable training result but the testing result is poor. This experiment shows that the supervised training strategy is more suitable for this type of application.

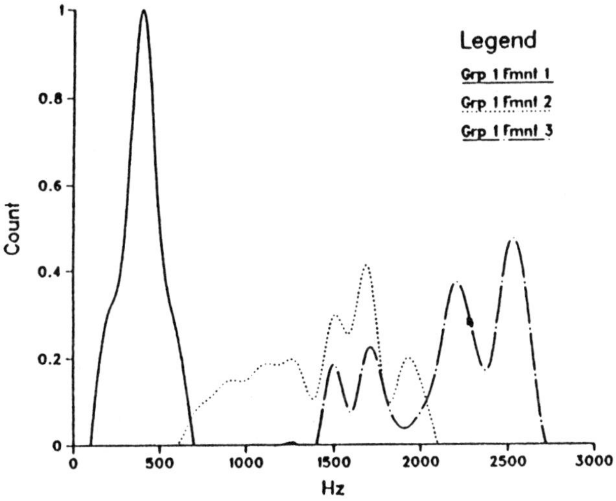

Fig. 3. Formant frequency distribution of group 1 speakers

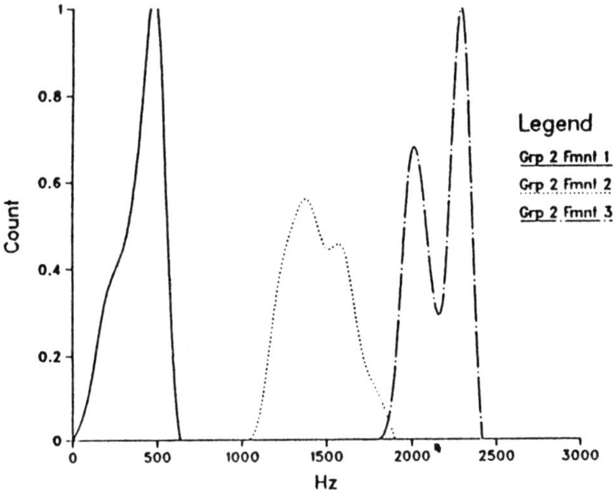

Fig. 4 Formant frequency distribution of group 2 speakers

IV. RESULTS AND COMPARISON

The following is a table of testing results which shows the percentage correct categorizations for the three ANNs studied. In the table, CL. is the competitive learning ANN, CP is the counter propagation ANN, and BP. is the back-propagation ANN. Furthermore, the number following each ANN indicates the training set used: "1" represents that the ANN was presented with the entire set of input data, while "2" indicates that the ANN was presented with half of the input data. Therefore, the "1" test rows are filled with N.A.'s.

For all the ANNs trained and tested, the three significant features (obtained by observing the associated weights) are the percentage of time during which only English is used, the second and the third formant frequencies, as expected. Another significant feature is the pitch frequency, which does not look apparently by inspecting the pitch histogram in Figure 2. This may be due to the fact that pitch frequency dictates intonation, and therefore it is not surprising to have different yet overlapping pitch frequency concentration as shown in Figure 2.

Table 1 Comparison of different neural network results

Type of ANN	CL. 1	CL. 2	CP. 1	CP. 2	BP. 1	BP. 2
TRAINING	90.9%	81.8%	90.9%	100%	100%	100%
TESTING	N.A.	45%	N.A.	64%	N.A.	90.9%

V. CONCLUSIONS

Three artificial neural networks were implemented to differentiate the twenty two speakers into two categories. Seven feature inputs were presented to the ANNs; these features were the first three average formant frequencies, the average pitch frequency, the percentage of time during which only English is used, the age at which English was first used, and the number of years during which English has been spoken. The important features, as observed by the ANN weights, are the percentage of time during which English is used, and the second formant frequency, and the pitch frequency. The back propagation ANN demonstrates superior performance over the competitive learning and counter propagation ANNs. The results of this experiment are promising even though a considerable amount of work remains to be accomplished. This research demonstrates the significance of artificial neural networks in recognizing of the accents of native and nonnative English speakers. It is believed that the approach and results shown in this paper can be used to construct a subsystem to improve the flexibility and capability of speech recognition systems.

REFERENCES

[1] F. M. Chreist, *Foreign Accent*, Prentice-Hall, Englewood Cliffs, 1964.

[2] T. Kohonen, *Self-Organization and Association Memory*, Second Edition. New York: Springer-Verlag, 1988.

[3] J. L. McClelland and D. E. Rumelhart, *Parallel Distributed Processing: Explorations in the Microstructure of Cognition*, Vols. 1 and 2, MIT Press, Cambridge, MA 1986.

[4] R. Hecht-Nielsen, *Neuralcomputing*, Addison Wesley, 1990.

[5] B. Kosko, *Neural Networks in Signal Processing*, Prentice Hall, 1990.

[6] R. A. Clinkenbeard and X. Feng, "An Unsupervised Learning and Fuzzy Logic Approach for Software Category Identification and Capability Planning," *Proceedings, 1992 International Joint Conference on Neural Network (IJCNN)*, Vol. 2, pp 1223-1228, June, 1992.

[7] R. Hecht-Nielsen, "Theory of the Backpropagation Neural Network," *IEEE IJCNN*, Vol. 1, pp. 593-595, 1989.

[8] *NeuralWorks Professional II/Plus User's Manual*, NeuralWare, Inc., Pittsburgh, PA, 1991.

[9] D. DeSieno, "Adding a Conscience to Competitive Learning," *Proceedings, International Conference on Neural Networks*, Vol 1, pp. 117-124, IEEE Press, New York.

[10] Alan V. Oppenheim and Ronald W. Schafer, *Discrete-Time Signal Processing*, Prentice-Hall, Englewood Cliffs, New Jersey 1989.

[11] L. R. Rabiner and R. W. Schafer, *Digital Processing Of Speech Signals*, Prentice-Hall, Englewood Cliffs, New Jersey, 1978.

The Use of Trapezoidal Function in a Linguistic Fuzzy Relational Neural Network for Speech Recognition

Carlos A. Reyes-Garcia and Wyllis Bandler
Department of Computer Science
The Florida State University
Tallahassee, Fl 32306-4019

Abstract: *In this paper we describe the use of trapezoidal functions as part of the implementation of a fuzzy relational neural network model. In the model, the input features are represented by their respective fuzzy membership values to linguistic properties. The membership values are calculated with trapezoidal functions. The weights of the connections between input and output nodes are described in terms of their fuzzy relations. The output values during training are obtained with the* max-min *composition, and are given in terms of fuzzy class membership values. The learning algorithm used is a modified version of the gradient-descent back-propagation algorithm. The classification of unknown patterns is made with the relational square product. The system is tested on a speech recognition problem.*

1 Introduction:

The implementation we describe in this article corresponds to the model of a general pattern classifier based on a neural network architecture which uses fuzzy sets in the form of linguistic properties for both input/output data and the structure of the classifier itself.

The system proposed here is based on two different models. The general system architecture, and the use of Nn-dimensional vectors to represent the fuzzy membership values of the input to linguistic properties was inspired by the work presented by Pal in [1, 2]. The idea of using a relational neural network as a pattern classifier was taken from the general classifier presented by Pedrycz in [3]. The implemented sistem has been tested on a speech recognition problem, where classes are ill-defined and have imprecise input specifications.

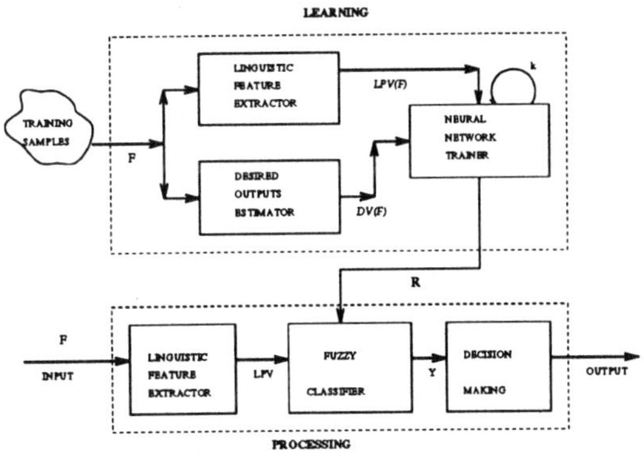

Figure 1: Block Diagram of the pattern classifier

2 Pattern Classification

The goal of a general pattern classifier is to determine the class or category of each pattern. There are four basic approaches by which the patterns may be classified, they are: (a) Pattern Matching, (b) Stochastic Models, (c) Knowledge-Based Systems, and (d) Connectionist Models. The system described here belongs to the kind of connectionist models. Most of the existing fuzzy neural network models only partially use the elements of fuzzy set theory and techniques, either in the learning process or in their structure [3]. The system proposed in this work is based upon fuzzy set operations in both the structure of the neural network and in the learning process. The use of linguistic variables is implemented in order to provide the system with the capability of handling input information in both exact and fuzzy forms. Following the Pal's idea of a general recognizer [2], the model is divided in two main parts, one for learning and another for processing (fig 1).

3 The Learning Phase

It was previously said that each input feature F_j can be expressed in terms of membership values to lingustic properties. In this case an input pattern $\vec{\mathbf{F}}_i = [F_{i1}, F_{i2}, ..., F_{in}]$ containing n features, may be represented as a Nn-dimensional vector [2]. i.e. as a $5n$ dimensional vector (see fig. 2)

0-7803-1901-X/94 $4.00 ©1994 IEEE

$$\vec{\mathbf{F}}_i = [\mu_{verylow(F_{i1})}(\vec{\mathbf{F}}_i), \mu_{low(F_{i1})}(\vec{\mathbf{F}}_i), \mu_{med(F_{i1})}(\vec{\mathbf{F}}_i), \mu_{high(Fi1)}(\vec{\mathbf{F}}_i), \mu_{veryhigh(F_{i1})}(\vec{\mathbf{F}}_i), \ldots, \mu_{veryhigh(F_{in})}(\vec{\mathbf{F}}_i)] \quad (1)$$

3.1 Fuzzy Sets and the Membership Functions

In typical classifiers, an element r either belongs or does not belong to a given class A [4]. The characteristic function of A is expressed as

$$\mu_A(r) = \begin{cases} 1, & \text{if } r \in A \\ 0, & \text{otherwise} \end{cases}$$

On the other hand, in everyday problems, the classes are generally ill-defined, overlapping, or fuzzy. A pattern may belong to more than one class with a non-zero degree of membership. In fuzzy set theory, a fuzzy set **A** has a characteristic function taking its values in the interval [0, 1]. $\mu_{\mathbf{A}}(r)$ is the grade of membership of $r \in \Re$ in **A**. **A** is defined as

$$\mathbf{A} = \{(r, \mu_{\mathbf{A}}(r))\},\ r \in \Re,\ \mu_{\mathbf{A}}(r) \in [0, 1]$$

The assignment of the membership function of a fuzzy set is subjective in nature and, in general, reflects the context in which the problem is viewed [5]. According to Kosko [6], in practice, triangular and trapezoidal shapes help capture the modeler's sense of fuzzy numbers and simplify computations. Supported on our experience we have selected the trapezoidal function for this application. An input pattern $\vec{\mathbf{F}}_i$ is expressed in terms of linguistic properties in order to divide the dynamic range of each feature into N overlapping partitions (in practice 3, 5, or 7), or fuzzy intervals, corresponding to the assigned linguistic properties (fig 2). To compute the parameters needed by the T function we find first the upper (F_{jmax}) and lower (F_{jmin}) bounds of the range of feature F_j considering all the M pattern points present in the training sample. The calculation of membership values of the input features to the linguistic properties is done in a very elegant and straigthforward fashion, as given by the following equations

$$X = \frac{F_j}{D} * N,$$

$$i = INT(X),$$

and

$$d = X - i$$

where $D = F_{jmax} - F_{jmin}$, i is the gratest integer such that $X - i \geq 0$, d is the decimal part of X, and N is the number of linguistic properties in which the feature space is going to be divided. The membership value of feature F_j to the corresponding linguistic properties is given by the following function

$$\mu_i(F_j) = 1$$
$$\mu_{i+1}(F_j) = d, if(i < n-1)$$
$$\mu_{i-1}(F_j) = 1 - d, if(i > 0)$$

the boundary conditions are; i) if $i = n - 1, \mu_{i+1}(F_j) = 0$, and ii) if $i = 0, \mu_{i-1}(F_i) = 0$. with the application of this function the input feature F_j will have a degree of membership value to only three of the linguistic overlapping partitions, in the general case, and to only two in the boundary cases. The membership value to the remaining properties will be zero. In this way feature F_j will allways have very strong membership to one of the linguistic properties (i.e. $\mu_i(F_j = 1)$). In this application, when $N = 5$, F_j is represented by the linguistic properties *very low, low, medium, high, very high.* And for $N = 7$ the linguistic properties are *very low, low, more or less low, medium, more or less high, high, very high.*

The system proposed here belongs to the supervised learning kind of systems. The supervised system approach attempts to estimate an unknown function $f : x \longrightarrow y$ from observed vector samples $(x_i, y_i), \ldots, (x_m, y_m)$ by minimizing an unknown expected error. The error is defined as the *difference between the desired output minus the actual output* of the system. The *supervision* determines the desired behavior by means of a *teaching* signal [6].

To define the output membership function, we first define the equation to calculate the weighted distance of the training pattern $\vec{\mathbf{F}}_j$ to the k_{th} class in an l-class problem domain as in [1]

$$z_{ik} = \sqrt{\sum_{j=1}^{n} \left[\frac{F_{ij} - o_{kj}}{v_{kj}}\right]^2},\ for\ k = 1, \ldots, l \quad (2)$$

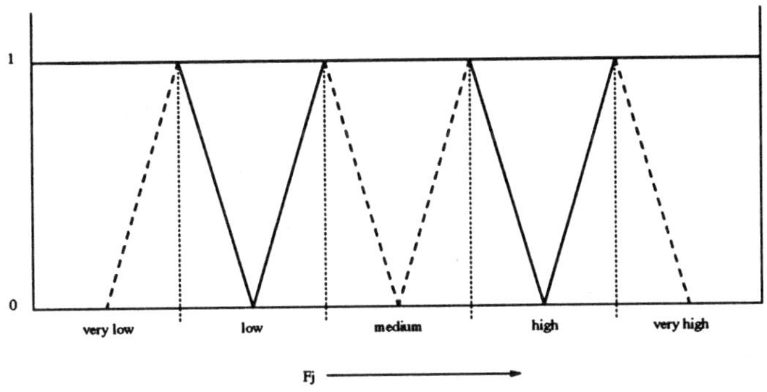

Figure 2: Overlapping structure of the T function for 5 linguistic properties

where F_{ij} is the jth feature of the ith pattern vector, C_k is the kth class. o_{kj} denotes the mean, and v_{kj} denotes the standard deviation of the jth feature for the kth class. The membership value of the ith pattern to class C_k is defined as follows

$$\mu_k(\vec{\mathbf{F}}_i) = \frac{1}{1+(\frac{z_{ik}}{f_d})^{f_e}},\ \mu_k(\vec{\mathbf{F}}_i) \in [0,1] \quad (3)$$

where f_e is the exponential fuzzy generator, and f_d is the denominational fuzzy generator controlling the amount of fuzzines in this class-membership set. In this case, the higher the distance of the pattern from a class, the lower its membership to that class.

3.2 The Neural Network Trainer

Neural networks and fuzzy systems estimate input-output functions. Both are trainable dynamical systems. Unlike statistical estimators, they estimate a function without a mathematical model. They learn from experience with numerical and sometimes linguistic data. Neural and fuzzy systems encode sampled information in a parallel-distributed framework [6]. Supervised neural networks can learn new patterns and recall old ones simultaneously. Supervised feedforward models provide the most tractable, most applied neural networks. The neural network model discused here is based on the fuzzy neural structure proposed by Pedrycz in [3]. As was previously mentioned, the model works exclusively with set-thoretic operations.

3.3 The Relational Neural Network

Let $\mathbf{X} = \{x_1, x_2, \ldots, x_n\}$ be a finite

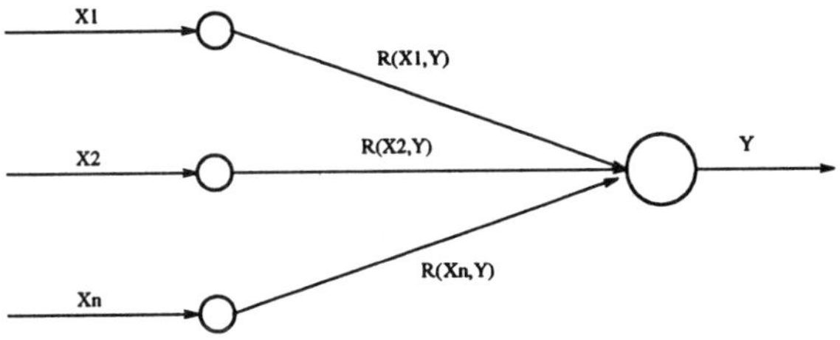

Figure 3: A basic n-input single output node of the network

set of input nodes and let $\mathbf{Y} = \{y_1, y_2, \ldots, y_l\}$ represent the set of output nodes in an l-class problem domain. When the max-min composition operator denoted $X \circ R$ is applied to a fuzzy set X and a fuzzy relation R, the output is a new fuzzy set Y, we have

$$Y = X \circ R \quad (4)$$

$$Y(y_j) = max_{x_i}(min(X(x_i), R(x_i, y_j)))$$

$$Y(y_j) = \bigvee_{x_i \in \mathbf{X}} [X(x_i) \wedge R(x_i, y_j)] \quad (5)$$

where X is a fuzzy set, Y is the resulting fuzzy set and R is a fuzzy relation $R : X \times Y \longrightarrow [0,1]$ describing all relationships between input and output nodes. We will take the whole neural network represented by expression 5 as a collection of l separate n-input single-output cells (fig 3). In order to provide the single cell in the model with a rough analogy to the conventional neuron, a threshold or bias $v \in [0,1]$ is incorporated. In this way, the entire unit interval of admissible values at the output node is obtained. The single element is described by

$$Y(y) = max_{x_i}[max(min(X(x_i), R(x_i, y_j))), v(y)] \quad (6)$$

3.4 Learning in a Fuzzy Neural Network

Learning in neural networks occurs through the modification of the strength of synaptic connections between cells. In supervised learning, a pattern is presented or clamped to the input layer, and a desired, or target, response pattern is clamped to the output layer. If the actual response from the network does not matches the target pattern, the network is corrected by modifying the link weights to reduce the difference between the observed and target patterns [7].

To evaluate the performance of the network it is necesary to introduce some kind of optimization index that reflects the nature of the framework of the problem being solved. For a complete description of the learning algorithm used here we refer the reader to [3] For the relational neural network Pedrycz [3] defines a performance index called equality index, which is

$$T(y) \equiv Y(y) = \begin{cases} 1 + T(y) - Y(y), & \text{if } Y(y) > T(y) \\ 1 + Y(y) - T(y), & \text{if } Y(y) < T(y) \\ 1, & \text{if } Y(y) = T(y) \end{cases} \quad (7)$$

In a problem with n input patterns, there are n input-output pairs (x_{ij}, t_i) where t_i is the target value when the input is $\mathbf{X}_{ij}$. In this case an overall performance index is estimated as the sum of the n equality indexes $y_i \equiv t_i$,

$$Q = \sum (y_i \equiv t_i)$$

In [3] Pedricz also discusses the learning scheme for the structure of a neural network with n-inputs and single output, and proposes to complete the process of learning separately for each output node. The updating procedure is made independent of the size of the training set. The learning algorithm is a version of the gradient-descent-based backpropagation algorithm. Once the training has been terminated, the output of the trainer is the updated relational matrix, which will contain the knowledge needed to map unknown patterns to their corresponding classes.

4 The Processing Phase

After the learning phase has been completed, the classification of unknown patterns may be started. In this moment the fuzzy processing section will have available useful information, collected and learned in the previous phase, to be used by its modules. The extraction of features from unknown patterns is similar to the one described in section 4.1. It uses the T function to calculate the values for the Linguistic Properties Vector (LPV). The LPVs, along with the final relational matrix, is used to classify each unknown pattern vector to its corresponding class. The classification is performed with the relational square product as defined in [10]. The relational square product, $X \Box R$ is applied to the fuzzy set X and the fuzzy relation R to estimate how true it is that x_i has just exactly those features which characterize class y_j. The output of the square product is expressed by

$$Y(y_j) = X(x_{ij} \Box R(x_{ij}, y_j)$$

$$Y(y_j) = min_{x_{ij}}(X(x_{ij} \leftrightarrow R(x_{ij}, y_j))$$

and by the Lukasiewicz implication

$$Y(y_j) = min_{x_{ij}}(1 - |X(x_{ij}) - R(x_{ij}, y_j)|)$$

The output is a class vector $Y(y_j)$ which contains the fuzzy membership value of the unknown pattern to each of the classes. The criterion applied to produce the output of the system, is to take the highest value in the class vectors $Y(y_j)$ and assign the index j as the corresponding class. If j is equal to the expected class, the output is computed as a perfect match.

FUZZY RELATIONAL NEURAL NETWORK		
CLASS	N=5	N=7
/a/	94.0 %	94.0 %
/e/	88.0 %	85.0 %
/i/	90.0 %	91.0 %
/o/	77.0 %	86.0 %
/u/	92.0 %	92.0 %
OVERALL	88.2 %	89.6 %

Table 1: Recognition scores for the fuzzy relational neural network.

5 Implementation and Results: As was previously mentioned, the difficulties in performing

CLASS	BAYES CLASSIFIER	CONVENTIONAL NEURAL NETWORK		FUZZY NEURAL NETWORK	
	Percent	m = 10	m = 20	m = 10	m = 20
/ae /	41.6 %	55.5 %	44.4 %	51.2 %	55.5 %
/ a /	91.1 %	86.6 %	88.8 %	51.2 %	80.0 %
/ e /	71.1 %	92.3 %	86.5 %	92.4 %	85.9 %
/ i /	93.0 %	81.4 %	81.4 %	81.9 %	91.5 %
/ o /	71.1 %	86.6 %	85.5 %	89.5 %	81.3 %
/ u /	94.7 %	88.1 %	90.7 %	86.8 %	86.6 %
OVERALL	79.2 %	84.6 %	82.8 %	84.2 %	83.6 %

Table 2: Recognition scores between various models.

effective automatic speech recognition lie in the inherent ill-definedness of boundaries among classes. These characteristics make the speech recognition problem particularly suited to be dealt with by the use of fuzzy neural networks [9]. The current model has been implemented in C++ on Sun Sparc workstations. It has been trained on two different sets of 400 vowel sounds, 80 of which correspond to each of the phonemes $/a/$, $/e/$, $/i/$, $/o/$, and $/u/$. The testing of the system has been done on two different sets of 743 vowel sounds. Both the training and testing data sets were taken from data collected by Kohonen *et al.* Each data set (one for training, and one for testing interchangeablly) consists of 1962 cepstral coefficient vectors, 743 of which correspond to vowel sounds, picked up from continuous Finnish speech by the same speaker. Each vector has a dimensionality of 20 and has been labeled to represent a phoneme [8]. For simulation purposes, the data sets were used with 10 and 9 cepstral coefficients, for $N = 5$ and $N = 7$ respectively, making the dimensionality of the input vectors 50 and 63 respectively. We show the results for the cases of input vectors with 5 and 7 linguistic properties per feature. In both cases, the classification method used was the square product composition.

a) For $N = 5$, the parameters used were; $f_d = 6, f_e = 3.0, k = 25$. The inital relational values and the initial bias values were set as 0.1. b) For $N = 7$, the parameters used were; $f_d = 4, f_e = 3.0, k = 20$. The inital relational values and the initial bias values were set as 0.15. The percentage of correct matches are shown in Table 1.

Attempting to give an idea of the performance of the proposed system compared to another systems, we include results obtained with some other models. In ref [1] Pal reports the comparison of percent correct recognition scores on a test set of 871 Indian Telegu vowel sounds, between the Bayes classifier and various neural network models. The neural network models used by Pal consist of three hidden layers with m nodes in each such layer. Here we show the results reported for a conventional neural network, and a fuzzy version with linguistic input proposed by Pal in [1]. Both models were tested for 10 and 20 nodes in each hidden layer. The reported results of the compared models are in Table 2.

Conclusions: Given the simplicity of the model implementation, the results obtained up to this time are very encouraging. With the use of the T function the impreciseness of the speech information is reduced by the generation of 3, 5, or 7 subregions for each acoustic feature. The use of the max-min composition operation facilitates implementation of the learning task and its performance. The relational square product provides an accurate way to classify unknown patterns. Based on the observed results, we are convinced that an improved fuzzy relational neural network model might bring an effective, reliable and compact speech recognizer.

References

[1] Pal, S.K., "Multilayer Perceptron, Fuzzy Sets, and Classification," in *IEEE Trans. on*

Neural Networks, vol 3, No 5, Sep 1992, pp 683-697.

[2] Pal, S.K. and Mandal, D.P., "Linguistic Recognition Systems Based on Approximated Reasoning," in *Information Science*, vol 61, No 2, 1992, pp 135-161.

[3] Pedrycz, W., "Neurocomputations in Relational Systems," in *IEEE Trans. on Pattern Analysis and Mach. Intelligence*, vol 13, No 3, Mar 91, pp 289-296.

[4] Zadeh, L.A., "Fuzzy Sets," *Inform. Contr.*, vol 8, 1965, pp 338-353.

[5] Kandel, A., *Fuzzy Techniques in Pattern Recognition,* John Wiley & Sons, New York, 1982.

[6] Kosko, B., *Neural Networks and Fuzzy Systems,* Prentice Hall, New Jersey, 1992.

[7] Cox, E., "Integrating Fuzzy Logic into Neural Nets," in *AI Expert*, June 1992, pp 43-47.

[8] Kohonen, T., Kangas, J., Laaksonen, J. and Torkkola, K., "The Learning Vector Quantization Program Package," Version 2.1, Helsinki University of Technology, Lab. of Comp. and Info. Sci., SF-021150 Espoo, 1992.

[9] Reyes, C.A. and Bandler, W.,"Una Introduccion al Reconocimiento Automatico del Habla," Technical Report, Dept. of CS, FSU, 93-041, Tallahasee, Fl, 1992.

[10] Bandler, W. and Kohout, L.J., "Mathematical Relations," in Sing, Mandan G., editor, *Systems & Control Encyclopedia*, Pergamon Press, Oxford, 1987, pp 4000-4008.

RBF Models for Detection of Human Speech in Structured Noise

John D. Hoyt
Engineering Research Facility
Federal Bureau of Investigation
Quantico, VA 22135

Harry Wechsler
Dept. of Computer Science
George Mason University
Fairfax, VA 22030

Abstract

This paper describes research to develop an efficient system that provides a binary decision as to the presence of speech in a short (one to three second) time sample of an acoustic signal. A method which is efficient and reliably detects human speech in the presence of structured noise (such as wind, music, traffic sounds, etc.) is described. There are methods which work well to detect speech in a communications environment, but previous methods can not distinguish speech from a quasi-periodic signal that have a spectral power density similar to speech (such as music).

Two separate feature sets are evaluated. Reliable detection is obtained down to signal to noise ratios (SNR) as low as 0 dB. The algorithm utilized is a statistical pattern classifier utilizing radial basis function (RBF) networks. Mel-cepstra and wavelet feature vectors are compared. A method of obtaining temporal feature information is described.

1. Introduction

The problem we address is that of detecting human speech in noise. For this research, noise is defined as any sound that is not speech (for simplicity, we ignore singing as either speech or non-speech). This collections of sounds we call structured noise, as it includes quasi-periodic signals, such as music; pure tones; impulse noise; and Gaussian like sounds, such as running water. Ideally our algorithm should detect the speech of anyone (speaker independent) speaking any phrase (word independent) in any language (language independent), and operate at low signal to noise ratios. It is desirable that any speech detection algorithm be capable of operating at near real time with minimal processing resources. We allow the detection system to operate with time segments of acoustic signals that are up to one second in duration. A simple diagram of this detection system is shown below.

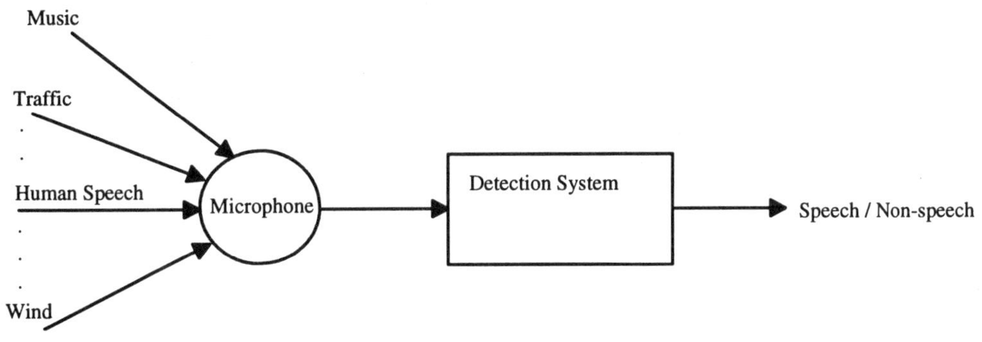

Figure 1: Diagram

It should be noted that our work is not speech recognition (converting speech to text given that the input signal is human speech), nor is our work speech enhancement (improving the intelligibility of a degraded speech signal). We view that speech detection would occur prior to either speech recognition or enhancement. Our problem domain model is that there is no meaningful *a priori* information of the presence of the signal class of interest (in our specific case, speech), and it is assumed that the presence of the signals of interest are of fairly low probability. Thus, the methodology developed here performs a sorting or filtering function for later stages of a larger signal processing system by passing on only those portions of a continuous sensor stream that have a high probability of containing signals of interest (again, in our case speech).

Existing speech detection algorithms were designed for a communications environment. They utilize various combinations of energy estimation, zero crossings, correlation functions, LPC coefficient and power change ratios, or bandpass filterbank signal to noise ratio thresholds [1] [2] [3]. These methods will not work when the noise has a long term power spectral density similar to speech and periodicity similar to speech (such as instrumental music).

0-7803-1901-X/94 $4.00 ©1994 IEEE

2. Data

The source of speech used for training and testing is the TIMIT acoustic - phonetic continuous speech corpus [4] developed by the Advanced Research Projects Agency (ARPA). This corpus consists of 630 different speakers which are divided approximately evenly between male and female, and between the eight major dialects of American English. Noise sources (rain, traffic sounds, rifle fire, birds songs, surf, etc.) are from a two volume compact disk (sound effects) [5] and from both compact disks and recordings from the reception of commercial FM radio stations (instrumental music - classical, jazz, and rock).

3. Previous Work

Previously we had evaluated speech detection utilizing both formant tracking methods and a radial-basis function classifier utilizing mel-cepstra feature vectors [6]. These speech detection methods provided reliable detection of speech at signal to noise ratios of at least +6 dB. However, we wish to refine our speech detection methods both for improved performance and for low power operation. For battery powered equipment, speech detection that requires at most a few miliwatts, is desired. We have developed a series of application specific CMOS integrated circuits that are capable of implementing a wavelet transform in real time with much lower power requirements than either the wavelet or windowed Fourier transform techniques on a conventional Von Neumann programmable computer [7]. Thus, this paper will compare wavelet derived features with features derived from mel-cepstra.

4. Radial Basis Function Classifier

As the distributions of the speech and non-speech acoustic signals are, in general, unknown, a nonparametric classifier is required. A block diagram of this algorithm is shown below in figure 2. This classifier was developed utilizing purely statistical methods with unsupervised clustering and supervised training data. Previous work by Ng and Lippmann had shown that Radial Basis Function (RBF) classifiers performed well in classification problems of high dimensionality and RBF classifiers train quickly, classify quickly, and require modest amounts of computational resources [8][9]. For a RBF classifier, the input feature vectors are projected by the basis functions onto a high dimensional space. In our classifier, these basis functions are hyper-elliptic Gaussian functions. A linear combination of these Gaussians defines a hyperplane that divides the output into the various classes [8][9]. K-means clustering was utilized to determine the RBF cluster means. The variance of each cluster is set equal to the Euclidean distance of all of the class members within a cluster. Additionally, the variance is calculated separately for each dimension in the feature space. The following figure shows the structure of our RBF network.

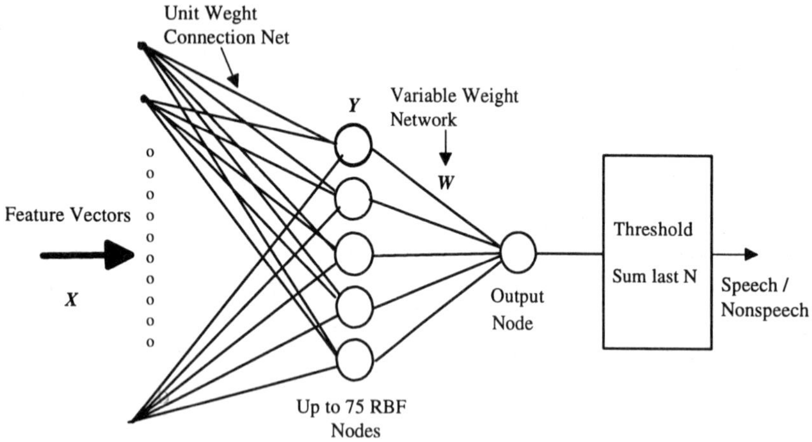

Figure 1: RBF Network

Each hidden layer node computes the following:

$$y_i = \Phi\left(\left\|\vec{X} - \vec{\mu_i}\right\|\right) = \exp\left[-\left(\frac{1}{h}\right)\left(\sum_k \frac{(x_k - \mu_{ik})^2}{2\delta_{ik}^2}\right)\right] \qquad (1)$$

The basis function means $\overrightarrow{\mu_i}$ are initially determined by k-means clustering. During training, those basis functions that do not meet a minimum threshold of autocorrelation (which we presently set to 1% of the highest autocorrelation value) through the training set are discarded and the remaining means are utilized to compute new clusters, cluster means, and variance. The basis function variances δ_i^2 are determined in each of the k dimensions by setting the variance equal to the mean of the distance from μ_{ik} and its N cluster members .

$$\overrightarrow{\delta_i^2} = \frac{1}{N}\Sigma_k\left(\overrightarrow{\mu_i} - \overrightarrow{x_k}\right)^2; \quad k \neq i, \; k \in \{1, \dots, N\} \qquad (2)$$

Training over the $x(p)$ training patterns and $C(p)$ class labels is performed via matrix inversion of the correlation matrix R and solving for the weights using the output matrix B and solving as follows [7]:

$$R_{il} = \sum_p y_i(p)y_l(p); B_{lj} = \sum_p y_l(p)d_j(p); \text{where } j = 1, \dots, p \text{ and } d_j(p) = \begin{cases} 1 \text{ if } C(p) = j \\ 0 \text{ otherwise} \end{cases} \qquad (3)$$

$$W = R^{-1}B \qquad (4)$$

Note that matrix R is square and that singularity problems are avoided by the step of discarding basis functions that do not have strong autocorrelation values. As we are interested in detecting speech over roughly a second interval, we threshold the output of our classifier to a zero / one value; store the most recent 32 outputs of the initial thresholding; and declare the signal as speech or non-speech based on the sum of these 32 values that exceed a threshold value.

5. Features

Mel-cepstra are generated by utilizing a 512 point Hamming window with 256 points of overlap between windows; each window undergoes a 512 point DFT; the log magnitude of the DFT is passed through a Mel scale filter bank; then the inverse DFT is taken [10]. Only the first 16 mel-cepstra coefficients are utilized as the training speech signals had very low values for higher coefficients. Mel-cepstra were selected as features as they have been very successful as the features for a large number of speech recognition systems [11].

Our wavelet features are generated by QMF 14 tap FIR filter pairs utilized in Mallat's pyramid decomposition [12]. We derived an exact solution to Mallat's equation for the spectral shape of the low pass filters needed for his pyramid decomposition. Utilizing the Parks-McClellan algorithm [10] an implementation for a 14 tap FIR low and high pass quadratic mirror filter pair is found [13]. Then the 14 floating point FIR coefficients are converted into integer canonical signed digit form [14]. Only wavelet coefficients for frequency components between 4K Hz and 62.5 Hz are utilized, as speech has very little energy outside these frequency bands [11]. Our audio data is all sampled at 16K Hz, thus to obtain the frequency bands from 4K Hz through 62.5 Hz, the data is recursively passed through the QMF filter pair 7 times. Each time the output of the QMF pair is down sampled by two. The first output is for 8K Hz to 4K Hz and is discarded. The remaining outputs are squared and averaged over the same time interval as the lowest frequency band. Thus each feature vector is of length 6 and corresponds to 128 samples of the original time series data.

6. Training and Testing

The RBF algorithm was trained on one second speech samples taken from twenty (10 male and 10 female) speakers chosen at random from the TIMIT training data as well as 25 non-speech samples chosen at random from the CBS compact disk set and commercial FM radio broadcasts [4][5]. All testing was performed on data that was not utilized in training. All data was preprocessed to remove periods of silence.

In the table below, noisy speech data was formed by adding TIMIT speech with digitized non-speech sounds. Six female samples and six male speech samples were taken at random from the TIMIT test data. The noise (non-speech) recordings were digitized from the CBS compact disk set and from music digitized from commercial FM radio broadcasts and compact disks. In all cases, the test speech and noise samples were not utilized in training. A 1964 song, *Leader of the Pack*, was also digitized for speech / non-speech testing. Vocal sections of this song are noted as LOP_V and non-vocal as LOP_M in the table below. Results in the table are given in percent of correct classification as either speech or non-speech. Music in the speech + music sections of the table below were four different instrumental sections - two classical and two jazz.

Clean Signals	% Correct	
Data	Mel-cepstra Features	Wavelet Features
clean speech	83.7%	91.7%
classical music	100%	100%
jazz / rock	100%	100%
cabin of 747	100%	100%
police siren	100%	100%
White Noise	100%	100%
Heavy Rain	100%	100%
LOP_V	100%	100%
LOP_M	100%	100%

Speech + Noise	% Correct	
Data	Mel-cepstra Features	Wavelet Features
speech + music 4:1 SNR	75.0%	91.7%
speech + music 2:1 SNR	33.3%	100%
speech + music 1:1 SNR	41.7%	91.7%
speech + rain 4:1 SNR	66.7%	91.7%
speech + rain 2:1 SNR	0%	83.3%
speech + rain 1:1 SNR	0%	0%
speech + WN 4:1 SNR	91.7%	66.7%
speech + WN 2:1 SNR	41.7%	0%
speech + WN 1:1 SNR	0%	0%

7. Conclusions

Our RBF models reliably distinguish between speech and environmental sounds. When speech is mixed with environmental sounds (music and the sound of heavy rain were tested), detection remains comparable to clean speech until the SNR is less than approximately 4:1 with both types of feature vectors. The wavelet derived features provided markedly better performance than the mel-cepstra feature vectors for detection of speech when mixed with environmental noise. Reliable detection was obtained down to a SNR of 0 dB for the environmental noises tested. White noise was also added to our test speech samples. Results were not indicative of the performance using additive environmental noise. We believe that this is due to the 1/f nature of spectral power estimates for the environmental noises utilized.

8. References

[1] W. Chan and D. Faconer, "Speech Detection for a Voice / Data Mobile Radio Terminal," *Proc. of IEEE Conf. on Comm.,* pp F8.7.1-F8.7.5, June 1983.

[2] J. Yang, "Frequency Domain Noise Suppression Approaches in Mobile Telephone Systems," *Proc. of IEEE ICASSP 1993, Vol II,* PP 363-366, April 1993.

[3] J. Burgett, "Description of the Readability Algorithm," UNCLASSIFIED Working Paper, Department of Defense, September 1986.

[4] *TIMIT Acoustic - Phonetic Continuous Speech Corpus*, NIST Speech Disk 1-1.1, NITS Order No. PB91-505065, October 1990.

[5] *The New CBS Sound Effects Library*, CBS Special Products, 51 W 52 St., NY, NY, 1977.

[6] J. Hoyt and H. Wechsler, "Detection of Human Speech in Structured Noise," IEEE ICASSP-94, April 1994.

[7] J. Hoyt, and H. Wechsler, "The Wavelet Transform - A CMOS VLSI ASIC Implementation," *Proc. of the 11th IAPR Conference D: Architectures for Vision and Pattern Recognition*, pp 19-22, IEEE Computer Society Press, September 1992.

[8] K. Ng and R. Lippmann, *A Comparative Study of the Practical Characteristics of Neural Networks and Conventional Pattern Classifiers*, Masters Thesis, MIT, May 1990.

[9] D. Hush and B. Horne, "Progress in Supervised Neural Networks, What's New Since Lippmann?", *IEEE Signal Processing Magazine*, January 1993.

[10] A. Oppenhiem and R. Schafer, *Discrete-Time Signal Processing*, Prentice Hall, 1989.

[11] J. Dieller, J. Proakis, and J. Hansen, *Discrete - Time Processing of Speech Signals*, Macmillan, 1993.

[12] S. Mallat, "A Theory for Multiresolution Signal Decomposition: the Wavelet Representation," *IEEE Transaction on Pattern Analysis and Machine Intelligence*, Vol. 11, No. 1, July 1989.

[13] D. Elliott, Ed., *Handbook of Digital Signal Processing Engineering Applications*, Academic Press, 1987.

[14] R. Jain, P. Yang, and T. Yoshino, "FIRGEN: A Computer-Aided Design System for High Performance FIR Filter Integrated Circuits," *IEEE Transactions on Signal Processing*, Vol. 39, No. 7, pp 1655-1668, July 1991.

ANALYSIS OF SPECTRAL FEATURE EXTRACTION USING THE GAMMA FILTER

Samel Çelebi, Jose C. Principe

Computational Neuroengineering Lab. CSE447
University of Florida, Gainesville FL3211
E-Mail: celebi@synapse.ee.ufl.edu,
principe@synapse.ee.ufl.edu

Abstract

We study the Focused Gamma Network and its special case TDNN for speech recognition from a signal representation point of view and show that these structures extract the features of the signals input to them in the form of Taylor's series approximation performed in the frequency domain.

Introduction

Classification of temporal patterns is one of the areas where artificial neural networks (ANNs) are frequently utilized. Speech recognition is a special case to this problem. In order to simplify the classification task undertaken by an ANN preprocessing of the temporal pattern is vital. The goal of the preprocessing should be to capture the features of the pattern and to express them in a low dimensional space. If this is achieved, then a big deal of computational and structural burden over the neural network can be removed.

One method suggested for the preprocessing of speech signals is the *Focused Gamma Network* [1][2]. This is a *generalized feedforward structure* with adjustable feedback which is responsible for changing the *time scale* (or alternatively the *memory depth*) of the preprocessor. Adjusting the time scale allows one to *focus* the representation space on the signal of interest such that a low dimensional, but a faithful representation is obtained. Well known *Time Delay Neural Network* (TDNN) [3] is a special case of the Gamma Network where the time scale is frozen to be unity. In their isolated word speech recognition task Tracey and Principe [1] showed that Gamma Network is superior to TDNN both in terms of the size of the neural network required and the time it took for the network to learn the given patterns. In this study we'll try to construct a mathematical basis for the analysis of the Gamma network and show that the features captured by the Gamma network are actually the Taylor's series coefficients of the Laplace transform of the temporal pattern.

0-7803-1901-X/94 $4.00

Gamma Network

Gamma network is a chain of identical lowpass filters each with transfer function $\lambda/(s+\lambda)$ for the continuous time and $\lambda/(z-(1-\lambda))$ for the discrete time. Although it is an *infinite impulse response* (IIR) system, feedbacks are restricted to be local. Choosing $\lambda>0$ for the continuous time and $0<\lambda<2$ for the discrete time will assure stability. The feedback parameter λ allows the change of time scale (or memory resolution) of the filter. This flexibility proves to be useful for representing signals with redundancies.

In their work Tracey & Principe [1] filter the speech signals using banks of constant Q bandpass filters. This seems to implement an artificial cochlea model [4]. Constant Q bandpass filters have a constant center frequency/bandwidth ratio, thereby providing high time resolution at high frequencies and high frequency resolution at low frequencies. Outputs of the bandpass filters are fed into a square law device followed by an envelope detector approximating the power spectrum of the signal in the band the filter is tuned to (Figure 1.). This low pass signal is further fed into the Gamma network whose outputs at each stage carried information regarding the features of the temporal signal to the neural network. In the next section we show that features extracted by the Gamma network are essentially the Taylor's series coefficients of the Laplace transform of the signal at its input.

Poisson Moments

Fairman and Shen [5] proposed that a distribution f(t) can be expanded in terms of the dirac delta function as follows

$$f(t) = \sum_{i=0}^{\infty} f_i(t_o)\, e^{-\lambda(t-t_o)} \delta^{(i)}(t-t_o) \qquad (1)$$

where $f_i(t_o)$ is defined by

$$f_i(t_o) = f(t) * p_i(t)\big|_{t=t_o}$$

$$p_i(t) = \frac{t^i}{i!} e^{-\lambda t} \qquad \lambda, t>0 \qquad (2)$$

'*' stands for the convolution operator. $f_i(t_o)$ can be viewed as the value at the $i+1^{st}$ tap of a cascade of identical low pass filters at time $t=t_o$. In

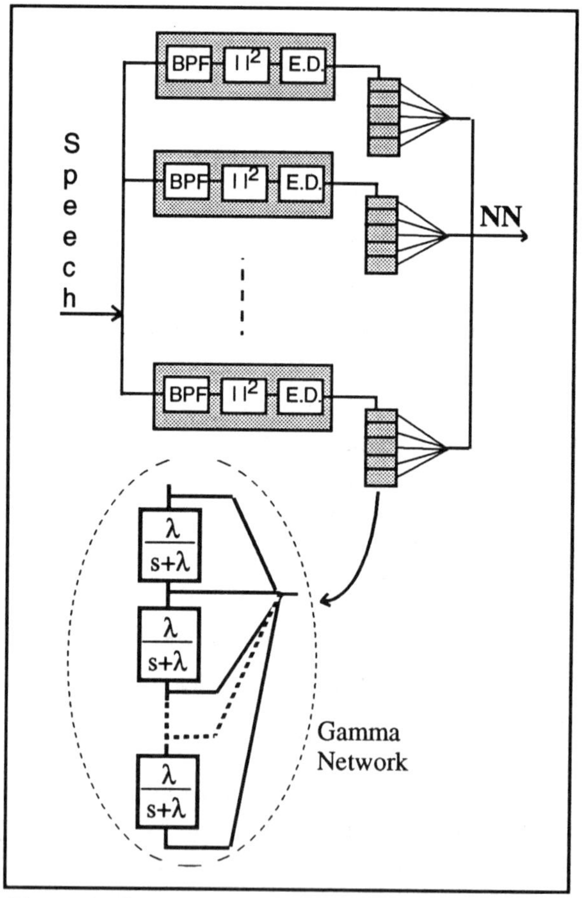

Figure 1. Preprocessing with the Gamma network

their studies on parametric system identification, Rao and Prasado [6] [7] refer to this quantity as the *Poisson Moment*. To maintain the consistency we will adopt the same name.

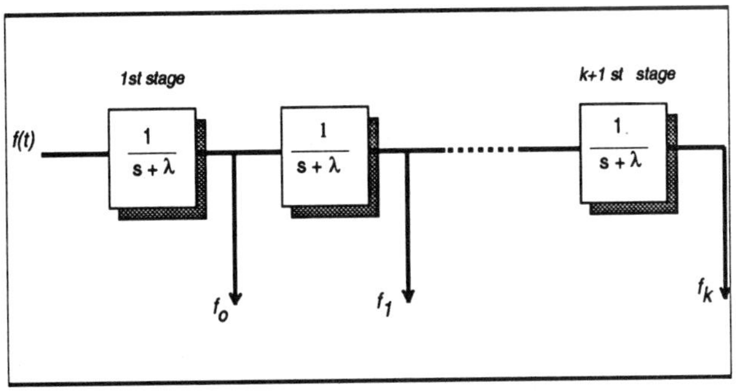

Figure 2. Poisson Moments

Taking the Laplace transform of both sides of (1) and using only a finite number of terms it can be shown that this is equivalent to [5]

$$e^{st_o}F(s) \approx \sum_{i=0}^{N} a_i (s+\lambda)^i \tag{3}$$

where $a_i = \frac{d^i}{ds^i}\{e^{st_o}F(s)\} = f_i(t_o)$

Equation (3) can be recognized as the Nth order Taylor's approximation of $e^{sto}F(s)$ around s=-λ. When one is concerned only with the magnitude spectrum |F(jw)| (as with the speech signals) the term e^{sto} has no significance in the analysis since it accounts for a delay. Incidentally, the Taylor series coefficients a_i are the Poisson Moments of f(t) which are physically measurable. Obviously these moments can be used as a feature vector representing F(s) around s=-λ. If λ is a complex number with an imaginary part λ_i and a relatively small real part λ_r this feature vector represents the frequency spectrum of f(t) around the frequencies $w=\lambda_i$. Due to the fact that Taylor's series approximation diverges at points away from the pivot point s=-λ, feature vector carries only local frequency information. However, a representation of the entire frequency axis can be attained by concatenating the feature vectors obtained around different λ_i (Figure 3.).

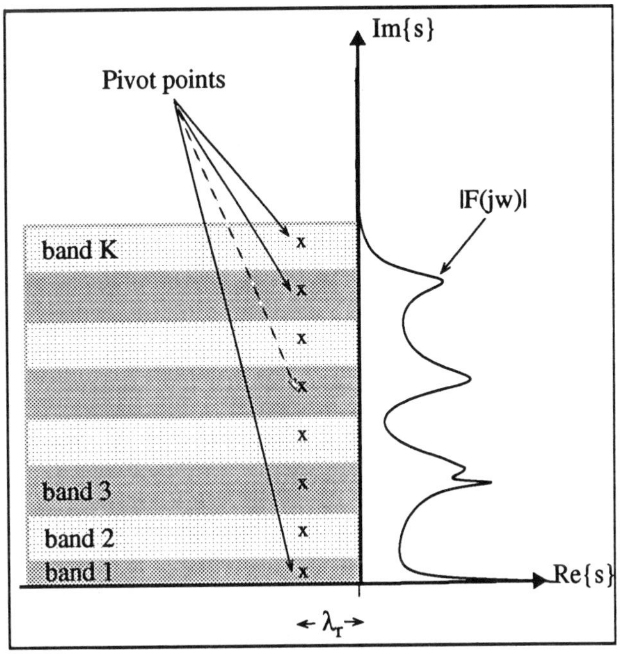

Figure 3. Taylor's expansion around various frequencies

Figure 4. and Figure 5. show the magnitude response of f(t) and a 4th order, band by band Taylor's approximation to it around values $\lambda=0.4+j\lambda_i$ where λ_i=0.5,1.5,2.5,3.5,...,7.5, respectively.

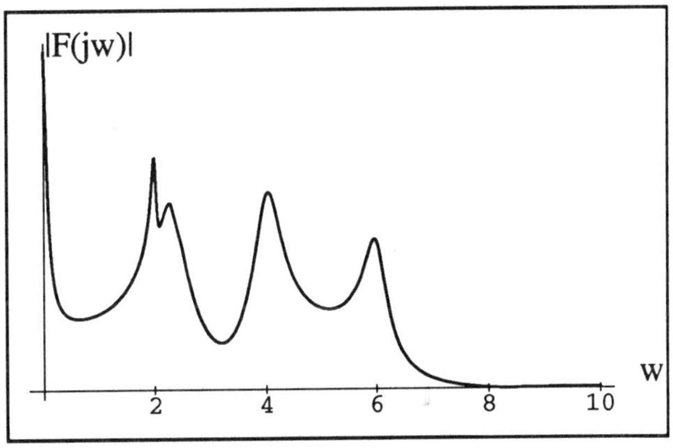

Figure 4. Magnitude response of f(t)

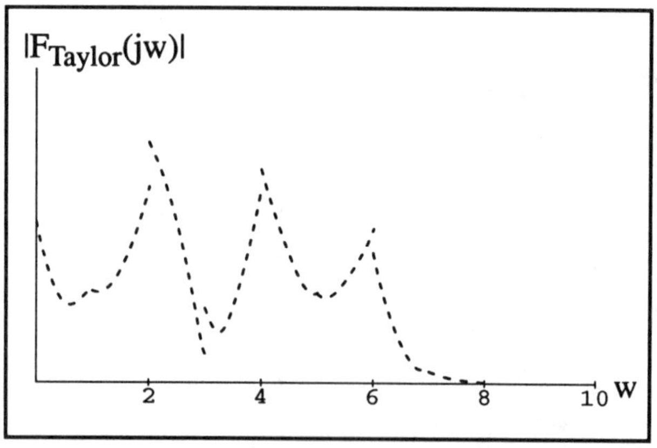

Figure 5. Band by band Taylor's approximation of |F(jw)|

Instead of expanding $e^{sto}F(s)$ around various center frequencies one can also frequency shift each band to the origin and expand it around real λ. In practice a constant Q bandpass filter followed by a mixer can be used to shift the frequency band of interest to the origin. The baseband signal at the output of the envelope detector can be fed into the Gamma network whose taps are sampled. These samples would represent the band of frequencies that the bandpass filter was tuned to. If the mixer is replaced with a cascade of a square-law device and an envelope detector, one can obtain an approximate representation for the power spectrum of the input signal. Actually that's what has been done in Tracey and Principe's study [1]. Gamma network captures the features of various bands of the input signal by simply sampling the output taps. This is a very simple and compact representation which can be fed into the ANN for classification.

For the discrete time Gamma Network the pivot point lies inside the unit circle (Figure 6.). Depending on the location of λ one can focus on different areas of the unit circle. In the TDNN network, which is a special case of the Gamma Network with λ=1, this flexibility does not exist. In the TDNN the pivot point is at the center of the unit circle and therefore all frequencies are treated equally. However, this is done at the expense of choosing the pivot far from the points on the unit circle. In that case a high order approximation is required for a faithful representation since Taylor's approximation diverges very quickly at points away from the pivot.

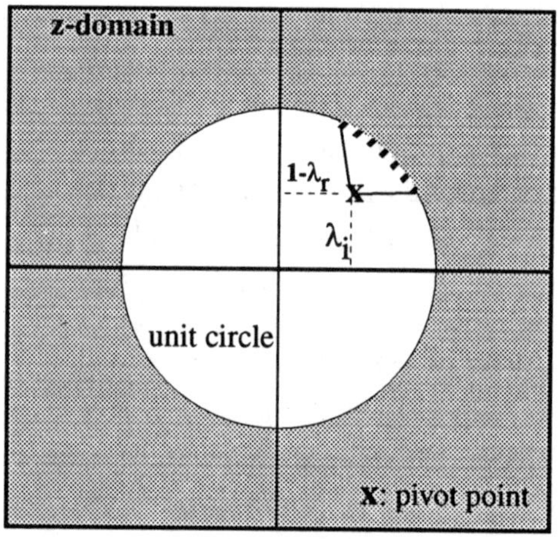

Figure 6. Taylor's approximation in the z-domain

Conclusions

With its adjustable time scale Gamma network proves to be an efficient tool in extracting the features of the temporal signals and expressing them in a low dimensional space. It is shown that these features which are obtained simply by sampling the tap outputs of the Gamma network are actually the Taylor's series coefficients of the temporal signal in the frequency domain. This fact may shed some light on the problem of selecting the optimum time scale, which may inspire future studies.

Acknowledgments:
This work has been partially supported by NSF grant ECS #920878.

References

[1] Tracey J.W., Principe J.C., 'Isolated-Word Speech Recognition Using the Focused Gamma Neural Network,' *World Congress on Neural Networks*, Portland, Oregon, vol III, pp. 87- 90, July 1993.

[2] Tracey J., 'Isolated Speech Recognition with the Focused Gamma Networks' Master Thesis, U. of Florida, 1992.

[3] Waibel, Alex, Hanazawa T., Hinton G., Shikano K., Lang K., 'Phoneme Recognition Using Time-delay Neural Networks,' *IEEE Trans. on Acoustics, Speech and Signal Processing*, vol. 37:3, pp. 328-339, 1989.

[4] Pickles J.O., *An Introduction to the Physiology of Hearing*,2nd edition, London:Academic Press, 1988.

[5] Fairman F.W., Shen D.W.C.,"Parameter Identification for Linear Time-Varying Dynamic Processes," *Proc. IEE*, vol. 117, no. 10, Oct. 1970.

[6] Saha D.C., Rao G.P., *Identification of Continuous Dynamical Systems- The Poisson Moment Functional Approach.* New York: Springer-Verlag, 1983.

[7] Saha D.C., Rao G.P., "A General Algorithm for Parameter Identification in Lumped Continuous Systems- The Poisson Moment Functional Approach," *IEEE Trans. Automatic Control*, vol. AC-27, no. 1, pp. 223-225, 1982.

Modeling Human Sound Localization with Hierarchical Neural Networks

Timothy R. Anderson, *Member, IEEE,* James A. Janko and Robert H. Gilkey

***Abstract*— Artificial neural networks were trained to identify the location of sound sources using head related transfer functions (HRTFs). The simulated signals were filtered clicks presented from virtual speakers placed at 15 degree steps in azimuth and 18 degree steps in elevation. After signals were passed through the HRTFs, quarter-octave spectra were computed. The inputs to the networks were either monaural spectra or binaural difference spectra. In some cases a broadband cross-correlation term was also provided. Back-propagation was used to train the networks. Separate networks were trained for each combination of spectral information. In some cases the networks achieved performance comparable to that of human observers in both accuracy and number of front-back reversals. With a hierarchy of neural networks accuracy better than human performance was obtained.**

I. Introduction

The Duplex Theory provides a simple, intuitive description of human sound localization. According to the model, the interaural difference in arrival time is used as the cue for sound location at low frequencies, while the interaural level difference is used at high frequencies. For each of these cues there is a relatively simple transformation that describes the relation between the value of the cue and the azimuth of a sound source located in the front half of the horizontal plane.

During the last few decades the Duplex Theory has been questioned on several levels. In addition to questions about whether interaural time and level cues can be strictly segregated into different frequency regions, there has been a growing awareness that other cues must also play a role in sound localization. Sounds synthesized with only interaural difference cues are typically localized inside the listeners head rather than at a location external to the listener. The fact that listeners typically perceive the elevation of a sound, as well as its azimuth, has also been difficult to explain within the Duplex Theory. Both externalization and vertical localization are believed to depend in part on changes in the shape of the monaural and binaural spectra, which are introduced by the filtering of the head, torso, and pinnae.

The Head Related Transfer Function (HRTF) describes the transfer function from the sound source to the tympanic membrane. A virtual source at the same position as the original source can be created by applying the appropriate HRTFs to the sounds delivered to the left and right headphones of an observer. That is, by recreating the spectral changes introduced by the torso, head, and pinnae, the sounds are externalized and vertical localization is possible.

While there seems to be general agreement that these spectral cues are relevant, there has been relatively little modeling work to explain how an observer might produce a localization judgment based on this information. It seems clear however, that some relatively complex pattern analysis must be applied to these spectra in order to "recognize" the source location. Because artificial neural networks have had considerable success in other pattern recognition tasks we applied them to the problem of localizing sounds in a 3-dimensional sound field.

Several simplifying decisions were made in this continuing investigation of the ability of these models to localize sounds. We used only simple stimuli and examined the HRTFs of only one subject, who is known to localize well. We employed a very simple and somewhat arbitrary model of the auditory periphery, the effects of internal noise, and the nature of the binaural interaction. Back-propagation was used to train the neural networks.

The work described in this paper attempts to answer three questions: 1) Can a neural network model trained to localize sounds, achieve performance similar to that of human listeners? 2) Will such a model

The first author is with Armstrong Laboratory, Bioacoustics and Biocommunications Branch, Wright-Patterson AFB, OH 45433-7901, USA. The other authors are with the Department of Psychology, Wright State University, Dayton, OH 45435-0001, USA.

0-7803-1901-X/94 $4.00 ©1994 IEEE

make errors similar to those made by humans? and 3) Is the performance of such a model in accord with expectations based on traditional models of binaural hearing?

II. Signal Representation

Figure 1 presents a block diagram of the preprocessing that was applied to the signal before the input to the neural network. A 20 microsecond click was used as the signal. The click was filtered with the HRTFs of subject SDO [4]. We used the HRTFs for 24 azimuth locations in 15 degree increments from -165 to +180 degrees and 6 elevations for each azimuth in 18 degree increments from -36 degrees to +54 degrees (144 source locations). In this coordinate system the zero elevation is a horizontal plane that runs through the subjects ears. Zero azimuth is straight ahead.

As Colburn and Durlach [1] emphasized, the performance of any binaural model is critically dependent on the assumed form of the internal noise. For these investigations, we assumed that each point in the left and right channels is subjected to a normally distributed gain and normally distributed delay, in a manner similar to the noise model in Durlach [2]. For the measurements reported here the standard deviation of the amplitude jitter was 0.25 and the standard deviation of the time jitter was 20 microseconds.

Rather than computing the cross-correlation in each frequency band, a single broadband cross-correlation was computed. The lag corresponding to the maximum correlation was used as an estimate of the interaural time difference.

A 1024-point FFT was performed and the logarithm of the power in each of 22 one-quarter-octave rectangular bands was computed, for both left and right channels. The difference of these log spectra was also computed.

III. Network Configuration

A feed-forward neural network with up to 23 inputs units (1 cross-correlation term and/or 22 spectral terms), 50 hidden units, and 30 output units (one for each azimuth and one for each elevation) was trained with a learning rate of 0.0625. This experiment used 14400 training vectors with 10 epochs through the training data. Test data consisted of an additional 14400 vectors.

IV. Baseline Results

Figure 2 summarizes the results of this experiment, comparing the responses of subject SDO with those of the neural network. The results shown for subject SDO were for the headphone listening condition of Wightman and Kistler [5]. Front-back confusions have been corrected. A front-back confusion occurs when the target position is in front and the judged position is in the back, or vice versa. The data from SDO were based on 72 locations; 36 of which were judged 10 times each; the other 36 were judged 6 times each. The data from the neural network (NET) were based on all 144 locations, each judged 100 times each. Each open circle represents the centroid of the responses at a particular location.

The azimuth component of the responses of SDO and the network were similar, in that they indicated good agreement between actual and judged azimuth. Both had a tendency to overestimate azimuths between 90 and 150 degrees and between -90 and -150 degrees. With regard to elevation, the match was not as good. SDO consistently overestimated the source elevation, while NET overestimated low source elevations and underestimated high source elevations. The pattern of the network's responses was partially determined by ceiling and floor effects. That is, the network could not produce responses greater than the highest elevation presented (54 degrees) or lower than the lowest elevation presented (-36 degrees). The human was not similarly constrained.

Table 1 shows the average angle of error for SDO and for NET, corrected for front-back confusions. The angle of error is the angle between the vector pointing at the actual source location and the vector pointing at the judged source location. After Wightman and Kistler [5], the results are broken out by source location, with 3 regions for azimuth (front, back, and side) and 3 regions for elevation (low, middle, and high). The results show that overall, the network performed slightly better than the human, although in the low-back region the network performed substantially worse, and in the high elevation region, substantially better.

Table 2 shows the percentage of front-back confusions for SDO and for NET. As in the previous table the results are broken out by region. The results show that overall, the network made more front-back reversals than the human, although at high elevations the network was less likely to make front-back confusions than the human, especially in the front region.

To gain a better understanding of the stimulus cues determining network performance, we considered three sources of stimulus information, cross-correlation (CC), monaural spectrum (LEFT or RIGHT), and binaural spectrum (DIFF). The results are presented in the "3-pole" coordinate system [3] in order to provide a more detailed description of the networks' performance. The right/left

(R/L) coordinate in this system is the angle between a location and the median plane (the vertical plane passing through the subject's nose and perpendicular to a line passing through the subject's ears). Performance in this dimension is often assumed to be determined by interaural difference cues. The front/back (F/B) coordinate is the angle between the location and the frontal plane (the vertical plane passing through the ears). Performance in this dimension may be determined by cues related to the degree of lowpass filtering introduced by the pinnae. The up/down (U/D) coordinate is the angle between the location and the horizontal plane (the horizontal plane passing through the ears). Performance in this dimension is often assumed to be determined by cues related to the detailed spectral modulations introduced by the pinnae.

Table 3 summarizes the rms error in each dimension of this coordinate system, for several different neural network models. Networks were trained with different combinations of input parameters. The row labeled DIFF+CC corresponds to a network with the same input parameters as NET. Notice that DIFF+CC performed similarly to SDO in the R/L and the U/D dimensions, but not as well in the F/B dimension. It can be seen that the individual parameters alone (CC, LEFT, RIGHT, and DIFF in Table 3) did not enable good network performance. It can also be seen that the cross-correlation term (CC) always helped in the R/L and F/B dimensions. The monaural spectra (RIGHT and LEFT) lead to good U/D performance, as would be expected from the current literature on elevation perception.

V. Hierarchical Neural Network

The auditory neurophysiological literature indicates that there are separate representations for monaural and binaural information within the auditory pathway. With this inspiration, we investigated a network configuration we call a Hierarchical Neural Network (HNN) as shown in Figure 3. This consisted of three networks each trained with one set of parameters, either LEFT, RIGHT, or CC. The 30 activations (24 azimuths and 6 elevations) from each of these trained networks were used as the input to a fourth arbitration or fusion network that consisted of 90 input units, 50 hidden units, and 30 output units. The arbitration network was also trained using back-propagation, with 14400 training vectors through 10 epochs, and tested with 14400 test vectors.

Table 3 shows the results of HNN and HNN without the CC network (HNN-C). The CC network provided benefit in the R/L and F/B dimensions, and no benefit in the U/D dimension. Note that the cross-correlation term had a similar effect in the first experiment. Also note, the HNN and HNN-CC performed as well or better (in all dimensions) than any network or SDO.

VI. Discussion

The neural network models made judgements that were similar to those of the human observer. The pattern of those judgement errors and front-back reversals was, to a first approximation, similar to that for the human observer. Better than human performance was achieved in all three dimensions using a hierarchical neural network. These results should be considered with some caution. Most of the parameters of the networks and the preprocessing stages were chosen arbitrarily. The influence of each of these on the form of the results should be examined. In particular, we believe that the form of the internal noise is likely to be important.

Future work will examine the effect of the noise parameters on the response of the neural network model. Experiments to examine the performance of this type of neural network model in binaural masking tasks are also planned.

VII. Acknowledgements

The authors would like to thank Dr. Frederic Wightman and Dr. Doris Kistler of the University of Wisconsin for providing the HRTFs and the response information for subject SDO. This work was sponsored in part by the Air Force Office of Scientific Research (AFOSR-91-0289 and AFOSR Task 2313V3) and the National Institutes of Health (DC-00786).

References

[1] S. Colburn and N. Durlach. Models of binaural interaction. In *Handbook of Perception*, volume IV, chapter 11, pages 467–518. Academic Press, 1978.

[2] N. Durlach. Equalization and cancellation theory of binaural masking-level differences. *J. Acoust. Soc. Am.*, 35(8):1206–1218, 1963.

[3] D. Kistler and F. Wightman. A model of head-related transfer functions based on principal components analysis and minimum-phase reconstruction. *J. Acoust. Soc. Am.*, 91(3):1637–1647, 1992.

[4] F. Wightman and D. Kistler. Headphone simulation of free-field listeneing. I: Stimulus synthesis. *J. Acout. Soc. Am.*, 85(2):858–867, 1989.

[5] F. Wightman and D. Kistler. Headphone simulation of free-field listeneing. II:Psycholphysical validation. *J. Acout. Soc. Am.*, 85(2):868–878, 1989.

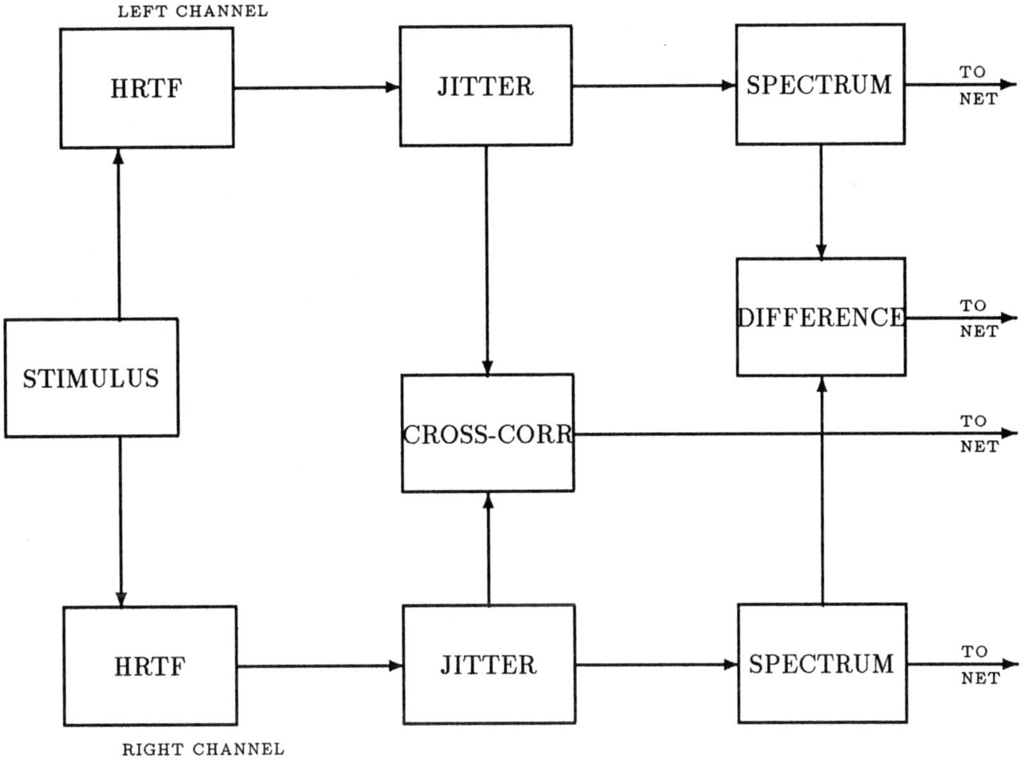

Figure 1: Preprocessing Scheme

	LOW		MIDDLE		HIGH		AVERAGE	
	SDO	NET	SDO	NET	SDO	NET	SDO	NET
FRONT	11.8	20.9	16.7	13.9	27.8	17.0	18.8	17.3
SIDE	11.7	16.9	14.5	11.2	24.5	17.5	16.9	15.2
BACK	11.3	20.1	17.2	12.6	24.9	16.8	17.8	16.5
AVERAGE	11.6	19.2	16.1	12.6	25.7	17.1	17.8	16.3

Table 1: Average Angle of Error in Degrees

	LOW		MIDDLE		HIGH		AVERAGE	
	SDO	NET	SDO	NET	SDO	NET	SDO	NET
FRONT	0	10	0	12	44	19	12	14
SIDE	34	20	20	16	22	23	25	20
BACK	0	10	2	5	18	12	6	9
AVERAGE	7	14	7	11	29	18	13	14

Table 2: Percent Front-Back Confusions

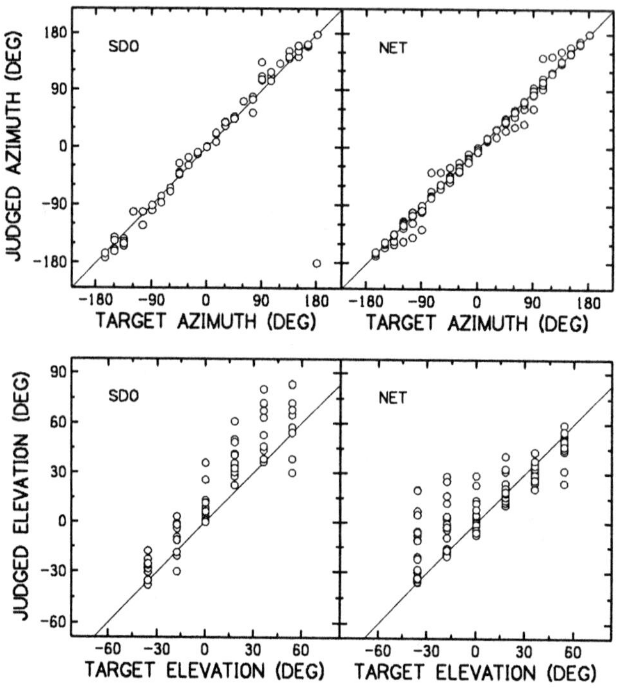

Figure 2: Response Data

	R/L	F/B	U/D
CC	11	51	45
LEFT	17	34	20
RIGHT	18	34	18
DIFF	13	44	26
DIFF+CC	8	38	26
HNN-CC	8	18	11
HNN	5	15	11
SDO	11	28	24

Table 3: RMS Error in Degrees

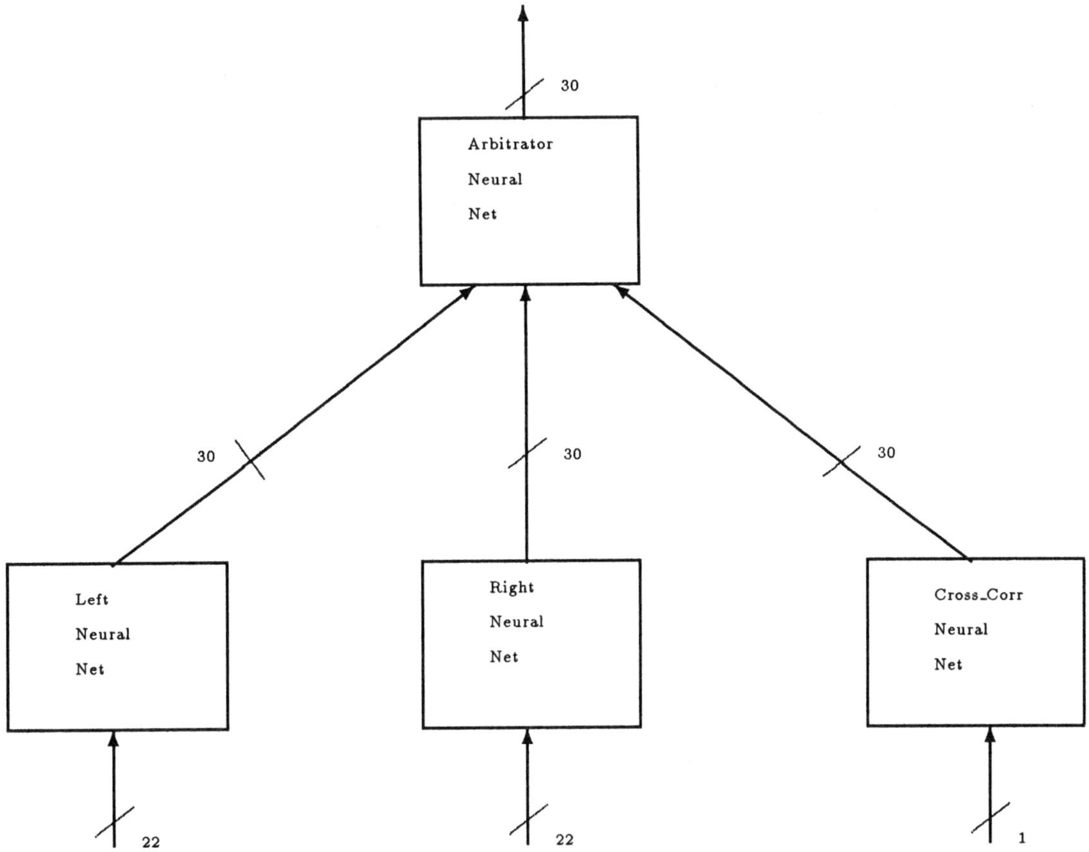

Figure 3: Hierarchical Neural Network

A Neural Network for N-Stage Optimal Control Problems

Roseli Francelin *
USP - ICMSC - SCE
13560 - São Carlos - SP - Brasil
e-mail: rafrance@icmsc.usp.br

Fernando Gomide †
UNICAMP - FEE - DCA
13081 - Campinas - SP - Brasil
e-mail: gomide@dca.fee.unicamp.br

***Abstract*— Neural nets have the potential to be a powerful tool in dealing with nonlinear systems. Different approaches about how neural nets can be incorporated in optimal control strategies have been proposed in terms of general gradient descent and back-propagation. In this paper a particular neural network to solve discrete time N-stage optimal control problems with a direct method to assign its weights is introduced, to systematically incorporate knowledge about the system's behavior. This method is based on the Bellmann's Optimality Principle and in the interchange of information which occurs during the synaptic chemical processing among neurons. This approach presents some advantages with regard to alternative approaches because of the ausence of exaustive training. Some important applications are addressed to illustrate the usefulness of the approach proposed.**

I. Introduction

The need to meet demanding control requirements in increasingly complex dynamical systems under significant uncertainties makes neural networks very attractive because of their ability to learn, to approximate functions, to classify patterns and because of their potential for massively parallel hardware implementation [1].

A number of different approaches for training a controller have been described in the literature. They include reinforcement learning [2], inverse control [11], [14] and optimal control [9], [11].

Optimal control problems can be solved by dynamic programming techniques. However, because of the large computational requirements of the standard computational algorithm a number of new procedures with reduced computational requirements have been developed.

Recently, an neural network with a two-layer feedback topology for solving discrete dynamic programming problems has been proposed [5]. The learning method implemented by this neural network is equivalent to the dynamic programming algorithm. A class of fuzzy decision making problems have also been solved by this approach [6]. In both in cases, Max and Min neuron models proposed in [8] have been utilized to construct the neural network.

In this paper generalized recurrent neurons models are introduced from which the Max and Min neurons of [8] can be obtained. Based on this new neuron model a modification of the approach proposed in [5] is presented. An artificial neural network to be used as controller for discrete time N-stage optimal control problems is proposed. The archictecture developed does not require iterative training algorithms for the weights adaptation. Prior knowledge is directly and systematically stored in the neural network. After this brief introduction, first, we recall the recurrence relation of dynamic programming process. Next, the neural network's characteristics are presented and the use of the proposed neural network is illustrated by using application examples. Finally conclusions and future work are addressed.

II. Optimal Control Systems and Dynamic Programming

We address the problem of designing an intelligent device (a controller, a decision maker, etc...) that drives, in N temporal stages, the state vector of a dynamic system from any initial point to any final point so as to minimize a certain objective function. We begin defining the plant by a general nonlinear discrete-timed dynamical equation

$$x(k+1) = f(x(k), u(k)), \quad k = 0, 1, \ldots, N-1; \qquad x(k) \in R^n, u(k) \in R^m \tag{1}$$

*Supported by CNPq grant # 300634/92-7
†Supported by CNPq grant # 300729/86-3

It is desired to determine a control law that minimizes the performance measure described in the general form,

$$J = h(x(N)) + \sum_{k=0}^{N-1} g(x(k), u(k)) \qquad (2)$$

where N is the especified final stage.

The difference equation (1) and the performance measure (2) may be a discrete approximation to a continuous system, or they may represent a system that is actually discrete. We are here considering the latter possibility. It is shown in [3] that, applying by dynamic programming to this problem (adopting a backward procedure), the following recurrence equation holds:

$$J^*_{N-k,N}(x(N-k)) = min_{u(N-k)}\{g(x(N-k), u(N-k)) + J^*_{N-(k-1),N}(f(x(N-k), u(N-k))\}, \quad k = 1, 2, \ldots, N$$

with initial value $J^*(x(N)) = h(x(N))$. The solution of this recurrence equation is an optimal control law or optimal policy, $u^*(x(N-k), N-k)$, $k = 1, 2, \ldots, N$, which is obtained by trying all admissible control values at each admissible state values.

The computational procedure assumes that the admissible state and control values are quantized into a finite number of levels. For a nth-order system the number of state grid points for each time t is $S = s_1 * s_2 * \ldots * s_n$ where $s_i = \frac{x_{imax} - x_{imin}}{\Delta x_i} + 1$; $i = 1, 2, \ldots, n$. It is assumed that the ratio $\frac{x_{imax} - x_{imin}}{\Delta x_i}$ is an integer. The admissible range of control values is quantized in exactly the same way; if C is the total number of quantized values of $u(k)$, then $C = c_1 * c_2 * \ldots * c_m$ where $c_i = \frac{u_{imax} - u_{imin}}{\Delta u_i} + 1$; $i = 1, 2, \ldots, m$. In what follows $x^{(i)}(k)(i = 1, 2, \ldots, S)$ and $u^{(j)}(k)(j = 1, 2, \ldots, C)$ denote the admissible quantized state and control values at stage k.

III. A Neural Network for N-Stage Optimal Control Problems

A. Generalized Model Neuron

The generalized model neuron is introduced bellow, because it is essential in building the neural network proposed in this paper. The neuron is an adaptive neuron in the sense that it goes through a learning and adaptation processes to improve its performance. The processing of the generalized neuron is divided into numeric and symbolic processing. By numeric processing we mean operations that a neuron can perform at numeric level, such as to compute the weighted sum of its inputs, whereas by symbolic processing, we mean the exchange of messages performed by the neurons before to perform an action.

The artificial, generalized neuron (Figure 1) is assumed to be a computational device which:

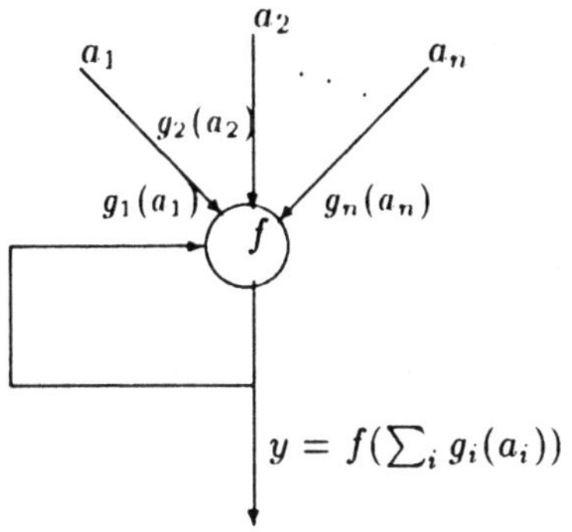

Figure 1: Generalized Neuron

- power averages its n inputs a_i, $v = \sum_{i=1}^{n} g_i(a_i)$, according to the weighting functions of the synapses linking the input neurons (pre-synaptic) n_i and the output neuron (post-synaptic) n_k, and
- recodes $v \in V$ into the axonic activation a_p of the post-synaptic neuron: $a_p = \begin{cases} f(v) & \text{if } v \geq \alpha \\ 0 & \text{otherwise} \end{cases}$ where α is the axonic threshold and f is the enconding function or transfer function.

The input $a = (a_1, a_2, \ldots, a_n)$ in the neuron n_k is transformed by the weight function G as follows:

$$a = (a_1, a_2, \ldots, a_n) \overset{G}{\mapsto} (g_1(a_1), g_2(a_2), \ldots, g_n(a_n))$$

where $g_i : R \mapsto R$; $i = 1, \ldots, n; a_i \mapsto w_i = g_i(a_i)$ Therefore, the weight function G is a function $G : R^n \mapsto R^n$ such that

$$\begin{aligned} a = (a_1, a_2, \ldots, a_n) &\mapsto w = (w_1, w_2, \ldots, w_n) = \\ G(a) &= (g_1(a_1), g_2(a_2), \ldots, g_n(a_n)) \end{aligned} \qquad (3)$$

The generalized neuron has a recurrent synapsis. The recurrent synapsis is established if axon of neuron n_j makes contacts with dendrites or the cell body of n_j itself. If the recurrent synapsis is located near the axon, then it may control the axonic threshold as a function of the n_j's activity itself. Based on this definition, we note that:

- If $g_i(a_i) = c_i a_i$ where c_i is a constant and

$$f(v) = \begin{cases} 1 & \text{for all } v \geq \alpha \\ 0 & \text{otherwise} \end{cases} \qquad (4)$$

then the neuron is a **binary neuron**, or the known McCulloch and Pitts neuron.

- If (4) is given and $f : V \mapsto [0,1]$

$$a_p = \begin{cases} 1 & \text{if } v \geq \alpha_2 \\ f(v) & \text{if } \alpha_1 \leq v \leq \alpha_2 \\ 0 & \text{otherwise} \end{cases} \quad (5)$$

  where α_1 and α_2 are axonic thresholds (in many applications they are furnished by a special type of neuron, called bias cell), then the neuron obtained is named **fuzzy neuron** [8].

- The Max-Neuron, proposed by Gomide and Rocha [8], can also be obtained as follows. Take the axonic threshold $\alpha_1(\tau) = 0$. Then at τ it is set equal to the firing level $a_p(\tau-1)$ at $\tau - 1$: $\alpha_1(\tau) = a_p(\tau-1)$ and the output $a_p(t)$ is given by:

$$a_p(\tau) = \begin{cases} \alpha_1(\tau) & \text{if } v(\tau) \leq \alpha_1(\tau) \\ v(\tau) & \text{otherwise} \end{cases}$$

  where $v(\tau)$ is the post-synaptic activation at τ. In this condition, the output $a_p(\tau)$ of the neuron at τ encodes $a_p(\tau) = \bigvee_{i=1}^{\tau} g_i(a_i)$. If $g_i = I$ for all i, then:

$$a_p(\tau) = \bigvee_{i=1}^{\tau} a_i \quad (6)$$

  where $\bigvee$ is the maximum operator and I denotes the identity function. A neuron that satisfy the above is named Max generalized neuron.

- Analogously, the Min-Neuron [8] can also be obtained. More details can be found in [7].

The neural network proposed here is a recurrent network constituted of two-layers (Figure 2). The first layer neurons are generalized neurons, named U-neurons and the second layer neurons are Max-Neurons (or Min-Neurons), named here as X-neurons. The first and second layers are named layer-U and layer-X, respectively. Since we are considering discrete problems, the inputs in the first layer neurons correspond the different discrete values $u(k)$ can assume, whereas the inputs in the second layer neurons correspond the different discrete values $x(k)$ can assume. The connections (weights) from X-neurons to U-neurons, as well as from U-neurons to X-neurons are determined by the symbolic processing of the neural network, to be described bellow.

U-neuron (Figure 3) is a generalized neuron that receives two synchronized input signals: $a1(u)$ and $a2(u)$ to provide an output s. These input signals can be vectors of suitable dimension. Supposing that the inputs $a1(u)$ and $a2(u) \in R^n$ and the correspondly weighting functions are: $\tilde{G}(a1(u)) = (\tilde{g}_1(a1_1(u)), \tilde{g}_2(a1_2(u)), \ldots, \tilde{g}_n(a1_n(u)))$ and

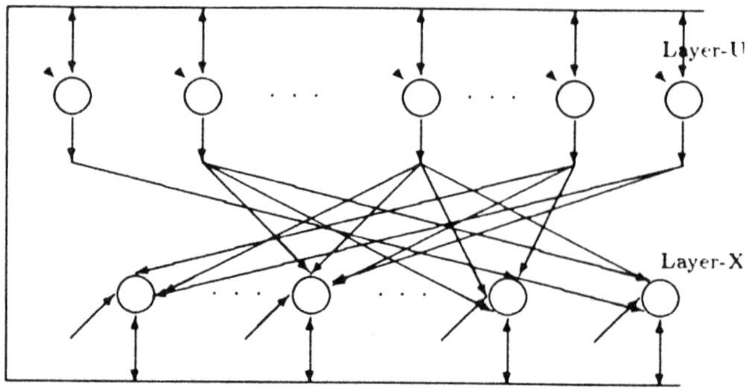

Figure 2: Neural Network for Optimal Control Problems

$\tilde{H}(a2(u)) = (\tilde{h}_1(a2_1(u)), \tilde{h}_2(a2_2(u)), \ldots, \tilde{h}_n(a2_n(u)))$, respectively, then the output s is given by:

$$s = f(\sum_{i=1}^{n} \tilde{g}_i(a1_i(u)) + \sum_{i=1}^{n} \tilde{h}_i(a2_i(u)))$$

where $f(\theta) = \begin{cases} \theta & \text{if } \theta \geq \alpha \\ 0 & \text{otherwise} \end{cases}$ and α is a threshold value for the U-neuron. A similar function is used by ASE proposed in [2].

In the neural network proposed here, the U-neuron weighting functions have the following meaning. The function $\tilde{G}(a_1(u))$ corresponds to that part of the objective function related with variable u at the Stage-$N-k$, being therefore furnished by the network designer. A function $\tilde{H}(a_2(u)))$ is such that, for the Nth-stage, $\tilde{H}(a_2(u))$ corresponds to that part of objective function related with the variable $x(N)$. Hence, this value is also known and is furnished to network during the initialization phase. For the $(N-k)^{th}$-stages, $k = 2, \ldots, N$, the weighting function $\tilde{H}(a_2(u))$ is defined as identity function.

A X-neuron (Figure 3) is a generalized Max-Neuron or generalized Min-Neuron, depending if the optimization problem to be solved is either a maximization or minimization problem, respectively. It receives synchronized input signals pairs: $(a1(x), a2(x))$ to provide an output s.

Supposing that $a1(x)$ and $a2(x) \in R^m$ and that the weighting functions are:

$$G(a1(x)) = (g_i(a1_i(x))) \text{ and } H(a2(x)) = (h_i(a2_i(x)))$$

for $i = 1, \ldots, m$ respectively, then the output s is given by:

$$s = \max_l\{a_l\} \text{ or } s = \min_l\{a_l\}$$

where $a_l = G(a1(x)) + H(a2(x))$ and l denotes the number of the X-neuron inputs.

In the DOCNN - Discrete Optimal Control Neural Network to be derived in the next section, the X-neuron weighting functions have the following meaning. The input signal $a1(x)$ is a fixed value for each X-neuron because it represents one among possible values that the variable x assumes at stage $N-k$. The function $G(a_1(x))$ corresponds to that part of the objective function related with variable x at the Stage-$N-k$ being, therefore, known. The input signal $a2(x)$ is unidimensional because it is the output of some U-neuron. The function $H(a_2(u))) = I$, where I denotes the identity function.

B. Symbolic Processing

Before to define the symbolic processing of a generalized neuron, the following concepts, described and detailed in [12], are introduced.

It is known that in the synaptic chemical processing, the production of a transmitter at the axonic terminals is dependent of both the pre and post-synapitc cells The proteins produced by the pre-synatic cell are called precursors, and those released by the post-synaptic neuron are called controllers. The genetic specification of the transmitter to be produced is dependent on signals provided by both the pre- and post- synaptic cells, and the activation of the reading of specified genes is governed by the camp produced by the activation of the post-synaptic receptors. The precursor produced at the pre-synaptic cell body must be transported to the axonic terminals. The same precursor may be used to produce different types of transmitters. This is because the final specification of a transmitter is dependent on the controllers produced by the post-synaptic cell. Let T denotes a transmitter, R a receptor and C a controller of a neuron. It is also known that the activation of the post-synaptic cell n_j due to transmitter T released by the pre-synaptic cell n_i activates control molecules C_j. This can be represented symbolically by

$$T_i \bigoplus R_j >> C_j \tag{7}$$

where $\bigoplus$ and $>>$ denote the conjunction and translation operations. Each especific coupling between a pre-syanptic transmitter and a post-synaptic receptor, in turn, activates different types of controllers C_j. These controllers exercise different types of action over the pre and post-synaptic cells,

$$T_i \bigoplus R_j >> C_j \mapsto action \tag{8}$$

Furthermore, the amount $q(C)$ of controllers triggered by the $T \bigoplus R$ binding is calculated as:

$$q(C) = (q(T) \oplus q(R)) \; o \; \mu(T,R) \tag{9}$$

where $q(T)$ is the amount of the T; $q(R)$ is the amount of the R and $\mu(T,R)$ is the degree of matching between T and R, $\oplus$ and o being operations to be defined, being in general, t-norms or t-conorms [12]. To simplify the notation, we represent the results given by the equations (7) - (9) by:

If $[(T_i)$ **and** $(R_j)]$ **then**
active (C_j),

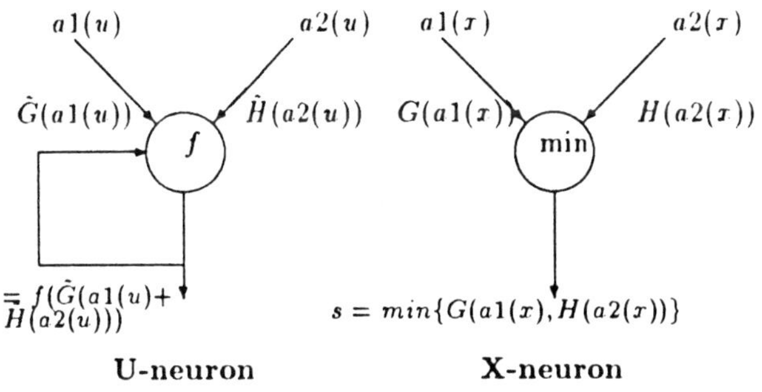

Figure 3: Neurons of the DOCNN

If $(C_j$ is active$)$ **then**
action: $q(C) = f(q(R), q(T))$

respectively.

Based on these concepts, the symbolic processing (Figure 4) of the neural network corresponding to the learning phase of the network, can to be defined. During this processing, the connections as well as the corresponding weights are established. Thus, consider the two different types neurons, that is, U-neuron and X-neuron.

The X-neuron sends the signal $a1(x)$ to the U-neuron, that is, $q(T(x)) = a1(x)$. Otherwise, the U-neuron receives this signal by his receptor ($q(R(u) = a1(x))$ and into his other input $a1(u)$, such that $a1(u) = q(T(u))$, actives his controller function, $C(u)$, computing: $q(C(u) = f(q(T(u)), q(R(u))$, where f is as in (1). Hence, the value $C(u))$ is a function of the input signals received by the U-neuron. Based on the value $C(u)$ the following test is performed:

If $(C(u))$ is feasible **then**
a connection from U-neuron to X-neuron
is established and the corresponding
weight is set equal to
$W(U-neuron, X-neuron) = 1$
else $W(U-neuron, X-neuron) = 0$.

In this way, the symbolic processing estimates the values $C(u)$ for all state-action pairs and makes use of these estimatives to select actions. A action here can be either activation of the controller function or activation of connections. This scheme is similar to one that occurs in a Q-learning system [13], in which estimations of $\hat{Q}$ are obtained for all state-action pairs and actions are selected based on these estimations.

In the symbolic processing the following actions can be performed: either the recurrent synapsis is actived and the signal $a2(u) = q(C(u))$ is sended to the U-neuron itself, or the feedback interconnections are actived and the signal

$q(T(u)) = C(u)$ is sended for all X-neuron in layer-X.

C. Numeric Processing

During the numeric processing (Figure 4), the U-neuron can perform the following actions: if its recurrent connection is actived then the output, $s(u)$, is:

$$s(u) = f(\sum_{i=1}^{n} \tilde{g}_i(a1_i(u)) + \sum_{i=1}^{n} \tilde{h}_i(a2_i(u)))$$

where $a1(u)$, $a2(u) = q(C(u))$ are the inputs and $\tilde{G}(a1(u))$ and $\tilde{H}(a2(u))$ the corresponding weighting functions.

If the feedback connections are actived, the degree of matching between a U-neuron and each one of X-neurons is computed, that is, the X-neuron whose amount of his receptor, $q(R(x))$, is approximately equal to the amount of the transmitter of U-neuron, $q(T(u))$, according to some norm, is identified and its output, $s(x)$ is sended to U-neuron. In this way, the DOCNN performs a similar procedure to one used by Kohonen [4] known as competitive learning. In DOCNN, the norm used is the euclidian norm. Hence, in this case, the output signal of the U-neuron, $s(u)$, is given by

$$s(u) = f(\sum_{i}^{n} \tilde{g}_i(a1(u)) + \sum_{i}^{n} \tilde{h}_i(a2(u))),$$

where $a1(u)$ and $a2(u) = s(x)$ are the inputs and $\tilde{G}(a1(u))$ and $\tilde{H}(a2(u)) = I$ the corresponding weighting functions.

The X-neuron receives the output signal of the U-neuron $a2(x) = s(u)$ and its other input, $a1(x) = q(T(x))$ with the corresponding weighting functions $H = I$ and G and computes one of its inputs, a_l:

$$a_l = I(s(u)) + \sum_{i}^{m} \tilde{g}_i(a1_i(u)).$$

Detailed DOCNN construction and processing algorithm can be found in [7].

IV. Application

Discrete Regulator Problems: In this section we consider a discrete system described by the state equation:

$$x(k+1) = A(k)x(k) + B(k)u(k)$$

where $u(k)$ and $x(k)$ can be variables satisfying constraints. The problem is to find an optimal policy $u^*(x(k), k)$ that minimizes the objective function

$$J = \frac{1}{2}x^T(NS)Hx(NS) + \frac{1}{2}\sum_{k=0}^{NS-1}[x^T(k)Q(k)x(k) + u^T(k)R(k)u(k)]$$

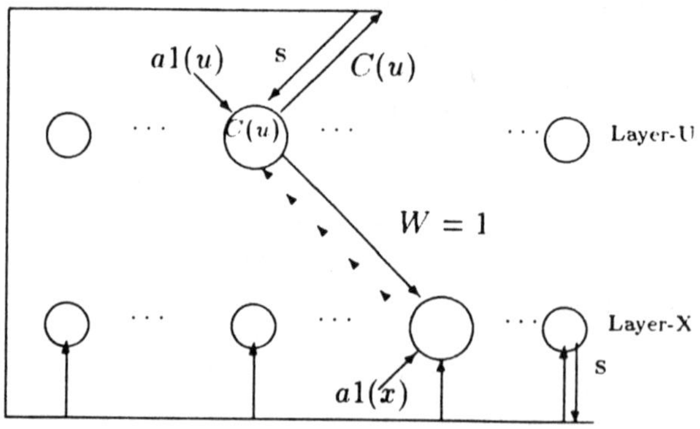

Figure 4: Symbolic and Numeric Processing

where H e $Q(k)$ are real symmetric positive semi-definite nxn matrices, $R(k)$ is a real symmetric positive mxm matrix and NS is a fixed integer greater than 0.

To simplify the notation in the derivation that follows, let us make the assumption that A, B, R and Q are constant matrices. Initially we remember that the allowable state and control values must be quantized. We will assume, without lost generally, that the state and control, $u(k)$, $x(k)$, respectively are quantized at the same values for all stages.

The weighting functions, $\tilde{G}(a1(u)), G(a1(x))$ must be determined at each stage for each U-neuron and X-neuron in the network. According with the definition of these functions, they correspond to the terms of the objective function that depend on of the variables u and x at a given stage. The weighting function $H(a2(u))$ corresponds the terms of the objective function that depend on the variable x at stage NS. Hence, we have:

For $k = NS-1$

$$\tilde{G}(a1(u)) = \tfrac{1}{2}u(NS-1)Ru(NS-1);$$
$$\tilde{H}(a2(u)) = \tfrac{1}{2}x(NS)Hx(NS);$$
$$G(a1(x)) = \tfrac{1}{2}x(NS-1)Qx(NS-1);\; H(a2(x)) = I.$$

For $k = NS-2, NS-3, \ldots, 0$

$$\tilde{G}(a1(u)) = \tfrac{1}{2}u(k)Ru(k);\; \tilde{H}(a2(u)) = I;$$
$$G(a1(x)) = \tfrac{1}{2}x(k)Qx(k);\; H(a2(x)) = I.$$

The processing of the network must be performed according to Main Algoritm proposed in [7].

A constrained linear quadratic control problem was solved to illustrate the uselfulness of the DOCNN. This problem has been considered by Parisini [10]. An approximate optimal solution is sought by constraining the control strategies to take on the structure of two chains (the feedback chain and the feed-forward chain) of multi-layer

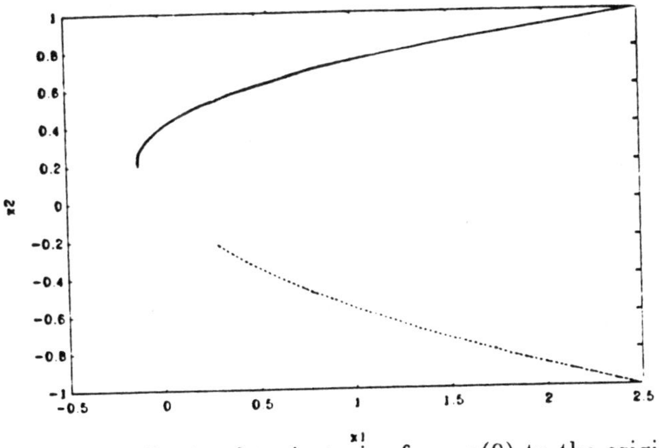

Figure 5: Optimal trajectories from x(0) to the origin

feed-forward neural networks. The dynamic system is:

$$x(k+1) = \begin{bmatrix} 0.65 & -0.19 \\ 0. & 0.83 \end{bmatrix} x(k) + \begin{bmatrix} 7 \\ 7 \end{bmatrix} u(k)$$

where $x(k) \in R^2$ and $u(k) \in R$. The objective function is:

$$J = \sum_{k=0}^{NS-1} u^2(k) + v_{NS}\|x(NS)\|^2$$

with $v_{NS} = 40$ and $NS = 10$.

We assume that the state variable $x = (x_1, x_2) \in R^2$ must be satisfy the following constraints:

$$-0.5 \leq x_1(k) \leq 3.5; \quad -1.0 \leq x_2(k) \leq 1.0$$

whereas the control variable $u \in R$ must be satisfy:

$$-0.5 \leq u(k) \leq 0.5$$

for all stage $k = 0, 1, \ldots, 9$. A DOCNN corresponding to this problem with a topology of $S = 107$ neurons in the Layer-U and $C = 300$ neuron in the layer-X has been simulated. Figure 5 shows the optimal neural trajectories in phase-plane obtained considering two different initial points: $x(0) = (2.5, 1.0)^T$ and $x(0) = (2.5, -1.0)^T$.

V. Conclusions and Future Work

In this paper a neural network to solve N-stage optimal control problems has been proposed has proposed based on a generalized recurrent neuron model. A direct method to assign the weights of neural network was presented and in this sense the network has capacity of auto-programming. The direct method is based on the Bellmann's Optimality Principle and in the interchange of information which occur during the synaptic chemical processing among neurons. This approach presents some advantages with regard to other schemes of learning that implement approximations of the standart algorithm from dynamic programming like as well as approaches that use sigmoidal functions and schemes of back-propagation type. Comparative analysis of the performance of the neural network proposed in obtaining solutions for more complex problems, as well as investigations of the potential of this new approach in neurocomputer implementations will be considered in the near.

References

[1] ANTSAKLIS, P. J., "Neural networks in control systems", *IEEE Control Systems Mag.*, vol 12, no. 2, pp. 8-10, April 1992.

[2] BARTO, A. G., SUTTON, R. S and ANDERSON C. W., "Neuronlike adaptive elements that can solve difficult learning control problems", *IEEE Trans. Syst., Man and Cybernetics*, vol. SMC-13, no. 5, pp. 834-846, Sept/Oct. 1983.

[3] KIRK, D. E., *Optimal Control Theory - An Introduction*, Prentice Hall, Inc., 1970.

[4] KOHONEN, T., *Self-Organization and Associative Memory*, Springer-Verlag, Berlin, 1984.

[5] FRANCELIN, R.A. and GOMIDE, F. A. C., "A neural network to solve discrete dynamic programming problems", *Proc. IEEE Int. Conf. Neural Networks - ICNN'93*, vol. II, pp. 1433-1438, March 1993.

[6] FRANCELIN, R.A. and GOMIDE, F. A. C., "A neural network for fuzzy decision making problems". *Proc. 2nd IEEE Int. Conf. on Fuzzy Systems*, vol. I, pp. 655-660, March 1993.

[7] FRANCELIN, R. A. and GOMIDE, F. A. C., "A neural network for discrete-time optimal control problems", *DCA/FEE/UNICAMP Tech. Report*, no. 9, Ago 1993.

[8] GOMIDE, F. and ROCHA, A. F., "Neurofuzzy controllers", *Proc. 2nd Int. Conf. on Fuzzy Logic and Neural Networks*, IIZUKA, JAPAN, 17-22, July 1992.

[9] NGUYEN, D. H. and WIDROW, B., "Neural networks for self-learning control systems", *IEEE Control Systems Mag.*, vol 10, no. 3, pp. 18-23, April 1990.

[10] PARISINI, T. and ZOPPOLI, R., *Backpropagation for N-stage optimal control problems*, IJCNN'91, vol. 2, pp. 1518-1529, Nov. 1991.

[11] PSALTIS, D., SIDERIS, A. and YAMAMURA, A. A., "A Multilayered Neural Network Controller", *IEEE Control Systems Mag.*, vol. 8, no. 2, pp. 17-21, April 1988.

[12] ROCHA, A. F., "Neural nets: a theory for brains and machines", *Lecture Notes in Artificial Intelligence*, Springer-Verlag, 1992, 393 pages.

[13] WATKINS, C.J.C.H., *Learning with delayed rewards*, PH.D. Thesis, Cambridge Univ. Phsychology Dept., 1989.

[14] WIDROW, B., *Adaptive Inverse Control*, in Adaptive Systems in Control and Signal Processing 1986, Intern. Federation of Automatic Control, July 1986.

k-Coloring Vertices Using a Neural Network with Convergence to Valid Solutions

Matthias Oliver Berger
RWTH Aachen, Lehrstuhl für Informatik IV, D-52056 Aachen

***Abstract*— This paper proposes a new algorithm using a maximum neural network model to k-color vertices of a simple undirected graph. Unlike traditional neural nets, the proposed network is guaranteed to converge to valid solutions with no parameter tuning needed. The power of the new method to solve this NP-complete problem will be shown in a number of simulations.**

I. Graph Coloring

Coloring an arbitrary graph with k colors is one of the fundamental problems in graph theory and combinatorics. The task is to color the vertices of a graph so that vertices which are connected by edges will have different colors. The conventional algorithms used to solve this problem suffer from the fact that efficiently finding a valid graph coloring is known to be very difficult: Graph coloring belongs to the class of NP-complete problems [2]. The following standard definitions will be used.

Definition 1 *A simple graph $G(V, E)$ consists of a finite set V of vertices and a specified two element subset of edges $E \in V^{(2)}$, where each edge corresponds to a different pair of distinct vertices. To simplify notation, the two element set $\{u, v\} \in E$ is denoted by uv and u and v are called adjacent vertices in G. An adjacency matrix $D_{|V|\times|V|} = ((d_{ij}))$ of a graph G describes the set E of G: $d_{ij} = 1$ if vertex i is adjacent to vertex j, 0 otherwise.*

It is assumed that G is undirected, i.e. the order between the two vertices of an edge is not important.

Definition 2 *$W \subset V$ is called independent if $W^{(2)} \cap E = \emptyset$. C is called a covering of G, if $C = \{W_1, \ldots, W_k\}$ and all sets $W_i \subset V$ are independent and $\bigcup_{i=1}^{k} W_i = V$ holds. If additionally $W_i \cap W_j = \emptyset$ for all $i \neq j$ then C is called a coloring of G. The chromatic number of G is denoted by $\chi(G)$ and is the minimal number of colors necessary to color G.*

A graph G is said to be k-colorable if all the vertices of G can be colored using k different colors such that no two adjacent vertices have the same color.

II. Hopfield Nets

A Hopfield neural network of order N comprises N fully connected computational units called neurons. Generally, Hopfield's neural net is considered to be able to solve combinatorial optimization problems in a very short time if it is realized using analog elements. The system minimizes an energy or cost function representing the optimization criteria. The model for each neuron i consists of an internal state u_i and an output V_i, where V_i is a fixed function of the internal state, i.e. $V_i = f(u_i)$ and I_i is the external input of the ith neuron. In general, any continuous, bounded, monotonic function may be taken as f.

The gradient descent method seeks the local minimum of a predefined Liapunov energy function E, which follows the quadratic form [3]

$$E = -\frac{1}{2}\sum_{i=1}^{N}\sum_{j=1}^{N} T_{ij}V_iV_j - \sum_{i=1}^{N} V_iI_i \qquad (1)$$

where N is the number of neurons in the system, T_{ij} is the symmetrical ($T_{ij} = T_{ji}$) synapse weight between the ith and the jth neurons with zero diagonal ($T_{ii} = 0$). The rate of change of the internal state or motion equation of the

0-7803-1901-X/94 $4.00 ©1994 IEEE

ith neuron given in [3] is

$$\frac{du_i}{dt} = -\frac{u_i}{\tau} - \frac{\partial E}{\partial V_i} \quad (2)$$

A. Maximum Neuron Model

This paper will use a two-dimensional modification of the Hopfield neural network model called the "maximum neuron model" [5] consisting of M clusters each with N neurons, resulting in $M \times N$ processing elements. The energy function extended for the two-dimensional case is written as

$$E = -\frac{1}{2}\sum_{m=1}^{M}\sum_{i=1}^{N}\sum_{m'=1}^{M}\sum_{j=1}^{N} T_{mim'j}V_{mi}V_{m'j} - \sum_{m=1}^{M}\sum_{i=1}^{N} V_{mi}I_{mi}$$

Only the one neuron in each cluster with the maximum internal state will have nonzero output, if there is more than one neuron with the same maximum input in any cluster, the neuron with the smallest subscript has nonzero output. The output of the other neurons in the same cluster become zero, so that always one and only one neuron in each cluster has nonzero output. The input/output function of the ith maximum neuron in the mth cluster is defined as $V_{mi} = 1$ if $u_{mi} = \max\{u_{m1}, \ldots, u_{mN}\}$ and $u_{mi} \geq u_{mj}$ for $i > j$, 0 otherwise. The convergence conditions for the maximum neuron model to a local minimum of the energy function E are given by

Theorem 1 *$\frac{dE}{dt} \leq 0$ is satisfied under two conditions (1) $\frac{du_{mi}}{dt} = -\frac{\partial E}{\partial V_{mi}}$ and (2) $V_{mi} = 1$ and $u_{mi} = \max\{u_{m1}, \ldots, u_{mN}\}$ and $u_{mi} \geq u_{mj}$ for $i > j$, $V_{mi} = 0$ otherwise*

For a proof, see [5]. The termination condition of the net is given as follows: As long as the system reaches a stable state or an equilibrium state, the procedure will terminate. The equilibrium state of the maximum neural model is defined as all firing neurons having the zero rate of change of the input per cluster.

III. Neural Network Representation

The graph coloring problem is defined as follows:

Instance: Given the adjacency matrix D of a simple, undirected graph $G(V, E)$ and $k \geq \chi(G)$.

Task: Find a valid k-coloring of G.

This leads to the following neural representation:

1. The problem is mapped on $k|V|$ variables V_{mi} with $V_{mi} = 1$ if vertex m is colored with color i, 0 otherwise.
2. Each variable V_{mi} is associated with the output $f(u_{mi})$ of a $|V| \times k$ maximum neural network with $|V|$ clusters and k neurons per cluster. The output of the mith neuron represents the ith out of the possible k colors for the mth vertex.
3. The optimization criteria are:
   (a) One and only one color is to be assigned to each vertex.
   (b) No two adjacent vertices should have the same color.

   The first criterion can be expressed by the cost function

   $$E_1 = \sum_{m=1}^{|V|}\left(\sum_{i=1}^{k} V_{mi} - 1\right)^2 \quad (3)$$

   which is positive if the first constraint is violated and zero if not. The second criterion can be expressed as cost function

   $$E_2 = \sum_{m=1}^{|V|}\sum_{\substack{m'=1\\ m'\neq m}}^{|V|}\sum_{i=1}^{k} d_{mm'}V_{mi}V_{m'i} \quad (4)$$

   where $d_{mm'}$ is the mm'th entry in the adjacency matrix D of G. E_2 is positive if two adjacent vertices are colored with the same color and zero if a G has a valid coloring. Note that the formulation of the criteria as cost functions is not unique.
4. When using a maximum neuron model, the first constraint E_1 can be eliminated, as the model itself already has the behaviour that one and only neuron is firing in each cluster of the network. Therefore, the computational energy E is given by

$$E = \frac{1}{2}E_2 = \frac{1}{2}\sum_{m=1}^{|V|}\sum_{\substack{m'=1\\ m'\neq m}}^{|V|}\sum_{i=1}^{k} d_{mm'}V_{mi}V_{m'i} \quad (5)$$

It is not required to tune any coefficient parameters in E.

5. The coupling weights and the external inputs are then defined as follows:

$$T_{mim'j} = -d_{mm'}\delta_{ij}(1-\delta_{mm'}) \quad (6)$$
$$I_{mi} = 0 \quad (7)$$

where δ denotes Kronecker's delta. $T_{mim'j}$ inhibits connections within each row of the neuron matrix.

6. Starting with random u_{mi}, the motion equation is computed until equilibrium state is reached. The motion equation is written as (decay term removed)

$$\frac{du_{mi}}{dt} = -\frac{\partial E}{\partial V_{mi}} = -\sum_{\substack{m'=1 \\ m'\neq m}}^{|V|} d_{mm'}V_{m'i} \quad (8)$$

7. The result is a valid k-coloring $\mathcal{C} = \{W_1,\ldots,W_k\}$ of G, where

$$W_i = \{m \in V | V_{mi} = 1\}$$

indicates the coloring. Note that $W_i \neq \emptyset$ not necessarily holds.

IV. Algorithm

The discrete network model described in the previous section was simulated on a sequential computer using parallel update. The internal states, neuron outputs and motions were represented as matrices. The pseudo-code for the algorithm is as follows ($m \in \{1,\ldots,|V|\}, i \in \{1,\ldots,k\}$).

1. `Fill internal state matrix` $U := ((u_{mi}))\forall m,i$ `with random integers.`
2. `Compute output matrix` $V := ((V_{mi}))\forall m,i$.
3. `Compute rate of change matrix` $\Delta U := ((\frac{du_{mi}}{dt}))\forall m,i$ `using eq.(8).`
4. `Terminate, if equilibrium is reached.`
5. `Else, using the first order Euler method, assign` $U := U + \Delta U$ `with parallel update.`
6. `Go to step 2.`

No.	$\|V\|$	$\|E\|$	$\chi(G)$	k
1	6	8	2	4
2	5	8	2	4
3	10	19	3	4
4	4	6	4	4
5	10	45	10	10
6	20	190	20	20

Table 1: Example graphs

No.	Hit rate	*Iterations*
1	100.0%	3.529
2	100.0%	4.698
3	100.0%	6.574
4	100.0%	3.867
5	100.0%	8.432
6	100.0%	10.541

Table 2: Simulation results

If the graph is k-colorable, the algorithm terminates with a valid solution, which is guaranteed by the model. Thus a 100% convergence rate to the global minimum is given. The coloring can be found in matrix V according to the model given in previous section.

V. Simulation Results and Discussion

The algorithm was implemented using C++. Several examples were used to test it, some results are presented in table 2. Each example graph was colored 1000 times, each time starting with new random internal states. The last column indicates the average number of iteration steps needed until convergence of the net was detected. Simulation examples are the graphs as given in table 1.

Note the convergence of the network to a valid solutions only. Whenever the proposed system converges, the corresponding configuration is always forced to be a valid solution, while none of the existing neural networks can guarantee it.

Comparing the results with those obtained by Takefuji and Lee [6], one immediately notes the superior convergence of the new algorithm. Takefuji and Lee use binary McCulloch-Pitts neurons with an energy function that has to control both optimization criteria as given by eq.(3) and eq.(4). Due to local minima, they cannot guarantee convergence to valid solutions of their model, which results in a number of heuristics to improve convergence. These heuristics are derived only from simulation experience and are not proven. Due to the number of additional terms, a tedious parameter tuning has to take place. Synchronous update is used, so that the algorithm is not guaranteed to terminate. Unfortunately, Takefuji and Lee do not give exact simulation results, so that a comparison with the algorithm presented here is rather difficult.

The graph coloring algorithm presented in [4] uses a different approach. Philipsen and Stok transform the problem into the maximum stable set problem, which results in a larger number of vertices and edges (in their example the number of vertices increases from 3 to 9 and the number edges increases from 2 to 15). The model used is the simulated annealing with a combination from mean field theory Potts and the sigmoid neurons, which means that they have to adjust the "temperature" of their system according to some "cooling schedule". They do not give details of their energy function nor of the graphs used in their simulation.

Dahl [1] uses a rather complicated energy function consisting of three terms. The three parameters α, β, γ require constant adjustment depending on the size of the maps to color. This is done to avoid local minima. Also, at various points in the time evolution of the net, Dahl had to truncate activation levels of the neurons.

VI. Conclusion

The vertex coloring problem is one of the difficult problems in graph theory. The problem is modeled in a Hopfield net divided into $|V|$ clusters each with k maximum neurons. The general principle of mapping optimization problems as well the particular neural representation is presented. The implementation of the parallel algorithm on a sequential machine using an asynchronous updating rule is given. The algorithm always terminates with a valid solution and has a guaranteed 100% convergence rate to the global minimum of the energy function.

To verify that the neural net proposed in this paper is actually useful, it is applied to a number of examples and its performance is compared with other neural graph coloring algorithms. The solution to the examples given in this paper prove that the proposed algorithm is superior to those. Its guaranteed convergence is a great advantage when compared with existing neural nets.

References

[1] Dahl, E.D., "Neural Network Algorithm for an NP-Complete Problem: Map & Graph Coloring", Proc. IEEE First Int. Conf. Neural Networks, vol. 3, pp.113–120, 1987

[2] Garey, M.R., and Johnson, D.S., *Computers and intractability*, W.H. Freeman, New York, 1979

[3] Hopfield, J.J., and Tank, D.W., "Neural computation of decisions in optimization problems", Biol. Cybern., vol. 52, pp.141–152, 1985

[4] Philipsen, W.J.M., and Stok, L., "Graph Coloring using Neural Networks", Proc. IEEE Int. Symp. Circuits Systems, vol. 3, pp.1597–1600, 1991

[5] Takefuji, Y., *Neural network parallel computing*, Kluwer Academic Publishers, Dordrecht, Netherlands, 1992

[6] Takefuji, Y., and Lee, K.C., "Artificial Neural Networks for Four-Coloring Map Problems and K-Colorability Problems", IEEE Trans. Circuits Systems, vol. 38, no. 3, pp.325–333, Mar. 1991

Impact of Energy Function on a Neural Network Model for Optimization Problems

Wei Lin†, José G. Delgado-Frias†, Gerald G. Pechanek+ and Stamatis Vassiliadis*

†Dept. of Electrical Engineering, State University of New York, Binghamton, NY 13902-6000

+IBM Microelectronics, Research Triangle Park, North Carolina

*IBM Corporation, AWS Division, Austin, Texas

Abstract

A neural network model for the solution of optimization problems is studied in this paper. Six different variations to the energy function that governs this network are presented and extensively evaluated. In order to evaluate these energy function the traveling salesman problem has been used. The evaluation consists of measuring (over a large number of simulations) the following parameters: number of times that the network converge to a valid solution, quality of generated solution, and the number of network update cycles to reach a solution.

1. Introduction

In a number of neural networks models an energy function is used to describe the condition of the system. This energy may be constantly changing, trapped at an energy value, or reach the system's minimum energy. Once a system has reached its minimum energy, such system is said to have arrived to its optimal state. In this case, the minimum energy state (or set of states) represents the solution to a problem which has been modeled using the neural network paradigm. Thus, the energy function of a system would help to evaluate the system performance. The neural network model proposed by Hopfield and Tank [1] is based on an electronic circuit consisting of inverting and non-inverting amplifiers, resistors, and capacitors. The circuit has an adjustable bias current to control the gain of the amplifiers. Each neuron has two outputs, excitatory and inhibitory, which can potentially be connected any neuron [1]. This paper is organized as follows. Section 2 introduces the traveling salesman problem and six different energy function approaches to solve this optimization problem. Section 3 provides the simulation steps. The behavior of different energy functions is discussed in the section 4 which includes the converge percentage, cycles, and distance. A measurement of random tour distance, optimal tour and the network results, quality of tour, is presented. Section 5 concludes this study.

2. Traveling Salesman Problem energy function

Traveling salesman problem (TSP) is defined as a salesman visiting N cities only once and coming back to the starting city having traveled a minimum distance. The importance of the TSP comes not only from the wealth of applications but also from the fact that it is typical of other problems of its genre: combinational optimization [2]. A neural networks solution to the TSP could be obtained by mapping the TSP constraints into a neural network energy function which is originated by Hopfield and Tank [1]. The Hopfield-Tank neural network model constrains this problem into a two dimension array. The rows indicate the cities, while the columns indicate the order. Each row and each column could only have one neuron turn on. The total number of on neurons is equal to the number of cities traversed.

Using different energy functions to fulfill the requirements to obtained a valid and better tour may produce different decision surfaces. This study compares the performance of those energy functions. Six energy functions which have been proposed by a number of researchers for solving TSP are presented in this study. To present these six energy functions, we use the Hopfield-Tank notation and have, therefore, transformed all the descriptions onto this notation.

2.1 Hopfield-Tank energy function

The Hopfield-Tank Energy function [1] for the TSP problem is

$$E = \frac{A}{2}\sum_{x}\sum_{i}\sum_{j\neq i} V_{xi}V_{xj} + \frac{B}{2}\sum_{i}\sum_{x}\sum_{x\neq y} V_{xi}V_{yi} + \frac{C}{2}\Big(\sum_{x}\sum_{i} V_{xi} - n\Big)^2 + \frac{D}{2}\sum_{x}\sum_{y\neq x}\sum_{i} d_{xy} V_{xi}(V_{y,i+1}+V_{y,i-1}) \qquad (1)$$

Where A, B and C are constraint terms for the neurons that are "on" in the rows, columns and the total number, respectively. The D term is used to ensured the quality of the tour by using distance constraints.

The proposed weights and bias current equations are

$$T_{xi,yj} = -A\delta_{xy}(1-\delta_{ij}) - B\delta_{ij}(1-\delta_{xy}) - C - Dd_{xy}(\delta_{j,i+1}+\delta_{j,i-1}) \qquad (2)$$

$$I_{xi} = C \times 1.5n \qquad (3)$$

where the δ is Kronecker impulse function [3]. If δ_{ij} with $i = j$, then $\delta_{ij} = 1$; otherwise, $\delta_{ij} = 0$. n indicates the number of cities. Motion equation is

0-7803-1901-X/94 $4.00 ©1994 IEEE

$$\frac{du_{xi}^{t+1}}{dt} = -\frac{u_{xi}^{t}}{\tau} + \sum_{y} \sum_{j} T_{xiyj} V_{yj} + I_{xi}$$

$$= -\frac{u_{xi}}{\tau} - A \sum_{j \neq i} V_{xj} - B \sum_{y \neq x} V_{yi} - C\left(\sum_{x} \sum_{j} V_{xj}\right) - D \sum_{y} d_{xy} (V_{y,i+1} + V_{y,i-1}) + I_{xi} \tag{4}$$

The activation function used here is

$$V_{xi} = \mathrm{Sig}(u_{xi}) = \frac{1}{2}\left(1 + \tanh\left(\frac{u_{xi}}{u0}\right)\right) = \frac{1}{1 + \exp\frac{-2u_{init}}{u0}} \tag{5}$$

Initial condition is set by

$$u_{init} = -\frac{u0}{2} \ln (N-1) \pm \text{Noise, where Noise} = 0.1 u_{init} \tag{6}$$

For the digital simulation, discrete time steps (δt) are used. The update equation is:

$$u_{xi}^{t+1} = u_{xi}^{t} + \frac{du_{xi}^{t}}{dt} \delta t \tag{7}$$

2.2 Bizzarri energy equation

Bizzarri [4] has proposed a modification to the original energy function in order to overcome some of the limitations of the networks. This limitations include low percentage convergence, sensitive parameters setting relationship. Bizzarri has added a new term to the energy function which becomes

$$E = \frac{A}{2} \sum_{x} \sum_{i} \sum_{j \neq i} V_{xi} V_{xj} + \frac{B}{2} \sum_{i} \sum_{x} \sum_{y \neq x} V_{xi} V_{yi} + \frac{C}{2} \left(\sum_{x} \sum_{i} V_{xi} - n\right)^2 + \frac{D}{2} \sum_{x} \sum_{y \neq x} \sum_{i} d_{xy} V_{xi} (V_{y,i+1} + V_{y,i-1}) + \frac{G}{2} \sum_{i} \sum_{x} (V_{xi} - 1)^2 \tag{8}$$

The introduction of the new term G was the result of observing that the excitatory terms such as A, B, and part of C, in the original Hopfield-Tank energy function produce weak force [4]. The G term could provide a large excitatory force without altering the behavior of the system [4].

The motion equation becomes

$$\frac{du_{xi}}{dt} = -\frac{u_{xi}}{\tau} - A \sum_{j \neq i} V_{xj} - B \sum_{y \neq x} V_{yi} - C\left(\sum_{x} \sum_{j} V_{xj} - n\right) - D \sum_{y} d_{xy} (V_{y,i+1} + V_{y,i-1}) - G (V_{xi} - 1) \tag{9}$$

Equation 5, 6, and 7 are used as activation function, initial condition and digital update respectively.

2.3 Kamgar-Parsi energy function

The Kamgar-Parsi [5] have proposed to split the C term constrain on whole permutation matrix into rows and columns constrains. The purpose of this change is to increase the success rate [5].

$$E = \frac{A}{2} \sum_{x} \sum_{i} \sum_{j \neq i} V_{xi} V_{xj} + \frac{B}{2} \sum_{i} \sum_{x} \sum_{y \neq x} V_{xi} V_{yi} + \frac{C}{2} \sum_{x} \left(\sum_{i} V_{xi} - 1\right)^2 + \frac{C}{2} \sum_{i} \left(\sum_{x} V_{xi} - 1\right)^2 + \frac{D}{2} \sum_{x} \sum_{y \neq x} \sum_{i} d_{xy} V_{xi} (V_{y,i+1} + V_{y,i-1}) - \sum_{x} \sum_{i} I_{xi} V_{xi} \tag{10}$$

Thus, motion equation becomes

$$\frac{du_{xi}}{dt} = -\frac{u_{xi}}{\tau} - A \sum_{j \neq i} V_{xj} - B \sum_{y \neq x} V_{yi} - C\left(\sum_{j} V_{xj} - 1\right) - C\left(\sum_{y} V_{yi} - 1\right) - D \sum_{y \neq x} d_{xy} (V_{y,i+1} + V_{y,i-1}) + I_{xi} \tag{11}$$

Equation 5, 6, and 7 are used as activation function, initial condition and digital update respectively.

2.4 Brandt et. al. energy function

Brandt, Wang, Laub, and Mitra [6] have proposed to exclude the C term by modifying the A and B terms to compensate for the excluded term. The A term represents the constraint that each row have exactly one non zero neuron, and the B term represents the constraint that each column have exactly one non zero neuron [6]. The total number of turn on neurons equal to cities number is embedding with A and B terms.

Brandt et. al. modification to Hopfield-Tank energy function is

$$E = \frac{A}{2} \sum_{x} \left(\sum_{i} V_{xi} - 1\right)^2 + \frac{B}{2} \sum_{i} \left(\sum_{x} V_{xi} - 1\right)^2 + \frac{D}{2} \sum_{x} \sum_{y \neq x} \sum_{i} d_{xy} V_{xi} (V_{y,i+1} + V_{y,i-1}) + \frac{v}{2} \sum_{x} \sum_{i} V_{xi} (1 - V_{xi}) \tag{12}$$

A new term v is introduced where $\frac{v}{2}\sum_{x}^{N}\sum_{i}^{N} V_{xi}(1-V_{xi}) = \frac{v}{2}(\frac{N^2}{2} - \sum_{x}^{N}\sum_{i}^{N}(V_{xi} - \frac{1}{2})^2)$. This term induces a gradient component that tends to force coordinate values away from $\frac{1}{2}$ [6]. Trajectories within the hypercube will tend toward the vertices. The activation function has been modified to

$$Sig(u_{xi}) = \frac{1}{1+\exp(-4\lambda\times(u_{xi} - 1/2))} \qquad (13)$$

where the λ represents the slope at the inflection point $\frac{1}{2}$.

Digital update equation Eq. 7 is utilized. For the initial condition, Brandt et. al. indicate that $V_{init} = \frac{1}{2} \pm$ Noise produces better results. Thus, from Eq. 13 we have that the initial values become

$$u_{init} = \frac{1}{2} \pm \text{Noise} \qquad (14)$$

2.5 Abe energy function

Abe [7] proposed a rearranged energy function. The original model C term may allow all the neurons on a column or row to be on. This in turn goes against the A and B terms constraints [7][8]. Due to the C term relatively weak in the original Hopfield-Tank neural networks TSP model, this term is embedded into the A and B terms. Thus, the energy function becomes

$$E = \frac{A}{2}\sum_{x}(\sum_{i} V_{xi} - 1)^2 + \frac{B}{2}\sum_{i}(\sum_{y} V_{yi} - 1)^2 + \frac{D}{2}\sum_{x}\sum_{y\neq x}\sum_{i} d_{xy} V_{xi}(V_{y,i+1} + V_{y,i-1}) \qquad (15)$$

A term and B term carry the constraint that $V_{xi} = 1$ holds for one x or i while varying them from 1 to n. D term constraint the distance.

Thus, the motion equation is

$$\frac{du_{xi}}{dt} = -\frac{u_{xi}}{\tau} - A(\sum_{i} V_{xi} - 1) - B(\sum_{y} V_{yi} - 1) - D\sum_{y\neq x} d_{xy}(V_{y,i+1} + V_{y,i-1}) + I_{xi} \qquad (16)$$

The weight equation and bias current are

$$T_{xi,yj} = -A\delta_{xy}(1-\delta_{ij}) - B\delta_{ij}(1-\delta_{xy}) - Dd_{xy}(\delta_{j,i+1} + \delta_{j,i-1}) \qquad (17)$$

$$I_{xi} = A$$

Eq. 5 as activation function is utilized and Digital update equation is similar to Eq. 7.

For the initial values, the following equation is used; the proposed relation is based on a theoretical investigation [7].

$$V_{xi} = \frac{1}{2} I + \text{Noise} \qquad (18)$$

The parameter settings are

$A = B$, $A > 2D \max_{x\,y} d_{xy}$, and each V_{xi} should be different.

2.6 Aiyer et. al. energy function

Aiyer, Niranjan, and Fallside [9] have proposed a modification on the original Hopfield-Tank energy function. By utilizing the eigen values of weights, they introduced a adjusting constant into the energy function to correct the landing error in the valid subspace. The energy function is proposed as

$$E = \frac{A}{2}\sum_{x}\sum_{i}\sum_{j\neq i} V_{xi}V_{xj} + \frac{B}{2}\sum_{i}\sum_{x}\sum_{x\neq y} V_{xi}V_{yi} + A1\sum_{x}\sum_{i} V_{xi}^2 + \frac{C}{2}((1 - \frac{2(An-A+A1)}{Cn^2})\sum_{x}\sum_{i} V_{xi} - n)^2$$
$$+ \frac{D}{2}\sum_{x}\sum_{y\neq x}\sum_{i} d_{xy} V_{xi}(V_{y,i+1} + V_{y,i-1}) \qquad (19)$$

Where A1 is added to increase one more degree of freedom to allow changes in the parameters without influencing the network behavior. The weights and bias current equations are

$$T_{xi,yj} = -A\delta_{xy}(1-\delta_{ij}) - B\delta_{ij}(1-\delta_{xy}) - 2A_1\delta_{xy}\delta_{ij} - C + \frac{2(An-A+A_1)}{n^2} - Dd_{xy}(\delta_{j,i+1} + \delta_{j,i-1}) \qquad (20)$$

$$I_{xi} = C\times n \qquad (21)$$

By adjusting the landing error, the bias current is set to its theoretical value which is C multiply with the cities number n. The activation function proposed is a piecewise linear function to mimic the sigmoid function.

$$G(u_i) = \begin{cases} 0 & \text{if } u_i \le -0.5 \\ u_i + 0.5 & \text{if } -0.5 \le u_i \le 0.5 \\ 1 & \text{if } u_i \ge 0.5 \end{cases} \quad , \qquad (22)$$

The purpose of this change is to achieve better quality of tour in less iterations due to the linearity assumption which is valid over a larger range than the hyperbolic tangent [9]. Equation 5 and 7 are used as Initial condition and digital update respectively.

3. Simulation and termination settings

In order to evaluate the different energy function, we have set a number of parameters. These parameters include a set of 10 10-city topology benchmarks [12], initial coordinates, and energy function parameters. Benchmarks 1 to 5 are uniform distribution topologies, Benchmarks 6, 7 and 8 are clusters topologies (the clustering center is generated by the uniform distribution), and Benchmarks 9 and 10 were symmetric topologies. (Benchmark 9 is symmetric in the X coordinate, while 10 (with a cluster) is symmetric in the Y coordinate.)

The conditions of our simulations steps are set as follows:

1. Generate the u_{xi} initial values according to each energy function specified value. These noise values are randomly generated and scaled to satisfy the constraints of each energy function. For each simulation, a new set of noise values is generated. The Activation^{-1} would be generated according to the specific activation function proposed for each energy function.
2. Select the energy function parameters according to the authors suggestions. Alone with the new functions, the authors have suggested the parameter values that should be used.
3. Calculate the motion equation ($\frac{du}{dt}$) for each neuron according to each energy function.
4. Apply the result of step 3 to the update equation Eq. 7 for each neuron.
5. Apply the result of step 4 to the activation function to generate the new output V_{xi} value for each neuron.
6. If termination criteria is met then the program is stopped. Otherwise steps 3 through 5 are repeated. The termination criteria is explained below.

The energy function has been partitioned into two terms

$$E = E_{penalty} + E_{min} \qquad (23)$$

The $E_{penalty}$ term is representative of constrains terms, such as A term, B term, etc. The E_{min} term is for the distance term, such as D term.

There are two conditions that cause the termination of the neural network operation.

A. Check if the network has converged to a valid tour; each column and each row contain only one neuron "on", and the total number of "on" neurons is equal to the number of cities. Check if the network energy function Eq. 23 is stable $E_{penalty} < 10^{-2}$.

B. The ceiling number of cycles has been reached. According to either a proposed ceiling cycles [4][10] or experimental observations [9] the ceiling number of cycles is assigned to each energy function. The ceiling numbers are listed in the [12]. Beyond the ceiling cycles, we would consider that the network does not converge. In test simulations, we have set these upper limits to a higher number with no visible impact on the performance of the network.

The η function [5] [12] is utilized in the simulation in order to increase the converge percentage. This function allows a converging network to reach a valid state faster.

4. Network behavior under different energy functions

In order to evaluate the impact of the proposed energy functions on the network, we have run 100 simulations per energy function and benchmark. The results are analyzed by using three measurements, namely average converge percentage, average cycles, and average distance. For the following figures, the symbols are indicating:

—□— Abe	—■— Brandt	—■— Aiyer
—◆— Bizzari	—◇— Kamgar-Parsi	—□— Hopfield

4.1 Convergence percentage

The convergence percentage provides information about the number of times that the network converge to a valid solution. Figure 1 shows this measurement for all the energy functions and the benchmarks.

From the converge percentage result, we have observed:

- Aiyer and Abe energy functions have the highest convergence percentages. For the 10 benchmarks, except benchmark 2 where Abe's energy function yields 85%, the convergence percentage is above 90%.
- For 7 out of 10 benchmarks, Aiyer energy function produces 100% convergence. Only at benchmarks 4, 5, and 10, Aiyer energy function produces 94%, 97%, and 96% respectively. Abe energy function produces 100%

convergence at benchmark 8 and 9. Both energy functions appear not to be influenced by the city topologies. (Abe energy function includes the distance in the parameters).

- Brandt energy function convergence percentage yields 100% at benchmark 5 and 8. All of convergence percentage are above 70% except at benchmarks 9 and 10 that are symmetric topologies. At symmetric topologies, Brandt energy function drops to 60% and 61%, respectively.
- Bizzarri energy function converge percentage is above 45%, except benchmark 4, 9 and 10. It appears that Bizzarri energy function is greatly affected by the symmetry of the topologies.
- Hopfield and Kamgar-Parsi energy functions have shown the lowest convergence rate. For benchmark 6, 7, and 8 (clustering topologies), Kamgar-Parsi energy function performs poorly (2%, 2%, and 1%, respectively). Both of these energy functions converge percentage below 30%.

It should be noted that Aiyer, et. al and Abe functions perform remarkable well.

4.2 Number of Cycles

The number of cycles to converge indicates the speed of the network converge to a valid tour. The faster the network converge, the lower number of cycles are consumed. Figure 2 shows the converge cycles for different energy functions and benchmarks.

From the average number of cycles to converge, we have observed

- The fastest average cycles to converge is produced by the Abe energy function. All of the average converge cycles are under 230 cycles. The number of cycles varies very little among different cities topologies.
- Hopfield energy function produces one of lowest converge cycles; in particular at benchmark 4 where only 80 cycles are needed. All the converge cycles are bellow 300 cycles except at benchmark 2 and 7 with 567 and 502 cycles, respectively.
- Kamgar-Parsi energy function's average converge cycles vary from 500 to 1100 cycles. The clustering cities topologies benchmarks increase the converge cycle factor. Two of the highest three cycles are produced in the clustering benchmark 6 and 7 with cycles 887.5 and 932, respectively.
- Bizzarri energy function needs an average of 802 cycles to converge on all cities topologies benchmarks. Due to the activating the η function at 800 cycles, the network repeatedly changed its status after 800 cycles. If the valid stationary state is reached, two cycles is the only additional cycles to converge after activating the η function. This indicates that the stationary state in this network are already reached at cycle 800. The η function activated cycles may could be decreased to reduce the cycles as long as the stationary state reached.
- Aiyer energy function consumes the second largest number of cycles to converge. Six out of ten benchmarks converged at 2002 cycles. One out of ten benchmarks is under 2002 cycles and three out of ten are slightly larger than 2002 cycles. Due to the activating the η function at 2000 cycles, this three larger cycles samples may suggest that a larger η function cycles may be necessary. This three benchmarks are 1, 2, and 4 with cycles 2006.16, 2014.31, and 2009.106, respectively.
- The Brandt energy function consumes the largest cycles to converge. Five out of ten benchmarks produced 2502 cycles to converge, and the other five benchmarks produced less than 2500 cycles (activating η function cycles). It could indicate that the η function cycles could be decreased.

4.3 Distance of average tour

One of the important parameters that need to be measured is the distance of the tour to where the network converged. This parameter is often referred as the quality of the solution. In order to fully compare the different energy functions, we have computed not only the average distance of the tours that the network has converged (C) but also the average random tour (C_{random}) and the optimal tour (C_{opt}). For the average random tour, tour distance for each benchmark has been computed by randomly constructing 10,000 tours. Figure 3 shows the quality of the tour by utilizing the following proposed equation [11]:

$$\text{Quality of tour} = \frac{C_{random} - C}{C_{random} - C_{opt}} \tag{24}$$

From Figures 3, we have observed that:

- Every energy function produces a better tour than the randomly selected tour.
- The best quality of tour is usually produced by at Aiyer energy function. There are only 3 benchmarks where Aiyer energy function is not the best; however, it is among the top. The worst tour is usually produced by Kamgar-Parsi energy function. At benchmark 6, 7 and 8 the quality of the tour is around 0.2.
- Bizzarri, and Brandt energy functions have good quality of the tours above 0.75 on every benchmark. Bizzarri energy function produces 5 out of 10 benchmarks above 0.9 quality; all the benchmarks, however, are above or about 0.8. Brandt energy function produces 5 out of 10 benchmarks above 0.9 quality, except by benchmark 6 that has 0.76, all the other benchmarks have a quality of 0.8 or higher.

- Hopfield energy function produces 2 out of 10 above 0.9 except by benchmarks 3 and 4 where the quality is 0.76 and 0.57, respectively, all the other benchmarks have a quality of 0.8 or higher.
- Kamgar-Parsi energy function produces quality above 0.4, except benchmarks 6, 7, and 8 where the quality is 0.209, 0.186 and 0.221, respectively. It appears that Kamgar-Parsi energy function is impacted by the cluster city topologies.

5. Concluding Remarks

In this paper we have described and evaluated six different energy functions that have been proposed for a neural network based on Hopfield-Tank model. This neural network is dedicated to the solution of optimal problems in particular the traveling salesman problem. In order to evaluate the energy functions 10 distinct benchmarks were created. The energy functions were evaluated by the tours they produce; specifically, convergence percentage, quality of the tour, number of cycles to reach a solution. In our study the energy function proposed by Aiyer et. al. provides the best performance (i.e. high percentage convergence and short distance tours).

References

[1] J. J. Hopfield and D. W. Tank, "Neural Computation of Decisions in Optimization Problems," *Biological Cybernetics*, Vol. 52, pp. 141 - 152, 1985.

[2] E. L. Lawler, J. K. Lenstra, A. H. G. Rinnooy Kan, and D. B. Shmoys, *The Traveling Salesman Problem*, pp. 1 - 2, John Wiley & Son press, 1985.

[3] A. H. Gee, S. V. B. Aiyer, and R. W. Prager, "An analytical framework for optimizing neural networks," *Neural Networks*, Vol. 6, pp. 79 - 97, 1993.

[4] A. R. Bizzarri, "Convergence properties of a modified Hopfield-Tank Model," *Biological Cybernetics*, Vol. 64, pp. 293 - 300, 1991.

[5] B. Kamgar-Parsi, and B. Kamgar-Parsi, "On Problem Solving with Hopfield Neural Networks," *Biological Cybernetics*, Vol. 62, pp. 415 - 423, 1990.

[6] R. D. Brandt, Y. Wang, A, J. Laub, and S. K. Mitra, "Alternative Networks for Solving the Traveling Salesman Problem and List-Matching Problem," *IEEE International Conference on Neural Networks*, Vol. II, pp. 333 - 340, 1988.

[7] S. Abe, "Theories on the Hopfield Neural Networks," *IEEE Proc. IJCNN89*, Vol. I, pp. 557 - 564, 1989.

[8] D. E. Van den Bout, T. K. Miller, "A Traveling Salesman Objective Function that Works," *IEEE International Conference on Neural Networks*, pp. II.299 - II.303, 1988.

[9] S. V. B. Aiyer, M. Niranjan, and F. Fallside, "A Theoretical Investigation into the Performance of the Hopfield Model," *IEEE Transactions on the Neural Networks*, Vol. 1, No. 2, pp. 204 - 215, June, 1990.

[10] G. W. Wilson and G. S. Pawly, "On the Stability of the Traveling Salesman Problem Algorithm of Hopfield and Tank," *Biological Cybernetics*, Vol. 58, pp. 63 - 70, 1988.

[11] P. W. Protzel, D. L. Palumbo, and M. K. Arras, "Performance and Fault-Tolerance of Neural Networks for Optimization," *IEEE Transactions on the Neural Networks*, Vol. 4, No. 4, pp. 600 - 614, July, 1993.

[12] W. Lin, J. G. Delgado-Frias, G. G. Pechanek, and S. Vassiliadis, "Energy Functions for a Neural Network Model for Optimization Problems: Evaluation and Eigen Value Analysis," *IBM Technical Report*, IBM Austin, December, 1993.

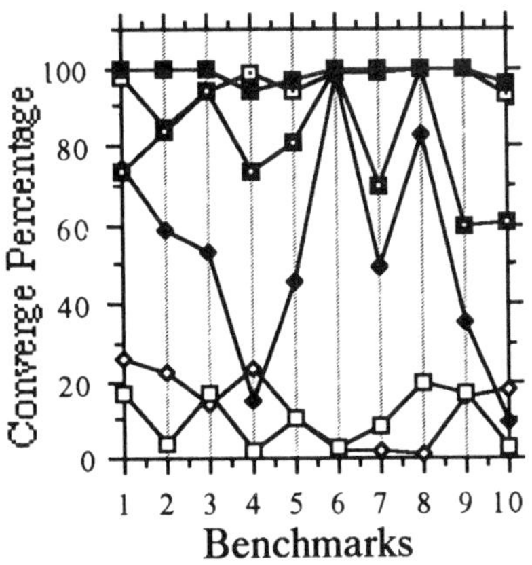

Figure 1. Different Energy function performance on the average converge percentage for each benchmarks

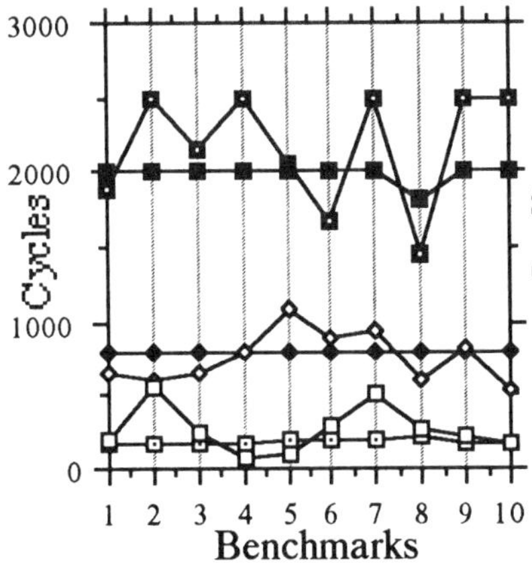

Figure 2. Different Energy function average converge cycles for each benchmarks

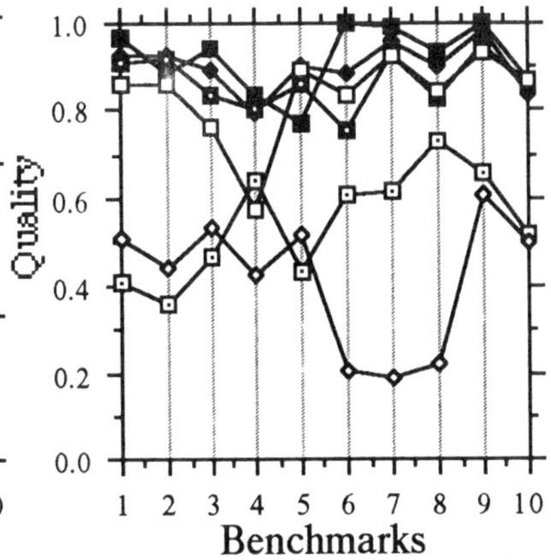

Figure 3. Different Energy function produced quality of tour for each benchmark

INTENTIONALLY LEFT BLANK

An Investigation of the Precision Impact on the Hopfield-Tank Neural Network Model for the TSP

Wei Lin+ José G. Delgado-Frias+ Stamatis Vassiliadis* Gerald G. Pechanek†

+Dept of Electrical Engineering
State University of New York
Binghamton, NY 13902-600

*IBM Corporation
AWS Division
Austin, Texas

†IBM Corporation
Triangle Research Park
North Carolina

Abstract

An advantage of the use of neural networks the utilization of a number of processing units to obtain the solution in short time. In the design of a neural network, different bit precisions alter the computer architecture and organization on design. In this paper, we study the impact of the precision by using the Hopfield-Tank Neural Network model for the Traveling Salesman Problem (TSP). In order to simulate the TSP problem using Hopfield-Tank model, we have used a number of previous studies to determine some of the required parameters. To investigate the influence of the precision, we have simulated the TSP problem in a MIPS R3000. We have considered in our investigation: five different bit precisions (8- 16- 24- 32- and double precision mantissas), three values of the sigmoid generation parameters, and convergency within 1000 neuron update cycles. We have run a total 7,080 simulations for the established benchmark in the MIPS-3000 machines; the simulation results are extensively discussed. Additionally, two novel approaches to measure the performance of the network, namely the average network performance and computational efficiency, are introduced and used in the evaluation of the performance of the model. Further information extraction is done by using *Dempster's rule of combination* for the average network performance and computational efficiency. Precision's influence and its boundary are provided in the conclusion.

1 Introduction

Hopfield and Tank have proposed a neural network approach to solve the traveling salesman problem (TSP) [1]. This approach is usually referred to as the Hopfield-Tank Model. The objective in the traveling salesman problem is to find a round-trip with short distance that visits all the cities of the problem only once. To map a N-city TSP, the Hopfield-Tank model uses a N^2 neuron array. In this array the columns stand for the sequence of cities to be visited and the rows represent the order in which these cities are visited. If the city is visited then the corresponding neuron is turned on, this is denoted by a logical "1". On the other hand, if the city is not visited the corresponding neuron is turned off, denoted by a logical "0".

To accomplish the desired result, the Hopfield-Tank model [1] uses the following equation:

$$\frac{du_{xi}}{dt} = -\frac{u_{xi}}{t} - A\sum_{j\neq i} V_{xj} - B\sum_{y\neq x} V_{yi} - C\sum_{x}\sum_{j}(V_{xj} - n) - D\sum_{y} d_{xy}(V_{y,i+1} + V_{y,i-1}) \quad (1)$$

where u_{xi} is the previous cycle neuron's input voltage, V_{xi} is the new neuron's output voltage, t is the RC time delay which could be set as 1, the A term is inhibitory connections within each row, the B term is inhibitory connections within each column, the C term is global inhibition which is the inhibitory of total turned on neurons, n is the number of cities, and the D term is the data term for the distance. The Sigmoid function:

$$V_{xi} = F_g(u_{xi}) = \frac{1}{2}\left[1 + \tanh\frac{u_{xi}}{u_0}\right] \quad (2)$$

where u_0 is the sigmoid factor [7].

Although Hopfield and Tank have been successful in their investigation of a 10-city problem, a number of researchers have not encountered their success [2, 3, 4, 5]. In particular, Wilson and Pawley have used a digital simulation of the continuous function in Eq. (1) using the following equation [3] before the application of the sigmoid generator.

$$(u_{xi})^{t+1} = (u_{xi})^t + \left(\left(\frac{du_{xi}}{dt}\right)\delta t\right) \quad (3)$$

where δt is the step size.

In order to investigate the precision and number representation impact on the Hopfield-Tank neural network model, we have developed a simulation program to vary the machine precision to the following number of bits: 8, 16, 24, 32, and double format. In addition to evaluate the influence of the sigmoid in the convergence of the network three different values of sigmoid factor (u_0) were chosen (namely, 0.005, 0.02, and 0.07). To study the Hopfield-Tank neural network model, sets of eight city positions for the TSP were created. An similar simulation steps and parameters setting are provided [7].

0-7803-1901-X/94 $4.00 ©1994 IEEE

This paper has been organized as follows. Section 2 provides the simulation results in terms of percentage of convergence, tour distance and number of cycles for each bit-precision. Overall performance of the Network is discussed in the section 3 with two different measurements, namely average performance and computational efficiency. In section 4, the performance and precision relation is provided by combining section 3 factors. Section 5 concludes this paper.

2 Simulation results

We have identified three estimation parameters to evaluate performance of the model. These are: percentage of convergence, number of cycles taken to converge to a valid tour, and distance of the tour. These estimation parameters are discussed in detail below. The symbols used in all the graphs are shown next which indicate the associated benchmarks.

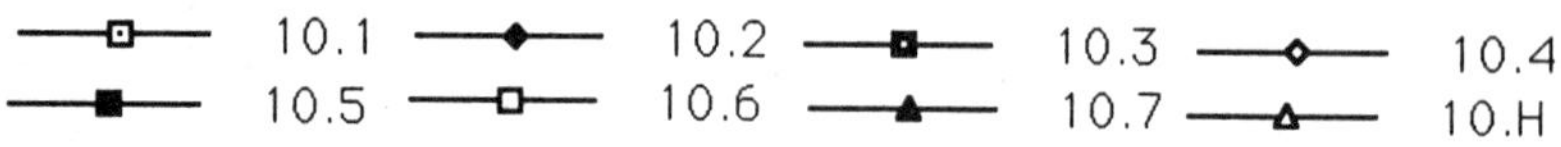

2.1 Percentage of convergence

The percentage of convergence is the number of times that a city-problem (with a fixed sigmoid and varying parameters) provides a valid solution within 1000 cycles over the total number of attempts. From the experiments, it was observed that the behavior of the network may not be easily predictable, as the convergence does not seem to follow any apparent pattern. Figure 1 show the percentage of convergence for different city tours, bit precisions, and sigmoid parameters. From these experiments, we have calculated the percentage of convergence. From 24 groups of experiments (3×8: 3 sigmoid factors, 8 10-city benchmarks), it was observed that eight-bit precision provides the poorest performance in 45.83% (11/24) of the cases. Table 1 provides a summary of the performance of the five bit-precisions.

Table 1. Performance by precision

Bit precision	8	16	24	32	double
performance	45.83%	95.8%	87.5%	95.8%	83.3%

The city-problem 10.6 (10-city TSP) performs well in all the simulations. The percentage of convergence tends to vary greatly from one city-problem to another. We decided to classify the TSPs into well-behaved and non-well-behaved city-problems. A well-behaved city problem is loosely defined as the TSP that has a large percentage of convergence (larger than or equal to 50%). Tables 2 provides a list of well behaved TSPs for 10-city problems.

Table 2. Well-behaved 10-city benchmark

sig	MIPS-3000				
0.005	10.2	10.4	10.5	10.6	10.Hop
0.02	10.2	10.4	10.5	10.6	10.Hop
0.07	10.2	10.4	10.5	10.6	

Convergence alone may not be enough to evaluate the network performance since network could have converged to a valid tour with large distance to travel.

2.2 Distance of the tour

The average distance of valid tours, that the model has converged to, was computed. This measure provides information on the "goodness" of the tour that the network converged to. The best solution will be the tour that gives the minimum distance. Figure 2 depict these results.

From these experiments it was observed:

- The average short distance for most of the 10-city TSP is obtained with the sigmoid factor of 0.07 with only two exceptions. This could be interpreted as the influence of the sigmoid values on the selection of the path.
- No single bit precision gives the best short average distance. It was observed however that for the non-well-behaved cities the short distance tends to be located at a bit-precision smaller than or equal to 24-bit. This observation points out that there may be some influence of the bit precision over the distance on non-well-behaved TSPs. However, no conclusive evidence can be found.

2.3 Number of cycles to converge

The number of cycles to converge is the amount of iterations that the model takes in order to converge to a valid tour. This parameter provide information on convergence speed which can be related to the computational requirements. The TSP that has the lowest number in this measurement would be preferred over others, since this would require less computational effort. A low number of cycles does not ensure that the best tour has been found. The average number of cycles was computed from the experiments. The results have been plotted as shown in Figure 3. Although no evidence of a common pattern is apparent with this parameter, it was observed from the experiments that:

- The lowest average number of cycles for the 10-city TSP is obtained at either 8-bit or 16-bit precision (see Table 3). There are three exceptions: city-1 with sigmoid 0.02 and 24-bit precision, city-4 with 0.02 sigmoid and 24-bit precision, and city-5 with .005 sigmoid and 32-bit precision.

Table 3. Lowest average cycles occur among precisions in MIPS 3000

Bit precision	8	16	24	32	double
percentage	50%	37.5%	8.33%	4.16%	0%

- No single sigmoid value always gives the lowest number of cycles for a given precision. However, for the well-behaved problems a 0.02 sigmoid gives the lowest number of cycles in 67% of the benchmarks.

3 Overall performance of the Network

In order to evaluate the overall performance of the neural TSP network, we have included two new measurements. These are the average performance on the three measurements (namely convergence, distance and cycles) and the computational efficiency on these three measurements. Before defining and computing the overall performance measurements, it is necessary to define the parameters that are used. These parameters are: percentage of convergence, distance ratio, and cycle ratio. The convergence percentage (c_p) is used as it was defined in the section 3; this parameter tends to be closer to one as the convergence improves. The distance ratio (dr) refers to the relation between the optimal distance and the actual distance of the tour.

$$d_r = \frac{\text{optimal distance}}{\text{average distance}}$$

where optimal distance is defined [5] as

$$\text{Optimal distance} = 0.708\sqrt{NA}$$

where N is the number cities and A is the area on which the cities are distributed. The distance ratio (d_r) is closer to one as the distance of the tour is closer to the optimal distance.

The cycle ratio (c_r) is defined as

$$c_r = \frac{\text{Time out - Average cycle} + 1}{\text{Time out}}$$

where time out cycles for this application is set to 1000 which refers to the number of cycles at which the computation is finished (called time out). As the average cycles tends to remain small the cycle ratio tends to be closer to one.

3.1 Average performance

This measurement gives the average of the three parameters. The average performance is expressed as

$$P = \text{average performance} = \frac{c_p + d_r + c_r}{3}$$

P is computed for all the benchmarks.

The 10-city problem shows the following features:

- In a well-behaved city-problem, the 96.6% average performance of the model are all above 0.65, with exception of 8 bit precision in 10.2 benchmark sigmoid equal to 0.005.
- For the well-behaved city-problem, the average performance are stable after 32 bit precision. The performance tends to be evenly distribution.
- For all the non-well-behaved city-problems with different bit precision, the average performance is below 0.65.
- The well-behaved city problems have their worst performance at 8-bit precision. The exceptions are: 10.5 at sigmoid factor 0.005, and 10.4 at sigmoid factor 0.07.
- The Average performance for the non-well-behaved tends to be similar for different bit precisions. Slightly better performance is observed at 8-bit precision. This is due to the number of cycles that is usually small for 8-bit precision non-well-behaved problems.

Figures 4 (a) to 6 (a) show the average performance for the 10-city benchmarks.

3.2 Computational efficiency

This gives a measurement of the computational efficiency of the three parameters. The computation efficiency is expressed as

$$EF = \text{Computational efficiency} = (c_p \times d_r \times c_r)$$

A large value of EF is obtained when the three value of c_p, d_r, and c_r are very similar; this in turn would provide information about the best and well balanced network. EF is computed for all the benchmarks. Figures 4 (b) to 6 (b) plot efficiency vs precision.

• It was observed that the non-well-behaved problems always have low performance.

4. Network Performance

An overall network performance information in terms of percision can be obtained by *Dempster's rule of combination* [6]. In general, evidence obtained in the same context from two different sources can be combined in several ways. The standard way [6] can be expressed by following equation.

$$M_{12}(A) = \frac{\sum_{B \cap C = A} M_1(B) M_2(C)}{1-K}$$

where $K = \sum_{B \cap C = \emptyset} M_1(B) M_2(C)$, and $M_{12}(\emptyset) = 0$.

Well-behaved benchmarks' EF and P are considered as $M_1(B)$ and $M_2(C)$ with different focus on the network performance from the same context (namely, cycles to converge, converge percentage, and converge distance). The $M_{12}(A)$ is extracting the further information of precisions from different sigmoid factors and benchmarks in terms of EF and P.

Figure 7 plots the result. From the operations, we observe:

- The poorest performance is at 8-bit precision. This may be due to error introduced by the small word size.
- 16-bit precision performs the best. However, the results are not always consistent.
- 24-bit precision has a poor performance as compared with 16, 32 and 56 bit precision.
- Bit precision 32 and 56 is a stable region with performance evenly distribution.

5. Concluding Remarks and Future Work

We have run a large number of simulations of the traveling salesman problem (TSP) using the Hopfield-Tank neural network model. From our investigation we can draw the following conclusions:

- Bit precision affects the network performance. In this experiment, the bit precision influences the network behavior; however, the 32-bit and 56-bit precisions perform better than the others. This indicates the boundary of precision may be considered at 32 bits.
- For some city benchmarks the model performs well. For well-behaved benchmarks the average performance is usually higher than 65%
- Non-well-behaved benchmarks consistently perform poorly under most of the conditions.

This study provides information both for the precision impact for Hopfield-Tank neural network and optimization network hardware designing. In a further study, the direction would be to explore more energy functions which utilize Hopfield-Tank type of neural network and provide better results [8].

References

[1] J. J. Hopfield and D. W. Tank, "Neural Computation of Decision in Optimization Problems," *Biological Cybernetics*, Vol. 52, pp. 141-152, 1985.

[2] R. Bizzarri, "Convergence Properties of a Modified Hopfield-Tank Model," *Biological Cybernetics*, Vol. 64 pp. 293-300, 1991.

[3] G. V. Wilson and G. S. Pawley, "On the Stability of the Traveling Salesman Problem Algorithm of Hopfield and Tank," *Biological Cybernetics*, Vol. 58, pp. 63-70, 1988.

[4] B. Kamgar-Parsi and B. Kamgar-Parsi, "On Problem solving with Hopfield Neural Networks," *Biological Cybernetics*, Vol. 62, pp. 415-423A, 1990.

[5] A. B. Kahng, "Traveling Salesman Heuristics and Embedding Dimension in the Hopfield Model," *IEEE International Joint Conference on Neural Networks*, pp. I513-I520, 1989

[6] G. J. Klir and T. A. Folger, *Fuzzy Sets, Uncertainty, and Information*, pp. 110-118, Prentice Hall, 1988.

[7] W. Lin, J. G. Delgado-Frias, G. G. Pechanek, and S. Vassiliadis, "Machine and Bit Precision Influence on the Hopfield-Tank Model for the TSP", *IJCNN '93 International Joint Conference on Neural Networks*, pp. 1516-1519, Nagoya, Japan, October 1993.

[8] W. Lin, J. G. Delgado-Frias, G. G. Pechanek, and S. Vassiliadis, "Energy functions for a Neural Network Model for Optimization Problems : Evaluation and Eigen Value Analysis," *IBM Technical Report*, IBM Austin, December, 1993.

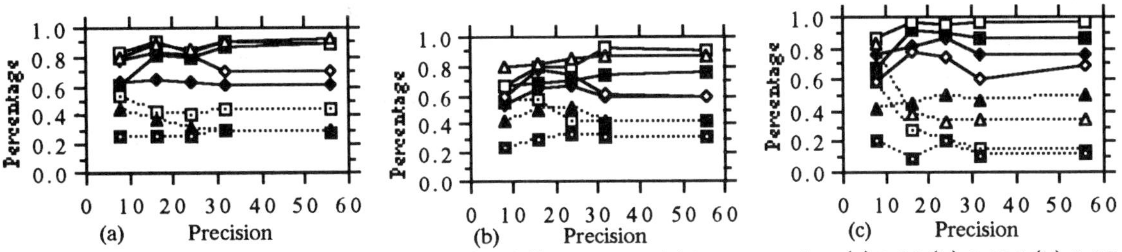

Figure 1. MIPS-3000, converge percentage, for different sigmoid factor equal to (a) 0.02 (b) 0.005 (b) 0.07

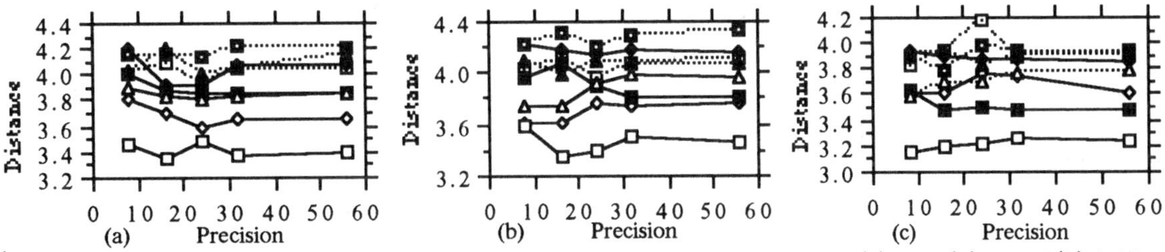

Figure 2. MIPS-3000, average distance, for different sigmoid factor equal to (a) 0.02 (b) 0.005 (b) 0.07

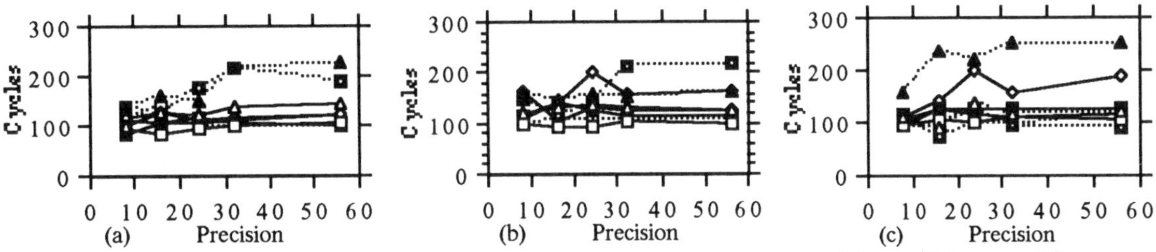

Figure 3. MIPS-3000, average cycle, for different sigmoid factor equal to (a) 0.02 (b) 0.005 (b) 0.07

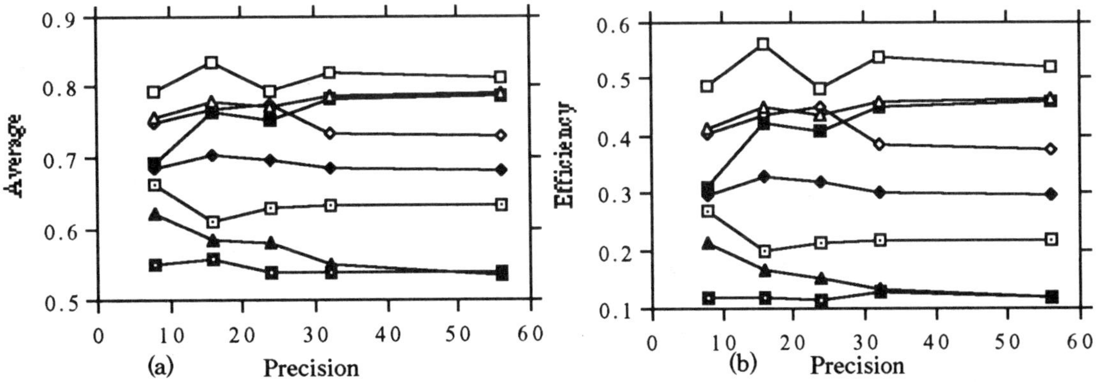

Figure 4. MIPS-3000 at sigmoid factor=0.02 (a) Average performance (b) Computation Efficiency

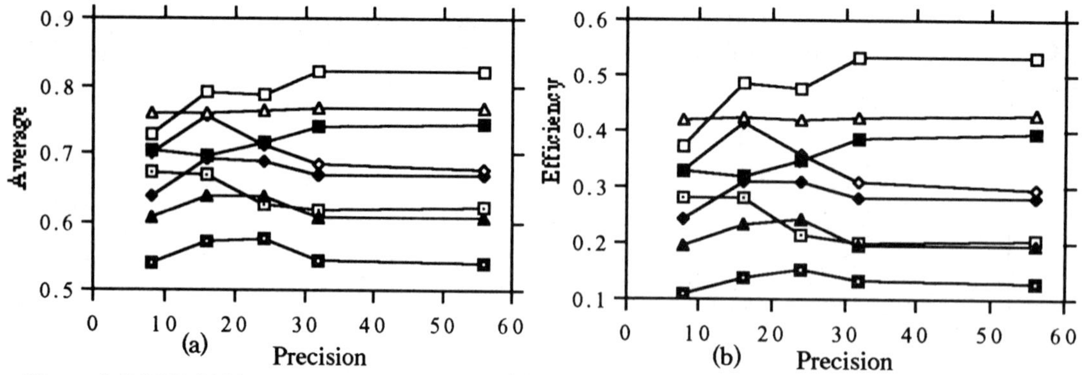

Figure 5. MIPS-3000 at sigmoid factor=0.005 (a) Average performance (b) Computation Efficiency

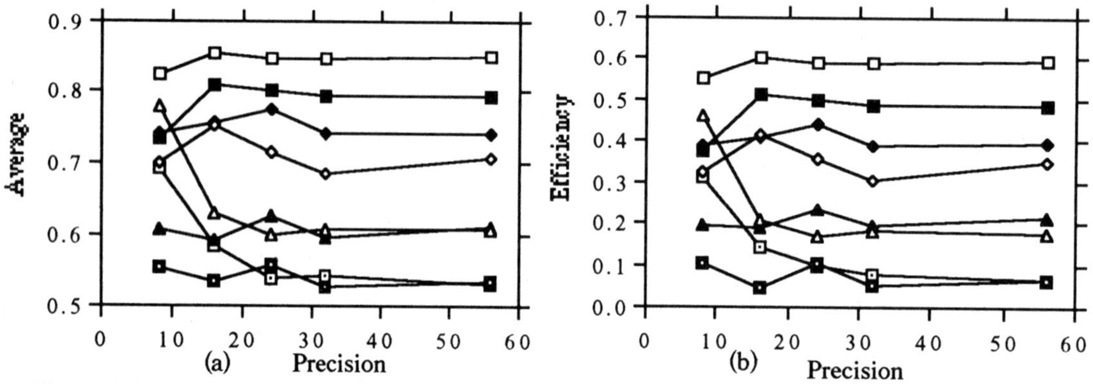

Figure 6. MIPS-3000 at sigmoid factor=0.07 (a) Average performance (b) Computation Efficiency

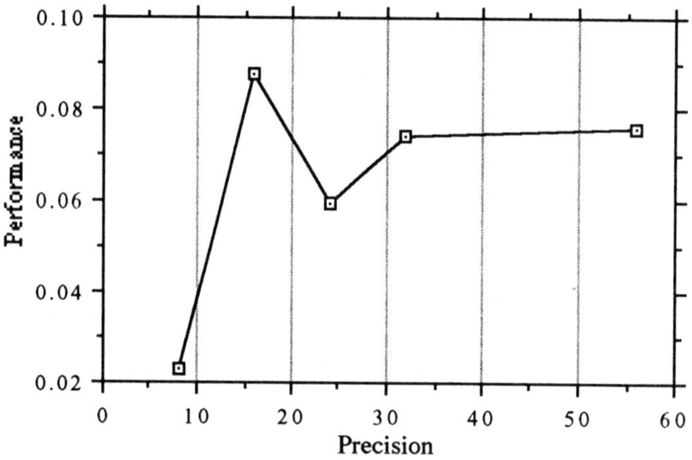

Figure 7. MIPS-3000 Performance vs Precision

Solving Traveling Salesman Problem by Real Space Renormalization Technique

Usami Yoshiyuki
Institute of Physics, Kanagawa University
Rokkakubashi 3-27-1, Kanagawa-ku Yokohama 221, Japan

ABSTRACT

Real space renormalization technique is applied, which is used in the study of critical phenomenon, to obtain approximate solution of traveling salesman problem. In the procedure we prepare in advance the basic optimized paths for 2x2 discrete space and store those as data set. In actual calculation considered space covering all cities is divided into square cell of the size 1/2x1/2, 1/4x1/4, 1/8x1/8..., step by step, and representative point is settled at the center of each cell, if there are cities in the area of cell. Thus all of position and path become discrete, finding shorter tour of TSP can be easily and quickly accomplished only by calling corresponding optimized path from data set.

Computer simulation was performed to the case of 532 USA cities data. On an average 37% longer path for 532 cities than the optimal one was obtained. The shortest tour among 20 different initial conditions was 29% longer one. Computational time was 0.0 sec by 60Mips workstation Sparc Classic. The results lead us to be able to compute several hundred cities TSP in real time with the use of personal computer.

Introduction

Traveling salesman problem has been drawn attention as an application problem of neural network theory in these several years since Hopfield applied his theory to this problem. He and Tank showed in their article that Hopfield's method could solve 30 cities TSP in short computational time with comparatively good accuracy. Many researchers have discussed about merit and demerit of Hopfield's model, however, following studies found difficulty in many aspect on solving TSP by this method [1-3]. On the other hand traveling salesman problem itself has been studied for many decades in both exact and approximate solving ways. Several works are summarized in Miller and Pekny's article[4], and famous data set of cities are collected by G.Reinelt and stored in FTP site *softlib.rice.edu*, etc.[5]. In relation to this work Padberg and Rinaldi obtained the optimal tour of 532 USA cities set by exact method with 6 hours by the super computer CYBER-205 in 1987[6]. Recently Matsuyama developed new approximate method which can apply to such large scale problem, and obtained good result in 3.7% accuracy for 532 cities USA data set with 2.8 hours by 10 Mips work station [7,8]. Generally, local exchange method for randomly chosen cities, or plus simulated annealing method is useful way to obtain approximate solution [9,10]. This method is very useful as in Matsuyma's work, 4.8% longer tour than the optimal tour of 532 USA cities set can be obtained in 20 minutes by 10 Mips work station. An approach to obtain approximate solution within very short time was developed by Bartholdi and Platzman named as space filling curves method [11]. Only several seconds are needed with the use of personal computer to calculate several hundred cities problem by this original algorithm. Note that Hopfield's type neural network theory has not been useful to solve such large cities problems by several reasons [1-3].

In this article we propose new method for solving large scale symmetric traveling salesman problem within quite short computer time. The idea is based on so called real space renormalization method which is used to study critical phenomena in statistical physics. By the use of this proposed algorithm, 532 cities problem could be solved in 0.0 sec with 37% accuracy by 60Mips workstation. Furthermore there are possibilities to calculate more quickly and more accurately, if we develop this algorithm further and build original hard architecture. In the following section we present the method and show an example of result applied to 532 USA cities set.

Algorithm

The whole calculation for solving TSP is divided into two parts in the algorithm as follows:

1. **Preparing template of basic cells.**
   Calculate optimized paths of 2x2 basic cells and save those as data set in advance before going into calculation of TSP.
2. **Allocate the templates for actual cells.**
   Divide considered space covering all cities into square cells with the size of 1/2x1/2, 1/4x1/4, 1/8x1/8, ... , and representative point is settled in each cell. For each cell, corresponding optimized path is called from data set.

We start to explain the algorithm in detail from procedure 1.

Procedure 1. Preparing template of basic cells.

Procedure 1 is a step preparing optimized paths of 2x2 basic cells. Let square space divide into the same 4 mini cells and call the whole square as basic cell. For the basic cell representative points can be settled at the center of each mini cells as black circles shown in Fig.1. White circles shown in Fig.1 are examples of edge points to neighborhood cells, which are incoming point into the cell or outgoing point.

All possible optimized paths are calculated, which connect incoming point through representative points and outgoing point in discrete space. The data is stored as data set, and will be called in actual calculation of TSP. Examples of those are shown as Fig.2.

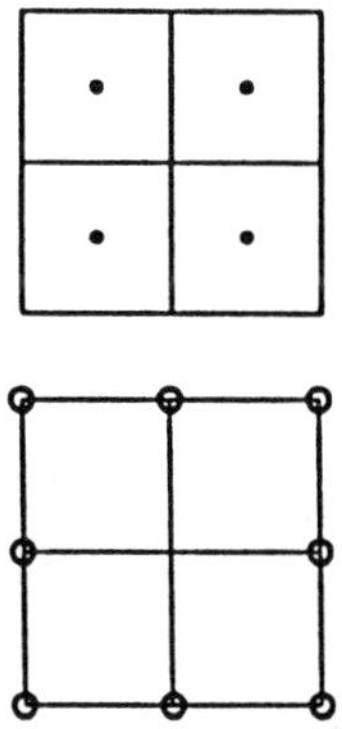

Fig.1
Basic Cell. Black circles in the upper square shows possible positions of representative point. White circles in the bottom are the ones for edge point.

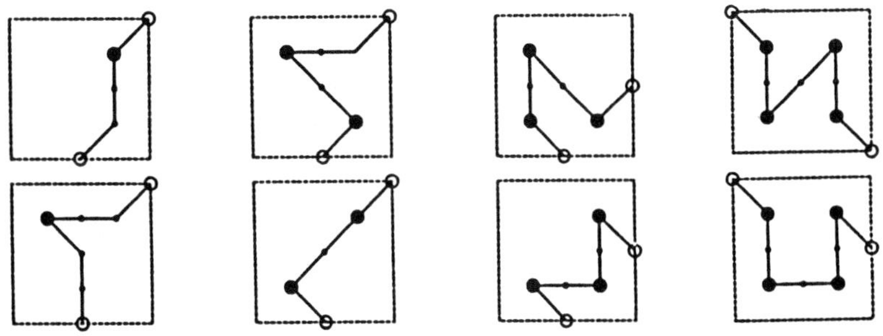

Fig.2
Examples of optimized paths connecting edge points and representative points in discrete space. Paths of all possible configuration are calculated and stored as data set.

Procedure 2. **Allocate the templates for actual cells.**

Procedure 2 is actual calculation. At first, square space covering all cities is set, and divided into 1/2x1/2 square cells as left hand figure of Fig.3.

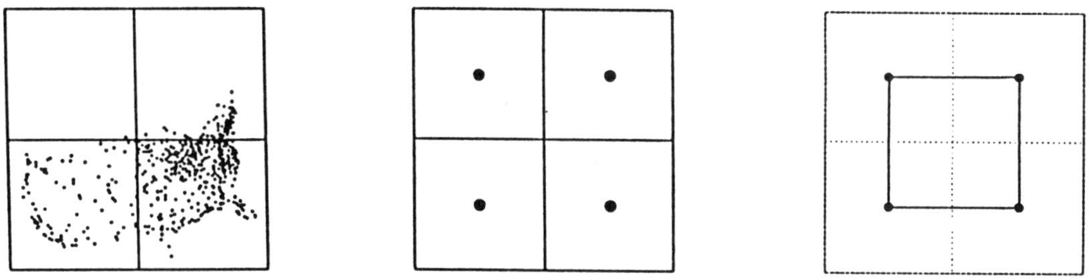

Fig.3 First step of actual calculation of renormalization process.

Fig.3 is an example applied to USA 532 cities set[6]. Now there are four mini cells. In a mini cell, if there are cities in the area of mini cell, representative point is settled in the center of the cell regardless of the number of cities. If there is not , no representative point is settled. Finally representative points are connected as right hand figure of Fig.3. Thus the first step of calculation is completed.

Next, dividing process is repeated again. Each mini cell is divided into 1/2x1/2 mini cells, i.e., 1/4x1/4 to the original square, now there are 16 cells as left hand figure of Fig.4. For each cell existence of cities in the area is checked, namely, if there are cities in a cell, representative point is settled regardless of the number of cities. Then optimized paths are called from data set and allocated, which connect edge points and all representative points in each cell. When the allocation process for all cells are completed, closed path connecting all representative points is automatically obtained as left hand side figure of Fig.4.

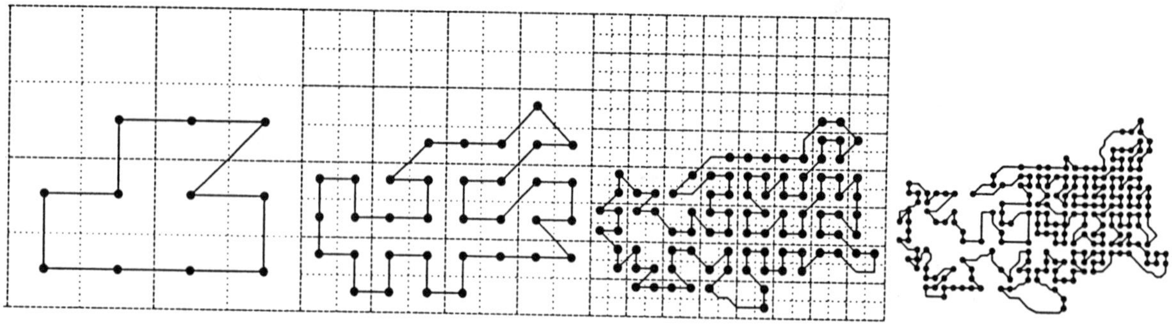

Fig.4 Renormalization process applied to 532 USA cities set.

Similar idea, namely, dividing space step by step and checking a certain quantity in coarse graining process, has been developed to study critical phenomenon in statistical mechanics. The method is called real space renormalization group technique, so we also use this name in this work. Actually the procedure looks like very similar to the method of real space renormalization group used in the study of fractal or percolation. We found the effectiveness of the method for TSP throughout this work as mentioned later.

The dividing space process and allocation of optimal path for each cell, renormalization process in short, are repeated several times in the same way as Fig.4, and stopped at adequate size. Final calculation searching shorter tour connecting actual position of cities is accomplished as follows: In the smallest cell at the final renormalization step there are only several cities. Error is not so large, if path is found in the way of connecting nearest cities from edge point step by step. So this method is applied to the final stage of the calculation. At the end of all procedures, tour connecting all cities is obtained as Fig.5.

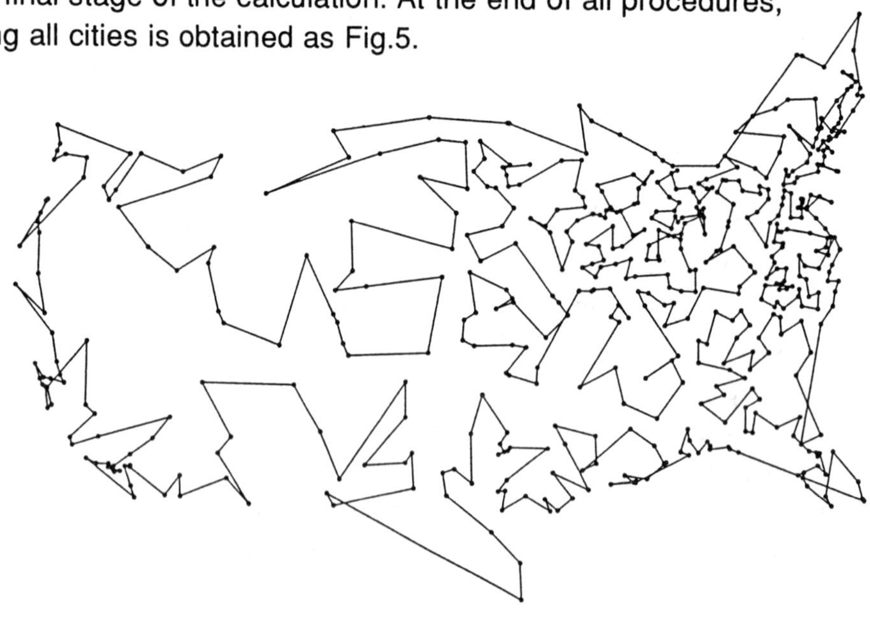

Fig.5 Final result obtained by the present method for 532 USA cities set.

Result

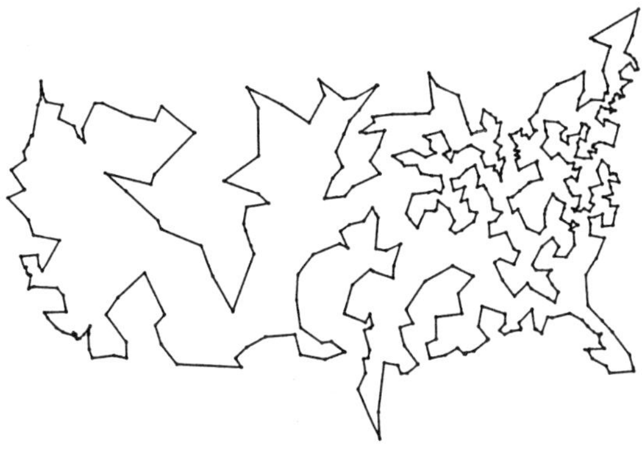

Fig.6 The optimal tour of 532 USA cities set by Padberg and Rinaldi[6].

Computational time solving 532 USA cities TSP was very short, 0.0 sec which was measured by UNIX "time" command of 60Mips workstation Sparc Classic. This computer shows almost similar performance to Sparc Station2, and slightly faster than 66Mz 486DX2 PC/AT IBM compatible machine. On an average 37% longer solution than the optimal one [6] was obtained for 20 different initial conditions.

One remarkable characteristic of the method is that there is no parameter at all in the algorithm. Only initial condition, whichi is ralative location of the initial square framework to original position of cities, is controllable. So 20 different locations of square framework to cities set were calculated and averaged in this work. The shortest tour was 29% longer and the longest was 40% longer than the optimal one among these 20 examples.

The optimal tour of Padberg and Rinaldi's is shown as Fig.6, which is taken from the data of their article [6]. They spent 6 hours to solve it rigorously by super computer. It can not be said that 30-40% error is small, however, if we need rough estimation of tour within quite short time such as real time, the present method might be useful. As mentioned in Introduction, Matsuyama developed algorithm obtaining 3.7% longer solution by 10 Mips work station [7]. Table listed below is the present result together with the data of his article.

Method	Time	Accuracy	Computer
* Present method	0.0 sec	37% (29%)	60Mips workstation
* Matsuyama's method	2.8 hours	3.7%	10Mips workstation
* Simulated Annealing[7,9]	20min	9.2%	10Mips workstation
* Durbin-Wilshaw's method[7,12]	170 hours	34%	10Mips workstation

Table 1. Simulation result based on the present algorithm applied to 532 USA cities set[6]. The other data are taken from Matsuyama's work[7]. Computational time of the present result was calculated by standard UNIX "time" command. In the table "37% accuracy" represents averaged value of 20 different initial conditions. "(29%) accuracy" represents the shortest tour among these 20 initial conditions.

Acknowledgments

We are studying about this algorithm further, and have a plan to publish those data. Request of information is convenient to ask to author's E-mail Address "princess@cc.kanagawa-u.ac.jp".

The Author gratefully acknowledges helpful information from Mr. A.Yoshikawa, Prof. M. Kubo and Prof. Y.Matsuyama. This work was financially supported by Tateisi Science and Technology Foundation. The author is grateful for this support.

Finally, note that author's name in the first page is written in the original manner; *Usami* (Family Name) *Yoshiyuki* (Own Name).

References

[1] G.V.Wilson and G.S.Pawley," On the Stability of the Traveling Salesman Problem Algorithm of Hopfield and Tank", Biol.Cybern.,**68**,(1988)63-70.

[2] K.P.Behzad and B Kamgar-Parsi, "On Problem Solving with Hopfield Neural Networks", Biol,Cybern., **62**(1990)415-423.

[3] K.Hinozawa, Y.Uchiyama and N.Sonehara, "An Inspection of Hopfield-Tank Type Neural Networks", Trans.IEICE, **J76-**D-2,7(1993)1471-1474. (*in Japanese*).

[4] D.L.Miller and J.F.Pekny. "Exact Solution of Large Asymmetric Traveling Salesman Problem, Science **251**,754-760(1991).

[5] TSP data sets can be obtained from library collected by Gerhard Reinelt, E-mail reinelt%augsopt.Uni-Augsburg.DE@relay.cs.net, or Robert E.Bixby E-Mail bixby@ rice edu.

[6] M.Padberg and G.Rinaldi, "Optimization of a 532-city Symmetric Traveling Salesman Problem by Branch and Cut", Oper.Res.Lett.,**6**(1987)1-7. M.Padberg and G.Rinald, addendum, *ibid*,9(1990)353.

[7] Y.Matsuyama,"Self-Organizing Neural Networks and Various Euclidean Traveling Salesman Problem", System and Computers in Japan **23**(1992)101-111. This article was also published as Japanese version; Y.Matsuyama, "Self-Organizing Neural Networks and Various Euclidian Traveling Salesman Problems", Trans.IEICE,**J74**-D-2,3(1991)416-425 (*in Japanese*).

[8] Y.Matsuyama and M.Kobayashi, "Minimum Learning Autonomous Cost Adjustment", Proc. IJCNN92 Beijing **1** (1992)326-334. Y.Matsuyama, "Self-Organization via Competition, Cooperation and Categorization Applied to Extended Vehicle Routing Problems", Proc. IJCNN-91-Seattle, **1**(1991)385-390.

[9] W.H.Press *et al.* "Numerical Recipes in C", Cambridge University Press(1988).

[10] S.Lin and B.Kernighan, " An effective heuristic algorithm for the traveling salesman problem", Operations Research, **21(**1973)498-516.

[11] J.J.Bartholdi III and L.K.Platzman, "An O(N log N) Planar Traveling Salesman Heuristic Based on Space filling Curves", Oper.Res.Lett.,**1**(1982)121-125. J.J.Bartholdi 3 and L.K.Platzman, "Heuristic Based on Space filling Curves for Combinatorial Problems in Euclidean Space", Managements Science, **34**(1988)291-305.

[12] R.Durbin and D.Willshaw, "An Analog Approach to the Traveling Salesman Problem Using an Elastic Net Method", Nature 326,16(1987)689-691.

Solving Vehicle Routing Problems Using Elastic Nets

Andrew I. Vakhutinsky and Bruce L. Golden

College of Business and Management
University of Maryland
College Park, MD 20742

Introduction

Using neural networks to find an approximate solution to difficult optimization problems is a very attractive prospect. The Traveling Salesman Problem (TSP), probably the best-known problem in combinatorial optimization, has been attacked by a variety of neural network approaches. Many of these results are summarized in [5]. The main purpose of this paper is to show how elastic network ideas can be applied to two TSP generalizations: the multiple traveling salesmen problem (MTSP) and the vehicle routing problem (VRP).

1 The Elastic Net Algorithm

This algorithm for solving the TSP [1, 2] can be briefly described as follows. We have a set of cities positioned on the plane at points X_i, $i = 1, \ldots, n$ and a set of dynamic variables Y_j, $j = 1, \ldots, m$ defining the *rubber band*. At the beginning of the algorithm, the rubber band is a small circle centered at the gravity center of the cities. Then, it is *stretched* towards the cities by tracking the minima of the energy function:

$$E = -\alpha K \sum_{i=1}^{n} \ln \sum_{j=1}^{m} e^{-\|X_i - Y_j\|/2K^2} + \beta \sum_{j=1}^{m} \|Y_j - Y_{j+1}\| \tag{1}$$

where $K \to 0$ and $\|a - b\| = (a_1 - b_1)^2 + (a_2 - b_2)^2$. The positions of the points defining the rubber band are updated according to the formula $\triangle Y = -K \nabla_Y E$. The right-hand side of equation (1) consists of two terms: the first one is responsible for the attraction of the points on the rubber band to the cities; the second one favors the shortest tour. We can think of K as the temperature and we are minimizing energy using some *cooling* schedule: $K \leftarrow (1 - \varepsilon)K$. An example of the process as it evolves is shown in Figure 1.

It was proved in [1] that when $K \to 0$, the local minima of the energy function is such that each city X_i is matched by at least one Y_j. Moreover, each X_i is matched by exactly one Y_j if certain conditions are satisfied (see [1, 6] for details).

2 The Multiple Traveling Salesmen Problem (MTSP)

The MTSP is a generalization of the TSP in which there are multiple salesmen. We are given a set of n cities in the plane. Each city must be visited by exactly one of the L Traveling Salesmen (TS) sharing the same depot $\mathcal{D}$. The objective is to minimize the total distance traveled by all salesmen.

As with the TSP, we introduce an appropriate energy function:

$$E = -\alpha K \sum_{i=1}^{n} \ln \sum_{v=1}^{L} \sum_{k=1}^{m/L} e^{-\|X_i - Y_{vk}\|/2K^2} + \beta \sum_{v=1}^{L} \sum_{k=1}^{m/L} \|Y_{vk} - Y_{v,k+1}\| \tag{2}$$

and track its minima while $K \to 0$. Here there are L rubber bands and Y_{vk} denotes the k-th point on the v-th rubber band. Equation (2) differs from equation (1) in the second term where the rubber band points are distributed evenly among the L routes and the length of each route is shortened independently of the others. The starting point of each route is the depot. This is implemented as follows:

0-7803-1901-X/94 $4.00 ©1994 IEEE

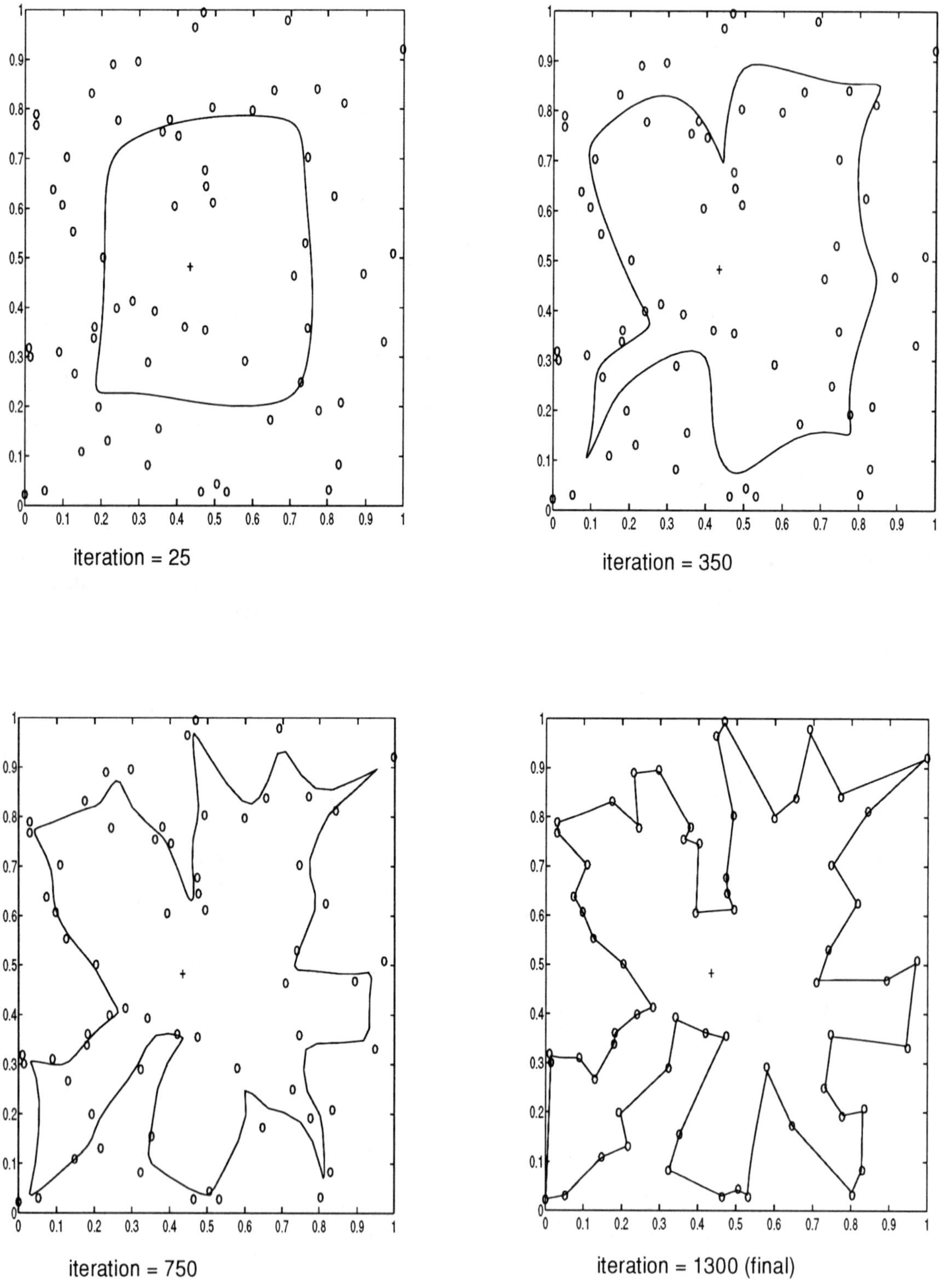

Figure 1: Evolution of TSP Tour over 64 Cities

do {
  $Y \leftarrow Y - K\nabla_Y E$;
  for $v = 1$ **to** L
    $Y_{v1} \leftarrow \mathcal{D}$;
  $K \leftarrow (1-\varepsilon)K$;
} **until** (all the cities are matched by the rubber band points).

At the very beginning of the algorithm we have L small loops going out of the depot. Their initial configuration and the evolution of the process are shown in Figure 2.

3 The Vehicle Routing Problem (VRP)

We define the VRP as follows: We are given a fleet of L vehicles located at depot $\mathcal{D}$. Each vehicle has the same capacity Q. City i is located at X_i in the plane and has a demand of q_i. For each vehicle, find a route which begins at the depot, visits a subset of cities, and returns to the depot without violating the capacity constraint. The objective is to minimize the total length of all routes.

It is easy to see that the VRP is an MTSP with additional capacity constraints. To take this into account, the algorithm for the MTSP was slightly modified. First, to predict which cities will be visited by a particular vehicle, we introduce a simple heuristic. We say that a city i is supposed to be served by a vehicle $\tilde{v} = v(i)$ if the $\tilde{v}$-th loop is the nearest to X_i or, more formally, if $\exists\, k^*$ such that

$$(\tilde{v}, k^*) = \arg\min_{(v,k)} \|X_i - Y_{vk}\|.$$

Next, we define a relative residual capacity of a vehicle $\tilde{v}$ as

$$r(\tilde{v}) \stackrel{def}{=} 1 - \sum_{i|v(i)=\tilde{v}} q_i/Q.$$

Now, consider the expression for the gradient of the MTSP energy function which can be obtained by differentiating the right-hand side of (2) with respect to y_{vk}. It is given by

$$\nabla_{vk} E_{MTSP} = \alpha \sum_i w_{i,vk}(x_i - y_{vk}) + \beta K(y_{v,k-1} + y_{v,k+1} - 2y_{vk}) \quad (3)$$

$$\text{where } w_{i,vk} = \frac{e^{-\|x_i - y_{vk}\|/2K^2}}{\sum_{ul} e^{-\|x_i - y_{ul}\|/2K^2}}.$$

To modify an updating rule for $\triangle Y$, we divide each term in the first summation of (3) by the inhibitor coefficient $h_v = 1 + e^{-r(v)/K^2}$ and obtain the expression

$$\triangle Y_{vk} = \alpha \sum_i \frac{w_{i,vk}}{h_v}(X_i - Y_{vk}) + \beta K(Y_{v,k-1} + Y_{v,k+1} - 2Y_{vk}), \quad (4)$$

which is used to evolve the solution to the vehicle routing problem (see Figure 3).

4 Computational Results

To test the code, several TSPs were solved with randomly generated cities in the unit square. The energy function had the following parameters: $\alpha = .2$, $\beta = 2.$, $K_{init} = .2$, $K_{fin} = .002$. The number of iterations to attract at least 1 point to each of the cities was about 2,000 and did not depend on the size of the problem. The problem size was varied from 30 cities to 80 cities. Each problem was randomly generated inside a unit square. Obtained solutions were compared to those produced by an exact branch-and-bound algorithm and were found to be within 2% of optimality. It was also found that the solutions obtained did not depend on the initial position of the rubber band.

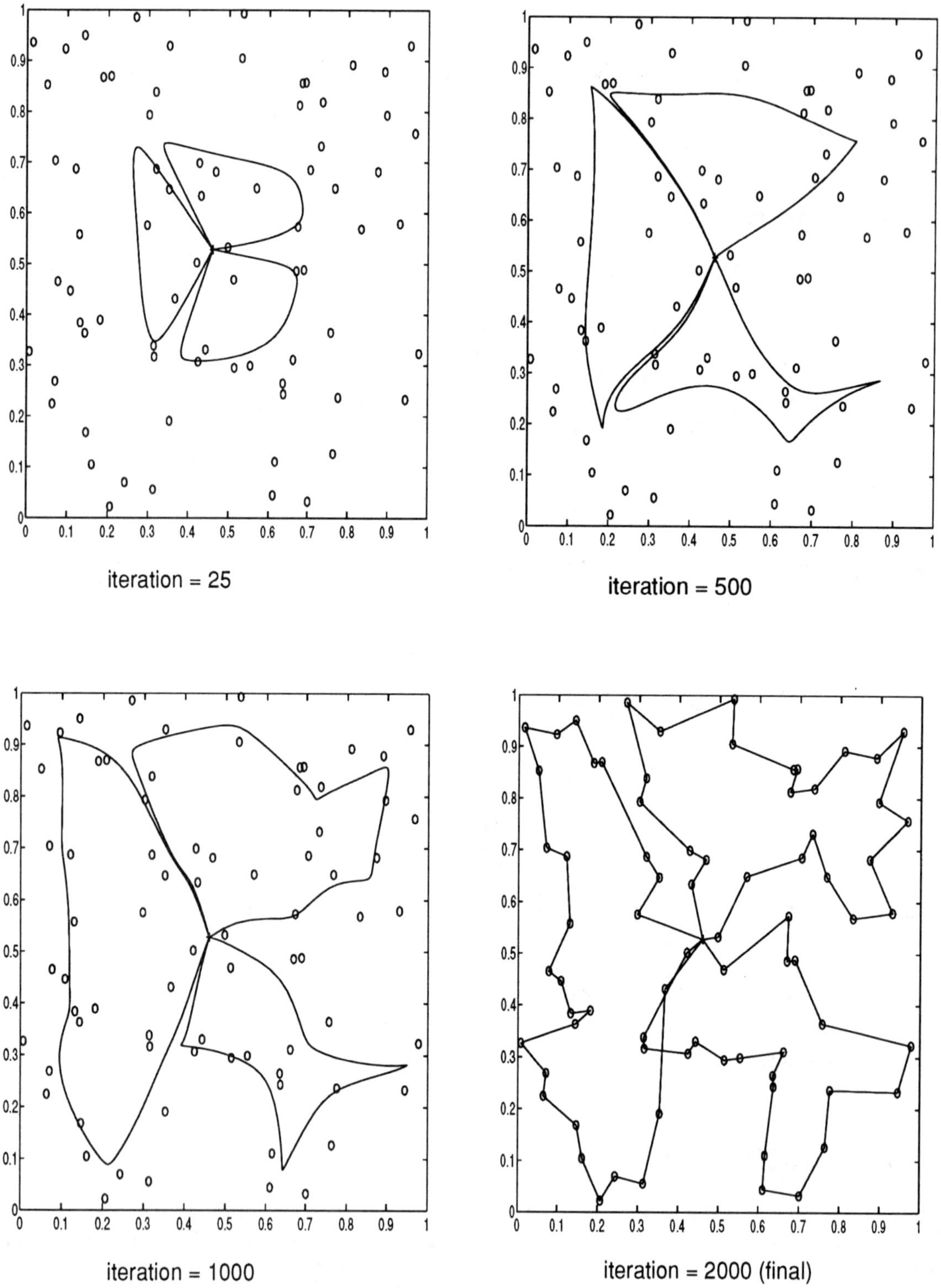

Figure 2: Evolution of the MTSP with 100 Cities and 3 Traveling Salesmen

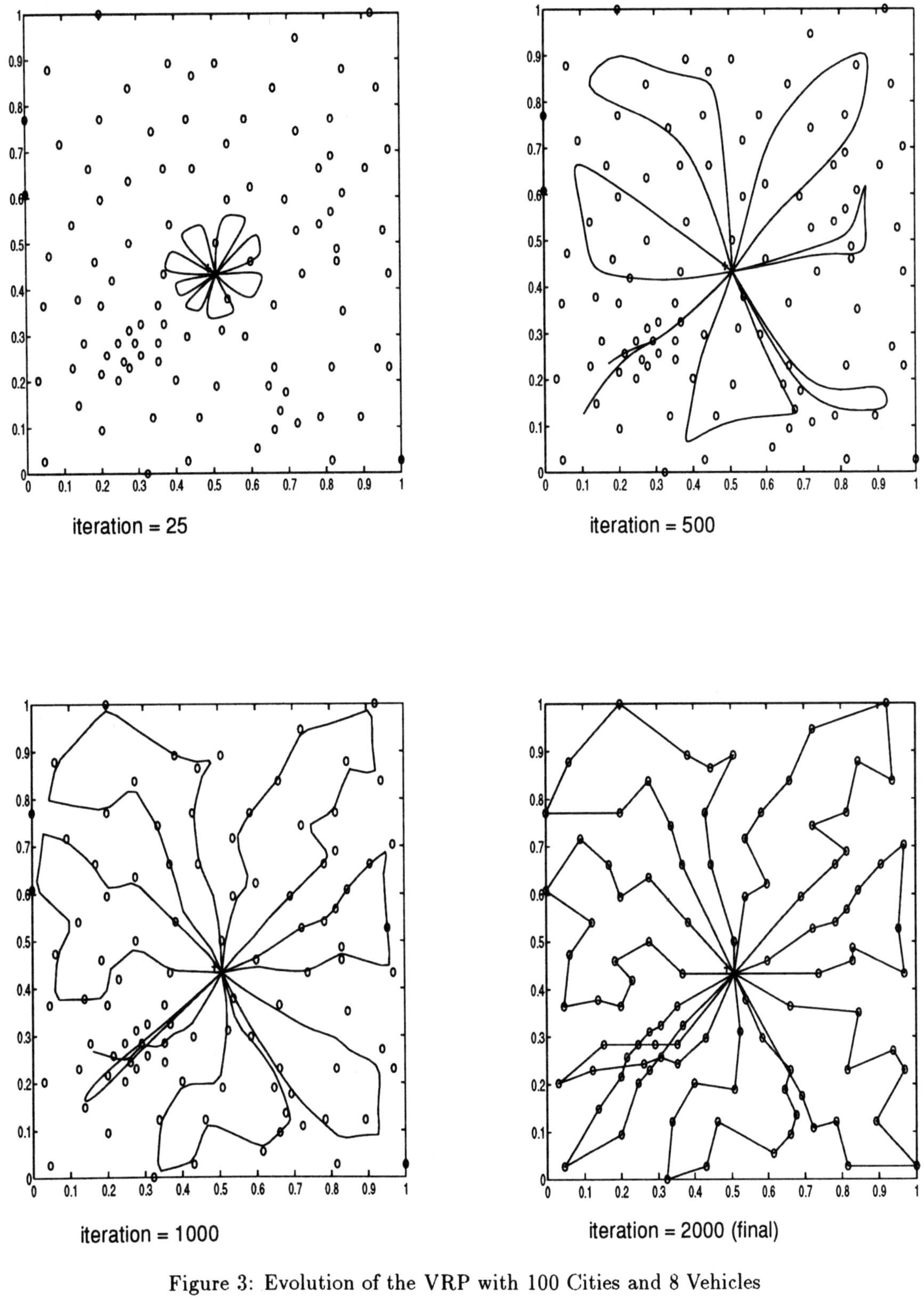

Figure 3: Evolution of the VRP with 100 Cities and 8 Vehicles

Problem number	Number of cities	Obtained solution	Capacity violation?	Number of routes	Eilon et al. solution
3	21	659	No	5	585
4	22	950	No	5	949
5	29	855	No	4	875
7	32	894	No	5	821
8	50	560	No	6	585

Table 1: Performance of the Elastic Net on the VRP.

To test the MTSP, we generated several random samples in the unit square with the depot chosen as the center. Our results turned out to be approximately 10% better than those in [4], but the computational time was worse. To test the VRP algorithm, several problems were taken from [3] and solved. Even though better solutions are now available , we compare the elastic network solutions with the best known solutions from 1971 (see Table 1). The results are comparable.

Conclusion

Although the elastic network algorithms are dominated by traditional operations research (OR) methods in terms of running time and solution accuracy, we point out that neural networks have been used to solve optimization problems for only ten years. Substantial improvements in performance are likely in the years ahead, especially as neural networks and traditional OR approaches are merged to form hybrid approaches.

In our elastic net algorithms, running times can easily be reduced by approximating the exponent with a more easily computable function.

Acknowledgment

The authors wish to thank R. Jonker and T. Volgenant for the use of their TSP code. This code uses branch and bound to solve traveling salesman problems with 100 to 200 cities optimally in a reasonable amount of computer time.

References

[1] R. Durbin, R. Szeliski and A. Yuille, 1989. An Analysis of the Elastic Net Approach to the Traveling Salesman Problem, *Neural Computation 1*, 348-358.

[2] R. Durbin and D. Willshaw, 1987. An Analogue Approach to the Traveling Salesman Problem Using an Elastic Net Method, *Nature 326*, 689-691.

[3] S. Eilon, C. D. T. Watson-Gandy and N. Christofides, 1971. *Distribution Management*, Hafner Publishing Company, New York.

[4] H. El-Ghaziri, 1991. Solving Routing Problems by a Self-Organizing Map, in T. Kohonen, K. Makiasara, O. Simula, J.Kangas (eds.), *Artificial Neural Networks*, North-Holland, Amsterdam, pp. 829-834.

[5] J.-Y. Potvin, 1993. The Traveling Salesman Problem: A Neural Network Perspective, *ORSA Journal on Computing 5*, 328-348.

[6] M.W. Simmen, 1991. Parameter Sensitivity of the Elastic Net Approach to the Traveling Salesman Problem, *Neural Computation 3*, 363-374.

Neural Network for combining Linear and Non-Linear modelling of Dynamic Systems

Per Printz Madsen
Ph.D, M.Sc.E.E.
Dept. of Control Engineering, Inst. of Elektronic Systems
Aalborg University, Fredrik Bajers vej 7 DK-9220 Aalborg Ø, Denmark
E-mail: ppm@control.auc.dk

Abstract

The purpose of this paper is to develop a method to combine linear models with MLP networks. In other words to find a method to make a non-linear and multivariable model, that performes at least as good as a linear model, when the training data lacks information. At the beginning the MLP network for predicting the output from a dynamic system is described. Then two methods are proposed to combine linear and non-linear modelling. The first method is the MLP network with linear path through and the second method is a linear model with non-linear error correction. Finally the two methods are tested. A thermal mixing process is used as a test system. This system is a multivariable and non-linear process. The test is partly based on a simulation of the process and partly on data from a physical process.

The results shows, that MLP networks with linear path through based on simulation, have a better performance than both a pure MLP network and a pure linear network. The optimal structure factor λ is about 0.5. In case the test is based on the physical process, it results in a small performance improvement. The linear model with non-linear error correction gives a larger performance improvment compared to the previous mentioned model, when the test is based on the physical process.

I. Introduction

Since Rumelhart et al in 1986 [1] described the Back-Propagation Error learning algoritme (BPE-algoritme) for Multi-Layer Perceptron neural networks (MLP). This type of network has been used in many applications, mainly for classification purpose. Another fast growing working field is the use of Artificial Neural Networks (ANN) for simulation and controlling of dynamic processes.

One of the important advantages of ANN of the type MLP is that these models are universal approximators [2]. In other words these models are able to approximate any multivariable and non-linear function. This fact is very important, when using this MLP-model for simulation of real world dynamic processes. It is possible to simulate any non-linear and multivariable system, when using MLP-networks as simulating tool. The major problem with the MLP-networks is that it is required, that the learning data which represents the system shows respect to both the dynamic and the non-linear behaviour of the system in the entire operation area. In case the learning data have lack of information, it often results in the fact, that the MLP network produces an even worse approximation to the process, than the approximation of a simple linear model. The explanation is, that linear models only requires learning data, which represents the dynamic behaviour in one working point in the operation area. Then the linear model, in a sense, fits in the best way to the linear approximation in that working point. In case the system is not too non-linear in the working area, the result will be, that this linear model is a good approximation in the entire working area.

A. The state space description

The MLP networks are static mappings from the input space to the output space. When using MLP networks for simulating and controlling of dynamic systems it is necessary to apply some dynamic capability to the static MLP network. One of the methods is to let the MLP network estimate a non-linear state space description of the system. This method is used in [3],[4] and in [5].

0-7803-1901-X/94 $4.00 ©1994 IEEE

This discrete state space model for a non-linear system is described by eqn. 1

$$\begin{aligned} \boldsymbol{x}(n+1) &= \boldsymbol{f}_{\mathrm{sys}}(\boldsymbol{x}(n), \boldsymbol{u}(n), \boldsymbol{d}(n), \boldsymbol{e}_x(n)) \\ \boldsymbol{y}(n) &= \boldsymbol{g}_{\mathrm{sys}}(\boldsymbol{x}(n), \boldsymbol{e}_y(n)) \end{aligned} \tag{1}$$

where n is the discrete time, $\boldsymbol{x}$ is the state, $\boldsymbol{u}$ is the input to the system, $\boldsymbol{d}$ is the measurable disturbance on the system and $\boldsymbol{e}_x$, $\boldsymbol{e}_y$ are white noise vectors. The state function $\boldsymbol{f}_{\mathrm{sys}}$ and the output function $\boldsymbol{g}_{\mathrm{sys}}$ are in general non-linear vector functions. If all the states can be measured (complete state information), it is possible to let an ANN estimate the deterministic part of the system functions $\boldsymbol{f}_{\mathrm{sys}}$ and $\boldsymbol{g}_{\mathrm{sys}}$. This can be done in two steps. First by using the state $\boldsymbol{x}(n)$, the input $\boldsymbol{u}(n)$ and the disturbance $\boldsymbol{d}(n)$ as input to the ANN and $\boldsymbol{x}(n+1)$ as the desired output. Secondary, if there is a difference between the state $\boldsymbol{x}$ and the output $\boldsymbol{y}$, you have to apply another ANN with the state as input, and the output $\boldsymbol{y}$ from the system as the desired output. If it is possible to minimize the difference between the output from the ANN and the desired output then these two networks in cooperation make a one-step predictor. In other words if $\boldsymbol{F}_{\mathrm{NN}}$ and $\boldsymbol{G}_{\mathrm{NN}}$ are the two network functions and $\hat{\boldsymbol{x}}$ is the predicted state and $\hat{\boldsymbol{y}}$ is the predicted output then: $\hat{\boldsymbol{x}}(n+1) = \boldsymbol{F}_{\mathrm{NN}}(\boldsymbol{x}(n), \boldsymbol{u}(u), \boldsymbol{d}(n))$ and $\hat{\boldsymbol{y}}(n) = \boldsymbol{G}_{\mathrm{NN}}(\boldsymbol{x}(n))$.

II. The used methods

On account of the neural networks of the type MLP are universal approximators, it is possible to adjust the weights in the network so that the network functions $\boldsymbol{F}_{\mathrm{NN}}$ and $\boldsymbol{G}_{\mathrm{NN}}$ approximate the deterministic part of $\boldsymbol{f}_{\mathrm{sys}}$ and $\boldsymbol{g}_{\mathrm{sys}}$ exactly or to any degree of accuracy if:

1. There is enough neurons in the hidden layer.
2. The learning algorithme is able to find the global minimum for the performance function.
3. The learning data contains enough information to describe the system functions $\boldsymbol{f}_{\mathrm{sys}}$ and $\boldsymbol{g}_{\mathrm{sys}}$ with respect to both the non-linear and the dynamic behaviours.

The solution to the first point can be: The optimal number of neurons can be chosen with respect to the test data set, where the test data set is different from the learning data set. Then the optimal number is: $N_{\mathrm{optimal}} = \{N \in [1, 2, \cdots] | \min P_{\mathrm{test}}(N)\}$ where $P_{\mathrm{test}}(N) = \sum_{i=1}^{A} (\boldsymbol{D}_{\mathrm{test}}(i) - \boldsymbol{F}_{\mathrm{NN}}(N, \boldsymbol{u}_{\mathrm{test}}(i)))^T (\boldsymbol{D}_{\mathrm{test}}(i) - \boldsymbol{F}_{\mathrm{NN}}(N, \boldsymbol{u}_{\mathrm{test}}(i)))$, $\boldsymbol{D}_{\mathrm{test}}(i)$ is the ith desired output and $\boldsymbol{u}_{\mathrm{test}}(i)$ is the ith input in the test data set. A is the number of input vectors in the test data set. The second point can cause problems in practical use. The BPE learning algorithm is often able to find a useable minimum, not necessarily a global minimum, for the performance function. The major problem is the third point. In linear system identification it is well known, that the frequency spectrum of the input signals must be sufficiently wide in order to identify the process. When using a Neural Network, in order to make a non-linear system identification, it is also demanded that the amplitude spectrum of the input signals is sufficiently wide, and that all combinations of frequencies and amplitudes are represented in the learning data. Often it is not possible, with respect to the amplitudes, to generate the learning data, which represents the entire working area for the process. In such case a linear system identification will, if the process is not too non-linear, give a better model than the Neural Network based model. In this situation MLP networks, with linear path through, will perform better, than MLP networks with only non-linear neurons in the hidden layer and no direct connection between the input layer and the output layer.

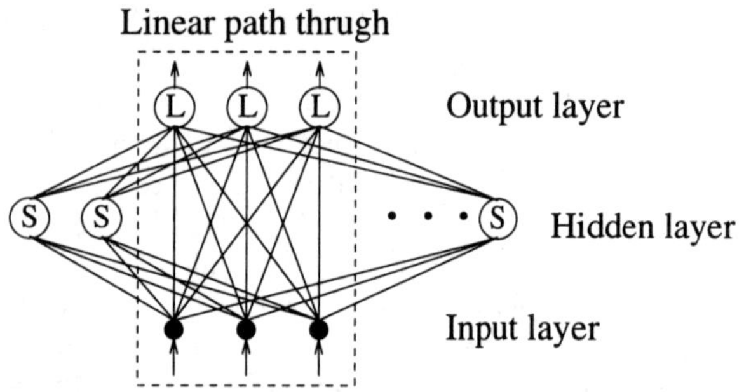

A. The MLP network with Linear path through

The network function of the MLP network, with linear path through, is described by eqn. 2.

$$\boldsymbol{F}_{\mathrm{NN}} = (1 - \lambda)\boldsymbol{w}_2 \boldsymbol{f}(\boldsymbol{w}_1 \boldsymbol{u}) + \lambda \boldsymbol{w}_L \boldsymbol{u} \tag{2}$$

where λ is the structure factor, $\boldsymbol{w}_2$ is a matrix, that contains the weights between the hidden layer and the output layer, $\boldsymbol{f}$ is a vector function, given by: $\boldsymbol{f}(\boldsymbol{x}) = [f_1(x_1), f_2(x_2), \cdots, f_N(x_N), -1]^T$ where f_n is the nth neuron function in the hidden layer and x_n is the nth element in the $\boldsymbol{x}$ vector, $\boldsymbol{w}_1$ is a matrix that contains the weights between the input layer and the hidden layer and $\boldsymbol{u}$ is the input vector to the network $\boldsymbol{u} = [u_1, u_2, \cdots, u_k, -1]$ where k is the number of input. The structure factor λ is the degree of simple linearity in the network. λ must be selected before starting the learning process.

- for $\lambda = 1$: $\boldsymbol{F}_{\text{NN}} = \boldsymbol{w}_L \boldsymbol{u}$ "A pure linear model".
- for $\lambda = 0$: $\boldsymbol{F}_{\text{NN}} = \boldsymbol{w}_2 \boldsymbol{f}(\boldsymbol{w}_1(\boldsymbol{u}))$ "A pure nonlinear MLP model'.

If the learning data are insufficient, then use λ near one. Otherwise if the data contains information above the non-linearities in the entire working area, then use λ near zero.

When using BPE-learning, the adjustments of the weights $\boldsymbol{w}$ are:

$$\Delta \boldsymbol{w}_1 = \eta(1-\lambda)\text{diag}(\boldsymbol{f}'(\boldsymbol{x}(i)))\boldsymbol{w}_2^T(\boldsymbol{D}(i) - \boldsymbol{F}_{\text{NN}}(\boldsymbol{u}(i)))\boldsymbol{u}^T(i) \quad (3)$$

$$\Delta \boldsymbol{w}_2 = \eta(1-\lambda)(\boldsymbol{D}(i) - \boldsymbol{F}_{\text{NN}}(\boldsymbol{u}(i)))\boldsymbol{Y}_1^T \quad (4)$$

$$\Delta \boldsymbol{w}_L = \eta\lambda(\boldsymbol{D}(i) - \boldsymbol{F}_{\text{NN}}(\boldsymbol{u}(i)))\boldsymbol{u}^T(i) \quad (5)$$

where η is the learning rate, $\boldsymbol{u}(i)$ is the ith input, $\boldsymbol{D}(i)$ is the desired output, $\text{diag}(\boldsymbol{f}'(\boldsymbol{x}))$ is a diagonal matrix whose elements in the principal diagonal are given by: $f'_{11}(\boldsymbol{x}) = f'_1(x)|_{x=x_1}$, $f'_{22}(\boldsymbol{x}) = f'_2(x)|_{x=x_2}$ and so on, where $f'_n()$ is the derived of the nth neuron in the hidden layer and x_n is the nth element in $\boldsymbol{x} = \boldsymbol{w}_1\boldsymbol{u}(i)$.

Eqn:3,4 and 5 are all trying to minimize the performance function in a manner of gradient descent. If λ is one, it is obvious, that only the linear path through will be adjusted, and by means of that find the "best" linear approximation to the system. On the other hand if λ is zero then only the non-linear part will be adjusted.

B. The linear model with non-linear error correction

When having a set of learning data, it is possible to find the optimal adjustment of the parameters in a linear model by linear regression. If the learning data represents a non-linear system, the error $\boldsymbol{y}_{\text{non-linear}}$ between the linear model and the learning data must be the non-linear part of the system. Figure 1 is illustrating this.

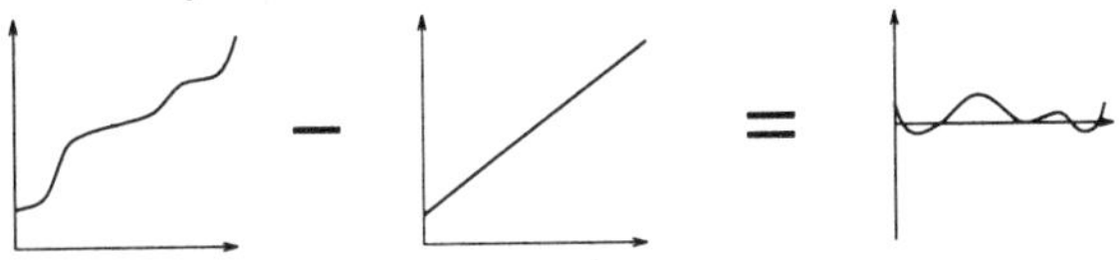

Figure 1: The difference between the non-linear system and the linear model, called the non-linear part of the system

The linear model of a MIMO-system is described by: $\boldsymbol{x}(n+1) = \boldsymbol{F}\boldsymbol{x}(n) + \boldsymbol{G}\boldsymbol{u}(n) + \boldsymbol{e}_x(n)$ and $\boldsymbol{y}(n) = \boldsymbol{H}\boldsymbol{x}(n) + \boldsymbol{e}_y(n)$. Where $\boldsymbol{F}$, $\boldsymbol{G}$ and $\boldsymbol{H}$ represent the deterministic linear part of the system. Figure 2 shows the learning methods for the neural net based non-linear error correction with complete state information. In this concept all states can be measured and the matrixes $\boldsymbol{F}$, $\boldsymbol{G}$ and $\boldsymbol{H}$ are known. These matrixes can be found by traditional linear system identification as described in [6].

The network will learn to correct the deterministic linear model to time $n+1$ as a function of $\boldsymbol{x}(n)$, $\boldsymbol{u}(n)$ and the error $\boldsymbol{y}_{\text{non-linear}}(n)$. The optimal one-step predictor is then given by eqn. 6.

$$\hat{\boldsymbol{y}}(n+1) = \boldsymbol{H}(\boldsymbol{F}\boldsymbol{x}(n) + \boldsymbol{G}\boldsymbol{u}(n)) + \boldsymbol{F}_{\text{NN}}(\boldsymbol{x}(n), \boldsymbol{u}(n), \boldsymbol{d}(n), (\boldsymbol{y}(n) - \boldsymbol{H}\boldsymbol{x}(n))) \quad (6)$$

where $\hat{\boldsymbol{y}}$ is the predicted output. If the state is chosen as output, then $\boldsymbol{H} = \boldsymbol{I}$. This causes that the neural network estimates the optimal non-linear "Kalman gain" or Kalman function and that the achieved predictor is a linear predictor with non-linear error correction.

Unfortunately all the states can't always be measured. In such case it is necessary to use a state observer and afterwards to do the learning and the prediction by means of the observed state.

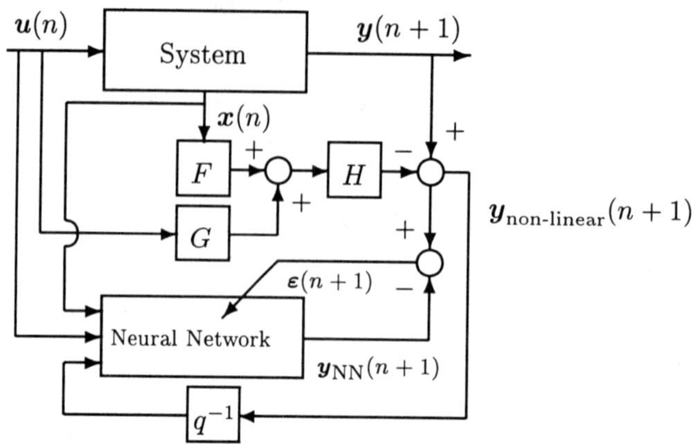

Figure 2: Learning methods for neural net based non-linear error correcting

III. EXAMPLE: THE THERMAL MIXING PROCESS

This section describes the process used for testing the proposed methods. Figure 3 shows, in principle, the

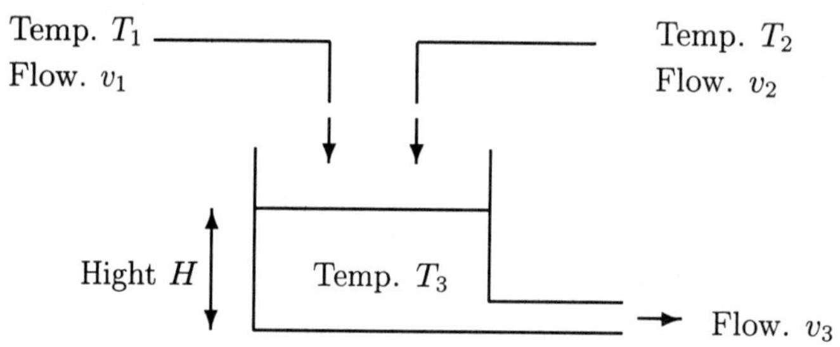

Figure 3: The thermal mixing process.

thermal mixing process. The inlet flows are the cold and the hot water supply. The flow and the temperature of the cold water are described by v_1 and T_1. The flow and the temperature of the hot water are described by v_2 and T_2. The water level and the temperature, in the mixing tank, are described by H and T_3. The disturbing outlet flow is described by v_3. All temperatures and flows are measured by fast sensors. The process is equipped with fast motor valves controlled by local feed-back loops. These local loops control the inlet water flow v_1 and v_2.

The mass balance for the tank is described by eqn. 7, and the energy balance for the tank is described by eqn. 8.

$$\frac{\partial H(t)}{\partial t} = \frac{v_1(t) + v_2(t) - v_3(t)}{A} \tag{7}$$

$$\frac{\partial T_3(t)}{\partial t} = \frac{v_1(t) \cdot (T_1(t) - T_3(t)) + v_2(t) \cdot (T_2(t) - T_3(t)}{A \cdot h(t)} \tag{8}$$

The non-linear discrete state-space model is described by eqn. 9.

$$\boldsymbol{x}(n+1) = \boldsymbol{f}(\boldsymbol{x}(n), \boldsymbol{u}(n), \boldsymbol{d}(n)) \text{ and } \boldsymbol{y}(n) = \boldsymbol{x}(n) \tag{9}$$

where the state is $\boldsymbol{x}(n) = [H(n), T_3(n)]^T$, the input is $\boldsymbol{u}(n) = [v_1(n), v_2(n)]^T$ and the measureable disturbance is $\boldsymbol{d}(n) = [v_3(n), T_1(n), T_2(n)]^T$.

The tests are based on four data sets.

Simulation: A learning and a test data set generated by a second-order Runge-kutta simulation of eqn. 7 and 8.

Practical: A learning and a test set collected from the physical thermal mixing process.

IV. Results and Discussion

In any case the MLP networks have 8 SIGMOID neurons $f(x) = 1/(1 + \exp(-x))$ in the hidden layer. The linear model with non-linear error correction uses a normal MLP network without linear path through and a second-order state space model with v_1 and v_2 as the input and with T_3 and H as the state vetcor. The numbers in table 1 and table 2 are the performance index $P_{\text{test}} = 1/A \sum^{A}(\boldsymbol{D}_{\text{test}} - \boldsymbol{F}_{\text{NN}})^T(\boldsymbol{D}_{\text{test}} - \boldsymbol{F}_{\text{NN}})$.

Simulation test: For λ about 0.5 the MLP network with linear path through shows performance improvement on both the temperature T_3 and the water level H compared to the pure MLP network, $\lambda = 0$, and the pure linear network, $\lambda = 1$. The linear model with non-linear error correction (table 2), compared with the linear state space model, shows significant improvement on both T_3 and H.

Practical test: The practial test of the MLP network with linear path through doesn't show significant improvement compared with both the pure MLP network, $\lambda = 0$, and the pure linear model, $\lambda = 1$. The explanation might be that this method dosn't work well when the data are noisy. The practial test of the linear model with non-linear error correction shows better performance on the temperature than the MLP network with linear path through does. This might mean that the separation of the linear part and the non-linear part of the system improve the performance when the data are noicy. The MLP network only does what it is best at, namely non-linear mapping. Otherwise if the test system is a linear process the desired output for the MLP network will be zero in all cases.

Table 1: MLP network with linear path through

λ		0	0.2	0.4	0.6	0.8	1
Simulation:	$T_3(n+1)$	$3.1 \cdot 10^{-3}$	$1.5 \cdot 10^{-3}$	$5.1 \cdot 10^{-4}$	$6.1 \cdot 10^{-4}$	$1.7 \cdot 10^{-3}$	$5.1 \cdot 10^{-3}$
Simulation:	$H(n+1)$	$1.0 \cdot 10^{-6}$	$2.3 \cdot 10^{-7}$	$5.9 \cdot 10^{-8}$	$1.7 \cdot 10^{-8}$	$2.5 \cdot 10^{-7}$	$7.9 \cdot 10^{-6}$
Practical:	$T_3(n+1)$	$2.5 \cdot 10^{-2}$	$3.0 \cdot 10^{-2}$	$2.2 \cdot 10^{-2}$	$2.1 \cdot 10^{-2}$	$2.3 \cdot 10^{-2}$	$2.7 \cdot 10^{-2}$
Practical:	$H(n+1)$	$7.4 \cdot 10^{-6}$	$7.0 \cdot 10^{-6}$	$6.8 \cdot 10^{-6}$	$7.1 \cdot 10^{-6}$	$6.6 \cdot 10^{-6}$	$8.0 \cdot 10^{-6}$

Table 2: Linear model with non-linear error correction

		The linear state space model	Model with non-linear error cor.
Simulation:	$T_3(n+1)$	$3.6 \cdot 10^{-2}$	$1.3 \cdot 10^{-4}$
Simulation:	$H(n+1)$	$7.6 \cdot 10^{-6}$	$1.3 \cdot 10^{-9}$
Practical:	$T_3(n+1)$	$4.7 \cdot 10^{-2}$	$1.6 \cdot 10^{-2}$
Practical:	$H(n+1)$	$1.0 \cdot 10^{-5}$	$7.1 \cdot 10^{-6}$

V. Conclusion

Two methods are proposed for combining linear models with neural network. The first method is called the MLP network with linear path through, the second method is called the linear model with non-linear error correction. The first method is a traditionel MLP network with a direct connection from the input layer to the output layer. The second method is a way to make a non-linear Kalman gain function based on the state, the input, the measurable disturbances and the previous prediction error. MLP networks with linear path through shows a performance improvement for λ about 0.5, when the data are deterministic, that is to say without noise. If the data are noisy "practical data" the performance improvement is small. The linear model with non-linear error correction has a better performance, concerning the temperature, than the previous mentioned model.

REFERENCES

[1] David S. Rumelhart and J.L. McClelland, *Parallel Distributed Processing*, vol. 1-2, MIT Press, 1986.

[2] Kurt Hornik, Maxwell Stinchcombe, and Halbert White, "Multilayer Feedforward Networks are Universal Approximators", *Neural Networks*, vol. 2, pp. 359–366, 1989.

[3] A J Robinson and F Fallside, "The Utility Driven Dynamic Error Propagation Network", *IEEE Conference on Neural Information Processing Systems - Natural and Synthetic*, 1987.

[4] O. Nerrand, P. Roussel-Ragot, L. Personnaz, and G. Dreyfus, "Neural Network Training Schemes for Non-linear Adaptive Filtering and Modelling", *IEEE Transactions on Neural Networks*, vol. 1, no. 1, pp. 63–66, january 1991.

[5] Kumpati S. Narendra and Kannan Parthasarathy, "Identification and Control of Dynamical Systems Using Neural Networks", *IEEE Transactions on Neural Networks*, vol. 1, no. 1, pp. 4–27, march 1990.

[6] Lennart Ljung and Torsten Söderström, *Theory and Practice of Recursive Identification*, The MIT Press, first edition, 1983.

ON SOLVING CONSTRAINED OPTIMIZATION PROBLEMS WITH NEURAL NETWORKS

Michael P. Glazos
School of Electrical Engineering
Purdue University
West Lafayette, IN 47907

Stefen Hui
Department of Mathematical Sciences
San Diego State University
San Diego, CA 92182

Stanislaw H. Żak
School of Electrical Engineering
Purdue University
West Lafayette, IN 47907

Abstract

We analyze a class of neural networks that solve convex programming problems. In carrying out the analysis we use concepts from the theory of differential equations with discontinuous right-hand sides and Lyapunov stability theory. We show that irrespective of the initial state of the network the state converges to a solution of the convex programming problem. The dynamic behavior of the networks is illustrated by two numerical examples.

1. Introduction

Recently, it has been shown that analog neural networks can be efficiently used to solve certain constrained optimization problems (see e.g. Chua and Lin (1984), Tank and Hopfield (1986), Kennedy and Chua (1988), Rodríguez-Vázquez et al. (1990), Cichocki and Unbehauen (1993), Lillo et al. (1993)). Such networks are particularly well suited for applications that require on-line optimization.

An approach commonly used in developing analog optimizers is to first convert the constrained optimization problem into an equivalent unconstrained optimization problem, and then design an analog network that solves the unconstrained problem. One method for converting a constrained optimization problem into an unconstrained optimization problem is the penalty function method. The idea behind the penalty function method is to replace the constrained optimization problem

$$\begin{aligned} &\text{minimize} \quad f(x) \\ &\text{subject to} \quad x \in \Omega \end{aligned}$$

with an unconstrained problem of the form

$$\text{minimize} \quad f(x) + \varsigma p(x) ,$$

where $f: \mathbb{R}^n \rightarrow \mathbb{R}$ is continuous on $\mathbb{R}^n$, $\Omega \subset \mathbb{R}^n$, ς is a positive constant, and $p: \mathbb{R}^n \rightarrow \mathbb{R}$ is continuous on $\mathbb{R}^n$ and satisfies

$$\text{(i)} \quad p(x) \geq 0 \quad \text{for all} \quad x \in \mathbb{R}^n ,$$

and

$$\text{(ii)} \quad p(x) = 0 \quad \text{if and only if} \quad x \in \Omega \quad \text{(Luenberger(1984))} .$$

Observe that the penalty term $\varsigma p(x)$ is intended to penalize the objective function $f(x)+\varsigma p(x)$ for any violated constraints. If for a finite value of the penalty parameter ς the solution of the unconstrained problem coincides with the solution of the constrained problem, then the penalty function $p(x)$ is said to be exact.

Rodríguez-Vázquez et al. (1990) recently proposed a class of neural networks for optimization problems whose design is based on concepts from the penalty function method. This class of analog optimizers is particularly attractive for two reasons. First, their design does not require the calculation of a penalty parameter. Second, these networks can be realized using switched-capacitor technology, and thus are suitable for monolithic implementation (Cichocki and Unbehauen (1993)). In light of these properties we feel that an analysis of the dynamics of these networks is in order. Since an analysis is not provided in Rodríguez-Vázquez et al. (1990), we do so here.

In this paper we analyze the dynamics of the analog networks proposed by Rodríguez-Vázquez et al. (1990) when applied to a class of constrained optimization problems.

0-7803-1901-X/94 $4.00 ©1994 IEEE

2. Problem Statement

We consider the constrained optimization problem

$$\begin{aligned} &\text{minimize} \quad f(x) \\ &\text{subject to} \quad g_i(x) \leq 0\,, \qquad i = 1, 2, \ldots, m, \end{aligned} \tag{1}$$

where $x \in \mathbb{R}^n$, $f: \mathbb{R}^n \to \mathbb{R}$, and $g_i : \mathbb{R}^n \to \mathbb{R}$, $i = 1, 2, \ldots, m$. Before proceeding further we first introduce some notation.

We let Ω denote the feasible region for problem (1), that is

$$\Omega \triangleq \bigcap_{i=1}^{m} \{x \mid g_i(x) \leq 0\}.$$

The collection of all interior (boundary) points of Ω is denoted by $\Omega^o(\partial\Omega)$. Also, we define

$$\Delta_i \triangleq \{x \mid g_i(x) = 0\}, \qquad i = 1, 2, \ldots, m\,,$$

and

$$\Delta \triangleq \bigcup_{i=1}^{m} \Delta_i\,.$$

We let Γ denote the collection of all relative minimum points for problem (1). Lastly, we introduce the index sets

$$I(x) \triangleq \{i \mid g_i(x) = 0\}$$

and

$$J(x) \triangleq \{i \mid g_i(x) > 0\}.$$

We assume the following:

A1. The sets $\{x \mid g_i(x) > 0\}$, $i = 1, 2, \ldots, m$, are nonempty.

A2. The functions f and g_i, $i = 1, 2, \ldots, m$, are convex over $\mathbb{R}^n$, and have continuous first partial derivatives on $\mathbb{R}^n$, i.e., $f \in C^1$ and $g_i \in C^1$, $i = 1, 2, \ldots, m$.

A3. The set Ω is nonempty and bounded.

A4. The constraints are everywhere regular, i.e., the vectors $\nabla g_i(x)$, $i \in I(x)$, are linearly independent for any $x \in \mathbb{R}^n$.

Remark 1. Note that there is no loss of generality to problem (1) by assuming A1. Indeed, when treating a constrained optimization problem we can simply ignore any constraints that are satisfied everywhere.

Remark 2. It follows from A2 that problem (1) is a convex programming problem. Specifically, we are asked to minimize a convex function f over a compact convex set Ω.

Remark 3. Problem (1) is well-posed in the sense that Ω is nonempty and the optimal value of f is not $-\infty$. Indeed, it follows from A2 and A3 that $f(\Omega)$ is compact.

Remark 4. It follows from A1-A4 that:

(i) The sets $\{x \mid g_i(x) < 0\}$, $i = 1, 2, \ldots, m$, are nonempty.

(ii) The points in Δ_i define a smooth $(n-1)$-dimensional surface in $\mathbb{R}^n$ that separates the regions $\{x \mid g_i(x) > 0\}$ and $\{x \mid g_i(x) < 0\}$, $i = 1, 2, \ldots, m$.

(iii) $\Omega^o = \bigcap_{i=1}^{m} \{x \mid g_i(x) < 0\}$, $\partial\Omega = \Omega \cap \Delta$, and both Ω^o and $\partial\Omega$ are nonempty.

The class of analog networks proposed by Rodríguez-Vázquez et al. (1990) for solving problem (1) is described by

$$
\tau \dot{x}(t) = h(x(t)) = \begin{cases} -\mu \sum_{i \in J(x(t))} \nabla g_i(x(t)) & \text{if } x(t) \notin \Omega \\ \\ -\nabla f(x(t)) & \text{if } x(t) \in \Omega, \end{cases} \tag{2}
$$

$$
x(0) = x_0,
$$

where τ and μ are positive design constants. We see from (2) that the function h is piecewise continuous over $\mathbb{R}^n$. Specifically, h is in general discontinuous on the surfaces $\Delta_1, \Delta_2, ..., \Delta_m$. As such, a rigorous analysis of the dynamics of the proposed networks cannot be carried out using only methods derived from the classical theory of differential equations. Rather, the fact that the function h is discontinuous on the surfaces $\Delta_1, \Delta_2, ..., \Delta_m$ requires that the analysis must utilize other methods, e.g., those proposed in Filippov (1988) and Utkin (1992).

Here, as in Filippov (1988), we take a solution of (2) to be a solution of the differential inclusion

$$
\tau \dot{x}(t) \in H(x(t)), \tag{3}
$$

where for each x, H(x) is the smallest closed convex set containing the cluster values of the function h(y) as $y \rightarrow x$, $y \notin \Delta$. That is, a solution of (2) is an absolutely continuous function x(t) defined on an interval or segment L for which $\tau \dot{x}(t) \in H(x(t))$ almost everywhere on L (Filippov (1988)). Observe that if the function h is continuous at a point x, i.e., $x \notin \Delta$, then H(x) consists of a single point, namely h(x), and the solution satisfies (2) in the usual sense. However, if $x \in \Delta$ then x lies on one or more of the surfaces $\Delta_1, \Delta_2, ..., \Delta_m$. Denoting the elements of I(x) by $i_1, i_2, ..., i_k$ it follows from A4 that for sufficiently small $\delta > 0$ the surfaces $\Delta_{i_1}, \Delta_{i_2}, ..., \Delta_{i_k}$ partition the δ-neighborhood of x into 2^k regions, $\mathcal{R}_1, \mathcal{R}_2, ..., \mathcal{R}_{2^k}$, in each of which the function h is continuous. Let h_j denote the function h restricted to the region $\mathcal{R}_j$. Then H(x) is the smallest closed convex set containing the set

$$
\bigcup_{j=1}^{2^k} \bigcap_{n=1}^{\infty} h_j(\{y \in \mathcal{R}_j \mid ||y-x|| \leq \frac{1}{n}\}).
$$

We note that a rigorous justification for using (3) to analyze the behavior of the proposed networks is provided in Chapter 2 of Filippov (1988).

Our goal is to show that all trajectories of system (2), irrespective of the initial condition x(0), converge to a solution of problem (1), where convergence is understood in the sense of the following definition.

Definition 1. A trajectory $x:[0, \infty) \rightarrow \mathbb{R}^n$ is said to *converge to a solution of problem (1)* if

$$
\lim_{t \rightarrow \infty} d(x(t), \Gamma) = 0,
$$

where

$$
d(x, \Gamma) \triangleq \inf_{y \in \Gamma} ||x-y||_2.
$$

Before proceeding with our analysis we first present a well-known property of the convex programming problem (1).

Theorem 1. Any relative minimum point of problem (1) is a global minimum point.

Remark 5. It follows from Theorem 1, A2, and A3 that Γ is both closed and bounded. Therefore, the infimum in the definition of $d(x, \Gamma)$ is achieved, i.e.,

$$
d(x, \Gamma) = \min_{y \in \Gamma} ||x-y||_2.
$$

3. Main Results

Before proceeding further we make a remark concerning the analysis of system (2). A phenomenon commonly occurring in systems such as (2) is the so-called sliding mode, where the motion of the system is confined to one or more of the discontinuity surfaces (Filippov (1988)). Consequently, we must consider two cases when analyzing the dynamic behavior of system (2).

The first case being when the motion of the system is not confined to any of the surfaces $\Delta_1, \Delta_2, \ldots, \Delta_m$. The second case being when the system is in a sliding mode on one or more of the surfaces $\Delta_1, \Delta_2, \ldots, \Delta_m$. We only need to consider these two cases, for every trajectory of system (2) is composed of these two types of motion.

Let

$$V(x) \triangleq \sum_{i=1}^{m} \max\{g_i(x), 0\},$$

or equivalently

$$V(x) = \begin{cases} \sum_{i \in J(x)} g_i(x) & \text{if } x \notin \Omega \\ \\ 0 & \text{if } x \in \Omega. \end{cases} \tag{4}$$

Remark 6. It follows from A2 that the function V is continuous and convex on $\mathbb{R}^n$. Also, by definition, $V(x) > 0$ for all $x \notin \Omega$, and $V(x) = 0$ for all $x \in \Omega$.

Lemma 1. V is a decreasing function of time when evaluated on any trajectory of system (2).

Proof. See Glazos et al. (1994).

Lemma 2. The set $\{x \mid V(x) \leq a\}$ is bounded for any $a \in \mathbb{R}$.

Proof. See Utkin (1992), p. 229.

Theorem 2. Every trajectory of system (2) reaches Ω in finite time and is thereafter confined to Ω.

Proof. See Glazos et al. (1994).

Let $F(x) \triangleq f(x) - f^*$, where f^* is the optimal value of f for problem (1).

Remark 7. It follows from A2 that the function F is convex over $\mathbb{R}^n$ and has continuous first partial derivatives on $\mathbb{R}^n$. Also, by definition, $F(x) = 0$ for all $x \in \Gamma$, and $F(x) > 0$ for all $x \in \Omega \backslash \Gamma$.

Lemma 3. F is a decreasing function of time when evaluated on any trajectory of system (2) while it is confined to Ω.

Proof. See Glazos et al. (1994).

Lemma 4. F tends to zero with time when evaluated on any trajectory of system (2).

Proof. See Glazos et al. (1994).

We are now ready to present the main result of the paper.

Theorem 3. Every trajectory of system (2) converges to a solution of problem (1).

Proof. By Theorem 2, every trajectory of system (2) reaches the feasible region Ω in finite time and is thereafter confined to Ω. By Lemma 4, $f(x(t)) \to f^*$ as $t \to \infty$ on any trajectory $x(\cdot)$. We are done since Ω is a compact convex set and f is a convex function.

4. Examples

Example 1

In this example we consider the quadratic programming problem

$$\begin{aligned} &\text{minimize} && \frac{1}{2} x^T Q x + c^T x \\ &\text{subject to} && Ax \leq b, \end{aligned} \tag{5}$$

where

$$Q = \begin{bmatrix} 4 & 1 \\ 1 & 2 \end{bmatrix}, \; c = \begin{bmatrix} -12 \\ -10 \end{bmatrix}, \; A = \begin{bmatrix} 5 & 1 \\ -5 & 1 \\ -1 & -2 \end{bmatrix}, \text{ and } b = \begin{bmatrix} 0 \\ 10 \\ 10 \end{bmatrix}.$$

Problem (5) clearly satisfies A1-A4, and one can easily verify that the point $x^* = [-19/22 \;\; 95/22]^T$ is a unique minimizer for this problem, i.e., $\Gamma = \{x^*\}$. Note that $x^* \in \Delta_1$. A phase-plane portrait for system (2) for problem (5) is shown in Figure 1. Observe that each of the trajectories in the phase-plane portrait converges to the point x^* while sliding along the surface Δ_1.

Example 2

In this example we consider the convex programming problem

$$\begin{aligned} &\text{minimize} && \frac{1}{2} x^T Q x + c^T x \\ &\text{subject to} && g_i(x) \leq 0, \;\; i = 1, 2, 3, \end{aligned} \tag{6}$$

where

$$\begin{aligned} g_1(x) &= x_1^2 + (x_2 - 4)^2 - 64, \\ g_2(x) &= (x_1 + 3)^2 + x_2^2 - 36, \\ g_3(x) &= (x_1 - 3)^2 + x_2^2 - 36, \end{aligned}$$

and Q and c are as defined in problem (5). One can easily verify that problem (6) satisfies A1-A4, and that the point $x^* = [1.776 \;\; 3.629]^T$ is a unique minimizer for the problem, i.e., $\Gamma = \{x^*\}$. Note that $x^* \in \Delta_2$. A phase-plane portrait for system (2) for problem (6) is shown in Figure 2. Note that each of the trajectories in the phase-plane portrait converges to the point x^* while sliding along the surface Δ_2.

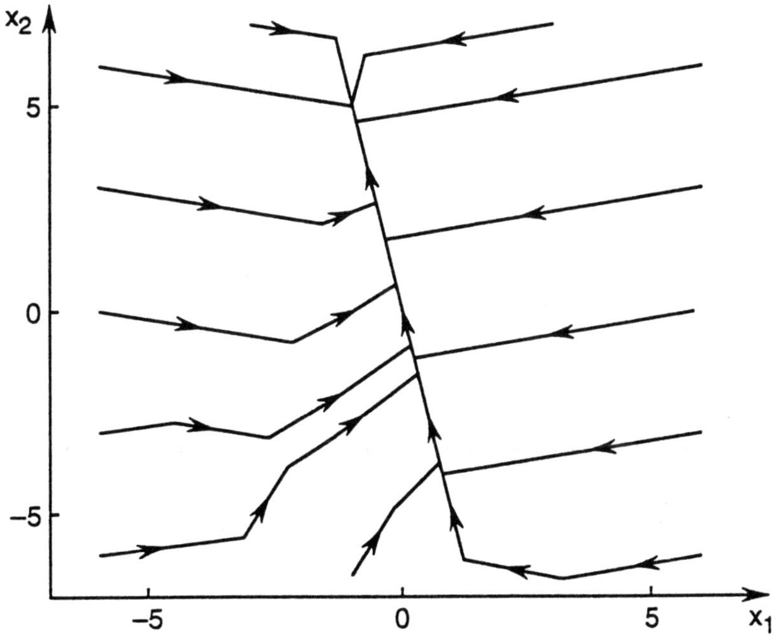

Figure 1. Phase-plane portrait for system (2) for problem (5).

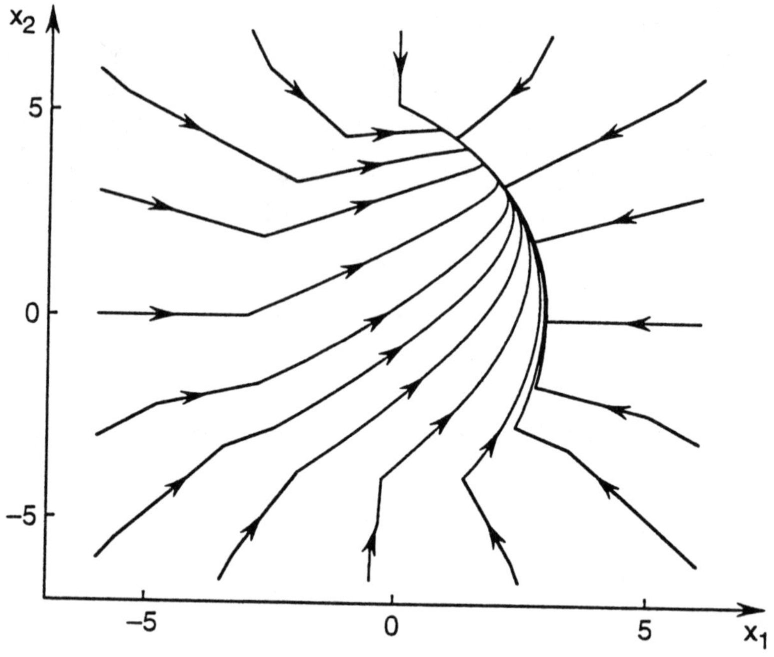

Figure 2. Phase-plane portrait for system (2) for problem (6).

References

Chua, L. O. and G.-N. Lin (1984). Nonlinear programming without computation. IEEE Trans. Circuits Syst., CAS-31, 182-188.

Cichocki, A. and R. Unbehauen (1993). Neural Networks for Optimization and Signal Processing, Wiley & Sons, Chichester.

Filippov, A. F. (1988). Differential Equations with Discontinuous Righthand Sides. Kluwer Academic Publishers, Dordrecht, The Netherlands.

Glazos, M. P., S. Hui, and S. H. Żak (1994). An analysis of neural networks that solve convex programming problems. Submitted for publication.

Kennedy, M. P. and L. O. Chua (1988). Neural networks for nonlinear programming. IEEE Trans. Circuits Syst., CAS-35, 554-562.

Lillo, W. E., S. Hui, and S. H. Żak (1993). Neural networks for constrained optimization problems. Int. J. Circuit Theory and Applications, 21, 385-399.

Luenberger, D. G. (1984). Linear and Nonlinear Programming (Second Edition). Addison-Wesley, Reading, Massachusetts.

Rodríguez-Vázquez, A., R. Domínguez-Castro, A. Rueda, J. L. Huertas, and E. Sánchez-Sinencio (1990). Nonlinear switched-capacitor "neural" networks for optimization problems. IEEE Trans. Circuits Syst., CAS-37, 384-397.

Tank, D. W. and J. J. Hopfield (1986). Simple "neural" optimization networks: An A/D converter, signal decision network, and a linear programming circuit. IEEE Trans. Circuits Syst., CAS-33, 533-541.

Utkin, V. I. (1992). Sliding Modes in Control and Optimization. Springer-Verlag, Berlin, Heidelberg.

Karhunen-Loeve Transform Using Neural Networks

Xianing Zhu (OCRON INC)
Shengwei Zhang (ExperVision INC)
A..G. Constantinides (Dept. of Electrical Engineering, Imperial College, London)

ABSTRACT

The optimality of Karhunen-Loeve Transform(KLT) over other transforms has been well known, together with the difficulty in implementing practical KLT systems. The wide applications of the transform deserve a new investigation on realizing such systems by using artificial neural networks. In this paper the KLT is known to be equivalent to a constrained optimization problem by maximizing covariance of output signals with the constraint of orthonormality. A neural network is then developed which can converge to the basis vectors of the transform.

1. Introduction

The Karhunen-Loeve Transform(KLT), also known as principal component analysis, is an optimal transform in the sense of mean-square-error and is useful in a variety of applications such as data compression, image processing and pattern recognition. KLT is an orthogonal transform whose basis vectors are eigenvectors of the specified covariance matrix of input data. For transforms of fixed basis vectors such as Fourier Transform, the intrinsic structure of the basis can be employed to reduce the computational load, leading to the so-called Fast Fourier Transform(FFT). For KLT however, the basis depends on the data covariance matrix and thus may be changing from one data source to anther, or even changing at different times for a fixed source(nonstationary data). Up to now no fast computational algorithms of KLT are available for general purpose. Since its occurrence, KLT has been considered as theoretically optimal but practically infeasible transform, and has been used merely as a benchmark for other suboptimal transforms.

In this paper, we report some encouraging results on implementing KLT with neural networks. In view of the statistical orthogonal expansion feature of the transform matrix and the maximum covariance of the output signals, the design of the KLT is converted into an equivalent optimization problem to which a neural network is then dedicated. The transform matrix and the output covariance are required by the activity levels of corresponding neurons, and are obtained simultaneously when the neural network converges. The computation of the KLT has been observed within a few characteristic time constants of the network regardless dimensional changes, and the updating of the transform matrix is automatically achieved as a results of the dynamic following feature of the network.

2. Neural Algorithm for KLT

Let $X \in R^n$ denote the input data, $Y \in R^m$ the transformed data, and $T \in R^{mn}$ is the linear association between X and Y with the relation Y=TX. For more efficient representation we require that m<n and that X can be reconstructed by $\overline{X}=WY$ with minimal error, where W is the inverse transform.

Assume that X is zero-mean with correlation matrix Q. Then it is well known that the mean squared error $E[(X-\overline{X})^2]$ is minimized when the rows of T span the first m eigenvectors of Q, and the transformation Y=TX is named Karhunen-Loeve Transform(KLT)(Ahmed & Rao, 1975). In summary, the usual procedure of KLT is as follows.

(a). Estimate the data covariance matrix Q:

$$Q = E[[X-E[X]][X-E[X]]^T] \qquad (2.1)$$

where $X \in R^n$ is the input signals, and the superscript T denotes the matrix transposition. In some procedures Q is not explicitly calculated.

(b). Solve the following equations:

$$|Q - \lambda_i I| = 0 \quad i=1,2,.....m \qquad (2.2)$$

for the eigenvalues and

$$(Q - \lambda_i I)\phi_i = 0 \quad i=1,2,......m \qquad (2.3)$$

for eigenvectors, where $\phi_i \in R^n$, $1 \le i \le m$ are orthonormal, i.e., $\phi_i^T \phi_i=1$, i=1,......m, $\phi_i^T \phi_j=0$, $i \neq j$, i,j=1......m, m<n.

(c). Compute the KL expansion for signal data:

$$Y = \phi^T X \qquad (2.4)$$

Where $\Phi=[\phi_1 ..... \phi_m] \in R^{n \times m}$ is the transform matrix, and $Y \in R^m$ is the transformed signal. X can be easily reconstructed from Y by using the relation $X=\Phi Y$.

In the above procedure steps (a)(c) are straightforward, however in step (b) the computational load of eigenvalue and eigenvectors is heavy. Some iteration algorithms are available but they are far from satisfactory in real-time applications.

Since the conventional procedure of the eigenvector and eigenvalue computation as defined by equation (2.2)-(2.3) seems a difficult task for neural networks. Therefore KLT algorithm via neural networks also follows iteration algorithm method (Oja,1989, Sanger, 1989, 1990). Here, we converted it into an equivalent optimization problem, taking into account the requirements of the KLT that, the basis vectors be orthogonal, the output covariance be maximum, and the transformed signal components be uncorrelated. The last constraint, though not obvious, is necessary to reach the right solution. More precisely, the following optimization problem is established.

$$\text{Maximize} \quad \sum_{i=1}^{m} E[\,[y_i-E[y_i]]^T [y_j-E[y_j]]\,] \qquad (2.5)$$

$$\text{Subject to} \quad \phi_i^T \phi_i=1 \quad i=1,2,......m \qquad (2.6)$$

$$\phi_i^T \phi_j=0 \quad j<i, \; i,j=1,2,......m \qquad (2.7)$$

$$E[[y_i-E[y_i]][y_j-E[y_j]]^T]=0 \quad j<i, \; i,j=1,2,......m \qquad (2.8)$$

Where $y_i=\phi_i^T X$

A more useful form can be obtained by combining the definition of Q.

$$\text{Minimize} \quad -\sum_{i=1}^{m} \phi_i^T Q \phi_i \qquad (2.9)$$

$$\text{Subject to} \quad \phi_i^T \phi_i=1 \quad i=1,2,......m \qquad (2.10)$$

$$\phi_i^T \phi_j=0 \quad j<i, \; i,j=1,2,......m \qquad (2.11)$$

$$\phi_i^T Q \phi_j = 0 \; j<i \; i,j=1,2......m \qquad (2.12)$$

(2.10)-(2.12) construct $K=m+\frac{(m^2-m)}{2}\frac{(m^2-m)}{2}+\frac{(m^2-m)}{2}=m^2$ constraints, where (2.10) and (2.11) represent the orthonomal conditions of the basis vectors while (2.12) denotes the fact that the transformed signal components are uncorrelated. The search for optimality is on D =mn variables { ϕ_{11}, ϕ_{12}, ..., ϕ_{1n}, ϕ_{21}, ϕ_{22}, ..., ϕ_{2n}, ..., ϕ_{im1}, ϕ_{im2}, ..., ϕ_{mn}}.

A specially dedicated networks(Pratt & Barr, 1988; Zhang & Constantinides, 1992) can now be defined to solve the constrained problem. We Consider the following nonlinear programming problem:

Minimize $F(\Phi) + \frac{1}{2} C \| G(\Phi) \|^2$ (2.15)

Subject to $G(\Phi) = 0$ (2.16)

where $F: R^D \rightarrow R$ and $G: R^D \rightarrow R^k$ are given functions with $K \leq D$. The components of G are denoted $G_1 .....G_K$. where C is a scalar and $\| . \|$ denotes Euclidean norm. Then an augmented Lagrangian function can be formed:

$$L_C(\Phi, \Gamma) = F(\Phi) + \Gamma^T G(\Phi) + \frac{1}{2} C \| G(\Phi) \|^2 \quad (2.17)$$

where $\Gamma \in R^K$ is a vector whose components are the Lagrange multipliers.

Define $\nabla_\Phi L(\Phi, \Gamma) = [\frac{dL}{d\phi_1}, \frac{dL}{d\phi_2}, ..., \frac{dL}{d\phi_n}]^T$ and $\nabla \frac{d\Gamma}{dt} {}_\Gamma L(\Phi, \Gamma) = [\frac{dL}{d\gamma_1}, \frac{dL}{d\gamma_2}, ..., \frac{dL}{d\gamma_m}]^T$, respectively.

The dynamic equations of the neural network are expressed as follows:

$$\frac{d\Phi}{dt} = - \nabla_\Phi L_C(\Phi, \Gamma) = - \nabla F(\Phi) - \nabla G(\Phi)(\Gamma + C G(\Phi)) \quad (2.18)$$

$$\frac{d\Gamma}{dt} = \nabla_\Gamma L_C \nabla_\Gamma L_C(\Phi, \Gamma) = G(\Phi) \quad (2.19)$$

where $\nabla G = [\nabla G_1, \nabla G_2, ..., \nabla G_k]$, $\nabla F(\Phi)$ and $\nabla G_i(\Phi)$is the gradients of scaler functions similarly define as $\nabla_\Phi L(\Phi, \Gamma)$.

The reason why the augmented Lagramge function (not the Lagrange function) is used will be made clear later when we discuss the satbility of the network.

The equilibrium point (Φ^*, Γ^*) of the dynamic system, define by $\frac{d\Phi}{dt}|(\Phi^*, \Gamma^*) = 0$ and $\frac{d\Gamma}{dt}|(\Phi^*, \Gamma^*) = 0$, satisfies equations:

$$\nabla_\Phi L(\Phi^*, \Gamma^*) = \nabla F(\Phi^*) + \nabla G(\Phi^*) \Gamma^* = 0 \quad (2.22)$$

$$\nabla_\Gamma L(\Phi^*, \Gamma^*) = G(\Phi^*) = 0 \quad (2.23)$$

and thus provides a Lagrange solution to the optimization problem(Bertsekas, 1982).

Returning to our previous optimization problem for KLT, we find the following equivent problem:

$$\text{Minimize } -\sum_{i=1}^{m} \phi_i^T Q \phi_i + \frac{c}{2} [\sum_{i=1}^{m} (\Phi_i^T \phi_i - 1)^2 + \sum_{i=1}^{m} \sum_{j<i} (\phi_i^T \phi_j)^2 + \sum_{i=1}^{m} \sum_{j<i} (\phi_i^T Q \phi_j)^2] \quad (2.24)$$

Subject to $\phi_i^T \phi_i = 1 \quad i=1,2,......m$ (2.25)

$\phi_i^T \phi_j = 0 \quad j<i, \; i,j=1,2,......m$ (2.26)

$\phi_i^T Q \phi_j = 0 \; j<i \; i,j=1,2......m$ (2.27)

The Augmented Lagrangian function becomes:

$$Lc(\Phi,\Gamma) = -\sum_{i=1}^{m}\phi_i^T Q\phi_i + \sum_{i=1}^{m}\gamma_i(\phi_i^T\phi_i - 1) + \sum_{i=1}^{m}\sum_{j=1}^{i-1}\beta_{ij}\phi_i^T\phi_j + \sum_{i=1}^{m}\sum_{j=1}^{i-1}\eta_{ij}\phi_i^T Q\phi_j +$$

$$\frac{c}{2}\left[\sum_{i=1}^{m}(\phi_i^T\phi_i - 1)^2 + \sum_{i=1}^{m}\sum_{j=1}^{i-1}(\phi_i^T\phi_j)^2 + \sum_{i=1}^{m}\sum_{j=1}^{i-1}(\phi_i^T Q\phi_j)^2\right] \quad (2.28)$$

where γ_i, β_{ij} and η_{ij} are the Lagrange multipliers.

The Neural network is obtained as :

$$\frac{d\phi_i}{dt} = 2Q\phi_i - [2\gamma_i + C(\phi_i^T\phi_i)]\phi_i - \sum_{j=1}^{i-1}[\beta_{ij} + C(\phi_i^T\phi_j)]\phi_j -$$

$$\sum_{j=1}^{i-1}[\eta_{ij} + C(\phi_i^T Q\phi_j)]Q\phi_j \quad i=1,2,......m \quad (2.29)$$

$$\frac{d\gamma_i}{dt} = \phi_i^T \phi_i - 1 \quad i=1,2,......m \quad (2.30)$$

$$\frac{d\beta_{ij}}{dt} = \phi_i^T \phi_j \quad j<i, \; i,j=1,2,......m \quad (2.31)$$

$$\frac{d\eta_{ij}}{dt} = \phi_i^T Q\phi_j \quad j<i \; i,j=1,2......m \quad (2.32)$$

The following will show that the equilibrium point of the neural network is indeed the KLT basis, and can be made asymptotically stable by choosing suitable value for C. Further discussion about above neural networks bas been in the paper of Zhang and Constantinides(1992).

We are now ready to show that the equilibrium point of the neural network provides the KLT basis vectors and the ouput variance. The equilibrium point (Φ^*, Γ^*) defined by $\frac{d\Phi}{dt}|(\Phi^*, \Gamma^*)=0$ and $\frac{d\Gamma}{dt}|(\Phi^*, \Gamma^*)=0$ satisfies equations:

$$Q\phi_i^* = \gamma_i^*\phi_i^* + \frac{1}{2}\sum_{j=1}^{i-1}\beta_{ij}^*\phi_j^* + \frac{1}{2}\sum_{j=1}^{i-1}\eta_{ij}^* Q\phi_j^* \quad i=1,2,......m \quad (2.33)$$

$$\phi_i^{*t}\phi_i^* = 1 \quad i=1,2,......m \quad (2.34)$$

$$\phi_i^{*t}\phi_j^{*}=0 \qquad j<i,\ i,j=1,2,......m \qquad (2.35)$$

$$\phi_i^{*t}Q\phi_j^{*}=0 \qquad j<i\ \ i,j=1,2......m \qquad (2.36)$$

Left multiplying equation (2.33) with ϕ_i^{*T} and taking into account the orthonormal features of the basis vectors represented by (2.34)-(2.36) we obtain

$$\phi_i^{*T}Q\phi_j^{*} = \gamma_i^{*} \qquad i=1,2,......m \qquad (2.37)$$

Denote two diagonal matrices as E=diag[1,......,1], Λ=diag[γ_1^{*} ,...., γ_m^{*}], and Φ^{*}=[ϕ_1^{*}..... ϕ_m^{*}]. Then the equations (2.37) and (2.34)-(2.35) possess a compact form as follows.

$$\Phi^{*T}Q\Phi^{*} = \Lambda \qquad (2.38)$$

$$\Phi^{*T}\Phi^{*} = E \qquad (2.39)$$

(2.38) and (2.39) show that ϕ_j^{*} i=1,.....,m, are the orthonormal eigenvectors of the covariance matrix Q, and hence are the basis vectors of the KLT. Notice that γ_i^{*} i=1,2,.....m are the eigenvalues of Q and therefore are the output variance.

The stability analysis is completed visa the Liapunov function method. Define a Liapunov function for the network as

$$E(\Phi,\Gamma)=\frac{1}{2}\|\nabla_\Phi L_c(\Phi,\Gamma)\|^2+\frac{1}{2}\|G(\Phi)\|^2 \qquad (2.40)$$

The differential of E with respect to time along the trajectory of the neural network can be easily deduced as:

$$\frac{dE}{dt}=\frac{\partial E}{\partial \Phi}\frac{d\Phi}{dt}+\frac{\partial E}{\partial \Gamma}\frac{d\Gamma}{dt}=-(\frac{d\Phi}{dt})^T\nabla^2_{\Phi\Phi}L_c(\Phi,\Gamma)(\frac{d\Phi}{dt}) \qquad (2.41)$$

Thus a sufficient condition to keep the network stable is that $\nabla^2_{\Phi\Phi}L_c(\Phi,\Gamma)>0$.

The analysis of $\nabla^2_{\Phi\Phi}L_c(\Phi,\Gamma)>0$ on the entire state is complicated, if not impossible. Fortunately, analysis of local property is available which shows that the optimal solution(KLT basis) is at least an asymptotically stable state with a reasonable domain of attraction.

The cost function $F(\Phi)$ and the constraint $G(\Phi)$ are both quadratic, and are Lipschitz continuous in the entire space. From proposition 1 of (Bertsekas, 1976) there exists a constant C* >0 such that, for any C > C*, $\nabla^2_{\Phi\Phi}L_c(\Phi^*,\Gamma^*)$ is positive definite. In fact, this claim can be extended to an open neighbor around (Φ^*,Γ^*). Thus (Φ^*,Γ^*) is an asymptotically stable state.

It is worth pointing out that, as long as the input data are enough so that the estimated covariance matrix Q is of full rank, the KLT basis is unique and thus our neural system has a unique equilibrium point.

There is no guideline in estimating C* but our empirience shows that setting $C = 2\max_i q_{ii}$ or C = trace { Q } is quite satisfactory.

3. Conclusions

By using the optimality and orthonormality features of KLT, we have transformed the computation of KL basis into an equivalent optimization problem. A neural computing algorithm is then developed which can converge to the basis from arbitrary initial states within the attraction domain. The neural network can be realized either by analog circuitry or by processing arrays(Fischer, 1990). In contrast to other neural algorithm(Sanger, 1989), the presented network provided both KL basis and output variance. The latter is useful in dynamically determining the compression rate.

References

Ahmed, N. & Rao, K. R. (1975). Orthogonal Transforms for Digital Signal Processing. New York: Springe-Verlag.

Bertsekas, D. P. (1976). Multiplier methods: A Survey, Automatica, 12, 133-145.

Bertsekas, D. P. (1982). Constrained optimization and language Multiplier Method. New York: Academic Press.

Fisher, H. (1990).Automatic differentiation: Paralle computation of function, gradient, and Hessian matrix. Parallel Computing 13, 101-110, 1990.

Oja, E. (1989). Neural Networks, Principal Components, and Subspaces. International Journal of Neural Systems, 1(1), 61-68.

Platt, J. C. & Barr, A. H. (1988). Constrained Differential Optimization, in D. Z. Anderson (Ed.) Neural Information Processing Systems, New York: American Institute of Physics.

Sanger, T. D. (1989). Optimal Unsupervised Learning in a Single-Layer Linear Feedforward. Neural Network, neural Networks, 2, 459-473.

Sanger, T. D. (990). Analysis of Two-Dimensional Receptove fields Learned by the general Hebbian Algorithm in Response to random Input. Biological Cybernetics. 63(3), 221-229.

Zhang, S. & Constantinides, A.G.(1992), Lagrange Programming Neural Networks, IEEE Transactions on Circuits and Systems. 39(7), 441-452.

Time-Varying Two-Phase Optimization for Neural Network Learning

Hyeon Myeong, Jong-Hwan Kim*

Abstract—**A two-phase neural network solves exact feasible solutions when the problem is a constrained optimization programming. The time-varying programmming neural network is a kind of modified steepest-gradient algorithm which solves time-varying optimization problems. In this paper, a time-varying two-phase optimization neural network is proposed which uses the merits of the two-phase neural network and the time-varying neural network. The training of multi-layer neural networks is regarded as a time-varying optimization problem, and the proposed algorithm is applied to system identification using a multi-layer neural network. Furthermore, we considered the case where the weights have some constraints in the learning of the neural network.**

I. Introduction

In the viewpoint of optimization theory, Kennedy and Chua [3] developed a network which satisfies both the K-T optimality condition and penalty function theorem. Yet the equilibrium point of the network may converge to only an approximate solution that is outside the feasible region when the solution of the constrained problem is on the boundary of the feasible region.

Maa and Shanblatt [1] proposed a two-phase optimization neural network as an alternative approach to the solution infeasibility problem inherent in the Kennedy and Chua network. It operates under different dynamics as the phase is changed by a predetermined timing switch. In the second phase, it satisfies the K-T optimality condition, so the equilibrium point is precisely a global minimizer to a convex program. When we deal with a time-varying optimization problem which arises frequently in many practical problems, static optimization techniques must include effects from time-varying characteristics of the problem. A time-varying nonlinear programming neural network was proposed by Feng and Zhao [2], who had taken the time-variation of the time-dependent function into consideration.

In this paper, a time-varying two-phase (TVTP) optimization neural network is proposed which uses the merits of the two-phase neural network and the time-varying neural network. As the training of multi-layer neural networks can be regarded as a time-varying optimization problem, the proposed algorithm is applied to the identification of dynamic plants using a multi-layer neural network. The practical case where the weights are constrained when we implement fast digital neural network hardware is considered and its usefulness is demonstrated through computer simulations.

*Dept. of Electrical Engineering, Korea Advanced Institute of Science and Technology (KAIST), 373-1 Kusung-dong, Yusung-gu, Taejonshi 305-701, Republic of Korea. Corresponding author's e-mail address : johkim@vivaldi.kaist.ac.kr

II. Time-Varying Two-Phase NN

The time-varying constrained program is defined as

Time-varying program (TVP) : Minimize $f(x,t)$ subject to constraints

$$g_1(x) \leq 0, \cdots, g_r(x) \leq 0, \quad h_1(x) = 0, \cdots, h_m(x) = 0. \tag{1}$$

The proposed algorithm is described by the next theorem.

Theorem 1 *Assume that the time-dependent function satisfies the following inequality (2) where μ is a positive constant.*

$$\|(\frac{\partial^2 f(x,t)}{\partial x \partial x^T})^{-1}\| < \frac{1}{\mu}, \quad \forall x, t \tag{2}$$

Let

$$\begin{aligned} \dot{x}(t) &= -\alpha(x,t)G(x) \\ \alpha(x,t) &= \alpha_0 + \frac{\partial f/\partial t}{\|G(x)\|^2} \end{aligned} \tag{3}$$

where $\alpha_0 > 0$, $\alpha(x,t) \neq 0$ (when $\alpha = 0$, α keeps the previous non-zero value) and

$$G(x) = \nabla f + s[\sum_{i=1}^{r} g_i^+ \nabla g_i + \sum_{j=1}^{m} h_j \nabla h_j] \tag{4}$$

for $0 \leq t < t_1$, and

$$G(x) = \nabla f + \sum_{i=1}^{r} \nabla g_i (s g_i^+ + \lambda) + \sum_{j=1}^{m} \nabla h_j (s h_j + \mu) \tag{5}$$

for $t \geq t_1$, where $\dot{\lambda} = \epsilon(s g_i^+)$, $\dot{\mu} = \epsilon(sh)$ and t_1 is a switching time. If df/dt is uniformly continuous, then $x(t)$ converges to $\bar{x}$.

The proof for convergence is based on the Lemmas 1, 2 and Theorem 1 in [2] and is omitted here.

As we selected $\alpha(x,t)$ not to be 0, $x(t)$ converges only if $G(x)$ equals to 0. So the proposed time-varying two-phase network always satisfies the optimality condition for the solution when $x(t)$ converges.

0-7803-1901-X/94 $4.00 ©1994 IEEE

III. TVTP FOR NN LEARNING

In the training of the multi-layer NN, the variables which can be adjusted are the weights in each layer. So the problem of training a NN can be formulated as follows :

Find the weights $\bar{w}$ in each layer that minimize the error between the output of the plant and the output of the NN.

$$\begin{aligned}\bar{w} &= \min_w f(w,t) = \min_w \frac{1}{2}(y-\hat{y})^2 \\ &= \min_w \frac{1}{2}(F(u(t)) - NN[w,u(t)])^2\end{aligned}$$

where w is the weights in each layer, y is the output of the plant, $\hat{y}$ is the output of the multi-layer neural network, $F(\cdot)$ is the function of the plant, and $NN[\cdot]$ is the function of the multi-layer neural network.

When we have no constraints in w, the problem is principally the same as the unconstrained minimization for a time-varying nonlinear problem. Using theorem 1, the algorithm can be described as follows :

$$\begin{aligned}\dot{w} &= -\alpha(w,t)\frac{\partial f}{\partial w} \\ \alpha(w,t) &= \alpha_0 + \frac{\partial f/\partial t}{\|\partial f/\partial w\|^2}\end{aligned} \quad (6)$$

where $\alpha_0 > 0$, $\alpha(w,t) \neq 0$. When $\alpha = 0$, α keeps the previous non-zero value.

The term $\partial f/\partial w$, i. e., $\nabla_w f$ is the same as the gradients in the conventional error back propagation (EBP) algorithm. And the term $\partial f/\partial t$ can be approximated as

$$\frac{\partial f(w,t)}{\partial t} \approx \frac{f(w,t) - f(w,t-\Delta t)}{\Delta t}$$

where $f(w,t-\Delta t) = (y(t-\Delta t) - \hat{y}(t-\Delta t))^2$, and $\hat{y}(t-\Delta t)$ is obtained from $w(t)$.

When we have some constraints, we can easily implement them using the previous time-varying two-phase algorithm.

The schematic diagram of the TVTP learning architecture is shown in Figure 1. TDL in Figure 1 denotes a tapped delay line whose output vector has for its elements the delayed values of the input signal. Both neural networks NN($W(t)$) have the same structure but different inputs in order to estimate $\partial f(w,t)/\partial t$.

IV. FAST DIGITAL NN WITHOUT MULTIPLIERS

Among hardware implementations of artificial NNs, digital approach is the most popular because it has several advantages over the analog implementation. One of the major problems of digital architecture implementing NNs, affecting both performance and chip area, is the presence of multipliers. As M. Marchesi et al. [4] indicated, the multiplications between inputs and weights can be the bottle-neck of the hardware system. A possible solution is to avoid multiplications using integer weights whose values are power-of-two or sums of power-of-two. Using such weights, it is possible to substitute multiplications with simple shifts or shift-and-add operations, which are much faster and require less hardware. M. Marchesi et al. introduced multilayer perceptrons with such weights and presented a learning procedure based on back-propagation. They first make the network learn using the conventional EBP algorithm until convergence and then take another learning steps to obtain admissible weights whose values are power-of-two. If we could obtain valid weights during the first learning procedure without requiring additional learning steps, it would be more efficient.

In the previous section, we have shown that it is possible to train NNs with constraints in weights. Thus we will apply the proposed time-varying two-phase algorithm to this problem.

First, we must construct mathematical representations of the constraints in order to use the proposed algorithm. Let us denote with W_S the set of admissible weight values :

$$W_S \equiv \{x | x = R \cdot 2^{-p}, R \in \{-1,0,1\}, p \in \{0,1,\cdots,S\}\} \quad (7)$$

where S is the number of bits that can be shifted. It can be noted that this definition constrains the weights absolute value to be less than or equal to one, which is easily obtained by normalizing weights and offsets. Let $x_i \equiv -\log_2|w_i|$. Then x_i is always a nonnegative integer when $w_i \in W_S$. So the constraints that force x_i to be an integer can be formulated as follows (Fig. 2).

$$g_i(w) = \mu_k(x_i) - M \leq 0 \quad (8)$$

where $\mu_k(x_i) = \{4(x_i-k)(1-x_i+k)\}^2$, k is a maximum integer not greater than x_i, and M is a very small positive constant. Then the gradient of the constraint is

$$\nabla g_i(w) = \frac{32}{\log 2}\cdot\frac{1}{|w_i|}\cdot(x_i-k)(x_i-k-1)(1+2k-2x_i). \quad (9)$$

This method is somewhat similar to the nonlinear integer programming techniques presented in [6].

Now that we have obtained $g_i(w)$ and $\nabla g_i(w)$, we can build the learning algorithm as follows :

$$\begin{aligned}\dot{w}(t) &= -\alpha(w,t)G(w) \quad (10)\\ G(w) &= \begin{cases}\nabla f + s[\sum_{i=1}^N g_i^+ \nabla g_i] & (0 \leq t < t_1)\\ \nabla f + \sum_{i=1}^N \nabla g_i(s g_i^+ + \lambda) & (t \geq t_1)\end{cases}\end{aligned}$$

As the offsets are not constrained, they are updated by $G(w) = \nabla f$. The overall learning procedure consists of the following steps.

1) Make the network learn using the proposed TVTP algorithm until convergence and until no significant improvement can be achieved. In this stage, weights are forced to have admissible values belonging to W_S while offsets can have arbitrary continuous values.

2) Round weights w_i to the nearest term belonging to W_S. We recalculate weights as $|w_i|_{new} = 2^{-y_i}$, where y_i is the integer nearest to $x_i = -\log_2|w_i|$.

Table 1. After procedure 1.

	w_{i1}	w_{i2}	θ
w^1_{1j}	-4.230275	-4.170734	0.027421
w^1_{2j}	-1.330536	-1.320387	0.425910
w^2	-2.949088	3.700967	-0.519345

Table 2. After procedure 3.

	w_{i1}	w_{i2}	θ
w^1_{1j}	-5.000000	-5.000000	0.856122
w^1_{2j}	-1.250000	-1.250000	-0.314223
w^2	-2.500000	5.000000	1.266355

3) Starting from the network having new weights calculated in 2) and offsets, perform a TVTP learning step with weights fixed. Only offset values are updated in this stage until convergence.

To give some insight into this learning procedure, we illustrate following examples through computer simulations.

V. Computer simulations

A. Example 1 : XOR problem

A simple *XOR problem* is used to investigate the effect of constrained weights. As the inputs are discontinuous and so is the error function $E = \frac{1}{2}\sum_i (y_i - \hat{y}_i)^2$, we cannot change the learning rate according to the equation $\alpha(t) = \alpha_0 + \frac{\partial E/\partial t}{\|\cdot\|}$. In this example, we fixed the learning rate and considered only the effect of constraints. The parameters we used have the following values : $s = 1000$, $\alpha_0 = 10.$, $M = 0$, $S = 6$. The neural network architecture is $N^2_{2,2,1}$ which is shown in Figure 3.

We normalized weights and offsets by a factor of 1/10 and each look up table (LUT) that computes sigmoidal output is scaled up by 10 to yield values corresponding to the nonscaled case. The plot of error function E during procedure 1 is shown in Figure 4(a). Learning dynamics were changed to phase 2 at $k = 3345$ epoch and iterated until $k = 5000$. Weights and offsets obtained are shown in Table 1. After procedure 2, we apply procedure 3 to obtain admissible weights and offsets. The plot of E during procedure 3 is shown in Figure 4(b) and the final weights and offsets are shown in Table 2. The result is quite satisfactory compared with the NN with unconstrained weights.

B. Example 2 : Identification of a dynamic plant

In this example, we can use the advantage of the time-varying learning rate since the error function is continuous. The same plant model described by *Example 4* in the reference [5] is used here. A neural network belonging to the class $N^3_{5,10,10,1}$ is to be trained under the prescribed learning procedures to obtain an identification model with admissible weights. The parameter values used in this simulation are $s = 1000$, $\alpha_0 = 10.$, $M = 0$, $S = 6$ and the normalization factor is 1/5. Figure 5(a) shows the outputs of the plant and the NN model and Figure 5(b) is the plot of error function $E = \frac{1}{2}(y - \hat{y})^2$ during procedure 1. The input was changed to $u(k) = 0.8\sin(2\pi k/250) + 0.2\sin(2\pi k/25)$ at $k = 5,000$ from an initial input of $u(k) = \sin(2\pi k/250)$. After performing the learning for 10,000 steps, the NN undergoes procedures 2 and 3. Figure 5(c) shows the each output of the plant and the NN during procedure 3.

We now test the NN with admissible weights and offsets obtained by such procedures. Figure 5(d) is the simulation result without on-line adaptation. As we can see in this figure, the performance of this NN is somewhat satisfactory compared with the Fig. 16 in [5]. Thus the usefulness of the TVTP algorithm when the weights are constrained has been demonstrated through this example.

VI. Conclusions

In this paper, application of a two-phase neural network in time-varying nonlinear programming was presented. It can achieve an exact feasible solution with some assumptions such as convexity, inequality condition, and uniform continuity of the time derivative of the minimizing function.

The training of multi-layer neural network using a time-varying two-phase optimization neural network was simulated with a good performance. The proposed algorithm was shown to have the following characteristics : it has a good adaptability in on-line learning and is less sensitive to a learning step size than the conventional EBP method. It was successful to train the neural network with some constraints in the weights which arises in the practical implememtation of the NN hardware. We described the proposed learning procedures and demonstrated its usefulness through computer simulations.

References

[1] C. Y. Maa and M. A. Shanblatt, "A Two-phase optimization neural network," *IEEE Trans. neural networks*, vol.3 (no.6), pp.1003-1009, 1992

[2] C. B. Feng and Y. Zhao, "Time-varying nonlinear programming and its realization via neural networks," *ACC*, pp.978-982, 1992

[3] M. P. Kennedy and L. O. Chua, "Neural networks for nonlinear programming," *IEEE Trans. circuits and syst.*, vol.35 (no.5), pp.554-562, 1988

[4] M. Marchesi, G. Orlandi, F. Piazza, "Fast Neural Networks Without Multipliers," *IEEE Trans. neural networks*, vol.5, (no.1), pp.53-62, 1993

[5] K. S. Narendra and K. Parthasarathy, "Identification and control of dynamical systems using neural networks," *IEEE Trans. neural networks*, vol.1 (no.1), pp.4-26, 1990

[6] S. S. Rao, Optimization theory and applications, A Halsted Press Book, pp.517-566, 1979

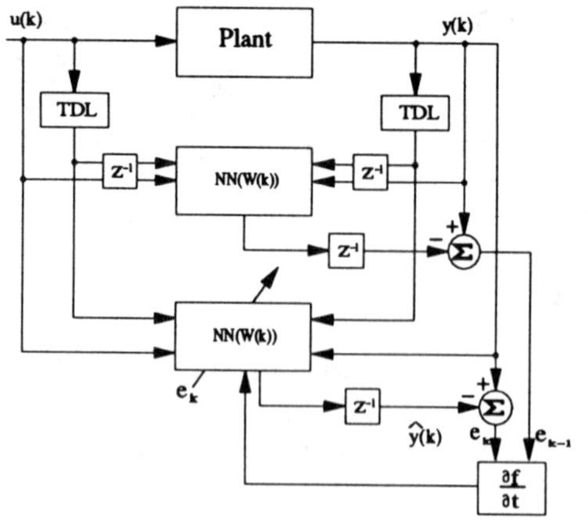

Fig. 1. schematic diagram of the TVTP learning architecture

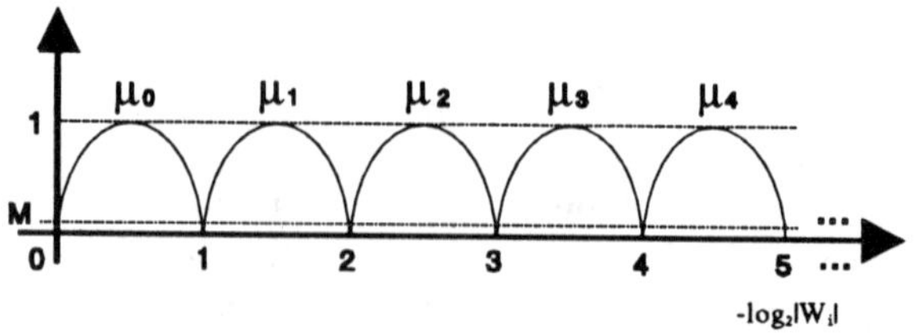

Fig. 2. Membership value $\mu_k(x_i)$ of admissible weight is not greater than M.

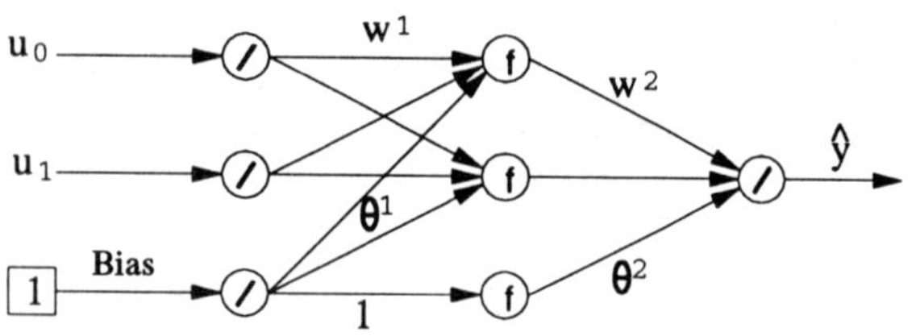

Fig. 3. neural network architecture in XOR problem

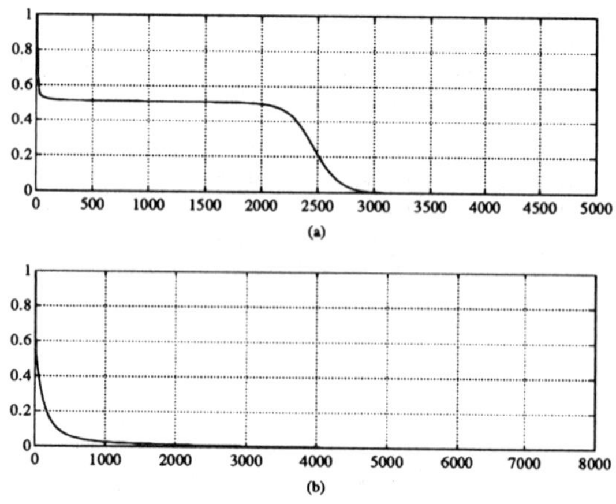

Fig. 4. Example 1 : (a) plot of E during procedure 1. (b) plot of E during procedure 3.

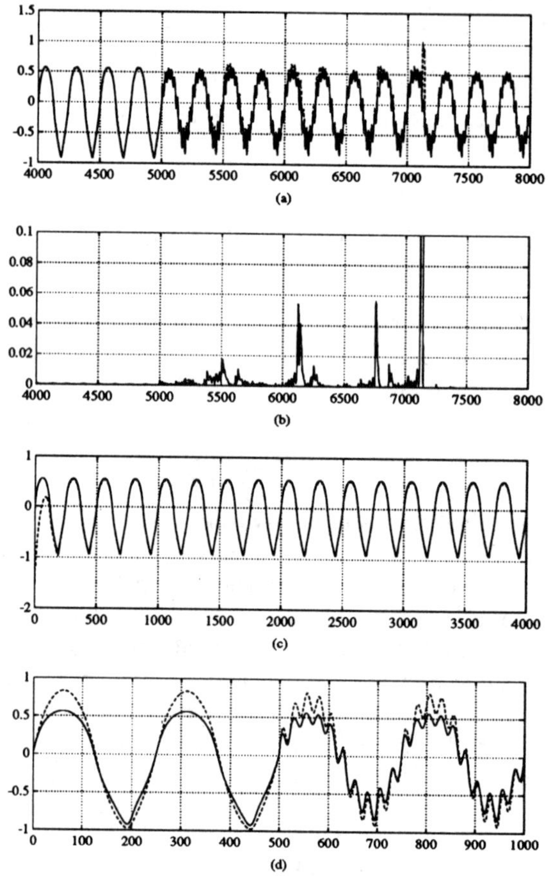

Fig. 5. Example 2 : Dynamic plant learning (a) outputs of plant and NN model when the input was changed at $k = 5000$ during procedure 1. (b) plot of error function in (a). (c) outputs of plant and NN model during procedure 3. (d) outputs of plant and NN model when no adaptation is carried out after procedure 3.

Theoretical Characterizations of Possibilities and Impossibilities of Hopfield Neural Networks in Solving Combinatorial Optimization Problems (Extended Abstract)

Satoshi Matsuda
Computer and Communication Research Center,
Tokyo Electric Power Company
1-3, Uchisaiwai-cho, 1-Chome, Chiyoda-ku, Tokyo, 100 Japan

ABSTRACT: The asymptotical stability and unstability conditions of the solutions and nonsolutions are proved for corners of Hopfield neural hypercube in solving typical combinatorial optimization problems, i.e., traveling salesman problem, N-queen problem and Hitchcock problem. These conditions make the theoretical characterizations of many possibilities and impossibilities of Hopfield neural networks in solving combinatorial optimization problems.

1. INTRODUCTION

Many trials to solve the combinatorial optimization problems by Hopfield neural networks have been made, however, few theoretical analysis of the dynamics of networks are made, and the choices of weights of constraints and optimization requirements are made by trial and error. These prevent Hopfield networks from being applied to practical optimization problems. In the previous paper[(2)], by taking traveling salesman problem as an example, the asymptotical stability and unstability conditions of the solutions satisfying constraints of the problem, and unstability condition of nonsolutions not satisfying constraints were proved. It was shown that these conditions derived many properties of the network, e.g., the theoretical limitation of networks without self-connections(w_{ii}=0), made theoretical explanations to many phenomena, and obtained best solution easily. Thus these conditions characterize the fundamental properties, or possibilities and impossibilities, of the dynamics of Hopfield neural networks.

Then, one wonders if it is possible for other combinatorial optimization problems, or TSP is an exception? In this paper, similar conditions, which will theoretically derive many properties similarly for TSP, are proved for new formalization of N-queen and Hitchcock problem. It suggests similar conditions seem to be possible for many or almost all the problems. It would be toward a unified theory of many optimization problems.

2. TRAVELING SALESMAN PROBLEMS

The dynamics and energy E of Hopfield neural network are defined as usual:

$$\frac{du_i}{dt} = \Sigma_j w_{ij} v_j + h_i \qquad (w_{ij} = w_{ji}), \qquad\qquad v_i = \frac{1}{2}\,(1 + \tanh(u_i/x_0))$$

$$E = -\frac{1}{2}\Sigma_i \Sigma_j w_{ij} v_i v_j - \Sigma_i h_i v_i$$

where u_i, v_i and h_i are an internal value, output value and threshold of neuron i respectively, and w_{ij} is a weight of connection from neuron j to i ($w_{ij} = w_{ji}$ and generally $w_{ii} \neq 0$). It is well known that $dE/dt \leq 0$, that is, networks converge to energy minima at last.

Hopfield and Tank[(1)] applied Hopfield network to solve a combinatorial problem, traveling salesman problem, and showed good solutions were obtained in a short time. The traveling salesman problem is formalized as usual:

$$E_T = \frac{A}{2}\Sigma_i(\Sigma_x v_{xi} - 1)^2 + \frac{A}{2}\Sigma_x(\Sigma_i v_{xi} - 1)^2 + \frac{B}{2}\Sigma_x \Sigma_i v_{xi}(1 - v_{xi}) + \frac{D}{2}\Sigma_x \Sigma_y \Sigma_i d_{xy} v_{xi}(v_{y\,i-1} + v_{y\,i+1}) \rightarrow \min. \qquad \cdots (1)$$

The first and second terms are constraint conditions, the last term is an optimization condition, and the third term, which makes neurons to converge to 0 or 1, i.e., a corner of unit hypercube, is a binary value constraint. In general a corner $V \in \{0,1\}^N$ is also called a solution or nonsolution if it satisfies all the constraints or not respectively.

To obtain good solutions it is necessary to choose the values of A, B, D and initial values of neurons adequately, however, these choices are made almost by trial and error at present. In the previous paper [2] the asymptotical stability and unstability conditions of solution and nonsolutions were proved for TSP represented as (1).

Prop. 1) [2] For Hopfield network having (1) as an energy function, followings hold:
(a) Any solution $V \in \{0,1\}^N$ is asymptotically stable if

$$2D \cdot \max_{xy, yz \in \beta(V)} \{ d_{xy} + d_{yz} \} < B,$$

and unstable if not

$$2D \cdot \max_{xy, yz \in \beta(V)} \{ d_{xy} + d_{yz} \} \leqq B.$$

(b) All the solutions are asymptotically stable if

$$2D \cdot \max_{xy, yz \in \beta(V),\ V \in \Gamma} \{ d_{xy} + d_{yz} \} < B,$$

and there is an unstable solution if not

$$2D \cdot \max_{xy, yz \in \beta(V),\ V \in \Gamma} \{ d_{xy} + d_{yz} \} \leqq B.$$

(c) All the solutions are asymptotically stable if

$$2D \cdot \max_{x, y, z} \{ d_{xy} + d_{yz} \} < B.$$

(d) There is no asymptotically stable solution if

$$4D \cdot \max_x \{ \min_y \{ d_{xy} \} \} > B,$$

where $\Gamma \subseteq \{0,1\}^N$ is a set of all solutions, and $\beta(V)$ is a set of all branches between two cities in the tour path the solution V means.

Prop. 2) [2] For Hopfield network having (1) as an energy function, all the nonsolutions are unstable if

$$A > \max\{ B/2,\ B/4 + D \cdot \max_{x, y} \{ d_{xy} \} \}.$$

Since networks converge to asymptotically stable corners and can not converge to unstable corners, these conditions make dynamics of the network considerably clear. For example, as shown in the previous paper [2], it means, by setting the values of A, B and D as above, that one can make all the solutions satisfying some quality asymptotically stable, nonsolutions unstable, and get the best solution easily, however, one cannot make only best solution asymptotically stable in general. In addition, these conditions derive many properties of the network, e.g., the theoretical limitation of the network without self-connections($w_{ii}=0$), and give theoretical explanations to many phenomena. They also suggest new effective formalizations of the problems. Actually we introduce new formalizations of N-queen and Hitchcock problems later.

3. N-QUEEN PROBLEMS

N-queen problem is a famous combinatorial optimization problem, which Hopfield network is applied to. It can be formally defined as:

$$\begin{aligned} E_Q = \ & A_1/2\ \Sigma_i (\Sigma_j v_{ij} - 1)^2 + A_1/2\ \Sigma_j (\Sigma_i v_{ij} - 1)^2 \\ & + A_2/2\ \Sigma_i \Sigma_j v_{ij} \Sigma_k (v_{i+k,\,j+k} + v_{i-k,\,j-k}) + A_2/2\ \Sigma_i \Sigma_j v_{ij} \Sigma_k (v_{i-k,\,j+k} + v_{i+k,\,j-k}) \\ & + B/2\ \Sigma_i \Sigma_j v_{ij} (1 - v_{ij}) \quad \rightarrow \min. \qquad \cdots (2) \end{aligned}$$

where v_{ij} means the presence of queen at a position (i, j) in chessboard, and $A_1, A_2 > 0$, $B \geqq 0$. All the terms are constraint conditions, especially, the last is a binary value constraint.

Th. 1) For Hopfield network having (2) as an energy function, any solution $V \in \{0,1\}^N$ is asymptotically stable if $B>0$, and unstable if $B<0$.
pr) Since $\Sigma_j V_{aj} - 1 = 0$ and $\Sigma_i V_{ib} - 1 = 0$ for any solution V and integer a and b,

$$\begin{aligned} \partial E / \partial v_{ab}(V) = \ & A_1(\Sigma_i V_{ib} - 1) + A_1(\Sigma_j V_{aj} - 1) \\ & + A_2 \Sigma_k (V_{a+k,\,b+k} + V_{a+k,\,b-k}) + A_2 \Sigma_k (V_{a-k,\,b+k} + V_{a-k,\,b-k}) + B(1/2 - V_{ab}), \\ & \begin{cases} \geqq B/2 & (\text{ if } V_{ab}=0\ ) \\ = -B/2 & (\text{ if } V_{ab}=1\ ). \end{cases} \end{aligned}$$

If $B>0$, $\partial E/\partial v_{ab}(V) > 0$ for $V_{ab}=0$, and $\partial E/\partial v_{ab}(V) < 0$ for $V_{ab}=1$. Hence V is asymptotically stable. If $B<0$, V is unstable. Q.E.D.

Th. 2) For Hopfield network having (2) as energy function, all the nonsolutions are unstable if

$$A_1 > A_2 + B/4 \quad \text{and} \quad A_2 > B/2.$$

pr) For any nonsolution $V=(V_{ii})$, there is integer a or b satisfying at least one of

① $\Sigma_i V_{ib} - 1 \geqq 1$, ② $\Sigma_j V_{aj} - 1 \geqq 1$,

③ $\Sigma_i V_{ib} - 1 = -1$, ④ $\Sigma_j V_{aj} - 1 = -1$,

⑤ $V_{ab}\Sigma_k (V_{a+k,b+k} + V_{a-k,b-k}) \geqq 1$, ⑥ $V_{ab}\Sigma_k (V_{a-k,b+k} + V_{a+k,b-k}) \geqq 1$.

In the case ①, by the assumption, there exists integer a such that $V_{ab}=1$. So, since

$$\begin{aligned}\partial E/\partial v_{ab}(V) &= A_1(\Sigma_i V_{ib} - 1) + A_1(\Sigma_j V_{aj} - 1) \\ &\quad + A_2\Sigma_k(V_{a+k,b+k} + V_{a+k,b-k}) + A_2\Sigma_k(V_{a-k,b+k} + V_{a-k,b-k}) + B(1/2 - V_{ab}) \\ &\geqq A_1 + 0 + 0 + 0 - B/2,\end{aligned}$$

if $A_1>B/2$, $\partial E/\partial v_{ab}(V)>0$, so V is unstable. Similarly for the case ②. For the case ⑤ and ⑥, we can similarly show that V is unstable if $A_2>B/2$.

For the case ③, since we can assume that ① and ② do not hold, it is immediate that there also exists integer a such that $\Sigma_j V_{aj} - 1 = -1$. And since we can also assume that ⑤ and ⑥ do not hold, $\Sigma_k(V_{a+k,b+k} + V_{a+k,b-k}) \leqq 1$ and $\Sigma_k(V_{a-k,b+k} + V_{a-k,b-k}) \leqq 1$. Therefore, since

$$\begin{aligned}\partial E/\partial v_{ab}(V) &= A_1(\Sigma_i V_{ib} - 1) + A_1(\Sigma_j V_{aj} - 1) \\ &\quad + A_2\Sigma_k(V_{a+k,b+k} + V_{a+k,b-k}) + A_2\Sigma_k(V_{a-k,b+k} + V_{a-k,b-k}) + B(1/2 - V_{ab}) \\ &\leqq -2A_1 + 2A_2 + B/2,\end{aligned}$$

if $A_1>A_2+B/4$, $\partial E/\partial v_{ab}(V)<0$, so V is unstable. Similarly for ④. Hence, summarizing three conditions above, we have $A_1>A_2+B/4$ and $A_2>B/2$. Q.E.D.

Thus, it is also possible to make all the solutions asymptotically stable, nonsolutions unstable for N-queen problem. Note that $A_1 \neq A_2$ seems a key to unstabilities of nonsolutions.

4. HITCHCOCK PROBLEMS

Hitchcock Problem is another famous combinatorial optimization problem, which Hopfield network is applied to. It can be formalized as

$$\begin{aligned}E_H = {} & A/2 \sum_{x=1}^{n}\sum_{i=1}^{s_x}\Big(\sum_{y=1}^{m}\sum_{j=1}^{d_y} v_{xiyj} - 1\Big)^2 + A/2 \sum_{y=1}^{m}\sum_{j=1}^{d_y}\Big(\sum_{x=1}^{n}\sum_{i=1}^{s_x} v_{xiyj} - 1\Big)^2 \\ & + B/2 \sum_{x=1}^{n}\sum_{y=1}^{m}\sum_{i=1}^{s_x}\sum_{j=1}^{d_y} v_{xiyj}(1 - v_{xiyj}) + C/2 \Big(\sum_{x=1}^{n}\sum_{y=1}^{m} c_{xy}\sum_{i=1}^{s_x}\sum_{j=1}^{d_y} v_{xiyj}\Big)^2 \rightarrow \min. \quad \cdots (3)\end{aligned}$$

where s_x is the number of products supplier x ($x=1,\cdots,n$) has, and d_y is the number of products consumer y ($y=1,\cdots,m$) demands. c_{xy} is the unit cost of transportation from supplier x to consumer y. $v_{xiyj}=1$ means i-th product of supplier x is transportated to satisfy j-th demand of consumer y. Note that (3) is different from one in Takeda and Goodman[3], and makes us a present of next theorems.

Th. 3) For Hopfield network having (3) as an energy function, followings hold:

(a) Any solution $V \in \{0,1\}^N$ is asymptotically stable if

$$2Cc_V \cdot \max_{(x,y)\in\gamma(V)}\{c_{xy}\} < B,$$

and unstable if not

$$2Cc_V \cdot \max_{(x,y)\in\gamma(V)}\{c_{xy}\} \leqq B.$$

(b) All the solutions are asymptotically stable if

$$2Cc_V \cdot \max_{(x,y)\in\gamma(V),\ V\in\Gamma}\{c_{xy}\} < B,$$

and there is an unstable solution if not

$$2Cc_V \cdot \max_{(x,y)\in\gamma(V),\ V\in\Gamma}\{c_{xy}\} \leqq B.$$

(c) All the solutions are asymptotically stable if

$$2Cc_V \cdot \max_{x,y}\{c_{xy}\} < B$$

(d) There is no asymptotically stable solution if

$$2Cc_V \cdot \max_x \{ \min_y \{ c_{xy} \} \} > B$$

where $\Gamma \subseteq \{0,1\}^N$ is a set of all the solutions, and $\gamma(V) = \{(x,y) \mid \exists i \exists j (V_{xiyj}=1)\}$, i.e., a set of all the pairs (x,y) such that the solution V means a transportation of products from supplier x to consumer y, and $c_V = \Sigma_x \Sigma_y c_{xy} \Sigma_i \Sigma_j V_{xiyj}$, i.e., transportation cost of a solution V.

pr) We prove only (a) here, others are immediate from (a). Since $\Sigma_y \Sigma_j V_{asyj} - 1 = 0$ and $\Sigma_x \Sigma_i V_{xibt} - 1 = 0$ for any solution V and any integer a, b, s and t,

$$\partial E/\partial v_{asbt}(V) = A(\Sigma_y \Sigma_j V_{asyj} - 1) + A(\Sigma_x \Sigma_i V_{xibt} - 1) + B(1/2 - V_{asbt}) + Cc_{ab} \Sigma_x \Sigma_y c_{xy} \Sigma_i \Sigma_j V_{xiyj}$$

$$= \begin{cases} Cc_{ab}c_V + B/2 & (\text{if } V_{asbt}=0) \\ Cc_{ab}c_V - B/2 & (\text{if } V_{asbt}=1) \end{cases}$$

If $V_{asbt}=0$, $\partial E/\partial v_{asbt}>0$ always holds, and when $V_{asbt}=1$, if $2Cc_{ak}c_V<B$, $\partial E/\partial v_{asbt}<0$. Hence if $2Cc_V \cdot \max_{xy \in \beta(V)} \{ c_{xy} \} < B$, V is asymtotically stable. If $2Cc_V \cdot \max_{(x,y) \in \beta(V)} \{ c_{xy} \} \leq B$ does not hold, $\partial E/\partial v_{ab}(V)>0$ and $V_{ab}=1$ for some a and b. Hence V is unstable. Q.E.D.

Th.4) For Hopfield network having (3) as energy function, all the nonsolutions are unstable if

$$A > \max\{ B/2 - 2C \cdot \min\{(c_{xy})^2\},\ B/4 + C/2 \max\{(c_{xy})^2\} \cdot \min\{ n \cdot \max\{s_x\},\ m \cdot \max\{d_y\} \} \}.$$

pr) For any nonsolution $V=(V_{ii})$, at least one of the followings holds:

① $\exists x \exists i (\Sigma_y \Sigma_j V_{xiyj} - 1 \geq 1)$ ② $\exists y \exists j (\Sigma_x \Sigma_i V_{xiyj} - 1 \geq 1)$

③ $\exists x \exists i (\Sigma_y \Sigma_j V_{xiyj} - 1 = -1)$ ④ $\exists y \exists j (\Sigma_x \Sigma_i V_{xiyj} - 1 = -1)$

In the case ①, there exists integer a, s, b and t such that $V_{asbt}=1$. Therefore, since

$$\partial E/\partial v_{asbt}(V) = A(\Sigma_y \Sigma_j V_{asyj} - 1) + A(\Sigma_x \Sigma_i V_{xibt} - 1) + B(1/2 - V_{asbt}) + Cc_{ab} \Sigma_x \Sigma_y c_{xy} \Sigma_i \Sigma_j V_{xiyj}$$
$$\geq A + 0 - B/2 + 2Cc_{ab} \cdot c_{ab}$$
$$\geq A - B/2 + 2C \cdot \min\{(c_{xy})^2\},$$

if $A > B/2 - 2C \cdot \min\{(c_{xy})^2\}$, $\partial E/\partial vak(V)>0$, so V is unstable. Similarly for the case ②.

For ③, first of all, since we can assume that ① or ② does not hold, it is immediate that there exist a, s, b and t such that $\Sigma_y \Sigma_j V_{asyj} - 1 = -1$ and $\Sigma_x \Sigma_i V_{xibt} - 1 = -1$. Hence

$$\partial E/\partial v_{asbt}(V)$$
$$= A(\Sigma_y \Sigma_j V_{asyj} - 1) + A(\Sigma_x \Sigma_i V_{xibt} - 1) + B(1/2 - V_{asbt}) + Cc_{ab} \sum_{x=1}^{n} \sum_{y=1}^{m} c_{xy} \sum_{i=1}^{s_x} \sum_{j=1}^{d_y} V_{xiyj}$$
$$\leq -2A + B/2 + Cc_{ab} \cdot \max\{c_{xy}\} \cdot \min\{n \cdot \max\{s_x\}, m \cdot \max\{d_y\}\}$$
$$\leq -2A + B/2 + C \cdot \max\{(c_{xy})^2\} \cdot \min\{n \cdot \max\{s_x\}, m \cdot \max\{d_y\}\}.$$

Therefore, if $A > B/4 + C \cdot \max\{(c_{xy})^2\} \cdot \min\{n \cdot \max\{s_x\}, m \cdot \max\{d_y\}\}/2$, $\partial E/\partial v_{asbt}(V)<0$. So V is unstable since $V_{asbt}=0$. Similarly for the case ④. Q.E.D.

Thus, it has also been shown to be possible to make all or good solutions asymptotically stable, and nonsolutions unstable for Hitchcock problems. Similarly for TSP, these theorems will derive many theoretical characterizations of the dynamics of networks, however, we here only point out that Th.3(a) suggests asymptotically stable corners can be 'more sharply' restricted only to very good solutions than Prop.1(a) for TSP,

5. CONCLUSION

The asymptotical stability and unstability conditions of the solutions and nonsolutions are proved for corners of Hopfield neural hypercube in solving typical combinatorial optimization problems, i.e., traveling salesman problem, N-queen problem and Hitchcock problem. Similarly for TSP shown in the previous paper [2], these will make other theoretical characterizations of many possibilities and impossibilities of Hopfield neural networks in solving combinatorial optimization problems. It suggests similar conditions seem possible for many or almost all problems. And it would be toward the general theory on many combinatorial optimization problems.

References:

(1)Hopfield, J.J. and D.W.Tank: "Neural" computation of decisions of optimization problems, Biol. Cybern. 52, 141-152 (1985)

(2)Matsuda, S.:The stability of the solution in Hopfield neural network — the case of travelling salesman problem —, Proc. of IJCNN'93-Nagoya, 1524-1527 (1993)

(3)Takeda, M. and J.W.Goodman: Neural network for computation:number representation and programming complexity, Appl.Opt.25, 3033 (1986)

A Stability criterion for Hopfield Networks based on Popov Theorem

D. Sbarbaro
Department of Electrical Engineering - Casilla 53-C
University of Concepción, Concepción-Chile

Abstract

A Hopfield network is considered as a nonlinear system with multiples nonlinearities (so called Lurie systems). A frequency domain criterion is formulated to prove global asymptotic stability of the equilibrium point of the system, this condition is expressed as a inequality over the whole range of frequency. This known result is applied to analyse the global asymptotic stability of a Hopfield network, obtaining conditions for testing the stability of the equilibrium points and their regions of attractions. These conditions do not require symmetric interconnection matrices.

1 Introduction

The stability properties of Hopfield networks have been studied considering the Lyapunov direct methods. On the other hand, several researchers have investigated the stability of autonomous feedback control systems with more than one nonlinearity. The nonlinear elements are always separated by intermediate energy storage elements, these type of systems has been called Lurie systems. The conditions for absolute stability of these systems were studied by Popov and extended by other researchers to systems with more than one linearity [1][3]. This paper outline the application of these known results to analyse the stability of Hopfield networks, obtaining sufficient conditions for the asymptotic stability of its equilibrium points.

The paper is organized as follow: Section 2 describes the structure of a Hopfield network. Section 3 describes the stability theorem for Lurie systems. Section 4 describes the results for the Hopfield networks based on Popov theorem, and finally in section 5 some conclusions are given.

2 Hopfield Network Structure

The continuous time Hopfield network is defined by a set of n scalar equations described in vector notation as

$$\frac{dU}{dt} = AU + WG(U) + B \tag{1}$$

where $U = [u_1, \ldots, u_n]^T$, $A = diag[a_1, \ldots, a_n]$, $a_i < 0, W \in R^{n \times n}$ (we do not require W to be symetric), and $G = diag[g_1, \ldots, g_n]$.

[0]Submitted to the IJCNN, Orlando, U.S.A. 1994

0-7803-1901-X/94 $4.00 ©1994 IEEE

The nonlinear function $g_i(.)$, $i = 1, 2, \ldots, n$ are assumed to satisfy the following conditions:

$$\begin{array}{llr} i) & u_i g_i(u_i) > 0 & \forall u_i \in R \\ ii) & \lim_{|u_i| \to \infty} = sgn(u_i) & \\ iii) & \frac{g_i(u_i)}{u_i} \geq \frac{g_i(v_i)}{v_i} & \forall |u_i| \leq |v_i| \\ iv) & g_i'(u_i) = \frac{dg_i(u_i)}{du_i} & \forall u_i \in R \end{array} \tag{2}$$

In order for a state $U^* \in R^n$ to be an equilibrium state of the system (1), it is necessary and sufficient that

$$AU^* + WG(U^*) + B = 0 \tag{3}$$

we assume that a given U^* is an isolated equilibrium state, i.e. there exist an $r > 0$ such that the region

$$\mathcal{B}(U^*, r) \subset R^n \ni \mathcal{B} = \{U : \|U - U^*\| < r\} \tag{4}$$

contains no equilibria other than U^*.

For a given equilibrium point U^*, with coordinate transformation $X = U - U^*$ [2], equation (1) can be written as

$$\frac{dX}{dt} = AX + W\tilde{G}(U) \tag{5}$$

where $\tilde{G}(X) = G(X + U^*) - G(U)$. Obviously, $X = 0$ defines an equlibrium point of (5) and $\tilde{G}(0) = 0$

3 The Lurie systems and its stability

A nominal description of a Lurie system, with multiple non-linearities $f_1, f_2, \ldots, f_m$ composing a vector non-linearity F, is defined by

$$\begin{array}{l} \frac{dX}{dt} = \tilde{A}X + \tilde{B}F(Y) \\ Y = \tilde{C}X \end{array} \tag{6}$$

where $X \in R^n$, $\tilde{A} \in R^{nxn}$, $\tilde{B} \in R^{mxn}$, $Y \in R^m$, and $\tilde{C} \in R^{mxn}$. The nonlinearity $F \in N_K$, where N_K is the family of all non-linearities $f : R^m \to R^m$ with the following properties:

$$\begin{array}{ll} i) & F(Y) \in C(R^m) \\ ii) & F(0) = 0 \\ iii) & f_i(y_i)y_i^{-1} \in (0, k_i) \quad \forall\, y_i \in R, \quad y_i \neq 0\ \forall i = 1, \ldots, m \end{array} \tag{7}$$

and the motion $\mathcal{X}(t, X_0, F)$ of 6 through X_0 at t=0 exist, and is defined on R_+ and is unique for every $X_0 \in R^n$.

The system described by (1) is a Lurie system with $m = n$, $\tilde{A} = A$, $\tilde{C} = I$, $\tilde{B} = W$, and $F = G$. The global stability of the system (6) has been studied by several researchers [1] [3], and the main result can be sumarized in the following theorem, which gives a sufficient condition for the system to be globally asymptotically stable.

Theorem 1 *The system (6) is globally asymptotically stable if there exist a positive matrix K such that*

1) The elements of K satisfy the inequality iii) of (7).

2) The matrix inequality

$$T(j\omega) = I - \frac{1}{2}[K\tilde{C}(j\omega I - \tilde{A})^{-1}\tilde{B} + \tilde{B}^T(-j\omega I - \tilde{A}^T)^{-1}(K\tilde{C})^T] > 0 \quad (8)$$

holds for all real ω.

3) A *is asymptotically stable.*

Theorem 1 can be considered as a multivariable version of Popov theorem.

4 Stabilty results of a Hopfield network based on Popov Theorem

The following relation are obtained for matrix A[1]

$$A = A^T \quad \text{and} \quad (j\omega I - A)^{-1} < -A^{-1}, \quad \forall \omega \in R_+. \quad (9)$$

Thus, applying the results obtained for the Lurie system, the following results are obtained for Hopfield networks.

Theorem 2 *The equilibrium point* U^* *of the system (5) is globally asymptotically stable if*

$$T = I + \frac{1}{2}[KA^{-1}W + W^T(A^T)^{-1}(K)^T] > 0 \quad (10)$$

where $K = G'(U^*)$

Proof:

If $K = G'(U^*)$, then exist an interval defined by $l_i \leq x_i < h_i$, where $l_i \in R$ and $h_i \in R$, such that

$$0 \leq x_i \tilde{g}_i(x_i) \leq k_i x_i^2, \quad \forall i = 1, \ldots, m \quad (11)$$

Using inequality (9) and Theorem 1, condition 2),

$$T = I + \frac{1}{2}[KA^{-1}W + W(A^T)^{-1}K^T] > 0 \quad (12)$$

is a sufficient condition for the system to be asymptotically stable in a neighbourhood of the equilibrium point U^*.◇

Theorem 3 *For a given equilibrium point* U^*, *there can exist no other equilibrium point of the system defined by (5) in the same quadrant, if*

$$T = I + \frac{1}{2}[HA^{-1}W + W^T A^{-1}(H)^T] > 0 \quad (13)$$

where $H = diag[\frac{g_1(u_1^*)}{u_1^*}, \ldots, \frac{g_1(u_1^*)}{u_1^*}]$.

Proof:

[1] $A \leq B$, if only if $a_{ij} \leq b_{ij}$, $\forall i \in \{i, \ldots, n\}$ and $j \in \{1, \ldots, n\}$

If $h_i = \frac{g_i(u_i^*)}{u_i^*}$ means that

$$0 \le x_i \tilde{g}_i(x_i) \le h_i x_i^2, \qquad \forall i = 1, \ldots, m \tag{14}$$

for all x_i, see figure 1, such that

$$\begin{array}{ll} -u_i^* \le x_i \le \infty & if \quad u_i^* > 0 \\ -\infty \le x_i \le u_i^* & if \quad u_1^* < 0. \end{array} \tag{15}$$

By Theorem 1, (12) is a sufficient condition for stablishing the asymptotic stability of $X = 0$ in the region defined by (15), i.e. for all U in the same quadrant of the equilibrium point U^*. Thus, as $X = 0$ is asymptotically stable in this region, there is no other equilibrium point in it. ◇

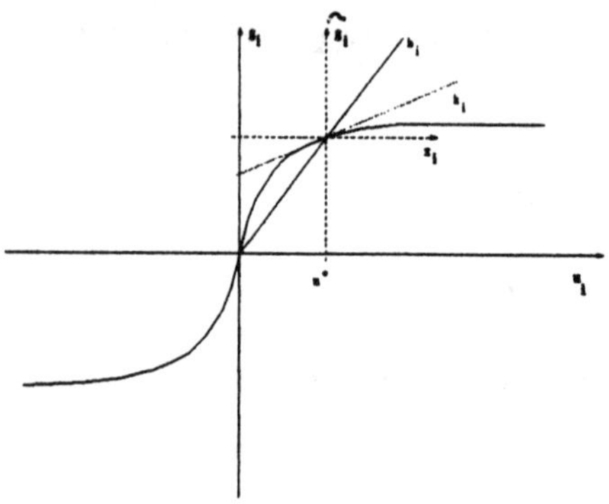

Figure 1: Nonlinearity and the change of coordinates

The conditions giving by Theorem 2 and Theorem 3 are interrelated because $G'(U^*) \le H$. Thus, if the system meets the condition of Theorem 3, then it satisfy the conditions of Theorem 2 as well. Equations (12) and (13) are equivalent to the conditions obtained in [2].

5 Conclusions

In this paper the conditions obtained to analyse the stability of a Lurie system were applied to analyse the asymptotic stability of the Hopfield network equilibrium points, demonstrating no only the effect of the matrices involved, but also the importance of the nonlinear function. The stability conditions and confinement of the stability region to an especific quadrant are reduced to test the positivity of a matrix, which depends on the matrices of the system and the nonlinearities. Further work is underway to extend these results to different network architectures, including discrete time Hopfield networks.

References

[1] E. Ibrahim and Z. Rekasius, "A stability criterion for nonlinear feedback systems," *IEEE Transactions on Automatic Control*, vol. 9, pp. 154–159, 1964.

[2] S. I. Sudharsanan and M. Sundareshan, "Equilibrium chracterization of dynamical neural networks and systematic synthesis procedure for associative memories," *IEEE Transactions on Neural Networks*, vol. 2, pp. 509–521, 1991.

[3] L. Grujic and D. Petkovski, "On robustness of lurie systems with multiple non-linearities," *Automatica*, vol. 23, no. 3, pp. 327–334, 1987.

Behavioral Testability and Test Pattern Generation of the Hopfield Network Model

Cesare Alippi, Franco Fummi, Vincenzo Piuri, Mariagiovanna Sami, Donatella Sciuto
Dipartimento di Elettronica e Informazione, Politecnico di Milano
piazza L. da Vinci 32, I-20133 Milano, Italy

Abstract

The problem of testability and test pattern generation at the highest abstraction level, i.e., based on the network's behavior, is here considered for Hopfield networks. Complete testability is proved. A test pattern generation approach based on creation of an equivalent Finite State Machine is presented, functional test pattern generation having being proved to allow very high coverage of logic-level faults in the case of FSMs. An efficient algorithm, using BDDs, is finally described.

1. Introduction

Recent literature has made evident a trend towards qualitative evaluation of system testability at the highest, i.e. behavioral, abstraction model. Such an approach can provide guidelines for choice of subsequent implementation alternatives; recent published examples are provided, e.g. by [1, 2] and, in the neural network domain, by [3]. Even more relevant efforts have been dedicated to the problem of functional-level test pattern generation (usually, the term "behavioral" is in this case adopted only for microprocessors). The justification of such trend can be found both in the extreme complexity of VLSI devices, making conventional techniques unmanageable, and in the possibility of creating test patterns as far as possible independent of the final silicon implementation. In particular, the functional test generation approach has been proved very rewarding in the case of Finite-State Machines; test patterns derived for a purely functional error model and on the basis of the state table only have experimentally given very high fault coverage for different types of implementation technologies (e.g., random logic, PLA) and for related fault models [4, 5, 6].

In the present paper, the functional approach is adopted both to evaluate testability and to provide efficient test pattern generation for Hopfield networks. We start from the standard Hopfield paradigm definition [7]:

$$x_i(t) = f_i\,(\Sigma_{j=1}^{N}\ w_{ij}\, x_j(t\text{-}1) - \theta_i) \qquad (1)$$

where $x_i(t)$ is the output of the i-th neuron at time t, $x_j(t\text{-}1)$ the output of the j-th neuron at the previous iteration, w_{ij} is the interconnection weight between neurons i and j, θ_i is the bias of neuron i, and f_i is the non-linear activation function (usually taken as the signum or step function).

We assume that learning has been perfected, so the values of the weights w_{ij} are determined and the network is able to reach a steady output for any input pattern. Without loss of generality, we consider that the possible values of x_i are only $\{0, 1\}$. We restrict our present analysis to the parallel-type recalling procedure of the Hopfield networks: the initial input $x_i(t_0)$ is set in each neuron simultaneously; the network evolves towards the final steady state so that, at each iteration, the output updating is performed within each neuron simultaneously.

In our analysis, we distinguish between errors in the network's outputs due to faults and errors which are intrinsic in the neural paradigm due to incomplete classification and generalization capabilities provided by the actual learning procedure. In the presence of the second class of output errors, even if they are related to an undesired neural behavior, testability and testing can be considered as in the desired behavior since the undesired behavior is part of the whole nominal behavior generated by the adopted learning procedure. Therefore, we concentrate our attention on the identification of erroneous outputs due to faults.

No assumption is made on the implementation technology as well as on the supporting architecture, excepting for the request of explicit synchronization with respect to a time base.

The first problem in testing is the preliminary evaluation of the *testability* of the whole system at behavioral level [1, 2], i.e., the possibility of providing and propagating the necessary test patterns for error

0-7803-1901-X/94 $4.00

excitation (*controllability*) and the possibility of observing the results generated by the circuit under test (*observability*). In [3], we adopted a behavioral approach at the abstraction level of the neural operators for the case of multi-layered feed-forward networks. In Section 2, we discuss this figure of merit of the neural paradigm for Hopfield networks, i.e., in the presence of feedback loops.

A subsequent, even more important problem, is that of test pattern generation. Hopfield networks of large dimensions have already been implemented [8]; moreover, such different implementation approaches as analog, digital and mixed solutions have been presented in the literature. A low level test generation approach would involve separate test pattern generation for each implementation alternative; moreover, such procedure would be very complex both for a digital implementation (the Hopfield network is a sequential one) and, even more, for an analog implementation.

In Section 3, we introduce an FSM modeling approach for Hopfield networks. It will be seen that such model allows a very efficient test pattern generation with reference to the "single-transition" fault model adopted for FSM functional testing [9]. In fact, complete coverage can be reached by a procedure whose complexity is linear with the number of states. Thus, we achieve test patterns valid for any implementation satisfying to the above recalled restrictions (parallel recall, explicitly synchronous operation). Section 4 presents a detailed description of the behavioral test procedure generation.

2. Testability analysis

The testability issue for any system can be summarized as the possibility of total *controllability* and *observability*, where by controllability we denote the possibility of propagating arbitrary test patterns from the system's inputs to the component whose possible error must be tested, while by observability we denote the possibility of propagating the results produced by the component under test up to the system's outputs.

In the case of the Hopfield network, *behavioral testability* can be seen as the possibility of forcing the network into an arbitrary state and of verifying the correct transition to its next state. By nature, an arbitrary state can be applied as an input configuration, i.e., the machine is completely controllable.

In the same way, the outcome of the transition, i.e., the next state, can be directly read on the network outputs, so that the machine is completely observable.

As a consequence, ***any Hopfield network affords complete behavioral testability***. Actual testability will then depend on the architectural and technological solutions; behavioral testability constitutes an upper bound for lower-level (e.g., gate-level) testability (it is respected in particular if one-to-one mapping of operators onto components is adopted).

3. FSM modeling of the Hopfield network

The classical definition of a finite state machine M is a quintuple $<S, I, O, \delta, \lambda>$, where S is the non-void and finite set of states, I is the finite input alphabet, δ is the next state function defined as $\delta: S \times I \rightarrow S$ and λ is the output function, defined as $\lambda: S \rightarrow O$ (we adopt here the Moore model). Operation of an FSM at the *functional* level is best described by a state diagram or (which is equivalent) a state table.

Gate-level testing of FSMs involves relevant difficulties in test pattern generation [11]; on the other hand, recent papers have proved that test approaches based on a *functional error model* - namely, the so-called ***single-transition fault model*** - and developing test patterns on the basis of the information provided by the state diagram only actually grant very good fault coverage even for lower-level (i.e., logic level) faults. We will now prove, first of all, that the Hopfield network is well representable by an equivalent FSM, and then we develop an FSM-based functional test generation approach valid for Hopfield networks.

Description of the Hopfield paradigm by using a FSM can be performed by introducing the following mapping between neural and FSM entities.

Each state of the Hopfield network, i.e., each output pattern x, is associated with one state s of the FSM; the output x_i of the i-th neuron coincides with the i-th bit of the state coding s.

The output alphabet O coincides with the set of states S.

The input alphabet I can actually be taken to be the void set; in fact, operation of the Hopfield net proceeds by forcing an initial state (coinciding with the input pattern) and then having the network evolve in an *autonomous* way (without presenting any further input patterns), controlled by the synchronization signal only, until a steady state is reached. This justifies our assumption of a void input alphabet to the associated FSM model.

As for the next state function δ, defined now as $\delta: S \rightarrow S$, given any state s_i, the next state s_j is computed by application of equation (1). Two instances may occur; either $s_j \neq s_i$, and equation (1) is applied again at the next step, or $s_j = s_i$, i.e., a steady state has been reached and computation stops until a new pattern is presented. Considering the operation of a Hopfield network whose weight matrix W has been perfected and for which *parallel* recall approach is adopted, given any input pattern I_i^* the network operates in a deterministic way, so that the associated FSM will evolve through a sequence of states $s_j \equiv I_{i_*}^*$, s_i^1, s_i^2, ... s_i^a, s_i^a being the steady state associated I_i^*.

The output function λ is the identity function since the Hopfield output coincides with the state; therefore, the output alphabet is identical to the set of state coding.

When learning has been perfected, an *n*-input Hopfield network presents a number of *attracting states* (*attractors*), i.e. the steady states reached by the network when an input pattern is applied (usually, this involves transition through a number of non-steady states). If learning has been perfected by using center-of-class patterns all orthogonal to each other, only the desired attractors will be present [7]; otherwise, spurious attractors will in general appear in the system's behavior.

$$W = \begin{bmatrix} 2 & 2 & 0 & -2 \\ 2 & 2 & 0 & -2 \\ 0 & 0 & 2 & 0 \\ -2 & -2 & 0 & 2 \end{bmatrix} \qquad \text{(a)}$$

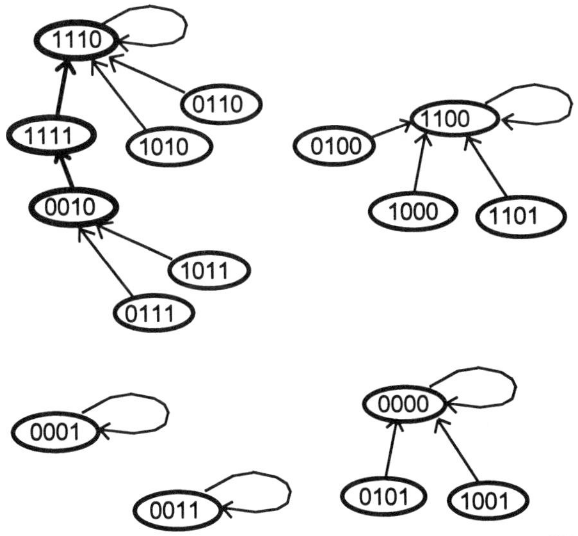

(b)

Figure 1 - The state graph for an Hopfield network: the weight matrix of the Hopfield network (a), the state graph (b).

Considering as an example a four-neuron Hopfield network characterized by the weight matrix W in fig.1a, application of the input pattern *0010* leads to creation of the state sequence *0010*, *1111*, *1110* (steady state), that can be represented as an oriented path in a state graph. Correct operation of the network grants that each state will be traversed only once. Thus, the state graph segment obtained is a simple directed path from the initial state s_i to the related attractor s_i^a.

Whenever we apply to the network an input pattern corresponding to any intermediate state s_i^k of a previously identified path, the state sequence created starting from s_i^k coincides with the subsequence s_i^k, s_i^{k+1}, ..., s_i^a of the complete path (this happens, e.g., if the input pattern is *1111*).

If another input pattern I_j is applied leading to the same attractor s_i^a, the directed path associated with such an input will either converge with the previous one in the final state, or else share with it a final segment (obviously including the final state). For example, for the steady state *1110*, the first case is achieved starting from the input state *1010*, leading to sequence *1010*, *1110*, while the second one is generated by the input state *1011*, leading to state *0010*.

By applying all input patterns leading to the same steady state s_i^a, an acyclic directed subgraph is built containing all and only the initial states sharing s_i^a as attractor. An example is given by the subgraph where the states converge to the steady state *1110* in figure 1. This subgraph is similar to an *n*-ary tree; however, the oriented paths are not directed from the root (in our case, the attractor *1110*) to the leaves, but they are in the reverse direction.

Similar subgraphs can be created for each attractor in the neural paradigm. Given the determinism of the parallel recall approach, these subgraphs are disjoint. The complete graph representing the FSM behavior is given by the union of all the above subgraphs; therefore, it is similar to a forest (see fig. 1b).

This basic characteristic does not change even in the presence of spurious attractors. When only expected attractors are present in the neural paradigm, the set of possible states is partitioned into disjoint subsets each associated with an expected attractor. Similarly, the state graph is partitioned into disjoint subgraphs: each of them is associated with an attractor and contains all and only the initial states leading to such an attractor. Each possible state belongs to exactly one subgraph.

When spurious attractors occur in the neural definition, the set of states is again partitioned into disjoint sets: in figure 1, only *1110* and *1100* are expected attractors while *0000*, *0001* and *0011* are spurious ones. States not associated with expected attractors are partitioned into subsets associated with the spurious attractors. As far as definition of the FSM is concerned, there is no differences between these two types of subsets.

Note that, as far as testing is concerning, spurious attractors and the related subgraphs will be treated in principle just as expected attractors and the related states subgraphs.

All the about assumed that the whole input space of the Hopfield network was meaningful, i.e., that all 2^n binary configurations over $x_1...x_n$ could be forced as initial states. As a consequence the associated FSM contains exactly 2^n different states. If on the contrary the input space is partitioned into a set of allowable patterns X_A and a set of unacceptable patterns X_U, states associated with patterns in X_A may appeared in the state graph in any position (ether as leaves or as nodes internal to a path or as roots) while states associated with patterns in X_U may never appear as leaves or roots. They will ether be internal to a path or not appear at all and the state graph, which may therefore consist of less than 2^n states.

4. Test pattern generation for the FSM model of the Hopfield network

By analyzing the state transition graph of the FSM modeling the Hopfield network, we can derive a strategy for creating the test procedure. Testing of an FSM at behavioral level aims at verifying if all allowed transitions between states (i.e., all transitions defined in the state graph) are correctly performed. If we adopt a single state transition fault model, an error can alter only one transition either in its output and/or in its next-state [4].

Due to the characteristics of the Hopfield networks, the starting state s_i of the transition under test can always be reached and controlled. In fact, if the starting state belongs to X_A, it can be directly set as the initial state of the network at time t_0. Otherwise, a pattern in X_A associated with a state s_k and such that a path from s_k to s_i exists in the state graph must be selected and applied to the network. The path from s_k to s_i constitutes the *set-up sequence* for the transition under test. The application of a set-up sequence allows testing at the same time all traversed transitions, since each transition is directly observable.

After the network has been set in the starting state for the transition under test, testing such a transition means simply performing an iteration of the neural computation according to equation (1) and observing the output result. The transition has been correctly performed if the state reached coincides with the expected one.

The set of input patterns that must be applied to the network, to test all transitions in the state graph, is the *test procedure* of the network at behavioral level. Obviously, it is not unique due to the arbitrary order of examination of the transitions.

To minimize the time required to test a device implementing the Hopfield network, we need to minimize the number of patterns belonging to the test procedure. Each test pattern is composed of a set-up sequence (which can be empty) and the transition under test. A test pattern completely included into another one can be discarded; for example (see figure 1) test pattern *0111,0010*, which tests the transition outgoing from state *0111*, is completely included in the test pattern *0111,0010,1111,1110*, which tests the transition outgoing from state *1111*.

The minimum test set is composed of all the input patterns corresponding to the leaves: in this case the Hopfield network is constrained to reach the steady state and thus to traverse and test all admissible transitions.

In our example, the minimum test procedure is given by the following 11 patterns: *0001*, *0011*, *0100*, *0101*, *0110*, *0111*, *1000*, *1001*, *1010*, *1011*, *1101*.

Generation of the minimum test procedure implies complete exploration of the state graph of the FSM associated with the Hopfield network. An explicit description may require a large amount of memory and a long time to verify if a state has been already examined; these requirements exponentially grow according to the size of the Hopfield network (i.e., with the number of neurons). To minimize the storage and the computation time we suggest to adopt an implicit approach for describing and managing the FSM

Thus, the deterministic approach, previously described, is converted into a random approach that performs a pseudo-exhaustive analysis of the admissible input patterns (states). A possible test pattern is randomly generated and simulated until the steady state is reached. All the traversed transitions are thus tested and set-up sequences are no longer necessary. For example the randomly generated input *0010* (see figure 1) enables testing of all transitions between state *0010* and the steady state *1110*. If the randomly generated input (in this case *0010*) is not a leaf, it will be removed from the test set when one of its predecessors will be randomly generated (in this case *1011* or *0111*). Note that the direct generation of the input configurations corresponding to the leaves is not feasible due to the impossibility of explicitly describing the state transition graph of the FSM.

The use of Binary Decision Diagrams (BDDs) for testing [12, 13] is becoming more and more popular, in particular because BDDs allow to implicitly enumerate

FSM's states [14]. The following description, of the proposed algorithm, relates to the standard operations on Reduced Ordered BDDs (ROBDDs) defined in [10].

BDDs are binary trees composed of nodes representing *variables*; each node has a pair of outgoing edges representing its possible binary values (*1* or *0*); edges can connect a node to another one or to a leaf. A path starting from the root of the BDDs and ending into a TRUE (1) leaf can be seen as an *algebraic product*; all the variables, traversed by the path, assume the value of the associated incoming edges. For example, figure 2 (a) shows the BDD for the product *0010*; that can be derived looking at the unique path starting from the root (node 0) and ending into the TRUE leaf (with the convention of left edge equal to 1 and right edge to 0). A set of binary configurations may be represented by a single BDD built by *or-ing* the BDDs of the single configurations.

Let us define **S** as the BDD representing all possible states (i.e., 2^n if all input patterns are allowable). At the beginning of the algorithm, **S** is composed of a single node (the *TRUE* node) that represents the inclusion in **S** of all possible input configurations. Such a circumstance dramatically highlights the efficiency of BDDs in relation to explicit techniques for storing binary information: only one node represent 2^n objects. If only a subset of the possible 2^n configurations is allowed, the **S** set includes only the admissible inputs. Let us define **E** as the BDD representing the set of *already explored states*: at the first step of the algorithm **E** is the *FALSE* node since no node has been explored yet. Note that **E** is the complement of **S**: definition of two BDD's is useful to clearly describe the algorithm, but only one must be used in the actual implementation of the algorithm.

The proposed approach uses the activation function *f* to analyze the network evolution until the steady state is reached. At each clock tick, the network changes state or remains in the final steady state: our exploration algorithm generates a BDD **C** for the current state by using *n-1* times the *apply-and* operation on BDD's, as defined in [10] Such an operation performs the algebraic *and* operation between two BDDs. One represents the current product and the other the current variable. The complexity of the *apply* operation is quadratic with the dimension of the two involved BDD's, but in this case one of the two BDDs has size equal to *1* (the variable) and the number of nodes of the other one is smaller than *n*. Thus, the final complexity for the construction of **C** is $n(n+1)/2$.

Whenever a new state is reached, its BDD **C** is compared with the set **E** of already explored states: if **C** is included in **E**, the exploration terminates and a new input pattern is selected; otherwise, the current state **C** is added to **E** by using the *apply-or* operation (see [10]) and a new current state is computed via the activation function *f*.

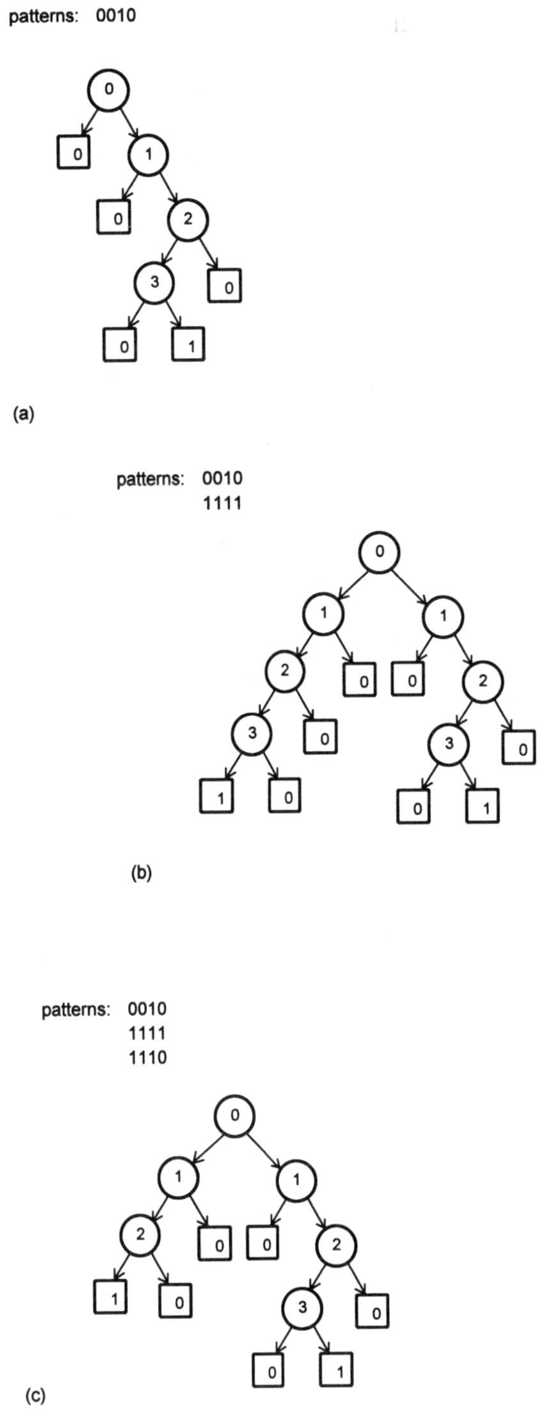

Figure 2 - The BDD's trees for compact pattern generation: the tree after the first pattern (a), the second one (b), and the third one (c).

Verifying that **C** is included in **E** is performed by the *intersect* operation (see [10]). If the intersect operation is successful, and the current state is also a test pattern, such a pattern can be removed from the test set since it means the inclusion of the sequence, starting from **C**, into the sequence starting from the current input. Complexity of the *intersect* operation is linear with the number of nodes of the smaller BDD involved (in this case **C**). Since the number of nodes in **C** is always equal to *n*, the above verification is performed in a very efficient way.
Generation of a new input pattern can be easily performed by traversing, in a random way, **S** from the root to a leaf. Also complexity of this operation is proportional to *n* (length of every path in **S** is at most equal to *n*).

The use of BDDs allows to generate the test patterns by analyzing the set of states reached by each input pattern.

5. Concluding remarks

The approach here presented allows to design a test procedure for a Hopfield network independently of final implementation. Previous research has proved the functional approach chosen to be effective in the case of FSMs; thus, given the common logical fault model, the same rate of fault coverage can be deduced for digital implementations of Hopfield networks. Simulations will be carried out to check whether the same extends to fully analog implementations.

All results presented here relate to the parallel-recall approach; at present, research is under way to determine an efficient extension to the case of sequential recall.

6. References

[1] C.H. Chen, C. Wu, D.G. Saab, "BETA: behavioral testability analysis", *Proc. ICCAD*, Santa Clara, 1991

[2] M. Bombana, G. Buonanno, P. Cavallaro, D. Sciuto, G. Zara, "A multi--level testability assistant for VLSI design", *Proc. EuroDAC 92*, Hambourg, Germany, 1992

[3] V. Piuri, M. Sami, D. Sciuto, R. Stefanelli, "A behavioral approach to testability of neural networks", *Proc. IJCNN '92*, Baltimore, 1992

[4] K.T. Cheng, J.Y. Jou, "Functional Test Generation for Finite State Machines", *Proc. IEEE ITC*, 1990

[5] I. Pomeranz, S.M. Reddy, "On Achieving a Complete Fault Coverage for Sequential Machines Using the Transition Fault Model", *Proc. IEEE DAC*, 1991

[6] G. Buonanno, F. Fummi, D. Sciuto, "Functional Fault Model and Gate Level Coverage for Sequential Architectures", *Proc. IEEE ICCD*, 1993

[7] J. Hertz, A. Krogh, R.G. Palmer, *Introduction to the Theory of Neural Computation*, Addison-Wesley Publishing Co., 1991

[8] *Proc. WCNN93,* Portland, 1993

[9] K.T. Cheng, J.Y. Jou, "A Single State-Transition Fault Model for Sequential Machines", *Proc. IEEE ICCAD*, 1990

[10] K.S. Brace, R.L. Rundell, R.E. Bryant, "Efficient Implementation of a BDD Package", *Proc. 27th ACM/IEEE DAC*, 1990

[11] M. Abramovici, M.A. Breuer, A.D. Friedman, *Digital Systems Testing and Testable Design*, Computer Science Press, 1990

[12] S.B. Akers, "Binary Decision Diagram", *IEEE Transactions on Computers*, June 1978

[13] R.E. Bryant, "Graph-Based Algorithms for Boolean Function Manipulation", *IEEE Transactions on Computers*, August 1986

[14] H.J. Touati, H. Savoj, B. Lin, R. Brayton, A. Sangiovanni-Vincentelli, "Implicit State Enumeration of Finite State Machines using BDD's", *Proc. IEEE ICCAD*, 1988

"Hopfield-Style Neural Networks and the TSP"

William J. Wolfe, Michael H. Parry, James M. MacMillan

University of Colorado at Denver
Campus Box 109
Denver, Colorado 80217
wwolfe@cudnvr.denver.colorado.edu

Abstract

We describe the results of our TSP neural model, using a linearization of the Hopfield model and an orthogonal projection onto the feasible subspace, including the definition of a region of *parameter space* that ensures exclusive convergence to tours. Our TSP results are relatively good for up to 30 cities, achieving a large number of optimal tours, but scaling remains a problem. For a particular 100 city problem the results are not very good, giving tours that are 80-90% longer than the optimal tour. We compare the performance of the network to the sequential nearest city algorithm, and provide several ideas for improving the performance of the network, including a *divide and conquer* approach. The relationship of TSP networks to lateral inhibition networks is also described.

1. Introduction

In this paper we describe our approach to the Traveling Salesman Problem (TSP), but first we give an overview of Hopfield-style networks, including a description of how the TSP is related to lateral inhibition networks. In the long run our research is aimed at uncovering subtle aspects of parallel distributed representations, independent of hardware implementation issues. We have chosen the TSP as a representative optimization problem, and we expect that better parallel algorithms will be a side effect, but our primary concern is the nature of the knowledge representation.

The majority of Hopfield-style networks are motivated by either of three apparently distinct scenarios : 1) optimization problems, such as the TSP; or 2) biological observations, such as lateral inhibition; or 3) a set of stable states, such as Content Addressable Memories (CAM). The optimization approach begins with an energy function (and usually a characterization of the desired stable states), and derives the connection strengths. The biological approach begins with connection strengths that model observations of neural tissue, while the energy function and stable states can be deduced. The CAM approach begins with specific stable states and derives the connection strengths (usually via Hebbian reinforcement). In the end, each case sits under the same theoretical umbrella with an energy function, a symmetric connection strength architecture, and a set of stable states.

From the biological point of view, questions concerning optimality of a network are usually a secondary matter. Intuitively, an organism would be wasting its efforts if it were fine-tuning its responses to inherently noisy signals. For example, [1] describes a two dimensional lateral inhibition network that converges to a *bubble* of active units. We wondered what preferences the network had for *where* the center of the bubble would be, based on initial activations of the neurons and bubble radius [2]. We tested several 1-dimensional cases for which optimal performance means the network converges to a *cluster* of active units corresponding to the largest k-wide sum of contiguous initial activations. That is, the network should converge to the *nearest* corner that represents a k-wide cluster (ie : a corner with k contiguous 1's, with wrap around, and 0 for the rest of the components). Intuitively, the network should find the largest k-wide *area* under the *curve* of initial activations. Although it was relatively easy to derive network parameters that guaranteed exclusive stability for k-wide clusters, the network was optimal only about 30% of the time (using random initial activations, with slightly better results using samples of a smooth curve). This and similar experiments led us to conclude that relatively simple networks are far from optimal. Interestingly enough, however, is the fact that k-wta networks [3,4], designed to pick the k largest initial activations without regard to the contiguous/cluster constraint, work optimally 100% of the time, but this is a very special case as explained in [2].

Although lack of optimality in a biologically-inspired network seems harmless and possibly desirable, lack of optimality in a TSP network is near fatal. We found it curious that optimization networks have sub-

0-7803-1901-X/94 $4.00

networks resembling biologically motivated ones. For example, the inhibitory rows and columns of a TSP network are a form of lateral inhibition. This motivated us to experiment with the Assignment Problem (AP) using an architecture of mutually inhibitory rows and columns [5]. The AP network did not perform optimally (randomly initialized two dimensional grid of neurons), although again about 30% of the trials on 10x10 grids were optimal. Further, we found that techniques we came up with to improve the performance of the AP network mapped onto corresponding improvements in the TSP network. This raised our suspicions that the poor performance of a standard TSP network could have its roots in the lack of optimality of lateral inhibition style networks, and we now conjecture that this principle might be of general concern for *all* optimization networks.

So we worked on improvements of the AP network and then mapped them onto the TSP network. The common factor in both the TSP and the AP is the identical set of feasible states : 1 active unit per row and column. As we investigated these feasible states we found that we could express them in terms of a subspace $\mathcal{F}$ of $\mathcal{R}^{k^2}$, and further, that there was a relatively easy way to construct an orthogonal projection into this subspace. This projection, when *spliced* with the ordinary neural update, provides significant improvements in the performance of the AP and the TSP. In the following sections we will provide the details of this approach.

An interesting distinction between the AP and the TSP, however, is that optimal performance of the AP requires convergence to the nearest feasible corner [2, 5] (as in the k-wide-cluster problem mentioned above), whereas the TSP requires convergence to the lowest energy feasible state. It seems that this is related to why the TSP network performs better when the initializations are near, but not at, the center of the cube [14].

2. Projection onto the Feasible Subspace

Before describing our neural model for the TSP, we can independently describe the operator that projects activation vectors onto the feasible subspace $\mathcal{F}$. We define $\mathcal{F}$ as containing all $\mathbf{a} \in \mathcal{R}^{k^2}$ that have the property that when written in a kxk array the sum of any row or column is 0. With this representation, instead of using *min* = 0 we use *min* = -1/(k-1), and *max* = 1. That is, the components of a feasible corner have a single 1 in each row and column, and -1/(k-1) elsewhere. Consequently the size of the k^2-cube has been changed. Altering the k^2-cube in this way has the advantage of making $\mathcal{F}$ a vector *subspace* of $\mathcal{R}^{k^2}$. The space of *doubly stochastic* kxk matrices [6] is similar to $\mathcal{F}$ except that they have a sum of 1 for every row and column. In fact, the corresponding Birkoff-von Neumann Theorem [5] assures us that our set of feasible corners spans $\mathcal{F}$. $\mathcal{F}$ intersects this k^2-cube in a region called the feasible *polytope* [12]. Given a vector **a** with components a_{ij} we can can compute the orthogonal projection **p** onto $\mathcal{F}$ via :

$$p_{ij} = a_{ij} - \text{grid}^{avg} + \text{row}_j^{avg} + \text{col}_i^{avg}.$$

Where grid^{avg} is the average value of all the activations, row_j^{avg} is the average value of the activations in the same row as a_{ij}, and col_i^{avg} is the average value of the activations in the same column as a_{ij}. This computation can be implemented as a neural network of its own with the following connection strength architecture :

external inputs	= 0,
self-connections	$= +[(k-1)/k]^2$,
inhibition on rows and columns	$= -(k-1)/k^2$,
all other connections	$= +1/k^2$.

That is, if we let a_{ij} be the activations of this kxk grid of connected neurons, then p_{ij} is the *net input* to neuron ij. Computing the projection using these averages is a significant simplification of the alternate way described in [5]. The projection is derived from the fact that $\mathcal{R}^{k^2}$ decomposes into the direct sum [5] :

$$\mathcal{R}^{k^2} = \mathcal{F} \oplus \mathcal{E}_c \oplus \mathcal{E}_r \oplus \mathcal{D}.$$

Where $\mathcal{E}_c$ is the space spanned by vectors whose columns are constant values while the sum of any row is 0. That is, the first row of an element of $\mathcal{E}_c$ must sum to 0, but is otherwise arbitrary, and the remaining rows are copies of the first row. Similarly, $\mathcal{E}_r$ is the space whose rows are constant while the sum of any column is 0 (ie : $\mathcal{E}_r$ is the *transpose* of $\mathcal{E}_c$). $\mathcal{D}$ is the space spanned by the constant vector (ie : $\mathcal{D}$ contains the diagonal of the k^2-cube).

We assume that **a** sits inside the modified k^2-cube, but the projection can take it outside the cube. In practice we fix this by *clipping* each component after a projection. That is, if an activation is greater than *max* we set it equal to *max*, and if it is less than *min* we set it equal to *min*. In practice the components of the projected vector are rarely larger than *max*, but often smaller than *min*. After the clip the vector is not necessarily in the polytope but it is near the polytope and in the k^2-cube.

A similar projection concept is described in [7-10], including a more sophisticated way of projecting into the polytope, without clipping, but we have not investigated this improvement yet.

3. TSP Neural Model

In our model we update the activations synchronously with a *linearized* version of the original Hopfield model called *interactive activation* [2, 4, 5, 11, 14]. Let a_i be the activation of the ith neuron and e_i its external input :

$$\begin{array}{ll} a_i(t+1) = a_i(t) + \eta\ \Delta a_i(t), & \\ \Delta a_i(t) = net_i(t)\ [max - a_i(t)] & \text{if } net_i(t) \geq 0, \\ \Delta a_i(t) = net_i(t)\ [a_i(t) - min] & \text{if } net_i(t) < 0, \\ net_i(t) = \Sigma_j a_j(t)\ w_{ij} + e_i, & \\ \eta > 0 \text{ is the step size.} & \end{array}$$

For the TSP we need a two dimensional representation, so we begin with a kxk grid of neurons, with the usual indexing : the vertical axis is labeled with upper case letters (X) for *cities* and the horizontal axis is labeled with lower case letters (i) for *stops*. As usual, neuron Xi corresponds to having city X appear, or not appear, in the ith position of a tour. Activations (a_{Xi}) are restricted to the in the range $min \leq a_{Xi} \leq max$, and consequently the activation vector (**a**) is a point in or on the k^2-cube.

When **a** converges to a feasible state, there is one active neuron in each row and column. Thus, there are 2^{k^2} corner states but only k! feasible states. Thus, we want the network to converge to feasible states but moreover, we want a strong preference for shorter tours. To this end we define symmetric connection strengths as follows :

$$w_{Xi,\,Yj} = \begin{cases} -1 & X = Y \quad \text{xor} \quad i = j \\ -\alpha\, d[X,Y] & j = i+1 \quad \text{or} \quad j = i-1 \end{cases}$$

There are no self connections, and all external inputs are zero. The inhibitory rows and columns represent the constraint that each city be visited once and only once. The neighboring columns are connected in proportion to the distance d[X,Y] between the corresponding cities. The last column is connected to the first in a wrap around fashion, implying that the arithmetic i+1 and i-1 is done modulo k. We assume $\alpha > 0$ and consider it one of the two critical parameters of the network design (the other is *min*).

The connections between neighboring columns represent the intuition that it is usually a good idea to pick the nearest city when asked to find a successor or predecessor to a given city. That is, neurons representing nearer cities will receive less inhibition than farther cities. In a sense, these connections are encoding a *distributed nearest city* strategy. Intuitively, this indicates a limiting behavior of the network since a nearest city algorithm (interpreted in the traditional sense of serial processing) is generally suboptimal [12]. The difficulty with this intuition is that the neural representation brings the nearest city effect into action throughout the city selection process, active at *all* cities and *all* stops *simultaneously*, whereas the serial approach picks cities one stop at a time. It is unclear how these distinct nearest city heuristics should be compared, since one is inherently a parallel-distributed processing concept and the other is a sequential concept. Later we compare our neural results to a sequential nearest city algorithm.

Note that any pair of neurons that do not share a common row or column, and are not in neighboring columns, are not connected. More importantly, there are many connection strengths of the same nonzero value, other that the -1 connections. That is, the connection strengths between columns is repeated as you move horizontally along the grid. Therefore all right/left shifted representations of a tour are equivalent and consequently a single tour is represented by k distinct feasible states. It is difficult to say whether this redundancy is beneficial or detrimental. Intuitively speaking, it seems beneficial since it provides more ways to obtain the optimal tour, but in another sense it may cause the network to pursue *all* of them in a simultaneous manner, resulting in some alternative final convergent state that sits somewhere in the middle. Finally, it is interesting to the consider the case of cities that are placed uniformly on a circle : the connection strength architecture is completely homogeneous. That is, each neuron *sees* the same distribution of connection strengths, and consequently the connections strengths are not only repeated as we move horizontally across the grid, but also vertically (a study of homogeneous networks is presented in [2]). Our neural networks run excellently for such circular city configurations and the reason must be related to this homogeneous architecture but we have yet to identify the exact causal relationship.

3. (α, *min*) Stability Region

We now describe a bounded region R of (α, *min*)-space where the network always converges to a feasible solution. For parameter choices inside R the network always converges to a tour, while increasing the value of α generally improves the quality of the tours. Since R is bounded we cannot increase α indefinitely : as α increases to the point where the parameters are outside R there is an increasing number of non-feasible states. Intuitively, as α is increased the energy of the shorter tours are being lowered, giving them wider and deeper basins of attraction, but as α leaves R local minima pop up at nearby non-feasible states which begin competing for convergence.

R is bounded by the *min*-axis and two hyperbolas, $h_1(\alpha)$ and $h_2(\alpha)$. The derivation of these boundaries is described in detail in [14] and is too long to describe here. We will just give the results, but the basic idea is to set the activations to an arbitrary feasible state and compute bounds on the values of α and *min* that ensure that the net input to an active neuron is positive and the net input to an inactive neuron is negative (ie : stability criteria). This is difficult to analyze because the bounds are a function of the distances between the cities. To define $h_1(\alpha)$ and $h_2(\alpha)$ we need the following definitions. For any configuration of euclidean cities let :

$$d_{max} = \text{maximum}_{XY} \{d[X,Y]\}$$
$$d_{min} = \text{minimum}_{XY} \{d[X,Y]\}$$

$$s_{min} = \text{minimum}_X \{\Sigma_Y d[X,Y] - \text{maximum}_Z \{d[X,Z]\}\}$$
$$s_{max} = \text{maximum}_X \{\Sigma_Y d[X,Y]\}.$$

Now define :

$$h_1(\alpha) = -(\alpha\, d_{max}) \;/\; (k-1 + \alpha\, s_{min})$$
$$h_2(\alpha) = -(1+\alpha\, d_{min}) \;/\; (2k-3 + 2\,\alpha\, s_{max}).$$

For $\alpha > 0$, $h_1(\alpha)$ goes through the origin and monotonically decreases toward the asymptote $min = -d_{max}/s_{min}$ while $h_2(\alpha)$ intersects the *min* axis at $min = -1/(2k-3)$ and monotonically increases toward the asymptote $min = -d_{min}/(2s_{max})$. Since the magnitude of d_{max}/s_{min} is greater than the magnitude of $d_{min}/(2s_{max})$ the hyperbolas intersect at a unique point (α_0, min_0) for some $\alpha_0 > 0$ and $min_0 < 0$. This cusp-like point is where α is at its largest possible value, and this is where we initially operate our TSP network.

It is important to recall that the *ideal* value of *min* is -1/(k-1), since that puts the feasible corners of the hypercube in $\mathcal{F}$. In practice min_0 turns out to be slightly larger than -1/(k-1) : $-1/(k-1) < min_0 < 0$.

4. TSP Results

First we tired our model, without the projection operator, on 10 to 30 cities. When we set $\alpha = \alpha_0$, $min = min_0$, and $\eta = 1/k$, the network always provided a tour, although in some cases the convergence time was quite long. The quality of the tours, however, was very poor. We observed that initializing the network as close to the origin as possible had beneficial effects, but the tours were still relatively poor.

The projection operator dramatically improved the results, although the final activations for the active units did not approach the full value of 1.0, converging to a value in the range from 0.6 to 0.8 [14]. The latter effect is an artifact of the *project and clip* procedure, but caused no difficulty otherwise. With the projection the tours improved yet again when value of α was doubled to $\alpha = 2\alpha_0$, without encountering nonfeasible states. For example, for the 10 cities from [15] we get the optimal tour about 80% of the time, while the other 20% are near optimal. For the special case where 10 cities are in an equally spaced circular arrangement we get the optimal tour 98% of the time. For 10 randomly placed cities we get the optimal tour only about 30% of the time, but we would describe the vast majority of the other 70% of the trials as near optimal. From these experiments it is easy to conclude that the relatively high 80% optimal for the 10 cities of [15] is a consequence of the fact that those cities are near circular in placement. It appears that when the cities are near circular the competing corners that represent near optimal tours are sufficiently higher in energy than the corners that represent the optimal tour.

Encouraged by these statistics we approached a particular 100 city problem defined in the literature [12] ([13] has the exact coordinates for the 100 cities). Although we got tours on every trial, they were relatively poor, having tour lengths approximately 80-90% larger than the optimal tour. It was interesting to compare our results to the *sequential* nearest city algorithm described in [12]. This nearest city algorithm creates a tour by starting at a city and picking the nearest city for the next step, and so on. This is done for each of the cities as the starting point and the best result is selected. This algorithm generates a tour for the 100 cities that is 16% longer than the optimal tour. Since it did so much better than our neural approach, which has a similar but *different* nearest city encoding, we conjectured that the neural approach, intuitively speaking, gets confused between the many nearest neighbor sub-tours, mixing them up to create a very sub-optimal combination of pieces, and the effect grows worse with the number of cities. Since we observed near optimal performance for 30 or fewer cities we decided to experiment with a *divide and conquer* approach : apply the neural network to 4 subsets of 25 nearby cities (essential breaking the square where the cities are placed into quadrants), and run the neural network separately on these subsets and then use simple rules to combine the results into a 100 city tour. We are still refining this approach but it is safe to say that it easily leads to tours that are at least as good as the sequential nearest city approach.

It is easy to conjecture that the trouble with scaling up to 100 cities or more has its roots in the *localness* of the connections between columns. For example, to include connection strengths at *two* columns away would imply that we use a measure of whether a city should sit in a tour *two* stops from a given city, perhaps computing all the two-stop paths between cities. We have not tried such an approach, but it seems intuitively plausible that doing a little more pre-computation on the city statistics would lead to a better network. Going another step we could compute all the three-stop paths, and so on, with the ultimate case being equivalent to computing the shortest tour before running the network! Incremental improvements in the network along these lines would still be of theoretical interest.

Many times we watched the network converge and observed a curious phenomenon that usually occurred about midway through a run. The network seemed to connect the outer lying cities as though it were implementing a *convex-hull* approach, forming an almost circular pattern, but when it neared final convergence the cities that were left out were then inserted in the convex-hull at seemingly random places, providing the majority of the tour length error. This is consistent with our original conjecture that some of the difficulty with the TSP network resides in the inhibitory rows and columns, since this effect is strongest toward the end of a run. It is also consistent with the excellent results for circular cities. This led us to conjecture that there may be a way to stop the convergence prematurely, in the convex-hull stage, and then use a simple insertion rule. We did this on cases of 10 to 30 randomly placed cities and it appears to improve the results, but we have not yet done enough experimentation to be confident.

5. References

[1] T. Kohonen, "Self-Organization and Associative Memory", Series in Information Sciences, Vol. 8, Springer-Verlag, 1988.

[2] W. J. Wolfe, J. Rothman, E. Chang, W. Aultman, G. Ripton, "Harmonic Analysis of Homogeneous Networks", Technical Report TR-33, University of Colorado, Department of Computer Science and Engineering, May, 1993.

[3] E. Majani, R. Erlanson, Y. Abu-Mostafa, "On the K-Winner-Take-All Network", Advances in Neural Information Processing Systems 1, D. Touretzkey editor, Morgan Kaufmann Publishers, 1989.

[4] W. J. Wolfe, D. Mathis, C. Anderson, J. Rothman, M. Gottler, G. Brady, R. Walker, G. Duane, G. Alaghband, "K-Winner Networks", IEEE Transactions on Neural Networks, Vol. 2, No. 2, March, 1991.

[5] W. J. Wolfe, J. MacMillan, G. Brady, R. Mathews, J. Rothman, D. Mathis, M. Orosz, C. Anderson, G. Alaghband. "Inhibitory Grids and the Assignment Problem", IEEE Transactions on Neural Networks, pp. 319 - 331, Vol. 4, No. 2, March, 1993.

[6] V. Chvatal, "Linear Programing", W. H. Freeman and Company, 1983.

[7] S. V. Aiyer, M. Niranjan, F. Fallside, "A Theoretical Investigation into the Performance of the Hopfield Model", IEEE TNN, Vol. 1, No. 2, June, 1990, pp 204-215.

[8] S. V. Aiyer, "Solving Combinatorial Optimization Problems Using Neural Networks", University of Cambridge, Department of Engineering Technical Report, CUED/F-INFENG/TR 89, Cambridge, England, October, 1991.

[9] A. Gee, "Problem Solving With Optimization Networks", Ph. D. Thesis, University of Cambridge, Department of Engineering Technical Report, CUED/F-INFENG/TR 150, Cambridge, England, October, 1991.

[10] A. Gee, S. V. Aiyer, R. Prager, "An Analytical Framework for Optimizing Neural Networks", Neural Networks, Vol. 6, pp. 79-97, 1993.

[11] J. L. McClelland, D. E. Rumelhart, "An Interactive Activation Model of Context Effects in Letter Perception : Part 1. An Account of Basic Findings", Psychological Review 88 : 375 - 407, 1981.

[12] E. L. Lawler, J. Lenstra, A. Rinnooy-Kan, D. Shmoys, "The Travelling Salesman Problem", John Wiley & Sons, 1985.

[13] P. Krolak, W. Felts, G. Marble, "A Man-Machine Approach Toward Solving the Traveling Salesman Problem", Communications of the ACM, Vol. 14, No. 5, May, 1971.

[14] W. J. Wolfe, J. MacMillan, G. Brady, J. Rothman, M. Orosz, "Neural Projection for the TSP", Technical Report TR-24, University of Colorado, Department of Computer Science and Engineering, October, 1992.

[15] J. J. Hopfield, D. W. Tank, "'Neural' Computation of Decisions in Optimization Problems". Biol. Cybern. 52, 141-152, 1985.

Two Approaches to Nonlinear Systems Optimal Control by Using Neural Networks

L. Acosta, A. Hamilton, L. Moreno, J.L. Sánchez, J.D. Piñeiro, J.A. Méndez
University of La Laguna. Dep. of Applied Physics. La Laguna. Tenerife. Spain.

Abstract

In this paper we present two methods based on Neural Networks (NN) for resolution of nonlinear systems optimal control with arbitrary performance index. In this paper we have used the minimum time index as an example.

Both methods solve the optimal problem for a region of the state space by means of a multistage optimization through a NN chain. Each NN has a fully connected feedfoward multilayer structure and the training algorithm for the NN chain is the Back Propagation (BP).

The chain structure is different for each method, as well as the discretization procedure: classical and Block Pulse Function (BPF).

Problem formulation

Let us consider a general system:

$\underline{x} \in \Re^n$ state

$\underline{u} \in \Re^n$ input(commands)

$\dot{\underline{x}} = \underline{f}(\underline{x},\underline{u},t)$ continuous system equation

If we discretize it, a function which represents the discrete system dynamic equation is obtained: $\Phi(\underline{x}_i,\underline{u}_i,t_i) = 0$.

In these conditions we attempt to tackle, for any state space initial point, the command sequence which generates a trajectory that minimizes, in N stages, the cost function given by:

$$\mathcal{J} = \sum_{i=0}^{N-1} h(\underline{x}_i,\underline{u}_i,t_i) + h_N(\underline{x}_N) \tag{1}$$

We solve the problem using a set of N NN to obtain the command sequence and time intervals $\{(\underline{u}_i,t_i)^o, i=0,..,N-1\}$ that minimize the cost function (1) for any initial point $\underline{x}_0 \in \mathcal{A}$, where $\mathcal{A}$ is a compact set of state space [1].

We solve this optimal problem by means of two different approaches. The first one consists in a set of NN that generates the command and time in each stage, and in the second approach, the set of NN gives the state in each stage.

First Method

We take the method proposed in [2] and we generalized it for minimum time problems making that each NN also provides the stage time interval [3].

The system evolution equation can be expressed by means of classical discretization like forward or backward difference in the following way:

$$\underline{x}_{i+1} = \underline{f}(\underline{x}_i,\underline{u}_i,t_i) \quad with \quad i = 0,\dots,N-1 \tag{2}$$

We will generate the command and time from the current state by means of a NN $\underline{v}_i = (\underline{u}_i,t_i) = \tilde{\gamma}(\underline{w}_i,\underline{x}_i)$ where $\underline{w}_i$ is the synaptic weight vector of the i-th network. The next state is obtained by means of (2). The calculation process is outlined in the figure:

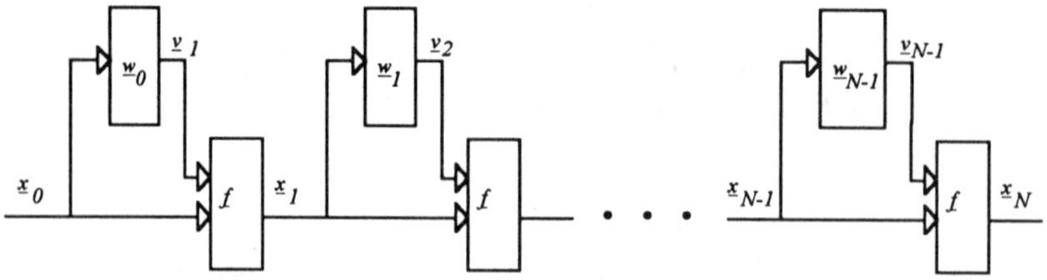

So the cost function takes the form $\mathfrak{J} = \mathfrak{J}(\underline{w}, \underline{x}_0)$ where $\underline{w} = [\underline{w}_0, \ldots, \underline{w}_{N-1}]$. To eliminate $\underline{x}_0$ dependence we choose it from a random uniform distribution on region $\mathcal{A}$, and we average the cost function with respect to $\underline{x}_0$.

Now, our problem is to find $\underline{w}^o$ which minimizes $\mathrm{E}_{\underline{x}_0}[\mathfrak{J}(\underline{w}, \underline{x}_o)]$.

We use a multilayer feedforward fully connected NN. For the i-th net we have:

$$z_q^i(s) = \sum_{p=1}^{n_s^i - 1} w_{pq}^i(s) y_p^i(s-1) + w_{0q}^i(s); \quad y_q^i(s) = g(z_q^i(s)) \ \ \text{where} \begin{cases} i = 0, \ldots, N-1 & \textit{net number} \\ s = 1, \ldots, L_i & \textit{layer number} \\ q = 1, \ldots, n_s & \textit{neuron number} \end{cases} \tag{3}$$

We use the hyperbolic tangent as the activation function (output range (-1,1)) in the neurons except last layer one which generates the time output. In order to obtain non-negative output we choose the sigmoid function $g(z) = D/(1+e^{-z})$, with output range (0,*D*). The constant *D* must be small for obtaining good time resolution ($D \cong 0.1$).

The training algorithm used is BP:

$$\underline{w}(k+1) = \underline{w}(k) - \alpha(k)\, \nabla_{\underline{w}} \mathrm{E}_{\underline{x}_0}\{\mathfrak{J}(\underline{w}(k), \underline{x}_0)\} + \eta(k)[\underline{w}(k) - \underline{w}(k-1)] \tag{4}$$

where k is the training stage and α and η are correction factors.

We define:

$$\delta_q^i \equiv \frac{\partial \mathfrak{J}(\underline{w}, \underline{x}_0)}{\partial z_q^i(s)}; \qquad \underline{\lambda}_i \equiv \nabla_{\underline{x}_i} \mathfrak{J}(\underline{w}, \underline{x}_0)$$

The partial cost derivative with respect to each weight is as follows:

$$\frac{\partial \mathfrak{J}}{\partial w_{pq}^i} = \delta_q^i(s) y_p^i(s-1) \tag{5}$$

We find formulas which allow recursive algorithms to obtain the gradient value:

$$\underline{\lambda}_N^{\mathrm{T}} = \frac{\partial \mathfrak{J}}{\partial \underline{x}_N} = \frac{\partial h_N(\underline{x}_N)}{\partial \underline{x}_N} \tag{6}$$

$$\underline{\lambda}_i^{\mathrm{T}} = \frac{\partial h}{\partial \underline{x}_i} + \underline{\lambda}_{i+1}^{\mathrm{T}} \frac{\partial \underline{f}}{\partial \underline{x}_i} + \sum_{q=1}^{n_1^i} \delta_q^i(1) w_{pq}^i(1) \qquad \textit{for } i < N \tag{7}$$

$$\delta_q^i(L_i) = g'(z_q^i(L_i)) \left[\frac{\partial}{\partial \underline{v}} h(\underline{x}_i, \underline{v}_i) + \underline{\lambda}_{i+1}^{\mathrm{T}} \frac{\partial}{\partial \underline{v}} \underline{f}(\underline{x}_i, \underline{v}_i) \right]_q \tag{8}$$

$$\delta_q^i(s) = g'(z_q^i(s)) \sum_{h=1}^{n_{s+1}^i} \delta_h^i(s+1) w_{qh}^i(s+1) \qquad s = 1, \ldots, L_i \tag{9}$$

The training process begins computing $\underline{\lambda}_N$ (6), next in the *N-1* net, we obtain the last layer δ with (8) and the previous layer δ with (9). When we have the first layer δ we can compute $\underline{\lambda}_{N-1}$ (7), and so on with previous nets. Then we calculate cost derivative with respect to each weight (5) and then we correct them with (4).

Example

Consider the following nonlinear system:

$$\begin{cases} \dot{x}_1 = x_2 \\ \dot{x}_2 = a(b - x_1^2)x_2 + x_1 + cu \end{cases} \quad (10) \quad \text{applying forward difference} \quad \begin{cases} x_{1i+1} = x_{1i} + t_i x_{2i} \\ x_{2i+1} = x_{2i} + t_i\left[a(b - x_{1i}^2)x_{2i} + x_{1i} + cu_i\right] \end{cases}$$

To observe the minimum-time trajectories with the origin as their final state we use the following cost function:

$$\mathcal{J} = \sum_{k=0}^{N-1} T_k + V_N \left\|\underline{x}_N\right\|^2$$

Parameters are $a=1$, $b=1$, $c=1$ y $V_N=100$.

Fig 1: Initial point modification. 1st method

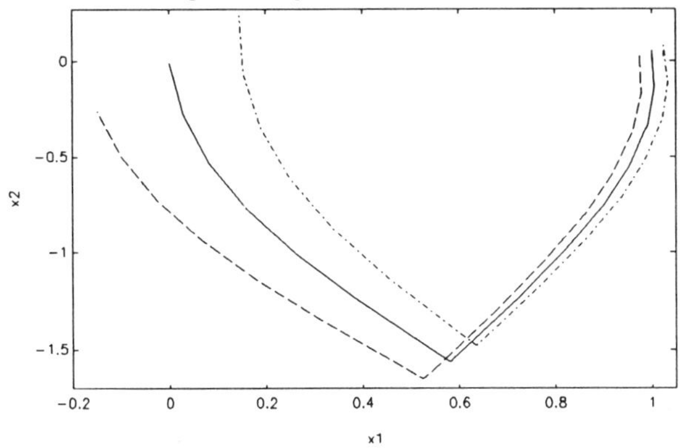

In accordance with considered activation functions, time varies from 0 to 0.1 and commands from -1 to 1. The number of stages is 30, all networks contain two hidden layers of five units, and α and η values are 10^{-4} and 0.8 respectively. The result of this method depends on the training region.

In case of deviation from the trajectory due to a disturbance, the system reproduces the same time-command sequence. So, system will not follow an optimal trajectory. In fig 1 we show the optimal trajectory for the training point (1,0) (continuous line); and the trajectories when we disturb the initial point: (0.975,-0.025) and (1.025,0.025). These disturb trajectories doesn't reach the final state (0,0). In other words, a small modification in initial state produces great deviation in the final state. This makes the method few robust.

Second Method

As a consequence of the first method mentioned problem, we developed a new NN structure [4]. Now each NN produces the next state from the previous one $\underline{x}_{i+1} = \tilde{\underline{\gamma}}(\underline{w}_i, \underline{x}_i)$ *with* $i = 1, \ldots, N$. The following diagram shows the process:

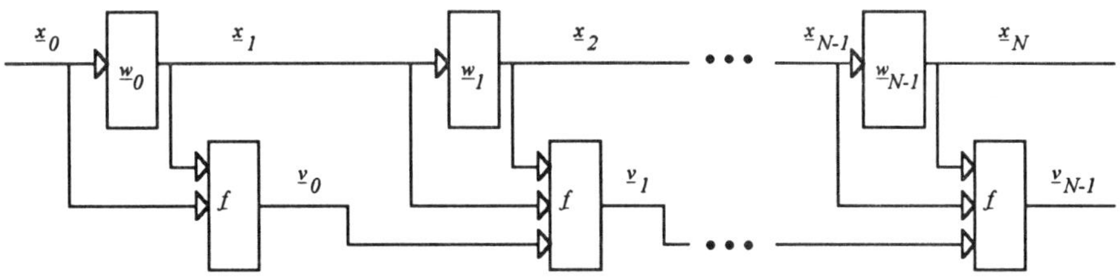

Since the NN chain is trained to produce the state in each stage, if a deviation appears, the structure forces the system to return to the optimal trajectory. So, this method is more robust than the previous one for disturbances.

In order to apply this structure, it is necessary to express the system dynamic equation in the following form:

$$\underline{v}_i = (\underline{u}_i, t_i) = \underline{f}(\underline{x}_i, \underline{x}_{i+1}, \underline{u}_{i-1}, t_{i-1}) \quad (11)$$

This expression calculates the time and command which cause the state transition in the system.

We choose the same kind of networks and training algorithm than in the previous method. To find the adjustment to be applied we must determine the cost partial derivatives with regard to each weight.

So, we define:

$$\delta_q^i \equiv \frac{\partial \mathfrak{I}(\underline{w},\underline{x}_0)}{\partial z_q^i(s)}; \qquad \underline{\lambda}_i \equiv \nabla_{\underline{v}_i} \mathfrak{I}(\underline{w},\underline{x}_0) \quad \text{then} \quad \frac{\partial \mathfrak{I}}{\partial w_{pq}^i} = \delta_q^i(s) y_p^i(s-1) \tag{12}$$

The expression for δ and λ becomes:

$$\delta_q^i(L_i) = g'(z_q^i(L_i)) \left[\frac{\partial \mathfrak{I}}{\partial \underline{x}_{i+1}} \right]_q \tag{13}$$

$$\delta_q^i(s) = g'(z_q^i(s)) \sum_{j=1}^{n_{s+1}^i} \delta_j^i(s+1) w_{pj}^i(s+1) \quad for \ s = 1,\ldots,L_i - 1 \tag{14}$$

$$\underline{\lambda}_N^{\mathrm{T}} = 0 \tag{15}$$

$$\underline{\lambda}_i^{\mathrm{T}} = \frac{\partial h(\underline{x}_i,\underline{v}_i)}{\partial \underline{v}_i} + \underline{\lambda}_{i+1}^{\mathrm{T}} \frac{\partial \underline{f}(\underline{x}_{i+1},\underline{x}_{i+2},\underline{v}_i)}{\partial \underline{v}_i} \quad for \ i < N \tag{16}$$

$$\frac{\partial \mathfrak{I}}{\partial \underline{x}_N} = \frac{\partial h_N(\underline{x}_N)}{\partial \underline{x}_N} + \underline{\lambda}_{N-1}^{\mathrm{T}} \frac{\partial \underline{f}(\underline{x}_{N-1},\underline{x}_N,\underline{v}_{N-2})}{\partial \underline{x}_N} \tag{17}$$

$$\left[\frac{\partial \mathfrak{I}}{\partial \underline{x}_i} \right]_q = \sum_{j=1}^{n_1^i} \delta_j(1) w_{qj}^i(1) + \left[\frac{\partial h(\underline{x}_i,\underline{v}_i)}{\partial \underline{x}_i} + \underline{\lambda}_{i-1}^{\mathrm{T}} \frac{\partial \underline{f}(\underline{x}_{i-1},\underline{x}_i,\underline{v}_{i-2})}{\partial \underline{x}_i} + \underline{\lambda}_i^{\mathrm{T}} \frac{\partial \underline{f}(\underline{x}_i,\underline{x}_{i+1},\underline{v}_i)}{\partial \underline{x}_i} \right]_q \tag{18}$$

The weight correcting process begins computing (17). Then we can calculate last layer δ of the $N-1$ net with (13), and previous layers δ with (14). We calculate (16) for $i=N-1$, keeping in mind (15). Then we can apply (18) to obtain cost partial derivative with regard to $\underline{x}_{N-2}$, and so on recursively. When we have all the δ we can correct the weights with (4).

In the first training stages the NN can produce state transitions that imply high command and negative time. To avoid this situation we modify cost function to strongly weight negative time and high command.

To obtain expressions in form (11) we apply two discretization types:

- Classical discretization based on forward difference.
- BPF development, which consists in the representation of the problem variables by means of variable width pulses e_i [5]:

$$y = \sum Y_i e_i \quad with \ i = 1,\ldots,N$$

where N is the subinterval number. The coefficients Y_i are chosen to minimize mean quadratic error. As we will show, this discretization method presents better behavior.

The expressions in the form (11) of the system equations (10) for classical and BPF discretization are as follows:

$$\begin{cases} t_i = \dfrac{x_{1i+1} - x_{1i}}{x_{2i}} \\ u_i = \dfrac{1}{c}\left[x_{2i} \dfrac{x_{2i+1} - x_{2i}}{x_{1i+1} - x_{1i}} - a(1 - b x_{1i}^2) x_{2i} - x_{1i} \right] \end{cases}$$

$$\begin{cases} t_i = \dfrac{2}{x_{2i+1}} \left[x_{1i+1} - x_{1i} - \dfrac{t_{i-1}}{2} x_{2i} \right] \\ u_i = \dfrac{1}{c t_i}\left[-c t_{i-1} u_{i-1} + 2(x_{2i+1} - x_{2i}) - ab(t_{i-1} x_{2i} + t_i x_{2i+1}) + b(t_{i-1} x_{2i} x_{1i}^2 + t_i x_{2i+1} x_{1i+1}^2) - (t_{i-1} x_{1i} + t_i x_{1i+1}) \right] \end{cases}$$

We use a structure composed by 6 NN with one hidden layer of 5 neurons. We use the same initial weight for both discretizations.

The forward difference discretization obtain a good trajectory but the states are grouped in its descending part (fig 2). On the other hand, in BPF discretization, states are distributed along the trajectory (fig 3) giving a better defined one.

Fig 2: Evolution with training number.

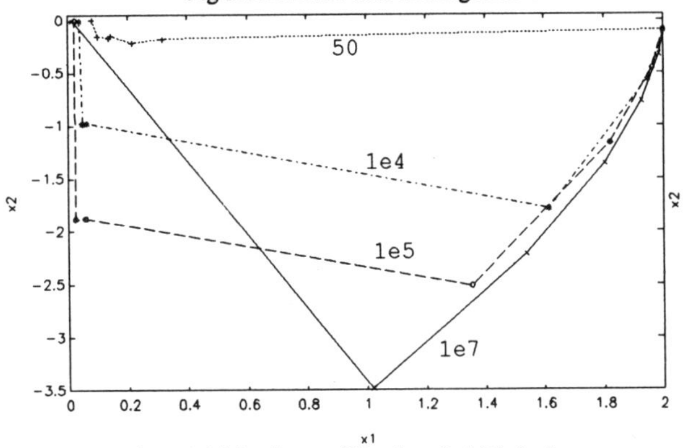

Fig 3: Evolution with training number.

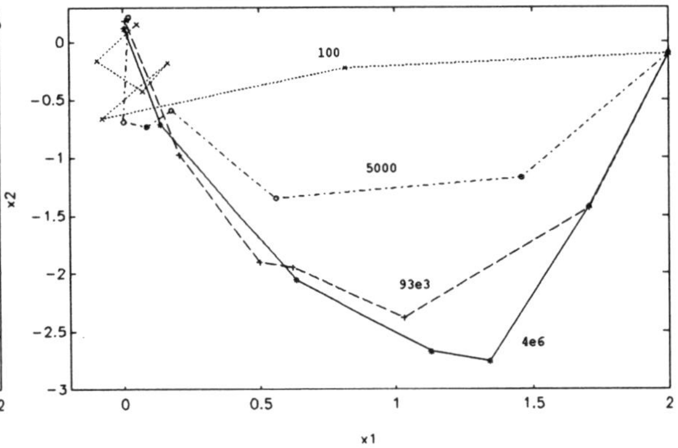

Fig 4: Initial point modification. 2nd Method.

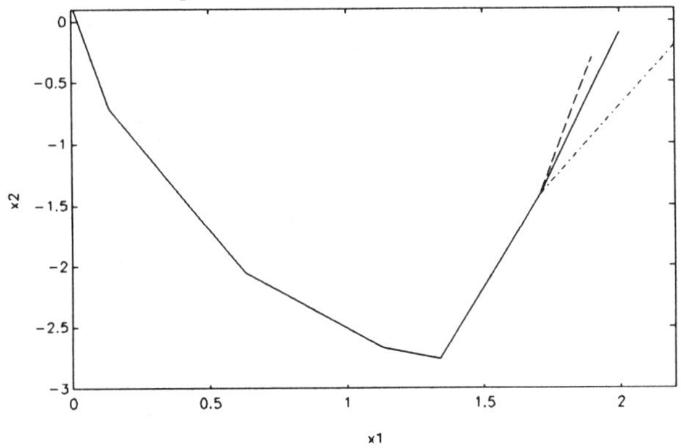

As we have mentioned above, in this method when a trajectory state is disturbed, system quickly returns to the optimal one. This is showed in fig 4 where the initial point has been modified. This is the main advantage of the second method.

Conclusions

We have carried out the application of two NN structures to nonlinear optimal control problems with arbitrary indexes of performance, including minimum time.

We have obtained the expressions for the training process in the proposed methods.

We have shown that the second method structure of NN chain is the more adequate in case of disturbance. In addition, this second method allows different kinds of discretization, giving BPF the best trajectory definition.

Acknowledgment

This work is being supported by the Comisión Interministerial de Ciencia y Tecnología of Spain, project number TAP92-0508.

Bibliography

[1] Narendra K.S., Parthasarathy K. "Identification and Control of Dynamic Systems Using Neural Networks." IEEE Trans. Neural Networks, 1990, 1, pp. 4-27.

[2] Parisini T., Zoppoli R. "Multi-Layer Neural Networks for the Optimal Control of Nonlinear Dynamic Systems." 1st IFAC Symposium on Design Method of Control Systems, pp 612-617, Zurich, Sep. 4-6, 1991.

[3] Hamilton A. "Políticas Óptimas para Sistemas No Lineales Mediante Programación Dinámica y Redes Neuronales." Master Degree Thesis. Universidad de La Laguna. 1992.

[4] L. Moreno, L. Acosta, A. Hamilton, J. Sánchez, J. Piñeiro, J. Merino "Neural Networks Based Minimum-Time Optimal Control of Nonlinear Systems" World Congress on Neural Networks, pp III-327, Portland, July 11-15, 1993.

[5] Rao G.P. "Piecewise constant orthogonal functions and their application to systems and control." Springer Verlag. 1983.

OPTIMAL RADAR PULSE SCHEDULING USING A NEURAL NETWORK

Alberto Izquierdo-Fuente (*), J.R. Casar-Corredera (**)

(*) ETSI. Telecomunicación - Universidad de Valladolid
C/ Real de Burgos s/n 47011 VALLADOLID SPAIN
Tf: +34 83 423260

(**) Dpto. Señales, Sistemas y Radiocomunicaciones. ETSI Telecomunicación-UPM
Ciudad Universitaria 28040 MADRID SPAIN
Tf: +34 1 5495700 (Ext. 206)

ABSTRACT

In a multifunction radar, the maximum number of targets which can be managed (maintain their tracks) is one of the main performance figures. The interleaving algorithms exploit the dead times between the transmitted and the received pulses to allocate new tracking tasks (transmit and receive pulses) thus increasing the capacity of the system.

Generally speaking, the interleaving of N targets is a complex problem (NP-complete type) and sub-optimal solutions are usually employed to satisfy the real-time constraints of the radar system.

In this paper we design an optimal interleaving algorithm based on a Hopfield network. We describe the general problem, define the network and select the criteria to design the weights. Finally as an example, we simulate a simple scenario with five targets.

INTRODUCTION

A multifunction radar, which is based on an electronically phased array, can steer the antenna beam to any direction almost instantaneously. Because of that, a multifunction radar can carry out simultaneously two kind of tasks: Surveillance and Tracking.

Once the surveillance tasks have been defined, the objective is to maximize the number of targets to track on the available time (total time minus surveillance time). Since we have an estimate of the range (distance) of the targets we know the dead time between the transmitted pulse and the received (reflected) pulse. Therefore we can interleave other pulses in these intervals.

The problem of interleaving the transmitted and received pulses of N targets is NP-complete. We have N! possibilities to order the pulses, and sometimes only one is feasible. The computational burden increases with the number of targets and usually sub-optimal solutions are employed.

These solutions sort the targets with a fixed criterion like the Farina & Studer algorithm [1], which orders the targets by decreasing range and try to allocate each received pulse next on the right of previous one. Other solutions like that of the Correlation algorithm [2] find the first available time slot in the temporal frame to allocate the next task.

In Fig. 1 we present a typical example of an interleaving algorithm, where pri represents the interval between consecutive transmitted pulses.

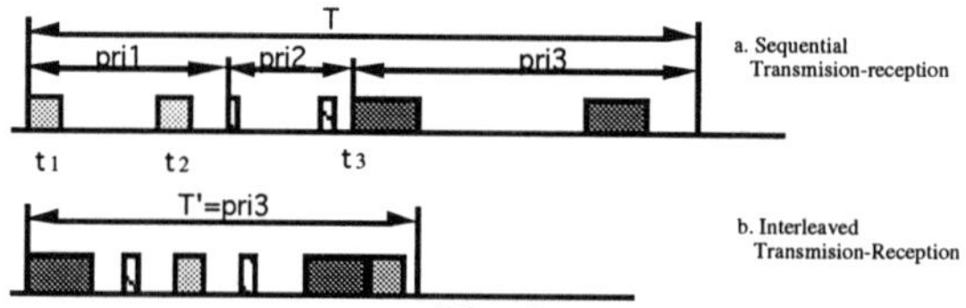

Fig. 1

We have three tasks to interleave. If the tasks are not interleaved (sequential scheduling) they spend a total time T= pri1 + pri2 + pri3. On the other hand, we can interleave tasks 1 and 2 in the dead time of task 3. Note the reduction in the necessary time from T to T'.

This paper handles the interleaving problem from a neural network viewpoint. For a given time interval, usually the pri of the farthest target, we want to find an algorithm which maximises the number of allocated pulses probing on all possible ordinations of the targets.The solution given by our algorithm should be the transmission order and the delay for each target in relation to a common time reference.

INTERLEAVING BASED ON NEURAL NETWORKS

The problem can be formulated in the following terms:

Input information

N tasks to allocate, having each one two τ_i µs wide pulses (transmit & receive), separated T_i sec.(gap)

Constraints

a) Neither of the pulses can be overlapped.
b) A task can be delayed T_r seconds provided the corresponding received pulse can be also scheduled. in the available time interval.

Output information

Order and relative delay for each task allocated.

To pre-process this information, we can simplify the input information, assuming:

a) The time axis is discrete, with Ts sec. slots.
b) The pulses have a constant width τ=Ts (time slot)
c) Gap between pulses T_i has to be an integer number of times the basic time slot: T_i=k*Ts
d) Delay for each task has to be an integer number of times the basic time slot: T_r=j*Ts
e) Available time interval has to be an integer number of times the basic time slot: T_t=i*Ts

Now we can figure out a paradigm as that shown in Fig.2. Where the neural network is built with L levels, each level having N neurons. Each level represents a time slot and the neurons at that level the tasks candidates to be scheduled in that slot. In this way we will have a neural network with N*L elements where neuron (i,j) corresponds to time slot j and task i.

The resulting paradigm is a dynamic Hopfield network where the weights are designed with the input information (gaps) and the constraints (overlap and maximum delay), and the final state of the neurons contain the output information.

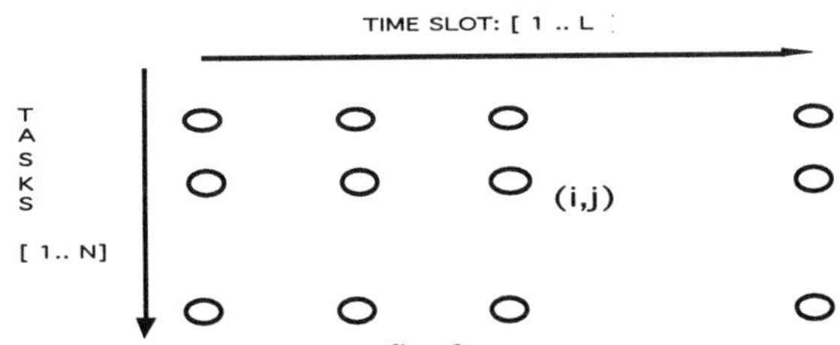

fig. 2

We only represent the transmitted pulse position since the received pulse position is the transmitted position plus the gap. After convergence, there will be as many neurons activated as tasks to allocate. For each row of neurons there will be only one activated neuron, which will indicate the scheduled position of the transmitted pulse.

Design of Weights

1) The $2L^2$-L weights that connect every pair of the neurons will be either null or negative,

2) Let T1 and T2 be two tasks. Let us assume that the transmitted pulse of T1 is allocated in the time slot represented by neuron Ni (i-th slot) and that the transmitted pulse of T2 is allocated in the time slot represented by neuron Nj (j-th slot). We will assign a null to the weight which links Ni and Nj if no one of the transmitted and received pulses overlap. Otherwise, we will assign a negative value to the weight.

3) For a task, assuming that the transmitted pulse is allocated in the position represented by the neuron N_i, we assign negative values to all the weights of that neuron, if the received pulse position exceeds the available time.

4) On the other hand, as only one neuron can be activated per task, we will assign negative weights between the neurons of a same task.

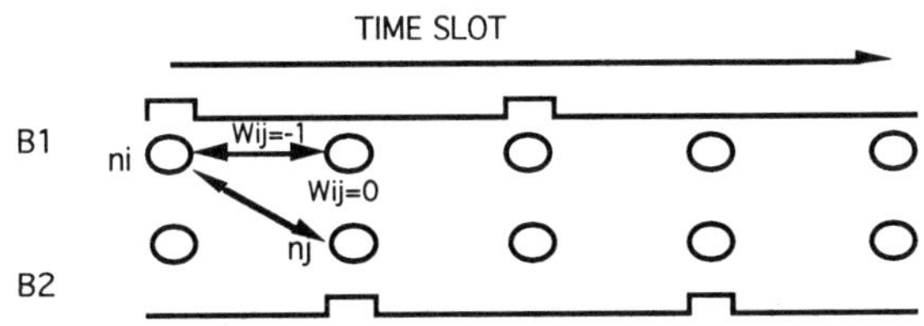

fig. 3

Dynamic node equations

Neurons are activated asynchronously with a random pattern as follows:

$$u_{(i,j)} = f\left(\sum_{k=1}^{k=N}\sum_{l=1}^{M} w_{(i,j)}u_{(i,j)} + v_{(i,j)}\right)$$

where:

u(i,j) neuron output state (i,j)
v(i,j) neuron input excitation (i,j)
w(i,j) weights from neuron (i,j) to all neurons

We assume that all neurons are activated in an initial input state. All arrangement of tasks are allowed.

$$U = \begin{bmatrix} 1 & \cdots & 1 \\ \vdots & & \vdots \\ 1 & \cdots & 1 \end{bmatrix}$$

The input excitation is equal for all neurons and decreases gradually after N iterations.

$$if \quad k = nN \quad v_{(i,j)} = v_{(i,j)} - \Delta v \quad n = [1,2,...]$$

In this way, we manage to cold the network until we obtain one of the possible solutions. Note that for v(i,j)=0, only those neurons which satisfy the constraints can be activated.

Finally the function f(), is a hard-limiter:

$$f(u) = \begin{cases} 0 & u < 0 \\ 1 & u \geq 0 \end{cases}$$

EXAMPLE

As an example we have designed a network for N=5 tasks and a time axis with L=14 slots. Thus the total number of neurons will be N*L = 60 neurons.
The targets (tasks) are sorted in range decreasing order, with gaps from one to five time slots, as we can see in figure 4 (where $\mathbb{T}$ represents the transmitted pulse and $\mathbb{R}$ the received pulse).

TASKS \ TIME SLOTS	1	2	3	4	5	6	7	8	9	10	11	12	13	14
1	T		R											
2	T			R										
3	T				R									
4	T					R								
5	T						R							

fig. 4

The initial input state is given by:

$$U = \begin{bmatrix} 1 & 1 & 1 & 1 & 1 & 1 & 1 & 1 & 1 & 1 & 1 & 1 & 1 & 1 \\ 1 & 1 & 1 & 1 & 1 & 1 & 1 & 1 & 1 & 1 & 1 & 1 & 1 & 1 \\ 1 & 1 & 1 & 1 & 1 & 1 & 1 & 1 & 1 & 1 & 1 & 1 & 1 & 1 \\ 1 & 1 & 1 & 1 & 1 & 1 & 1 & 1 & 1 & 1 & 1 & 1 & 1 & 1 \\ 1 & 1 & 1 & 1 & 1 & 1 & 1 & 1 & 1 & 1 & 1 & 1 & 1 & 1 \end{bmatrix}$$

For setting the weights we used the values:

$$W = \begin{cases} 0 \\ -1.5 \end{cases}$$

We have performed, in a random way, 10*5*14 iterations, beginning with an input excitation v=1,5 and decreasing it in steps of 0.1 every 60 iterations.

In Fig. 5 we show the evolution versus time of the output state for a specific simulation experiment.

v = 1.4

$$U = \begin{bmatrix} 0 & 1 & 0 & 0 & 1 & 1 & 0 & 0 & 0 & 0 & 0 & 0 & 0 & 0 \\ 1 & 0 & 0 & 0 & 1 & 1 & 1 & 0 & 0 & 0 & 0 & 1 & 1 & 0 \\ 1 & 0 & 1 & 0 & 0 & 1 & 0 & 1 & 0 & 0 & 1 & 0 & 0 & 0 \\ 0 & 1 & 0 & 1 & 0 & 0 & 0 & 1 & 1 & 0 & 0 & 0 & 0 & 0 \\ 1 & 0 & 1 & 0 & 1 & 0 & 0 & 0 & 1 & 0 & 0 & 0 & 0 & 1 \end{bmatrix}$$

v = 1.3

$$U = \begin{bmatrix} 0 & 1 & 0 & 0 & 0 & 0 & 0 & 0 & 0 & 0 & 0 & 0 & 0 & 0 \\ 0 & 0 & 0 & 0 & 1 & 0 & 1 & 0 & 0 & 0 & 0 & 0 & 1 & 0 \\ 0 & 0 & 1 & 0 & 0 & 0 & 0 & 0 & 0 & 0 & 0 & 0 & 0 & 0 \\ 0 & 1 & 0 & 0 & 0 & 0 & 0 & 0 & 0 & 0 & 1 & 0 & 0 & 0 \\ 1 & 0 & 1 & 0 & 0 & 0 & 0 & 0 & 0 & 0 & 1 & 0 & 0 & 0 \end{bmatrix}$$

v = 1.2

$$U = \begin{bmatrix} 0 & 1 & 0 & 0 & 0 & 0 & 0 & 0 & 0 & 0 & 0 & 0 & 0 & 0 \\ 0 & 0 & 0 & 0 & 1 & 0 & 0 & 0 & 0 & 0 & 0 & 0 & 1 & 0 \\ 0 & 0 & 1 & 0 & 0 & 0 & 0 & 0 & 0 & 0 & 0 & 0 & 0 & 0 \\ 0 & 0 & 0 & 0 & 0 & 1 & 0 & 0 & 0 & 0 & 0 & 0 & 0 & 0 \\ 0 & 0 & 0 & 0 & 0 & 0 & 0 & 0 & 0 & 0 & 0 & 0 & 0 & 0 \end{bmatrix}$$

v = 1.1

$$U = \begin{bmatrix} 0 & 1 & 0 & 0 & 0 & 0 & 0 & 0 & 0 & 0 & 0 & 0 & 0 & 0 \\ 0 & 0 & 0 & 0 & 1 & 0 & 0 & 0 & 0 & 0 & 0 & 0 & 1 & 0 \\ 0 & 0 & 1 & 0 & 0 & 0 & 0 & 0 & 0 & 0 & 0 & 0 & 0 & 0 \\ 0 & 0 & 0 & 0 & 0 & 1 & 0 & 0 & 0 & 0 & 0 & 0 & 0 & 0 \\ 0 & 0 & 0 & 0 & 0 & 0 & 0 & 0 & 0 & 0 & 0 & 0 & 0 & 0 \end{bmatrix}$$

v = 1.0

$$U = \begin{bmatrix} 0 & 1 & 0 & 0 & 0 & 0 & 0 & 0 & 0 & 0 & 0 & 0 & 0 & 1 \\ 0 & 0 & 0 & 0 & 1 & 0 & 0 & 0 & 0 & 0 & 0 & 0 & 0 & 0 \\ 0 & 0 & 1 & 0 & 0 & 0 & 0 & 0 & 0 & 0 & 0 & 0 & 0 & 0 \\ 0 & 0 & 0 & 0 & 0 & 1 & 0 & 0 & 0 & 0 & 0 & 0 & 0 & 0 \\ 0 & 0 & 0 & 0 & 0 & 0 & 0 & 0 & 0 & 0 & 0 & 0 & 0 & 0 \end{bmatrix}$$

v = 0.9

$$U = \begin{bmatrix} 0 & 0 & 0 & 0 & 0 & 0 & 0 & 0 & 0 & 0 & 0 & 0 & 0 & 1 \\ 0 & 0 & 0 & 0 & 1 & 0 & 0 & 0 & 0 & 0 & 0 & 0 & 0 & 0 \\ 0 & 0 & 1 & 0 & 0 & 0 & 0 & 0 & 0 & 0 & 0 & 0 & 0 & 0 \\ 0 & 0 & 0 & 0 & 0 & 1 & 0 & 0 & 0 & 0 & 0 & 0 & 0 & 0 \\ 0 & 0 & 0 & 0 & 0 & 0 & 0 & 0 & 0 & 0 & 0 & 0 & 0 & 0 \end{bmatrix}$$

v = 0.8

$$U = \begin{bmatrix} 0 & 0 & 0 & 0 & 0 & 0 & 0 & 0 & 0 & 0 & 0 & 0 & 0 & 1 \\ 0 & 0 & 0 & 0 & 1 & 0 & 0 & 0 & 0 & 0 & 0 & 0 & 0 & 0 \\ 0 & 0 & 1 & 0 & 0 & 0 & 0 & 0 & 0 & 0 & 0 & 0 & 0 & 0 \\ 0 & 0 & 0 & 0 & 0 & 1 & 0 & 0 & 0 & 0 & 0 & 0 & 0 & 0 \\ 0 & 0 & 0 & 1 & 0 & 0 & 0 & 0 & 0 & 0 & 0 & 0 & 0 & 0 \end{bmatrix}$$

v = 0.5

$$U = \begin{bmatrix} 0 & 0 & 0 & 0 & 0 & 0 & 0 & 0 & 0 & 0 & 0 & 0 & 0 & 1 \\ 0 & 0 & 0 & 0 & 1 & 0 & 0 & 0 & 0 & 0 & 0 & 0 & 0 & 0 \\ 0 & 0 & 1 & 0 & 0 & 0 & 0 & 0 & 0 & 0 & 0 & 0 & 0 & 0 \\ 0 & 0 & 0 & 0 & 0 & 1 & 0 & 0 & 0 & 0 & 0 & 0 & 0 & 0 \\ 0 & 0 & 0 & 1 & 0 & 0 & 0 & 0 & 0 & 0 & 0 & 0 & 0 & 0 \end{bmatrix}$$

Fig.5

The final solution turns out to be that shown in Fig. 6

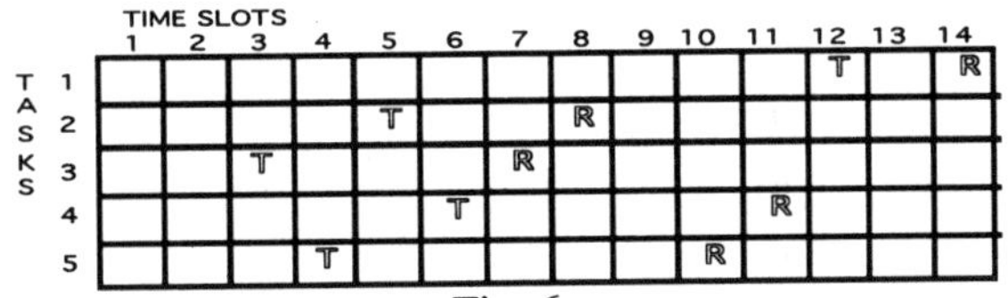

Fig. 6

Finally we present a final state set for different random patterns.

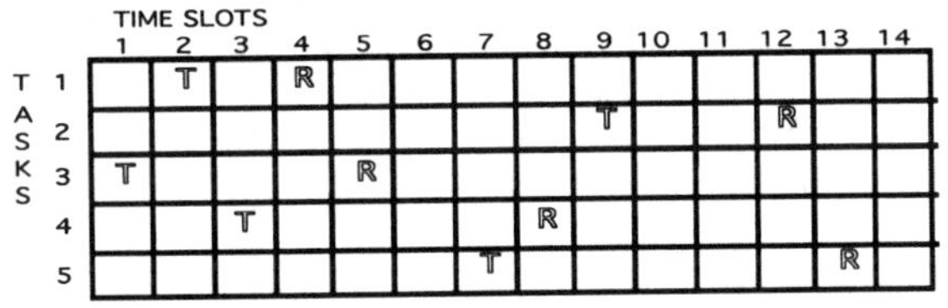

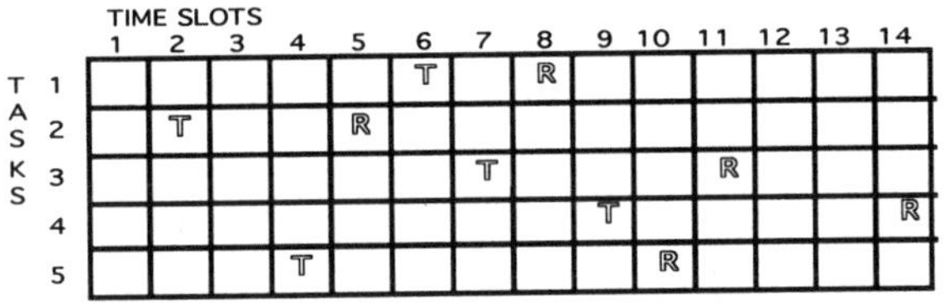

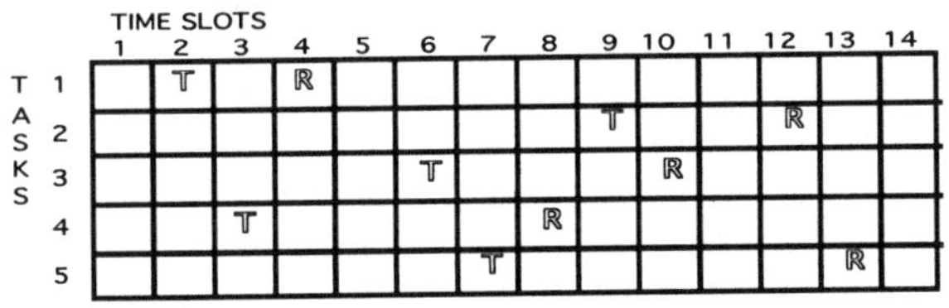

CONCLUSIONS

We have presented a new approach to interleaving based on a Hopfield´s neural network. Under some simplifications we have designed the network layout and we have established a criterion for designing weights and neuron activations (colding process . For a simple example and a set of random patterns the results have been shown to be excellent. More complex scenarios have been tested with similar results.

The next step will be to evaluate the computational burden and efficiency in relation to classical algorithms.

REFERENCES

[1] A. Farina and P. Neri. " Multitarget interleaved tracking for phased-array radar " IEE Proc. Vol 127 Pt. F, No 4 Aug. 1980

[2] Alberto Izquierdo y J.R. Casar Corredera. " Análisis y selección de algoritmos de entrelazado de pulsos para radares multifunción". VII Simposium Nacional de la Unión Científica de Radio.URSI-92. Málaga (Spain). Sept, 1992. pp. 934-938.

[3] Richard P. Lippmann. " An introduction to computing with neural nets" IEEE ASSP Magazine April 1987

[4] Don R. Hush and Bill Horne. " An overview of neural networks: Part I / Part II" Revista Informática y Automática. Vol 25, Num. 1-2. March-June 1992.

LEARNING WITHOUT LOCAL MINIMA

J. Barhen[1,2] , N. Toomarian[1], and A. Fijany[1]

California Institute of Technology
Pasadena, CA 91109

Abstract: A computationally efficient methodology for overcoming local minima in nonlinear neural network learning is presented. This methodology is based on the newly discovered TRUST global optimization paradigm. Enhancements to the backpropagation schema in feedforward multilayer architectures, and to adjoint-operator learning in recurrent networks are discussed. Extensions to TRUST now formally guarantee reaching a global minimum in the multidimensional case. Results for a standard benchmark are included, to illustrate the theoretical developments.

Introduction

Much of the promise of neural networks lies in the hope that they will learn. Generally, the development of learning algorithms is based upon the minimization of an energy-like "neuromorphic" function or functional. In the past, attention has largely focused on error-backpropagation algorithms for "feedforward" [1] architectures. Recently, considerable efforts have been devoted to the more complex "recurrent" networks [2-5]. The introduction of adjoint-operator formalisms for modeling static [6] and time-dependent [7] phenomena has opened new avenues in terms of computational efficiency and relevance to real-time applications. The main emphasis of most research to date has been on how to best obtain the gradients [8] of the aforementioned neuromorphic function or functional with respect to the various parameters of the neural architecture. Heretofore, local minimization techniques have provided the main operational tools for implementing the corresponding algorithms, with the notable exception of stochastic paradigms such as the "Boltzmann Machine" [9] or "diffusion" processes [10].

One of the fundamental limitations of artificial neural network learning by gradient descent is the susceptibility to local minima during training. This paper presents a new approach to learning, in which the gradient descent mechanism is replaced by a methodology based upon a recently developed global optimization scheme, acronymed TRUST [11]. The deterministic TRUST algorithm formulates global optimization in terms of the flow of a special nonlinear dynamical system. TRUST can be applied both to backpropagation learning and to recurrent networks, even those with terminal (i.e., non-lipschitzian) dynamics. Originally [11], our methodology could only guarantee convergence to a global minimum for 1-dimensional problems, eventhough in practice, for all n-dimensional applications, a global minimum was always reached. Here, we present a simple extension

(1) Jet Propulsion Laboratory, 4800 Oak Grove Dr., Tel. (818)354-9218, Fax (818)393-5013, (2) Applied Physics Department

0-7803-1901-X/94 $4.00 ©1994 IEEE

to TRUST, which now formally guarantees convergence to global minima in the multi-dimensional case. We demonstrate, on a standard benchmark, that our approach indeed overcomes encountered local minima, and thereby provides a globally optimal solution to learning problems under consideration.

Globally Optimal Learning

Let $E(p)$ be a scalar function of the single variable p defined over an interval of interest. Consider the nonlinear transformation

$$\Omega(p,p^*) = \ln \frac{1}{1+e^{-[\hat{E}(p)+\varepsilon]}} - \frac{3}{4}\rho(p-p^*)^{4/3}\ H[\hat{E}(p)] \tag{1}$$

where H denotes the Heaviside function, p^* is a fixed value of p, the selection of which will be discussed below, and $\hat{E}(p)$ represents an offset of $E(p)$ by the amount $E(p^*)$. The positive parameters ε and ρ will be specified in the sequel. To highlight the two basic concepts which underlie the TRUST formalism, we rewrite Eq. (1) as

$$\Omega(p,p^*) = \Omega_s(p,p^*) + \Omega_\rho(p,p^*) \tag{2}$$

The sub-energy tunneling function, Ω_s, is defined as the first term in the right-hand-side of Eq. (1). It has the same relative ordering of local and global minima as $E(p)$ since

$$\frac{\partial \Omega_s}{\partial p} = 0 \iff \frac{dE}{dp} = 0$$

Furthermore, Ω_s is monotonically increasing in terms of both $E(p)$ and $\hat{E}(p)$. We want Ω_s to have the following effects: first, it should suppress $\hat{E}(p)$ to zero for $E(p) > E(p^*)$; second, it should leave $\hat{E}(p)$ nearly unmodified for $E(p) < E(p^*)$. These requirements determine possible values for the parameter ε. Figure 1 illustrates the action of Ω_s on the function $E(p) = [\sin 2p - p - 1]^2$ with $p^* \simeq -6.80678$ and $\varepsilon = 2$. We see that Ω_s preserves all properties relevant for optimization. The term Ω_ρ induces a terminal repeller [12] effect.

The basic idea driving our approach to globally optimal learning is to construct a dynamical system which switches autonomously between two phases: (1) a tunneling phase, where the system flows under the action of a terminal repeller, over a sub-energy surface flattened to near zero level for all values of $E(p)$ above a threshold $E(p^*)$; (2) a gradient descent phase, during which the repeller effect is switched off, and which starts whenever a lower energy valley has been reached, to obtain a new threshold $E(p^*)$. For actual neural learning, E is a function of a parameter vector $\bar{p}$ [including, e.g., the synaptic weights]. For the sake of simplicity, the following discussion is limited to one dimension. In this vein, upon application of gradient descent to the Ω functional, we obtain

$$\dot{p} = -\frac{dE(p)}{dp}\frac{1}{1+e^{\hat{E}(p)+\varepsilon}} + \rho(p-p^*)^{1/3} H[\hat{E}(p)] \tag{3}$$

We assume that the optimization is to take place in a specified domain, D, which, in the multidimensional case, will be taken as a hyperparallelepiped. In the one-dimensional case, D is simply the interval $[p_L, p_U]$. To initiate the optimization process, p^* is chosen to be lower limit of D, i.e., $p^* = p_L$. This point need not be a local minimum. A repeller is placed at p^*, and the dynamical system (3) is given the initial condition $p^* + \xi$, where ξ is a very small perturbation. In the one dimensional case, ξ is chosen to be positive, so that the system flows in the positive direction, i.e., toward the upper limit of D.

The selection of p^* defines a threshold called the zero sub-energy limit, $E(p^*)$, above which $\Omega_s(p, p^*)$ is nearly zero in value and approximately flat. If $E(p^* + \xi) < E(p^*)$, the algorithm immediately enters a gradient descent phase, in which the state of the dynamical system flows down the gradient and reaches its first local minimum at $p = p^{1(*)}$. At this point, we set $p^* = p^{1(*)}$ in (3), and perturb p to $p^* + \xi$. Since $p^{1(*)}$ is a local minimum, $E(p) \geq E(p^*)$ in a neighborhood of p^*. Consequently, the repelling term is active. The repeller located at p^* drives the solution across the flattened sub-energy surface, which in effect pushes the system uphill on the surface of the associated objective function. The dynamical system remains in the repelling phase until it reaches a lower valley, where $\hat{E}(p) < 0$. In effect, this phase tunnels through all of the state space region with functional values that lie above the last found local minimum, $E(p^{1(*)})$. A lower valley of $\Omega_s(p, p^*)$ is a lower value of $E(p)$ as well. As the dynamical system enters the next valley, the algorithm automatically switches to the second phase, where the terminal repeller term is zero and gradient descent takes over, leading to further minimization of $E(p)$. The system will equilibrate at the next lower local minimum, $p^{2(*)}$. We set $p^* = p^{2(*)}$ and repeat the process. If $E(p^* + \xi) \geq E(p^*)$ when the optimization procedure is initiated, the dynamical system will initially enter the tunneling phase. The tunneling will proceed to a lower valley, at which point the algorithm enters a gradient descent phase and follows the behavior discussed above.

The two-phase descent-and-tunneling process continues until a suitable stopping criterion is satisfied. Here, as soon as the lowest local minimum, p^*_G, in D has been reached, the optimization cycle is repeated by placing a repeller at p^*_G and perturbing the system to initiate the next tunneling phase. In this case, the sub-energy transformation flattens $E(p)$ in the entire domain of interest, since $E(p^*_G)$ is the lowest objective function value in D. The perturbed dynamical system, which is now in the repeller tunneling phase, will eventually flow beyond the upper boundary of D. Thus, when the state flows out of the domain boundary, i.e., when $p > p_U$, the last local minimum found is the global minimum of the function in D.

Multidimensional Global Optimization and Learning Example

The multidimensional global optimization in [11] was carried out by generalizing Eq. (3) to a vector-differential equation. In a departure from that paradigm, we consider here an approach whereby the M-dimensional learning error function (typically $M = N^2, N$ being the number of neurons in the network) is represented in terms of a single variable. To achieve such a representation, Kolmogorov embeddings [13] could be envisioned, but they result in a computationally complex nonsmooth transform. On the other hand, multidimensional embeddings based on the dense covering of the real plane by Archimedes' spiral are known [14]. Using the latter transformation, we can write:

$$E[\,\mathrm{w}_1, \cdots \mathrm{w}_\mu, \cdots \mathrm{w}_M] = E[\alpha_1(\omega), \cdots \alpha_\mu(\omega), \cdots \alpha_M(\omega)]$$

Each synaptic weight w_μ has been expressed in terms of a single parameter w, using the Archimedes spiral representation. Specifically, for a 2-dimensional case, we can write

$$\mathrm{w}_1 = \alpha\omega\cos\omega \qquad \text{and} \qquad \mathrm{w}_2 = \alpha\omega\sin\omega$$

where α is a constant controlling the precision of the computation. TRUST, the fastest known [11] 1-D global optimization algorithm can now readily be applied to the function $E(w)$.

To illustrate the power of such an approach, we consider the following learning error function:

$$f(\,\mathrm{w}_1,\ \mathrm{w}_2) = \left\{\sum_{i=1}^{5} i\cos[(i+1)\ \mathrm{w}_1 + i]\right\}.\left\{\sum_{j=1}^{5} j\cos[(j+1)\ \mathrm{w}_2 + j]\right\}$$

This function is displayed in Fig. 2, and is shown to exhibit a rather complex structure. For weights in the interval [-10, +10], it possesses 760 local minima. We measure the cost of the global minimization in terms of the number of function evaluations. Then, *under identical operating conditions*, we find that the respective costs of the best stochastic method (Aluffi-Pentini), tunneling (Levy-Montalvo), and interval algorithm (Walster) were 241215, 12160 and 7424, respectively. TRUST, on the other hand reached the global minimum after only 269 function evaluations.

ACKNOWLEDGMENTS

This research was carried out at the Center for Space Microelectronics Technology, Jet Propulsion Laboratory, California Institute of Technology. Support for the work came from the Innovative Science and Technology Office of the Ballistic Missiles Defense Organization, and from the Office of Basic Energy Sciences of the U.S. Department of Energy, through an agreement with the National Aeronautics and Space Administration.

REFERENCES

1. Rumelhart, D. E., et al., 1986, *Parallel and Distributed Processing*, MIT Press.
2. Pearlmutter, B. A., 1989,"Learning State Space Trajectories in Recurrent Neural Networks", *Neural Computation, 1* (2), 263-269.
3. Williams, R. J., and Zipser, D., 1989, "A Learning Algorithm for Continually Running Fully Recurrent Neural Networks", *Neural Computation, 1*, (2), 270-280.
4. Barhen, J., Gulati, S., and Zak, M., 1989, "Neural Learning of Constrained Nonlinear Transformations",*IEEE Computer*, 22(6), 67-76.

5. Pineda, F., 1990, "Time Dependent Adaptive Neural Networks", *Adv. Neur. Inf. Proc. Sys.*, 2, 710-718.
6. Barhen, J., Toomarian, N., and Gulati, S., 1990b, "Application of Adjoint Operators to Neural Learning", *Appl. Math. Lett.*, 3 (3), 13-18.
7. Toomarian, N. and Barhen, J., 1992, "Learning a Trajectory Using Adjoint Functions and Teacher Forcing", *Neural Networks, 5*, 473-484.
8. Rohwer, R., 1991, "Time Trials on Second Order and Variable-Learning Rate Algorithms", *Adv. Neur. Inf. Proc Syst., 3*, 977-983.
9. Hinton, G., 1989, "Deterministic Boltzmann Learning Performs Steepest Descent in Weight Space", *Neural Computation, (1)*, 143-150.
10. Guillerm, T.J., Cotter, N.E., 1991, "A Diffusion Processfor Global Optimization in Neural Networks," *IEEE INNS, 1*, 335-340.
11. Cetin, B., Barhen, J., and Burdick, J., 1993, "Terminal Repeller Unconstrained Subenergy Tunneling for Fast Global Optimization", *Journal of Optimization Theory and Applications, 77* (1), 97-126.
12. Zak, M., 1989, "Terminal Attractors in Neural Networks", *Neural Networks, 2*, (4), 259-274.
13. Fisher, A.J., 1986, "A New Algorithm for Generating Hilbert Curves", *Software-Practice and Experience, 16*(1), 5-12 (1986).
14. Cherrualt, Y. and A. Guillez, 1983, *Comptes Rendus de l'Academie des Sciences, Paris, 296*(I), 175-178.

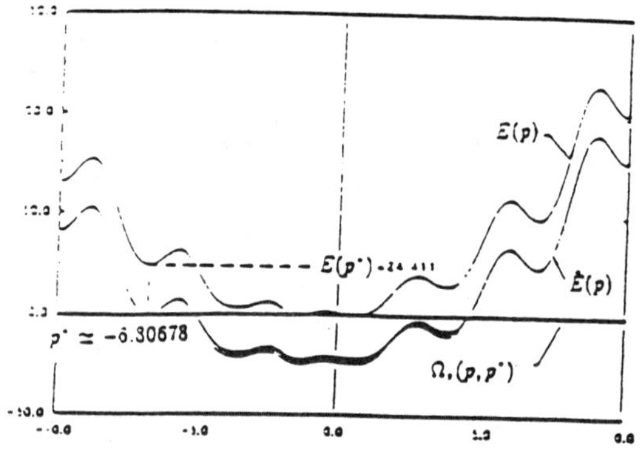

Figure 1: Example of Subenergy Tunneling Transformation

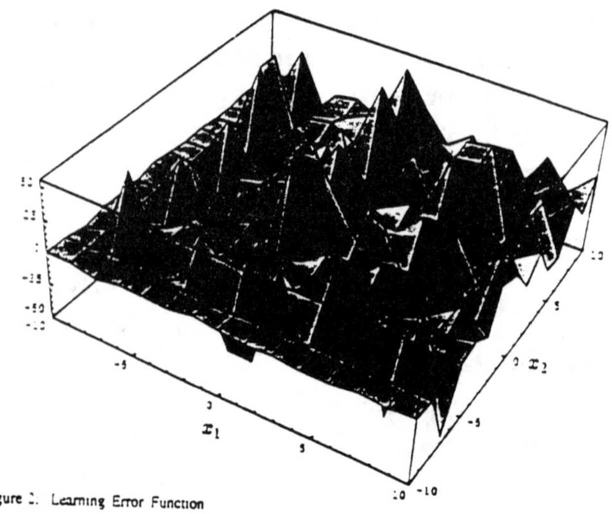

Figure 2. Learning Error Function

Pathfollowing Approach to Globally Optimal Vector Quantizer Design

Fu-lai Chung and Tong Lee*
Dept. of Electronic Engineering
The Chinese University of Hong Kong
Shatin, Hong Kong.

Wilson Chan
Dept. of Electronic Engineering
City Polytechnic of Hong Kong
83 Tatchee Avenue, Kowloon, Hong Kong.

Abstract

Continuation method, also known as pathfollowing method, is applied to the problem of globally optimal vector quantization, and a novel algorithm is proposed. The superiority of the proposed algorithm in codebook quality, computational efficiency, and algorithmic simplicity is demonstrated through experiments in image coding.

I. Introduction

Vector quantization (VQ) is a simple and yet powerful source coding technique which provides large reductions in bit rate while least compromising the signal quality [2]. Mathematically, vector quantization is defined as a mapping, $Q: R^k \rightarrow C$, from a k-dimensional input vector space R^k to a finite subset $C = \{\bar{c}_i | i = 1, 2, \ldots, M\} \in R^k$ called codebook and its objective is to minimize the difference between input vectors $\vec{x}_p$ and the mapped codevectors $\bar{c}_i$. A good codebook is hence the key to VQ. Among the commonly used design algorithms, the Linde-Buzo-Gray (LBG) algorithm [4] is perhaps the most well-known one. The performance of this algorithm is always considered as suboptimal because it is simply a local descent method for which a prescribed distortion function is decreased monotonically by updating the codebook entries iteratively. Unfortunately, due to the highly non-linear nature of the problem, the distortion function is generally non-convex and may exhibit many local minima [1]. Therefore, the resulted codebook designed does not guarantee minimum distortion, and the mapped codevectors are not necessarily good approximations to the original signal vectors. To tackle this problem, Zeger *et al.* [8] have recently proposed a class of stochastic relaxation based VQ algorithms. These algorithms have been shown to improve the quality of the designed codebooks, but inevitably, increase the computational and algorithmic complexity.

In this letter, a novel approach taking use of the so-called pathfollowing or continuation methods [3,6] to attain globally optimal VQ design is presented and a new algorithm called continuation method VQ (CMVQ) algorithm is proposed. In section II, a brief introduction to continuation methods is given and the CMVQ algorithm is derived. Its performance is demonstrated through image coding simulations in Section III.

---

* To whom all communications should be directed

0-7803-1901-X/94 $4.00 ©1994 IEEE

II. Vector Quantization Using Continuation Methods

A. *Overview of Continuation Methods*

Although continuation methods (CM) [6] have been studied extensively by mathematicians to solve a system of non-linear equations for more than two decades, it is not until recently that they have received considerable attentions as an engineering tool to solve nonlinear problems [5,7]. The advantages of CM are globally convergent and, under certain conditions, exhaustive [6]. Its underlying concept is to define a parameterized homotopy function $h(\mathbf{x},t)$ in such a way that it deforms a simple problem with known solution into the desired problem, i.e.,

$$h(\mathbf{x},t) = (1-t)g(\mathbf{x}) + tf(\mathbf{x}) = 0 \tag{1}$$

where $\mathbf{x}$ is the solution parameters to be determined, $t \in [0,1]$ is a homotopy parameter, $f(\mathbf{x})=0$ is the system of equations to be solved, and $g(\mathbf{x})=0$ is a simple system of equations with known solutions. Thus the homotopy function $h(\mathbf{x},t)$ defines a path from the known solution when $t=0$ to the desired solution when $t=1$ in the $\mathbf{x}$ parameter space. With such function defined, continuation methods are the numerical tools used to follow this path and hence they are also known as pathfollowing methods [3]. For discrete type CM [7], the path can be followed by incrementing and fixing t and then solving $h(\mathbf{x},t)=0$ by iterative optimization process. If the increment Δt is chosen sufficiently small, then the iterative process will generally converge since the starting value $\mathbf{x}^{(n-1)}$ will be close to the solution $\mathbf{x}^{(n)}$ of $h(\mathbf{x},t_n)=0$ at the n-th instance. The main theoretical problem is then to determine the sequence $\{0 = t_0 < t_1 \cdots < t_n < \cdots < t_L = 1\}$ such that $\mathbf{x}^{(n-1)}$ is always in the basin of attraction of $\mathbf{x}^{(n)}$. This method will be applied to the problem of globally optimal VQ design in next subsection.

B. *A Continuation Method Vector Quantization (CMVQ) Algorithm*

As exemplified in [7], the system of equations for the desired problem $f(\mathbf{x})=0$ can be formulated as the stationary points of the problem's objective function space. For the VQ problem, suppose there are N input vectors in a training set $S = \{\vec{x}_p | p = 1,2,\cdots,N\}$ and M codevectors in a codebook $C = \{\vec{c}_i | i = 1,2,\cdots,M\}$ where M<N. The objective is to minimize the within groups sum of squared error

$$D(S,C) = \sum_{i=1}^{M} \sum_{x_p \in S_i} d_2(\vec{x}_p, \vec{c}_i) = \sum_{i=1}^{M} \sum_{x_p \in S_i} \left\| (\vec{x}_p - \vec{c}_i) \right\|^2 \tag{2}$$

where $S_i = \{\vec{x}_p \in S | d_2(\vec{x}_p, \vec{c}_i) \le d_2(\vec{x}_p, \vec{c}_j) \forall j \ne i\}$ is the set of input vectors nearest to $\vec{c}_i$. By evaluating $\partial D(S,C) / \partial \vec{c}_i = 0$, we have the desired problem f characterized by

$$\sum_{x_p \in S_i} (\vec{x}_p) - |S_i| \cdot \vec{c}_i = 0 \tag{3}$$

where $|\cdot|$ is the cardinality operator. In fact, eq.(3) is essentially the centroid computation step of the LBG algorithm. Consider now a much simpler VQ problem where a training set S^M consists of only M vectors randomly chosen from S. By evaluating $\partial D(S^M, C) / \partial \vec{c}_i = 0$, we have the system of equations

$$\sum_{x_p \in S_i^M}(\bar{x}_p) - \left|S_i^M\right| \cdot \bar{c}_i = 0 \tag{4}$$

where $S_i^M = \{\bar{x}_p \in S^M | d_2(\bar{x}_p, \bar{c}_i) \le d_2(\bar{x}_p, \bar{c}_j) \forall j \ne i\}$. Obviously, $\{\bar{c}_i = \bar{x}_i \forall i\}$ is a solution to this problem. Thus, the homotopy function is defined as

$$h(\bar{c}_i, t) = (1-t)[\sum_{x_p \in S_i^M}(\bar{x}_p) - \left|S_i^M\right| \cdot \bar{c}_i] + t[\sum_{x_p \in S_i}(\bar{x}_p) - \left|S_i\right| \cdot \bar{c}_i] \tag{5}$$

By setting equation (5) to zero and taking the known solution into account, a new codevector updating law

$$\bar{c}_i = \frac{1}{1 + t\left|\{S_i - S_i^M\}\right|}(\bar{x}_i + \sum_{x_p \in \{S_i - S_i^M\}} t \cdot \bar{x}_p) \tag{6}$$

is derived. The homotopy parameter t can be considered as a weighting factor in this centroid computation step and in fact, it is such weighted operations to produce "intermediate" results that are of higher potential for obtaining better final codebook. By fixing an appropriate homotopy parameter sequence and applying the LBG iterative process with the codevector updating law replaced by equation (5) at each fixed t, a continuation method VQ (CMVQ) algorithm is proposed. In this paper, linear homotopy parameter sequence $\{t_n = n \cdot \Delta t | n = 0, 1, \cdots, (1/\Delta t)\}$ is adopted for the sake of simplicity. As justified by the simulation results reported in next section, such simple sequence is good enough for obtaining final codebooks superior to those of the simulated annealing VQ (SA-C) algorithm, a global algorithm proposed in [8].

III. Simulation Results

The Lena and Peppers standard monochrome 256×256 images were used to measure the performances of the CMVQ algorithm. Corresponding to nonoverlapping extraction using 2×2 block size, a total of 16384 training vectors was obtained for each image and three codebooks sizes (M=16, 64, 256) were chosen to simulate. In Table I, the performance in terms of SNR and execution time of the proposed algorithm is recorded. For comparisons, results obtained from the LBG algorithm and the SA-C algorithm proposed in [8] are included here. All quoted readings for execution time are based DECstation 3100 (14.3 MIPS). For the homotopy parameter sequence, Δt was chosen as 0.1. For the SA-C algorithm, the initial temperature and Kirkpatrick constant were set to be 10 and 0.6 respectively. From the table, it can be observed that the execution time consumed by CMVQ is much shorter than that of SA-C and more importantly the superiority of CMVQ's codebook quality is maintained as well. Although the CMVQ algorithm has to perform ten LBG-like iterative processes for Δt=0.1, its execution time is only about twice of the LBG algorithm. Thus, the proposed algorithm is an attractive alternative to vector quantizer design.

IV. Conclusions

As supported by the simulation results, the proposed CMVQ algorithm is distinctive in codebook quality, algorithmic simplicity, and reduced demand in computational power. However, the theoretical problem of obtaining a homotopy parameter sequence to ensure the algorithm globally convergent has not yet been addressed. Further, applying continuous type continuation methods [6] to this problem has been omitted in this study. All these have been left for further researches.

References

[1] R.M. Gray and E.D. Karnin, "Multiple Local Optima in Vector Quantizers," *IEEE Trans. on Information Theory*, vol.IT-28, no.2, pp.256-261, Mar. 1982.

[2] R.M. Gray, "Vector Quantization," *IEEE ASSP Magazine*, vol.1, pp.4-29, 1984.

[3] J. Guddat, F. Guerra Vazquez, and H.Th. Jongen, *Parametric Optimization : Singularities, Pathfollowing and Jumps*. Chichester:Wiley, 1990.

[4] Y. Linde, A. Buzo, and R.M. Gray, "An Algorithm for Vector Quantizer Design," *IEEE Trans. on Communications*, vol.COM-28, pp.84-95, Jan. 1980.

[5] A. Morgan, *Solving Polynomial Systems Using Continuation for Engineering and Scientific Computation*. Englewood Cliffs, NY:Prentices-Hall, 1987.

[6] S.L. Richter and R.A. DeCarlo, "Continuation Methods : Theory and Applications," *IEEE Trans. on Circuits and Systems*, vol.CAS-30, no.6, pp.347-352, 1983.

[7] V.L. Stonick and S.T. Alexander, "Globally Optimal Rational Approximation Using Homotopy Continuation Methods," *IEEE Trans. on Signal Processing*, vol.40, no.9, Sept. 1992.

[8] Zeger, J. Vaisey, and A. Gersho, "Globally Optimal Vector Quantizer Design by Stochastic Relaxation," *IEEE Trans. on Signal Processing*, vol.40, no.2, Feb. 1992.

Table I. Performance of the proposed CMVQ algorithm in image coding

Image	Codebook Size	SNR (dB) LBG	SNR (dB) CMVQ	SNR (dB) SA-C	Execution Time (Sec.) LBG	Execution Time (Sec.) CMVQ	Execution Time (Sec.) SA-C
Lenna	16	10.07	11.32	10.53	19	32	9767
	64	17.41	20.13	20.05	46	103	7976
	256	23.34	23.56	23.33	310	496	6771
Peppers	26	11.10	11.66	11.64	19	37	13131
	64	18.95	19.72	17.78	75	96	6091
	256	22.37	23.20	22.38	310	536	5672

The Capacity of Convergence-Zone Episodic Memory

Mark Moll, Risto Miikkulainen, Jonathan Abbey

***Abstract*— Human episodic memory provides a seemingly unlimited storage for everyday experiences, and a retrieval system that allows us to access the experiences with partial activation of their components. This paper presents a computational model of episodic memory inspired by Damasio's idea of Convergence Zones. The model consists of a layer of perceptual feature maps and a binding layer. A perceptual feature pattern is coarse coded in the binding layer, and stored on the weights between layers. A partial activation of the stored features activates the binding pattern which in turn reactivates the entire stored pattern. A worst-case analysis shows that with realistic-size layers, the memory capacity of the model is several times larger than the number of units in the model, and could account for the large capacity of human episodic memory.**

I. Introduction

Human episodic memory is characterized by an extremely high capacity. New memories are formed every few seconds, and many of those persist in the memory for years, even decades (Squire 1987). Another significant characteristic of human memory is content-addressability. Most of the memories can be retrieved simply by activating a partial representation of the experience, such as a sound, a smell, or a visual image.

Although several artificial neural network models of episodic memory have been proposed (Hopfield 1982; Kanerva 1988; Kortge 1990; Miikkulainen 1992), they fall short of explaining the simultaneous huge capacity and content-addressability of human memory. For example in the Hopfield model of N units, $N/4 \log N$ patterns can be stored with a 99% probability of correct retrieval when N is large (Hertz et al. 1991; Keeler 1988; McEliece et al. 1986) This means that storing and retrieving, for example, 10^8 memories would require in the order of 10^{10} nodes and 10^{20} connections. Given that the human brain is estimated to have about 10^{11} neurons and 10^{15} synapses (Jessell 1991), this is clearly unrealistic.

Despite vast amount of research in human memory, no clear understanding has yet emerged on exactly where and how the memory traces are represented in the brain. There is evidence for both localized encoding and for distributed encoding (Squire 1987). Damasio (1989b, 1989a) proposed a general framework, based on observations of typical patterns of injury-related memory deficits, that can potentially account for much of the data. The main idea is that the memory system is organized in a hierarchy of associational regions, or convergence zones, with each region serving as a basis for higher-level associations. The hierarchy is grounded in the sensory modality regions, and becomes more abstract and general as one moves from the sensory cortical regions to the forebrain. The low-level and intermediate regions contain object representations, and the high-level regions contain representations for complete episodes, in terms of the lower-level entities.

This paper presents a new episodic memory model loosely based on the convergence zone idea. The model consists of a number of perceptual maps and a binding layer (a convergence zone). An episodic experience appears as a pattern of local activations across the perceptual maps, and is encoded as a coarse-coded (Rosenfeld and Touretzky 1989; Touretzky and Hinton 1988) pattern in the binding layer. The connections between the maps and the binding layer store the encoding so that the complete perceptual pattern can later be regenerated from partial activation. The details of the low-level neural implementation are left open in this paper. The goal is to analyze the behavior of the model at the functional level, and derive general results about its capacity and physical size.

Mark Moll is with the Department of Computer Science, University of Twente, P.O. Box 217, 7500 AE Enschede, The Netherlands.

Risto Miikkulainen is with the Department of Computer Sciences, The University of Texas at Austin, Austin, TX 78712, USA.

Jonathan Abbey is with Applied Research Laboratories, P.O. Box 8029, Austin, TX 78713, USA

A worst-case analysis of the model shows that: (1) with realistic-size maps and binding layer, the capacity of the convergence-zone memory is extremely high, exceeding the number of units in the model by a factor of 5; and (2) the majority of the neural hardware is required in the perceptual processing; the binding layer needs to be only a fraction of the size of the perceptual maps. Such results suggest how an extremely high capacity could be achieved in the human episodic memory with very little extra hardware beyond the perceptual maps.

II. Storage and Retrieval

The model consists of two layers of real-valued units (the feature map layer and the binding layer), and bidirectional binary connections between the layers (figure 1). Perceptual experiences are represented as vectors of feature values, such as color=`red`, shape=`round`, size=`small`. The values are encoded as units on the feature maps. There is a separate map for each feature domain, and each unit on the map represents a particular value for that feature. For instance, on the map for the color feature, the value `red` could be specified by turning on the unit in the lower-right quarter (figure 1). The feature map units are connected to the binding layer with bidirectional binary connections (i.e. the weight is either 0 or 1). An activation of units in the feature map layer causes a number of units to become active in the binding layer, and vice versa. In effect, the binding layer activation is a compressed, distributed encoding of the value-unit perceptual representation.

Initially, all connections are inactive at 0. A perceptual experience is stored in the memory through the feature map layer in three steps. First, those units that represent the appropriate feature values are activated at 1. Second, a subset of m binding units are randomly selected in the binding layer as the compressed encoding for the pattern, and activated at 1. Third, the weights of all the connections between the active units in the feature maps and the active units in the binding layer are set to 1 (figure 1). Note that only one presentation is necessary to store a pattern.

To retrieve a pattern, first all binding units are set to 0. The pattern to be retrieved is partially specified in the feature maps by activating a subset of its feature units. For example, in figure 2a the memory is cued with the two leftmost features. The activation propagates to the binding layer through all connections that have been turned on so far. The set of binding units that a particular feature unit turns on is called the binding constellation of that unit. All binding units in the binding encoding of the pattern to be retrieved are active at 2 because they belong to the binding constellation of both retrieval cue units. A number of other units are also activated at 1, because each cue unit takes part in representing multiple patterns, and therefore has several other active connections as well. Only those units active at 2 are retained; units with less activation are turned off (figure 2b).

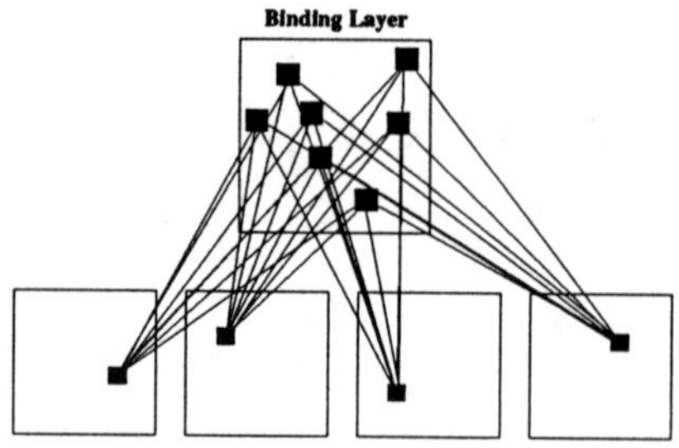

Figure 1: **Storage.** The weights on the connections between the appropriate feature units and the binding representation of the pattern are set to 1.

The activation of the remaining binding units is then propagated back to the feature maps (figure 2c). A number of units are activated at various levels in each feature map, depending on how well their binding constellation matches the current pattern in the binding layer. Chances are that the unit that belongs to the same pattern than the cues has the largest overlap and becomes most highly activated. Only the most active unit in each feature map is retained, and as a result, a complete, unambiguous perceptual pattern is retrieved from the system (figure 2d).

III. Retrieval Errors

If there are n units in the binding layer and m units are chosen as a representation for a pattern, the number of possible different binding representations is equal to $\binom{n}{m}$. If n is sufficiently large and m is relatively small compared to n, this number is extremely large, suggesting that the convergence-zone memory could have a very large capacity.

However, due to the probabilistic nature of the storage and retrieval processes, there is always a chance that the retrieval will fail. The binding constellations of the retrieval cue units may overlap significantly, and several spurious units may be turned on at the binding layer. When the activation is propagated back to the feature maps, some random unit in a feature map may have a binding constellation that matches the spurious units very well. The "rogue" unit may receive more activation than the correct unit, and a wrong feature value may be retrieved. As more patterns are stored, the binding constellations of feature units become larger, and

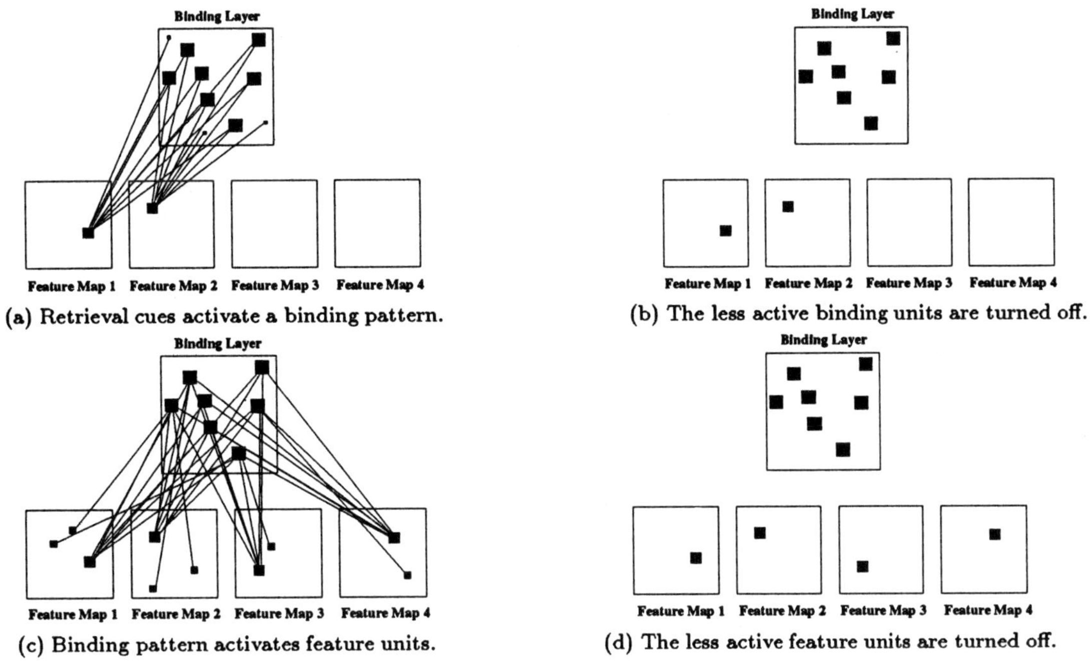

(a) Retrieval cues activate a binding pattern.

(b) The less active binding units are turned off.

(c) Binding pattern activates feature units.

(d) The less active feature units are turned off.

Figure 2: **Retrieval.** A stored pattern is retrieved by presenting a partial representation as a cue. The size of the square indicates activation level of the unit.

erroneous retrieval becomes more likely.

To determine the capacity of the convergence-zone memory, the chance of retrieval error must be computed. Below, a probabilistic formulation of the model is first given, and bounds for retrieval error are then computed.

IV. Probabilistic Formulation

Let Z_i be the size of the binding constellation of a feature unit after i patterns have been stored on it and let Y_i be its increase after storing the ith pattern on it. Obviously, $Y_1 = m$. To obtain the distribution of Y_i when $i > 1$, note that the new active connections belong to the intersection of a randomly chosen subset of m connections among all n connections of the unit, and its all remaining inactive connections (a set with $n-z$ elements, where z is the binding constellation at the previous step). Therefore, $Y_i, i > 1$ is hypergeometrically distributed with parameters $m, n-z$, and n:

$$\mathrm{P}(Y_i = y | Z_{i-1} = z) = \binom{n-z}{y}\binom{z}{m-y} \Big/ \binom{n}{m}. \qquad (1)$$

The constellation size Z_i is then given by

$$Z_i = \sum_{k=1}^{i} Y_k. \qquad (2)$$

Let I be the number of patterns stored on a particular feature unit after p patterns have been stored in the entire memory. I is binomially distributed with parameters p and $\frac{1}{f}$, where f is the number of units in a feature map:

$$I \sim \mathrm{B}(p, \frac{1}{f}). \qquad (3)$$

Let Z be the binding constellation of a particular feature unit after p patterns have been stored in the memory. It can be shown that $\mathrm{E}(Z) = n(1-(1-\frac{m}{nf})^p)$. The binding constellation of a feature unit, given that at least one pattern has been stored on it, is denoted by Z'; obviously $\mathrm{E}(Z') > E(Z)$. The variable Z' can be used to denote the binding constellation of a retrieval cue, which necessarily must have been used once, assuming that the retrieval cues are valid. Let Z'_j be the binding constellation of the jth retrieval cue and let X_j be the number of units in the intersection of the first j retrieval cues. Then $X_1 = Z'_1$. To get X_j for $j > 1$, we remove from consideration the m units all retrieval cues necessarily have in common (because they belong to the same stored pattern), and randomly select $z-m$ units from the total set of $n-m$ units and see how many of them belong to the current intersection of $x_{j-1} - m$ units. This is a hypergeometric distribution with parameters $z-m, x_{j-1}-m$, and $n-m$:

$$\mathrm{P}(X_j = x_j + m | Z'_j = z, X_{j-1} = x_{j-1}) = \binom{x_{j-1}-m}{x_j - m}\binom{n-x_{j-1}}{z-x_j} \Big/ \binom{n-m}{z-m}. \qquad (4)$$

The intersection is taken over the binding constellations of all j retrieval cues.

The number of units in common between a potential rogue unit and the j retrieval cues is denoted by R_{j+1} and is also hypergeometrically distributed, however with parameters z, x, and n because we cannot assume that the rogue unit has at least m units in common with the cues:

$$P(R_{j+1} = r | Z = z, X_j = x) = \binom{x}{r}\binom{n-x}{z-r} \Big/ \binom{n}{z}. \quad (5)$$

The correct unit in a feature map where a retrieval cue was not presented will receive an activation X_{j+1}. The correct unit will be retrieved if $X_{j+1} > R_{j+1}$, which is usually the case because $E(X_{j+1}) > E(R_{j+1})$. In each feature map there are $(f-1)$ potential rogue units, so the conditional probability of successful retrieval is $(1 - P(R_{j+1} > X_{j+1} | X_{j+1}, Z, X_j))^{(f-1)}$, not addressing tie-breaking. Unfortunately, it is very difficult to compute p_{success}, the unconditional probability of successful retrieval, because the distribution functions of Z, X_j, X_{j+1} and R_{j+1} are not known. But it is possible to derive bounds for p_{success} and show that with reasonable values for n, m, f, and p, the memory is reliable.

V. Lower bound for memory capacity

Memory capacity can be defined as the maximum number of patterns that can be stored in the memory so that the probability of correct retrieval with a given number of retrieval cues is greater than α (a constant close to 1). In this section, worst-case bounds for the chance of successful retrieval will be derived. The analysis consists of three steps: (1) bounds for the number of patterns stored on a feature unit; (2) bounds for the binding constellation size; and (3) bounds for the intersections of binding constellations. Given particular values for the system parameters, it is then possible to give a lower bound for the capacity of the model.

1. Number of patterns stored on a feature unit. Since I has a binomial distribution (with parameters p and $\frac{1}{f}$), Chernoff bounds can be applied:

$$P(I \le (1-\delta)\frac{p}{f}) \le \left[\frac{e^{-\delta}}{(1-\delta)^{1-\delta}}\right]^{\frac{p}{f}}, 0 < \delta < 1, \quad (6)$$

$$P(I \ge (1+\delta)\frac{p}{f}) \le \left[\frac{e^{\delta}}{(1+\delta)^{1+\delta}}\right]^{\frac{p}{f}}, \quad \delta > 0. \quad (7)$$

The formal parameter δ determines the tradeoff between the tightness of the bounds and the probability of satisfying them.

2. Size of the binding constellation. Instead of choosing exactly m different units for the binding representation of each pattern, let us select k not-necessarily-distinct units in such a way that the *expected* number of different units is m. This will make the analysis easier at the cost of larger variance, so that the bounds derived will also be valid for the actual process.

Let us assume i patterns are stored on a unit, which is equivalent of selecting ki units from the binding constellation at random. Let Z_v be the expected size of the binding constellation after v units have been selected. Then

$$Z_v = \tilde{Z} + (n - \tilde{Z})(1 - (1 - \frac{1}{n})^{ki-v}), \quad (8)$$

where $\tilde{Z}$ is the size of the binding constellation formed by the first v selected units. Now, $E(Z_v | Z_{v-1}) = Z_{v-1}$, and the sequence of variables $Z_0, \ldots, Z_{ki}$ is a martingale. Moreover, it can be shown that $|Z_v - Z_{v-1}| \le 1$, and bounds for Z can be obtained from Azuma's inequality (see e.g. Alon and Spencer 1992):

$$P(Z < n(1 - (1 - \frac{1}{n})^{ki_l}) - \lambda\sqrt{ki_l}) < e^{-\lambda^2}, \quad (9)$$

$$P(Z > n(1 - (1 - \frac{1}{n})^{ki_u}) + \lambda\sqrt{ki_u}) < e^{-\lambda^2}, \quad (10)$$

where i_l is the lower bound for I obtained from equation 6, and i_u the upper bound from equation 7. Similar bounds can be derived for Z'.

3. Intersection of binding constellations. The process of forming the intersection of j binding constellations incrementally one cue at a time can also be formulated as a martingale process. Let X_j denote the expected number of elements in the intersection of two sets, after the first j elements of the first set have been checked (the elements of the second set are assumed to be known at all times). Then

$$X_j = \tilde{X} + \frac{(n_1 - j)(n_2 - \tilde{X})}{n - j}, \quad (11)$$

where $\tilde{X}$ is the number of elements in the intersection of the second set and the set formed by the first j elements of the first set, and n_1, n_2 and n are the sizes of the first, second, and the superset. If n_1 and n_2 are both smaller than $\frac{1}{2}n$, Azuma's inequality can be applied. Taking the intersection of the previous step as the first set, the binding constellation of the jth cue as the second set, and the binding layer as the common superset, this approach gives us the following upper bound for X_j:

$$P(X_j > \frac{(x_{j-1,u} - m)(z'_u - m)}{(n - m)} + m + \lambda\sqrt{x_{j-1,u} - m}) < e^{-\lambda^2/2}, \quad \lambda > 0, \quad (12)$$

where z'_u and $x_{j-1,u}$ are upper bounds for Z' and X_{j-1} and are assumed to be less than $\frac{1}{2}n$. Then X_j is at its upper bound, a potential rogue unit has the largest chance of taking over. In this case, R_{j+1} has the upper bound

$$\mathrm{P}(R_{j+1} > \frac{x_{j,u}z_u}{n} + \lambda\sqrt{x_{j,u}}) < e^{-\lambda^2/2}, \quad \lambda > 0, \quad (13)$$

where z_u and $x_{j,u}$ are upper bounds for Z and X_j. A lower bound for X_{j+1} while using an upperbound for X_j is then given by

$$\mathrm{P}(X_{j+1} < \frac{(x_{j,u}-m)(z_l-m)}{(n-m)} + m - \lambda\sqrt{x_{j,u}-m}) < e^{-\lambda^2/2}, \qquad \lambda > 0. \qquad (14)$$

If the resulting lower bound is smaller than m, m can be used instead.

The above analysis ignores correlations between binding constellations. The correlations originate from storing the same partial pattern multiple times and tend to increase the size of the intersections. The chance that two random patterns have more than one feature in common in j features is equal to $(1-(1+\frac{j}{f-1})(1-\frac{1}{f})^j)$, which is negligible for sufficiently large values of f.

We can now use equations 6–14 to derive a lower bound for the probability of successful retrieval with given system parameters n, m, F, j, f, and p. The retrieval is successful if $r_{j+1,u}$, the upper bound for R_{j+1}, is lower than $x_{j+1,u}$, the lower bound for X_{j+1}. Under this constraint, the probability that none of the variables in the analysis exceeds its bounds is a lower bound for successful retrieval.

Obtaining the upper bound for X_j involves bounding $3j-1$ variables: I and Z' for the j cues and X_j for the $j-1$ intersections. Computing $x_{j+1,l}$ and $r_{j+1,u}$ each involve bounding 3 variables (I, Z, and X_{j+1}; I, Z', and R_{j+1}). There are $F-j$ maps, each with one $x_{j+1,l}$ bound and $f-1$ different $r_{j+1,u}$ bounds (one for each rogue unit). The total number of bounds is therefore $3j-1+3f(F-j)$. Setting the righthand sides of the inequalities 6–14 equal to a small constant β, a lower bound for successful retrieval is obtained:

$$p_{\text{success}} > 1-(3j-1+3f(F-j))\beta. \qquad (15)$$

For example, assuming each unit in the model corresponds to a vertical column in the cortex, it is reasonable to assume feature maps with 10^6 computational units (Sejnowski and Churchland 1989). We can further assume that the system has 15 feature maps, 10 of which is used to cue the memory, and the binding layer consists of 10^5 units, with 150 used for each binding pattern. Assuming full connectivity between the feature units and the binding units, there are 1.5×10^{12} connections in the system.

If we store 0.85×10^8 patterns in the memory, z'_u and $x_{j-1,u}$ are less than $\frac{1}{2}n$, the chance of partial overlap of more than 1 feature is less than 0.45×10^{-10}, and the analysis above is valid. Setting $\beta = 0.5\times10^{-9}$ yields bounds $r_{j+1,u} < x_{j+1,l}$ with $p_{\text{success}} > 99\%$. In other words, 0.85×10^8 memories can be stored in the memory with 99% probability of successful retrieval. Such a capacity is approximately equivalent of storing one new memory every 17 seconds for 70 years, 16 hours a day.

VI. Conclusion

Mathematical analysis shows that an extremely high number of episodes can be stored in the convergence-zone memory with reliable content-addressable retrieval. Moreover, the convergence zone itself requires only a tiny fraction of the hardware required for perceptual representation. These results provide a possible explanation for why human memory appears almost unlimited, and why memory areas appear small compared to the areas devoted to low-level perceptual processing.

The model makes use of the combinatorics and the clean-up properties of coarse coding in a neurally-inspired architecture. The storage capacity of the model appears to be at least two orders of magnitude higher than that of the Hopfield model with the same number of units, while using two orders of magnitude fewer connections. However, direct comparison is difficult because the stored patterns in the Hopfield model are much larger (contain more information), and its $N/4\log N$ capacity result only indicates how many patterns are stable instead of estimating the probability of correct retrieval with a partial pattern as a cue.

The convergence-zone episodic memory model could be extended to make it more accurate as a model of actual neural processes. For instance, lateral inhibitory connections between units within a feature map could be added to select the unit with the highest activity. A similar extension could be applied to the binding layer; instead of only one unit multiple units should stay active. A variation of the Hebbian learning mechanism (Hebb 1949; Miller and MacKay 1992) could be used to implement the storage mechanism. Such research could lead to a practical implementation of the convergence zone memory, and perhaps even to a hardware implementation. Another important research direction is to analyze the behavior of the model as a psychological model, that is, to observe and characterize its memory interference effects and compare them with experimental results on human episodic memory.

Acknowledgements

We would like to thank Greg Plaxton for pointing us to martingale analysis on this problem. This research was supported in part by NSF grant #IRI-9309273.

References

Alon, N., and Spencer, J. H. (1992). *The Probabilistic Method.* New York: Wiley.

Damasio, A. R. (1989a). The brain binds entities and events by multiregional activation from convergence zones. *Neural Computation*, 1:123–132.

Damasio, A. R. (1989b). Time-locked multiregional retroactivation: A systems-level proposal for the neural substrates of recall and recognition. *Cognition*, 33:25–62.

Hebb, D. O. (1949). *The Organization of Behavior: A Neuropsychological Theory.* New York: Wiley.

Hertz, J., Krogh, A., and Palmer, R. G. (1991). *Introduction to the Theory of Neural Computation.* Reading, MA: Addison-Wesley.

Hopfield, J. J. (1982). Neural networks and physical systems with emergent collective computational abilities. *Proceedings of the National Academy of Sciences, USA*, 79:2554–2558.

Jessell, E. R. K. (1991). Nerve cells and behavior. In Kandel, E. R., Schwartz, J. H., and Jessell, T. M., editors, *Principles of Neural Science*, 18–32. Elsevier.

Kanerva, P. (1988). *Sparse Distributed Memory.* Cambridge, MA: MIT Press.

Keeler, J. D. (1988). Comparison between Kanerva's SDM and Hopfield-type neural networks. *Cognitive Science*, 12:299–329.

Kortge, C. A. (1990). Episodic memory in connectionist networks. In *Proceedings of the 12th Annual Conference of the Cognitive Science Society*, 764–771. Hillsdale, NJ: Erlbaum.

McEliece, R. J., Posner, E. C., Rodemich, E. R., and Venkatesh, S. S. (1986). The capacity of the hopfield associative memory. *IEEE Transactions on Information Theory*, 33:461–482.

Miikkulainen, R. (1992). Trace feature map: A model of episodic associative memory. *Biological Cybernetics*, 66:273–282.

Miller, K. D., and MacKay, D. J. C. (1992). The role of constrains in hebbian learning. CNS Memo 19, Computation and Neural Systems Program, California Institute of Technology, Pasadena, CA.

Rosenfeld, R., and Touretzky, D. S. (1989). A survey of coarse-coded symbol memories. In Touretzky, D. S., Hinton, G. E., and Sejnowski, T. J., editors, *Proceedings of the 1988 Connectionist Models Summer School*, 256–264. San Mateo, CA: Morgan Kaufmann.

Sejnowski, T. J., and Churchland, P. S. (1989). Brain and cognition. In Posner, M. I., editor, *Foundations of Cognitive Science*, chapter 8, 315–356. Cambridge, MA: MIT Press.

Squire, L. R. (1987). *Memory and Brain.* Oxford, UK; New York: Oxford University Press.

Touretzky, D. S., and Hinton, G. E. (1988). A distributed connectionist production system. *Cognitive Science*, 12:423–466.

An Embedded Connectionist Approach for the Inverse Shortest Paths Problem

C.W. Tong and K.P. Lam

Department of Systems Engineering
The Chinese University of Hong Kong
Shatin, N.T., Hong Kong

Abstract

A type of connectionist network, called the binary relation inference network, has been recently applied to solve constrained optimization problems, such as the shortest path problem, assignment problem, etc. The inherently parallel operating nature of the network promises a potential speedup in solving the problems. In some situations where the problems cannot be solved directly with the network, it is possible to have the network acting as an embedded real-time engine to solve the involved subproblems. In this paper, the possibility of embedding the network to solve the inverse shortest paths problem is explored. Limitations in incorporating the network are discussed and remedies are suggested.

1 The Inverse Shortest Paths Problem

Shortest path problems find presence in many applications, as in traffic control, communications network routing, etc. As an example, in a fire services department, it is always the goal to have the fire-fighters arriving at the scene in the shortest time possible. The traffic planner has to choose a route from a usually densely populated road map. There are many well established algorithms, such as Floyd's, Dijkstra's [1], in finding the shortest path between two nodes in a graph if all the arc costs in the graph are known.

However, in many practical cases, some of the arc costs are usually unknown. As in the previous example, the exact values of the road costs depend on factors like road length, maximum traveling speed, the frequency of traffic jams, etc.; and some of these factors may even be time varying. As a result, the shortest path determined may not be the optimum. On the other hand, daily drivers on the road would have a priori knowledge (or expert's knowledge) of some of the shortest routes available; but they have no idea on how the costs are being assigned to the roads. In such cases, it is desirable to modify the road costs, such that the a priori optimal routes are incorporated as the shortest paths in the map. The inverse shortest paths problem arises as the need to estimate the unknown arc costs in a graph, and hence to determine all of the possible shortest paths, based on the given expert's knowledge of some shortest routes.

Reference [2] described another similar but interesting situation in seismic tomography. Semisic perturbations from earthquake observations are used to determine the transmission characteristics between different points in the geologic zone. Different geologic zones correspond to different nodes in a graph while the transmission characteristics between the zones will correspond to the costs of the paths among the nodes. Similar to the previous situation, it is required to calculate the costs from the given shortests paths, which correspond to the semisic perturbations from the earthquake observations.

These problems are instances of the inverse shortest paths problem which can be formulated mathematically as follows.

1.1 Problem statement

Let a graph with n vertices $\{v_i\}_{i=1}^{n}$, m arcs $\{a_i\}_{i=1}^{m}$, each arc being associated with an non-negative cost c_i be denoted by the triple $G = (V, A, C)$ where V is the set of vertices, A is the set of arcs and C is the set of costs. Each arc a_i is defined by its source vertex $v_{s(i)}$ and destination vertex $v_{d(i)}$, denoted as $a_i = (v_{s(i)}, v_{d(i)})$. A path p_j in G is given by a set of consecutive arcs $p_j = (a_{j_1}, a_{j_2}, \ldots, a_{j_{l(j)}})$ where $l(j)$ is the number of arcs in path p_j and $d(j_i) = s(j_{i+1})$ for $i = 1, \ldots, l(i) - 1$. The cost of path p_j is given by $\sum_{i|a_i \in p_j} c_i$.

Given a graph G, and a set of p paths $P = \{p_i\}_{i=1}^{p}$, the inverse shortest path problem requires the costs c_i to be modified such that all p_js are to be the shortest paths in the graph. In other words, find c_i' such that

$$\sum_{j|a_j \in q_i} c_j' \geq \sum_{j|a_j \in p_i} c_j' \qquad (i = 1, \cdots, p), \tag{1}$$

and

$$c_i' \geq 0, \qquad (i = 1, \cdots, m) \tag{2}$$

where q_i is any path with the same source and destination vertices as in p_i.

There are a number of characteristics observed in the problem.

- The solution is not unique.
- The number of inequalities involved in Eq. (1) is generally very large. This depends on the number of given paths p, the connectivity of the graph which determines the number of possible paths between a vertex pair in the graph.
- There would also be a large of number of redundancies in Eq. (1).

The problem can be solved by formulating it into an optimization problem and applying the many available optimization techniques. In [2] and [3], an additional constraint in minimizing the changes in the costs is imposed to the formulation. The objective of these approaches is to minimize the cost changes while satisfying the shortest path requirements in Eq. (1) and Eq. (2).

Section 3 of this paper describes an alternative approach using an embedded connectionist network, called the binary relation inference network. The basics of the binary relation inference network would be reviewed first in Section 2.

2 Finding all-pair shortest paths with a Binary Relation Inference Network

Based on a connectionist approach, the binary relation inference network has been proposed to solve the all-pair shortest path problem with analog processing units [4]. A binary relation inference network is formed by the interconnection of self contained computational units. Figure 1 shows the interconnections

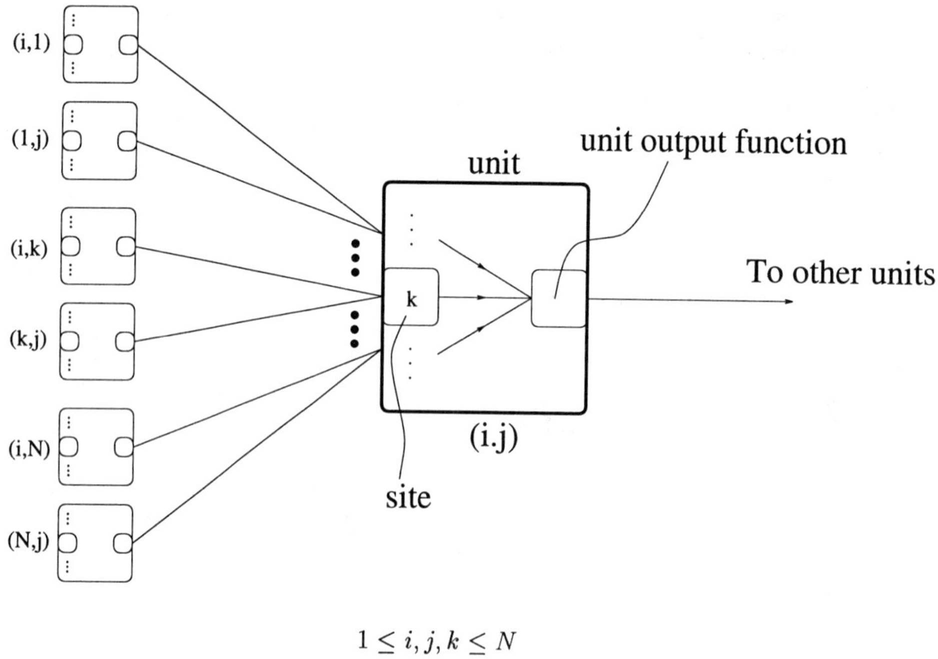

Figure 1: 'Neuronal' interpretation of a basic unit in a binary relation inference network

in a general binary relation inference network defined on N objects. Each unit, denoted by (i, j), represents a binary relation between two objects x_i and x_j. In each unit, the site function defines the inference operations on two incoming signals. The value of the corresponding relation $R_2(i, j)$ is then determined by resolving the conflict among all the possible site outputs.

The asynchronous and parallel operating nature of the binary relation inference network promises a significant potential speedup in solving many problems. The inference network has been applied to solve shortest path problems, transitive closure problems, and assignment problems [5].

In solving the shortest path problem [6], the unit function $g(i,j)$ and site function S_k^{ij} are required to be specified as

$$\begin{aligned} S_k^{ij} &= g(i,k) + g(k,j) \\ g(i,j) &= \min_k \{S_k^{ij}, g(i,j)\} \end{aligned} \tag{3}$$

and the network has been proven to converge to the global minimum, with the unit output $g(i,j)$ being the shortest path distance between objects x_i and x_j.

3 The Embedded Approach

3.1 The Formulation

In the proposed approach for solving the inverse shortest path problems, the costs are revised to drive the costs of the paths in P to be smaller than the costs of the shortest paths obtained from the graph G. As a result, the given paths in P will become the shortest path between the corresponding vertex pair. The objective function in this formulation is

$$\min_{c_j} \sum_{i=1}^{p} \Big(\sum_{j|a_j \in \Omega(s(i),d(i))} c_j - \sum_{j|a_j \in p_i} c_j - \varepsilon \Big)^2 \tag{4}$$

where $\Omega(s(i), d(i))$ is the shortest path between $v_{s(i)}$ and $v_{d(i)}$ in (V, A, C). The necessary constraint is the non-negativeness of the costs in Eq. (2). ε is a small positive constant, introduced to ensure the uniqueness of p_i being the shortest path in the solution. A widely used technique in solving general constrained nonlinear programming problem, the penalty function transformation is selected to solve the problem. The transformed unconstrained problem is then solved with the General Conjugate Gradient-Golden Section Acceptable Point(GCG-GSAP) [7].

With the penalty function transformation, the constrained optimization problem is turned into the optimization of an unconstrained function.

$$\min_{\mathbf{c}} f(\mathbf{c}, \tau) = \min_{\mathbf{c}} \left\{ \sum_{i=1}^{p} \left(\sum_{j|a_j \in \Omega(s(i),t(i))} c_j - \sum_{j|a_j \in p_i} c_j - \varepsilon \right)^2 + \frac{1}{\tau} \sum_{i=1}^{m} (\psi_i c_i)^2 \right\} \tag{5}$$

where

$$\psi_i = \begin{cases} 0 & c_i \geq 0 \\ c_i & c_i < 0 \end{cases}$$

The solution of the constrained problem is obtained from the solutions of a sequence of the unconstrained problem with decreasing values of τ and as $\tau \to 0$.

In evaluating the objective function in Eq. (5), it is needed to find the shortest paths for all the source-destination vertex pairs of the paths in P. As the analog operating inference network provides an efficient means in solving all pair shortest path problem, it is incorporated in the algorithm. Figure 2 shows pictorially how the inference network is embedded in the algorithm in solving the inverse shortest paths problem. The embedded inference network helps finding the shortest path in evaluating the objective function.

3.2 The Algorithm

The following describes the proposed algorithm in solving the inverse shortest path problem. For additional details on the conjugate gradient algorithm, see [8].

1. Initialization

   With Eq. (5), transform the constrained optimization problem in Eq. (4) into an unconstrained problem.

   Set $\tau = 0.1$

   Set the initial solution $\mathbf{c}$ to the given set of costs C.

2. Solving the unconstrained problem:

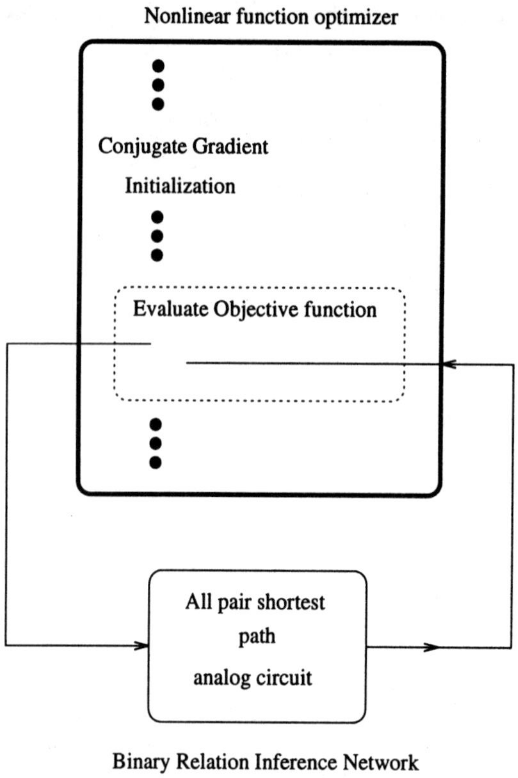

Figure 2: Embedded approach for the inverse shortest paths problem

(a) Initialization
$k = 0$
Take the current set of costs be $\mathbf{c}^k$.
Set $\mathbf{s}^0 = -\mathbf{g}^0$, g is the gradient of $f(\mathbf{c}, \tau)$.

(b) Let $\mathbf{c}^{k+1} = \mathbf{c}^k + \lambda_k \mathbf{s}^k$ where λ_k is determined by the GSAP algorithm

(c) If $\| \mathbf{g}^{k+1} \| < \varepsilon$, optimum reached and

$$\mathbf{c}^* = \mathbf{c}^{k+1}, f^* = f(\mathbf{c}^{k+1})$$

(d) To reduce the effect of roundoff errors, at a predetermined number of iterations, $RESET$, ω_{k+1} is set to 0. This brings the search to discard information accumulated during the previous iterations.
If $k > RESET$, let $\mathbf{c}^0 = \mathbf{c}^{k+1}$, $\mathbf{s}^0 = -\mathbf{g}^{k+1}$, $k = 0$, goto step b; otherwise goto step e

(e) Set $\mathbf{s}^{k+1} = -\mathbf{g}^{k+1} + \omega_{k+1}\mathbf{s}^k$, where

$$\omega_{k+1} = \frac{(\mathbf{g}^{k+1} - \mathbf{g}^k) \cdot \mathbf{g}^{k+1}}{(\mathbf{g}^{k+1} - \mathbf{g}^k) \cdot \mathbf{s}^{k+1}}$$

If $\mathbf{g}^{k+1} \cdot \mathbf{s}^{k+1} > 0$, reset as in step d

(f) $k = k + 1$

(g) Goto step b.

This solved $\mathbf{c}$ for a particular τ.

3. $\tau = \tau \times 0.09$
If $\tau > 1e - 6$, goto step 2. Otherwise stop.

As there is no explicit expression for the gradient, g^k, of the objective function $f(\mathbf{c}, \tau)$, the gradient is evaluated using the forward differences in the objective function..

4 Implementation Results

The data in the test run would be generated as follows:

1. Generate all the shortest paths in the graph with the given costs
2. The set of costs are altered in a randomized manner, as a result, some of the previous generated paths will not be the shortest paths

As an example, consider a problem on a 5-node graph with bi-directional arcs. The arc costs are:

c_{12}	10	c_{14}	4	c_{23}	20	c_{25}	2	c_{35}	12
c_{13}	8	c_{15}	6	c_{24}	∞	c_{34}	15	c_{45}	∞

with known shortest paths

p_1	=	1,2	p_6	=	2,1,4
p_2	=	1,3	p_7	=	2,5
p_3	=	1,4	p_8	=	3,4
p_4	=	1,2,5	p_9	=	3,5
p_5	=	2,5,3	p_{10}	=	4,3,5

Running on a PC, the solution time is 1.05s with the following modified costs

c_{12}	7.60	c_{14}	8.95	c_{23}	20	c_{25}	1.56	c_{35}	7.78
c_{13}	8.73	c_{15}	9.16	c_{24}	∞	c_{34}	10.05	c_{45}	∞

The updated arc costs indeed have the given paths incorporated as the shortest paths. There are 263 evaluations of the objective function, with 120 involved in determining the gradient.

5 Discussion

In this paper, the analog binary relation inference network is shown to be able to perform as an embedded engine in solving the inverse shortest paths problem. It was found to be an efficient means to find all-pair shortest paths, during the continuous evaluation of the objective function required for the nonlinear optimization process.

The solution time can be improved by removing the overheads in interfacing the host computer with the inference network. The overheads exist in two major areas:

1. Control of the network operations

   As the inference network operates with analog signals, values of the costs have to be converted to analog values. In the current implementation, this is accomplished with an data acquisition add-on card on the host computer, a PC. The add-on card also provides the digital interface to the inference network in reading the routes. To cope with the operating range of the analog inference network, the set of costs need to be scaled before converting to analog signals and applied to the inference network. The measured time for converting and initializing the network is 0.15ms.

2. Interpretation of the results

   The route indices obtained from the inference network only indicate the index of the contributing site in a shortest path, and they need to be converted to the corresponding node index in the graph. The measured time for finding the routes of the shortest paths is 0.8ms.

When compared with the running time of the network, 10μs, these overheads lower the anticipated performances that can be obtained from the inference network. A suggested system for removing the overheads from the host computer is shown in Figure 3. The system is interfaced to the host computer as 3 memory blocks, one for storing the costs, one for the resulting costs of the shortest paths and one for the route indices. Solving a shortest path problem would then require initializing the memory block with the arc costs, waiting for the end of operation in the inference network, and reading results from the other two memory blocks. This will remove most of the overheads in operating the inference network as an embedded engine.

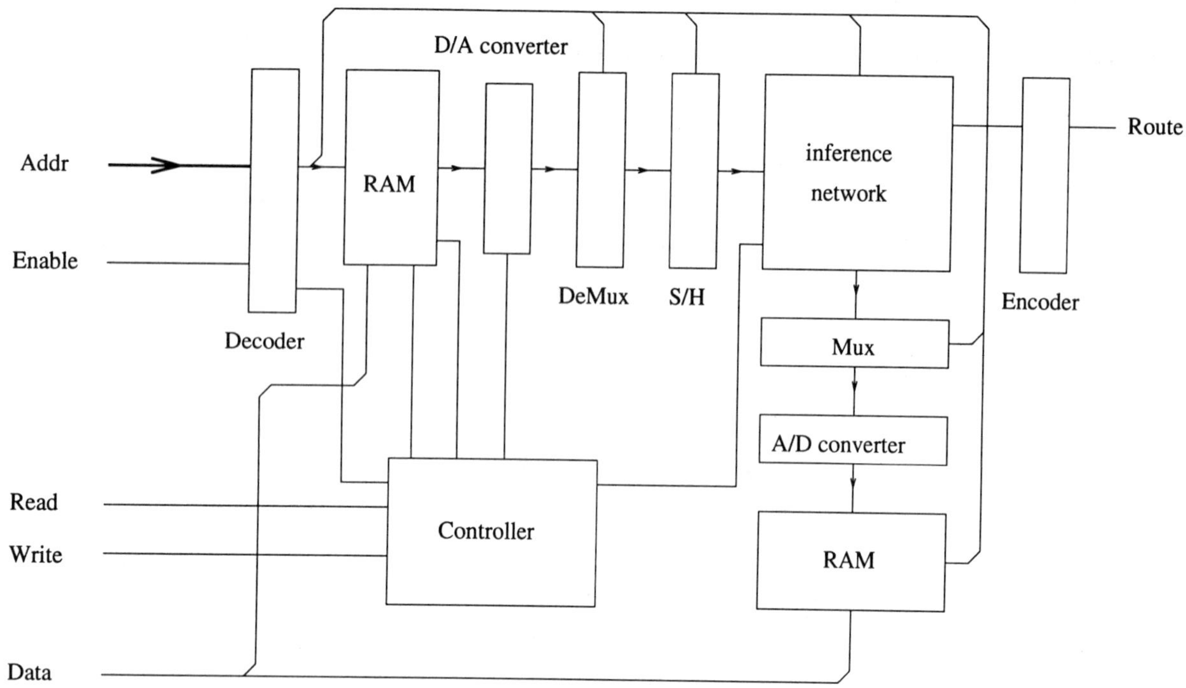

Figure 3: A system for solving shortest path problems

References

[1] Alfred V. Aho, John E. Hopcroft, and Jeffrey D. Ullman. *Data structures and algorithms.* Addison-Wesley, Reading, Mass., 1983.

[2] D. Burton and Ph.L. Toint. On an instance of the inverse shortest paths problem. *Mathematical Programming*, 53:45–61, 1992.

[3] Patrick S.L. Koh. On Computing Shortest Paths from known Shortest Paths. Technical Report AR-92-03, City Polytechnic of Hong Kong, 1992.

[4] C.W. Tong and K.P. Lam. Analog Implementations of a Binary Relation Inference Network for Minimum Cost Path Problems. In *IEEE International Conference on Neural Networks*, pages 1081–1085, 1993.

[5] Crystal Jinghua Su. *A Binary Relation Inference Network For Constrained Optimization.* PhD thesis, University of British Columbia, 1992.

[6] K.P. Lam and C.J. Su. On a Binary Relation Inference Network. In *Proc. of the IEEE 5th International Parallel Processing Symposium*, pages 250–255, 1991.

[7] G.E. Johnson and M.A. Townsend. An Acceptable-Point algorithm for Design Optimization. In R.C Johnson, editor, *Optimum Design of Mechanical Elements*, pages 488–507. Wiley-Interscience, 1980.

[8] William H. Press. *Numerical recipes in C: the art of scientific computing.* Cambridge, 1988.

A Hierarchical Approach for Solving Large-Scale Traveling Salesman Problem

Dong C. Park, Anthony L. Figueras, and Carl Chen
Intelligent Computing Research Lab
Department of Electrical and Computer Engineering
Florida International University
Miami, FL 33199
e-mail: parkd@cherry.fiu.edu

Abstract

A hierarchical approach which combines an unsupervised learning algorithm and a recursive Hopfield neural network is proposed for solving the large-scale Traveling Salesman Problem (TSP). For a TSP with given number of cities, an unsupervised learning algorithm was first used to find the clusters for decomposing the given problem and then a recursive version of the Hopfield Network was applied to the centroids of the clusters. The proposed recursive Hopfield Network was also applied to cities in each cluster in order to find an optimal path. A final tour was obtained by connecting together the resultant paths of each cluster.

1 Introduction

The Traveling Salesman Problem has been studied extensively in literature for many years. There has been many attempts to improve upon the original HT algorithm. The HT algorithm for solving the Traveling Salesman Problem is characterized by the following energy function [1],

$$\begin{aligned} E &= A/2\sum_X\sum_i\sum_{j\neq i} V_{Xi}V_{Xj} + B/2\sum_i\sum_X\sum_{j\neq i} V_{Xi}V_{Yi} \\ &+ C/2\left(\sum_X\sum_i V_{Xi} - n\right)^2 + D/2\sum_X\sum_{Y\neq X}\sum_i d_{XY}V_{Xi}(V_{Y,i+1}+V_{Y,i-1}). \end{aligned} \tag{1}$$

An optimal tour solution can be obtained when the energy function is minimized. The algorithm was first used to find the optimum closed-loop tour for 10 cities in [1]. There are 181,440 total distinct paths and the solutions found were within the best $10^{-3}\%$ of all paths compared to random paths with a good choice of the coefficients A, B, C, and D.

Van den Bout and Miller attempted to improve the results of Hopfield and Tank by performing neuron state normalization and annealing [4]. Here, the energy function, compared to that of the HT algorithm, is reduced down to two terms, with the A, B, C, and D coefficients being replaced by a penalty parameter, d_p, to get

$$E = \frac{d_p}{2}\sum_i\sum_X\sum_{Y\neq X} v_{Xi}v_{Yi} + \frac{1}{2}\sum_X\sum_{Y\neq X}\sum_i d_{XY}v_{Xi}(v_{Y,i+1}+v_{Y,i-1}). \tag{2}$$

It should be noted that there is no term to penalize a city which is not visited or is visited more than once.

0-7803-1901-X/94 $4.00 ©1994 IEEE

This is handled by using a normalized Boltzmann Distribution to represent the value of each neuron state:

$$v_{Xi} = \frac{e^{-E_{Xi}/T}}{\sum_j e^{-E_{Xj}/T}}, \tag{3}$$

where E_{Xi} is the mean field of a city X occupying a position i, and is given by [4]

$$E_{Xi} = d_p \sum_{Y \neq X} v_{Yi} + \sum_{Y \neq X} d_{XY}(v_{Y,i+1} + v_{Y,i-1}). \tag{4}$$

So, tour positions with higher mean fields are less likely to be occupied than those with lower mean fields, which correspond to shorter tours with fewer violated constraints. This procedure is equivalent to the operations performed by a Hopfield network, with the temperature corresponding to the inverse of the gain of the neuron [4].

Annealing is also used to improve tour solutions [4]. The temperature, T, was varied until a critical temperature T_c was found. Using T_c for the neuron updating produces the best results. If T_c was known beforehand, then annealing would not be necessary. The difficulty of finding valid tours is eliminated by the normalization process. It was also found that the solution quality was dependent on the initial state of the network (i.e. formation of seed points) and the temperature (i.e., neural gain). By eliminating seed points and by permitting groups of neurons to have different temperatures, the network found the **optimum tour in 30% of the trials**.

Jayadeva and Bhaumik also attempted to improve upon the HT algorithm by implementing a varying parameter controlling algorithm [5]. The original HT algorithm often converges to invalid solutions, which have been attributed to improper choice of parameters and energy functions. The authors have claimed that the Hopfield Network essentially performs only one iteration of a Sequential Unconstrained Minimization Technique (SUMT). They improve the performance of the original HT algorithm solution by varying the parameters A, B, C, and D with each SUMT iteration.

The constraints are basically the same as in the original HT algorithm. The expression below has to be minimized for each SUMT iteration:

$$Min \ \sum_{i=1}^{N} \sum_{j=1, j\neq 1}^{N} d_{ij} \sum_{k=1}^{N} V_{i,k}(V_{j,k-1} + V_{j,k+1}) + \sum_{i=1}^{N} \sum_{j \neq i} \sum_{k} (a_{pijk})^{-1} V_{i,k} V_{j,k}$$
$$+ \sum_i \sum_j \sum_{k \neq j} (b_{pijk})^{-1} V_{i,j} V_{i,k} + c_p{}^{-1} \left(\sum_i \sum_j V_{i,j} - N \right)^2 \tag{5}$$

where $V_{i,j}$ is the output of neuron (i,j), d_{ij} is the distance from city j to city i, and a_{pijk}, b_{pijk}, and c_p are scalar parameters which vary from one SUMT iteration to the next. The index p denotes the SUMT iteration. If we set $a_{pijk}{}^{-1} = A/D$, $b_{pijk}{}^{-1} = B/D$, and $c_p = C/D$, we get the well-known energy function of the HT algorithm, which uses fixed values for these parameters.

Starting with $A_{pijk} = a = B_{pijk} = b = C_{pi} = c = D_{pj} = d = 1$ and increasing the parameters a, b, and c by 10% after each SUMT iteration, Jayadeva and Bhaumik achieved a better convergence and also a reduction in the number of iterations needed to converge. The solutions they obtained were highly dependent on the initial state of the network. If the initial starting state is not good, then a poor tour should be obtained.

In our approach, the original HT algorithm is employed. We chose the HT algorithm with up to a 10-city TSP since the HT algorithm for a problem with more cities hardly produces good results in our simulation. By applying the algorithm recursively to a 10-city problem, an attempt is made to improve the solution quality obtained by the HT algorithm in our approach. Since the initial state of the neurons and the parameters A, B, C, and D are essential for obtaining good solutions, we have chosen to set very specific initial states and A, B, C, D parameters for problems with different number of cities. In Section 2, we explain our recursive approach to the HT algorithm of a simple example. A clustering algorithm for decomposing a given large-scale TSP is discussed in Section 3. Section 4 shows the experiments and corresponding results we obtained. We give our conclusions in Section 5.

2 Recursive Hopfield-Tank Algorithm

Assume that a 10-city TSP is given. First, the Hopfield Network is used to produce a tour from a given starting city to a given ending city. The tour obtained is then improved upon, if possible, by applying a

4-city Hopfield network (H4) to this tour. H4 is first applied to the 1st through 4th cities, then to the 2nd through 5th cities, then to the 3rd through 6th cities, and so on. The tour obtained from this recursive process is then submitted to a 5-city Hopfield network (H5), which performs a recursive operation similar to that of H4. This is repeated for 6 cities (H6), 7 cities (H7), and again for 4 cities (H4). A pseudocode representing the recursive processes is shown below.

```
function RecurHop (N, Cities, CityArray)
   for K=0 to Niterations do
      for I=0 to I < (Cities-(N-1)) do
         Run Hopfield Neural Network
      endfor
   endfor
end
```

Above, N is the number of cities the recursive operation is occurring for (i.e., N=4 denotes RecurHop is H4, N=5 denotes RecurHop is H5, and so on). *Cities* denotes the number of total cities in the problem, *CityArray* holds the coordinates of the cities, and *Niterations* denotes the number of iterations the recursive procedure is run for. The functions "UpdateSum" and "CalcEnergy" simply perform the calculations involved in a Hopfield Network, as stated in Eq.(1).

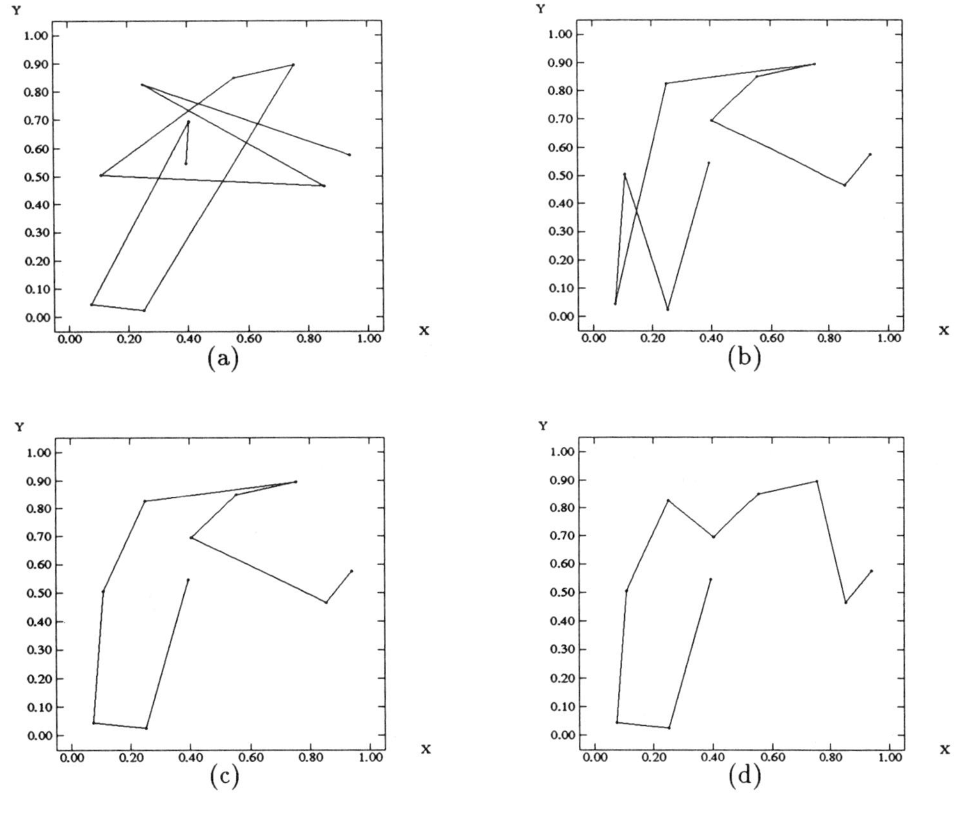

Figure 1: (a) Initial 10-city Hopfield tour (dist=5.021217), (b) tour after running through H4 (dist=3.892595), (c) tour after running through H5 (dist=3.111533), and (d) tour after running through H6, H7, and second H4 (dist=2.736338).

The main advantage of these recursive Hopfield networks is that they are capable of escaping from a local minimum solution. As an example, we are given an initial solution in Figure 1(a) for a 10-city TSP after applying the HT algorithm. This solution results in a tour distance of 5.021217, as depicted in Figure 2. By applying H4 to the initial solution, Figure 1(a), the resulting tour shows improved results, Figure 1(b), with a reduced tour distance of 3.892595 (Figure 2). Again, an improved tour is obtained after applying H5 to the solution of H4 (Figure 1(c), tour distance of 3.111533 seen in Figure 2), after applying H6 to the solution of H5 (Figure 1(d), tour distance of 2.736338 seen in Figure 2), H7 to the solution of H6 (Figure 1(d), tour distance of 2.736338 seen in Figure 2), and H4 to the solution of H7 (Figure 1(d), tour distance of 2.736338 seen in Figure 2). The final tour distance of 2.736338 was found to be the global minimum for the given 10-city TSP.

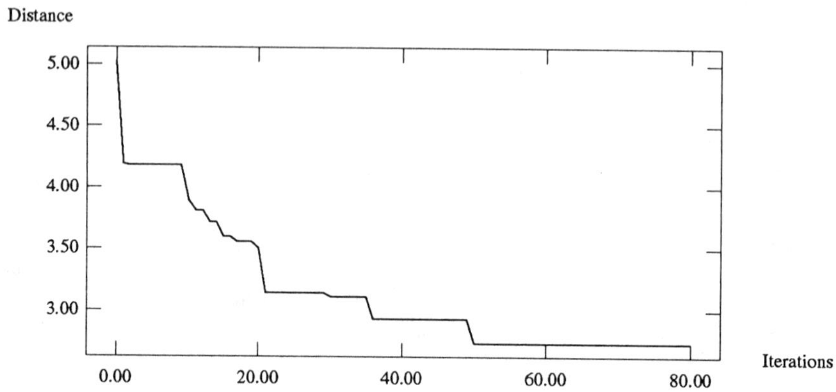

Figure 2: Total distance plot for iterations of original and recursive Hopfield networks (iteration 0 is original Hopfield, iterations 1-10 are H4, iterations 11-30 are H5, iterations 31-50 are H6, iterations 51-70 are H7, and iterations 71-80 are second H4).

3 Clustering Algorithm

The Centroid Neural Network (CNN) was used to estimate optimal centroids of the related cluster groups to each training data pattern [6]. The synaptic vectors in the CNN converge to the centroids of clusters as learning proceeds. However, the CNN finds locally optimal synaptic vectors for each data presented and consequently converges to the centroids of clusters much faster than conventional algorithms.

One of the advantages of the CNN is that it does not require a schedule for learning coefficients. The CNN rather finds its optimal learning coefficients in each representation of training data. The CNN can also reward and punish by optimal learning coefficients for winner and loser, respectively. The CNN also does not require the total number of iterations which is required in advance for other conventional unsupervised competitive learning algorithms.

Because of its stated advantages, the CNN algorithm was used to classify the cities in the Traveling Salesman Problem to groups of 10 cities maximum per group. Given N sets of data, $\{\mathbf{x}(i), i = 1, \cdots, N\}$, and M number of classes, each of the data is classified as one of the M classes. The main step of the algorithm, which is based on the *K-means* clustering algorithm, is characterized by weight adaptation of a winning neuron, j, and a losing neuron, i, as follows:

$$\mathbf{w}_j(n+1) = \frac{1}{N_j+1}[N_j\mathbf{w}_j(n) + \mathbf{x}(n)] = \mathbf{w}_j(n) + \frac{1}{N_j+1}[\mathbf{x}(n) - \mathbf{w}_j(n)] \quad (6)$$

$$\mathbf{w}_i(n+1) = \frac{1}{N_i-1}[N_i\mathbf{w}_i(n) - \mathbf{x}(n)] = \mathbf{w}_i(n) - \frac{1}{N_i-1}[\mathbf{x}(n) - \mathbf{w}_i(n)] \quad (7)$$

4 Experiments and Results

The Hopfield Network was applied to the centroids of the groups output by the CNN, producing a centroid tour. Given the starting city of the first group and the ending city of the last group, an algorithm was written to find the starting and ending cities of each of the internal groups The Hopfield Network was then applied to each of the groups, and by connecting the starting city to the ending city of each group we obtained the final tour for the total number of cities. This entire procedure, including that of the recursive Hopfield networks as described in Section 2, was automated to run in one program execution. For problems containing less than 10 cities, the program input the entire set of city coordinates directly into the Hopfield networks. For problems containing more than 10 cities, the program invoked a function that recursively performed the CNN on the set of city coordinates until it was broken down into two or more groups of cities, where each group had at most 10 cities in it. The invoked function then input each new group of city coordinates separately into the Hopfield networks, as was described in the previous paragraph.

4.1 100-city TSP

For a 10-city traveling salesman problem, where the starting and ending cities are fixed, there are 40,320 possible tours. In most of our cases, tours obtained were within the top 400 shortest tours. For the example tour shown in Figure 1, the final solution was the optimum tour. For a 100-city TSP in Figure 3(a), the CNN was used to cluster the cities into 12 smaller groups, as in Figure 3(b), since some groups initially output by the CNN have more than 10 cities, they are decomposed again (the circles shown in Figure 3(b) are to show which cities are in the same group, but the circle centers do not necessarily correspond to the CNN group centroids). The Hopfield Network was then applied to the centroids of the groups and to each group, as shown in Figure 3(c). As we can see in the final result shown in Figure 3(d), the result appears to indicate a good tour. The result for a 200-city TSP, shown in Figure 4, implies that the proposed approach can handle large-scale TSP cases.

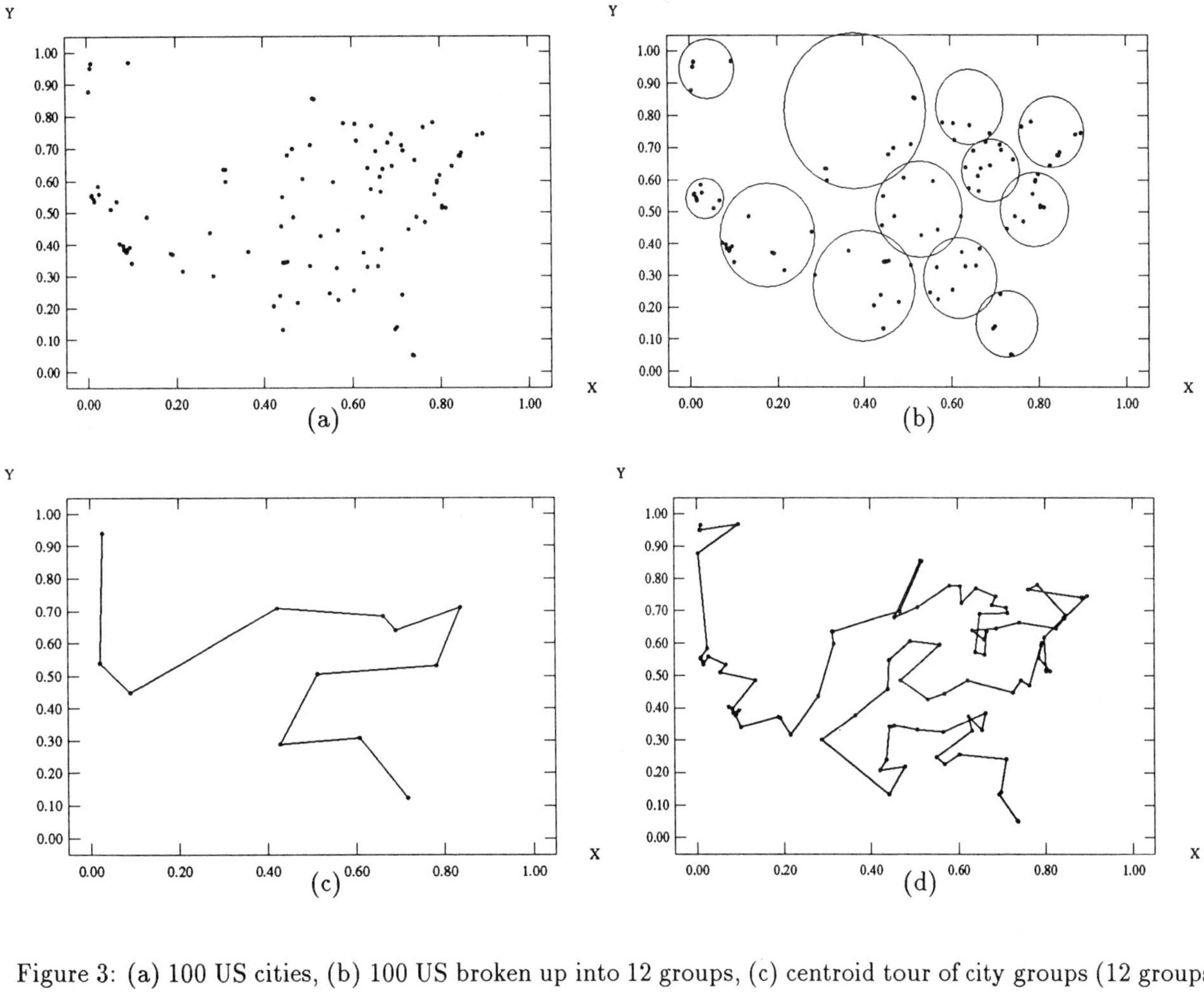

Figure 3: (a) 100 US cities, (b) 100 US broken up into 12 groups, (c) centroid tour of city groups (12 groups), and (d) final tour of 100 US cities.

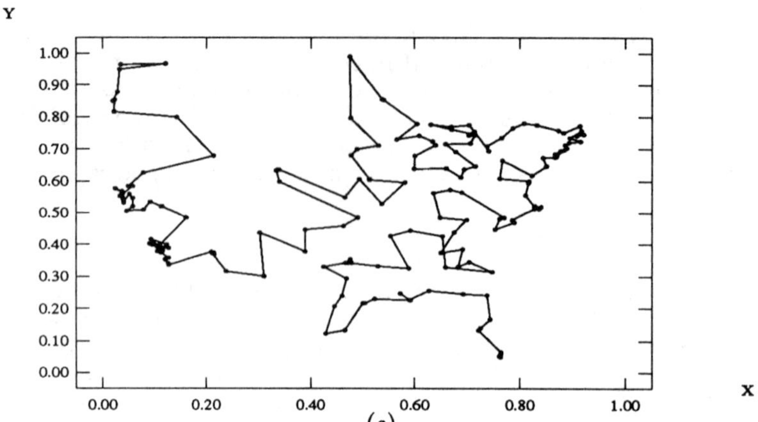

(c)

Figure 4: Final tour of 200 US cities.

5 Conclusions

An approach for solving the large-scale TSP was proposed. It combined an unsupervised learning algorithm and a recursive version of the Hopfield Network. A very common problem with the original HT algorithm for solving the TSP was that tours would sometimes converge to a local minimum. The HT algorithm is also very sensitive to the coefficients chosen, making it almost impossible to solve a TSP of more than 50 cities, and the HT algorithm also requires N^2xN^2 matrix computations for an N-city problem. However, our approach can solve most practical-sized problems with minimum computation since the problem is decomposed to smaller-sized ones. Exemplar problems with 100 and 200 cities were solved with our approach. The results show that our approach is very advantageous.

Acknowledgements

The research described in this paper was supported in part by the National Science Foundation grant CDA-9313624. We thank ICRL members at FIU for fruitful discussions. We especially thank Cheuk Man Tong for his helpful assistance.

References

[1] J.J. Hopfield and D.W. Tank. "Neural Computation of Decisions in Optimization Problems," *Biological Cybernetics.* Vol. 52, pp 141-152, 1985.

[2] J.J. Hopfield and D.W. Tank. "Computing with Neural Circuits: A Model," *SCIENCE.* Volume 233, pgs 625-633, 1986.

[3] A.R. Bizzarri. "Convergence properties of a modified Hopfield-Tank model," *Biological Cybernetics.* Volume 64, pp 293-300, 1991.

[4] S.W. Van den Bout and T.K. Miller III. "Improving the Performance of the Hopfield-Tank Neural Network through Normalization and Annealing," *Biological Cybernetics.* Vol. 62, pp 129-139, 1989.

[5] Jayadeva and B. Bhaumik. "Optimization with neural networks:arecipe for improving convergence and solution quality," *Biological Cybernetics.* Vol. 67, pp 445-449, 1992.

[6] D. C. Park and T. V. Dinh. "Centroid Neural Network Algorithm for Unsupervised Competitive Learning," *(Submitted for publication).*

Solving a Near-Maximal Graph Planarization Problem Using Strictly Digital Neural Networks with Virtual Slack-Neurons

Katsuhiko Murakami, Tohru Nakagawa, and Hajime Kitagawa
Department of Information and Control Engineering
Toyota Technological Institute, Nagoya, 468 Japan

Abstract— **This paper presents a neural network parallel algorithm for solving a near-optimum graph planarization problems using SDNN/V (Strictly Digital Neural Networks enhanced with Virtual Slack-Neurons). The proposed algorithm generates a near-maximal planar subgraph from a nonplanar or a planar graph within $O(1)$ time. The problem can be defined as a "Set Selection Problem" based on the "between-l-and-k-out-of-n" design rule in SDNN/V algorithm. The results of solving the graph planarization problem using a simulator of SDNN/V show that the computation time in parallel execution is only three steps to get one of near-optimum solutions. Our algorithm has a mechanism that our neural network should wait some changes until at least one neuron in each constraint satisfaction set will be "ON" state. In case of this problem, the obtained solutions are not always maximal subgraphs. In order to improve the quality of solutions, this paper presents a numbering method for neurons in order of importance within each constraint satisfaction set. As a result of simulation, this paper shows that the numbering method has an effect on the quality of solutions to be improved up to 20% from 2% which is the earlier percentage of the maximal subgraphs in solutions.**

I. Introduction

Recently, some studies on solving large scale combinatorial optimization problems, including the NP-complete problem (Nondeterministic Polynomial), using neural networks has been growing. Unfortunately, there are few papers that have solved the problems within $O(1)$ time in highly parallel algorithms [3][8][13], and also a few parallel algorithms have been reported to solve the graph planarization problem such as [2][3][13]. The graph planarization problem is to yield the maximal planar subgraph from a nonplanar graph or a planar graph, and to yield a maximal planar subgraph from a nonplanar graph. The problem is an NP-complete problem [1]. We have been solving various problems to prove that our parallel algorithms based on SDNN [8]–[12] or SDNN/V [13][14] provide highly parallel processing. The number of neurons needed in previous SDNN is decreased in SDNN/V enhanced with "*virtual slacks*" [13]. Virtual slacks have been newly introduced in SDNN/V, and CS programming, constraint sets programming, based on "between-l-and-k-out-of-n" rule is facilitated by the range of "l" and "k". The number of edges in a given graph determines the number of neurons required. In our new algorithm, only $2 \times M$ neurons are required, where M is the number of edges in a graph. We have solved a planarization problem for N-sided polygon, and presented that the computation time in parallel execution is only 3 steps which is $O(1)$ time and the solutions are always maximal subgraphs [13].

As extension of this problems, We have been trying to solve other planarization problems for embedding a near-maximal planar subgraph from a nonplanar or a planar subgraph using SDNN/V. The simulation results show that our neural networks have always converged to one of global-minima in only 3 steps within $O(1)$ time, but all solutions are not always maximal subgraphs because the used constraint conditions are insufficient to get the maximal subgraphs. In order to improve the quality of solutions, Takefuji *et al.* introduced hill-climbing [7], but it is not effective in improving the quality of solutions as we have examined the algorithm proposed by them. A neuron priority of activity in a constraint set, which is named "numbering order," will be defined in parallel manner. And, we will introduce three different types for numbering order of neuron activity in CS programming, that is, i) numbering the neurons in randomized order, ii) numbering in decremental order of the number of intersecting constraint sets, iii) numbering in decremental order of the length of each edge to be appeared. This paper presents that the method of numbering is effective to improve the quality of solutions in this algorithm.

II. SDNN/V Algorithm for Graph Planarization Problems

In the SDNN/V algorithm with virtual slacks, solving the problem is to describe it with the CS programming based on the "between-l- and-k-out-of-n" design rule, and

0-7803-1901-X/94 $4.00 ©1994 IEEE

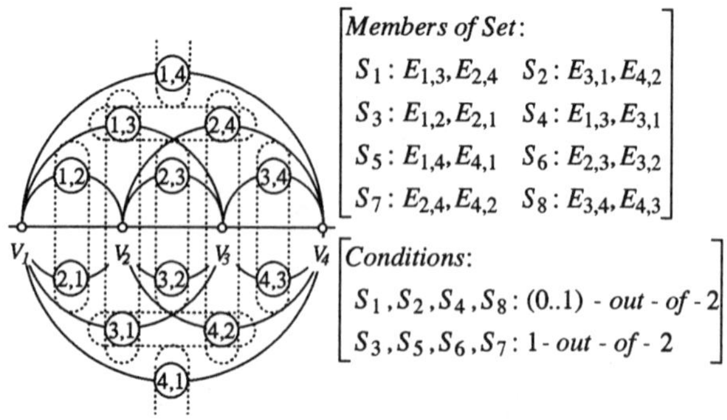

Fig. 1. A CS program of 8 intersecting sets of 12 neurons for embedding a maximal planar subgraph with 4 vertices and 6 edges on a single layer.

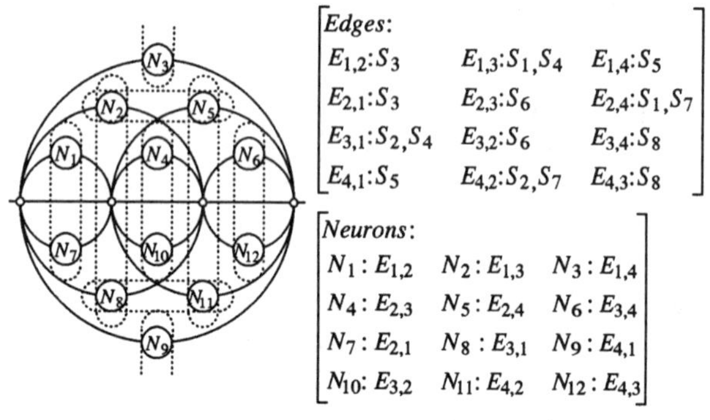

Fig. 2. An assignment of the neuron number in Fig. 1.

this algorithm allows us to describe the most simplified CS program using an expression of $(l_x..k_x)$-out-of-n for each set of S_x. Fig. 1 shows a CS program of graph planarization for embedding a maximal planar subgraph on a single layer from a graph of 4-sided polygon where (i,j) means the $(i,j)^{th}$ neuron which plays the role of a edge $(E_{i,j})$ from i^{th} vertex (V_i) to the jth vertex (V_j). Members of Set mean edges $(E_{i,j})$ which are included in each set (S_i). Conditions show the design rule which constrains each set (S_i). Actually on CS programming, each neuron required to solve the problem is numbered in sequential. As shown in Fig. 2, each edge $(E_{i,j})$ is assigned to each neuron (N_i), and each neuron is numbered at random in no relation with the number of set included in. In case of planarization problem in the nonplanar graph, the number of required neurons and sets can be estimated. The sum of required neurons is $V\times(V-1)$, while required sets is $V\times(V^3-6\times V^2+17\times V-12)/12$. Note that V is the number of vertices. This algorithm for solving N-sided polygon problem gets one of global-minima within only three parallel steps, and also each obtained planar subgraph is always the best that the total number of embedded edges is exactly equal to $3\times(V-2)$.

III. Numbering the Neurons

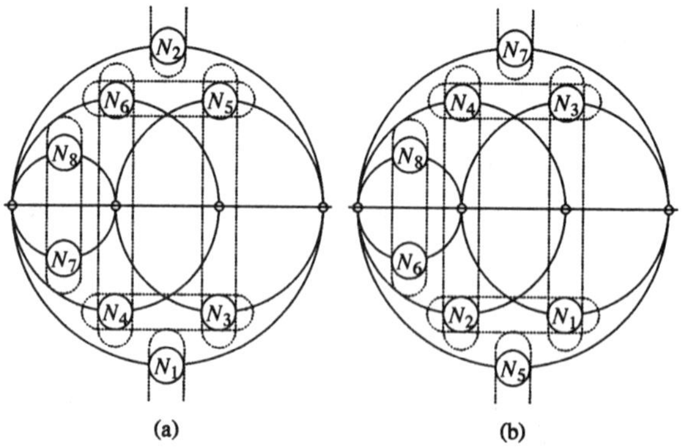

Fig. 3. (a) Numbering the neurons in decremental order of the length of each edge. (b) Numbering in decremental order of the number of intersecting sets.

We have introduced the numbering order of neurons to improve the quality of solutions. In SDNN/V algorithm, the numbering order of neurons, which is required to describe problems with CS programming, gives a static priority of activity to update the status of neurons in parallel execution. In Fig. 2, each neuron is numbered in randomized order without relation to the number of intersecting sets on a neuron. In addition to the above numbering order, we have been introduced other two numbering methods. One is related to the length of each edge, which is the number of cross points with the other edges, and the other is related to the number of intersecting sets in SDNN/V algorithm in order to research whether numbering neurons is effective to improve the quality of solutions. The neurons are numbered in these two methods as shown in Fig. 3 as case to solve a problem for the subgraph of 4 vertices and 4 edges on a single layer. Fig. 3(a) shows that it is numbered in decremental order of the length of each edge, and Fig. 3(b) shows that it is numbered in decremental order of the number of intersecting sets. The length of each edge is the distance from start point to end point of each edge, such as in Fig. 2(a) the length of N_1 and N_2 is 3, N_3 - N_6 is 2, and other neurons are 1. The number of intersecting sets is what number of sets a neuron assigns, that is, added one to the number of intersected edges to each edge. As shown in Fig. 3(b), the number of intersecting sets of N_1, N_2, N_3, and N_4 in the subgraph of 4 vertices and 4 edges on a single layer are 2, and other neurons are 1.

IV. Simulation Results

We had performed the simulation in three types of the numbering order of neurons with relation to CS programming in order to search the effect of the solution quality

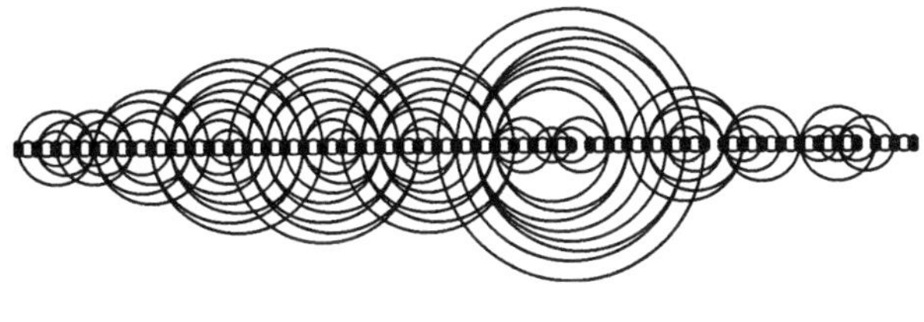

Fig. 4. Graph in the single-row representation with 48 vertices and 105 edges

Fig. 5. Solutions of graph in Fig. 4.

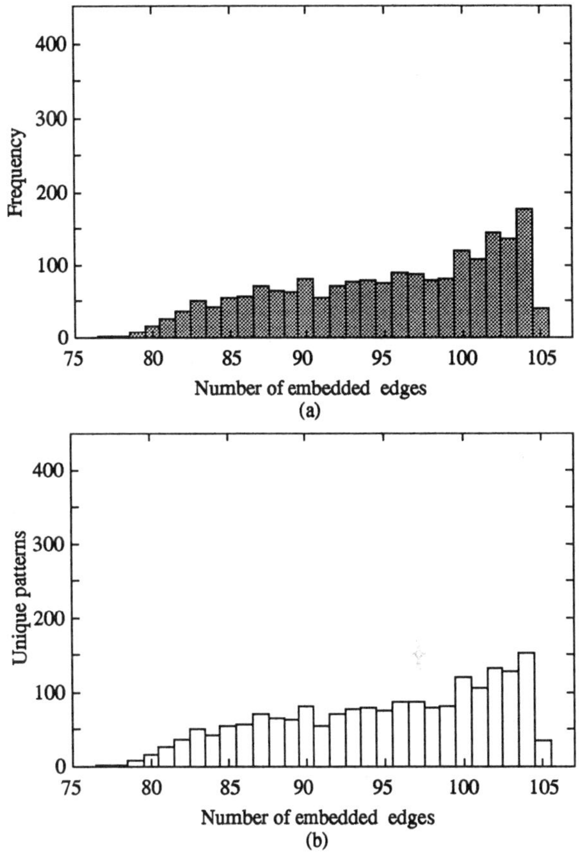

Fig. 6. The numbering is randomized order. (a) The relation between the frequency and the number of embedded edge for the problem in Fig. 4. (b) The relation between the number of patterns and the number of embedded edges for the problem in Fig. 4.

improvement given by them in SDNN/V algorithm. Then the graph problem which we have used in simulation is with 48 vertices and 105 edges [7]. This graph is given by US-continental map where it contains 48 (states) vertices and 105 edges and which is known to be planar, and Fig. 4 shows that it is presented in the single row. Fig. 5 shows one of the maximum solutions with 105 edges embedded which have solved by SDNN/V algorithm. This algorithm has converged at one of global-minima in only three parallel steps on an average of 2000 cases.

Figs. 6(a) and 7(a) show that the relation between the frequency and the number of embedded edge for the problem in Fig. 4. In Fig. 6(a), the rate of maximum solutions is about 2%. In this case, in spite of randomized numbering order 2% maximum solutions are found. Because a simulator of SDNN/V have function which have been waiting until one at least of neurons assigned each set is changed in one parallel step. In same as above case, the numbering of neurons in decremental order according to the length of each edge is no more improved the quality solution. In Fig. 7(a), the numbering of neurons is decremental order according to the number of intersecting sets and the rate of maximum solutions is improved to about 20 percentage, From above the result, it is found that the numbering order of neurons have an effect to improve the quality of solutions in our algorithm, and numbering of neurons in decremental order of intersecting sets is mostly effective to improve the quality of solutions. Figs. 6(b) and 7(b) show the relation between the frequency of patterns and the number of edges embedded in a solution in each of Fig. 6(a) and 7(a).

The simulation result using the method of numbering the neurons in decremental order of the intersecting sets presents the consistent improvement in the solutions as shown in Fig. 7(a). We found that the numbering order of neurons is effective to the improvement the quality of solutions in the SDNN/V algorithm.

V. Conclusions

This paper reports that SDNN/V algorithm using ***virtual slacks*** for solving graph planarization problems has converged at one of global-minima within $O(1)$ time in parallel execution using $O(N^2)$ neurons. Because this algorithm has the proposed mechanism that our network will wait some changes until at least one neuron in each

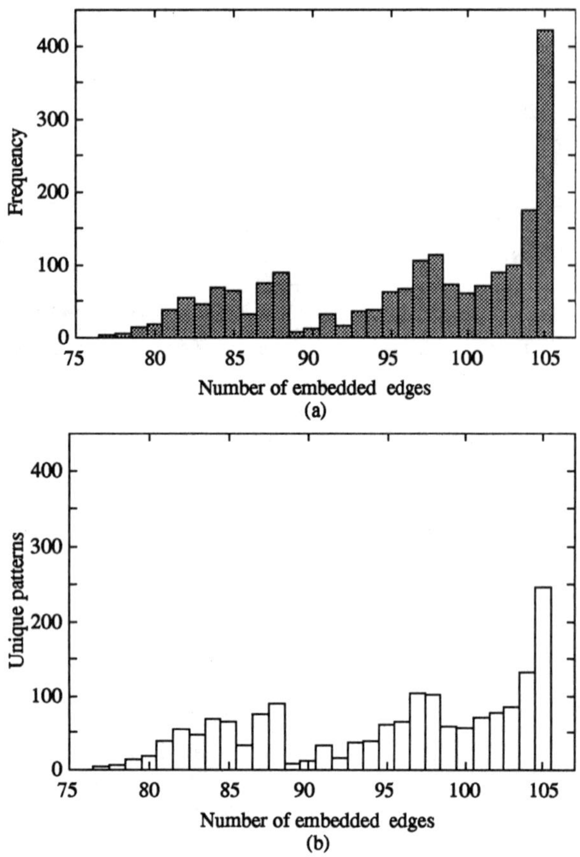

Fig. 7. The numbering is decremental order of the number of intersecting sets. (a) The relation between the frequency and the number of embedded edge for the problem in Fig. 4. (b) The relation between the number of patterns and the number of embedded edges for the problem in Fig. 4.

constraint satisfaction set will be "ON" state. All simulation results show that the numbering method in some order of neuron importance has affected to improve the quality of solutions in graph planarization problems, and especially in the case of the numbering method in decremental order, the effectiveness is the best to improve the quality of solutions. The parallel algorithm in this paper can be applied to designing printed circuit boards or VLSI circuits, and be extended for finding a maximum independent set of a circle graph and for predicting the secondary structure in ribonucleic acids (RNA). As a next step, we are working on RNA secondary structure prediction as one of attractive applications using SDNN/V algorithm.

References

[1] M. R. Garey and D. S. Johnson, "Computers and Intractability : A Guide to the Theory of NP-Completeness," *W. H. Freeman and Company*, 1979.

[2] R. Jayakumar, K. Thulasiraman, and M. N. S. Swamy, "O(n^2) algorithms for grpah planarization," *IEEE Trans. on Computer Aided Design*, vol. 8, no. 3, Mar. 1989.

[3] Y. Takefuji, and K. C. Lee, "A Near-Optimum Parallel Planarization Algorithm," *Science*, vol. 245, pp. 1221 - 1223, Sept. 1989.

[4] Y. Takefuji and K. C. Lee, "A parallel algorithm for tiling problems," *IEEE Trans. on Neural Networks*, vol. 1, no. 1, Mar. 1990.

[5] Y. Takefuji and K. C. Lee, "A super parallel sorting algorithm based on neural networks", *IEEE Trans. on Circuit Syst.*, vol. 37, no 7, 1990

[6] Y. Takefuji, L. L. Chen, K. C. Lee, and J. Huffan, "Parallel Algorithms for Finding a Near-Maximum Independent Set of a Circle Graph," *IEEE Trans. on Neural Networks*, vol. 1, no. 3, pp. 263 - 267, Setp. 1990.

[7] Y. Takefuji, "Neural Network Parallel Computing," *Kluwer Academic Publishers*, 1992.

[8] T. Nakagawa, E. W. Page, and G. A. Tagliarini, "SDNN: A Computation Model for Strictly Digital Neural Networks and its Application," *Proc. 5th AAAIC'89, ACM/SIGART Dayton*, Oct. 1989.

[9] T. Nakagawa and H. Kitagawa, "SDNN: An O(1) Parallel Processing with Strictly Digital Neural Networks for Combinatorial Optimization in Large Scale N-Queen Problem," *Proc. ICANN'89, Finland*, Jun. 1991.

[10] T. Nakagawa, H. Kitagawa, E. W. Page, and G. A. Tagliarni, "SDNN-3: A Simple Processor Architecture for O(1) Parallel Processing in Combinatorial Optimization with Strictly Digital Neural Networks," *Proc. IJCNN'91, Singapore*, vol. 3, pp. 2444 - 2449, Singapore, 1991.

[11] K. Murakami, T. Nakagawa, and H. Kitagawa, "Solving Four-Coloring Map Problems using Strictly Digital Neural Networks," *Proc. IJCNN'91, Singapore*, vol. 3, pp. 2440 - 2443, Singapore, 1991.

[12] T.Nakagawa, K.Murakami, and H.Kitagawa, "Strictly Digital Neurocomputer Based on a Paradigm of Constraint Set Programming for Solving Combinatorial Optimization Problems," *Proc. IEEE ICNN'93, San Francisco*, vol. 2, pp. 1086 - 1091, San Francisco, 1993.

[13] T. Nakagawa and K. Murakami, "Evaluation of Virtual Slack-Neurons for Solving Optimization Problems in Circuit Design Using Neural Networks Based on the Between-l-and-k-out-of-n Design Rule," *Proc. WCNN'93 Portland*, vol. 1, pp. 122 - 125, Portland, 1993.

[14] K. Murakami, T. Nakagawa, and H. Kitagawa, "A High-speed and Low-cost Parallel Convergence in Coloring Map Problems with Virtual Slack-Neurons," *Proc. WCNN'93, Portland*, vol. 4, pp. 421 - 424, Portland, 1993.

Near Optimal Solutions to the Grid Connection Problem

Sundararajan Vedantham
Department of Computer Science,
Sanjoy Das
Department of Electrical & Computer Engineering,
S. Sitharama Iyengar
Department of Computer Science,
Louisiana State University, Baton Rouge LA 70803.

Abstract *Stochastic optimization using simulated annealing has found wide applications in combinatorial optimization of NP-Complete problems in recent years, especially in VLSI related problems. The Grid Connection Problem is a combinatorial optimization problem that is proven to be NP-Complete. In this paper the simulated annealing algorithm has been applied to the Grid Connection Problem. We also propose an algorithm for the Grid Connection Problem based on certain heuristics. Results of our simulations show that while both algorithms do yield good solutions, those of the simulated annealing are superior to those of the heuristic algorithm, with rare exceptions.*
Keywords: *Combinatorial Optimization, NP-Complete problems, Simulated Annealing, Global Minima, Heuristics.*

1. Introduction

The problem of connecting a given set of points, called active points located on a grid, by means of straight lines to one of the edges of the grid is NP-Complete [1] for three or more dimensions [2]. It is also NP-Complete for two-dimensional problems when certain restrictions apply [2]. Consequently, seeking out a globally optimal solution is rendered computationally infeasible and one is motivated to look for a near optimal solution to the problem in a reasonable amount of computational time rather than perform a near-exhaustive search on the entire solution space. To the best of our knowledge, there is no algorithm that attempts to obtain such near-optimal connections. In this paper we propose two algorithms for the same purpose, which are discussed at length in sections 2 and 3. In the remainder of this paper, we shall, for the sake of conciseness, refer to the problem as the Grid Connection Problem (GCP). In this section, we provide a formal definition for the Grid Connection Problem.

An instance of the Grid Connection Problem is (i) an n-dimensional grid of size $l_1 \times l_2 .. l_n$, and (ii) a set of active points at specific locations in the grid, $\Sigma = \{P_i(x_1, x_2, .. x_n) | \, x_j$ is an integer and $1 \leq x_j \leq l_j.\}$. Each point in Σ is to be connected by means of a straight line to one of the several faces of the grid. An intersection of the straight line connections between any two points constitutes a violation. When portions of two straight line connections coincide for a certain (integral) length, the total number of violations is simply this length. Figure 1. shows a 6×6 grid with six active points and with violations at four different points as indicated by arrows. The objective of the GCP is to connect all active points in the grid to the sides with the least possible number of violations. The relevance of GCP in VLSI routing is immediately obvious.

2. A Heuristic Algorithm

In this section, we present a heuristic algorithm which is, in a restricted sense, greedy. Our algorithm can be applied to problems of any dimension. We observe that points that are closer to the center of the grid are potentially capable of causing a larger number of violations than those that are near the faces of the grid. Also, reducing the length of a line connecting an active point to a face should result in lower number of violations. Hence we propose the following two heuristics:

1. *Points that are closer to the center of the grid are lower in the priority list of the algorithm than those near the faces of the grid.*
2. *The algorithm has a preference for connecting points to the face of the grid that is closest.*

0-7803-1901-X/94 $4.00 ©1994 IEEE

Within the framework of these two heuristics, the algorithm performs as follows. In the first pass it tries to connect as many points as possible without any violation. In subsequent passes it tries to connect the unconnected active points with increasing number of violations. An outline of the heuristic algorithm is provided below :

$\Sigma = \{P_j(x_{1j}, x_{2j},\ldots, x_{nj}) / P_j \textit{ is an active point.}\}$
$max = 0$
while $(\Sigma \neq \Phi)$ {
  $\forall P_j \in \Sigma$ *let* $(C_1^j, C_2^j,\ldots, C_n^j) = (F, F,\ldots, F)$
  while *(another connection is possible)* {
    pick $P_j \in \Sigma$ *such that* $\forall\, i\; x_k^i = min(x_1^j, x_2^j,\ldots, x_n^j)$
      $\leq min(min(x_1^i, x_2^i,\ldots, x_n^i))$ *and* $C_k^j = F$
    if (*violations with* P_j *connected along* k^{th} *coordinate* $= max$)
      connect P_j *along* k^{th} *coordinate*
      $\Sigma = \Sigma - \{P_j\}$
    else
      $C_{kj} = T$
  }
  $max = max+1$
}

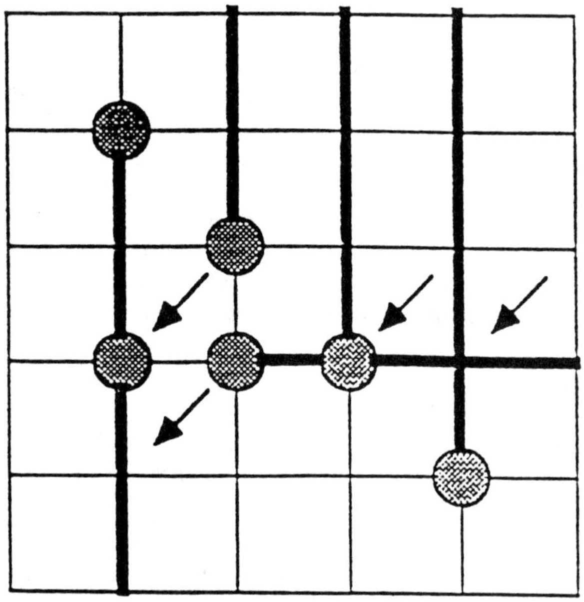

Figure 1. A 6×6 two dimensional instance of GCP with 6 active points and 4 violations.

At any stage in the algorithm, Σ is the set of unconnected active points. As points get connected, they are removed from Σ. The variable *max* contains the maximum number of violations that is permitted while connecting an active point. It is initialized to zero before the first pass of the algorithm and incremented by one at the beginning of each subsequent pass of the algorithm. This increment implies that after exhausting all the points that could be connected with a specific number of violations, the algorithm should then attempt to connect the remaining active points with one more allowable violation, in the next pass. For each unconnected active point P_j in Σ the algorithm maintains an n-tuple of flags ($C_1^j, C_2^j,\ldots, C_n^j$). At the beginning of each pass, it is updated to $(F, F,\ldots, F)$. If the point P_j cannot be connected along a certain direction, say the kth direction, during a certain pass of the algorithm, the latter should then not attempt to connect it again along the same direction in the remainder of the algorithm. This is done by updating the corresponding flag C_k^j to T. When the algorithm picks a point for connection along any direction, it checks to see if the corresponding flag is F. The algorithm halts only after Σ is empty i.e. when all the active points have been connected. Having provided a formal description of the heuristic algorithm, we now provide an upper bound on its worst case time complexity.

Lemma. *The worst case time-complexity of the heuristic algorithm is* $O(N^5dn)$.

Proof: The maximum number of violations can occur in an instance of GCP only when all the active points are aligned and their straight line connections coincide for the maximum possible length. Such a case occurs only in the highly improbable situation of all the active points being in adjacent locations. If N is the number of active points and d the length of the grid along the dimension through which the connections run, then clearly the number of violations is Σ. To obtain this many number of violations, obviously the algorithm has to go through the same number of passes. In each pass of the algorithm it can perform a maximum of N iterations, each with n steps, where n is the dimensionality of the grid. Since each iteration is of $O(N^2)$, the worst case time complexity is $O(N^5dn)$. ■

Results obtained by executing the heuristic algorithm on different instances of the GCP (for various grid sizes and active points densities) are presented in Section 4.

3. Simulated Annealing for Grid Connection

The problem of connecting active points in a grid by means of straight lines is particularly suitable for simulated annealing [3] for it is trivially shown to be strongly irreducible, by the facts that it has only a finite number of possible configurations and that each configuration is attainable from any other configuration with a finite number of moves [4] [5] [6] [7] [8]. Our choice of simulated annealing as an approach is also partially motivated by the fact that it has very few requirements, and can be adapted easily to any other version of the problem merely by changing the energy function or the move selection strategy accordingly. We devote this section to a description of our approach. An outline of the well known *double loop* version of simulated annealing algorithm is presented below.

```
T = T_max
C = Initial configuration
while   (stopping condition is not satisfied) {
        for i = 1 to maximum # of iterations {
                move(C,C_new)
                ΔE = Energy(C_new ) - energy(C)
                if (ΔE < 0) or (e^(-ΔE/T) > random(0,1))
                        C = C_new
        }
        T = αT
}
```

3.1 Initial Configuration

The initial configuration was generated randomly. A greedy algorithm was also tried to generate the initial configuration but was later abandoned in favor of a random configuration as the former proved to be ineffective in reducing the amount of computation time.

3.2 Annealing Schedule

A good annealing schedule is of critical importance. Experimentally we found out that for an instance of GCP with n active points, a value of T_{max} numerically equal to $n/4$ itself yields the best possible result. Any higher value for T_{max} does not result in any improvement on the outcome of the algorithm, whereas any further reduction in the starting temperature results in a deterioration of the quality of the final solution.

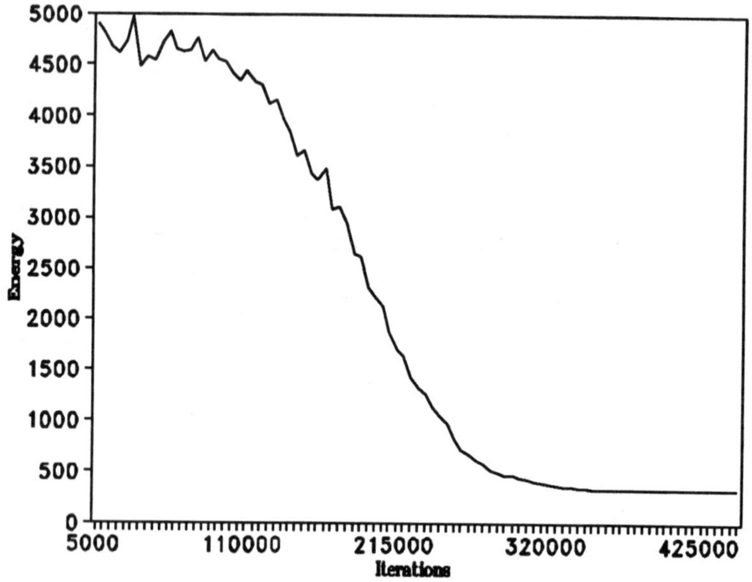

Figure 3. A sample annealing curve.

We adopted the well known *double loop* version of simulated annealing. We chose a simple geometric cooling schedule. Our results suggest that an optimal value for α (the cooling factor) is 0.9. A sample annealing curve from our simulation experiments is shown in Figure 3. We bring the algorithm to a stop when the slope of the annealing curve reaches zero, rather than basing it purely on a prefixed temperature value. Between each temperature drop we found that letting the algorithm iterate $5n$ times (where n is the number of active points on the grid) allows thermal equilibrium to be established without executing far too many iterations.

3.3 Move Generation

A move in simulated annealing results in a transition from the current configuration to a neighboring configuration within the solution space. Depending upon the control parameters, the new configuration may or may not be accepted. At each stage of the algorithm, the total number of violations is taken to be the energy of the system that needs to be minimized. Moves are generated by randomly picking an active point, and changing the face to which it is connected by rolling a die. This alteration defines the new configuration. Variation on the number of violations is calculated. A decrease in the number of violations leads to the acceptance of the move. If the move has resulted in an increase of the energy level, the move is accepted if the $e^{-\Delta E/T}$ value is greater than a random number picked between 0 and 1. It is easily seen that moves resulting in higher energy level will be accepted easily at higher temperature and the probability of such moves being accepted will continue to decrease as the temperature is decreased.

4. Simulation Results

In this section, we discuss the results of the simulations we carried out. Table 1 below, presents the results of the simulation using the heuristic algorithm.

No:	Grid Size	No. of Active points	Active Points Density %	Heuristic Algorithm No. of Violations		
				Min	Max	Avg
1	10	50	5	0	2	0.8
2		100	10	0	5	1.7
3		200	20	7	25	12.9
4		400	40	42	79	62.6
5	15	169	5	3	22	11.1
6		338	10	40	67	55.2
7		676	20	152	238	196.8
8		1352	40	553	720	631.5
9	20	400	5	43	90	68.3
10		800	10	151	259	224.7
11		1600	20	748	949	852.1
12		3200	40	3313	3819	3512.4

Table 1. Results of the simulation using the Heuristic Algorithm.

We considered grids of three different size. They were 10×10×10 (1000 points), 15×15×15 (3380 points), and 20×20×20 (8000 points). For each grid size, we ran the simulations with active points to the total grid size ratio (*active points density*) of 5, 10, 20 and 40 percent. These active points were randomly located on the grid. At each percentage level we ran the simulation ten times in order to get a clear idea of each algorithm's performance. The minimum, maximum and the average number of violations encountered for each algorithm was noted.

Table 2 below presents the results obtained for the same set of conditions by simulated annealing. The initial average number of violations is the average number of violations obtained during the initial configuration for the ten runs executed, when the active points were connected to any one of the six sides randomly. Minimum and maximum number of violations are the least and most number of violations observed at the end of the experiment among the ten trials carried out. The last column in the table presents the average number of violations observed in the final solutions of the ten trial runs. Comparing Tables 1 and 2, we observe that the heuristic algorithms performs slightly better than simulated annealing when the active points density is extremely high, whereas annealing yields much better results than the heuristic algorithm for all other cases. Table 2 also presents the details of the cooling schedule. For each configuration, we provide the average maximum and minimum temperature for each case and the average number of iterations it took to converge to the solution.

5. Conclusions

We presented two algorithms that yield a near optimal solution for the Grid Connection Problem. Experiments carried out using the algorithms show that simulated annealing performs better than the heuristic algorithm proposed in most of the cases. In cases where the active points density is very high, the heuristic algorithm performs marginally better than the simulated annealing algorithm. Since the GCP problem itself has been posed very recently, there are, to the best of our knowledge, no other algorithms available for comparison. As a direction for further research, one might consider situations where neighbouring lines connecting active points, that run parallel are also considered as violations (of a less serious nature) even though they do not intersect each other. One could also apply either algorithm to a restricted version of GCP where the active points can be connected only to a limited number of faces.

Grid Size	No. of active points	Active Points Density %	No. of Violations				Avg. Temperature		Avg. No. of Iterations
			Initial Avg	Min	Max	Avg	Initial	Final	
10	50	5	34	0	0	0	12.0	0.3694	8325
	100	10	118.2	0	0	0	25.0	0.2361	22250
	200	20	420.1	2	7	4.5	50.0	0.0758	61900
	400	40	1327.3	72	88	79	100.0	0.0640	141200
15	169	5	227.9	0	0	0	42.0	0.2051	42842
	338	10	840.5	0	6	2.8	84.0	0.0759	113399
	676	20	2716.4	63	100	82.8	169.0	0.0584	256880
	1352	40	7539.4	702	829	785.2	338.0	0.0394	587444
20	400	5	921.7	0	1	0.2	100.0	0.1172	128800
	800	10	3161.9	24	39	33.7	200.0	0.0440	323200
	1600	20	9852.9	503	539	525.3	400.0	0.0376	714400
	3200	40	25604.8	3250	3489	3357.2	800.0	0.0213	1638400

Table 2. Results of the simulation using the simulated annealing algorithm.

Bibliography

[1] M. R. Garey and D. S. Johnson, "Computers and Intractability: A Guide to the Theory of NP Completeness", *W. H. Freeman & Co., San Francisco*, 1979.

[2] Y. Birk and J. B. Lotspiech, "On Finding Non-intersecting Straight Line Connections of Grid Points to the Boundary", *IBM Technical Report*, 1989.

[3] S. Kirkpatrick, C. Gelatt and M. Vecchi, "Optimization by Simulated Annealing", *Science*, vol 14, 1983.

[4] F. Romeo and A. L. Sangiovanni-Vincentelli, "Probabilistic Hill-climbing Algorithms: Properties and Applications", *Proc. Chapel Hill Conf. on VLSI*, May 1985.

[5] E. H. L. Aarts and P. J. M. Van Laarhoven, "Statistical Cooling : A General Approach to Combinatorial Optimization Problems", *Phillips Journal of Research*, 1985.

[6] M. Metropolis, A. Rosenbluth, M. Rosenbluth, M. Teller, E. Teller, "Equation of State Calculations by Fast Computing Machines", *J. Chem Phys.* 1953.

[7] M. D. Huang, F. Romeo and A. L. Sangiovanni-Vincentelli, "An Efficient General Cooling Schedule for Simulated Annealing", *Proc. I.E.E.E. Intl. conf on Computer Aided Design*, 1986.

[8] S. R. White, "Concept of Scale in Simulated Annealing", *Proc. I.E.E.E. Intl. Conf. on Comp. Des.*, Nov. 1984.

A Lagrangian relaxation network for graph matching

Anand Rangarajan and Eric Mjolsness
Department of Computer Science
Yale University
P. O. Box 208285 Yale Station
New Haven, CT 06520-8285

Abstract

We present a Lagrangian relaxation network for graph matching. The problem is find a *permutation matrix M* that minimizes a distance between the two graphs. We adopt a *deterministic annealing* approach which is similar to a *Lagrangian decomposition* approach in that the row and column constraints of the permutation matrix are satisfied separately and Lagrange multipliers are used to equate the two "solutions." A fixpoint preserving transformation is applied to the graph matching constraint. A *symmetry-breaking* term is added in order to obtain a permutation matrix and is reversed via another fixpoint preserving transformation. The resulting network performs minimization with respect to the Lagrange parameters and maximization with respect to the match matrix variables. Simulation results are shown on 100 node random graphs and for a wide range of connectivities.

1 Introduction

Graph matching is an important part of object recognition systems in computer vision. The problem of matching structural descriptions of an object to those of a model can be posed as weighted graph matching [14], [10], [7]. Good, approximate solutions to inexact, weighted graph matching are usually required. The focus is then shifted from brittle, symbolic, subgraph isomorphism distance metrics to an "energy" based distance between graphs which is minimized by the right relabelling of the vertex labels of one graph with respect to the other.

Neural network approaches to graph matching [12] share the feature of other recent approaches to graph matching [13], [1], [2] that they are not restricted to looking for the right isomorphism. Instead, a measure of the distance between the two graphs is minimized. Graph isomorphism is a special case and is achieved when the distance is zero.

In this work, we follow the *deterministic annealing* framework formulated in [11] and [6]. The motivation for examining this particular approach stems from its ability to generalize to inexact, weighted graph matching. We set up our problem as follows: given graphs G and g, find a *permutation matrix M* that minimizes the distance between the two graphs. A permutation matrix is a zero-one matrix whose rows and columns sum to one. Permutation matrix constraints can be formulated quite naturally in the framework of deterministic annealing. Essentially, the row or column constraints are *winner-take-alls* and either set (but not both sets) of constraints can be exactly imposed using deterministic annealing methods. Our approach is similar to a *Lagrangian decomposition* approach [4], [5] in that the row and column constraints are satisfied separately and Lagrange multipliers are then used to equate the two "solutions." This is

0-7803-1901-X/94 $4.00 ©1994 IEEE

not the only way to satisfy both the row and column constraints and our method (for obtaining a permutation matrix) is equivalent w.r.t fixpoints to the one presented in [15]. A fixpoint preserving transformation [9] is applied to the graph matching distance, allowing us to express the combination of the graph matching distance constraint and the permutation matrix constraint using terms that are linear in the permutation matrix M. Due to the unavoidable symmetries involved in graph matching (resulting in multiple global minima), we add a *symmetry-breaking* term in order to obtain a permutation matrix. The symmetry-breaking term is reversed via another fixpoint preserving transformation. Then the network performs minimization with respect to the Lagrange parameters and maximization with respect to the permutation matrix variables. We tested the algorithm on the graph isomorphism problem with 100 node random graphs.

2 A deterministic annealing energy function for graph matching

The graph matching problem can be formulated in terms of the adjacency matrices of the two graphs. Given the adjacency matrices G_{ab} and g_{ij} of two graphs $G(V,E)$ and $g(v,e)$, respectively, the problem is to find the permutation match matrix M such that the distance between the two graphs is minimized. The adjacency matrices G_{ab} and g_{ij} of the two undirected graphs can be represented as symmetric, sparse matrices with zero diagonal entries. The problem then is

$$\min_M \sum_{ai}\left(\sum_b G_{ab}M_{bi} - \sum_j M_{aj}g_{ji}\right)^2$$

$$\text{subject to } \sum_a M_{ai} = 1, \sum_i M_{ai} = 1$$

with $M_{ai} \in \{0,1\}$. We apply a fixpoint preserving transformation [9] which transforms $X^2 \rightarrow 2X\mu - \mu^2$. The maximum of $2X\mu - \mu^2$ w.r.t μ is X^2. The distance is transformed to

$$D(M,\mu) = \qquad (1)$$
$$\sum_{ai}\mu_{ai}\left[\sum_b G_{ab}M_{bi} - \sum_j M_{aj}g_{ji}\right] - \tfrac{1}{2}\sum_{ai}\mu_{ai}^2.$$

The basic idea is to start with two match matrices $M_{ai}^{(1)}$ and $M_{ai}^{(2)}$ which have the respective properties

$$\sum_a M_{ai}^{(1)} = 1, \text{ and } \sum_i M_{ai}^{(2)} = 1 \qquad (2)$$

always satisfied. Assuming that the claim in (2) can be established, the new objective is

$$\min_{M^{(1)},M^{(2)}} \max_\mu D(M^{(1)},M^{(2)},\mu) = \qquad (3)$$
$$\sum_{ai}\left[\mu_{ai}\left(\sum_b G_{ab}M_{bi}^{(1)} - \sum_j M_{aj}^{(2)}g_{ji}\right) - \tfrac{1}{2}\mu_{ai}^2\right]$$
$$\text{subject to } M_{ai}^{(1)} = M_{ai}^{(2)} \qquad (4)$$

with respect to $M_{ai}^{(1)}$ and $M_{ai}^{(2)}$, $\forall\, a,i$. The constraint in (4) is set up using Lagrange parameters λ.

As mentioned in the Introduction, we follow the deterministic annealing framework of [11] and [6]. An energy function is constructed with four ingredients: (i) the graph matching constraint expressed through the reversed neurons μ, (ii) the winner-take-all on $M^{(1)}$ and $M^{(2)}$ expressed via a Potts glass [11], (iii) equating the two "solutions" through the Lagrange parameters λ and (iv) symmetry breaking whose strength depends on the parameter γ. The free energy which guarantees (2) and which, at its fixed points, minimizes (3) subject to (4) is

$$F(\mu,\lambda,U^{(1)},M^{(1)},U^{(2)},M^{(2)}) =$$
$$+\sum_{ai}\left[\lambda_{ai}\left(M_{ai}^{(1)} - M_{ai}^{(2)}\right) + \tfrac{\gamma}{8}\left(M_{ai}^{(1)} - M_{ai}^{(2)}\right)^2\right]$$
$$+\sum_{ai}\left[\mu_{ai}\left(\sum_b G_{ab}M_{bi}^{(1)} - \sum_j M_{aj}^{(2)}g_{ji}\right) - \tfrac{1}{2}\mu_{ai}^2\right]$$
$$+\tfrac{\gamma}{4}\sum_{ai}\left[M_{ai}^{(1)}(1-M_{ai}^{(1)}) + M_{ai}^{(2)}(1-M_{ai}^{(2)})\right]$$
$$+\tfrac{1}{\beta}\left(\sum_{ai}U_{ai}^{(1)}M_{ai}^{(1)} - \sum_i \log\sum_a \exp\left\{U_{ai}^{(1)}\right\}\right)$$
$$+\tfrac{1}{\beta}\left(\sum_{ai}U_{ai}^{(2)}M_{ai}^{(2)} - \sum_a \log\sum_i \exp\left\{U_{ai}^{(2)}\right\}\right)$$

where $U^{(1)}$ and $U^{(2)}$ are dummy variables involved in enforcing the constraints.

We now define a change of variables to simplify the above free energy. Consider

$$\sigma_{ai} \stackrel{\text{def}}{=} \frac{M^{(1)}_{ai} + M^{(2)}_{ai}}{2}, \; \tau_{ai} \stackrel{\text{def}}{=} M^{(1)}_{ai} - M^{(2)}_{ai}.$$

Here σ is another reversed neuron (arising from the fixpoint preserving transformation applied to the symmetry breaking term) that reexpresses the symmetry breaking constraint so that the energy function is still linear in $M^{(1)}$ and $M^{(2)}$. The fixed points of the free energy w.r.t $U^{(1)}$, $U^{(2)}$, $M^{(1)}$ and $M^{(2)}$ can be evaluated by direct differentiation. These variables can be eliminated from F and after dropping the terms $\sum_{ai} M^{(1)}_{ai}$ and $\sum_{ai} M^{(2)}_{ai}$, we get

$$\begin{aligned} F(\mu,\lambda,\sigma) &= \frac{1}{2}\sum_{ai}\mu_{ai}^2 - \frac{\gamma}{2}\sum_{ai}\sigma_{ai}^2 \qquad (5)\\ &+\tfrac{1}{\beta}\textstyle\sum_i \log\sum_a \exp(-\beta[\sum_b G_{ab}\mu_{bi} + \lambda_{ai} - \frac{\gamma}{2}\sigma_{ai}])\\ &+\tfrac{1}{\beta}\textstyle\sum_a \log\sum_i \exp(+\beta[\sum_j g_{ij}\mu_{aj} + \lambda_{ai} + \frac{\gamma}{2}\sigma_{ai}]).\end{aligned}$$

This is the final free energy used in this paper.

Note that τ does not appear in the free energy. The energy function in (5) has to be minimized w.r.t the reversed neuron μ (which is almost like another Lagrange parameter) and the Lagrange parameter λ and maximized w.r.t σ. When the fixed-points are evaluated (partial derivatives with respect to μ_{ai} and λ_{ai} are set to zero), we get

$$\begin{aligned} \frac{\partial F}{\partial \mu_{ai}} &= \mu_{ai} - \textstyle\sum_b G_{ab}M^{(1)}_{bi} + \sum_j M^{(2)}_{aj} g_{ji} &= 0\\ \frac{\partial F}{\partial \lambda_{ai}} &= -M^{(1)}_{ai} + M^{(2)}_{ai} &= 0\\ \frac{\partial F}{\partial \sigma_{ai}} &= -\gamma(\sigma_{ai} - \tfrac{M^{(1)}_{ai}+M^{(2)}_{ai}}{2}) &= 0\end{aligned}$$

where

$$M^{(1)}_{ai} = \frac{\exp\left(-\beta\left[\sum_c G_{ac}\mu_{ci} + \lambda_{ai} - \frac{\gamma}{2}\sigma_{ai}\right]\right)}{\sum_b \exp\left(-\beta\left[\sum_c G_{bc}\mu_{ci} + \lambda_{bi} - \frac{\gamma}{2}\sigma_{bi}\right]\right)}$$

$$M^{(2)}_{ai} = \frac{\exp\left(\beta\left[\sum_k g_{ik}\mu_{ak} + \lambda_{ai} + \frac{\gamma}{2}\sigma_{ai}\right]\right)}{\sum_j \exp\left(\beta\left[\sum_k g_{jk}\mu_{ak} + \lambda_{aj} + \frac{\gamma}{2}\sigma_{aj}\right]\right)}$$

which can be seen to satisfy the constraints (3) and (4).

Thus we have obtained a free energy which expresses the graph matching and permutation matrix constraints. In the next section, we describe the algorithm that minimizes the above energy function.

3 The Lagrangian relaxation algorithm

In Appendix A, we show that the energy function in (5) is weakly convex w.r.t the reversed neurons μ and the Lagrange parameters λ. Also, note that if the second term on the right of (1) is dropped, μ reverts to being a Lagrange parameter and we are left with the isomorphism problem. We will have more to say about this in the next section.

It remains to find a saddle-point of the energy function. While minimizing the energy function, the objective is not to find the Lagrange parameters – rather the main objective is to satisfy the constraints in (3) and (4). To this end, we use the merit function [8] rather than the energy function to determine the line search parameter. Also, the $l^{(2)}$ norm of the constraint violation can be directly obtained from the merit function and used for setting convergence thresholds. Since the energy function is weakly convex, the merit function (and therefore the $l^{(2)}$ norm as well) are guaranteed not to increase for gradient descent dynamics [8].

The Lagrangian relaxation algorithm is implemented as follows:

1. Set $\beta = \beta^{(0)}$.
2. Run a conjugate-gradient algorithm w.r.t μ and λ in $F(\mu,\lambda,\sigma)$ until the $l^{(2)}$ norm is lower than $l^{(2)}_{\text{thr}}$. Use the merit function for determining the line search parameter.
3. Set $\sigma_{ai} = \frac{M^{(1)}_{ai}+M^{(2)}_{ai}}{2}$ + random noise. This performs symmetry breaking.
4. Change β according to $\beta^{(k+1)} = (1-\delta)\beta^{(k)} + \delta\beta_{\max}$ and return to step 2 unless all M_{ai} have converged ($M_{ai}(1-M_{ai}) < \epsilon$).

From the algorithm description, it can be seen that while the energy function is minimized w.r.t the Lagrange parameters at each temperature setting, only one iteration of the σ variables is executed. We converged on this algorithm after much experimentation.

4 Simulation results

We are first interested in testing our method on the isomorphism problem which requires that the distance between the two graphs be zero. This can be achieved by dropping the second term of (1) and treating μ as a Lagrange parameter instead of as a reversed "neuron" [9] arising from the fixpoint preserving transformation. Henceforth, we deal with the isomorphism case exclusively, but point out that the graph matching case can be easily recovered by adding back the second term of (1).

We ran the Lagrangian relaxation algorithm on 100 node undirected, random graphs ($N = 100$) and for a wide range of connectivities. The results are presented in Figures 1 and 2. In all experiments, we used the following parameters: $\delta = 0.01$, $\beta^{(0)} = 1.0$ and $\beta_{\text{max}} = 100$. The symmetry breaking parameter γ was set to $N/20$. The bifurcations (due to symmetry breaking) start occurring at $\beta = \frac{2N}{\gamma} = 40$ for fully connected graphs. The $l^{(2)}$ norm threshold ($l^{(2)}_{\text{thr}}$) was set to 0.02 and ϵ to 0.001.

Our method always gave a correct permutation matrix for all the examples except for three failures at an average connectivity percentage of 1%. From Figures 1 and 2, it can be seen that the number of iterations and the relaxation time are large for both extremely small connectivities and moderate to large connectivities.

5 Conclusions

We have formulated a Lagrangian relaxation algorithm for graph matching. The algorithm was tested on the graph isomorphism problem. We are currently testing our algorithm on weighted graph matching problems. We are also investigating the possibility of using weighted, graph matching as a distance measure for unsupervised learning of graph-like structures [3].

A Non-negative definiteness of the Hessian

In this section, we show that the Hessian with respect to the Lagrange parameters is non-negative definite. In order to ensure this, we require for any x and y,

$$
\begin{aligned}
D = \sum_{aibj} [x_{ai} \left(\frac{1}{\beta} \frac{\partial^2 F}{\partial \mu_{ai} \partial \mu_{bj}} \right) x_{bj} \\
+ 2 y_{ai} \left(\frac{1}{\beta} \frac{\partial^2 F}{\partial \lambda_{ai} \partial \mu_{bj}} \right) x_{bj} \\
+ y_{ai} \left(\frac{1}{\beta} \frac{\partial^2 F}{\partial \lambda_{ai} \partial \lambda_{bj}} \right) y_{bj}] \geq 0
\end{aligned}
$$

Now

$$
\begin{aligned}
\frac{\partial^2 F}{\partial \mu_{ai} \partial \mu_{bj}} &= \delta_{ab,ij} - \sum_c G_{ac} \frac{\partial M^{(1)}_{ci}}{\partial \mu_{bj}} - \sum_k \frac{\partial M^{(2)}_{ak}}{\partial \mu_{bj}} g_{ki} \\
\frac{\partial^2 F}{\partial \lambda_{ai} \partial \lambda_{bj}} &= -\frac{\partial M^{(1)}_{ai}}{\partial \lambda_{bj}} - \frac{\partial M^{(2)}_{ai}}{\partial \lambda_{bj}} \\
\frac{\partial^2 F}{\partial \lambda_{ai} \partial \mu_{bj}} &= -\frac{\partial M^{(1)}_{ai}}{\partial \mu_{bj}} - \frac{\partial M^{(2)}_{ai}}{\partial \mu_{bj}}
\end{aligned}
$$

where $\delta_{ab,ij}$ is the Kronecker delta function. Now define

$$
w_{ai} \stackrel{\text{def}}{=} \sum_b (G_{ab} + \delta_{ab}) x_{bi} + y_{ai}
$$

$$
v_{ai} \stackrel{\text{def}}{=} \sum_j (g_{aj} + \delta_{ij}) x_{aj} + y_{ai}
$$

Then the expression for D can be shown to be:

$$
\begin{aligned}
D = \sum_i \left[\sum_a w^2_{ai} M^{(1)}_{ai} - \left(\sum_a w_{ai} M^{(1)}_{ai} \right)^2 \right] \\
+ \sum_a \left[\sum_i z^2_{ai} M^{(2)}_{ai} - \left(\sum_i z_{ai} M^{(2)}_{ai} \right)^2 \right]
\end{aligned}
$$

For any i, setting $f_a = w_{ai} \sqrt{M^{(1)}_{ai}}$ and $g_a = \sqrt{M^{(1)}_{ai}}$ and using the Schwartz inequality

$$
\left(\sum_a f^2_a \right) \left(\sum_a g^2_a \right) \geq \left(\sum_a f_a g_a \right)^2
$$

with equality occurring when $f_a = hg_a$ and h is an arbitrary non-zero constant, we get

$$\left(\sum_a w_{ai}^2 M_{ai}^{(1)}\right)\left(\sum_a M_{ai}^{(1)}\right) \geq \left(\sum_a w_{ai} M_{ai}^{(1)}\right)^2$$

$$\Rightarrow \sum_a w_{ai}^2 M_{ai}^{(1)} \geq \left(\sum_a w_{ai} M_{ai}^{(1)}\right)^2$$

using the fact that $\sum_a M_{ai}^{(1)} = 1$ is always satisfied.

Similarly, for any a,

$$\sum_i z_{ai}^2 M_{ai}^{(2)} \geq \left(\sum_i z_{ai} M_{ai}^{(2)}\right)^2$$

Therefore $D \geq 0$ with equality occurring for those $w_{ai} = s_i$, $\forall\ a$ and $z_{ai} = t_a$, $\forall\ i$, and s_i, t_a are arbitrary. Thus the Hessian is non-negative definite.

References

[1] H. A. Almohamad. A polynomial transform for matching pairs of weighted graphs. *J. Applied Math. Modeling*, 15(4), April 1991.

[2] H. A. Almohamad and S. O. Duffuaa. A linear programming approach for the weighted graph matching problem. *IEEE Trans. Patt. Anal. Mach. Intell.*, 15(5):522–525, May 1993.

[3] S. Gold, E. Mjolsness, and A. Rangarajan. Clustering with a domain specific distance measure. In J. Cowan, G. Tesauro, and J. Alspector, editors, *Advances in Neural Information Processing Systems 6*. Morgan Kaufmann, San Francisco, CA, 1994.

[4] M. Guignard and S. Kim. Lagrangean decomposition: A model yielding stronger Lagrangean bounds. *Mathematical Programming*, 39:215–228, 1987.

[5] K. Jörnsten and M. Näsberg. A new Lagrangian relaxation approach to the generalized assignment problem. *European Journal of Operational Research*, 27:313–323, 1986.

[6] J. J. Kosowsky and A. L. Yuille. The invisible hand algorithm: Solving the assignment problem with statistical physics. Technical Report 91–1, Harvard Robotics Laboratory, 1991.

[7] M. Lades, J. C. Vorbrüggen, J. Buhmann, J. Lange, C. von der Malsburg, R. P. Wurtz, and W. Konen. Distortion invariant object recognition in the dynamic link architecture. *IEEE Trans. Computers*, 42(3):300–311, March 1993.

[8] D. Luenberger. *Linear and Nonlinear Programming.* Addison–Wesley, Reading, MA, 1984.

[9] E. Mjolsness and C. Garrett. Algebraic transformations of objective functions. *Neural Networks*, 3:651–669, 1990.

[10] E. Mjolsness, G. Gindi, and P. Anandan. Optimization in model matching and perceptual organization. *Neural Computation*, 1:218–229, 1989.

[11] C. Peterson and B. Söderberg. A new method for mapping optimization problems onto neural networks. *International Journal of Neural Systems*, 1(1):3–22, 1989.

[12] P. D. Simić. Constrained nets for graph matching and other quadratic assignment problems. *Neural Computation*, 3:268–281, 1991.

[13] S. Umeyama. An eigendecomposition approach to weighted graph matching problems. *IEEE Trans. Patt. Anal. Mach. Intell.*, 10(5):695–703, Sept. 1988.

[14] C. von der Malsburg. Pattern recognition by labeled graph matching. *Neural Networks*, 1:141–148, 1988.

[15] A. L. Yuille and J. J. Kosowsky. Statistical physics algorithms that converge. Technical Report 92–7, Harvard Robotics Laboratory, 1992.

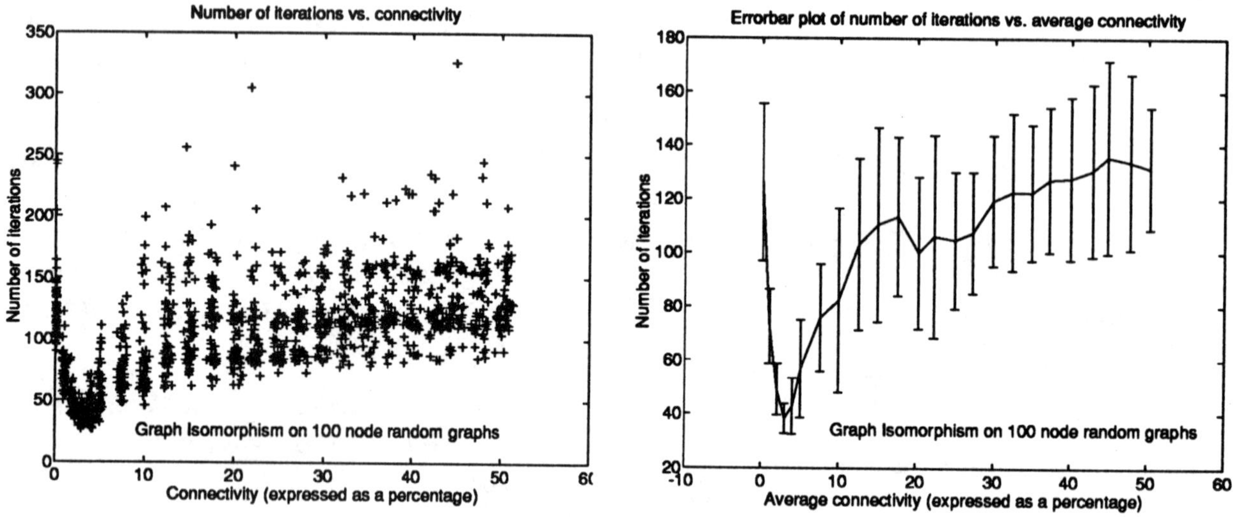

Figure 1: Number of iterations vs. connectivity percentage

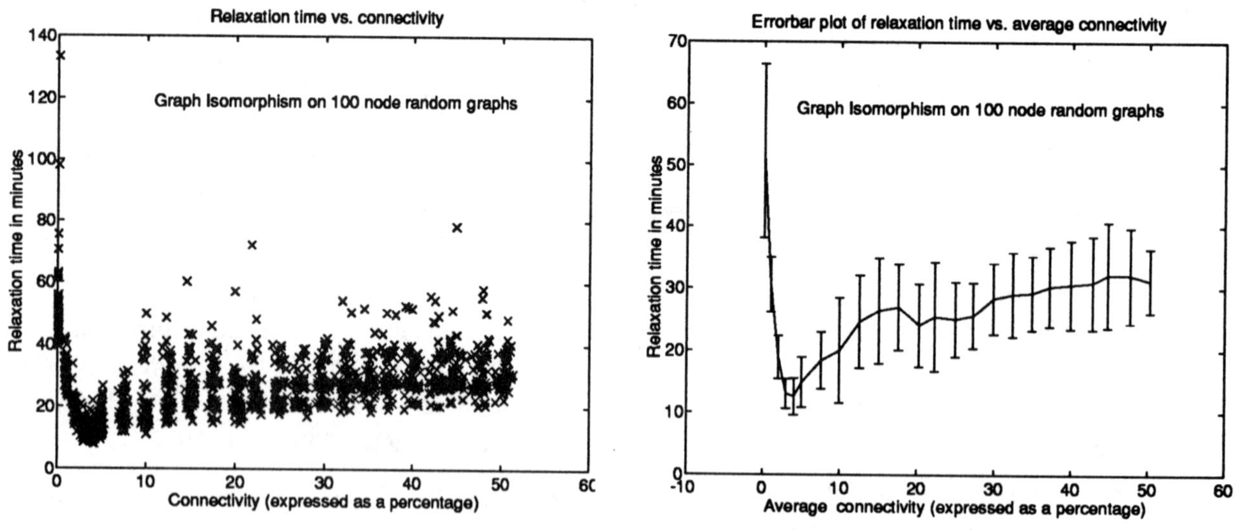

Figure 2: Relaxation time vs. connectivity percentage

PROCESS OPTIMIZATION USING NEURAL NETWORKS

Yi Yang*, Yizong Cheng*, Renhong Zhao** and Rakesh Govind**
* Department of Computer Science, University of Cincinnati, Cincinnati, OH 45221
**Department of Chemical Engineering, University of Cincinnati, Cincinnati, OH 45221

1. Introduction

Optimization of chemical processes can result in decreased energy consumption, improved productivity, better product quality, and generally increased profits. Most chemical plants achieve optimal operation by gradually varying process conditions experimentally and exploring a localized feasible region around the current operating point. Major concerns are cost and time involved in attempting to achieve "optimal operation". This paper presents a systematic methodology using neural networks to improve the efficiency of a sequential search process for achieving optimal process operating conditions. An example, developed by Ultramax Corporation, Cincinnati, is presented to illustrate the approach.

2. Development of Process Models

Most industrial processes are constrained by the fact that they allow only sequential experiments to be run and generally it is not possible to run several experiments in parallel. In traditional design-of-experiments methodology, as in the Taguchi method, it is implicitly assumed that several experiments can be run at the same time to obtain all the needed process data. However, for an operating process, it is generally desired to minimize the number of experiments needed to achieve optimal operation.

Box and Draper's [1] factorial evolutionary operation (EVOP) methodology for process improvement introduced the concept of sequential experimentation. It was followed by a computer-based sequential optimization approach, ULTRAMAX (Ultramax Corporation, Cincinnati, OH), which used a model building approach to reduce noise senstivity and enhance convergence. However, the Ultramax approach relied on a polynomial model, which requires extensive data for evaluating the polynomial coefficients as the degree of polynomial is increased to achieve accuracy in modeling complex process behavior. Using low-order polynomials simplifies the process of fitting the polynomial to experimental data, but often results in decreased model accuracy.

Equation-based models, based on fundamental principles of process behavior, require detailed understanding of all process effects. Often, development of equation-based models requires detailed understanding obtained through process experimentation. Empirical models, as used in the Ultramax approach, suffer from tradeoffs between empirical model complexity and model accuracy.

3. Neural Network Models

In this paper, a neural network model is developed for a process using actual process observations. Neural networks represent parallel architecture models where the process information is distributed between a large number of processors and connections. Neural networks can directly use experimental data to calculate the weights without requiring an explicit mathematical correlation. In this paper, neural network models are used to improve the efficiency of sequential search for process optimization.

3.1 Initialization of Neural Networks

For any existing process, operating data on input and output variables usually exists. Further experimentation may have to be conducted to obtain additional experimental data. To prevent extrapolation of data over a wide range, experimental data should be obtained at the minimum and maximum values of the input process variables.

The initial weights in the neural network model are generated using the algorithm proposed by Grogono [2]:

$$r_k = \frac{Seed_k}{2^{16} - 1} \quad (1)$$

and

$$Seed_{k+1} = (25173 x Seed_k + 13849) Mod(2^{16}) \quad (2)$$

In the example presented in this paper, $Seed_0$ are arbitrarily selected as 1. By using equations (1) and (2) repetitively, a set $[r_k]$ is obtained which are a pseudo-random sequence in the range of [0,1]. This

0-7803-1901-X/94 $4.00 ©1994 IEEE

sequence can be transformed to another sequence R_k located in [-0.5,0.5] using the following transformation:

if $r_k > 0.5$, then $R_k = r_k - 1$
if $r_k \leq 0.5$, then $R_k = r_k$

The transformed pseudo-random numbers R_k are used as initial weights in the neural network model.

3.2 Neural Network Model Constraints

Most process variables are bounded by safety constraints. Due to model errors, safety factors are used to set constraints on model variables based on the actual process safety limits. The constraint on the jth model input variable, ym_j can be expressed as

$$(yp_{jL} + \delta m_{jL}) \leq ym_j \leq (yp_{jU} - \delta m_{jU}) \quad (3)$$

where yp_{jL} and yp_{jU} are the minimum and maximum process variable values, bounded by safety constraints, and $\delta m_{jL} > 0$ and $\delta m_{jU} > 0$ are the safety factors to compensate for model errors. Safety factors are assigned values based on process experience and can be changed during process optimization as accuracy of the neural network model improves.

3.3 Training of Neural Network

A three layer backpropagation neural network is used as the process model. A sigmoid function is used for activation of the hidden and output nodes with the activation values being continuous numbers in the range [0,1]. There are two methods for training the neural network model: (1) Limited Horizon method where only few current data are used to train the network; and (2) Infinite Horizon method where all the experimental data are used to train the network. The infinite horizon method minimizes the effect of errors in a few experimental runs as well as the impact of noise in the measurement data.

The transformation of neural network signals to actual process variable values is achieved by the following equations:

$$a_j = \frac{(x_j - x_{j\,\min})}{(x_{j\,\max} - x_{j\,\min})} \quad (4)$$

$$y_k = y_{k\,\min} + o_k(y_{k\,\max} - y_{k\,\min}) \quad (5)$$

where x_j is the jth process variable input to the neural network and a_j is the activation value for the jth input node in the network. x_{jmax} and x_{jmin} are the maximum and minimum values for the process variable. For neural network output, o_k, the corresponding process variable value is y_k, with y_{kmin} and y_{kmax} being the minimum and maximum bounds for the process variable, respectively. The maximum and minimum values for the process variables are obtained from process knowledge and experience, and can be changed dynamically during optimization.

In the process example, the infinite horizon method is used for training the neural network. The error difference between two successive training passes is used to determine convergence, i.e.,

$$|E(n+1) - E(n)| \leq 4x10^{-7} \quad (6)$$

where E(n) is the error in the nth training pass and E(n+1) is the error in the subsequent $(n+1)^{th}$ training pass.

4. Neural Network Model Inversion

The objective in optimization is to find the feasible process inputs for achieving "optimal" values of the process output(s) or objective function. This requires determination of the neural network input activation values for maximizing or minimizing the specified objective function. This inversion of the neural network model is achieved by using a grid search technique. The main advantages of using grid search technique are: (1) feasibility of solution can be easily checked; (2) can locate the global or near global optimum solution of the model; (3) method is simple to implement and does not require derivatives; and (4) method is computationally robust.

The grid search technique involves the following steps: (1) Subdivide the allowable range of each input process variable $[x_{jmin}, x_{jmax}]$ into a finite number of steps to generate several input process variable values $[x_{jmin}, x_{jmin}+\Delta_j, x_{jmin}+ 2\Delta_j, ... x_{jmax}]$, where Δ_j is the step size selected for the jth input variable; (2) For all combinations of input process variable values, calculate the objective function using the converged neural network model; (3) search all the calculated values of the objective function to locate the desired maximum or minimum value and consequently the values of the process input variables corresponding to the "optimal" value of the objective function; and (4) refine the values of the process input variables by decreasing the step size for each input process variable in the neighborhood of the "optimal" values and repeating the entire grid search method.

It is important to note that during the grid search for the "optimal" values of the input process variables, only the neural network model is used and no experiments are performed using the actual process.

5. Process Optimization Procedure

The process optimization procedure can now be described as follows: (1) Problem Formulation which involves defining the process input variables, the objective function or measure of process performance and the allowable minimum and maximum values (feasible region) for each variable based on process understanding and/or safety constraints; (2) Model Generation by determining converged values of neural network weights using either prior process data or data generated by the process using extreme values of the input process variables. The neural network weights are initialized using the algorithm presented earlier and convergence is checked by comparing the error in each training pass. (3) Model Recommendation by using the converged neural network model and the grid search technique to recommend the "optimal" process input variable values; and (4) Sequential Search in which the recommended "optimal" values of the process input variables are used to experimentally determine the actual objective function value, and this data is then used in conjunction with the prior data to retrain the neural network model. The retrained neural network model is then used to recommend another set of "optimal" process inputs using the grid search technique and the process is repeated resulting in a sequential strategy for locating the process optimum.

The accuracy of the neural network model improves as more actual process data is used to retrain the model. The performance of the neural network optimization procedure is quantified by the number of experimental process runs required to obtain the actual value of the objective function.

6. Process Example

The following example [3], provided by Ultramax Corporation, Cincinnati, involves the optimization of a chemical reactor. The process input variables are crude feed rate, reactant feed rate and reactor temperature. The process dependant variables are: viscosity of product, solids content in the output stream and reactor pressure. The quality of product is quantified by its viscosity and solids content, and a performance loss function has been formulated as the objective function.

The process constraints are as follows: (1) Crude feed rate must be larger than 25K gallons per hour to meet the required production rate; (2) Reactor temperature must be less than 190°F to prevent undesireable reactions at higher temperatures; (3) Product viscosity should be maintained at a desired value of 850K centipoise with a tolerance deviation of ±50K centipoise; (4) Product solids content has a desired value of 45 weight percent with a tolerance deviation of ±2.5 weight percent; and (5) Reactor pressure must be less than 320 psi for safety reasons.

The performance loss function is specified as follows:

$$obj = Min\left\{\left[\frac{y1-850}{50}\right]^2 + \left[\frac{y2-45}{2.5}\right]^2\right\} \qquad (7)$$

where y1 is the product viscosity in centipoise and y2 is the product solids content in weight percent. Note that the denominator in each term of the objective function represents the tolerance level for the product variable.

The process constraints can be written as follows:

$$x1 \geq 25 \qquad (8)$$

$$x2 \geq 0 \qquad (9)$$

$$0 \leq x3 \leq 190 \qquad (10)$$

$$y3 \leq 320 \qquad (11)$$

where x1 is the crude feed rate, x2 is reactant feed rate, x3 is reactor temperature and y3 is reactor pressure.

To simulate the actual running of the process, the following equations are used:

$$y1 = \frac{6,800}{(1+x1/25)(1+12.5/x2)(1+x3/185)} + 5(VNRV) \qquad (12)$$

$$y2 = \frac{360}{(1+25/x1)(1+x2/12.5)(1+x3/185)} + 0.25VNRV \qquad (13)$$

$$y3 = \frac{2,400}{(1+25/x1)(1+12.5/x2)(1+185/x3)} + VNRV \quad (14)$$

where VNRV is a normal random variable with values in the range [0,1]. VNRV simulates measurement noise for the variables. These process simulation equations are used only to obtain the value of the objective function for any recommended values of the process input variables. In the actual case, these process simulation equations will be replaced by the actual process with direct measurement of the process output variables.

The following two initial experiments are performed to generate initial process performance data for the training of the three-layer neural network model with three input nodes, three hidden nodes and three output nodes:

$$X(1) = [x1=25.5,\ x2 = 13.5,\ x3 = 165] \quad (15)$$

$$X(2) = [x1=26.5,\ x2 = 14.5,\ x3 = 175] \quad (16)$$

To calculate the neural network node activation values, the following maximum and minimum values for each process input variable are used:

$$x1 = [25.1, 27.1] \quad (17)$$
$$x2 = [12.1, 14.6] \quad (18)$$
$$x3 = [164, 189] \quad (19)$$

A neural network learning rate of 0.25 is used for training the three-layer neural network model.

Once the neural network is trained, the grid search technique is used to locate the input process variable values that would minimize the performance loss (objective function). The step sizes used in the grid search technique are Δ_1=0.1; Δ_2 = 0.1 and Δ_3 = 1.0 for input variables x1, x2, and x3 respectively. The neural network model is used to simulate the process and determine the values of the objective function. The safety constraint on reactor pressure (y3) is used in conjunction with a safety factor of 11, which sets the maximum allowable value of y3 as (320-11) = 309 psi. Hence a modified constraint y3 $\leq$ 309 is used to determine the feasible outputs.

The values of the process input variables that minimizes the calculated values of the performance loss are then recommended as the "optimal' values to operate the process. After the process is operated (process simulation equations) the actual value of the objective function is determined, and this actual data is then used in conjunction with the previous data to retrain the neural network model.

Figures 1 through 6 show the performance of the neural network sequential optimization procedure, with each run number denoting the number of actual process experimentation (use of process simulation equations). It can be seen that the neural network sequential optimization technique attains the optimum in 5 runs and remains stable after reaching the optimum value.

To compare the neural network optimization procedure with a polynomial (quadratic)-based sequential optimizer in which the last three actual process data are used to fit a quadratic function model between the input process variables and the objective function value. As more data are generated, previous data points are deleted and replaced by the current data. The performance of the quadratic model sequential optimizer is also shown along with the neural network approach. Clearly, a quadratic function model takes longer to achieve the optimum value than a neural network model-based process optimizer. Further, as shown in Figures 1 through 6, the quadratic-function sequential optimizer oscillates while the neural network results are very stable.

6. Conclusions

A neural network model-based sequential process optmizer has been presented which is capable of optimizing a real operating process using process inputs and outputs to develop a neural network model. A grid search technique is used to obtain the "optimal" input process variable values. Comparison with a quadratic function model sequential optimizer shows that the neural network approach attains the "optimum" in a few experimental runs and remains stable after achieving the optimum.

7. References

[1] Box, G.E.P and N.R. Draper, *Evolutionary Operations*, J. Wiley & Sons, New York, NY, 1969.

[2] Grogono, Peter, *Programming in Pascal*, Addison-Wesley, 1980.

[3] *Ultramax Optimization Technology User's Guide*, Ultramax Corporation, Cincinnati, OH, 1987.

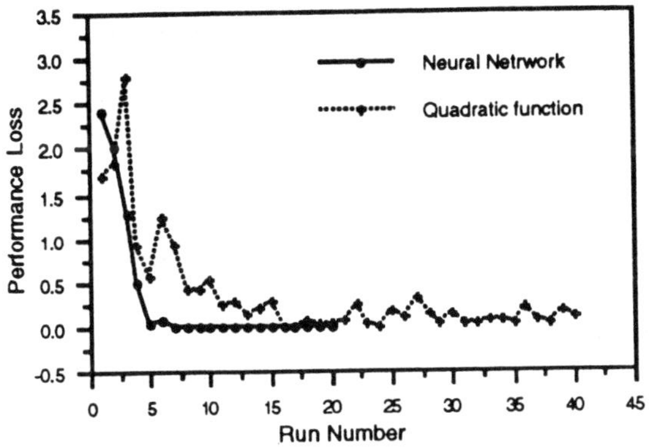

Figure 1. Performance Loss versus the run number

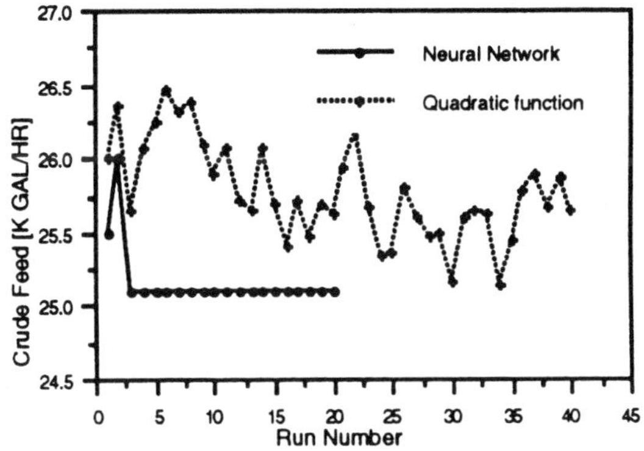

Figure 2. Crude feed rate (x1) versus the run number

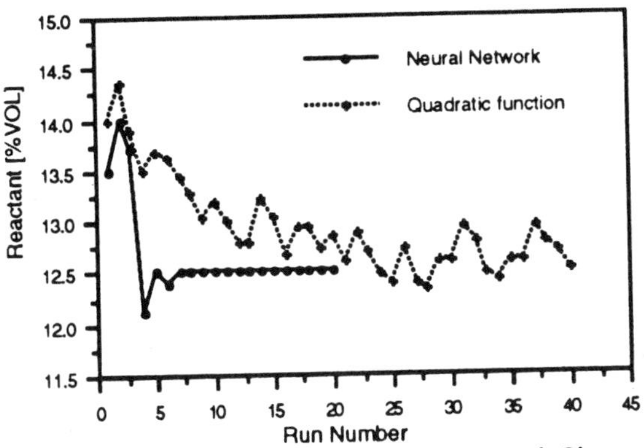

Figure 3. Reactant feed rate (x2) versus the run number

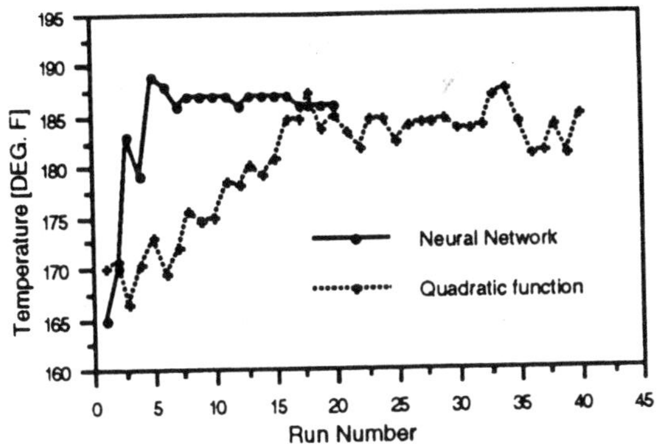

Figure 4. Reactor temperature (x3) versus the run number

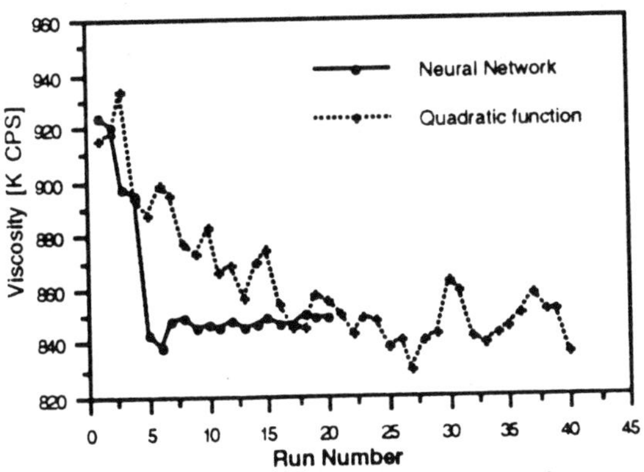

Figure 5. Product viscosity (y1) versus the run number

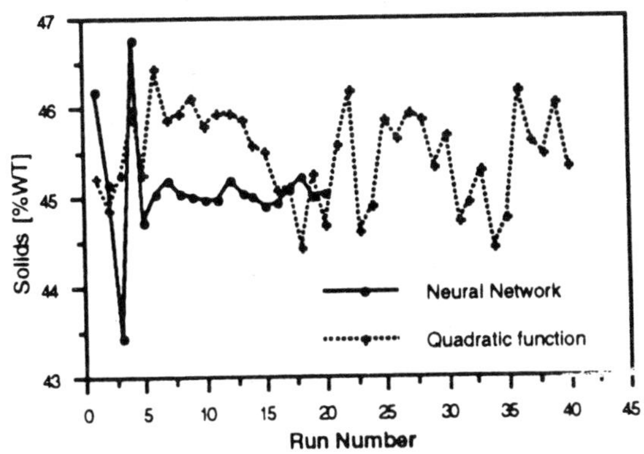

Figure 6. Product solids (y2) versus the run number

Initialising the Continuous Hopfield Net

W. K. Lai, *Student Member* IEEE and G. G. Coghill, *CEng*, *Member* INNS, *Member* IEE.

Abstract— **In this paper, we will compare some of the commonly used initialising schemes for the Hopfield Neural Net. This is demonstrated by solving an optimization problem which is representative of a class of problems that can be found in many application areas, such as engineering, medicine and finance. We also introduce a new initialising scheme which may not only be used for this particular application, but in other areas as well. Simulation results are provided to validate each approach.**

I. Introduction

Neural networks have been used in many different areas of applications. One promising area which has received growing attention is that optimization. In almost every case, a neural network model known as the Hopfield Net has been used. This is a fully connected, single layered network with feedbacks to every other processing element, except to itself. The architecture of such a neural network is shown in figure (1).

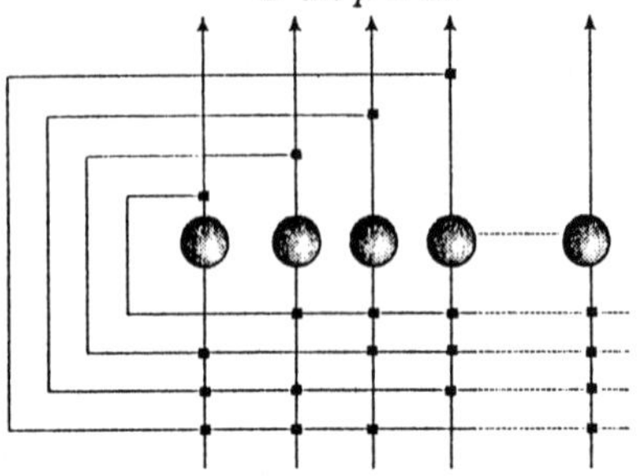

Fig. 1. Architecture of the Hopfield Net. The black squares at the intersections represent the interconnection weights between the outputs of each neuron to the inputs of others.

Ever since it was used to solve an optimization problem known as the Travelling Salesman Problem in 1985, many other new application areas have followed. However, the dynamics of this approach to solve any optimization problem is very much dependent upon the overall energy function of the network, and this has been shown [1] to be of the general form,

$$E = -\frac{1}{2}\sum_i \sum_j T_{ij} V_i V_j - \sum_i V_i I_i \qquad (1)$$

where,

V_i represents the output of neuron i and
T_{ij} is the interconnection weight between the i and j neuron pair.

Researchers working with this particular neural network model, especially for such an application, have noted that the network is especially sensitive to the system parameters. Many different approaches have been suggested to help overcome this sensitivity. This may come in the form of modifications to the fundamental architecture of the network (Aiyer *et al.* [2]), heuristics to determine the best set of parameters (Raeth [3], Hedge *et. al* [4], etc), modifications of the updating rules (Bhaumik [5]) etc. However, these are only some of the network's system parameters which may be modified, and they can be generally grouped into three major areas: the operating parameters, changes to the distance terms and last but not least, changes to the initial conditions. Except for a few well accepted initialisation heuristics, there is not much work reported on supplying some form of global information to the network at the beginning, so as to assist the network in avoiding those invalid regions in the search space. Examples of such regions are network configurations which translate to incomplete tours, two or more subtours, visiting any one city more than once, etc. In general, most practitioners of this neural net model have usually relied on ad hoc initialisation techniques and in most cases, this is based on the approach of Hopfield and Tank. In this paper we attempt to provide a comparison of some of the popular initialisation techniques. Although this will only be verified on one particular application, we believe that the results may also be applicable to other application areas. In this respect, we have elected to conduct our investigation on the well-known optimization problem, commonly known as as the travelling salesman problem (TSP).

A. The TSP Revisited

The travelling salesman problem (TSP), fundamentally involves an imaginary salesman who must visit all the N cities in his itinerary once, and returns to his home city at the end of the trip. In addition, and perhaps more importantly, he must attempt to minimize the total distance travelled. Mathematically, this can be expressed as,

The work of W. K. Lai is partially supported by a scholarship from the *New Zealand Ministry of External Relations & Trade*.
G. G. Coghill is a Senior Lecturer in the Department of Electrical & Electronic Engineering, University of Auckland, Private Bag 92109, Auckland, New Zealand.

$$\text{Min} \sum_i \sum_j d_{ij} x_{ij} \quad (2)$$

Subject to,

$$\sum_i x_{ij} = 1 \quad (3)$$

$$\sum_j x_{ij} = 1 \quad (4)$$

$$\sum_{i \in \mathcal{Q}} \sum_{j \in \bar{\mathcal{Q}}} x_{ij} \geq 1, \qquad \mathcal{Q} \subset \mathcal{V}, \quad \mathcal{Q} \neq \phi \quad (5)$$

$$x_{ij} = \begin{cases} 1 & \text{if the edge (i,j) is in the tour,} \\ 0 & \text{otherwise.} \end{cases} \quad (6)$$

where V is the set of cities and $\bar{\mathcal{Q}} = \mathcal{V} - \mathcal{Q}$.

B. The Neural Network Approach

Clearly, if we can map this problem in terms of the energy function of the neural network, the Hopfield Net may then be used to find good solutions to the problem. Typically, the major objective function of the problem is assigned to this energy function, with the constraints included as additional penalty terms.

Mapping the TSP into a Hopfield Net and after some simple algebraic manipulation, the equivalent interconnection weights of this neural net may be shown to be,

$$T_{ij} = -\alpha_1 \delta_{xy}(1 - \delta_{ij}) - \alpha_2 \delta_{ij}(1 - \delta_{xy}) - \alpha_3 - \alpha_4 d_{xy}(\delta_{j,i+1} + \delta_{j,i-1}) \quad (7)$$

with the external inputs,

$$I_{xi} = \alpha_3 n \quad (8)$$

The parameters α_1, α_2, α_3 and α_4 shown here, define the relative importance of each of the associated terms in the overall energy function and individually, may only take up positive values.

The trajectory of the neural net in the search space is governed by the equation of motion which may be derived from the interconnectivity equation shown previously.

$$\frac{du_{xi}}{dt} = -\frac{u_{xi}}{\tau} - \alpha_1 \sum_{j \neq i} V_{xj} - \alpha_2 \sum_{y \neq x} V_{yi} - \alpha_3 \sum_x \sum_i V_{xi} - \alpha_3 n - \alpha_4 \sum_y d_{xy}(V_{y,i+1} + V_{y,i-1}) \quad (9)$$

The next step is to configure the initial state of the network and to update this until it converges to a steady state. In the next section, we will briefly outline some of the common heuristics used for initialisation.

II. Initial Network Configuration

A. Original H&T (*OHT*)

Hopfield and Tank first suggested the following initialisation technique in their seminal work on the TSP [1]. In this case, given that the final valid states should consist of only N neurons switched-on, then the mean of the initial operating points of the network can be shown to be,

$$V_i^{t0} \approx \frac{1}{N}$$

$$\hat{u} = -\frac{1}{2} u_0 \ln\left(\frac{1 - V_i^{t0}}{V_i^{t0}}\right)$$

However, to avoid the network getting stuck at this particular configuration, it is customary to introduce a small amount of random noise. This is usually in the range of $\pm 10\%$ of the initial value. It then follows that both the initial inputs and outputs have to be,

$$u_{ij}^{t0} = \hat{u} + \mathbf{rand}(\delta \hat{u})$$

$$V_{ij}^{t0} = 1/2(1 + \tanh(u_{ij}^{t0})/(u_0))$$

where,

$-0.1\hat{u} \leq \mathbf{rand}\ (X) \leq +0.1\hat{u}$,

u_0 denotes the slope of the transfer function (sigmoid), and

$1 \leq i, j \leq N$

B. Center of Hypercube (*COH*)

The center of the solution hypercube is another popular heuristic which has been used to initialise the neural net. Numerous applications have used such a starting point as the basis for the search of optimum solutions in the solution space [6, 7].

$$V_{ij}^{t0} \approx 0.5$$

$$u_{ij}^{t0} = \mathbf{rand}\ (\psi)$$

where,

$-0.0004 \leq \mathbf{rand}\ (\psi) \leq +0.0004$

C. Sinusoidal Bias (*WILSB*)

Although this third technique is not as well known as the previous two, nevertheless, it has its own merits. In this case, the heuristic has the ability to incorporate both ordering and direction information based on the location of the individual cities into the initial network configuration [8].

$$V_{ij}^{t0} = \frac{1}{2}\left(1+\tanh\left(\frac{u_{ij}^{t0}}{u_0}\right)\right)$$

$$\hat{u}_{ij} = \cos\left(\arctan\left(\frac{y_i-0.5}{x_i-0.5}\right)+\frac{2\pi(j-1)}{N}\right) * \sqrt{(x_i-0.5)^2+(y_i-0.5)^2}$$

$$u_{ij}^{t0} = \beta * \hat{u}_{ij} * \mathbf{rand}\ (\psi)$$

where,

$$-\alpha\hat{u}_{ij} \leq \mathbf{rand}\ (\psi) \leq +\alpha\hat{u}_{ij}$$

Wilson *et al.* have suggested a good value for both α and β to be 10 % or 0.1.

The following figure (fig. 2) compares the typical initial outputs obtained with each of the techniques described above. The second row in figures (a) and (b) gives a magnified view of each of these outputs. Notice that the scale used here are no longer similar.

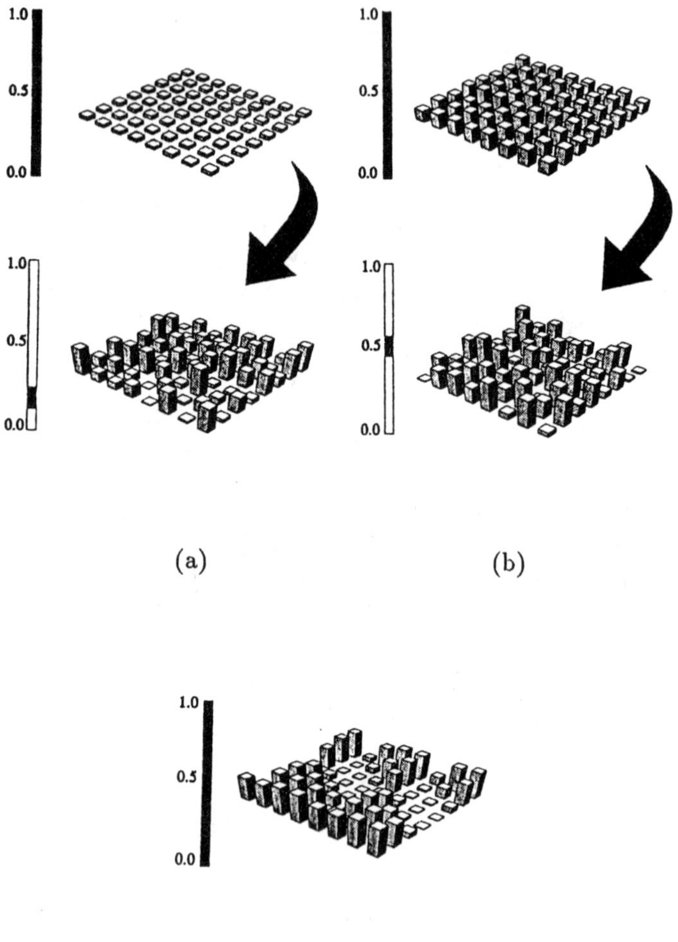

Fig. 2. Typical initial outputs of the network obtained with (a) random initialisation and (b) initialised at the center of the solution hypercube (c) sinusoidal bias.

In the first experiment, the Hopfield Net was used to solve a 8-city TSP and all the three heuristics described were investigated. The same set of network parameters, as well as the same data set were used throughout this exercise. 500 different runs were tested with each heuristic and the results noted. This is summarized in table (1).

Heuristic	# runs	% Valid
OH&T	500	66.2
COH	500	50.6
WILSB	500	1.2

Table 1. Comparing the quality of solutions obtained through two different initialisation techniques.

III. A New Approach

For problems such as the travelling salesman problem (TSP), there usually exist several other minima, as well as the optimum. Unfortunately, not all of these network configurations representing unique "*solutions*" are necessarily valid. In consequence, we believe that the initial starting point is especially important. This is because the neural net will converge to the nearest minimum within the basin of attraction of the starting point. With the same set of network parameters, the network may converge to a valid configuration with one set of initial conditions, while it may converge to an invalid one for a different set. This has been very evident in the discussion as well as from the simulation results in the previous section. Fortunately, this may be alleviated to a certain extent by either making modifications to the dynamics of the network as suggested by some researchers [2], or by careful selection of the network parameters, as suggested by others [4].

Randomly initialising the neural net has been the most commonly used strategy, if not for its simplicity, then it may be because of its universal suitability for most, if not all the known applications. However, the influence that the initial inputs (and outputs) have on the efficiency of the network in converging to valid solutions may have been largely overlooked.

If we can identify what the invalid configurations are, we may then bias the initial inputs so that they are well beyond the radius of attraction of the invalid states. Extensive simulations have shown that if the mean of the initial inputs of one group of neurons is larger than the remainder by as much as 20 %, the network would be largely attracted to that particular initial configuration. This is especially true if the initial conditions have been such that this is near a valid configuration, and the network was not strongly biased for minimal tour lengths. In a recent article, a variation of this argument was used to investigate the fault-tolerance of the network [9]. In this case, the second group of neurons have been set to the largest possible value and the results have shown that the network will converge to a valid solution based around such a "*selected*" initial configuration.

We now suggest that this information may be used to advantage. In problems where valid configurations may be easily identified, the initial conditions are chosen so that the network is directed to give valid solutions. For the travelling salesman problem, valid solutions may be translated as meaning that only single neurons may fire in each unique location in the matrix of neurons. As an example, consider a three city problem. Since each neuron represents the order in which the city is to be visited in the tour, there can only be a limited number of possible valid configurations. This is illustrated in figure (3) which shows some of the possible combinations of the two-dimensional array of neurons. It is clear that multiple firings of neurons in each column or row can only result in invalid tours. Consequently, it is important that the initial configurations should be well away from such areas, to avoid the unfortunate event that the trajectory of the search gets trapped within that sphere of influence.

0	1	0
0	1	0
0	0	1

Invalid

0	0	1
1	0	0
0	1	0

Valid

0	1	0
0	0	1
1	0	0

Valid

0	1	0
1	0	1
1	0	0

Invalid

Fig. 3. Some examples of valid and invalid network configurations.

We will now proceed to describe a novel initialisation approach based on the discussion so far which may be used to effectively initialise the Hopfield Net. The two-tier initialization technique has been used already on a different application [10].

D. Two Tier Approach (*2TIER*)

This is basically an extension of the simple random initialisation as proposed by Hopfield and Tank, but with the major difference of avoiding invalid sectors of the search space. In this respect, it is very essential that we have some idea of what these regions are beforehand.

$$\hat{u} = -\tfrac{1}{2}u_0 \ln\left(\frac{1-V_{ij}^{t0}}{V_i^{t0}}\right)$$

$$u_{ij}^{t0} = \hat{u} + \textbf{rand}\ (\delta\hat{u})$$

where,

$$V^{t0} = \begin{cases} \dot{V}_{ij}^{t0} \approx \frac{1}{N} & \textit{First Tier} \\ \ddot{V}_{ij}^{t0} = \dot{V}^{t0} + \varphi\dot{V}^{t0} & \textit{Second Tier} \end{cases}$$

with,

$0.0 \leq \varphi \leq 1.0$, and

$1 \leq i,j \leq N$

The neurons representing valid configurations were first randomly selected and subsequently initialized with the higher mean. The remainder were initialized with the second (and lower) mean. In both cases the outputs were randomly distributed at ± 10 % from their mean. As a result, the initial network configuration is biased towards those valid configurations. The two tier initialization scheme is illustrated in figure (4). The shaded neurons have been initialised with respect to the upper (or second) tier.

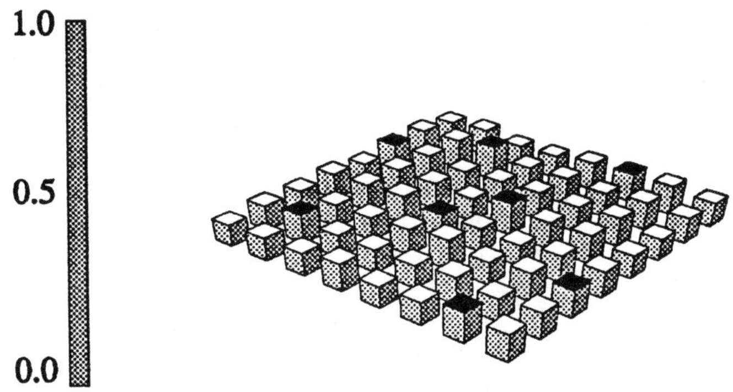

(a)

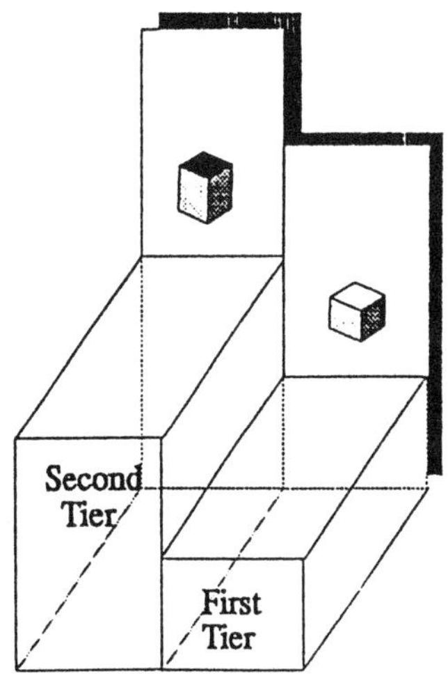

(b)

Fig. 4. Two tier initialization (a) An example of the initial output state of the network. Some of the neurons have been assigned with values from the second tier while the others from the lower tier. (b) Symbolic representation of the two tiers.

However, further simulation results show that if the two-tier initialization is such that the minimum of the upper tier is more than or equal to maximum of the lower tier, the initial operating point will be biased strongly towards one configuration. Such a situation can be compared to a fault in the network with several neurons exhibiting erroneous outputs. Under these conditions the final network solution would revolve around these faults. Such a scenario has been extensively investigated in a recent article by a major research group from NASA [9]. The network will be unable to escape from the attractive forces of the nearest minimum, even if it has been strongly biased to move away from that corner of the hypercube towards a better solution. From further experimentation, a good value for the mean of the upper tier was found to be about 50 % more than the upper limit of the lower tier.

With this technique, the network now makes use of additional information which would be lost if the inputs had been randomly initialized with no regard to such valid configurations.

IV. Simulation Results

The new two-tier initialisation technique was compared with that of the other heuristics described in the preceding sections. Altogether two additional data sets were used. For each technique, the results from 500 runs were generated and the results summarized in table(2). In addition to the number of successful runs, we have also monitored the quality of the solutions obtained.

Heuristic	neurons	runs	Valid (%)	Distances	
				Avg.	Min.
OH&T	64	500	66.2	2.927	1.986
COH	64	500	50.6	2.478	1.986
WILSB	64	500	1.2	4.107	3.673
2TIER	64	500	70.4	3.105	1.986
OH&T	81	500	33.4	2.955	2.314
COH	81	500	24.0	2.774	2.314
WILSB	81	500	0.0	-	-
2TIER	81	500	40.4	3.249	2.314
OH&T	100	500	23.8	3.468	2.752
COH	100	500	17.0	3.245	2.691
WILSB	100	500	0.0	-	-
2TIER	100	500	32.6	3.820	2.691

Table 2. Comparing the quality of solutions obtained to the new two tier initialisation technique

V. Conclusions

For the 3 existing initialisation heuristics, even though *COH* does consistently provide qualitatively better solutions than *OH&T*, it converges to valid solutions less frequently. On the other hand, while *WILSB* has performed rather poorly, we believe that this may be because the individual neurons were initialised to the full spectrum of the output value, i.e. 0.0 – 1.0. Certainly, this is in stark contrast to the range of the initial outputs with the other approaches. For the new initialization technique, a significant improvement in converging to valid solutions is apparent, even though there is a slight deterioration in the average of the results. However, it must be remembered that this technique has only been designed to increase the efficiency of convergence to valid solutions. In other words, its primary function is to avoid those invalid regions of the search space. The simulation results shown here have strongly validated this. Unlike the sinusoidal bias technique (*WILSB*), it may also be used in other situations, especially those in which the valid regions of the search space can be easily identifiable.

An interesting area of further investigation is to combine the novel two tier technique used here with the sinusoidal technique mentioned earlier in an attempt to improve both the efficiency and quality of the solutions.

References

[1] J. J. Hopfield and D. W. Tank, "Neural computation of decisions in optimization problems," *Biological Cybernetics*, vol. 52, pp. 141 – 152, 1985.

[2] S. V. B. Aiyer, M. Niranjan, and F. Fallside, "A theoretical investigation into the performance of the Hopfield model," *IEEE Trans. Neural Networks*, vol. 1, no. 2, pp. 204 – 215, 1990.

[3] P. G. Raeth, "An experiment with 3-D surface maps to illustrate neural network performance," in *Proc. International Neural Network Conference*, (Paris, France), pp. 733 – 737, 1990.

[4] S. U. Hedge, J. L. Sweet, and W. B. Levy, "Determination of parameters in a Hopfield/Tank computational network," *Proc. IEEE Intl. Conf. on Neural Networks*, pp. 291 – 298, 1988.

[5] Jayadeva and B. Bhaumik, "Optimization with neural networks: A recipe for improving convergence and solution quality," *Biological Cybernetics*, vol. 67, pp. 445 – 449, 1992.

[6] K. B. Sriram and L. M. Patnaik, "Neural network approach for the 2-dimensional assignment problem," *IEE Electronics Letters*, vol. 26, pp. 809 – 810, 7th. June 1990.

[7] H. Kita, H. Odani, and Y. Nishikawa, "Solving a placement problem by means of an analog neural network," *IEEE Trans. Industrial Electronics*, vol. 39, no. 6, pp. 543 – 551, 1992.

[8] G. V. Wilson and G. S. Pawley, "On the stability of the travelling salesman problem algorithm of Hopfield and Tank," *Biological Cybernetics*, vol. 58, pp. 63 – 70, 1988.

[9] P. W. Protzel, D. L. Palumbo, and M. K. Arras, "Performance and fault-tolerance of neural networks for optimization," *IEEE Trans. Neural Networks*, vol. 4, no. 4, pp. 600 – 614, 1993.

[10] W. K. Lai and G. G. Coghill, "A neural network for standard cell placement," *IEEE Trans. Systems, Man and Cybernetics*, 1993. Submitted for publication.

Neural Networks for the Set Covering Problem: An Application to the Test Vector Compaction

M. Aourid and B. Kaminska

Ecole Polytechnique de Montréal
Electrical Engineering Department
CP 6079, Succ. A, Montréal
Québec, Canada.

Abstract:

A new neural network architecture is proposed and evaluated for the set covering problem. The network is designed by using the connections between nonlinear and integer programming problems. This connection is based on the concavity and penalty function methods. The general objective function obtained, which combines the objective function and constraints, is fixed as the energy of the system. The network obtained was then applied to a practical problem in VLSI systems. The simulation results for the network show that the system can converge rapidly within a few neural time constants even for large scale problems.

I. INTRODUCTION

In integer optimization, modeling with boolean variables represents an important and widely used technique, the idea being to decide if an event x may or may not occur. In mathematics applications, several examples follow such as, the knapsack, traveling salesman, covering, sequencing and scheduling problems [1]. To solve such problems, a number of heuristics have been proposed [2]-[4]. The majority of cases, good solutions are yielded by heuristics, however they are never optimal. In this paper, based to our earlier work [6] a new neural network is introduced for solving the set covering problem. This problem has been applied to airline crew scheduling, various deliverly and distribution problems, logic design for computers, problems related to database and information retrieval, and many others. Recently, we have established an equivalence between test vector compaction (TVC) and the set covering problem (SCP), see [7] for further details on the compaction problem. The design of the model is based on the connection between the concave nonlinear and integer programming problems. The objective function for the concave problem is associated with a certain parameter μ which must be chosen appropriately to guarantee the equivalence. The linear constraints are incorporated in the objective function by using the penalty methods. The penalized terms are multiplied by a penalty parameter α that must be increased during the network computation. Specifically, an unconstrained problem is obtained. The general objective function for the unconstrained problem is considered to be the energy of the network. Consequently, for this energy function, we design and synthesize the network by applying Newton's equation [6],[8].

The paper is organized as follows: In section 2, we give a formulation of the set coverign problem. Section 3 describes the synthesis of the proposed network. The simulation results are given in section 4 and finally, conclusion follows in section 5.

II. FORMULATION OF THE 0-1 LINEAR PROGRAMMING PROBLEM

The set covering problem is defined by (1). Where d_{ji} is 0 or 1, and each a_i is a positive integer. The computational results for large scale set covering are reported in Balas [9], Etchebery [10]and others. Problem with n = 50-100 and m = 1000-2000 seem to be solvable in reasonable time. The most existed algorithms are based on the branch-and-bound type. An other method proposed by Nemhausser[11] consists on problem reduction by preprocessing. Based on our earlier work [6] and on [12] we can show easily that (SC) is equivalent to CM given in (2)

0-7803-1901-X/94 $4.00 ©1994 IEEE

$$SC:\quad \min f(x) = \sum_{i=1}^{n} a_i x_i$$

$$S.T. \begin{cases} \sum_{i=1}^{n} d_{ji} x_i \geq 1, & j = 1, 2, \ldots, m \\ x_i = 0 \text{ or } 1 \end{cases} \tag{1}$$

$$CM:\quad \min F_\mu(x) = \sum_{i=1}^{n} a_i x_i + \mu x_i (1 - x_i)$$

$$S.T. \begin{cases} Dx \geq e \\ 0 \leq x \leq e \end{cases} \tag{2}$$

where μ is large enough and e is a vector of ones. $D=[d_{ji}]$ is an mxn matrix and $x=[x_1,\ldots,x_n]$ is the unknown variable of the problem. To ensure the equivalence between (SC) and (CM), we must choose an appropriate μ such that F_μ becomes concave [6].

III. NEURAL NETWORK SYNTHESIS

The paradigms of neural networks in optimization applications consist in finding an energy function in which the lowest energy state corresponds to the solution of the optimization problem. An appropriate choice for the total energy function of a constrained problem is to incorporate all the constraints into the objective function by the penalty function, such that the minimum of the total objective function corresponds exactly to the solutions we are looking for. In this way, we obtain an energy function for the problem (P) defined as:

$$E(x, \mu, \alpha) = F_\mu(x) + \alpha P(x) \tag{3}$$

where α is a positif real and increasing parameter, called a penalty multiplier, P(x) is a nonnegative function and can be choosing as:

$$P(x) = \frac{1}{2} \sum_{j=1}^{m} \left[\min \left(0 , \sum_{k=1}^{n} d_{jk} x_k - 1 \right) \right]^2 \tag{4}$$

For this purpose, the (CM) is now equivalent to:

$$\min_{x \in I^n} E(x, \mu, \alpha) = \sum_{i=1}^{n} a_i x_i + \mu \sum_{i=1}^{n} x_i (1 - x_i) + \frac{\alpha}{2} \sum_{j=1}^{m} \left[\min \left(0, \sum_{i=1}^{n} d_{ji} x_i - 1\right) \right]^2 \tag{5}$$

Where I^n is the unit hypercube that represents the only constraints and can be ommited for the simple reason that by using the sigmoid function in the network these constraints hold every time.

Consequently, we can now derive the equations of motion for the system and the architecture by using the

Newton equation [9], [8], which give:

$$\begin{cases} c_i \dfrac{du_i}{dt} = -a_i - \mu(1-2x_i) - \alpha \sum_{j=1}^{m} d_{ji} \min(0, \sum_{k=1}^{n} d_{jk} x_k - 1) \\ x_i = g(u_i) \qquad for\ i=1,\ldots,n \end{cases} \tag{6}$$

These equations represent a set of nonlinear differential equations that govern the dynamics of the system. The activation function considered here is a sigmoid-like function with asymptotes 0 and 1, and is defined by:

$$x = g(u) = \begin{cases} 0 \quad if\ u < 0 \\ \dfrac{1}{2}\left(1 + \sin\left(\pi\left(\dfrac{u}{u_0} - \dfrac{1}{2}\right)\right)\right) \quad if\ 0 \le u \le u_0 \\ 1 \quad if\ u > u_0 \end{cases} \tag{7}$$

g is a continuously differentiable and monotonically increasing function which describes the input/output characteristics for each neuron i. The constant u_0 associated with each neuron represents, by analogy with the biological neuron, the threshold or the bias for the neuron. Note that when u_0 is very small, the function g tends to the Heaviside function and all solutions are integers.

According to the results given above we can show that the network is asymptotically stable in the Lyapunov sens. To show this we give the following theorem.

Theorem 1: The energy function given in (3) is a Lyapunov function in I^n for the network.

Proof: A Lyapunov function is positive definite, has continuous partial derivatives and its time derivative along any state trajectory is negative semidefinite.

Since $x^T(e-x)$ and P(x) are positive definite, then E(x) is also positive definite in I^n. In addition, E(x) is continuously differentiable. Thus it remains to show that E(x) is monotone nonincreasing along the trajectories.

Since g(.) is a monotonic increasing function and c_i is positive, then we can show that $dE/dt \le 0\ \forall\ t$. Therefore, the energy function E(x) is monotone nonincreasing along the trajectories, and hence it is a Lyapunov function for the network.

VI. SIMULATION RESULTS

To show the effectiveness of the proposed network, we have simulated equation (7) on a digital computer. To simulate time evolution, we used the fourth-order Runge-kutta method with step size $\nabla t=0.0001$. The regime for adapting the penalty parameter is as follows:

$$\begin{cases} \alpha_k = \alpha_{k-1} + 1 \\ \alpha_0 = 0 \end{cases}$$

We choose this sequence for the simple reason to make α_k to vary slowly. The parameters of the network have been fixed for all simulation examples and for all i=1,...,n as:

capacitors: $C_i=10^{-5}$Farad, resistances:$R_i=10^5$ Ohm, initial conditions: $x_i(0)=0$, and the bias for each neuron $u_0=0.01$.

We include two illustrative examples below.

Example 1: Let us consider the following set covering problem with 15 variables and 21 constraints:

$$\min f(x) = x_1 + x_2 + x_3 + x_4 + x_5 + x_6 + x_7 + x_8 + x_9 + x_{10} + x_{11} + x_{12} + x_{13} + x_{14} + x_{15}$$

$$\text{Subject to } \begin{cases} Dx \geq e \\ x_i \; 0 \text{ or } 1 \quad \text{for } i = 1,2,\ldots,15 \end{cases}$$

$$D = \begin{pmatrix} 1&0&1&1&1&1&0&1&0&1&0&0&1&0&0 \\ 1&0&0&0&1&0&1&0&1&0&0&0&0&0&1 \\ 1&0&1&0&1&1&1&1&0&0&0&0&0&1&0 \\ 1&1&1&0&0&0&1&0&0&0&0&1&0&0&1 \\ 0&1&0&1&0&0&0&0&1&1&1&0&0&0&0 \\ 0&0&0&0&0&1&0&0&1&0&0&0&0&0&1 \end{pmatrix} \quad \text{and} \quad e = \begin{pmatrix} 1\\1\\1\\1\\1\\1 \end{pmatrix}$$

The optimal solution for this problem by using CPLEX program [13] is $x_1=x_9=1$ and other variables are 0. When applaying our approach, the state variables $u_i(t)$ for $\mu=12$ are shown in Fig.1. Note that, the network converges to the global minimum after 9 iterations. To make this clear, solution variables x_i (output of the activation function) generated by the network are given in Table 1.

Table 1: Solutions variables for 16 iterations

k	Output of different neurons														
	x_1	x_2	x_3	x_4	x_5	x_6	x_7	x_8	x_9	x_{10}	x_{11}	x_{12}	x_{13}	x_{14}	x_{15}
0	0	0	0	0	0	0	0	0	0	0	0	0	0	0	0
1	0	0	0	0	0	0	0	0	0	0	0	0	0	0	0
2	0	0	0	0	0	0	0	0	0	0	0	0	0	0	0
3	0	0	0	0	0	0	0	0	0	0	0	0	0	0	0
4	0	0	0	0	0	0	0	0	0	0	0	0	0	0	0
5	1	0	0	0	0	0	0	0	0	0	0	0	0	0	0
6	1	0	0	0	0	0	0	0	0	0	0	0	0	0	0
7	1	0	0	0	0	0	0	0	0	0	0	0	0	0	0
8	1	0	0	0	0	0	0	0	0	0	0	0	0	0	0
9	1	0	0	0	0	0	0	0	1	0	0	0	0	0	0
10	1	0	0	0	0	0	0	0	1	0	0	0	0	0	0
11	1	0	0	0	0	0	0	0	1	0	0	0	0	0	0
12	1	0	0	0	0	0	0	0	1	0	0	0	0	0	0
13	1	0	0	0	0	0	0	0	1	0	0	0	0	0	0
14	1	0	0	0	0	0	0	0	1	0	0	0	0	0	0
15	1	0	0	0	0	0	0	0	1	0	0	0	0	0	0

From this result we can see that the network converges correctly to the optimal solution and the solution is asymptotically stable. In the next example we applied our network to the test vectors compaction problem.

Example 2: The test vector compaction can be defined as: Given an ATPG (Automatic Test Pattern Generator) [14] and a combinational circuit with m faults, the ATPG may generate a test set to ensure maximum fault coverage (i.e. to detect large numbers of faults). The question here is if it is possible to eliminate some test vectors without compromising the fault coverage [15]. To show this, we take the benchmark circuit C432 from ISCAS-85 [16]. The C432 has 524 collapsed faults. The ATPG applied to this circuit generates 76 vectors. Consequently, we construct a matrix D, such that:

$$d_{ji} = \begin{cases} 1 & \textit{if fault } f_j \textit{ is detected by vector } v_i \\ 0 & \textit{if not} \end{cases}$$

D is a 524x76 matrix that defines the functional constraints. Before solving the problem we reduce the size of the constraint by computing the equivalent faults [15]. This procedure is called preprocessing. So we obtain a reduced problem, see table 2.

Table 2: Matrix size D(mxn) before and after preprocessing

	Number of vectors:n	Number of fault: m
Before preprocessing	76	524
After preprocessing	76	196

According to table 2, we see that preprocessing procedure is very usfull in the sens that it allows us to reduce the number of constraints by eliminating the redundent constraints. In the following table we give the comparison between CPLEX's results and our approach for the circuit C432 after preprocessing.

Table: Compaction of test set size

	CYPLEX	Our Approach
Solution	52	56

We can see that the network reduces the test size by 20 (i.e. 76-56). The solution given by CPLEX is the optimal (global) one. In our case we have fixed μ at 12 and the initial conditions at 0 for simplicity. However, to reach a global minimum by our approach it suffices to vary the parameter μ [6].

V. CONCLUSION

The application of artificial neural networks in optimization problems, and especially in combinatorial optimization, continues to be a very promising field. However, the results obtained up to now are limited by the size of problems and the quality of the solution space. To improve the design of the network, and consequently of the solutions, we have combined the techniques of ANN with those of mathematical programming in such a way as to exploit the advantages of both. We have showed by simulation results that the network can find the optimal solution within a few neural time constants even for large scale problems.

Bibliography:

[1] G.L. Nemhauser, L.A. Wolsey, Integer and Combinatorial Optimization, J.Wiley, 1988

[2] P.J.M Van Laarhoven, A.H.L. Aarts, Simulated Annealing: Theory and Applications, Kluwer Academic Publishers, 1992

[3] F.Glover, " Tabu Search ", CAAI Report 88-3, University of Colorado, Boulder 1988.

[4] J.J. Hopfield, J.W. Tank, " Neural Computation of Decisions in Optimization Problems " Biol. Cybern. 52, 141-152, 1985.

[5] D. W. Tank, J. J. Hopfield, " Simple `Neural` Optimization Networks: an A/D Converter, Signal Decision Circuit, and a Linear Programming Circuit ", IEEE Trans. on CAS, Vol.33, No.5, pp. 533-541, 1986.

[6] M. Aourid, B. Kaminska," Minimization of Pseudo-Boolean Programming Problem Under Linear Constraints by Using Neural Networks" Submitted to IEEE Trans. on Neural Networks.

[7] I. Pomeranz et. al.," COMPACTEST: A Method to Generate Compact Test Sets for Combinational Circuits" 1991 Inernational Test Conference, pp. 194-203.

[8] M. Aourid and B. Kaminska, "Neural Networks for Solving the Quadratic 0-1 Programming Problem Under Linear Constraints", ICNN'93 San Francisco, Vol. III, pp. 1092-1095

[9] E. Balas and A. Ho, "Set Covering: Algorithms Using Cutting Planes, heuristics, and Subgradient Optimization: A Computational Study", Mathematical programming 12 (1980), pp.37-60
[10] J. Etcheberry, " The Set Covering Problem: A New Implicit Enumeratin Algorithm", Operations Research, Vol.25, No.5, 1977, pp.760-772.
[11] R. Garfinkel and G. Nemhausser, Integer Programming, (Wiley, New York) 1969.
[12] F. Giannessi, F. Niccolucci, " Connections between Nonlinear and Integer Programming Problems", Symposia Mathematica - Vol. XIX, Convegno dell'Aprile 1974.
[13] CPLEX, Using the CPLEX Callable Library and CPLEX Mixed Integer Library, 1992 Cplex Optimization.
[14] P. Goel, " An Implicit Enumeration Algorithm to Generate Tests for Combinational Logic Circuits", IEEE Trans. on Computers, Vol. C-30, pp. 215-222, Mar. 1981.
[15] M. Aourid and B. Kaminska, "On the Equivalence Between Test vector Compaction and the Set Covering problem", submitted to IEEE Trans. on Computers.
[16] F. Berlez and H. Fujiwara, " A Neutral Netlist of 10 Combinational Benchmark Designs and a special Translator in Fortran", ISCAS, June 1985.

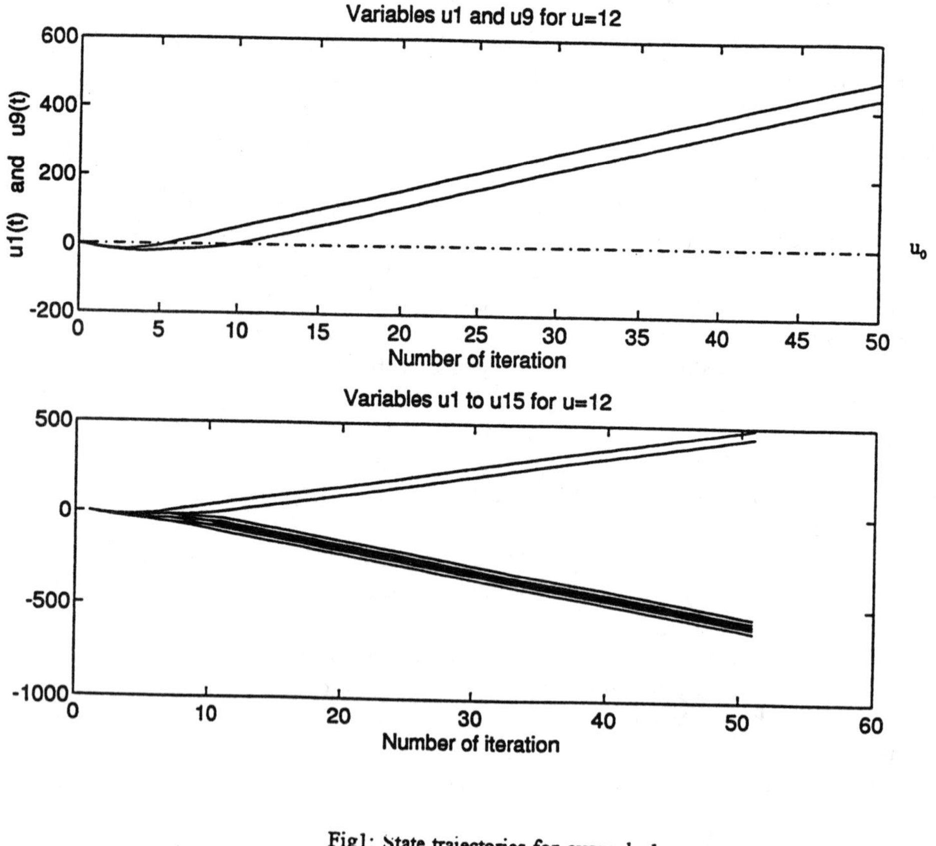

Fig1: State trajectories for example 1

INTENTIONALLY LEFT BLANK

Dynamic Neural Network with Heuristics

Jeon Gue Park, Jong Man Park, Dou Seok Kim, Chong Hyun Lee,
Sang Weon Suh, and Mun Sung Han

Systems Engineering Research Institute
Korea Institute of Science and Technology
P.O.Box 1, Yusung, Taejon,
305-600 Korea
e-mail: jgpark@phoenix.seri.re.kr

ABSTRACT

With the deterministic nature and the difficulty of scaling, Hopfield-style neural network is readily to converge to one of local minima in the course of energy function minimization, not to escape from those undesirable solutions. Wilson and Pawley[11] criticizes those defects of the Hopfield networks, and many researchers, who want to find the global minimum of the Traveling Salesman Problem(TSP), have introduced various approaches to solve such conditions using heuristics, genetic algorithms, hybrid algorithms of some methods, etc.

We introduce a simple heuristic algorithm which embedds the classical local search heuristics into the optimization neural network. The proposed algorithm is characterized with the best neighbors selection, which is used in the dynamic scheduling[8] and in ordering the update sequence of neurons, and with the decidability check which is used to guarantee the near-optimal solution. The proposed algorithm enhances both the convergence speed and the quality of solutions.

1 Introduction

The TSP is a well-known *NP-complete* problem and is a Hamiltonian cycle which asked for a tour which has minimum cost. Using dynamic programming, the worst case time complexity will not be any better than $O(n^2 2^n)$. And none of the conventional methods has found satisfactory results to solve such NP-complete problems.[5]

The explosive nature of NP-complete problems says that the problems are practically unsolvable when the sizes are large. But in many practical situations, the near optimum is sufficiently useful to some limited applications. In this point of view, Hopfield and Tank proposed a neural network model for solving optimization problem, and simulated the TSP as an example[3]. Though lots of researchers have tried to improve the Hopfield/Tank algorithm, no satisfactory refinement has been found. Most of those modified algorithms include the modification of the Hopfield/Tank original formula, the hybrid algorithms combining the neural network with the classical optimization methods such as divide-and-counquer, branch-and-bound, deterministic local search, etc. [9, 1, 8, 6, 7, 2, 10, 11]

Above all, their general approaches are as follows :

1. To determine proper values of the parameters involved
2. To set good objective function
3. To choose good transfer function
4. To determine the connection strength T_{ij} and bias I_i according to 1.
5. To get the global minima by simulating the neuro-dynamics based on T_{ij} and I_i

In general, the basic idea of these approaches is to find the global minima, keeping the characteristics of the Lyapunov function. In the original paper of Hopfield/Tank[3, 4], the energy function for TSP of the analog neural networks is defined as follows :

$$E = \frac{A}{2}\sum_{x}\sum_{i}\sum_{j \neq i} V_{xi}V_{xj} + \frac{B}{2}\sum_{i}\sum_{x}\sum_{y \neq x} V_{xi}V_{yi} + \frac{C}{2}\left(\sum_{x}\sum_{i} V_{xi} - n\right)^2$$

$$+\frac{D}{2}\sum_{x}\sum_{y \neq x}\sum_{i} d_{xy}V_{xi}\left(V_{y,i+1} + V_{y,i-1}\right)$$

The energy function evaluated and minimized on the state space of the $2N$ corners of the N-dimensional hypercube by $V_i = 0$ or 1, has local minima if and only if each row contains no more than one 1, each column no more than one 1, and there are n entries of 1 in the entire matrix.

In the process of minimization, the offset hyperbolic tangent form of the gain curve is chosen to resemble the real neural input-output relation as well as the characteristics of a simple transistor amplifier. Thus they describe the dynamics of the optimization neural networks as following equation :

$$\frac{du_{xi}}{dt} = -\frac{u_{xi}}{\tau} - A\sum_{j \neq i} V_{xj} - B\sum_{y \neq x} V_{yi} - C\left(\sum_{x}\sum_{j} V_{xj} - n\right) - D\sum_{y} d_{xy}\left(V_{y,i+1} + V_{y,i-1}\right)$$

$$V_{xi} = g\left(U_{xi}\right) = \frac{1}{2}\left(1 + \tanh\frac{U_{xi}}{U_0}\right)$$

Unfortunately, the deterministic nature of the Hopfield/Tank network, which minimizes a global energy function, is heavily dependent on initial values of parameters and variables. With this nature, the original network is apt to converge to local minima, never to escape from this stationary point. Thus, it is very important to use appropriate ranges of randomized initial states and of some multipliers. Furthermore when the TSP is simulated with neural networks, the inter-relationships among the variables are very complex to be refined decisively.

2 Dynamic Neural Network with Heuristic

As we introduce several concepts to find the global or near optimum, our modified network is not any more dependent on the initial values or parameters. The main idea is summed up in the following three heuristics: the neuro-dynamics scheduling, the selective attention to the city of maxinum possibility to be fired and to the best neighbors, and finally the decidability check. In Han's paper[8], the concept of scheduling and the selective attention to the city of maximum possibility are explained with its detailed algorithm.

Hence we introduce here the best neighbor and the decidability check.

Best Neighbors Selection : The word 'dynamic' results from our new scheduling scheme by the weights and priority mechanism. Once a city is visited(or fired), the network refers to the distance matrix and gives weight to the two cities of minimum inter-city distance among its neighbors not visited yet. The effects of this modification not only give the visit priority to the cities of minimum inter-city distance, but also control the whole visiting sequence in Hamiltonian cycle. Figure 1 shows the relationship among the city visited and the two cities of minimum inter-city distance; When a city X is fired, then the first city Z and the second city Y of minimum distances are selected for ordering the update sequences, as long as the selected cities are not fired yet, and for weighting the connection strengths. The best neighbors selected is used in the dynamic scheduling[8] and in ordering the update sequence of neurons.

if a city is visited

for (the city visited) X

$$Z \leftarrow min_{1 \le i \le n} \{distance\,(X, X_i)\}$$
$$Y \leftarrow min_{1 \le i \le n} \{distance\,(X, X_i)\}\; where Z \neq Y$$

where $X, Y, Z, and X_i\ (i = 1, .., n)$ *are cities and* n *is number of cities*

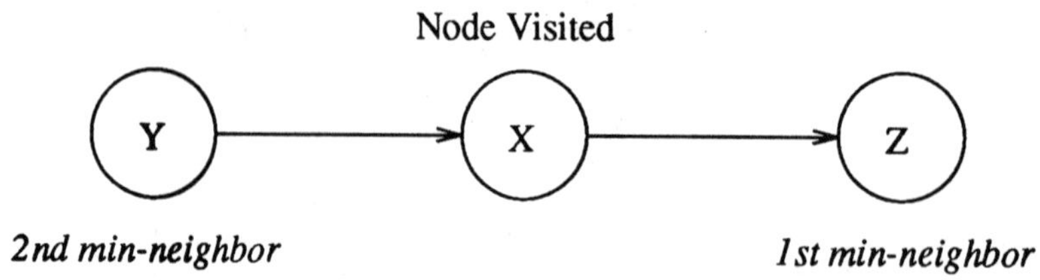

Figure 1. Ordering the city visited and its neighbors of minimum distances

Decidability Check : As for the combinatorial optimization problems, one can hardly know the decided path of TSP is optimum. In this point of view, we introduce a heuristics what is called *goodness value.* While the above trial is proceeding, we check the validity and consistency of the given tour; that is every row and column contains only one 1 respectively and there are exactly n entries of 1 in the entire matrix. If those conditions are satisfied, we check the number of wrong decisions that occured on the tour, refering to the distance matrix. The wrong decision means the network fails to select the next city of minimum distance. During this process, the occurrence of right decisions is enumerated and this enumerated number is just goodness value. The goodness means the best neighbors condition above mentioned, $Y \rightarrow X \rightarrow Z$. If the goodness value goes over some limit ε, we decide that the tour is acceptable. In this paper, we set ε to about 7 of its maximum 10. The value of ε is due to the idea that the near optimum is sufficiently useful to some practical applications.

```
GoodnessValue ← 0
for every city fired, X
        if the city X is placed in such a position that the path
           Y → X → Z is locally minimal
                then GoodnessValue ← GoodnessValue + 1
if GoodnessValue > ε
        then terminate
        else re-schedule and re-tour
```

3 Simulation and Results

Results in this section refer to parameter sets at or near $A, B = 100, C = 1000, u_0 = 0.02, n = 5, 10, 15, 20, 25, 30, 50, and 100$, and the step constant 10^{-5}. In five cities example, we use the distance matrix in Table 1. As we can see, all the distances are in the very simple format of 10^{-2} for easy calculation of optimum solution for a given size of cities. And for the examples of larger size of cities, the similar uniform distribution distance matrices are used.

Figure 2 and Table 2 demonstrates the solution quality of the three algorithms; the original one, the scheduled one[8], and the proposed one. The proposed algorithm enhance the convergence speed and the quality of solution of the other two algorithms. For fairness, we used the same initial values and parameters for all three algorithms, and did not try to tune the initial parameters.

	A	B	C	D	E
A	∞	0.04	0.01	0.08	0.09
B	0.04	∞	0.04	0.01	0.08
C	0.01	0.04	∞	0.01	0.10
D	0.08	0.01	0.01	∞	0.05
E	0.09	0.08	0.10	0.05	∞

Table 1: Distance Matrix of five cities example, optimum tour length=0.19

algorithm/cities	5	10	15	20	25	30	50	100
Original	0.23	0.50	0.98	1.08	1.81	1.90	3.23	5.21
Scheduled	0.21	0.45	0.94	0.99	1.59	1.53	2.82	5.07
Proposed	0.19	0.32	0.81	0.85	1.23	1.25	1.83	4.07

Table 2: Tour Length Comparison of the three algorithms

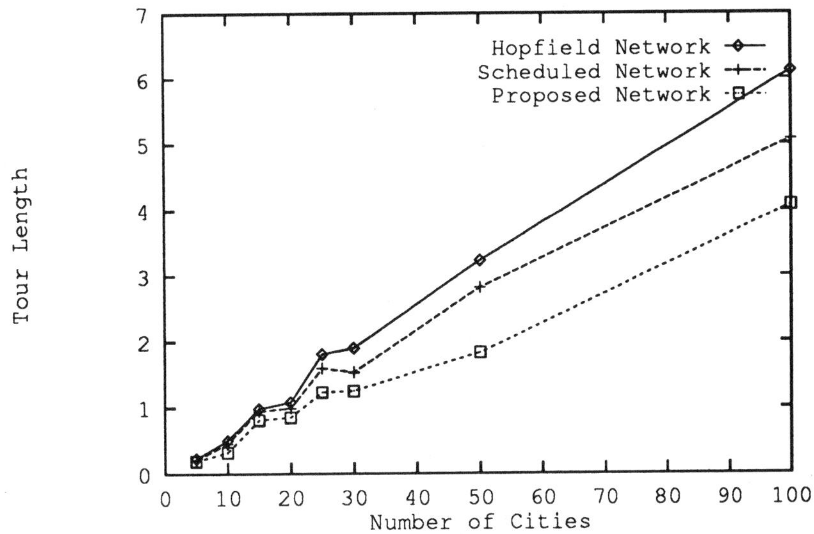

Figure 2. Tour Length Comparison of the three algorithms

In Table 3 compares the number of iterations between the original Hopfield/Tank neural network and our scheduled neural network when complete the convergence. It shows that the scheduled network converges in some constant time though the size of the cities grows. But in case of the original network, the larger the size of cities is the slower the convergence is, as expected.

algorithm/cities	5	10	15	20	25	30	50	100
Original	221	447	1501	4063	7890	15650	50110	129430
Scheduling	202	392	437	481	262	333	399	389

Table 3: Iterations in original and scheduled/proposed neural network

4 Conclusion

In this paper, we introduced a heuristic method to enhance the convergence speed and the scaling behavior of the Hopfield neural networks. The main idea is embedding the classical deterministic local search techniques into the optimization neural networks. Though it is not satisfactory, the modified algorithm shows great improvements over the original Hopfield networks, and is no longer dependent on the initial values or parameters.

At the same time, we confirm that there are lots of remains to be discussed such as the conditions search for better scheduling, the global strategy which integrates the local search heuristics to find optimum solution, the comparison with existing heuristic-emdedded neural networks, etc.

References

[1] Y. P. Simon Foo and H. Szu. Solving large-scale optimization problems by divide-and-conquer neural network. In *International Joint Conference on Neural Network*, volume 1, pages 507–511, 1989.

[2] A. Tsirukis G. Reklaitis and M. Tenorio. Generalized hopfield networks and nonlinear optimization. In *Neural Information Processing System*, volume 2, pages 355–362, 1985.

[3] J. Hopfield and D. Tank. Neural computation of decisions in optimization problems. *Biological Cybernetics*, 52:141–152, 1985.

[4] J. Hopfield and D. Tank. Simple neural optimization networks: An a/d converter, signal decision circuit and linear programming circuit. *IEEE Trans. on Circuits and Systems*, CAS-33:533–541, 1986.

[5] E. Horowitz and S. Sahni. *Fundamentals of Computer Algorithm.* Computer Science Press, 1978.

[6] B. Kamgar-Paris and B. Kamgar-Paris. An efficient model of neural networks for optimization. In *International Joint Conference on Neural Network*, volume 3, pages 785–790, 1987.

[7] R. Lister. Segment reversal and the traveling salesman problem. In *International Joint Conference on Neural Network*, volume 1, pages 424–427, 1990.

[8] C. H. Lee M. S. Han and J. G. Park. Scheduling the neuro-dynamics in hopfield-tank neural network. In *World Congress on Neural Network*, volume 4, pages 358–362, 1993.

[9] A. J. Laub R. D. Brandt, Y. Wang and S. K. Mitra. Alternative networks for solving the traveling salesman problem and the list-matching problem. In *International Conference on Neural Network*, volume 2, pages 333–340, 1988.

[10] H. Szu. Fast tsp algorithm based on binary neuron output and analog neuron input using the zero-diagonal interconnect matrix and necessary and sufficient constraints of the permutation matrix. In *International Joint Conference on Neural Network*, volume 2, pages 259–266, 1987.

[11] G. Wilson and G. Pawley. On the stability of the travelling salesman problem algorithm of hopfield and tank. *Biological Cybernetics*, 58:63–70, 1988.

Comparison of Neural Network and Genetic Algorithms for a Resource Allocation Problem

Yuri Owechko and Soheil Shams

Hughes Research Laboratories
3011 Malibu Canyon Rd. RL69
Malibu, CA 90265
owechko@maxwell.hac.com, shams@maxwell.hac.com

Abstract

We compare neural network and genetic algorithm solutions of a resource allocation problem and discuss the relative asymptotic scaling of the two approaches in terms of time and space complexity. We show that for this problem neural networks and genetic algorithms perform similarly.

1. Introduction

Artificial Neural Networks (NN) and Genetic Algorithms (GA) have demonstrated a high degree of effectiveness at solving difficult combinatorial optimization problems.[1,2,3,4,5] Neural networks used for optimization fall in the category of unsupervised feed-back models, such as the Hopfield net[6], elastic net[7], self-organizing feature maps[8], and constraint net[9]. It has been shown recently that the underlying computation performed by these networks can be viewed as a "natural" optimization of the effective free energy in statistical mechanics.[10] Genetic algorithms, on the other hand, find good solutions to optimization problems using the Darwinian principles of natural selection.[11]

In this paper we compare the NN and GA techniques for solving a realistic resource allocation optimization problem. This problem consists of the assignment of weapons of various types to different-valued targets so as to cause maximum total damage. A target can also be damaged indirectly by assigning a weapon to another target linked to it. A GA solution of this Weapon-Target-Allocation (WTA) problem has been developed by the C^3I group in the Systems Sector of GM-Hughes Electronics.[12] We have reformulated this problem as a quadratic optimization problem and derived a Hopfield neural network solution. The computational complexity of each approach has been determined and compared. We have also explored trade-offs in parallel implementations of each approach. The problem definition will be presented in detail in the following section. In section 3 the mapping of the problem onto the neural network is discussed. The relative performance of the two approaches are discussed in Section 4. Concluding remarks are presented in Section 5.

2. Problem Definition

As mentioned in the introductory section, the specific resource allocation problem we are considering involves generating an assignment of N_w weapons to N_t targets in such a way that the total residual target strength is minimized. In this scenario each target i has an initial strength value v_i. A weapon j assigned to a target i will reduce the target strength by a factor P_{ij}. In our formulation, the assignment variable X_{ij} is defined as having a value of one if weapon j is assigned to target i, and zero otherwise. The percentage of direct damage caused to a specific target i based on a specific assignment matrix X_{ij} can now be calculated as

$$d_i = 1 - \prod_{j=1}^{N_w} \left(1 - P_{ij} X_{ij}\right). \tag{1}$$

An interesting complication arises when we consider the interdependence relationship among various targets. In a realistic scenario, a target i might be dependent on a different target j to a certain degree a_{ij}, where a_{ij} is an element of the connectivity matrix **A**. Therefore, if target j is damaged, target i will also incur some indirect damage proportional to a_{ij}. Of course this indirect damage can be propagated back from target j to target k who is dependent on j by a factor of a_{jk} (see Figure 1). Consequently, the total damage associated with a specific target i can be calculated as

$$w_i = d_i + e_i(1 - d_i), \tag{2}$$

0-7803-1901-X/94 $4.00 ©1994 IEEE

where e_i is the total indirect damage factor for target i. Note that e_i affects only the portion of target i remaining after direct damage.

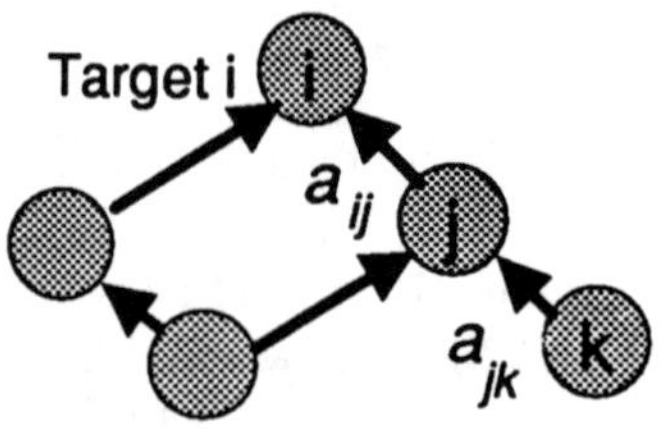

Fig. 1. Dependency graph for targets in weapon allocation problem.

The indirect damage e_i is calculated as

$$e_i = \sum_{k=1}^{N_t} a_{ik} d_k + \sum_{k=1}^{N_t} \sum_{l=1}^{N_t} a_{ik} a_{kl} (1 - d_k) d_l + \sum_{k=1}^{N_t} \sum_{l=1}^{N_t} \sum_{m=1}^{N_t} a_{ik} a_{kl} a_{lm} (1 - d_l)(1 - d_k) d_l + \cdots . \tag{3}$$

This equation can be simplified by defining $b_{jk} = a_{jk}(1 - d_j)$ and rewriting (3) as

$$e_i = \sum_{k=1}^{N_t} a_{ik} d_k + \sum_{k=1}^{N_t} \sum_{l=1}^{N_t} a_{ik} b_{kl} d_l + \sum_{k=1}^{N_t} \sum_{l=1}^{N_t} \sum_{m=1}^{N_t} a_{ik} b_{kl} b_{lm} d_l + \cdots . \tag{4}$$

Equation (4) can now be put into a matrix-vector form and further simplified as

$$\mathbf{e} = \mathbf{Ad} + \mathbf{ABd} + \mathbf{AB}^2\mathbf{d} + \cdots, \qquad \text{or}$$

$$\mathbf{e} = \mathbf{A}(\mathbf{I} - \mathbf{B})^{-1}\mathbf{d}, \qquad \text{where } b_{ij} = a_{ij}(1 - d_i). \tag{5}$$

An obvious constraint on the matrix A is that no target is dependent on other targets more than 100%. With this constraint we can see that the total damage caused to a target i is limited to the range $0<w_i<1$.

In this weapon allocation scenario, each target i has a specific value v_i. The objective of the allocation algorithm is to assign the weapons to targets such that the total target value is minimized. Stated differently, we would like to find an assignment that will maximize the total damage D, defined as

$$D = \sum_{i=1}^{N_t} w_i v_i \tag{6}$$

This can be achieved using a neural network system where each neuron represents one of the elements of the assignment matrix **X**. Therefore, the state of neuron X_{ij}, after network convergence, determines whether weapon j is assigned to target i or not. The formulation of an appropriate neural network to solve this optimal allocation problem is presented in the next section.

3. Neural Network Solution of Weapon Allocation Problem

Cohen and Grossberg[13] as well as Hopfield[14], published seminal papers on the dynamics and Lyapunov functions of neural networks. Specifically, Hopfield studied a fully connected neural network governed by the set of differential equations

$$\frac{du_i}{dt} = -\frac{u_i}{\tau} + \sum_{j}^{n} T_{ij} X_j + I_i \tag{7}$$

where X_i=g(u_i) is the activation value of neuron i, g() is the sigmoidal neuron transfer function, T_{ij} is the weight matrix, τ is the neuron time constant, and I_i is an external input. He showed that a Lyapunov or "energy" function for the system is given by

$$E^H = -\frac{1}{2}\sum_i^n\sum_j^n T_{ij}X_iX_j - \sum_i^n I_iX_i + \frac{1}{\tau}\sum_i^n\int_0^{X_i} g^{-1}(V)dV \tag{8}$$

The above quantity monotonically decreases as the system evolves in time. Therefore, if one can map parameters of an optimization problem to the weight matrix T and input vector I so that minima in E^H correspond to valid solutions, the neural network can then be used to solve the problem by allowing the network to evolve until it reaches equilibrium. We mapped the WTA problem to the above form and included terms for both the objective (maximizing target damage) and constraints (limited number of weapons, assign each weapon to only one target, and neuron values of 1 or 0). Terms higher than quadratic order in the X_i variables were neglected so as to allow the term by term matching of the objective function with the NN energy function (Eq. (8)). In the general case, the resultant weight matrix is of size $(N_tN_w)^2$ which accounts for every combination of weapons and targets. In practice, the weight matrix, however, reflects the sparseness of the target connectivity graph, aside from an additive constant. Since weapon dependency graphs for realistic scenarios tend to be quite sparse, the storage requirements can be significantly reduced from the general case. As discussed in Section 5, taking into account the indistinguishability of weapons of the same type will result in further dramatic decreases in the storage requirements.

4. Comparison of Neural Network and Genetic Algorithm

4.1 Relative Performance

The NN was tested on three WTA scenerios of increasing size supplied by Hughes Systems Sector. The small, medium, and large problems consisted of 16 targets/6 weapons (N_t/N_w), 50 targets/20 weapons, and 100 targets/20 weapons, respectively. Weapons consisted of two types with differing destructive effects on three types of targets. The small 16/6 problem was used for initial testing of the NN and for attempts to understand the nature of the energy surface for the WTA problem. The medium and large problems are closer to realistic problem sizes and were used for comparison with GA solutions. The quality of the NN solution is dependent on several parameter settings, including the sigmoid gain β, time constant τ, and the objective and constraint weighting factors λ_{obj} and λ_{con}. The small 16 target problem was used to determine "good" parameter values which were then scaled proportionally for larger problems.

A useful method for studying the energy surface was to examine 2-D cross-sections of the 96-dimensional configuration space for the 16/20 problem. The domains of the plots were chosen so as to contain two randomly selected solutions to the WTA problem, $\mathbf{X_1}$ and $\mathbf{X_2}$. Specifically, the domain was constructed as $\mathbf{X}=c_1\mathbf{X_1}+c_2\mathbf{X_2}$. We then plotted $E_{tot}(X)$ as a function of c_1 and c_2, as shown in Fig. 2. A typical energy surface for the low gain case (β=0.01) is shown in Fig. 2a. As discussed by Hopfield, for low gain the energy is dominated by the last term in Eq. 8 and the problem-specific terms are negligible. The energy surface becomes a bowl and all neuron values tend towards 0.5. In Fig. 2b, β is increased to 2 and the objective portion of the energy function is set to zero. Note that, as desired, minima occur for (c_1,c_2)=(1,0) and (0,1) which correspond to the $\mathbf{X_1}$ and $\mathbf{X_2}$ solutions. The two solutions have equal energy values since the objective weighting factor (λ_{obj}) is zero. In Fig. 2c the objective factor is set equal to the constraint factor, resulting in the $\mathbf{X_1}$ and $\mathbf{X_2}$ solutions having different energies. Note also that the locations of the energy minima are shifted slightly from the valid solutions. (Thresholding the neuron activation values results in valid solutions). Finally, note that if the objective factor is too large, as in Fig. 2d, the energy is not minimized near an allowable solution and invalid solutions result even after thresholding. By making many such plots for this problem, we found that for a large range of parameters the energy landscape appears to be relatively smooth and devoid of local minima at illegal solutions. This was borne out in the simulations where it was not difficult to avoid illegal solutions.

Both the NN and the GA were used to solve the medium and large WTA problems. In the case of the NN, the relative values of the constraint and objective factors were not changed from the small problem. However, we did scale them as the problem size increased. We also found that adding a small amount of noise improved the consistency of the NN solutions. In Fig. 3 histograms of NN, GA, and random solutions are plotted. For the parameters used, in which the objective term was heavily weighted, approximately half of the NN runs resulted in valid solutions. The NN solutions are consistently four standard deviations better than random solutions. For the 50 target/20 weapon problem the NN and GA solutions are very close in performance. The robustness of the two solutions are similar also, e.g. uncertainty in the target dependency matrix had similar effects on both. The GA outperformed the NN on the 100 target/20 weapon problem, which may be due to the searching of a much larger solution space by the NN (see Section 5).

4.2 Computational Complexity

The comparison between the quality of the results obtained by each technique was discussed in the previous section. In this section we will analyze the remaining issues of computational complexity and parallelization methods for each approach. Serial C language implementations of both the GA and NN WTA solutions were executed on a DEC Alpha computer. Table 1 shows the timing results.

No. Targets/No. Weapons	Neural Network Execution Time (sec.)	Genetic Algorithm Execution Time (sec.)
50/20	6	7
100/20	23	28

Table 1. - Execution times of NN and GA programs written in C on DEC Alpha computer. No parallelization was done.

In order to assess the scaling characteristics of each approach, we have calculated the computational complexity of each algorithm based on the following parameter values: P - the population size of the GA; m - the number of generations used in the GA (which we assume to be on the same order as the number of iterations used by the NN to converge to a solution); N - the number of elements in the solution assignment matrix (which is the number of neurons used in the NN and the chromosome size used in the GA), e.g. $N=N_wN_t$ when unique weapons are assigned to each target; and μ - the sparsity factor of the NN interconnection network. The computational complexity of the neural network is rather simple to calculate since it is essentially a series of matrix-vector products. Table 2 shows the various asymptotic complexities associated with the use of the NN.

	Neural Network	Neural Network ($\mu \approx 1/\sqrt{N}$)
Space Complexity	$O(\mu N^2)$	$O(N^{3/2})$
Time Complexity	$O(m\mu N^2)$	$O(mN^{3/2})$
Parallel Implementation[1]	$O(mN)$	$O(mN)$
Parallel Implementation[2]	$O(m\mu N)$	$O(mN^{1/2})$
Parallel Implementation[3]	$O(m)$	$O(m)$

Table 2 - Computational complexities associated with the implementation of the NN algorithm. The parallel implementations assume N processing elements: (1) N systolic processors.[15] (2) N-processor DREAM machine.[16] (3) N fully-interconnected analog electronic[17] or optical[18] processors.

	Genetic Algorithm
Space Complexity	$O(PN)$
Time Complexity	$O(mPN)$
Parallel Implementation[1]	$O(m\nu PN)$
Parallel Implementation[2]	$O(mN)$
Parallel Implementation[3]	$O(m)$

Table 3 - The complexities associated with the implementation of the genetic algorithm. The parameter ν indicates the degree of the interconnectivity used in the parallel processing architecture. The range of values for ν are between one (in case of a single bus broadcast architecture) to $1/P$ in case of a fully interconnected (crossbar) architecture: (1) P processors in master/slave architecture. (2) Assumes recombination of genetic material takes place between P locally connected processors. (3) Same as 2 except PN processors are used.

The calculation of the computational complexity of the genetic algorithm is more difficult as it requires a number of different operations (e.g., reproduction, selection, crossover, etc.). The complexities outlined in Table 3 for the GA were arrived at under the assumption that an efficient "tournament" selection algorithm for the reproduction phase is employed with a computational complexity of $O(P)$.[19] It should be noted here that the constant multiplicitive factor for the GA complexity is much larger than that of the neural net.

5. Conclusions

In interpreting the relative performance of the NN and GA it should be kept in mind that the NN formulated here assumes *distinguishable* weapons. The GA, on the other hand, assumes *indistinguishable* weapons where each weapon is labeled only by its type. The solution space searched by the NN is therefore of much higher dimension than the one searched by the GA. For the 50 target/20 weapon problem, the NN search space is larger by 13 orders of magnitude. This fact may be the reason for the lower performance of the NN on the larger problem shown in Fig. 3b. We are currently modifying the NN to incorporate the assumption that weapons are labeled only by their type. At the very least this modification will greatly reduce the storage and processing requirements of the NN solution and improve the scaling performance.

In conclusion, our experience with NNs and GAs in solving this particular WTA problem has shown both approaches to be competitive in terms of both performance and implementation scaling characteristics. However, this cannot be said for other application areas. In cases where the optimization objective function cannot be transformed into the Hopfield energy function, a GA approach might be more suitable. On the other hand, NN appear to be more suitable for efficient implemention in dedicated hardware for real-time embedded applications.

Acknowledgments

This work was partially supported by Hughes Systems Sector. We wish to thank B. H. Soffer, S. T. Toborg, and W. Przytula for helpful discussions and K. Steinhoff for assistance with the GA program code.

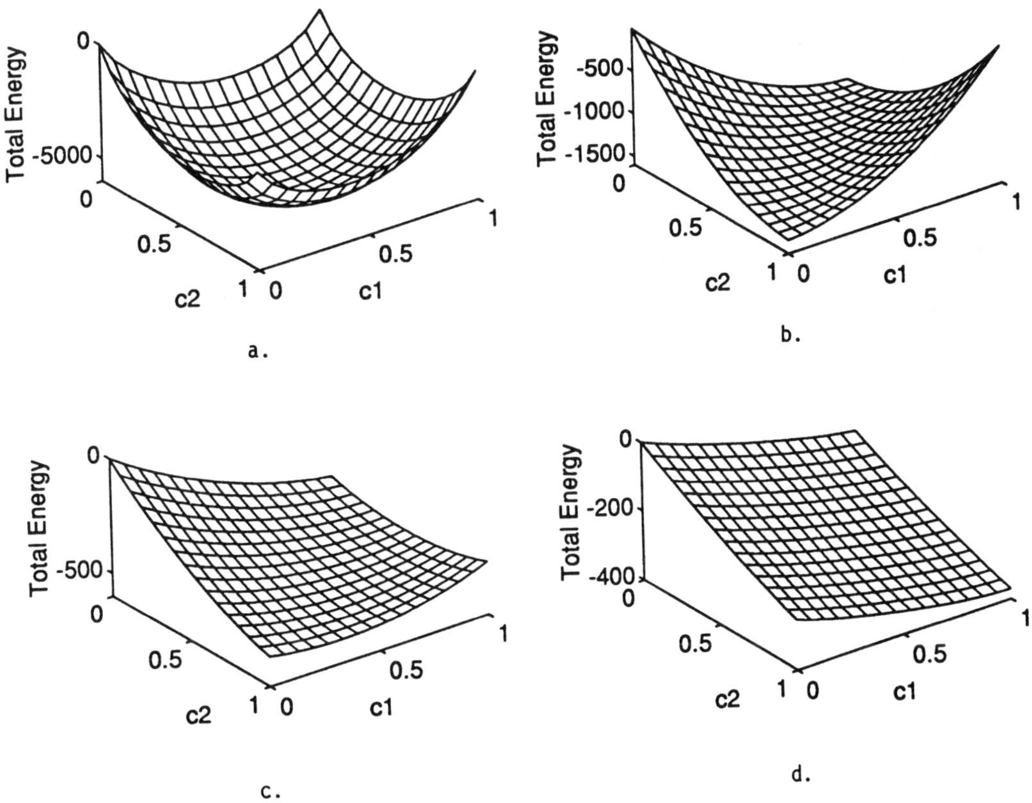

Fig. 2. Energy surfaces plotted on 2-D planes through the space of neuron activation values. The total energy including objective and constraint terms is plotted as a function of c_1 and c_2 where the neuron activation vector is given by $\mathbf{X}=c_1\mathbf{X}_1+c_2\mathbf{X}_2$, and $\mathbf{X}_1$ and $\mathbf{X}_2$ are two random valid solutions to the WTA problem. The relative weighting of the constraint and objective terms (λ_{con} and λ_{obj}) are varied in the four plots. a. $\lambda_{con}=20$, $\lambda_{obj}=0$ (low neuron gain). b. $\lambda_{con}=20$ $\lambda_{obj}=0$ (high neuron gain). c. $\lambda_{con}=\lambda_{obj}=20$. d. $\lambda_{con}=0$, $\lambda_{obj}=20$.

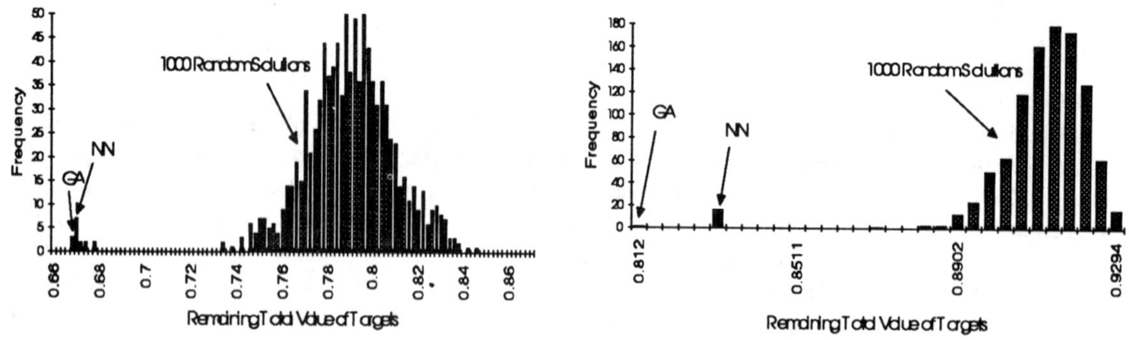

a. b.

Fig. 3. Histograms of solutions to weapon-target allocation problem using neural network (NN), genetic algorithm (GA), and random selection. a. 50 targets and 20 weapons. b. 100 targets and 20 weapons.

References

[1]B. Fu and P. Hajela, "Minimizing Distortion in Truss Structures - A Hopfield Network Solution," Computing Systems in Engineering. 4(1): pp. 69-74, 1993.

[2]A. Hemani and A. Postula, "Cell Placement by Self-Organization,"Neural Networks. 3: 377-383, 1990.

[3]P. Simic and S. Shams, "Solving the Assignment and Scheduling Problems Using Cnet," Technical Report CALT-68-1892, California Institute of Technology, 1992.

[4]N. Funabiki and Y. Takefuji, "Neural Network Approach to Topological Via-Minimization Problems," IEEE Trans on Computer-Aided Des. of Integ. Circ. & Sys. 12(6): pp. 770-779, 1993.

[5]G. A. Tagliarini, J. F. Christ, and E. W. Page, "Optimization Using Neural Networks," IEEE Trans. Comp. Vol. 40, 1347-1358 (1991).

[6]J. J. Hopfield and D. W. Tank, "'Neural' Computation of Decisions in Optimization Problems," Biol. Cybern., Vol. 52, 141-152 (1985).

[7]R. Durbin and D. Willshaw, "An Analogue Approach to the Traveling Salesman Problem Using an Elastic Net Method," Nature. 326: 689-691, 1987.

[8]T. Kohonen, Self-Organization and Associative Memory. Springer-Verlag, 1987.

[9]P. D. Simic, "Constrained Nets for Graph Matching and Other Quadratic Assignment Problems," Neural Computation. 3: 268-281, 1991.

[10]P. D. Simic, "Statistical Mechanics as the Underlying Theory of 'Elastic' and 'Neural' Optimizations," Networks. 1: 89-103, 1990.

[11]D. E. Goldberg, Genetic Algorithms in Search, Optimization, and Machine Learning, Addison-Wesley, 1989.

[12]K. Steinhoff, "Examination of a Resource Allocation Problem with a Desktop Tool," Internal Hughes Report, 16 December 1992, CSN IV-1-3-10.

[13]S. Grossberg, Studies of Mind and Brain: Neural Principles of Learning, Perception, Development, Cognition, and Motor Control, Reidel, 1982.

[14]J. J. Hopfield, "Neurons With Graded Response Have Collective Computational Properties Like Those of Two-State Neurons," Proc. Natl. Acad. Sci. USA, Vol. 81, 3088-3092 (1984).

[15]D. Hammerstorm, "A VLSI Architecture for High-Performance, Low-Cost, On-chip Learning, "Proceedings of the Inter. Joint Conf. on Neural Networks, San Diego, Vol. 2, pp. 537-544, 1990.

[16]S. Shams, "Implementing Arbitrarily Interconnected Neural Networks on the DREAM Machine,"Proceedings of the World Congress On Neural Networks, Portland, OR, Vol. 4, pp. 869-873, 1993.

[17]M. Holler, S. Tam, H. Castro and R. Benson, "An Electrically Trainable Artificial Neural Network (ETANN) with 10240 "Floating Gate" Synapses," Proceedings of the Inter. Joint Conf. on Neural Networks, Washington D.C., Vol. 2, pp. 191-196, 1989.

[18]Y. Owechko, "Cascaded-Grating Holography for Artificial Neural Networks," Appl. Opt. Vol. 32, 1380-1398 (1993).

[19]D. E. Goldberg and K. Deb. "A Comparative Analysis of Selection Schemes Used in Genetic Algorithms." In Foundations of Genetic Algorithms. Ed. G. J. E. Rawlins, San Mateo, CA, Morgan Kaufmann Publishers, pp. pp. 69-93, 1991.

Connectionist Approach for Clustering

G.Phanendra Babu and M.Narasimha Murty
Department of Computer Science and Automation
Indian Institute of Science, Bangalore - 560012,(India)

November 24, 1993

Abstract

This paper presents a stochastic connectionist approach for cluster analysis. Clustering problem is formulated as a real-parameter function optimization problem and is solved using the proposed approach. As the proposed connectionist approach performs stochastic search, it avoids getting stuck in a local minimum, and guarantees asymptotic convergence to optimal solution. The amenability of connectionist approaches to massive parallelization enables to obtain linear speedup with available parallel hardware. Several data sets are clustered using the proposed approach and the partitions obtained are (near)optimal in nature. Results pertaining to some important data sets are presented.

1 Introduction

Cluster analysis is inevitable where the underlying classification knowledge pertaining to the data under consideration is not available. Due to its potential use in many areas, such as Exploratory data analysis, image segmentation and databases, many methods and algorithms have been proposed in the literature to suit the requirements[1]. The main aim of clustering methods is to group similar patterns, characterized by a similarity measure, such that patterns in a group have similar characteristics compared to patterns in different groups. We emphasize the difference between clustering method or approach and clustering algorithm[1]. The clustering approach generally decides the criterion function to be optimized, such as squared-error criterion, whereas clustering algorithm is a procedure such as the K-Means algorithm to optimize the criterion function. We confine our dicussion to

Partitional methods specify a mathematical criterion function that indirectly imposes a structure on the data[1]. Algorithms such as K-Means, and ISODATA are used to minimize the defined criterion. Most of the algorithms proposed are of gradient descent type and converge to a locally optimal partition. The applications of squared-error criterion are extensive and hence it has been given much attention in the literature. The problem associated with algorithms that optimize squared-error criterion, also called *within group sum of squared error criterion*, is that they converge to a locally optimal partition. Many engineering applications demand optimal partition of the data in order to reduce long term loss due to non-optimal partition. One way of finding optimal partition is to enumerate all possible partitions and select an optimal one. The number of possible partitions for a given data set of size N and K clusters, is given by stirling approximation:$S(N,K) = \frac{1}{K!}\sum_{j=1}^{K}(-1)^{K-j}\binom{K}{j}j^N$. In the case $K = 2$, the number of partitions is $S(N,2) = 2^{N-1} - 1$ and this clearly indicates the exponential complexity involved in the exhaustive enumeration. In order to reduce the computational burden involved in exhaustive enumeration, other heuristic methods such as branch and bound that

0-7803-1901-X/94 $4.00

guarantee optimal partition have been investigated. But these methods consume prohibitive amount of computational time for large or moderate sized data. In this paper, we investigate the applicability of a connectionist approach to solve clustering problem efficiently.

This paper is organized as follows: Section 2 presents the problem formulation and Section 3 presents a brief description of connectionist approaches for solving optimization problems, followed by the new stochastic connectionist approach for solving nonlinear programming problem(NPP). Section 3 explores the applicability of this approach to the clustering problem. Experimental results are presented in Section 4.

2 PROBLEM FORMULATION

In this section, we give the formulation of the squared-error criterion as a nonlinear programming problem(NPP). This formulation needs to optimize real-valued parameters, i.e., obtaining optimal cluster centers such that the optimal partition is obtained. We slightly alter the formulation given by Gordon and Henderson[2] and make it as an NPP.

Let $X = \{x_1, \ldots, x_N\}$ be N patterns, $x_i \in \Re^d, \forall i$,
$C_1, \ldots, C_K$ be the K clusters, and $C_1 \cup C_2 \ldots \cup C_K = X$
$C_i \cap C_j = \emptyset$
$o_1, \ldots, o_K$ be K centroids of K clusters respectively, and $o_i \in \Re^d, \forall i$
$o_i = \frac{\sum_{j=1}^{N} u_{ji} x_j}{|C_i|}, \forall i$
squared error criterion is defined as:

$$J(o_1, \ldots, o_K) = \sum_{i=1}^{N} \sum_{c=1}^{K} u_{ic} d_{ic} \qquad (1.1)$$

where $d_{ic} = (x_i - o_c)^T (x_i - o_c)$, and $U = [u_{ij}]_{N \times K}$

In the above formulation, U represents the pattern association matrix and $\sum_c U_{ic} = 1$, for each pattern i. The association, $u_{ic} \in \{0, 1\}$ specifies whether a pattern i belongs to cluster $c(u_{ic} = 1)$ or not$(u_{ic} = 0)$. $u_{ic} = 1$ implies that i^{th} pattern is nearer to cluster center o_c compared with other cluster centers $o_l, l \neq c$, so $d_{ic} < d_{il}, \forall l \neq c$.

The criterion function given in equation 1.1 is a continuous variable vector function, and is nonconvex$(K > 1)$ and of multimodal type. Now the problem is to obtain a set of optimal centroids that characterizes the global minimum of $J()$.

In the next section, we present a connectionist approach which is amenable to high parallelization and performs parallel stochastic line search converging to a globally optimal solution.

3 CONNECTIONIST APPROACH FOR GLOBAL OPTIMIZATION

In optimization theory, finding global optimal solution of nonlinear programming problems is termed as the global optimization problem. Many approaches have been proposed in the literature to solve the global optimization problem[3]. Connectionist approaches or neural networks provide a rich set of models for solving the global optimization problem[4]. We use the term connectionist approach rather than neural networks. Connectionist approaches make use of interconnection of processing elements often termed as neurons or nodes and solve problems in the context of learning, knowledge representation, and search[4].

A connectionist model that has been used to solve nonlinear quadratic functions is Hopfield neural network. The problem associated with Hopfield network is that it converges to a local optimal solution. Most of the work done in this direction, i.e., employing connectionist methods to solve the global optimization problem, assumed that node in the network is very basic and is a simple processing element. It is quite convincing in the case of learning and knowledge representation, because even if a few nodes in the network fail, the performance of the entire network as a whole will not degrade much, but in the context of optimization it is not the case. Even the failure of a single node during optimization process leads to wrong or incorrect solution(s) because of missing variable values. With this fact in mind, we assume that the node can be full fledged processing unit capable of executing certain set of instructions. In fact this necessitates to investigate a compromise between the capability of the node verses parallelization achievable. With this assumption of increased processing capability, we show how broader range of problems can be solved using connectionist approaches. The reason behind using the term connectionist approaches against neural networks, is basically exploiting the advantages provided by these approaches in optimization rather than biological fidelity of assuming a node to be simple processor.

Apart from Hopfield network, we can extend Boltzmann machine, a stochastic version of Hopfield network, to optimize real-valued parameter functions[5]. This approach has been successfully employed to solve the global optimization problem and could optimize large scale problems involving 400 variables with 2^{1950} local minima. In that study each node is assumed to have higher capability than that of a simple thesholding processor. Even in sequential simulation, that approach has showed excellent scalability with respect to number of variables. Network is fully connected, i.e., each node is connected to every other node and can be viewed as a graph $G = \{V, E\}$, where V is a set of nodes and E represents a set connections associated with nodes, $\{v_i, v_j\} \in E$. Each connection is associated with a weight, called connection weight, w_{ij} and these weights are assumed to be symmetric $w_{ij} = w_{ji}$. Each node corresponds to a variable and outputs a real value representing the corresponding variable value. All weights are equated to 1. The connections here are used to get the values of other variables from other nodes. Every node performs stochastic line search along its direction, and by the parallel operations of all nodes, the network converges to a global optimal solution. The objective function to be optimized should be coded into each node. Let the function be $f()$. There are no restrictions on the type of function being optimized. The value $f^t_{|x_i=a}$ denotes the function value computed at node i using the other variable values at time step t.

$$f^t_{x_i=a} = f(x^t_1, \ldots, x^t_{i-1}, a, \ldots, x^t_n)$$

Initially network is set with some random values, that fall in the feasible reason. The bound constraints that specify the range of each variable can be used to restrict the search space to a bounded space as against including them into the objective function using penalty functions. In general bound constraints can be described by $\mu \leq x \leq \nu$, where μ and ν are lower and upper bound vectors respectively. Each node generates a neighborhood value, x_{i_n} to the current output by adding Gaussian noise to the current output value, x_{i_c} and is generated as follows:

$$x^t_{i_n} = g(x^t_{i_c} + N(0, \sigma^2_i))$$

where $N(0, \sigma^2_i)$ generates a normal random number with variance σ^2_i, t denotes the current time step, and function $g()$ checks for the violation of bound constraints[7] and is given by:

$$\begin{aligned} g(y_i) &= y_i \text{ if } \mu_i \leq y_i \leq \nu_i \\ &= \mu_i \text{ if } y_i < \mu_i \\ &= \nu_i \text{ if } y_i > \nu_i \end{aligned}$$

The change in the function value with the proposed change in variable x_i value is given by:

$$\Delta f^t_i = f^t_{i_{|x_i=x_{i_n}}} - f^t_{i_{|x_i=x_{i_c}}} \quad (1)$$

The new value is set as current output following the node update rule:

$$\begin{aligned} x_{i_c}^{t+1} &= x_{i_n}^t \quad \text{if} \quad \Delta f_i^t < 0 \quad \text{else} \\ &= x_{i_n}^t \quad \text{if} \quad \exp(-\tfrac{\Delta f_i^t}{T}) > rand(0,1) \quad \text{else} \\ &= x_{i_c}^t \end{aligned}$$

where function $rand(0,1)$ generates a uniform random number between 0 and 1, and the parameter T is called *temperature*. This temperature term controls the stochasticity in node update rule. We can directly see the relevance of this approach to Boltzmann machine(BM) and this update rule is an extension of node update rule in BM for discrete optimization problems. Initially network is started at high temperatures and is allowed to reach thermal equilibrium characterized by the steady state distribution over possible solutions in the search space. In thermal equilibrium at temperature T, the probability that the network will be in a state x is given by Boltzmann distribution:

$$\pi_T(x) = \frac{1}{Z_T}\exp(-\frac{f(x)}{T}) \tag{2}$$

where $Z_T = \int_{\Re^n} \exp(-\frac{f(x)}{T})$.

As temperature $T \to 0$ the distribution π_T approximates to global minima. The network has to be started at a high temperature and should be annealed down slowly. ature should be decreased slowly. Detailed convergence result has been presented else where[6]

4 Clustering with connectionist approach

In the proposed network architecture, each node represents a d dimensional cluster center. This indicates that the output of each node is a real-valued vector. The vectorized node output values can be communicated to other nodes with the available network communications facilities or with the help of a specialized hardware to support parallel transfer of vector output. The values of variables can be mapped onto [0,1] range to facilitate analog circuit realization[7]. The node update rule discussed earlier has to be extended to accommodate vector valued states. The neighborhood values are generated as follows:

$$x_{i_j}(l) = g(x_{i_0} + N(0,\sigma_l^2)), 1 \le l \le W$$

where σ_l^2 is the variance in the lth dimension. It is evident that the stochastic search is performed by sampling the neighborhood. This process consumes excessive computational time that increases with the increase in dimensionality. We can make use of gradient knowledge, in order to increase the speed of search, and the stochastic line search is done along the gradient direction. Assume that the gradient at vector x_{i_0} is $\vec{C_{i_0}} = -\frac{\partial f}{\partial x_{i_0}}$. The neighborhood points are generated along gradient direction.

$$x_{i_j} = g(x_{i_0} + \frac{\vec{C_{i_o}}}{||\vec{C_{i_0}}||}N(0,\sigma^2))$$

Here variance, σ^2 is estimated using the normal distribution property $P(x - 2\sigma \le Xx + 2\sigma) \approx 0.95$, so $\sigma = \frac{||\vec{C}||}{2}$. In clustering problem, we can obtain partial derivative with respect to a cluster center. The gradient direction $\vec{C_i}$ at node i can easily be computed, and is done as follows:

1. assign patterns to nearest cluster centers,
2. compute new cluster center C'_{i_0}.

The gradient now is $\vec{C}_i = C'_{i_0} - C_{i_0}$. The network is initialized with initial cluster centers and is annealed down by starting at a high starting temperature T_0, and initial variance σ_0^2. We use exponentially decreasing temperature schedule. The temperature and variance are decreased by multiplying with $\alpha_T(< 1)$ and $\alpha_\sigma(< 1)$ respectively.

5 Experimental Results and Analysis

Several data sets have been extensively tested using the proposed approach. In most of the cases (near)optimal solutions are obtained. All simulations are carried out on a PC/AT 386 machine. The network is run in asychronous mode[4], by allowing randomly selected half of the nodes in the network to update their output values in each iteration. Here an iteration is defined as one complete asychronous update. At each temperature value fifty iterations are performed. Initial temperature is set to a sufficiently high value such that it satisfies the following criterion: $E(J(X)^2) - E(J(X))^2 \ll T$[4], where $E()$ gives expectation of function values over all configurations or solutions. Final temperature, T_f is selected by observing the convergence of network till zero temperature limit, and selecting a value where there will not be any further change in the state of the network. We should bear in mind that data has to be made available with every node, making this approach not suitable for large data sets. One way of avoiding this problem is to maintain a central shared memory for the data, such that all nodes when they are updating can access data from the shared memory.

We present the results obtained using two standard data sets: 1. British towns data(BTD) and 2. German towns data(GTD)[8]. The results for BTD and GTD are presented in Tables 1 and 2 respectively. Statistics pertaining to 10 different runs are presented. In all trails, we used asynchronous parallel execution of the network in each iteration, i.e., from time t to time $t + 1$ half of the total number of nodes are allowed to update their output values. So all operations done in parallel are accounted as a single operation while computing time of execution. The average execution time over 10 runs is provided in tables. These results are compared by running well known clustering algorithm for 100 times and considering best value obtained. These results clearly demonstates the utility of the proposed method.

6 Conclusions

In this paper, we investigated the applicability of a new stochastic connectionist approach for solving the clustering problem. The major advantage of this approach over other stochastic methods is that it utilizes gradient knowledge and performs stochastic search along the gradient direction. This makes end user to obtain a desired partition, that is better than or equal to a specified objective function value very quickly. The results obtained for two standard data sets have been presented.

References

[1] A.K. Jain and R.C. Dubes. *Algorithms for Clustering Data.* Prentice-Hall, Englewood, Cliffs, NJ, 1988.

[2] A.D. Gordon and J.T. Henderson. Algorithm for euclidean sum of squares classification. *Biometrics*, 33:355–362, 1977.

[3] L.C.W. Dixen and (Eds.) Szego, G.P. *Towards Global Optimization 2.* North-Holland, Amsterdam, 1978.

[4] E. Aarts and J. Korst. *Simulated Annealing and Boltzmann Machine: a stochastic approach to combinatorial optimization and neural computing.* John Wiley & sons Ltd., New York, 1989.

[5] G.P. Babu and M.N. Murty. Connectionist approach for global optimization. *submitted to ICNN'94.*

[6] G.P. Babu and M.N. Murty. Connectionist approach for pattern clustering. *submitted to IEEE Trans. on PAMI.*

[7] A. Bouzerdoum and T.R. Pattison. Neural network for quadratic optimization with bound constraints. *IEEE Transactions on Neural Networks*, 4(2):293–304, 1993.

[8] H. Spath. *Cluster analysis Algorithms.* Ellis Horwood, Chichester, U.K., 1980.

Table 1. BTD: Results obtained over 10 Monte-Carlo runs. The control parameters are $T_0 = 75.0, T_f = 55.0, \alpha_T = 0.90, \sigma_0^2 = 3.0, \sigma_f^2 = 1.0$, and $\alpha_\sigma = 0.95$.

Number of clusters	Objective function values Min. J()	Max. J()	Avg. J()	S.D	N_Best	Avg. time per run(secs)	Min. value(100 trails) in K-means
2	336.15	336.15	336.15	0.00	10	6.65	336.15
3	227.22	227.22	227.22	0.00	10	7.87	227.22
4	180.91	180.91	180.91	0.00	10	9.31	180.91
5	160.23	160.55	160.26	0.09	9	10.69	160.33
6	141.46	146.62	142.50	1.62	7	11.98	144.81
7	126.27	140.05	129.37	4.3	3	13.28	134.54
8	113.50	119.38	115.70	2.19	2	14.80	128.19
9	103.28	106.50	104.63	1.34	2	16.03	124.92
10	92.92	113.58	98.84	6.45	1	17.56	124.74

*. N_Best is the number of times the minimum objective function value is obtained.

Table 2. GTD: Results obtained over 10 Monte-Carlo runs. The control parameters are $T_0 = 15000.0, T_f = 3500.0, \alpha_T = 0.90, \sigma_0^2 = 30.0, \sigma_f^2 = 15.0$, and $\alpha_\sigma = 0.85$.

Number of clusters	Objective function values Min. J()	Max. J()	Avg. J()	S.D	N_Best	Avg. time per run(secs)	Min. value(100 trails) of K-means
2	121425.75	121425.75	121425.75	0.00	10	5.13	121425.75
3	77008.63	77008.63	77008.63	0.00	10	6.07	77008.63
4	49600.59	49600.59	49600.59	0.00	10	7.08	49600.59
5	38716.02	39452.81	39231.77	337.63	3	8.07	38716.01
6	30535.39	32531.50	31072.33	835.61	7	9.15	30535.39
7	24432.57	24453.97	24434.70	6.42	9	10.17	24432.56
8	21483.02	21507.15	21492.21	9.41	5	11.09	22832.05
9	18550.43	18571.83	18552.57	6.42	9	11.99	20562.61
10	16307.96	16524.66	16400.80	89.10	4	13.32	20358.27

Constrained optimization with use of two-dimensional maximum neurons

Percy P.C. Yip and Yoshiyasu Takefuji
Department of Electrical Engineering and Applied Physics
Case Western Reserve University
Cleveland, OH44106.

Abstract

A special neuron, which we call two-dimensional maximum neuron is proposed. This type of neuron can eliminate the row and column constraints that occur in many problems, such as the stable marriage problem. A parallel processing algorithm to find the stable marriage matching using the proposed two-dimensional maximum neurons is described and the result is now reported.

I. Introduction

In 1985, Hopfield and Tank [1] reported on the use of interconnected sigmoidal neurons for solving constrained optimization problems. They defined an energy function such that when the system converges to the minimum energy state, it corresponds to a solution of the problem. The equation of motion obtained in that way contains several tuning parameters which affect the convergence of the system [2]. There is no guidance of the choice of those parameters. It is conceivable that the more parameters there are in the equation of motion, the more difficult it is to obtain the solution. With the use of the proposed 2-D maximum neurons, we can eliminate the row and column constraints. It means, we can reduce the number of parameters by 2 in most problems. We illustrate the use of such 2-D maximum neuron by the 'Stable Marriage Problem [3]'.

Since the introduction of the 'Stable Marriage Problem', many people working in a wide range of disciplines, including computer science, mathematics, economics, game theory, management science and operations research started to study and have introduced many additional variants of this basic problem [4]. Some parallel algorithms for solving this problem have been reported [5-7]. However, no parallel algorithm with worst case complexity better than $O(n^2)$ is known. Here we descibe the use of the 2-D maximum neurons for this task. We describe the stable marriage problem in the next section and then represent matching states by states of neurons. A parallel algorithm using the 2-D maximum neurons for the stable marraige problem is then described and simulation results are reported.

II. The task

In a stable marriage problem, there are equal-sized sets of men and women. The matching is a one-one mapping. Assume there are n men and n women, and so n couples are formed. If these n couples are chosen such that there exists a man and a woman who are not actually married, but they both prefer each other to their actual marriage partners, then the matching is said to be unstable. If no such pair exists, it is called a stable marriage matching.

0-7803-1901-X/94 $4.00

We can represent the matching by a state of n x n neurons, as shown in Figure 1, such that the row represents man and column represents woman. If $V_{ij} = 1$, it means that the ith man and j^{th} woman is a matched couple.

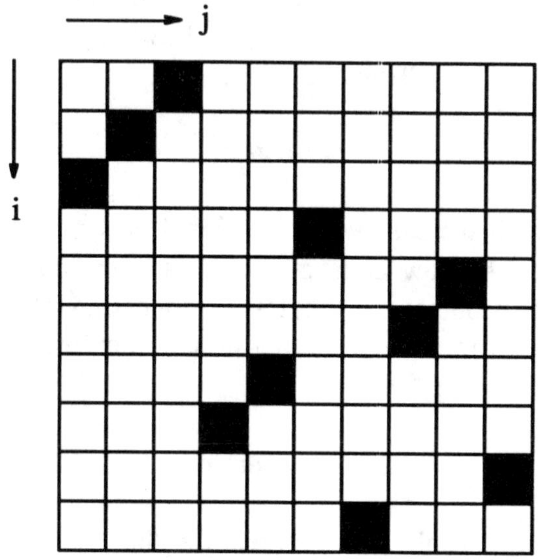

Figure 1 Representation of the problem (A filled black block indicates $V_{ij} = 1$)

The one-one mapping can then be represented by local constraints.

$$\sum_i V_{ij} = 1 \tag{1}$$

$$\sum_j V_{ij} = 1 \tag{2}$$

III. A parallel algorithm with use of 2-D maximum neurons

A 2-D maximum neuron is now introduced. U_{ij} and V_{ij} are the input and the output of the $(i,j)^{th}$ neuron respectively. The inputs of the neighbors of each neuron are compared asynchrously until each row and each column has one and only one neuron fired. The neurons are updated according to Equation (3).

$$\text{If } U_{ij} = \underset{k}{\text{MAX}}(U_{ik}) \text{ and } U_{ij} = \underset{l}{\text{MAX}}(U_{lj})$$
$$\text{then } V_{ij} = 1 \text{ and } V_{ik} = 0 \text{ and } V_{lj} = 0 \tag{3}$$

If $(i,j)^{th}$ neuron is fired (i.e $V_{ij} = 1$), the neurons in i^{th} row and the neurons in j^{th} column are disabled and they will not compete with other neurons. These operations go on asynchrously until each row and each column has exactly one neuron fired.

With this special 2-D maximum neuron, the system is updated until there is exactly 1 neuron fired in each row and in each column. Hence the local constraints can be eliminated and do not appear in the equation of motion.

There is one global constraint that assures the matching is stable. We have to encode the preference of each individual into the equation of motion to assure the matching is stable. In our simulation, Men's preferences to women are represented by a preference matrix M and Women's preferences to men are represented by another preference matrix W. M_{ij} is the preference of the jth woman that i^{th} man gives. W_{ij} is the preference of the ith man that the jth woman gives. If $M_{ij} > M_{ik}$ the ith man prefers the jth woman to the kth woman. If $W_{ij} > W_{kj}$ the jth woman prefers the ith man to the kth man.

Using these neurons, and the preference matrices to represent the problem, the equation of motion is given by (4)

$$\frac{\partial U_{ij}}{\partial t} = A\sum_{k\neq j}\sum_{l\neq i} g(i,j,k,l)V_{ik}V_{lj} \qquad (4)$$

If $V_{ik} = 1$ and $V_{lj} = 1$ and $M_{ij} > M_{ik}$ and $W_{ij} > W_{ij}$
then $g(i,j,k,l) = 1$ else $g(i,j,k,l) = 0$ (5)

IV. Simulation results

For each size of couples, 50 sets of preference matrices M_{ij} and W_{ij} were randomly generated and for each set of preference matrices, 50 random runs were performed. The relationship between the average number of iterations and problem size is tabulated in Table 1. It was found that the system always converged to a stable matching. An example of the problem with size 10 and a solution is given in Figure 2, and the statistcial relationship between the cumulative frequency of convergence and the number of iterations for that example is illustrated in Figure 3.

Table 1 Average iteration steps for different sizes

size	**average iteration**	frequency of convergence
10	6	100 %
20	12	100 %
30	15	100 %
40	20	100 %
50	22	100 %
70	27	100 %
100	32	100 %

Men's preference

8	4	10	9	5	3	2	1	7	6
1	9	5	8	10	3	6	4	7	2
9	6	1	5	4	2	7	8	10	3
4	9	7	8	5	10	2	6	1	3
2	7	8	9	3	6	1	4	10	5
3	7	9	1	6	4	8	5	10	2
3	6	2	9	10	1	5	4	8	7
6	3	7	9	1	2	10	8	5	4
8	10	9	6	2	5	1	3	4	7
6	5	9	8	1	3	10	4	2	7

Women's preference

6	5	6	7	6	6	7	7	7	7
5	8	9	9	9	9	10	10	10	9
9	9	5	6	5	5	6	6	6	6
8	7	8	5	4	4	4	4	4	4
1	1	1	1	8	8	9	9	9	8
3	3	3	3	2	2	2	3	3	3
10	10	10	10	10	10	5	5	5	5
4	4	4	4	3	3	3	2	2	2
2	2	2	2	1	1	1	1	1	1
7	6	7	8	7	7	8	8	8	10

A solution

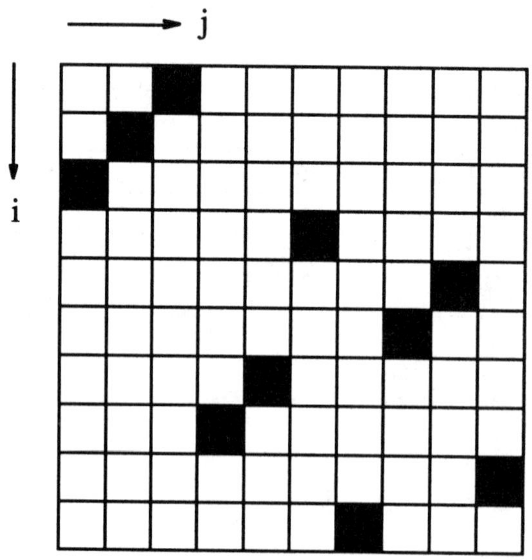

Figure 2 An example of preference matrices of size 10 and a solution

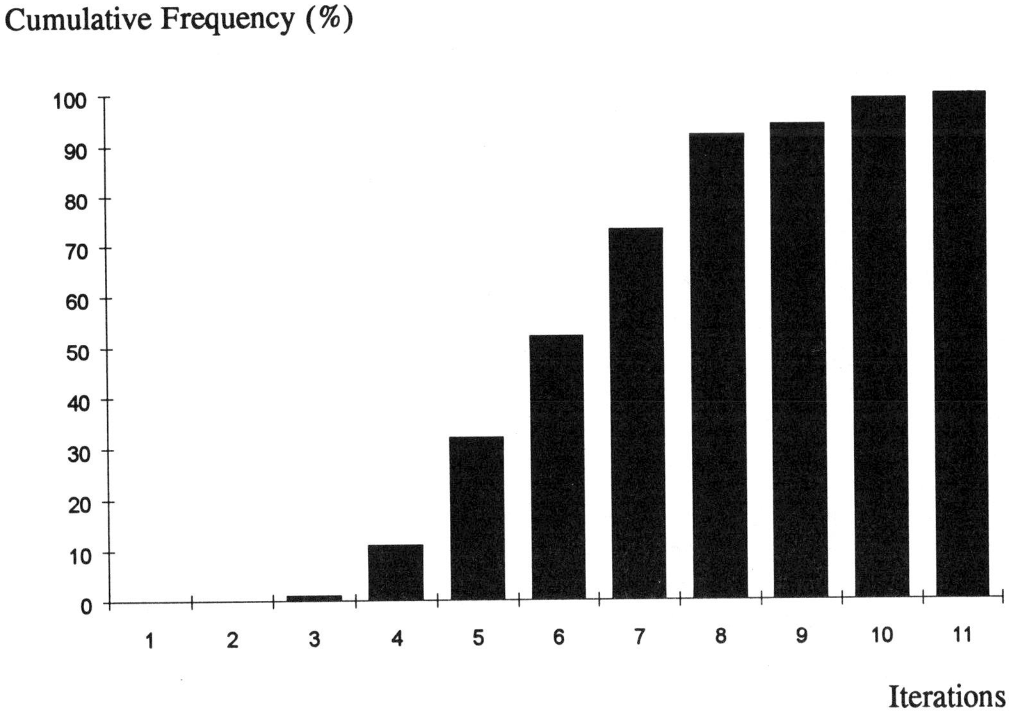

Figure 3 Cumulative frequency of convergence by iteration steps

V. Conclusion

A 2-D maximum neuron has been introduced. The use of this type of neuron can eliminate the row and column constraints for those one-one mapping problems and so simplify the equation of motion. A parallel algorithm with the use of the 2-D maximum neurons has been described in solving the stable marriage problem.

References

[1] J. J. Hopfield and D. W. Tank, "Neural computation of decisions in optimization problems," *Biological Cybernetics*, vol. 52, pp.141-152, 1985.

[2] G. V. Wilsonand G. S. Pawley, "On the stability of the travelling salesman problem algorithm of Hopfield and Tank," *Biological Cybernetics*, vol. 58, pp.63-70, 1986.

[3] D. Gale and L. S. Shapley, "College admissions and the stability of marriage," *American Mathematical Monthly*, vol. 69, pp.9-15, 1962.

[4] D. Gusfield and R. W. Irving, *The Stable Marriage Problem Structure and Algorithms*. MIT Press, 1989.

[5] M. E. C. Hull, "A parallel view of stable marriages," *Information Processing Letters*, vol. 18, pp.63-66, 1984.

[6] S. S. Tseng and R. C. T. Lee, "A parallel algorithm to solve the stable marriage problem," *BIT*, vol. 24, pp.308-316, 1984.

[7] S. S. Tseng, "The average performance of a parallel stable marriage algorithm," *BIT*, vol. 29, pp.448-456, 1989.

Connectionist Approach for Global Optimization

G.Phanendra Babu and M. Narasimha Murty
Department of Computer Science and Automation,
Indian Institute of Science, Bangalore, INDIA.

Abstract: *A connectionist approach for global optimization is proposed. The standard function set is tested. Results obtained, in the case of large scale problems, indicate excellent scalability of the proposed approach.*
Indexing Terms: Neural Networks, Function optimization

Locating global optimal value of a given non-convex function is a difficult task, but this problem arises in many engineering applications. Gradient descent methods fail to find global optimum as they have a tendency to get stuck in a local optimum. In this letter, we present a stochastic connectionist approach(CA) for solving the global optimization problem. We confine our discussion to non-linear programming problems(NPP). Let $f : R^n \to R$ be a non-linear function with constraint set C that defines a feasible region. We assume that the chosen problem is a minimization problem. Using penalty function approach, we can obtain an unconstrained optimization problem: $J(x) = f(x) + \mu p(x)$, where $p(x)$ is a penalty function and μ is a multiplying factor. The second term, with appropriate μ value, constrains the solution vector, x, to lie in the feasible region defined by the constraints. The penalty function penalizes $J()$ whenever solution, x, falls outside the feasible region. The aim of global optimization methods is to find global optimum, $x^* \in R^n$, of $J()$.

$$J(x^*) \leq J(x), \forall x \in R^n$$

Many attempts[1] have been made to solve this problem. A stochastic optimization method called simulated annealing(SA) that adopts annealing behavior of physical systems has also been studied in this context[2,3]. Another approach for solving optimization problems is based on Connectionist or Neural Network models. As these models involve many processing units that operate in parallel, these models are endowed with powerful search capability. A processing unit can be a simple unit such as an RC circuit[4] or it can be a full-fledged processor that can execute a defined set of instructions. Hopfield neural network[4] and its stochastic version Boltzmann Machine(BM)[5] have been used to solve optimization problems. Here we extend the BM to solve NPP.

In the proposed approach, the network is fully connected, i.e., each node is connected to all other nodes. Node in the network is expected to process a set of instructions. The number of nodes in the network is equal to the number of variables. All connection weights are equal to 1. Each node is labeled with a variable, and each node performs stochastic line search along its direction. The value of function can be computed by each node by gathering output values of all other variables. All computational units perform parallel search in the feasible region in order to locate global optimum x^*. The node update rule is an extension of that of BM in real-valued parameter space. Output of each node i is updated as follows:

0-7803-1901-X/94 $4.00 ©1994 IEEE

$$x_{in} = x_{ic} + N(0,\sigma^2)$$
$$\Delta J := J_{|x_i=x_{ic}} - J_{|x_i=x_{in}}$$
$$x_{ic} = x_{in} \text{ if } \Delta J > 0 \text{ else}$$
$$:= x_{in} \text{ if } exp(\tfrac{\Delta J}{T}) > \text{rand}(0,1)$$

where x_{ic} is current node output value, x_{in} is the neighborhood of x_{ic} and T is temperature. $N(0,\sigma^2)$ is normal random variate with zero mean and σ^2 variance and rand(0,1) generates uniform random number between 0 and 1.

The above state transition rule allows occasional hill climbing avoiding getting stuck in a local optimum. T controls the stochasticity in the node update process. At high temperatures, all proposed uphill movements will be accepted. As the temperature decreases, the number of accepted uphill movements decreases. Another control parameter, σ, that controls the neighborhood generation, plays an important role in the convergence process. In general neither large values of σ nor small values of σ are suitable[2]. The parameters $\alpha_T(<1)$ and $\alpha_\sigma(<1)$ are used to reduce T and σ respectively, when the network reaches equilibrium. Equilibrium can be reached by running the net for certain number of iterations at a fixed value of T. As $T \rightarrow 0$ and $\sigma \rightarrow 0$, the network converges to global optimal solution. One should select initial values of $T(T_0)$ and $\sigma(\sigma_0)$ and decrease ratios α_T and α_σ carefully. The parameter selection procedures of SA are also applicable to this approach. We used asynchronous parallel execution of network and at each time half of the total number of nodes are updated. All function evaluations performed in parallel are considered as a single function evaluation.

Experimental Results: Most of the algorithms proposed in the literature for global optimization are evaluated against the standard function test suit given in [1]. Since the proposed model can be viewed as a network model of SA, we compare the performance of this model with that of SA[2] and Tree annealing(TA)[3]. The criterion used for comparison is the number of objective function evaluations. For each test function, 100 Monte-Carlo runs were made and the results are presented in Table 1(Percentages in brackets represent success rate). Shekel's function set, S5, S7, and S10, created some problem in converging to global optimum as these functions possess deep local minima. The same difficulty has also been reported by Vanderbilt and Louie[2], and by Bilbro and Snyder[3].

Scalability: Function's tested are of low dimensional type. But in real-life we encounter functions with many variables. So scalability to support large scale function optimization is also an important criterion. In order to test the performance of this approach, we have considered two functions, one is Function 19[6] and the other is COS function[7]. Functions are given below.

Function.19: $f(x) = \frac{1}{10}\{\sin^2(3\pi x_1) + \sum_{i=1}^{n-1}(x_i - 1)^2[1 + \sin^2(3\pi x_{i+1})] + (x_n - 1)^2[1 + \sin^2(2\pi x_n)]\}$ where $-10.0 \leq x_i < 10.0, \forall i$ and $f^* = 0.0$

COS function: $f(x) = 0.1\sum_{i=1}^{n}\cos(5\pi x_i) - \sum_{i=1}^{n} x_i^2$ where $-1 \leq x_i < 1, \forall i$ and $f^* = n/10.0$

The number of local minima in these functions increases exponentially as the number of variables increases. Function 19 has 30^n local minima, whereas COS function has 5^n local minima. We run the program till global optimum is obtained with a precision of 10^{-4}. Results for sequential and asynchronous parallel execution of the network are shown in Figures 1 and 2. It can be observed that the number of objective function evaluations, in the case of asynchronous parallel execution, are almost constant even as *the number of variables increases*. We can infer that the CA has excellent scalability.

References

[1] Dixen, L.C.W., and Szego, G.P.(Eds)(1978). *Towards Global Optimization 2*, North-Holland, New York.

[2] Vanderbilt, D. and Louie, S.G.(1984)."A Monte Carlo simulated annealing approach to optimization over continuous variables," *Journal of Computational Physics,* Vol. 56, pp. 259-271.

[3] Bilbro, G.L. and Snyder, W.E.(1991)."Optimization of function with many minima,"IEEE Trans. on SMC, Vol.21, No.4, pp. 840-849.

[4] Tank, D.A., and Hopfield, J.J.(1986)."Simple neural optimization networks: An A/D converter, signal decision circuit, and a linear programming circuit," *IEEE Trans. on Circuits and Systems,* Vol.33, pp. 533-541.

[5] Hinton, G.E., Sejnowski, T.J., Ackley, D.H.(1984). "Boltzmann machine: Constraint satisfaction networks that learn," Carnegie-Mellon University, Tech. Rep. CMU-CS-84-119.

[6] Renpu Ge and Yongfeng Qin(1990)."The Globally convexized filled functions for global optimization," *Applied Mathematics and Computation*, Vol.35, pp.131-158.

[7] Breiman, L., and Cutler, A.(1993)."Deterministic algorithm for global optimization," *Journal of Mathematical Programming,* Vol.58, pp.179-199.

Function	SA	TA	CA
GP	557(100%)	6375	321(100%)
RCOS	-	4172	782(96%)
H3	1224(100%)	1113	1097(93%)
H6	1914(62%)	17262	1276(81%)
S5	3910(54%)	3700(40%)	2569(48%)
S7	3421(64%)	2426(60%)	2571(59%)
S10	3078(81%)	3463(50%)	2437(72%)

Table.1. Comparision of the number of function evaluations.

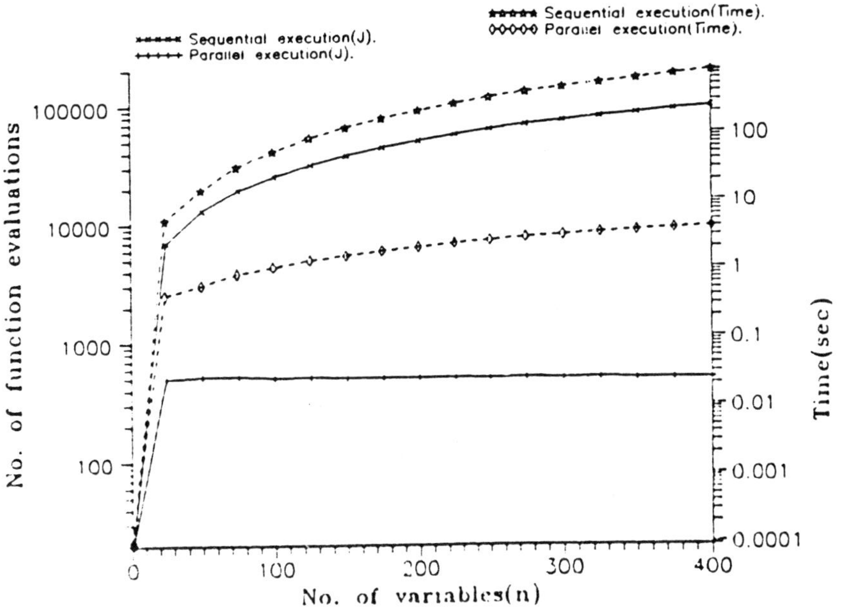

Figure.1.

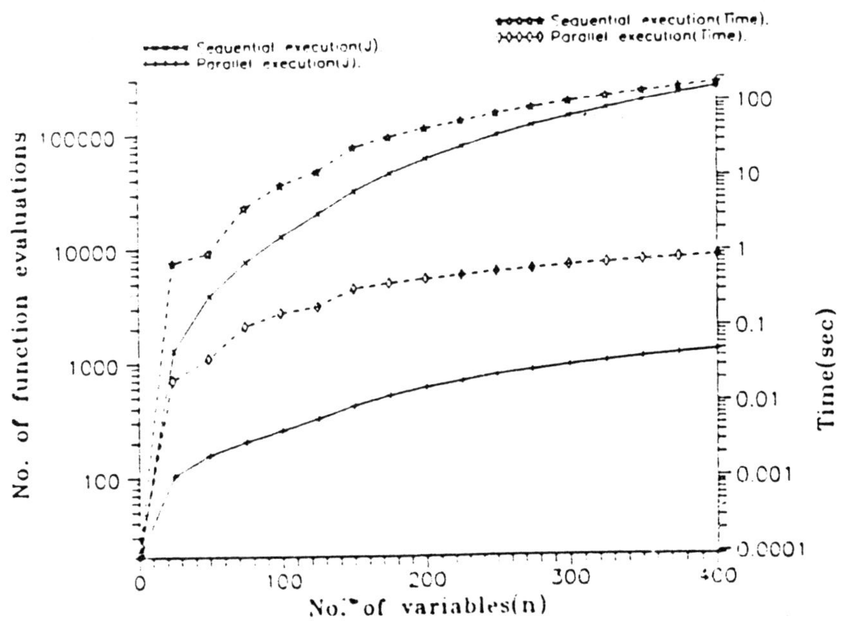

Figure.2.

A Hopfield Neural Network Solution to the TCM Partitioning Problem[1]

Tom Hameenanttila and Jo Dale Carothers
Dept. of Electrical and Computer Engineering
The University of Arizona
Tucson, AZ 85721

Abstract

In this paper the problem of circuit partitioning for multichip module packaging realizations is considered. A Hopfield-type neural network is designed for use in solving the previously proposed TCM partitioning problem, to which only heuristic solutions have been applied thus far. It is expected that the global nature of the Hopfield neural network's operation will make it a useful tool as the problem complexity is increased.

1 Introduction

A great deal of recent research has been directed towards the physical design and manufacture of multichip modules (MCM's), a form of digital system packaging. Multichip modules comprise a set of silicon dies, each placed directly on a routing substrate which serves as the media through which connections are made. MCM's have gained increased prominence in high-performance digital packaging as circuit designs have pushed the limits of printed circuit board realizations. Since transmission delay bounds the speed of modern digital circuitry, MCM realizations represent a great increase in computational power. Thermal Conduction Modules (TCM's) are a special type of MCM that are used by IBM in mainframe designs.

Research into the creation of tools for the automated design of MCM realizations is much less advanced. Multichip modules represent a new class of design problem, separated from printed circuit board and IC layout design by several distinguishing characteristics. The most fundamental of these is the interdependence of the geometry of partitioning, placement, and routing problems and the electrical and thermal constraints of the problems. This interdependence of design constraints necessitates a global approach to design which is not taken in conventional circuit design or package design [5].

While heuristic techniques generally take a step-by-step approach to a design problem, the nature of the Hopfield neural network model is to do the opposite. Used in optimization, Hopfield networks consider problem objectives and constraints simultaneously whether or not they have a direct intuitive connection. This characteristic of Hopfield networks motivates their consideration as tools for aspects of MCM design. Hopfield networks have been used successfully to solve other complex optimization problems [3].

The specific design problem considered here (proposed in [6]) is that of circuit partioning for eventual realization in a Thermal Conduction Module (TCM), a specific MCM design. In this paper, the TCM partitioning problem is described and the method currently applied to its solution is discussed. The challenges in applying Hopfield networks to the problem are detailed afterwards, and a prototype network design is presented. Preliminary results have been obtained on simple test cases and simulation results are summarized.

2 The TCM Partitioning Problem

The problem defined in [6] is that of placing functional units of a circuit, represented in the form of a graph, on available chip slots in a TCM. The objective is to minimize wire length between chip slots, while satisfying both chip

[1]This work was supported in part by the University of Arizona Foundation.

slot area and inter-node timing constraints.

The TCM is an early MCM design [2] which is used in IBM's mainframe designs. The chip slots on the TCM are regularly placed and equal in area. Although more advanced MCM's relax these geometric constraints, the TCM serves as an excellent starting point for development of automated design tools for solving the difficult partitioning problem.

The problem is presented as follows: Given a circuit $G = (V, E)$ and a set of chip slots S_{TCM}, we seek a mapping $T : V \rightarrow S_{TCM}$ which minimizes

$$\sum_{i,j \ni T(v_i) \neq T(v_j)} d_{T(v_i),T(v_j)} a_{ij} \qquad (1)$$

where d_{ij} is the wiring distance between chip slots s_i and s_j and a_{ij} is one if two nodes v_i and v_j are adjacent and zero if not. Minimization of the objective is subject to the following constraints:

$$c_{ij} D(T(v_i), T(v_j)) \leq T_c \quad \forall v_i \neq v_j \in V \quad (2)$$

$$\sum_{i \ni T(v_i) = s_j} a_i \leq A_j \quad \forall s_j \in S_{TCM} \quad (3)$$

where T_c is the cycle time required, $D()$ is the transmission delay between two chips slots, a_i is the area of circuit node i and A_j is the area of chip slot j. The term c_{ij} is one if v_i and v_j must have lower delay than T_c between them and zero otherwise.

In [6], the problem is simplified by assuming a constant distance between all chips slots on the TCM. This simplification removes the placement aspect of this problem entirely, and allows a heuristic preprocessing step to be applied to the circuit graph to cluster circuit nodes into "supernodes" based on timing constraints. After this, the well-known K&L graph partitioning algorithm is used to partition the graph of supernodes. The algorithm has been modified to handle the area constraint.

Much of the problem statement above may be encoded into a Hopfield neural network in a straightforward manner. However, the area constraint takes a mathematical form which is somewhat unusual. Rather than requiring that a specific number of Boolean variables evaluate to true, or putting an inequality bound on the number, the area constraint shown above is an inequality constraint on a linear combination of Boolean variables. This constraint requires a special technique to allow a successful encoding. One such method is detailed below.

3 An Approach to Dealing with Linear Combination Inequality Constraints

The Hopfield neural network model is applied to optimization by encoding a problem stated in terms of a set of binary-valued variables to the binary-valued (or continuous-valued between 0 and 1) outputs of the neurons in the network and simulating the network dynamics with synapse weights set to encourage convergence to stable states which represent solutions to the problem. Energy functions to be minimized (optimized) are generally confined to be of the quadratic form:

$$E = -\frac{1}{2} \sum_{i=1}^{N} \sum_{j=1}^{N} T_{ij} V_i V_j - \sum_{i=1}^{N} V_i I_i \qquad (4)$$

which Hopfield has shown to be a Lyapunov function of the system, a local minimum of which the Hopfield model converges given a symmetric weight matrix T_{ij} with a non-negative diagonal [4].

The typical method of dealing with inequality constraints, proposed by Tagliarini [7], is the use of "slack neurons," which participate in the network dynamics but do not contribute to the problem solution encoded into the network. Slack neurons can be used to formulate an inequality energy term in the form of an equality. However, if the inequality constraint is not a bound on the number of neurons which should be on within some set of neurons but rather a bound on the value of a linear combination of those neurons (as shown in equation (3) above), the slack neuron method cannot be used.

This is noted in [1], in which the use of a continuous-valued slack neuron is proposed to express the constraint of equation (3) as follows, where V_i represent hypothesis neurons and Z_i represent slack-neurons:

$$d_i Z_i - \sum_{j=1}^{n} V_j x_{ij} = 0 \qquad (5)$$

The output values of all Z_i are continuous between 0 and 1 but saturate beyond that point. The term above may be squared to form an objective term which increases when the linear combination of V_j outputs grows to be too large, but remains close to zero if the bound is met, given appropriate behavior of the slack neurons. This method is termed in [1] as the "slack variable" method and is used to improve convergence of a slack neuron formulation of the solution to the N-Queens problem.

The slack variable method is used here to meet the area constraint of the TCM partitioning problem.

4 The Hopfield Neural Network Implementation

The energy equation for convergence to a solution of the TCM partitioning problem is given below. The problem was encoded into the network as follows: if the network is visualized as a two-dimensional array of neurons, each with two indices, then output of V_{ij} will indicate that circuit node i has been placed in chip slot j when high. One continuous slack neuron Z_j exists for each chip slot, to realize the area constraint.

The energy equation

$$E = E_A + E_B + E_C + E_D \qquad (6)$$

is the sum of three constraint terms, E_A, E_C, E_D, and one objective term, E_B. It is the consideration of these terms as a sum by the network which facilitates the global approach to the partitioning problem.

The four terms are as follows:

$$E_A = \frac{A}{2}\sum_{i=1}^{N}\left(\sum_{j=1}^{C} V_{ij} - 1\right)^2 \qquad (7)$$

$$E_B = \frac{B}{2}\sum_{i=1}^{N}\sum_{i'=1}^{N}\sum_{j=1}^{C}\sum_{j'=1}^{C} d_{jj'} a_{i'} V_{ij} V_{i'j'} \qquad (8)$$

$$E_C = \frac{C}{2}\sum_{i=1}^{N}\sum_{i'=1}^{N}\sum_{j=1}^{C}\sum_{j'=1}^{C} h(D(j,j') - c_{ii'}T_c) V_{ij} V_{i'j'} \qquad (9)$$

$$E_D = \frac{D}{2}\sum_{j=1}^{C}\left(\sum_{i=1}^{N} a_{ij} V_{ij} - A_j Z_j\right)^2 \qquad (10)$$

The notation of Section 2 is used in the above equations wherever applicable. E_A above enforces the constraint that no node be present in more (or less) than one chip slot. E_B creates a tendency to minimize the number of circuit interconnections passing between chip slots; thus realizing the problem objective. E_C enforces the timing constraint between those nodes which have a maximum allowable delay between them; in the simplified problem this amounts to keeping any such nodes in the same chip slot. The function h is defined as follows:

$$h(x) = \begin{cases} 1 & \text{if } x > 0 \\ 0 & \text{if } x \leq 0 \end{cases}$$

Energy term E_D enforces the area constraint, as discussed above.

5 Simulation Results

The above equations combined to form an energy equation E which can be couched in terms of Hopfield's canonical form (equation (3)). To simulate the network dynamics on a computer, the time derivative of the motion equation was calculated using the relationship

$$\frac{dU_{ij}}{dt} = -\frac{dE}{dV_{ij}}. \qquad (11)$$

The resulting time derivative was used in conjunction with the Euler approximation using a small Δt value to continually update neuron activation values until it was detected that the constraints of the problem were met. The network was simulated further to allow for a further decrease in E without constraint violations, and then stopped. A "hill-climbing" term was included in the motion equation to aid in avoiding local minima.

The convergence of the slack variable method of [1] was initially tested with a degenerate form of the TCM problem; the parameters a_i were set to one for each circuit node. This allowed the slack variable method to be compared directly with the conventional slack neuron method. Graphs representing circuits to be partitioned were generated. Partitioning was done into six slots, each holding up to two vertices.

It was observed that the characteristics of the networks changed very rapidly as the constant B controlling the objective term was modified. The convergence rate of both networks dropped dramatically with an increase in the objective term constant. The improvement in the quality of the solutions generated by the network changed far less dramatically.

The slack variable method performed much better than the slack neuron method in terms of convergence to a valid solution, and somewhat better in terms of solution quality. Figs. 1 and 2 show the data for the graph described above. Data points were averaged from 500 simulation runs each. It was determined from these test runs that a value between 0.1 and 0.2 results in the highest rate of convergence to valid solutions while providing high-quality solutions. (Note that the lower the number of interchip connections, the higher quality the solution since interchip connections are slower then intrachip connections.)

The area parameters were returned to the TCM partitioning problem in the next portion of the simulation. (This means that different vertices in the graph could have different area requirements.) Graphs with individual node areas were partitioned into non-homogeneous sets of slots, also with associated sizes.

To minimize the effect that problem specifics have on the behavior of the network,

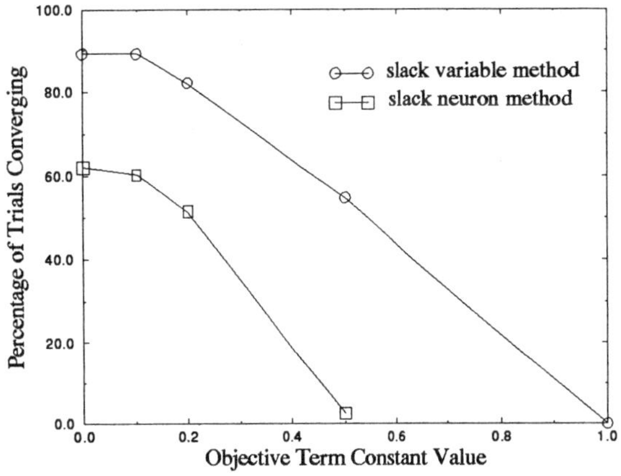

Figure 1: Convergence of the slack neuron and slack variable methods

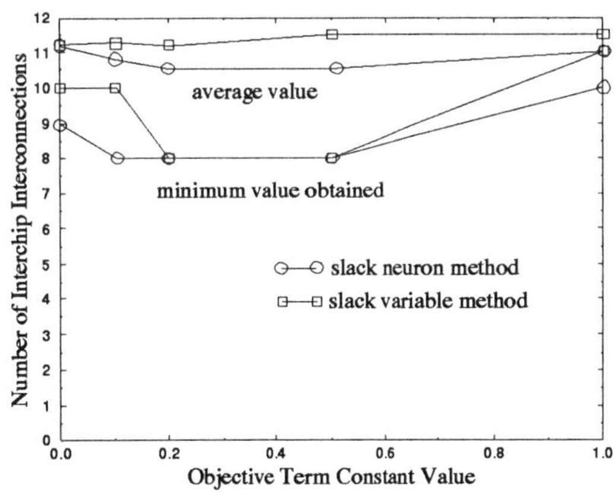

Figure 2: Solution quality of the slack neuron and slack variable methods

all node areas were normalized to the value of the largest node area before the data was passed to the network. (Needless to say, chip slot areas were normalized using the same factor.) The threshold at which area constraint term values were considered to be zero was dynamically adjusted to input data by setting the threshold value at one fifth of the smallest node area present in the simulation (after normalization). This does not ensure against undetected area overflow in solutions, but errors of this low magnitude should be insignificant at the high level design stage, at which most system parameters are estimated.

The simulation data describing the network

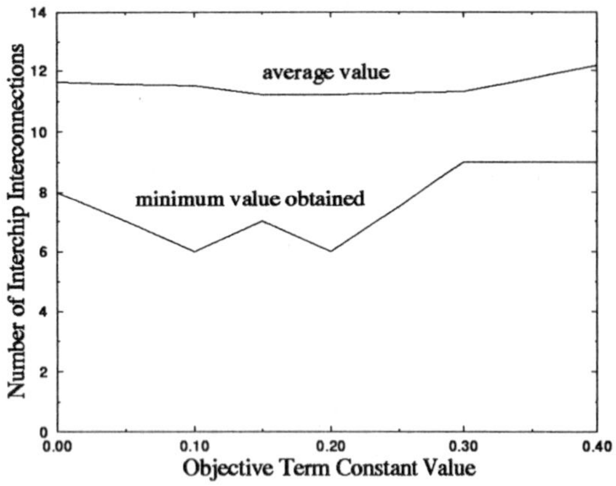

Figure 3: Solution quality of the slack variable method with area values

behavior for a representative graph is shown in Fig. 3. It is very similar to that of the simplified problem. Convergence is affected drastically by increases in the objective constant, but solution quality is improved very little.

5 Conclusion

The slack variable method appears to be a reasonable approach to dealing with inequality constraints of linear combinations of variables as found in this problem. This is important, as this type of constraint will be seen often in MCM design problems. In addition, the slack variable method allows for easy implementation of variable area parameters whereas the slack neuron method restricts the problem to all vertices having equal area. It is also possible to use the preprocessing step proposed by Shih et al. as a front end for the neural network. This would have the effect of speeding up convergence, allowing large problems to be solved faster, and removing or simplifying the timing constraint. This solution would not compromise the global aspect of the network approach, since only problem constraints are addressed by it. In conclusion, these results represent preliminary work on the application of neural networks to the optimization of multichip module partitioning. In ongoing work, extensive testing and the addition of further problem constraints, e.g. thermal constraints, that have not been previously solved, even with heuristics, are underway. Due to the nature of neural networks, it is felt that they may prove to provide a better exploration of the design space and may be better able to handle the additional constraints than the currently limited heuristic approach.

References

[1] Abe, S. "Convergence of Hopfield Neural Networks with Inequality Constraints." *Proceedings of the IEEE IJCNN*, 1992, Vol. 1, pp. 869-874.

[2] Blodgett, A. J., and Barbour, D. R. "Thermal Conduction Module: A High-Performance Multilayer Ceramic Package." *IBM Journal of Research and Development*, Vol. 26, No. 1, January 182, pp. 30-36.

[3] Gassen, D. W., and Carothers, J. D. "A Hopfield Network for Solving a Complex Scheduling Problem in Behavioral Synthesis." *Proceedings of the IEEE IJCNN*, 1993, Vol. 2, pp. 1537-1540.

[4] Looi, C-K. "Neural Network Methods in Combinatorial Optimization." *Computers Operations Research*, Vol. 19, No. 3/4, 1992, pp. 191-208.

[5] Sherwani, Naveed. *Algorithms for VLSI Physical Processing Design Automation.* Kluwer Academic Publishers, Boston, 1993.

[6] Shih, M., Kuh, E. S., and Tsay, R-S. "System Partitioning for Multi-Chip Modules Under Timing and Capacity Constraints." *IEEE Multi-Chip Module Conference*, 1992, pp. 123-126.

[7] Tagliarini, G. A. and Page, E. "Learning in Systematically Designed Networks," *Proceedings of the IEEE IJCNN*, 1989, Vol. 1, pp. 497-502.

Hopfield Energy of the Random Neural Network

Erol Gelenbe
Department of Electrical Engineering,
Duke University
Durham, N.C. 27709-0291

Abstract

Hopfield's seminal work on energy functions for neural networks and other early work [2, 3, 4] has drawn much attention to neural heuristics for combinatorial optimization. These heuristics are often very time consuming, because of the need for randomization or Montecarlo simulation during the search for solutions. The Random Neural Network (RNN) model [8, 19] has the nice property of being analytically solvable, and therefore computationally fast, so that any application of the model is based on obtaining solutions to a simple system of fixed-point equations. In this paper we first introduce the Binary Random Network model and show that it has a Hopfield Energy which it minimizes and which can be used for optimization problems. We illustrate this by the search for heuristic solutions to the Minimum Node Covering Problem (MCP) for graphs, which we also then proceed to solve using the full (rather than binary) RNN. We then turn to a defintion of Hopfield Energy for the RNN model, and prove that it is minimized at each fixed-point iteration used in solving the RNN model's equations. This is again illustrated in relation t the MCP.

1 Introduction

Since the seminal papers of the early eighties [2, 5, 3, 4], the study of emergent collective properties of artificial neural networks has created an exciting area for research.

For instance, it is well known that for the Hopfield Network with symmetric weights, as well as for other models [4], each individual state change of the network has the effect of reducing an appropriately defined cost or energy function (Hopfield [6], Rumelhart et al. [7]). This elementary but subtle observation has spawned a large body of work on using neural networks to provide heuristic solutions to computationally intractable or very difficult optimization problems. This is usually achieved by designing a Hopfield – or other appropriate neural - network whose energy function mimics a cost function which embodies the optimization problem to be solved. Much work has followed upon these initial results, including [9, 10, 11, 12, 13, 15, 16, 17, 18].

The Random Neural Network Model (Gelenbe 1989,90) [8, 19]) is a novel "spike" based neural network which has convenient closed form solutions for network state. It has been used for a variety of image processing applications [24, 25]. It has also been applied to a variety of combinatorial optimization problems for which it has provided polynomial-time solutions which are more effective than conventional greedy heuristics, and much faster than those provided by other techniques such as Simulated Annealing and the Boltzmann Machine [23, 22, 27, 28].

Based on this work it is of interest to determine whether the Random Neural Network (RNN) has an "energy function" representation which would relate it to Hopfield's formulation, as well as to cost functions of optimization problems of interest. This is done in the present paper.

We first recall the main features and properties of the RNN model. Then we then show that it has an interesting energy function and a related minimizing property, which may be used – in particular – to solve optimization problems. In order to illustrate this useful property, we discuss a well known NP-complete optimization problem – the Minimum Graph Covering Problem (MCP). We then show how the full RNN can be set up to solve heuristically the MCP. We provide experimental comparisons with the exact solution, and with the conventional greedy algorithm for the problem.

0-7803-1901-X/94 $4.00

1.1 The Random Neural Network Model

In the random neural network model [8, 19] signals in the form of spikes of unit amplitude circulate among the neurons. Positive signals represent excitation and negative signals represent inhibition. Each neuron's state is a non-negative integer called its potential, which increases when an excitation signal arrives to it, and decreases when an inhibition signal arrives. The state of the n-neuron network at time t, is represented by the vector of non-negative integers $k(t) = (k_1(t), ..., k_n(t))$, where $k_i(t)$ is the potential or integer state of neuron i. We will denote by k and k_i arbitrary values of the state vector and of the $i-th$ neuron's state. Neuron i will "fire" (i.e. become excited and send out spikes) if its potential is *positive*. The spikes will then be sent out at a rate r_i, with independent, identically and exponentially distributed inter-spike intervals. Spikes will go out to some neuron j with probability P^+_{ij} as excitatory signals, or with probability P^-_{ij} as inhibitory signals. A neuron may also send signals out of the network with probability $d(i)$, and: $d(i) + \sum_{j=1,...,n} P^+_{ij} + P^-_{ij} = 1$.

Let $\omega^+_{ij} = r_i P^+_{ij}$, and $\omega^-_{ij} = r_i P^-_{ij}$. Here the "omega's" play a role similar to that of the synaptic weights in connexionist models, though they specifically represent rates of excitatory and inhibitory spike emission. They are non-negative. Exogenous (i.e. those coming from the "outside world") excitatory and inhibitory signals also arrive to neuron i at rates Λ_i, λ_i, respectively. This is a "recurrent network" model, *i.e.* an network which is allowed to have feedback loops, and the network has an arbitrary topology.

Computations related to this model are based on the probability distribution of network state $p(k,t) = Pr[k(t) = k]$, or with the marginal probability that neuron i is excited $q_i(t) = Pr[k_i(t) > 0]$. As a consequence, the time-dependent behaviour of the model is described by an infinite system of *Chapman-Kolmogorov* equations for discrete state-space continuous Markovian systems.

Information is carried by the *frequency* at which spikes travel. Thus, neuron j, if it is excited, will send spikes to neuron i at a frequency $\omega_{ij} = \omega^+_{ij} + \omega^-_{ij}$. These spikes will be emitted at exponentially distributed random intervals. In turn, each neuron behaves as a non-linear *frequency demodulator* since it transforms the incoming excitatory and inhibitory spike trains' rates into an "amplitude", which is $q_i(t)$ the probability that neuron i is excited at time t. Intutively speaking, each neuron of this model is also a frequency modulator, since neuron i sends out excitatory and inhibitory spikes at rates (or frequencies) $q_i(t)r_iP^+_{ij}$, $q_i(t)r_iP^-_{ij}$ to any neuron j. The stationary probability distribution associated with the model is the quantity used throughout the computations:

$$p(k) = \lim_{t\to\infty} p(k,t), \quad q_i = \lim_{t\to\infty} q_i(t), \quad i = 1, ..., n. \tag{1}$$

Theorem 1. **[8, 19]** q_i satisfies the system of equations

$$q_i = \lambda^+(i)/[r(i) + \lambda^-(i)] \tag{2}$$

where the $\lambda^+(i), \lambda^-(i)$ for $i = 1, ..., n$ are given by a system of nonlinear simultaneous equations:

$$\begin{aligned} \lambda^+(i) &= \sum_j q_j r(j) p^+(j,i) + \Lambda(i), \quad \lambda^-(i) \\ &= \sum_j q_j r(j) p^-(j,i) + \lambda(i) \end{aligned} \tag{3}$$

Another important result guarantees that we can always find the quantities q_i because the $\lambda^+(i)$ and $\lambda^-(i)$ can always be computed [26].

2 Hopfield Energy of the RNN

In this section we construct and energy function of the RNN. Consider the $s-th$ computational step of the fixed-point iteration for (2):

$$q_i(s+1) = \frac{\Lambda(i) + \sum_{j=1}^n q_j(s)\omega^+_{ji}}{\lambda(i) + r(i) + \sum_{j=1}^n q_j(s)\omega^-_{ji}} \tag{4}$$

The fixed-point values of the q_i, $i = 1, \ldots, n$ which would then be used in solving an optimization problem, can be obtained by this iteration. The energy minimizing properties of the RNN are summarized in the following definition and result.

Definition The Hopfield Energy $H(s)$ of the RNN at step $s = 0, 1, 2 \ldots$ is defined as:

$$\begin{aligned} H(s) &= -\sum_{i=1}^n [q_i(s)\Lambda(i) + \sum_{j=1}^n q_i(s)q_j(s)\omega^+_{ji} \\ &- \sum_{j=1}^n q_i^2(s)q_j(s)\omega^-_{ji} - q_i^2(s)(r_i + \lambda_i)] \end{aligned} \tag{5}$$

It is interesting to see how this energy function definition differs from the classical approach of Hopfield. Note the additional terms which are squared in one state variable and linear in the other. It is not difficult to see that for optimization problems in the variables $\{0, 1\}$ a cost function with such terms is identical to a cost function with only quadratic terms, since $V^2 = X$ if $V = 0$ *or* 1. Therefore, the above energy function can correspond to a a quadratic cost function of the form:

$$C = -\sum_{i=1}^{n}[V_i\Lambda(i) + \sum_{j=1}^{n} V_iV_j\omega_{ji}^{+} - \sum_{j=1}^{n} V_iV_j\omega_{ji}^{-} - V_i(r_i + \lambda_i)] \quad (6)$$

The quadratic cost representation is motivated by the "usual" formulation of optimization problems with neural networks. However there may be cases where the more complex formulation of $H(s)$ can benefit the specific problem at hand. Let us now state and prove our main result.

Theorem 2. The RNN minimizes its Hopfield Energy and its state converges to a minimum energy value, *i.e.* $[H(s+1) - H(s)] \leq 0$, for each $s = 0, 1, \ldots$.

Proof The proof of this important property is simple. Write:

$$H(s+1) - H(s) = -\sum_{i=1}^{n}[q_i(s+1) - q_i(s)] [\Lambda(i) + \sum_{j=1}^{n} q_j(s)\omega_{ji}^{+} - \sum_{j=1}^{n} q_i(s)q_j(s)\omega_{ji}^{-} - q_i(s)(r_i + \lambda_i)] \quad (7)$$

Notice however that:

$$q_i(s+1) - q_i(s) = \frac{\Lambda(i)+\sum_{j=1}^{n} q_j(s)\omega_{ji}^{+} - \sum_{j=1}^{n} q_i(s)q_j(s)\omega_{ji}^{-} - q_i(s)(r_i+\lambda_i)}{\lambda(i)+r(i)+\sum_{j=1}^{n} q_j(s)\omega_{ji}^{-}}$$

Hence:

$$H(s+1) - H(s) = -\sum_{i=1}^{n} \frac{[q_i(s+1)-q_i(s)]^2}{\lambda(i)+r(i)+\sum_{j=1}^{n} q_j(s)\omega_{ji}^{-}} \leq 0.$$

completing the proof.

2.1 An Example: Minimum Cover for Graphs

In order to illustrate the use of the Hopfield Energy, consider the well known minimum cover problem (MCP) for graphs. This is an NP-complete problem [1] which is formulated as follows.

Method	Mini	Exc	T
n=20	$\pi = 0.5$		
GR	72%	0.28	0s
RN	100%	0	3s
n=20	$\pi = 0.25$		
GR	68%	0.40	0s
RN	96%	0.04	0s
n=20	$\pi = 0.125$		
GN	84%	0	0s
RN	100%	0	0s
n=50	$\pi = 0.5$		
GR	16%	1.20	0s
RN	52%	0.52	32s
n=50	$\pi = 0.25$		
GR	24%	1.28	0s
RN	60%	0.4	20s
n=50	$\pi = 0.125$		
GR	12%	1.52	0s
RN	80%	0.2	9s
n=100	$\pi = 0.5$		
GR	20%	1.28	0s
RN	60%	0.52	3'40s
n=100	$\pi = 0.25$		
GR	0%	2.04	0s
RN	48%	0.56	2'00s
n=100	$\pi = 0.125$		
GR	4%	2.72	0s
RN	56%	0.52	1'10s

Table 1:

n=100	$\pi = 0.0625$		
	Mini	Exc	T
Method			
GR	4%	2.88	0s
RN	76%	0.36	35s

Table 2:

	Mini	Exc	T
	n=20		
GR	79%	0.23	0s
RN	99%	0.01	3s
	n=50		
GR	21%	1.27	0s
RN	73%	0.28	32s
	n=100		
GR	7%	2.23	0s
RN	60%	0.49	3'40s

Table 3:

Suppose that we are given a non-directed graph G whose nodes are N = {1,..., n}, and which is described by its binary adjacency matrix $A = \{a_{ij}\}$. A cover of G is any subset K of N such that for any arc of the graph represented by $a_{ij} = 1$, either node i or node j is in K. Thus K contains at least one of the "end nodes" of any arc of the graph. A cover is said to be minimal if there is no smaller cover (in number of nodes).

A simple quadratic cost function which we can immediately propose for the MCP is based on identifying what is desirable, and what is to be avoided, in the construction of a cover. Obviously, for every arc we need at least one of its end nodes be included in the cover. But there is no need for both end nodes to be included. Let V_i be a binary variable which will be 1 if node i is in the cover, and which will be 0 otherwise. Thus a cost function C of the form can be written:

$$C = \sum_{i,j=1}^{n} V_i(1 - V_j)a_{ij} \tag{8}$$

C states that for each arc, one of the end nodes, and only one of them, is needed. Clearly C should be maximized when we solve the MCP.

Let us now construct a heuristic random network model for the minimum graph covering problem as follows. This heuristic network is in fact inspired by the well-known greedy algorithm for the MCP which will be described below. Each node i in the graph is "represented" by two neurons, call them i, and i^*: the first of these will be "on" if the network recommends that i be included in the cover, while the second will have the opposite role.

The neurons will be interconnected by weights as follows:

- The firing rate for neuron i is set to $r(i) = 2n$, and $p^-(i, i^*) = 1$, so that $\omega^-_{i,i^*} = 2n$ and all other $\omega^-_{i,j} = \omega^+_{i,j} = 0$.
- The firing rate for neuron i^* is $r(i^*) = D(i)$, where D(i) is the degree of node i. Furthermore $p^+(i^*, j) = 1/D(i)$ for any neighbour j of i, *i.e.* with $a_{ij} = 1$.
- $\Lambda(i) = D(i)$, so that neuron i is being excited proportionally to node i's degree – this is the aspect of the random network which mimics the greedy algorithm discussed below.
- $\Lambda(i^*) = 1$, to provide external excitation to neuron i^*.
- All other weights and rates are set to zero.

Using (2), and after some simplification, one obtains:

$$q_i = \frac{D(i)}{2n} + \frac{1}{2n}\sum_{1}^{n} \frac{a_{ij}}{D(j) + q_j} \tag{9}$$

The procedure we use for deriving an approximate solution to the MCP is then:

- **Step 1.** Solve (9) by a fixed point iteration, and select the node i whose probability q_i is highest; that node is included in the cover. Go to Step 2.
- **Step 2.** Remove that node from the graph, and remove all edges which originate at that node. If the resulting graph has no edges, stop. If the resulting graph still has edges, then for the new reduced graph go back to Step 1.

Notice that this is inspired from the simple Greedy Algorithm heuristic for the MCP, which is as follows:

- **Step 1.** Choose the node which has the largest value of $D(i)$ – the degree. Place that node in the cover. Go to Step 2.
- **Step 2.** Remove that node from the graph, and remove all the arcs which originate at that node. If the resulting graph has no edges, stop. If the resulting graph still has edges, then for the new reduced graph go back to Step 1.

Both of the methods described above have been tested on a set of randomly generated graphs, and compared when possible with the exact solution consisting of an enumerative search for the optimum. The number of arcs in the graphs has been varied with the following values: $n = 20, 50, 100$. The enumerative exact approach could not be carried out for 100 nodes because of the excessive computation times which are involved with such large problems.

Once the size of the graphs is fixed at a value, the random generation is carried out as follows. A probability value π is fixed; this is the probability that for any pair of nodes i, j there is an edge (i, j). In other words, π will be the probability that we will draw $a_{ij} = 1$ for each i, j.

We have taken different values of $\pi = 0.125, 0.25, 0.5$ and $n = 20, 50, 100$. These results are presented in Table 1. For $n = 100$ we also present an evaluation with $\pi = 0.0625$ in Table 2. On the other hand, Table 3 summarizes results for a set of 400 graphs of three different sizes. Clearly, small values of π will lead to sparsely interconnected graphs, while larger values will lead to very densely connected graphs. For each pair (n, π) we have generated 25 graphs at random in this manner, and the results which are tabulated below are average values over this set. The two MCP heuristics – using the RNN as described above, and the greedy algorithm – are compared with respect to the following criteria. "Mini" is the percentage of cases where the method obtains the minimum cover, while "Exc" is the average number of nodes in excess of the minimum for the set of 25 graphs, for a given (n, π) pair. T is the computation time on a workstation for each method. For the case with $n = 100$, it was impossible to run the enumerative solution to seek the minimum cover. Therefore "Mini" and "Exc" in this case refer to the values in comparison with the results obtained by the best of the two heuristics for each particular graph.

The results clearly show that the heuristic RNN easily outperforms the greedy heuristic in all cases, and that this performance improvement is particularly substantial when the graph is "sparse" (*i.e.* small values of π.

Let us re-examine the RNN for the MCP. We constructed a $2n$-neuron network, with a neuron i^* which should be "off" when neuron i is "on", for $i = 1, \ldots, n$.

From the network description in Section 4, the equations for the q_i , q_{i^*} become:

$$q_i = \frac{D(i) + \sum_{j=1}^{n} q_{j^*} a_{ji}}{2n}, \tag{10}$$

$$q_{i^*} = \frac{1}{D(i) + 2nq_i}. \tag{11}$$

As a consequence, the Hopfield Energy of the network is:

$$\begin{aligned} H(s) &= -\sum_{i=1}^{n}[q_i(s)D(i) + q_{i^*} \\ &+ \sum_{j=1}^{n} q_j(s)q_{i^*}(s)a_{ij} - 2nq_i^2(s)q_{i^*}(s) \\ &- 2nq_i^2(s) - D(i)q_{i^*}^2(s)] \end{aligned} \tag{12}$$

which, using (6) corresponds to a quadratic cost function C to be minimized by binary variables V_i, V_{i^*}:

$$\begin{aligned} C &= -\sum_{i=1}^{n}[V_i D(i) + V_{i^*} \\ &+ \sum_{j=1}^{n} V_{i^*} V_j a_{ij} - 2nV_i V_{i^*} - 2nV_i \\ &- D(i)V_{i^*}] \end{aligned} \tag{13}$$

This is a plausible cost function for the MCP. Indeed it may be written as:

$$\begin{aligned} C &= \sum_{i=1}^{n}\{2nV_i - V_i D(i) + [D(i) - 1]V_{i^*} \\ &- \sum_{j=1}^{n} V_{i^*} V_j a_{ij} + 2nV_i V_{i^*}\} \end{aligned} \tag{14}$$

where the first term states that there should be as few nodes as possible in the minimum cover, while the second and third terms state that we should favour nodes which have a large degree. The fourth term states that we would like to have only one of each end node of an edge in the cover, while the last term states that we cannot have the same node both in and out of the cover.

Though this cost function is more elaborate than a much simpler one such as (8), it does provide a more detailed representation of the problem's constraints and is a good tool for this optimization, as indicated by the experimental results we have obtained.

References

[1] Garey, M.J., Johnson, D.S. *"Computers and Intractability, A Guide to the Theory of NP-Completeness"*, W.H. Freeman and Co., New York, 1979.

[2] Hopfield, J.J. "Neural networks and physical systems with emergent collective computational abilities", *Proc. National Acad. Sci. USA*, Vol. 79, pp. 2554-2558, 1982.

[3] Cohen M.A., Grossberg S., "Absolute stability of global pattern formation and parallel memory storage by competitive neural networks", *IEEE Trans. Sys. Man Cyber.*, Vol. 13, No. 5, 1983.

[4] Hummel, R.A., Zucker, S.W., "On the foundations of relaxation labeling processes", *IEEE Transactions on Pattern Analysis and Machine Intelligence*, Vol. PAMI-5, No. 3, pp. 267-287, 1983.

[5] Hopfield, J.J. "Neurons with graded response have collective computational properties like those of two-state neurons", *Proc. National Acad. Sci. USA*, Vol. 81, pp. 3088-3092, 1983.

[6] Hopfield, J.J., Tank, D. " "Neural" computation of decisions in optimization problems", *Biological Cybernetics*, Vol. 52, pp. 141-152, 1985.

[7] D.E. Rumelhart, J.L. McClelland and the PDP Research Group (1986) *"Parallel Distributed Processing"*, Volumes 1 & 2, MIT Press, 1986.

[8] Gelenbe E., "Random neural networks with negative and positive signals and product form solution", *Neural Computation*, Vol. 1, No. 4, pp 502-511, 1989.

[9] Aarts E.H.L., Korst J.H.M., "Boltzmann machines for traveling salesman problems", *European Journal of Operational Research*, No. 39, pp 79-95, North-Holland, 1989.

[10] Abe S., "Theories on the Hopfield neural networks", *Proc. International Joint Conference on Neural Networks (IJCNN'89)*, Washington D.C., Vol. I, pp 557-564, June 1989.

[11] Abe S., "Determining weights of the Hopfield neural networks", *Proc. International Conference on Artificial Neural Networks (ICANN'91)*, Helsinki, pp 1507-1510, June 1991.

[12] Abe S., "Global convergence and suppression of spurious states of the Hopfield neural networks", *Trans. IEEE Circuits & Systems I*, in press.

[13] Ackley D.H., Hinton G.E., Sejnowski T.J., "A learning algorithm for Boltzmann machines", *Cognitive Science*, No. 9, pp 147-169, 1985.

[14] Aiyer S.V.B., Niranjan M., Fallside F., "A Theoretical Investigation into the Performance of the Hopfield Model", *IEEE Transactions on Neural Networks*, Vol. 1, No. 2, pp 204-215, June 1990.

[15] Aiyer S.V.B., Niranjan M., Fallside F., "On the optimization properties of the Hopfield model", *Proc. International Conference on Neural Networks (ICNN'90)*, pp 245-249, 1990.

[16] Akiyama Y., Yamashita A., Kajiura M., Aiso H., "Combinatorial Optimization with Gaussian Machines", *Proc. International Joint Conference on Neural Networks (IJCNN'89)*, Washington D.C., Vol. I, pp 533-540, 1989.

[17] Joppe A., Cardon H.R.A., Bioch J.C., "A neural network for solving the traveling salesman problem on the basis of city adjacency in the tour", *Proc. International Joint Conference on Neural Networks (IJCNN'90)* , San Diego, California, Vol. III, pp 961-964, June 1990.

[18] Wilson G.V., Pawley G.S., "On the stability of the traveling salesman problem algorithm of Hopfield and Tank", *Biological Cybernetics*, No. 58, pp 63-70, 1988.

[19] Gelenbe E., "Stability of the random neural network model", *Neural Computation*, Vol. 2, No. 2, pp. 239-247, 1990.

[20] Gelenbe E., Stafylopatis A., Likas A., "An extended random network model with associative memory capabilities", *Proc. International Conference on Artificial Neural Networks (ICANN'91)*, Helsinki, June 1991.

[21] Gelenbe, E., Stafylopatis, A., "Global behaviour of homogenous random neural systems", *Applied Math. Modelling*, **15** (1991), pp. 535–541.

[22] Pekergin, F. "Optimization Combinatoire avec le Réseau Neuraonal Aléatoire", Doctoral Thesis, EHEI – University of Paris V, Paris, 1992.

[23] Gelenbe E., Batty, F. "Minimum graph vertex covering with the Random Neural Network", in Balci, O., Sharda, R., and Zenios, S.A. (eds.), *Computer Science and Operations Research, New Developments and their Interfaces*, pp. 139-148, Pergamon Press, Oxford, 1992.

[24] Atalay V., Gelenbe E., Yalabık N., "The random neural network model for texture generation", *International Journal of Pattern Recognition and Artificial Intelligence*, Vol. 6, No. 1, pp 131-141, 1992.

[25] Atalay V., Gelenbe E., "Parallel algorithm for colour texture generation using the random neural network model", *International Journal of Pattern Recognition and Artificial Intelligence*, Vol. 6, No. 2-3, pp 437-446, 1992.

[26] Gelenbe E., "Learning in the recurrent random neural network", *Neural Computation*, Vol. 5, No. 1, pp 154-164, 1993.

[27] Gelenbe, E., Koubi, V., Pekergin, F. "Dynamic random neural approach to the Traveling Salesman Problem", *Proc. of the IEEE Annual Symposium on Systems, Man and Cybernetics (SMC)*,La Baule, September 1993.

[28] Koubi, V. "Le Problème du Voyageur de Commerce et le Réseau Neuronal Aléatoire", Doctoral Thesis, EHEI – University of Paris V, Paris, 1994 – in preparation.

A Simulated Annealing Approach to Job Shop Scheduling using Critical Block Transition Operators

Takeshi Yamada†, Bruce E. Rosen‡[1], and Ryohei Nakano†
yamada@cslab.ntt.jp, rosen@ringer.cs.utsa.edu, nakano@cslab.ntt.jp

†NTT Communication Science Laboratories
2 Hikaridai Seika-cho Soraku-gun, Kyoto 619-02 Japan
‡Division of Mathematics, Computer Science and Statistics
The University of Texas at San Antonio, San Antonio, Texas, 78249

***Abstract*—The Job Shop Scheduling Problem is one of the most difficult NP hard combinatorial optimization problems. This research investigates finding optimal and near optimal schedules using simulated annealing and a recently developed schedule permutation procedure. New schedules are generated by permuting operations within existing schedules. Simulated annealing probabilistically chooses one of the new schedules and probabilistically accepts or rejects it, allowing importance sampling search over the job shop schedule space. The initial and (minimum) final temperatures are adaptively determined *a priori*, and a reintensification strategy that improves the search by the resetting the current temperature and state. Experimental results show this simple and flexible method can find near optimal schedules and often outperforms previous SA approaches.**

I. Introduction

The $n \times m$ *minimum-makespan* general job shop scheduling problem (JSSP) can be described by a set of n jobs $\{J_j\}_{1 \leq j \leq n}$ that is to be processed on a set of m machines $\{M_r\}_{1 \leq r \leq m}$. The processing of job J_j on machine M_r is the operation $O_{j,r}$. Each job has a technological sequence of machines to be processed. Operation $O_{j,r}$ requires the exclusive use of M_r for an uninterrupted duration $p_{j,r}$, its processing time. The maximum time required to complete all the jobs on all machines is called the makespan L. The objective when solving or optimizing this general problem is to determine the processing order of all operations $\{O_{j,r}\}_{1 \leq j \leq n}$ on each machine M_r which minimizes L. The general job shop scheduling problem is not only NP-hard but is extremely hard to solve optimally. An indication of this is given by the fact that one 10×10 problem formulated in 1963 [1], remained unsolved for over 20 years.

Besides exhaustive search algorithms based on branch & bound algorithms, several approximation algorithms have been developed. The most popular ones in practice are based on priority rules and active schedule generations [2]. Adams *et al.* [3] developed a more sophisticated *shifting bottleneck* procedure which has been shown to be very successful. Also stochastic approaches such as simulated annealing [4] [5] and genetic algorithms [6] [7] have been applied recently with good success.

II. Background

A. Critical Block

A convenient representation known as the *disjunctive graph* model describes a job shop scheduling problem by a disjunctive graph $G = (V, C \cup D)$, where

- V is a set of nodes, representing the operations of the jobs together with two special nodes, a *source* $\circ$, and a *sink* $\star$, representing the beginning and end of the schedule respectively,
- C is a set of conjunctive arcs, representing the technological sequences (order) of the operations, and
- D is a set of disjunctive arcs, representing each pair of operations that must be performed on the same machines.

The processing time for each operation $O_{j,r}$ is the weighted value $p_{j,r}$ attached to the corresponding node.

Figure 1 shows an example of the disjunctive graph of a 3×3 problem. Circles represent the nodes, or operations. Solid arrows represent the conjunctive arcs, and dashed bidirectional arrows represent the disjunctive arcs. A complete schedule is obtained by defining an ordering between all operations on the same machine. In the disjunctive graph model, this is done by turning all undirected (disjunctive) arcs into directed ones. A selection S defines a feasible schedule if and only if the resulting directed graph $G(S) = (V, C \cup S)$ is acyclic. In this case, S is called a *complete selection*[2]. The makespan, $L(S)$, is given by the length of longest weighted path from the source to the sink in this graph. That path is called the *critical path* $\mathcal{P}$, and is composed of a sequence of *critical operations*. A subsequence of consecutive operations on $\mathcal{P}$ is called a *critical block* if

[1]This research was performed while the author was a visiting scientist at NTT Communication Science Laboratories and this work is based upon work supported by the National Science Foundation under grant No. (INT-931186).

[2]Without loss of generality, selections and their associated schedules will both be referred to by the symbol S.

1. all critical operations in that critical block are on the same machine, and
2. an operation (if it exists) on the same machine preceding (succeeding) the first (last) critical operation of the critical block is not on the critical path.

The critical path can be redefined as the sequence of critical blocks $\{B_i\}$, from the source to the sink:
$\mathcal{P} = (\circ, B_1, \ldots, B_j, \ldots, B_k, \star)$ where k is the number of critical blocks in $\mathcal{P}$.

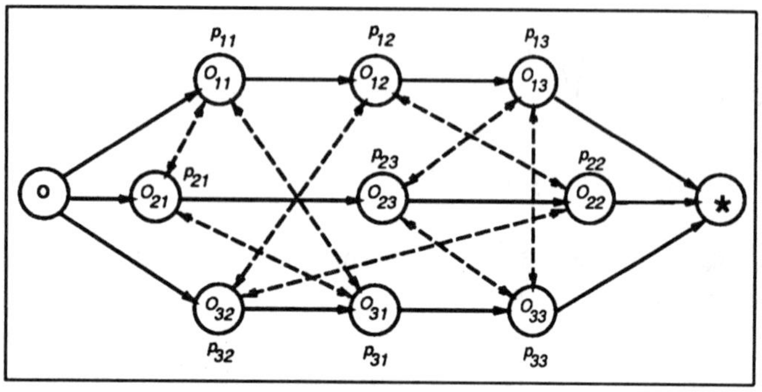

Fig. 1: The disjunctive graph G of a 3×3 problem.

B. The Critical Block Neighborhood

For the job shop scheduling task, a neighborhood $N(S)$ of a schedule S can be defined as the set of solutions, or feasible schedules, that can be reached from S by exactly one transition, a single perturbation of S. For example, one neighborhood employed in a simulated annealing approach by [4] and [5] utilizes a transition operator that exchanges a pair of consecutive operations in a critical block (Adjacent Swapping (AS) neighborhood). The transition operator was originally defined by *Balas* [8] in his branch and bound approach.

A very powerful transition operator also employed in a branch & bound search was proposed by [9] and [10]. The transition operator permutes the order of operations in a critical block by moving an operation to the beginning or the end of the critical block. Based on this idea, a *critical block neighborhood* $N^C(S)$ is defined for a schedule S as follows:

Let $B_j = (u_{1,j}, \ldots, u_{i,j}, \ldots, u_{l_j,j})$ represents the j'th critical block on $\mathcal{P}$. Here $u_{i,j}$ represents the i'th operation and l_j represents the number of operations in the sequence $(l_j = |B_j|)$.
The transition operators are $\mathcal{S}^b$ and $\mathcal{S}^a$, where

- $\mathcal{S}^b(S, u_{i,j})$, $1 < i \leq l_j$ creates a new selection by moving the i'th operation, $u_{i,j}$, within critical block B_j of schedule S to the front of B_j, and
- $\mathcal{S}^a(S, u_{i,j}), 1 \leq i < l_j$ creates a new selection by moving the i'th operation, $u_{i,j}$, within critical block B_j of schedule S to the rear of B_j.

The selections obtained by the applications of $\mathcal{S}^b$ or $\mathcal{S}^a$ are called *before* or *after* candidates respectively. Figure 2 shows an example of two permutations of a critical block by the transition operators.

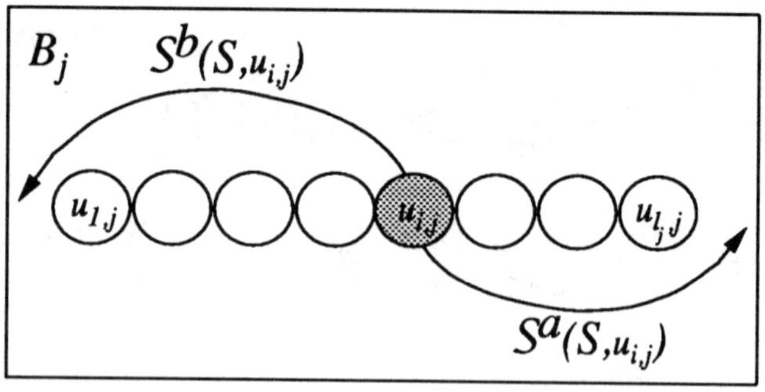

Fig. 2: Permutations of a critical block B_j when applying $\mathcal{S}^b(S, u_{i,j})$ or $\mathcal{S}^a(S, u_{i,j})$.

The set of all selections derived from S by the application of $\mathcal{S}^b$ and $\mathcal{S}^a$ are described as follows:

$$N'^C(S) = \{\mathcal{S}^b(S, u_{i,j}) \mid l_j > 1, i = 2, .., l_j, j = 1, .., k\}$$
$$\bigcup \{\mathcal{S}^a(S, u_{i,j}) \mid l_j > 1, i = 1, .., l_j - 1, j = 1, .., k\}$$

Since some selections in $N'^C(S)$ might contain cyclic arcs, and are therefore infeasible schedules, the critical block neighborhood is defined as

$$N^C(S) = \{S' \in N'^C(S) \mid S' \text{ is a complete selection}\}$$

If S does not contain any critical blocks of length greater than one, S must be optimal. Alternatively S will contain at least one critical block of length greater than one. $N'^C(S)$ may contain infeasible schedules, however $N^C(S)$ will never be empty, because the exchanging two consecutive operations in a critical block never leads to a cycle [4]. Therefore at least two schedules generated, $\mathcal{S}^b(S, u_{2,j})$ and $\mathcal{S}^a(S, u_{l_j-1,j})$, are always guaranteed to be feasible.

The neighborhood $N^C(S)$ is effective because any transition not on the critical path $\mathcal{P}$ will never shorten the makespan since $\mathcal{P}$ still exists as a path in the resulting schedule. Moreover, at least one of the operations different from the first or last operation in a block B_j in S must be processed before or after all other operations of B_j in S' when $L(S') < L(S)$ and S and S' are complete selections (See [10]).

Often, a schedule's makespan may be reduced by reassigning operations by shifting them to the left as follows. Consider two operations, $O_{j,r}$ and $O_{k,r}$, in a schedule which utilize the same machine M_r. Assume $O_{k,r}$ is processed prior to $O_{j,r}$ and machine M_r has an idle period longer than $p_{j,r}$ before processing $O_{k,r}$. Then $O_{j,r}$ may be reassigned to be processed prior to $O_{k,r}$. Such a reassignment is called a *permissible left shift*. When no permissible left shifts can be applied to a schedule, it is called an *active schedule* [11]. It is often useful to make an inactive schedule $S' \in N^C(S)$ active, if the resulting new schedule will be different from S.

C. Simulated Annealing

The general SA procedure is defined below.

1. Choose an initial (high) temperature T_0 and a random state x_0. $T_{k=0} \leftarrow T_0$, $x \leftarrow x_0$
2. Calculate the cost function value of the starting state. $E \leftarrow f(x_0)$
3. For each iteration k, $k = 1 \ldots k_f$ do the following:
   (a) Choose a new state x', using a generating function. $x' \leftarrow g(x)$
   (b) Calculate the cost of x'. $E' \leftarrow f(x')$
   (c) Set $x \leftarrow x'$ and $E \leftarrow E'$ with probability determined by the acceptance function h.
   (d) Reduce the temperature T by annealing (e. g. $T_{k+1} \leftarrow \gamma T_k$, $0 < \gamma < 1$).
   (e) When T is lower than a sufficiently small value T_f, exit the loop.
4. Return x and E as the (near) optimal state and function cost value.

For combinatorial optimization problems, a uniform random distribution is often used to generate new states

$$\text{Prob}(g(x) = x_j) = 1/n, \; x_j \in N(x) \quad j = 1, \ldots, n. \tag{1}$$

where n is the number of states that can be directly generated by the generating function, i.e. $n = |N(x)|$.

The acceptance probability function $h(x)$ is based on the chances of accepting a new state x' relative to the current state x, i.e. the difference of their function values

$$h(x') = \min(1, e^{-(f(x') - f(x))/T}) \tag{2}$$

The practical annealing schedule, T_k, most often used to find the global minimum is of the form

$$T_k = T_0 e^{-ck} \tag{3}$$

where c is a positive constant, and k is the number of annealing steps.

III. Critical Block Simulated Annealing

Critical Block Simulated Annealing (CBSA) is a method of searching the job shop scheduling space. For the job shop scheduling problem, a state x is defined by a particular schedule S, and the cost $f(x)$ is defined by the makespan $L(S)$. The algorithm is described below.

Algorithm – Critical Block Simulated Annealing –

set S = A randomly generated initial schedule
set initial step number $k = 0$
set $T_{k=0}$ = initial temperature T_0
do
  do
    Pick $S' \in N^C(S)$
    Accept S' probabilistically according to the Metropolis Criterion distribution, i.e. choose S' with probability one if $L(S') \leq L(S)$, and $e^{-(L(S') - L(S))/T}$ otherwise
    if S' is accepted **then do**
      set $S = S'$
      Increase k
      Decrease T_k according to the annealing schedule
    end if
  until S' is accepted
until termination (i.e. T_k is sufficiently small or k is sufficiently large or the minimal makespan or lower bound is found)
Print the best schedule found and its makespan

A. Reintensification

Often during the search process 1) the system state wanders far from states that are leading to the global minima, or 2) the system state may become trapped in a deep local minima. Then all schedules generated from the current schedule will have longer makespans. If the acceptance temperature is low, it may be difficult for the system to escape from this local minimum and continue the search.

Occasionally a reintensification strategy may be applied to improve the search. This reintensification is similar to reannealing [12], [13] which is used in numerical function optimization to occasionally reset the system temperature and the state of the system after a sufficiently long period of time without finding a new global minima.

It is useful to reintensify the search when a large number of acceptances have occurred without improving the problem makespan, or when the recent *acceptance to generated ratio* (AG ratio) becomes lower than a prescribed threshold, indicating that the system is caught in a minimum. The reintensification process replaces the current state (schedule) with the best state found so far, removing the system state from a local minimum if it has become trapped in a basin of attraction.

Reintensification also alters the annealing temperature to a more current and appropriate value. A new annealing temperature is calculated from the root mean square of the differences between the functional cost of best state and states in the best neighborhood. If the new resulting temperature is greater than the current temperature, then the current temperature is reset to the new temperature.

B. Annealing Parameters

Simulated annealing algorithms often require some parameter specific values be determined *a priori*. These annealing parameters include the initial and final temperatures (T_0, T_f), and the number of annealing steps (k_f). An appropriate temperature reduction function is also needed. Since both inverse logarithmic and inverse linear annealing schedules are too slow for practical consideration, it is useful to apply the exponential annealing schedule given in equation 3, with constant c determined by

$$c = -\log(T_f/T_0)/k_f. \quad (4)$$

For example, if the annealing schedule is defined so that $T_0 = 1$, $T_f = 10^{-20}$ and $k_f = 10000$, then
$c = -\log\,(10^{-20})/10000 = 0.0046$.

Since scheduling problems have different characteristics, constraints, and differing degrees of difficulty, different annealing schedules must be chosen to fit different problems. Because the initial and final lower bound temperatures are problem dependent parameters, they are difficult to determine *a priori*. By defining these temperatures in terms of the desired *uphill acceptance to generated (AG)* ratios, the temperatures can be determined adaptively from problem independent values. The initial uphill *AG* ratio should be relatively large so that a large number of uphill transitions are accepted. Later, at the end of the annealing schedule, the final uphill *AG* ratio should be small forcing most schedules having inferior makespans to be rejected.

The adaptive determination of the initial or final temperature can be incorporated in a short *warmup* sequence at the beginning of a simulation. A desired uphill *AG* threshold are chosen *a priori* which are used to adaptively determine the annealing temperatures. The reverse annealing process is implemented by starting at a sufficiently low temperature such that no uphill states are accepted, and increasing the temperature by a small percentage until the actual uphill *AG* ratio is greater than or equal to the desired threshold. This approach is similar to that defined by Aarts [14] (p59), however only *uphill* generated and accepted states determine the *AG* ratio. T_f provides a lower bound for the final temperature. This value would only be arrived at if all generated states would be accepted but realistically never occurs. For the initial temperature, T_0, an uphill *AG* threshold of 50% was found to be appropriate. For the final temperature, T_f, an uphill *AG* threshold of 0.2% proved most effective.

The total number of annealing steps k_f can be chosen empirically, but should be governed by the desired 1) to have reasonable small differences between successive temperatures, and 2) to have non-excessive trial run times, i.e. at most one or four hour per trial, and 3) to generate as many potential schedules as possible within the time limits.

If reintensification is to be used, two parameters must be specified to determine when it must be performed. The first parameter, the reintensification frequency R, determines how often reintensification should be performed. Reintensification can be applied after a set number of new schedules are accepted without finding an improved makespan. The second parameter is an *AG* threshold limit. Reintensification is performed when the current *AG* ratio falls below this value.

IV. Simulation Results

The performance of the CBSA algorithms was tested by running several simulation trials with and without reintensification. For the reintensification trials, two reintensification frequencies $R = 3,000$ and $R = 10,000$ were tested, both with an AG ratio threshold of 10^{-3}. Although reintensification violates the theoretical ergodicity of simulated annealing by resetting the state of the system, performances were found to be improved when reintensification was incorporated into the system.

Table 1 shows the minimum makespans of the first ten trials when the CBSA algorithm (with R=3,000) was initially applied to the difficult MT10×10 job shop scheduling problem[1]. Different random number seeds were used in each trial, resulting in each trial starting from a different randomly generated schedule. The CBSA algorithm was executed for a warm up period to generate new schedules and to gather acceptance rate statistics. The statistics were used to adaptively determine appropriate values for T_0 and T_f. T_f given in equation 4 was used to determine reasonable values for c.

The table also shows the number of actual schedules evaluated, the number of new schedules generated, and the cpu time for each of the trials. Since new schedules are often regenerated from the same current schedule, their makespans need not be reevaluated. Hence the actual number of schedules evaluated is always less than or equal to the number of generations. Optimal schedules are indicated by a star ⋆.

The last temperature (T_l) of the successful runs shown can vary considerably depending upon when the algorithm terminated. In table 1 the algorithm was terminated when an optimal solution was found, or when k was equal to k_f. Since T_f was determined from accepted, rather than generated states, any solution found on or before the last generation k_f will have an actual final temperature T_l larger than the initially determined T_f. The adaptively determined a priori final temperatures (not shown) were uniformly small, with mean 2.14 and standard deviation of 1.51 respectively.

Table 1: Ten Trials using the Simulated Annealing Method ($R = 3,000$).

No.	Best	e ×10³	g ×10³	T_0	T_l	Time
1	⋆930	481	548	51.84	06.19	38m00s
2	⋆930	510	537	44.83	10.61	41m28s
3	⋆930	507	580	47.04	06.20	40m08s
4	⋆930	344	332	49.40	17.33	28m45s
5	⋆930	367	404	44.76	07.89	28m40s
6	⋆930	459	472	47.09	14.83	37m59s
7	⋆930	372	405	38.69	09.07	29m08s
8	⋆930	649	711	38.76	09.57	51m39s
9	⋆930	317	352	36.83	08.41	25m00s
10	938	459	1000	54.39	00.50	36m06s

e: Evaluations, g: Generations

Although the last MT10×10 trial did not find the optimal solution, it did terminate with a makespan of 938. Trial ten's initial temperature, which was adaptively determined, was the highest of all of the trials. Hence it is likely that the system spent excessive amounts of annealing time performing random search at high temperatures. The cpu time and the number of function evaluations performed during the execution of trial ten was quite comparable with those of the successful trials. It is likely that the the system state became caught in a deep local minimum, allowing few if any new states to be explored.

Figure 3 shows the time evolution of the makespans of two typical trials with and without reintensification. The abscissa shows the number of schedules generated, and the ordinate shows the makespan differences between the current and optimal schedules. The highly oscillatory behavior of the reintensification trial is due to reintensification.

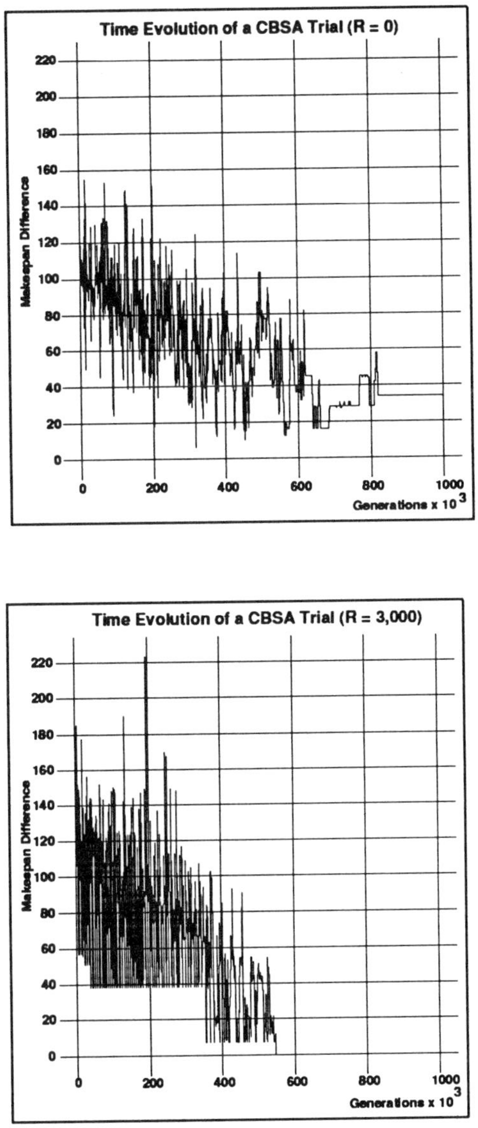

Fig. 3: Successive makespan differences between the current and optimal solution of the MT10×10 problem, without reintensification ($R = 0$) and with reintensification ($R = 3,000$).

The power of a reintensification and Critical Block neighborhood structure is illustrated in table 2 where the comparative performances of 10 trials of the CBSA and the simulated annealing using adjacent swapping neighborhood (ASSA) by Van Laarhoven *et al.* [4] are shown.

Table 2: Comparisons between CBSA and ASSA.

Method	$R=0$		$R=3,000$		$R=10,000$	
CBSA	930	945	930	938	930	938
	937.8	4.2	930.8	2.4	933.1	3.8
	(41 m 13 s)		(44 m 36 s)		(42 m 44 s)	
ASSA	938	972	930	951	934	970
	951.6	10.2	939.5	5.1	944.4	10.2
	(49 m 9 s)		(35 m 43 s)		(40 m 46 s)	

top left: mininum, top right: maximum, down left: mean, down right: standard deviation, (average cpu time)

All performances conditions were identical, except for the reintensification frequencies, (R=0 (no reintensification), R=3,000, and R=10,000), and the neighborhood structure. The performances are best when R=3,000 and the CBSA is used. Here R were chosen ad hoc. The values of R=3,000 appeared reasonable for the $MT10\times10$ problem, and has also used for the other benchmark problems. Clearly this is one parameter that may have to be tuned to the data.

A set of benchmark problems has been established to judge the effectiveness of algorithms on the JSSP. [3] Table 3 shows the makespan performances of the CBSA and various other algorithms on ten difficult benchmark problems.

The LB column indicates the lower bound of the problem if the optimal makespan is unknown. The *CBSA* column indicates the best makespan found from 5 CBSA trials. (Each trial used a reintensification frequency $R = 3,000$ and was run for one million generations or until the known optimal minimum makespan or lower bound was found.) The column headings *Laar* and *Appl* indicate the best performances of Applegate [16] and Van Laarhoven et. al. [4] respectively.

V. Discussion

It is clear that simulated annealing as a local optimization method is well suited for approximating optimal job shop schedules. Applying simulated annealing with the critical block generation method has had good results. When scheduling the MT10×10 problem, optimal solutions were frequently found.

According to Aarts [14] , the success of an approximation algorithm depends on a number of aspects including performances, ease of implementation, and applicability and flexibility. Experimental results show this method, possessing the simplicity and flexibility of SA, can find near optimal schedules for the difficult benchmark problems and can outperform the existing SA adjacent swapping approach as applied to job shop scheduling problems. The performance of the CBSA algorithms has been shown on a benchmark set of difficult job shop scheduling problems. This approach might be further improved by augmenting the essence of the simulated annealing and generating algorithm with other powerful heuristic based methods. For example, augmenting the method with Genetic Algorithms to

[3] We are grateful for the benchmark problem set given to us by D. Applegate [15].

Prob.	$n \times m$	LB	CBSA Methods				Larr	Appl
			best	mean	std.	Time		
abz7	20×15	654	671	679.00	6.57	$3h35m25s$		668
abz8	20×15	635	679	689.20	7.36	$3h58m34s$		687
abz9	20×15	656	701	712.00	6.07	$3h39m57s$		707
la21	15×10	1040	1050	1054.60	3.01	$1h07m02s$	1063	1053
la24	15×10	—	943	947.20	3.31	$0h48m01s$	952	935
la25	15×10	—	985	987.80	2.40	$1h11m16s$	992	977
la27	20×10	1235	1262	1266.00	2.76	$2h07m02s$	1269	1269
la29	20×10	1120	1188	1193.20	4.66	$2h31m10s$	1203	1195
la38	15×15	1184	1209	1214.00	2.76	$2h03m59s$	1215	1209
la40	15×15	—	1235	1248.80	11.48	$1h29m25s$	1234	1222

std.: standard deviation, Time: cpu time (average of five trials)

parallelize this algorithm may improve performance characteristics.

References

[1] J.F. Muth and G.L. Thompson. *Industrial Scheduling*. Prentice-Hall, Englewood Cliffs, N.J., 1963.

[2] S. S. Panwalkar and Wafix Iskander. A survey of scheduling rules. *Oper. Res.*, 25(1):45–61, 1977.

[3] J. Adams, E. Balas, and D. Zawack. The shifting bottleneck procedure for job shop scheduling. *Manage. Sci.*, 34(3):391–401, 1988.

[4] P.J.M. van Laarhoven, E.H.L. Aarts, and J.K. Lenstra. Job shop scheduling by simulated annealing. *Oper. Res.*, 40(1):113–125, 1992.

[5] H. Matsuo, C.J. Suh, and R.S. Sullivan. A controlled search simulated annealing method for the general jobshop scheduling problem. *Working Paper, 03-04-88, Department of Management, The University of Texas at Austin*, 1988.

[6] T. Yamada and R. Nakano. A genetic algorithm applicable to large-scale job-shop problems. In *Proc. 2nd PPSN (Brussels,Belgium)*, 1992.

[7] R. Nakano and T. Yamada. Conventional genetic algorithm for job shop problems. In *Proc. 4th ICGA (San Diego,CA.)*, pages 474–479, 1991.

[8] E. Balas. Machine sequencing via disjunctive graphs: an implicit enumeration algorithm. *Oper. Res.*, 17:941–957, 1969.

[9] J. Grabowski, E. Nowicki, and S. Zdrzalka. A block approach for single machine scheduling with release dates and due dates. *European Journal of Operational Research*, 26:278–285, 1986.

[10] P. Brucker, B. Jurisch, and B. Sievers. A branch & bound algorithm for the job-shop scheduling problem. *Discrete Applied Mathematics (to appear)*.

[11] B. Giffler and G.L. Thompson. Algorithms for solving production scheduling problems. *Oper. Res.*, 8:487–503, 1969.

[12] L. Ingber and B. E. Rosen. Genetic algorithms and very fast simulated reannealing: A comparison. *Mathematical and Computer Modeling*, 16(11):87–100, 1992.

[13] B. Rosen. Function optimization based on advanced simulated annealing. *Workshop on Physics and Computation, PhysComp 92*, 1992.

[14] E.H.L. Aarts and J.H.M. Korst. *Simulated Annealing and Boltzmann machines.* Wiley, Chichester, 1989.

[15] D. Applegate. Jobshop benchmark problem set. Personal Communication, 1992.

[16] D. Applegate and W. Cook. A computational study of the job-shop scheduling problem. *European Journal of Operational Research*, 3(2):149–156, 1991.

The Ordering-Oriented Hopfield Network

Joe-E Hu
Industrial and Manufacturing Engineering
Wayne State University
Detroit, Michigan 48202, USA

Pepe Siy
Electrical and Computer Engineering
Wayne State University
Detroit, Michigan 48202, USA

Abstract - The Travelling Salesman Problem (TSP) is a well known problem which can be solved using Hopfield Networks. The TSP solution with Hopfield Networks is based on the uniqueness constraint. This is, each city must be visited once and only once while trying to minimize the travelling distance. But in the real world applications, usually there are other equally important constraints needed to be considered. For example, an ordering constraint in how cities are to be visited. This paper proposes a modified Hopfield neural network architecture that can solve a new class of optimization problem, called "The Picking Stone Problem (PSP)". The PSP requires not only the uniqueness but also the ordering constraints. The neural network implementation to solve PSP tends to turn on neurons which satisfy the ordering constraint and this constraint is essential in solving stereo correspondence problem in binocular vision and can be applied to many other pattern recognition problems. In this paper we define the PSP, formulate its computational complexity, propose the ordering-oriented neural network architecture, discuss the performance of the proposed network by the traditional random initialization method, and propose a new initialization method to improve the performance of the network.

I. INTRODUCTION

The travelling salesman problem (TSP) is a classical problem in combinational optimization. The task is to find the shortest possible tour through a set of N cities that passes through each city exactly once. It is generally believed that the computational power needed to solve it grows exponentially with the number of the cities [1].

Hopfield and Tank proposed a hardwired analog computational network to solve the TSP. [2,3] But in the practical applications, the constraints used to solve a problem may be more complicated than TSP. For example, if you are travelling by bus, yet the cities that you would like to visit are not directly connected to each other, then you must travel in certain order along the road in order to satisfy the uniqueness requirement. Based on the Hopfield network solution of the TSP, we propose another class of optimization problem, the picking stone problem (PSP), which requires both the uniqueness and ordering constraints. We develop an ordering-oriented Hopfield network to solve the PSP problem. The proposed network can be modified to accommodate more constraints and then be applied to solve the stereo correspondence problem [4].

This paper is organized as follows. In Section 2, we describe the picking stone problem definition. In section 3, the mathematical formulation of the problem is derived. In Section 4, the neural network architecture is proposed to solve the PSP problem. In Section 5, the performance of the network is analyzed. In Section 6, a new initialization method is proposed to improve the performance of the network. In Section 7, the conclusions are made.

II. THE PICKING STONE PROBLEM (PSP)

The definitions of Picking Stone Problem (PSP) are stated as follows:

Suppose you ask a person to pick one stone from each of the X stone sets labelled from 1 to X, where each stone set contains the same number of stones labelled from 1 to i. It is required that the number of stones in each stone set must be greater than or equal to the number of stone sets (i>=X), and there should be at least two stone sets (X>=2). The person who picks the lightest total weights of the X stones wins the game, if he obeys the following special rules. 1. He must pick one stone per stone set. We can call this rule as the uniqueness constraint. 2. The stones in each set are labelled from 1 to i, if a person who picks the stone j from set Y, then from set Y+1, he must pick the stone with the label larger than j, and from set Y-1, he must pick the stone with label smaller than j. We can call this rule as the ordering constraint because the decision to pick a stone is based not only on the weights but also on the relative locations with the picks in the neighboring stone sets. This rule also implies that the positions of stones in a valid picking set are in a diagonal distribution across all the stone sets. 3. He can start to pick from any stone set. That is, he can pick stones in random sequences of the stone sets as long as he obeys the above rules.

For example, as shown in Fig. 1, there are four sets of stones. In each set, there are seven stones labelled from 1 to 7 and the weights of the stones are shown below each stone. If we pick the #2 stone in the 1st set, the #3 stone in the 2nd set, the #5 stone in the 3rd set, and the #7 stone in the 4th set, we get the best set possible. Any other valid picks have more weights than the above set. If we pick the lightest stone in every stone set, although we can get the lightest weights but we violate the PSP rule of ordering constraint in this example.

0-7803-1901-X/94 $4.00 ©1994 IEEE

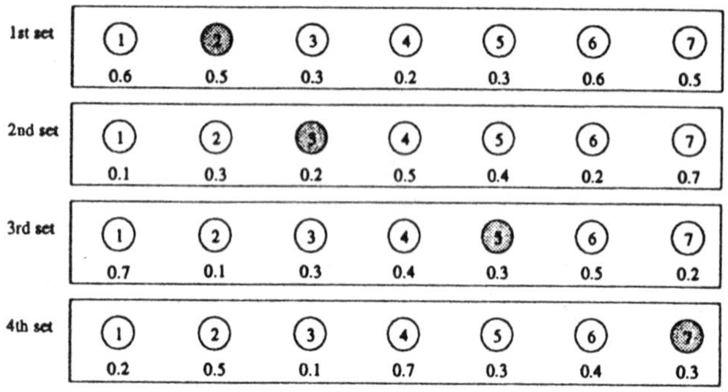

Fig. 1. A Picking Stone Problem example. There are four sets of stones. Each stone set has seven stones labelled from one to seven. The number under each stone indicates its weight. The light dotted stones are the set with the lowest weights in all possible valid picking combinations.

III. THE MATHEMATICAL FORMULATION AND COMPUTATION COMPLEXITY OF THE PSP.

In order to derive the mathematical equation to calculate the number of all possible valid picking sets of the PSP, we have to start from the basis frames which are the PSP with two stone sets. From Fig. 2, we can observe that the number of valid picking sets for basis frame is a straight forward summation as discussed in the next paragraph.

Before we start the discussion, let's first define the term PSP(X,i) as a PSP with X stone sets and i stones in each set,

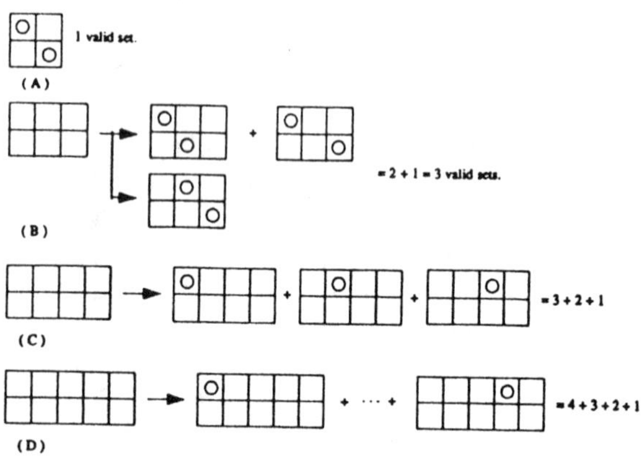

Fig. 2. From the condition (A) through (D), we can derive the conclusion for the basis frames. If there are i stones in each stone set, then the number of valid sets is the summation from 1 to (i-1).

S(m,n) as the nth stone in the mth stone set, PSP(2,i) as the basis frames, and VS(X,i) as the number of valid picking sets for PSP(X,i). For PSP(2,2) as shown in Fig. 2(A), there is only one possible set. For PSP(2,3) as shown in Fig. 2(B), it can be decomposed to two subproblems. One is to fix S(1,1) as a pick, then there are two possible sets based on this pick. Another is to fix S(1,2) as a pick, then there is only one possible set based on this pick. Thus, there are three valid sets for PSP(2,3). For PSP(2,4) as shown in Fig. 2(C), it can be decomposed to three subproblems. They are to fix S(1,1), S(1,2), and S(1,3) as a pick respectively, then count the valid sets for the corresponding pick. The PSP(2,5) is treated in the same manner. From the above discussion, we can find that to count the valid sets VS(2,i) for basis frames PSP(2,i) is nothing but to evaluate the following equation:

$$VS(2,i) = \sum_{p=1}^{i-1} P \qquad (1)$$

For example to count VS(2,6) is to calculate 1+2+3+4+5 which is 15. The equation for basis frames is very important because all the PSP can be decomposed to basis frames thus we are able to calculate the valid picking sets for any PSP.

Through analyzing the PSP(3,i), we can easily derive the general equation for calculating VS(X,i) for any PSP(X,i). For PSP(3,3), there is only one possible set as shown in Fig. 3(A).

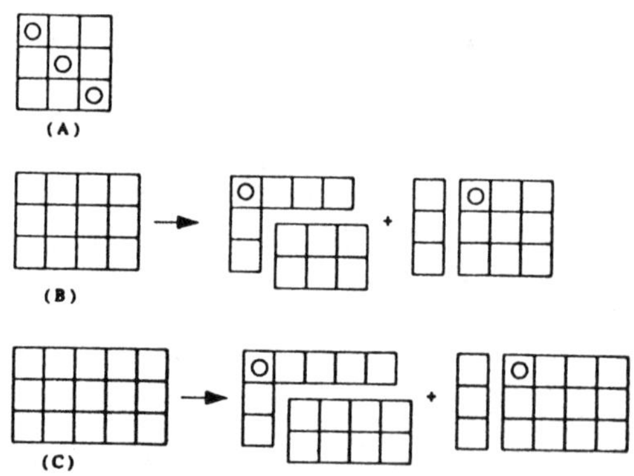

Fig. 3. The analysis of PSP(3,i). (A). VS(3,3)=1. (B). VS(3,4)= VS(2,3)+VS(3,3). (C). VS(3,5)=VS(2,4)+VS(3,4)

The PSP(3.4) can be decomposed to two subproblem as shown in Fig.3(B). One is to fix S(1,1) as a pick. If we do so, then it is the same as to figure out PSP(2,3). Another is not to pick S(1,1). If we do so, it is the same as to figure out the problem for PSP(3,3). For PSP(3,5), it can be decomposed to PSP(2,4) if we fix S(1,1) as a pick and to PSP(3,4) if we do not pick S(1,1) as shown in Fig. 3(C). We know how to calculate VS(2,i) for basis frames. Thus VS(3,5) can be easily calculated as VS(3,5) = VS(2,4) + VS(3,4) = VS(2,4) + VS(2,3) + VS(3,3). The same method can be applied to higher dimension. For example, VS(4,6)= VS(3,5) + VS(4,5) = VS(3,5) + VS(3,4) + VS(4,4). We know all VS(3,i) can be derive from VS(2,i). Thus it is solved.

Based on the above analysis, we can derived the general solution for VS(X,i) in a recursive equation as shown in equation 2.

$$VS(X, i) = VS(X-1, i-1) + VS(X, i-1) \quad (2)$$

where X <= i, VS(X,i)=1 when X=i, VS(2,i) is defined in equation 1, and VS(X,i)=0 when X=1.

Now the next question is what is the computational complexity for a random PSP? Here are the results for several PSPs based on equation 2.

VS(10,15)=3003

VS(20,30)=30045015

VS(40,60)= We use Multiflow Trace mini-super computer to run the simulation program for three days and still can not get the result.

From the above figures, it shows that PSP is a non-trivial problem. An Optimizing neural network is presented to solve PSP. This ordering-oriented architecture is then applied to the stereo correspondence problem.

IV. THE ENERGY FUNCTION AND ARCHITECTURE OF ORDERING-ORIENTED HOPFIELD NETWORK FOR SOLVING PSP.

The energy function for the ordering-oriented Hopfield network to solve the PSP is

$$\begin{aligned} E = {} & \frac{A}{2}\sum_{X}\sum_{i}\sum_{j\neq i}V_{X,i}V_{X,j} + \frac{B}{2}\sum_{i}\sum_{X}\sum_{X\neq Y}V_{X,i}V_{Y,i} \\ & + \frac{C}{2}\left(\sum_{X}\sum_{i}V_{X,i} - n_i\right)^2 \\ & + \frac{D}{2}\sum_{X}\sum_{i}\frac{1}{Normalization}\sum_{j>i}d_{X+1,j}V_{X,i}V_{X+1,j} \\ & + \frac{D}{2}\sum_{X}\sum_{i}\frac{1}{Normalization}\sum_{k<i}d_{X-1,k}V_{X,i}V_{X-1,k} \\ & + \frac{E}{2}\sum_{X}\sum_{i}\frac{1}{Normalization}\sum_{Y<X}\sum_{j>i}V_{Y,j}V_{X,i} \\ & + \frac{F}{2}\sum_{X}\sum_{i}\frac{1}{Normalization}\sum_{Y>X}\sum_{j<i}V_{Y,j}V_{X,i} \\ & + G\sum_{X}\sum_{i}d_{X,i}V_{X,i} \end{aligned} \quad (3)$$

where X,Y represent the Xth and Yth stone sets, i, j, and k represent the ith, jth, and kth stones in a stone set, $V_{X,i}$ indicates the output voltage of a neuron at location (X,i), $d_{X,i}$ is the weight for the ith stone in the Xth stone set, and A, B, C, D, E, F, and G are the weighting parameters. The normalization is required because the number of interconnections for each neuron is different.

The first term (with parameter A) is 0, if and only if no more than one stone is picked in every stone set. The 2nd term (with parameter B) is 0, if and only if there is no more than one stone is picked with the same stone label. The 3rd term (with parameter C) is 0, if n stones are picked. The 4th and 5th terms (with parameters D) are minimized when the total weights of the solution set is minimized. The 6th and 7th terms (with parameters E and F) are the inhibiting terms to implement the ordering constraint. For any stone (X,i), it inhibits the stones in its upper right and lower left areas as shown in Fig. 4 (A) and (B). If any neuron is turned on in the these areas while neuron (X,i) is turned on, then the solution set violates the ordering constraint. The 8th term is a bias term that injects a negative current proportional to the weight of each stone. So the stone with small weight will be more likely to be picked.

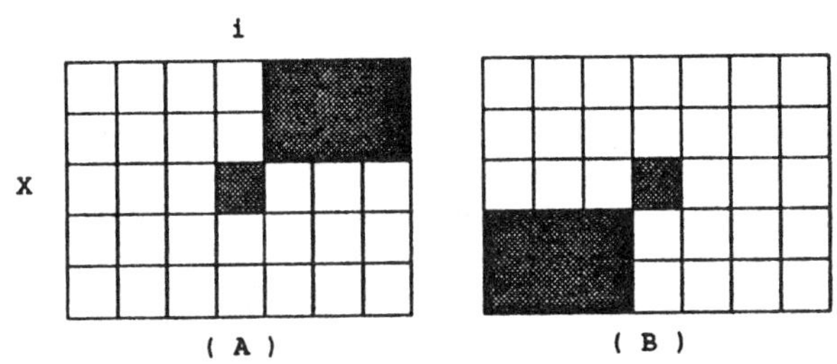

Fig. 4 (A) and (B) describe the inhibiting areas for implementing the ordering constraint.

According to the energy function, we can define the strength (conductance) of the interconnections between neurons. After the computation process being performed by the network system, the locations of those neurons which are turned on give us a set of solution.

V. THE PERFORMANCE ANALYSIS OF THE ORDERING ORIENTED HOPFIELD NETWORK.

The performance of the ordering-oriented neural network should be analyzed in terms of (1) the success rate (probability) that a test can obtain valid picking set, (2) how close the valid results compared to the global minimum obtained from exhaustive search in terms of the Average Departure (AD) rate which is the ratio of the difference between the average result and the global minimum to the global minimum. That is,

AD=(average_result-global_minimum)/(global_minimum) (4)

Both of the above two analyses are subject to different E and F values in equation 3. An extensive performance evaluation of the ordering-oriented Hopfield network has been conducted. The experiment uses ten randomly generated PSP(10,14). From equation 3, we know that E and F are ordering constraint parameters. The larger the E and F, the more likely a well ordered set will be picked. The simulation program initializes both E and F to 100 and increased by 100 at each subsequent trial until E and F reach 1000 to show the effects of different ordering strength. It is well known that the initial value of each neuron in Hopfield network tends to favor certain result, so 10 initial value sets for the network are randomly generated to test the average result. Thus, for each of the ten PSP(10,14), ten different ordering weights and ten different initial neuron values are used to test it. There are total 1000 tests in the experiment. The results are shown in Table 1. The first column of the table is the label of a PSP, the second column is the ordering weights, the third column is the exhaustively searched minimum of the PSP set, the fourth column is the average result of successful tests from different initial neuron values, the fifth column is the average error rate compared to the minimum using equation 4, the sixth column is the number of successful tries (maximum 10).

From the table, we can observe that we can always get valid PSP solutions by increasing the ordering weights E and F. When E and F is small, for example 100 or 200, we have high probability that the system can not pick a valid set. But from the error rate we can find that as we increase the ordering weights, the error rate may be increased too. That is because if the system emphasizes ordering too much, it tends to pick a valid set without putting deserved attention to the total weights of the solution set. That is why if we have small E and F value, although with low successful rate, we usually can get lower and better error rate than the results with higher E and F values.

VI. THE PROPOSED INITIALIZATION METHOD TO IMPROVE PERFORMANCE OF THE ORDERING-ORIENTED HOPFIELD NETWORK.

There are many theorems to improve the performance of the Hopfield network in terms of the departure rate. But most of the methods, for example simulated annealing [5], heavily relies on the temperature scheduling which is a very time consuming process. Although these methods can achieve better results, but they sacrifice speed. Ways to improve the performance that may benefit all kinds of Hopfield network without sacrificing speed have been studied.

A different initialization method is proposed. The proposed method initializes the neurons in the network with a value reversely proportional to the weight of the stone they represent. The lighter the stone, the larger the initialization value is assigned to it. The initialization equation is given by equation 5.

$$\mu_{X,i} = S \times (-d_{X,i} + 0.5) \times 2 \qquad (5)$$

where $\mu_{X,i}$ is the initial input voltage for the neuron (X,i), S is a scale down constant to keep initial value small and to prevent the initial value from saturating the network. The weight of the stone $d_{X,i}$ is normalized between 1 and 0, the term $(-d_{X,i} + 0.5) \times 2$ distributes the initial values to the range between 1 and -1 in an reverse order proportional to the stone's weight. The initial values generated by equation 5 favor the neurons representing low-weight stones.

The ten test sets used in section V is tested again by the proposed pre-determined initialization method. The last three columns in Table 1 are the results obtained using the above initialization method. Since the initial values are fixed and not random, there is no need to test it ten times for a given ordering weight E and F. It is either a successful try or a failure as shown in the 9th column of table 1. The result obtained from the neural network is shown in the 7th column. The departure rate is listed in the 8th column. The average departure rate of the random initialization method is 19% while for the proposed pre-determined method it is 11%. That is, it achieves an average improvement of 47% compared to the departure rate from the randomly initialized method.

VII. CONCLUSION

In this paper, the PSP is defined, formulated, and analyzed. From the analysis, we can find the need for a fast solution instead of using exhaustive search. From the testing results of the ordering-oriented neural network, PSP can be solved within reasonable error range. From the Table 1, we can understand the dynamics between different ordering weights in the energy function and results. The proposed initialization method may be applied to various Hopfield networks to improve their performances. This ordering oriented neural network can be modified easily to integrate all the major constraints in stereo vision to solve the stereo correspondence problem[4]. We are currently working on its applications in other fields.

VIII. REFERENCES

[1] R. Durbin, R. Szeliski, and A. Yulle, "An Analysis of the Elastic Net Approach to the Travelling Salesman Problem." Neural Computation, 1, pp. 348-358, Massachusettes Institute of Technology, 1989.

[2] J. J. Hopfield and D. W. Tank, "Computing with Neural Circuits: A Model," Science, vol. 233, pp. 625-632, Aug. 1986.

[3] J. J. Hopfield and D. W. Tank, "Computation of Decisions in Optimization Problems," Biological Cybernetics, 52, pp. 141-152, 1985.

[4] J. E. Hu and P. Siy, "Stereo Correspondence through Multiple Constraints Neural Networks," Proc. IEEE Intl. Conf. on Neural Networks, San Francisco, CA, March 28 - April 1, 1993.

[5] D. E. Rumelhart, J. L. McClelland, and the PDP Research Group, "Parallel Distributed Processing," vol. I and II, The MIT Press, 1986.

Test Set	Weight of Order	Global Minimum	Average Result	Average Error Rate	# Success / 10 tries	Result	Error Rate	# Success / 1 try
1	100	3.748	3.748	0.0	10	3.748	0.0	1
1	200	3.748	3.748	0.0	10	3.748	0.0	1
1	300	3.748	3.748	0.0	10	3.748	0.0	1
1	400	3.748	3.748	0.0	10	3.748	0.0	1
1	500	3.748	3.748	0.0	10	3.748	0.0	1
1	600	3.748	3.748	0.0	10	3.748	0.0	1
1	700	3.748	3.748	0.0	10	3.748	0.0	1
1	800	3.748	3.748	0.0	10	3.748	0.0	1
1	900	3.748	3.748	0.0	10	3.748	0.0	1
1	1000	3.748	3.748	0.0	10	3.748	0.0	1
2	100	3.169	N.A.	N.A.	0	N.A.	N.A.	0
2	200	3.169	3.432	0.083	8	3.395	0.071	1
2	300	3.169	3.428	0.082	9	3.395	0.071	1
2	400	3.169	3.428	0.082	9	3.395	0.071	1
2	500	3.169	3.461	0.092	9	3.395	0.071	1
2	600	3.169	3.538	0.116	9	3.395	0.071	1
2	700	3.169	3.605	0.138	9	3.395	0.071	1
2	800	3.169	3.642	0.149	10	3.395	0.071	1
2	900	3.169	3.667	0.157	10	3.395	0.071	1
2	1000	3.169	3.667	0.157	10	3.691	0.165	1
3	100	3.473	N.A	N.A	0	N.A	N.A	0
3	200	3.473	3.699	0.065	7	N.A	N.A	0
3	300	3.473	3.722	0.072	9	3.679	0.059	1
3	400	3.473	3.721	0.071	10	3.679	0.059	1
3	500	3.473	3.747	0.079	10	3.679	0.059	1
3	600	3.473	3.854	0.110	10	3.679	0.059	1
3	700	3.473	3.857	0.110	10	3.679	0.059	1
3	800	3.473	3.857	0.110	10	3.679	0.059	1
3	900	3.473	3.876	0.116	10	3.679	0.059	1
3	1000	3.473	3.896	0.122	10	3.679	0.059	1
4	100	2.757	3.002	0.089	4	N.A	N.A	0
4	200	2.757	3.489	0.266	8	3.061	0.110	1
4	300	2.757	3.728	0.352	10	3.061	0.110	1
4	400	2.757	3.867	0.403	10	3.061	0.110	1
4	500	2.757	4.026	0.460	10	3.563	0.292	1
4	600	2.757	4.026	0.460	10	3.563	0.292	1
4	700	2.757	4.088	0.483	10	3.581	0.299	1
4	800	2.757	4.109	0.490	10	3.581	0.299	1
4	900	2.757	4.130	0.498	10	3.581	0.299	1
4	1000	2.757	4.130	0.494	10	3.581	0.299	1
5	100	2.217	2.508	0.131	2	N.A	N.A	0
5	200	2.217	2.589	0.168	10	2.527	0.083	1
5	300	2.217	2.623	0.183	10	2.630	0.127	1
5	400	2.217	2.623	0.183	10	2.630	0.127	1
5	500	2.217	2.625	0.184	10	2.630	0.127	1
5	600	2.217	2.628	0.185	10	2.630	0.127	1
5	700	2.217	2.612	0.178	10	2.630	0.127	1
5	800	2.217	2.612	0.178	10	2.630	0.127	1
5	900	2.217	2.596	0.171	10	2.630	0.127	1
5	1000	2.217	2.580	0.164	10	2.630	0.127	1
6	100	3.183	3.569	0.121	2	N.A	N.A	0
6	200	3.183	4.151	0.304	9	3.447	0.083	1
6	300	3.183	4.544	0.428	10	3.587	0.127	1
6	400	3.183	4.870	0.530	10	3.587	0.127	1
6	500	3.183	4.856	0.526	10	3.587	0.127	1
6	600	3.183	4.908	0.542	10	3.587	0.127	1
6	700	3.183	4.933	0.550	10	3.587	0.127	1
6	800	3.183	4.933	0.550	10	3.587	0.127	1
6	900	3.183	5.005	0.572	10	3.587	0.127	1

Test Set	Weight of Order	Global Minimum	Average Result	Average Error Rate	# Success / 10 tries	Result	Error Rate	# Success / 1 try
6	1000	3.183	5.005	0.472	10	3.587	0.127	1
7	100	2.713	2.985	0.100	10	N.A	N.A	0
7	200	2.713	3.026	0.115	10	2.789	0.028	1
7	300	2.713	3.058	0.127	10	2.789	0.028	1
7	400	2.713	3.140	0.157	10	2.789	0.028	1
7	500	2.713	3.140	0.157	10	2.713	0.0	1
7	600	2.713	3.289	0.212	10	2.713	0.0	1
7	700	2.713	3.267	0.204	10	2.789	0.028	1
7	800	2.713	3.332	0.228	10	2.789	0.028	1
7	900	2.713	3.360	0.238	10	2.987	0.101	1
7	1000	2.713	3.414	0.258	10	2.987	0.101	1
8	100	3.485	3.621	0.039	9	N.A.	N.A.	0
8	200	3.485	3.594	0.031	10	3.564	0.023	1
8	300	3.485	3.594	0.031	10	3.564	0.023	1
8	400	3.485	3.663	0.051	10	3.662	0.051	1
8	500	3.485	3.734	0.071	10	3.662	0.051	1
8	600	3.485	3.734	0.071	10	3.662	0.051	1
8	700	3.485	3.734	0.071	10	4.064	0.166	1
8	800	3.485	3.774	0.083	10	4.064	0.166	1
8	900	3.485	3.841	0.102	10	4.064	0.166	1
8	1000	3.485	3.841	0.102	10	4.064	0.166	1
9	100	2.470	2.587	0.047	1	N.A.	N.A.	0
9	200	2.470	3.306	0.339	10	N.A	N.A	0
9	300	2.470	3.343	0.353	10	N.A	N.A	0
9	400	2.470	3.395	0.375	10	N.A	N.A	0
9	500	2.470	3.331	0.348	10	N.A	N.A	0
9	600	2.470	3.371	0.365	10	N.A	N.A	0
9	700	2.470	3.411	0.381	10	N.A	N.A	0
9	800	2.470	3.411	0.381	10	N.A	N.A	0
9	900	2.470	3.411	0.381	10	3.289	0.332	1
9	1000	2.470	3.420	0.381	10	3.289	0.332	1
10	100	2.635	2.687	0.020	5	N.A.	N.A.	0
10	200	2.635	2.699	0.024	10	2.848	0.081	1
10	300	2.635	2.699	0.024	10	2.848	0.081	1
10	400	2.635	2.781	0.055	10	2.848	0.081	1
10	500	2.635	2.760	0.047	10	2.848	0.081	1
10	600	2.635	2.760	0.047	10	2.848	0.081	1
10	700	2.635	2.863	0.087	10	3.143	0.193	1
10	800	2.635	2.921	0.109	10	3.143	0.193	1
10	900	2.635	2.921	0.109	10	3.143	0.193	1
10	1000	2.635	3.025	0.148	10	3.143	0.193	1

Table 1. The performance of Ordering Oriented neural network.

A Neural Network Approach to Broadcast Scheduling in Multi-hop Radio Networks

Gangsheng Wang and Nirwan Ansari
Center for Communications and Signal Processing Research
Department of Electrical and Computer Engineering
New Jersey Institute of Technology, University Heights, Newark, NJ 07102

Abstract— **The problem of scheduling interference-free transmissions with maximum throughput in a multi-hop radio network is NP-complete. The computational complexity becomes intractable as the network size increases. In this paper, the scheduling is formulated as a combinatorial optimization problem. An efficient neural network approach, namely, mean field annealing, is applied to obtain optimal transmission schedules. Numerical examples show that this method is capable of finding an interference-free schedule with (almost) optimal throughput.**

I. Introduction

A RADIO network consists of a set of stations which communicate with each other using broadcast radio. Packet radio networks and cellular mobile telephone networks are two typical examples. The stations in a multi-hop radio network share radio channels. To avoid interference, the neighboring stations are assigned different channels among a set of available channels, and stations at a distance might reuse the same set of channels without causing interference. In time division multiplexing access (*TDMA*) systems, the channel assignment is scheduled in a frame format consisting of fixed-length time slots, where each transmission is allocated a time slot in such a way that transmissions scheduled to the same time slot will not interfere with each other. In a frame, each station must be assigned at least one slot for transmission. For a broadcast schedule where the transmission time of stations is arranged, there might exist two types of interferences: primary and secondary. A primary interference occurs when a station receives transmissions designated to it from different stations simultaneously. A secondary interference occurs when a station receiving a particular transmission intended for it is within the range of another transmission for other stations. Therefore, broadcast scheduling in a TDMA system should try to provide an optimal schedule which has the maximum number of interference-free transmissions.

Several scheduling algorithms have been proposed in the literature [1]-[4]. In [1], the authors showed that the broadcast scheduling problem is NP-complete and proposed a heuristic scheduling algorithm. In [2], extensive simulations and comparisons were made among the scheduling algorithms [1]-[4]. It has been shown that the algorithm described in [1] provides the best performance in term of throughput.

For NP-complete problems, an exact search for the best solution is very difficult, if not impossible. Instead of searching for the best solutions, some approximation algorithms are used to find near-optimal solutions. In this paper, an efficient approximation method, *mean field annealing* (MFA), is applied to finding optimal schedules in multi-hop radio networks.

II. Problem Formulation

A radio network can be described by a directed graph $G = (S, A)$, where S is the set of stations and A is the set of arcs between stations. For any two stations $i, j \in S$, arc $(i,j) \in A$ if and only if station j is in the transmission range of station i. All stations are assumed to have the same transmission range R, and use the same frequency band for transmission. Station i and j are neighbors if station i is in the transmission range of station j and vice versa. Under these assumptions, a radio network can be described by an undirected graph $G = (S, A)$, where if $(i,j) \in A$, then $(j,i) \in A$, and station i is called a one-hop neighbor of station j and vice versa. Station k is a two-hop neighbor of station i if $(i,j) \in A$, $(j,k) \in A$, but $(i,k) \notin$ A.

The number of time slots in a frame is set to be equal to the number of stations N in a radio network. We define that

$$a_{ij} = \begin{cases} 1 & \text{if station } j \text{ is a one-hop or two-hop} \\ & \text{neighbor of station } i, \\ 0 & \text{otherwise,} \end{cases}$$

and

$$s_{kl} = \begin{cases} 1 & \text{if station } l \text{ transmits in the } k\text{-th slot} \\ & \text{in a frame,} \\ 0 & \text{otherwise,} \end{cases}$$

where $a_{ii} = 1 \; \forall i$. The schedule should be chosen to avoid both primary and secondary interferences.

This work was supported, in part, by the New Jersey Institute of Technology under Grant No. 421250.

Thus, the problem constraint becomes

$$\sum_{i \neq j} a_{ij} \cdot s_{ki} \cdot s_{kj} = 0. \quad (1)$$

The throughput (transmissions/slot)

$$\gamma_{\mathbf{s}} = \frac{1}{N} \sum_{k=1}^{N} \sum_{i=1}^{N} s_{ki}. \quad (2)$$

N is the total number of stations in a radio network. Therefore, the broadcast scheduling problem can be formulated as a constrained optimization problem as follows:

find the optimal schedule $\mathbf{s}^{\mathbf{opt}}$ such that

$$\gamma_{\mathbf{s}^{opt}} = \max_{\mathbf{s}} \quad \gamma_{\mathbf{s}} = \max_{\mathbf{s}} \frac{1}{N} \sum_{k=1}^{N} \sum_{i=1}^{N} s_{ki}, \quad (3)$$

subject to

$$\sum_{k=1}^{N} \sum_{i=1}^{N} \sum_{j=1}^{N} a_{ij} \cdot s_{ki} \cdot s_{kj} (1 - \delta_{ij}) = 0, \quad (4)$$

where

$$\delta_{ij} = \begin{cases} 1 & \text{if } i = j, \\ 0 & \text{otherwise.} \end{cases}$$

III. The MFA Algorithm to Optimize Broadcast Schedules

For a binary neural network, MFA uses the thermal averages of neurons to approximate the stochastic process of simulated annealing. This approximation provides an efficient method to search for optima [5]. The MFA procedure can be briefly summarized as follows:

Formulate energy function $E(\mathbf{s})$
Initialize $< s_i >_T = \frac{1}{2} \pm \Delta$ *(Δ is a small positive number)*
$T \leftarrow T_c$ *(Critical temperature)*
While (Criteria of terminating iterations are not satis-
fied)
do until (equilibrium is reached)
for(i=1,i≤ M, i++)
update neuron i:
$< s_i >_T = \frac{1}{2}[1 + tanh(\frac{1}{T} \cdot h_i^{MFT})]$,
$h_i^{MFT} = -\frac{\partial E(< s_i >_T)}{\partial (< s_i >_T)}$.
$T \leftarrow \alpha T$ $(\alpha < 1)$

$< s_i >_T$ is the thermal average of neuron i and M is the total number of neurons.

A. Energy function

$$\begin{aligned} E(\mathbf{s}) &= \frac{w_1}{2} E_1 + \frac{w_2}{2} E_2 + w_3 E_3 \\ &= -\frac{w_1}{2N} \sum_{i=1}^{N} \sum_{j=1}^{N} s_{ij}^2 + \frac{w_2}{2} \sum_{i=1}^{N} \sum_{j=1}^{N} \sum_{k=1}^{N} a_{ij} s_{ki} s_{kj} \\ &\quad \cdot (1 - \delta_{ij}) + w_3 \sum_{i=1}^{N} \sum_{j=1}^{N} s_{ij} (1 - s_{ij}). \end{aligned} \quad (5)$$

There are $N \times N$ neurons. E_1 in (5) corresponds to the negative throughput; E_2 to the constraint (4), and E_3 is used to force all neurons to their steady states {0,1}. The state with the minimum energy corresponds to the optimal schedule. The constraints E_2 and E_3 must be appropriately weighed. If they are heavily weighed, the MFA algorithm might lead to poor solutions which satisfy the constraints but provide less throughput. On the other hand, less weighed constraints would result in invalid solutions. Appropriately selected weights w_1, w_2, w_3 will result in global optimal schedules. In our simulations, the weights are chosen empirically, and we use

$$w_2 = 2w_3, \qquad w_1 = 5Nw_3. \quad (6)$$

B. Critical Temperature

Each neuron is updated according to:

$$v_{ij}^{(n)} = \frac{1}{2} + \frac{1}{2} tanh[-\frac{1}{T} \frac{\partial E(v^{(n-1)})}{\partial v_{ij}^{(n-1)}}] \qquad \forall i, j, \quad (7)$$

where $v_{ij} =< s_{ij} >_T$, and $< \cdot >$ is the averaging operator. $v = (v_{ij})$ is the neuron matrix of dimension $N \times N$, and n stands for the n-th iteration.

From (7), it is seen that iterations starting at too high a temperature result in trivial solutions. Starting at too low a temperature, on the other hand, might force the system into a poor or invalid solution. Critical temperature is defined as the temperature at which fast state transitions begin.

For the scheduling problem,

$$\begin{aligned} v_{ij}^{(n)} &= \frac{1}{2} + \frac{1}{2} tanh[-\frac{1}{T} \frac{\partial E(v^{(n-1)})}{\partial v_{ij}^{(n-1)}}] \\ &= \frac{1}{2} + \frac{1}{2} tanh\{-\frac{1}{T}[-\frac{W_1}{N} v_{ij}^{(n-1)} + W_2 \sum_{k=1}^{N} c_{jk} \\ &\quad \cdot v_{ik}^{(n-1)} (1 - \delta_{jk}) + W_3 (1 - 2v_{ij}^{(n-1)})]\}. \end{aligned} \quad (8)$$

It is seen from Eq. (8) that the state of each neuron remains relatively unchanged at high temperatures.

The iteration procedure in Eq. (8) should start at a temperature (the critical temperature) at which fast transition begins as illustrated in Fig. 1 until steady state is reached. Thus,

$$|\frac{1}{T_c}\frac{\partial E}{\partial v_{ij}^{(0)}}| = \alpha,$$

where $0.1 \leq \alpha \leq 0.2$ is chosen, at which state transition becomes rapid. Since all neurons v_{ij} are initialized to $0.5 \pm \Delta$, we chose

$$\begin{aligned} T_c &= \frac{1}{\alpha}|\frac{\partial E}{\partial v_{ij}^{(0)}}| \\ &= \frac{1}{\alpha}|-\frac{W_1}{N}v_{ij}^{(0)} + W_2\sum_{k=1}^{N} c_{jk}v_{ik}^{(0)}(1-\delta_{ij}) \\ &\quad +W_3(1-2v_{ij}^{(0)})| \\ &\approx \frac{1}{\alpha}|-\frac{0.5W_1}{N} + W_2\sum_{k=1}^{N} 0.5c_{jk}(1-\delta_{ij})|. \quad (9) \end{aligned}$$

Thus,

$$T_c \geq \frac{1}{2\alpha}[-\frac{W_1}{N} + W_2 \cdot \underset{j}{min} \sum_{k=1}^{N} c_{jk}(1-\delta_{jk})],$$

or

$$T_c \leq \frac{1}{2\alpha}[-\frac{-W_1}{N} + W_2 \cdot \underset{j}{max} \sum_{k=1}^{N} c_{jk}(1-\delta_{jk})].$$

The lower bound for the temperature is taken as

$$T_c = \frac{1}{2\alpha}[-\frac{W_1}{N} + W_2 \cdot \underset{j}{min} \sum_{k} c_{jk}(1-\delta_{jk})]. \quad (10)$$

The derived critical temperature is suitable only for the synchronous mode, in which all $v_{ij}^{(n)}$ are updated simultaneously using the previous $v^{(n-1)}$. For the asynchronous mode, each neuron is sequentially updated. The critical temperature for asynchronous iteration can be estimated by a *trial-and-error* method, i.e., the iteration starts at a very high temperature and the temperature is gradually lowered. At each temperature, each neuron is sequentially updated once. At the end of each iteration, the average absolute value

$$AAE = \frac{1}{N^2}\sum_i\sum_j |v_{ij}^{(n)} - v_{ij}^{(n-1)}| \quad (11)$$

is checked. At high temperatures, $AAE \ll \alpha$ for some constant α. When $AAE \geq \alpha$, significant state transitions begin. Therefore, when $AAE \geq \alpha$, the trial process ends, at which point the corresponding temperature is critical.

C. Annealing Schedule

The annealing schedule reflects the way the temperature is reduced, and the following empirical annealing schedule

$$T_{n+1} = 0.9 \cdot T_n \quad (12)$$

is adopted in our simulations.

D. Stopping Criterion

At a very low temperature, all neurons converge to either 0 or 1. Let

$$error = \frac{1}{N^2}\sum_i\sum_j v_{ij}^{(n)}(1-v_{ij}^{(n)}). \quad (13)$$

Thus, the iterative process may stop either when the error is approaching 0 (in our case, error ≤ 0.01) or when the temperature reaches 0. The final values of neurons represent the schedule.

IV. Numerical Examples and Results

To demonstrate the feasibility of the proposed method, networks of different sizes are considered. The topologies of the networks are randomly selected. Fig. 2 shows two of the networks with 15 and 40 stations. The resulting broadcast schedules obtained by MFA are shown in Table 1, where $s_{ij} = 1$ means that station j can transmit at the i-th slot. Since the algorithm in [1] always provides the highest throughput among other algorithms [1]-[4], we only compare our results with [1]. The throughput achieved by both of the algorithms for different networks are plotted in Fig. 3, which shows that the MFA algorithm provides better performance. For the 15-station network, both of the schedules achieve the global maximum throughput. For the other two networks, even though we are unable to conclude that the schedules obtained by MFA provide the global maximum throughput, they do achieve higher throughput than the other schedules. Like the algorithm in [1], the MFA scheduling algorithm generates an uneven allocation of time slots among stations. The reason is that the uneven schedules yield higher throughput than their evenly distributed counterparts.

If an additional term,

$$\frac{w_4}{2}\sum_i(\sum_k s_{ki} - \frac{1}{N}\sum_a\sum_b s_{ab})^2, \quad (14)$$

is introduced in the energy function, a more even schedule is expected. However, the even schedules might not provide maximum throughputs.

V. Conclusion

The broadcast scheduling in a multi-hop radio network is formulated as a combinatorial optimization problem. It is mapped into an unconstrained optimization framework such that it can be solved by the efficient neural network-based approach, mean field annealing. (Almost) optimal schedules are consistently obtained, and in many cases, the proposed approach achieves larger throughput than the state-of-art method mentioned in [1].

References

[1] A. Ephremides and T. V. Truong, "Scheduling Broadcasts in multihop radio network," *IEEE Trans. on Commun.*, COM-38, pp. 456-460, April, 1990.

[2] K. Hung and T. Yum, "Fair and efficient transmission scheduling in multihop packet radio networks," Proc. of GLOBECOM'92, pp. 6-10, Phoenix, AZ, Dec. 1992.

[3] R. Ramaswami and K. Parhi, "Distributed scheduling of broadcasts in a radio network," Proc. of INFOCOM'89, pp. 497-504, April 1989.

[4] I. Chlamtac, "On broadcasting in radio networks - problem analysis and protocol design," *IEEE Trans. on Commun.*, COM-33, pp. 1240-1246, December, 1985.

[5] C. Peterson and J. Anderson, "Neural networks and NP-complete optimization problems: a performance study on the graph bisection problem," *Complex Systems*, Vol. 2, pp. 59-71, 1988.

[6] C. Peterson and E. Hartman, "Explorations of the mean field theory learning algorithm," *Neural Networks*, Vol. 2, pp. 475-494, 1989.

[7] F. Kamoun and M. K. Mehmet Ali, "A neural network shortest path algorithm for optimum routing in packet-switched communications networks," *Proceedings of 1991 IEEE Global Telecommunications Conference*, Phoenix, Arizon, December 2-5, 1991, p. 120-124.

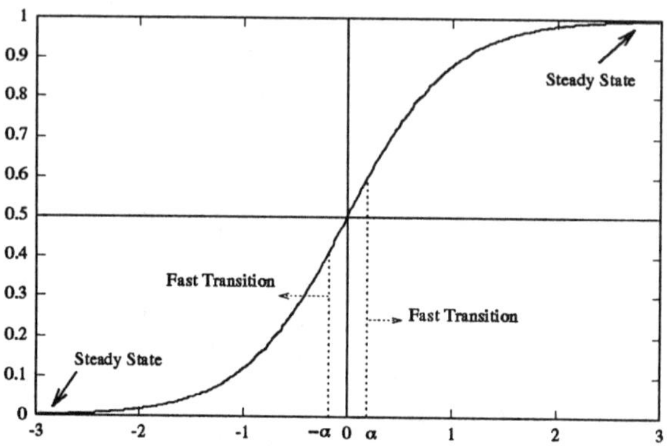

Fig. 1. The plot of $v_{ij}^{(n)}$ vs. $\frac{1}{T}\frac{\partial E}{\partial v_{ij}^{(n-1)}}$ – illustration of fast state transition.

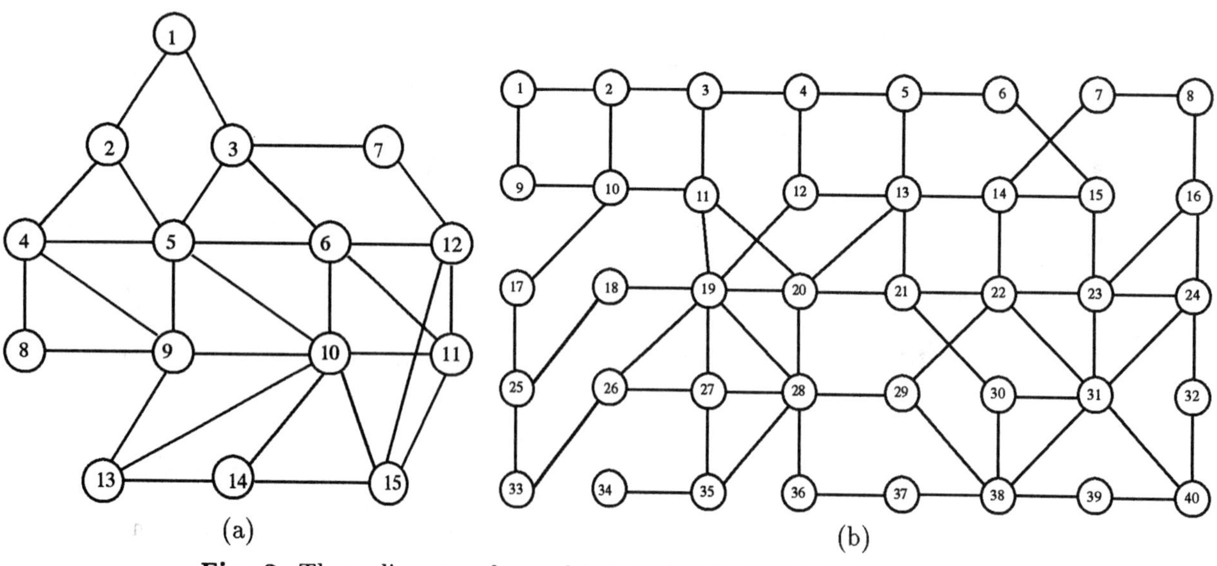

Fig. 2. The radio networks used in the simulation. (a) the 15-station network and (b) the 40-station network.

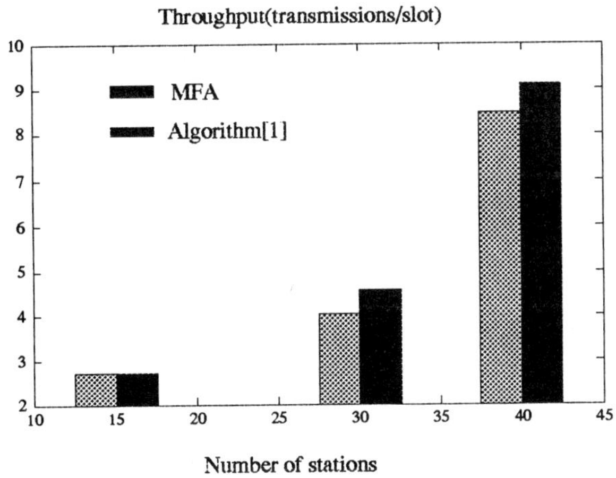

Fig. 3. The Througput for both of MFA and Algorithm [1].

time slot \ station	1	2	3	4	5	6	7	8	9	10	11	12	13	14	15
1	1	0	0	0	0	0	0	1	0	0	0	0	0	0	1
2	0	1	0	0	0	0	1	0	0	0	0	0	1	0	0
3	0	0	1	0	0	0	0	1	0	0	0	0	0	1	0
4	0	0	0	1	0	0	1	0	0	0	0	0	0	1	0
5	0	0	0	0	1	0	0	0	0	0	0	0	0	0	0
6	0	0	0	0	0	1	0	1	0	0	0	0	0	0	0
7	0	1	0	0	0	0	1	0	0	0	0	0	0	1	0
8	1	0	0	0	0	0	0	1	0	0	0	0	0	1	0
9	1	0	0	0	0	0	0	0	1	0	0	1	0	0	0
10	1	0	0	0	0	0	0	0	0	1	0	0	0	0	0
11	1	0	0	0	0	0	0	1	0	0	1	0	0	0	0
12	1	0	0	0	0	0	0	1	0	0	0	1	0	0	0
13	0	1	0	0	0	0	0	0	0	0	0	1	1	0	0
14	0	0	0	0	0	0	1	1	0	0	0	0	0	1	0
15	1	0	0	0	0	0	0	1	0	0	0	0	0	0	1

(a)

time slot \ station	1	2	3	4	5	6	7	8	9	10	11	12	13	14	15	16	17	18	19	20	21	22	23	24	25	26	27	28	29	30	31	32	33	34	35	36	37	38	39	40
1	1	0	0	1	0	0	0	1	0	0	0	0	0	0	1	0	1	0	0	0	1	0	0	0	0	1	0	0	0	0	0	1	0	1	0	1	0	0	0	0
2	0	1	0	0	0	1	0	1	0	0	0	1	0	0	0	0	0	0	0	0	0	1	0	0	0	0	0	0	0	0	0	1	1	1	0	1	0	0	0	0
3	0	0	1	0	0	1	0	1	1	0	0	0	0	0	0	0	0	0	0	0	1	0	0	0	0	0	0	0	0	0	0	1	1	1	0	1	0	0	0	0
4	1	0	0	1	0	0	0	1	0	0	0	0	0	0	1	0	1	0	0	0	1	0	0	0	0	1	0	0	0	0	0	1	0	1	0	1	0	0	0	0
5	1	0	0	0	1	0	0	1	0	0	1	0	0	0	0	0	0	0	0	0	0	0	0	0	0	0	0	0	0	1	0	1	1	1	0	1	0	0	0	0
6	0	0	1	0	0	1	1	0	1	0	0	0	0	0	0	0	0	0	0	0	1	0	0	1	0	0	0	0	0	0	0	0	1	1	0	1	0	0	1	0
7	0	0	1	0	0	1	1	0	1	0	0	0	0	0	0	0	0	0	0	0	1	0	0	1	0	0	0	0	0	0	0	0	1	1	0	1	0	0	1	0
8	0	0	1	0	0	0	0	1	1	0	0	0	0	0	1	0	0	0	0	0	1	0	0	0	0	0	0	0	0	0	0	1	1	1	0	1	0	0	0	0
9	0	0	1	0	0	1	0	1	1	0	0	0	0	0	0	0	0	0	0	0	1	0	0	0	0	0	0	0	0	0	0	1	1	1	0	1	0	0	0	0
10	0	0	0	1	0	1	0	1	0	1	0	0	0	0	1	0	0	0	0	0	1	0	0	0	0	0	0	0	0	0	0	1	1	1	0	1	0	0	0	0
11	1	0	0	0	0	1	0	1	0	0	1	0	0	0	0	0	0	0	0	0	0	0	0	0	0	0	0	0	0	1	0	1	1	1	0	1	0	0	0	0
12	1	0	0	0	0	1	0	1	0	0	0	1	0	0	0	0	0	0	0	0	0	1	0	0	0	0	0	0	0	0	0	1	1	1	0	1	0	0	0	0
13	0	0	1	0	0	0	0	1	1	0	0	0	1	0	0	0	0	0	0	0	0	0	0	0	0	0	0	0	0	0	0	0	1	1	0	1	0	0	0	1
14	1	0	0	1	0	0	0	0	0	0	0	0	0	1	0	1	1	0	0	0	0	0	0	0	0	1	0	0	0	0	0	0	0	1	0	1	0	0	0	1
15	1	0	0	1	0	0	0	1	0	0	0	0	0	0	1	0	1	0	0	0	1	0	0	0	0	1	0	0	0	0	0	1	0	1	0	1	0	0	0	0
16	0	0	1	0	0	1	0	0	1	0	0	0	0	0	0	1	0	0	0	0	1	0	0	0	0	0	0	0	0	0	0	0	1	1	0	1	0	0	0	1
17	1	0	0	1	0	0	0	1	0	0	0	0	0	0	1	0	1	0	0	0	1	0	0	0	0	1	0	0	0	0	0	1	0	1	0	1	0	0	0	0
18	0	0	1	0	0	1	0	1	1	0	0	0	0	0	0	0	0	1	0	0	1	0	0	0	0	0	0	0	0	0	0	1	0	1	0	1	0	0	0	0
19	1	0	0	0	0	1	0	1	0	0	0	0	0	0	0	0	1	0	1	0	0	1	0	0	0	0	0	0	0	0	0	1	0	1	0	0	1	0	0	0
20	1	0	0	1	0	0	0	1	0	0	0	0	0	0	1	0	0	0	0	1	0	0	0	0	0	0	0	0	0	0	0	1	1	1	0	0	1	0	0	0
21	0	0	1	0	0	1	0	1	1	0	0	0	0	0	0	0	0	0	0	0	1	0	0	0	0	0	0	0	0	0	0	0	1	1	0	1	0	0	0	1
22	1	0	0	0	0	1	0	1	0	0	0	1	0	0	0	0	0	0	0	0	0	1	0	0	0	0	0	0	0	0	0	1	1	1	0	1	0	0	0	0
23	1	0	0	0	1	0	1	0	0	0	1	0	0	0	0	0	0	0	0	0	0	0	1	0	0	0	0	0	0	0	0	0	1	1	0	1	0	0	1	0
24	0	0	1	0	0	1	1	0	1	0	0	0	0	0	0	0	0	0	0	0	1	0	0	1	0	0	0	0	0	0	0	0	1	1	0	1	0	0	1	0
25	0	0	1	0	0	1	0	1	1	0	0	0	0	0	0	0	0	0	0	0	1	0	0	1	1	0	0	0	0	0	0	1	0	1	0	1	0	0	0	0
26	1	0	0	1	0	0	0	1	0	0	0	0	0	0	1	0	1	0	0	0	1	0	0	1	0	1	0	0	0	0	0	1	0	1	0	1	0	0	0	0
27	0	0	1	0	0	1	0	1	1	0	0	0	0	0	0	0	0	0	0	0	1	0	0	0	1	0	1	0	0	0	0	1	0	0	0	0	1	0	0	0
28	0	0	1	0	0	1	0	1	1	0	0	0	0	0	0	0	0	0	0	0	0	0	0	0	0	0	0	1	0	1	0	1	1	0	0	0	0	0	0	0
29	0	0	0	0	0	1	0	1	1	0	0	1	0	0	0	0	0	0	0	0	0	0	0	0	0	0	0	0	1	0	0	0	1	1	0	0	0	0	0	1
30	1	0	0	0	0	1	0	1	0	0	0	1	0	0	0	0	0	0	0	0	0	0	0	0	0	0	0	0	0	1	0	1	1	1	0	1	0	0	0	0
31	1	0	0	0	0	1	0	1	0	0	0	1	0	0	0	0	0	0	0	0	0	0	0	0	0	0	0	0	0	0	1	0	1	1	0	1	0	0	0	0
32	0	0	1	0	0	1	0	1	1	0	0	0	0	0	0	0	0	0	0	0	1	0	0	0	0	0	0	0	0	0	0	1	1	1	0	1	0	0	0	0
33	0	0	0	0	0	1	0	1	1	0	0	1	0	0	0	0	0	0	0	0	0	1	0	0	0	0	0	0	0	0	0	1	1	1	0	1	0	0	0	0
34	0	0	1	0	0	1	0	1	1	0	0	0	0	0	0	0	0	0	0	0	1	0	0	0	0	0	0	0	0	0	0	1	1	1	0	1	0	0	0	0
35	0	0	1	0	0	1	0	1	1	0	0	0	0	0	0	0	0	0	0	0	1	0	0	0	0	0	0	0	0	0	0	1	1	0	1	0	1	0	0	0
36	0	0	1	0	0	1	0	1	1	0	0	0	0	0	0	0	0	0	0	0	1	0	0	0	0	1	0	0	0	0	0	0	0	1	0	1	0	0	1	0
37	0	0	1	0	0	1	0	1	1	0	0	0	0	0	0	0	0	0	0	0	1	0	0	0	0	0	0	0	0	0	0	0	1	1	0	0	1	0	0	1
38	1	0	0	0	0	0	0	1	0	0	0	1	0	0	1	0	0	0	0	0	0	0	0	0	0	0	0	0	0	0	0	1	1	1	0	0	0	1	0	0
39	0	0	1	0	0	1	1	0	1	0	0	0	0	0	0	0	0	0	0	0	1	0	0	1	0	0	0	0	0	0	0	0	1	1	0	1	0	0	1	0
40	0	0	1	0	0	1	0	1	1	0	0	0	0	0	0	0	0	0	0	0	1	0	0	0	0	0	0	0	0	0	0	0	1	1	0	0	1	0	0	1

(b)

Table 1. Schedules Obtained by MFA. (a) The Schedule for the 15-station Network. (b) The Schedule for the 40-station Network.

A Solution of Combinatorial Optimization Problem by Uniting Genetic Algorithms with Hopfield's Model

Hiroyuki Shirai , Atsushi Ishigame , Shunji Kawamoto and Tsuneo Taniguchi

Department of Electrical & Electronic Systems, University of Osaka Prefecture
1-1 Gakuen-cho, Sakai, Osaka, 593 Japan

Abstract

It is important to solve a combinatorial optimization problem because of its utility. In this paper, we propose a method of solving combinatorial optimization problems by uniting Genetic Algorithms (GAs) with Hopfield's model(Hp model). We also apply it to Traveling Salesman Problem (TSP). GAs are global search algorithms. On the other hand, in Hp model the range of a search is neighborhood of the initial point. Then Hp model is local search Algorithm. By using these natures that make up for defects of each other, we unite GAs with Hp model. Then we can overcome some difficulties, such as coding and crossover in GAs and setting up the initial point and parameter in Hp model. The availability of our proposed approach is verified by simulations.

1 Introduction

Many approaches for combinatorial optimization problems have ever been proposed, because it is important in practical uses. However, there is no efficient approach as number of combination increasing. Recently, Genetic Algorithms (GAs) [1] are paid attention as it giving solutions of combinatorial optimization problems. GAs that imitate processes of life evaluations are kinds of optimum algorithms. And Hopfield's neural network model [2] is also one of optimum algorithms, and imitates an analogy with the neural network of human brains. Both GAs and Hopfield's model (Hp model) have something in common. First of all, they are models of life principles, and of highly parallel processing. On the other hand, in these algorithms there are some differences that are worthy of notice. The most important difference is as following point. In operations of GAs, we set up the initial point and the searching point are settled step by step. Then GAs are global search Algorithms. On the other hand, in Hp model the range of a search is neighborhood of the initial point. Then Hp model is local search Algorithm. In this difference, both approaches are complementary to each other. Therefor some studies concerned with combinations of these two approaches have been reported [4][5].

In this paper we propose new approaches in which GAs and Hp model are united to solve combinatorial optimization problems for performing global search effectively. It is expected to the efficient convergence to the solution owing to Hp model to which informations of gene in GAs are given. In our approaches, we define a matrix for uniting conditions of each neuron in Hp model and consider the matrix as the gene of GAs. Elements of the matrix are defined as symbols of "0, 1" and GAs' operations are applied the matrix of gene. These approaches are applied to Traveling Salesman Problem (TSP) which is one of a combinatorial optimization problems. The key to solution of TSP has ever been studied with GAs and Hp model [2][6][7]. Both applications with GAs and Hp model have had some difficulties, such as coding and crossover in GAs and setting initial points and parameters in Hp model. However, by applying our proposed approaches, we can overcome these difficulties, and get good solutions of TSP.

0-7803-1901-X/94 $4.00 ©1994 IEEE

2 Genetic Algorithms

GAs are search algorithms based on the mechanics of natural selection and natural genetics, and different from common optimization method on some points. One of these differences is that GAs are grovel search Algorithms. In GAs, a set of genes in natural genetics is referred to as string. The mechanics of GAs is simple, involving nothing more complex than genetic operators which are eliminating strings, copying strings, swapping and changing partial strings. Each of these operators are referred to as selection, reproduction, crossover and mutations. These basic operators in GAs are explained as follows.
(1)Coding : GAs require the natural parameter set to be coded as a finite-length string over some finite alphabet. How to code in strings is learned to a designer.
(2)Setting up of searching group : We make a long number of strings on the basis of the string decided in operation (1).
(3)Calculation of fitness value of each strings : We calculate the fitness value of each string with objective (fitness) function according to the problem type.
(4)Selection and Reproduction : Reproduction is a process in which individual strings are copied according to their objective function values. Eliminating strings according to their fitness values means that strings with a lower value have a lower probability of contributing and inversely, coping strings with a higher value have a higher probability of contributing.

These operations are artificial versions of natural selection. By going through these operation (3) $\sim$ (4), the average of fitness value of searching group become higher. But only these operator, each fitness value can't become higher than the best fitness value in initial searching group. Therefor the next two operations are important in GAs.
(5)Crossover : We select some pair of strings. Crossover is applied to these pair of string on a position. An integer position (k) along the string is selected uniformly at random between 1 and the string length (n) minus one. Two new strings on the under-rightside are created by snapping all characters between position $k+1$ and n inclusively.
(6)Mutations : Mutations is the occasional random alteration of the value of a string position. The mutations operator protects against irrecoverable loss.

In GAs, methodology is to improve the fitness value of a searching group by repeating (3) $\sim$ (6). When we solve TSP with GAs, it is important how to code well in this problem (TSP). And according to the above, we must decide how to perform operations as crossover and mutations. If we fail in this coding, it is difficult to find out optimum solutions.

3 Hopfield's model

This network can be implemented as a single layer of binary-valued (0, 1) neurons. Each neuron is symmetrically connected to all other neurons in the network but not back to itself. And it can converge in the minimum value of the total network energy. The Hopfield network is useful for optimization task.

3.1 Structure of Hopfield's model

We illustrate a structure of Hp model in Fig.1

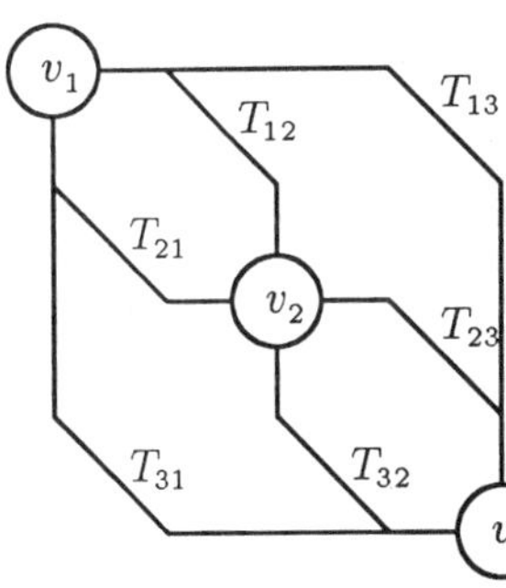

Fig.1 A conceptual picture of Hp model

The output of i-th neuron v_i is defined as eq.(1)

$$v_i = \frac{1}{2}\{1+\tanh(\frac{x_i}{\mu_0})\}$$
$$x_i = \sum_{j=1}^{N} T_{ij}v_j + I_i \qquad (1)$$
$$(i = 1, \cdots, N)$$

Where I_i is the threshold value and T_{ij} is the weight of connection between i and j neuron. In

Hp model we assume all connection strengths are symmetric ($T_{ij} = T_{ji}$). Then the energy defined by eq.(2) decreases with time going (step by step) and converge in the minimum.

$$E = -\frac{1}{2}\sum_{i=1}^{N}\sum_{j=1}^{N} T_{ij} v_i v_j - \sum_{i=1}^{N} I_i v_i \qquad (2)$$

When we solve TSP with Hp model, whether we can solve TSP or not depends on initial values and parameters of the network. So, Hp model said to have the defect that it is easy to converge in the local minimum.

4 Uniting GAs with Hp model

How to unit GAs with Hp model and to apply our proposal to TSP are explained as follows.

4.1 The application of Hp model

4.1.1 Setting up the network

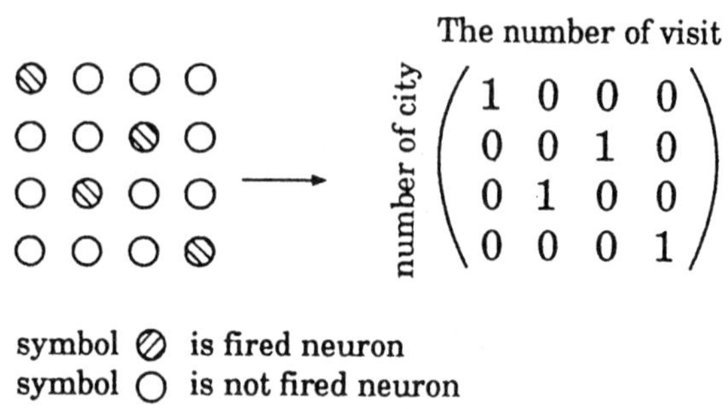

Fig.2 5×5 matrix

In the case of n cities problem, we make a n×n neuron matrix. For example, we illustrate a 5×5 matrix in Fig.2. In this network each neuron is connected to all other neurons (fired neuron = symbol "1" and not fired = symbol "0"). In this matrix, a row is the number of the city and a column is the number of the visit. If the city was visited, the neuron of this matrix is fired as shown in Fig.3.

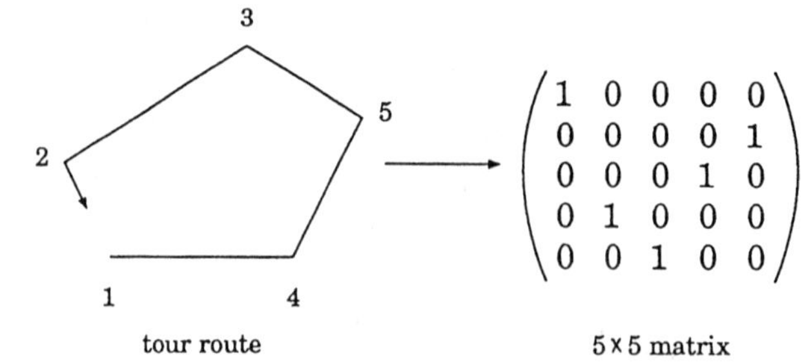

Fig.3 A tour route and matrix

4.1.2 Decision of input-output relations

Solving TSP, it is necessary to satisfy the following conditions.
1. Not visit the same city more than one time
2. Not visit more than one city at the same time
3. Distance of the tour must be shortest

The evaluation function is defined as eq.(3), so that above three conditions are satisfied.

$$\begin{aligned} E_1 = \; & \frac{A}{2}\sum_{x=1}^{N}\sum_{i=1}^{N}\sum_{\substack{j=1\\ j\neq i}}^{N} V_{xi}V_{xj} \\ & +\frac{B}{2}\sum_{x=1}^{N}\sum_{i=1}^{N}\sum_{\substack{y=1\\ y\neq x}}^{N} V_{xi}V_{yj} \\ & +\frac{C}{2}\left(\sum_{x=1}^{N}\sum_{i=1}^{N} V_{xi} - n\right)^2 \\ & +\frac{D}{2}\sum_{x=1}^{N}\sum_{i=1}^{N}\sum_{y=1}^{N} d_{xy}V_{xi}(V_{y,i+1}V_{y,i-1}) \end{aligned} \qquad (3)$$

In Hp model, the energy function becomes eq.(4) that is extended in two dimensions.

$$E_2 = -\frac{1}{2}\sum_{x=1}^{N}\sum_{i=1}^{N}\sum_{y=1}^{N}\sum_{j=1}^{N} T_{xi,yj}V_{xi}V_{yj} - \sum_{x=1}^{N}\sum_{i=1}^{N} V_{xi}I_{xi} \qquad (4)$$

By putting $E_1 = E_2$, we decided parameters T_{xi}, T_{yj}, I_{xi}. Next, T_{xi}, T_{yj}, I_{xi} are substituted into eq.(5) which is rewritten as discrete equation for eq.(1).

$$\begin{aligned} U_{xi}(k) &= \sum_{y=1}^{N}\sum_{j=1}^{N} T_{xi,yj}V_{xi}(k-1) + I_{xi} \\ V_{xi}(k) &= \frac{1}{2}\{1+\tanh(\frac{U_{xi}(k)}{\mu_o})\} \end{aligned} \qquad (5)$$

Then, we get eq.(6) which decides relations between input and output.

$$
\begin{aligned}
U_{xi}(k) &= -A\sum_{\substack{j=1\\ j\neq i}}^{N} V_{xj}(k-1) - B\sum_{\substack{y=1\\ y\neq x}}^{N} V_{yi}(k-1) \\
&\quad -C\{\sum_{y=1}^{N}\sum_{j=1}^{N} V_{yj}(k-1) - n\} \\
&\quad -D\sum_{y=1}^{N} d_{xy}\{V_{y,i+1}(k-1) + V_{y,i-1}(k-1)\}
\end{aligned}
$$

$$
V_{xi}(k) = \frac{1}{2}\{1+\tanh(\frac{U_{xi}(k)}{\mu_0})\} \qquad (6)
$$

Though Hp model acts following eq.(6), it is necessary to satisfy the condition in which the only one neuron in each row and column of this matrix must be fired, so that the condition of this neuron may be the solution of TSP. In order to satisfy these conditions, we take following method (See Fig.4).

Step.1 one neuron which has the largest value in n×n matrix is fired

Step.2 removing one row and one column in which the fired neuron in Step.1 is belonged

Step.3 one neuron which has the largest value in n-1×n-1 matrix is fired

Step.4 repeating operations from Step 1 to Step 3 for n-1 times

Step 5 1×1 neuron remained is fired

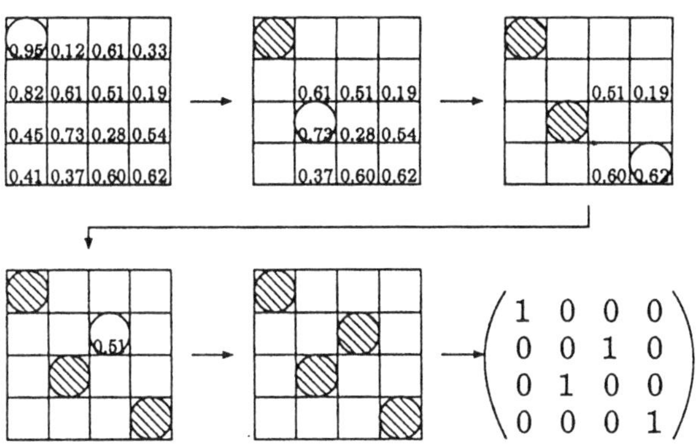

Fig.4 The converging process of Hp model

By using this method, we have always a solution of TSP. But there remains a serious difficulty here. The solution gotten by the method is not necessarily always the optimal solution. We propose a way to overcome this difficulty by uniting GA with Hp model.

4.2 Application of GAs

(1) Coding : It is proposed that the matrix type gene which is the same form as the neuron matrix of Hp model. As an example, a matrix of gene (n=5) is illustrated in Fig.5.

number of visit

number of city

$$
\begin{pmatrix}
1 & 0 & 0 & 0 & 0\\
0 & 0 & 0 & 0 & 1\\
0 & 0 & 0 & 1 & 0\\
0 & 1 & 0 & 0 & 0\\
0 & 0 & 1 & 0 & 0
\end{pmatrix}
$$

Fig.5 A matrix of gene

(2) Setting up searching group : Symbols "0,1" are chosen at random in the matrix decided by (1). The gene matrix is initial point of Hp model.

(3) Calculation of fitness value of each gene matrix : As a result of input the initial gene matrix to Hp model, the neuron matrix converge to the form of solution of TSP (= new gene matrix). A tour distance is gotten by a new gene matrix. The tour distance, which is the shortest of all tour distances in GAs' populations, is considered as a gene which has the highest fitness value.

(4) Selection and Reproduction : A gene of lower fitness value is exchanged for a gene of higher fitness value.

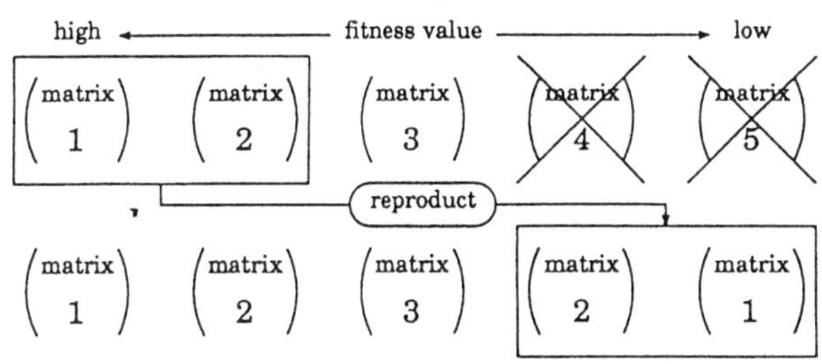

Fig.6 Selection and reproduction

(5) Crossover : An integer position K is selected at random between 1 and $n-1$ (shown in Fig.7).

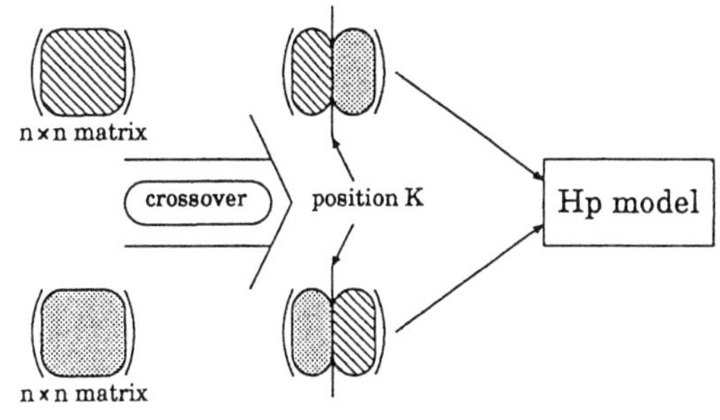

Fig.7 Crossover

Two new matrices on the under-rightside are created by swapping all characters between position $K+1$ and n.

(6) Mutations : One position in the matrix is selected at random and its value is reversed (or changed) as shown in Fig.8.

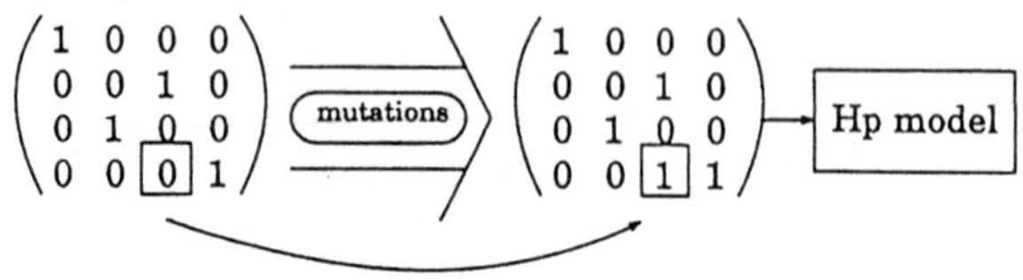

Fig.8 Mutations

(7) Mutations for TSP : This operation is applied in the matrix which has the highest fitness value.

1. One column which is selected at random is picked out and an integer position K is also selected at random and one column is put in position K (shown in Fig.9).

2. Two columns which are selected at random are picked out and an integer position K is also selected at random. And two columns are put in position K as it is or after changing the order (shown in Fig.10).

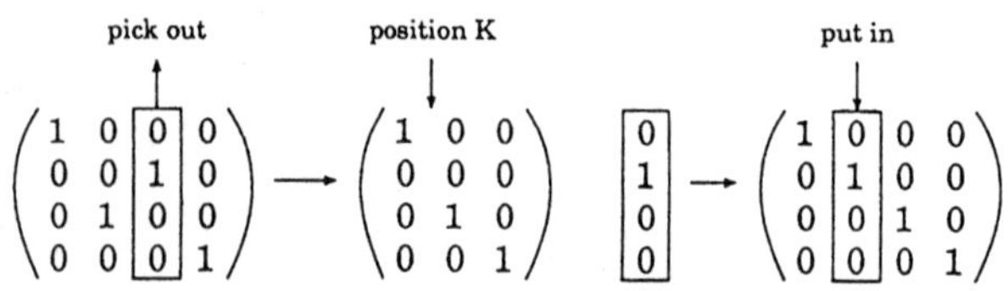

Fig.9 Mutations for TSP 1

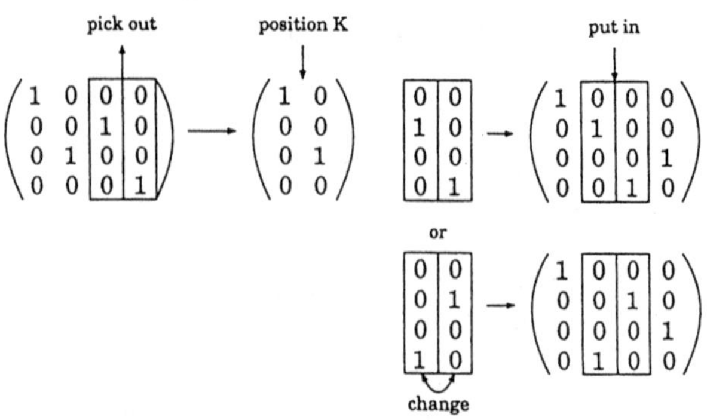

Fig.10 Mutations for TSP 2

(8) Check operation : When the solution of GAs is converged some degree, following two operations are carried out.

⟨unbinding small lope⟩

Two orders which are side by side are reversed. And if the round distance of tour becomes shorter, this new state is adopted (shown Fig.11).

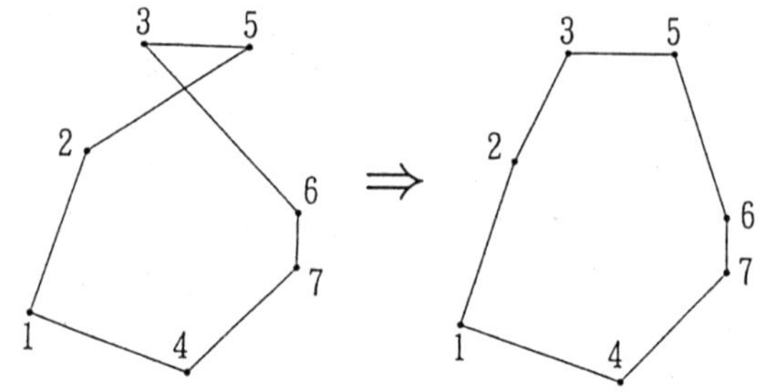

Fig.11 Unbiding small loop

⟨unbinding large lope⟩

The cross points are searched for in turn, if they are found out, following operation is applied. 4 cities which concerned about the cross point are found. In the matrix, the order of inside in the matrix is reversed by repeating this operation. Then the large lope is unbinded (shown in Fig.12).

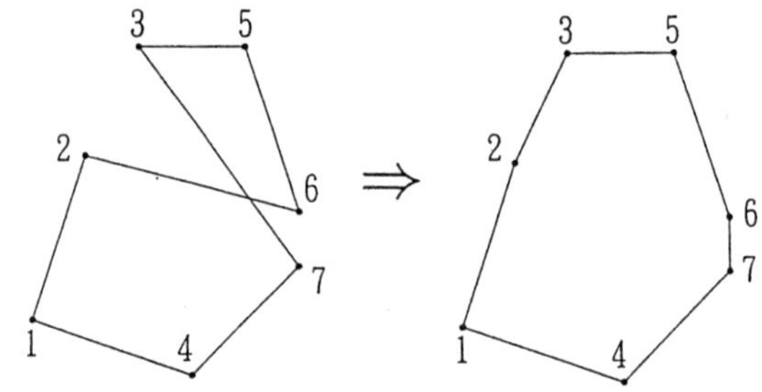

Fig.12 Unbiding large loop

5 Simulation

1) GAs+Hp model (the approach explained in section 4)

2) GAs+Hp model (the approach of element (1,1) is to be forced to fire in the matrix of TSP)

In the approach 1), there exist different gene matrices (the number is "2n") for a solution of TSP. So we had better decide the city at the start point. That is to say, the model matrix, in which the element of (1,1) is forcibly decided as symbol "1", is used. By this method there exist only two different gene matrices for a solution of TSP and the effects of GAs can be enhanced.

3) Modified GAs

The local search by Hp model is not carried out.

In this method, GAs' operations are applied after matrices for TSP solutions are given as a initial gene group, and crossover (5) and mutations (6) of GAs are not operated. The simulation results of the proposed three methods are shown as follows. The location of 30 cities are decided at random. In GAs the population is set at 10. Selection and reproduction, crossover and mutations rates are 30%, 40% and 1%, respectively. These parameters are decided by trial and error. Even if these parameters are changed a little, the similar results are also obtained. The process of searches by three methods are illustrated in Fig.13. It shows the effectiveness of uniting GAs with Hopfield's model.

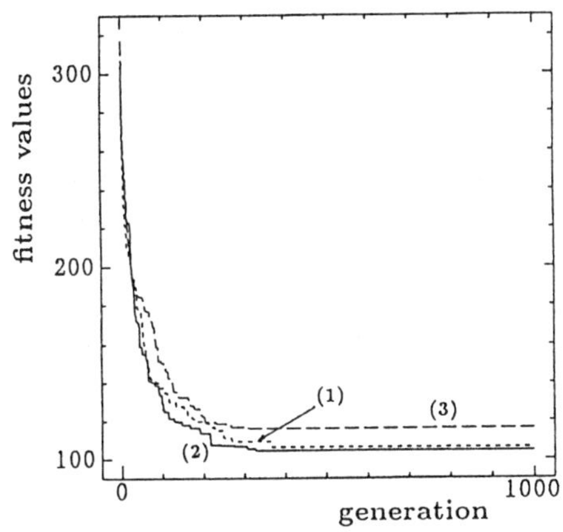

Fig.13 The process of searches

As the best result is given by the method 2), in which the effect of GAs is improved, we notice that our proposed approach depend heavily on GAs and its performance can be improved by using Hp model. The best solution of TSP in this simulation is illustrated in Fig.14.

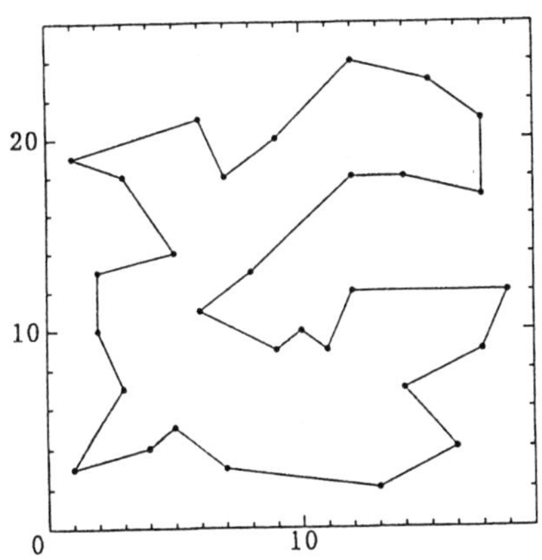

Fig.14 The best solution of TSP

6 Conclusion

We propose new approaches in which GAs is united with Hp model by using the nature of making up for defects of each other algorithms. And the effectiveness of our proposed approach is verified by solving TSP. Because of both two natures that GAs are global search algorithm and Hp model is local search one, we can get a good travelling rote by uniting them well. And by using our approach, some difficulties such as mutations and crossover in GAs and setting up the initial point in Hp model for solving TSP can be overcome.

For future subjects, we intend to improve our approach and apply other combinatorial optimization problems.

References

[1] D.E.Goldbarg, *Genetic Algorithms in Search, Optimization and Machine Learning,* Addison-Wesley (1989).

[2] J.J.Hopfield and D.E.Tank, *"Neural" computation of decisions in optimization problems,* Bio. Cybern., Vol.52, pp.141–152 (1985).

[3] A.Maren, C.Harston and Robert Pap, *Handbok of Neural Computing Applications,* Academic Press, Inc. (1990).

[4] S.Yasiki, T.Shimizu and N.Matsumoto, *Consideration of Blended System of Hopfield Model and Genetic Algorithms,* Technical Report of IEICE, NC92-146, pp.139–146 (1993). (in Japanese)

[5] E.Aiyoshi and A.Yoshikawa, *Evolution and Genetic Algorithms for Global Optimization,* Mathematical Sciences, No.353, pp.38–44 (1992). (in Japanese)

[6] J.Grefenstette, R.Gopal, B.Rosmaita and D.V.Gucht, *Genetic Algorithms for the Traveling Salesman Problem,* Proc. the First Int. Conf. on GAs and Their Applications, pp.160–168 (1985).

[7] E.Aarts and J.Korst, *Simulated annealing and Bolzmann machines,* Jhon Wiley & Sons (1989).

Neural Network Estimators: Application To Ship Position Estimation

D. G. Lainiotis, K. N. Plataniotis
Florida Institute of Technology
Department of Electrical and Computer Engineering
150 W. University Blvd., Melbourne Fl. 32901, USA

ABSTRACT- Ship motion prediction is an important practical problem in design of many ocean systems i.e. fire controls, air craft landing and take off. As such the problem has received considerable attention in the past and various attempts for designing estimators via the statistical methodology were made in the past. In this paper the design of the ship position estimator via neural networks is considered. The ship position estimation is viewed as an adaptive estimation problem for partially unknown systems. New powerful neural estimators based on dynamic recurrent neural networks are applied to the solution of the ship position problem. The new proposed neural estimators, and the state of the art statistical filters, are comparatively evaluated via extensive simulations. The results show that the neural algorithms have excellent performance, achieving significant computational savings due to their massively parallel structure.

I. INTRODUCTION

The accurate on-line estimation of ship motion is essential to many ship related problems such as ship steering [1], dynamic positioning [2], marine oil exploration [3], off shore platforms, and aircraft landing and take off [4]. Based upon predicted ship motion, the necessary control commands for the control of highly qualified ships like hovercrafts are calculated and generated. Ship motion prediction is also essential when accurate control of position mechanisms for guns or missiles is required. Especially when tracking of a maneuvering target is the objective there is a considerable amount of delay in transmitting information regarding the motion to the position mechanism. It is obvious that accurate predictions are required before an appropriate tracking command can be issued [3],[8],[14].

In the past several studies have been carried out for the solution of the ship position problem, most of them utilizing the Kalman Filter approach, or other least-squares estimation methods [1],[3]. However the design of a statistical estimator like the Kalman Filter requires the definition of a linear model describing the motion of the ship. More specifically, it requires a state-space representation of this motion. In most cases, the model equations are derived from the ship motion spectral density which corresponds to a particular sea-ship condition, the wave excitation input, and a gaussian random noise as driving input. In other words the sea-state magnitude, the ship speed, the ship heading with respect to the waves, and the disturbance pattern of the sea waves are incorporated in the model [5], [6]. The unknown wave excitation input transforms the problem to an adaptive estimation one reducing the effectiveness of the traditional filtering techniques.

Recently, the emerging technology of neural networks [15] has been successfully applied to the solution of the estimation problem [16]-[20]. Given the difficulties the conventional estimators encounter, neural solutions constitute a unique and novel alternative. The trained multilayer perceptrons with their massive parallelism, capability to approximate arbitrary continuous functions, and significant ability, appear to offer a new promising tool in adaptive filtering research.

In this paper the estimation of the ship motion based on a linear state space model that includes the wave-excitation input is proposed. Specifically, the paper is organized as follows. In Section II, the general formulation of the ship motion dynamics is presented. In Section III, new adaptive neural estimators are tested in extensive simulations on the ship motion model. Comparisons with conventional statistical methods in a variety of simulation experiments are also provided. Conclusions are given in Section IV.

II. SHIP MOTION DYNAMICS

The motion of the ship can be described by a set of differential equations. As it was mentioned above, the model depends on the sea-state magnitude, the ship speed and the ship heading with respect to the waves. For a rigid ship travelling with a constant forward speed and in the direction which makes an arbitrary angle with regard to sinusoidal waves, its motion can be described by a set of second-order linear differential equations of the form:

$$a\ddot{q}(t) + b\dot{q}(t) + cq(t) = \xi(t) \quad (1)$$

where, q(t) represent a vector of surge, sway and heave motions or variations of roll, pitch and yaw orientations, $\xi(t)$ represents the sea-wave excitation, and a,b,c are constants that represents the virtual mass, damping and restoring stiffness, and are determined by the dimensions and shape of the ship.

0-7803-1901-X/94 $4.00 ©1994 IEEE

The above linear model can be obtained using the power spectral density function under different sea-wave excitation[5]. The most important part of the equation is the representation of the periodic sea-wave excitation. The wave excitation can be approximated by the superposition of sinusoidal waves[6].

$$\xi(t) = \Sigma A_i \cdot \sin(\omega_i \cdot t + b_i) \tag{2}$$

where, Ai is the amplitude of wave excitation, ωi is the frequency, b_i the phase of each different wave.

In most of the cases, the amplitude and the frequency of the waves are considered to be time-invariant. When the ship is moving with forward speed, there exist certain relation between the actual wave frequencies, and the frequencies encountered by the ship[6]. Following this relation, the direct influence of the waves on the ship is given as follow

$$\xi_e(t) = \Sigma A_i \cdot \sin(\omega_{ei} \cdot t + b_i) \tag{3}$$

$$\omega_{ei} = \omega_i - \frac{\omega_i^2}{g} \cdot v \cdot \cos(x) \tag{4}$$

where, w_{e_i} is the transformed wave frequency, v is the forward speed of the ship, x is the angle between the ship heading and the wave direction, and g is the standard gravitational acceleration.

Moreover since the energy of each individual wave component rapidly decreases as the frequency of the wave increases, the above expression can be simplified further. Truncating the high frequency components the expression takes the following form:

$$\xi_e(t) = \sum_{i=1}^{N} A_i \cdot \sin(\omega_{ei} \cdot t + b_i) \tag{5}$$

It is reported in numerous studies [1], [5],[6],[7] that a value of 3 for N, is sufficient to approximate the wave excitation input, in the case of small ships. After all the approximations and transformations, the equation for the ship motion in the equivalent state space representation can be written as follows:

$$\dot{x}(t) = \begin{bmatrix} 0 & 1 \\ -\frac{c}{a} & -\frac{b}{a} \end{bmatrix} \cdot x(t) + \begin{bmatrix} 0 \\ \frac{1}{a} \end{bmatrix} \cdot \xi_e(t) + w(t)$$

$$z(k) = \begin{bmatrix} 1 & 0 \end{bmatrix} \cdot x(k) + v(k) \tag{6}$$

where, x(t) is the state vector which represents the ship motion. It is a 2 x 1 vector defined as follows:

$$x(t) = \begin{bmatrix} q(t) \\ \dot{q}(t) \end{bmatrix} \tag{7}$$

ξe(t) is the truncated wave excitation input, w(t) is the state random noise, z(k) is the measurement vector, v(k) is a random noise which corrupts the measurements.

The position and velocity of the ship are usually measured by on-board sensors. Since all the states are not measurable, and the measurements always contain noise, filters are employed to estimate the actual position of the ship. The objective is to obtain the optimal, in the mean square sense, state estimate $\hat{x}$(k/k) of the state x(k/k), given the measurement record, Z(k) = {z(1),z(2),., z(k)}.

III. SHIP POSITION ESTIMATORS

In the past Kalman Filter based techniques, or other statistical filters have been used in connection with state space models in order to provide meaningful and accurate estimates of the ship motion. If the sea-wave excitation (sea condition) is known in advance, and all other dynamic and statistical specifications of the above model meet the assumptions of the Kalman Filter, then this filter is the optimal estimator and provides the most accurate estimate.

However, it is highly unlikely to know the actual wave excitation input function which directly influences the ship motion. Since the states of the ship are determined by the actual encountered wave excitation input is of great practical importance to derive an estimator that can handle successfully this uncertainty. Due to the uncertainty in the wave excitation input function as given equations (3)-(5) the ship position estimation can be viewed as an adaptive estimation problem where the unknown parameter vector in the model summarizes the uncertainty in the amplitude of the wave excitation and/or the encounter frequencies. It is difficult to estimate the states of the above model using statistical filters when all these parameters must be identified simultaneously without any constraints. Therefore the current methodology is to treat only the corresponding amplitudes as parameters Even in this case, when a mismatch occurs between the actual model and the model used by the designer, the Kalman filter fails.

A more robust statistical filter, namely the Adaptive Lainiotis Filter [8]-[14], was successfully used in this situation. Unlike the Kalman Filter, this new filter, due to its adaptive nature, identifies in real time, the actual model and provides the appropriate solutions [8],[14].

Motivated by the recent interest on neural networks application to state estimation problem [16]-[20] a dynamic neural estimator was used in [20] to provide estimates of the current and future ship position. The estimator was an input recurrent multilayer recurrent neural network, trained using back-propagation technique, to provide estimates of the ship position. Since in that analysis the comparative evaluation between neural and the statistical filters was the main objective, the dynamic model of the ship motion was completely known.

The trained multilayer perceptron as state estimator was proved to enjoy certain advantages over the conventional filters derived through the statistical methodology [18],[20]:

- It can handle any assumption or uncertainty concerning the statistics of the actual data generation model. It does not depend on any assumption about the stochastic input. To the contrary the Gaussian nature of the noises in the model, and the independence between the state and the noises, are fundamental assumptions behind any feasible filter derived using statistical methodologies.
- Due to its massive parallel structure and high speed the neural estimator can take full advantage of the new hardware capabilities. That makes the neural and not the statistical estimator the preferable choice for real time signal processing, and automatic control applications.

In this work the wave excitation input is assumed partially or completely unknown. Since the actual model is not available a different approach is used. Several networks are trained independently using different variations of the wave excitation input in the model. Each one of the networks trained with data pairs obtained using different assumptions about the amplitudes and the frequencies in eq. (5). Due to this training methodology each network converges to a different solution. When the training is over, a bank of different neural estimators is available to be applied to the solution of the ship position estimation. In the actual operation phase a nonlinear selection mechanism is used to select at every time instant the neural estimator that provides the best estimate.The new estimator is an extension of the Adaptive Lainiotis Filter to neural networks.

The new adaptive neural estimators are compared with the Adaptive Lainiotis Filter (the most advanced statistical filter for adaptive estimation) in a variety of different uncertainty scenarios.

The following simulation experiments are performed:

A. SIMULATION I

In this first experiment, the adaptive neural estimator is compared with the ALF. It is supposed for comparison purposes that the dynamic model is partially known. The encounter frequencies in the wave excitation input are known. The only unknown element in this experiment is the actual amplitude in equation (8). The statistical estimator is matched to the actual statistical model of the ship dynamics. The experimental set-up is given below:

1) System Model:

$$\dot{x}(t) = \begin{bmatrix} 0 & 1 \\ -0.36 & -0.06 \end{bmatrix} \cdot x(t) + \begin{bmatrix} 0 \\ 1 \end{bmatrix} \cdot \xi_e(t) + w(k) \qquad (8)$$

$$z(k) = \begin{bmatrix} 1 & 0 \end{bmatrix} \cdot x(k) + v(k), \qquad (9)$$

$$\xi_e(t) = \sum_{i=1}^{3} a_{2i-1} \cdot \sin(\omega_i \cdot t) + a_{2i} \cdot \cos(\omega_i \cdot t) \qquad (10)$$

where: $a_{2i-1} = A_i \cos(b_i)$, $a_{2i} = A_i \sin(b_i)$, sampling interval, 0.4 sec, total measurement time, 60 sec, amplitudes of the wave excitation inputs $A_i = 0.75$, constant excitation frequency $\omega_i = \pi/4$, different phases $b_i = 2\pi/3$; $b_2 = \pi/3$; $b_3 = \pi/6$, zero mean gaussian plant noise with covariance Q=0.001, and white gaussian measurement noise with covariance, R=0.1 The initial state x(0) is assumed Gaussian with mean value 0.1,and variance 1.0

In order to estimate the state of the above model the following estimators had been used in this first experiment:

2) statistical estimator: Adaptive Lainiotis Filter (ALF)

The ALF filter employs two Kalman filters matched to the above dynamic and statistical model. The first KF assumes that the amplitude is A_i=0.5, and the second one uses the value A_i=1.5. Moreover, the filter starts its recursive cycle assuming initial state estimate, $\hat{x}(0/0) = 0.1$, and initial covariance, $P(0/0) = 1$.

3) adaptive neural estimator

The adaptive neural estimator uses two trained recurrent neural networks. The first one was trained with data from eq. (8)-(10) assuming that the actual amplitude value was A_i=0.5. The second one was trained using data generated under the alternative hypothesis about the amplitude, namely A_i=1.5. The detailed configuration for each one of the recurrent networks are summarized below:

4) input recurrent neural network

network topology:

- two input nodes: the current and the previous measurements are used as input signals.
- two output nodes: the estimates of the system states. The neural network has so many output nodes, as the states of the model.
- two hidden layers with 5-5 hidden nodes respectively

learning parameters:

- learning rate: 0.005, momentum: 0.2

training procedure:

- backpropagation training algorithm
- the target vector during training is the state vector which is generated running the above model for a given value of the unknown amplitude.
- the network tries to minimize the square error between the current output and the target vector.
- each training set consists of 100 input/output pairs (z(k), x(k)).
- the test data record consists of a sequence of data points produced separately from the training record.
- the training procedure is terminated if the training error tolerance is less than 0.01 or if the number of iterations of the training set is more than 5000.

Observations:

Since there is no theoretical analysis to justify the performance of the neural estimators Monte Carlo techniques are used to verify the results. The figure of merit used to compare performance is the mean square error averaged over 100 Monte Carlo runs.Namely, the following performance index, is used

$$MSE = \frac{1}{mc} \cdot \sum_{i=1}^{mc} (x(k) - \hat{x}(k|k))^2 \tag{11}$$

From the figures it is obvious that the Adaptive Lainiotis Filter as well as the adaptive neural estimator perform very well. In Fig.2,3 the performances of the estimators in the estimation of the ship position and the errors over 100 Monte Carlo runs, using the same performance index shown above are given. (Fig. 1-4)

B. SIMULATION II

In a second experiment, a simple recurrent neural network is compared with the Adaptive Lainiotis Filter under a different uncertainty scenario. This time the amplitude is known but the encounter frequencies are assumed unknown. The system model that generates the test data during the operation phase is that of equations (8)-(10). In this simulation study a recurrent neural network is trained without knowing the exact wave excitation input. However in the operation phase this network is used to provide estimates of the model states. The configuration of the two estimators used in the experiment are summarized below:

1) statistical estimator: Adaptive Lainiotis Filter (ALF)

The ALF filter employs two Kalman filters matched to the statistics of the actual model. The first KF has complete knowledge of the actual dynamics. Its knows the exact form of the wave excitation input. The second one is simply assumed that there is no wave input in the model. Moreover, the filter starts its recursive cycle assuming initial state estimate, $\hat{x}(0/0) = 0.1$, and initial covariance, $P(0/0) = 1$.

2) input recurrent neural estimator

network topology:

- two input nodes: the current and the previous measurements are used as input signals.
- two output nodes: the estimates of the system states. The neural network has so many output nodes, as the states of the model.
- two hidden layers with 5-5 hidden nodes respectively.

learning parameters:

- learning rate: 0.005, momentum: 0.2

training procedure:

- backpropagation training algorithm.
- the target vector during training is a state vector which is generated running the model of eq. (8)-(10) assuming as wave input a random input uniformly distributed over the interval [-0.5,0.5].
- the network tries to minimize the square error between the current output and the target vector.
- each training set consists of 100 input/output pairs (z(k), x(k)).
- the test data record consists of a sequence of data points produced separately from the training record using the actual wave excitation pattern.
- the training procedure is terminated if the training error tolerance is less than 0.01 or if the number of iterations of the training set is more than 5000.

Observations:

As was expected the Adaptive Lainiotis filter identifies the actual model and uses the matched Kalman filter to estimate the state of the model. The neural estimator also successfully estimate the ship position despite the minimum information used for its training. It must be emphasized that the neural estimator does not require any information about the inputs to the model statistical or deterministic. The performance of the statistical filter depends on the information about the possible variations of the unknown elements. If the actual parameter vector is far away from the trajectory values used in the filters bank its performance deteriorates. These possibility will be explored in a final simulation study (Fig. 5-7).

C. SIMULATION III

In this final experiment the two adaptive methodologies are compared using a more difficult uncertainty scenario. The filters must provide state estimates without any knowledge about the wave excitation input. This time uncertainty exists in both the amplitude and frequencies.The encounter frequencies are unknown for both the neural and the statistical estimator.The configuration of the two estimators are summarized below:

1) statistical estimator: Adaptive Lainiotis Filter (ALF)

The ALF filter employs two Kalman filters matched to the above dynamic and statistical model. The first KF assumes that the amplitude is A_i=0.5, and the second one uses the value A_i=1.5. However none of the above filters in its bank knows the exact form of the wave input. Both the filters are assume that only the part of the eq.(10) associated with the cosine input is present. The filter starts its recursive cycle assuming initial state estimate, $\hat{x}(0/0) = 0.1$, and initial covariance, $P(0/0) = 1$.

2) adaptive neural estimator

The adaptive neural estimator uses two trained recurrent neural networks. The first one was trained with data from eq. (8)-(10) assuming that the actual amplitude value was A_i=0.5. The network did not know the exact form of the input. The network assumed that it was a random input uniformly distributed over the interval [-0.5,0.5]. Similar to this the second recurrent net was trained using data generated under the alternative hypothesis about the amplitude, namely A_i=1.5.During its training the wave input was assumed uniformly distributed over the interval [-1.5,1.5]. The detailed configuration for each one of the recurrent networks are summarized below:

3) input recurrent neural network

network topology:

- two input nodes: the current and the previous measurements are used as input signals.
- two output nodes: the estimates of the system states. The neural network has so many output nodes, as the states of the model.
- two hidden layers with 5-5 hidden nodes respectively.

learning parameters:

- learning rate: 0.005, momentum: 0.2

training procedure:

- backpropagation training algorithm.
- the target vector during training is a state vector which is generated running the state space model for a given form of the unknown input.
- the network tries to minimize the square error between the current output and the target vector.
- each training set consists of 100 input/output pairs (z(k), x(k)).
- the test data record consists of a sequence of data points produced separately from the training record. The actual model as described in simulation I was used to produce the test data record.
- the training procedure is terminated if the training error tolerance is less than 0.01 or if the number of iterations of the training set is more than 5000.

Observations:

In this final experiment the neural adaptive estimator performs better than the corresponding statistical one. The state estimates and the estimation errors summarized over 100 Monte Carlo trials are summarized in Fig. 8-11.

Summarizing the results from the above simulation studies the following conclusions can be drawn:

- The neural estimator provides a very reliable solution to the estimation problem The proposed adaptive neural estimator provides accurate and consistent results despite the significantly less information used for its training.

- In more realistic situations where the actual model is not completely known the neural estimator outperforms the conventional estimators. However advanced statistical filters like the Adaptive Lainiotis Filter (ALF) can be used successfully in some cases. On the other hand the adaptive neural estimator was proved the best choice for all the different uncertainty scenarios used in this study.

- The ability of the neural network based estimator to provide accurate solutions to the ship position problem under more realistic assumptions, and its massively parallel structure and high speed, makes it the preferable choice for such real time signal processing applications.

IV. CONCLUSIONS

The real time ship motion estimation was considered in this paper. The approach taken, was to design a neural network based estimator, that can handle more realistic scenarios about the underlying physical model. A comparison with an advanced statistical estimator ALF, was provided. Simulation experiments were carried out in order to assess the performance of the proposed neural estimator. In the ship motion estimation problem the neural network estimator shows excellent performance, though it was derived using minimal information about the dynamics of the model.

REFERENCES

[1] R.E. Reid, A.K. Tugcu, B.C. Mears, *"The use of wave filter design in Kalman Filter state estimation for the automatic steering problem of a tanker in a seaway"*, IEEE Transactions on Automatic Control, Vol. AC-20, No. 7, pp. 917-922, 1984.

[2] T. M. Weiss, T. W. Devries, *"Ship motion measurement filter design"*, IEEE Journal of Ocean Engineering, Vol. OE-2, No. 4, October 1977, pp. 325-330.

[3] M.S. Triantafyllou, M.Bodson, M. Athans, *"Real time estimation of ship motion using Kalman Filtering technique"*, IEEE Journal of Ocean Engineering, Vol OE-8, pp. 8-20, January 1983.

[4] M.M. Siolar, B.F. Doolin, *"On the feasibility of real time prediction of aircraft carrier motion at sea"*, IEEE Transactions of Automatic Control, Vol. AC-28, pp. 350-356, March 1983.

[5] R. Bhattacharyya, *"Dynamics of Marine Vehicles"*, Wiley N.Y., 1978.

[6] J.C. Chung, Z. Bien, Y.S. Kim, *"A note on ship-motion prediction based on wave-excitation input estimation"*, IEEE Journal of Ocean Engineering, Vol. OE-15, No. 3, July 1990, pp. 244-250.

[7] B. Friedland, *"Estimating angular velocity from output of rate integrating gyro"*, IEEE Transactions on AES-11, July 1975, pp. 551-555.

[8] D.G. Lainiotis et al., *"Real time ship motion estimation using Lainiotis Filters"*, IFAC Workshop, CAMS-'89, Expert Systems in Marine Automation, pp. 293-301, 1989.

[9] D.G. Lainiotis, *"Optimal adaptive estimation: Structure and parameter adaptation"*, IEEE Transactions on Automatic Control, Vol. AC-16, pp. 160-170, April 1971.

[10] D.G. Lainiotis, "Partitioning: A unifying framework for adaptive systems, I-Estimation", Proceedings of IEEE, Vol. 64, pp. 1126-1142, August 1976.

[11] D.G. Lainiotis, *"Optimal Nonlinear Estimation"*, International Journal of Control, Vol. IJC-14, pp. 11137-1148, 1971.

[12] D.G. Lainiotis, "Joint detection, estimation and system identification" Inform. Control J.,vol. 19, pp. 75-92,1972.

[13] D.G. Lainiotis, S.K. Katsikas, *"Linear and Nonlinear Lainiotis filters Survey"*, in IFAC Workshop, CAMS-'89, Expert Systems in Marine Automation Proceedings, pp. 280-293, 1989.

[14] D.G. Lainiotis, C.J. Charalampous, P. Gianakopoulos, S. Katsikas, *"Real time ship motion estimation"*, Proceedings Oceans '92, pp. 283-287, Newport, Rhode Island, 1992.

[15] D.E. Rumelhart, J.L. McClelland, *"Parallel Distributed Processing Explorations into the Microstructure of Cognition, Vol. 1"*, M.I.T. Press, 1986.

[16] J.P. De Gruyenaece, H.M. Haffer, *"A comparison between Kalman Filters and recurrent neural networks"*, Proceedings of IJCNN-92, Vol. IV, pp. 247-251, 1992.

[17] A.J. Kanekar, A. Feliachi, *"State estimation using artificial neural networks"*, Proceedings of IEEE Systems and Engineering Conference, pp. 552-556, 1990.

[18] D.G.Lainiotis,K.N. Plataniotis, D. Menon, C.J. Charalampous, *"Heave Compensation via Neural Networks"*, Intelligent Engineering Systems through Artificial Neural Networks, Vol. 3, pp 143-148, ASME Press, 1993.

[19] D.G.Lainiotis,K.N. Plataniotis, D. Menon, C.J. Charalampous, *"Adaptive Heave Compensation via Neural Networks"*, in IEEE OCEANS'93 Proceedings, Vol. I, pp 243-248, 1993.

[20] D.G.Lainiotis,K.N. Plataniotis, D. Menon, C.J. Charalampous, *"Neural Network Application to Ship Position Estimation"*, in IEEE OCEANS'93 Proceedings, Vol. I, pp 243-248, 1993.

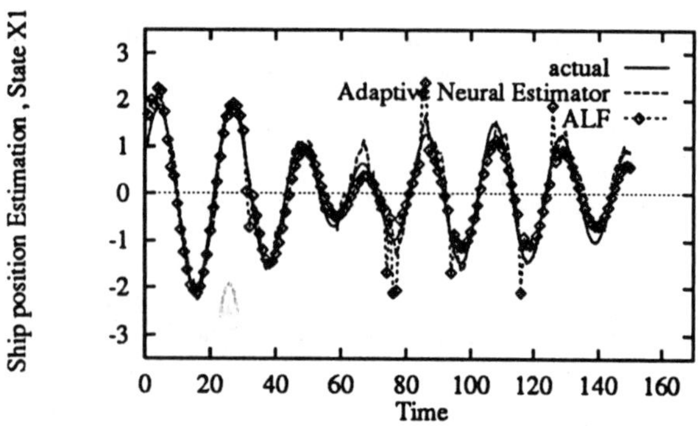

Fig. 1. Ship Position Estimation, Adaptive Neural Network vs. ALF

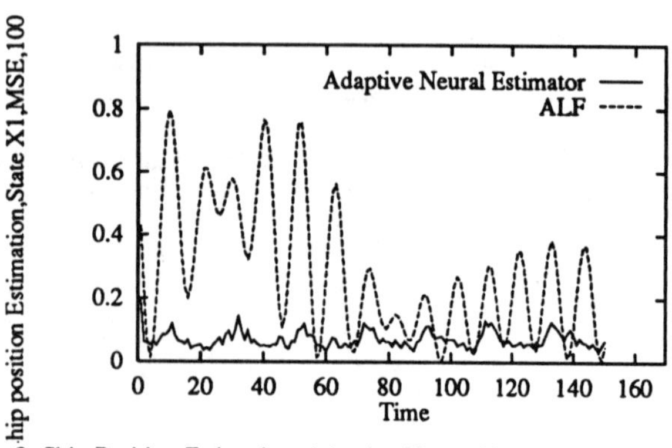

Fig. 2. Ship Position Estimation, Adaptive Neural Networks vs. ALF, MSE Evaluation, 100 MCRs

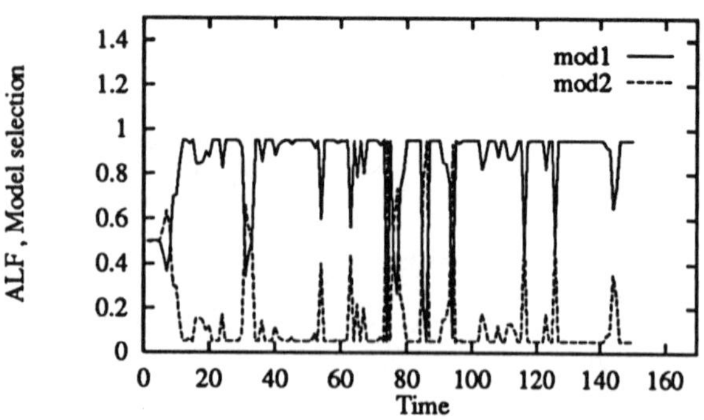

Fig. 3. Ship Position Estimation, ALF, Model Selection

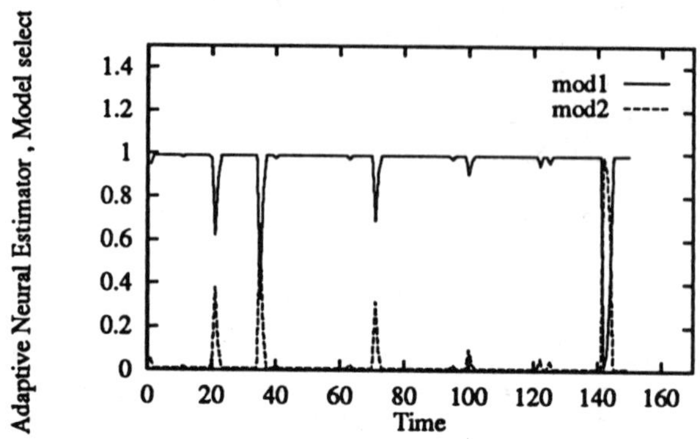

Fig. 4. Ship Position Estimation, Adaptive Neural Estimator, Model Selection

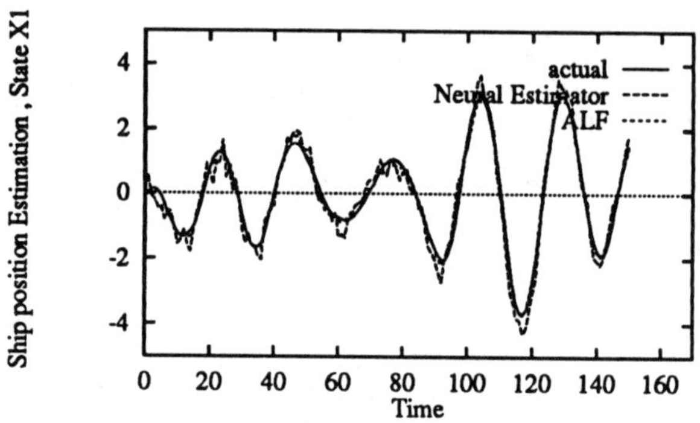

Fig. 5. Ship Position Estimation, Recurrent Neural Network vs. ALF

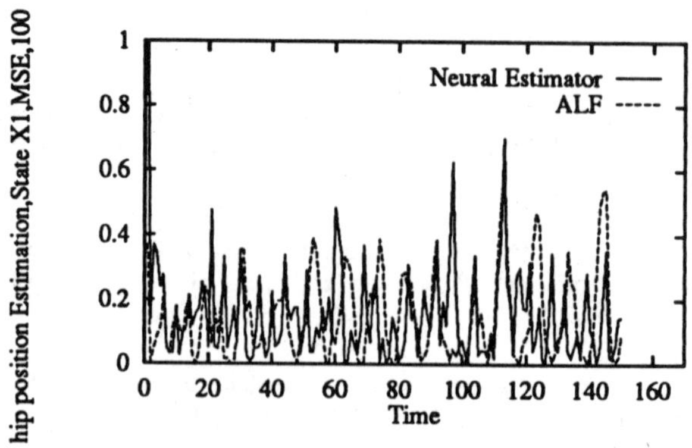

Fig. 6. Ship Position Estimation, Recurrent Neural Networks vs. ALF, MSE Evaluation, 100 MCRs

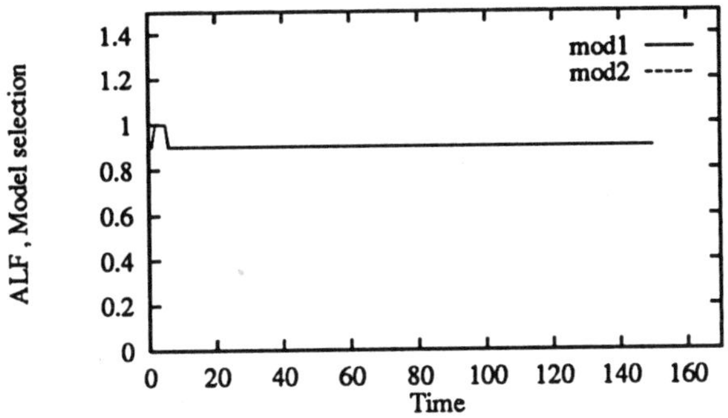

Fig. 7. Ship Position Estimation, ALF, Model Selection

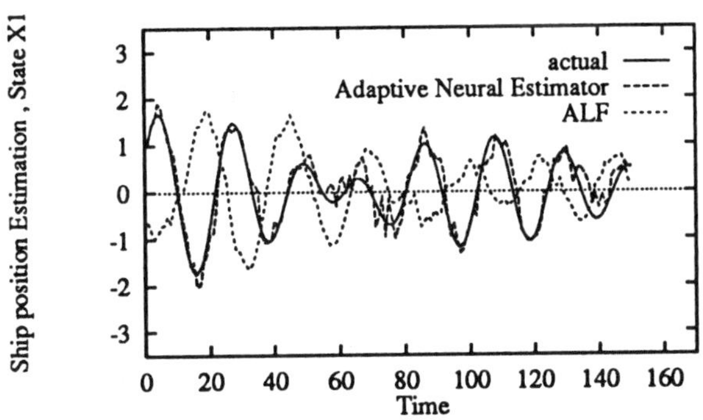

Fig. 8. Ship Position Estimation, Adaptive Neural Network vs. ALF

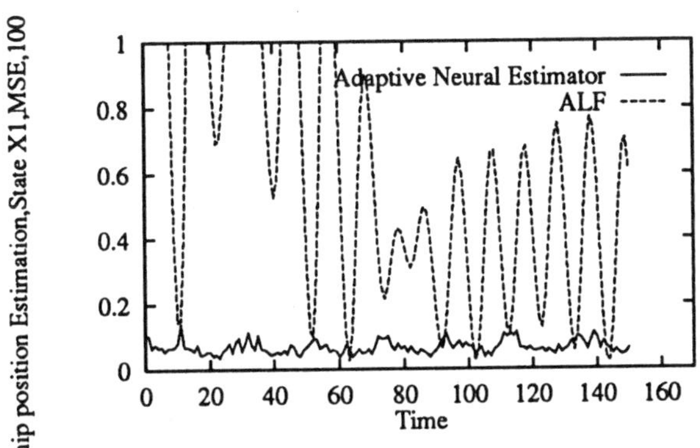

Fig. 9. Ship Position Estimation, Adaptive Neural Networks vs. ALF, MSE Evaluation, 100 MCRs

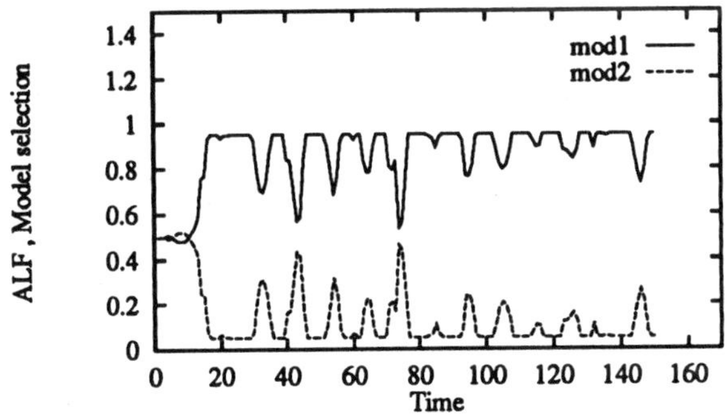

Fig. 10. Ship Position Estimation, ALF, Model Selection

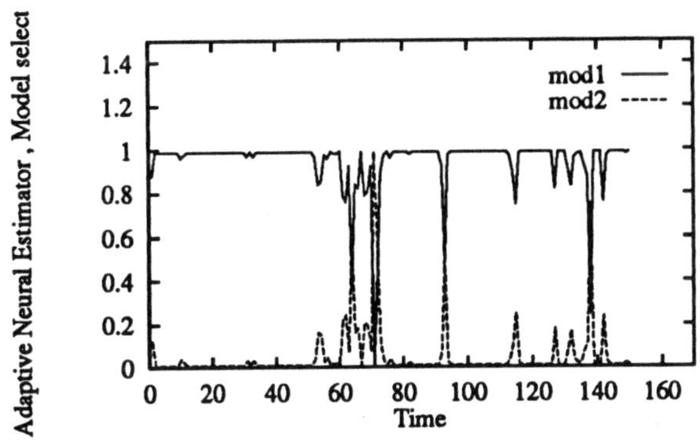

Fig. 11. Ship Position Estimation, Adaptive Neural Estimator, Model Selection

System Identification and Noise Cancellation via Neural-Net Computing

Gwang-Hoon Park and Yoh-Han Pao, Fellow, IEEE

Department of Electrical Engineering and Applied Physics
Case Western Reserve University, Cleveland, Ohio 44106, U.S.A.

Abstract

We report on highly favorable results obtained in use of neural-net computing in the learning of processes and in the cancellation of noise in signals obscured by noise. In the first instance, we demonstrate ability to accurately learn models of linear and nonlinear functional mappings in noisy environments. In the case of noise cancellation, we report on the ability to extract a signal from noisy background.

I. Introduction

Adaptive linear algorithms can be used effectively in different types of tasks provided the systems being identified, monitored or controlled are reasonably linear. On the other hand, there are no general adaptive algorithms for nonlinear environments. The few algorithms which have been used in nonlinear environments work only on a system by system basis. Therefore, there is a need for a general adaptive algorithm with sufficient stability for application to both linear and nonlinear system environments without the need for significant change of the structure of the algorithm from system to system.

Neural network algorithms can be applied to both linear and nonlinear environments. Examples of applications to digital signal processing include noise cancellation using a Hopfield net[6] and nonlinear system identification[3]. Our present study is consonant with those studies with different problem context.

This paper describes and demonstrates two neural net computing digital signal methodologies. These methods can be used in the tracking of both linear and nonlinear systems without significant modification of the structure of the method. The first approach is for linear and nonlinear system identifications especially in noisy environments. The second implementation is to cancel noise in linear or nonlinear noise environments for circumstances where the desired true signals are never available, not even in training because of noise corruption.

In both cases, the network structure is identical for both linear and nonlinear environments and is independent of the input signals.

II. Network Learning Algorithm

Feedforward Perceptron-like neural-nets were used in this work. However in the nets used in this investigation, there is no hidden layer. The approach is called the Functional-Link net approach[1,7,8] and is a highly efficient one. That approach can be interpreted in terms of a single hidden-layer perceptron, except that the lower layer weights do not need to be learned [9,10]. Instead they are selected in a specific manner, as components of vectors randomly distributed in parameter space.

III. Neural-net Computing Approach to System Identification

The problem considered in this section is the identification of an unknown system(filter), which has linear or nonlinear characteristics, using neural-net computing. For the purpose of this discussion, the input signals and the noise are taken to be zero mean signals. The suggested approach is shown in Figure 3-1.

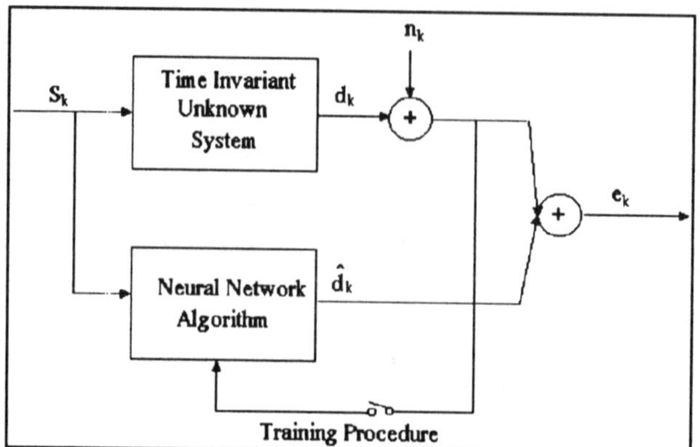

Figure 3-1 System identification using a neural network

In Figure 3-1, the random input sequence S_k to the unknown system is assumed to be known and is also supplied to the neural-net. The plant noise n_k is added to the system output d_k, so the exact value of unknown system output cannot be measured. The unknown system is assumed to be time-invariant and stable with unknown values of parameters. The neural-net approach can be seen to be divided into two procedures; the training and the identification procedures. The training procedure allows the network to settle with the estimated optimum weights vector $\mathbf{W}'$ using relatively small amounts of output and input signal pairs such as $\{ (d_k + n_k), (S_k, S_{k-1}, S_{k-2}, \cdots, S_{k-(M-1)}) \}, k = 1,2,\cdots,L$, where L is the length of training procedure. The number of training pairs needs not be large and is typically small in comparison with the total length of transmitted signal. In the training procedure, $(d_k + n_k)$ is used as a target signal, and the TDL form of input signal vector $\mathbf{S}_k$ and their functional expansions are used as input signals. This approach can be applied to identify both linear and nonlinear time invariant systems without any change in the architecture because the net is capable of synthesizing nonlinear mappings as well as linear ones using functional expansions.

The performance of the neural-net in the system identification problem is checked by the linear and nonlinear unknown system models.

As an example of linear time-invariant system identification, we assume that the unknown system has the following characteristics;

$$d_k = 0.921 \cdot S_k + 0.107 \cdot S_{k-1} + 0.336 \cdot S_{k-2} + S_{k-3} + 0.336 \cdot S_{k-4} + 0.107 \cdot S_{k-5} + 0.921 \cdot S_{k-6} \quad (3\text{-}1)$$

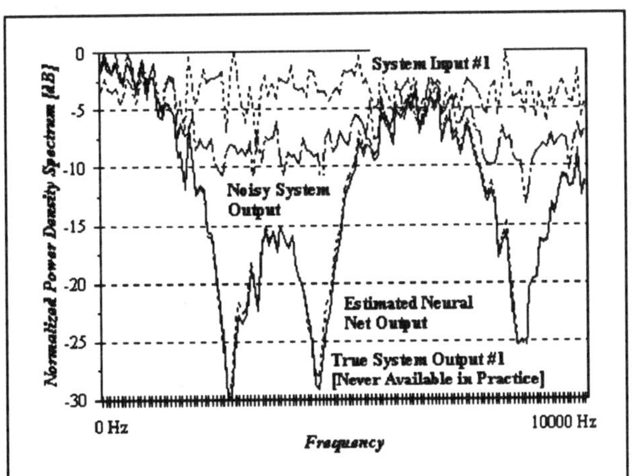

Figure 3-2 Normalized power density spectra of system input, output, noisy output and estimated signals by neural-net in linear system identification

The first input signal S_k to this unknown system is a white Gaussian random signal which has zero mean and 0.003 variance. The normalized power density spectra of the first input signal, unknown system output, and noisy system output signals are shown in Figure 3-2. For this example, the SNR between the system output and the additive white Gaussian noise is 0.76 dB .

In the suggested approach, 100 iterations of 1000 samples of input output pairs were used in the training procedure. The estimated result is also shown in Figure 3-2.

The exponential convergence rate of the system error is shown as a function of the training iterations in Figure 3-3. In this figure, the system error does not converge to zero. That means the net is trying to identify the desired system output using the system input, instead of identifying the given noisy output as the target signal. This is what is needed.

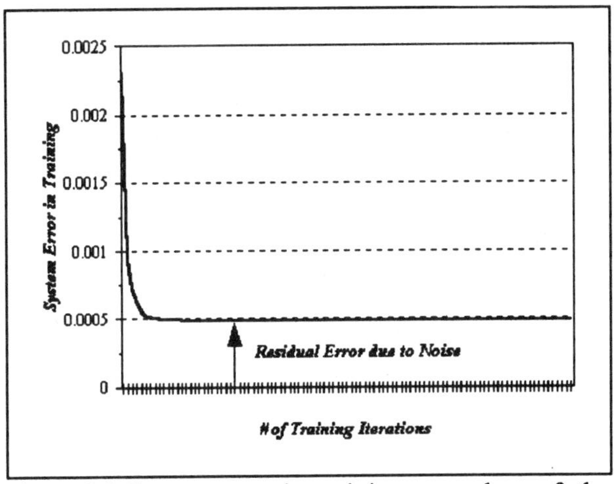

Figure 3-3 System error in training procedure of the neural network algorithm (convergence rate)

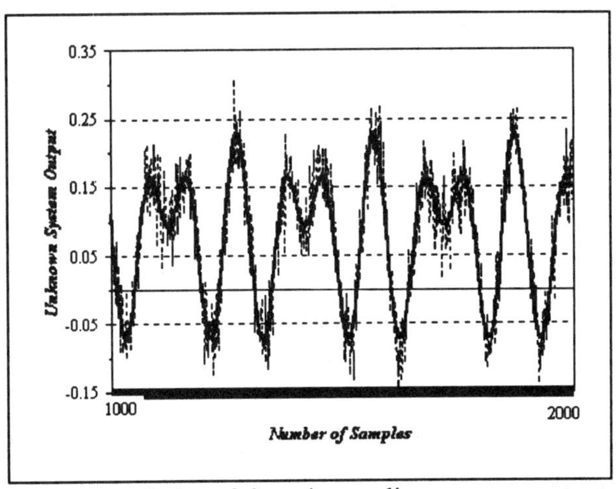

Figure 3-4 Display of the noisy nonlinear system output

As an example of noisy nonlinear system identification, the unknown system output to be identified is taken to be defined by using the difference equation;

$$d_{k+1} = 0.15d_k + 0.3d_{k-1} + 0.6S_k^3 + 0.18S_k^2 - 0.24S_k \quad (3\text{-}2)$$

The first input to the nonlinear system is a sinusoid such as;

$$S_k = 0.7 \cdot \sin(2 \cdot \pi \cdot k/300) \quad (3\text{-}3)$$

Another input was used to verify that the neural-net algorithm did indeed identify the system rather than just learn the input sequence. That second input consisted of two sinusoids.

$$S_k = 0.7 \cdot \sin(2 \cdot \pi \cdot k/300) + 0.3 \cdot \sin(2 \cdot \pi \cdot k/30) \quad (3\text{-}4)$$

The SNR between system output and noise was taken to be approximately 9.73 dB. The first noisy system output is depicted in Figure 3-4.

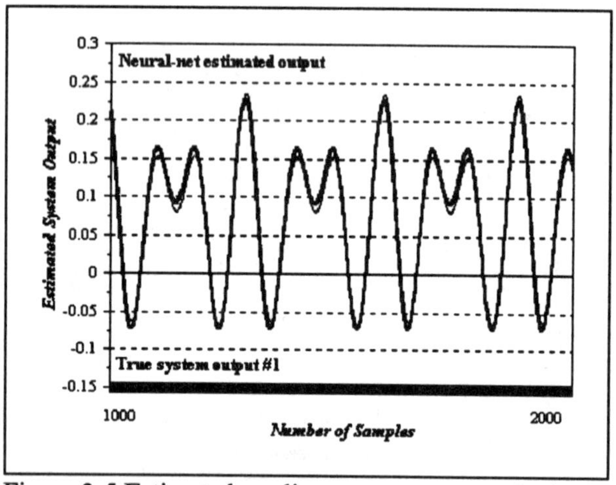

Figure 3-5 Estimated nonlinear system output for input 1 obtained with the neural network

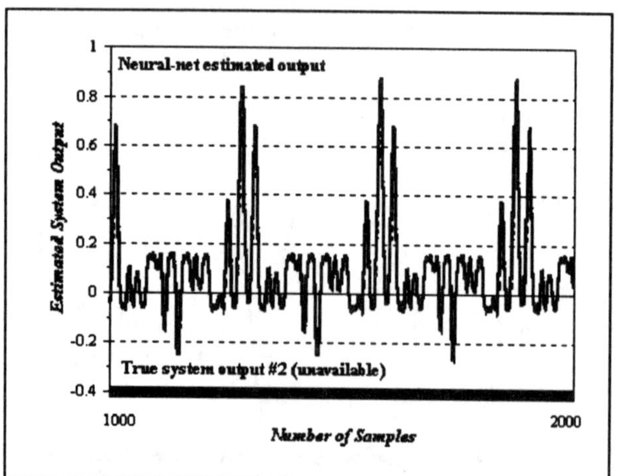

Figure 3-6 Estimated nonlinear system output for input 2 obtained with the neural network

After training with 100 iterations of the first 1000 samples, the estimated system output is obtained. The unknown system output and estimated system output are shown in Figure 3-5. Even when the input is changed to the second input (a sum of two sinusoids), the neural-net performed satisfactorily using the same weights as before, obtained in the noisy environment. This is shown in Figure 3-6. The estimated values of the system output are so close to the true system output that the difference is not easily discerned in the Figure. This is remarkable considering that the true system output was never available in the training procedure. The above results indicate that the neural-net computing approach is suitable for use in both linear and nonlinear system identification problems, in noise environments.

IV. A Neural-net Computing Approach to Noise Cancellation

In digital signal processing, it is important to be able to separate signals from background noise. In this section, we describe an approach towards implementing a neural-net for the recovery of an unknown target signal from a high level of interference noise. The most widely used approach to noise cancellation is based on the two sensor scenario [2,4,5]. One sensor(the primary sensor) measures the signal that consist of the desired signal embedded in the noise. The second sensor(the reference sensor) measures additional information on the background noise. The signal measured in the reference sensor is used for canceling the noise which corrupted the desired signal in the primary sensor. In order to get appropriate results in the two sensor problem, the reference signal must contain as little as possible of the desired signal so as not to cancel the desired signal along with corrupting noise. This section assumes that the signal at the reference sensor does not contain any of the desired signal. A block diagram of noise cancellation procedure is shown in Figure 4-1.

In Figure 4-1, signal P_k at the primary sensor is composed of the desired signal S_k and noise n^1_k which is the output of an unknown environment of noise n_k with the transfer function **W**, whereas the reference sensor measured signal is almost wholly consisted of the noise signal n_k. The weight coefficients of $\mathbf{W}'$ are trained in the manner shown in Figure 4-1. The purpose of $\mathbf{W}'$ is to provide an estimate of n^1_k so that $e_k = P_k - n^{1'}_k$ is an estimated signal S'_k of the desired signal. When S_k is assumed to be uncorrelated with both n_k and $n^1{}_k$, the mean square error $E\{e_k^2\}$ is obtained by following equations;

$$E\{e_k^2\} = E\{(P_k - n^{1'_k})^2\}$$

$$= E\{S_k^2\} + E\{(n^{1_k} - n^{1'_k})^2\} \quad (4\text{-}1)$$

After adjusting the response of W' with the adaptive algorithm, the minimized $E\{e_k^2\}$ does not affect the signal energy $E\{S_k^2\}$ at any frequency.

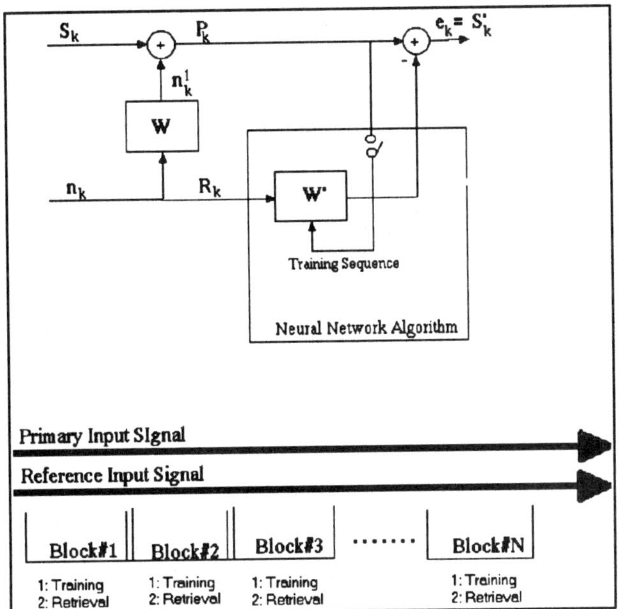

Figure 4-1 The neural network approach to noise cancellation

In Figure 4-1, We assume that the properties of the noise environment transfer function **W** changes relatively slowly with time, as would be the case for a room transfer function. We note that **W**, the transfer function between n_k and $n^1{}_k$, can be nonlinear. The short-term time invariant assumption influences our choice of the training and noise cancellation procedure(retrieval). An example of this short-time processing method is time dependent processing of speech using the short time Fourier representation in which short segments of the signal are isolated and processed as if they were short segments of a sustained signal with fixed properties. The neural-net is divided into the training procedure and the retrieval process in short segments and these two processes are repeated as needed. Specially, we divide the concurrent data streams into blocks of associated time-indexed pairs. Time invariance of **W** is assumed to be valid within the duration of each block. These block-frames will commonly overlap one another. After each block-frame is stored with P_k (primary) and $\mathbf{R}_k$ (reference), $k=1,2,\cdots,L$, the network is allowed to settle in the training procedure. The neural-net is trained with segments of $\mathbf{R}_k$ and P_k pairs with length M, which is considerably shorter than the stored L observed length of each block frame. The neural-net does it's best to learn a single set of weights which would allow it to estimate P_k given $\mathbf{R}_k$ for all such pairs. One approach is to load the kth set of M observations of the reference input, $R_{k-(M-1)}, R_{k-(M-2)}, R_{k-(M-3)}, \cdots, R_k$, and then estimate the corresponding output P_k' using the primary input P_k as a target signal. After the estimate is obtained, the second set of reference input, $R_{k-(M-2)}, R_{k-(M-3)}, \cdots, R_{k+1}$, is loaded and P_{k+1}' is estimated using the target signal P_{k+1}. This procedure would be performed a total of L times to obtain the estimates of each block sequence in one learning period. The network would settle iteratively with the above learning period. The training of the network would fail in that task precisely because P_k contains the desired signal S_k. So, in the retrieval process, the estimated transfer function $\mathbf{W}'$, obtained after the network is allowed to settle, provides an estimate $n^{1'}{}_k$ of the noise signal $n^1{}_k$ in the primary signals such that the error signal $e_k = P_k - f(\mathbf{W}^T \cdot \mathbf{R}_k)$ is infact the estimated desired signal S_k'. The primary problem with this approach is that it does not take into account the truncation of the observation sequences which cause the block effect. This block effect can be solved by overlapping M samples between the boundaries of each block frame.

This learning procedure works because what is being learned is the effect of **W** on n_k. The trains of input and related output signals are almost incidental, just means for learning the weight $\mathbf{W}'$.

A neural-net approach to the noise cancellation problem is implemented and its performance is shown in linear and nonlinear noise environments. Two examples were used to check the performance: white Gaussian noise cancellation and nonlinear interference cancellation problems. In the white Gaussian noise cancellation problem, we assume that the desired signal S_k is produced by sending a white Gaussian random signal through a bandpass filter whose low cutoff frequency is 8 Hz, high cutoff frequency is 11 Hz, and the sampling frequency is 200 Hz. The reference noise signal n_k is also a white Gaussian random signal which has zero mean and 0.0536 variance. The transfer function of the noise environment between reference noise n_k and $n^1{}_k$ is unavailable to the observer and assumed to be;

$$n^1{}_k = 0.1842 \cdot n_k + 0.0214 \cdot n_{k-1} + 0.0672 \cdot n_{k-2} + 0.2 \cdot n_{k-3} + 0.0672 \cdot n_{k-4} + 0.0214 \cdot n_{k-5} + 0.1842 \cdot n_{k-6} \quad (4\text{-}2)$$

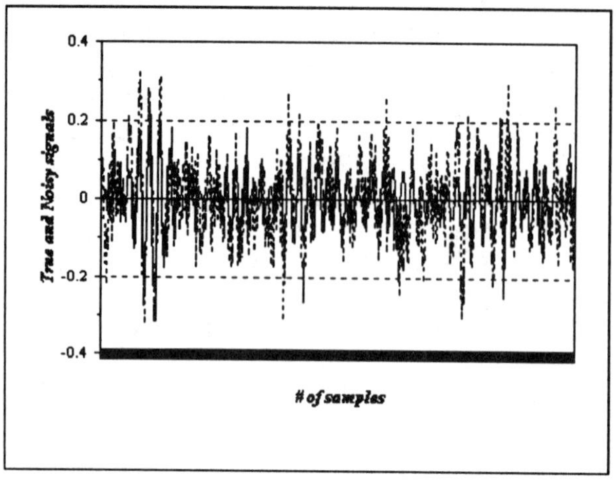

Figure 4-2 White Gaussian signal S_k and the noisy signal P_k

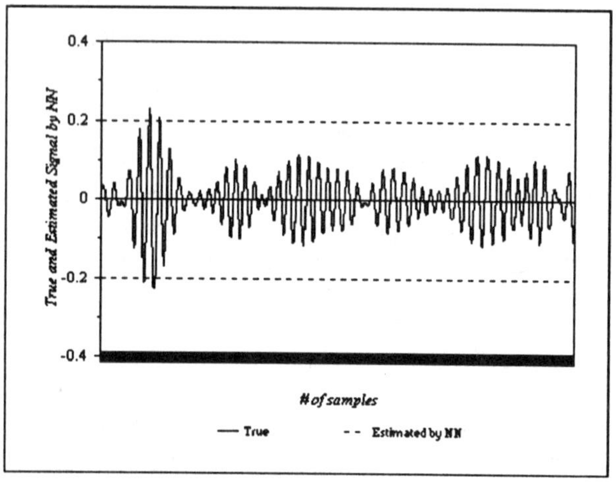

Figure 4-3 Estimated signal using a neural network in the white Gaussian noise cancellation problem

The white Gaussian signal S_k and noisy signal P_k are generated according to Figure 4-1 and the SNR in P_k is assumed to be approximately -2.54 dB. This is shown in Figure 4-2. In the neural-net algorithm, pairs of 1000 samples of noise input $\mathbf{R}_k$, and noise corrupted signal P_k are used in each block in the training and retrieval process. In each block sequence, maximum iterations are set to 100 in the training process. The convergence rate between system error and training iterations in the first block sequence is similar with Figure 3-3. This convergence means that the neural-net attempts to find the unknown noise transfer function $\mathbf{W}$ of n^1_k, instead of attempting to find P_k (the desired signal S_k corrupted by noise n^1_k), using the reference input $\mathbf{R}_k$. A comparison of the true and estimated signal are shown in Figure 4-3. In the figure, agreement is so close that the difference can not be readily discerned.

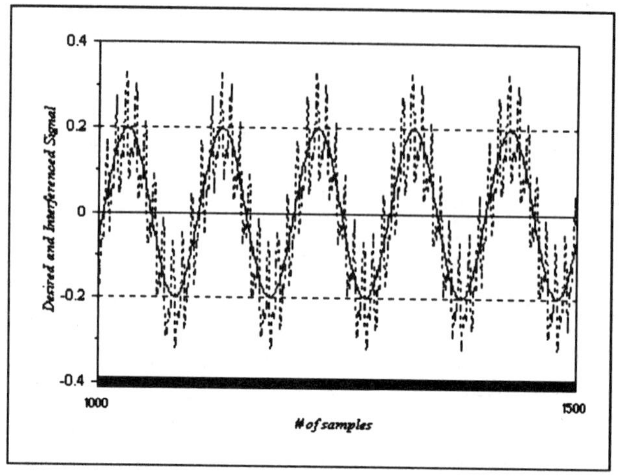

Figure 4-4 Desired S_k and nonlinearly corrupted signal P_k in the nonlinear interference cancellation problem

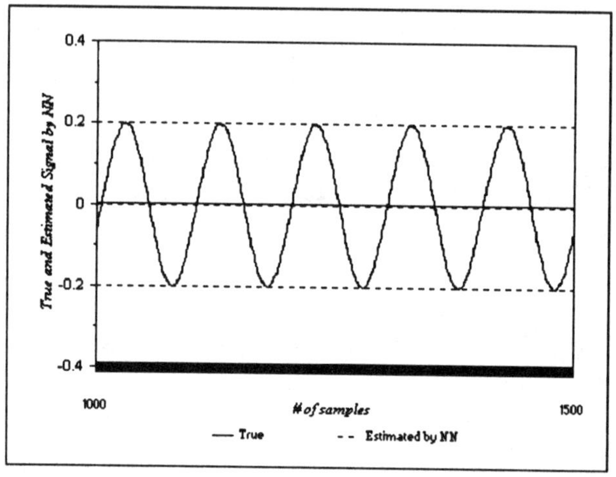

Figure 4-5 Estimated signal obtained with the neural network algorithm in the nonlinear interference cancellation problem

In the nonlinear interference cancellation problem, the desired signal S_k and reference noise n_k are assumed as follows;

$$S_k = 0.2 \cdot \sin(2 \cdot \pi \cdot 10 \cdot k/1000) \qquad (4\text{-}3)$$

$$n_k = 0.285 \cdot \sin(2 \cdot \pi \cdot 100 \cdot k/1000) \qquad (4\text{-}4)$$

The unknown nonlinear noise transfer function between n_k and n^1_k is assumed to be ;

$$n^1_k = 0.3 \cdot n_k + 0.6 \cdot n_{k-1}^2 + 0.9 \cdot n_{k-2}^3 - 0.6 \cdot n_{k-3}^2 - 0.3 \cdot n_{k-4} \qquad (4\text{-}5)$$

We note that nonlinearity in this case refers to nonlinear distortion of the 'noise' n_k in one of the paths. The desired S_k and the nonlinearly corrupted signal P_k

are shown in Figure 4-4, and the SNR in P_k is assumed to be approximately 4.72 dB. The estimated signal S'_k is shown in Figure 4-5. From the above examples, the neural-net can be shown to be used with acceptable stability in nonlinear noise environment as well as linear situation without modification to the structure of the algorithm.

V Conclusion

This paper introduces feedforward type of neural network approaches which can be used in system identification and noise cancellation tasks. In system identification and noise cancellation problems, it is assumed that the unknown systems change relatively slowly with time and the training set signals are considered to be unknown because of noise corruption. Simulation results show that neural-nets can learn a model of a system transfer function (linear or nonlinear) even when training data are corrupted by noise. In noise cancellation, the neural-net effectively learns how to estimate what is required to cancel out the background noise even though different environment transfer functions can severely distort the common background noise differently along different paths.

Reference

[1]. Pao, Y. H., 1989, *Adaptive Pattern Recognition and Neural Networks*, Addison-Wesley Publishing.

[2]. Feder, M., Oppenheim, A. V. and Weistein, E., 1989, "Maximum likelihood noise cancellation using the EM algorithm", *IEEE trans. on Acoustics, Speech, and Signal Processing*, Vol. 37, No. 2, pp. 204-216.

[3]. Narendra, K. S. and Parthasarathy, K., 1990, "Identification and control of dynamical systems using neural networks", *IEEE trans. on Neural Networks*, Vol. 1, No. 1, pp. 4-26.

[4]. Schwartz, M. and Shaw, L., 1975, *Signal Processing, Discrete Spectral Analysis, Detection, and Estimation*, McGraw-Hill.

[5]. Widrow, B. and S. D. Stearns, S. D., 1983, *Adaptive Signal Processing*, McGraw-Hill.

[6]. Zhao, X. and Mendel, J. M., 1988, "An artificial neural minimum-variance estimator", *IEEE International Conference on Neural Network*, Vol. 2, pp. 499-506.

[7]. Pao Y. H., Park, G. H., and Sobajic, D. J., 1994 "Learning and Generalization Characteristics of the Random Vector Functional Link Net", *Neurocomputing*, vol. 6, no. 1.

[8]. Pao, Y. H. and Takefuji, Y., 1991, "Functional-link net computing: Theory, system architecture, and functionlities", Special issue of *Computer* on Computer Architectures for Intelligent Machines, IEEE Computer Society Press, vol. 3, pp. 76-79, also published in Readings in *Computer Architectures for Intelligent Systems* (expanded version), J. Herath (ed.), in press

[9]. Igelnik B. and Pao, Y. H., 1994, "Mathematical Concepts Underlying the Functional-Link Approach", *WCINNS*, June, Sandiego, CA

[10]. Pao, Y. H., Phillips, S. M. and Sobajic, D. J., 1992, "Neural-net computing and the intelligent control of systems", Special Intelligent Control issue of *International Journal of Control*, vol. 56, no. 2, pp. 263-289, Taylor and Francis, LTD., London, U.K.

Neural Network Architectures for Short-Term Load Forcasting

Kwang Y. Lee, Tae-Il Choi, Chao-Chee Ku, and June Ho Park

Abstract— **Different neural network architectures are presented for short-term load forecasting. The fully connected recurrent neural network(FRNN), where all neurons are coupled to one another, is difficult to train and to converge in a short time. The diagonal recurrent neural network (DRNN) is a modified model of FRNN. It requires fewer weights than FRNN and rapid convergence has been demonstrated. A dynamic Backpropagation Algorithm coupled with adaptive learning rate guarantees even faster convergence. Many experiments are conducted to provide the one-day ahead load forecast, and the results are compared. The effect of temperatures and Functional-Link Net mapping are also studied by including them as the network's inputs. The forecasting accuracy for weekend load can be improved by using a seperate weekend load model.**

I. Introduction

There are many classes of load forecasting models reported in literature [1]. Some load models which use no weather information have been presented by time sequence [2]. The other load models have included the effects of weather variables on the power system load [3]. The former is based on the extrapolation and the load behavior is represented by fourier series or trend curves in terms of time functions. The weather sensitive load is mostly predicted using the correlation techniques and the non-weather sensitive load is modeled by the method mentioned above. Recently, a new method of adaptively identifying the load model was developed, which reflects the stochastic behavior without the aid of weather variables [4]. They decomposed the load model into three components: the nominal load, the residual load and the type load. The parameters of the model are adapted to the load variations.

Kwang Y. Lee, Tae-Il Choi, Chao-Chee Ku are with the Department of Electrical Engineering, Pennsylvania State University, University Park, PA 16802
June Ho Park is with the Department of Electrical Engineering, Pusan National University, Pusan 609-735, Korea.

Recently, the artificial neural network (ANN) has been used for forecasting time series. Both the backpropagation algorithm for the training of feedforward ANN [5] and dynamic backpropagation algorithm for the training of recurrent ANN are proposed [6] as methodologies for electric load forecasting. A nonlinear load model is suggested and the parameters of the nonlinear load model are estimated using backpropagation and dynamic backpropagation algorithms. Although the ANN is a very promising tool for load forecasting, several key issues must be addressed before it can be effectively used. The load profile is dynamic in nature with temporal, seasonal and annual variations. During the course of this study, several attempts were made to enhance the accuracy of the forecast by selecting different structures of neural networks. A simple ANN can often outperform several complex and extensive forecasting systems, which was demonstrated in references [4] and [5] using the same data.

There are two distinct load patterns; weekday and weekend patterns. The weekend pattern includes Saturday, Sunday, and Monday loads. Comparing weekday loads with Saturday loads, the level of Saturday loads is relatively low during p.m. The level of Monday loads during a.m. influenced by Sunday loads is also low. The weekday loads at a fixed hour are similar to each other due to daily periodic patterns of the customers, but vary slowly during the year. Factors changing loads are economical, sociological, seasonal and meteorological effects. However, since load variations are slow, loads are sufficiently predicted by the appropriate technique in prediction algorithm.

0-7803-1901-X/94 $4.00 ©1994 IEEE

II. Artificial neural networks

A generic feedforward neural network (FNN) is shown in Fig. 1, which has input, hidden, and output layers of processing elements. Processing elements in an ANN are also known as *neurons*. These neurons are interconnected by means of information channels called interconnections. Each neuron can have multiple inputs, while there can be only one output. Inputs to a neuron could be from external stimuli or could be from output of other neurons. Copies of the single output that comes from a neuron could be input to many other neurons in the network. It is also possible that one of the copies of a neuron's output could be input to itself as a feedback. In this case, the network is called self recurrent neural network (SRNN). There is a connection strength, *synapses*, or weight associated with each connection.

When the weighted sum of the inputs to a neuron exceeds a certain threshold, the neuron is fired and an output signal is produced. The network can recognize input patterns once the weights are adjusted or tuned via some kind of learning process. The *backpropagation* learning algorithm is the most frequently used method in training the feedforward neural networks (FNN). In order to train the self recurrent neural networks (SRNN), a modified learning algorithm called *dynamic backpropagation* learning algorithm [6] is used.

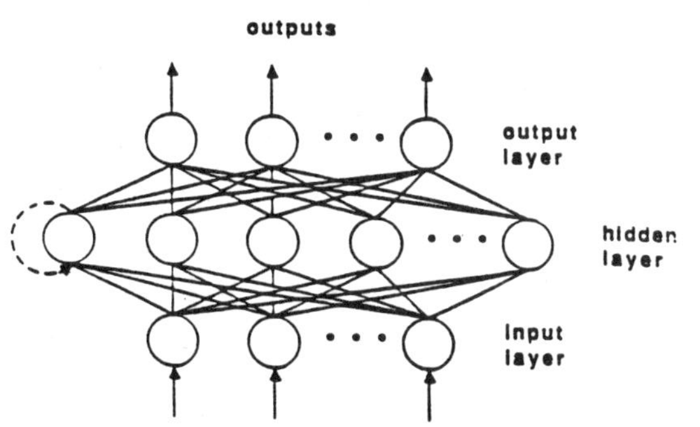

Figure 1: Artificial Neural Network (with diagonal recurrent neurons shown in dotted line)

III. Dynamic backpropagation algorithm

An error function for a pattern p can be defined as

$$E_p = \frac{1}{2}\sum_j (t_{pj} - o_{pj})^2, \quad (1)$$

and $E = \sum_p E_p$ is the overall measure of the error for all patterns, $p = 1, 2, \ldots, P$. Here t_{pj} is the target output for j-th component of the output pattern for pattern p and o_{pj} is the corresponding network output. The self recurrent neural network [6] is specified as

$$o_{pj} = f_j(net_{pj}), \quad (2)$$

$$net_{pj} = \sum_k w_{jk} o_{pk} + w_{jd} z^{-1}(o_{pj}), \quad (3)$$

where f_j is a differentiable and nondecreasing function (sigmoid type), w_{jd} is the weight for the delayed feedback, w_{jk} is input or output weight, and z^{-1} is a unit delay operator.

To obtain a rule for adjusting weights, the gradient of E_p with respect to input or output weight w_{ji} is used and it is represented as follows:

$$-\frac{\partial E_p}{\partial w_{ji}} = \delta_{pj}(o_{pi} + w_{jd} z^{-1} \frac{\partial o_{pj}}{\partial w_{ji}}), \quad (4)$$

where δ_{pj} is the equivalent error defined for the output layer as

$$\delta_{pj} = (t_{pj} - o_{pj}) f_j'(net_{pj}), \quad (5)$$

and for a unit in an arbitrary hidden layer as

$$\delta_{pj} = f_j'(net_{pj}) \sum_k \delta_{pk} w_{kj}, \quad (6)$$

where δ_{pk} is the equivalent error backpropagated from the next layer, and f_j' is the derivative of the sigmoid function f_j. The output gradient is generated by the *dynamic* or *recurrent* equation as follows:

$$\frac{\partial o_{pj}}{\partial w_{ji}} = f_j'(net_{pj})(o_{pi} + w_{jd} z^{-1} \frac{\partial o_{pj}}{\partial w_{ji}}). \quad (7)$$

For the hidden or output layer, o_{pi} is the i-th component of the input, which can be the output from the previous layer. It can be noted that if $w_{jd} = 0$, then (4) is for the usual feedforward network.

For the recurrent weight w_{jd}, the error gradient is represented as follows:

$$-\frac{\partial E_p}{\partial w_{jd}} = \delta_{pj}(z^{-1}(o_{pj}) + w_{jd} z^{-1} \frac{\partial o_{pj}}{\partial w_{jd}}), \quad (8)$$

where δ_{pj} is similarly defined as (5) or (6), and the output gradient is generated by the dynamic or recurrent equation as follows:

$$\frac{\partial o_{pj}}{\partial w_{jd}} = f_j'(net_j)(z^{-1}(o_{pj}) + w_{jd} z^{-1} \frac{\partial o_{pj}}{\partial w_{jd}}). \quad (9)$$

If the self recurrent neurons are only in the hidden layer, not in the output, then the network is called a diagonal recurrent neural network (DRNN)[7]. Thus the rule of adjusting weights is defined as

$$\Delta w_{ji}(n+1) = \eta(-\frac{\partial E_p}{\partial w_{ji}}) + \alpha \Delta w_{ji}(n), \quad (10)$$

where η is the learning rate, α is the momentum factor, and Δ represents the changes in weight.

IV. Load forcasting using ANN

Two different methods of application of ANN are presented for the short-term load forecasting. The first method is a *static mapping* in the sense that the 24-hour load vector is forecasted simultaneously using the previous load patterns. The second method is a *dynamic approach* in the sense that the 24-hour load is forecasted sequentially using the previous-time forecasts. However, when the recurrent neural network is used to the second method, the current state memorizes the previous state, which makes this approach truly a *dynamic approach*.

A. Simultaneous forecasting

In general, the load model for one-day ahead forecasting can be represented as a nonlinear mapping of previous loads in each pattern:

$$y(i) = F_p(W_i, Y(i-1)), \quad p = 1, 2, \ldots, P, \quad (11)$$

where

$y(i) = \{y(i,t) : t = 1, 2, \ldots, 24\}$: load for day i
$y(i,t)$: the actual load at day i, time t
$Y(i-1) = [y(i-1)^T, y(i-2)^T, \ldots, y(i-k)^T]^T$
k: index for data length
W_i: the weight vector for day i
$F_p(\cdot,\cdot)$: nonlinear vector function for pattern p
P: the number of patterns.

In contrast to conventional approaches, the nonlinear function is used with the weight vector to represent the load model. The weight vector W_i can be thought of as the storage that contains a certain load pattern, and $F_p(\cdot,\cdot)$ is the general nonlinear function that can comprise all loads in each pattern.

To estimate the load for day i, the index i is replaced by $i-1$ in (11) and a number of latest loads can be used to adjust the weight. Both weekday and weekend patterns can be trained using this model. Often, the forecasting errors in weekend are higher than those in weekdays. To improve the forecasting accuracy, additional inputs such as temperature can be added, or the Functional-Link Net mapping can be utilized [8].

Once the weight vector for day i is estimated, the load is forecasted using the estimated weights in (11)

The above scheme worked well when enough number of patterns are classified and the results were fair except at peak time hours [5].

B. Sequential forecasting

The autocorrelation function of the load shows peaks at the multiples of 24 hour lags, which indicates that the load at a fixed hour of a day has strong correlation with that for any other day, independent of the day of the week, including weekend [5]. Thus the following sequential load model is proposed:

$$\begin{aligned} y(i,t) \quad = \quad & F_p(W(i,t), y(i,t-1), \ldots, y(i,t-m), \\ & y(i-1,t), \ldots, y(i-1,t-m), \\ & \vdots \\ & y(i-n,t), \ldots, y(i-n,t-m)), \\ & \qquad p = 1, 2, \ldots, P \quad (12) \end{aligned}$$

where n and m indicate the data length.

Note that this model differs from the usual time-series model. Since it includes loads for both previous times and previous days, it better represents the daily and hourly variations than the first model. Another advantage of this model is that training is easier since it has a single output, as compared to the first model which has the 24×1 vector output. The load patterns can be classified into weekday pattern and weekend pattern. The weight vector $W(i,t)$ can be estimated at each time using previous load data for each pattern in a way similar to the first model, i.e., i is replaced by $i-1$ for training.

After the weight vector for day i, time t is estimated, the load is forecasted with the load data of previous days as well as the forecasted load data for the same day, day i, at previous time steps. It should be noted that the estimate $\hat{y}(i,t-1), \ldots, \hat{y}(i,t-m)$ are used as inputs to the model to obtain $\hat{y}(i,t)$. This is because we need to forecast the entire 24 hour loads for the one-day-ahead forecasting problem. The first model is a *static* mapping while the second is a *dynamic* model. The feedforward neural network can be used for both models. However, when the recurrent neural network is used, the internal states memorize previous states, and, thus, less neurons can be used to capture the dynamic behavior than the feedforward neural network. This will be demonstrated numerically in the following section.

V. Simulation results

Case studies for the proposed method were carried out for a one-day ahead forecasting of hourly electric loads using historical data of Puget Sound Power and Light Company.

A. Comparison between FNN and DRNN

Several structures of ANN with the backpropagation and dynamic backpropagation learning algorithms were tested. The learning rate η and the momentum constant α in (10) was fixed to 0.5. The tolerance of adjusting the weight vector was 0.005. One hidden layer was used with various numbers of neurons. The data lengths m and n were changed to compare the result. For example, if m is 1 and n is 3, inputs to the ANN are load for time t and $t-1$ of three previous days, and the forecasted load for time $t-1$ of the future forecasting day, totalling 7 inputs. The neural network with one hidden layer was simulated and 7, 15, and 1 neurons were used in the input, hidden, and output layers, respectively. The results were analyzed in detail on an hourly base for one day (July 31, 1991). Both FNN and DRNN resulted in small percentage error, where DRNN shows the smaller error of 0.867% compared to 0.982% for FNN. The average iteration number is also smaller for DRNN, 99 compared to 115 for FNN. In Table 1 the results for one week (July 22 - July 28, 1991) and one month (July 1991) are compared. The DRNN shows better results of 1.624% for one week compared to 1.674% for FNN, and 1.911% for one month compared to 1.954% for FNN. Fig. 2 shows the comparison of actual load and forecasted load for one month by using DRNN. In Table 2 different structures for input and neurons are compared for one month by using DRNN and FNN, respectively (July 1991). The DRNN shows better results than FNN, and the input structure with m=1 and n=3 shows the best result. Therefore the DRNN is used throughout the subsequent experiment. It was shown that the minimum number of hidden neurons for a one-hidden layer network is 2N+1, where N is the number of inputs. Thus, this rule was followed as a basis to make comparison.

B. Different structures for input and neurons

Since it is known that two hidden layers are sufficient for any kind of nonlinear mapping, two hidden layers with DRNN are tested with various numbers of inputs and neurons. For two hidden layer, the 2N+1 rule is no longer applicable; but the number is evenly devided between the layers. The learning rate η, the momentum constant α, and the tolerance are the same as in the previous method. With two hidden layers of $15-15-15-1$ neuron structure, the input structure of m=1 and n=7 shows a good result comparable with the input structure of m=1 and n=3 for the one hidden layer (Table 2). Both structures are tested for a one-day-ahead load forecasting for one year from September 1990 to August 1991. The percent relative error is 2.251% and 2.274%, for one and two hidden layers, respectively. Test results shows that one hidden layer is enough. Thus, the results from one hidden layer are used to examine the seasonal effects for four representative months in four seasons. These months are February, May, July and October for Winter, Spring, Summer and Fall, respectively. The minimum values of the standard deviation and percent relative error are found in Summer, which are 50.21$[MW]$ and 1.726%, respectively, and the maximum values are found in Fall, which are 81.84$[MW]$ and 2.642%, respectively.

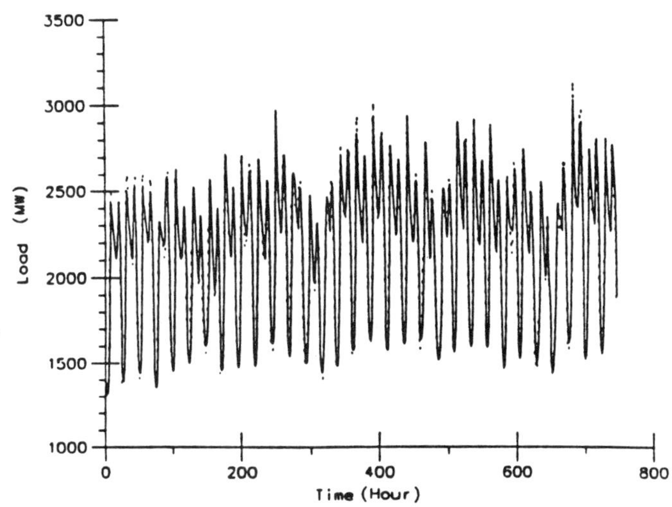

Figure 2: Comparison of actual load and forecasted load using DRNN for July, 1991. (solid:actual load; dot:fore casted load)

C. Weekday and weekend models

As mentioned before, the load behavior for weekdays (Tuesday through Friday) shows the same pattern and is different from the weekend load pattern. Most classic approaches used several different models according to the load pattern. For example, in [5,6] the load model is divided into weekday and weekend models. The weekend model is further classified into several load types.

Table 3 shows the comparison between the use of one model and the use of two models, one for weekday and another for weekend. Here again, the one hidden layer with the input structure of m=1 and n=3 is used for both models. It can be concluded that two different models can be used to improve the forecasting accuracy for weekend load and the total accuracy for one month (July 1991) can also be improved. However, this results in a slight increase in error for weekday, mainly in the border of the blocks (cf. 1.689% vs. 1.498%).

Table 1: Comparison of forecasting results for one week and one month in persentage error

	FNN		DRNN	
hour	week	month	week	month
1	0.726	1.079	0.983	1.189
2	1.280	1.378	1.272	1.347
3	1.023	1.130	0.962	1.115
4	0.905	1.156	0.969	1.142
5	2.426	2.071	1.902	1.931
6	1.398	2.163	1.135	2.112
7	1.286	2.930	1.266	2.527
8	3.510	3.779	3.824	3.783
9	3.110	3.628	3.530	3.790
10	1.142	1.887	0.981	1.879
11	1.270	1.507	1.177	1.463
12	1.691	1.800	1.523	1.725
13	0.878	1.159	0.804	1.179
14	0.799	1.049	0.821	1.052
15	0.737	0.983	0.750	0.991
16	0.338	0.747	0.364	0.744
17	1.537	1.406	1.409	1.267
18	1.116	1.076	1.124	1.116
19	1.312	1.440	0.880	1.285
20	1.577	1.425	1.584	1.441
21	0.608	0.910	0.524	0.856
22	3.480	2.503	3.371	2.431
23	5.270	5.836	4.685	5.396
24	2.742	3.800	3.127	4.068
total	1.673	1.954	1.624	1.911

D. *Temperature effects and functional link net mapping*

Weather variables are playing an important role in changing the load patterns. Thus, often loads are classified as weather sensitive load and non-weather sensitive load. Temperature data is obviously a very important factor affecting the load. However, its value is often limited to the confidence level on weather forecasting. Therefore, unless the weather forecasting is very accurate, much care should be made on the use of temperature data. Additional inputs using temperature or Functional-Link Net mapping [8] are experimented to improve the forecasting and Table 4 shows the results. With the structure of m=1 and n=0, two temperatures for time t and $t-1$ of the future forecasting day are added to the best input structure defined in Table 2; and with the structure of m=1 and n=1, four temperatures for time t and $t-1$ of previous day and future forecasting day are added. But the results are not improved. For the use of Functional-Link Net mapping, three inputs of $L(1)^2, L(2)^2, L(1) \times L(2)$ are added to the inputs, where $L(1)$ is the load for time $t-1$ of the future forecasting day and $L(2)$ is the load for time t of the previous day. Only the accuracy of the weekend forecasting is slightly improved. Table 4 shows that the inclusion of temperature data does not improve the forecasting accuracy; and the effect of mixed bag data (part depends on the weather and other independent of the weather) was not shown through out the year.

Table 2: Comparison of results for different structures of input and neuron

input stru.	neuron stru.	s.dev	p.err
m=0 n=3	3-8-8-1	224.44	8.142
m=0 n=4	4-8-8-1	204.53	7.213
m=0 n=5	5-8-8-1	178.67	5.541
m=1 n=1	3-8-8-1	91.61	3.162
m=1 n=2	5-8-8-1	80.21	2.760
m=1 n=3	7-8-8-1	60.42	2.120
m=1 n=4	9-9-9-1	58.97	2.051
m=1 n=5	11-11-11-1	56.33	1.998
m=1 n=6	13-13-13-1	54.67	1.979
m=1 n=7	15-15-15-1	54.12	1.912
m=1 n=8	17-17-17-1	55.00	1.946
m=1 n=9	19-19-19-1	88.72	2.459
m=2 n=1	5-8-8-1	103.35	3.179
m=2 n=2	8-8-8-1	85.43	2.925
m=2 n=3	11-11-11-1	62.91	2.386
m=2 n=4	14-14-14-1	64.19	2.417
m=2 n=5	17-17-17-1	63.64	2.420
m=3 n=0	3-8-8-1	120.02	4.382
m=3 n=1	7-8-8-1	92.45	3.004
m=3 n=2	11-11-11-1	81.29	2.927
m=3 n=3	15-15-15-1	64.57	2.509
m=4 n=0	4-8-8-1	111.98	4.381
m=4 n=1	9-9-9-1	86.98	3.156
m=4 n=2	14-14-14-1	78.61	3.076
m=4 n=3	19-19-19-1	92.75	3.188
m=4 n=4	24-24-24-1	223.35	7.159
m=5 n=0	5-8-8-1	122.43	4.950
m=5 n=1	11-11-11-1	85.69	3.187
m=5 n=2	17-17-17-1	81.29	3.149
m=5 n=3	23-23-23-1	148.02	4.508

Table 3: Comparison between one model and two models for one month

model	one model		two model	
index	s.dev	p.err	s.dev	p.err
weekday	40.52	1.498	47.42	1.689
weekend	68.81	2.487	63.00	2.173
one month total	54.17	1.911	54.64	1.896

Table 4: Additional inputs using temperature and Functional Link Net mapping

model	weekday		weekend	
index	s.dev	p.err	s.dev	p.err
w/o add.input	47.42	1.689	63.00	2.173
2 temp. m=1 n=0	48.26	1.729	64.06	2.200
4 temp. m=1 n=1	71.61	2.076	64.33	2.241
3 F-L.N.M.	68.32	1.986	61.96	2.169

VI. Conclusion

Artificial neural network method is applied to the short-term load forecasting of one-day ahead hourly electric loads in several different ways. Several structures for input and neurons are tested with one hidden layer to compare between the DRNN and FNN. The dynamic approach using DRNN performs better than FNN in the sense that it uses less number of neurons and weights, converges faster, and gives better results. One hidden layer is shown to be enough to get the comparable result compared with two hidden layers.

Since the load profile is dynamic in nature with temporal, seasonal and annual variations, many structures for inputs and neurons need to be tested experimentally to get the best forecasting result. The forecasting accuracy for weekend load is improved by using two different models (weekday and weekend). Additional inputs using temperature and Functional Link Net mapping can be used to improve the forecasting results with careful investigation. The forecasting error is about 2% for the percent relative error and thus shows a promise for the use of artificial neural network method in load forecasting.

References

[1] IEEE Committee Report, "Load forecasting bibliography phase I, " *IEEE Trans. on Power Appr. and Sys.*, vol. PAS-99, pp. 53-58, 1980.

[2] W. R. Christiaanse, "Short-term load forecasting using general exponential smoothing," *IEEE Trans. on Power Appr. and Sys.*, vol. PAS-90, pp. 900-910, 1971.

[3] M. Nakamura, "Short term load forecasting using weekday load models and bias models," *Proc. PICA Conference*, pp. 37-42, 1984.

[4] J. H. Park, Y. M. Park and K. Y. Lee, "Composite modeling for adaptive short-term load forecasting", *IEEE Trans. on Power Sys.*, vol. 6, pp. 450-457, May 1991.

[5] K. Y. Lee, Y. T. Cha and J. H. Park, "Short-term load fore- casting using an artificial neural network", *IEEE Trans. on Power Sys.*, vol. 7, pp. 124-132, Febuary 1992.

[6] K. Y. Lee, Y. T. Cha and C. C. Ku, "A Study on Neural Net- works for Short-Term Load Forecasting", *Proc. of Applications of Neural Networks to Power Systems '91*, pp. 26-30, Seattle, WA, July 1991.

[7] C. C. Ku and K. Y. Lee, "Diagonal Recurrent Neural Network Based Control Using Adaptive Learning Rates", *Proc. 31st IEEE Conf. on Decision and Control*, Tucson, Arizona, pp. 3485-3490, Dec. 16-18, 1992.

[8] Y. H. Pao, "Adaptive Pattern Recognition and Neural Net- works", Addison-Wesley, Reading, MA, 1989.

[9] C. C. Ku and Y. Lee, "Diagonal Recurrent Neural Networks for Dynamic System Control", *accepted for publication in IEEE Transactions on Neural Networks.*

[10] C. C. Ku and K. Y. Lee, "Diagonal Recurrent Neural Net- works for Controller Designs", *Proc. of Applications of Neural Networks to Power Systems '92*, April 19-22, 1993, Yokohama, Japan.

A DECOMPOSITION APPROACH TO FORECASTING ELECTRIC POWER SYSTEM COMMERCIAL LOAD USING AN ARTIFICIAL NEURAL NETWORK

George Mbamalu, Ferial and M. E. El-Hawary

Technical University of Nova Scotia
P. O. Box 1000, Halifax, Nova Scotia
Canada, B3J 2X4
Tel. (902) 420-7625
Fax (902) 422-7535
email elhawary@tuns.ca

Abstract- Different methods have been proposed and subsequently used in forecasting the power system load. Most of the reported work treat the system load at the bulk power level. In practice, the system load is decomposed into user-based sectors. These are domestic, commercial, industrial and municipal load sectors. Each sector is governed and influenced by phenomena inherent to that sector. Thus the load consumption characteristic for a sector is unique due to different socio-economic functions that take place in that sector. We use a multilayer neural network with a back propagation algorithm to forecast the commercial sector load portion resulting from decomposing the system load of the Nova Scotia Power Inc. system. To minimize the effect of weather on the forecast of the commercial load, it is further decomposed into four autonomous sections of six hour durations. The optimal input for a training set is determined based on the sum of the squared residuals of the predicted loads. The input patterns are made up of the immediate past four or five hours load and the output is the fifth or the sixth hour load. The results obtained using the proposed approach provide evidence that in the absence of some influential variables such as temperature, a careful selection of training patterns will enhance the performance of the artificial neural network in predicting the power system load.

Key Words: Power System Load Forecasting, Estimation and Prediction.

I. INTRODUCTION

One of the primary tasks of an electric utility is to accurately predict load requirements at all times. Results obtained for different classes of load forecasting are applied to different operational and management needs. For example long-term load forecasting (one to ten years ahead monthly and yearly values) is applied to capacity expansion, inter-tie tariff setting and long-term capital investment return problems. While results from short-term load forecasting (one day to one month ahead hourly and daily values) are applied in unit commitment, maintenance and generating units dispatch problems. Thus there is a need for accurate load forecasting techniques in general.

Various load forecasting techniques have been proposed and successfully applied to predict the different classes of power system load requirements. Methods based on time series analysis [2-7] exploit the inherent relationship between the present hour load, weather variables and the previous past hours loads. The autoregressive (AR), moving average (MA) and the mixed autoregressive and moving average (ARMA) models are prominent in the time series approach, and they require massive amount of data in order to produce optimal models. In the absence of such data, these approaches may produce inadequate models. Also these algorithms require frequent update with the availability of new information. The time series approach may perform poorly for data with inherent special events.

The performance of the weather-sensitive load forecasting models depends to a great extent on the accuracy of the weather prediction model in use. The non-weather-sensitive AR, MA, and ARMA models [2,5 and 7], treat the weather variables as constants. In some cases, this may result in suboptimal results, however the propagation of errors inherent to the weather prediction model will be eliminated.

Efforts to forecast power system loads using artificially intelligent methods [8 and 9], and artificial neural networks (ANN) [10-13] have shown promising and encouraging results. The methods of [8] and [9] use rules that are similar to operators' judgement in order to forecast the system load. The emphasis here is to identify linking relationships between the changing load pattern and the weather variables responsible for the change.

In order to develop optimal decision variables (weights), the ANN based approaches proposed in [10-13] establish links between the input (training data) to the output (target data). The performance of the ANN techniques depends highly on the relationship between the pattern used in training the weights and the expected forecast pattern. If the diversity or the inconsistency between the training pattern and the expected forecast pattern is strong, the forecast errors of the ANN technique may be relatively high.

Traditionally, the power system load has been decomposed into three sub-components indicated as: trend, cyclic and seasonal loads [7], time series and non-weather sensitive models were used to obtain adequate forecast. Another effort [14] decomposes the power system load into nominal, the type, and the residual loads. The Kalman filter, the exponential smoothing and the autoregressive models were used to estimate model parameters. As a result of varying

0-7803-1901-X/94 $4.00 ©1994 IEEE

industrial and commercial activities different ANN models were proposed and used [10] to predict the power system load.

We approach the load forecasting problem by decomposing the power system load into four principal sectors: residential, commercial, municipal and industrial loads. Our proposed approach treats each sector load independently with due consideration of its unique operational characteristics. Each sector is investigated and an appropriate ANN structure that considers the socio-economic events taking place in the sector is developed. It has been noted previously that the performance of the ANN forecasting technique depends on the consistency of the link between the training patterns and the expected forecast patterns. By decomposing the load into sectors, it is obvious that pattern consistency within each sector will be relatively high.

In addition, the daily loads are divided into four different sections, each composed of six consecutive hourly loads. The objective is to marginalize the effect of the weather variables on the performance of the artificial neural network. The results reported in this paper are focussed on commercial sector loads.

II. THE NEURAL NETWORK TRAINING STRUCTURE

A neural network consists of a number of simple, but highly interconnected processing units. A major objective of the neural network is to achieve good performance through dense interconnections of elements. This can be achieved through an adequate structuring of the network, appropriate training data set selection and using appropriate learning rule.

A popular learning rule is the Generalized Delta Rule (GDR), which is basically a mean squared error minimization algorithm. It emphasizes the difference between the neural network's computed output and the desired output. The network weights or synaptic strengths are adjusted in proportion to the sum of the squared error between the neural network outputs and the desired outputs, in a manner that reduces the error in the direction of the gradient. The error inherent to the training of the neural network structure can be stated as:

$$E = \frac{1}{2}(D_K - O_K)^2 \qquad (1)$$

Here the desired output for the neuron K is D_K, and the computed output of neuron K is O_K.

Through the weight or synaptic strength W_{ij}, the output of neuron i is connected to the input of neuron j. For any neuron K that is not an input neuron, its output is defined as:

$$O_K = f\left(\sum_i W_{iK} O_i\right) \qquad (2)$$

Where f is a differentiable and non-decreasing function, the sum includes all neurons in the adjacent layer. The function f is a sigmoid function of the type:

$$f(m) = \frac{1}{(1+e^{-m})} \qquad (3)$$

The delta rule used in adapting the weights is obtained by taking the gradient of E with respect to the weights W_{ij}

$$\frac{-\partial E}{\partial W_{ij}} = \delta_j O_i \qquad (4)$$

where δ_j can be defined for the final neural network output unit or for the output unit of a hidden layer.

The value of δ_j is defined as:

$$\delta_j = (D_j - O_j)\left(f'\left(\sum_i W_{ik} O_i\right)\right) \qquad (5)$$

For a hidden layer, δ_j is defined as:

$$\delta_j = f'\left(\sum_i W_{iK} O_i\right) \sum_K \delta_k W_{jK} \qquad (6)$$

where f' is the derivative of the non-decreasing function. Using equation (4), we obtain the GDR as:

$$\Delta W_x(n+1) = \Gamma \delta_j O_i + \alpha \Delta W_{ij}(n) \qquad (7)$$

where Γ is the parameter associated with the learning rate, α is the well known momentum term, and n is the iteration index.

III. SECTOR LOAD CHARACTERISTICS

Typical week day commercial load patterns are characterized by one daily peak load during the morning hours between 11:00 am and 12 noon. This is typical of a projectile oriented commercial economy where activity increases significantly in the morning, attaining its maximum at about midday. Subsequently, the activity trend changes to its downward climb, accompanying significant decrease in commercial activities. The lowest commercial activities occur at about 4:00 am or 6:00 am in the early morning.

Developing temperature dependent load forecasting models for the Nova Scotia Power INC is limited because of lack of comprehensive hourly temperatures for the entire Province. To avoid this difficulty, we decided to sectionalize the weekday commercial load. Section activities can be accurately described using monotonically increasing or decreasing functions of time. The sectionalized weekday commercial loads are shown in Figure (1) for the winter, and Figure (2) for the summer.

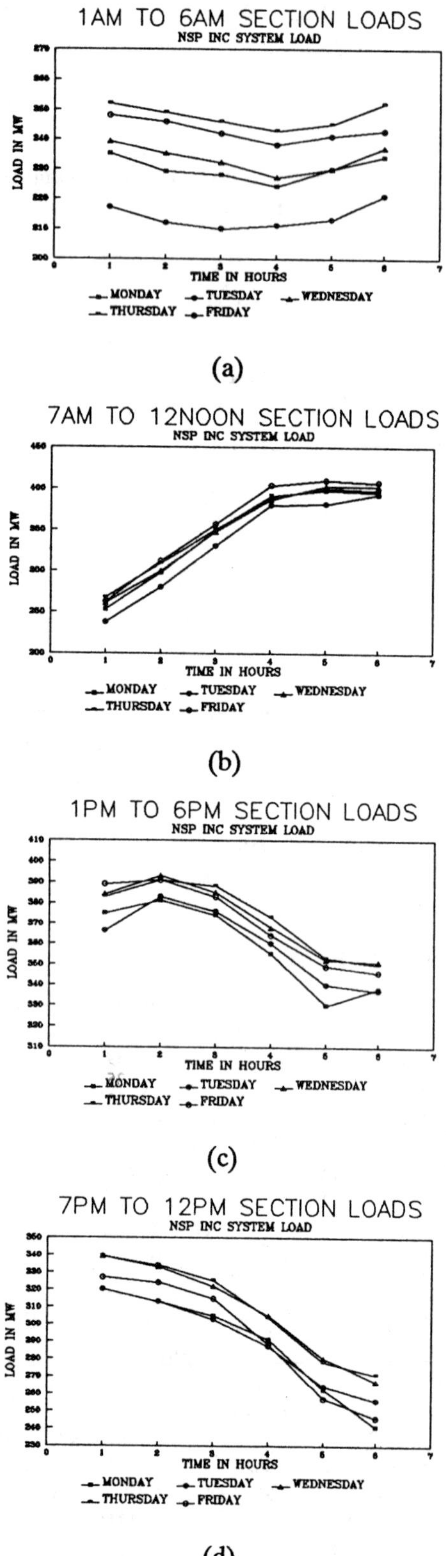

Figure (1) Sectionalized Winter Loads

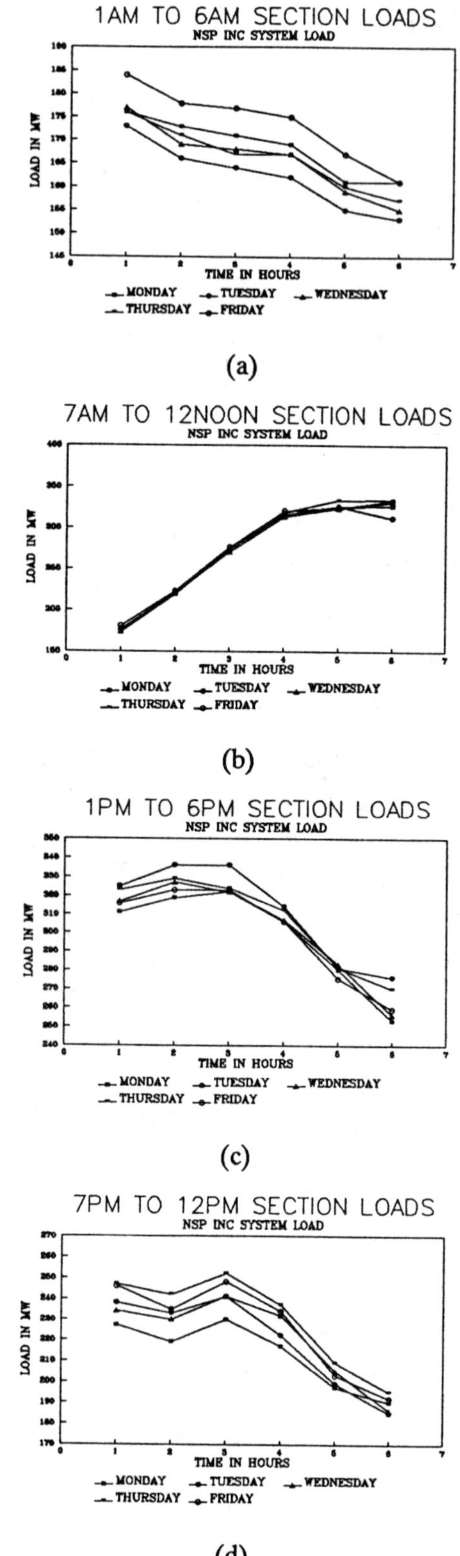

Figure (2) Sectionalized Summer Loads

IV. COMPUTATIONAL EXPERIENCE

An optimal forecast for the winter commercial activities occurring between the hours of 1:00 am and 6:00 am was not attained using the proposed ANN. However, an optimal forecast results when the training sets were reduced to three sets. With the exception of the winter commercial activities occurring between 7:00 pm to 12:00 pm, the proposed ANN structure produced optimal forecasts using five inputs, one output and six training sets. For the winter loads between 7:00 pm to 12:00 pm, four inputs, one output and six training sets were used to produce an optimal forecast.

The convergence of the ANN was improved when the activities were described using monotonically increasing or decreasing functions of time. The following are testing statistics:

- For activities between 1:00 pm and 6:00 pm described in Figures (1-c), winter and (2-c), summer the ANN converged after 18 CPU minutes.
- For activities between 7:00 pm and 12:00 pm, described by functions of Figures (1-d), winter, and (2-d) summer, the proposed ANN structure converged after 1.30 hours of computational time.
- But for 1:00 am to 6:00 am, winter, Figures (1-a), and 7:00 am to 12:00 noon both winter (1-b) and summer (2-b), the proposed ANN converged after 3 CPU hours.
- For activities described by functions of 1:00 am to 6:00 am summer, Figure (2-a), our proposed ANN structure converged after 4.5 CPU hours.

WINTER FORECASTS

The results obtained using the proposed ANN structure with back propagation algorithm and winter weekday load data are shown in Figure (4). The results are remarkable and encouraging given the fact that temperature influence was not included. From Table (1), the prediction errors associated with the proposed ANN structures varied up to a maximum of 15.5%. A prediction error above 10.0% occurred during the second week of prediction with activities described by functions of Figure (1-d).

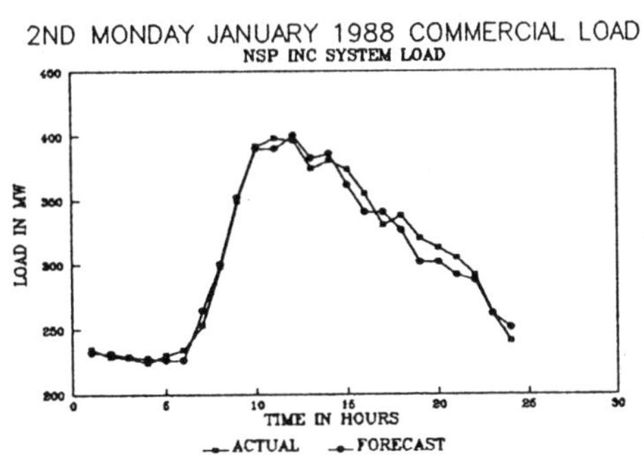

(a)

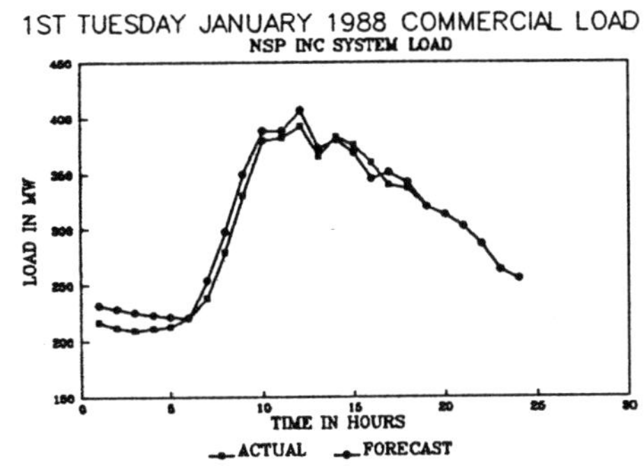

(b)

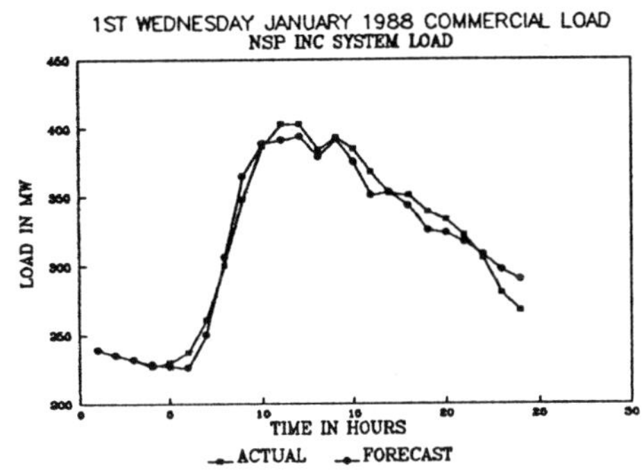

(c)

Figure (3) Winter Load Forecasts

Table (1)
Representative Weekday Winter Commercial Load Forecast
A = Actual, P = Predicted, % E = % Error

	MON.			TUE.			WED.		
T	A	P	% E	A	P	% E	A	P	% E
1	235	232	1.2	217	232	6.9	239	339	0.0
2	229	230	8.7	212	229	8.0	235	235	0.0
3	228	229	0.4	210	226	7.6	232	232	0.0
4	224	227	1.3	211	223	5.7	227	229	0.8
5	230	226	1.7	213	222	4.2	230	227	1.3
6	234	226	3.4	221	221	0.0	237	226	4.6
7	253	265	4.5	238	254	6.7	261	250	4.2
8	298	300	0.7	280	298	6.4	300	306	2.0
9	349	352	1.1	331	350	5.7	348	365	4.9
10	392	390	0.5	380	388	2.1	387	389	0.5
11	398	390	2.0	382	389	1.8	403	391	3.0
12	396	400	1.0	393	407	3.5	403	394	2.2
13	375	383	2.1	366	373	1.9	384	379	1.3
14	381	386	1.3	383	381	0.5	393	392	0.3
15	374	362	3.2	376	369	1.9	385	375	2.6
16	355	340	4.2	360	346	3.9	368	351	4.6
17	330	340	3.3	340	351	3.2	352	353	0.3
18	338	326	3.5	337	343	1.8	351	343	2.2
19	320	301	5.9	320	320	0.0	339	325	4.1
20	313	301	3.8	313	313	0.0	333	323	2.9
21	305	291	4.4	303	303	0.0	322	317	1.5
22	291	287	1.4	287	287	0.0	305	308	0.9
23	262	262	0.0	264	264	0.0	280	296	6.0
24	241	251	4.1	256	256	0.0	267	290	8.7

For the activities described by Figure (1-c), the maximum error associated with the proposed ANN structure is less than 8.0%. While a majority of the errors are less than 5.0%. The other two functions produced prediction errors that are below 10.0 % .

SUMMER FORECASTS

The results obtained using the proposed ANN structure with back propagation algorithm and summer weekday load data are shown in Figure (4). From Table (2), the prediction errors associated with the proposed ANN structures varied up to a maximum of 11 %. A prediction error of 11.0 % occurred during the second week of prediction with activities described by functions of Figure (2-b).

For activities described by Figures (2-a) and (2-c), the maximum error associated with the approach is less than 8.5%. While a majority of the errors for the activities are less than 5.0 %. We observed a maximum prediction error of 9.6 %, and a minimum prediction error of 0.0% for the activity described by Figure (2-d).

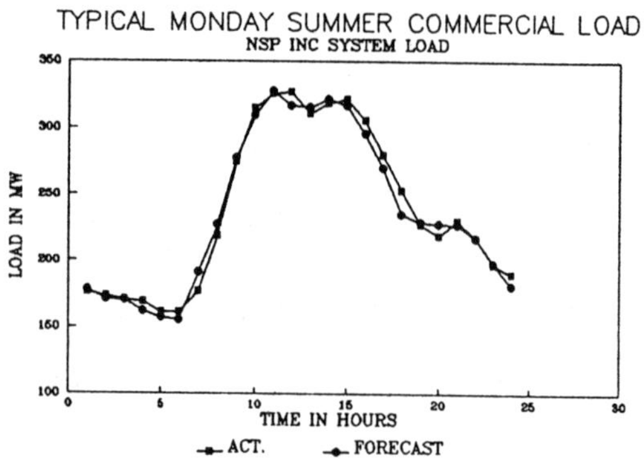

(a)

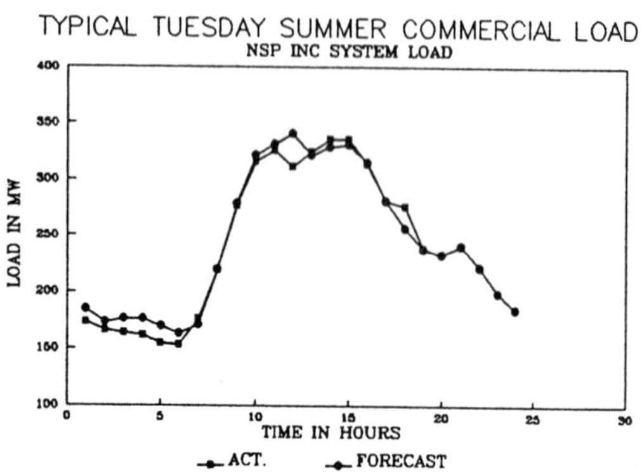

(b)

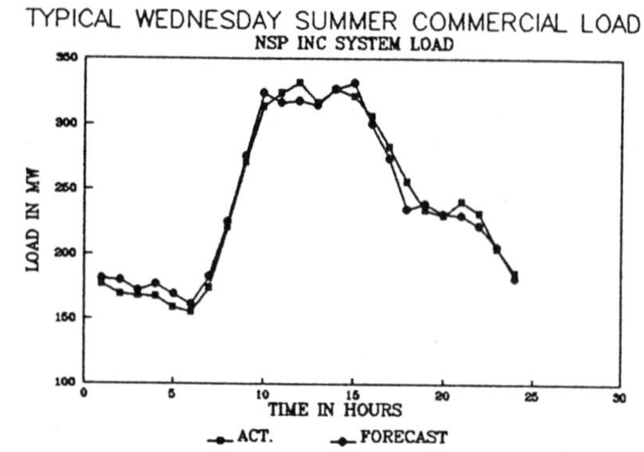

(c)

Figure (4) Summer Load Forecasts

Table (2)
Representative Weekday Summer Commercial Load Forecast
A = Actual, P = Predicted, % E = % Error

	MON.			TUE.			WED.		
T	A	P	%E	A	P	%E	A	P	%E
1	176	178	1.1	173	185	6.9	177	181	2.2
2	173	171	1.2	166	173	4.5	169	180	6.8
3	171	170	0.6	164	176	7.2	168	172	2.5
4	169	162	4.1	162	176	8.8	167	177	6.1
5	161	157	2.5	155	169	9.5	159	169	6.4
6	161	155	3.7	153	164	6.9	155	161	3.8
7	177	191	7.8	171	176	2.9	174	183	5.4
8	219	227	3.8	220	220	0.0	221	224	1.6
9	275	278	1.2	279	277	0.7	271	276	1.9
10	315	310	1.7	322	316	1.8	314	324	3.3
11	326	327	0.5	332	326	1.8	324	317	2.0
12	327	317	3.1	341	312	8.5	332	318	4.3
13	311	316	1.7	322	325	1.0	317	315	0.5
14	319	322	1.0	329	336	2.0	327	327	0.0
15	322	317	1.6	331	336	1.6	322	332	3.0
16	306	296	3.4	315	313	0.4	307	301	2.0
17	280	270	3.6	281	281	0.0	283	274	3.0
18	253	234	7.2	257	276	7.4	256	235	8.2
19	227	228	0.7	238	238	0.0	234	239	2.1
20	219	228	4.4	233	233	0.0	230	231	0.6
21	230	227	1.4	241	241	0.0	241	230	4.3
22	217	217	0.0	222	222	0.0	232	222	4.1
23	197	198	0.7	199	199	0.0	205	206	0.3
24	190	181	4.7	185	185	0.0	186	182	1.9

V. CONCLUSIONS

We presented a method that uses the ANN with the back propagation algorithm to forecast the commercial load of a power utility. The effect of weather on the weekday commercial load is minimized by dividing the daily commercial load into four short sections of 6 hours duration each. The resulting autonomous sections are used to develop an ANN structure that is used in training the weights and subsequent commercial load forecasting. The proposed ANN structure demonstrates that the artificial neural network can be used to produce reasonable forecasts of the power system commercial load when temperature data is not available.

VI. REFERENCES

[1] Lippmann, Richard P. "An Introduction to Computing with Neural Nets", IEEE ASSP Magazine, April 1987, pp. 4-22.

[2] Mbamalu, G.A.N. and El-Hawary, M.E. "Load Forecasting Via Suboptimal Seasonal Autoregressive Models and Iteratively Reweighted Least Squares Estimation", IEEE Trans. Power Systems, Vol. 8, No. 1, February 1993, pp. 343-348.

[3] Barakat, E.H. and Eissa, M.A.M. "Forecasting Monthly Peak Demand in Fast Growing Electric Utility: A Composite Multi-regression-Decomposition Model", IEE Proc., Vol. 136, Pt. C, No. 1, January 1989. pp35-41.

[4] Moghram, I. and Rahman, S. "Analysis and Evaluation of Five Short-Term Load Forecasting Techniques", IEEE Trans. Power Systems, Vol. 4, October 1989, pp. 1484-1491.

[5] El-Hawary, M.E. and Mbamalu, G.A.N. "Short-Term Power System Load Forecasting Using the Iteratively Reweighted Least Squares Algorithm", Electric Power Systems Research, 19 (1990) pp. 11-22.

[6] Elrazaz, Z.S. and Mazi, A.A. "Unified Weekly Peak Load Forecasting for Fast Growing Power System", IEE Proc. Vol. 136, Pt. C, No. 1, January 1989, pp. 29-34

[7] Barakat, E.H. Qayyum, M.A, Hamed, M.N, and Al Rashed, S.A. "Short-Term Peak Demand Forecasting in Fast Developing Utility with Inherent Dynamic Load Characteristics", IEEE Trans., Power Systems, Vol. 5, No. 3, August 1990. pp. 813-824.

[8] Ho, Kun-Long, et. al.,"Short Term Load Forecasting of Taiwan Power System Using a Knowledge-Based Expert System", IEEE Trans. Power Systems, Vol. 5, No. 4, November 1990, pp. 1214-1221.

[9] Rahman, S. and Bhatnagar, R. "An Expert System Based Algorithm for Short Term Load Forecast" IEEE Trans. Power Systems, Vol. 3, No. 2, May 1988, pp. 392-399.

[10] Lee, K.Y., Cha, Y.T. and Park, J.H. "Short-Term Load Forecasting Using an Artificial Neural Network", IEEE Trans. Power Systems, Vol. 7, No. 1, February 1992, pp. 124-132.

[11] Lu, C.N., Wu, H.T. and Vemuri, S. "Neural Network Based Short Term Load Forecasting", IEEE Trans. Power Systems, Vol. 8, No. 1, February 1993, pp. 336-342.

[12] Park, D.C, El-Sharkawi, M.A., Marks II, R.J., Atlas, L.E. and Damborrg, M.J. "Electric Load Forecasting Using an Artificial Neural Network" IEEE Trans. Power Systems, Vol. 6, No. 2, May 1991, pp. 442-449.

[13] Ho, Kun-Long, et. al. "Short term Load Forecasting Using a Multilayer Neural Network with an Adaptive Learning Algorithm" IEEE Trans. Power Systems, Vol. 7, No. 1, February 1992, pp. 141-149.

[14] Park, J.H., Park, Y.M., and Lee, K.Y. "Composite Modeling For Adaptive Short-Term Load Forecasting" IEEE Trans. Power Systems, Vol. 6, No. 2, May 1991, pp. 450-457.

Adaptive Dynamic Neural Network Estimators

D. G. Lainiotis, K. N. Plataniotis
Florida Institute of Technology
Department of Electrical and Computer Engineering
150 W. University Blvd., Melbourne Fl. 32901, USA

Abstract - The problem of state estimation for linear or nonlinear models with unknown parameters is very important in many engineering problems. As such it has been addressed extensively through the use of statistical methodologies i.e. ALF, EKF, etc. In this paper the solution to the problem of adaptive estimation for unknown state variable or chaotic models through the use of adaptive dynamic neural estimators is proposed. The proposed adaptive neural estimators are developed and their advantages are discussed. Extensive computer simulations of the application of the proposed adaptive neural estimator to state estimation as well as chaotic series prediction illustrate the effectiveness of the adaptive neural solution.

I. Introduction

Estimation theory (filtering) has received considerable attention in the past four decades because of its practical significance in solving engineering and scientific problems. As a result of the combined research efforts of many scientists in the field numerous filtering algorithms, have been developed through the use of statistical methodologies. These can be classified in two major categories, namely linear and nonlinear filtering algorithms, corresponding to linear (or linearized) physical dynamic models, and nonlinear physical models [1]-[8].

The two more serious problems facing the systems engineering community nowadays is model uncertainty and nonlinearity [2],[3],[7]. In real world situations it is not possible to represent, adequately, system characteristics such as nonlinearity, time delay and/or time varying parameters. The need to deal with increasingly complex nonlinear systems, and the tremendous increase in computing power has recently led to a reevaluation of the conventional estimation methods. Nonlinear and adaptive filtering has been established as an important theoretical and applied research area [7]. The need for new estimation methods that can handle more realistic assumptions, and can take advantage of the new hardware capabilities is quite apparent [10].

A great deal of effort has been devoted in the past for the problem of adaptive nonlinear estimation. Numerous filters have been obtained using statistical methodologies, and extending the basic linear theory to nonlinear as well as adaptive systems. Among them the so called Extended Kalman Filter (EKF) [1], [7],and the Adaptive Lainiotis Filter (ALF) [2]-[9] are the most notable. However, a generally applicable optimal nonlinear filter and its practical implementation are not known.

Recently, the emerging technology of neural networks [9]-[12] has been successfully applied to the solution of the adaptive estimation problem [13]-[21]. Given the difficulties the conventional estimators encounter, neural solutions constitute a unique and novel alternative [21]. The trained multilayer perceptrons with their massive parallelism, capability to approximate arbitrary continuous functions, appear to offer a new promising tool in estimation theory.

In this paper a general framework for neural estimators is proposed. Trained multilayer networks are integrated with traditional adaptive techniques to design a neural adaptive filter capable of providing robust and accurate solutions to a broad class of adaptive and nonlinear problems.

The paper is organized as follows: In section II a short description of the adaptive estimation problem for linear and nonlinear state space models as well as for chaotic signals are given. The structure of the neural network as state estimator is also discussed followed by the proposed framework for the adaptive neural estimators. Section III presents the first part of the experimental results where the effectiveness of the proposed methodology is illustrated via simulations. In this section the adaptive neural estimator is used to predict the values of an partially unknown chaotic system. Section IV demonstrates the robustness of the new method as state estimator using a series of adaptive state space models. Finally, section V contains a summary of this work.

II. Adaptive Systems

In general, the state space model for an adaptive stochastic nonlinear system in discrete time has the following form

$$x(k+1) = f(k, x(k), u(k), \theta(k), w(k)) \quad (1)$$

$$z(k) = h(k, x(k), \theta(k), v(k)) \quad (2)$$

where

0-7803-1901-X/94 $4.00 ©1994 IEEE

x(k) is the n dimensional state of the system which the initial value x(0) is coming from a known probability density function
u(k) is the system's deterministic input vector
z(k) is the system's output vector (measurement)
f(), h() are in general arbitrary non linear functions
w(k), v(k) are stochastic inputs to the system, plant and measurement noises
$\theta(k)$ is the unknown parameter vector, that summarizes the uncertainty in the above system

From the above state space model it can be seen that in a discrete adaptive system there are two mapping for a neural network to identify. One is the mapping f() which maps the past system state and the inputs (deterministic and stochastic) to the new state x(k+1). The second is mapping h() which transforms the state x(k) into the measurable output z(k).

A different mapping is the network's objective when it is used to predict the next values of a chaotic dynamic time series. It is well known that chaotic signals are usually generated by the state evolution of chaotic nonlinear systems. In a discrete time the state evolution of a chaotic signal is generally described by the following equation

$$x(k+1) = f(k, x(k), \theta(k)) \quad (3)$$

In chaotic systems in discrete space, the signal's states may be are attracted to and remain on a compact subset of the state space, known as attractor, for a given set of initial values x(0),and parameters θ. In chaotic signal analysis the network's objective is to identify the mapping f() which maps the current state of the chaotic model to the next one.

Various filters and algorithms have been developed in the past extending the original linear theory for certain nonlinearities and for allowing adaptation in model parameters. However, these algorithms require sufficient a priori information of the system, are quite complex, and in most of the cases suboptimal as well [1],[4],[7]-[8].

Recently neural networks have been used to estimate states of dynamic systems. Recurrent neural networks seem to be an answer to these filtering problems where the applicability of other statistical estimators like the Kalman filter is limited.

In this work recurrent multilayer perceptrons trained via the backpropagation rule, have been used as neural state estimators. The standard architecture of the multilayer perceptron consists of an input layer, one or more hidden layers and an output layer. The input layer consists of simple distributing nodes, while the other two or more layers have sigmoidal non linear nodes. When the network is used to provide estimates of the systems's state a buffered delayed version of the output signals (measurements) are fed to the input nodes, since the actual states are used as desired vectors in the output nodes. In an infinite dimension environment an alternative technique that uses residuals (pseudo-innovation process) between actual and predictive measurements as additional input to the neural network has also successfully used. In this context the neural structure can be viewed as an input recurrent dynamic network that allows information to flow from the output nodes to the input nodes capturing the transient characteristics of the dynamic physical system. During training the weights of the network are calculated iteratively using the steepest descent based backpropagation rule in order to minimize a quadratic function of the error. After training the network is ready to be used as estimator. There is a large amount of experience to indicate that the neural estimator performs exceptionally well in many practical applications.

The trained multilayer perceptron as state estimator enjoys certain advantages over the conventional filters derived through the statistical methodology [18],[20].

- It can handle any assumption or uncertainty concerning the statistics of the actual data generation model. It does not depend on any assumption about the stochastic input. To the contrary the Gaussian nature of the noises in the model, and the independence between the state and the noises, are fundamental assumptions behind any feasible filter derived using statistical methodologies.

- Due to its massive parallel structure and high speed the neural estimator can take full advantage of the new hardware capabilities. That makes the neural and not the statistical estimator the preferable choice for real time signal processing, and automatic control applications.

The main disadvantage of the neural estimation methodology described above is that the designer must have complete knowledge of the system's dynamics during the training phase [18]-[21]. The training procedure is performed in a supervised manner, whereby a desired output signal is used to computed the error [9]-[12]. If state estimation in a state space model is the objective, full knowledge of the model dynamics is required.

However, the ideal model to be used in training is rarely known. Almost all real plants can be characterized as a system with partially known dynamics since nobody can fully realize an actual system with a mathematical model [4]. In the context of adaptive filtering where models with structure or parameter uncertainty are used, the designer never knows the exact dynamics of the physical model. In a similar situation when nonlinear non stationary signals are used the desired outputs may vary in time.

Due to the above difficulties the designer is forced to use an evaluation criterion describing the overall performance of the network in an approximate correct training set. This method requires large training periods with slow training and significant performance and/or robustness degradation.

A different approach is proposed here. Instead of using one network to map approximate dynamics of an adaptive system, several networks are trained independently using different variations of the actual adaptive model. Each one of the networks trained with data pairs obtained using different parameter vectors $\theta(k)$ in the nonlinear system that generates the data. Due to this training methodology each network converges to a different solution. When the training is over, a bank of different neural estimators is available to be applied to the solution of the nonlinear filtering problems. In the mean time another set of multilayer perceptrons are used to provide one step ahead predictions of the systems measurements.In the actual operation phase a nonlinear selection mechanism is used. The adaptive algorithms compares residuals between true and predicted measurements to identify at every time instant which neural estimator provides the best estimate.

The adaptive neural methodology described above uses the Lainiotis partitioning theorem [3]-[5], and it is an extension of the Adaptive lainiotis Filter (ALF) to neural networks. In this case however, instead of a bank of statistical filters operating around trajectory points, trained multilayer perceptrons are used [21]. The adaptive neural estimation scheme integrates the robustness of the neural estimator with the effectiveness and attractiveness of the partitioning theory. In the next section simulation studies were carried out to test the effectiveness of the new algorithm.

III. CHAOTIC TIME SERIES PREDICTION

The classic time series prediction problem is the one step ahead prediction of the logistic function (Feigenbaum map) [13] in its discrete form:

$$x(k+1) = ax(k)\,(1-x(k)) \tag{4}$$

The behavior of the time series generated by the above equation depends critically upon the value of the parameter a. If a<1 the map has a single fixed point at the origin, and from a random initial value in the closed interval [0 1] the time series collapses to a constant value. For a>3 the map generates periodic attractor. Beyond the value a=3.6 the map becomes chaotic. The time series passes every test for randomness, having the spectrum of a white noise process. It is well known in the neural network literature that the future value of the time series can be predicted perfectly once the actual data generation model is learned by a neural network. In the first simulation experiment the objective is the prediction of the map's future values when the critical parameter a is unknown. The experimental set-up is summarized below:

In order to estimate the state of the above model the following estimators had been used in this first experiment:

SIMULATION III. 1

A. adaptive neural estimator:

- a bank of three recurrent multilayer perceptrons, each one trained with data obtained using a different value of the parameter a in equation (4)
- the candidate networks are trained as follows:
- the network one uses data obtained with a=3.6
- the network two uses data obtained with a=3.8
- the network three uses data obtained with a=4.0

For each one of the three perceptrons in the adaptive estimator bank the following set -up is used.

B. recurrent multilayer perceptron

network topology:

- two input nodes: the current and the previous value of the time series are used as input signals
- one output node: the one step ahead value of the time series
- two hidden layers with 4-1 hidden nodes respectively

learning parameters:

- learning rate: 0.05, momentum: 0.1

Training procedure:

- backpropagation training algorithm
- the target vector is the actual one step ahead value of the chaotic signal.
- the network tries to minimize the square error between the current output and the target vector
- training data sets of 100 points are produced by running the system equation (4) using every time a random selected initial condition from the closed interval [0 1].
- the training procedure is terminated if the training error tolerance is less than 0.01 or if the number of iterations of the training set is more than 2500
- the test data record consists of a sequence of data points produced separately from the training record using a new initial condition The test data set is generated using the value a=4.

Since there is no theoretical analysis to justify the performance of the neural estimators Monte Carlo techniques are used to verify the results. The figure of merit used to compare performance is the mean square error averaged over 100 Monte Carlo runs.Namely, the following performance index, is used

$$MSE = \frac{1}{mc} \cdot \sum_{i=1}^{mc} (x(k) - \hat{x}(k/k))^2 \qquad (5)$$

The performance of the adaptive estimator is given in Fig. 1-4. For comparison purposes the performance of a neural estimator which had been trained using the parameter value a=3.6 is also given. This neural estimator is called 'mismatched'

SIMULATION III.2

The most difficult part in the design of the adaptive estimator is to select values for the parameter a. In the first experiment the actual value of the parameter used to generate the test data was included in the design. In this second experiment the adaptive estimator uses three networks each of them trained using the values a=3.6,a=3.9,a=4.5 respectively. It can be noticed that the real value a=4 is not included in the set. Moreover the performance of the adaptive estimator is compared with that of a simple "mismatched' neural estimator which was trained using random values from the interval (3.5,4.5). The networks' configurations are the same as above. In Fig. 5-8, it can been seen that the adaptive neural estimator correctly recognizes the candidate model which is closer to the correct one (Fig. 8). The 'mismatched' estimator fails completely (Fig. 6).

In order to verify the results obtained previously similar experiments are performed for the two dimension Henon map [21]. Its equation is given by:

$$x(k+1) = 1 - 1.4x^2(k) + 0.3x(k) \qquad (6)$$

The Henon map form is qualitatively similar to that of the Feigenbaum (logistic) map.

SIMULATION III.3

In the third simulation the unknown parameter is the value of the constant term in equation (6). The set -up for the adaptive estimator is now

C. adaptive neural estimator:

- a bank of three recurrent multilayer perceptrons, each one trained with data obtained using a different value of the constant term in equation (6)
- each one of the candidate networks is trained using a different value of the parameter a
- the network one uses data obtained with a=1.4
- the network two uses data obtained with a=0.8
- the network three uses data obtained with a=1.0

The same configuration as before is used for the multilayer perceptrons. The performance of the adaptive estimator is compared with that of a 'mismatched' estimator trained using the parameter value a=0.6. The results are depicted in Fig. 9-12.

SIMULATION III.4

In last experiment the robustness of the estimators with respect to the parameter values used in the design is investigated. The adaptive estimator is designed without any network trained with the exact value a=1. The following values are used in the training phase, a=0.6, a=0.9, a=1.2. The 'mismatched' estimator is a simple recurrent network trained using random values from the interval (0,1) as constant term in equation (6). According to the results depicted in Fig. 13-16 the 'mismatched' estimator cannot tolerate the ignorance about the constant term in the model and fails completely. To the contrary the adaptive estimator correctly identifies that the second net which was trained with value 0.9 is the closest to the actual model. The Adaptive estimator uses it to provide the estimates.

Observations:

- The adaptive neural estimator learned to emulate the logistic map and was able to accurately predict the time series on a novel testing set, obtained independently of the training set using different initial conditions

- The adaptive algorithm successfully detected the actual data generation model, and selected the appropriate trained neural estimator from its bank to provide the necessary estimation. In the more realistic design of experiments III.3,and III.4 the network identifies the model that is closer to the actual model.

- The decision about the parameter value during the training phase is crucial for the performance of the estimator. All the 'mismatched' estimators failed to provide accurate results.

IV. ADAPTIVE STATE ESTIMATION

The neural networks' ability to represent nonlinear dynamic systems has served as initiative for their application to nonlinear filtering problems. In this section we investigate the performance of the adaptive neural estimator in nonlinear state estimation problems. Moreover since the major advantage of the proposed new algorithm is its ability to adapt in changing environments in all the simulation studies it will be assumed that more than one dynamic models generate the data.

SIMULATION IV.1:

The objective of this experiment is to illustrate the effectiveness of the recurrent neural network as estimator and assess the attractiveness of the adaptive neural estimator for changing actual models. Two different state space models are used in this numerical example. The first system is a signal observed in noise as follows:

$$x(k+1) = 1.7exp(-2x^2(k)) + 0.1w(k) \quad (7)$$

$$z(k) = x^3(k) + 0.1v(k) \quad (8)$$

where w(k), v(k) are independent standard white Gaussian sequences, and the initial state x(0) is assumed Gaussian with zero mean and variance 0.25.

The second system is a linear state space model with state dependent noises. The equations of the this system are:

$$x(k+1) = 0.5x(k) + 0.5\tanh\ (x(k) + 0.5w(k)) \quad (9)$$

$$z(k) = x(k) + 0.5x^3(k)v(k) \quad (10)$$

with w(k), v(k) are independent standard white Gaussian sequences, and the initial state x(0) is assumed Gaussian with zero mean and variance 0.25.

It must be emphasized that all the statistical filters have restricted applicability in chaotic nonlinear systems like the one in eq. (7),(8). Moreover there is no feasible statistical filter that can be used to estimate the state of the system in eq. (9),(10).

An adaptive neural estimator is applied to this problem. The adaptive estimator has in its bank two multilayer perceptrons. The Network I is trained using data which are generated running the equations (7),(8). The Network II is trained using the data which have been produced from the system of equations (9),(10). After training the recurrent nets are used as neural filters. To test the efficiency of the proposed algorithm in a time varying environment we assume that the data generation model is not the same during the actual operation phase. Specifically, in the first half of the testing period the measurements are coming from the first model. In the remaining time the second model is used to provide the actual measurements. The objective of the adaptive network is to correct identify the active model, and then use its decision to provide the best estimate of the current state. The detailed configuration of the recurrent nets used by the adaptive estimator is summarized below:

A. input recurrent neural network

network topology:

- two input nodes: the current and the previous measurements are used as input signals
- one output node: the estimates of the system states. The neural network has so many output nodes, as the states of the model
- two hidden layers with 4-4 hidden nodes respectively

learning parameters:

- learning rate: 0.05, momentum: 0.2

Training procedure:

- backpropagation training algorithm
- the target vector during training is a state vector which is generated running the equations of one model
- the network tries to minimize the square error between the current output and the target vector
- each training set consists of 200 input/output pairs (z(k), x(k)).
- the training procedure is terminated if the training error tolerance is less than 0.01 or if the number of iterations of the training set is more than 5000
- the test data record consists of a sequence of data points produced separately from the training record. In order to generate the test data both the models are used.

The performance of the adaptive estimator and the mean square averaged over 100 Monte Carlo runs are given in Fig. 17-19. The adaptive algorithm correct identifies the change in the data generation process during the operation phase and uses the appropriate trained neural network in its bank to provide the estimate.

SIMULATION IV.2

In this last simulation test a linear, and a highly nonlinear state space models are used to test the performance of the adaptive algorithm. The first one is described by the following equations:

$$x(k+1) = 0.588x(k) + w(k) \quad (11)$$

$$z(k) = x(k) + v(k) \quad (12)$$

where w(k), v(k) are independent white Gaussian sequences with variance 0.25, and the initial state x(0) is assumed standard white Gaussian.

The second one is the model described by the equations (9)-(10). During the actual operation phase in the first half of the testing period equations (11)-(12) are used to generate the data. From the data point 100 until the end the alternative model is used. The adaptive estimator has two networks in the bank. Network I is trained with data from model (11)-(12), and network II is trained according to the model (9)-(10). The same configuration as in simulation IV.1 is used during training. The graphs if Fig. 20-22 summarizes the results of this last experiment. It is obvious that the adaptive neural estimator can operate in an changing environment. In both experiments the algorithm had successfully identify the model change in a limited number of steps.

V. CONCLUSIONS

The problem of adaptive estimation via neural networks was addressed in this paper. New adaptive neural estimators were proposed and applied in numerous problems. The results can be summarized as follows:

- The neural estimator provides reliable and consistent solutions to the estimation problem, especially in nonlinear or chaotic models.
- In realistic situations where the actual model is not completely known or changes during the implementation phase an adaptive neural estimator must be used. The adaptive neural estimator can efficiently detect the active model and use the recurrent perceptrons in its bank to provide the best estimate.

In conclusion, the neural estimator with its capability to provide accurate solutions to adaptive estimation problem under more realistic assumptions, and its massively parallel structure and high speed, constitutes a new promising tool in estimation theory.

RREFERENCES

[1] B.D.O Anderson, J.B. Moore **Optimal Filtering**, Prentice Hall, 1979.

[2] D.G. Lainiotis, *"Optimal Nonlinear Estimation"*, International Journal of Control, Vol. IJC-14, pp. 11137-1148, 1971.

[3] D.G. Lainiotis, *"Optimal Adaptive Estimation: Structure and Parameter Adaptation"*, IEEE Transactions on Automatic Control, Vol. AC-16, pp. 160-170, 1971.

[4] D.G. Lainiotis, "Partitioning: A Unifying Framework for Adaptive Systems, I-Estimation", Proceedings of IEEE, Vol. 64, pp. 1126-1142, 1976.

[5] D.G. Lainiotis, "Joint detection, estimation and system identification" Inform. Control J.,vol. 19, pp. 75-92,1972.

[6] D.G. Lainiotis, J. G. Deshpande "Parameter estimation using splines" J. Information Sciences, vol. 7, 1974.

[7] D.G. Lainiotis, S.K. Katsikas, *"Linear and Nonlinear Lainiotis filters Survey"*, in IFAC Workshop, CAMS-'89, Expert Systems in Marine Automation Proceedings, pp. 280-293, 1989.

[8] K. Watanabe **Adaptive Estimation and Control: The Partitioning Approach**, Prentice Hall, 1992.

[9] D.E. Rumelhart, J.L. McClelland, **Parallel Distributed Processing: Explorations into the Microstructure of Cognition, Vol. 1**, M.I.T. Press, 1986.

[10] B. Kosko **Neural Networks for Signal Processing**, Prentice Hall, 1992.

[11] L.V. Fausett **Fundamentals of Neural Networks: Architectures,Algorithms,and Applications**, Prentice Hall, 1993.

[12] D.R Hush, B.G. Horne *"Progress in Supervised Neural Networks"*, IEEE Signal Processing Magazine, pp 8-39,1993.

[13] D. Lowe, A.R. Webb *"Time Series Prediction by Adaptive Networks: A Dynamic System Perspective"*, IEE Proceedings Part F, Vol. 138, pp 17-24,1991.

[14] Y.H. Pao, G.H. Clark, D.J. Sobajic *"System Identification and Noise Cancellation: A Quantitative Comparative Study of Kalman Filtering and Neural Network Approaches"*, Proceedings of ACC-91, Vol. I, pp. 1408-1411, 1991.

[15] Q. Sun, A.T. Aluani, T.R. Rice, J.E. Gray *"A Neural Network Computation Algorithm for Discrete Time Linear System State Estimation"*, Proceedings of IJCNN-92, Vol. I, pp. 443-448, 1992.

[16] J.P. De Gruyenaece, H.M. Haffer, *"A Comparison between Kalman Filters and Recurrent Neural Networks"*, Proceedings of IJCNN-92, Vol. IV, pp. 247-251, 1992.

[17] A.J. Kanekar, A. Feliachi, *"State Estimation using Artificial Neural Networks"*, Proceedings of IEEE Systems and Engineering Conference, pp. 552-556, 1990.

[18] D.G.Lainiotis,K.N. Plataniotis, D. Menon, C.J. Charalampous, *"Heave Compensation via Neural Networks"*, Intelligent Engineering Systems through Artificial Neural Networks, Vol. 3, pp 143-148, ASME Press, 1993.

[19] D.G.Lainiotis,K.N. Plataniotis, D. Menon, C.J. Charalampous, *"Adaptive Heave Compensation via Neural networks"*, IEEE OCEANS'93 Proceedings, Vol. I, pp 243-248, 1993.

[20] D.G.Lainiotis,K.N. Plataniotis, D. Menon, C.J. Charalampous, *"Neural Network Application to Ship Position estimation"*, IEEE OCEANS'93 Proceedings, Vol. I, pp 243-248, 1993.

[21] K.N. Plataniotis, **Adaptive State Estimation via Neural Networks**, Ms Thesis, Florida Institute of Technology,1992.

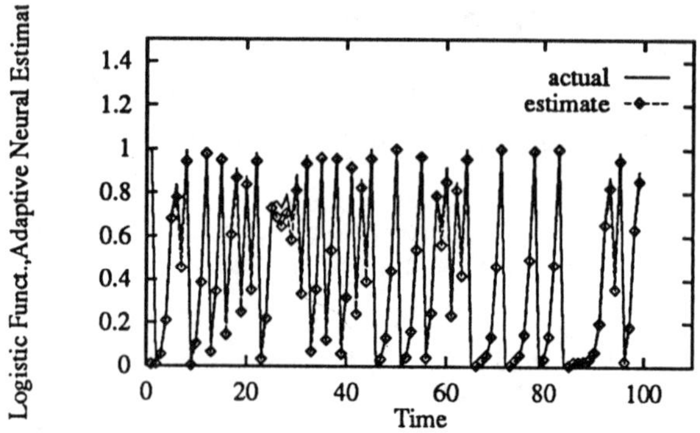

Fig. 1. Simulation III.1, Logistic Map, Adaptive Neural Estimator, One Step Ahead prediction

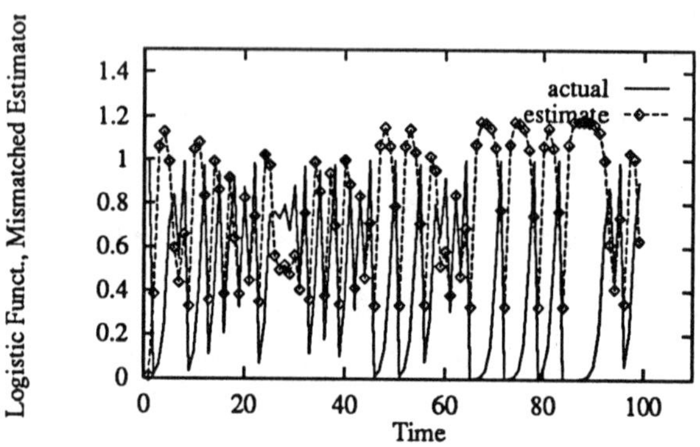

Fig. 2. Simulation III.1, Logistic Map, Mismatched Estimator, One Step Ahead Prediction

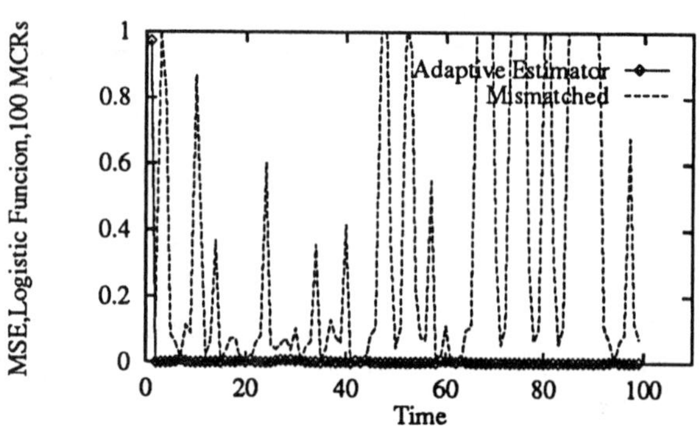

Fig. 3. Simulation III.1, Logistic Map, MSE, Comparative Evaluation, 100 MCRs

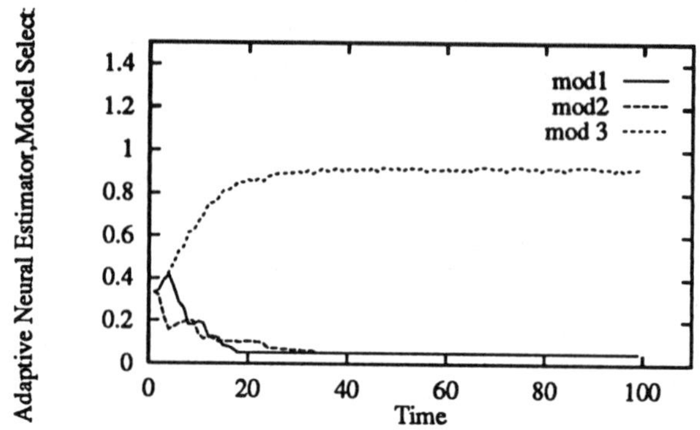

Fig. 4. Simulation III.1, Logistic Map, Adaptive Estimator, Model Selection

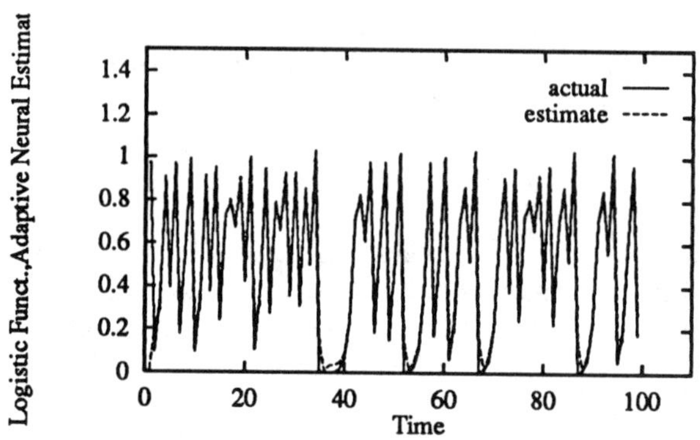

Fig. 5. Simulation III.2, Logistic Map, Adaptive Neural Estimator, One Step Ahead prediction

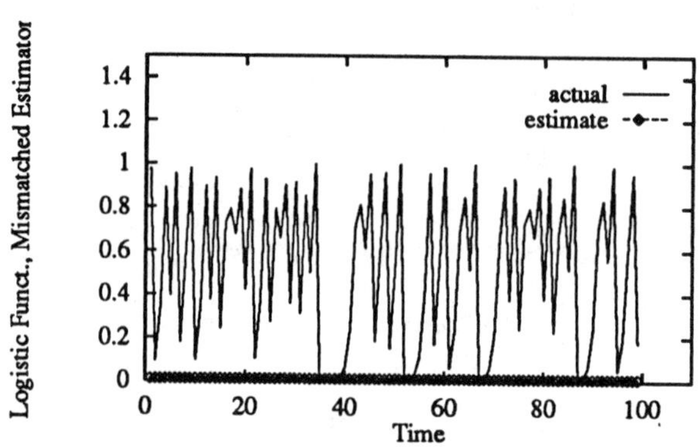

Fig. 6. Simulation III.2, Logistic Map, Mismatched Estimator, One Step Ahead Prediction

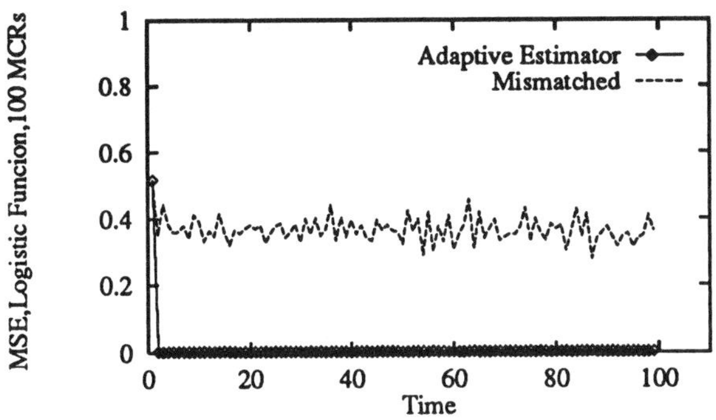

Fig. 7. Simulation III.2, Logistic Map, MSE, Comparative Evaluation, 100 MCRs

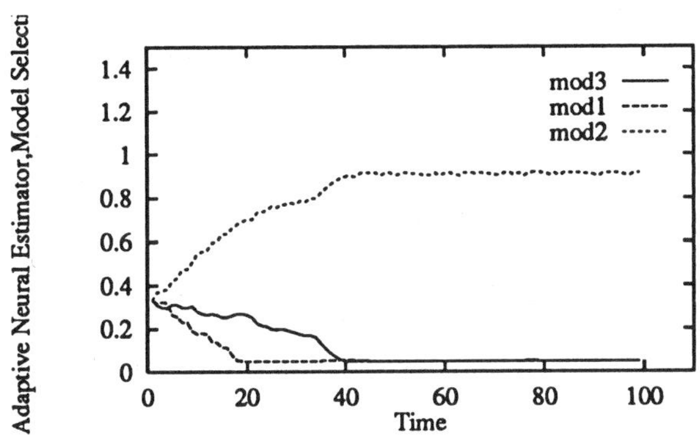

Fig. 8. Simulation III.2, Logistic Map, Adaptive Estimator, Model Selection

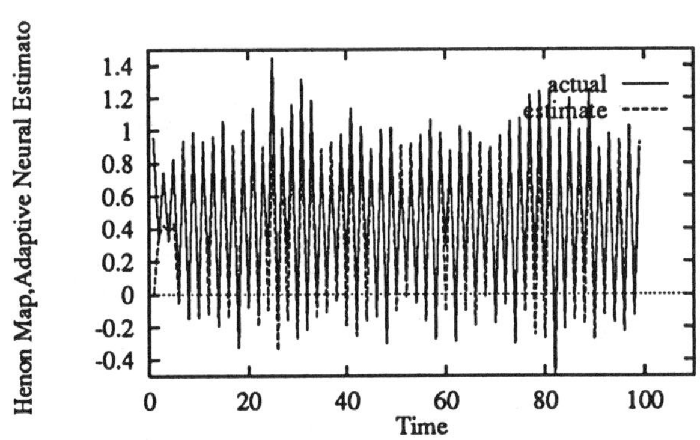

Fig. 9. Simulation III.3,Henon Map, Adaptive Neural Estimator, One Step Ahead prediction

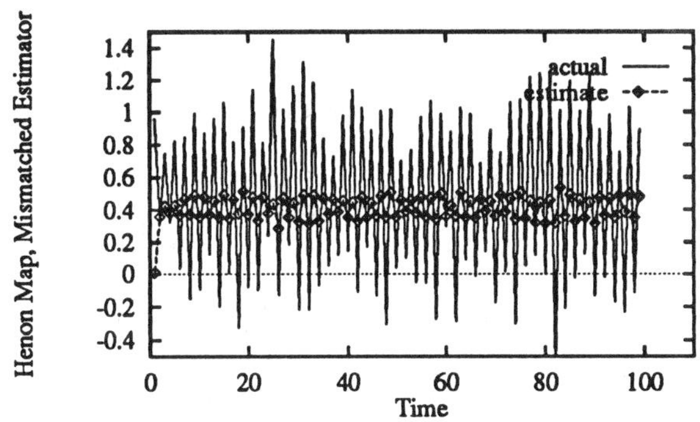

Fig. 10. Simulation III.3,Henon Map, Mismatched Estimator, One Step Ahead Prediction

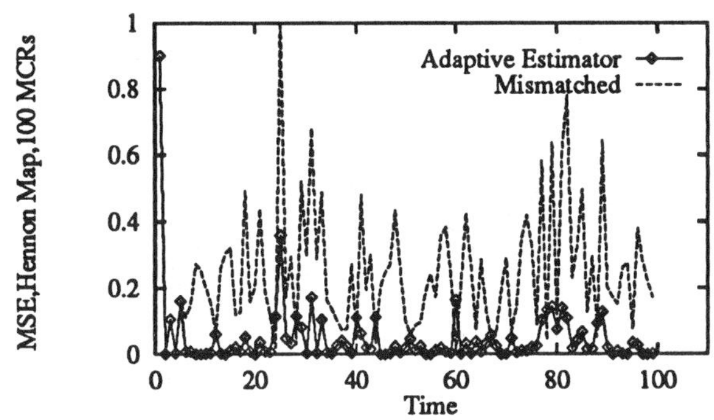

Fig. 11. Simulation III.3,Henon Map, MSE, Comparative Evaluation, 100 MCRs

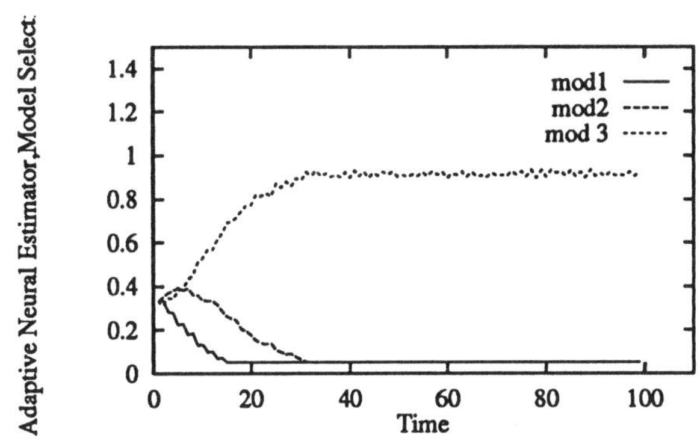

Fig. 12. Simulation III.3,Henon Map, Adaptive Estimator, Model Selection

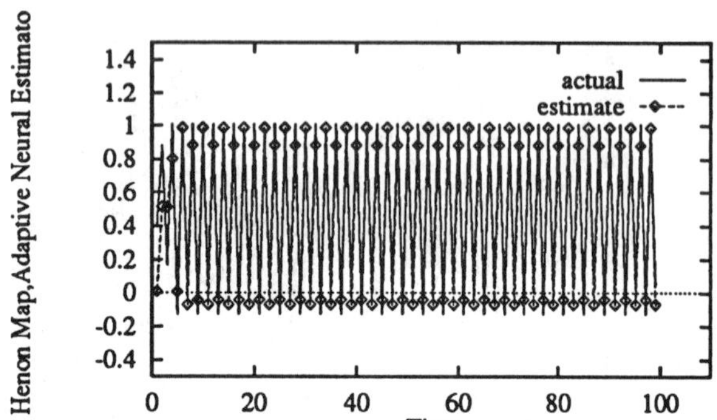

Fig. 13. Simulation III.4,Henon Map, Adaptive Neural Estimator, One Step Ahead prediction

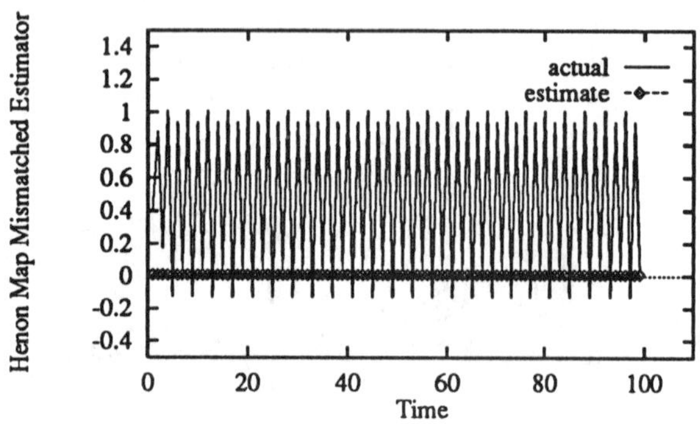

Fig. 14. Simulation III.4,Henon Map, Mismatched Estimator, One Step Ahead Prediction

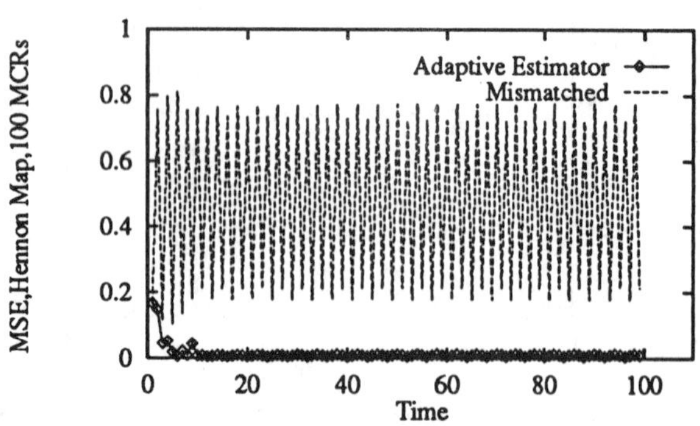

Fig. 15. Simulation III.4, Henon Map, MSE, Comparative Evaluation, 100 MCRs

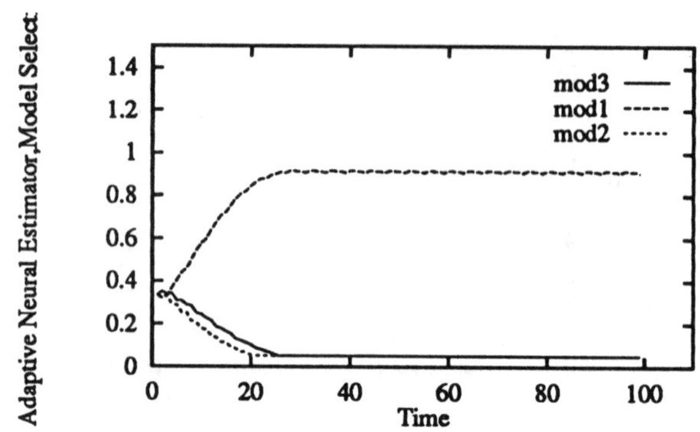

Fig. 16. Simulation III.4, Henon Map, Adaptive Estimator, Model Selection

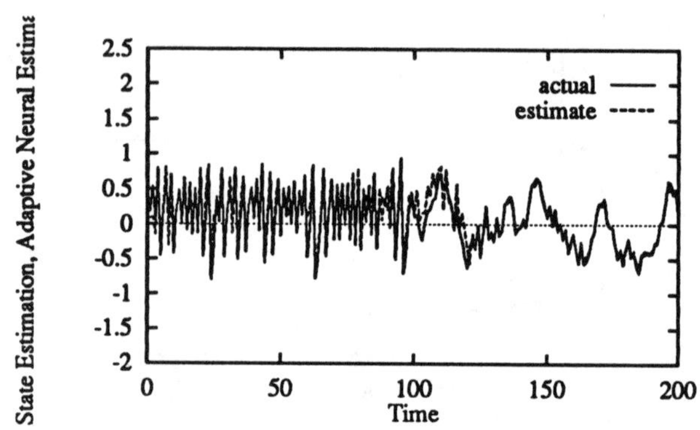

Fig. 17. Simulation IV.1, State Space Model, Adaptive Estimator

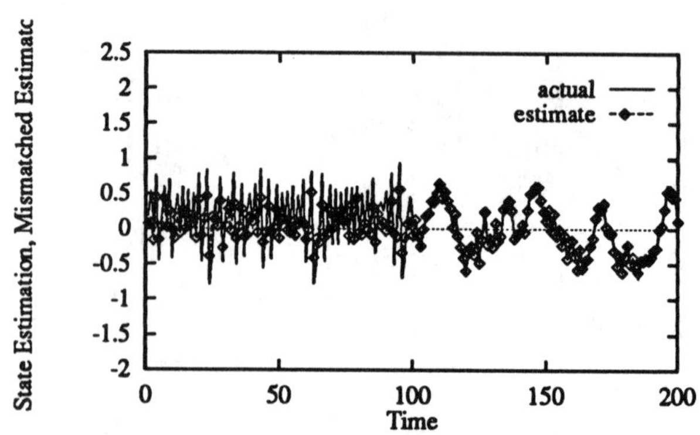

Fig. 18. Simulation IV.1,State Space Model, Mismatched Estimator

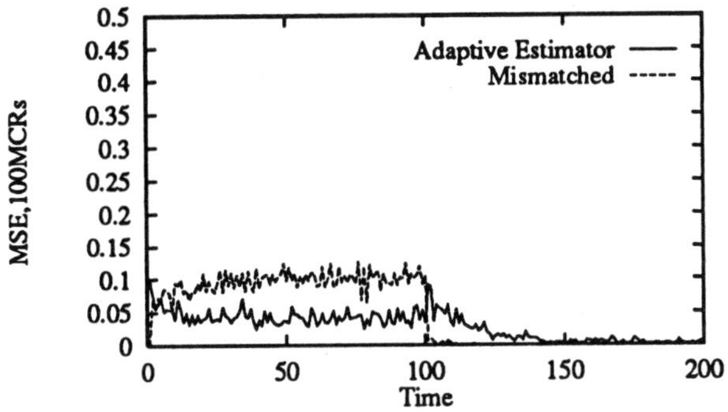

Fig. 19. Simulation IV.1,State Space Model, MSE, Comparative Evaluation, 100 MCRs

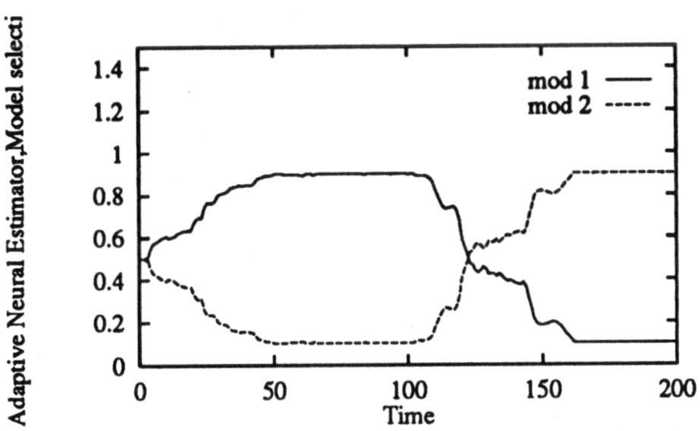

Fig. 20. Simulation IV.1, State Space Model, Adaptive Estimator, Model Selection

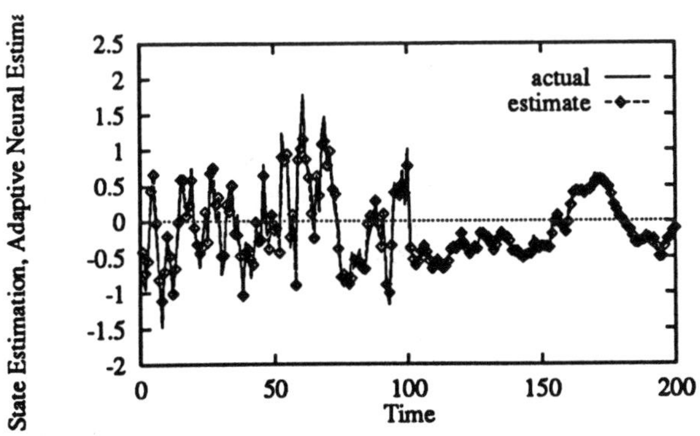

Fig. 21. Simulation IV.2, State Space Model, Adaptive Estimator

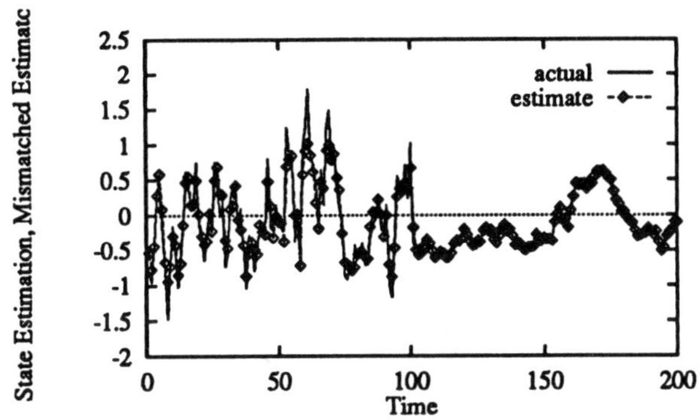

Fig. 22. Simulation IV.2,State Space Model, Mismatched Estimator

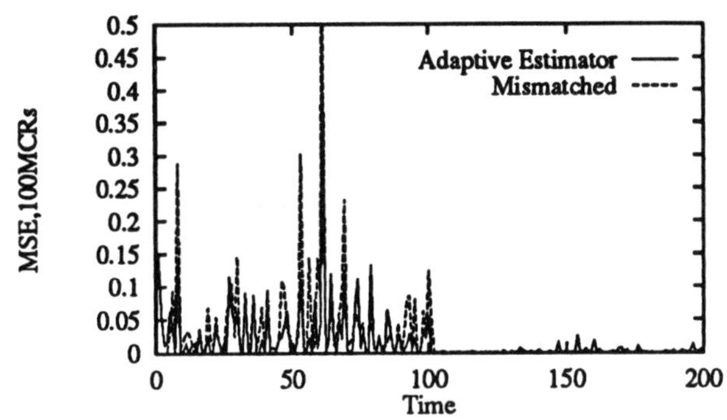

Fig. 23. Simulation IV.2,State Space Model, MSE, Comparative Evaluation, 100 MCRs

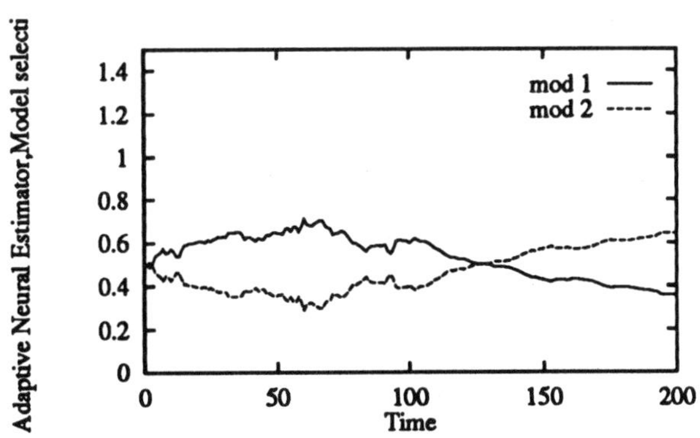

Fig. 24. Simulation IV.2, State Space Model, Adaptive Estimator, Model Selection

Low Power Analog Chips For The Computation of The Maximal Principal Component

Fathi M. A. Salam *Shanti S. Vedula* *Gamze Erten*
Circuits and Systems *and* Artificial Neural Networks Laboratories
Department of Electrical Engineering
Michigan State University, East Lansing, MI, 48824.
email: salam@ee.msu.edu

Abstract: Test results of two prototype circuit implementations that compute the maximal principal component are described. The implementations are designed to be compact and operate in the subthreshold regime for low power consumption. The prototypes use direct realization of a nonlinear self-learning circuit models which we have developed.

1. INTRODUCTION

Principal component analysis (PCA) is a common method of studying multi-dimensional data. Its primary goal is to locate a set of vectors that capture the statistical properties of the incoming set of signals. These vectors are the eigenvectors of the covariance matrix of the original input. The eigenvector corresponding to the highest eigenvalue, also called the maximal principal component often has the highest information content.

The computation of the Principal Components has been realized in the form of an unsupervised learning for a single layer linear network [1]-[2]. There are limits to the direct realization of this linear algorithm since the basic building blocks of analog circuits are naturally nonlinear. The key view adopted here is to reconstruct the algorithm in the nonlinear domain to make a circuit implementation feasible.

In this paper, we briefly summarize some of our results and present some new test data of a prototype chip. We present two compact circuit implementations and compare some of their features. Moreover, we describe the non-conventional techniques used to accommodate unidirectional current processing. The feedback structure of the circuits feeds back the output (current) signal to readjust bias currents of transconductance amplifiers. This adaptive adjustment enhances the robustness of the circuit and decreases its sensitivity to mismatches. These feedback circuit designs are suitable for the subthreshold operation since they improve sensitivity to mismatch.

2. CIRCUIT MODEL

Motivated by Oja and Sanger's rule [1] [2], we proposed a nonlinear circuit model in [7]. Using transconductance amplifiers or differential pairs as building blocks [6], the circuit model is

$$\eta_{ij}\dot{z}_{ij} = -\alpha_i z_{ij} + v_i I_{diff_j} \qquad (1)$$

*Acknowledgment: This work is supported in part by ONR Grant N00014-92-J-1441 and the Michigan Research Excellence Fund (REF).

$$w_{ij} = tanh(z_{ij}) \qquad (2)$$

$$I_{diff_j} = tanh(\xi_j) \qquad (3)$$

$$v_i = W_i^T I_{diff} \qquad (4)$$

where z_{ij} is the jth element of the vector z_i, η_{ij} is its time constant, α_i is a positive constant (pseudo-eigenvalue), w_{ij} is the jth weight of the vector W_i, and ξ_j is the jth element of the input vector ξ. Basically, the input vector is passed through the nonlinearity $tanh(.)$ and so is the state z_{ij} which is passed through a similar sigmoidal nonlinearity.

In vector form, system (1-4) can be rewritten as:

$$\eta_i\dot{z}_i = -\alpha_i z_i + [I_{diff} I_{diff}^T]W_i \qquad (5)$$

The equilibria are at:

$$0 = -\alpha_i S^{-1}(W_i) + [\overline{I_{diff} I_{diff}^T}]W_i \qquad (6)$$

where *overline* denotes the time-average. Note that using a tanh function ensures global stability and bounds W_i. Also, as the bound is sufficiently small, we have $S^{-1}(W_i) \approx W_i$. Hence,

$$\alpha_i W_i = [\overline{I_{diff} I_{diff}^T}]W_i \qquad (7)$$

where the ordered constants $\alpha_1 > \alpha_2 > ... > \alpha_m > 0$ act as pseudo-eigenvalues.

This is the equilibrium weight vector equation. The stability of the equilibrium is due to the cubic (inverse sigmoidal) function. In addition to direct circuit implementation, this model eliminates the need for the term $v_i^2 W_i$ in [1, 2], which would require a multiplication of possibly three terms.

3. MOS CIRCUIT REALIZATION

We presented a circuit realization of our circuit model in [7] and demonstrated that the weights converged for several input signals. We used external op-amps to convert the weights, which in this case were small currents, into voltages. In order to increase the accuracy of our measurements, we measured the states z_i, the voltages across the capacitors, which by equation (2) should provide the same information as the weights. The circuit realization is shown in Fig.1.

We implemented a variation of our model to find the maximal principal component of *three* dimensional data.

The circuit schematic for the three stage circuit is shown in Fig.2. The modular nature of both models allows them to be exploited for processing higher dimensional data.

While the two versions are very compatible in architecture and similar in processing (see below), the circuit shown in Fig.1 has two main advantages:

1. more compact structure, and
2. more reliable operation by eliminating a stage prone to transistor size mismatches and current variations.

We conducted several experiments to test the performance of both implementations of the PCA chip. Each experiment was conducted twice, and the two figures included for each indicate the results.

In the first experiment, we applied *sine* signals to both circuit configurations, each signal having a *peak-to-peak* amplitude of $15mV$ and a frequency of $2kHz$. We observed that the z_i values are analogous with respect to each circuit implementation.

In the second experiment, we applied the signals with the amplitudes in the increasing order. We observe that the z_i values are also in increasing order (Fig.3 and Fig.4) and when we switch the input signals, the z_i signals also switch accordingly.

In contrast to the time varying z_i signals obtained so far, it is desirable to have the z_i values, and hence the weights, W_i approach constant voltages. It would then be possible to apply these *converged* weights to process test patterns or signals. With this end result in mind, we carried out the third experiment and observed that the weights approach constant values as the frequency of the input signals is increased (Fig.5 and Fig.6). Similarly, an equivalent result can be obtained if the capacitive values in the circuit are externally increased.

The last experiment was carried out to determine the circuit parameter improvements necessary to expand the architecture beyond three dimensions. The reference voltage for the input transamps, the bias voltage and the reference voltage for the weight transamps are the key parameters useful in preventing *clipping* of the z_i signals. Fig.7 shows the effect of V_{ref} for the input transamps. Although the z_i voltages follow the input signals in general, there is a slight discrepancy with respect to the *dc* levels and amplitudes. This is attributed to the transistor mis-matches. These effects of such circuit anomalies become more prominent as the number of stages, i.e., the dimensionality of the input space increases. To alleviate these problems, the reference voltages of the input transamps and the *weight* transamps for each of the stages have been separated from each other.

4. APPLICATION TO IMAGE ENHANCEMENT USING COLOR BANDS

Primary applications of PCA are in speech signals and image processing. We now decribe an image processing application that can be realized with the three dimensional version of this chip.

The commonly used algorithm for principal component transformation of multispectral imagery which exploits the high correlation between channels was proposed by Ready and Wintz [8]. Using a similar procedure, the three dimensional chip we have presented can process an image with three color bands (RGB - Red Green Blue) in real-time. The final output is a single-channel signal that condenses the information content of a noisy color image into a single image with the highest possible signal-to-noise ratio [8]. The proposed set-up is shown in Fig.8. The three color bands associated with each pixel are input to the PCA chip, and the z_i values determine the principal component. The dot product of this vector and the local spatial average of the three dimensional image signal determines the scalar image value at the pixel.

An additional advantage that emerges from this application is the reduction in the value of the capacitance needed, which can result in the formation of an even more compact structure that can process multiple pixels in parallel.

5. CONCLUSIONS

Two prototypes of compact realization of a nonlinear model for computing the maximal component are presented and compared. The power consumption of the prototypes is in the order of microwatts. The processing is achieved efficiently, in terms of hardware, using unidirectional currents only.

REFERENCES

[1] J. Hertz, A. Krogh, R.G. Palmer, *Introduction to the Theory of Neural Computation*, Addison Wesley.

[2] T.D. Sanger, "Optimal Unsupervised Learning in a Single-layer Linear Feedforward Neural Network", *Neural Networks*, vol.2, pp 459-473, 1989.

[3] H.Chen, R. Liu, "An On-Line Unsupervised Learning Machine for Adaptive Feature Extraction", *Proc., IEEE Symposium On Circuits and Systems*, Chicago, Illinois, vol.1, 1993, pp. 535-538.

[4] P. Hasler, L. Akers, "Circuit Implementation of a Trainable Neural Network using the Generalized Hebbian Algorithm with Supervised Techniques", *Intl. Joint Conf. on Neural Networks*, Baltimore, Maryland, vol.1, 1992.

[5] J. Donald, L.A. Akers, "A Neural Processing Node with On-Chip Learning", *Proc., IEEE Symposium On Circuits and Systems*, Chicago, Illinois, vol.4, 1993, pp. 2748-2751.

[6] C.A. Mead, *Analog VLSI and Neural Systems*, Addison-Wesley.

[7] F.M.A. Salam and S.S. Vedula, "Data-Driven Subthreshold Analog Circuit that Computes Principal Components", *IEEE Midwest Symposium on Circuits and Systems*, Detroit,1993.

[8] P. Ready and P. Wintz, "Information extraction, SNR improvement, and data compression in multispectral imagery", *IEEE Trans. Comm.*, vol COM-21, Oct 1973.

[9] S.S. Vedula, F.M.A. Salam, and G. Erten, "Subthreshold Analog Circuit for Computing the Maximal Principal Component of 3-D Data" *IEEE Symposium on Circuits and Systems*, London, 1994.

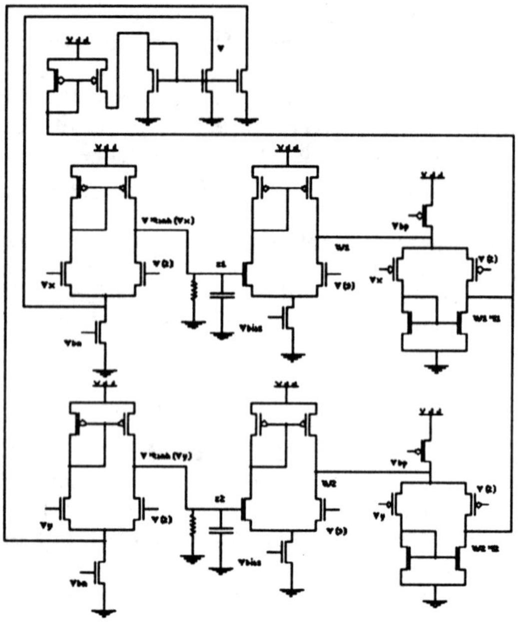

Figure 1. Schematic of the Circuit (2-D Implementation)

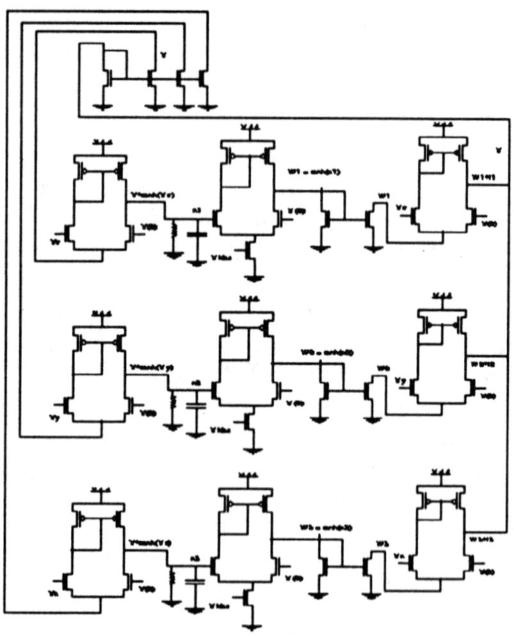

Figure 2. Schematic of the Circuit(3-D Implementation)

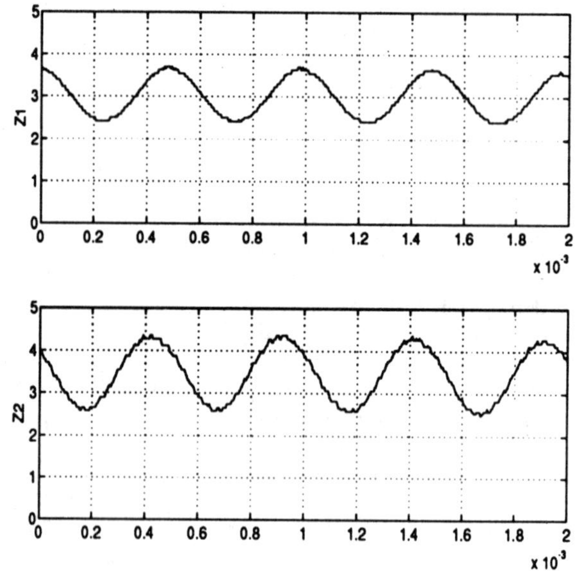

Figure 3. Z1,Z2 for $10mV$ and $20mV$(p-p) input signals at 2kHz

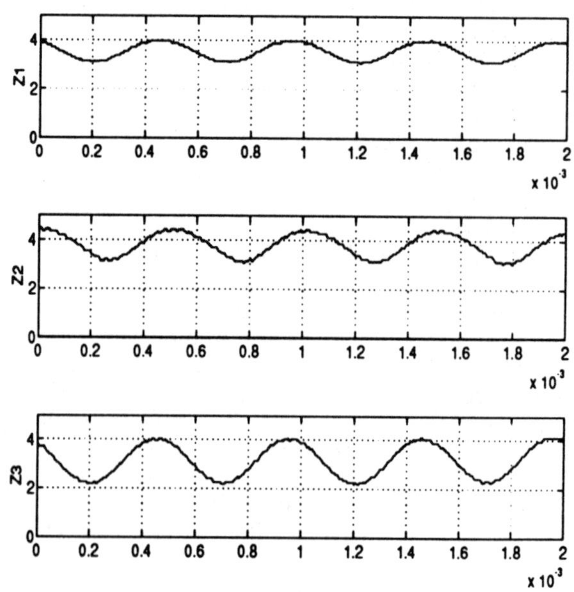

Figure 4. Z1,Z2,Z3 for $10mV$, $20mV$ and $33mV$(p-p) input signals

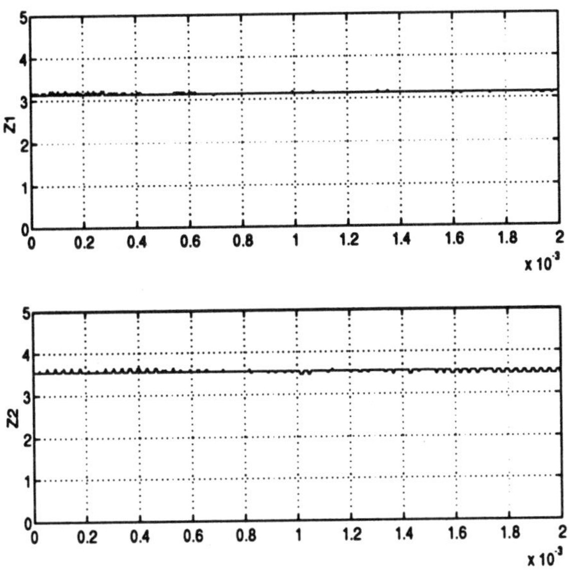

Figure 5. Z1,Z2 for $10mV$ and $20mV$(p-p) input signals at 100kHz

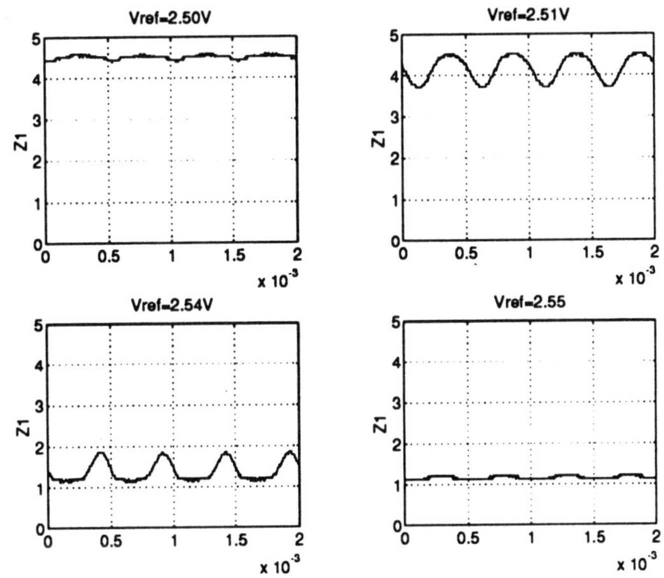

Figure 7. Response of Z1 to change in the V_{ref} of the input transamps

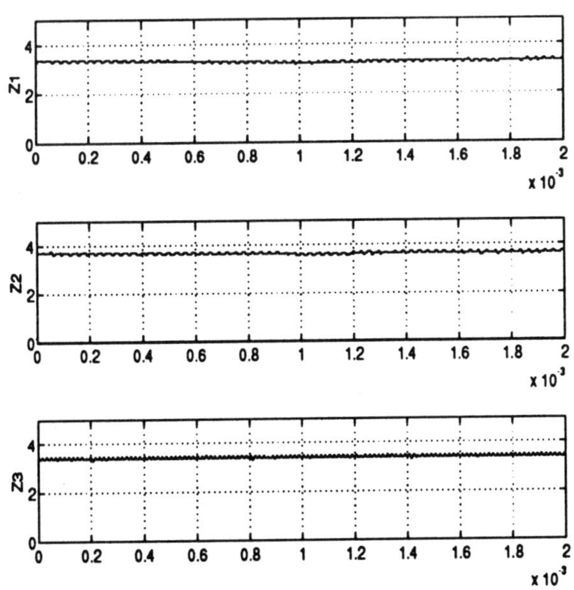

Figure 6. Z1,Z2,Z3 for $33mV, 20mV$ and $10mV$(p-p) input signals at 60kHz

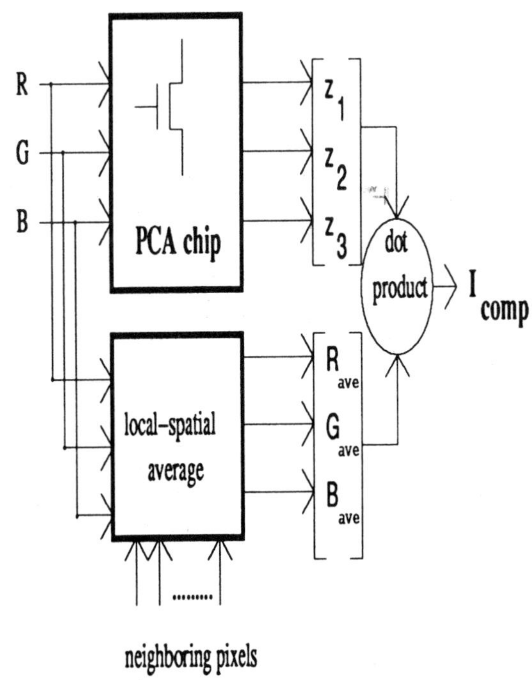

Figure 8. Circuit set-up for color image processing using the PCA chip

A NEUROCONTROLLER TO STABILIZE A SPECIFIC CLASS OF NONLINEAR CONTROL SYSTEMS

M.M.Bayoumi and Y.Long

Department of Electrical and Computer Engineering
Queen's University, Kingston, Ontario, Canada K7L 3N6

Abstract: This paper deals with the state feedback stabilization problem of nonlinear affine systems. Our purpose is to provide a method for constructing a control Lyapunov function that will be used to stabilize such a system using the neural network approach.

1. INTRODUCTION

Feedback stabilization of nonlinear systems is a problem that has recently received a great deal of attention. Some of these investigations have shown the existence of feedback controller with varying degrees of smoothness. These methods have been derived using Lyapunov techniques whereas others were based on geometric or linearization methods. Sliding mode techniques were also used by other authors. Thus necessary and sufficient conditions were obtained for the stabilization of certain nonlinear systems[1]...[14]. Of special interest are the works of Artstein[11], Sontag[10], and Tsinias[9] where stabilization of nonlinear systems based on Lyapunov-like techniques have been addressed.

Lyapunov techniques have long been used in studying control problems for systems described by the different equation dx/dt=f(x,u). In the paper[12] by Sontag, the relation between the property of asymptotic controllability and the existence of a positive definite continuous function V whose derivative can be made negative by appropriate choices of controls was addressed. It is shown that a control system in R^n is asymptotically controllable to the origin if and only if such a function V exists.

Most of the discussions on the Lyapunov approach have been centred on the construction of the Lyapunov function, based on the given system and a suggested feedback control scheme. How to utilize the Lyapunov function to design a nonlinear system controller is a challenging task. In order to make this task tractable, many researchers have concentrated on a wide class of affine systems. Due to the particular structure of the affine systems, it can be characterized in terms of a computable control Lyapunov function, which can be used by the feedback controller to stabilize the dynamic system[9]-[11]. In the paper by Tsinias[9], sufficient conditions for the existence of a control Lyapunov function are provided. This guarantees stabilization at a specified equilibrium point by means of a feedback law, which is smooth except possibly at the equilibrium. In recent years, the use of neural networks for modelling and controlling nonlinear systems has attracted a great deal of attention[15]-[17]. The learning ability of the neural network has provided a convenient means of modelling the nonlinear system and/or nonlinear controllers. However, the stability issue of the closed loop system is still an open question even though neural networks may have been properly trained.

In this paper, we show how to construct a control Lyapunov function with the help of a neural network. Once the neural network has been trained, the closed loop system will be stable. The main advantage of this approach is that it becomes easy to construct an appropriate control Lyapunov function to stabilize the system for a large class of dynamic systems.

0-7803-1901-X/94 $4.00 ©1994 IEEE

2. SYSTEM MODEL AND CONTROLLER DESIGN

Consider a single input affine nonlinear system described by

$$\dot{x} = f(x) + g(x)u \qquad x \in R^n,\ u \in R \tag{1}$$

where f and g are smooth vector fields and f(0)=0. We say that the system eq(1) satisfies a Lyapunov condition, if there exists a neighbourhood U of $0 \in R^n$ and a real function V: U→R such that

- (i) V is continuous on U and has continuous derivative DV with respect to the state x on the region U except at x=0.
- (ii) V is positive definite, namely, V(0)=0 and V(x)>0 for x∈U, x≠0.
- (iii) For very x∈U, x≠0, the following holds:

$$(DVg)(x) = 0 \rightarrow (DVf)(x) < 0 \tag{2}$$

where DV is defined as

$$DV = \left(\frac{\partial V}{\partial x_1}, \frac{\partial V}{\partial x_2}, \ldots\ldots, \frac{\partial V}{\partial x_n}\right) \tag{3}$$

The real function V: U→R with the above properties is called a control Lyapunov function.

The system eq(1) is asymptotically stable at zero, if there exists a feedback law u=r(x), which is smooth for x≠0 near zero and such that x=0 is an asymptotically stable equilibrium point for the closed-loop system

$$\dot{x} = f(x) + g(x)r(x) \tag{4}$$

According to [9]-[11], the existence of the control Lyapunov function is necessary and sufficient for asymptotic stabilization of the nonlinear system eq(1). Sontag[10] has provided an explicit formula for the stabilizing feedback law as

$$w = r(x) = \begin{cases} 0 & \text{for } x\text{: } (DVg)(x) = 0 \text{ and } (DVf)(x) < 0 \\ -\left(\dfrac{DVf + \sqrt{(DVf)^2 + (DVg)^2}}{DVg}\right)(x) & \text{otherwise} \end{cases} \tag{5}$$

The feedback law will be analytic for x≠0 and asymptotically stabilizes eq(1) at zero.

For the affine system discussed above, the stabilization with a continuous and analytic feedback law is then reduced to the construction of the control Lyapunov function. Since the control Lyapunov function depends on the dynamics of the system, systematically constructing the control Lyapunov function is a difficult task. The ability of neural networks to approximate large classes of nonlinear functions with sufficient accuracy makes them ideal candidates for use in constructing such Lyapunov functions. Due to the fact that V(x) is analytic if f(x) and g(x) are analytic, we know that such a neural network exists. Hence a stabilizing law can be obtained from that neural network. For ease of discussion, we assume that:

Assumption 1: There exists a control Lyapunov function V(x) for the system eq(1) in U.

Assumption 2: The Lyapunov function V(x) can be exactly represented by a multi-layer neural network (without bias weights since V(0)=0)

Assuming that V(x) is a control Lyapunov function for the system eq(1) and that V(x) can be represented as

$$V = x^T A \Phi(Bx) \tag{6}$$

where the elements of the matrices $A \in R^{n \times m}$ and $B \in R^{m \times n}$ are the weights of the neural network. The function Φ: $R^m \rightarrow R^m$ is defined as

$$\Phi(z) = (\phi(z_1), \ldots, \phi(z_m))^T \qquad z \in R^m \tag{7}$$

where ϕ: R → R is the sigmoid function of the neural network with $\phi(0)=0$.

For the function V(x), its derivative with respect to time can be expressed as

$$\dot{V} = (DVf)(x) + (DVg)(x)u \tag{8}$$

with

$$DV = [A\,\Phi(Bx)]^T + x^T A\,\Phi'(Bx)\,B \tag{9}$$

where

$$\Phi'(Bx) = \frac{\partial \Phi}{\partial (Bx)}$$
$$\Phi'(z) = diag(\phi'(z_1),\ \ldots,\ \phi'(z_m))^T \qquad z \in R^m \tag{10}$$

A nonlinear recursive least square algorithm will be used to estimate the parameters of the matrices A and B [19]. Let the matrices A and B be represented as $A=\{a_{ij}\}$ and $B=\{b_{ij}\}$. We can define the parameter vector for the recursive least square estimation as

$$\theta = (a_{11},\ \ldots,\ a_{nm}, b_{11},\ \ldots,\ b_{mn})^T \tag{11}$$

The parameter vector θ will then be updated as

$$\hat{\theta}(k) = \hat{\theta}(k-1) + P(k-1)\Psi(k-1)e(k) \tag{12}$$

$$P^{-1}(k-1) = P^{-1}(k-2) + \Psi(k-1)\,\Psi^T(k-1) \tag{13}$$

with $P(-1)=\alpha I$ and $\alpha>0$. The error e(k) is defined as

$$e(k) = (e_1(k)\quad e_2(k))^T \tag{14}$$

where $e_1(k)$, $e_2(k)$, which correspond to V(k) in eq(6) and dV(k)/dt in eq(8) respectively, are defined as follows:

$$e_1(k) = \begin{cases} 0 & \text{if } V(k) \ge 0 \\ -V(k) & \text{if } V(k) < 0 \end{cases}$$

$$e_2(k) = \begin{cases} -(DVf)(X)|_{x=x(k)} & (DVg)(x)|_{x=x(k)} \text{ and } (DVf)(x)|_{x=x(k)} > 0 \\ 0 & \text{otherwise} \end{cases} \tag{15}$$

where $V(k)=V|_{x=x(k)}$. The matrix $\Psi(k)$: $R^{2mn \times 2}$ can be expressed as

$$\Psi(k) = (\Psi_1(k),\ \Psi_2(k)) \tag{16}$$

with

$$\Psi_1(k) = \frac{\partial V}{\partial \theta}|_{x=x(k)} = [\frac{\partial V}{\partial a_{11}},\ \ldots,\ \frac{\partial V}{\partial a_{nm}}, \frac{\partial V}{\partial b_{11}},\ \ldots,\ \frac{\partial V}{\partial b_{mn}}]^T\ |_{x=x(k)}$$
$$\Psi 2(k) = \frac{\partial (DVf)}{\partial \theta}|_{x=x(k)} = [\frac{\partial (DVf)}{\partial a_{11}},\ \ldots,\ \frac{\partial (DVf)}{\partial a_{nm}}, \frac{\partial (DVf)}{\partial b_{11}},\ \ldots,\ \frac{\partial (DVf)}{\partial b_{mn}}]^T\ |_{x=x(k)} \tag{17}$$

If the matrix B is represented as

$$B = [B_1^T\ \ B_2^T\ \ \ldots\ \ B_m^T]^T \tag{18}$$

where B_i, i=1, ..., m, is a 1 x n vector and if the vector G(x,u) is decomposed according to

$$G(x,u) = [g_1(x,u)\ \ \ldots\ \ g_n(x,u)]^T \tag{19}$$

then it is easy to show that for i=1, ..., n and j=1, ..., m

$$\frac{\partial V}{\partial a_{ij}} = x_i \phi(B_j x) \tag{20}$$

$$\frac{\partial (DVf)}{\partial a_{ij}} = f_i(x)\phi(B_j x) + x_i \phi'(B_j x) B_j f(x) \tag{21}$$

For i=1, ..., m and j=1, ..., n, we have

$$\frac{\partial V}{\partial b_{ij}} = (\sum_{k=1}^{n} x_k a_{ki}) \phi'(B_i x) x_j$$

$$\frac{\partial (DVf)}{\partial b_{ij}} = \left(\sum_{k=1}^{n} f_k(x) a_{ki}\right) \phi'(B_i x) x_j + \left(\sum_{k=1}^{n} x_k a_{ki}\right) \left[\phi'(B_i x) f_j(x) + \phi''(B_i x) x_j B_i f(x)\right] \tag{22}$$

The neural network will be trained as follows:

1. Generate a set of states $x \in U$ randomly.
2. Calculate (DVf)(x) and (DVg)(x). If (Dvg)(x)=0 and (Dvf)(x)>0, go to step 3, otherwise go to step 4.
3. Update the neural network based on the nonlinear recursive least square algorithm given by eq(11) and eq(12).
4. Exit if the exit criterion is satisfied, otherwise return to step 1.

3. SIMULATIONS

The proposed control method is demonstrated here for various nonlinearities and initial points. The value of m is 12 and the initial weights of the neural network were selected as random numbers lying in the range [-0.5, +0.5].

System 1:

$$\begin{aligned} \dot{x}_1 &= x_2 + 0.3\sin(x_1 x_2) \\ \dot{x}_2 &= x_1 + x_2 + 0.5x_1^2 + 0.2x_2^2 + u \end{aligned} \tag{23}$$

During the training phase, the components of the state vector x were selected to lie in the range [-2,2]. After training, the system response for various initial conditions have been depicted in Fig.1 - Fig.4.

System 2:

$$\begin{aligned} \dot{x}_1 &= \frac{0.5x_1}{1 + x_1^2 + x_2^2} + x_2 + 2u \\ \dot{x}_2 &= 0.2x_1 + u \end{aligned} \tag{24}$$

In this case, the system is unstable around its equilibrium point (0,0). The state vector x was selected to lie in the range [-1,1] and the system responses are shown in Fig.5 - Fig.8.

It should be noted that the rate of convergence is not as fast as that of the control algorithm given in [19]. However, the control signals are made continuous and the chattering effect is eliminated except at the zero state.

4. CONCLUSIONS

In this paper, we propose a method for implementing the feedback stabilization theorem which is given by Artstein. The neural network approach has proven to be a viable one.The simulations illustrated that the construction of the Lyapunov function using the method suggested can be very effective and definitely feasible.

REFERENCES

[1] M.Kelemen (1986), "A stability property", IEEE Trans. Aut. Control, AC-31, pp.766-768

[2] W.Hahn (1967), "Stability of motion", New York, Springer-Verlag.

[3] A.Aeyels (1985), "Stabilization of a class of nonlinear systems by a smooth feedback control", Sys. Contr. Lett., Vol.5, pp.289-294.

[4] W.M.Boothby and R.Marino (1989), "Feedback stabilization of planar nonlinear systems", Sys. Contr. Lett., Vol.12, p.87-92.

[5] C.I.Byrnes and A.Isidori (1988), "Local stabilization of minimum phase nonlinear systems", Sys. Contr. Lett., Vol.11, pp.9-17.

[6] M.Kawski (1989), "Stabilization of nonlinear systems in the plane", Sys. Contr. Lett. Vol.12, pp.169-176.

[7] H.J.Sussmann (1979), "Subanalytic sets and feedback control", J. Diff. Eqs., Vol.31, pp.31-52.

[8] E.D.Sontag and H.J.Sussmann (1980), "Remarks on continuous feedback", in Proc. IEEE Conf. Decision and Control, pp.916-921.

[9] J.Tsinias (1989), "Asymptotic feedback stabilization: A sufficient condition for the existence of control Lyapunov functions", Sys. Contr. Lett., Vol.15, p.441-448.

[10] E.D.Sontag (1989), "A 'universal' construction of Artstein's theorem on nonlinear stabilization", Sys. Contr. Lett., Vol.13, pp.117-123

[11] Z.Artstein (1989), "Stabilization with relaxed controls", Nonlinear Anal. Math. Appl.7, pp.1163-1173.

[12] E.D.Sontag (1983), "A Lyapunov-like characterization of asymptotic controllability", SLAM J. Control and Optimization, Vol.21, No.3, May 1983.

[13] R.W.Brockett (1983), "Asymptotic stability and feedback stabilization", in: R.W.Brockett, R.S.Millman and H.H.Sussmann, Eds., Differential Geometric Control Theory (Birkhauser, Basel-Boston).

[14] M.Vidyasagar (1980), "Decomposition techniques for large-scale systems with nonadditive interactions: Stability and stabilizability", IEEE Trans. Auto. Contr., AC-25, pp.773-779.

[15] K.S.Narendra and K.Parthasarathy (1990), "Identification and control of dynamical systems using neural networks", IEEE Trans. on Neural Networks, pp.4-27.

[16] F.C.Chen (1991), "A dead-zone approach in nonlinear adaptive control using neural networks", Proceedings of the 30th IEEE Conference on Decision and Control, pp.156-161.

[17] D.A.Hoskins, J.N.Hwang and J.Vagners (1992), "Iterative inversion of neural networks and its application to adaptive control", IEEE Trans. on Neural Networks, pp.292-301.

[18] G.C.Goodwin and K.S.Sin (1984), "Adaptive filtering, Prediction and control", Prentice Hall, pp.308-311.

[19] Y.Long and M.M.Bayoumi (1992), "A neural network based regulator", Internal report, Queen's University, Kingston Ontarion.

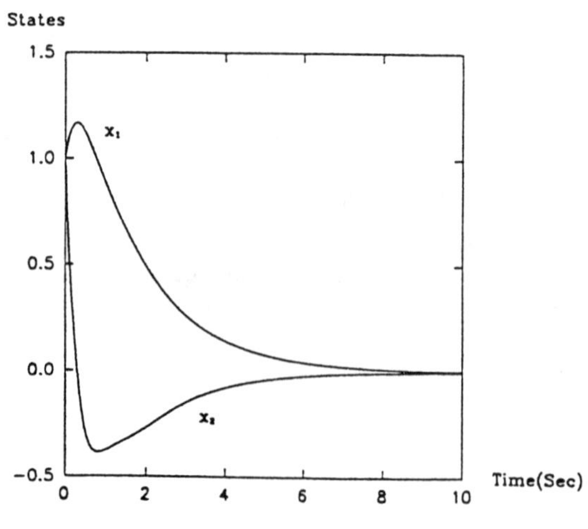

Figure 1 The response to system 1, $x_o = (1.0, 1.0)^T$

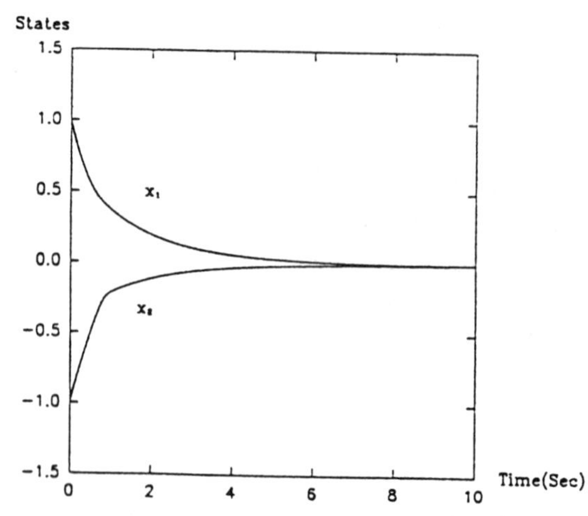

Figure 2 The response to system 1, $x_o = (1.0, -1.0)^T$

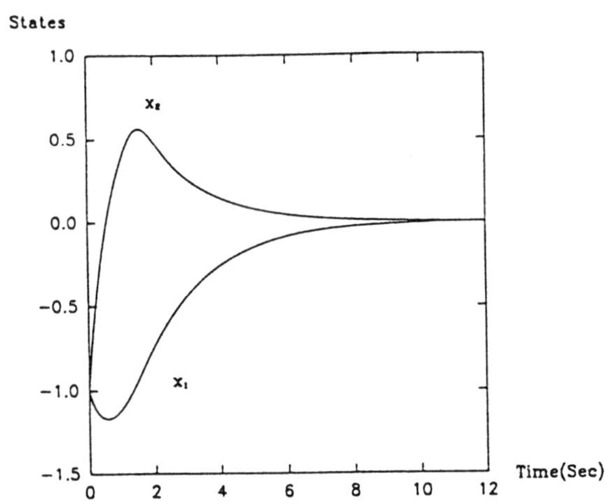

Figure 3 The response to system 1, $x_o = (-1.0, -1.0)^T$

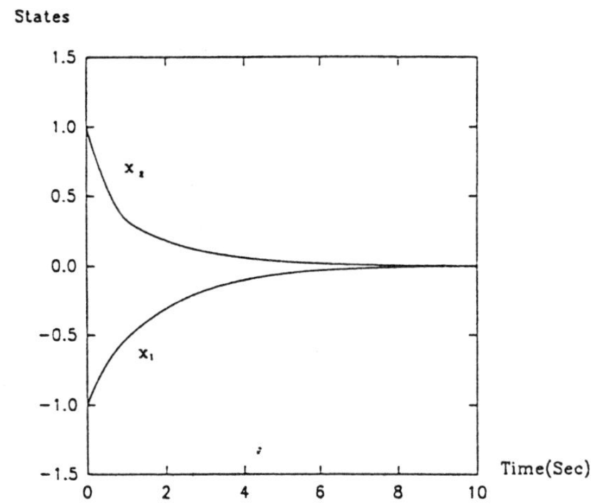

Figure 4 The response to system 1, $x_o = (-1.0, 1.0)^T$

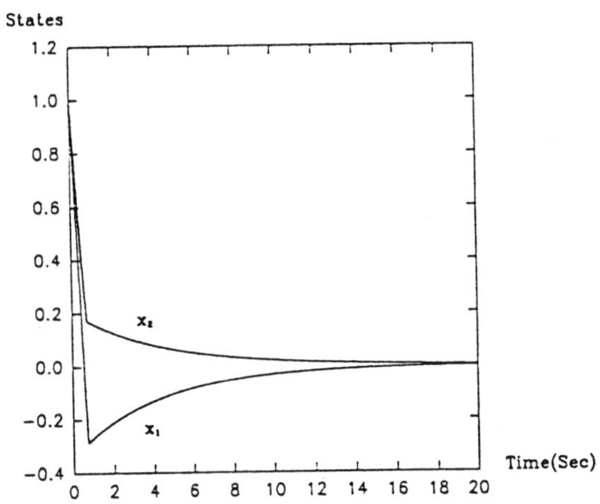

Figure 5 The response to system 2, $x_o = (1.0, 1.0)^T$

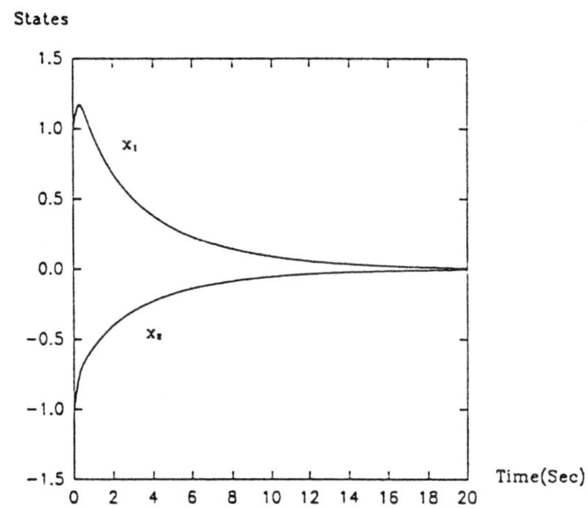

Figure 6 The response to system 2, $x_o = (1.0, -1.0)^T$

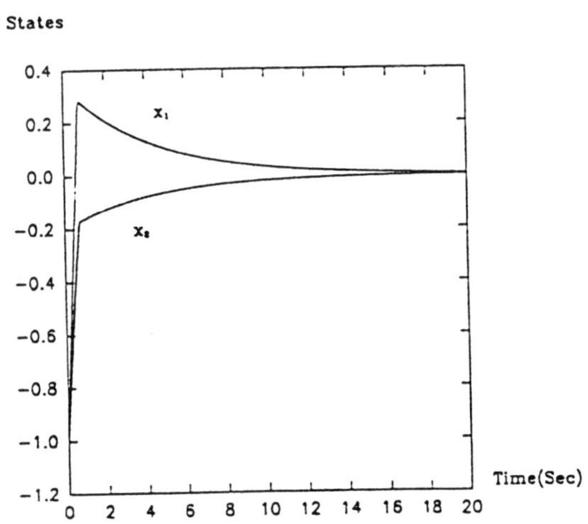

Figure 7 The response to system 2, $x_o = (-1.0, -1.0)^T$

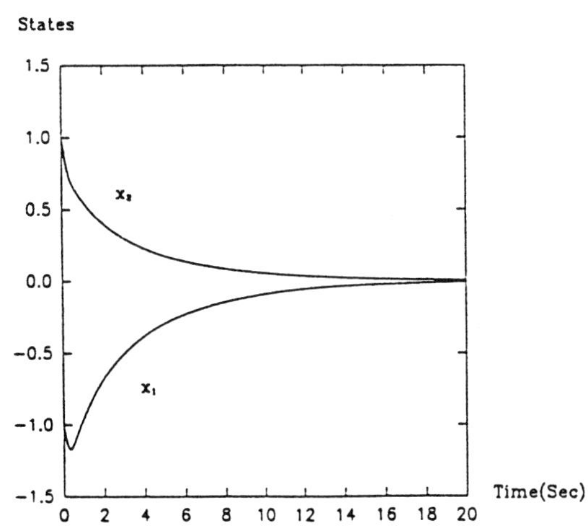

Figure 8 The response to system 2, $x_o = (-1.0, 1.0)^T$

INTENTIONALLY LEFT BLANK

The Convergent Learning of Three-Layer Artificial Neural Networks for Any Binary-to-Binary Mapping†

Jung H. Kim
Center for Adv. Comp. Studies
University of SW Louisiana
Lafayette, LA 70504
kim@cacs.usl.edu:318-231-6732

Sung-kwon Park
Electronic-Comm. Eng.
Hanyang University
Seoul, Korea 133

In Sook Kim
Biology Dept.
University of SW Louisiana
Lafayette, LA 70504

ABSTRACT

In this paper, the learning algorithm called Expand-and-Truncate Learning (ETL) is proposed to train three-layer binary neural networks (BNN) with guaranteed convergence for any binary-to-binary mapping. The most significant contribution of this paper is the development of learning algorithm for three-layer BNN which guarantees the convergence, automatically determining a required number of neurons in the hidden layer. Furthermore, the learning speed of the proposed ETL algorithm is much faster than that of Back propagation learning algorithm in a binary field. Neurons in the proposed BNN employ a hard-limiter activation function, only integer weights and integer thresholds. Therefore, this will greatly facilitate actual hardware implementation of the proposed BNN using currently available digital VLSI technology.

1. Introduction

Recently, the Back Propagation Learning (BPL) algorithm has been applied to many binary-to-binary mapping problems. However, since the BPL algorithm searches the solution in continuous space, the BPL algorithm applied to binary-to-binary mapping problems results in long training time and inefficient performance. Typically, the BPL algorithm requires an extremely high number of iterations to obtain even a simple binary-to-binary mapping [GrMi92]. Also, in the BPL algorithm, the number of neurons in the hidden layer required to solve a given problem is not known a priori. Since the number of neurons in the input and the output layer is determined by the dimensions of the input and output vectors, respectively, the abilities of three-layer neural networks depend on the number of neurons in the hidden layer. Therefore, one of the most important problems in application of three-layer neural networks is to determine the necessary number of neurons in the hidden layer. It has been widely recognized that Stone-Weierstrass's theorem does not give a practical guideline in determining the required number of neurons [Cott90].

In this paper, the geometrical learning algorithm called Expand-and-Truncate Learning (ETL) is proposed to train a three-layer BNN for any binary-to-binary mapping problem. The neuron in the proposed BNN employs a hard-limiter activation function, only integer weights, and integer threshold. This will greatly facilitate hardware implementation of the proposed BNN using currently available VLSI technology. Also notice that there hasn't been an efficient learning algorithm for three-layer neural networks which employs a hard-limiter activation function.

2. Preliminaries

Suppose that a set of n-bit training input vectors is given and a binary desired output is assigned to each training input vector. An n-bit input vector can be considered as a vertex of an n-dimensional hypercube. Also, assume that these two classes of training input vectors (i.e. vertices) can be separated by an $(n-1)$-dimensional hyperplane which is expressed as a net function,

†This research is partly supported by NSF Grants IRI-9318328 and ADP-04, and Board of Regents of Louisiana grants LEQSF-RD-A-28 and LEQSF-RD-A-37.

0-7803-1901-X/94 $4.00 ©1994 IEEE

$$net(X,T) = w_1x_1 + w_2x_2 + \ldots + w_nx_n - T = 0 \quad (1)$$

where w_i's and T are constant. In this case, the set of training inputs is said to be linearly separable (LS), and the $(n-1)$-dimensional hyperplane is the separating hyperplane. The $(n-1)$-dimensional separating hyperplanes can be established by an n-input neuron with a hard-limiter activation function. Actually a neuron function bears more information than a hyperplane. A neuron assigns either one or zero to each side of a hyperplane, while a hyperplane merely defines a border between two groups of vertices. In order to match a separating hyperplane with a neuron, we need to properly assign either one or zero to each side of the separating hyperplane.

If a given binary-to-binary mapping function has the property of linear separability, then the function can be realized by only one neuron. However, if the given function is not a LS function, then more than one neuron is required to realize the function. The main problem is how to decompose the linearly inseparable function into two or more LS functions, and how to combine these LS functions. In this paper, we propose a method to decompose any linearly-inseparable function into multiple LS functions based on a geometrical approach, and to combine these LS functions to produce desired outputs. Our proposed method will show that any binary-to-binary mapping function can be realized by three-layer BNN with one hidden layer.

3. Learning the Hidden Layer

In this section, the geometrical learning algorithm called Expand-and-Truncate Learning (ETL) is proposed to decompose an arbitrarily linearly inseparable function into multiple LS functions. For any binary-to-binary mapping, ETL will determine the required multiple LS functions, each of which is realized by a neuron in the hidden layer.

ETL finds a set of separating hyperplanes based on a geometrical analysis of the training inputs, so that inputs located between two neighboring hyperplanes have the same desired outputs. Since a separating hyperplane can be established by a neuron with a hard-limiter activation function, the number of required neurons in the hidden layer is equal to that of required hyperplanes.

Fundamental ideas behind the proposed ETL algorithm is introduced using a simple example. For instance, let us consider a function of three input variables, $f(x_1, x_2, x_3)$. If inputs are {000,010,011,111}, then $f(x_1, x_2, x_3)$ produces output 1. If inputs are {001,100}, then $f(x_1, x_2, x_3)$ produces output 0. If input vertices are {101,110}, then we don't care what $f(x_1, x_2, x_3)$ produces. In other words, the given example can be considered as having six training inputs. An n-bit input can be considered as a vertex in an n-dimensional hypercube. A 3-bit input can be considered as a vertex of a unit cube. The vertex whose desired output is 1 and 0 is called a *true vertex* and a *false vertex*, respectively.

Definition: *A set of included true vertices (SITV)* is a set of true vertices which can be separated from the rest vertices by a hyperplane.

ETL algorithm begins by selecting a true vertex. The first selected true vertex is called as a core vertex. The first vertex will be selected based on the clustering center found by the modified k-nearest neighboring algorithm. In this example, the first true vertex selected is {000}. Then, the hyperplane $-2x_1 - x_2 - 2x_3 + 1 = 0$ will separate SITV {000,010} from the other training vertices {001,100,011,111}. This hyperplane is geometrically expanded to add to SITV possibly more input vertices which produce the same output, while keeping the linear-separability. This step will reduce the total number of required hyperplanes, i.e., the number of required neurons. To choose an input vertex to be included in SITV, it is logical to choose the nearest true vertex to the vertices in SITV in the Euclidian distance sense. There could be more than one. The reason to choose the nearest vertex first is that as the chosen vertex gets closer to the vertices in SITV, the probability that the vertices in SITV are separated from the rest vertices becomes higher. The nearest true vertex can be easily found by considering the Hamming disdance (HD) from the vertices in SITV. In the given example, the nearest true vertex is

{011}. Let's call this vertex a trial vertex. Expand the hyperplane to include a trial vertex {011} such that the hyperplane separates the true vertices in SITV {000,010,011} from the other training vertices {001,100,111}. To determine whether such a hyperplane exists and find the hyperplane, a geometrical approach is proposed next.

Consider a reference hypersphere (RHS),

$$(x_1 - \frac{1}{2})^2 + (x_2 - \frac{1}{2})^2 + \cdots + (x_n - \frac{1}{2})^2 = \frac{n}{4}, \qquad (2)$$

Notice that the center of the RHS is the center of the n-dimensional hypercube, and all the 2^n vertices are on the RHS. Now consider another n-dimensional hypersphere which has its center at $(\frac{C_1}{C_0}, \frac{C_2}{C_0}, \cdots, \frac{C_n}{C_0})$ and its radius r. C_0 is the number of elements in SITV including the trial vertex. C_i is calculated as follows: $C_i = \sum_{k=1}^{C_0} v_k^i$, where v_k is an element in SITV, and v_k^i is the ith bit of v_k. Notice that the point $(\frac{C_1}{C_0}, \frac{C_2}{C_0}, \cdots, \frac{C_n}{C_0})$ in the n –dimensional space represents the center of gravity of all elements in SITV.

If SITV is linearly separated from the other training vertices, there must exist a hypersphere to include SITV and exclude the other training vertices. To find such a hypersphere, consider the hypersphere whose center is located at the center of gravity of all elements in SITV. If this hypersphere separates, this one can do with the minimum radius. On the other hand, a hypersphere with its center away from it must have a longer radius in order to include all the elements in SITV. This will obviously increase the chance of including non SITV elements. Hence, the hypersphere whose center is the center of gravity, is called as a separating hypersphere which is expressed as

$$(x_1 - \frac{C_1}{C_0})^2 + (x_2 - \frac{C_2}{C_0})^2 + \cdots + (x_n - \frac{C_n}{C_0})^2 = r^2 \qquad (3)$$

When this separating hypersphere intersects RHS, an $(n-1)$-dimensional hyperplane is found. By subtracting Eq. (3) from Eq. (2) and multiplying by C_0, we obtain the separating hyperplane as

$$(2C_1 - C_0)x_1 + (2C_2 - C_0)x_2 + \cdots + (2C_n - C_0)x_n - T = 0$$

where T is a constant.

That is, if there exists a separating hyperplane which separates SITV from other training vertices,

$\sum_{i=1}^{n}(2C_i - C_0)v_t^i - T \geq 0$ for each vertex v_t in SITV, and

$\sum_{i=1}^{n}(2C_i - C_0)v_r^i - T < 0$ for each vertex v_r from the rest vertices.

Therefore, each vertex v_t in SITV and each vertex v_r satisfy

$$\sum_{i=1}^{n}(2C_i - C_0)v_t^i > \sum_{i=1}^{n}(2C_i - C_0)v_r^i.$$

Let $t_{\min}$ be the minimum value of $\sum_{i=1}^{n}(2C_i - C_0)v_t^i$ among all vertices in SITV, and $f_{\max}$ be the maximum of $\sum_{i=1}^{n}(2C_i - C_0)v_r^i$ among the rest vertices.

If $t_{\min} > f_{\max}$, then there exists a separating hyperplane which is

$$(2C_1 - C_0)x_1 + (2C_2 - C_0)x_2 + \cdots + (2C_n - C_0)x_n - T = 0$$

where $T = \left\lceil \frac{t_{\min} + f_{\max}}{2} \right\rceil$ and $\lceil x \rceil$ is the smallest integer greater than or equal to x. If $t_{\min} \leq f_{\max}$, then there does not exist a separating hyperplane, thus the trial vertex is removed from SITV.

To include more true vertices, another true vertex is chosen using the same criteria as earlier, and tested if the new trial vertex can be added to SITV. This procedure continues until no more true vertices can be added to SITV. If all true vertices are included in SITV, the given function is a LS function, and only one neuron is required for the function. However, if all true vertices can not be included in SITV, more than one neuron is required for the given function. The method to find the other required hyperplanes, i.e., the other neurons, is described next.

The reason why the first hyperplane could not expand to add more true vertices to SITV, is due to the existence of false vertices around the hypersphere. That is, these false vertices block the expansion of the first hypersphere. In order to train more vertices, the expanded hypersphere must include the false vertices in addition to the true vertices in SITV of the first hypersphere. For this reason, *false vertices are converted into true vertices, and true vertices which are not in SITV are converted into false vertices.* Here the desired output for each vertex is only temporarily converted. That is, the conversion is needed only to obtain the separating hyperplane. Now, expand the first hypersphere to add more true vertices to SITV, until no more true vertices can be added to SITV. When the expanded hypersphere meets with RHS, the second hyperplane (i.e. neuron) is found.

If SITV includes all true vertices, then the geometrical learning is converged. Otherwise, the training vertices which are not in SITV are converted again, and the same procedure repeats again. The above procedure can get stuck even when there are more true vertices still left to be included. Consider the case that when ETL tries to add any true vertex to SITV, no true vertex can be included. In this case, ETL converts the not-included true vertices and false vertices into the false vertices and true vertices, respectively. When ETL tries to include any true vertex, no true vertex can be included even after conversion. Hence, the procedure is trapped and it can not proceed any more. This situation is due to the limited degree of freedom in separating hyperplanes using only integer coefficients (i.e. weights). If this situation does not occur until SITV includes all true vertices, the proposed ETL algorithm is converged with finding all required neurons in the hidden layer.

If the above situation (i.e. no true vertex can be included even after conversion) occurs, ETL declares the true vertices in SITV as "don't care" vertices in order to consider these vertices no more in the finding of other required neurons. Then, ETL continues by selecting a new core vertex based on the clustering center among the remaining true vertices. Until all true vertices are included, ETL proceeds in the same way as explained earlier. Therefore, the convergence of the proposed ETL algorithm is always guaranteed. The selection of core vertex is not unique in the process of finding separating hyperplanes. Accordingly, the number of separating hyperplanes for a given problem can vary depending upon the selection of the core vertex and the orderings of adding trial vertices. By trying all possible selections, the minimal number of separating hyperplanes can always be found. Figure 1 shows the structure of BNN for the 3-bit function example. Table 1 analyzes the outputs of neurons in the hidden layer for input vertices. In Table 1, notice that linearly inseparable input vertices are transformed into a linearly separable function in the hidden layer.

4. Learning an output layer

After all required hyperplanes (i.e. all required neurons on the hidden layer) are found, one output neuron is needed in the output layer, to combine the outputs of the neurons in the hidden layer. In this section, we will discuss how to combine the outputs of hidden neurons in order to produce the desired output.

Definition: A hidden neuron is defined as *a converted hidden neuron*, if the neuron was determined by converted true vertices which are originally false vertices and converted false vertices which are originally true vertices. If all required hidden neurons are found using only one core vertex, then every even-numbered hidden neuron is a converted hidden neuron, such as the second neuron in Fig. 1.

If ETL finds all required separating hyperplanes with only one core vertex, the weights and threshold of one output neuron are set as follows. The weight of the link from the odd-numbered hidden neuron to the output neuron is set to 1. The weight of the link from the even-numbered neuron to the output neuron is set to -1, since each even-numbered neuron is a converted hidden neuron. By setting the threshold of the output neuron to 0 (1) if the hidden layer has an even (odd) number of neurons, the three-layer BNN always produce the correct output to each training input. Figure 1 shows the weights and the threshold of the output neuron for the given example, since ETL finds all required hyperplanes with only one core vertex {000}.

If ETL uses more than one core vertex to find all required hyperplanes, the weights and threshold of the output neuron cannot be determined straight-forwardly as above. For further discussion, we need the following definition.

Definition: A positive successive product (PSP) function is defined as a boolean function which can be expressed as $B(h_1, h_2, \ldots, h_n) = h_1 \mathrm{O}\, (h_2 \mathrm{O}\, (\ldots \mathrm{O}\, (h_{n-1} \mathrm{O}\, h_n))\ldots)$ where the operator O is either logical AND or logical OR. A PSP function can also be expressed as

$$B(h_1, h_2, \ldots, h_n) = h_1 \mathrm{O}\, (B(h_2, h_3, \ldots, h_n)), \text{ and } B(h_{n-1}, h_n) = h_{n-1} \mathrm{O}\, h_n$$

An example of a PSP function is $B(h_1, h_2, \ldots, h_7) = h_1 + h_2(h_3 + h_4(h_5 + h_6\, h_7))$
From the definition of a PSP function, it can be easily shown that a PSP function is always a positive unate function [Muro71]. Note that a LS function is always a unate function, but a unate function is not always a LS function.

Theorem 1: A PSP function is a LS function.

The proofs of Theorem 1 as well as other Theorems are given in [Kim93]. Theorem 1 means that a neuron with a hard-limiter activation function can map any PSP function since a PSP function is a LS function. Using a PSP function, an output neuron function can be expressed as the function of the outputs of the hidden neurons.

A neuron is supposed to assign one to the side of a hyperplane having true vertices, and zero to the other side. However, in ETL a converted hidden neuron assigns one to the side of a hyperplane having original false vertices and zero to the other side having original true vertices. Therefore, without transforming the outputs of converted hidden neurons, an output neuron function can not be a PSP function of the outputs of hidden neurons. In order to make a PSP function, the output of each converted hidden neuron is complemented and fed into the output neuron. Complementing the output of a converted hidden neuron is identical to multiplying by (-1) the weight from this neuron to the output neuron and subtracting this weight from the threshold of the output neuron. That is, if the output neuron is realized by the weight-threshold $\{w_1, w_2, \cdots w_j, \cdots w_n; T\}$ whose inputs are $h_1, h_2, \cdots h_j' \ldots h_n$, then the output neuron is also realized by weight-threshold $\{w_1, w_2, \ldots -w_j, \cdots w_n; T - w_j\}$ whose inputs are $h_1, h_2, \ldots h_j, \ldots h_n$.

Theorem 2: After the hidden neurons are determined by ETL, an output neuron function can always be expressed as a PSP function of the outputs of hidden neurons if the output of each converted hidden neuron is complemented.

Theorem 2 shows that an output neuron function is a LS function of the outputs of hidden neurons. The way to determine the weights of the output neuron is to find a PSP function, and then transform the PSP function into the net function. For an n variable PSP function $f(h_1, h_2, \ldots, h_n)$, there exists a systematic method to generate a net function, $net(H, T)$. The systematic method is given next.

First, the method starts from the innermost net function net_n. The net_n is set to $h_n - 1$ since $net_n \geq 0$ if $h_n = 1$ and $net_n < 0$ if $h_n = 0$. Let's find the next net function net_{n-1}. If the operation between h_n and h_{n-1} is a logical OR, then $net_{n-1} = (-Min[net_n])\, h_{n-1} + net_n$, where $Min[net_n]$ is the minimum value of net_n. Since $Min[net_n] = Min[h_n - 1] = -1$, $net_{n-1} = h_{n-1} + h_n - 1$. If the operation between h_n and h_{n-1} is a logical AND, then $net_{n-1} = (Max[net_n] + 1)h_{n-1} + net_n - (Max[net_n] + 1)$, where

$Max[net_n]$ is the maximum value of net_n. Since $Max[net_n] = Max[h_n - 1] = 0$, $net_{n-1} = h_{n-1} + h_n - 2$. Continuing this process, the net function $net(H,T)$ is determined. The connection weight between the output neuron and the ith hidden neuron is the coefficient of h_i in the net function, and the threshold of the output neuron is the constant in the net function.

From the above discussion, we can formally state the following theorem.

Theorem 3: For any generation of binary-to-binary mapping, the proposed ETL algorithm always converges and finds the three-layer BNN whose hidden layer has as many neurons as separating hyperplanes.

5. Conclusion

In this paper, the learning algorithm called Expand-and-Truncate Learning (ETL) is proposed to train multi-layer BNN for any binary-to-binary mapping. The ETL algorithm is implemented in C language (about 2,500 lines). We have shown that for any generation of binary-to-binary mapping, the proposed ETL algorithm always converges and finds the three-layer BNN, by automatically determining a required number of neurons in the hidden layer. The learning speed of ETL is much faster than that of BPL for the generation of binary-to-binary mapping. The neuron in the proposed BNN employs a hard-limiter activation function, only integer weights and integer thresholds. Therefore, this will greatly facilitate actual hardware implementation of the proposed BNN using currently available digital VLSI technology.

Reference

[GrMi92] Gray, D. L. and A. N. Michel, "A training Algorithm for Binary Feedforward Neural Network", IEEE trans. on Neural Networks, March 1992, pp 176-194.

[Cott90] Cotter, N. E., "The Stone-Weierstrass Theorem and Its Application to Neural Networks", IEEE Trans. on Neural Network, Dec. 1990.

[Kim93] Kim, J. H. and S. K. Park, "The Geometrical Learning of Biological Neural Networks", to appear at IEEE Trans. on Neural Networks.

[Muro71] Muroga, S., "Threshold Logic and Its Applications", John Wiley & Sons, Inc. 1971.

[Park91] Park, S., J. H. Kim, and H. Chung, "A Learning Algorithm for Discrete Multilayer Perceptron", Proc. of Intl. Symp. on Circuit and System, Singapore, June 1991.

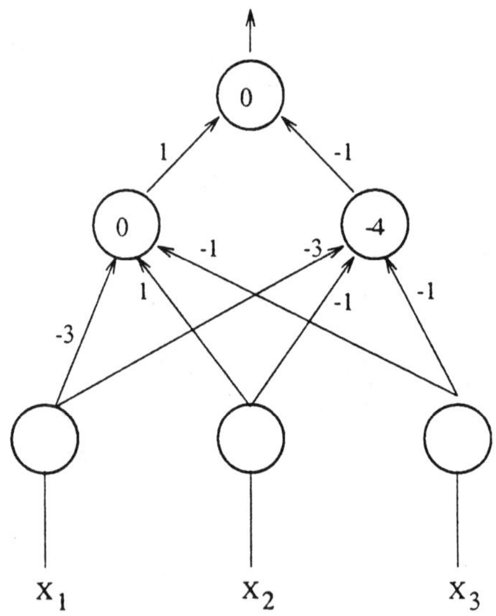

Fig. 1. The three-layer BNN for the given example.

Input	Desired output	Hidden layer		Output neuron
		1st neuron	2nd neuron	
000, 010, 011	1	1	1	1
001, 100	0	0	1	0
111	1	0	0	1

Table 1. The analysis of the hidden layer for the given example

Image Compression Using a Feedforward Neural Network

Rudy Setiono and Guojun Lu

Abstract— **We present an image compression technique using a feedforward neural network. The neural network has three layers: one input layer, one hidden layer and one output layer. The inputs of the neural network are original image data, while the outputs are reconstructed image data which are close to the inputs. If the amount of data required to store the hidden unit values and the connection weights to the output layer of the neural network is less than the original data, compression is achieved. In our experiments, we achieved a compression ratio of about 10 with good reconstructed image quality.**

The neural network construction algorithm we used has an attractive feature that each addition of a hidden unit to the network will always improve the image quality. Thus our compression scheme is flexible in the sense that the user can trade between image quality and compression ratio depending on the application requirements.

I. Introduction

Because digital images require large amount of data to represent, image compression is needed in order to store and transmit images economically. Many image compression techniques and standards have been proposed [1], [2]. Recently, several authors [3], [4], [5], [6], [7] have proposed methods for image compression using neural network techniques. In these methods, the image is normally subdivided into small square blocks of pixels which are then used as the patterns to train the neural network. The size of each block is typically $4 \times 4, 5 \times 5, 6 \times 6$ or 8×8. A simple and yet very interesting method for image compression using feedforward neural network was proposed by Sicuranza et al. [8]. A network with a single hidden layer is employed. The number of units in the input and output layers is equal to the number of pixels in a block. The smaller the number of units in the hidden layer is, the higher the compression ratio that can be obtained. However, a network with small number of hidden units may result in an unsatisfactory reconstructed image. For their experiments, Sicuranza et al. subdivided an image of 256×256 pixels into $6 \times 6, 5 \times 5$ and 4×4 blocks. Nine, six, and four hidden units were used respectively in order to achieve an immediate compression ratio of about 4. The reconstructed image that were obtained had signal to noise ratio (SNR) values that ranged between 19.4 and 20.5 dB. A similar approach has also been reported by Cotrell et al. [9] who used blocks of 8×8 pixels for training the neural network.

In this paper, we shall report on an algorithm that we have developed for constructing a feedforward neural network and its application to image compression. The algorithm is similar to the Dynamic Node Creation of Ash [10]. It starts with a network that contains only a single hidden unit in the hidden layer. The network is trained and if the weights obtained after training do not give a network with the desired accuracy then one more hidden unit is added and the network is retrained. This process is repeated until a final network with the desired accuracy has been obtained. The advantage of this approach is obvious. We have eliminated the need to determine *a priori* the number of hidden units needed in the network.

In the Dynamic Node Creation algorithm, the network is always trained using the standard backpropagation method. It is well known that the backpropagation method is very slow to converge. We use a variant of the quasi-Newton method in conjunction with the network construction algorithm to reduce the training time. When a line search procedure is incorporated into the quasi-Newton method, we show that the error function of the neural network is non-increasing throughout the execution of the neural network construction algorithm.

Our experimental results show that when this algorithm is applied to image compression, it is able to achieve better compression performance than those obtained by Sicuranza et al. The algorithm is also

The authors are with Department of Information Systems and Computer Science, National University of Singapore, Kent Ridge, Singapore 0511, Republic of Singapore

0-7803-1901-X/94 $4.00 ©1994 IEEE

tinue adding hidden units to the network in order to obtain better quality image at the cost of reducing the compression ratio. In Section 2 we will describe our neural network construction algorithm and in Section 3 we will discuss the application of this algorithm to image compression.

II. Neural network construction algorithm

Let us consider a feedforward neural network with an input layer, an output layer and h hidden units in the hidden layer. The problem of training this neural network can be cast as an unconstrained optimization problem. The objective function to be minimized is the error function defined as follows:

$$F^h(w,v) := \frac{1}{2}\sum_{i=1}^{k}\left\|\left(\sum_{j=1}^{h}\sigma(x^iw^j)v^j\right)-t^i\right\|^2, \quad (1)$$

where

k = fixed integer number of given samples $x^i \in \mathbb{R}^n$.
x^i = given n-dimensional vectors samples.
$t^i \in \mathbb{R}^m$ is the target value for $x^i, i = 1,2,\ldots,k$. For our image compression application $t^i = x^i$ for all $i = 1,2,\ldots,k$ and $m = n$, the dimensionality of the patterns.
v^j = m-vector weights of outgoing arcs from hidden units, $j = 1,2,\ldots,h$.
w^j = n-vector weights of incoming arcs to hidden units, $j = 1,2\ldots,h$.
$\sigma(\xi)$ is the monotonically increasing sigmoidal function

$$\sigma(\xi) = 1/(1+e^{-\xi}), \quad (2)$$

and
$\|z\|$ denotes the usual 2-norm, ie. for any vector $z \in \mathbb{R}^n$, $\|z\|^2 = \sum_{i=1}^{n}(z_i^2)$.

Note that the product x^iw^j is to be interpreted as a dot product between the vectors x^i and w^j.

Let us define the error

$$e_\ell^i = S_\ell^i - t_\ell^i, \quad \forall i = 1,2,\ldots,k, \ \forall \ell = 1,2,\ldots,n, \quad (3)$$

where we have defined the n-dimensional vector

$$S^i = \sum_{j=1}^{h}\sigma(x^iw^j)v^j. \quad (4)$$

By applying the chain rule, the components of the gradient of the function $F^h(w,v)$ can be computed efficiently as follows:

$$\frac{\partial F^h(w,v)}{\partial w_q^p} = \sum_{i=1}^{k}\sum_{\ell=1}^{n}[e_\ell^i \times v_\ell^p \times \sigma(x^iw^p)\times (1-\sigma(x^iw^p)) \times x_q^i]$$

$$\frac{\partial F^h(w,v)}{\partial v_q^p} = \sum_{i=1}^{k}[e_q^i \times \sigma(x^iw^p)]$$

for all $p = 1,2,\ldots,h$ and $q = 1,2,\ldots,n$.

A neural network training algorithm such as the backpropagation method [11] will terminate at a stationary point of the function $F^h(w,v)$. Let $(\overline{w},\overline{v}) \in \mathbb{R}^{2n\times h}$ be a point such that $\nabla F^h(\overline{w},\overline{v}) = 0$ and suppose that the network with h hidden units corresponding to this set of weights fails to give a reconstructed image with satisfactory quality. Let us define $F^{h+1}(w,v)$ to be the error function (1) that corresponds to a network with $h+1$ hidden units. Let $w^{h+1} \in \mathbb{R}^n$ be a randomly generated vector and

$$v^{h+1} = -\sum_{i=1}^{k}\sigma(x^iw^{h+1})\overline{e}^i / \sum_{i=1}^{k}\left(\sigma(x^iw^{h+1})\right)^2, \quad (5)$$

where

$$\overline{e}^i = \sum_{j=1}^{h}\sigma(x^i\overline{w}^j)\overline{v}^j - t^i.$$

It can be shown that

$$F^{h+1}(w^{h+1},v^{h+1}) = F^h(\overline{w},\overline{v}) - \left\|\sum_{i=1}^{k}\sigma(x^iw^{h+1})\overline{e}^i)\right\|^2 / \left(2\sum_{i=1}^{k}(\sigma(x^iw^{h+1}))^2\right).$$

The above equation ensures that, if the network with h hidden units gives an error value (cf. Eq. (1)) that is too large, we can always add a new hidden unit to the network and reduce this error. By keeping the weights of the original network and carefully selecting a set of value for the weights on the arcs connecting the new hidden unit to the output units, the value of the error function is guaranteed to decrease even before the new network with $h+1$ hidden units is retrained. The algorithm is summarized below.

1. Set the initial number of hidden units h to 1.
2. Initialize $w^1, v^1 \in \mathbb{R}^n$ randomly.
3. Find a point that minimizes the error function (1). Denote this solution by $(\overline{w},\overline{v})$.
4. If this solution meets a prespecified accuracy, then stop.
5. Add one unit to the hidden layer and pick $w^{h+1} \in \mathbb{R}^n$ randomly and set v^{h+1} according to equation (5). Set $h = h+1$ and use the point $(\overline{w}, w^{h+1}, \overline{v}, v^{h+1})$ as a starting point for minimizing the function (1) for the new expanded network.
6. Go to Step 3.

III. Application to image compression

In this section we report the results obtained from applying our neural network construction described in the previous section on the familiar image of Lena (Figure 1a).

We have implemented the algorithm using FORTRAN language. The program was run on a DECsystem 5000 machine running ULTRIX V4.2A operating system. The original image of 512×512 pixels on a gray scale of 8 bits was subdivided into blocks of 4×4 giving a total of 16,384 patterns available for neural network training and construction. Due to this large number of patterns, it is imperative that a quick converging neural network training algorithm is chosen.

Watrous [12] experimented with two different variants of the quasi-Newton methods namely DFP (Davidon-Fletcher-Powell) and BFGS (Broyden-Fletcher-Goldfarb-Shanno) methods for neural network training. It was shown that BFGS method is more efficient than DFP method and is much more superior than the traditional backpropagation method in terms of the number of floating point operations required. We have selected another variant of the quasi-Newton method for unconstrained minimization to find a local minimum point of the function (1). This method is based on the combination of Symmetric Rank One (SR1) method and BFGS method. We have tested this combined SR1/BFGS method on a wide range of nonlinear optimization problems and found that this new method we used is slightly faster than the straightforward BFGS method [13].

To measure the quality of the reconstructed image, the peak signal to noise ratio (PSNR) of the image is usually computed. The PSNR is defined as

$$\text{PSNR} = 10 \log \left(\frac{k \times n \times (255)^2}{\sum_{i=1}^{k} \sum_{\ell=1}^{n} \left(x_\ell^i - \tilde{t}_\ell^i \right)^2} \right), \quad (6)$$

where $n = m \times m$, and $\tilde{t}_\ell^i = \left(\sum_{j=1}^{h} \sigma(x^i w^j) v^j \right)_\ell$.

We run the program until a network with 8 hidden units had been constructed. Figure 2 shows the progression of the neural network construction algorithm where the total error is plotted against the number of iteration. The figure also shows the number of hidden units in the network. The total numbers of iteration and function evaluations needed by the algorithm SR1/BFGS to find a local minimum point of the error function (1) with $h = 1, 2, \ldots, 8$ are depicted in Figure 3. From this figure, it can be concluded that for most iterations of SR1/BFGS method, only one function evaluation is needed. In our implementation of this quasi-Newton method, an inexact line search procedure is used (for details see [14]) where each time the error function (1) is evaluated, its gradient will also be evaluated. Hence the total number of function evaluations shown in Figure 3 also reflects the total number of gradient evaluation. The line search procedure also ensures that the function value decreases at each iteration.

The PSNR values (cf. Eq. (6)) corresponding to the different number of hidden units are depicted in Figure 4.

The activation value at each of the hidden unit, which is a real number between zero and one, is normally quantized using a small number of bits. Table 1 summarizes the effect of quantizing the hidden unit outputs $\sigma(x^i w^j)$ obtained from the network with 3 hidden units using different number of bits. The column ρ gives the compression ratios while the values in the column ρ' indicate the compression ratio that can be achieved after applying run-length coding [15] on the quantized data. Let us assume that b bits are used for quantization, then the compression ratio ρ is computed using the following equation

$$\rho = \frac{8 \times 512 \times 512}{T_{NN}}, \quad (7)$$

where T_{NN} is the total number of bits required to store the compressed image

$$T_{NN} = \left(\frac{512 \times 512}{m \times m} \times b \times h \right) + (m \times m \times h \times r(b)).$$

The second term in the right hand side of the above equation represents the total number of bits required to store the weights $v^j, j = 1, 2, \ldots h$, where each of the $m \times m$ components of v^j is assumed to be stored as $r(b)$ bits real number. We have set $r(b) = 32$, $h = 3$ and $m = 4$ to compute the compression ratio ρ in Table 1.

No. of Bits	PSNR	ρ	ρ'
2	20.8005 dB	24.01	24.01
3	25.1020 dB	14.08	15.84
4	27.7405 dB	10.58	12.69
5	28.7546 dB	8.48	10.60
6	29.4458 dB	7.07	9.09
7	29.6521 dB	6.06	7.95
8	29.7687 dB	5.31	7.08

Table 1. PSNR and compression ratio from a network with 3 hidden units using various quantization bits.

The reconstructed image of 'Lena' after compression with three hidden units and six quantization bits is shown in Figure 1(b).

IV. Summary

We have described a single hidden layer feedforward neural network construction algorithm and its application to image compression. The compressed image is stored as the activation values of the hidden units. With a small number of hidden units in the network, high compression ratio can be achieved. The neural network construction algorithm we proposed has an attractive feature that each addition of a hidden unit to the network will always improve the reconstructed image quality. This feature allows the user to trade between required image quality and compression ratio. The results from our implementation of the algorithm are promising.

References

[1] G.K. Wallace. (1991) The JPEG still picture compression standard, *Communications of the ACM*, 34:4, 31-44.

[2] D. Gall. (1991) MPEG: a video compression standard for multimedia applications, *Communications of the ACM*, **34:4** , 47-58.

[3] D. Anthony, E. Hines, J. Barham and D. Taylor. (1990) A comparison of image compression by neural networks and principal component analysis. *Proc. International Joint Conference on Neural Networks*, San Diego, I-339-I-344.

[4] L.O. Chua and T. Lin. (1988) A neural network approach to transform image coding. *Int. J. Circuit Theory and Applications,* **16**, 317-324.

[5] T. Li, L. Fang, and K.Q-Q. Li. (1993) Hierarchical classification and vector quantization with neural trees, *Neurocomputing,* **5**, 119-139.

[6] N. Sonehara, M. Kawato, S. Miyake, and K. Nakane. (1989) Image data compression using a neural network model, *Proc. Inter. Joint Conference on Neural Networks*, II-35-II-41.

[7] E. Wan, P. Ning and B. Widrow. (1990) Neural tree structured vector quantization, *Proc. International Joint Conference on Neural Networks*, Washington D.C., II-267-II-270.

[8] G.L. Sicuranza, G. Ramponi and S. Marsi. (1990) Artificial neural network for image compression, *Electronics Letters,* **26:7**, 477-479.

[9] G.W. Cotrell, J.B. Theeten and W. Krauth. (1987) Learning internal representations from gray-scale images: An example of extensional programming. *Procs. Cognitive Science Society Annual Conference*, 461-473.

[10] T. Ash. (1989) Dynamic node creation in backpropagation networks. *Connection Science,* **1:4**, 365-375.

[11] D.E. Rumelhart and J.L. McClelland. (1990) *Parallel Distributed Processing*, MIT Press, Cambridge, Massachusetts.

[12] R.L. Watrous. (1987) Learning algorithm for connectionist networks: Applied gradient method of nonlinear optimization, *Proceedings of IEEE First International Conference on Neural Networks*, II-619-II-627.

[13] P.K.H. Phua and R. Setiono. Combined quasi-Newton updates for unconstrained optimization. Technical Report TR41/92, DISCS. National University of Singapore (1992).

[14] D.F. Shanno and K.H. Phua. (1980) Remark on algorithm 500. *ACM Transaction on Mathematical Software,* **6**, 618-622.

[15] W.K. Pratt. (1978) *Digital Image Processing.* New York: John Wiley & Sons.

Figure 1a. The original image of Lena.

Figure 1b. The reconstructed image of Lena.

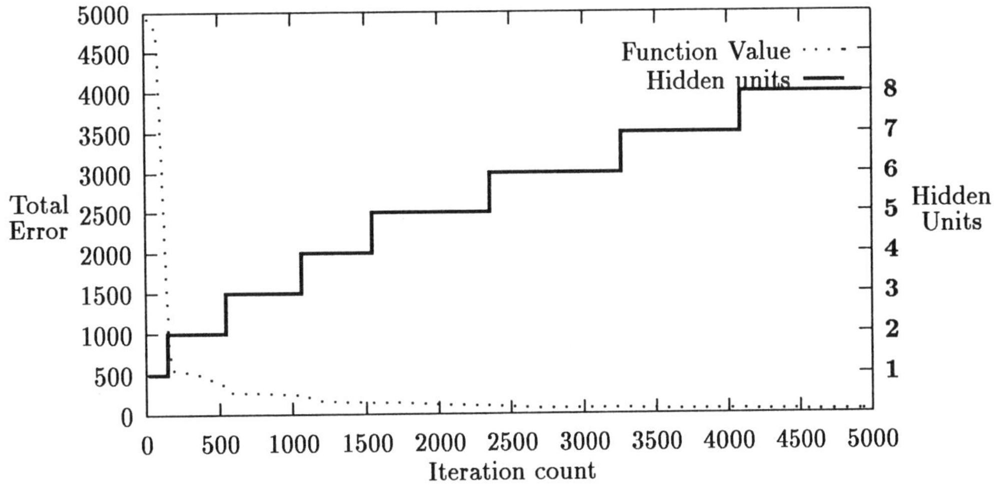

Figure 2. Total error vs. Iteration counts.
The bold line shows the number of hidden units.

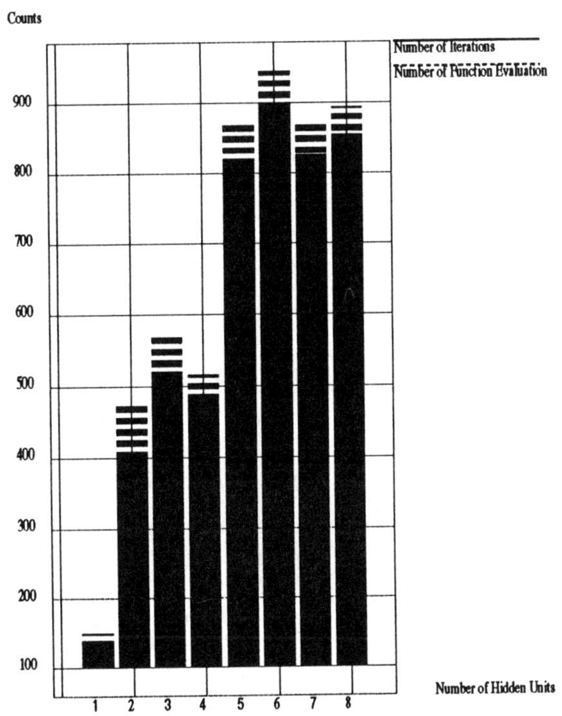

Figure 3: Number of iterations and function evaluations required to find a local minimum of the error function (1) for the network with h = 1, 2, ... 8 hidden units.

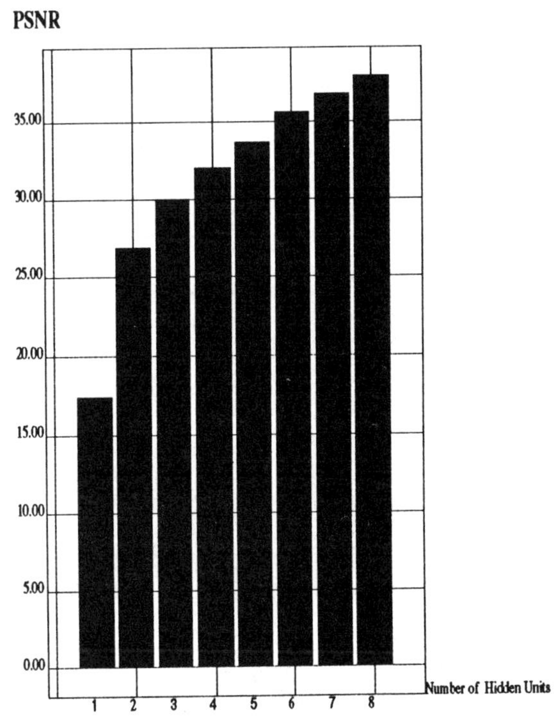

Figure 4: The Peak Signal to Noise Ratio obtained from network with h = 1, 2, ... 8 hidden units.

MODEL REFERENCE ADAPTIVE CONTROL OF NONLINEAR DYNAMICAL SYSTEMS USING MULTILAYER NEURAL NETWORKS

S. Jagannathan, F. L. Lewis, and O. Pastravanu*
Automation and Robotics Research Institute
7300 Jack Newell Blvd. South
Fort Worth, Texas 76118
(817) 794-5957

*Visiting Professor from Technical University of Iasi,
Str, Horia 7-9, 6600 Iasi, Romania.

Abstract

A multilayer discrete-time neural net (NN) controller is presented for the model reference adaptive control of a class of multi-input multi-output (MIMO) dynamical systems. No initial learning phase is needed and the tracking error between the output of the nonlinear plant and a linear model converges within a very short time. This weight tuning paradigm is based on the well-known delta rule but includes a modification to the learning rate parameter plus a correction term. It guarantees tracking as well as bounded NN weights in non-ideal situations, so that a persistency of excitation condition on the internal signals is not needed. Simulation results are presented in order to verify the theoretical conclusions.

1. INTRODUCTION

Neural Networks have been increasingly employed for the adaptive control of nonlinear systems as these networks do not require apriori knowledge of the system to be controlled. The NN-based adaptive control of nonlinear systems is investigated by many researchers both in continuous and discrete-time [Narendra & Parthasarathy, 90; Chen & Khalil, 91; Jagannathan & Lewis, 93a]. Specifically, some results exists for the direct adaptive control of nonlinear discrete-time systems that guarantee tracking performance through Lyapunov based approach [Jagannathan & Lewis, 93a]. On the other hand, an indirect model reference adaptive controller design with NN having multilayers for discrete-time nonlinear systems is treated in [Narendra & Parthasarathy, 90].

Persistent problems that remain to be adequately addressed in using discrete-time neural nets for direct model reference adaptive control (MRAC) include ad hoc controller structures and the inability to guarantee satisfactory performance of the system. Uncertainty on how to initialize the NN weights leads to the necessity for preliminary off-line tuning. In addition, the backpropagation tuning algorithm requires the evaluation of sensitivity derivatives along the network signal paths which is highly time consuming, and often impossible in closed-loop uncertain systems.

Research Supported by the NSF Grant IRI-9216545 and EPRI Grant RP8030-09.

To confront all these issues head on, in our previous paper [Jagannthan & Lewis, 93a] a novel learning scheme is investigated for a multilayer discrete-time NN whose weights are tuned on-line with no learning phase needed. The weight tuning mechanisms guarantee convergence of the NN weights when initialized at zero, even though there do not exist 'ideal' weights such that the NN perfectly reconstructs a certain required function.

In this paper, the results presented in our previous paper is extended to MRAC of a class of discrete-time systems so that PE is not needed. The controller ensures good tracking performance, as shown through a Lyapunov's stability approach, so that convergence to a stable solution is guaranteed. It is found that the maximum permissible tuning rate for the NN weight tuning decreases as the NN size increases; this is a major drawback. Therefore it is demonstrated that a projection algorithm can easily correct the problem allowing larger nets to be more quickly tuned. Simulation results are given to demonstrate the theoretical conclusions.

2. BACKGROUND

Let R denote the real numbers, R^n denote the real n-vectors, $R^{m \times n}$ the real m x n matrices. Let S be a compact simply-connected set of R^n. With maps $f : S \to R^k$, define $C^k(S)$ as the space such that f is continuous. We denote by $\|.\|$ any suitable vector norm. Given a matrix $A = [a_{ij}]$, $A \in R^{n \times m}$ the Frobenius norm is defined by

$$\| A \|_F^2 = \mathrm{tr}(A^T A) = \sum_{i,j} a_{ij}^2,$$

with tr () the trace operation. The Frobenius norm $\| A \|_F$, denoted by $\| A \|$ throughout this paper until unless specified explicitly, is nothing but the vector 2-norm over the space defined by stacking the matrix columns into a vector, so that it is compatible with the vector 2-norm, that is, $\| Ax \| \le \| A \| . \| x \|$.

2.1 Neural Networks

A general function $f(x) \in C^k(S)$ can be written, according to the Stone-Weirstrass Theorem [Park & Sandberg, 91], using a three-layer NN as

$$f(x) = W^T \sigma (V^T x) + \varepsilon(k), \qquad (2.1)$$

with $\varepsilon(k)$ a small neural net functional reconstruction error vector, $\sigma(.)$ be the hidden layer activation function and the input and output layer activation functions considered to be linear. If there exists N_2 and constant ideal weights W and V such that $\varepsilon = 0$ for all $x \in S$, then f(x) is said to be in the functional range of the neural net. In general, given a constant real number $\varepsilon_N \geq 0$, f(x) is within ε_N of the neural net range if there exists N_2 and constant weights so that for all $x \in R^n$, equation (2.1) holds with $\| \varepsilon \| \leq \varepsilon_N$.

In general, equation (2.1) can be rewritten for an n-layer NN as

$$f(x) = W_n^T \varphi_n[W_{n-1}^T \varphi_{n-1}(.....\varphi_1(x(k))] + \varepsilon(k), \qquad (2.2)$$

where W_n, W_{n-1} ,...., W_2, W_1 are the constant ideal weights and $\varphi_{n-1}(.)$, $\varphi_{n-2}(.)$,...., $\varphi_2(.)$, $\varphi_1(.)$ denote vectors of activation functions for the n - 1 hidden layers, with $\varphi_n(.)$ the vector of activation functions for the output layer. For notational convenience, the vector of activation functions of the input layer at the instant k is denoted as $\varphi_1(k) = \varphi(x(k))$. Then, the vectors of hidden and output layer activation functions are denoted by

$$\varphi_{m+1}(k) = \varphi(W_m^T \varphi_m(k)); \; \forall m = 1, ..., n-1. \qquad (2.3)$$

2.2 Dynamics of an MIMO System

Consider a mnth-order multi-input and multi-output discrete-time nonlinear system, to be controlled, given by

$$x_1(k+1) = x_2(k)$$

$$\vdots$$

$$x_{n-1}(k+1) = x_n(k)$$

$$x_n(k+1) = f(x(k)) + u(k) + d(k), \; y(k) = x_1(k), \qquad (2.4)$$

with state $x(k) = [x_1^T(k), .., x_n^T(k)]^T$ with $x_i(k) \in R^m$, control input $u(k) \in R^m$, output $y(k) \in R^m$, and $d(k) \in R^m$ a disturbance vector acting on the system at the instant k with $\| d(k) \| \leq d_M$ a known constant. A reference system is chosen as

$$\bar{x}(k+1) = \bar{A}\bar{x}(k) + \bar{B}r(k), \bar{y}(k) = \bar{x}_1(k), \qquad (2.5)$$

with state $\bar{x}(k) = [\bar{x}_1^T(k), ..., \bar{x}_n^T(k)]^T$, and $\bar{A}$ and $\bar{B}$ are appropriately dimensioned matrices. $\bar{A}$ and $\bar{B}$ are selected so that an asymptotically stable reference model is obtained. A bounded reference input $r(k) \in R^m$ is selected so that the output of the plant $y(k) \in R^m$ follows the output of the model $\bar{y}(k) \in R^m$ under the assumption that the plant is controllable and the state vector of the plant is accessible. In other words, the aim is to determine the control input u(k) for all $k \geq k_0$ so that

$$\lim_{k \to \infty} \| y(k) - \bar{y}(k) \| \leq \delta, \qquad (2.6)$$

for some specified constant $\delta \geq 0$.

Define the tracking error as

$$e(k) = y(k) - \bar{y}(k) = x_1(k) - \bar{x}_1(k), \qquad (2.7)$$

and select the control input u(k) as

$$u(k) = -\hat{f}(x(k)) + \bar{A}\bar{x}(k) + \bar{B}r(k) + k_v e(k+n-1), \qquad (2.8)$$

with the asymptotically stable gain matrix k_v, and $\hat{f}(x(k))$ an estimate of $f(x(k))$. Then, the closed-loop error system becomes

$$e(k+n) = k_v e(k+n-1) + \tilde{f}(x(k)) + d(k), \qquad (2.9)$$

where the functional estimation error is given by

$$\tilde{f}(x(k)) = f(x(k)) - \hat{f}(x(k)). \qquad (2.10)$$

Denoting $\bar{k} = k + n - 1$, and changing variables as $k = \bar{k}$,, then (2.9) can be rewritten as

$$e(k+1) = k_v e(k) + \tilde{f}(x(k)) + d(k). \qquad (2.11)$$

This is an error system wherein the tracking error is driven by the functional estimation error. In this paper, equation (2.11) is used to focus on selecting NN tuning algorithms that guarantee the stability of the tracking error e(k).

3. NN CONTROLLER DESIGN

Approaches such as σ-modification [Polycarpou & Ioannu, 91], or e-modification [Narendra & Annaswamy, 87] are available for the robust adaptive control of continuous systems wherein the persistency of excitation condition is not needed. However, modification to the standard weight tuning mechanisms in discrete-time without the necessity of PE is, to our knowledge, yet to be investigated in the NN control community. In this paper an approach similar to e-modification is derived for discrete-time model reference adaptive control of dynamical systems.

Assume that there exist some constant ideal weights W_n, .., W_2 and W_1 for a n-layer NN so that the nonlinear function in (2.4) can be written as (2.2) where $\| \varepsilon(k) \| < \varepsilon_N$, with the bounding constant ε_N known. Unless the net is "minimal", suitable 'ideal' weights may not be unique. The best weights may then be defined as those which minimize the supremum norm over S of $\varepsilon(k)$. This issue is not a major concern here, as it is needed to know only the existence of such ideal weights; their actual values are not required. For notational convenience define the matrix of all the ideal weights as $Z = \begin{bmatrix} W_n \\ \cdot \\ \cdot \\ W_1 \end{bmatrix}$, with padding by zeros as required for dimensional consistency. Then, some bounding assumptions can be stated.

Assumption 1

The ideal weights are bounded by known positive values so that

$\| W_1 \| \leq W_{1max}$, $\| W_2 \| \leq W_{2max}$,..,

$\| W_n \| \leq W_{nmax}$ or $\| Z \| \leq Z_{max}$. ■

3.1 Structure of the NN Controller and Error System Dynamics

Define the NN functional estimate by

$$\hat{f}(x(k)) = \hat{W}_n^T(k)\varphi_n(\ldots\hat{W}_2^T(k)\varphi_2(\hat{W}_1^T(k)\varphi_1(x(k)))) \tag{3.1}$$

with $\hat{W}_n(k)$,.., $\hat{W}_2(k)$ and $\hat{W}_1(k)$ the current values of the weights. The vector of input layer activation functions is given by $\hat{\varphi}_1(k) = \varphi_1(k) = \varphi(x(k))$. Then the vector of activation functions of the hidden and output layer with the actual weights at the instant k is denotedby

$$\hat{\varphi}_{m+1}(k) = \varphi(\hat{W}_m^T\hat{\varphi}_m(k)); \forall m = 1, ..., n-1. \tag{3.2}$$

Fact 2

The activation functions are bounded by known positive values so that

$\| \hat{\varphi}_1(k) \| \leq \varphi_{1max}$, $\| \hat{\varphi}_2(k) \| \leq \varphi_{2max}$, ..,

and $\| \hat{\varphi}_n(k) \| \leq \varphi_{nmax}$. ■

The error in the weights or weight estimation errors are defined by

$$\tilde{W}_n(k) = W_n - \hat{W}_n(k), .., \tilde{W}_2(k) = W_2 - \hat{W}_2(k),$$
$$\tilde{W}_1(k) = W_1 - \hat{W}_1(k), \tilde{Z}(k) = Z(k) - \hat{Z}(k), \tag{3.3}$$

where $\hat{Z}(k) = \begin{bmatrix} \hat{W}_n \\ \cdot \\ \hat{W}_1 \end{bmatrix}$ and the hidden-layer output errors are defined as

$$\tilde{\varphi}_2(k) = \varphi_2 - \hat{\varphi}_2(k),.., \tilde{\varphi}_n(k) = \varphi_n - \hat{\varphi}_n(k). \tag{3.4}$$

Select the control input u(k) in (2.4) to be

$$u(k) = -\hat{W}_n^T(k)\hat{\varphi}_n(k) + \bar{A}\bar{x}(k) + \bar{B}r(k) + k_v e(k), \tag{3.5}$$

where the functional estimate (3.1) is provided by a n-layer NN and denoted in (3.5) by $\hat{W}_n^T(k)\hat{\varphi}_n(k)$. Then, the closed-loop tracking error dynamics become

$$e(k+1) = k_v e(k) + e_i(k) + W_n^T\tilde{\varphi}_n(k) + \varepsilon(k) + d(k), \tag{3.6}$$

where the identification error is given by

$$e_i(k) = \tilde{W}_n^T(k)\hat{\varphi}_n(k). \tag{3.7}$$

The next step is to determine the weight updates so that the tracking performance of the closed-loop error dynamics is guaranteed.

3.2 Weight Updates for Guaranteed Tracking Performance

A novel NN weight tuning paradigm that guarantees the stability of the closed-loop system (3.6) is presented in this section. It is required to demonstrate that the tracking error e(k) is suitably small and that the NN weights $\hat{W}_i(k)$; $\forall i = 1,..., n$ remain bounded, for then the control u(k) is bounded.

In this paper, an improved algorithm discussed for a STR/MRAC in [Jagannathan & Lewis, 93b] is extended to a multilayer discrete-time NN so that PE is not needed. In fact, the following theorem shows the tuning algorithm that overcomes the need for PE in the case of a multilayer NN.

Theorem 3.1

Let the reference input r(k) be bounded and the NN functional reconstruction error and the disturbance bounds, ε_N, d_M, respectively, be known constants. Consider the weight tuning provided for the input and hidden layers as

$$\hat{W}_i(k+1) = \hat{W}_i(k) - \alpha_i\hat{\varphi}_i(k)\hat{y}_i^T(k) - \Gamma \| I - \alpha_i\hat{\varphi}_i(k)\hat{\varphi}_i^T(k) \| \hat{W}_i(k), \quad \forall i = 1, ..., n-1, \tag{3.8}$$

and the weight update for the output layer is given by

$$\hat{W}_n(k+1) = \hat{W}_n(k) + \alpha_n\hat{\varphi}_n(k)e^T(k+1) - \Gamma \| I - \alpha_n\hat{\varphi}_n(k)\hat{\varphi}_n^T(k) \| \hat{W}_n(k), \tag{3.9}$$

with $\Gamma > 0$ a design parameter. Then, the tracking error e(k) and the NN weight estimates $\hat{W}_i(k)$; $\forall i = 1, ..., n$ are globally uniformly ultimately bounded provided the following conditions hold:

(1) $\alpha_i\varphi_{imax}^2 \; < 2, \forall i = 1, ..., n-1,$
$\qquad\qquad < 1, i = n,$ (3.10)

(2) $0 < \Gamma < 1$, (3.11)

(3) $k_{vmax} < \frac{1}{\sqrt{\sigma}}$, (3.12)

where σ is given by

$$\sigma = \frac{1}{\eta}[1 + \Gamma^2 \| I - \alpha_n\hat{\varphi}_n(k)\hat{\varphi}_n^T(k) \|^2 + 2\alpha_3\Gamma\varphi_{nmax}^2 \| I - \alpha_3\hat{\varphi}_n(k)\hat{\varphi}_n^T(k) \|] \quad (3.13)$$

with η in (3.13) given by

$$\eta = \frac{1}{(1 - \alpha_n\varphi_{nmax}^2)}. \quad (3.14)$$

Proof: Select the Lyapunov function candidate

$$J = e^T(k)e(k) + \sum_{i=1}^{n} \frac{1}{\alpha_i}\mathrm{tr}(\widetilde{W}_i^T(k)\widetilde{W}_i(k)) \quad (3.15)$$

Considering the input and hidden (3.8), output (3.9) layer weight updates as well as the tracking error dynamics (3.6), using these in the first difference of (3.15) and completing the squares for $\| \widetilde{Z}(k) \|$, one may obtain

$$\Delta J \le -[1 - \eta k_{vmax}^2][\| e(k) \|^2 - \frac{2\gamma k_{vmax}}{[1 - \eta k_{vmax}^2]} \| e(k) \| - \frac{(\rho + c_0 Z_{max}^2)}{[1 - \eta k_{vmax}^2]}]$$

$$- \sum_{i=1}^{n-1} [2 - \alpha_i\hat{\varphi}_i^T(k)\hat{\varphi}_i(k)] \| \widetilde{W}_i^T(k)\hat{\varphi}_i(k) - \frac{[(1 - \alpha_i\hat{\varphi}_i^T(k)\hat{\varphi}_i(k)) - \Gamma \| I - \alpha_i\hat{\varphi}_i(k)\hat{\varphi}_i^T(k) \|]}{[2 - \alpha_i\hat{\varphi}_i^T(k)\hat{\varphi}_i(k)]} W_i^T\hat{\varphi}_i(k) \|^2 - [1 - \alpha_n\hat{\varphi}_n^T(k)\hat{\varphi}_n(k)] \| e_i(k) - \frac{[k_v e(k) + (\alpha_n\hat{\varphi}_n^T(k)\hat{\varphi}_n(k) + \Gamma \| I - \alpha_n\hat{\varphi}_n(k)\hat{\varphi}_n^T(k) \|)}{[1 - \alpha_n\hat{\varphi}_n^T(k)\hat{\varphi}_n(k)]} (W_n^T\widetilde{\varphi}_n(k) + \varepsilon(k) + d(k))] \|^2$$

$$- \Gamma(2 - \Gamma)c_{min}[\| \widetilde{Z}(k) \| - \frac{(1 - \Gamma)}{(2 - \Gamma)}\frac{c_{max}}{c_{min}} Z_{max}]^2, \quad (3.16)$$

where

$$\gamma = \eta(W_{nmax}\widetilde{\varphi}_{nmax} + \varepsilon_N + d_M) + \Gamma \| I - \alpha_n\hat{\varphi}_n(k)\hat{\varphi}_n^T(k) \| \hat{\varphi}_{nmax}W_{nmax}, \quad (3.17)$$

$$\rho = [\eta(W_{nmax}\widetilde{\varphi}_{nmax} + \varepsilon_N + d_M) + 2\Gamma \| I - \alpha_n\hat{\varphi}_n(k)\hat{\varphi}_n^T(k) \| \hat{\varphi}_{nmax} W_{nmax}](W_{nmax}\widetilde{\varphi}_{nmax} + \varepsilon_N + d_M) + \sum_{i=1}^{n-1} [(\alpha_i\hat{\varphi}_{imax}^2 + 2\Gamma \| I - \alpha_i\hat{\varphi}_i(k)\hat{\varphi}_i^T(k) \|) + \frac{[(1 - \alpha_i\hat{\varphi}_{imax}^2) - \Gamma \| I - \alpha_i\hat{\varphi}_i(k)\hat{\varphi}_i^T(k) \|]^2}{(2 - \alpha_i\hat{\varphi}_{imax}^2)}] \hat{\varphi}_{imax}^2 W_{imax}^2, \quad (3.18)$$

$$c_0 = \frac{c_{max}}{c_{min}}\frac{1}{(2 - \Gamma)}[(1 - \Gamma)^2 c_{max} + \Gamma^2(2 - \Gamma)c_{min}], \quad (3.19)$$

with c_{max} and c_{min} denote the maximum and minimum singular value of the diagonal matrix whose elements are given by

$$\frac{1}{\alpha_i} \| I - \alpha_i\,\hat{\varphi}_i(k)\,\hat{\varphi}_i^T(k) \|, \forall i = 1, .., n. \quad (3.20)$$

Then $\Delta J \le 0$ as long as (3.10) through (3.12) hold and the quadratic term for e(k) in (3.16) is positive, which is guaranteed when

$$\| e(k) \| > \frac{1}{(1 - \eta k_{vmax}^2)}[\gamma k_{vmax} + \sqrt{\gamma^2 k_{vmax}^2 + [\rho + c_0 Z_{max}^2](1 - \eta k_{vmax}^2)}], \quad (3.21)$$

with γ and ρ in (3.21) are given in (3.17) and (3.18) respectively.

Similarly completing the squares for $\| e(k) \|$ in (3.16), the first difference is

$$\Delta J \le -[1 - \eta k_{vmax}^2][\| e(k) \| - \frac{\gamma k_{vmax}}{[1 - \eta k_{vmax}^2]}]^2 - \Gamma[(2 - \Gamma)c_{min} \| \widetilde{Z}(k) \|^2 - 2(1 - \Gamma)c_{max} \| \widetilde{Z}(k) \| Z_{max} - (\Gamma c_{max} Z_{max}^2 + \frac{\gamma^2 k_{vmax}^2}{(1 - \eta k_{vmax}^2)} + \rho)]$$

$$- \sum_{i=1}^{n-1} [2 - \alpha_i\hat{\varphi}_i^T(k)\hat{\varphi}_i(k)] \| \widetilde{W}_i^T(k)\hat{\varphi}_i(k) - \frac{[(1 - \alpha_i\hat{\varphi}_i^T(k)\hat{\varphi}_i(k)) - \Gamma \| I - \alpha_i\hat{\varphi}_i(k)\hat{\varphi}_i^T(k) \|]}{[2 - \alpha_i\hat{\varphi}_i^T(k)\hat{\varphi}_i(k)]} W_i^T\hat{\varphi}_i(k) \|^2 - [1 - \alpha_n\hat{\varphi}_n^T(k)\hat{\varphi}_n(k)] \| e_i(k) - \frac{[k_v e(k) + (\alpha_n\hat{\varphi}_n^T(k)\hat{\varphi}_n(k) + \Gamma \| I - \alpha_n\hat{\varphi}_n(k)\hat{\varphi}_n^T(k) \|)}{[1 - \alpha_n\hat{\varphi}_n^T(k)\hat{\varphi}_n(k)]} (W_n^T\widetilde{\varphi}_n(k) + \varepsilon(k) + d(k))] \|^2 \quad (3.22)$$

where ρ is given in (3.18). Then $\Delta J \le 0$ as long as (3.10) through (3.12) hold and the quadratic term for $\| \widetilde{Z}(k) \|$ in (3.22) is positive, which is guaranteed when

$$\| \widetilde{Z}(k) \| > \frac{\Gamma(1 - \Gamma)c_{max}Z_{max}}{\Gamma(2 - \Gamma)} + \frac{\sqrt{\Gamma^2(1 - \Gamma)^2 c_{max}Z_{max}^2 + \Gamma(2 - \Gamma)c_{min}\theta}}{\Gamma(2 - \Gamma)}, \quad (3.23)$$

where

$$\theta = [\Gamma^2 c_{max}Z_{max}^2 + \frac{\gamma^2 k_{vmax}^2}{(1 - \eta k_{vmax}^2)} + \rho]. \quad (3.24)$$

From (3.21) or (3.23), it can be concluded that the tracking error e(k) and the error in weight estimates $\widetilde{Z}(k)$ are globally uniformly ultimately bounded. ■

Note that the NN reconstruction error bound ε_N and the bounded disturbances d_M increase the bounds on $\| e(k) \|$ and $\| \widetilde{Z}(k) \|$ in a very interesting way. Note that small tracking error bounds may be achieved by placing the closed-loop poles inside the unit circle and near the origin through the selection of the largest eigenvalue, k_{vmax}. On the other hand, the NN weight error estimates are fundamentally bounded by Z_{max}, the known bound on the ideal weights Z. The parameter Γ offers a design tradeoff between the relative eventual magnitudes of $\| e(k) \|$ and $\| \widetilde{Z}(k) \|$; a smaller Γ yields a smaller $\| e(k) \|$ and a larger $\| \widetilde{Z}(k) \|$, and vice versa.

It is important to note that the problem of initializing the net weights (referred to as symmetric breaking [Rumelhart et. al., 90]) occurring in other techniques in the literature does not arise, since when $\widehat{W}_i(0)$; $\forall i = 1,...n$ is taken as zero (with nonzero thresholds) the PD term of $k_v e(k)$ stabilizes the plant, on an interim basis, for instance in certain restricted class of nonlinear systems. Thus, the NN controller requires no learning phase.

3.3 Projection Algorithm

The theorem reveals that the delta rule based update tuning mechanisms have a major drawback. Since $\widehat{\varphi}_i(k) \in R^{N_{pi}}$, with N_p the number of hidden-layer neurons in the ith layer and the maximum value of each hidden-node output in the ith layer is taken as unity (as for the sigmoid), then the bounds on the adaptation gain in order to assure stability of the closed-loop system are given by

$$0 < \alpha_i < \frac{2}{N_p}, \ \forall i = 1, ..., n-1,$$
$$0 < \alpha_i < \frac{1}{N_p}, \ i = n. \tag{3.25}$$

In other words, the upper bound on the adaptation gain at each layer for the case of delta rule decreases with an increase in the number of hidden-layer nodes in that particular layer, so that learning must slow down for guaranteed performance. This behavior has been noted in the literature [Mpitsos & Burton, 92; Kung et. al, 91] but never to our knowledge explained.

This major drawback can be easily overcome by modifying the update rule at each layer using a projection algorithm [Astrom & Wittenmark, 89]. To wit, replace the constant adaptation gain at each layer by

$$\alpha_i = \frac{\xi_i}{\zeta_i + \| \widehat{\varphi}_i(k) \|^2}, \ \forall i = 1, ..., n \tag{3.26}$$

where

$$\zeta_i > 0, \ \forall i = 1, ..., n \tag{3.27}$$

and

$$0 < \xi_i < 2, \ \forall i = 1, ..., n-1$$

$$0 < \xi_i < 1, \ \forall i = n, \tag{3.28}$$

are constants. Note that ξ_i, $\forall i = 1, ..., n$ is now the new adaptation gain at each layer and it is always true that

$$\frac{\xi_i}{\zeta_i + \| \widehat{\varphi}_i(k) \|^2} \| \widehat{\varphi}_i(k) \|^2 < 2, \ \forall i = 1, ..., n-1$$
$$< 1, \ \forall i = n, \tag{3.29}$$

hence guaranteeing (3.10) for every N_p at each layer.

From the bounds indicated for the adaptation gains in both (3.10) and (3.29), it is interesting to note that the upper bound on the adaptation gains for the input and hidden layers is 2 whereas for the output layer the upper bound is given by 1. It appears that the hidden layers act as pattern extractors [Rumelhart et. al., 90]. In other words, the hidden layers of a multilayer NN are employed for the identification of the nonlinear plant and the output layer is used for controlling the plant.

4. SIMULATION RESULTS

In order to illustrate the performance of the NN controller, a discrete-time nonlinear system is considered and the objective is to control this MIMO system by using the improved NN controller. it is shown that the improved weight tuning mechanism with the projection algorithm makes the NN weights bounded, and can allow fast tuning even for large NN.

Note that the NN controllers derived herein require no a priori knowledge of the dynamics of the nonlinear system, not even the structure of the system being controlled, unlike conventional adaptive control, nor is any learning phase needed.

Consider the first order multi-input multi-output discrete-time nonlinear system described by

$$\begin{bmatrix} x_1(k+1) \\ x_2(k+1) \end{bmatrix} = \begin{bmatrix} \dfrac{x_2(k)}{1 + x_1^2(k)} \\ \dfrac{x_1(k)}{1 + x_1^2(k)} \end{bmatrix} + \begin{bmatrix} u_1(k) \\ u_2(k) \end{bmatrix},$$
$$y(k) = \begin{bmatrix} y_1(k) \\ y_2(k) \end{bmatrix} = \begin{bmatrix} x_1(k) \\ x_2(k) \end{bmatrix}. \tag{4.1}$$

The objective is to track the output of the linear stable reference model given by

$$\begin{bmatrix} \overline{x}_1(k+1) \\ \overline{x}_2(k+1) \end{bmatrix} = \begin{bmatrix} 0.6 & 0.2 \\ 0.1 & -0.8 \end{bmatrix} \begin{bmatrix} \overline{x}_1(k) \\ \overline{x}_2(k) \end{bmatrix} + \begin{bmatrix} r_1(k) \\ r_2(k) \end{bmatrix},$$
$$\overline{y}(k) = \begin{bmatrix} \overline{y}_1(k) \\ \overline{y}_2(k) \end{bmatrix} = \begin{bmatrix} \overline{x}_1(k) \\ \overline{x}_2(k) \end{bmatrix}, \tag{4.2}$$

where $r_1(k)$ and $r_2(k)$ are the reference inputs.

The elements in the diagonal gain matrix were chosen as $k_v = \begin{bmatrix} 0.1 & 0 \\ 0 & 0.1 \end{bmatrix}$ and a sampling interval of 10 msec was considered. A three-layer NN was selected with 2 input, 6 hidden and 2 output nodes. Sigmoidal activation functions were employed in all the nodes in the hidden layer. The initial conditions for the plant and the model were chosen to be $[2, -2]^T$ and $[0.1, 0.6]^T$ respectively. The weights were initialized to zero with a initial threshold value of 3.0. No learning is performed initially to train the networks.

The response of the NN controller with weight tuning in (3.8) and (3.9) and (3.26) is illustrated in Figure 4.1. The design parameters are selected as $\xi_1 = \xi_2 = 1.0$, $\xi_3 = 0.7$ with $\zeta_1, \zeta_2, \zeta_3$ chosen as 0.001. The parameter Γ is selected to be 0.01. Note that with the developed weight tuning the weights are guaranteed to be bounded without the need of the PE condition.

5. CONCLUSIONS

A multilayer neural net controller was presented for the model reference adaptive control of nonlinear dynamical systems based on the well-known delta rule. The NN offers guaranteed performance without the persistency of excitation condition on internal signals. In addition, it was found that the adaptation gain in the case of the delta rule at each layer must decrease with an increase in the number of hidden-layer neurons in that layer so that learning must slow down for large NN.

The constant learning rate parameters employed in these weight tuning updates have to be modified to obtain a projection algorithm so that the learning rate is independent of the number of hidden-layer neurons. At low adaptation gains, as expected, a smooth and slow convergence was observed with a slight degradation in tracking performance. On the other hand at large adaptation gains, oscillatory behavior was seen with a good tracking performance and faster convergence.

REFERENCES

Astrom, K, J., & B. Wittenmark (1989), Adaptive control, Addison-Wesley Company, Reading Massachusetts.

Chen, F., & Khalil, K., H. (1992), Adaptive control of nonlinear systems using neural networks, International Journal of Control, 55(6), 1299-1317.

Jagannathan, S., & Lewis, F. L. (1993a), Multilayer discrete-time neural network controller with guaranteed performance, Submitted to IEEE Trans. on Neural Networks.

Jagannathan, S., & Lewis, F. L. (1993b), Robust STR/MRAC for a class of Discrete-time Dynamical Systems", Submitted to Automatica.

Kung, S. Y., Diamantras, K., Mao, W. D., and Taur, J. S. (1991), Generalized perceptron networks with nonlinear discriminant functions, Neural Network Theory and Applications, Edited by Mammone & Zeevi, Academic Press Inc., San Diego, 245-279.

Mpitsos, G. J., & Burton. Jr., R. M. (1992), Convergence and Divergence in Neural Networks: Processing of Chaos and Biological Analogy, Neural Networks, 5, 605-625.

Narendra, K. S., & Annaswamy, A. M. (1987), A new adaptive law for robust adaptation without persistent adaptation", IEEE Trans. Automatic Control, AC-32(2), 134-145.

Narendra, K. S., & Parthasarathy, K. (1990), Identification and control of dynamical systems using neural networks, IEEE Trans. Neural Networks, 1, 4-27.

Park, J., & Sandberg, I. W. (1991), Universal approximation using radial-basis-function networks, Neural Computation, 3, pp. 246-257.

Polycarpou, M., & Ioannu, P. A. (1991), Identification and control using neural network models:design and stability analysis", Tech. Report 91-09-01, Dept. Elect. Engg. Sys., Univ. S. California.

Rumelhart, D. E., Hinton, G. E., & Williams, R. J. (1990), Learning internal representations by error propagation, Readings in Machine Learning, Edited by J. W., Shavlik et.al., Morgan Kaufmann Publishers Inc., (pp. 115-137).

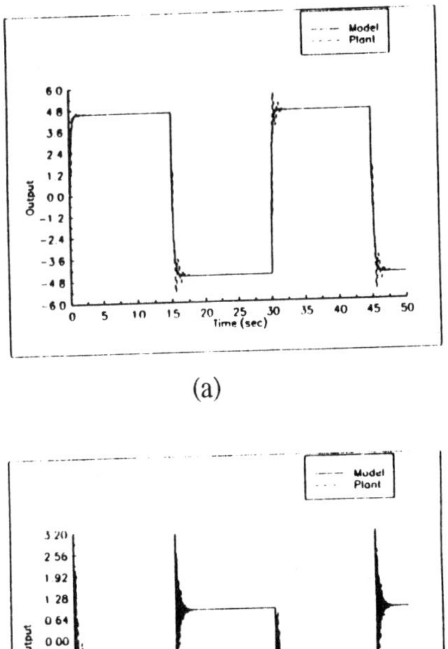

(a)

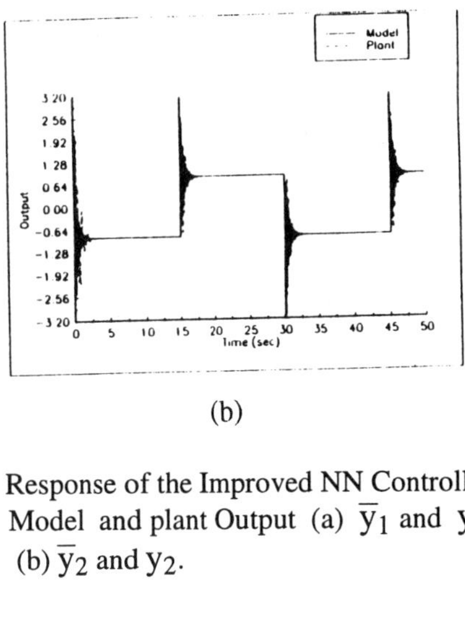

(b)

Figure 4.1: Response of the Improved NN Controller. Model and plant Output (a) $\bar{y}_1$ and y_1 (b) $\bar{y}_2$ and y_2.

A NEURAL NETWORK FOR ANALOGICAL REASONING

by: Yehuda Salu.
Department of Physics and CSTEA. Howard university, Washington DC, 20059

ABSTRACT: Analogical reasoning is one of the fundamental mental processes. It is a multi-step procedure that involves retrieval and manipulation of stored information, and generation of new inferences. Presented here is a model neural network, that encodes and stores information, so that it can be easily accessed in analogical reasoning processes. Learning rules that the network uses for incorporating new inferences are formulated. The interactions between the network and an external controller, that controls the execution of the various steps of the analogical reasoning process, are described, and an example that illustrates how these principles operate in a typical analogical reasoning problem is given. Some of the learning rules that the network employs are different from those currently utilized in other connectionist models of the brain. Whether the brain really employs these new learning rules is an intriguing open question.

1. INTRODUCTION

1.1 ANALOGIES

Since ancient times, humans have been relying on analogies to guide their reactions to the environment. Old scriptures from different cultures contain analogies, that offer insights to given situations based on previously-experienced unrelated events. Analogies are commonly used, consciously and subconsciously, in a variety of mental activities, and they are one of the tools that AI employs in problem solving. One dictionary definition of analogy is: "inference that if two or more things agree with one another in some respects they will probably agree in others." (1). Another definition, aimed at the utilization of analogies by machines, states: "Analogy is a **mapping** between elements of a **source** domain and a **target** domain,.... Analogy becomes useful in some context when a reasoner is familiar with the source, and can map familiar elements or relations from the source into unfamiliar (or unknown) elements or relations in the target. These mapped elements are **analogical inferences**..." (2).

There are many forms of reasoning by analogy, but they all consist of the same three basic steps: First, gaining access to an (appropriate) analog; second, mapping some part of the information from that analog source to the target; and third, the side effects of analogical reasoning in terms of the production of more general rules and representations (3).

1.2 KNOWLEDGE REPRESENTATION

These three steps are operations on a data structure whose elements may be regarded as having two roles: concepts and factors. **Concepts consist of factors**. A factor may belong to several concepts. A concept may be a factor of other concepts. A data structure that consists of concepts and factors can be represented by a layered semantic network. This report introduces one such network. The nodes of the network represent factors and concepts. The arcs of the network connect pairs of nodes; an arc from node **A** in a lower layer to node **B** in a higher layer indicates that **A** is a factor of **B**.

1.2.1 BASIC FACTORS: **Basic factors** are innate to the system. There are two kinds of basic factors; basic features and basic relations. A **basic feature** cannot be decomposed into other factors. It is represented by a node that can only be activated by causes from the outside of the network. A **basic relation** is represented by a node that can be activated by a combination of other nodes, but the specification of that combination is pre-determined. For example, in a network that models the visual system, a retinal rod cell is a basic feature. It can only be activated by light from the outside. A complex cell in the primary visual cortex, that responds to a light bar in a specific orientation, is a basic relation. It is pre-wired to respond to a specific combination of light points. There are, presumably,

0-7803-1901-X/94 $4.00 ©1994 IEEE

other neurons that represent basic relations, such as 'spatial-sameness-neurons', that fire when two spatial stimuli at different parts of the retina are 'the same', or 'temporal-sameness-neurons', that fire when the 'same' event occurs at different times. The basic features and the basic relations are the innate building blocks with which the network constructs its concepts and its perception of the external world. Together with the learning rules and the retrieval mechanisms, these basic factors determine the mental capabilities of the network.

1.2.2 EXEMPLARS AND PROPERTIES: There are several **conditional relationships** between factors and concepts that are captured by the network. A factor may be an **exemplar** of a concept, or a **property** of a concept.

DEFINITION: Let node **A** be a factor of node **B**. **A** is an **exemplar** of **B** if **B** was active whenever **A** was active. In other words, **A** has been a sufficient condition for **B**. When **B** has several exemplars that have been active at different times, it is called the **class** or the **label** to which **A** belongs.

A may become an exemplar of class **B** in three ways. First, by arbitrary assignment. Second, due to a property; **A** contains a property, due to which it qualifies as a member of **B**. Third, by association; **A** has been associated with a key concept **C**. This association makes **A** eligible to belong to **B**.

Examples:

1. Arbitrary assignment: Inanimate nouns in some languages (e.g. French, Hebrew) belong to one of two gender classes. These affiliations are arbitrary.
2. By property: The class of green objects. Each member has the color green.
3. By association: The class of cigarette smokers. Each member has been associated with cigarette smoking.

Except for cases of arbitrary assignment, a concept is assigned to a class if the concept has any one of a list of properties or associations that defines that class. If a class has just one defining property or association, this property or association is also a necessary condition for each exemplar of the class.

DEFINITION: Let node **A** be a factor of node **B**. **A** is a **property** of **B** if whenever **B** was active **A** was active. In other words, **A** has been a necessary condition for **B**.

A property may be also a sufficient condition for its concept. More commonly, a group of properties, as a whole, is a sufficient condition to a concept, while any part of this group is not a sufficient condition. Such a group of properties will be called **a specific clue**. A specific clue is represented by a node, placed in between the properties and their concept. The properties send their arcs to the specific clue, and the specific clue sends an arc to the concept.

Properties, as factors, are necessary conditions for their concepts. If **A** is a property of **B**, and **B** is a property of **C**, then **A** is also a property of **C**. However, **A** will have an arc only to **B**, and not to **C**.

A chain of classes is a sequence of classes in which each member is an exemplar of the next member. When a concept is an exemplar of a chain of classes, the arcs of the network only record its membership in the directly superior class. e.g. there will be arcs between 'dove' and 'bird', and between 'bird' and 'animal', but not between 'dove' and 'animal'. If a chain of classes has a common defining property, this property will have an arc only to the class at the top of the chain, e.g. 'breathing' will have an arc to 'animal' but not to 'bird' or 'dove'. This arcs management method saves on 'network material' without compromising the contents of the stored information.

If **A** is a factor of **B**, **A** may be an exemplar, a property, or an exemplar and a property of **B**. The arc that connects nodes **A** and **B** encodes the relationship between them.

2. THE REASONER

The reasoner is capable of performing a variety of reasoning tasks, such as generalization and reasoning by analogy. It consists of two components: The semantic neural network, which learns and stores the semantic information, and the controller, which manipulates these data according to the specific reasoning task. The controller activates the nodes that represent the initial state, activates the data retrieval processes, evaluates the retrieved data, decides on the termination of the reasoning process, and initiates recruitment of nodes to represent new concepts, that are the outcome of analogical reasoning. The network's structure and dynamics facilitate the operation of the controller.

2.1 THE NEURAL NETWORK

2.1.1 STRUCTURE: The nodes of the network, that represent concepts and factors, are arranged in layers. There are two kinds of nodes; innate and recruited. The innate nodes consist of the basic feature nodes, the basic relation nodes, and innate specific-clue nodes. The basic feature nodes fill the first (bottom) layer. Arcs connect the appropriate innate nodes. All the other nodes and arcs are recruited into the network, as the external world is experienced and learned. Information can flow in two directions: from factors to concepts (up), and from concepts to factors (down). Connected nodes are linked by two directional arcs, one in the up and the other in the down direction. The direction of information flow in the network at any given time is determined by the external controller. All nodes act like standard artificial neurons. Their firing status is determined by the weighted sum of their input signals, and by the threshold, which is 1 for all the nodes.

2.1.2 DYNAMICS: The weights of the two directional arcs that connect a factor node and its concept node encode the conditional relationships that exist between the nodes. The weight between an exemplar and its directly superior class is set to 1. The weight between a concept and its directly inferior feature is 1. Since all the firing thresholds are set to 1, these weights ensure that when information flows up, each exemplar will activate its class labels, and when information flows down, each concept will activate its features. The other weights are set in such a way, that when the entire set of factors that define a concept is present, this concept will be activated. When only a part of this set of factors is present, the appropriate concept may be retrieved by **vector completion.** In vector completion, the controller gradually **modulates** the intensity of the signals, till previously silent nodes fire. The modulation can be accomplished by increasing the strengths of the signals, increasing the weights of the arcs, or decreasing the thresholds. The network has to be constructed in a special way that makes modulation by the controller possible. More details about modulation are given in (4,5).

2.2 THE CONTROLLER:

The controller has a repertoire of basic operations that it can exercise on the data base. The starting point of any reasoning process is activating the nodes that represent the input factors. These nodes constitute the initial condition of the problem. Then, information flows in the network as directed by the weights, and activates the concepts that are made of the input factors. The controller then decides whether the retrieved information is satisfactory, or there is a need for a reasoning process, such as vector completion. Vector completion is a simple reasoning process, which is accomplished by modulation, as explained above.

2.2.1 MAPPING AND SOURCE SELECTION. Analogical reasonings are more complicated processes, and they consist of cycles of basic operations. In some problems only the target is given, while in others both the target and the source are given. In both cases, the controller first activates the nodes that represent the initial state of the particular problem.

Then, the controller has to define the mappings between factors of the two concepts. A pair of mapped factors must have a common feature or a common relation. In other words, the two factors must belong to the same class. So, the controller starts with a factor of the target, finds its class, and then activates other members of that class. These members are potential mappings of the original target's factor. A way to achieve this retrieval in the network is to enable information flow up, starting at the factors of the target. This will result in the retrieval of the class labels. Then, information flow is enabled in the down direction, retrieving other exemplars of these classes. These exemplars are possible mappings of the original target's factors. When both the source and the target are given, some of the retrieved factors, which do not belong to the given source, are eliminated. If the source is not given, enabling information flow in the up direction, with or without modulation, will activate concepts that contain these retrieved factors. One of these activated concepts may be selected as the analogical source to the given target.

The controller has means for determining which is the most appropriate source when several sources are retrieved, and which are the most appropriate mappings between the factors of the source and the target. These determinations may be based on the distance between the retrieved and the target entities, and they vary from one analogical reasoning process to another (2).

2.2.2 LEARNING AND INFERENCES. In learning the external world, the brain receives patterns of factors, parses them, and records the information in its network as inter-connected concepts. In the network presented here, learning is accomplished by two mechanisms: 1. changing weights of arcs, including adding new arcs between existing nodes, and 2. recruiting new nodes and their arcs. A node that represents a class label can always add new exemplars, and a node that represents a property can add more concepts to which it belongs. However, once a concept node is defined as the representation of a conjunction of a given set of factors, it cannot add any new factors to its original set, because that will change its meaning. More details about these learning mechanisms are given in (5,6), where a new network, the Binary Diamond, is described. The Binary Diamond learns the environment one event at a time, and forms its concepts in a way similar to that of the brain. The Binary Diamond recruits its nodes and arcs so that the precise conditional relationships between factors and concepts are recorded. Its structure and dynamics facilitate regular data retrieval, and vector completion by modulation. In analogical reasoning, inferences are made based on retrieved analogical mappings. In addition to the learning rules that are used to form concepts from information that comes from the outside (5,6), learning rules for consolidating analogical inferences are also needed.

Once the final mappings are determined, the controller recruits nodes and arcs to represent new concepts. These concepts embody the inferences that are the product of the analogical reasoning process. This may be viewed as the learning phase of the analogical reasoning process, since changes in the network occur now. There are three basic mechanisms that are used for recording the inferred information, and they are very similar to those used by (4,5,6).

Let **T** indicate a factor of the target, and **S** indicate its mapped factor in the source.

1. If **S** is an exemplar of class **C**, then also **T** becomes an exemplar of class **C**. This is accomplished by establishing the appropriate arc between **T** and **C**.
2. If **P** is a property of **S** then **P** becomes also a property of **T**. This is accomplished by establishing the appropriate arc between **T** and **P**.
3. If **S**, together with **A** and **B**, are the factors of the concept **C** in the source, then a new concept **N** is recruited in the target. The factors of **N** are **A**, **B**, and **T**. The new concept **N** is the analog of **C**.

Figure 1. illustrates these three basic mechanisms.

All three mechanisms rely on the mapping between **T** and **S**. **S** acts as a pointer to the nodes of the source that will become associated with node **T**. Mechanisms 1 and 2 are of the Hebbian type, and they are reminiscent to classical conditioning. Mechanism 3 is a non-Hebbian recruitment mechanism.

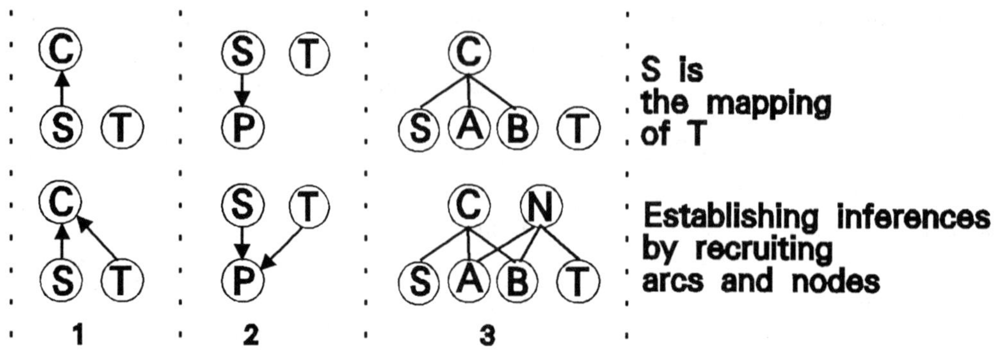

Figure 1. The three inference mechanisms. Arrows indicate weights of 1 in the corresponding direction. In 1 and 2 only arcs are recruited, while in 3 a node and arcs are recruited.

3. EXAMPLE

As an example that illustrates the data structure of the network and the operation of the controller in an analogical reasoning process, consider the following situation. The network already stores information about a hammer pushing a nail into a wall, and a knife cutting bread. The target is to push a hook into the wall. A solution is found by analogical reasoning, employing a controller and a semantic neural network. Figure 2 depicts the network. An arrow indicates a relationship between an exemplar and its class label. A solid line indicates an old relationship between a concept and its feature. Dashed lines indicate information that the network acquires during the process of analogical reasoning. The basic properties in this network are: [knife], [hook], [nail], [hammer], [wall], and [bread]. The basic relations are: [cut], [knock], [cause], [to_two], and [into]. The analogical reasoning is carried out in steps as follows (where: [a] --> [b] indicates that concept [a] activated concept [b]. The notation [a] <--> [b] indicates that [a] and [b] are analogs):

1. The initial condition is activated; nodes [hook], [into], and [wall] are activated. A node representing [hook into wall] is recruited and connected to its three factors.
2. Information is allowed to propagate up, and the class labels are activated: [hook] --> [sharp]; [into] --> [shape change]; [wall] --> [flat].
3. Information is allowed to propagate down, modulation takes place, and exemplars of the previously activated class labels are now retrieved: [sharp] --> [nail], [knife], [hook]; [change] --> [into], [to-two]; [flat] --> [wall], [bread]. Possible analogical mappings are stored: [hook] <--> [knife], [nail]; [into] <--> [to-two], [cause]; [wall] <--> [bread].
4. Information is allowed to propagate up. Several nodes are activated. [knife], [cut], [bread] --> [knife cut bread]; [nail], [into], [wall] --> [nail into wall].
5. The controller selects [nail into wall] over [knife cut bread] due to its greater similarity to the target.
6. Information is allowed to propagate up in vector completion. Another concept is activated: [nail into wall] --> [hammer knock nail cause nail into wall].

6 Information is allowed to propagate down, and features are retrieved. [hammer knock nail cause nail into wall] --> {[cause]}, {[hammer knock nail] --> [hammer], [knock], [nail]}, {[nail into wall] --> [nail], [into], [wall]}.

7. Recruitment takes place, and a selected solution is constructed using the inference rules of 2.2.2. In this example rule 3 is used three times. [hammer knock nail], [hammer], [knock], and [nail] <--> [hook] recruits [hammer knock hook]. [nail into wall], [into], [wall], and [nail] <--> [hook] recruits [hook into wall]. and [hammer knock nail cause nail into wall], [cause], [hammer knock nail] <--> [hammer knock hook], and [nail into wall] <--> [hook into wall] recruit [hammer knock hook cause hook into wall], which is a solution to the problem.

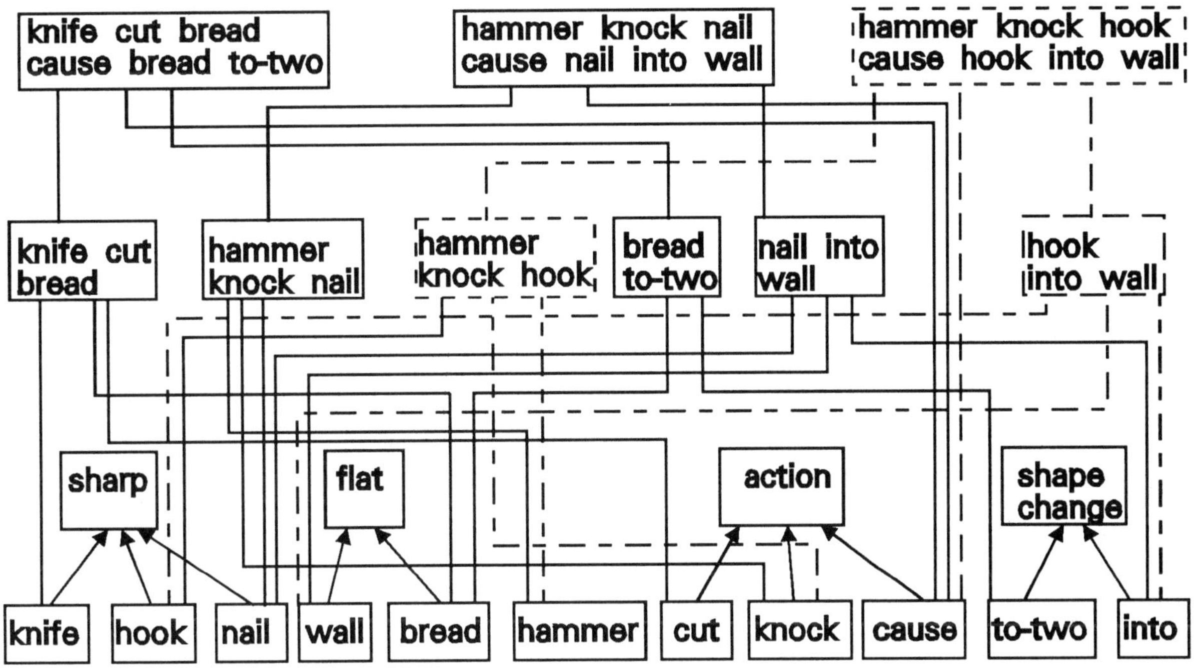

Figure 2. Solid lines = old information. Dashed lines = information gained by analogical reasoning.

4. DISCUSSION

There is a school of thought that models the brain as a connectionist network, in which neurons represent concepts, and mental activities are represented by the activation of patterns of neurons. Analogical reasoning is a fundamental process that the brain employs in a wide variety of mental activities. The work presented here illustrates how analogical reasoning can be implemented in a neural network. It uses an architecture and learning mechanisms, that have been found to be effective in other neural network applications. The work suggests that in advanced reasoning processes, the system may need to have two distinct components; memory and controller. This work concentrates on the memory component, while the controller is treated in an ad-hoc manner. It should be possible to implement the controller too in a neural network. The biological actuality of the basic principles of the model have to be tested in biological systems.

5. REFERENCES

1. Webster's New Collegiate Dictionary, 1975.

2. R.P. Hall, Computational approaches to analogical reasoning: A comparative analysis. Artificial Intelligence, 39, pp 39-120, 1989.

3. S. Vosniadou and A. Ortony. Similarity and analogical reasoning: a synthesis. in S. Vosniadou and A. Ortony (eds.) Similarity and Analogical Reasoning,Cambridge University Press, pp1-15, 1989.

4. Y. Salu A neural network that stores and retrieves information like the brain. in Cotterill R.M. (ed) Models of Brain Function. Cambridge University Press. pp 553-561. 1989

5. Y. Salu and J. Tilton. Non-parametric analysis of LANDSAT maps using neural nets and parallel computers. SPIE Vol 1623 AIPR Workshop, pp 174-183, 1991.

6. Y. Salu and J. Tilton. Classification of multispectral image data by the binary diamond neural network and by non-parametric, pixel-by-pixel methods. IEEE Transactions on Geoscience and Remote Sensing, Vol 31, pp 606-617, 1993.

Authors Index

Authors Index

Authors Index

Authors Index

Authors Index

Authors Index

The following papers were not included in their appropriate categories due to unforeseen last minute changes in the program.

TEMPORAL FUZZINESS IN COMMUNICATIONS SYSTEMS

Stamatios V Kartalopoulos, Ph.D.
AT&T Bell Laboratories
101 Crawfords Corner Rd
Holmdel, NJ 07733

ABSTRACT

Communication systems are real-time deterministic, well defined systems that transport voice/data signals from point A to point B reliably. However, the transmitted signal is subject to significant distortion by the very harsh environment, the medium, and the system itself. Despite this, data reaches its destination crispily or error-free. To achieve the high quality of error-free data, mechanisms that affect the quality of signal are addressed a priori and countermeasures are developed so that the potentially "fuzzifiers" are removed or "de-fuzzified". Here, the fuzzification-defuzzification process of the signal in real-time communication systems is addressed in the context of *temporal fuzziness* or fuzziness in the time domain. Temporal fuzzy factors that affect the operation of communication systems and their signal transmission are illustrated, analyzed, and the de-fuzzification process is discussed.

1. INTRODUCTION

Communication systems are real-time deterministic, well defined systems that transport voice/data from point A to a remote point B reliably.[1] Between the two points, a number of communication systems are inter-networked. A communication system, macroscopically, appears to be a synchronous real-time, deterministic system. However, microscopically, it is a distributed operating system that consists of many concurrent (micro)-programmed sequential processors (or ASICs) to control its many operations that describe its internal structure and protocol specification.

Fuzziness in communication systems may sound like a paradox. To understand this paradox, let us follow a signal departing from point A, with destination point B. As it departs, an adventurous travel begins: it is subject to algorithmic manipulations (equalization, digital processing, analog to digital conversion), to transformations (sound to electronic, to photonic, to electromagnetic waves), it suffers from external influences (electromagnetic, environmental), etc. The result is a distorted or *fuzzy* signal. To date, sophisticated techniques have been developed to de-fuzzify (or recover) a fuzzified signal, documented in many transmission and information textbooks.[2]

In addition to algorithmic and environmental influencies to transmitted data, there is another serious contributor to data integrity, the system itself. The technology used in the system, its architecture, its implementation, the networking and the interface specifications, all affect data integrity. In addition, a large number of discrete events take place that may influence the integrity of the signal and the system's transmission efficiency. For example, when a request to initiate a call is made, there is a stupendous number of events that take place. A request to initiate a call must successfully be detected. A large number of network communications transactions must successfully take place for a communication path from point A to point B in the network to be established. Moreover, during data transmission, data may either be corrupted or partially lost due to system misbehavior: the system may loose temporarily synchronization, some critical part may become marginal, etc.; i.e. some condition emerges that fuzzifies data. Consequently, a robust system design should be able to either avoid data corruption or be able to detect data corruption and restore. In this case, a number of de-fuzzification (and error correction) processes take place, transparent to the user. This paper focuses on the third source of data fuzzification.

2. THE LOGICS PUZZLE

The traditional **combinatorial** logic is a static crisp boolean (0-1) logic; similarly, **sequential** logic is a boolean logic that decides the *next* event or state from the current one; hence this is also considered a crisp static logic. On the other hand, *fuzzy logic*[3] is a non-crisp logic where the variables, in contrast to boolean, are *fuzzy*; nevertheless, this logic is also static. The **temporal logic**[4] is an extension of the traditional logic where the *notion* of time or the *time interval* is a key variable. However, temporal logic is also a crisp logic. Mapping the different logic algebras in a matrix, see figure 1, the puzzle piece missing is under FUZZY and TEMPORAL. This logic, recently formulated[5], is known as **Temporal Fuzzy Logic.**

	STATIC	DYNAMIC
CRISP	B_L	T_L
FUZZY	F_L	?

B_L = Binary logics
T_L = Temporal logic
F_L = Fuzzy logic

Figure 1. The Logics Puzzle

3. FUNDAMENTALS OF TEMPORAL FUZZY LOGIC

Temporal Fuzzy Logic addresses the type of propositional logic where statements are not *crisp*, in contrast to binary (yes-no, 1-0) logic, but with a lot of uncertainty,[6] and time-variant. As an example, consider the statement: *If runner A is fast, runner B is faster than A, and runner C is slower than B, then, what is the relationship between runners A and C?*

Now, assume that at some specified initial time, the normalized speed profiles or membership functions of runners are SLOW, MODERATE, and FAST, as shown in figure 2 (solid lines). Now, in contrast to many other examples seen in the literature, all parameters in this example are functions of time, such as performance of runners and population of runners. Hence the distributions that define SLOW, MODERATE and FAST are functions of time. I.e., the membership functions are functions of time.

In real life, numerous other time dependant membership functions may found. It is not overstated If I'd say that most real life cases are functions of time (this is an ancient philosopher's discovery). Temporal fuzzy logic assumes such functions.

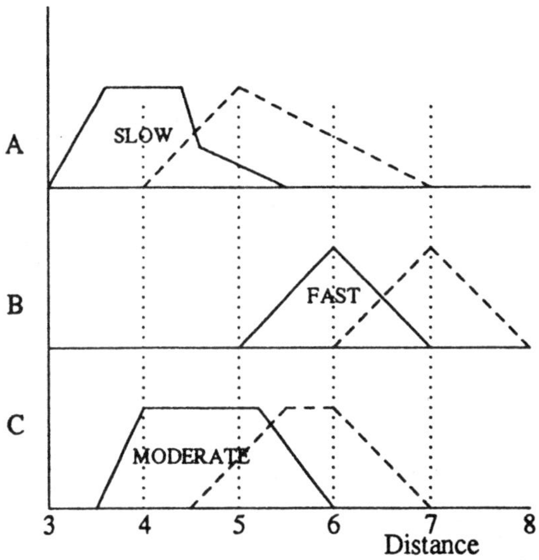

Figure 2. Membership Functions:
Speed Profiles at t=0 (solid) and t=T>0 (dashed)"

In temporal fuzzy logic the membership function is expressed by:

$\mu_{\tilde{F}}(x,t)$ 1

and, the grade of membership of $\mu_{\tilde{F}}(x,t)$ at $t=t_i$ by:

$\mu_{\tilde{F}}(x_i,t_i)$ 2

Here, we consider normalized fuzzy logic only, hence:

$\sup_{x\in E} r\,\mu_{\tilde{F}}(x,t) = 1$ 3

In addition, Temporal Fuzzy Logic defines a rate of confidence $\Re$ (see Appendix). The rate of confidence is used to further increase certainty during the de-fuzzification process. It is also an index of the **trend** of events. The language herein, although similar to other logics, uses additional symbolism. Appendix A lists the temporal fuzzy operators and their meaning.

A typical linguistic statement in temporal fuzzy logic is also expressed with **If ... Then** statements as in regular fuzzy logic, however, the essence of time is explicitly stated as follows:

If
  A is almost true at t=i
and
  B is almost false at t=i+2
then
  F at t=i+3

where F is an activity, and t is the dimension of time measured in small equal discrete increments, or small equal intervals. Discrete time is a mathematical convenience that allows for algorithmic description and the usage of a clock for the problem at hand. Thus, i+2 means two time intervals (or two clock ticks) latter than i.

Using temporal fuzzy logic symbolism as in Appendix A, the above statement is expressed by:

$$[M^{\alpha}\mu_A(x,t_i)]\,W^2\varnothing[M_{\alpha}\wedge(1-\mu_B(x,t_{i+3}))]\rightarrow\bigcirc F \qquad 4$$

In the above, the first bracket evaluates the grade of membership at point x_i, and at time t_i and stores it in location α. Then, it waits for two intervals doing nothing: $W^2\varnothing$), and then, in the second bracket, a number of events take place: it computes the grade of membership B at instant t+3, it computes the almost true value of μ_B, it recalls the value of μ_A from location α, and it computes the intersection of the two memberships. Finally, if the result is true (as expected), execution of F is the next event.

The difference between the linguistic statements and equation 4 is that the latter expresses the problem statement in a mathematical notation whereby the grade of memberships are explicitly calculable in the time domain. In fact, relation 4 "designs" a virtual circuit that computes the problem at hand.

4. TEMPORAL FUZZINESS IN COMMUNICATIONS SYSTEMS

In communication systems time plays a significant role in the de-fuzzification process of signals. Then, based on the rules of the particular problem and the previous (history) and/or current grades of memberships, inferences are made and certain control activities take place.

The next section briefly describes a communication system, where the On-Hook/Off-Hook process takes place, as one of the fuzzification influencies in data handling.

4.1 A Voice/Data Communication System

The communication system under consideration, in principle, consists of the following major functions, figure 3:

- **Channel units**: each terminates an analog voice or digital data signal. Analog voice is pulse code modulated (PCM) at 64 Kbps.
- **The On-Hook/Off-Hook Detector**: This circuitry detects the state of the external apparatus (i.e. telephone, modem). When the apparatus goes Off-Hook, it is sensed by the detector.
- **A time compressor/multiplexer**: A number of 64 Kbps PCM signals are time compressed and multiplexed into a higher bit rate; this is known as *time division multiplexing* (TDM).
- **The High-speed interface unit**: it synchronizes to the received bit-stream from a remote system, and it transmits/receives high-speed bipolar signals.
- **A Time-Slot Interchanger (TSI)**: it constitutes a space-time crosspoint of multiplexed channels.
- **The Controller**: it controls the flow through the cross-connect dynamically, it monitors the system performance, it provisions the various units of the system, it provides maintenance and telemetry, it monitors the operation of the system and it executes call processing based on the On-Hook/Off-Hook state of the channel units.

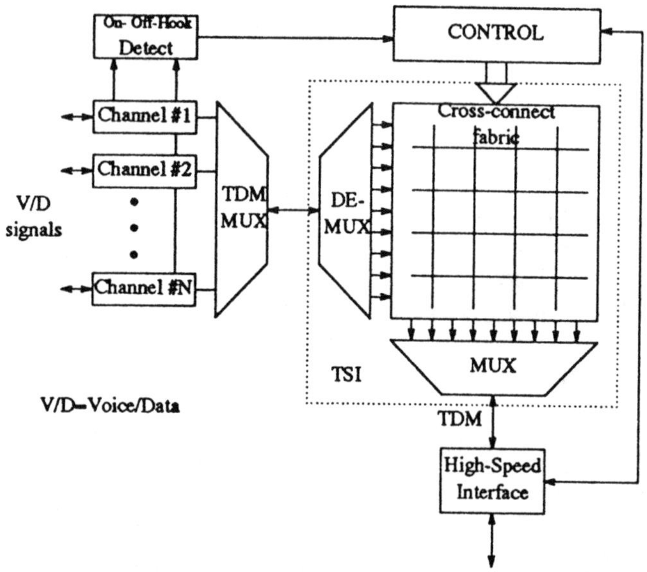

Figure 3. Functional Architecture of the TDM System

4.2 On-Hook or Off-Hook?

The TDM system described above detects transitions from the On-Hook to Off-Hook state of the channels. Initially, this transition may exhibit a degree of uncertainty in the time domain; hence, it is a temporal fuzzy variable. When this condition is defuzzified, i.e. the system is certain of the transition, then it requests from the network an end-to-end communication path. Figure 4a illustrates a continuous linear function of the On-to-Off-Hook state where the x-axis, although in the time domain, represents cumulative time, and figure 4b the diagrammatic representation of the fuzzy change of state in three sequential confidence levels, or membership functions, Low, Medium, and High. In our application, the controller determines the confidence level of all three different time intervals (see rules); hence temporal fuzzy logic is transformed to temporal combinatorial fuzzy logic.

Prior to requesting a communication path, the system constructs a time-dependency (or history) of that state for a predetermined period of time. Then, depending on the membership grades within that time period it decides whether a path should be requested or not. This process is also repeated when a voice/data channel becomes inactive, or "On-Hook"; in this case the path is disconnected.

4.2.1 Temporal fuzzification: As an example, consider that a telephone goes Off-Hook. This represents a change in the telephone state from a logic 1 to logic 0. Now, for many reasons, that are beyond the purpose of this paper, the change of state may be uncertain, i.e. the state may change temporarily, or it may oscillate for a very short period and then reach a steady state. Hence, there is temporal fuzziness in the change of state of the telephone, and in the decision making process of the system. Hence the question: to what degree is the telephone Off-Hook? Figure 5 illustrates a situation of temporal fuzziness with respect to the change of state from On-to-Off-Hook and also the degree of confidence of the change of state. Here, we consider the case where the degree of confidence is a linear function of time, (see also figure 4).

The function of the temporal fuzzy signal is described by:

$$F(t) = \sum_{ij} r_H^i(t) + r_L^j(t) \qquad 4$$

where $r_H^i(t)$ is a random number that indicates the i_{th} length (in time units) at state 1, and $r_L^j(t)$ is the j_{th} length at state 0. In our particular case, t takes discrete values (in increments of 10 msecs). For example, $r_H^2(t)=50$ indicates that the second high level segment is 50 msecs.

4.2.2 Rules and Temporal Defuzzification: In our communication system, for robustness, we have set simple defuzzification rules. Here, the rules of the temporal fuzzy problem in linguistic statements are:

1. If L & $\overline{M}$ then,
   if r_H & $\bar{r}_L$,
   then, next
   if $\Re > 0$ then,
   repeat 1 until $\Re$=0 (or L=1),
   else t=0,

2. If M & previous L then,
   if r_H & $\bar{r}_L$,
   then, next
   if $\Re > 0$ then,
   repeat 2 until $\Re$=0 (or M=1),
   else t=0, go to 1

3. If H & (previous) M & (previous) L, then,
   if r_H & $\bar{r}_L$,
   then, next
   if $\Re > 0$ then,
   repeat 3 until $\Re$=0 (or H=1),
   then, next
   declare Off-Hook steady state and request a communication path
   else t=0, go to 1

where L=Low, M=Medium, H=High, &=AND operator and $\Re$ = rate of confidence.

The above linguistic statements are expressed with temporal fuzzy notation as:

$$\Phi_{\mu_L(x,t_i)\wedge(\mu_{\bar{M}}(x,t_i)}[\bigcirc(r_H \wedge \bar{r}_L \wedge \Re > 0 U \Re = 0)], \rightarrow$$
$$\bigcirc[\Phi_{\mu_M(x,t_{i+A})\wedge(\mu_L(x_A,t_A)}[\bigcirc(r_H \wedge \bar{r}_L \wedge \Re > 0 U \Re = 0)]], \rightarrow$$
$$\bigcirc[\Phi_{\mu_H(x,t_{i+B})\wedge\mu_L(x_B,t_B}[\bigcirc(r_H \wedge \bar{r}_L \wedge \Re > 0 U \Re = 0)]] \rightarrow \bigcirc F_{Off-Hook}$$

where $F_{Off-Hook}$ is the final activity **declare Off-Hook state valid**. This activity invokes a request for a communication path.

When the path has been requested, assigned and connected, and when the state changes from Off-Hook to On-Hook, then the reverse process takes place, and the path is de-assigned and disconnected.

5. SUMMARY

In this paper, linear temporal fuzziness encountered in data/voice communication systems has been identified and analyzed, and the rules and the de-fuzzification process described. The temporal fuzzy logic has been briefly described and it has been applied in the exemplar communication system. In addition, expressions that describe the threshold conditions that should be met to defuzzify, infer and control the data flow, beyond doubt, have also been developed. Identifying *fuzzifiers*, i.e. factors that fuzzify data, and incorporating de-fuzzification mechanisms in the system, an assurance is made of the robust signal/data processing and safe data transport from point A to point B, a requirement and a characteristic of communication systems.

6. APPENDIX: TEMPORAL FUZZY OPERATORS

1. **The Rate of Confidence:** It indicates the direction of confidence of a fuzzy variable in the time domain. This is expressed by:

$$\Re_{\bar{F}} = -\eta \frac{\mu_{\bar{F}}(x_i) - \mu_{\bar{F}}(x_{i+1})}{\delta t} \mu_{\bar{F}}(x_i)$$

where x_i and x_{i+1} are the values of x measured at time points t_i and t_{i+1} and η is a scalar, the confidence index.

2. The Time Expansion Operator, D^λ: Then, $\underset{\lambda}{\tau} = D^\lambda \tau = (\lambda\tau)_{time-units}$

3. The Time Compression Operator, D_λ: Then, $\underset{\lambda}{\tau} = D_\lambda \tau = (\frac{\tau}{\lambda})_{time-units}$

4. The "O" for **next**, i.e. $O\mu_A(x,\tau)$: $\mu_A(x,\tau)$ becomes true at the next instance or at the next tick of a clock. Then, $O\mu_A(x,\tau_i)=\mu_A(x,\tau_{i+1})$

5. The "□" for **henceforth**; i.e. $\Box\mu_A(x,t_i)$: $\mu_A(x,t_i)$ will be true henceforth, or for i=i,i+1,...

6. The "◊" for **eventually**; i.e. $\Diamond\mu_A(x,t)$: $\mu_A(x,t)$ eventually will be true.

7. The "U" for **until**; i.e. $\mu_A(x,t)U\mu_B(x,t)$: $\mu_A(x,t)$ will be true until $\mu_B(x,t)$ is.

8. The "$\wp$" for **precedes**; i.e. $\mu_A(x,t_i)\wp\mu_B(x,t_j)$, $i\leq j$: $\mu_A(x,t_i)$ will be true prior to $\mu_B(x,t_i)$

9. "Δ=" for **event**; $\Delta=\mu_A(x,t)$: the event $\mu_A(x,t)$ is about to occur.

10. The "∂" for **while**; i.e. $\mu_A(x,t)\partial\mu_B(x,t)$: $\mu_A(x,t)$ will become true *iff* $\mu_B(x,t)$ is true and it stays true for as long as $\mu_B(x,t)$ is true.

11. The "¢" for **concurrence**; i.e. $\mu_A(x,t)¢\mu_B(x,t)$: when $\mu_A(x,t)$ becomes true then (synchronously) $\mu_B(x,t)$ becomes true; the reverse is also true.

12. The "**W**" for **wait**; i.e. **W** $\mu_A(x,\tau_i)$: calculate the grade of membership $\mu_A(x,\tau_i)$ and wait until another condition terminates the validity of this operator.

13. The "W^n" for **wait for n**; i.e. $W^n\mu_A(x,t_i)$: wait for n consecutive intervals and calculate the grade of membership $\mu_A(x,t_i)$.

14. The "$\overset{n}{\rightarrow}$" for **shift-in n times**; i.e. $[\mu_A(x_i,t_i)]\overset{n}{\rightarrow}X$: shift the grades of membership $\mu_A(x_i,t_i)$ n consecutive times in X, where $X=\{x_1,...,x_m\}$, $n\leq m$.

15. The "$\alpha\{\ \}$" for **contents** of α location; i.e. $\alpha\{x_i\}$: the contents of α are x_i.

16. The "M^α" for **store in address** α; i.e. M^α $\mu_A(x_i,t_i) = \alpha\{\mu_A(x_i,t_i)\}$: store the value of $\mu_A(x_i,\tau_i)$ in location α.

17. The "M_α" for **recall from address**; i.e. M_α: get the contents from location α. If $\alpha\{\mu_A(x_i,t_i)\}$, then: $M_\alpha = \mu_A(x_i,t_i)$,

18. The "∅" for **null** or **empty set**.

19. The "L^n[.]" for **loop**; i.e. $L^n[F_{op}]$: do $[F_{op}]$ recursively n times, where $[F_{op}]$ is a predefined fuzzy operation.

20. The "Φ^n[.]" for **while do**; i.e. $\Phi^n_A[F_{op}]$: while A is true do F_{op} n times recursively,

21. the equality of A^i with B^j: Then, $A^i = B^j \leftrightarrow \mu_A(x,t_i) = \mu_B(x,t_j)$

22. the containment of A^i in B^j: Then, $A^i \subset B^j \leftrightarrow \mu_A(x,t_i) \leq \mu_B(x,t_j)$

23. the complement of A: Then, $\bar{A} = (compl.)A \leftrightarrow \mu_{\bar{A}}(x,t_i) = 1-\mu_A(x,t_i)$

24. the union of A^i and B^j: Then, $A^i \cup B^j \leftrightarrow \mu_{A^i\cup B^j}(x,t) = \max\{\mu_A(x,t_i),\mu_B(x,t_j)\}$

25. the intersection of A^i and B^j: Then, $A^i \cap B^j \leftrightarrow \mu_{A^i\cap B^j}(x,t) = \min\{\mu_A(x,t_i),\mu_B(x,t_j)\}$

7. REFERENCIES

1. Transmission Systems for Communications, 5th edition, 1982, Bell Telephone Laboratories, Inc.
2. H.G. Brierley, "Communications Engineering", Edw. Arnold, London, UK, 1986.
3. B. Widrow and A.D. Stearns, "Adaptive Signal Processing", Prentice Hall, Englewood Cliffs, New Jersey, 1955.
4. L.A. Zadeh, "Fuzzy Sets", Information and Control, vol. 8, 1965, pp. 338-353.
5. L.A. Zadeh, "A Theory of Approximate Reasoning", in J. Hayes, D. Michie, and L.I. Mikulich, Eds., *Machine Intelligence*, vol. 9, New York, Halstead Press, 1979, pp.149-194.
6. Z. Manna, and A. Pnueli, "The Temporal Logic of Reactive and Concurrent Systems-Specification", Springer Verlag, New York, 1992.
7. J.G. Thistle, and W.M. Wonham, "Control Problems in a Temporal Logic frame work", Int. J. Control, vol 44, 1986, pp. 943-976.

8. N. Rescher, and A. Urquhart, "Temporal Logic", Springer Verlag, Library of Exact Philosophy, New York, 1971.

9. J. S. Ostroff, "Temporal Logic for Real-Time Systems", Research Studies Press, Ltd, London, and John Wiley & Sons, Inc, New York, 1989.

10. S. V. Kartalopoulos, "Temporal Fuzzy Logic", Submitted for publication.

11. S.V. Kartalopoulos, "A Plateau of Performance?", special issue on Fuzzy and Neural Networks, IEEE Communications Magazine, vol. 30, no.9, 1992, pp 13-14.

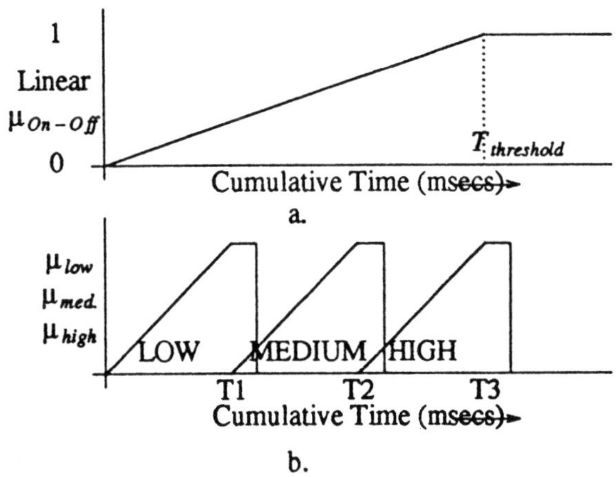

Figure 4. Membership Functions of the On-to-Off-Hook State

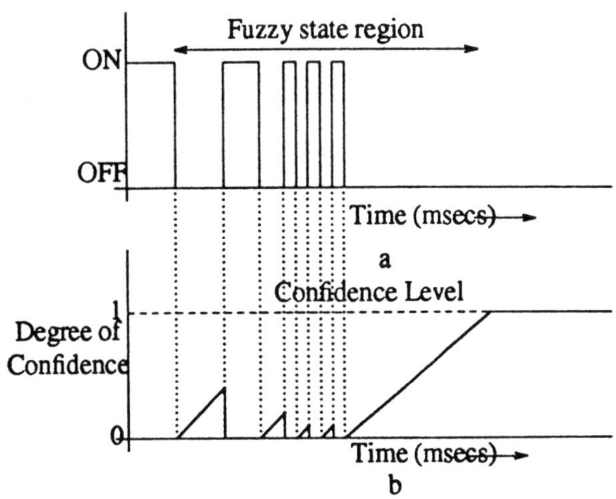

Figure 5. a. Temporal Fuzzy Signal and b. Certainty Level

Determining Overlap of Classes in the n-dimensional Boolean Space

Antônio de Pádua Braga[1] and Igor Aleksander

***Abstract* — This paper presents a solution to the problem of determining the distribution of the n-dimensional Boolean space in relation to two arbitrary patterns which are separated by a fixed distance *h* in such space. The estimation of such distribution allows the evaluation of the amount of overlap between the two corresponding *r-spheres*, which is a measure of the correlation between the classes determined by the patterns. This work is significant for applications in pattern recognition as well as for works on storage capacity and retrievability of patterns in Boolean neural networks.**

I. INTRODUCTION

Sphere packing has been concerning scientists in the field of Information Theory since the late 40's and early 50's when the first works were published on the subject [1]. The problem in sphere packing is to determine how *n* code words, which represent the centres of the spheres, can be located in the Euclidean Space E^n so that the *n* correspondent congruent spheres of radius *r* (or *r-spheres*) do not overlap and cover as much of E^n as possible. The aim of the research in Information and Coding Theory is therefore to determine the representation of the *n* code words in such a way that the *n* congruent and disjoint spheres have maximum volume.

In most cases in the Neural Networks field there is not freedom to represent elements of the training set as code words in order to maximise sphere's volume. Elements of the training set are determined by the problem under study and can be located anywhere in E^n. Nevertheless, the knowledge of the amount of overlap between two arbitrary spheres is an important issue when determining the storage capacity and retrievability of patterns in Boolean Neural Networks [2,3,4,5,6]. The overlap in this case, gives an idea of which is the percentage of the whole space that is *dubious* in relation to the centres of the two *r-spheres*.

The aim of this paper is to present some ideas to allow the prediction of the amount of overlap between two *r-spheres* in the n-dimensional Boolean space. The results enable a comparision with the previous work of Kanerva on the same subject [2,3]. Such comparision shows that for small values of *r*, the results of the two models are similar and quite accurate but, when *r* is large, the model presented here tends to be more precise when compared with computer results. Kanerva's model of Sparse Distributed Memory (SDM) uses small *r-spheres* and the expressions developed for that model are quite precise in the range of *r* demanded to prove the ideas behind SDM. The work presented here extends the one developed for SDMs in the sense that it is precise in the whole range of variation of *r*, being useful for SDMs as well as for any other model of Boolean Neural Networks.

II. THE THIRD SIDE OF THE TRIANGLE

The problem addressed in this section is known as the "problem of the third side of the triangle" [2,3], due to the geometrical analogy which exists between a triangle in a plane and the relative distances among three arbitrary points in the Boolean space. It is important to note that Hamming instead of Euclidean Distances are used as metric measures in this work. Although the rules of Euclidean Geometry cannot be directly applied to solve the problem, the geometrical analogy shown in Figure 1 helps to visualise it.

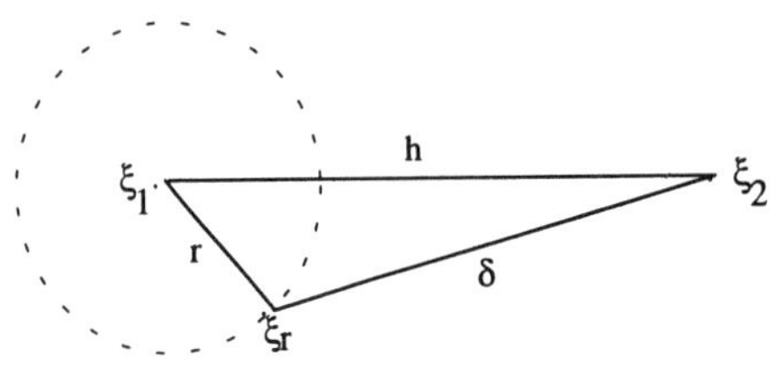

Figure 1. Geometrical view of the "problem of the third side of the triangle". What is the distribution of δ ?

---

[1]On leave from Universidade Federal de Minas Gerais, Brazil, and supported by CNPq grant 202286/91-6

Address for correspondence: Department of Electrical Engineering, Imperial College, Exhibition Road, London SW7 2BT, England

It is aimed here to determine how the patterns that are at fixed distance r of ξ_1 are distributed in the space in relation to ξ_2. By the triangle and circle analogy of Figure 1, it is suggestive that such distribution starts from a minimum, increases to a maximum and then returns to the minimum in the same way that a Binomial Distribution does. It was observed that under certain circumstances the Binomial approximation yields relatively good results, but there are other situations where this rule does not apply and the Binomial approximation is poor. It is shown in the next sections that such distribution resembles much more a Hypergeometric then a Binomial distribution and that the patterns at fixed distance of ξ_1 are seen by ξ_2 as clusters sparsely scattered in the space. Each cluster boundary defines a set of patterns that are at distance r from ξ_1 and distance δ from ξ_2.

III. SIMPLEST CASE : $0 \le r \le h$ and $0 \le r \le (n-h)$

In this situation, the radius r in relation to ξ_1 is smaller than h and $(n-h)$. The procedure to obtain a pattern at distance r from a fixed pattern ξ_1 is to invert r bits in its field of n bits. Using this procedure it is possible to obtain a maximum of $\binom{n}{r}$ different patterns at distance r from ξ_1. Figure 2, where ξ_1 and ξ_2 are seen divided into two fields, facilitates the visualisation of this process in relation to ξ_2. All the bits in the *h-field* are different and all the bits in the *(n-h)-field* are equal when ξ_1 and ξ_2 are compared. Therefore, every pattern at distance r from ξ_1 should keep a known relationship with ξ_2 depending on whether the r bits were taken from the *h-field*, from the *(n-h)-field* or from both at the same time.

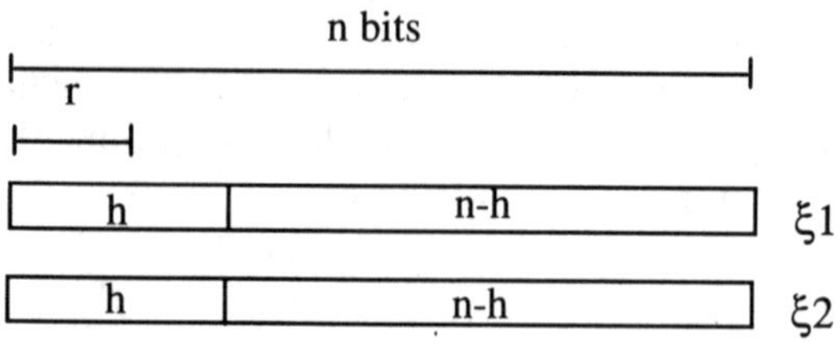

Figure 2. Patterns ξ_1 and ξ_2 are separated by a distance h in the space $\{0,1\}^n$.

It can easily be seen that if all r bits are taken from the *h-field*, the patterns generated are at a distance $(h-r)$ from ξ_2 and if they are taken from the *(n-h)-field*, they shall be located at a distance $(h+r)$ from ξ_2. In the case they are taken from both fields at the same time, the distance δ is given by $h+r-2hr$, where hr is the number of bits taken from the *h-field*. In general, expression (1) gives the value of δ as a function of h, r and hr.

$$\delta = h + r - 2hr \tag{1}$$

Therefore, the number of patterns in each cluster at distance δ from ξ_2 is a function of the number of patterns which can be generated from ξ_1 after inverting hr bits in the *h-field* and *(r-hr)* in the *(n-h)-field*. The size of each cluster can be calculated by the following expression:

$$T_r = \binom{n-h}{r-hr} \times \binom{h}{hr} \tag{2}$$

with hr varying from 0 to r for this particular case.

As it can be noticed from expression (2), the distribution of δ resembles a Hypergeometric distribution. The main difference between the Hypergeometric and the distribution of δ is that the second is a discrete distribution with gaps between subsequent clusters, being bounded by the upper and lower limits of δ. For example, if $n=100$, $h=20$ and $r=8$, it is obtained that the distribution of δ is formed by 9 clusters at distances 28, 26, 24, 22, 20, 18, 16, 14 and 12 and that each cluster has a different number of patterns as can be seen from Figure 3.

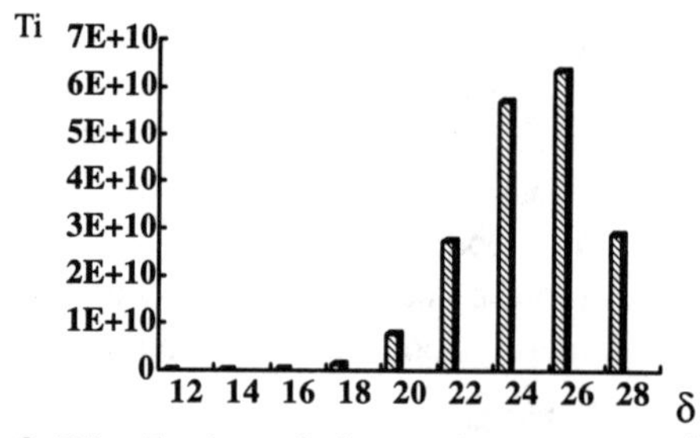

Figure 3. Distribution of clusters in relation to ξ2 when n=100, h=20 and r=8.

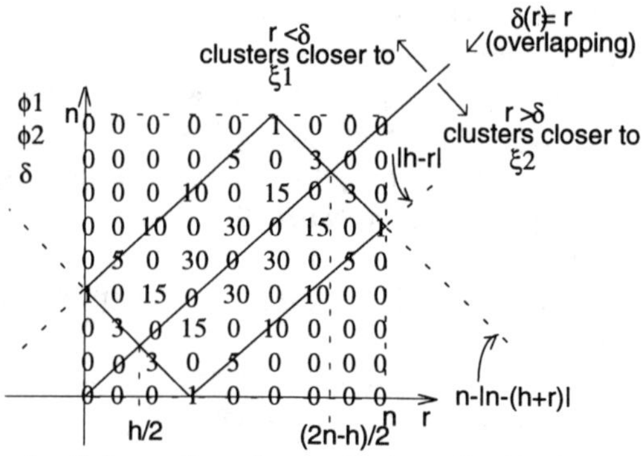

Figure 4. Schematic view of the distribution of clusters as defined by expressions (4) and (5) for $n=8$ and $h=3$.

IV. GENERAL SOLUTION

Based on the reasoning developed in the previous section, it is possible to find a general solution to obtain the distribution of δ when n, h and r are known. Expressions (1) and (2) are general solutions, but the bounds of hr and δ demand a more careful analysis in the different situations that may appear. Table I shows the values of the bounds of δ for each possible relation of n, h and r. From a simple inspection in the table, it is possible to deduce that the lower bound of δ is defined by $|h-r|$ and its upper bound by $n-|n-(h+r)|$. From expression (1) the bounds of h_r are then obtained:

$$hr_{lower} = \frac{h+r-n+|n-(h+r)|}{2} \quad (4)$$

$$hr_{upper} = \frac{h+r-|h-r|}{2} \quad (5)$$

The intersections of the functions $\phi_1(r)=|h-r|$ and $\phi_2(r)=n-|n-(h+r)|$ occurs at $r=0$ and $r=n$, which creates an envelope for the clusters within the range $0 \le r \le n$. A detailed description of the regions in the plane formed by the two functions can be seen in Figure 4, together with an example for the case where $n=8$ and $h=3$. It is also interesting to observe that any pattern at distance $r<h/2$ is considered to belong to class ξ_1 and any pattern at distance $r>(2n-h)/2$ is considered to belong to class ξ_2. Picking-up patterns in the range $h/2 < r < (2n-h)/2$ can result in a classification in class ξ_1 or class ξ_2 with different expectations as a function of r. For example, considering Figure 4, if a random pattern is picked-up at radius 2, there are 25 patterns which are closer to ξ_1 and 3 which are closer to ξ_2, among the total of 28 patterns. On the other hand, if a random pattern is picked-up at radius 5, there are only 16 patterns closer to ξ_1 among the total of 56. Therefore, the chance to pick-up a pattern closer to ξ_1 at radius 2 is $25/28$ and at radius 5 it decreases to $16/56$. Having a pattern recognition task in mind, it could be interpreted as if a random noise of 25% (radius 2 for this case) is added to ξ_1, the chance that the noisy pattern is classified as more similar to ξ_1 than to ξ_2 in terms of Hamming Distance is $25/28$. The probability of the noisy pattern being classified as more similar to ξ_1 decreases with the increase of the amount of noise added to the original pattern, being zero for values of r greater than $(2n-h)/2$.

Table I. Bounds of δ for every possible range of h and r

h range	r range	δ(lower)	δ(upper)
$h>n/2$	$0\le r\le(n-h)$	$(h-r)$ $r<h$	$(h+r)$ $h+r<n$
$h>n/2$	$(n-h)<r\le h$	$(h-r)$ $r<h$	$2n-(h+r)$ $h+r>n$
$h>n/2$	$h<r\le n$	$-(h-r)$ $r>h$	$2n-(h+r)$ $h+r>n$
$h<n/2$	$0<r\le h$	$(h-r)$ $r<h$	$(h+r)$ $h+r<n$
$h<n/2$	$h<r\le(n-h)$	$-(h-r)$ $r>h$	$(h+r)$ $h+r<n$
$h<n/2$	$(n-h)<r\le n$	$-(h-r)$ $r>h$	$2n-(h+r)$ $h+r>n$
$h=n/2$	$0<r\le h$ $0<r\le(n-h)$	$(h-r)$ $r<h$	$(h+r)$ $h+r<n$
$h=n/2$	$h<r\le n$ $h<r\le(n-h)$	$-(h-r)$ $r>h$	$2n-(h+r)$ $h+r>n$

Figure 6 shows all possible situations of $\delta(r)$ for the space $\{0,1\}^8$, where a matrix was generated for each different value of h. The sizes and positions of the clusters were generated by counting the patterns using a computer program. The distributions generated by counting match those generated by expressions (1) to (5). The observation of Figure 6 also shows the change in shape and size of the parallelogram formed by functions $\phi 1$ and $\phi 2$. The amount of the total area occupied by it gives an idea of the amount of clusters which are scattered in the space. The greater is the area, the greater is the number of clusters on the average and the greater is the spreading of δ for fixed r. The normalized area can be calculated as follows:

$$a_n = \frac{\int_0^n n-|n-(h+r)|dr - \int_0^n |h-r|dr}{n^2} \quad (6)$$

$$a_n = 2p(1-p) \quad (7)$$

where $p = h/n$.

Function a_n has its maximum at the point $h=n/2$ ($p=0.5$), where it occupies half the total area, as can be seen in Figure 5. In other words, when the two patterns are orthogonal, the clusters are more sparsely distribbuted in the space. For large n it could be interpreted that when the patterns are orthogonal they are *indifferent* to each other, as pattern ξ_2 visualises the space at distance r of ξ_1 in the same way it does in relation to the entire space, or as a binomial distribution [2,3].

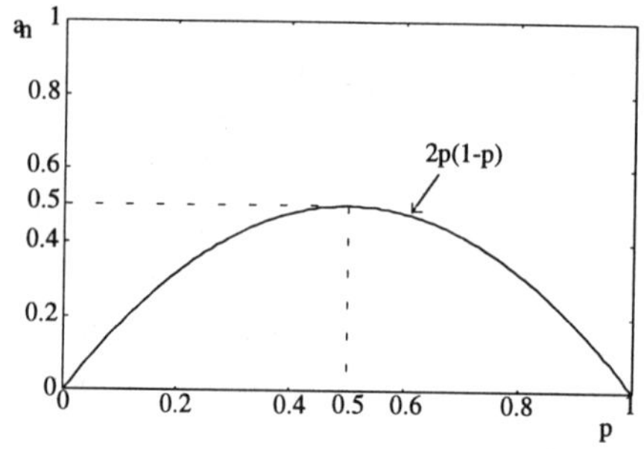

Figure 5. Normalized area a_n is maximum when $h=n/2$.

h=0

δ \ r	0	1	2	3	4	5	6	7	8
8	0	0	0	0	0	0	0	0	**1**
7	0	0	0	0	0	0	0	**8**	0
6	0	0	0	0	0	0	**28**	0	0
5	0	0	0	0	0	**56**	0	0	0
4	0	0	0	0	**70**	0	0	0	0
3	0	0	0	**56**	0	0	0	0	0
2	0	0	**28**	0	0	0	0	0	0
1	0	**8**	0	0	0	0	0	0	0
0	**1**	0	0	0	0	0	0	0	0

h=1

δ \ r	0	1	2	3	4	5	6	7	8
8	0	0	0	0	0	0	0	**1**	0
7	0	0	0	0	0	0	**7**	0	**1**
6	0	0	0	0	0	**21**	0	**7**	0
5	0	0	0	0	**35**	0	**21**	0	0
4	0	0	0	**35**	0	**35**	0	0	0
3	0	0	**21**	0	**35**	0	0	0	0
2	0	**7**	0	**21**	0	0	0	0	0
1	**1**	0	**7**	0	0	0	0	0	0
0	0	**1**	0	0	0	0	0	0	0

h=2

δ \ r	0	1	2	3	4	5	6	7	8
8	0	0	0	0	0	0	**1**	0	0
7	0	0	0	0	0	**6**	0	**2**	0
6	0	0	0	0	**15**	0	**12**	0	**1**
5	0	0	0	**20**	0	**30**	0	**6**	0
4	0	0	**15**	0	**40**	0	**15**	0	0
3	0	**6**	0	**30**	0	**20**	0	0	0
2	**1**	0	**12**	0	**15**	0	0	0	0
1	0	**2**	0	**6**	0	0	0	0	0
0	0	0	**1**	0	0	0	0	0	0

h=3

δ \ r	0	1	2	3	4	5	6	7	8
8	0	0	0	0	0	**1**	0	0	0
7	0	0	0	0	**5**	0	**3**	0	0
6	0	0	0	**10**	0	**15**	0	**3**	0
5	0	0	**10**	0	**30**	0	**15**	0	**1**
4	0	**5**	0	**30**	0	**30**	0	**5**	0
3	**1**	0	**15**	0	**30**	0	**10**	0	0
2	0	**3**	0	**15**	0	**10**	0	0	0
1	0	0	**3**	0	**5**	0	0	0	0
0	0	0	0	**1**	0	0	0	0	0

h=4

δ \ r	0	1	2	3	4	5	6	7	8
8	0	0	0	0	**1**	0	0	0	0
7	0	0	0	**4**	0	**4**	0	0	0
6	0	0	**6**	0	**16**	0	**6**	0	0
5	0	**4**	0	**24**	0	**24**	0	**4**	0
4	**1**	0	**16**	0	**36**	0	**16**	0	**1**
3	0	**4**	0	**24**	0	**24**	0	**4**	0
2	0	0	**6**	0	**16**	0	**6**	0	0
1	0	0	0	**4**	0	**4**	0	0	0
0	0	0	0	0	**1**	0	0	0	0

h=5

δ \ r	0	1	2	3	4	5	6	7	8
8	0	0	0	**1**	0	0	0	0	0
7	0	0	**3**	0	**5**	0	0	0	0
6	0	**3**	0	**15**	0	**10**	0	0	0
5	**1**	0	**15**	0	**30**	0	**10**	0	0
4	0	**5**	0	**30**	0	**30**	0	**5**	0
3	0	0	**10**	0	**30**	0	**15**	0	**1**
2	0	0	0	**10**	0	**15**	0	**3**	0
1	0	0	0	0	**5**	0	**3**	0	0
0	0	0	0	0	0	**1**	0	0	0

h=6

δ \ r	0	1	2	3	4	5	6	7	8
8	0	0	**1**	0	0	0	0	0	0
7	0	**2**	0	**6**	0	0	0	0	0
6	**1**	0	**12**	0	**15**	0	0	0	0
5	0	**6**	0	**30**	0	**20**	0	0	0
4	0	0	**15**	0	**40**	0	**15**	0	0
3	0	0	0	**20**	0	**30**	0	**6**	0
2	0	0	0	0	**15**	0	**12**	0	**1**
1	0	0	0	0	0	**6**	0	**2**	0
0	0	0	0	0	0	0	**1**	0	0

h=7

δ \ r	0	1	2	3	4	5	6	7	8
8	0	**1**	0	0	0	0	0	0	0
7	**1**	0	**7**	0	0	0	0	0	0
6	0	**7**	0	**21**	0	0	0	0	0
5	0	0	**21**	0	**35**	0	0	0	0
4	0	0	0	**35**	0	**35**	0	0	0
3	0	0	0	0	**35**	0	**21**	0	0
2	0	0	0	0	0	**21**	0	**7**	0
1	0	0	0	0	0	0	**7**	0	**1**
0	0	0	0	0	0	0	0	**1**	0

h=8

δ \ r	0	1	2	3	4	5	6	7	8
8	**1**	0	0	0	0	0	0	0	0
7	0	**8**	0	0	0	0	0	0	0
6	0	0	**28**	0	0	0	0	0	0
5	0	0	0	**56**	0	0	0	0	0
4	0	0	0	0	**70**	0	0	0	0
3	0	0	0	0	0	**56**	0	0	0
2	0	0	0	0	0	0	**28**	0	0
1	0	0	0	0	0	0	0	**8**	0
0	0	0	0	0	0	0	0	0	**1**

Figure 6. Distribution of the clusters at distance δ as a function of r and h. Elements M(x,y) hold the number of patterns at distance y from ξ_2 and radius x from ξ_1.

V. AMOUNT OF OVERLAP

The clusters which are in the overlap of the classes defined by ξ_1 and ξ_2 are those located in the sites where r=δ, or in the diagonal of the matrix. The observation of Figure 6 suggests a binomial distribution for the terms in the diagonal as a function of r when h is even. It can be shown by making δ=r in expression (1) and taking it to (2) :

$$T_r = \binom{n-h}{r-h/2} \times \binom{h}{h/2} \qquad (8)$$

Expression (8) can now be rewritten as an actual binomial term:

$$T_r = C \times \binom{n-h}{r-h/2} \qquad (9)$$

As can be observed from Figure 6, the terms in the overlap have a bell-shape, what suggests that it can be approximated using the standard form of the Normal Distribution Function [7] for large n. The best match found for such distribution in relation to the total number of patterns in the overlap was the Normal Distribution with mean $n/2$ and standard deviation $\sqrt{n-h}/2$. Each term of such distribution is equivalent to $T_r/N_o(h)$, where $N_o(h)$ is the total number of patterns in the overlap for the distance h. Therefore :

$$\frac{T_r}{N_o(h)} = \frac{1}{\sqrt{n-h}/2\,\sqrt{2\pi}}\, e^{-\frac{(r-n/2)^2}{2(\sqrt{n-h}/2)^2}} \qquad (10)$$

The percentage of the total number of patterns that is in the overlap is :

$$\varphi(h) = \frac{N_{o(h)}}{2^n} \qquad (11)$$

Therefore, using Stirling's Formula [7] for the factorials of expression (8) and making $r=n/2$ in the right side of expression (10), the function φ(h) can be obtained after taking the result obtained for No(h) to expression (11). The final result is shown in expression (12).

$$\varphi(h) = \begin{cases} 1 & h=0 \\ \sqrt{\dfrac{2}{\pi h}} & h \geq 1 \end{cases} \qquad (12)$$

Therefore, expression (12) determines the percentage of the space that is at the same distance from two arbitrary patterns ξ_1 and ξ_2 which are separated by even distance h (if h is odd $\rightarrow$ φ(h)=0). It is quite useful, as it provides a closed form to assess the amount of *dubious* patterns in the space as a function of the distance h. It is also significant to observe that the percentage of overlap does not depend on the number of dimensions n of the space, but only on the distance between the patterns. For example, if two patterns are at distance 14 in the space $\{0,1\}^{20}$, there is a percentage of approximately 21% of the total number of patterns that has the same distance from them. For the particular case of the space $\{0,1\}^{20}$, it corresponds to 223602 patterns of the total amount of 2^{20} possible. In the case of recurrent neural networks with probabilistic nodes [8], it estimates the chance of a node firing with hesitation, or that it will fire a random output. Figure 7 shows the graphics of φ(h) compared with experimental results for $n=20$.

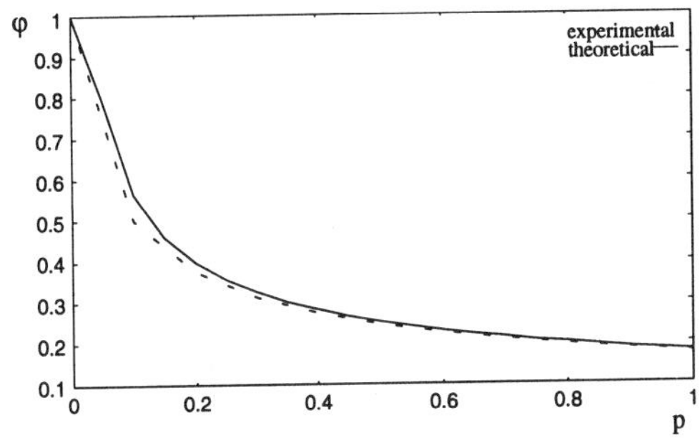

Figure 7. Comparison between experimental and theoretical results of φ(h) for $n=20$, where p is the ratio h/n.

For spheres with arbitrary radius r_1, the percentage of patterns $\theta(r_1)$ in the overlap can be obtained from the previous expressions :

$$\theta(r_1) = \varphi(h) \int_{-\infty}^{r_1} \frac{1}{\sqrt{n-h}/2\,\sqrt{2\pi}}\, e^{-\frac{(r-n/2)^2}{2(\sqrt{n-h}/2)^2}}\, dr \qquad (13)$$

$$\theta(r_1) = \frac{2}{\pi\sqrt{h(n-h)}} \int_{-\infty}^{r_1} e^{\frac{-2(r-n/2)^2}{(n-h)}} dr \qquad (14)$$

Kanerva [2,3] developed a similar expression to estimate the amount of overlap, which is :

$$g(p,u) = \int_{h/n}^{1} \frac{1}{2\pi\sqrt{u(1-u)}} e^{(-\frac{1}{2}\frac{C_p^2}{1-u})} du \qquad (15)$$

where $C_p = (r_p - n/2)\big/\sqrt{n/4}$.

As pointed out by Kanerva [2,6], expression (15) is precise for small values of *r*, as can be observed in Figure 8, where a comparision with expression (14) is made. For each point of the graphics in Figure 8 it was calculated the average of the absolute errors of the two expressions in relation to values generated by counting in a computer program, having *h* varying from *0* to *n* for each value of *r*. It can be seen that expression (14) is very precise for all the values of *r* and can be used as a general solution for whatever value *r* assumes. The difference between the results of the two expressions persists for larger values of n.

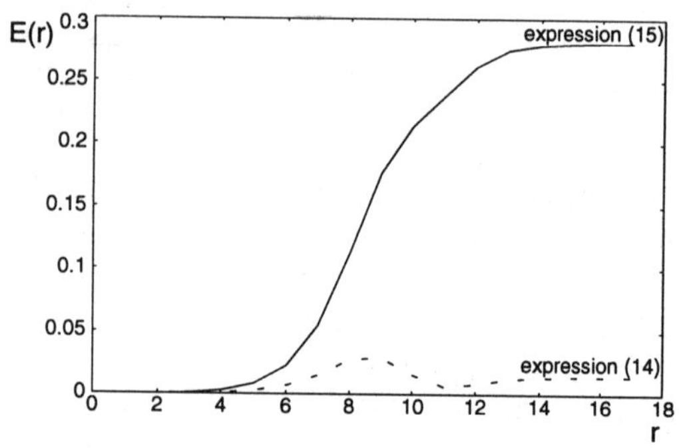

Figure 8. Average error of expressions (14) and (15) in relation to experimental results for *n=20*.

VI. CONCLUSIONS

This paper presented a general solution for determining how the n-dimensional space is distributed in relation to two arbitrary patterns which are separated by a fixed distance in such space. It was shown that such distribution is discrete with gaps between its subsequent elements. The discrete distribution can be determined by using the expressions and procedures presented in sections 2 and 3, which involves calculating its bounds, determining where the actual gaps are located and calculating each element of the distribution. In this way, it is possible to estimate how the space is divided into the classes characterized by the two patterns.

The procedures developed to estimate the discrete distribution allowed the deduction of expression (12), which is a closed form to determine the percentage of patterns in the overlap between the two classes. The closer are the patterns, the greater is the correlation between then and the greater is the overlap between the two classes. Therefore, the amount of overlap between the n-spheres given by expression (12) can be seen as a measure of the correlation between the *classes* determined by the two patterns.

The results presented in this work are key issues when determining storage capacity, retrievability of patterns and temporal properties of Boolean neural networks, as they present a more general and precise solution to the determination of the space distribution in relation to two arbitrary patterns.

REFERENCES

[1] Thompson, T. M., *From error-correcting codes through sphere packing to simple groups*, The Carus Mathematical Monographs, The Mathematical Association of America, 1983.

[2] Kanerva, P., *Self-propagating search: a unified theory of memory*, PhD Dissertation: Stanford University, 1984.

[3] Kanerva, P. , *Sparse Distributed Memory*, MIT Press, 1988.

[4] Braga, A. P., *On the information capacity of auto-associative RAM-based neural networks*; Proceedings of the ICANN-93, Amsterdam, 13-16 of September, 1993.

[5] Braga, A.P., *Predicting contradictions in the storage process of recurrent Boolean neural networks*, IEE Electronis Letters (Accepted for publication).

[6] Chou, P. A., *The Capacity of the Kanerva Associative Memory*, IEEE Transactions on Information Theory, Vol 35, Number 2, March, 1989, pp 281-298.

[7] Feller, W., *An introduction to probability theory and its applications*, John Wiley and Sons Inc., third edition, 1968.

[8] Aleksander, I., *Neural Systems Engineering : towards a unified design discipline?* IEE Computing and Control Engineering Journal, (1):259-265,1990.

The Dependence Identification Neural Network Construction Algorithm

John O. Moody and Panos J. Antsaklis
Department of Electrical Engineering
University of Notre Dame
Notre Dame, IN 46556

Abstract

An algorithm for constructing and training multilayer neural networks, dependence identification, is presented in this paper. Its distinctive features are that (i) it transforms the training problem into a set of quadratic optimization problems that are solved by a number of linear equations and (ii) it constructs an appropriate network to meet the training specifications. The architecture and network weights produced by the algorithm can also be used as initial conditions for further on-line training by backpropagation or a similar iterative gradient descent training algorithm if necessary. In addition to constructing an appropriate network based on training data, the dependence identification algorithm significantly speeds up learning in feedforward multilayer neural networks compared to standard backpropagation.

1 Introduction

The main tool for training multilayer neural networks is gradient descent, as used by the backpropagation (BP) algorithm developed by Rumelhart [7]. Gradient descent algorithms are susceptible to local minima, sensitive to initial conditions, and slow to converge. Gradient descent can work quite well with the appropriate set of of initial conditions and with a proper network architecture, but using random initial conditions and guessing at the network architecture usually leads to a slow and ponderous training process. The designer must specify the number of network layers and the number of neurons in the "hidden layers" when using basic backpropagation. A method of quickly specifying a network architecture and set of intitial weight values for possible further training through gradient descent would be extremely valuable.

The dependence identification algorithm (see also [4] and [5]) is proposed in section 2 of this paper. Section 3 gives examples of neural network construction, and concluding remarks appear in section 4.

2 Dependence Identification

This section details a method called *dependence identification* (DI) for constructing *multi-layer* neural networks. The method is based on the ability to easily solve single layer neural network training problems. Many methods exist [3] for training single layer neural networks including steepest descent, least mean squares, and the "perceptron training algorithm" (for single layer classification problems). In [8], Sartori and Antsaklis proposed quadratic optimization which transforms the nonlinear training cost function of a single layer network into a quadratic one. This method reduces the problem to solving a set of linear equations and is the method used in the examples of section 3.

The network is to be constructed and trained to approximate a function with m inputs and n outputs. The training set consists of p input/output patterns. The training patterns are stored in the following matrices:

$$U \in \mathbb{R}^{p \times m} \qquad\qquad D \in \mathbb{R}^{p \times n}$$

where U is the matrix of input patterns and D is matrix of desired output patterns. The network is constructed one layer at a time, using the rules for single layer network construction. The desired hidden layer outputs are equal to portions of the actual desired outputs. The hidden layer activations (outputs) for a layer are used as the input matrix U for the next layer.

2.1 The Algorithm

To construct the network, first attempt to create a single layer neural network using an appropriate single layer training algorithm. Compute the error of the single layer network. If the error is acceptable (less than a given tolerance) then training is complete and the solution is a single layer network, otherwise create a layer of hidden neurons each of which gets a subset of the complete set of training patterns matched correctly, i.e.,

every pattern should be classified correctly by at least one hidden layer neuron. To do this choose an $m \times m$ portion of U (it is assumed that there are more training patterns than there are inputs, i.e., $p > m$.), and the corresponding $m \times n$ portion of D. Use these patterns to solve a single layer neural network training problem as above. It is guaranteed that a unique zero error solution to this problem exists if the $m \times m$ portion of U is full rank; see [9]. Repeat this procedure until every pattern is matched by at least one hidden layer neuron. Patterns in U and D which are correctly matched by a single hidden layer neuron are linearly dependent after being operated on by the nonlinear neural activation function. This is the reason for the name dependence identification. The hidden layer outputs are then treated as inputs to form a new layer. Layers may be added to the network until a maximum number of layers has been added or the network error is within the desired tolerance.

Dependence identification is presented formally in Algorithm 2.1. The inputs to the algorithm include the training patterns U and D as well as the neural activation function ϕ $\{\phi : \mathbb{R} \rightarrow \mathbb{R}\}$, the maximum number of layers $h_{\max}$, and two tolerances ϵ_N and ϵ_p. The acceptable error for the entire network is given by ϵ_N. The other tolerance, ϵ_p, is used to determine whether the output of the network for an individual pattern is within bounds. Larger values for ϵ_p give fewer hidden layer neurons as discussed in section 2.2. The algorithm uses the notation $\Phi(A)$ to mean that every element of the matrix A should be operated on by the nonlinear activation function ϕ.

Algorithm 2.1 (Dependence Identification).

input $U \in \mathbb{R}^{p\times m}$, $D \in \mathbb{R}^{p\times n}$, $\phi : \mathbb{R} \rightarrow \mathbb{R}$, ϵ_N, ϵ_p, $h_{\max}$.
Set $h = 1$
repeat
  Solve $\min_{W_h} \operatorname{trace}\left((\Phi(UW_h) - D)^T(\Phi(UW_h) - D)\right)$, $W_h \in \mathbb{R}^{m\times n}$.
  Compute error:
  $e = \operatorname{trace}\left((\Phi(UW_h) - D)^T(\Phi(UW_h) - D)\right)$
  if $(e > \epsilon_N)$ **and** $(h < h_{\max})$ **then**
    Set G = **empty matrix,** $l = 0$
    Set $U_{\text{unmarked}} = U$, $D_{\text{unmarked}} = D$
    repeat
      Choose $u \subset U_{\text{unmarked}}$, $d \subset D_{\text{unmarked}}$ **where** $u \in \mathbb{R}^{m\times m}$, $d \in \mathbb{R}^{m\times n}$
      if less than m **patterns are unmarked then augment** u **and** d **with previously marked patterns.**
      Solve:
      $\min_g \operatorname{trace}\left((\Phi(ug) - d)^T(\Phi(ug) - d)\right)$, $g \in \mathbb{R}^{m\times n}$.
      Add the solution g **as new column(s) of** G.
      $l \leftarrow l + n$
      Mark all patterns which satisfy $U_{\text{unmarked}}\, g = V_{\text{unmarked}}$ **within the tolerance** ϵ_p.
    until all patterns have been marked.
    Find the hidden layer outputs:
    $H = \Phi(UG) \in \mathbb{R}^{p\times l}$.
    Add a zero column to G **with a single nonzero element corresponding to the constant input.**
    $W_h \leftarrow G$
    $U \leftarrow H$
    $m \leftarrow l$
    $h \leftarrow h + 1$
until $(e \leq \epsilon_N)$ **or** $(h = h_{\max})$
output W_i **for** $i = 1, \ldots, h$ **and the error** e

2.2 Hidden Layer Neurons

The dependence identification algorithm constructs a network which solves the ***single layer problem*** within the desired accuracy, if such a solution actually exists. The ***number of layers*** created can be bounded with the parameter $h_{\max}$. The ***number of hidden layer neurons*** depends on the number of layers and the desired accuracy. Several authors have shown (with different degrees of ease and generality) that p neurons in the hidden layer suffice to store p arbitrary patterns[1] in a two layer network; see [1], [6], and [9] for constructive proofs.

The bound on the number of hidden layer neurons created by dependence identification is proportional to the bound of p described above. Assume that the $m \times m$ portions of U are full rank and that the number of network layers is limited to two (one hidden layer). The U matrix has p rows, so it will be broken into at most ceiling($\frac{p}{m}$) linearly dependent groups[2] in order to form the hidden layer neurons. This bound is achieved when every group is made of at most m patterns. In practice the number of groups can be much smaller than ceiling($\frac{p}{m}$) since larger groups of linearly dependent patterns may be found. Every linearly dependent groups yields n hidden layer neurons (one for each output). An extra neuron which has a constant output is then added to the hidden layer in order to help form constant offsets and/or thresholds for the output layer. Thus the dependence identification algorithm has an upper bound of ceiling($\frac{p}{m}$)$n+1$ hidden layer neurons for a two network and assuming the $m \times m$ portions of U are full rank. The dependence identification algorithm assumes that one input is a constant used to form thresholds for the first layer's neurons. Thus for a SISO network $m = 2$ and $n = 1$ and the bound on the number of hidden layer neurons created by dependence identification is approximately one half the bound of p.

There may be situations where dependence identification determines a number of neurons and/or layers that may not be physically realizable due to hardware or software constraints. The number of layers may be limited by the parameter $h_{\max}$ in Algorithm 2.1, and the number of hidden layer neurons may be decreased by increasing the tolerance ϵ_p. This value is used to determine whether a pattern should be considered part of a linearly dependent set, i.e., if a pattern subset u, d and associate weight g satisfies $\Phi(ug) = d$, then another pattern $\hat{u}, \hat{d}$ is considered "linearly dependent" if the elements of $|\Phi(\hat{u}g) - \hat{d}|$ are all less than ϵ_p. Linear dependence is written in quotes here because the nonlinear activation function is being used to determine a pattern match. An example of hidden layer neuron reduction is given in section 3.2. Further discussion and implementation concerns regarding dependence identification can be found in [4].

3 Examples

Programs are written in C to perform backpropagation (BP) and dependence identification (DI) and are run on Sun SPARCstation 2 workstations. The single layer training problems are solved with quadratic optimization [8] and the block conjugate residual algorithm [2], [4]. Section 3.1 shows a comparison between networks constructed with dependence identification to networks trained through trial and error and back-propagation. Section 3.2 shows how the number of hidden layer neurons may be reduced by increasing the DI tolerance value ϵ_p. The overall error of the network is kept down, while the tolerance is increased, by recomputing the weights after each linearly dependent set of training patterns is found. Section 3.3 shows how dependence identification may be successfully used to construct a network architecture and set of initial conditions for further training by backpropagation.

3.1 Function Approximation Examples

Dependence identification has been tested on several multi-input/multi-output functions with the number of training patterns ranging as high as 2000. The functions were also trained using backpropagation with random initial conditions.

The activation function for the networks created by backpropagation (BP) and dependence identification (DI) for all three functions is $\phi(x) = \tanh(x)$. The training results are summarized in table 1. The column

---

[1]The bound of p assumes that one input to the network is constant, if the neural thresholds are handled differently then the bound is $p - 1$.

[2]The notation ceiling(x) means the smallest integer greater than or equal to x.

for network architecture has entries of the form $m - h - n$ where m is the number of network inputs, n is the number of outputs, and h is the number of hidden layer neurons.

	Training Method	Network Architecture	Square Error (Training)	Square Error (Test Set)	Time to Solution (seconds)
1 input/1 output Function	DI	$2 - 9 - 1$	0.2923	1.8023	0.0167
	BP	$2 - 10 - 1$	0.9993	3.8570	274.8
2 input/2 output Function	DI	$3 - 103 - 2$	0.3547	1.5508	15.14
	BP	$3 - 103 - 2$	0.7902	2.1196	4429.25
3 input/1 output Function	DI	$4 - 286 - 1$	0.4495	0.1221	291.13
	BP	$4 - 50 - 1$	1.2661	0.2475	3026.93

Table 1: Comparative results of network training methods.

The process of determining BP learning parameters, the number of hidden layer neurons, and the stopping requirement for backpropagation is a tedious trial and error procedure. The time required to actually determine an appropriate set of parameters is not included as part of the solution time for backpropagation. The times in table 1 are actual CPU times spent performing network construction and training. These times illustrate that even when the learning rates and network architecture are known, dependence identification computes an entire network with similar error in much less time than is required by the gradient descent performed by backpropagation. However the most important contribution of dependence identification is that the search for the appropriate parameters is eliminated and an appropriate network architecture is an output of the algorithm, not an input.

3.2 Increased Tolerance and Recomputed Weights

Hardware and/or memory restrictions may limit the number of hidden layers or hidden layer neurons that may be used in a particular neural network. Section 2.2 mentions that it is possible to decrease the number of hidden neurons created by the dependence identification algorithm by increasing the tolerance, ϵ_p, used to check whether or not a pattern should be included in a set of "linearly dependent" patterns. Unfortunately as the parameter ϵ_p is increased and the number of hidden layer neurons decreases, the overall error of the network tends to increase. The increase in network error can be combated by recomputing the weight matrix g (see Algorithm 2.1) for the entire set of linearly dependent patterns after this set has been found. Figure 1a shows how the number of hidden layer neurons decreases as the tolerance ϵ_p is increased from 0.05 to 5.00. The training patterns are for 1 input / 1 output function approximation example from section 3.1. The network is constrained to have three layers[3] ($h_{\max} = 3$). Note that in this example the dependence identification algorithm determines linear dependence on the basis of the quadratic error cost used by quadratic optimization [8] which allows the error tolerance to be increased past $\epsilon_p = 2$ up to $\epsilon_p = 5$. Figure 1a shows that *the number of hidden layer neurons can be successfully decreased with and without the recomputation of the weights.* The reason the number of hidden layer neurons is different when the weights are recomputed is that a three layer network is being constructed. The inputs produce a set number of neurons in the first hidden layer dependent on ϵ_p only, not on whether the weights are recomputed. The recomputation of weights produces different hidden layer activations (outputs) than those produced when the weights are not recomputed. Thus the *second hidden layer may have a different number of neurons when the weights are recomputed* since the inputs to the second hidden layer are different.

Figure 1b shows how the overall error of the network varies as the tolerance is increased. The network error is the final value of e in Algorithm 2.1. The figure shows how *recomputing the weight matrix helps to keep the overall error of the network from blowing up.* It also shows that there is no simple relationship between the overall error and the tolerance ϵ_p. For example, when ϵ_p increases from 3 to 4, the overall error when the weights are not recomputed actually decreases from about 9.2 to 3.2. However the trend is that the recomputation keeps the error down. The average error for the fourteen different tolerances used in the

[3] The networks in section 3.1 have two layers

a) Decrease of hidden layer neurons. b) Overall network error.

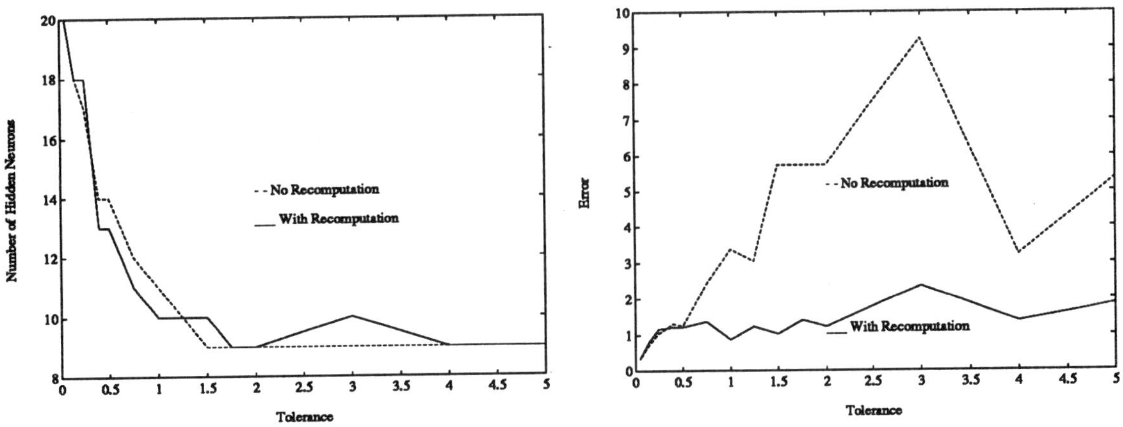

Figure 1: Effects of increasing tolerance ϵ_p.

figure is 3.47 when the weights are not recomputed and 1.25 when they are. It is possible that an error of 1.25 may be higher than the degree of approximation accuracy required for a particular problem. The next section shows how dependence identification can be used to identify an appropriate network architecture and set of initial conditions that will allow backpropagation to quickly decrease the overall network error.

3.3 Dependence Identification for Backpropagation Initial Conditions

Backpropagation is extremely sensitive to initial conditions and there are some problems that are inherently very difficult for backpropagation to solve due to a large number of local minima and relatively flat sections of the cost function. One of these difficult problems is the parity checker [10]. A parity checker receives a number of boolean inputs. In this example, the boolean values are 1 and -1. The parity checker has one boolean output which should be 1 when there is an odd number of 1's at the input and -1 when there are an even number of 1's at the input.

A six input parity checker is used in this problem. The number of network inputs is seven because one input is constant and is used to create biases. The number of training patterns is 64 which includes all possible combinations of six boolean inputs ($2^6 = 64$). Dependence identification is used to find an appropriate two layer network architecture of $7 - 7 - 1$. Networks are then trained using backpropagation with random initial conditions and with the initial conditions obtained from dependence identification. Table 2 shows the results. Patterns are considered to be identified correctly if the network has the proper sign, i.e, a desired output of 1 is classified correctly if the network output is positive and a desired output of -1 is classified correctly if the network output is negative. The entry for "% Error" is calculated as the number of missed patterns divided by 64.

The table shows that, by itself, dependence identification does not produce a very successful solution to the problem. However *the initial conditions it produces are quite good for improving the network with backpropagation*, bringing the error down from about 27% to just over 3%. When random initial conditions are used, *backpropagation is completely unsuccessful in learning the problem*, misclassifying more than half of the input space.

4 Conclusions

A new method of constructing feedforward multi-layer neural networks has been presented, and examples show that it works well for creating neural network approximations of continuous functions as well as providing a starting point for further backpropagation training. Dependence identification is a faster and more systematic method of developing initial network architectures than trial and error or pruning techniques used with gradient descent. Network size and construction time are conserved since dependence identifica-

Training Method	Correctly Classified Patterns	% Error
BP with initial conditions from DI	62	3.12%
Dependence Identification	47	26.56%
BP with random initial conditions	30	53.12%

Table 2: Results of parity checker training

tion builds a small network up instead of whittling a huge network down, and because it relies on the ability to quickly solve single layer training problems instead of ponderous gradient descents on entire multilayer networks.

Dependence identification relaxes the constraint that neural activation functions be continuously differentiable (assuming this is not a requirement of the particular single layer training method), and it determines the number of hidden layer neurons and layers as part of its operation. Dependence identification does not require trial and error with learning rates like backpropagation does. There may well be situations with specific applications where DI indicates a number of hidden layer neurons that can not be physically implemented (due to memory or hardware constraints). The number of hidden layer units can be decreased by increasing the tolerance ϵ_p in Algorithm 2.1. The number of layers can also be limited with the parameter $h_{\max}$. The speed of DI makes it appropriate for creating neural network architectures and initial weight values to be used in real applications.

References

[1] Baum E. B., "On the Capabilities of Multilayer Perceptrons," *J. Complexity*, vol 4, pp 193–215, 1988.

[2] Elman, H. C., "Iterative Methods for Large Sparse Nonsymmetric Systems of Linear Equations," Ph.D. thesis, Computer Science Dept., Yale University, New Haven, CT., 1982.

[3] Hertz, J., Krogh, A. and Palmer, R. G., *Introduction to the Theory of Neural Computation,* Addison-Wesley Publishing Company, 1991.

[4] Moody, J. O., "A New Method for Contructing and Training Multilayer Neural Networks," Master's thesis, Dept. of Electrical Engineering, University of Notre Dame, Notre Dame, IN., 1993.

[5] Moody, J. O., Antsaklis, P. J., "The Dependence Identification Neural Network Construction Algorithm," Technical report ISIS-93-005 of the ISIS Group at the University of Notre Dame, Notre Dame, IN., 1993.

[6] Nilsson N. J., *Learning Machines*, McGraw-Hill, 1965.

[7] Rumelhart, D. E., Hinton, G. E. and Williams, R. J., "Learning Internal Representations by Error Propagation," in Rumelhart, D. E. and McClelland, J. L., eds. *Parallel Distributed Processing: Explanations in the Microstructure of Cognition, vol 1: Foundation*, pp. 318–362, MIT Press, 1986.

[8] Sartori, M. A. and Antsaklis, P. J., "Neural Network Training via Quadratic Optimization", Proc of ISCAS, San Diego, CA, May 10–13, 1992.

[9] Sartori, M. A. and Antsaklis, P. J., "A Simple Method to Derive Bounds on the Size and to Train Multi-Layer Neural Networks", IEEE Trans. on Neural Networks, Vol 2, No 4, pp. 467–471, July 1991.

[10] Tesauro, G. and Janssens, B., "Scaling Relations in Backpropagation learning", *Complex Systems*, Vol 2 pp. 39–44, 1988.